THE MMPI-2

AN INTERPRETIVE MANUAL

SECOND EDITION

ROGER L. GREENE

Pacific Graduate School of Psychology

ALLYN AND BACON

Boston • London • Toronto • Sydney • Tokyo • Singapore

To Alex B. Caldwell
for his generosity in sharing
his MMPI-2 dataset

Executive Editor: Becky Pascal
Series Editorial Assistant: Susan Hutchinson
Marketing Manager: Joyce Nilsen
Manufacturing Manager: Megan Cochran

Copyright © 2000 by Allyn & Bacon
A Pearson Education Company
Needham Heights, MA 02494

Internet: www.abacon.com

Library of Congress Cataloging-in-Publication Data

Greene, Roger L.
    The MMPI-2 : an interpretive manual / Roger L. Greene. — 2nd ed.
      p.   cm.
    Rev. ed. of: The MMPI-2/MMPI. c1991.
    Includes bibliographical references and index.
    ISBN 0-205-28416-7
    1. Minnesota Multiphasic Personality Inventory.   I. Greene, Roger
L. MMPI-2/MMPI. II. Title.
    BF698.8.M5G74   2000
    155.2'83—DC21   99-20373
                                          CIP

Printed in the United States of America

10 9 8 7 6 5 4 3 2   03 02 01 00

CONTENTS

PREFACE

This revision of my *MMPI-2/MMPI Manual* is intended to provide clinicians and researchers who already are familiar with the MMPI-2 with the most current summary of the research. It also will serve as an introduction to the MMPI-2 for clinicians with no prior experience with the test. As with my original *MMPI Manual* and *MMPI-2/MMPI Manual,* this revision is intended to provide a summary of the extant research on the instrument and a step-by-step procedure for profile interpretation.

The chapters have been reorganized slightly from the *MMPI-2/MMPI Manual* and one chapter has been added. The expanded emphasis on the use of Content scales within the MMPI-2 has necessitated separating Chapter 5 into two chapters. Chapter 5 emphasizes the MMPI-2 Content and Content Component scales. Chapter 6 includes all of the Supplementary scales that are available for interpretation. Finally, all information relating to demographic variables other than adolescence has been collated into Chapter 9.

ACKNOWLEDGMENTS

I wish to express my appreciation to the reviewers who provided valuable feedback on the second edition of my *MMPI-2 Manual:* Mark Janus, Ohio State University; William Perry, University of California San Diego Medical Center; Robert Woody, University of Nebraska, Omaha; Eric A. Zillmer, Drexel University. Their comments and insights helped me to elucidate many issues and to clarify the content. Of course, I accept the ultimate responsibility for any inadequacies that remain.

I specifically would like to thank four individuals: Alex B. Caldwell, Ph.D., who generously provided access to the huge MMPI-2 dataset that is cited frequently throughout the text; David S. Nichols, Ph.D., who provided extensive feedback and insight on many issues; Christine Dassoff, M.L.I.S., who conducted the electronic searches of numerous databases; and Erin Holker, who obtained copies of the articles as they were needed. I also would like to thank countless clinicians, students, and clients who have raised numerous questions that constantly require me to explore the nuances of the MMPI-2.

Finally, I wish to thank the many individuals who gave me permission to reproduce copyrighted materials. Specific citations occur whenever such material is used in the book.

CHAPTER 1

The Evolution of the MMPI and MMPI-2

The Minnesota Multiphasic Personality Inventory (MMPI: Hathaway & McKinley, 1940) and its successor, the MMPI-2 (Butcher, Dahlstrom, Graham, Tellegen, & Kaemmer, 1989) are currently the most widely used and researched objective personality inventories. Dahlstrom, Welsh, and Dahlstrom (1975) include almost 6,000 references on the clinical and research applications of the MMPI in *An MMPI Handbook;* Buros' (1978) *The Eighth Mental Measurements Yearbook* contains more than 5,000 citations on the MMPI; and Lubin, Larsen, Matarazzo, and Seever (1985) report that the MMPI is the most frequently used test in professional settings. Watkins, Campbell, Nieberding, and Hallmark (1995) report similar findings for the MMPI-2 in professional settings. Butcher and Rouse (1996) found over 4,300 references to the MMPI over the last 20 years (1974–1994). They also found that references to the MMPI-2 were becoming more common with 50+ publications per year as it replaces the MMPI in research. Originally devised by Hathaway and McKinley in 1940, the MMPI provides an objective means of assessing psychopathology, which has been continued with the advent of the MMPI-2.

A person taking the MMPI-2 sorts 567 statements into one of three categories: "true," "false," or "cannot say." The person's responses to these statements are then scored on 10 clinical scales that assess major categories of psychopathology. In addition, 4 validity scales assess the person's test-taking attitudes. Table 1.1 illustrates the scale names and numbers of the 4 validity and 10 clinical scales. A

TABLE 1.1 MMPI Validity and Clinical Scales

SCALE NAME	NUMBER	ABBREVIATION	NUMBER OF ITEMS
Validity			
Cannot Say		*?*	
Lie		*L*	15
Infrequency		*F*	64
Correction		*K*	30
Clinical			
Hypochondriasis	*1*	*Hs*	33
Depression	*2*	*D*	60
Hysteria	*3*	*Hy*	60
Psychopathic Deviate	*4*	*Pd*	50
Masculinity-Femininity	*5*	*Mf*	60
Paranoia	*6*	*Pa*	40
Psychasthenia	*7*	*Pt*	48
Schizophrenia	*8*	*Sc*	78
Hypomania	*9*	*Ma*	46
Social Introversion	*0*	*Si*	70

standard profile sheet (see Profile 1.1) is used for plotting the person's scores on these validity and clinical scales.

Before proceeding further it is necessary to define what is meant by an MMPI or MMPI-2 *codetype* because this term will be used frequently before codetypes actually are discussed in Chapter 7. Since the items on the MMPI scales were selected empirically, which will be described shortly, it is *not* appropriate to say that the client is hypochondriacal because he or she has an elevated score on Scale *1* (Hypochondriasis). Rather it must be said that the client endorses the items *like* the hypochondriacal patients that were used in developing Scale *1* and any correlates of an elevated score also must be determined empirically. Consequently, it has become common practice to refer to the MMPI clinical scales by number (*1, 2, 3, 4, 5, 6, 7, 8, 9,* or *0*[1]) rather than by name to help clinicians avoid this interpretive error. Interpretation of the MMPI or MMPI-2 then is based on the codetype, which is the two highest elevated clinical scales at a T score of 65 or higher. An MMPI-2 codetype is defined by writing the numbers of the two scales involved with the most elevated one first. For example, if a client's two highest scores on the MMPI-2 are on Scales *2* and *7,* and both are above a T score of 65 but Scale *7* is higher than Scale *2,* then the client's codetype would be *7-2.* If the two highest clinical scales have identical T scores, they are listed in numerical order. In this example, if both Scales *2* and *7* had identical T scores of 75, the client's codetype would be *2-7.* If only one clinical scale is elevated to a T score of 65 or higher, the codetype is called a "Spike" codetype. If Scale *2* were the only clinical scale elevated to a T score of 65 or higher, the codetype would be a Spike *2.* There are 90 possible codetypes on the MMPI and MMPI-2 following this procedure. Finally, if no clinical scale is elevated above a T score of 65 or higher, it is called a "Within-Normal-Limits" codetype. Codetypes will be explored more completely in Chapter 7.

After a brief review of the history of objective personality inventories, the rationale underlying the development of the MMPI and the empirical methods used for item selection and scale construction will be described. Problems associated with interpreting the content of individual items as well as assessing test-taking attitudes will be discussed. Next, the appropriateness of the original norms for the MMPI for contemporary use (cf. Pancoast & Archer, 1989; Colligan, Osborne, Swenson, & Offord, 1983, 1989) will be discussed, followed by describing the development of the MMPI-2 (Butcher et al., 1989), the current revision of the MMPI. Finally, the relative merits of the MMPI and MMPI-2 will be discussed briefly and then the chapter will end with a quick overview of the interpretive process for the MMPI-2 that provides the rationale for the organization of the chapters within this text.

THE EARLY HISTORY OF OBJECTIVE PERSONALITY INVENTORIES

Personality assessment, like intellectual assessment, received its first major impetus during World War I when a need arose for assessment procedures to screen large numbers of individuals. In response to this demand, Woodworth and Poffenberger developed the Woodworth Personal Data Sheet (Woodworth, 1920), a self-rating scale for detecting neurotic individuals. They assembled 116 items reflecting neurotic symptoms to which a person answered "yes" or "no." The total number of positive answers resulted in a score that indicated whether the person should be interviewed individually by a psychiatrist. Some items were considered so pathognomonic that a "yes" response to any of them prompted an individual interview. The items were heterogeneous in content since they tapped every symptom of psychological nervousness that Woodworth and Poffenberger could identify. The items were chosen because Woodworth and Poffenberger thought that they assessed psychological maladjustment; no empirical or theoretical perspective was employed in selecting items to be included on the test. Although the Personal Data Sheet was developed too late to be very useful in selecting recruits, since the United States was already involved in World War I, it did identify those recruits who were emotionally unsuitable for service in the army under wartime conditions.

---

1. By convention, Scale *0* (Social Introversion) is called Scale "Zero," not Scale "Ten."

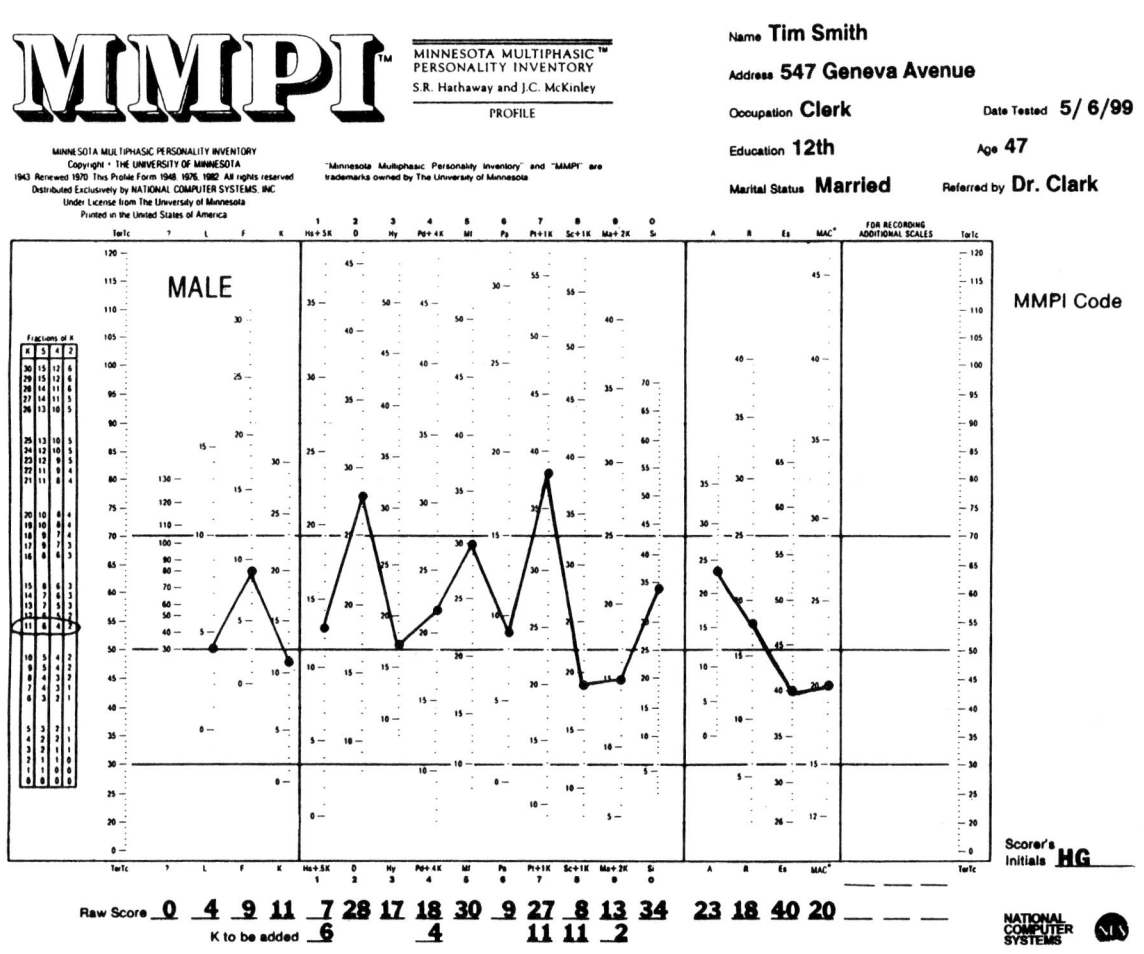

PROFILE 1.1

Note. Minnesota Multiphasic Personality Inventory (MMPI). Copyright 1943 (renewed 1970), 1948, 1976, 1982 by the Regents of the University of Minnesota. All rights reserved. MMPI and Minnesota Multiphasic Inventory are trademarks of the University of Minnesota. Reproduced by permission of the publisher.

The success of psychological testing during World War I stimulated the development in the next decade of several personality inventories similar to the Personal Data Sheet. Probably the best known of these instruments is the Bernreuter Personality Inventory (Bernreuter, 1933), which measures neuroticism, dominance, introversion, and self-sufficiency. Like other personality inventories of this era, the Bernreuter Personality Inventory was constructed on a rational rather than an empirical basis. That is, the test developer would include items on a particular scale that, on the basis of clinical experience, were thought to measure a specific trait or construct. Likewise, the test developer would determine the scoring direction for any particular item on a rational basis. For example, if the test developer felt that a "yes" response to the item "Do you daydream a lot?" indicated neuroticism, that item would be added to the neuroticism scale with "yes" as the "deviant" response. The total number of these "deviant" responses, responses that the test developer felt tapped the specific trait or construct being assessed, became the score on the scale.

Strong critiques (cf. Landis & Katz, 1934; Super, 1942) devastated the Bernreuter Personality Inventory and other rationally derived personality inventories of this era. For example, to investigate how certain groups would perform on the Bernreuter Personality Inventory, Landis and Katz (1934) administered the inventory to 224 patients with a known clinical diagnosis and examined their scores. On the neuroticism scale 39 percent of the neurotic patients scored above the 90th percentile; 23 percent of the schizophrenic patients and 21 percent of the manic-depressive patients, however, also scored above the 90th percentile. Thus, this scale is inadequate since in addition to identifying some neurotic patients correctly, it also misclassified several groups of psychotic patients as neurotic.

Furthermore, analyzing responses to individual items revealed additional problems. Bernreuter weighted a positive response to the items in the neurotic direction; however, Landis and Katz (1934) found that other groups endorsed some items as much or more frequently than neurotics. For example, the item "Are you critical of others?" elicited a "yes" response from 69 percent of the normal sample as compared with 32 percent of the neurotic sample and 39 percent

of the psychotic sample. Similarly, the item "Do you daydream frequently?" was answered "yes" by 43 percent of the normal sample, 40 percent of the neurotic sample, and 31 percent of the psychotic sample.

Other studies (cf. Page, Landis, & Katz, 1934) demonstrated that identifying psychotic individuals with a rationally derived scale is also difficult. Page et al. constructed a rationally based scale by selecting 100 commonly accepted schizophrenic symptoms and traits from the psychiatric literature. The 50 traits considered schizophrenic by at least 10 of the 12 psychiatrists who reviewed the list were combined into a questionnaire. Page et al. administered the questionnaire to 125 schizophrenic patients, 100 manic-depressive patients, and 240 normal individuals, who were matched for intelligence and social status. They found little difference in the average number of the "schizophrenic" traits reported by the three groups: schizophrenics ($M = 17.60$; $SD = 7.50$), manic-depressives ($M = 14.00$; $SD = 7.35$), and normals ($M = 18.00$; $SD = 6.35$). The normal individuals, in fact, actually acknowledged having more of the "schizophrenic" traits than the schizophrenic patients did.

In examining responses to individual items, Page et al. (1934) also found inadequacies. Only 14 of the 50 traits reliably differentiated one group from the other two groups. Even more striking, the normal individuals endorsed 11 of the 50 items more frequently than the schizophrenics did. Some of these 11 items were: "Are you often occupied with your own thoughts?" "Do you think it is possible for other people to influence your actions?" "Do your emotions change frequently without cause?"

Thus, the early personality inventories constructed on a rational basis were unsuccessful outside of a wartime setting. These shortcomings should not be interpreted as an indictment of the general procedure, however. In the last three decades several widely used personality tests have been developed at least partly on a rational basis, such as the Edwards Personal Preference Schedule (Edwards, 1959) and the Personality Research Form (Jackson, 1968). Wiggins (1966) also successfully constructed 13 content scales for the MMPI on a rational basis, which have been validated as veridical self-reports of psychopathology (Jarnecke & Chambers, 1977; Lachar & Alexander, 1978). Chapter 5 provides further information on Wiggins' content scales and the new content scales for the MMPI-2 (Butcher, Graham, Williams, & Ben-Porath, 1990). Wiggins (1973) provides an excellent, in-depth analysis of the relative merits of empirically and rationally derived scales.

CONSTRUCTION OF THE MMPI

Out of the psychometric wilderness of the early 1930s appeared two men, Starke Hathaway and J. C. McKinley, who, under the banner of empiricism, waged a new battle for the scientific advancement of personality assessment. They sought to develop a multifaceted or multiphasic personality inventory, now known as the MMPI, that would surmount the shortcomings of the previous personality inventories, some of which were described previously. Instead of using independent sets of tests, each with a special purpose, Hathaway and McKinley included in a single inventory a wide sampling of behavior of significance to psychologists. They wanted to create a large pool of items from which various scales could be constructed, in the hope of evolving a greater variety of valid personality descriptions than was currently available.

To this end, Hathaway and McKinley (1940) assembled more than 1,000 items from psychiatric textbooks, other personality inventories, and clinical experience. After deleting duplicate items and items that they considered relatively insignificant for their purposes, they arrived at a sample of 504[2] items. The items were written as declarative statements in the first-person singular, and most were phrased in the affirmative. Hathaway and McKinley (1940) arbitrarily classified the items under 25 headings as a convenience in handling and in an effort to avoid duplication (see Table 1.2). However, they did not attempt to

obtain any particular number of items for a category or to ensure that an item was actually properly classified in a category. Table 1.2 shows that some categories are heavily overrepresented and other categories are underrepresented.

Using these 504 items, Hathaway and McKinley (1940) next constructed a series of quantitative scales that could be used to assess various categories of psychopathology. In selecting items for a specific scale (e.g., Hypochondriasis), they used an empirical approach. The items had to be answered differently by the criterion group (e.g., hypochondriacal patients) as

TABLE 1.2   Content Categories for MMPI Items

CONTENT CATEGORY	NUMBER OF ITEMS
Social attitudes	72
Political attitudes, law and order	46
Morale	33
Affect, depressive	32
Delusions, hallucinations, illusions, ideas of reference	31
Family and marital	29
Phobias	29
Affect, manic	24
Habits	20
Religious attitudes	20
General neurologic	19
Sexual attitudes	19
Occupational	18
Lie	15
Obsessive, compulsive	15
Educational	12
Cranial nerves	11
Gastrointestinal	11
Vasomotor, trophic, speech, secretory	10
General health	9
Sadistic, masochistic	7
Genitourinary	6
Motility and coordination	6
Cardiorespiratory	5
Sensibility	5
Total	504

Note. The category names and sizes are from Hathaway and McKinley (1940).

2. Hathaway and McKinley did not provide a rationale for deleting insignificant items. Although potentially useful items may have been discarded, this procedure was acceptable at the time because they used an empirical method of item selection. The issue of their rationale for deletion of items, however, has become more relevant since item content is sometimes important in current usage of the MMPI. Wiggins' (1966) content scales are an example.

compared with normal groups. Since their approach was strictly empirical and no theoretical rationale was posited as the basis for accepting or rejecting items on a specific scale, it is not always possible to discern why a particular item distinguishes the criterion group from normal groups. Rather, items were selected solely because the criterion group answered them differently than other groups.

Scale *1* (Hypochondriasis) was constructed first (McKinley & Hathaway, 1940).[3] This choice was not simply fortuitous. Hypochondriasis is one of the simpler, more definite diagnostic categories, and hypochondriacs also were one of the largest groups of patients available to McKinley and Hathaway. Since the procedure for developing Scale *1* typifies the procedure for most of the clinical scales, it will be described in detail. Later, the development of the other clinical scales will be described only in cases in which the procedure differs.

The first step in developing Scale *1* was to select an appropriate criterion group. Using a diagnostic classification as the basis for the criterion group selection was logical because McKinley and Hathaway's intent was to develop an inventory to aid in differential diagnosis. They defined hypochondriasis as an abnormal neurotic concern over bodily health, excluding the symptomatic occurrence of hypochondriacal features in psychotic individuals. Using this definition, they selected 50 cases of pure, uncomplicated hypochondriasis as their criterion group.

The next step was to select groups of normal individuals. The primary normative group, which served as the reference group for determining the standard MMPI profile for over 50 years, consisted of 724 individuals who were friends or relatives of patients in the University Hospitals in Minneapolis. The only criterion for exclusion was if an individual was currently receiving treatment from a physician. This group reflected a fairly representative cross section for gender and marital status of the Minnesota population aged 16 to 55 in the late 1930s. Dahlstrom et al. (1975) reported that all of the persons in the primary normative group were white because very few members of any ethnic minority other than American Indian resided in Minnesota at that time. The normative groups for the MMPI-2 will be described later in this chapter, and the use of the MMPI and MMPI-2 with ethnic minorities will be described in Chapter 9.

Four additional normative groups were used in the development of Scale *1* and other clinical scales. Two normative groups were formed to assess whether "nuisance" variables such as age, socioeconomic class, or education were influencing differential item endorsement by members of the criterion group and the primary normative group. One group consisted of 265 precollege high school graduates who came to the University of Minnesota Testing Bureau for precollege guidance. The other was composed of 265 skilled workers from local Works Progress Administration projects. A third normative group consisted of 254 patients who were hospitalized for some form of physical disease in the general wards of the University Hospitals. None of the patients had obvious psychiatric symptomatology. The fourth general normative group consisted of 221 patients in the psychopathic unit of the University Hospitals, regardless of diagnosis.

Once the criterion group and the other normative groups were established, the process of item selection began. For the criterion group and each of the normal groups, the frequency of "true" and "false" responses was calculated for each item. An item was considered significant and was tentatively selected for a scale if the difference in frequency of response between the criterion group and the normative groups was at least twice the standard error of the proportions of "true/false" responses of the two groups being compared. For example, the response frequencies for two potential items for Scale *1* are provided in Table 1.3. In this example, only two groups, the criterion group of hypochondriacs and the original normative group, are compared; before any items were finally selected, the criterion group would be compared with the other normative groups as well.

The following formula (Ferguson, 1971) was used for the test of the significance of the difference between two independent proportions:

---

3. It is now customary to identify each scale by its number rather than its name. The use of the scale number reduces the emphasis placed on diagnostic labels like hypochondriasis, schizophrenia, and so on, and encourages the clinician to be aware of the empirical correlates of specific scores on each scale.

TABLE 1.3   Frequency of Response by Group for Two Possible Items for Scale *1* (Hypochondriasis)

	GROUP			
	Normals[a]		*Hypochondriacs*[b]	
Item	*True*	*False*	*True*	*False*
1. I have few or no pains.[c]	211 (81%)	51 (19%)	17 (34%)	33 (66%)
2. Much of the time my head seems to hurt all over.[c]	10 (4%)	252 (96%)	5 (10%)	45 (90%)

[a]$n = 262$
[b]$n = 50$
[c]Minnesota Multiphasic Personality Inventory (MMPI). Copyright 1943 (renewed 1970), 1948, 1976, 1982
by the Regents of the University of Minnesota. All rights reserved. MMPI and Minnesota Multiphasic Inventory are trademarks of the University of Minnesota. Reproduced by permission of the publisher.

$$Z = \frac{p_1 - p_2}{\sqrt{pq[(1/n_1) + (1/n_2)]}}$$

where

p = the proportion of "true" responses in the total group

p_1 = the proportion of "true" responses in the first sample

p_2 = the proportion of "true" responses in the second sample

$q = 1 - p$

n_1 = the number of persons in the first sample

n_2 = the number of persons in the second sample

Thus, the values of p and q for the first item would be the following:

$$p = \frac{211 + 17}{262 + 50} = \frac{228}{312} = .73$$

$$q = 1 - p = 1.0 - .73 = .27$$

Substituting these values in the preceding formula results in the following:

$$Z = .81 - .34/\sqrt{(.73)(.27)[(1/262) + (1/50)]} =$$
$$.47/.069 = 6.81$$

Checking a standard table of Z values shows that this Z value has a probability less than .001. Hathaway and McKinley considered significant any percentage difference of at least twice the standard error of the independent proportions, or any Z equal to or greater than $+2$. Since a Z of $+2$ has a probability slightly less than .05 using a two-tailed test, they essentially selected only items that were significant beyond the .05 level. Thus, the first item in the preceding example would be tentatively included in Scale *1*, and a "false" response would be the "deviant" answer because the hypochondriacal patients responded more frequently in the "false" direction. If this item also differentiated the hypochondriacal group from the other normative groups using an identical procedure, it would then be included on Scale *1*.

Using the same procedure for the second sample item would result in substituting the following values in the formula:

$$Z = .04 - .10/\sqrt{(.048)(.952)[(1/262) + (1/50)]} =$$
$$-.06/.033 = -1.82$$

This item would not be included on Scale *1* because the proportions of endorsement are not significantly different between the two groups.

Having selected items according to this procedure, Hathaway and McKinley then eliminated some of them for various reasons. First, the frequency of the criterion group's response was required to be greater than 10 percent for nearly all items; those items that yielded infrequent "deviant" response rates from the criterion group were excluded even if they were highly significant statistically because they represented so few criterion cases. Additionally, items whose responses appeared to reflect biases on variables such as marital status or socioeconomic status were excluded.

Finally, Hathaway and McKinley rejected a few more of the tentatively selected items that, after a rational inspection of the list, they concluded were not germane to the construct of hypochondriasis. Correlations between each item and the total score on the scale were not calculated nor were any other psychometric bases used in selecting items. The psychometric problems that later were discovered with some of the validity and clinical scales arose because these issues were not considered when each scale was constructed. These problems will be discussed later as appropriate when each scale is reviewed.

The preliminary Scale *1* consisted of 55 items that had been identified by this procedure. The next step was weighting or combining them into a scale. Evaluation of several methods of weighting individual items showed no advantage over using unweighted items. Therefore, each item simply received a weight of "one" in deriving a total score. In other words, a person's score on Scale *1* is equal to the total number of items that the individual answers in the same manner as the criterion group.

The responses of the normative group consisting of general psychiatric patients helped to refine Scale *1*. A fair number of these psychiatric patients obtained high scores on this scale, although the psychiatric staff had not noted the presence of hypochondriasis. To eliminate this potential source of bias, the responses of 50 patients who had no hypochondriacal symptoms but who obtained the highest scale scores on the preliminary Scale *1* were contrasted with the original criterion group of 50 hypochondriacal patients. Items showing a significant difference in frequency of endorsement between these two groups were located and combined into a separate grouping, known as the correction of Scale *1*. (This correction of Scale *1* should not be confused with the *K*-correction of Scale *1*, which will be discussed later.) For each of these correction items that an individual answered in the nonhypochondriacal direction, one point was subtracted from the total score on Scale *1*. Cross-validation revealed that the corrected score on Scale *1* was more effective in differentiating the groups than the original uncorrected score.

The normative group with physical disease also was used in developing Scale *1*. This group scored more like the normal group than like the hypochondriacal group on the corrected Scale *1*. Thus, their actual physical symptoms appeared to alter their total scores only moderately in the direction of hypochondriasis.

More recently, Scale *1* was modified again. In order to differentiate Scale *1* more clearly from Scale *3* (Hysteria), McKinley and Hathaway (1944) eliminated from Scale *1* those correction items that also appeared on Scale *3*, thus arbitrarily making Scale *1* into a somatic ailments scale. They also eliminated some of the original items from Scale *1* that did not separate hypochondriacs from normals under subsequent analyses. This final step resulted in the 33 items that are currently used on Scale *1* on the MMPI.

Soon after the development of Scale *1* (McKinley & Hathaway, 1940), five other clinical scales were developed: *2* (Depression) (Hathaway & McKinley, 1942); *7* (Psychasthenia) (McKinley & Hathaway, 1942); and *3* (Hysteria), *4* (Psychopathic Deviate), and *9* (Hypomania) (McKinley & Hathaway, 1944). The description of the construction of three other clinical scales—*5* (Masculinity-Femininity), *6* (Paranoia), and *8* (Schizophrenia)—was not published until 1956 (Hathaway, 1956), although these three scales had been used routinely for more than a decade. (More detailed information on each of these scales will be provided in Chapter 4.)

Scale *5* (Masculinity-Femininity) was developed somewhat differently than the other clinical scales. Some 55 items, mostly related to sexual orientation, were added to the MMPI item pool after the data already had been collected from the original normative sample.[4] Thus, the criterion group of male homosexuals who were used in developing Scale *5* could not be contrasted with the original normative group on

---

4. The addition of 55 items to the original 504 items on the MMPI would produce an item pool of 559 items. Since the MMPI contains only 550 items, it is not clear what happened to the other 9 items (W. G. Dahlstrom, personal communication, 1979).

these 55 items. Consequently, 54 male soldiers were used as one of the normative groups for this scale, and items that distinguished them from the male homosexuals were included on Scale *5*. In addition, items that differentiated men from women within the normative sample were included on this scale. The effects of these different construction procedures for Scale *5* will be explored more fully in Chapter 4.

In 1946 Scale *0* (Social Introversion) was added to the MMPI (Drake, 1946), completing the standard MMPI clinical profile. Scale *0* also was constructed differently from the other clinical scales. Drake selected MMPI items that differentiated 50 college students who scored above the 65th percentile on the Minnesota T-S-E Inventory (Evans & McConnell, 1941) from 50 students who scored below the 35th percentile.

The Minnesota T-S-E Inventory assesses introversion-extroversion in three areas: thinking (T), social (S), and emotional (E). Drake limited his initial work to the social introversion-extroversion area, or, more specifically, he investigated introversion-extroversion only in the social area as assessed by the Minnesota T-S-E Inventory. Although Drake conducted his analysis on men and women separately, their norms were so similar that he combined the normative data for the two genders into a single group before finally incorporating it into the standard MMPI profile. (This issue will be explored more fully in Chapter 4.)

INTERPRETATION OF INDIVIDUAL ITEM CONTENT

Individuals sometimes fail to provide a veridical self-report (one that accurately reflects how others perceive their behavior) in responding to personality inventory items. There are several possible reasons for their inaccurate self-description. First, although persons constructing test items generally assume that each item has essentially the same meaning to all persons taking the test, this assumption is not always appropriate. For example, for a test item such as "I have headaches frequently,"[5] persons may interpret "frequently" to mean once a day, once a week, or once a month and respond "true" or "false" accordingly. One client might endorse this item as being "true" since he

has headaches at least once a month; another might endorse this item as being "false" since she has headaches only once a week. The ambiguity inherent in any single item makes it extremely difficult to obtain a veridical self-description because the person answering a specific item and an observer rating the person on that item's content may interpret the item somewhat differently.

Second, although self-ratings provided through item responses can be useful because direct observations of behavior are often impractical, impossible, or inefficient, individuals vary in their self-awareness and in their ability or willingness to report the appropriate behaviors. Third, the rational method of test construction also requires that the test developer be knowledgeable about the relationship between persons' responses to individual items and the construct being assessed. The fallacies and errors in earlier rationally derived personality inventories suggest that it is very difficult for the test developer to have this depth of understanding of the dynamics of a personality inventory.

These problems can be demonstrated by the response of psychopaths to the MMPI item "I have been quite independent and free from family rule."[6] A test developer would likely make the a priori assumption that psychopaths would respond "true" to this item. In fact, psychopaths answered this item "false" more often than the normative groups. This response does not mean that this specific behavior is actually characteristic of psychopaths; rather it means that psychopaths say it is characteristic of them. As such it can be treated like any other verbalization the individual makes. It indicates how the person interprets the item and how the person thinks, perceives, and feels, even though it may actually be untrue. Although this statement is untrue, it still provides useful diagnostic information about the individual.

---

6. Ibid.

Another example is the response of hypochondriacs to the MMPI item "I have few or no pains."[7] They answered this item "false" more often than the normative group. Such a response does not necessarily mean that hypochondriacs actually experience more pain than other persons, but it does mean that they are more willing to say that it is true about themselves.

Although these issues unquestionably exist in the interpretation of the content of individual items on the MMPI, they do not invalidate it. The empirical approach to item selection used by Hathaway and McKinley, in fact, freed them of these problems because it assumes that the client's self-report is just that and makes no a priori assumptions about the relationships between the client's self-report and the client's behavior. Items are selected for inclusion in a specific scale only because the criterion group answered the items differently than the normative groups irrespective of whether the item content is actually an accurate description of the criterion group. Any relationship between clients' responses on a given scale and their behavior must be demonstrated empirically. The interested reader should consult Meehl's (1945) article, which explores this issue in greater depth, and the section on critical items in Chapter 6.

ASSESSMENT OF TEST-TAKING ATTITUDES

Because Hathaway and McKinley (1940) developed the MMPI under the banner of empiricism, they recognized that the honesty or frankness with which the client responds to the items needs to be assessed empirically each time the MMPI is administered rather than blithely assume that the client has answered the items appropriately. It is possible that a client might adopt a test-taking attitude other than that desired by the test developer. A client may decide, for whatever reason, to overreport (exaggerate, "fake bad") or underreport (deny, "fake good") the behavior being assessed by the test instrument, or a client may respond randomly to the test items because of an unwilling-

ness or inability to respond appropriately. In either case it is important for the interpreter of the test inventory to be aware of the possibility that the client has responded inappropriately. Previous test developers often paid lip service to the importance of appropriate test-taking attitudes, but they did not provide specific directions on how to develop or maintain those attitudes. More importantly, they did not provide a means of assessing whether those attitudes actually were present. In the development of the MMPI this problem was assessed directly through what are now called the validity scales.

Meehl and Hathaway (1946) were convinced of the necessity of assessing two dichotomous categories of test-taking attitudes: defensiveness ("faking-good") and plus-getting ("faking-bad").[8] (These two categories will be called *underreporting* and *overreporting* of psychopathology, respectively, throughout later sections of this book to avoid the connotations inherent in the terms *faking-good* and *faking-bad,* because it is not always clear whether the person's motivation for distorting responses is conscious or unconscious.)

Meehl and Hathaway (1946) considered three possible approaches to assess these two categories of test-taking attitudes. First, they could give the client an opportunity to distort the responses in a specific way and observe the extent to which the client did so. One way of implementing this approach would be to repeat items within the MMPI, phrased either identically or in the negative rather than the affirmative. A large number of inconsistent responses would suggest that the client was either unable or unwilling to respond consistently. Although Meehl and Hathaway rejected this solution, the old MMPI group booklet form included 16 identically repeated items that could be used to detect inconsistent responding. However, these 16 items were deleted and not replaced in developing the MMPI-2 so this solution has been rejected again.

Second, Meehl and Hathaway considered providing an opportunity for the client to answer favorably when a favorable response would almost certainly be

8. The term *plus-getting* describes the procedure of making a deviant response to an item on a scale, thus adding plus one to the total score on the scale.

untrue. This solution would involve developing a list of extremely desirable but very rare human qualities. If a client endorsed a large number of these items, it is highly probable that the responses would be dishonest. The *L* (Lie) scale was developed specifically for this purpose. Items for the *L* scale, based on the work of Hartshorne and May (1928), reflect behaviors that, although socially desirable, are all rarely true of a given individual. A large number of responses in the deviant direction on the *L* scale indicates response distortion.

The *F* scale was developed according to a variant of this second approach for assessing test-taking attitudes. Items for the *F* scale were selected primarily because they were answered with a relatively low frequency by a majority of the original normative group. In other words, if a client endorsed a large number of the *F* scale items, that person would be responding in a manner that was atypical of most people in the normative group. In addition, the items include a variety of content areas so that any specific set of experiences or interests for a particular individual would be unlikely to influence the person to answer many of the items in the deviant direction. The *F* scale effectively identified individuals who were intentionally faking pathology; however, schizoid individuals and persons who were overly pessimistic about themselves also obtained high scores. Therefore, additional procedures were needed to separate these two groups of persons from those who faked their psychopathology or misunderstood the items. Meehl and Hathaway thought the *L* scale would serve this function, which provided another reason for its use as a validity scale.

Third, Meehl and Hathaway considered using an empirical procedure to identify items that elicit different responses from persons taking the test in an appropriate fashion and those who have been instructed to "fake" psychopathology. Gough's Dissimulation scale (Gough, 1954, 1957), which was based on this procedure, will be described in Chapter 3.

Meehl and Hathaway adopted a variant of this third approach in developing a third validity scale, the *K* scale. Their task was to differentiate persons known to have psychopathology who were hospitalized and yet obtained normal profiles from normal individuals who for some reason obtained elevated profiles. They selected 25 male and 25 female patients diagnosed as having psychopathic personalities, alcoholism, and other behavior disorders who (1) had a T score of 60 or higher on the *L* scale, which would indicate some form of response distortion, and (2) had diagnoses indicating that they should have elevated profiles, but (3) had actual profiles in the normal range. Based on a comparison of this group with the original normative sample on all items, 22 items were selected that showed at least a 30 percent difference in the response rates of the two groups.

It was later found that these 22 items generally did an adequate job of identifying defensiveness in most patients; however, depressed and schizophrenic patients tended to get low scores. To counteract this tendency, 8 items were added and scored to differentiate these two groups from the original normative group. This final step resulted in the 30-item *K* scale, which is currently used. Meehl and Hathaway also empirically determined the proportions of *K* that when added to a clinical scale would maximize the discrimination between the criterion group and the normative group. Because Meehl and Hathaway determined the optimal weights of *K* to be added to each clinical scale in a psychiatric inpatient population, they warned that with maladjusted normal populations and other clinical populations, other weights of *K* might serve to maximize the identification of individuals with psychopathology. This issue of the optimal weights to be added to each clinical scale in different populations will be discussed in Chapter 3 when the *K* scale is examined in more depth.

APPROPRIATENESS OF MMPI NORMS

The issue of whether the items and norms for the MMPI developed in the early 1940s are appropriate for contemporary use has been raised repeatedly and debated widely (cf. Butcher, 1972; Colligan et al., 1983; Faschingbauer, 1979). Since the typical individual in the original Minnesota normative group was "about thirty-five years old, was married, lived in a small town or rural area, had had eight years of general schooling, and worked at a skilled or semiskilled trade (or was married to a man with such an occupation level)" (Dahlstrom, Welsh, & Dahlstrom, 1972,

p. 8), it seems apparent that there have been numerous changes in our society over the ensuing five decades.

Pancoast and Archer (1989) collated the existing literature on the performance of normal individuals on the MMPI to assess the adequacy of the norms based on the original Minnesota normative group. The mean MMPI profile for these normal men (Profile 1.2, squares) and women (Profile 1.3, squares) showed T scores near 55 for Scales *K* (Correction), *3* (Hysteria), *4* (Psychopathic Deviate), and *9* (Hypomania). Only on Scales *L* (Lie) and *1* (Hypochondriasis) did the mean T scores approach 50. Pancoast and Archer found that studies as early as 1949 demonstrated that normal individuals showed generally small but consistent variations from the mean scores of the original Minnesota normative group. Two conclusions can be drawn from the data summarized by Pancoast and Ar-

cher. First, the scores of normal individuals may have been slightly different from the original Minnesota normative group on the standard Validity and Clinical scales since the MMPI was first developed. Second, there have been only small changes in normal individuals across five decades as reflected by their mean T scores on the standard validity and clinical scales.

Greene (1990) examined the changes in the standard Validity and Clinical scales on the MMPI within four frequently occurring codetypes (Spike *4*, *2-4/4-2*, *2-7/7-2*, and *6-8/8-6*) in samples of psychiatric patients over a time span of 40 years. The mean MMPI profiles were virtually identical within all four codetypes for all four samples as can be seen in Table 1.4. The range in scores across all of the clinical scales in all four samples was 2 T points for the Spike *4* codetypes, 4 T points in the *2-4/4-2* code-

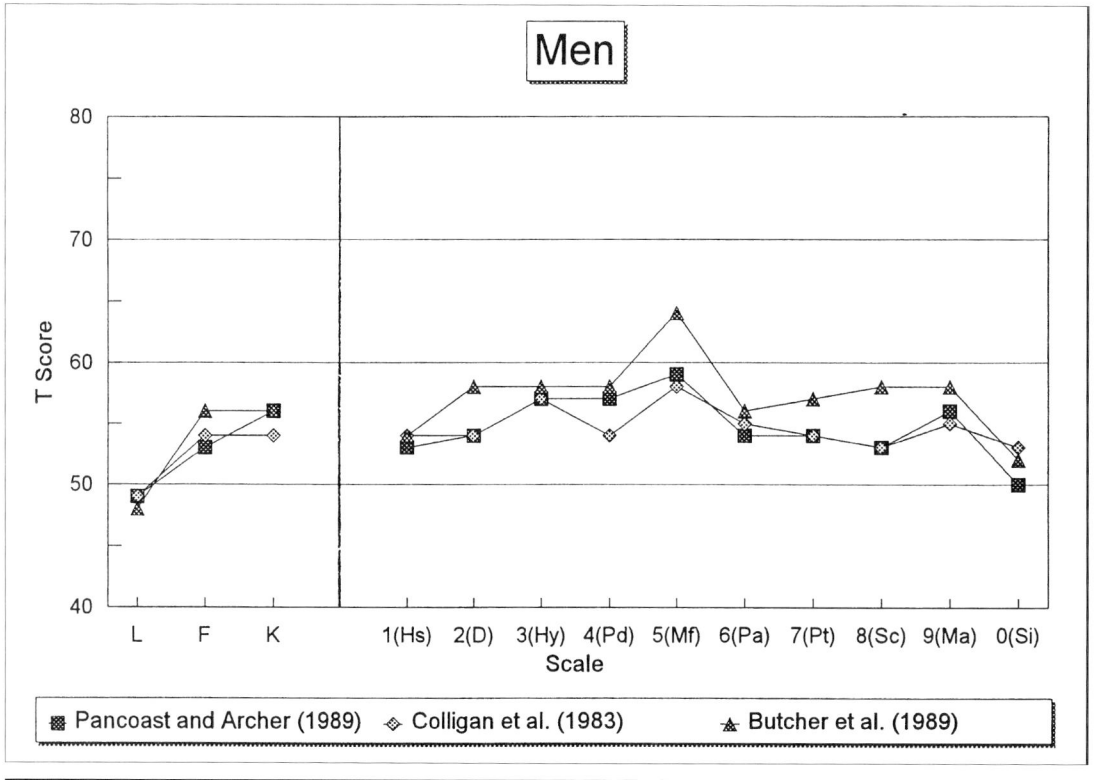

PROFILE 1.2

Note. Minnesota Multiphasic Personality Inventory-2 (MMPI-2). Copyright © 1942, 1943 (renewed 1970), 1989 by the Regents of the University of Minnesota. Reproduced by permission of the publisher. "MMPI-2" and "Minnesota Multiphasic Personality Inventory-2" are trademarks owned by the University of Minnesota.

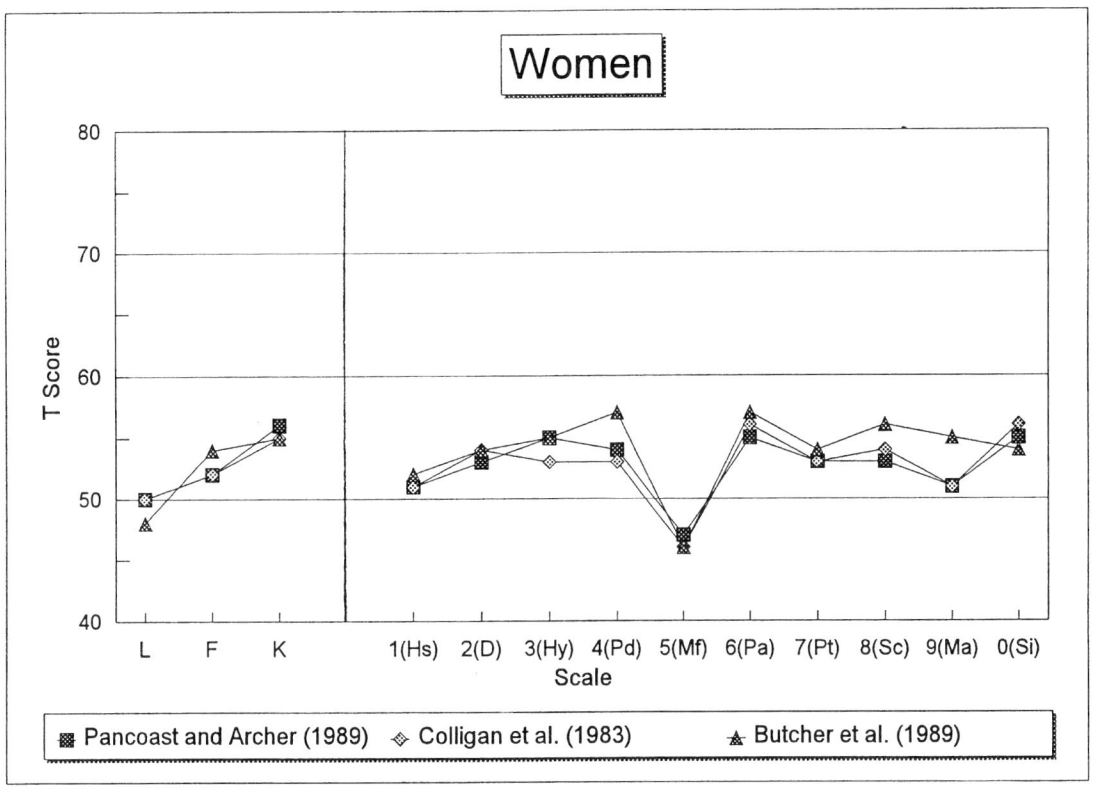

PROFILE 1.3

Note. Minnesota Multiphasic Personality Inventory-2 (MMPI-2). Copyright © 1942, 1943 (renewed 1970), 1989 by the Regents of the University of Minnesota. Reproduced by permission of the publisher. "MMPI-2" and "Minnesota Multiphasic Personality Inventory-2" are trademarks owned by the University of Minnesota

types, 5 T points in the *2-7/7-2* codetypes, and 9 T points in the *6-8/8-6* codetypes. The average difference between the highest and lowest score on all of the clinical scales was 2.2, 3.0, 2.5, and 5.5 T points for these four codetypes, respectively. It appears that the MMPI scale scores of psychiatric patients have been very stable over this time span. Greene's data did not address whether the empirical correlates of these codetypes remained unchanged across the 50 years that the MMPI has been in use. However, the stability of the MMPI scale scores across these years would at least suggest that the correlates probably have not changed. Of course, empirical data are needed to answer this question.

Table 1.4 also provides the mean MMPI-2 profiles for these same four codetypes in a sample of psy-chiatric inpatients (Greene & Schinka, 1995) and psychiatric outpatients (Caldwell, 1997a) collected over different time periods in the 1990s. These MMPI-2 profiles are very similar for all of the code-types except for the *6-8/8-6* codetypes in which the inpatients' scores are 5–10 T points higher than the outpatients' on a number of the scales. The stability in these MMPI-2 codetypes would be expected given the stability that was found for MMPI codetypes.

When the MMPI-2 profiles provided in Table 1.4 are compared to the corresponding MMPI profiles, there are differences found in each codetype. The MMPI-2 *2-4/4-2* codetypes are about 5 T points higher on Scale *F* (Infrequency) and 3–5 T points lower on Scales *K* (Correction), *3* (Hysteria), and *9* (Hypomania). The MMPI-2 *2-7/7-2* codetypes are

TABLE 1.4 MMPI and MMPI-2 Performance within Four Codetypes across Five Decades

SAMPLE	N	(%)	AGE	GENDER	L	F	K	1(Hs)	2(D)	3(Hy)	4(Pd)	5(Mf)	6(Pa)	7(Pt)	8(Sc)	9(Ma)	0(Si)
2-4/4-2				*MMPI*													
Minnesota 1950 Mean	68	(2.71%)	35.1	53%F 47%M	53	63	53	66	84	70	84	53	66	71	70	56	60
Minnesota 1960 Mean	245	(4.11%)	32.3	64%F 36%M	51	65	53	63	83	69	84	54	66	71	66	57	64
Missouri 1970 Mean	607	(5.77%)	38.1	22%F 78%M	51	62	51	61	82	66	83	56	64	68	66	58	60
Texas 1980 Mean	241	(5.29%)	33.0	50%F 50%M	50	64	51	63	82	67	84	53	66	70	70	58	62
				MMPI-2													
Texas 1992 Mean	72	(2.32%)	35.0	47%F 53%M	50	70	43	61	80	62	83	51	66	69	67	52	62
California 1997 Mean	855	(2.45%)	36.0	63%F 37%M	50	69	46	62	80	65	81	50	65	69	67	50	61
2-7/7-2				*MMPI*													
Minnesota 1950 Mean	157	(6.26%)	37.8	55%F 45%M	51	58	52	68	90	71	67	52	65	85	74	53	67
Minnesota 1960 Mean	381	(6.39%)	37.9	47%F 53%M	50	61	52	68	90	71	69	55	65	86	71	53	68
Missouri 1970 Mean	392	(3.72%)	40.3	25%F 75%M	50	63	49	66	90	68	70	58	66	85	74	54	69
Texas 1980 Mean	180	(3.95%)	33.6	44%F 56%M	49	63	50	66	89	69	70	56	67	85	75	54	69
				MMPI-2													
Texas 1992 Mean	172	(5.54%)	40.8	73%F 27%M	52	72	42	70	87	69	67	51	66	85	76	50	70
California 1997 Mean	1,931	(5.54%)	38.6	54%F 46%M	52	67	46	67	86	68	64	51	66	83	72	47	68

Spike 4   *MMPI*

	N		Age	Sex													
Minnesota 1950 Mean	70	(2.79%)	28.6	53%F / 47%M	52 / 51	54 / 56	61 / 60	52 / 54	55 / 57	58 / 60	75 / 77	53 / 51	56 / 56	56 / 58	59 / 57	57 / 56	49 / 50
Minnesota 1960 Mean	208	(3.49%)	26.5	51%F / 49%M	53 / 52	55 / 55	58 / 58	53 / 52	57 / 57	58 / 59	77 / 76	52 / 50	56 / 57	55 / 56	57 / 58	58 / 58	49 / 52
Missouri 1970 Mean	752	(7.15%)	34.0	25%F / 75%M	—	—	—	—	—	—	—	—	—	—	—	—	—
Texas 1980 Mean	201	(4.42%)	29.8	61%F / 39%M	—	—	—	—	—	—	—	—	—	—	—	—	—

MMPI-2

	N		Age	Sex													
Texas 1992 Mean	49	(1.58%)	34.7	39%F / 61%M	54	53	56	51	54	54	71	48	53	53	52	51	45
California 1997 Mean	1,258	(3.61%)	34.5	54%F / 46%M	54	51	58	51	51	54	70	49	54	52	53	50	45

6-8/8-6   *MMPI*

	N		Age	Sex													
Minnesota 1950 Mean	121	(4.83%)	32.9	69%F / 31%M	51	89	44	63	70	62	72	60	90	75	95	73	65
Minnesota 1960 Mean	137	(2.30%)	32.1	71%F / 29%M	53	94	46	69	70	65	74	61	89	74	91	72	65
Missouri 1970 Mean	686	(6.52%)	30.4	36%F / 64%M	49	93	43	70	76	67	79	60	95	81	101	75	65
Texas 1980 Mean	225	(4.94%)	28.3	52%F / 48%M	49	92	45	70	73	67	77	58	92	79	99	73	64

MMPI-2

	N		Age	Sex													
Texas 1992 Mean	427	(13.77%)	35.9	76%F / 24%M	52	109	36	78	80	73	78	54	101	85	102	68	71
California 1997 Mean	1,784	(5.12%)	34.0	44%F / 56%M	51	99	38	74	77	71	74	54	97	81	95	64	66

5–10 T points higher on Scale *F* (Infrequency) and 5–10 T points lower on Scale *K* (Correction). The MMPI-2 Spike *4* codetypes are about 5 T points lower on Scale *F* (Infrequency) and 3–5 T points lower on most of the clinical scales. Finally, the MMPI-2 *6-8/8-6* codetypes are 5–10 T points higher on Scales *F* (Infrequency), *2* (Depression), and *6* (Paranoia) and 5–10 T points lower on Scales *K* (Correction), *5* (Masculinity-Femininity), and *9* (Hypomania). The common pattern to these comparisons between the MMPI and MMPI-2 within the same codetype appears to be for T scores to be 5–10 T points higher on Scale *F* (Infrequency) and about 5 T points lower on Scales *K* (Correction), *3* (Hysteria), and *9* (Hypomania). The variations in the T scores on Scales *F* (Infrequency) and *K* (Correction) between the MMPI and MMPI-2 would be expected given that Hathaway and McKinley assigned the T scores to the validity scales arbitrarily and they recognized that these T scores were inaccurate (Hathaway & McKinley, 1951). The variations on the clinical scales usually do not affect the scales that are defining the codetype and, thus, would have only minor impact on the interpretation of the codetype. This complex issue of the relationship between MMPI and MMPI-2 codetypes will be explored in Chapter 7.

The finding that normal individuals and psychiatric patients have shown only minor changes on the standard validity and clinical scales of the MMPI and MMPI-2 across 50 years is very surprising, and would suggest that the MMPI may not be as outdated as many people have thought. The recent work of Colligan et al. (1983) in developing contemporary norms for the MMPI and the current restandardization of the MMPI that has resulted in the MMPI-2 also have examined the changes that have occurred since the MMPI was developed originally. These two projects will now be examined in turn.

A CONTEMPORARY NORMATIVE STUDY OF THE MMPI

Colligan and his colleagues (Colligan et al., 1983, 1989) investigated whether the original MMPI norms were appropriate for contemporary use. They essentially replicated the data-collection procedures employed by McKinley and Hathaway (1940) and gathered a representative sample of individuals living within 50 miles of the Mayo Clinic in Rochester, Minnesota. "Persons having chronic diseases (for example, diabetes) were excluded from the study, as were patients receiving cancer treatment, those with rheumatoid or other types of arthritis, those described as being chemically dependent, having a learning disability, or being mentally retarded, and persons undergoing psychotherapy" (Colligan et al., 1983, pp. 74–75).

Their final sample consisted of 1,408 white individuals (646 men and 762 women), whose mean age was in their mid-40s and who had a mean of 13 years of education. Nearly three-fourths of them were married. These individuals were somewhat older and better educated than the original Minnesota normative sample that has been described previously. Colligan et al. also selected a subset of these individuals "in proportion to the age and sex in the general population of adult whites in the United States, as determined by the 1980 census" (1983, p. 87) so that they could make more direct comparisons with the original normative group because the population of the United States had increased in age and become better educated in the ensuing four decades.

Profiles 1.2 (diamonds) and 1.3 (diamonds) provide the mean profile for these contemporary men and women, respectively, plotted on the *original* MMPI norms. As can be seen in these two profiles, the men average 3 to 8 T score points higher on the Clinical scales and the women average 1 to 6 T score points higher (except on Scale *5* [Masculinity-Femininity] where they are 4 points lower) on the Clinical scales than the original Minnesota normative group.

Two basic points can be made based on the data presented in Profiles 1.2 and 1.3. First, there are some differences in MMPI performance across the five decades that the MMPI has been in use, although these differences are not as substantial as might have been expected, given the changes in our society in the last 50 years. When the data in these two profiles reported by Colligan et al. (1983) (diamonds) are compared with Pancoast and Archer (1989) (squares), there is further support for the statement that the scores of normal individuals may have been slightly different from the original Minnesota normative group on the standard Validity and Clinical scales since the MMPI was first developed. Second, it appears that these changes average less than one-half standard deviation (5 T points) and these small changes in profile elevation are not likely to have major impact on the clinical interpretation of the MMPI.

Colligan et al. (1983) continued the procedure of using K-corrected scores and they used the same correction weights on the same Clinical scales (Scales *1* [Hypochondriasis], *4* [Psychopathic Deviate], *7* [Psychasthenia], *8* [Schizophrenia], and *9* [Hypomania]) that had been suggested by Meehl and Hathaway (1946). However, they made one major change in the method whereby raw scores are transformed into T scores. The results of using different methods to compute T scores will be explored further in the next chapter.

There has been only limited research with the Colligan et al. (1983) norms. Colligan, Osborne, Swenson, and Offord (1985) reported the frequency with which codetypes occurred in four clinical samples, and the concordance between their contemporary norms and the original MMPI norms. Concordance of codetypes between the two sets of norms ranged from 40 to 60 percent for women and from 50 to 70 percent for men, whereas agreement on single scales ranged from 66 to 79 percent for women and from 69 to 79 percent for men.

Miller and Streiner (1986) reported the concordance between profiles generated by contemporary norms and the original MMPI norms in a large sample of psychiatric patients. They found that 48.4 percent of the profiles showed no changes in the two highest clinical scales, and another 15.1 percent of the profiles had the two highest clinical scales reversed. Thus, 63.5 percent of the profiles had the same codetype using the two sets of norms. In 23.6 percent of the profiles, the highest clinical scale remained the same while another clinical scale became the second highest scale. A totally unique codetype was produced in 9.4 percent of the profiles. Although it is important to know the concordance between codetypes generated by the two sets of norms, the primary issue remains whether the original or contemporary norms more accurately reflect external correlates.

Over the ensuing years Colligan and his colleagues have provided contemporary norms for Barron's (1953) Ego Strength scale (Colligan & Offord, 1987a), Welsh's (1956) Anxiety and Repression scales (Colligan & Offord, 1988a), MacAndrew's (1965) Alcoholism scale (Colligan & Offord, 1987b), Wiggins' (1966) Content scales (Colligan & Offord, 1988b), and the *F–K* index (Osborne, Colligan, & Offord, 1986).

Tables for converting raw scores into T scores so that the clinician can compare a patient's performance with a *contemporary* adult sample are available in Colligan et al. (1983, 1989). Separate tables are provided for men and women, so the clinician should be careful to use the correct table. Hsu and Betman (1986) have provided tables for converting the T scores for the original MMPI normative group into Colligan et al.'s (1983) contemporary norms and vice versa. Colligan et al. (1983) also illustrate a standard profile sheet for use with their contemporary norms (p. 421).

DEVELOPMENT OF THE MMPI-2

The MMPI-2 (Butcher et al., 1989)[9] represents the restandardization of the MMPI that marks the advent of a new era of clinical usage and research of this venerable inventory. Restandardization of the MMPI was needed to provide current norms for the inventory, develop a nationally representative and larger normative sample, provide appropriate representation of ethnic minorities, and update item content where needed. Continuity between the MMPI and the MMPI-2 was maintained because new criterion groups and item derivation procedures were *not* used on the standard Validity and Clinical scales. Thus, the items on the Validity and Clinical scales of the MMPI are essentially unchanged on the MMPI-2 except for the elimination of 13 items based on item content (see Table 1.5) and the rewording of 68 items.

The profile forms for the original MMPI (Profile 1.1) and the MMPI-2 (Profile 1.4) also are virtually identical. A quick comparison of Profiles 1.1 and 1.4 will not reveal any readily apparent differences between the two forms. Only on closer examination are any differences seen on the MMPI-2 profile form: the Cannot Say (*?*) scale has been moved to the bottom

---

9. There were several minor errors in the first printings of the *MMPI-2 Manual* that were corrected in subsequent printings (see page 24).

TABLE 1.5 Thirteen MMPI Items Dropped from the Standard Validity and Clinical Scales of the MMPI-2

F Scale

14. I have looseness in my bowels (diarrhea) once a month or more.
53. A minister can cure disease by praying and putting his hand on your head.
206. I am very religious (more than most people).
258. I believe there is a God.

Scale 1 (Hs)

63. I have had no difficulty in starting or holding my bowel movements.

Scale 2 (D)

58. Everything is turning out just as the prophets of the Bible said it would.
95. I attend religious services almost every week.
98. I believe in the second coming of Christ.

Scale 5 (Mf)

69. I am very strongly attracted by members of my own sex.
70. I used to like drop-the-handkerchief.
249. I believe there is a Devil and a Hell in afterlife.
295. I liked "Alice in Wonderland" by Lewis Carroll.

Scale 0 (Si)

462. I have had no difficulty starting or holding my urine.

Note. Minnesota Multiphasic Personality Inventory (MMPI). Copyright 1943 (renewed 1970), 1948, 1976, 1982 by the Regents of the University of Minnesota. All rights reserved. MMPI and Minnesota Multiphasic Inventory are trademarks of the University of Minnesota. Reproduced by permission of the publisher.

of the page, T scores of 65 are considered to be clinically significant instead of T scores of 70, and the T score distributions have been truncated at 30 so that T scores below 30 do not occur. (T scores also are truncated at 30 in the tables converting raw scores to T scores so information is not lost in using the standard profile form [see Table A.1 in Appendix A]).

In the development of the MMPI-2, the Restandardization Committee (Butcher et al., 1989) started with the 550 items on the original MMPI (i.e., they first deleted the 16 repeated items). They reworded 141 of these 550 items to eliminate outdated and sexist language and to make these items more easily understood. Many of these items were omitted on the original MMPI because clients did not understand them. Greene (1991, p. 57) provides examples of these items. Rewording these items did not change the correlations of the items with the total scale score in most cases (Ben-Porath & Butcher, 1989). The Restandardization Committee then added 154 provisional items that resulted in the 704 items in Form AX, which was used to collect the normative data for the MMPI-2.

When finalizing the items to be included on the MMPI-2, the Restandardization Committee deleted 77 items from the original MMPI in addition to the 13 items deleted from the standard Validity and Clinical scales and the 16 repeated items. Consequently, most special and research scales that have been developed on the MMPI are still capable of being scored unless the scale has an emphasis on religious content or the items are drawn predominantly from the last 150 items on the original MMPI. The content areas for these 77 items that were not retained plus the 13 items deleted from the standard Validity and Clinical scales can be seen in Table 1.6. Levitt (1990) also has grouped these 77 items into logical content categories and listed the actual items within each category.

TABLE 1.6 Content Areas of MMPI Items *Not* Retained on the MMPI-2

CONTENT AREA	NUMBER OF ITEMS
Interests/hobbies	17
Religion	16
Interpersonal relationships	14
Negative affects	12
Bodily functions	9
Miscellaneous	5
Sexuality	5
Sensory functions	4
Substance abuse	3
Blushing	3
Dreaming	2
Total	90

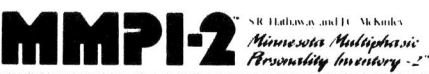

MMPI-2 ™ S R Hathaway and J C McKinley
*Minnesota Multiphasic
Personality Inventory -2™*

Profile for Basic Scales

Minnesota Multiphasic Personality Inventory-2
Copyright © by THE REGENTS OF THE UNIVERSITY OF MINNESOTA
1942, 1943 (renewed 1970), 1989. This Profile Form 1989.
All rights reserved. Distributed exclusively by NATIONAL COMPUTER SYSTEMS, INC
under license from The University of Minnesota.

"MMPI-2" and "Minnesota Multiphasic Personality Inventory-2" are trademarks owned by
The University of Minnesota. Printed in the United States of America.

Name **Cherie Jones**

Address **2894 Albion Way**

Occupation **Secretary**   Date Tested **3/4/99**

Education **13th** Age **27** Marital Status Single

Referred by **Dr. Smiley**

MMPI-2 Code **26'43-1078/59** **F-KL**

Scorer's Initials **HG**

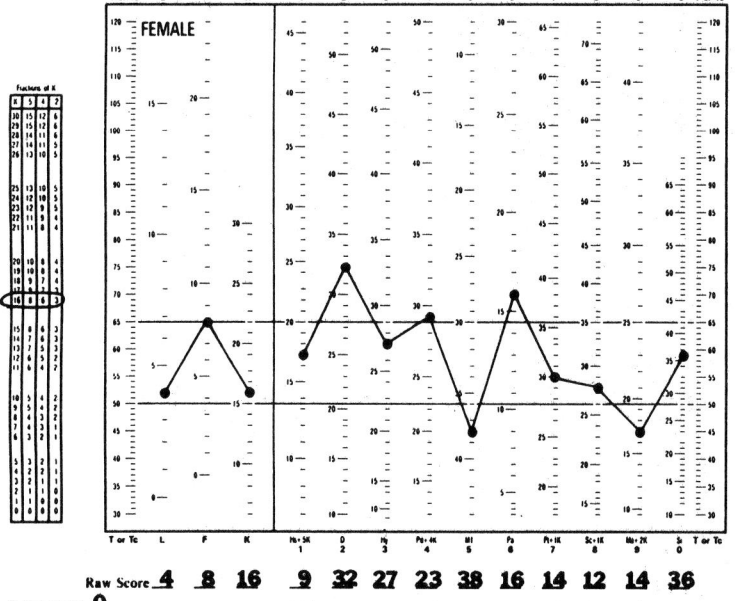

	L	F	K	Hs+.5K 1	D 2	Hy 3	Pd+.4K 4	Mf 5	Pa 6	Pt+1K 7	Sc+1K 8	Ma+.2K 9	Si 0	
Raw Score	4	8	16	9	32	27	23	38	16	14	12	14	36	
? Raw Score 0														
K to be Added			8				6			16	16	3		
Raw Score with K			17		29					30	28	17		

PROFILE 1.4

Note. Minnesota Multiphasic Personality Inventory-2 (MMPI-2). Copyright © 1942, 1943 (renewed 1970), 1989 by the Regents of the University of Minnesota. Reproduced by permission of the publisher. "MMPI-2" and "Minnesota Multiphasic Personality Inventory-2" are trademarks owned by the University of Minnesota

The Restandardization Committee included 68 of the 141 items that had been rewritten, and they incorporated 107 of the provisional items to assess major content areas that were not covered in the original MMPI item pool. The rationale for including and dropping items from Form AX that resulted in the 567 items on the MMPI-2 has not been made explicit to date. Table 1.7 illustrates the changes that were made in the transition from the 566 items on the MMPI to the 567 items on the MMPI-2.

The MMPI-2 was standardized on a sample of 2,600 individuals who resided in seven different states (California, Minnesota, North Carolina, Ohio, Pennsylvania, Virginia, and Washington) to reflect national census parameters on age, marital status, ethnicity, education, and occupational status. The demographic characteristics of this sample can be seen in Table 1.8.

The normative sample for the MMPI-2 varies significantly from the original normative sample for the MMPI in a number of areas: years of education,

TABLE 1.7 Changes in Items from the MMPI to the MMPI-2

	NUMBER OF ITEMS
MMPI	566
Drop 16 repeated items	–16
Drop 13 items from the standard validity and clinical scales	–13
Drop 77 items from the last 167 items	–77
Total	460
Add 86 items for the new scales	+86
Add 21 unscored items	+21
MMPI-2	567

representation of ethnic minorities, and occupational status. The individuals in the normative sample for the MMPI-2 also are more representative of the United States as a whole because national census pa-

TABLE 1.8 Demographic Variables for the MMPI-2 Normative Sample

VARIABLE	N	PERCENTAGE	CENSUS	VARIABLE	N	PERCENTAGE	CENSUS
Gender				*Education*			
Female	1,462	56.2%		Part high school	129	5.0%	33.5%
Male	1,138	43.8		High school	640	24.6	34.4
				Part college	651	25.0	15.7
Ethnicity				College graduate	700	26.9	8.7
White	2,117	81.4%	85.0	Postgraduate	480	18.5	7.8
Black	314	12.1	10.5				
Native American	77	3.0	0.5	*Marital Status*			
Hispanic	73	2.8	—	Married	1,717	66.0%	59.0%
Asian American	19	.7	1.5	Never married	518	19.9	25.9
Other			2.5	Divorced	220	8.5	5.7
				Widowed	89	3.4	7.2
Age				Separated	56	2.2	2.3
18–19	50	1.9%	5.4%				
20–29	641	24.7	25.2	*Occupation*			
30–39	769	29.6	19.3	Professional	1,060	40.8%	15.6%
40–49	401	15.4	14.0	Managerial	277	10.7	11.2
50–59	321	12.3	14.3	Skilled	215	8.3	25.5
60–69	277	10.7	11.5	Clerical	365	14.0	27.2
70–79	120	4.6	7.5	Laborer	205	7.9	20.6
80–89	21	.8	3.1	None of the above	463	17.8	—
				(Missing data)	15	.6	—

Note. Adapted from Butcher et al. (1989).

rameters were utilized in their collection. However, they still varied from the census parameters on years of education and occupational status. The potential impact of this higher level of education and occupation in the MMPI-2 normative sample on codetype and scale interpretation has been a focus of ongoing concern (Caldwell, 1990; Helmes & Reddon, 1993). However, Schinka and LaLone (1997) developed a census-matched subsample within the MMPI-2 restandardization sample and found only one difference that exceeded 3 T score points between these two samples on the standard Validity and Clinical scales, Content scales, and Supplementary scales. A more complete discussion of the impact of demographic variables on MMPI-2 scores will occur in Chapter 9.

Profiles 1.2 and 1.3 (triangles) illustrate the average scores for men and women on the standard Validity and Clinical scales in the MMPI-2 normative sample when plotted on the *original* MMPI norms. The MMPI-2 normative sample scores are about 3 to 5 T points higher on most of these scales. Only on

Scales *L* (Lie), *1* (Hypochondriasis), and *0* (Social Introversion) are their scores nearly identical. Thus, the transition to the MMPI-2 norms will mean that the new profiles are slightly less elevated when compared to the original MMPI norms. It also should be noted that the average scores for the standard Validity and Clinical scales for the MMPI-2 in Profiles 1.2 and 1.3 correspond very closely to those reported by Colligan et al. (1983) (diamonds) and Pancoast and Archer (1989) (squares).

It also is possible to compare the average scores of the MMPI-2 normative group on the Wiener and Harmon (Wiener, 1948) Obvious and Subtle subscales (see Chapter 3 for a discussion of these subscales) with the original Minnesota normative group (see Profiles 1.5 and 1.6). It is readily apparent in Profiles 1.5 and 1.6 that the MMPI-2 normative group and the original Minnesota normative group have almost identical scores on the obvious subscales (excluding *Ma–O*), whereas their scores are very different on the subtle subscales (excluding *D–S*).

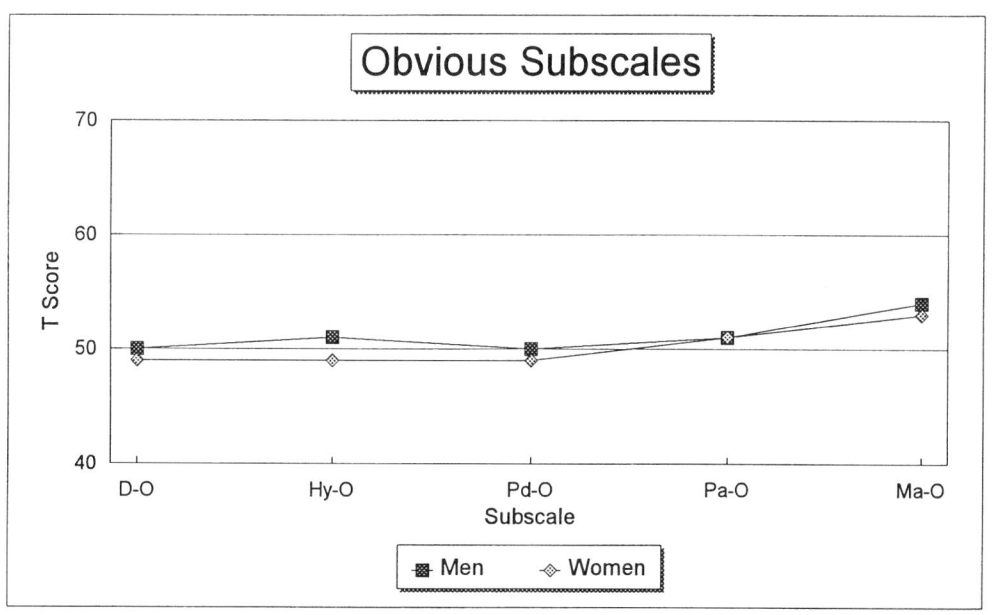

PROFILE 1.5

Note. Minnesota Multiphasic Personality Inventory-2 (MMPI-2). Copyright © 1942, 1943 (renewed 1970), 1989 by the Regents of the University of Minnesota. Reproduced by permission of the publisher. "MMPI-2" and "Minnesota Multiphasic Personality Inventory-2" are trademarks owned by the University of Minnesota.

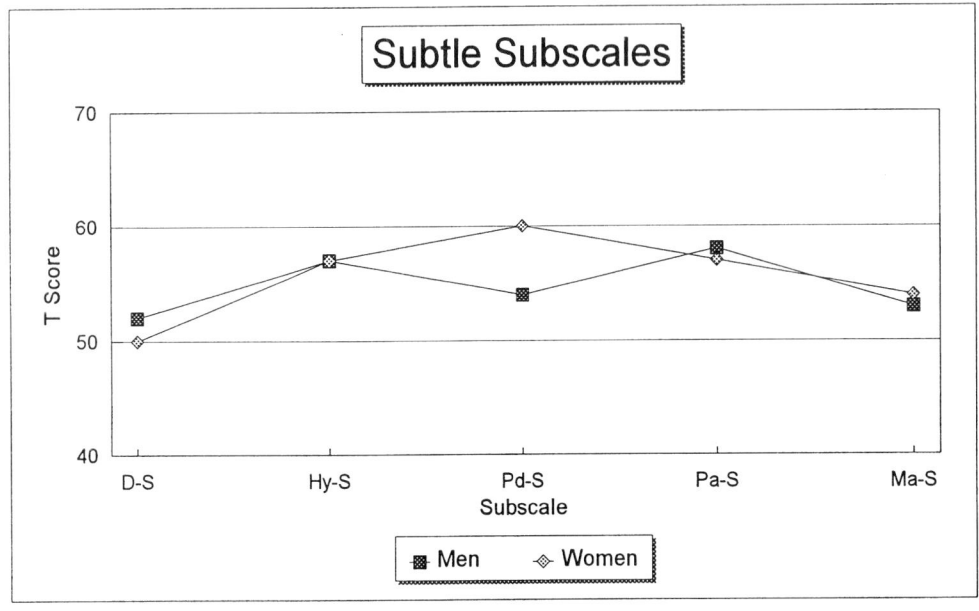

PROFILE 1.6

Note. Minnesota Multiphasic Personality Inventory-2 (MMPI-2). Copyright © 1942, 1943 (renewed 1970), 1989 by the Regents of the University of Minnesota. Reproduced by permission of the publisher. "MMPI-2" and "Minnesota Multiphasic Personality Inventory-2" are trademarks owned by the University of Minnesota..

Thus, the differences between the MMPI-2 normative group and the original Minnesota group in Profiles 1.2 and 1.3 predominantly reflect the influence of the subtle items on these five subscales. It does not appear that the relatively high level of education and occupational status characteristic of the MMPI-2 normative group adversely affected scores on the obvious subscales because these scores are very similar to the original Minnesota normative group. The stability or consistency of the scores on the obvious subscales over five decades is not unexpected given that the symptoms, signs, and behaviors characteristic of major categories of psychopathology have not changed. That is, the major symptoms of depression in 1940 such as depressed mood, decreased libido, weight loss, and memory problems still are the major symptoms of depression in the 1990s. Again, it can be noted that the scores of the MMPI-2 normative group on the Wiener and Harmon Obvious and Subtle subscales correspond very closely to those reported by Colligan et al. (1983).

The *K*-correction procedure, which will be described in detail in Chapters 2 and 3, continues to be used with the MMPI-2 with the same *K*-weights being used on the same Clinical scales. However, in a major departure from the MMPI, the method for transforming raw scores into T scores was changed for all Clinical scales except Scales *5* (Masculinity-Femininity) and *0* (Social Introversion) and the new Content scales. The implications of this change in method to compute T scores will be discussed in Chapter 2.

A number of Supplementary scales are available to assist the clinician in interpreting the standard Validity and Clinical scales on the MMPI-2. Most of these Supplementary scales will be familiar to the clinician who has used the MMPI: Barron's (1953) Ego Strength scale; Gough, McClosky, and Meehl's (1951) Dominance scale; Gough, McClosky, and Meehl's (1952) Social Responsibility scale; Kleinmuntz's (1961a) College Maladjustment scale; MacAndrew's (1965) Alcoholism scale; Megargee,

Cook, and Mendelson's (1967) Overcontrolled Hostility scale; and Welsh's (1956) Anxiety and Repression scales. These scales have had a few minor changes made in them at the item level. Ten new scales are represented in the Supplementary scales: two gender-role scales (Gender Role—Feminine; Gender Role—Masculine), two post-traumatic stress disorder scales (Post Traumatic Stress Disorder—Keane; Post Traumatic Stress Disorder—Schlenger), two addiction scales (Addiction Admission and Addiction Potential), a marital distress scale (Marital Distress), and three Validity scales (Back *F;* True Response Inconsistency; Variable Response Inconsistency). The three new Validity scales will be discussed in Chapter 3; the remainder of the Supplementary scales will be reviewed in Chapter 6.

A total of 15 new Content scales have been developed for the MMPI-2 (Butcher, Graham, Williams, & Ben-Porath, 1990). These scales are Anxiety, Fears, Obsessions, Depression, Health Concerns, Bizarre Mentation, Anger, Cynicism, Antisocial Practices, Type A, Low Self-Esteem, Social Discomfort, Family Problems, Work Interference, and Negative Treatment Indicators. Component scales also have been developed for the new content scales to facilitate their interpretation (Ben-Porath & Sherwood, 1993). These new content and content component scales will be described in Chapter 5.

Unlike the MMPI, which was used with all ages, *the MMPI-2 is to be used only with adults 18 years of age and older.* Adolescents are to be tested with the MMPI-A (Butcher et al., 1992), which is designed specifically for them. The use of the MMPI with adolescents and the MMPI-A will be discussed in Chapter 9.

MMPI VERSUS MMPI-2

In many respects the question of whether the clinician should utilize the MMPI or the MMPI-2 is unnecessarily restrictive. Because only 13 MMPI items were deleted from the standard Validity and Clinical scales, the MMPI and the MMPI-2 are virtually identical on these scales. The rewording of the items on the MMPI-2 that removed sexist and outdated language has resulted in clients omitting fewer items and raising fewer questions about the meanings of words, which allevi-

ates a number of potential problems in administration. One major change in item content between the MMPI and MMPI-2 was the deletion of all but one religious item on the MMPI-2. If the clinician believes that the religious items would be important for evaluating a specific client, it would be necessary to administer the MMPI. Several content areas such as alcohol and drug abuse, suitability for treatment, and work-related problems also were added to the MMPI-2 that were not well represented in the MMPI. Most clients will find the items in the MMPI-2 booklet more "user friendly," and it would behoove clinicians to use the MMPI-2 items rather than the MMPI items. The raw scores on MMPI-2 also can be transformed into T scores on the MMPI if the clinician desires to do so by using Appendix K (pp. 157–161) of the *MMPI-2 Manual* (Butcher et al., 1989) or Appendix F of this text. The University of Minnesota Press has announced that it will discontinue the publication and distribution of the original MMPI on September 1, 1999, which will relieve the clinician of the burden of deciding whether to administer the MMPI or MMPI-2.

The differences between the normative groups for the MMPI and MMPI-2 that were described earlier and the different method used for calculating T scores on the MMPI-2, which will be described in Chapter 2, have altered the relationships among the Clinical scales and, thus, the relative frequencies with which high-point scales and codetypes occur has changed. Concordance rates for codetypes between the MMPI-2 and MMPI are reported to range from 57 to 70 percent in clinical samples (Butcher et al., 1989), and appear to be similar to those reported for the Colligan et al. (1983) norms when compared to the original MMPI norms. An important question about the MMPI-2 involves whether the correlates of codetypes that were derived on the MMPI can be applied to the MMPI-2. For example, if a client has a *2-4/4-2* codetype on the MMPI-2, can the clinician use the correlates of a *2-4/4-2* codetype that were developed on the MMPI for interpreting the profile? An associated question is even more difficult to answer. If the client has a *2-8/8-2* codetype and would have had a *2-4/4-2* codetype if MMPI T scores rather than MMPI-2 T scores had been used, are correlates of the former or latter codetype, or even some other codetype, more appropriate for this client? Clearly such questions require an empirical answer, but studies of the correlates of specific MMPI-2 codetypes still are very sparse given that the MMPI-2 has been in existence for almost a decade. Exploration of this complex issue will be deferred until Chapter 7.

INTERPRETATION OF THE MMPI-2

The interpretation of the MMPI-2 is a multistage process and it is important that each step be undertaken sequentially. The first task for the clinician is to establish the proper conditions for the administration of the MMPI-2 to ensure the cooperation of the client in the assessment process (Chapter 2). Then the clinician needs to determine the validity of this specific administration of the MMPI-2 (Chapter 3). If the items have been endorsed consistently and accurately to produce a valid MMPI-2 profile, the clinician next must understand the interpretation of the individual Clinical scales (Chapter 4) as well as the resulting codetype (Chapter 7). Finally, the clinician can examine the Content and Supplementary scales and the individual items to determine how they amplify the description of the codetype (Chapters 5 and 6). This entire process will be illustrated as it is followed by a clinician and the computer in interpreting the MMPI-2 profiles for two clinical cases (Chapter 8).

The clinician also must consider whether demographic variables will alter the interpretation of the MMPI-2 profile (Chapter 9). The use of the MMPI and its revision, the MMPI-A, with adolescents illustrates how age impacts the interpretation of the profile (Chapter 10).

CURRENT STATUS OF THE MMPI-2

There are a number of major reviews of the MMPI-2 (Butcher, Graham, & Ben-Porath, 1995; Butcher & Rouse, 1996; Caldwell, 1997c; Greene, Gwin, & Staal, 1997; Helmes & Reddon, 1993; Weed & Butcher, 1992) that provide summaries from a variety of perspectives on this venerable instrument, which will not be summarized here. These reviews provide the interested reader with an excellent starting point for looking at the current status of the MMPI-2. Butcher et al. (1995) and Greene et al. (1997) also outline the general steps that researchers need to follow and issues that need to be addressed in conducting research with the MMPI-2. Hopefully researchers will heed the advice dispensed in these reviews in order to enhance the quality of the data that are being collected.

MMPI-2 ERRATA

There has not been a mechanism developed to date whereby any errors that are found in the MMPI-2 are brought to the attention of users in a systematic manner. As a consequence, the several very minor errors that do exist are not likely to be known by most clinicians. These errors in the MMPI-2 that have been identified up to the time of the publication of this text are collated in Table 1.9. It is particularly important that clinicians verify that these corrections have been made if their MMPI-2s are scored by computer. The most reliable method for checking computer scoring is to hand score the scales listed in Table 1.9 for several MMPI-2s using the items listed in Appendix B of this text and to make sure that the raw scores match exactly.

The University of Minnesota Press will be releasing new profile forms for the MMPI-2 and a new edition of the *MMPI-2 Manual* (Butcher et al., 1989) in the spring of 2000 that will be correcting these errors.

TABLE 1.9   MMPI-2 Errata

SCALE	ERROR	CORRECTION
1 (Hypochondriasis) + .5*K*		
Men	$M = 12.78$; $SD = 3.86$	$M = 12.84$; $SD = 3.82$
Women	$M = 13.69$; $SD = 4.05$	$M = 13.70$; $SD = 4.05$
	Latest printing of *MMPI-2 Manual*	*MMPI-2 Manual* (2000)
4 (Psychopathic Deviate) + .4*K*		
Men	$M = 22.65$; $SD = 4.67$	$M = 22.69$; $SD = 4.63$
Women	$M = 22.21$; $SD = 4.65$	$M = 22.22$; $SD = 4.52$
	Latest printing of *MMPI-2 Manual*	*MMPI-2 Manual* (2000)
Pd_1 (Familial Discord)		
Men	$M = 1.78$	$M = 1.79$
Pd_2 (Authority Conflict)		
Men	$M = 3.29$; $SD = 1.52$	$M = 3.48$; $SD = 1.50$
Women	$M = 2.35$; $SD = 1.34$	$M = 2.55$; $SD = 1.29$
T Scores	First printings of *MMPI-2 Manual*	Subsequent printings
Pd_3 (Imperturbability)		
Men	$M = 3.64$; $SD = 1.71$	$M = 3.83$; $SD = 1.69$
Women	$M = 3.37$; $SD = 1.73$	$M = 3.58$; $SD = 1.71$
T Scores	First printings of *MMPI-2 Manual*	Subsequent printings
Pd_4 (Social Alienation)		
Men	$M = 3.74$; $SD = 1.89$	$M = 3.93$; $SD = 1.90$
Women	$M = 3.98$; $SD = 1.93$	$M = 4.18$; $SD = 1.89$
T Scores	First printings of *MMPI-2 Manual*	Subsequent printings
7 (Psychasthenia) + 1*K*		
Men	$M = 26.43$; $SD = 5.00$	$M = 26.53$; $SD = 4.81$
Women	$M = 27.70$; $SD = 5.10$	$M = 27.72$; $SD = 5.07$
	Latest printing of *MMPI-2 Manual*	*MMPI-2 Manual* (2000)
8 (Schizophrenia) + 1*K*		
Men	$M = 26.40$; $SD = 5.92$	$M = 26.50$; $SD = 5.73$
Women	$M = 26.25$; $SD = 5.97$	$M = 26.27$; $SD = 5.93$
	Latest printing of *MMPI-2 Manual*	*MMPI-2 Manual* (2000)
9 (Hypomania) + .2*K*		
Men	$M = 19.93$; $SD = 4.29$	$M = 19.95$; $SD = 4.28$
	Latest printing of *MMPI-2 Manual*	*MMPI-2 Manual* (2000)
0 (Social Introversion)	Item 328 False	Item 328 True
Men	Item 358 False	Item 358 True
Women	$M = 25.86$; $SD = 8.57$	$M = 24.74$; $SD = 8.84$
T Scores	$M = 27.98$; $SD = 9.18$	$M = 26.90$; $SD = 9.46$
	First printings of *MMPI-2 Manual*	Subsequent printings

(continued)

TABLE 1.9 MMPI-2 Errata (continued)

SCALE	ERROR	CORRECTION
VRIN (Variable Response Inconsistency)		
Men	$M = 4.52$; $SD = 2.39$	$M = 5.07$; $SD = 2.62$
Women	$M = 4.47$; $SD = 2.28$	$M = 5.04$; $SD = 2.51$
	First printings of *MMPI-2 Manual*	Subsequent printings
GF (Gender Role—Feminine)	Item 203 False	Item 203 True
Men	$M = 27.32$; $SD = 4.70$	$M = 27.93$; $SD = 4.72$
Women	$M = 36.86$; $SD = 3.85$	$M = 37.68$; $SD = 3.88$
T Scores	Latest printings of *MMPI-2 Manual*	*MMPI-2 Manual* (2000)
GM (Gender Role—Masculine)	Item 331 True	Item 331 False
Men	$M = 37.49$; $SD = 4.56$	$M = 37.87$; $SD = 4.87$
Women	$M = 28.81$; $SD = 6.16$	$M = 28.83$; $SD = 6.51$
T Scores	Latest printings of *MMPI-2 Manual*	*MMPI-2 Manual* (2000)
MAC-R (MacAndrew Alcoholism)	Item 387 False	Item 387 True
Men	$M = 21.72$; $SD = 4.32$	$M = 20.81$; $SD = 4.37$
Women	$M = 19.78$; $SD = 3.65$	$M = 18.85$; $SD = 3.69$
T Scores	First printings of *MMPI-2 Manual*	Subsequent printings
Appendix K	First printing of *MMPI-2 Manual*	Subsequent printings

Note. The later printings of the *MMPI-2 Manual* containing these corrections have Appendix A starting on page 57. The corrected hand-scoring template indicates that it was reprinted in June 1995 for *Si* (Social Introversion) and in September 1995 for *MAC-R* (MacAndrew Alcoholism).

CHAPTER 2

Administration and Scoring

Administering and scoring the MMPI-2 are usually straightforward procedures that can be handled by a competent psychometrician. The apparent ease of MMPI-2 administration sometimes leads clinicians to underestimate the importance of establishing appropriate conditions for taking the MMPI-2, clarifying the test instructions if necessary, and unobtrusively monitoring the client's progress. Occasionally clinicians inappropriately relegate the task of MMPI-2 administration to a secretary or clerk, who may administer the test incorrectly. The ease of MMPI-2 administration does not absolve the clinician of the responsibility for ensuring that it is handled properly.

Before administering the inventory for the first time, the clinician should read the *MMPI-2 Manual* (Butcher et al., 1989) and Chapter 1 of *An MMPI Handbook* (Dahlstrom et al., 1972). The *Handbook,* the definitive reference on the MMPI, is particularly useful when the clinician anticipates any unusual circumstance in administration or whenever a more general text omits answering any question. Although the *Handbook* addresses issues in the administration of the MMPI, the clinician should realize that the suggestions also are appropriate for the MMPI-2.

Once administered, the MMPI-2 can be scored either by hand or by computer through commercial scoring services. This chapter will describe the procedures for scoring and profiling the MMPI-2; examples of a clinician's interpretation of the MMPI-2 profile and several computer interpretive services will be provided in Chapter 8. This chapter also will address several related issues, such as the various forms of the MMPI-2, T score derivation, the *K*-correction procedure, and linear and uniform T scores.

ADMINISTRATION

The first issue in the administration of the MMPI-2 or any other psychological test is ensuring that the client

is invested in the process. A few extra minutes spent answering any questions the client may have about why the MMPI-2 is being administered and how the results will be used in determining the course of treatment will pay excellent dividends. Fischer (1994) has described the process of individualizing psychological assessment in which the client and the clinician collaborate to obtain the desired information. Finn (1996) has written a splendid text on making the assessment process with the MMPI-2 therapeutic for the client, which should be mandatory reading for all clinicians. The major thesis of his text is that the clinician should determine what the client wants to learn from the assessment process and then make sure that the client gets that feedback. He also provides specific examples of how clients can be given feedback about troublesome behaviors and symptoms that will be very insightful for the clinician who is just learning this process. If clinicians will follow the procedures suggested by Fischer and Finn, they should find that validity issues become virtually a nonexistent process, because it does not makes sense for a client to try to invalidate the MMPI-2 if he or she genuinely wants to learn something from its administration and is an active participant or collaborator in the process.

Reading level is a crucial factor in determining whether or not a person can complete the MMPI-2; inadequate reading ability is a major cause of inconsistent patterns of item endorsement. Butcher et al. (1989) suggest that most clients who have had at least *eight* years of formal education can take the MMPI-2 with little or no difficulty because the items are written on an eighth-grade level or less. A number of authors (Dahlstrom, Archer, Hopkins, Jackson, & Dahlstrom, 1994; Paolo, Ryan, & Smith, 1991; Schinka & Borum, 1993) have studied the readability of MMPI-2 items in the last few years. Although they found that their results varied depending upon the specific method used to assess readability, there was general concurrence that the *average* readability of the MMPI-2 and MMPI-A is in range of the *fifth to sixth* grade. The scales requiring the highest reading levels were *9* (Hypomania), the three Content scales of *ASP* (Antisocial Practices), *CYN* (Cynicism), and *TPA* (Type A), and a number of the Harris and Lingoes (1955) subscales: Hy_2 (Need for Affection), Pa_3 (Naivete), Sc_5 (Lack of Ego Mastery, Defective Inhibition), Ma_1 (Amorality), Ma_2 (Psychomotor Acceleration), Ma_3 (Imperturbability), and Ma_4 (Ego Inflation). Most of these scales had at least 25 percent of their items that required more than an eighth-grade reading level. It is important to realize that these estimates of the required grade level are very conservative because they are based on assessing the readability of individual MMPI-2 items or groups of items. They are *not* based on the difficulty of understanding what is meant by saying either "true" or "false" to a specific item. The reader can assess this problem directly by trying to understand exactly what is meant by saying "false" to an MMPI-2 item that is worded in the negative. For example, what does a client actually mean when he or she says "false" to the MMPI-2 item "I do not always tell the truth?"[1] Schinka and Borum did suggest that clients be asked to read MMPI-2 items 114, 226, and 445 if they have completed less than a tenth-grade education to determine whether their reading skills are adequate. Dahlstrom et al. also noted that the instructions for both the MMPI-2 and MMPI-A actually were more difficult than the items on the test so clinicians should be sure the client fully understands them.

This issue of the reading level required to complete the MMPI-2 becomes more serious when it is realized that most freshman-level college texts are written at the ninth-grade level. Despite the increased years of education of most people, reading level can still be a potential problem. Clients with limited educational opportunity still may be able to take the MMPI-2 if their reading level is adequate. If there is

any reason to suspect that a person's reading level may be deficient, the clinician should ascertain the person's reading level by administering a brief reading test. Dahlstrom et al. (1994) recommended that the Gray Oral Reading Test (GORT-3: Wiederholt & Bryant, 1992) be used if a screening instrument for reading ability is needed. Reading level becomes especially important among ethnic minorities who, despite their fluency in speaking English, may be unable to read English. Anyone who cannot read may be defensive about revealing this deficiency; at times persons have responded to all 567 items even though they were unable to read them.

Although less important than reading ability, a person's age and intelligence also can affect his or her ability to complete the MMPI-2. The *MMPI-2 is to be administered to persons who are 18 years of age and older,* while the *MMPI-A is to be administered to adolescents 18 years of age and younger.* Sometimes with persons who are 18 years old it is not clear whether they should be administered the MMPI-A or the MMPI-2. The *MMPI-A Manual* (Butcher et al., 1992) states that "a suggested guideline would be to use the MMPI-A for those 18-year-olds who are in high school and the MMPI-2 for those who are in college, working, or otherwise living an independent adult lifestyle" (p. 23). For example, an 18-year-old who is married and supporting herself probably could be given the MMPI-2, while an 18-year-old who is single and still living at home with his parents might be given the MMPI-A. This decision must be made carefully because the MMPI-A and MMPI-2 have slightly different item pools even on the standard Validity and Clinical scales, because 58 items were deleted on the MMPI-A compared to 13 items on the MMPI-2 in the transition from the MMPI. Shaevel and Archer (1996) found substantial differences that could range as high as 15 T points in the performance of 18-year-olds depending upon whether MMPI-2 or MMPI-A norms were used. They suggested that both an MMPI-2 and MMPI-A profile be plotted in those clients for whom it is unclear which set of norms is most appropriate using the foregoing guidelines. More information on the performance of 18-year-olds on the MMPI-2 will be provided in Chapter 9. There is no upper age limit for the MMPI-2 with persons in

---

1. Minnesota Multiphasic Personality Inventory-2 (MMPI-2). Copyright © 1942, 1943 (renewed 1970), 1989 by the Regents of the University of Minnesota. Reproduced by permission of the publisher. "MMPI-2" and "Minnesota Multiphasic Personality Inventory-2" are trademarks owned by the University of Minnesota.

their 70s well represented in the MMPI-2 normative group. Persons who score below a Wechsler Adult Intelligence Scale—Revised (Wechsler, 1980) IQ of 70 probably will be unable to complete the MMPI-2.

Even when a person has inadequate reading skills or an IQ below 70, the clinician need not automatically abandon the idea of administering the MMPI-2, because such persons sometimes can complete the inventory if it is presented orally. An audio-cassette-taped version of the MMPI-2 serves this purpose that is available in English and Spanish. The cassette tape should be utilized any time that the items are to be presented orally rather than having someone read the MMPI-2 items to the client. In addition to the amount of time that is required for the person reading the items, it is difficult for the person to maintain a standardized procedure. Edwards, Holmes, and Carvajal (1998) found few significant differences between MMPI-2s read by an examiner and administered by the booklet in college students. However, these students had T scores 5 to 7 points lower on Scales 6 (Paranoia) and 8 (Schizophrenia), which suggests that they were reluctant to endorse items that might reflect more severe psychopathology in the presence of an examiner. Dahlstrom et al. (1972) reported that taped administrations of the MMPI were effective with IQs as low as 65 and reading comprehension levels as low as the third grade.

Brauer (1993) translated the MMPI into American Sign Language (ASL) and found adequate linguistic equivalence between the two forms. Brauer (1992) also found no systematic effects among different signers on a set of 38 critical items from the MMPI. The use of the Brauer-Gallaudet ASL version of the MMPI-2 with deaf individuals seems warranted based on this limited research.

Few explicit guidelines exist regarding how much assistance the clinician can provide for a client who has marginal reading skills. It seems reasonable to give standard dictionary definitions of terms if the client asks. The clinician should refrain, however, from administering the MMPI-2 by reading the items aloud because this practice is a significant change from standardized administration and its effects are unknown. Hopefully, future research will compare the responses obtained when the clinician reads items aloud with responses obtained in the standard administration. Until such research is conducted, the clinician should consider administering some other personality instrument to persons with limited intelligence or reading ability unless standard definitions provide adequate clarification or the taped version can be used.

Psychiatric impairment rarely precludes taking the MMPI-2 unless the client is extremely agitated and unable to sit still long enough to complete the test. Clients who are severely depressed or noncommunicative frequently can complete the MMPI-2, providing the clinician with valuable information that might otherwise be unavailable. Such clients usually feel pleased that they can complete the task and relieved that other clients have had experiences similar to their own, as evidenced by items referring to such experiences on the MMPI-2.

After determining that the person is capable of completing the MMPI-2, the clinician should ensure that the individual is seated comfortably and provided with a pencil for taking the test. If a pencil is used in taking the MMPI-2, the client can easily change any responses if so desired. Few problems generally occur in administration so the MMPI-2 can be given to small groups of individuals as long as there is sufficient room so that each person's privacy can be respected.

Giving a brief explanation of why the test is being administered and what uses will be made of the results, as well as answering any other questions that the client may have about testing, will pay tremendous dividends in avoiding invalid profiles. Clients also should be told whether they will be provided with feedback on their results. In most, if not all, instances, clients should be provided with such feedback, which will enhance their motivation to complete the MMPI-2 in an appropriate manner. Friedman, Webb, and Lewak (1989, pp. 43–47) provide illustrations of common questions asked about taking the MMPI with their suggested answers. The client should read the instructions, the clinician should answer any questions about them, and then the client should proceed at his or her own pace in completing the test. More than 90 percent of the persons taking the MMPI-2 will not need any explanation of the instructions, and they will complete the test in 60 to 90 minutes.

One common question asked by clients is whether they should report prior feelings or current ones. The clinician should clarify that *the client should report current feelings and experiences.* Clients also occasionally questioned the appropriateness of the content of some MMPI items, particularly those related to gender, bodily functions such as elimination, and religion (Butcher & Tellegen, 1966; Walker & Ward, 1969). Most of these objectionable items have been deleted from the MMPI-2, so there should be few objections to item content. Clients who raise objections to item content frequently can be reassured by being told that their answers will remain confidential and that their answers to groups of items, rather than individual items, are what is important. If this reassurance is insufficient, the client may be allowed to omit an objectionable item. The number of such omissions must be minimized, however, because the validity of the entire test becomes an issue if the client omits more than 10 items (see Chapter 3).

If the client still objects to many items, the clinician may need to use some other personality instrument. Exploring more fully the reasons for the client's reluctance to complete the MMPI-2 also might be useful. Clients are most likely to object to item content when the MMPI-2 is being used for personnel selection; they may have legitimate questions about the relevance of such items to job performance. In such situations, the clinician should explain how the results from the MMPI-2 will be used and how they are relevant to personnel selection.

Once or twice during the test session, the clinician should unobtrusively check on the client's progress. If possible, and particularly if the client appears confused, the clinician should verify that the client is placing the answers correctly on the answer sheet. The clinician should be available throughout the test session in case any questions arise.

Although it is preferable to have the client complete the MMPI-2 in a single session, it is *not* mandatory to do so. In such a case the client should be encouraged to complete the MMPI-2 within a few days at most in order to minimize the possibility of any significant changes in the client's current status during the testing period. Some clients are relieved to know that they may complete the MMPI-2 across

several days because its length may appear formidable if it is to be completed in one session. Awareness of the client's need to complete the MMPI-2 across several days will increase the likelihood of obtaining a valid MMPI-2.

COMPUTER ADMINISTRATION

The MMPI-2 can also be administered by computer wherein the client sits in front of a terminal and responds to the items as they are presented on the screen. Because the MMPI-2 items are copyrighted, clinicians must lease the software to be used on the computer from the test distributor.

Honaker (1988) has provided a critical review of the comparability of hand and computer MMPI administrations and concluded that (1) computer administration is generally viewed in a more positive light and takes less time to complete, (2) individuals are ranked similarly across the two procedures, and (3) computer administration may produce lower overall profiles. Honaker describes a number of methodologic issues that must be addressed before clinicians can assume that booklet- and computer-administered MMPIs or MMPI-2s yield equivalent scores. Watson, Thomas, and Anderson (1992) performed a meta-analysis of comparisons of booklet- and computer-administered MMPIs and found that computer-administered MMPIs consistently had slightly lower T scores on most of the standard Validity and Clinical scales. These differences averaged only 0.73 T point, however, and would have no practical impact on the interpretation of the MMPI because they would reflect less than one item and are smaller than the standard error of measurement in all comparisons. In a similar meta-analysis Finger and Ones (1998) concluded that booklet- and computer-administered MMPIs were psychometrically equivalent.

Watson, Manifold, Klett, Brown, Thomas, and Anderson (1990) also reported that computer-administered MMPIs were completed much faster than booklet-administered MMPIs, and that their subjects preferred the computer-administered MMPI. It appears safe to conclude that computer-administered MMPI-2s will be essentially equivalent to booklet-administered MMPI-2s because of the extremely small differences in T scores between the two modes of administration.

There has been some interest shown in computer-adaptive administration of the MMPI-2 (Ben-Porath, Slutske, & Butcher, 1989; Roper, Ben-Porath, & Butcher, 1991, 1995). The essence of computer-adaptive administration involves deleting the remaining items on a scale once it is clear that the person is not endorsing them in the deviant direction. Computer-adaptive administration of the MMPI-2 results in a time savings because individuals are not administered items that they have indicated are not applicable to them. In addition to saving time, it seems that clients should be more satisfied with the assessment process because it is tailored for them. For example, if the items on Scale *2* (Depression) were rank-ordered as an index of depression, once the person had not endorsed the first 5 to 10 items, the remaining items would not need to be administered. Since the MMPI-2 Validity and Clinical scales are multidimensional, this method of adapting the administration is not appropriate. One alternative would be to stop administering the items once it is no longer possible to achieve a T score of 65 or higher on a specific scale, the "countdown method." The order in which the items are presented typically is based on their frequency of endorsement in the MMPI-2 normative sample (Butcher et al., 1989) with the least frequently endorsed items administered first. Since a man has to endorse 26 of the 57 items on Scale *2* to achieve a T score of 66, once he has answered 32 items in the nondeviant direction it is no longer possible to achieve a T score of 65 or higher so the remaining items would be deleted. If the researcher is interested in knowing the degree of elevation above a T score of 65, all of the remaining items on Scale *2* would be administered. If the researcher is only interested in whether Scale *2* is at or above a T score of 65, the remaining items could be deleted once he has endorsed 26 of them. This latter alternative is viable when the research is only interested in the MMPI-2 codetype and not the actual elevation of the scales.

Computer-adaptive administrations of the MMPI-2 have resulted in a reduction of nearly 28 percent of the items that were administered with more items needing to be administered in clinical samples as would be expected because they are more likely to elevate scales at or above a T score of 65 (Ben-Porath et al., 1989; Roper et al., 1991, 1995). The results in all of these studies were comparable to booklet-administered MMPI-2s. Further exploration of computer-adaptive administration of the MMPI-2 seems warranted because of its ability to provide comparable information frequently with considerable time savings for individuals.

Honaker (1988; Honaker, Harrell, & Buffaloe, 1988) and Butcher (1987) provide excellent overviews of the issues that are involved in the use of computers with the MMPI that should be consulted by the clinician interested in this topic.

TEST FORMS

The MMPI-2 exists in many different forms: softcover, hardcover, audiocassette tape, and computer. All of these forms have the items in the same order with the same item numbers. Since the MMPI-2 is a restricted test, only professionals with appropriate training may purchase the test materials. MMPI-2 booklets are available in either softcover or hardcover both of which have the 567 items in the same item order, unlike the MMPI in which the group booklet form (softcover) and Form R (hardcover) have the last 200 items in different orders. The softcover booklet of the MMPI-2 is preferable in situations in which clients may mark on or otherwise deface the booklet, because it is less expensive than the hardcover booklet. The hardcover booklet is useful in situations such as a hospital where the client may not have a desk or table readily available on which to work.

Several answer sheets can be used with the MMPI-2 booklets, some of which are designed for computer scoring and others which are designed to be read by optical scanners. When purchasing MMPI-2 test materials for the first time, the clinician should ensure that the answer sheet is appropriate for the test booklet and hand or computer scoring as desired.

Once the client has completed the MMPI-2, the clinician should inspect the answer sheet for any problems, such as an omitted item, an item marked both "true" and "false," marking all or most of the items "true" or "false," or an item for which the client changed the response but failed to show clearly which answer was intended. Occasionally, a client will even omit an entire column of items. Usually the client can readily correct these problems; then scoring of the responses can begin.

HAND SCORING

Scoring can be accomplished either by computer (discussed later in this chapter) or by hand.[2] The first step in hand scoring is to examine the answer sheet carefully and indicate omitted items and double-marked items by drawing a line through both the "true" and "false" responses to these items with a brightly colored ink pen. Also, cleaning up the answer sheet is helpful and facilitates scoring. Responses that were changed need to be erased completely if possible, or clearly marked with an "X" so that the clinician is aware that the item has not been endorsed by the client.

There is one scale that must always be scored without a template. The *?* (Cannot Say) scale score is the total number of items not marked and double marked. All of the Validity and Clinical scales on all hand-scored answer sheets are scored by placing a plastic template over the answer sheet with a small box drawn at the scored (deviant) response—either "true" or "false"—for each item on the scale. The total number of such items marked equals the client's raw score for that scale; this score is recorded in the proper space on the answer sheet. One scale—Scale 5 (Masculinity-Femininity)—is scored differently for men and women, and unusually high or low scores on

this scale might indicate that the wrong template was used. Among women, for example, a raw score of less than 30 is unusual, and such raw scores should at least arouse a suspicion that the wrong template was used in scoring the scale. All scoring templates are made of plastic and they must be kept away from heat.

Plotting the profile is the next step in the scoring process. In essence, the clinician transfers all the raw scores from the answer sheet to the appropriate column of the profile sheet (see Profile 2.1). Some precautions must be taken and data calculations performed. First, separate profile sheets are used for men and women as with the scoring templates for Scale *5;* an unusually high or low score plotted for Scale *5* should alert the clinician to the possibility that the wrong profile sheet was selected.

Second, each column on the profile sheet is used to represent the raw scores for a specific scale. Each dash represents a raw score of 1 with the larger dashes marking increments of 5. Thus, the clinician notes the client's raw score on the scale being plotted and makes a point or dot at the appropriate dash. In Profile 2.1, since the client has a raw score of 7 on the *L* (Lie) scale, the clinician finds the dark dash marked 5 on this scale and then counts up 2 more dashes and makes a point or dot at 7. A similar procedure is followed for the other two Validity scales. Once the clinician has plotted the client's scores on the three Validity scales, a solid line is drawn to connect them. The raw score on the *?* (Cannot Say) scale is merely recorded in the proper space in the lower left-hand corner of the profile sheet.

A similar procedure is followed to plot the ten Clinical scales except that five of the Clinical scales (*1* [Hypochondriasis], *4* [Psychopathic Deviate], *7* [Psychasthenia], *8* [Schizophrenia], and *9* [Hypomania]) are *K*-corrected and a fraction of *K* is added to the raw score before the client's score is plotted. (The rationale and procedure for the *K*-correction will be described in the next section.) For these five scales that are *K*-corrected, the clinician plots the raw score on the scale with *K* added. Thus, on Scale *1* the client's *raw score (8) plus one-half (.5) of the raw score of K* (.5*14 = 7) is 15 (see Profile 2.1), so the clinician finds the dark dash marked 15 and makes a point or dot there. Once the clinician has plotted the client's

---

2. There were several minor errors in the first printing of the *MMPI-2 Manual:* Two items (328 and 358) on Scale *0* (Social Introversion) were incorrectly keyed as "false" rather than "true," one item (387) on *MAC-R* (MacAndrew Alcoholism—Revised) was incorrectly keyed as "false" rather than as "true," one item (331) on *GM* (Gender Role—Masculine) was incorrectly keyed as "true" rather than as "false," and one item (203) on *GF* (Gender Role—Feminine) was incorrectly keyed as "false" rather than as "true." These errors caused the first versions of the MMPI-2 hand-scoring answer keys and computer-scoring programs to have similar errors. It is important that clinicians determine that these items are being scored correctly. The hand-scoring stencil for *MAC-R* indicates in the bottom left-hand corner that it was revised in September 1995.

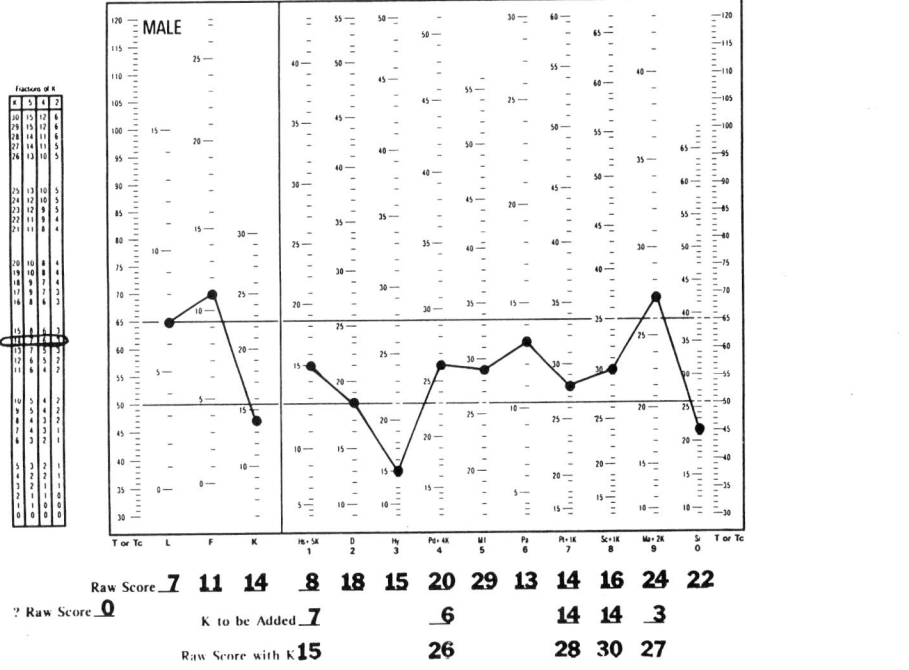

Profile for Basic Scales

Minnesota Multiphasic Personality Inventory-2
Copyright © by THE REGENTS OF THE UNIVERSITY OF MINNESOTA
1942, 1943 (renewed 1970), 1989. This Profile Form 1989.
All rights reserved. Distributed exclusively by NATIONAL COMPUTER SYSTEMS, INC.
under license from The University of Minnesota.

"MMPI-2" and "Minnesota Multiphasic Personality Inventory-2" are trademarks owned by
The University of Minnesota. Printed in the United States of America.

Name **John Brown**

Address **6411 Chicago Street**

Occupation **Janitor**   Date Tested **4/ 8/99**

Education **9th** Age **47** Marital Status Married

Referred by **Dr. Nichols**

MMPI-2 Code **96-145872/0:3   F'L-K**

Scorer's Initials **HG**

	L	F	K	Hs+.5K 1	D 2	Hy 3	Pd+.4K 4	Mf 5	Pa 6	Pt+1K 7	Sc+1K 8	Ma+.2K 9	Si 0
Raw Score	7	11	14	8	18	15	20	29	13	14	16	24	22
? Raw Score 0													
K to be Added			7				6			14	14	3	
Raw Score with K				15			26			28	30	27	

24001

PROFILE 2.1

Note. Minnesota Multiphasic Personality Inventory-2 (MMPI-2). Copyright © 1942, 1943 (renewed 1970), 1989 by the Regents of the University of Minnesota. Reproduced by permission of the publisher. "MMPI-2" and "Minnesota Multiphasic Personality Inventory-2" are trademarks owned by the University of Minnesota.

scores on the ten Clinical scales, another solid line is drawn to connect them. The clinician should note that the Validity and Clinical scales are *not* connected, because the determination of the validity of the MMPI-2 is independent of or precedes the evaluation of the Clinical scales.

The left and right columns of the profile for basic scales provide the T score equivalents for the raw scores on each scale (see Profile 2.1). For example, the client's raw score of 7 on the *L* (Lie) scale is equivalent to a T score of 65. Similarly, the client's raw score with *K* of 15 on Scale *1* (Hypochondriasis) is equivalent to a T score of 57. The profile form for the basic scales provides a direct means of converting the raw scores on the standard Validity and Clinical scores into the appropriate T scores. The development and use of T scores will be described later.

Hand scoring of the MMPI-2 is to be discouraged for a variety of reasons. First, hand scoring is extremely time consuming and clinicians will be tempted not to score all of the possible MMPI-2 scales in order to save time. There currently are 129 different scales and indexes that are scored on the National Computer Systems Extended Score Report for the MMPI-2. If it takes only ten seconds to score each scale or index, the clinician will spend over 20 minutes simply scoring the MMPI-2. Second, hand scoring is prone to error even when clinicians are very careful as will be discussed later. National Computer Systems requires the client's responses to be entered twice and to be identical before scoring proceeds in order to ensure that the data have been input accurately. Third, hand scoring of the two inconsistency scales on the MMPI-2 (Variable Response Inconsistency [*VRIN*] and True Response Inconsistency [*TRIN*]) requires that the clinician copy 138 of the client's responses on to an additional answer sheet before scoring these two scales, which introduces another opportunity for errors to be made. In fact, hand scoring the *VRIN* and *TRIN* scales several times is sufficient to convince most clinicians to use computer scoring of the MMPI-2. The extra time required to hand score the *VRIN* and *TRIN* scales may tempt clinicians to omit scoring these two scales, which are vital in assessing the validity of the MMPI-2 as will be demonstrated in the next chapter.

K-CORRECTION

As noted in Chapter 1, Meehl and Hathaway (1946) developed the *K* scale to identify individuals who were defensive in endorsing the MMPI items. They determined that the raw scores on five scales, when transformed into *K*-corrected form, enhanced the ability of these scales to discriminate their respective criterion groups from other groups of respondents (see Chapter 3). This *K*-correction process is a standard step in plotting the MMPI and it was *not* changed in the restandardization of the MMPI-2.

The standard profile sheet can be used only to plot directly *K*-corrected profiles. In order to use this profile sheet correctly, the clinician must add to five of the Clinical scales the proper fractions of the client's raw score on the *K* scale. The five Clinical scales in question and their *K*-corrections are *1* (Hypochondriasis) + .5*K; 4* (Psychopathic Deviate) + .4*K; 7* (Psychasthenia) + 1*K; 8* (Schizophrenia) + 1*K;* and *9* (Hypomania) + .2*K*. Thus, in Profile 2.1 in which *K* = 14, the following amounts were added to Scales *1, 4, 7, 8,* and *9,* respectively: 7, 6, 14, 14, and 3.

The clinician does not need to calculate the values of the *K*-correction because a table on the left side of the profile sheet provides all needed fractions of *K* for all possible raw scores on the *K* scale. Circling the raw score of the *K* scale and the other numbers on this same row in the table on the profile sheet facilitates locating the appropriate fractions of *K* to be added to each of the *K*-corrected scales (see Profile 2.1).

LINEAR T SCORES

Inspection of the completed profile sheet provides the clinician with a standard score (T score) as well as a raw score for each scale. T scores among normals have a mean of 50 and a standard deviation of 10. Thus, a T score of 70 indicates that a score is two standard deviations above the mean, and a T score of 30 is two standard deviations below the mean. Knowing the client's T score on a scale is important for two reasons. First, it shows how the client scored compared to the group of normals on whom the MMPI-2 was standardized. For example, knowing that a male client has a raw score of 26 on Scale *5* (Masculinity-

Femininity) means virtually nothing, but the fact that the client has a T score of 50 on this scale tells the clinician that the client's score on this scale is at the mean of the MMPI-2 normative group.

Second, T scores enable the clinician to compare the client's scores on the various scales with one another. For example, knowing that a male client has a raw score of 26 on Scale *5* and 46 on Scale *0* (Social Introversion) means very little; knowing that the client has a T score of 50 on Scale *5* and 70 on Scale *0*, however, allows the clinician to determine the relative deviation and the interpretive importance of these two scales in this specific client.

Since the T score equivalent of each raw score can be read directly from the profile sheet when the raw score is plotted, the clinician need not perform any calculations to convert raw scores to T scores. The following equation was used to obtain the linear T score equivalents of each raw score:

$$T = 50 + 10\left(\frac{X - M}{SD}\right)$$

X = the client's raw score

M = the mean score on the scale in normals

SD = the standard deviation on the scale in normals

In converting raw scores to T scores, fractions were rounded to the nearest whole number. For example, if a man answered 35 items on Scale *5* (Masculinity-Femininity) of the MMPI-2 in the deviant direction or like the criterion group on whom the scale was constructed, substituting 35 in the foregoing formula would produce a T score of 68 (see Profile 2.1):

$$T = 50 + 10\left(\frac{35 - 26.01}{5.08}\right) = 50 + 10(1.8) = 50 + 18 = 68$$

Similarly, if a man answered 21 items on Scale *5* in the deviant direction, substituting this raw score in this formula would produce a T score of 40:

$$T = 50 + 10\left(\frac{21 - 26.01}{5.08}\right) = 50 + 10(-1.0) = 50 - 10 = 40$$

The previously described procedure was used to develop T scores for all of the Validity and Clinical

scales on the original MMPI. These T scores are known as linear T scores because they are linear transformations of the raw scores that maintain the underlying distributions of the raw scores. Inherent in the use of T scores on the MMPI is the assumption that they have similar meanings from one clinical scale to the next (i.e., a T score of 75 on Scale *4* [Psychopathic Deviate] has the same probability of occurrence as a T score of 75 on Scale *8* [Schizophrenia]). This assumption is valid, however, only if the scales involved have similar distributions. If the underlying raw score distributions for each scale are not similar, then a T score of 70 will not be equivalent to the 97.7 percentile.

Colligan, Osborne, and Offord (1980) examined the raw score distributions of the standard Validity and Clinical scales in the Hathaway and Briggs (1957) "purified" sample of the original Minnesota normative group that was used to derive the T scores on the standard profile sheet for the MMPI. They found that most of these scales showed significant skewness to the right, with from 4.8 to 8.0 percent of these normal individuals scoring above a T score of 70 instead of the 2.3 percent that would be expected with a normal distribution. Colligan et al. recommended that Scales *1* (Hypochondriasis), *2* (Depression), *7* (Psychasthenia), *8* (Schizophrenia), and *9* (Hypomania) in women and Scales *1* (Hypochondriasis), *2* (Depression), *4* (Psychopathic Deviate), *7* (Psychasthenia), *8* (Schizophrenia), and *9* (Hypomania) in men should be interpreted more conservatively because of the increased frequency with which elevations occurred in normal individuals.

UNIFORM T SCORES

The MMPI-2 Restandardization Committee (Butcher et al., 1989) realized the importance of ensuring that the same T score elevation would have similar meaning or equal probability of occurring across scales, and they developed uniform T scores to meet this need. Uniform T scores were developed for all Clinical scales on the MMPI-2 (except Scales *5* [Masculinity-Femininity] and *0* [Social Introversion], which retained linear T scores) and the new Content scales (see Chapter 5). Linear T scores were retained on Scales *5*

TABLE 2.1 Illustration of the Process of Creating Uniform T scores

Targeted Uniform T Score	Percentile	SCALE *1* (HYPOCHONDRIASIS)		SCALE *2* (DEPRESSION)		Composite
		Men	Women	Men	Women	
79	99	83	83	82	77	81
68	95	69	70	69	69	69
63	90	63	64	64	64	64
58	80	57	57	58	58	58
54	70	53	53	54	55	54
51	60	50	50	51	51	51
49	50	48	48	48	48	48

Note. Targeted uniform T scores are provided in Table 4 of Tellegen and Ben-Porath (1992).

and *0* because these two scales were derived in a different manner than the other clinical scales and the distribution of raw scores was less skewed (Butcher et al., 1989).

These uniform T scores were developed in a three-step process (Tellegen & Ben-Porath, 1992). First, non-*K*-corrected linear T score distributions were determined by gender for each of the eight Clinical scales. This step resulted in 16 distributions of linear T scores. Second, the associated linear T score was determined for each percentile in each of the 16 distributions. Finally, composite or average T scores were determined for each percentile. These composite T scores were then used to create uniform T scores for each of the eight Clinical scales. Uniform T scores result in a similar probability of occurrence of a particular T score across these eight Clinical scales while maintaining the underlying positive skew in the distribution. An easy means of understanding uniform T scores is to realize that they are equivalent percentiles across these scales.

Table 2.1 provides an illustration of the process of creating uniform T scores for two scales. In this illustration, the composite or average T score for the 95th percentile was 69, which would become the uniform T score for the 95th percentile on both scales in men and women. Similarly, the composite T score for the 80th percentile was 58, which would become the uniform T score for that percentile. It can be seen that the adjustments from linear T scores that are being made using uniform T scores are only a few T points.

The net result of uniform T scores is to make the distribution of T scores more similar across the Clinical scales than would be found using linear T scores. Figure 2.1 illustrates these minor changes in the shape of the distribution of linear and uniform T scores for Scales 8 (Schizophrenia) and 9 (Hypomania) for women.

Table 2.2 illustrates the relationship between uniform and linear T scores for a man on Scales *1* (Hypochondriasis) and *6* (Paranoia) that are taken from Appendices A and K of the *MMPI-2 Manual* (Butcher et al., 1989), respectively. Uniform T scores are consistently 3 to 10 T points lower than linear T scores throughout the distribution on Scale *1* when the scores are *K*-corrected and nearly identical when the scores are non-*K*-corrected. In both comparisons on Scale *1* the differences between uniform and linear T scores become larger at T scores of 80 and higher. Uniform T scores are about 6 T points lower than linear T scores on Scale *6* up to T scores of 60 and then very similar to T scores of 90.

Table 2.3 provides a comparison of non-*K*-corrected and *K*-corrected linear and uniform T scores in the range of 60 to 80 by gender for all eight Clinical scales. Non-*K*-corrected linear T scores for women on Scale *1* (Hypochondriasis) are consistently 2 to 4 T points lower than uniform T scores. Otherwise non-*K*-corrected linear T scores always are slightly higher than uniform T scores with differences ranging as high as 15 T points on Scale *2* (Depression) in men. The mean difference between the non-*K*-corrected

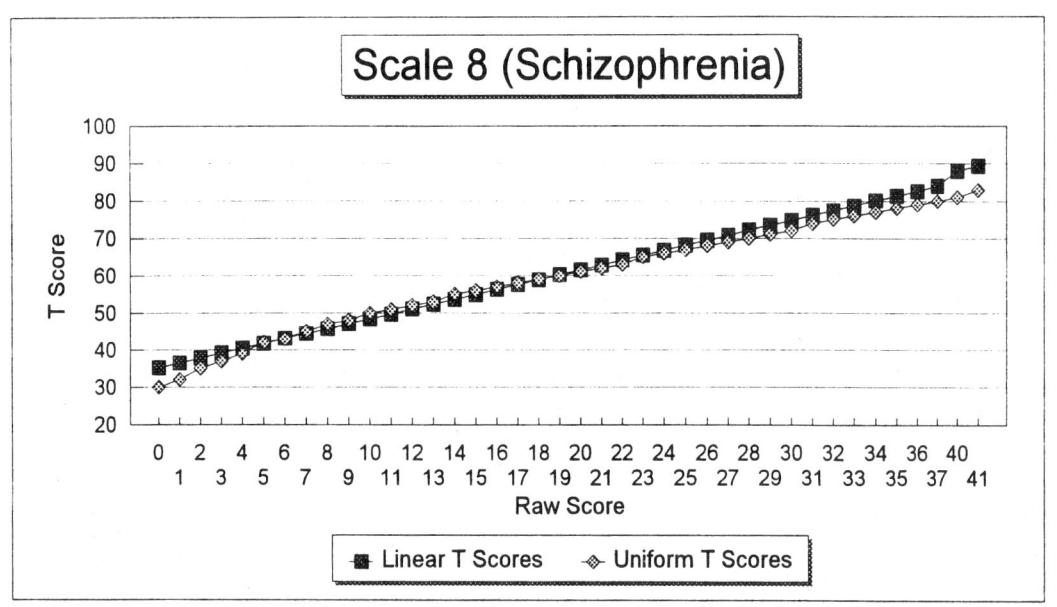

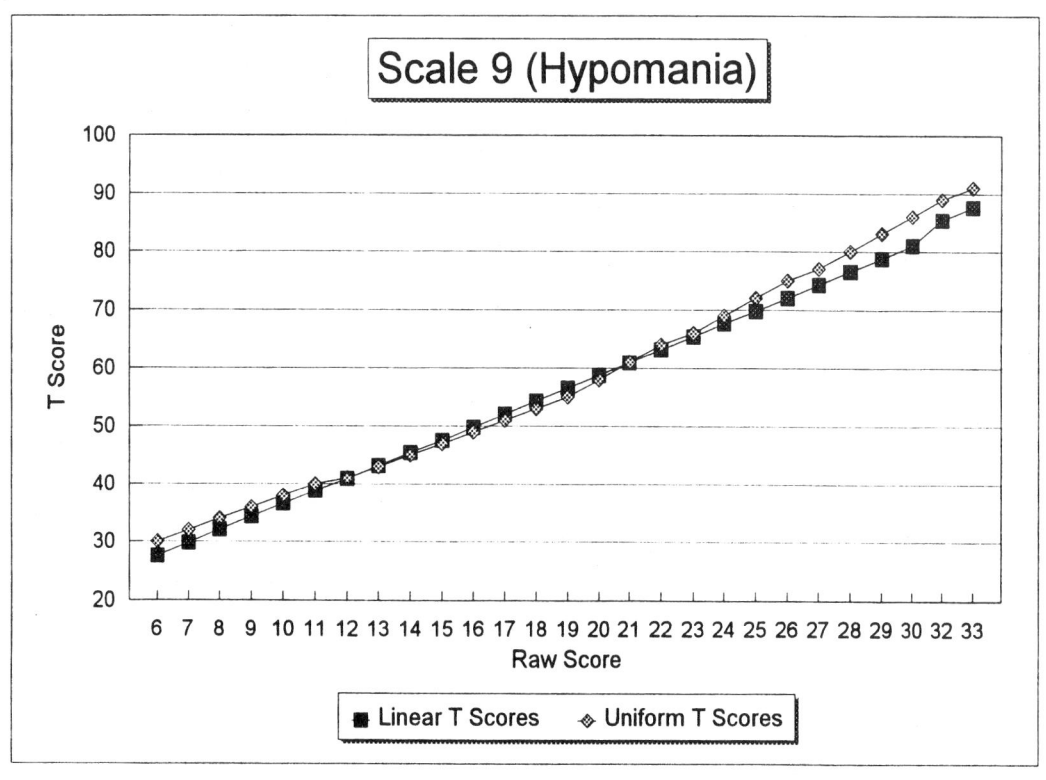

FIGURE 2.1 Comparison of Linear and Uniform T Scores

Note. Minnesota Multiphasic Personality Inventory-2 (MMPI-2). Copyright © 1942, 1943 (renewed 1970), 1989 by the Regents of the University of Minnesota. Reproduced by permission of the publisher. "MMPI-2" and "Minnesota Multiphasic Personality Inventory-2" are trademarks owned by the University of Minnesota.

TABLE 2.2   Comparisons between Linear and Uniform T Scores for a Male Client

| | SCALE *1* (HYPOCHONDRIASIS) | | | | SCALE *6* (PARANOIA) | |
| | *T Score (with* K) | | *T Score (without* K) | | *T Score* | |
Raw Score	Linear	Uniform	Linear	Uniform	Linear	Uniform
0			40	34		
2			44	42	33	30
4	31	31	49	49	38	32
6	36	33	53	54	44	37
8	41	37	58	59	50	42
10	47	42	62	63	56	49
12	52	48	67	67	62	57
14	57	54	72	71	67	64
16	62	59	76	75	73	72
18	67	64	81	79	79	79
20	72	68	85	83	85	86
22	77	73	90	87	91	94
24	82	77	94	91	97	101
26	88	81	99	95	102	108
28	93	86	104	99	108	116
30	98	90	108	103	114	120
32	103	94	113	107	120	
34	108	99				
36	113	103				
38	118	108				
40	120	112				

Note. These uniform and linear T scores may be found in Appendices A (Table A-2) and K (Table K-2) of Butcher et al. (1989), respectively. There were a number of errors in Appendix K in the first printing of the *MMPI-2 Manual.* Clinicians must be sure that they have a correct version of Appendix K.

uniform and linear T scores is 4 T points in men and 1 to 3 T points in women. It does appear that the linear T scores that are reported for Scale *2* in men and Scale *4* (Psychopathic Deviate) in men and women may still be in error in Appendix K of the *MMPI-2 Manual* (Butcher et al., 1989). The relationship between *K*-corrected linear and uniform T scores is very similar to what was found with non-*K*-corrected T scores except that the differences are slightly larger averaging 7 T points in men and 2 to 4 T points in women. These differences as a result of the *K*-correction process reflect that the MMPI-2 normative group had significantly higher raw scores on the *K* scale (Men: $M = 15.30$; $SD = 4.76$; Women: $M = 15.03$; $SD = 4.58$)

than the MMPI normative group (Men: $M = 13.13$; $SD = 5.43$; Women: $M = 12.35$; $SD = 5.07$). Thus, it seems appropriate to conclude that the primary differences between the T scores on the MMPI and MMPI-2 reflect the larger contribution of the *K*-correction process on the MMPI-2 more than the transition from linear to uniform T scores.

These comparisons between these two procedures for transforming raw scores on the MMPI-2 clinical scales into T scores illustrate that: (1) uniform transformations will reduce the overall profile elevation about 2 to 7 T points; and (2) the relationships among any pair or set of scales may be altered by these changes in relative elevation and distribution of

TABLE 2.3 Comparison of Linear and Uniform T Scores on the MMPI-2

Men	MMPI NON-*K*-CORRECTED LINEAR T SCORES								
Uniform T Score	1(Hs)	2(D)	3(Hy)	4(Pd)	6(Pa)	7(Pt)	8(Sc)	9(Ma)	Mean
80	82	95	81	91	81	80	84	81	84
75	76	87	77	84	75	75	78	78	79
70	70	82	73	79	70	71	74	75	74
65	63	75	69	74	67	66	67	69	69
60	59	70	65	68	64	61	61	65	64

Women	MMPI NON-*K*-CORRECTED LINEAR T SCORES								
Uniform T Score	1(Hs)	2(D)	3(Hy)	4(Pd)	6(Pa)	7(Pt)	8(Sc)	9(Ma)	Mean
80	78	80	79	88	81	77	82	80	81
75	71	77	75	83	77	74	78	77	76
70	66	73	72	78	72	71	72	73	72
65	62	69	67	73	68	64	66	69	67
60	58	63	64	68	65	59	59	65	63

Men	MMPI *K*-CORRECTED LINEAR T SCORES								
Uniform T Score	1(Hs)	2(D)	3(Hy)	4(Pd)	6(Pa)	7(Pt)	8(Sc)	9(Ma)	Mean
80	87	95	81	88	81	86	91	85	87
75	80	87	77	84	75	81	86	78	81
70	75	82	73	79	70	77	80	76	77
65	68	75	69	74	67	72	74	73	72
60	63	70	65	69	64	67	69	68	67

Women	MMPI *K*-CORRECTED LINEAR T SCORES								
Uniform T Score	1(Hs)	2(D)	3(Hy)	4(Pd)	6(Pa)	7(Pt)	8(Sc)	9(Ma)	Mean
80	78	80	79	87	81	80	85	84	82
75	73	77	75	82	77	76	80	79	77
70	69	73	72	78	72	71	75	74	73
65	64	69	67	73	68	67	69	70	68
60	59	63	64	69	65	62	64	66	64

Note. The raw scores for these clinical scales for each uniform T score can be found in Tellegen and Ben-Porath (1992). These linear T scores may be found in Appendix K of the *MMPI-2 Manual* (Butcher et al., 1989). There were a number of errors in Appendix K in the first printing of the *MMPI-2 Manual*. The corrected version of Appendix K is reprinted in this text as Appendix F.

the T scores. The overall lowering of the profile elevation in many respects has been compensated for by using a T score of 65 on the MMPI-2 to indicate clinical significance rather than a T score of 70 as was used on the MMPI. However, these changes in the elevation of specific clinical scales may alter their rank ordering using uniform T scores, which would result in a different codetype than would be obtained with linear T scores. The effects of using uniform T scores on codetypes will be examined in Chapter 7.

COMPUTER SCORING

Computer scoring of the MMPI-2 eliminates the need for the clinician to go through all of the preceding steps for scoring and plotting the profile. Computer scoring also encourages the clinician to use the Content and Supplementary scales (see Chapter 5) since no extra time is required. Various computer-scoring services are available; clinicians will need to determine which service is most appropriate for their clinical setting. There are three basic types of computer-scoring services: The MMPI-2 can be administered, scored, and interpreted (if desired) on a personal computer in the clinician's office; the clinician can use a personal computer and a modem to transmit the client's responses to the MMPI-2 to another computer to be scored and have the results transmitted back to the clinician's personal computer; or the clinician can mail the answer sheet in for computer scoring. Clinicians need to ensure that they are using an answer sheet for the MMPI-2 that is compatible with whatever computer-scoring service is to be used, since different answer sheets are employed.

The scoring templates for the MMPI-2 are copyrighted so that computer scoring has to be authorized by the University of Minnesota Press. Clinicians should make sure that any computer-scoring services that they use have been authorized for such purposes. At the time of the writing of this text, there are only two authorized sources for the commercial scoring of the MMPI-2: Caldwell Report and National Computer Systems.

ERRORS IN SCORING

Few if any errors in scoring generally occur with the MMPI-2. Occasionally, the clinician miscounts the number of deviant responses on a specific scale. Greene (1980) reported that at least 70 percent of the hand-scored answer sheets for two samples of MMPI clients—Clinic Clients and University Students—had no errors on any of the 14 Validity and Clinical scales, and another 12 to 14 percent had errors on only one scale (see Table 2.4). For a third group—Medical Patients—whose answer sheets were computer scored, 100 percent of the answer sheets were scored perfectly.

TABLE 2.4 Percentage of Answer Sheets Scored Incorrectly

Number of Scales Scored Incorrectly	GROUP[a]		
	Clinic Clients	University Students	Medical Patients
0	70%	82%	100%
1	14	12	0
2	6	2	0
3	6	4	0
4+	4	0	0

[a]$N = 50$ for each group.
Note. See Greene (1980, pp. 22–25) for a more complete description of these groups.

When an error did occur, in the preceding two samples, it was most likely a result of the clinician counting only one fewer deviant item than the client actually answered (see Table 2.5). Consequently, errors in scoring should have a negligible effect on the interpretation of the profile. This statement is not meant to suggest that clinicians do not need to be concerned about scoring the MMPI or the MMPI-2; when clinicians exercise reasonable care, however, few substantial errors in scoring occur.

Other than miscounting the number of deviant responses, the other likely source of error, as already mentioned, is using the scoring template for the opposite gender in scoring Scale 5 (Masculinity-Femininity).

TABLE 2.5 Percentage of Answer Sheets Scored Incorrectly with Errors of Varying Magnitude

Magnitude of Error[a]	GROUP	
	Clinic Clients	University Students
−3	2.6%	0.0%
−2	7.7	7.1
−1	82.1	85.7
+1	2.6	7.1
+2	5.1	0.0

[a]A negative magnitude indicates that the clinician counted fewer deviant items than the client actually answered.

Unusually high or low scores on Scale 5 should alert the clinician to the possibility that the wrong scoring template or profile form was used, particularly if such a score seems inappropriate for the individual being tested.

INTERPRETING THE PROFILE

Once the MMPI-2 has been scored and plotted on the standard profile sheet, the process of interpreting the profile can begin. The first step involves translating the T scores on each scale into more usable informa-tion. The next two chapters will present interpreta-tions of various T score elevations on each of the Validity and Clinical scales both individually and in some combinations with each other. Chapter 7 will provide the correlates of the Clinical scale(s) with the highest elevation at or above a T score of 65 (i.e., the codetype or high-point pair of the profile). The corre-lates of the codetype are the core of the process of in-terpreting the profile. Finally, Chapter 8 will present illustrations of integrating all of this information to complete the process of profile interpretation.

CHAPTER 3

Validity Indexes and Validity Configurations

The MMPI was one of the first personality tests to offer a means of directly assessing a client's test-taking attitude. Thus, the first step in interpreting an MMPI-2 profile is to examine the various Validity scales and indexes to determine the client's test-taking attitude. If these validity indexes reveal an inappropriate attitude, the entire profile may be invalid and the interpretation of the profile should be tentative at best.

In this chapter the process for assessing the validity of an MMPI-2 profile will be described using the traditional Validity scales of L (Lie), F (Infrequency), and K (Correction). The correlates of each traditional Validity scale also will be provided. This chapter will emphasize additional MMPI-2 Validity scales such as the Variable Response Inconsistency (*VRIN:* Butcher et al., 1989), Infrequency-Psychopathology (*F*[*p*]: Arbisi & Ben-Porath, 1995), and Superlative (*S:* Butcher & Han, 1995) scales. Finally, the research on simulation of psychopathology, detection of response sets, and subtle and obvious items on the MMPI and MMPI-2 will be reviewed. The effects of the setting in which the MMPI-2 is administered and demographic variables such as age and education, which can drastically alter scores on these Validity scales, will be discussed in Chapter 9.

A NOTE ON THE CONCEPT OF VALIDITY ON THE MMPI-2

The concept of validity traditionally has meant the degree to which a test actually measures what it purports to measure (Anastasi, 1968). For example, a graduate school aptitude test is valid to the extent that it can identify students who will succeed in graduate school. The test's validity would be assessed by the relationship between scores on the test and some index of success in graduate school, such as grade point average or completion of a graduate degree. Similarly with the MMPI-2, the overall relationship of the test to some external criterion (i.e., the accuracy with which the MMPI-2 can predict some other variable such as length of hospitalization or psychiatric diagnosis) would be a measure of its validity.

The concept of validity on the MMPI-2 also has a second, somewhat different meaning. It describes the test-taking attitudes of an individual client, that is, whether or not the client has endorsed the test items in some distorted manner. If the client has provided a consistent and accurate self-description when responding to the MMPI-2 items, the profile is considered to be valid. Consequently, it is possible for a client to provide a valid MMPI-2 on one occasion, an invalid MMPI-2 at another time, and a valid MMPI-2 on a third testing. Because in this second sense validity actually can refer to the consistency with which the client has endorsed the items, as well as the accuracy with which the client has described himself or herself, the clinician needs to be aware of the multiple meanings of the concept of validity on the MMPI-2.

The usage of the concept of validity to refer to the consistency of item endorsement within a single administration of the MMPI-2 would be described more appropriately by the term *reliability*. The usage of the concept of validity also to refer to the accuracy of the self-description by the client further complicates this issue, because a client can provide a consistent pattern of item endorsement that is distorted in some manner so as to make himself or herself look more or less psychopathological. The term *validity* of the MMPI-2, however, has a long history of usage, and attempting to convince several generations of clinicians to use more appropriate terms is probably unrealistic. Therefore, the clinician needs to understand the multiple meanings of the concept of validity on the MMPI-2.

STEPS IN ASSESSING MMPI-2 VALIDITY

Assessing the validity of a specific administration of the MMPI-2 to a client is a process that involves multiple steps, which need to be carried out in a sequential manner.[1] An overview of these steps is provided in Figure 3.1. The clinician will see the various meanings of the concept of validity that are raised at each of these steps and they are explained later.

The clinician also may be surprised that the traditional Validity scales of the MMPI-2 (Scales *L* [Lie], *F* [Infrequency], and *K* [Correction]) are introduced at a

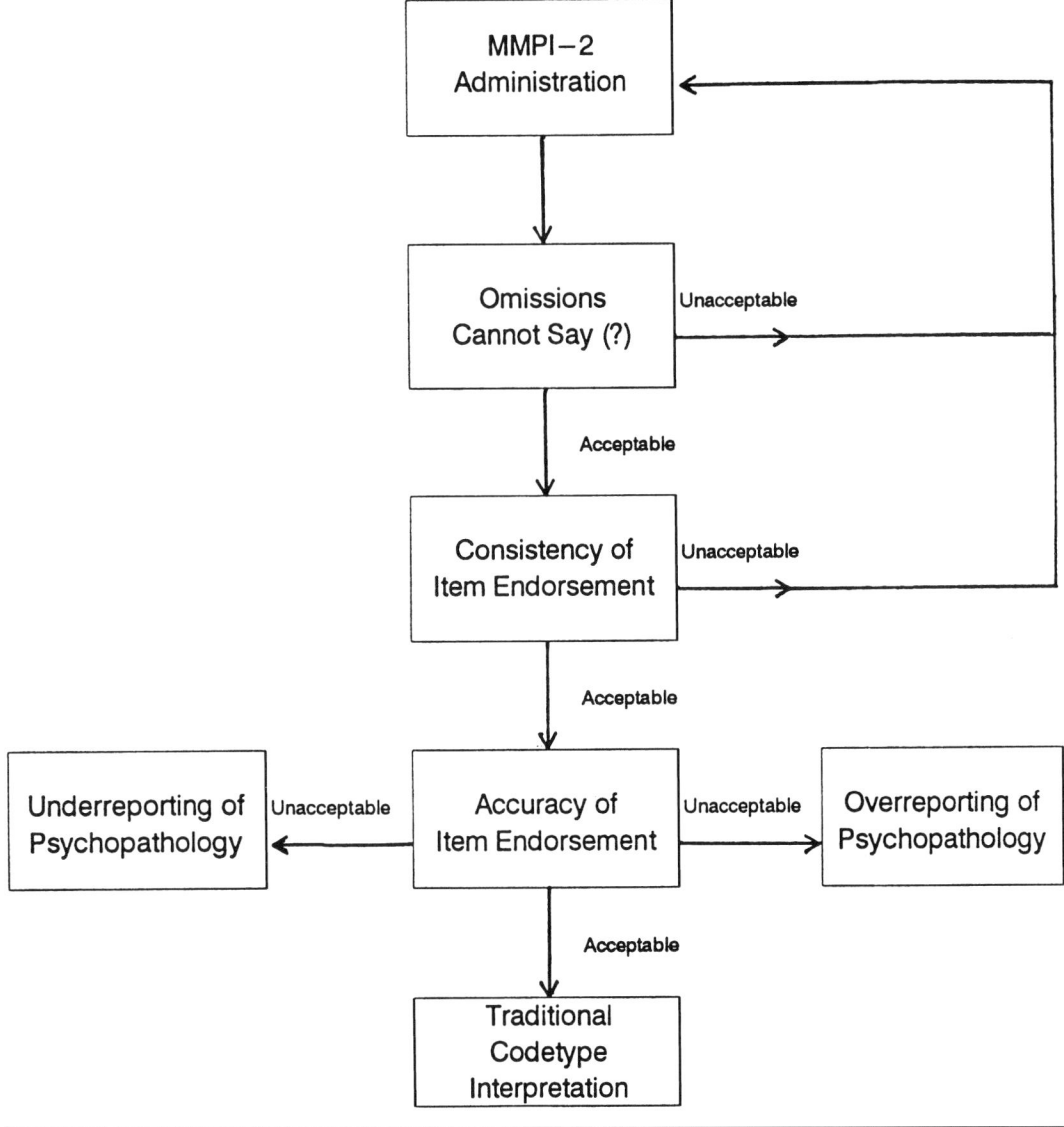

FIGURE 3.1   Steps in Assessing MMPI-2 Validity

1. A condensed version of this section can be found in Greene (1997).

very late stage in this process. Hopefully, the rationale for this revised process for determining the validity of an individual administration of the MMPI-2 will become clearer in the next few pages. The first step in assessing the validity of this specific administration of the MMPI-2 is to evaluate the number of items omitted (Figure 3.1), which is discussed in the next section.

Item Omissions

Cannot Say (?) Scale.   The *?* scale consists of the total number of items that the client omits, that is, fails to answer or answers both "true" and "false." Therefore, the *?* scale is *not* composed of a specific set of items as the other Validity and Clinical scales are; the client potentially can omit any one or combination of the 567 items. Thus, the term *scale* is a misnomer because it comprises no specific items.

In standard scoring procedures omitted items are considered to be answered in the nondeviant direction because only items answered in the deviant direction are counted. Thus, the effect of omitted items is potentially to lower the elevation of the overall profile and of any scale on which the items were omitted, since if the client had answered the item a deviant response might have been given.

Table 3.1 lists the 25 most frequently omitted MMPI items in medical patients referred for a psychiatric evaluation (Colligan & Offord, 1986) and psychiatric patients (Hedlund & Won Cho, 1979) as well

TABLE 3.1   Frequency of Omission of MMPI Items

MAYO CLINIC MEDICAL PATIENTS (COLLIGAN & OFFORD, 1986)									MISSOURI PSYCHIATRIC PATIENTS (HEDLUND & WON CHO, 1979)								
Women (N = 6,581)			Men (N = 4,700)			Total (N = 11,281)			Women (N = 3,168)			Men (N = 7,356)			Total (N = 10,524)		
ITEM	N	%	ITEM	N	%	ITEM	N	%	ITEM	N	%	ITEM	N	%	ITEM	N	%
58	262	4.0	177	180	3.8	58	437	3.9	513	378	11.9	513	999	13.6	513	1377	13.1
441	225	3.4	58	175	3.7	177	394	3.5	58	351	11.1	58	868	11.8	58	1219	11.6
513	224	3.4	70	150	3.2	295	358	3.2	441	234	7.4	483	579	7.9	483	732	7.0
295	215	3.3	295	143	3.0	513	354	3.1	558	228	7.2	558	460	6.3	558	688	6.5
177	214	3.3	60	136	2.9	70	343	3.0	483	153	4.8	53	447	6.1	53	579	5.5
520	199	3.0	369	136	2.9	520	334	3.0	42	148	4.7	287	425	5.8	287	567	5.4
540	194	2.9	520	135	2.9	441	329	2.9	295	145	4.6	70	416	5.7	295	546	5.2
70	193	2.9	513	130	2.8	369	323	2.9	287	142	4.5	98	414	5.6	98	543	5.2
369	187	2.8	483	128	2.7	471	311	2.8	476	137	4.3	295	401	5.5	400	519	4.9
471	187	2.8	455	126	2.7	534	311	2.8	168	135	4.3	400	390	5.3	249	507	4.8
534	185	2.8	534	126	2.7	540	308	2.7	53	132	4.2	249	376	5.1	70	476	4.5
558	185	2.8	471	124	2.6	483	300	2.7	249	131	4.1	415	366	5.0	415	475	4.5
542	179	2.7	517	120	2.6	558	289	2.6	98	129	4.1	168	330	4.5	168	465	4.4
562	178	2.7	353	118	2.5	237	286	2.5	232	129	4.1	232	310	4.2	232	439	4.2
237	176	2.7	299	117	2.5	455	285	2.5	400	129	4.1	471	299	4.1	476	416	4.0
544	174	2.6	540	114	2.4	542	285	2.5	485	129	4.1	115	285	3.9	471	401	3.8
483	172	2.6	237	110	2.3	60	281	2.5	255	119	3.8	373	284	3.9	115	387	3.7
477	171	2.6	453	110	2.3	299	274	2.4	415	109	3.4	476	279	3.8	255	385	3.7
232	168	2.6	542	106	2.3	562	274	2.4	364	108	3.4	255	266	3.6	42	380	3.6
514	167	2.5	199	104	2.2	232	271	2.4	101	103	3.3	413	265	3.6	373	373	3.5
475	166	2.5	441	104	2.2	517	270	2.4	115	102	3.2	562	254	3.5	441	356	3.4
536	165	2.5	451	104	2.2	544	266	2.4	471	102	3.2	514	248	3.4	562	355	3.4
548	165	2.5	558	104	2.2	539	264	2.3	562	101	3.2	50	244	3.3	364	350	3.3
553	165	2.5	232	103	2.2	548	264	2.3	50	100	3.2	364	242	3.3	413	349	3.3
20	163	2.5	545	103	2.2	453	261	2.3	387	95	3.0	42	232	3.2	50	344	3.3
M		7.6			5.9			6.9			5.2			4.8			4.9
SD		12.8			10.4			11.9			6.4			6.1			6.2

as the means and standard deviations for the *?* scale. The psychiatric patients were somewhat more likely to omit items than the medical patients, although they tended to omit the same items. Table 3.2 provides the content of these items that both groups of patients were likely to omit. A majority of these items have religious content and several used outdated language such as "drop-the-handkerchief" or "marks in deportment." All of these religious items were deleted from

TABLE 3.2 Content of Frequently Omitted MMPI Items

ITEM NUMBER	ITEM CONTENT
53	A minister can cure disease by praying and putting his hand on your head.
58	Everything is turning out just like the prophets of the Bible said it would.
70	I used to like drop-the-handkerchief.
98	I believe in the second coming of Christ.
177	My mother was a good woman.
249	I believe there is a Devil and a Hell in afterlife.
287	I have very few fears compared to my friends.
295	I liked "Alice in Wonderland" by Lewis Carroll.
369	Religion gives me no worry.
400	If given the chance I could do some things that would be of great benefit to the world.
441	I like tall women.
471	In school my marks in deportment were quite regularly bad.
476	I am a special agent of God.
483	Christ performed miracles such as changing water into wine.
513	I think Lincoln was greater than Washington.
534	Several times I have been the last to give up trying to do something.
558	A large number of people are guilty of bad sexual conduct.

Note. Minnesota Multiphasic Personality Inventory (MMPI). Copyright 1943 (renewed 1970), 1948, 1976, 1982 by the Regents of the University of Minnesota. All rights reserved. MMPI and Minnesota Multiphasic Inventory are trademarks of the University of Minnesota. Reproduced by permission of the publisher.

the MMPI-2 and two of these items (177, 471) were reworded on the MMPI-2. It would be expected that these deletions and rewording of the items on the MMPI-2 would make omissions less of a problem than they were on the MMPI.

Table 3.3 lists the 25 most frequently omitted MMPI-2 items in the MMPI-2 normative group (Butcher et al., 1989) and psychiatric patients (Caldwell, 1997a) as well as the means and standard deviations for the *?* scale. As expected, items are less frequently omitted on the MMPI-2 than the MMPI with an average of only 1 to 2 items being omitted in both samples. The most frequently omitted MMPI-2 item (215; 2.4%) in the psychiatric sample would not rank in the top 25 items omitted from the MMPI. The psychiatric patients were slightly more likely to omit items than normal individuals, although these differences are very small. They still generally omit the same items. Table 3.4 provides the content of these items that both of these groups were likely to omit. The content of these items tends to be more diverse than was found on the MMPI. Three of the items (12, 268, and 470) have sexual content. The sole remaining religious item (132) on the MMPI-2 also is omitted frequently.

Clopton and Neuringer (1977) showed how randomly omitting six different numbers of items (5, 30, 55, 80, 105, and 130) affects MMPI profile elevation and distorts profile configuration. The MMPI Clinical scales dropped an average of .45, 2.74, 5.61, 7.70, 9.09, and 11.54 T points, respectively, when these six quantities of random items were omitted. More important, the codetype of the profile (the two most highly elevated Clinical scales) changed in 1, 8, 4, 8, 10, and 17 profiles, respectively, from a group of 30 profiles at each level of item omission. Thus, omitting only 30 items changed the codetype for more than 25 percent of their MMPI profiles, and when 130 items were omitted, more than half of the codetypes changed. Berry et al. (1997) found similar results on the MMPI-2 when different numbers (0, 5, 10, 15, 20, 25, 30) of frequently omitted items were deleted. The MMPI-2 Clinical scales declined about 2 T points with 10 omitted items, which is a negligible effect, but codetype changes occurred in 25% of the profiles with 10 omitted items and 39% of the profiles with 30 omitted items. Consequently, profile

TABLE 3.3   Frequency of Omission of MMPI-2 Items

MMPI-2 NORMATIVE GROUP (BUTCHER ET AL., 1989)									CALDWELL CLINICAL SAMPLE (CALDWELL, 1997A)								
Women (N = 1,462)			Men (N = 1,138)			Total (N = 2,600)			Women (N = 26,425)			Men (N = 26,118)			Total (N = 52,543)		
ITEM	N	%	ITEM	N	%	ITEM	N	%	ITEM	N	%	ITEM	N	%	ITEM	N	%
211	29	2.0	261	16	1.4	211	41	1.6	215	636	2.4	215	616	2.4	215	1,252	2.4
19	23	1.6	132	15	1.3	217	37	1.4	559	551	2.1	211	412	1.6	211	943	1.8
217	22	1.5	217	15	1.3	261	36	1.4	211	531	2.0	261	329	1.3	559	837	1.6
261	20	1.4	538	13	1.1	19	35	1.3	12	439	1.7	217	288	1.1	12	648	1.2
132	19	1.3	19	12	1.1	132	34	1.3	560	371	1.4	559	286	1.1	261	638	1.2
559	18	1.2	211	12	1.1	500	28	1.1	87	361	1.4	132	270	1.0	132	616	1.2
500	16	1.1	434	12	1.1	538	26	1.0	132	346	1.3	443	259	1.0	158	596	1.1
560	16	1.1	500	12	1.1	559	26	1.0	158	338	1.3	158	258	1.0	443	584	1.1
268	15	1.0	473	11	1.0	268	22	0.8	443	325	1.2	88	233	0.9	217	577	1.1
76	14	1.0	13	10	0.9	473	21	0.8	268	322	1.2	268	227	0.9	268	549	1.0
88	13	0.9	384	10	0.9	434	20	0.8	261	309	1.2	13	220	0.8	87	547	1.0
531	13	0.9	544	10	0.9	548	20	0.8	470	290	1.1	12	209	0.8	88	520	1.0
538	13	0.9	443	9	0.8	76	19	0.7	217	289	1.1	335	209	0.8	560	504	1.0
269	12	0.8	470	9	0.8	470	19	0.7	88	287	1.1	473	200	0.8	470	465	0.9
357	11	0.8	548	9	0.8	531	19	0.7	434	273	1.0	71	191	0.7	13	460	0.9
515	11	0.8	557	9	0.8	567	19	0.7	278	251	0.9	87	186	0.7	434	442	0.8
548	11	0.8	563	9	0.8	88	18	0.7	15	250	0.9	6	183	0.7	71	437	0.8
567	11	0.8	71	8	0.7	269	18	0.7	71	246	0.9	470	175	0.7	473	416	0.8
87	10	0.7	158	8	0.7	544	18	0.7	13	240	0.9	406	174	0.7	335	412	0.8
113	10	0.7	491	8	0.7	13	17	0.7	345	234	0.9	444	174	0.7	278	410	0.8
212	10	0.7	559	8	0.7	158	17	0.7	406	230	0.9	112	171	0.7	406	404	0.8
350	10	0.7	567	8	0.7	212	17	0.7	357	220	0.8	357	169	0.6	6	402	0.8
436	10	0.7	6	7	0.6	436	17	0.7	6	219	0.8	434	169	0.6	357	389	0.7
470	10	0.7	56	7	0.6	560	17	0.7	473	216	0.8	113	168	0.6	444	381	0.7
473	10	0.7	212	7	0.6	71	16	0.6	444	207	0.8	246	166	0.6	15	376	0.7
M		1.0			0.9			1.0			1.7			1.3			1.5
SD		2.9			3.0			2.9			4.9			4.0			4.5

distortion seems likely when 10 or more items are omitted on the MMPI-2, even though profile elevation may be reduced only slightly. As the number of omitted items approaches 30, the profile essentially becomes uninterpretable.

It is clearly preferable to minimize the number of omitted items. Initially explaining to the client the reasons for and importance of completing the MMPI-2 will help obtain the client's full cooperation in completing the test. If the client omits more than 10 or 15 items, the clinician can ask the client to review the omitted items and respond to them based on whether each is *mostly true* or *mostly false*. If the client still omits more than 10 items, the clinician can question the client about the reasons for not responding. A fi-

nal solution is to construct an augmented profile, which is discussed later in this chapter.

A major issue concerning omitted items is the client's motivation for doing so. Is the client *unwilling* to answer the omitted items or is the client *unable* to answer them? Distinguishing these two categories of omitted items would be useful (Brown, 1950). In the former instance the client probably would have given a deviant response if he or she had actually answered the items; when this assumption is tenable, construction of an augmented profile might be considered. In the latter instance ignoring the omitted items seems preferable because they are probably irrelevant for this particular client. Unfortunately, no one, including Brown (1950), has provided criteria by

TABLE 3.4 Content of Frequently Omitted MMPI-2 Items

ITEM NUMBER	ITEM CONTENT
12	My sex life is satisfactory.
19	When I take a new job, I like to find out who it is important to be nice to.
87	I have met problems so full of possibilities that I have been unable to make up my mind about them.
132	I believe in a life hereafter.
158	It makes me uncomfortable to put on a stunt at a party even when others are doing the same sort of things.
211	I have been inspired to a program of life based on duty which I have since carefully followed.
215	I brood a great deal.
217	My relatives are nearly all in sympathy with me.
261	I have very few fears compared to my friends.
268	I wish I were not bothered by thoughts about sex.
406	I would certainly enjoy beating criminals at their own game.
434	If I was in trouble with several friends who were as guilty as I was, I would rather take the whole blame than give them away.
443	I do not try to cover up my poor opinion or pity of people so that they won't know how I feel.
470	A large number of people are guilty of bad sexual conduct.
473	The one to whom I was most attached and whom I most admired as a child was a woman (mother, sister, aunt, or other woman).
500	Although I am not happy with my life, there is nothing I can do about it now.
538	Most men are unfaithful to their wives now and then.
559	The people I work with are not sympathetic with my problems.
560	I am satisfied with the amount of money I make.
567	Most married couples don't show much affection for each other.

Note. Minnesota Multiphasic Personality Inventory-2 (MMPI-2). Copyright © 1942, 1943 (renewed 1970), 1989 by the Regents of the University of Minnesota. Reproduced by permission of the publisher. "MMPI-2" and "Minnesota Multiphasic Personality Inventory-2" are trademarks owned by the University of Minnesota.

which these two categories of omitted items can be distinguished. A clinician may be able to make this distinction by interviewing the client extensively. This procedure, however, is time-consuming and often impractical or impossible. Fortunately, most clients omit few items, and so the problem rarely occurs.

Although high scores on the ? scale occur infrequently, research is needed to establish the causes of excessive omissions when they do occur. The work in this area to date has resulted in conflicting findings. Dahlstrom et al. (1972) suggested that defensive procedures are one significant cause of elevated scores on the ? scale. However, Tamkin and Scherer (1957) found that high scores on the ? scale did not seem to represent a defensive, evasive attitude in their psychiatric sample. Moreover, Eaddy (1962) found that intolerance of ambiguity and desire for uncertainty were not related to level of item omission on the ? scale among college sophomores. Although the relative infrequency with which most clients omit items makes this area of research slow and time-consuming, more research is sorely needed in a variety of clinical populations.

Greene, Davis, and Morris (1993) reported data on 339 and 57 alcoholic patients who completed the MMPI on two or three different admissions to treatment, respectively. These admissions were separated by approximately two to three years. Both groups of patients omitted an average of about eight items each time they took the MMPI. Only 3.0% (79/2,665) of the same items were omitted by the patients who had taken the MMPI twice, and only 3.5% (17/488) and 8.1% (37/459) of the same items were omitted between the first and second and second and third administrations of the MMPI, respectively. No patient who took the MMPI three times omitted the same item on all three administrations. These data suggest that item omissions on the MMPI are more likely to occur for idiosyncratic reasons rather than any systematic attempt to avoid endorsing the item content.

In scoring a client's MMPI-2, the clinician should ascertain how many of the omitted items are among those commonly omitted items, which are listed in Tables 3.3 and 3.4. These items probably have no particular significance for this client and can be ignored as long as they are not excessive (< 11). Clients who omit idiosyncratic items, that is, those items that are *not* omitted commonly, should be interviewed, if possible, to evaluate their inability to endorse these specific items because most clients are capable of doing so.

For example, suppose that a male psychiatric patient omitted the following 14 MMPI-2 items: 12, 87, 98, 135, 158, 168, 173, 215, 232, 261, 338, 473, 559, and 567. Since 98 percent (Table 3.5) of psychiatric patients omit 12 or fewer items, this patient has omitted more items than most psychiatric patients. When Table 3.4 is consulted, he omitted 8 items that psychiatric patients commonly omit (12, 87, 158, 215, 261, 473, and 559). He also omitted 7 idiosyncratic items: 98, 135, 168, 173, 232, 338, and 567. The clinician could interview the patient about his inability to endorse these latter 6 items.

Hathaway and McKinley (1967) arbitrarily converted raw scores on the *?* scale of the original MMPI to T scores. They assigned a raw score of 30 on the *?* scale to a T score of 50; thus, 30 omitted items should be an average score for the reference population. Assuming that a client could omit 1 item in 5 (110 items total) and still have an interpretable profile, Hathaway and McKinley assigned a raw score of 110 to a T score of 70. Actually a raw score of 30 on the *?* scale occurs about 5 percent of the time (Greene, 1991); that is, a raw score of 30 is nearly a T score of 70, not a T score of 50 as Hathaway and McKinley (1967) assumed. Similarly, a raw score of 100 on the *?* scale occurs about .5 percent of the time, which is approximately a T score of 80, not 70 as Hathaway and McKinley suggested. Thus, the *?* scale T score equivalents on the standard profile sheet of the original MMPI are of questionable accuracy, and the clinician should use

the foregoing T score equivalents that are more accurate estimates of the frequency with which items are omitted on the original MMPI. Clinicians who were taught the MMPI must realize that the frequency with which items are omitted, which they may have learned from the standard MMPI profile sheet, are extremely misleading. Carrying these notions about the frequency of item omission forward to the MMPI-2 is even more serious because items are omitted less frequently on the MMPI-2 than the MMPI.

There are two small changes on the MMPI-2 that may affect the *?* scale. First, the *?* scale is not included on the standard profile sheet for the MMPI-2 (see Profile 2.1, p. 33); instead the number of omitted items is simply noted at the lower left-hand corner of the sheet. This change means that T score equivalents are not provided for the *?* scale. Second, the instructions for administering the MMPI-2 discourage clients from omitting items. Both of these changes may cause clinicians to underestimate the importance of checking for item omissions. Consequently, clinicians will need to be more intentional in checking each client's answer sheet to determine the exact number of item omissions and then determine the T score equivalent for this number of item omissions. If only the first 370 items of the MMPI-2 are administered because the clinician is only interested in obtaining a client's scores on the standard Validity and Clinical scales, the clinician should *not* count the nonadministered items as being omitted.

The first step in determining the validity of this specific administration of the MMPI-2 involves ascertaining the number of omitted items, as outlined in Figure 3.1. Table 3.5 provides the quantitative data that are needed to use the flowchart for the MMPI-2 normative sample (Butcher et al., 1989) and clinical (Caldwell, 1997a) and personnel (Caldwell, 1997b) samples. Omitting items is fairly uncommon in all three samples and the setting in which the MMPI-2 is administered does not appreciably affect the number of items that are omitted. It might be expected that individuals in a personnel setting would be more likely to omit items, but item omissions actually are somewhat less frequent in this setting. This finding would suggest that the revision of the MMPI-2 has eliminated a number of the items that had been found

TABLE 3.5 Cutting Scores for Assessing Frequency of Item Omissions by Setting

?			PERCENTILE						
	30	50	70	84	93	98	99.2	99.7	99.9
Normal[a]			0	1	3	10	16	22	26
Clinical[b]			0	2	5	12	18	24	27
Personnel[c]		0	1	3	5	11	12	16	23

[a]Butcher et al. (1989).
[b]Caldwell (1997a).
[c]Caldwell (1997b).

objectionable on the original MMPI (Butcher & Tellegen, 1966).

One general comment needs to be made about the use of the flowchart provided in Figure 3.1, because it applies at all choice points. No specific percentile for any scale or index has been suggested as indicating that the MMPI-2 profile is acceptable or unacceptable. Instead the clinician is provided with the range of percentiles for each scale or index and the clinician must decide whether to be more or less stringent in making a decision at each choice point. Cutting scores in the range of the 93rd (1.5 standard deviations above the mean) to 99th (2.0 standard deviations above the mean) percentiles typically will be appropriate in most settings. However, the relative costs of false positive (identifying a normal individual as a patient) or false negative (identifying a patient as a normal individual) decisions must be weighed in each clinical setting to determine the optimal cutting score within this range.

No reliability data on the *?* scale have been reported.

Table 3.6 provides interpretations of four levels of item omissions. A summary of the potential causes of excessive item omissions are presented in Table 3.7 as well as some possible solutions for these problems. Most of these solutions allow for the client to correct the problem of omissions on the MMPI-2 so that the clinician then can proceed with the assessment of the consistency of item endorsement. Consequently, this step ensures that an excessive number of items have not been omitted once any reasons that the client might have for omitting items have been identified and corrected.

Constructing an Augmented Profile. A clinician occasionally will be faced with a situation in which the client omitted a sizable number of items and it is not possible to have the client complete these items. For example, when the MMPI-2 is administered as a screening procedure, it may not be possible to interview the client again or have the client retake the omitted items. One way of handling such circumstances is to augment the obtained profile. There are no well-defined criteria as to when a profile should be augmented. Augmenting is probably unnecessary if

TABLE 3.6 Interpretation of Levels of Elevation on the Cannot Say (?) Scale

RAW SCORE	INTERPRETATION
0–2	1. *Normal.* Scores in this range indicate clients who are omitting a few items characteristically omitted by the individual's reference group or omitting a few items that have idiographic significance. The specific items omitted and their content should be scanned.
3–5	2. *Mild.* Scores in this range indicate clients who have omitted slightly more items than is typical of most individuals. The scales from which the items have been omitted should be checked. There is little probability of profile distortion unless all omitted items are from a single scale (Appendix E).
6–25	3. *Moderate.* Scores in this range indicate clients who have omitted more items than is typical. If possible, the client should be encouraged to complete these items. Constructing an augmented profile might be considered. The profile may be of questionable validity as the number of omitted items approaches 25.
26+	4. *Marked. The Profile Is Very Likely To Be Invalid.* These clients are unwilling or unable to complete the MMPI-2 in an appropriate manner. They may be overly cautious in trying not to reveal any significant information about themselves, obsessionally unable to come to any decision about numerous items, or simply so defiant and uncooperative that they will not answer the items. If possible, the clinician should have the client complete the omitted items or retake the entire test. A client who fails to complete the MMPI-2 or who is only given the first 370 items does not automatically fall into this category.

TABLE 3.7 Potential Causes of and Solutions for Excessive Item Omissions

CAUSE	SOLUTION
1. Client is unsure of frequency of occurrence of item content.	1. Emphasize to client that item responses indicate "mostly" true and "mostly" false.
2. Client has been careless in completing the test.	2. Encourage client to take sufficient time to respond to all items.
3. Client is very defensive and unwilling to endorse any items that might be "controversial."	3. Explain that answers to individual items are less important than scores on scales; reassure client that responses to items are confidential.
4. Client is not familiar with item content.	4. None; actually very few of such items for most people.

fewer than 5 items have been omitted, and probably inappropriate if more than 20 to 30 items have been omitted. Consequently, augmenting the profile may be considered between these two extremes if it is not possible to have the client retake the omitted items, *although clinicians should be well aware that there are no empirical data to justify this procedure.*

There are two methods of augmenting the profile. The first is based on the assumption that the client systematically avoided answering the omitted items and that, if the client had responded to them, the response would have been in the deviant direction. The process basically involves determining which items were omitted from which scales and adding one point for each omitted item to the raw score on the appropriate scale. (Appendix E of this book lists the scales on which each MMPI-2 item is scored. Karol [1985] has provided this same information in tabular form for the MMPI that may facilitate determining the scales on which each item is scored.)

Since some items are scored on more than one scale and may even be scored in the opposite direction from one scale to the next, it is possible for the omitted items to be scored as if the client responded both "true" and "false" to them. This "double" scoring of items is a logical inconsistency in this method of constructing an augmented profile; however, if it appears that the client systematically avoided the omitted items, this method represents an appropriate attempt to salvage as much clinical data as possible from an otherwise lost cause.

An example of this method of augmenting the profile might be that a male client omitted 10 items when taking the MMPI-2 (Table 3.8). By checking Appendix E, the clinician can determine which scales contained these items. To construct the augmented profile, the clinician would then add one point for each omitted item to the raw score of the appropriate scale. For example, two points would be added to the raw score for Scale 7 (Psychasthenia) since 2 omitted items (33 and 242) appear on this scale. A similar procedure would be followed for the other items and scales (Table 3.8). The clinician would then plot the augmented profile on the standard profile sheet. If the *K* scale has been augmented, all the *K*-corrected scales (*1* [Hypochondriasis], *4* [Psychopathic Deviate], *7*, *8* [Schizophrenia], and *9* [Hypomania]) also would have to be augmented if a *K*-corrected profile is being plotted.

In addition, the clinician should indicate on the profile sheet that the profile has been augmented using standard procedures. In this example, in which only 10 items were omitted, augmenting the profile

TABLE 3.8 Example of the Procedure for Constructing an Augmented Profile

Items	MMPI-2 Item Number	SCALE	
		True	False
1.	33		2, 7
2.	40	3	
3.	48	F, 8	
4.	75		2
5.	118		2
6.	177	5	8
7.	178		2
8.	185	0	3, 4
9.	189		2, 0
10.	242	7, 8, 9	

changed the two highest Clinical scales from Scales *7* (Psychasthenia) and *0* (Social Introversion) to Scales *2* (Depression) and *7* (Table 3.9). Since the codetype based on which Clinical scales are most elevated in the profile is a central feature of MMPI-2 interpretation, this shift in the codetype can have a significant effect on the interpretation of the profile.

The second method of augmenting the profile is based on the assumption that the client did not systematically avoid the omitted items and would not have answered all the omitted items in the deviant direction. This method would be appropriate if, for example, the client had insufficient time to complete the MMPI-2 and omitted a number of the later items.

After determining, in the fashion described previously, which scales contained the omitted items, the clinician would calculate the proportion of items on each of these scales that the client answered in the deviant direction. Then for each scale the clinician would multiply this proportion times the number of omitted items, assuming that the client would answer the same proportion of the omitted items in the deviant direction.

Using the same example as earlier (Tables 3.8 and 3.9), the client answered 27 of the 57 items on

Scale *2* (Depression) in the deviant direction and omitted 5 items. Thus, the client answered 27/52, or .519 of the items in the deviant direction. Multiplying .519 times the number of omitted items (5) yields 2.60; this figure, which would be rounded to the nearest whole number (3), would be added to the raw score for Scale *2*. A similar process would be followed for each scale on which items were omitted. As with the first method of augmenting the profile, the clinician would then plot the augmented profile, adjusting the *K*-corrections if the *K* scale were augmented and noting on the profile sheet that the profile was augmented by this procedure.

Consistency of Item Endorsement

After the number of items omitted has been checked and found to be in the acceptable range or corrected in one of the manners described earlier, the next step in the process of assessing the validity is to verify the consistency of item endorsement (see Figure 3.1). Consistency of item endorsement verifies that the client has endorsed the items in a reliable manner for this specific administration of the MMPI-2. It is necessary to ensure that the client has endorsed the items consistently before it is appropriate to determine the accuracy with which the client has endorsed the items.

Another way of understanding the difference between the consistency and accuracy of item endorsement, which may clarify why they are distinct steps in this process of assessing the validity of an individual profile, is to conceptualize the consistency of item endorsement as being independent of or irrelevant to item content, whereas the accuracy of item endorsement is dependent on or relevant to item content. Thus, measures of the consistency of item endorsement assess whether the individual has provided a reliable pattern of responding to the items throughout the test regardless of their content, whereas measures of the accuracy of item endorsement assess whether the individual has attempted to distort his or her responses to the items in some specific manner. There are a number of reasons that the client might provide an inconsistent pattern of item endorsement: poor reading skills; limited intellectual ability; limited comprehension of English because it is a second language; medical, neurologic, or psychiatric conditions

TABLE 3.9 Standard and Augmented Scale Scores

Scale	STANDARD PROFILE		AUGMENTED PROFILE	
	Raw Score (with K*)*	T *Score*	*Raw Score (with* K*)*	T *Score*
L	1	39	1	39
F	7	58	8	61
K	11	41	11	41
1 (Hs)	17	62	17	62
2 (D)	27	68	32	78
3 (Hy)	22	52	24	57
4 (Pd)	28	62	29	64
5 (Mf)	31	60	32	62
6 (Pa)	13	61	13	61
7 (Pt)	39	77	41	81
8 (Sc)	37	69	40	74
9 (Ma)	16	41	17	43
0 (Si)	45	72	47	75

that severely impair attention and concentration; unwillingness to comply with the assessment process; and so on.

The consistency of item endorsement on the MMPI is assessed by the Test-Retest (*TR*) index (Dahlstrom et al., 1972) and the Carelessness (*CLS*) scale (Greene, 1978). The *TR* index is the total number of the 16 repeated items on the MMPI that the client has endorsed inconsistently. These 16 repeated items from Scales *6* (Paranoia), *7* (Psychasthenia), *8* (Schizophrenia), and *0* (Social Introversion) were added to the MMPI to facilitate scoring of the IBM answer sheet. If a client endorses a number of these repeated items in a different manner on their second occurrence, this inconsistency quickly becomes apparent and it is easy to demonstrate this inconsistency to the client. These 16 repeated items were omitted from the MMPI-2 so the *TR* index cannot be scored on the MMPI-2. The *CLS* scale consists of 12 pairs of empirically selected items that were judged to be psychologically opposite in content. Further information on the *CLS* scale can be found in Greene (1991).

The consistency of item endorsement on the MMPI-2 is assessed by the Variable Response Inconsistency (*VRIN*) and True Response Inconsistency (*TRIN*) scales. Each of these scales will be examined in turn followed by several other methods of assessing the consistency of item endorsement.

Variable Response Inconsistency* (VRIN) *Scale. The Variable Response Inconsistency (*VRIN*) scale consists of 67 pairs of items that have similar or opposite item content. These pairs of items are scored if the client is inconsistent in his or her responses. Table 3.10 provides two examples of pairs of items on the *VRIN* scale and the inconsistent response(s). For example, if a client endorses item 99 "false" and item 138 "true," it is scored as an inconsistent response.

Table 3.10 also shows that few normal individuals or clients endorse this particular pair of items inconsistently. If a client endorses item 6 "true" and item 90 "false" or item 6 "false" and item 90 "true," it is scored as an inconsistent response. Slightly more normal individuals and clients are likely to endorse this pair of items inconsistently. The *VRIN* scale actually consists of 49 pairs of unique items, since two

TABLE 3.10 Examples of Scored Responses on the Variable Response Inconsistency (*VRIN*) Scale

	138. I believe that I am being plotted against.			
	Normal Individuals		*Clients*	
99. Someone has it in for me.	*True*	*False*	*True*	*False*
True	2.0%	3.7%	14.8%	9.7%
False	0.0	94.3	4.8	70.7

Deviant Responses: 99F–138T.

	90. I love my father or (if your father is dead) I loved my father.			
	Normal Individuals		*Clients*	
6. My father is a good man.	*True*	*False*	*True*	*False*
True	91.2%	1.3%	85.3%	3.3%
False	5.5	2.0	5.5	5.9

Deviant Responses: 6T–90F; 6F–90T.

Note. N = 401 normal individuals; N = 1,500 clients.

separate response patterns are scored for 18 of these 67 item pairs as with items 6 and 90.

Berry and his colleagues (Berry et al., 1991; Berry, Wetter, Baer, Larsen, Clark, & Monroe, 1992; Gallen & Berry, 1996, 1997; Wetter, Baer, Berry, Smith, & Larsen, 1992) have demonstrated the utility of the *VRIN* scale in the identification of inconsistent responding on the MMPI-2. Using a self-report methodology, they also found that 29 to 60 percent of clients randomly endorsed 12 to 38 items, which suggests that this problem may be more prevalent than most clinicians would like to think.

Table 3.11 illustrates the distribution of scores on the *VRIN* scale if the client randomly "endorsed" the MMPI-2 items. Since only one of the four possible combinations of "true" and "false" response patterns is scored on each of the 67 pairs of items on the *VRIN* scale, the average score in such random sorts is 16.75 (67/4). As can be seen in Table 3.11, 8.4 percent of these randomly endorsed MMPI-2s are at or below a

TABLE 3.11 Assessing Random Responses on the MMPI-2 with the *VRIN* Scale and the $|F - F_B|$ Index

	VRIN		$|F - F_B|$		VRIN + $|F - F_B|$			$F + F_B + |F - F_B|$		
Raw Score	Frequency	Cumulative Percent	Frequency	Cumulative Percent	Raw Score	Frequency	Cumulative Percent	Raw Score	Frequency	Cumulative Percent
0			27	1.1	8	2	0.1	36	1	0.0
1			58	3.4	9	1	0.1	38	4	0.2
2			62	5.9	10	4	0.3	40	7	0.5
3			86	9.3	11	3	0.4	42	15	1.1
4			108	13.6	12	5	0.6	44	24	2.0
5			124	18.6	13	6	0.8	46	50	4.0
6	1	0.0	159	25.0	14	13	1.4	48	81	7.3
7	3	0.2	157	31.2	15	15	2.0	50	111	11.7
8	7	0.4	181	38.5	16	41	3.6	52	154	17.9
9	20	1.2	210	46.9	17	57	5.9	54	192	25.6
10	27	2.3	156	53.1	18	55	8.1	56	253	35.7
11	57	4.6	207	61.4	19	78	11.2	58	253	45.8
12	96	8.4	188	68.9	20	90	14.8	60	265	56.4
13	172	15.3	179	76.1	21	90	18.4	62	254	66.6
14	228	24.4	144	81.8	22	131	23.6	64	198	74.5
15	283	35.8	121	86.7	23	140	29.2	66	186	81.9
16	315	48.4	101	90.7	24	163	35.8	68	160	88.3
17	286	59.8	73	93.6	25	177	42.8	70	110	92.7
18	275	70.8	54	95.8	26	164	49.4	72	77	95.8
19	254	81.0	34	97.2	27	165	56.0	74	35	97.2
20	188	88.5	30	98.4	28	161	62.4	76	32	98.5
21	109	92.8	14	98.9	29	148	68.4	78	20	99.3
22	78	96.0	13	99.4	30	130	73.6	80	14	99.8
23	50	98.0	5	99.6	31	108	77.9	82	2	99.9
24	26	99.0	3	99.8	32	114	82.4	86	1	100.0
25	16	99.6	2	99.8	33	94	86.2	88	1	100.0
26	7	99.9	2	99.9	34	84	89.6			
28	2	100.0	2	100.0	35	61	92.0			
					36	65	94.6			
					37	47	96.5			
					38	29	97.6			
					39	15	98.2			
					40+	44	100.0			
	M = 16.74		M = 10.05			M = 26.80			M = 59.95	
	SD = 2.44		SD = 4.83			SD = 8.60			SD = 7.58	

Note. N = 2,500 for each comparison.

score of 12, which is the recommended cutting score for the *VRIN* scale in the *MMPI-2 Manual* (Butcher et al., 1989).

The interpretation of four levels of elevation of the *VRIN* scale is provided in Table 3.18.

True Response Inconsistency* (TRIN) *Scale. The True Response Inconsistency (*TRIN*) scale consists of 23 pairs of items. The *TRIN* scale is very similar to the *VRIN* scale except that the scored response on the *TRIN* scale is either "true" or "false" to both items in each pair. Table 3.12 provides two examples of pairs of items on the *TRIN* scale and the inconsistent response(s). For example, if a client endorses both items 40 and 176 "true," it is scored as an inconsistent response. Similarly, if a client endorses both items 125 and 195 either "true" or "false," it is scored as an inconsistent response. Table 3.12 also shows that few normal individuals or clients endorse either of these pairs of items inconsistently.

The *TRIN* scale has 14 pairs of items to which the inconsistent response is "true" and 9 item pairs to which the inconsistent response is "false." Scoring the *TRIN* scale is somewhat complicated. One point is *added* to the client's score for each of the 14 item pairs

TABLE 3.12 Examples of Scored Responses on the True Response Inconsistency (*TRIN*) Scale

40. Much of the time my head seems to hurt all over.	176. I have very few headaches.			
	Normal Individuals		Clients	
	True	*False*	*True*	*False*
True	.5%	7.2%	4.5%	11.4%
False	72.1	20.2	68.6	15.5

Deviant Responses: 40T–176T.

125. I believe that my home life is as pleasant as that of most people I know.	195. There is very little love and companionship in my family as compared to other homes.			
	Normal Individuals		Clients	
	True	*False*	*True*	*False*
True	2.7%	84.1%	11.3%	51.6%
False	3.7	9.5	20.4	16.7

Deviant Responses: 125T–195T; 125F–195F.

Note. Minnesota Multiphasic Personality Inventory-2 (MMPI-2). Copyright © 1942, 1943 (renewed 1970), 1989 by the Regents of the University of Minnesota. Reproduced by permission of the publisher. "MMPI-2" and "Minnesota Multiphasic Personality Inventory-2" are trademarks owned by the University of Minnesota.
N = 401 normal individuals; *N* = 1,500 clients.

that are scored if endorsed "true," whereas one point is *subtracted* for each of the 9 item pairs that are scored if endorsed "false." Then 9 points are added to this score. (Nine points are added to the score so that it is not possible to obtain a negative score on the *TRIN* scale. If a client endorsed none of the 14 "true" item pairs and all 9 of the "false" item pairs, a score of –9 would be obtained. Adding 9 points avoids this problem.)

For example, if a client endorsed three of the "true" item pairs on the *TRIN* scale, and six of the "false" item pairs, the score would be 6 (3 – 6 + 9). If a client endorsed eight of the "true" item pairs on the *TRIN* scale, and two of the "false" item pairs, the score would be 15 (8 – 2 + 9). The former client with a relatively low score of 6 on the *TRIN* scale has a propensity to say "false" to the items regardless of their content, whereas the latter client with a score of 15 is tending to say "true" to the items.

Scores on the *TRIN* scale should *not* be used to determine whether a client has endorsed the items consistently. High scores on the *TRIN* scale reflect that clients tend to be "yea-sayers," whereas low scores are obtained by clients who are "nay-sayers," regardless of the item content. The implications of these two response styles on the interpretation of the MMPI-2 profile and the empirical correlates of high and low scores on the *TRIN* scale will need to be determined.

A final comment about the *TRIN* scale needs to be made for those clinicians who use the computer scoring of the MMPI-2 provided by National Computer Systems. The Extended Score Report for the MMPI-2 indicates a score of 9 on the *TRIN* scale by placing an asterisk at a T score of 50. Otherwise, a "T" or "F" is plotted at the appropriate T score based on the client's raw score. Since only T scores above 50 are possible on the *TRIN* scale, there needs to be a mechanism whereby high and low scores are differentiated. Scores from 10 to 19 are indicated by placing a "T" at the appropriate T score. For example, if a woman's raw score on the *TRIN* scale was 15, a "T" would be plotted at a T score of 95. Scores from 0 to 8 are indicated by placing an "F" at the appropriate T score. Thus, if a man's raw score was 3, an "F" would be plotted at a T score of 92. This procedure may be clearer if the standard profile form for the Supplementary scales is examined (Profile 6.1, page 244).

$|F - F_B|$ *Index.*   The F (Infrequency) scale and the Back F (F_B: Back Infrequency) scale are composed of items that were endorsed infrequently (less than 10 percent of the time) by the normative sample on the MMPI and MMPI-2, respectively. Each of these scales will be described in more detail later in this chapter. Since the items on both scales are endorsed infrequently, clients would be expected to endorse approximately the same number of items on each scale. Consequently, the *absolute* value of the difference between the number of items that the client has endorsed on each scale can be used as a measure of the consistency of item endorsement.

Table 3.11 provides the distribution of this measure of the consistency of item endorsement for randomly endorsed MMPI-2s. Exactly 75 percent of these randomly endorsed MMPI-2s have a score of 7 or higher on this index, and the mean is approximately 10. Less than 26 percent of these randomly endorsed MMPI-2s with scores on the *VRIN* scale in the intermediate range (8 to 15) had scores of 6 or lower on this index. Thus, the clinician can be fairly confident that the client has endorsed the items consistently if this index is 6 or lower when the *VRIN* scale is in the intermediate range of 8 to 15.

The clinician also can add the score on the *VRIN* scale to the index of $|F - F_B|$ to provide a second measure of consistency of item endorsement for scores in the intermediate range of 8 to 15. Less than 15 percent of the randomly endorsed MMPI-2s had scores of 20 or less on this index (Table 3.11). Only 31.1 percent of the scores in the intermediate range on the *VRIN* scale had scores of 20 or lower. Consequently, the clinician can use scores of 20 or lower on this index (the raw score on the *VRIN* scale plus the index of $|F - F_B|$) to indicate that the client has endorsed the items consistently.

Finally, the clinician can add the raw scores on the F and F_B scales to the index of $|F - F_B|$ to provide a third measure of consistency of item endorsement for scores in the intermediate range on the *VRIN* scale. None of these randomly endorsed MMPI-2s had scores lower than 36 on this index (Table 3.11), which the clinician could use as another means of assessing consistency of item endorsement for these intermediate scores on the *VRIN* scale.

A number of studies (Cramer, 1995; Gallen & Berry, 1996, 1997; Paolo & Ryan, 1992) have evaluated the effectiveness of the index of $|F - F_B|$ to identify randomly endorsed MMPI-2s. These studies have found that the index of $|F - F_B|$, when used in combination with either the *VRIN* scale (Gallen & Berry, 1996) or plus the raw scores of the F and F_B scales (Cramer, 1995; Gallen & Berry, 1997), had the highest hit rates in distinguishing among profiles with differing numbers of random items compared to the *VRIN*, F, and F_B scales individually. However, Paolo and Ryan found that the index of $|F - F_B|$ did not contribute unique variance beyond that provided by the *VRIN*, F, and F_B scales individually. Even in those studies in which the index of $|F - F_B|$ in conjunction with other scales had the highest hit rates, the increments in the number of randomly endorsed MMPI-2s that were identified were small. It appears that the index of $|F - F_B|$ will be most useful when used in conjunction with other scales when they do not provide a definitive decision as to whether the items have been endorsed consistently.

Randomly Endorsed MMPI-2s.   One method of trying to simulate inconsistent patterns of item endorsement has utilized groups of randomly endorsed MMPI-2s ("true" and "false" are assigned randomly to each item). Even a cursory inspection of [this] profile (p. 125) arouses the clinician's suspicions of an inconsistent response style. Subsequent examination of several validity indices confirms the high probability of such an inconsistent response style. In general, the larger the number of items on the Validity scale/index being used, the better the detection of randomly endorsed MMPI-2s. Since the F (Infrequency) scale consists of 60 infrequently endorsed items, randomly endorsing the MMPI-2 items should produce raw scores around 30 (i.e., a T score > 120). Thus, the F scale tends to be one of the most reliable indicators of randomly endorsed MMPI-2s (Carlin & Hewitt, 1990; Dahlstrom et al., 1972; Rogers, Dolmetsch, & Cavanaugh, 1983; Sewell & Rogers, 1994). Similarly, the F_B (Back Infrequency) scale consists of 40 infrequently endorsed items, and randomly endorsing the items should produce a raw score around 20 and a T score greater than 120.

A second method of simulating inconsistent responses involves generating groups of profiles based on patterns of item endorsements such as TFTF, TTFTTF, FFTFFT, and so on. These profiles are identified almost as easily as randomly endorsed MMPI-2s, and again the larger the number of items on the Validity scale/index, the better these profiles are detected (Dahlstrom et al., 1972; Nichols, Greene, & Schmolck, 1989). Huba (1986) has developed a statistical test to assess whether the individual switches between "true" and "false" responses more or less often than would be expected by chance. The test requires computer scoring of the inventory to look for all specific sequences of stereotyped responses. Table 3.13 provides these data for the MMPI-2 normative group and a sample of psychiatric patients (Caldwell, 1997a). Only 4.49% of the normal individuals had revised Z scores greater than +1.96 or less than –1.96 (i.e., more than plus or minus two standard deviations) whereas 6.64% of the psychiatric patients exceed these same revised Z scores. The revised Z statistic appears to reflect more accurately the typical pattern of endorsing the MMPI-2 items because of their nonrandom order. This test is particularly promising since it correlates nearly 0.00 with both of the *VRIN* and *TRIN* scales and, therefore, provides another independent measure for the consistency of item endorsement (Table 3.14). The low correlations between the measures of consistency of item endorsement and the infrequency scales also should be noted in both normal individuals and psychiatric patients.

Reaction Time. The advent of computer-administered MMPI-2s makes it possible to examine the reaction time of the person in responding to each item. Very rapid reaction times would suggest that the person has not taken the time to read the items carefully and should be suggestive of inconsistent item endorsement. Research that evaluates such a hypothesis and provides guidelines for interpreting the obtained reaction times will be needed. In addition, any changes in the person's reaction time across the 567 items could be measured easily by blocks of items to see if there are changes in the client's motivation. Research to test other response styles also is feasible. For example, persons who have very slow reaction times may be trying to overreport or underreport psychopathology because they are trying to make sure that they are providing the "correct" response to each item. Popham and Holden (1990), Holden and Kroner (1992), and Brunetti, Schlottmann, Scott, and Hollrah (1998) provide an introduction to these issues on the MMPI-2.

TABLE 3.13 Distribution of Z Scores for Runs Test in Assessing Inconsistency of Item Endorsement

		NORMAL INDIVIDUALS (BUTCHER ET AL., 1989)				PSYCHIATRIC PATIENTS (CALDWELL, 1997A)			
		(N = 2,589)				(N = 50,966)			
		Z		REVISED Z		Z		REVISED Z	
Range		N	%	N	%	N	%	N	%
−2.50	–	84	3.24	2	0.01	1,145	2.25	225	0.44
−2.24	−2.49	66	2.55	11	0.42	762	1.50	160	0.31
−1.96	−2.23	79	3.05	30	1.16	1,226	2.41	304	0.60
−1.64	−1.95	140	5.41	59	2.28	2,120	4.16	697	1.37
−1.15	−1.63	373	14.41	172	6.64	5,161	10.13	2,541	4.99
1.14	−1.14	1,656	63.96	2,029	78.37	34,229	67.16	38,153	74.86
1.15	1.63	95	3.67	152	5.87	2,962	5.81	4,541	8.91
1.64	1.95	39	1.51	59	2.28	1,129	2.22	1,647	3.23
1.96	2.23	13	0.50	24	0.93	704	1.38	909	1.78
2.24	2.49	10	0.39	14	0.54	403	0.79	554	1.09
2.50	–	34	1.31	37	1.43	1,125	2.21	1,235	2.42

TABLE 3.14 Intercorrelations among Inconsistency and Infrequency Scales

Normal Individuals (Butcher et al., 1989)

Inconsistency Scales			Infrequency Scales		
	TRIN	*Z'*		*F_B*	*F(p)*
VRIN	.029	.087	*F*	.595	.561
TRIN		−.004	*F_B*		.532

Inconsistency Scales with Infrequency Scales

	F	*F_B*	*F(p)*
VRIN	.362	.382	.251
TRIN	.150	.219	.131
Z'	.202	.175	.086

Psychiatric Patients (Caldwell, 1997a)

Inconsistency Scales			Infrequency Scales		
	TRIN	*Z'*		*F_B*	*F(p)*
VRIN	.053	.089	*F*	.844	.696
TRIN		.018	*F_B*		.631

Inconsistency Scales with Infrequency Scales

	F	*F_B*	*F(p)*
VRIN	.371	.339	.285
TRIN	.193	.214	.193
Z'	.155	.164	.081

Note. F = Infrequency scale; *F_B* = Back Infrequency scale; *F(p)* = Infrequency-Psychopathology scale; *TRIN* = True Response Inconsistency scale; *VRIN* = Variable Response Inconsistency scale; *Z'* = Revised Z score for Runs test.

Clinical Case 3-1. Jerry was a 32-year-old, single man who had completed high school as a special education student. He came to his local county mental health agency requesting services for work-related problems. His supervisor thought that Jerry was "lazy," while Jerry characterized his supervisor as being "mean." He was well oriented and his thought processes were logical and coherent. He discussed his work problems easily without any sense of distress or concern. Psychological testing was requested in order to better understand any psychological factors that might be contributing to his work problems.

Jerry's MMPI-2 Profile (Profile 3.1, solid circles) was a *6-8* codetype that matched the prototypic *6-8/8-6* codetype (Profile 3.1, open circles) very closely. Following the flowchart presented in Figure 3.1 (p. 43), Jerry omitted no items so consistency of item endorsement would be assessed next. Jerry had a raw score of 21 (T score of 111) on the *VRIN* scale that clearly indicates that he had endorsed the items inconsistently. (A raw score of 14 is beyond the 99.9th percentile in all samples [Table 3.17].) If measures of the consistency of item endorsement were not examined, the clinician would be likely to conclude that Jerry had serious psychological problems and might even be psychotic (see description of *6-8/8-6* codetype in Chapter 7). His scores on the MMPI-2 Content scales (Profile 3.2) also seem to confirm this picture of serious psychological problems. Subsequently, he was administered a reading test that showed that he read at the 4th grade level. In retrospect the clinician might have been alerted to a potential problem with reading comprehension by the fact that he had graduated from high school as a special education student. This case illustrates the importance of assessing the consistency of item endorsement every time that the MMPI-2 is administered. It also will be shown later (Table 3.39, p. 114) that nearly 34 percent of *6-8/8-6* codetypes are a result of an inconsistent pattern of item endorsement.

Inconsistency Scales versus Infrequency Scales. One advantage of the *VRIN* scale over infrequency scales (*F, F_B*, and *F[p]*, which will be discussed later in this chapter) in the assessment of the consistency of item endorsement is that the *VRIN* scale is not affected by the presence of psychopathology. Elevations on infrequency scales can represent either an inconsistent pattern of item endorsement *or* the person's acknowledgment of the presence of psychopathology, however infrequent it may be, *or* the person's overreporting of psychopathology. In contrast, the *VRIN* scale is relatively unaffected by the type and severity of psychopathology as can be seen in the similar means and standard deviations in the MMPI-2 normative group (Men: *M* = 5.07; *SD* = 2.62; Women: *M* = 5.04; *SD* = 2.51) and the Caldwell (1997a) psychiatric patients (Men: *M* = 5.29; *SD* = 3.19; Women: *M* = 5.37; *SD* = 2.94), and its low correlations with the infrequency scales (Table 3.14). The *VRIN* scale also is not affected by overreporting (Wetter et al., 1992) of psychopathology because the person has to

MMPI-2 PROFILE FOR VALIDITY AND CLINICAL SCALES

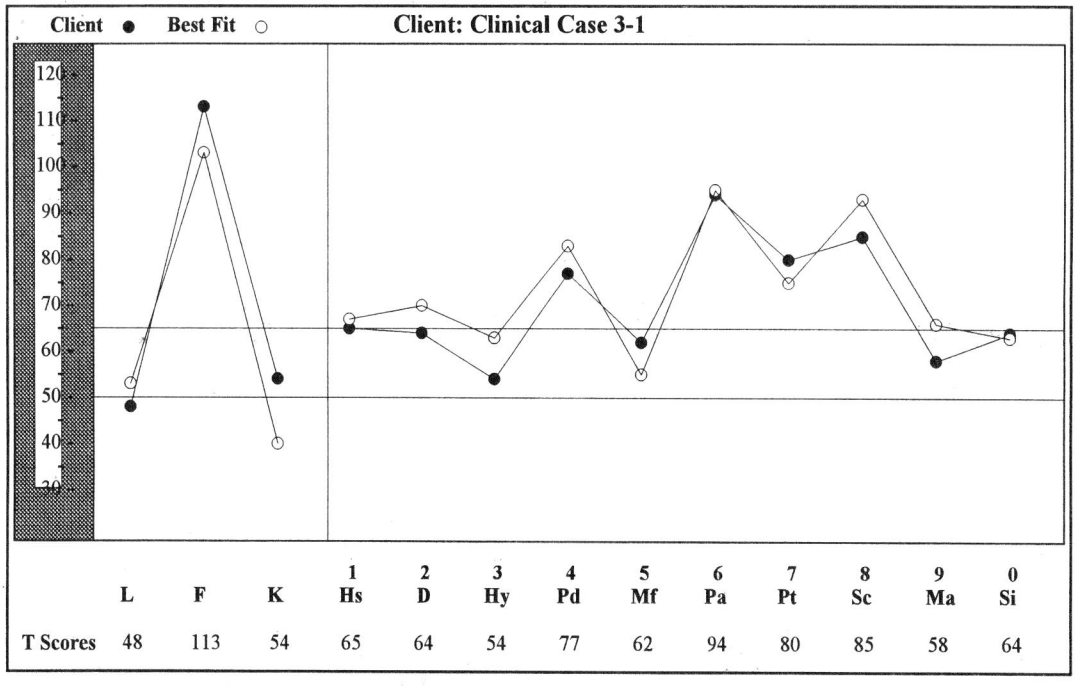

	L	**F**	**K**	**1** **Hs**	**2** **D**	**3** **Hy**	**4** **Pd**	**5** **Mf**	**6** **Pa**	**7** **Pt**	**8** **Sc**	**9** **Ma**	**0** **Si**
T Scores	48	113	54	65	64	54	77	62	94	80	85	58	64

PROFILE 3.1

Note. Minnesota Multiphasic Personality Inventory-2 (MMPI-2). Copyright © 1942, 1943 (renewed 1970), 1989 by the Regents of the University of Minnesota. Reproduced by permission of the publisher. "MMPI-2" and "Minnesota Multiphasic Personality Inventory-2" are trademarks owned by the University of Minnesota.

endorse the items consistently to alter his or her responses. In fact, a potential indicator of an underreported MMPI-2 profile is one in which the person has been *more* consistent than would be expected. Consequently, the *VRIN* scale can provide an independent estimate of the consistency of item endorsement. The *VRIN* scale will detect some profiles with inconsistent responses that would be considered consistent by infrequency scales, and also can demonstrate that the person has been endorsing the items consistently despite elevated scores on the F, F_B, and $F(p)$ scales (see Evans & Dinning, 1983; Gallucci, 1985; Maloney, Duvall, & Friesen, 1980; Wetter et al., 1992). These findings indicate that the *VRIN* and infrequency scales are *not* measuring identical processes in test-taking attitudes (Fekken & Holden, 1987) and, consequently, cannot be simply substituted for one another.

Changes in Consistency of Item Endorsement within an Administration. In discussing the consistency of item endorsement so far, it has been assumed that the client has followed the same pattern of item endorsement for all 567 items. This assumption may not always be appropriate, since clients' motivation and ability to concentrate may change as they go through the test. Since only one of the four possible combinations of "true" and "false" response patterns are scored on each of the 67 pairs of items on the *VRIN* scale (i.e., scoring is not symmetrical), the probability of endorsing any single pair of items is .25, not .50. Consequently, an individual still may have a low score on the *VRIN* scale despite inconsistently endorsing a large number of the items toward the end of the MMPI-2, because the first item in a pair has been *endorsed appropriately.* For example, a cli-

MMPI-2 PROFILE FOR CONTENT SCALES

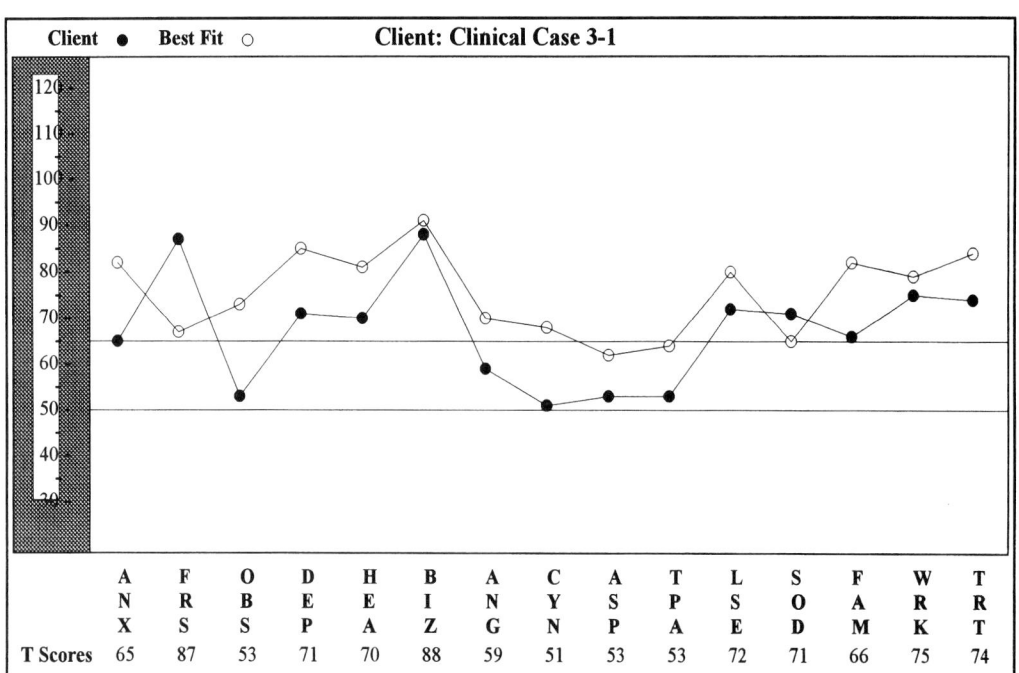

	Client ●	Best Fit ○		Client: Clinical Case 3-1											
	A N X	F R S	O B S	D E P	H E A	B I Z	A N G	C Y N	A S P	T P A	L S E	S O D	F A M	W R K	T R T
T Scores	65	87	53	71	70	88	59	51	53	53	72	71	66	75	74

PROFILE 3.2

Note. Minnesota Multiphasic Personality Inventory-2 (MMPI-2). Copyright © 1942, 1943 (renewed 1970), 1989 by the Regents of the University of Minnesota. Reproduced by permission of the publisher. "MMPI-2" and "Minnesota Multiphasic Personality Inventory-2" are trademarks owned by the University of Minnesota.

ent could endorse the first 400 items consistently and then endorse the remainder of the items inconsistently and produce a relatively low score on the *VRIN* scale. Berry and his colleagues (Berry et al., 1991; Berry et al., 1992) have examined the ability of measures of consistency of item endorsement to detect persons who were instructed to respond randomly after completing the first 100, 200, 300, 400, or 500 items appropriately. They found that the *F*, *F_B*, and *VRIN* scales were effective at detecting persons who endorsed the items randomly, and that these measures were more accurate as the number of items that were endorsed randomly increased.

All items for the MMPI-2 standard Validity and Clinical scales occur in the first 370 items. If inconsistent responding is observed after item 370, clinicians still could score and interpret the standard scales. If blocks or groups of items were assessed for consistency of item endorsement rather than for the entire 567 items, those items up to the point at which the patient started responding randomly could be scored. One of the few advantages of hand scoring the *VRIN* scale is that the clinician can evaluate whether inconsistent responses tend to be distributed evenly throughout the MMPI-2 or begin to occur after some specific point in the test.

As shown in Table 3.15, the items on the *VRIN*, *F*, and *F_B* scales are fairly evenly distributed throughout the MMPI-2 so clinicians could determine when clients start to make inconsistent responses. This approach might be particularly appropriate for intermediate scores on the *VRIN* scale for which it is more difficult to make an assessment of the consistency of item endorsement.

TABLE 3.15   Distribution of F, F_B, and $VRIN$ Items by Blocks of 100 and an Example of a Client Who Endorsed the Items Inconsistently

Item Numbers	NUMBER OF ITEMS ON SCALE			CLINICAL CASE 3–2		
	F	F_B	$VRIN$	F	F_B	$VRIN$
1–100	16	0	4	1	0	0
101–200	17	0	6	1	0	1
201–300	17	2	9	4	0	1
301–400	10	13	9	0	5	3
401–500	0	11	10	0	6	2
501–567	0	14	11	0	7	0
Total	60	40	49	6	18	7

Note. There are only 49 unique item pairs on *VRIN*, since two response patterns are scored on 18 item pairs.

Clinical Case 3-2.   Maria was a 34-year-old, married Hispanic woman with a high school education. She had a long history of drinking that finally resulted in her being placed in an inpatient alcohol treatment program. She was administered the MMPI-2 approximately 10 days after admission as part of a standard assessment battery given to all patients.

Her *4-2* codetype (Profile 3.3, solid circles) is one of the most frequently encountered codetypes in alcohol treatment programs (Greene & Garvin, 1988) and it matches closely the prototypic *2-4/4-2* codetype (Profile 3.3, open circles). The MMPI-2 Content scales (Profile 3.4), which tend to be concentrated in the last 150 items (see Chapter 5), were elevated rather significantly and did not fit her clinical picture at all. Specifically her high point on the Bizarre Mentation (*BIZ*) scale clearly was not accurate because there was no evidence of any type of psychotic process throughout her hospitalization.

MMPI-2 PROFILE FOR VALIDITY AND CLINICAL SCALES

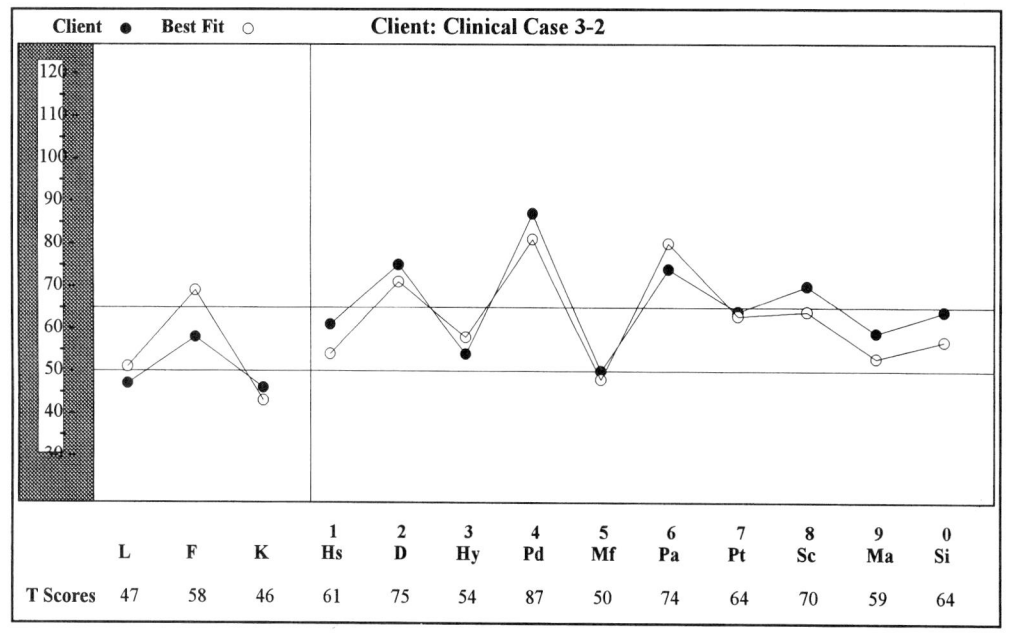

	L	F	K	1 Hs	2 D	3 Hy	4 Pd	5 Mf	6 Pa	7 Pt	8 Sc	9 Ma	0 Si
T Scores	47	58	46	61	75	54	87	50	74	64	70	59	64

PROFILE 3.3

MMPI-2 PROFILE FOR CONTENT SCALES

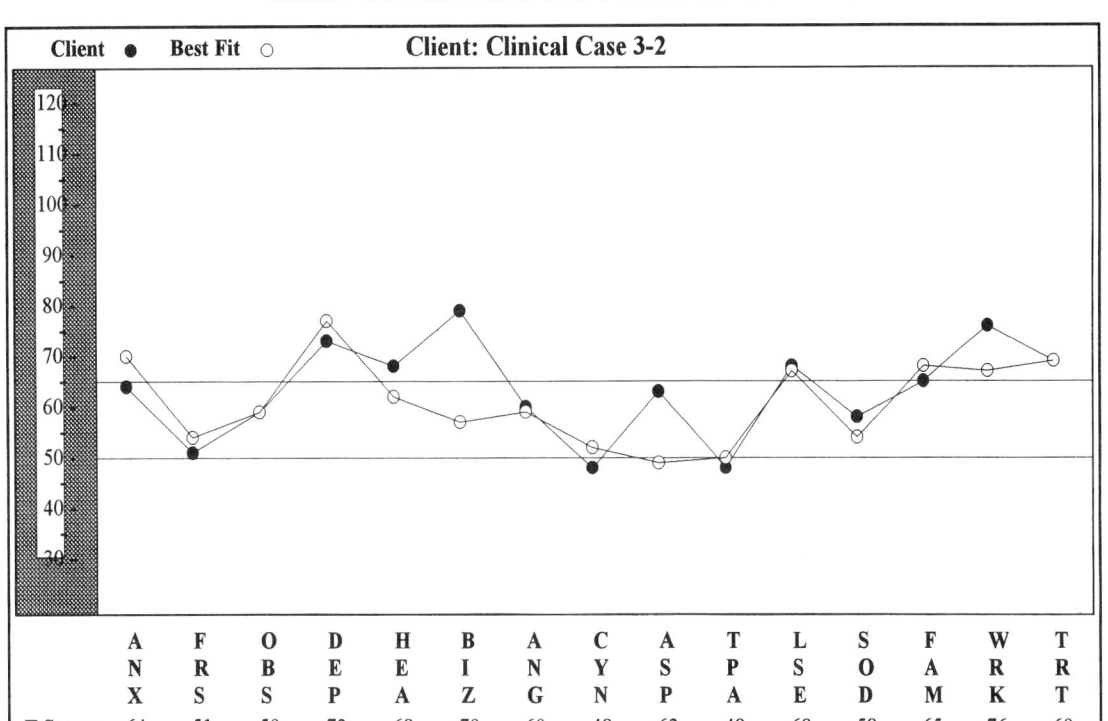

	A N X	F R S	O B S	D E P	H E A	B I Z	A N G	C Y N	A S P	T P A	L S E	S O D	F A M	W R K	T R T
T Scores	64	51	59	73	68	79	60	48	63	48	68	58	65	76	69

PROFILE 3.4

Following the flowchart for assessing the validity of the MMPI-2 presented in Figure 3.1 (p. 43), Maria omitted no items so consistency of item endorsement would be assessed next. Table 3.15 also shows Maria's pattern of item endorsement on the *VRIN, F,* and F_B scales. It is apparent that she started to endorse the items inconsistently somewhere between items 300 and 400, since she endorsed almost one-half of the F_B items in each block of 100 items after endorsing very few of the *F* items. When asked about her performance on the MMPI-2, she related that she became "tired" as she went through the items and responded in a "hurry" toward the end of the test. The standard Validity and Clinical scales still appeared to provide a good clinical description of her because they are based on the first 370 items, as was noted earlier.

This clinical case illustrates the importance of routinely evaluating whether the patient's motivation for taking the MMPI-2 may have changed across the 567 items. Berry et al.'s (1992) finding that 29 to 60 percent of clients randomly endorsed 12 to 38 items also underlines the importance of examining for changes in motivation across the MMPI-2 items, since it seems logical to assume that these random responses are more likely to occur toward the end of the test.

Effects of Demographic Variables on Consistency of Item Endorsement. The variables of age and gender have virtually no impact on any of the scales that measure the consistency of item endorsement (Table 3.16). Scores on the *VRIN* scale are slightly higher in 18- and 19-year-olds than the other age

TABLE 3.16 Effects of Demographic Variables on Scales Measuring Inconsistency of Item Endorsement in the Caldwell Clinical Dataset

		AGE						
		18–19	*20–29*	*30–39*	*40–49*	*50–59*	*60–69*	*70+*
Scale/Index	N =	959	10,979	16,201	12,927	5,703	1,737	498
VRIN	M =	6.2	5.0	5.1	5.2	5.4	5.5	5.6
$\lvert F - F_B \rvert$	M =	3.7	3.0	3.1	3.2	3.3	3.1	3.0
TRIN	M =	9.1	9.0	9.0	9.0	9.0	9.2	9.2

		EDUCATION (YEARS)						
		1–8	*9–10*	*11–12*	*13–14*	*15–16*	*17–18*	*19+*
Scale/Index	N =	1,457	2,215	14,449	10,395	9,524	4,315	3,058
VRIN	M =	6.6	6.2	5.5	5.0	4.7	4.7	4.6
$\lvert F - F_B \rvert$	M =	3.6	3.9	3.3	3.1	2.9	2.9	2.7
TRIN	M =	9.4	9.2	9.1	8.9	8.9	8.9	8.8

		GENDER	
		Men	*Women*
Scale/Index	N =	25,203	25,763
VRIN	M =	5.1	5.3
$\lvert F - F_B \rvert$	M =	3.3	3.0
TRIN	M =	9.0	9.0

Standard Deviation	N = 50,966
VRIN	2.87
$\lvert F - F_B \rvert$	2.62
TRIN	1.45

groups, but this same pattern is not seen on the $\lvert F - F_B \rvert$ index or the *TRIN* scale. There is a steady decline on all three measures of consistency of item endorsement as the years of education increase; individuals with fewer years of education are more likely to endorse the items inconsistently. These data underscore the importance of making sure that persons with less than a high school education have adequate reading skills to complete the MMPI-2. They also indicate that many people with less than a high school education can take the MMPI-2 quite appropriately.

Summary. Now that the *VRIN* and *TRIN* scales and the index of $\lvert F - F_B \rvert$ have been explained as measures of the consistency of item endorsement on the MMPI-2, the next step in the implementation of the flowchart in Figure 3.1 (p. 43) can be described. Table 3.17 provides the quantitative data necessary to determine whether the items have been endorsed in a consistent manner, and Table 3.18 provides interpretations of four levels of consistency of item endorsement. Scores on the *VRIN* and *TRIN* scales are very similar in normal individuals (Butcher et al., 1989) and psychiatric (Caldwell, 1997a) and personnel (Caldwell, 1997b) samples, while scores on the $\lvert F - F_B \rvert$ index are somewhat higher in the psychiatric patients than the other two samples. Again, a specific score on these scales and index has *not* been selected to indicate that

TABLE 3.17 Cutting Scores for Assessing Consistency of Item Endorsement by Setting

	PERCENTILE											
VRIN	2	7	16	30	50	70	84	93	98	99.2	99.7	99.9
Normal[a]	0	1	2	3	4	6	7	9	11		12	13
Clinical[b]	0	1	2	3	5	6	8	9	11	12	13	14
Personnel[c]			0	1	2	3	4	6	8	10	12	13
	PERCENTILE											
$|F - F_B|$	2	7	16	30	50	70	84	93	98	99.2	99.7	99.9
Normal[a]		0		1	2	3	4	5	8	9	10	12
Clinical[b]		0		1	2	4	5	7	10	12	14	16
Personnel[c]			0		1	2	3	4	6	8	14	17
	PERCENTILE											
TRIN	2	7	16	30	50	70	84	93	98	99.2	99.7	99.9
Normal[a]	6	7		8		9		10	11	12	13	14
Clinical[b]	6		7	8		9	10	11	12	13	14	15
Personnel[c]		7		8			9		10		11	12

[a]Butcher et al. (1989).
[b]Caldwell (1997a).
[c]Caldwell (1997b).

the items were endorsed inconsistently. The clinician will have to decide which cutting score is most appropriate given the specific patient and the setting in which the MMPI-2 is administered. Once it has been determined that the items have been endorsed consistently, the clinician then can proceed to the next step to assess the accuracy of item endorsement.

A summary of the potential causes of inconsistency in item endorsement is presented in Table 3.19 as well as some possible solutions for these problems. Most of these solutions allow for the MMPI-2 to be readministered so that a consistent pattern of item endorsement can be obtained and the clinician then can proceed with the assessment of the accuracy of item endorsement. Consequently, this step ensures that the items have been endorsed consistently once any problems have been identified and corrected.

ACCURACY OF ITEM ENDORSEMENT

After item omissions and consistency of item endorsement have been checked, the next step in the process of assessing the validity of the MMPI-2 is to verify the accuracy of item endorsement (Figure 3.1, p. 43). Accuracy of item endorsement verifies whether the client has adopted a response set either to overreport ("fake-bad," malinger, make socially undesirable responses, etc.) or underreport ("fake-good," be defensive, make socially desirable responses, etc.) either the presence or severity of psychopathology.

As noted in Chapter 1, the terms *overreporting* and *underreporting* of psychopathology will be used throughout this book rather than the terms indicated parenthetically because a client's motivation for over-reporting or underreporting may range from being very conscious and intentional to being out of awareness and unconscious. Since the client's test data reveal only that the items have been endorsed inaccurately, it is necessary to determine the client's motivation for inaccurate item endorsement from a clinical interview and a review of the client's reasons for taking the MMPI-2.

Several issues about overreporting and underreporting of psychopathology must be made explicit

TABLE 3.18 Interpretation of Levels of Consistency of Item Endorsement

SCALE/INDEX

VRIN	$|F - F_B|$	Interpretation
0–2	0–1	1. *Low.* Scores in this range indicate clients who have endorsed the items more consistently than would be expected in most settings. The possibility of underreporting of psychopathology should be considered.
3–7	2–5	2. *Normal.* These clients have endorsed the items consistently.
8–10	6–9	3. *Marginal.* These clients may have endorsed the items inconsistently throughout the test or starting at some specific point in the test. Other means of assessing the consistency of item endorsement that were discussed in this Chapter should be reviewed.
11+	10+	4. *Marked.* These clients have endorsed the items inconsistently. The potential reasons for the inconsistent item endorsement should be determined, the problem corrected if possible, and the MMPI-2 readministered.

before the scales and indexes for assessing accuracy of item endorsement are discussed. First, it will be assumed that overreporting and underreporting represent a unitary dimension that is characterized by the overreporting of psychopathology at one end of the dimension and underreporting at the other (Figure 3.2). Consequently, accurate patterns of item endorsement gradually will shade into overreporting or underreporting of psychopathology as one moves up or down this dimension; there is no exact point at which the client's performance suddenly reflects either overreporting or underreporting of psychopathology. Instead, a probability statement can be made that this client's perfor-

mance has a particular likelihood of reflecting either overreporting or underreporting of psychopathology.

Second, it will be assumed that clients who are endorsing the items inaccurately will overreport or underreport psychopathology in general rather than a specific mental disorder or a set of symptoms. It is very difficult for clients to take the MMPI-2 in an accurate manner, as if they have a specific mental disorder that has been documented frequently (see Gough Dissimulation scale and Simulation as Role Playing later). The interested clinician is encouraged to take the MMPI-2 with a specific mental disorder in mind and see how well the scales and indexes designed to assess accuracy of item endorsement detect it.

Third, the presence of overreporting or underreporting of psychopathology *cannot* be taken as evidence that the client does or does not have actual psychopathology, because a client who actually has some specific mental disorder can overreport or underreport psychopathology. The scales and indexes to assess accuracy of item endorsement *cannot* determine whether the client actually has psychopathology, only whether the client has provided an accurate self-description.

Finally, the scales used to assess the consistency of item endorsement (*VRIN, F,* and F_B) are *not* appropriate to assess the accuracy of item endorsement (Gallucci, 1984), and the scales and indexes used to assess the accuracy of item endorsement are *not* appropriate to assess the consistency of item endorsement (Rogers, 1983). These two steps in assessing the validity of a specific administration of the MMPI-2 need to be understood as independent events using the scales and indexes that are appropriate at each step.

In assessing the accuracy of item endorsement, it is more efficient to discuss procedures for assessing overreporting of psychopathology and then underreporting because the same scales and indexes do not always work for both response sets. The reader should realize that it is *not* necessary to score all of these methods for assessing overreporting and underreporting of psychopathology for every client. Several methods will be illustrated within each response set. The reader will need to decide which method is most appropriate for his or her specific treatment setting and clients. Overreporting and underreporting of psychopathology will be examined in turn.

TABLE 3.19 Potential Causes of and Solutions for Inconsistent Item Endorsement

CAUSE	SOLUTION
1. Client has not been told why the MMPI-2 is being administered.	1. Explain why the MMPI-2 is being administered and how the data are to be used.
2. Inadequate reading ability or comprehension; inadequate educational opportunity.	2. Present the MMPI-2 orally by audiotape administration (see Chapter 2). Dahlstrom et al. (1972) reported that audiotape administrations are effective with reading and educational levels as low as the third grade.
3. Limited intellectual ability.	3. Present the MMPI-2 orally by audiotape administration (see Chapter 2). Dahlstrom et al. (1972) reported that audiotape administrations are effective with IQs as low as 65.
4. Too confused psychiatrically or neuropsychologically.	4. Readminister the MMPI-2 when the client is less confused.
5. Still toxic from substance abuse.	5. Readminister the MMPI-2 when the client is detoxified.
6. Noncompliant or uncooperative.	6. Be sure client understands the importance of the MMPI-2 for treatment and intervention and readminister the MMPI-2. If the client is still noncompliant, that issue becomes the focus of treatment.

Overreporting of psychopathology on the MMPI-2 can be assessed by infrequency (F, F_B, and $F[p]$) scales, the $F - K$ Dissimulation index, the Gough Dissimulation (Ds: Gough, 1954, 1957) scale, critical items (cf. Koss & Butcher, 1973; Lachar & Wrobel, 1979), and the Wiener and Harmon (Wiener, 1948) Obvious and Subtle subscales. All of these methods for assessing overreporting of psychopathology ex-cept for $F(p)$ are essentially identical as can be seen by most of the intercorrelations being greater than .80 in the Caldwell clinical dataset (Table 3.20). The higher correlations in the psychiatric patients than the normal individuals reflect that there are restricted ranges for these scales and indexes in the normal individuals. The deviant direction for 46 to 93 percent of the items on these scales is "true" (Table 3.21). Any

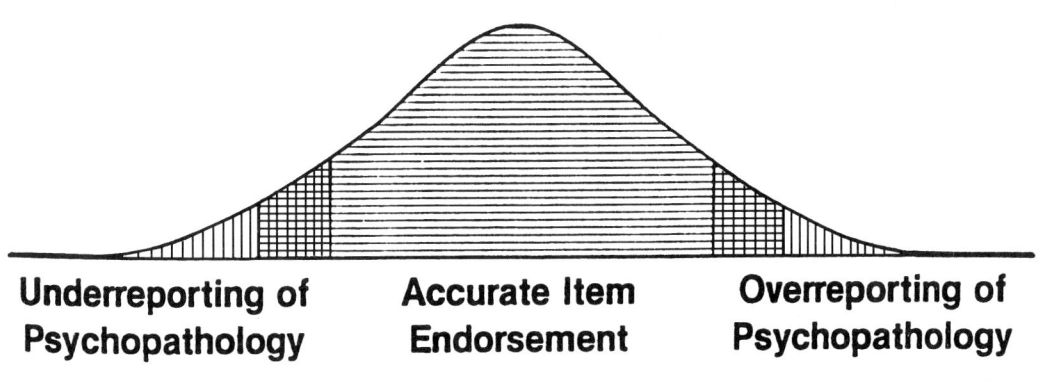

Underreporting of Psychopathology   **Accurate Item Endorsement**   **Overreporting of Psychopathology**

FIGURE 3.2

TABLE 3.20   Intercorrelations among Scales Measuring Overreporting of Psychopathology

Normal Individuals (Butcher et al., 1989)

	F_B	F(p)	KBSum	LWSum	F – K	Ds	Total O – S	True %
Infrequency								
F	.59	.57	.66	.67	.75	.61	.58	.45
F_B	–	.53	.72	.69	.62	.66	.63	.60
F(p)		–	.37	.37	.42	.36	.34	.29
Critical Items								
KBSum			–	.92	.79	.80	.82	.73
LWSum				–	.79	.84	.82	.72
Other Indexes								
F – K					–	.77	.84	.80
Ds						–	.79	.76
Total O – S							–	.78

Psychiatric Patients (Caldwell, 1997a)

	F_B	F(p)	KBSum	LWSum	F – K	Ds	Total O – S	True %
Infrequency								
F	.86	.75	.83	.84	.91	.84	.81	.71
F_B	–	.68	.85	.84	.83	.84	.81	.76
F(p)		–	.52	.54	.64	.58	.52	.49
Critical Items								
KBSum			–	.96	.89	.90	.93	.81
LWSum				–	.89	.92	.93	.79
Other Indexes								
F – K					–	.90	.92	.87
Ds						–	.90	.85
Total O – S							–	.84

Note. F = Infrequency; F_B = Back Infrequency; *F(p)* = Infrequency-Psychopathology; KBSum = total number of Koss and Butcher (1973) critical items endorsed; LWSum = total number of Lachar and Wrobel (1979) critical items endorsed; *F – K* = Gough (1950) Dissimulation index; *Ds* = Gough (1954) Dissimulation scale; Total O – S = total T score difference between the Obvious and Subtle subscales (Wiener, 1948); True % = percentage of all 567 items endorsed "true."

time all of these scales are elevated significantly the possibility of a tendency to endorse the items in the "true" direction should be considered by checking the percentage of items endorsed "true." Table 3.21 also provides a rating of the obviousness of the item content as a measure of a psychological problem (Christian, Burkhart, & Gynther, 1978). A rating of 4 indicates that the scale has obvious content, 3 neither obvious nor subtle content, and 2 subtle content. Thus, the infrequency scales have obvious content and the underreporting scales have subtle content.

Overreporting of Psychopathology

Infrequency (**F, F$_B$,** *and* **F[p])** *Scales.*
F *(Infrequency) Scale.*   The *F* scale consists of 60 items that were selected to detect unusual or atypical ways of answering the test items. Unlike most of the other scales, the *F* scale was not derived by comparing item endorsements between criterion and normal groups; it is made up of items that no more than 10 percent of an early subsample of the Minnesota normative sample answered in the deviant direction.

TABLE 3.21 Percentage of Items Endorsed "True" and Obviousness Ratings for Scales Assessing the Accuracy of Item Endorsement

Scales/Index	True %	OBVIOUSNESS[a]	
		Mean	Items
OVERREPORTING OF PSYCHOPATHOLOGY			
Infrequency			
Infrequency (F)	68.3	3.79	60
Back Infrequency (F_B)	92.5	3.92	20
Infrequency – Psychopathology (F[p])	66.7	3.67	22
Critical Items			
Koss & Butcher (1977)	84.6	3.77	68
Lachar & Wrobel (1979)	72.9	3.59	107
Gough Dissimulation (Ds)	82.8	3.54	32
Total Obvious – Subtle	46.2		
Obvious subscales			
Depression (D-O)	43.6	3.32	39
Hysteria (Hy-O)	37.5	3.30	32
Psychopathic Deviate (PD-O)	71.4	3.53	28
Paranoia (Pa-O)	87.0	4.07	23
Hypomania (Ma-O)	87.0	3.22	23
Subtle subscales			
Depression (D-S)	16.7	2.15	18
Hysteria (Hy-S)	3.6	2.34	28
Psychopathic Deviate (Pd-S)	18.2	2.63	22
Paranoia (Pa-S)	29.4	2.78	17
Hypomania (Ma-S)	65.2	2.54	23
UNDERREPORTING OF PSYCHOPATHOLOGY			
Lie (L)	0.0	2.41	15
Other Deception (ODecp)	54.5	2.14	33
Wiggins Social Desirability (Sd)	72.7	2.14	33
Superlative (S)	12.0	2.19	39
Correction (K)	3.3	2.28	30
Edwards Social Desirability (So)	21.6	2.04	37

[a]These ratings are based on Christian, Burkhart, and Gynther (1978).

The *F* scale can be called quite accurately a *frequency* scale, but the exact derivation of the label *F* is unknown. The scale taps a wide variety of obvious and unambiguous content areas, including bizarre sensations, strange thoughts, peculiar experiences, feelings of isolation and alienation, and a number of unlikely or contradictory beliefs, expectations, and self-descriptions (Dahlstrom et al., 1972). Examples of items on the *F* scale with the deviant answer indicated in parentheses are:

"There is something wrong with my mind." (true)

"No one cares much what happens to you." (true)

"Sometimes I feel as if I must injure either myself or someone else." (true)[2]

2. Minnesota Multiphasic Personality Inventory-2 (MMPI-2). Copyright © 1942, 1943 (renewed 1970), 1989 by the Regents of the University of Minnesota. Reproduced by permission of the publisher. "MMPI-2" and "Minnesota Multiphasic Personality Inventory-2" are trademarks owned by the University of Minnesota.

Most of the items on the F scale (35 of 60) are scored only on the F scale among the standard Validity and Clinical scales; 15 items overlap with Scale *8* (Schizophrenia), 9 items with Scale *6* (Paranoia), and 4 items with Scale *4* (Psychopathic Deviate). The F scale also shares 14 items with the Infrequency-Psychopathology ($F[p]$) scale, 10 items with the Bizarre Mentation (*BIZ*) scale, 5 items with the Mac-Andrew Alcoholism—Revised (*MAC-R*), 5 items with the Post Traumatic Stress Disorder—Keane (*PK*) scale, and 4 items with Post Traumatic Stress Disorder—Schlenger (*PS*) scale. Eight of the items on the F scale (12, 48, 120, 132, 204, 222, 264, and 288) do not meet the 10 percent or below criterion for either men or women in the MMPI-2 normative sample, and an additional 4 items (84, 174, 306, and 343) for men do not meet this criterion (Butcher et al., 1989). There also are 69 more items on the MMPI-2 that meet the 10 percent or below criterion; 37 of these items are found on the Back Infrequency (F_B) scale.

Five of the items on the F scale (20, 54, 112, 115, and 185) on the MMPI do not meet the 10 percent or below criterion for either men or women in the original Minnesota normative sample, and an additional 11 items for men and 3 for women do not meet this criterion (Dahlstrom et al., 1972). Most of these items, however, exceeded the criterion by only a few percentage points. There also are 38 more items that meet the 10 percent or below criterion that could have been included in the F scale but were not for unknown reasons.

Gravitz (1987) reported that normal job applicants endorsed a number of the MMPI items on the F scale more frequently than the 10 percent criterion of the original normative sample. More than 10 percent of the men and women endorsed MMPI items 112, 115, 199, and 206 in the deviant direction. The men also endorsed item 215 more than 10 percent of the time. Gravitz concluded that these changes in the frequency of item endorsement indicate that it may be necessary to renorm the MMPI. These same items also were endorsed more than 10 percent of the time by the MMPI-2 normative sample except for item 206, which was deleted.

Researchers have investigated the relationship between elevations on the F scale, validity of the profile, and extent of psychopathology. Hathaway and McKinley (1951) originally recommended that MMPI profiles should be ruled invalid if the raw score on the F scale exceeds 11 (T score > 70). Researchers quickly showed, however, that all profiles with a raw score greater than 11 on the F scale were not invalid. Kazan and Sheinberg (1945) reported that 35 of 37 male mental hygiene clinic patients with a raw score greater than 11 on the F scale were providing valid self-descriptions on the MMPI. Similarly, Schneck (1948) believed that 10 of 17 male prisoners with a raw score on the F scale greater than 11 were providing accurate responses, and their elevation on the F scale appeared to reflect the severity of their personality disturbance.

The next flurry of research investigated whether MMPI profiles with a raw score on the F scale greater than 16 (T score > 80) should be considered invalid. Preliminary research in this area indicated that persons with a raw score greater than 16 were likely to be diagnosed as having behavior disorders (Gynther, 1961; Gynther & Shimkunas, 1965a) in court-referred cases and as being psychotic in psychiatric samples (Blumberg, 1967; Gauron, Severson, & Englehart, 1962; Gynther & Shimkunas, 1965b).

Again, it appears that a specific raw score on the F scale cannot be used to consider profiles routinely as invalid because a majority of the persons in these studies were classified accurately. Instead, significant psychopathology tends to be correlated with raw scores greater than 16 on the F scale, although the exact correlates differ as a function of the setting in which the MMPI is given.

Finally, Gynther, Altman, and Warbin (1973b) examined the correlates of raw scores on the F scale greater than 25 (T scores > 98) in white and black hospital patients. They identified and cross-validated seven descriptors of the white patients: They were unable to understand proverbs, were monosyllabic, had delusions of reference, had auditory hallucinations, were disoriented for place, had short attention spans, and did not know why they were hospitalized.

Essentially the white patients with raw scores greater than 25 on the F scale could be described as confused psychotics, and their extreme profile elevations reflected the severity of their psychopathology. No descriptors could be cross-validated among the black patients (i.e., there were no replicable differences between black patients with raw scores greater than 25 versus those with raw scores equal to or less than 25). Obviously, the *F* scale was tapping different dimensions in black as compared to white patients. More information on the performance of blacks and other minority groups on the MMPI-2 is provided in Chapter 9.

Gynther, Lachar, and Dahlstrom (1978) developed an *F* scale for blacks that is designed to serve the same validity function as the standard *F* scale (i.e., to identify persons who endorse items that members of a normal population infrequently endorse). This *F* scale for blacks also is described in Chapter 9.

Other studies have investigated clients' responses to individual items on the *F* scale. Gynther and Petzel (1967) observed that psychotics and persons with behavior disorders were not differentiated by their raw scores on the *F* scale; they hypothesized that this occurred because these persons endorsed different subsets of items within the scale. They found, however, only one item that discriminated the two groups; therefore, their hypothesis was not supported.

McKegney (1965) observed that delinquent adolescents have elevated scores on the *F* scale and hypothesized that these elevations occurred because some of the items on the *F* scale are accurate responses for them. Hence, McKegney thought that delinquent adolescents were consistently endorsing only certain items on the *F* scale that are meaningful for them. Three professionals and three nonprofessionals familiar with adolescents identified 21 items on the *F* scale that they felt could be answered truthfully by delinquent adolescents.

McKegney (1965) also found that 21 items on the *F* scale were answered more frequently by delinquent adolescents than by normal adolescents. These items dealt with such content as stealing, misbehaving in school, and injuring others; the items directly tap the behaviors and attitudes that caused the adolescents to be labeled delinquent. McKegney reported that these two sets of 21 items were positively correlated, but he did not report how many or which items overlapped between the two sets.

Thus, it appears that high scores on the *F* scale among delinquent adolescents may result at least partially from the fact that some items are genuinely more applicable to juveniles than to the original normative group. Archer (1984, 1987, 1992, 1997) has noted that most adolescents have higher scores on the *F* scale than adults, which also suggests that a number of these items may not be infrequent items for adolescents.

Elevation of the *F* scale is correlated positively with the overall elevation of all of the MMPI-2 Clinical scales and particularly Scales *6* (Paranoia) and *8* (Schizophrenia), both in adult psychiatric patients and in adolescents (Dahlstrom et al., 1972). Elevation of the *F* scale also is a rough index of the severity of the psychological distress that the client is experiencing; higher scores indicate more severe distress. Clinicians should keep in mind, however, that the content of the items on the *F* scale is obvious, and clients may lower or raise their scores on the *F* scale virtually as desired.

Test-retest reliability coefficients for the MMPI *F* scale range from .80 to .97 for an interval up to two weeks and range from .45 to .76 for intervals from eight months up to three years (Dahlstrom et al., 1975). Test-retest reliability coefficients for the *F* scale on the MMPI-2 are .78 for men and .69 for women over a one-week interval (Butcher et al., 1989).

Scores on the *F* scale decrease only 1 to 3 T points in normal individuals (Butcher et al., 1989; Colligan et al., 1989), medical patients (Swenson, Pearson, & Osborne, 1973), and psychiatric patients (Caldwell, 1997a; Hedlund & Won Cho, 1979) from age 20 to 70 (Table 3.23). However, there is a 5 to 10 T point decrease in scores on the *F* scale from the teenage years to age 20 in normal individuals (Butcher et al., 1989; Butcher, Graham, Dahlstrom, & Bowman, 1990; Butcher et al., 1991) and psychiatric patients (Caldwell, 1997a). There are no gender differences in the endorsement of the items on the *F* scale items. Scores on the *F* scale also decrease 8 to 16 T points as years of education increase from less than 9 years to more than 18 years in normal individuals (Butcher et al., 1989) and psychiatric patients (Caldwell, 1997a).

The optimal cutting score on the *F* scale to identify students who are instructed to overreport psychopathology compared to students who have taken the MMPI-2 accurately has ranged from 16 (Sivec, Lynn, & Garske, 1994) to 29 (Austin, 1992). A cutting score of 16 on the *F* scale would classify nearly

10 percent of the psychiatric patients (Caldwell, 1997a; Table 3.24) as overreporting, while a cutting score of 29 would classify a little under 1 percent as overreporting. When students who are instructed to overreport psychopathology are compared with psychiatric patients who are presumed to have taken the MMPI-2 honestly, the optimal cutting score on the F scale has ranged from 16 (Bagby, Rogers, Buis, & Kalemba, 1994) to 27 (Graham, Watts, & Timbrook, 1991). A more in-depth analysis of this issue will be undertaken once all of the scales and indexes used to assess overreporting of psychopathology have been described.

A summary of the interpretation of four levels of the F scale is provided in Table 3.22.

F_B *(Back Infrequency) Scale.* The Back Infrequency (F_B) scale consists of 40 items on the MMPI-2 that no more than 10 percent of the MMPI-2 normative sample answered in the deviant direction. This scale is analogous to the standard F scale except that the items are placed in the last half of the test. Item 281 is the first item on the F_B scale, whereas item 361 is the last item on the standard F scale (Appendix B). The

scale taps a wide variety of content areas, including suicidality, hopelessness, alcohol- or drug-related problems, general fearfulness, and poor interpersonal and familial relations. Examples of items on the F_B scale with the deviant answer indicated in parentheses are:

> "The future seems hopeless to me." (true)
>
> "My life is empty and meaningless." (true)
>
> "Several times a week I feel as if something dreadful is about to happen." (true)[3]

Most of the items on the F_B scale (28/40) are scored only on the F_B scale among the standard Validity and Clinical scales; 10 items overlap with Scale 8 (Schizophrenia) and 2 items with Scales 6 (Paranoia) and 7 (Psychasthenia). The F_B scale also shares 7 items with the Infrequency-Psychopathology ($F[p]$)

---

3. Minnesota Multiphasic Personality Inventory-2 (MMPI-2). Copyright © 1942, 1943 (renewed 1970), 1989 by the Regents of the University of Minnesota. Reproduced by permission of the publisher. "MMPI-2" and "Minnesota Multiphasic Personality Inventory-2" are trademarks owned by the University of Minnesota.

TABLE 3.22   Interpretation of Levels of Elevation on the F (Infrequency) and F_B (Back Infrequency) Scales

T SCORE	INTERPRETATION
45 and below	1. *Low.* Scores in this range indicate clients who avoided acknowledging the socially unacceptable or disturbing content represented in these scales. They may be trying to underreport psychopathology, or they may be normal persons who are very conventional, unassuming, and unpretentious.
46–58	2. *Normal.* These clients are willing to acknowledge a typical number of unusual experiences.
59–80	3. *Moderate.* These clients are acknowledging the unusual experiences represented in these scales more than the typical person. The elevation reflects the extent and severity of the client's psychopathology, and how the client has adjusted to his or her psychopathology (i.e., an intact psychotic patient frequently falls in the middle of this range).
81–110	4. *Marked.* The profile may be invalid; other validity indicators should be evaluated to determine whether the client has overreported psychopathology. If the items have been endorsed accurately, the elevation reflects the severity of distress and extent of psychopathology the client is experiencing that will be readily apparent in a clinical interview. The client is likely to be diagnosed as having severe behavior disorders or being psychotic, depending on his or her age and type of treatment facility.
111 and above	5. *Extreme. The profile is very likely to be invalid.* Other validity indicators should be checked. These clients are likely to be severely disorganized and floridly psychotic if they have endorsed the items accurately; these characteristics are readily apparent in a clinical interview.

scale, 7 items with the Fears (*FRS*) scale, 6 items with the Depression (*DEP*) scale, and 3 items with the Bizarre Mentation (*BIZ*), Low Self-Esteem (*LSE*), Family Problems (*FAM*), and Negative Treatment Indicators (*TRT*) scales.

There are large differences between raw scores and their corresponding T scores on the F_B and F scales on the MMPI-2 (compare Profile 8.3, page 383, and Profile 8.5, page 385). For men a raw score of 16 is a T score of 108 on the F_B scale and a T score of 85 on the F scale, while for women a raw score of 12 is a T score of 89 on the F_B scale and a T score of 79 on the F scale. These differences in T scores occur because the items on the F_B scale (Men: $M = 1.86$; $SD = 2.44$; Women: $M = 1.94$; $SD = 2.58$) are much less likely to be endorsed than the items on the F scale (Men: $M = 4.53$; $SD = 3.24$; Women: $M = 3.66$; $SD = 2.91$). Although the items on the F scale were endorsed infrequently by the MMPI normative group, eight of these items (12, 48, 120, 132, 204, 222, 264, and 288) were endorsed by more than 10 percent of the MMPI-2 normative group. The items on the F_B scale were selected because they were endorsed infrequently by the MMPI-2 normative group.

The clinician should recall the use of the relationship between the raw scores on the F and F_B scales as a measure of consistency of item endorsement (page 54). In using this index, it is important to be aware of the differences in item content on these two scales even though these items are endorsed relatively infrequently. The items on the F scale primarily reflect more strange and atypical, frequently psychotic, behaviors and symptoms, while the items on the F_B scale emphasize suicidal ideation, hopelessness, and problems with relations. When a client endorses three to five more items on either scale, the clinician should consider whether this difference is the result of the client's accurate endorsement of the item content rather than an indication of inconsistent item endorsement.

Test-retest reliability coefficients for the F_B scale on the MMPI-2 are .86 for men and .71 for women over a one-week interval (Butcher et al., 1989). These coefficients are slightly higher than those reported for the F scale.

The effects of gender and age on the F_B scale are very similar to those reported earlier on the F scale so they will not be repeated here (Table 3.23). The effects of education are even larger on the F_B scale than on the F scale with scores decreasing 12 to 18 T points as years of education increase from less than 9 years to more than 18 years in normal individuals (Butcher et al., 1989) and psychiatric patients (Caldwell, 1997a).

The optimal cutting score on the F_B scale to identify students who are instructed to overreport psychopathology compared to students who take the MMPI-2 accurately has ranged from 11 (Sivec et al., 1994) to 23 (Graham et al., 1991). A cutting score of 13 would classify about 10 percent of the psychiatric patients (Caldwell, 1997a) in Table 3.24 as overreporting, while a cutting score of 23 would classify a little under 1 percent as overreporting. Similar variability in cutting scores on the F_B scale has been reported to identify students who are instructed to overreport psychopathology compared to patients who are presumed to have taken the MMPI-2 honestly, with cutting scores ranging from 13 (Bagby, Rogers, Buis, & Kalemba, 1994) to 27 (Graham et al., 1991). Again this issue will be explored in more depth later.

The levels of F_B scale elevation and their interpretation should be comparable to the standard F scale because the items were selected by a similar criterion. Consequently, the same interpretive statements are suggested for both F_B and F scales (Table 3.22).

Infrequency-Psychopathology (F[*p*]) *Scale.* The Infrequency-Psychopathology (*F*[*p*]) scale (Arbisi & Ben-Porath, 1995) consists of 27 items[4] on the MMPI-2 that no more than 20 percent of a sample of 706 men who were psychiatric inpatients, a second sample of 423 men and women who also were psychiatric inpatients, and the MMPI-2 normative sample endorsed in the deviant direction. This scale is analogous to the standard F scale except that the items were endorsed infrequently by a sample of psychiatric inpatients, hence the name of infrequency-psychopathology. The scale taps a wide

---

4. The listing of the items on the $F(p)$ scale is incorrect in Table 4 (p. 428) in Arbisi and Ben-Porath (1995). The listing of the items in the Appendix (p. 431) of that article is correct. The listing of the items in Appendix B.8 of this text is correct.

variety of heterogeneous content areas reflecting severe psychotic symptoms, very unusual habits, highly amoral attitudes, and identity confusion. Examples of items on the $F(p)$ scale with the deviant answer indicated in parentheses are:

"In walking I am very careful to step over sidewalk cracks." (true)

"There are persons who are trying to steal my thoughts and ideas." (true)

"I can't go into a dark room alone even in my own home." (true)[5]

Most of the items on the $F(p)$ scale (22/27) are scored on the standard Validity and Clinical scales; 14 items overlap with the F (Infrequency) scale, 7 items overlap with Scale 8 (Schizophrenia), and 4 items with the L (Lie) scale. The item overlap between the $F(p)$ and L scales potentially can confound the interpretation of the $F(p)$ scale if its elevation primarily is the result of these shared items because of the different variables that produce elevations on the L scale (see the discussion of the L scale below). The $F(p)$ scale also shares 7 items with the Back Infrequency (F_B) scale, 3 items with the Bizarre Mentation (*BIZ*) scale, and 2 items with the Fears (*FRS*) and Family Problems (*FAM*) scales.

Arbisi and Ben-Porath (1995, 1998) found that the $F(p)$ scale was better able to identify psychiatric patients who were overreporting psychopathology on the MMPI-2 than the F scale. They suggested that T scores over 100 (raw scores greater than 8 in men and 7 in women) on the $F(p)$ scale were likely indicators that the individual is overreporting psychopathology. Arbisi and Ben-Porath (1997) also reported that scores on the $F(p)$ scale were independent of diagnosis (Post Traumatic Stress Disorder, Major Depression, Substance Abuse, Schizophrenia, and Bipolar Disorder) among psychiatric patients, and that scores on the $F(p)$ scale were significantly lower than the scores on the F and F_B scales. However, the schizophrenic patients had scores on the $F(p)$ scale that

were nearly one-half standard deviation higher than the other four groups, which suggests that scores on the $F(p)$ scale may not be totally independent of more severe forms of psychopathology. Frederick (1998) and Ladd (1997) found that the items on the $F(p)$ scale were not likely to be endorsed by criminal forensic examinees or chemically dependent inpatients, respectively, supporting the generalizability of the scale to other settings and groups of patients.

No reliability data have been reported for the $F(p)$ scale.

There are no gender effects on the $F(p)$ scale and no age effects beyond the age of 20 (see Table 3.23). There is a 5 to 6 T point difference between psychiatric patients who are 18 to 19 years of age and older age groups. The effects of education are slightly smaller on the $F(p)$ scale than either on the F or F_B scales, although they still are quite substantial, with scores decreasing 14 T points as years of education increase from less than 9 years to more than 18 years in psychiatric patients (Caldwell, 1997a).

There have been no studies of the effectiveness of the $F(p)$ scale at identifying students who are instructed to overreport psychopathology because of its recent development. The optimal cutting score on the $F(p)$ has not been determined with most studies only reporting descriptive statistics. Arbisi and Ben-Porath (1995) suggested a cutting score of a T score of 100 on the $F(p)$ scale. A raw score of 7 would classify 2 percent of the psychiatric patients (Caldwell, 1997a) (see Table 3.24, pp. 75–76) as overreporting, while a raw score of 8 would classify less than 1 percent as overreporting.

A summary of the interpretation of four levels of the $F(p)$ scale will be provided in Table 3.25 (p. 76) as one of the primary scales to assess whether the person is overreporting psychopathology.

Additional Infrequency Scales.   Two additional infrequency scales have been developed for the MMPI-2: Fake Bad (*FBS:* Lees-Haley, English, & Glenn, 1991) and Inconsistent Response (*IR:* Sewell & Rogers, 1994). The *FBS* scale consists of 43 items endorsed infrequently by personal-injury malingerers and the *IR* scale consists of 16 items, eight of which are scored on the Infrequency-Psychopathology $F(p)$ scale, endorsed infrequently by psychiatric patients.

---

5. Minnesota Multiphasic Personality Inventory-2 (MMPI-2). Copyright © 1942, 1943 (renewed 1970), 1989 by the Regents of the University of Minnesota. Reproduced by permission of the publisher. "MMPI-2" and "Minnesota Multiphasic Personality Inventory-2" are trademarks owned by the University of Minnesota.

TABLE 3.23 Effects of Demographic Variables on Scales Measuring Overreporting of Psychopathology in the Caldwell Clinical Dataset

SCALE/INDEX	N =	AGE						
		18–19	*20–29*	*30–39*	*40–49*	*50–59*	*60–69*	*70+*
		959	*10,979*	*16,201*	*12,927*	*5,703*	*1,737*	*498*
Infrequency								
F[raw]	M =	9.1	6.5	6.5	6.9	7.1	6.5	5.7
F[T]	M =	65.9	57.6	57.8	59.0	59.8	57.7	55.3
F_B	M =	67.9	59.0	58.4	59.9	60.7	59.1	56.3
$F(p)$	M =	59.5	54.1	52.9	53.1	53.7	54.2	54.5
Critical Items								
KBSum	M =	26.2	18.9	19.8	21.0	21.9	19.8	16.7
LWSum	M =	34.8	26.1	27.4	28.8	30.2	27.8	24.1
Other Indexes								
$F – K$	M =	–4.2	–9.3	–9.6	–8.9	–8.4	–9.1	–10.0
Ds	M =	17.9	13.4	12.9	13.3	13.5	12.6	11.0
Total O – S	M =	69.3	26.9	27.5	34.4	42.5	35.9	26.4
SCALE/INDEX	N =	EDUCATION (YEARS)						
		1–8	*9–10*	*11–12*	*13–14*	*15–16*	*17–18*	*19+*
		1,457	*2,215*	*14,449*	*10,395*	*9,524*	*4,315*	*3,058*
Infrequency								
F[raw]	M =	10.0	10.3	7.8	6.5	5.6	5.2	4.9
F[T]	M =	68.9	69.4	61.8	57.7	54.8	53.4	52.2
F_B	M =	72.4	71.8	63.3	58.2	54.9	53.1	52.7
$F(p)$	M =	63.5	61.5	55.2	52.7	51.3	50.1	49.4
Critical Items								
KBSum	M =	26.6	27.6	23.3	19.9	17.2	16.0	15.1
LWSum	M =	36.4	37.0	31.7	27.6	23.9	22.5	21.2
Other Indexes								
$F – K$	M =	–3.9	–3.1	–7.0	–9.5	–11.3	–12.0	–12.5
Ds	M =	17.5	17.9	14.8	13.0	11.6	11.0	10.5
Total O – S	M =	76.5	81.0	53.3	29.1	10.4	1.8	–4.8

(continued)

TABLE 3.23 Effects of Demographic Variables on Scales Measuring Overreporting of Psychopathology in the Caldwell Clinical Dataset (continued)

		GENDER	
		Men	*Women*
SCALE/INDEX	N =	*25,203*	*25,763*
Infrequency			
F[raw]	$M =$	7.0	6.8
F[T]	$M =$	57.5	60.7
F_B	$M =$	59.3	60.2
$F(p)$	$M =$	53.1	54.5
Critical Items			
KBSum	$M =$	19.6	21.4
LWSum	$M =$	26.9	29.5
Other Indexes			
$F - K$	$M =$	–8.9	–8.9
Ds	$M =$	12.7	14.2
Total O – S	$M =$	31.0	36.3

STANDARD DEVIATION	$N = 50,966$
Infrequency	
F[raw]	6.0
F[T]	18.8
F_B	22.0
$F(p)$	13.8
Critical Items	
KBSum	16.0
LWSum	19.3
Other Indexes	
$F - K$	10.1
Ds	8.9

TABLE 3.24 Cutting Scores for Assessing Overreporting of Psychopathology by Setting

F	2	7	16	30	50	70	84	93	98	99.2	99.7	99.9
						PERCENTILE						
Normal[a]		0	1	2	3	4	6	9	12	14	16	17
Clinical[b]		0	1	3	5	8	12	17	24	28	32	35
Personnel[c]			0	1		2	3	4	7	11	24	27

F_B	2	7	16	30	50	70	84	93	98	99.2	99.7	99.9
						PERCENTILE						
Normal[a]				0	1	2	3	6	9	11	13	14
Clinical[b]				0	2	5	9	14	20	24	26	28
Personnel[c]						0		1	3	7	9	11

F(p)	2	7	16	30	50	70	84	93	98	99.2	99.7	99.9
						PERCENTILE						
Normal[a]				0		1	2	3	4	5	6	8
Clinical[b]				0	1	2	3	4	7	8	9	10
Personnel[c]				0		1	2	3	4	5	9	10

F − K	2	7	16	30	50	70	84	93	98	99.2	99.7	99.9
						PERCENTILE						
Normal[a]	−23	−20	−18	−15	−12	−9	−5	−1	3	7	9	11
Clinical[b]	−24	−22	−19	−16	−11	−5	1	7	15	20	25	28
Personnel[c]	−26	−25	−23	−22	−20	−17	−14	−11	−5	0	6	8

Ds	2	7	16	30	50	70	84	93	98	99.2	99.7	99.9
						PERCENTILE						
Normal[a]	2	3	5	6	9	12	15	19	24	27	29	32
Clinical[b]	1	2	4	7	11	17	22	28	35	39	42	44
Personnel[c]	0	1		2	4	6	8	11	16	19	22	25

K & B	2	7	16	30	50	70	84	93	98	99.2	99.7	99.9
						PERCENTILE						
Normal[a]	0	2	3	6	10	14	20	27	36	39	44	49
Clinical[b]	0	1	4	8	16	28	38	47	57	61	65	68
Personnel[c]		0		1	3	4	7	11	19	24	29	33

L & W	2	7	16	30	50	70	84	93	98	99.2	99.7	99.9
						PERCENTILE						
Normal[a]	3	5	7	11	15	21	27	35	45	50	56	62
Clinical[b]	2	5	8	14	24	37	49	60	73	80	85	89
Personnel[c]	0	1	2	4	6	9	12	18	27	40	47	49

(continued)

TABLE 3.24 Cutting Scores for Assessing Overreporting of Psychopathology by Setting (continued)

O & S	PERCENTILE											
	2	7	16	30	50	70	84	93	98	99.2	99.7	99.9
Normal[a]	−93	−74	−56	−33	−6	25	56	91	135	164	189	197
Clinical[b]	−105	−86	−63	−31	19	80	135	186	240	269	291	305
Personnel[c]	−120	−108	−97	−85	−66	−44	−20	7	52	85	108	124

True %	PERCENTILE											
	2	7	16	30	50	70	84	93	98	99.2	99.7	99.9
Normal[a]	26	29	31	34	37	41	45	49	54	57	60	62
Clinical[b]	25	27	29	32	37	42	48	53	59	63	66	69
Personnel[c]	23	25	26	28	31	33	36	40	44	49	52	54

Note. All scores are raw scores except for $|F - F_B|$, O − S, and F − K, which are difference scores.
[a]Butcher et al. (1989).
[b]Caldwell (1997a).
[c]Caldwell (1997b).

The *IR* scale correlates .75 or higher with the *F* (Infrequency), Back Infrequency (F_B), and $F(p)$ scales, while the *FBS* scale correlates .50 or lower with these same three scales. Since the *IR* scale overlaps substantially with the $F(p)$ scale, there is little reason to score both scales. It might be worth evaluating whether there is an increment in validity when the eight unique items on the *IR* scale are combined with the $F(p)$ scale. Additional research is needed to determine whether the *FBS* scale is specific to persons try-

TABLE 3.25 Interpretation of Levels of Overreporting of Psychopathology

SCALE/INDEX

F(p)	F − K	Interpretation
0–1	<−11	1. *Low.* Scores in this range indicate clients who have reported little emotional distress and few unusual behaviors or symptoms even though they are in a clinical setting. They clearly have not overreported psychopathology, although they may need to be evaluated as to whether they have underreported psychopathology.
2–3	>−12 < 2	2. *Normal.* These clients have endorsed the items accurately. Codetype interpretation may proceed with confidence.
4–8	> 1 < 21	3. *Moderate.* These clients either are experiencing and reporting a significant level of emotional distress or they may be embellishing the severity and extent of their psychopathology. Their clinical history and reasons for seeking treatment should be evaluated to assess whether they are commensurate with the level of distress that these clients are reporting. If they are accurately reporting their psychopathology, it will be readily apparent in their clinical interview and history.
> 8	> 20	4. *Marked.* These clients are overreporting the extent and severity of their psychopathology. They are very likely to terminate treatment prematurely despite what appears to be serious psychopathology.

Note. Clinicians may prefer to use another scale or index of overreporting from Table 3.24 that can be substituted for the scales in this table.

ing to malinger a personal injury because of its low correlations with other infrequency scales.

F − K *Index (Gough Dissimulation Index).* Another validity indicator, the $F - K$ index (Gough Dissimulation index), has been developed by combining two of the three traditional Validity scales. The reader is cautioned *not* to confuse the $F - K$ index (Gough Dissimulation index) with the Gough Dissimulation scale (*Ds*: Gough, 1954), which will be described in the next section. The *Ds* scale is a set of empirically derived items designed to assess overreporting of psychopathology, whereas the $F - K$ index utilizes the relationship between the standard Validity scales of F (Infrequency) and K (Correction) to assess overreporting.

Gough (1947, 1950) suggested that this index—the *raw* score of the F scale minus the *raw* score of the K scale—would be useful in screening MMPI profiles for accuracy of item endorsement. If the $F - K$ index was greater than +9, the profile was designated as overreporting (i.e., the client was trying to feign the presence of psychopathology). If the $F - K$ index was less than 0, the profile was classified as underreporting (i.e., the client was trying to deny the existence of any form of psychopathology). Intermediate scores on the $F - K$ index (0 to 9) indicated accurate item endorsement (i.e., valid profiles). Gough (1950) reported that the $F - K$ index readily detected overreporting profiles; in one sample it accurately classified 97 percent of the authentic profiles and 75 percent of the overreporting profiles.

Most studies of the $F - K$ index in identifying overreporting profiles on the MMPI have utilized normal persons who were instructed to overreport psychopathology. Numerous investigators working with students (Cofer, Chance, & Judson, 1949; Exner, McDowell, Pabst, Stackman, & Kirk, 1963; Hunt, 1948) have confirmed the ability of the $F - K$ index to identify students who are instructed to overreport psychopathology; some of these investigators (Exner et al., 1963; Hunt, 1948), however, also noted that the F scale alone identified overreporting profiles even more efficiently than the $F - K$ index.

Gallucci (1984) found that scores on the $F - K$ index corresponded directly with the presumed moti-

vation of veterans who were undergoing psychiatric evaluations to determine their eligibility for disability benefits. These veterans also seemed to dissimulate psychopathology in general rather than any specific psychiatric diagnosis.

Most studies (Austin, 1992; Graham et al., 1991; Woychyshyn, McElheran, & Romney, 1992) have confirmed the ability of the $F - K$ index on the MMPI-2 to identify students who are instructed to overreport psychopathology. Several of these investigators (Graham et al., 1991; Woychyshyn et al., 1992) also noted that the F scale alone identified overreporting as or even more efficiently than the $F - K$ index similar to what had been reported with this index on the MMPI. The optimal cutoff scores in these studies have ranged from 6 (Sivec et al., 1994) to 12 (Graham et al., 1991). Higher cutting scores on the $F - K$ index are required to distinguish between normal individuals who are trying to overreport psychopathology and patients with optimal cutting scores ranging from 7 (Bagby, Rogers, Buis, & Kalemba, 1994) to 27 (Graham et al., 1991).

Rothke, Friedman, Dahlstrom, Greene, Arredondo, and Mann (1994) have provided extensive tables of the distribution of the $F - K$ index in samples of patients with mental disorders, head-injured patients, disability claimants, job applicants for police and priest positions, and substance abusers as well as the MMPI-2 normative group. Substantial differences were observed in the $F - K$ index for these various samples. They suggested that clinicians using the $F - K$ index consider the specific diagnostic group being studied as well as the person's gender.

Table 3.24 (pp. 75–76) provides the cutting scores that can be used with the $F - K$ index in the assessment of overreporting of psychopathology in three different settings. A summary of the interpretation of four levels of the $F - K$ index is provided in Table 3.25 (p. 76) as one of the primary scales to assess whether the person is overreporting psychopathology.

Gough Dissimulation (Ds) Scale. The Gough Dissimulation (*Ds*) scale (Gough, 1954) consists of 74 items, later revised to 40 items (*Ds-r:* Gough, 1957), which significantly differentiated a group of neurotic patients from groups of college students and professional psychologists instructed to simulate the responses of neurotic patients in taking the MMPI. The items on the *Ds* and *Ds-r* scales on the MMPI-2 may be found in Appendix B-8. The *Ds-r* scale taps a wide variety of the prevailing stereotypes about neuroticism including nonspecific fears, inability to share with others, and isolation and avoidance of others. The *Ds-r* scale shares 5 items with the *F* (Infrequency) scale, 3 items with the Back Infrequency (F_B) scale, and no items with the Infrequency-Psychopathology *F(p)* scale. Examples of *Ds-r* scale items with the deviant answer indicated in parentheses are:

"Several times a week I feel as if something dreadful is about to happen." (true)

"No one seems to understand." (true)

"I find it hard to keep my mind on a task or job." (true)[6]

The psychologists and students scored three to four times higher than neurotic patients on the *Ds* scale. The professional psychologists were only slightly better at simulating neurosis than the students, and both groups were easily identified by the *Ds* scale. Gough's results suggest that professional psychologists endorse the same erroneous stereotypes about neuroticism that students without any training in psychopathology endorse. Apparently, formal training in psychopathology does not eliminate common stereotypes about neuroticism. Gough's findings underscore the advantage of empirically selecting items or empirically validating items selected to assess a specific behavior.

The interested reader can demonstrate this result by taking the MMPI-2 as a client with a specific "neurotic" disorder and then scoring the *Ds* scale. After scoring the *Ds* scale, the reader should examine the content of the items on the scale to gain an appreciation of the types of items that are stereotypically thought to reflect neuroticism.

6. Minnesota Multiphasic Personality Inventory-2 (MMPI-2). Copyright © 1942, 1943 (renewed 1970), 1989 by the Regents of the University of Minnesota. Reproduced by permission of the publisher. "MMPI-2" and "Minnesota Multiphasic Personality Inventory-2" are trademarks owned by the University of Minnesota.

Mehlman and Rand (1960) provided general support for Gough's findings that persons attempting to simulate psychopathology on the MMPI can be identified readily by their responses to the test items. They presented 45 MMPI items to clinical psychologists, graduate students in psychology, and undergraduates and asked them to indicate the Clinical scale on which each item was found. There were no differences between the groups in their ability to indicate the scale on which the item appeared, and all groups could accurately identify only about four or five items.

These results are not surprising since MMPI scales were formed empirically, not rationally. Because these persons could not guess which scales contained various items, the implication is that they also would be unable to distort their responses to simulate accurately those of a client who actually had a specific form of psychopathology and achieve an elevated score on the appropriate scale.

There are no gender effects on the *Ds* scale. There are few age effects on the *Ds* scale beyond the age of 20, although 18- and 19-year-olds have scores about 6 T points higher than the older age groups. There is a sizable decrease in scores on the *Ds* scale as years of education increase. Persons with educational levels below the 11th grade have scores 3 to 9 T points higher than those with more years of education.

Research with the *Ds* scale on the MMPI-2 has been limited by the fact that it is not recognized as one of the standard scales to be scored routinely. No consensus has been observed whether the original or revised version of the *Ds* scale should be used, although the MMPI-2 version of the revised MMPI scale (*Ds-r*) would seem to be the more viable alternative. Given these limitations, the few studies of the *Ds* scale have found it to be effective (Bagby, Rogers, & Buis, 1994; Bagby, Rogers, Buis, & Kalemba, 1994; Rogers, Bagby, & Chakraborty, 1993; Wetter, Baer, Berry, & Reynolds, 1994; Wetter, Baer, Berry, Robison, & Sumpter, 1993). Because Berry, Baer, and Harris (1991) in their meta-analysis of the MMPI found that the *Ds* scale had one of the largest effect sizes, it clearly needs to be used in evaluating whether the person is overreporting psychopathology.

Table 3.24 provides the cutting scores that can be used with the *Ds* scale in the assessment of overreporting of psychopathology in three different settings.

Wiener and Harmon Obvious and Subtle Subscales.   Examining endorsements to obvious versus subtle items has shown some promise in detecting overreporting and underreporting of psychopathology. In the early research in this area, Wiener and Harmon (Wiener, 1948) performed a rational inspection of MMPI items, identifying obvious items as those that they thought were easy to detect as indicating emotional disturbance, and subtle items as those that were relatively difficult to detect as reflecting emotional disturbance. This procedure resulted in the identification of 146 obvious and 110 subtle items.

The empirically determined deviant response for 65 (59 percent) of these subtle items was in the opposite direction from what would be expected by merely inspecting item content, whereas only 8 (5 percent) of these obvious items were scored in the opposite direction. These findings substantiate the subtle and obvious nature of these two groups of items, respectively. Although Wiener and Harmon had intended to develop obvious and subtle subscales for each Clinical scale, it was possible to do so for only five scales: Scales *2* (Depression), *3* (Hysteria), *4* (Psychopathic Deviate), *6* (Paranoia), and *9* (Hypomania). Thus, the total score on each of these five scales can be divided into an obvious score and a subtle score, which could be evaluated as to their respective contributions to the total score. The items on the obvious and subtle subscales for each of these five scales appear in Appendix B.3 of this text.

The other Clinical scales were composed primarily of obvious items so it was not possible to develop obvious and subtle subscales. These Clinical scales include the scales that require the most *K*-correction (Scales *1* [Hypochondriasis], *7* [Psychasthenia], and *8* [Schizophrenia]). Wiener and Harmon's preliminary work also suggested that elevation of the obvious scales tended to predict failure in school or vocational training, whereas the subtle scales were not significantly related to these criteria.

The available research does not suggest explicit criteria for defining an overreporting response set based on the obvious and subtle scales as was noted earlier. It probably is safe to assume that a client who achieves T scores of 90 or more on all five obvious scales and T scores near 40 on all five subtle scales is trying to overreport. The converse relationship between scores on the obvious and subtle subscales should arouse the suspicion of an underreporting response set. Since it will be assumed that overreporting and underreporting of psychopathology are a general process, one method for creating a criterion to assess these response sets would be to sum the differences between the obvious and subtle subscales (Greene, 1991, pp. 79–80).

Before the use of this total T score difference to assess accuracy of item endorsement is explored, several issues must be addressed. First, there are a number of obvious and subtle subscales that could be used to assess accuracy of item endorsement (see the section on Obvious and Subtle subscales later in this chapter). The Wiener and Harmon (Wiener, 1948) Obvious and Subtle subscales were selected because they have the longest history of usage in the MMPI field. The high degree of item overlap among the various obvious and subtle subscales and their high correlations suggest that any of these obvious and subtle subscales would work equally well.

Second, the question of whether large T score differences on the individual Clinical scales have any significance has not been explored (e.g., it is not clear whether a T score difference of +30 points on Scale *2* [Depression] has the same meaning as +30 points on Scale *9* [Hypomania]).

Finally, it must be explicit that these Obvious and Subtle subscales are *not* being used to predict specific external criteria since it is reasonably well known that the Obvious scales are better predictors of most criteria than Subtle scales (see the section on Obvious and Subtle subscales later in this chapter). Instead the total T score difference between the Obvious and Subtle subscales is being used as an index of the accuracy of item endorsement. This usage of the difference between the Obvious and Subtle subscales is in the same vein as the first approach to assess test-taking attitudes outlined by Meehl and Hathaway (1946), which was described in Chapter 1.

Table 3.24 provides the cutting scores that can be used with the total T score difference between the Obvious and Subtle scales in the assessment of overreporting of psychopathology in three different settings.

Critical Items.   Despite the inherent difficulties in understanding responses to individual MMPI items (difficulties that provided the original impetus for the empirical selection of items on the MMPI), clinicians have been unwilling to ignore the information that might be contained in those responses. The original set of "critical" items, which were thought to require careful scrutiny if answered in the deviant direction, was rationally or intuitively selected by Grayson (1951). Grayson's early work on critical items has since been followed by the development of other sets of critical items (Chapter 6). Since these critical items have obvious or face valid item content (Wrobel & Lachar, 1982), they provide another means of assessing the accuracy of item endorsement.

The Lachar and Wrobel (1979) critical items will be used to illustrate this procedure; any critical item set could be used to assess accuracy of item endorsement, and the clinician may prefer to use another set of these items that is described in Chapter 6. Regardless of the set of critical items that is used, the rationale for assessing accuracy of item endorsement will remain the same.

Lachar and Wrobel (1979) developed their critical items to be face-valid (obvious) descriptors of psychological concerns. They first identified 14 categories of symptoms that summarized problems that motivate people to seek psychological treatment and that help the clinician make diagnostic decisions. Then 14 clinical psychologists read each MMPI item and nominated items that would be face-valid indicators of psychopathology in one of these 14 categories. These items were empirically validated by contrasting item response frequencies for normals and psychiatric samples matched for gender and race. Lachar and Wrobel were able to validate 130 of the 177 items nominated.

After eliminating 19 items that were highly duplicative of item content in other items on the list, they arrived at a final list of 111 (20.2 percent) critical items out of a possible 550 MMPI items. All but four of the Lachar and Wrobel critical items appear on the MMPI-2. These critical items identified by Lachar and Wrobel appear in Appendix C of this text.

The total number of Lachar and Wrobel critical items that are endorsed by the client can become another index of the accuracy of item endorsement. A client who is trying to overreport psychopathology would be expected to endorse a large number of these items whereas a client who is trying to underreport

psychopathology would be expected to endorse few of them.

Table 3.24 provides the cutting scores that can be used with the Koss and Butcher (1973) and Lachar and Wrobel (1979) critical items in the assessment of overreporting of psychopathology in three different settings.

Clinical Case 3-3

Henry was a 28-year-old, married white man, who had completed two years of college before he took a full-time position with a local business. He appeared at an outpatient clinic to request treatment for his concerns about his jealousy of his wife's many friends. His mental status examination was unremarkable and he did not report any significant life stressors.

Henry's MMPI-2 Profile (Profile 3.5, solid line) was a 6-8 codetype that matched the prototypic 6-8/8-6 codetype (Profile 3.5, solid circles) very closely. Following the flowchart presented in Figure 3.1 (p. 43) for assessing the validity of an MMPI-2, Henry omitted no items and all measures of consistency of item endorsement were well within normal ranges (Table 3.17). (Henry had a raw score of 2 on the Variable Response Inconsistency [VRIN] scale, 1 on the $|F - F_B|$ index [absolute difference between the raw score on these two infrequency scales], and 11 on the True Response Inconsistency [TRIN] scale). In fact, he was slightly *more* consistent than would be expected for most psychiatric patients.

The next step in the flowchart is to assess the accuracy of item endorsement. All measures of overreporting of psychopathology were above the 98th percentile (see Table 3.24, pp. 75–76). (Henry had raw scores of 29 on the F [Infrequency] scale, 28 on the Back Infrequency (F_B) scale, 9 on the Infrequency-Psychopathology [$F(p)$] scale, 23 on the $F - K$ index [raw score of F – raw score of K], and 41 on the Gough Dissimulation [Ds] scale. He endorsed 69 of the Koss and Butcher critical items and 94 of the Lachar and Wrobel critical items. He had a total T score difference of +307 between the Wiener and Harmon Obvious and Subtle subscales.) Following the flowchart in Figure 3.1, Henry's MMPI-2 is classified as being overreported and the interpretive process would stop.

MMPI-2 PROFILE FOR VALIDITY AND CLINICAL SCALES

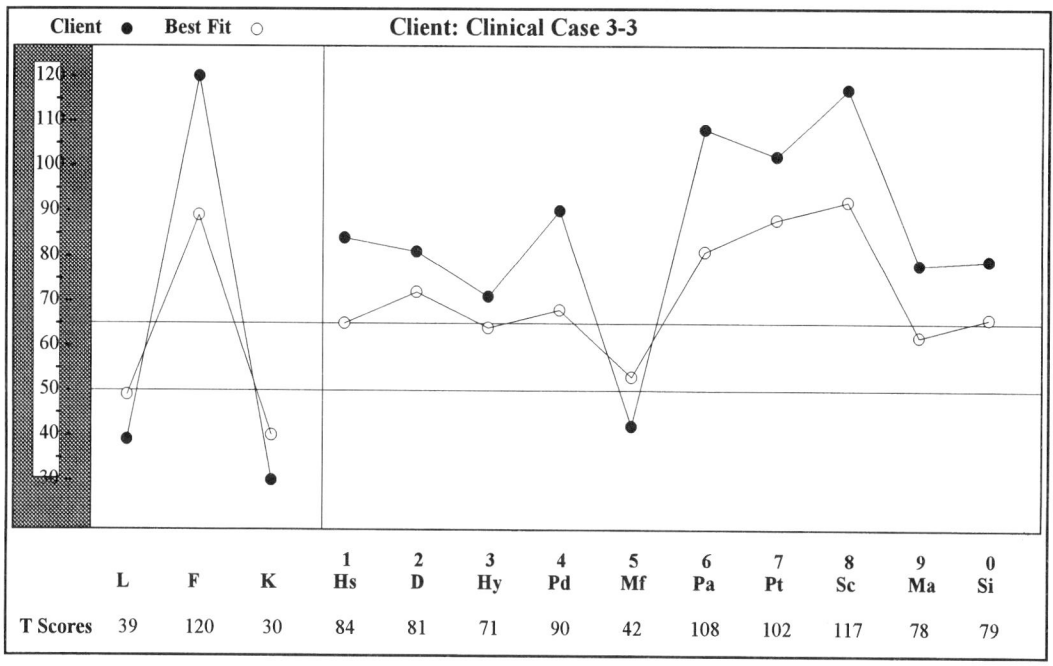

	L	F	K	1 Hs	2 D	3 Hy	4 Pd	5 Mf	6 Pa	7 Pt	8 Sc	9 Ma	0 Si
T Scores	39	120	30	84	81	71	90	42	108	102	117	78	79

PROFILE 3.5

Note. Minnesota Multiphasic Personality Inventory-2 (MMPI-2). Copyright © 1942, 1943 (renewed 1970), 1989 by the Regents of the University of Minnesota. Reproduced by permission of the publisher. "MMPI-2" and "Minnesota Multiphasic Personality Inventory-2" are trademarks owned by the University of Minnesota.

Although the MMPI-2 is uninterpretable because it has been overreported, the clinician must ascertain Henry's motivation for overreporting the severity of his psychopathology. When questioned about his approach to describing himself on the MMPI-2, Henry stated that he had found that people never seemed to take his concerns seriously and he wanted to make sure that the clinician understood that he really was upset by his jealousy of his wife's friends.

This case illustrates the importance of assessing the accuracy of item endorsement every time that the MMPI-2 is administered. If measures of the accuracy of item endorsement were not examined, the clinician would be likely to conclude that Henry had serious psychological problems and might even be psychotic (see description of *6-8/8-6* codetype in Chapter 7). His scores on the MMPI-2 Content scales (Profile 3.6)

also seem to confirm this picture of serious psychological problems. It will be shown later (Table 3.39, p. 114) that nearly 46 percent of *6-8/8-6* codetypes are a result of an overreported pattern of item endorsement.

Clinical Case 3-4

John was a 22-year-old, white man who had been hospitalized several times during the last two years. He had a long list of significant losses during these two years: a homosexual friend died of AIDS in March; his mother died in August; his fiancee died in an automobile accident in December while on her way to visit him in the hospital; and his father died in January. In addition, his best friend and twin cousins had committed suicide in this same two-year period.

MMPI-2 PROFILE FOR CONTENT SCALES

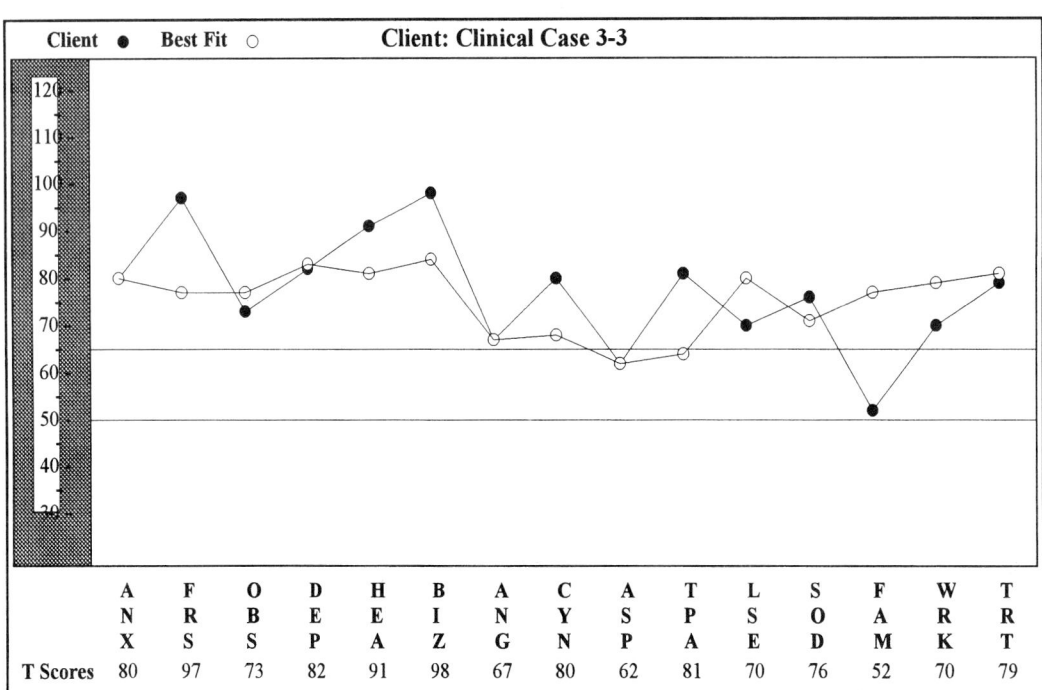

Client ●	Best Fit ○	Client: Clinical Case 3-3

	ANX	FRS	OBS	DEP	HEA	BIZ	ANG	CYN	ASP	TPA	LSE	SOD	FAM	WRK	TRT
T Scores	80	97	73	82	91	98	67	80	62	81	70	76	52	70	79

PROFILE 3.6

John had made three suicide attempts during this same period of time.

John was severely depressed and withdrawn upon admission to the hospital. He had auditory hallucinations that commanded him to commit suicide in order to join his deceased parents, fiancee, and friends. Given the severity of his depression it was remarkable that he could even complete the MMPI-2. After it had taken him almost an hour to answer the first 20 items, he was told that it was not necessary to finish the test. He insisted that he was going to finish it, which he did over the next five days. This determination was vital in his progress and recovery during hospitalization. He was diagnosed as having a Major Depressive Disorder, Recurrent, severe with mood-congruent psychotic features.

John's MMPI-2 Profile (Profile 3.7, solid circles) was a *6-8/8-6* codetype that was somewhat more

elevated than the prototypic *6-8/8-6* codetype (Profile 3.7, open circles). Following the flowchart presented in Figure 3.1 for assessing the validity of an MMPI-2, John omitted no items and all measures of consistency of item endorsement were well within normal ranges (Table 3.17). (John had a raw score of 1 on the Variable Response Inconsistency [*VRIN*] scale and 9 on the True Response Inconsistency [*TRIN*]).

The next step in the flowchart is to assess the accuracy of item endorsement. All measures of overreporting of psychopathology were above the 93th percentile (see Table 3.24, pp. 75–76). (John had raw scores of 30 on the *F* [Infrequency] scale, 5 on the Infrequency-Psychopathology [*F(p)*] scale, 21 on the *F − K* index [raw score of *F* − raw score of *K*], and 31 on the Gough Dissimulation [*Ds*] scale. He endorsed 76 of the Lachar and Wrobel critical items, and he had a total T score difference of +238 between the

MMPI-2 PROFILE FOR VALIDITY AND CLINICAL SCALES

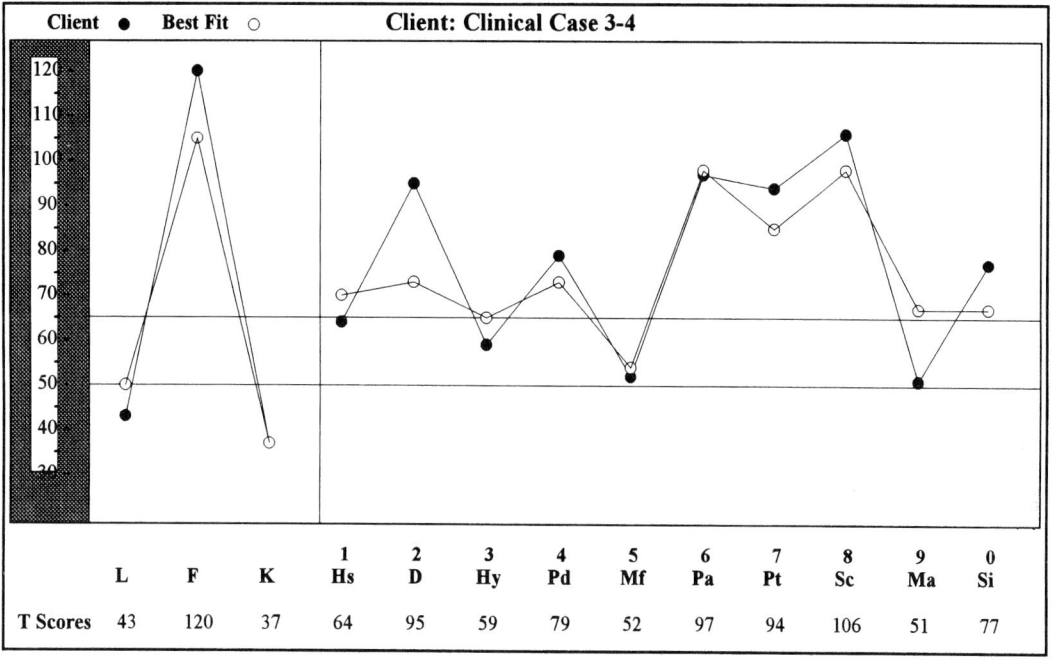

	L	F	K	1 Hs	2 D	3 Hy	4 Pd	5 Mf	6 Pa	7 Pt	8 Sc	9 Ma	0 Si
T Scores	43	120	37	64	95	59	79	52	97	94	106	51	77

PROFILE 3.7

Wiener and Harmon Obvious and Subtle subscales.) Given the severity of stressors with which John is dealing, these elevations are a more accurate reflection of his level of distress consistent with his psychiatric diagnosis rather than simply the overreporting of psychopathology. The reader also might note that John's scores on many of these measures actually are somewhat lower than Henry's, whose case was described earlier.

This case illustrates the severity and extent of psychopathology that should be seen when these measures of overreporting are elevated to a significant degree. The client's stressors and psychopathology should be obvious in a clinical interview as they were in John's case. The differentiation between accurate reporting and overreporting of psychopathology actually becomes easier as the scores on the measures of overreporting become more elevated.

The clinician should begin to suspect overreporting of psychopathology any time that these measures are elevated beyond the 90th percentile and the client's psychopathology is not readily apparent in the clinical interview and history.

Comparison of Clinical Cases 3-1, 3-3, and 3-4. Figure 3.3 juxtaposes the MMPI-2 profiles for Clinical Cases 3-1, 3-3, and 3-4 so that clinicians can directly compare them. Although these three profiles are produced by three different patterns of item endorsement (inconsistent item endorsement, overreporting of psychopathology, and the accurate reporting of severe psychopathology, respectively), they are very similar to each other and cannot be differentiated by simply looking at the profile. The importance of going through each step of the flowchart for assessing the validity of each administration of the MMPI-2 cannot

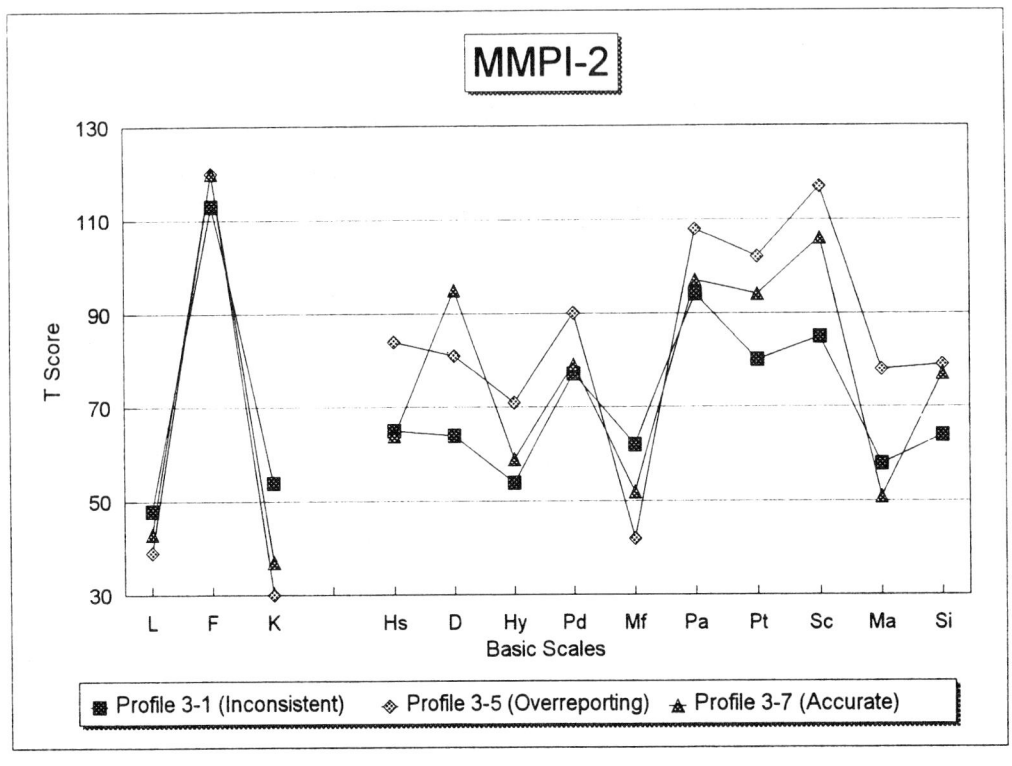

FIGURE 3.3
Note. Minnesota Multiphasic Personality Inventory-2 (MMPI-2). Copyright © 1942, 1943 (renewed 1970), 1989 by the Regents of the University of Minnesota. Reproduced by permission of the publisher. "MMPI-2" and "Minnesota Multiphasic Personality Inventory-2" are trademarks owned by the University of Minnesota.

be emphasized too strongly so that clinicians are aware of the test-taking attitude of the client.

Meta-Analyses of Overreporting of Psychopathology. There are a number of reviews of the MMPI and MMPI-2 assessment of overreporting of psychopathology that can be consulted by the interested reader (Berry, 1995; Faust, 1995; Franzen, Iverson, & McCracken, 1990; Greene, 1988a, 1997; Schret-len, 1988). In addition two separate meta-analyses of overreporting were conducted on the MMPI (Berry et al., 1991) and MMPI-2 (Rogers, Sewell, & Salekin, 1994). Berry et al. found that the F and Ds scales and the $F - K$ index had the largest effect sizes on the MMPI, while Rogers et al. found that the F scale, the $F - K$ index, and the total T score difference on the obvious and subtle subscales (Wiener, 1948) had the largest effect sizes

on the MMPI-2. In both studies, the effect sizes exceeded 2.00, which are quite substantial in magnitude. Cohen (1988) defines an effect size of 0.80 as large when two groups are being compared, which reflects a difference of slightly less than one standard deviation between the means of the two groups.

Table 3.26 provides a summary of the results of the four most commonly used scales and indexes on the MMPI-2 to assess overreporting of psychopathology. When college students who are instructed to overreport psychopathology are compared with college students who take the MMPI-2 accurately, all of these scales are very effective at making what is a very easy discrimination, although the F scale has the largest effect size. Similar results are found when adults are given the same instructions, although the effect sizes are significantly smaller, but still very substantial, on all four scales. When college students who are instructed to overreport psychopathology are compared with psychiatric patients who are presumed to be taking the MMPI-2 accurately, the effect sizes are smaller again except for the $F - K$ index. Even in these comparisons, however, the effect sizes still are very large by Cohen's standard. There is a sizable range in the optimal cutting scores across these various studies so that it is difficult to reach any definitive conclusions. Cutting scores around 20 on both the F (Infrequency) and Back Infrequency (F_B) scales, in the range of 10 to 12 on the $F - K$ index, and around 17 on the Ds scale are fairly typical. The positive and negative predictive power for these four scales ranges from 70 to 90 percent, which is quite good. These figures for positive predictive power are somewhat misleading though because the base rate or prevalence of overreporting in most of these studies was around 50 percent. If the base rate was decreased to a more appropriate range, say 10 to 20 percent, the positive predictive power would decrease to around 20 percent, while negative predictive power would increase to around 95 percent. Butcher, Graham, and Ben-Porath (1995) also have noted the importance of using positive and negative predictive power rather than sensitivity and specificity when evaluating a specific MMPI-2 scale. Baldesserini, Finkelstein, and Arana (1983) provide an excellent overview of the relationships among base rate or prevalence and positive and negative predictive power that all clinicians should know.

Few studies (Iverson, Franzen, & Hammond, 1995; Rogers, Sewell, & Ustad, 1995) actually have studied overreporting of psychopathology within psychiatric samples, which is the real test of these scales and indexes rather than analogue studies with college students. Both Iverson et al. and Rogers et al. reported similar effect sizes and cutting scores that were found with college students, which is reassuring. This arena is one in which additional research is needed because it is the one in which clinicians must be making their decisions as to whether this person is overreporting psychopathology.

Nicholson, Mouton, Bagby, Buis, Peterson, and Buigas (1997) used receiver operating characteristic curves to compare seven measures of overreporting of psychopathology. They found that all seven measures were effective at discriminating between college students who were instructed to overreport psychopathology and general psychiatric patients and forensic patients who took the MMPI-2 accurately. The strongest indictors of overreporting in these comparisons were the F (Infrequency) scale, the $F - K$ index, and the Infrequency-Psychopathology ($F[p]$) scale.

There have been a number of studies that have examined whether specific diagnoses can be overreported on the MMPI-2. These studies will be reviewed later in the section on Simulation as Role Playing.

Effects of Demographic Variables on Scales and Indexes Assessing Overreporting of Psychopathology. There are no effects of age on any of these scales and indexes beyond the age of 20 (Table 3.23). There is a consistent pattern, however, for the 18- and 19-year-olds to score about one-half of a standard deviation higher than the other age groups. This pattern of 18- and 19-year-olds scoring more like adolescents than like people in their 20s will be seen repeatedly as the other scales of the MMPI-2 are discussed. There also are no gender differences on any of these eight scales and indexes used to assess whether the person is overreporting psychopathology. The effects of demographic variables will be examined more systematically in Chapter 9, and the performance of adolescents will be discussed in Chapter 10.

There are essentially no differences in the scores between persons with 8 years or less of education and persons with 9 or 10 years of education on all of these scales and indexes. Beyond 10 years of education, however, there is a consistent pattern for scores to decrease as the number of years of education increases. There are more than 16 to 18 T points' difference between the performance of persons with 19 or more years of education and persons with 10 years of education or less on the three infrequency scales (F, F_B, and $F[p]$) and 8 to 10 T points on the other four measures. This pattern of the substantial effects of education on the scores of MMPI-2 scales also will be seen repeatedly and will be examined more fully in Chapter 9.

Summary.   Although the point should be self-evident, any measure of overreporting of psychopathology is confounded with measures of psychopathology be-

TABLE 3.26 Effect Sizes and Positive and Negative Predictive Power for Scales and Indexes Assessing Overreporting of Psychopathology

	Base Rate	F: Cutting Score	F: d	F: PPP	F: NPP	F_B: Cutting Score	F_B: d	F_B: PPP	F_B: NPP	F–K: Cutting Score	F–K: d	F–K: PPP	F–K: NPP	Ds: Cutting Score	Ds: d	Ds: PPP	Ds: NPP
Normal Individuals Responding Accurately or Overreporting Psychopathology																	
Students																	
Austin (1992)	0.53	29	1.99	92.1	93.8					11	4.43	72.5	100.0				
Bagby et al. (1994a)	0.45	20	3.64	92.9	90.5	16	3.34	92.4	86.9	11	3.75	90.3	90.3	16	2.75	83.3	84.9
Bagby et al. (1994b)	0.39	16	2.89	82.8	94.0	13	2.35	77.6	85.5	7	3.75	84.6	96.4	18	1.92	80.0	78.6
Graham et al. (1991)	0.50	27	4.26	97.9	94.2	23	3.10	97.7	87.5	12		95.9	94.1				
Lim & Butcher (1996)	0.50	26		95.8	92.3	22		100.0	92.6	12		100.0	96.2				
Sivec et al. (1994)	0.51	16	4.68	96.6	94.9	11	3.20	93.3	93.1	6	3.45	98.3	95.0	35*	3.95	100.0	80.6
Timbrook et al. (1993)			6.32														
Mean	0.48	22	3.96	92.7	93.0	17	3.00	91.6	88.5	10	3.85	90.1	94.4	17	2.87		
Adults																	
Berry et al. (1996)	0.50	29	3.87	73.2	100.0	25	2.86	73.2	100.0	25	2.90	73.2	100.0	35*	2.70	83.3	100.0
Rogers et al. (1993)	0.54	28	1.52	100.0	68.4	17	1.43	100.0	76.5	14	1.55	100.0	72.2	15	1.35	100.0	76.5
Wetter et al. (1994)	0.39		3.56				2.86				2.31				2.56		
Mean	0.48	28	2.98	78.0	84.2	21	2.38	78.8	88.9	19	2.25	78.4	86.5	15	2.20		
Normal Individuals Overreporting Psychopathology versus Patients Responding Accurately																	
Students																	
Bagby et al. (1994a)	0.30	20	2.44	66.3	94.0	11	1.90	66.3	91.6	11	2.40	67.0	94.0	16	2.25	65.2	91.0
Bagby et al. (1994b)	0.38	16	2.36	74.6	93.9	13	2.35	78.9	85.7	7	3.75	79.7	96.2	18	1.92	75.0	78.0
Graham et al. (1991)	0.50	27	1.99	88.7	93.6	27	1.61	88.7	93.6	12		85.5	93.3				
Lim & Butcher (1996)	0.50	26		92.0	92.0	22		86.8	91.5	12		85.7	95.5				
Sivec et al. (1995)	0.62	18	2.96	93.9	92.3												
Timbrook et al. (1993)			4.49														
Mean	0.46	21	2.85	80.8	93.5	19	1.95	78.0	90.3	10	3.08	77.6	94.7		2.09		
Adults																	
Wetter et al. (1994)			1.41				0.86				1.36						
Iverson et al. (1995)															1.01		
Inmates vs. Patients	0.35	18	3.00	96.2	94.3	11	1.67	89.5	81.7	11	2.78	95.8	90.9				
Inmates vs. Inmates	0.51	18	2.74	100.0	90.0	11	1.69	100.0	71.1	11	2.73	95.8	83.9				
Rogers et al. (1995)	0.46	25	2.45	91.2	94.6	18	1.66	92.0	78.3	18	2.02	82.9	88.9	22	1.28		
Mean	0.44	20	2.73	95.3	93.3	13	1.67	93.4	77.8	13	2.51	90.4	88.5	22	1.28		

Normal Individuals Reporting Specific Diagnoses or Responding Accurately

Diagnosis / Study	d	d	n	PPP	NPP	n	d	PPP	NPP	d	n	PPP	NPP	n	d	PPP	NPP
Borderline Personality Disorder																	
Sivec et al. (1995)	0.52	4.90															
Depression																	
Sivec et al. (1995)	0.50	5.30															
Posttraumatic Stress Disorder																	
Wetter et al. (1993)	0.50	1.51	19	73.9	82.4	13	1.13	69.6	76.5	1.64	15	83.3	77.3	35*	1.73	83.3	77.3
Schizophrenia																	
Bagby et al. (1997a)		3.99					2.16			3.33					2.42		
Bagby et al. (1997b)																	
Undergraduate Students		2.30					1.77			2.31					1.93		
Residents		1.97					0.99			1.73					1.32		
Graduate Students		1.91					0.76			1.79					1.46		
Sivec et al. (1994)	0.50	5.81	16	96.6	98.2	11	3.87	93.3	96.4	4.35	6	98.3	98.3	35*	4.11	100.0	82.9
Rogers et al. (1993)	0.29	0.92	28	90.0	85.7	17	0.74	61.1	88.2	0.91	14	58.8	85.7	15	1.12	64.7	88.6
Wetter et al. (1993)	0.52	2.30	21	91.7	100.0	16	2.47	88.0	100.0	3.58	16	95.5	95.0	33*	2.91	95.0	86.4
Somatoform Disorder																	
Sivec et al. (1994)	0.50	1.71	16	94.1	68.3	11	1.23	86.7	62.8	1.26	6	96.6	65.5	35*	1.55	100.0	55.8
Borderline Personality Disorder																	
Wetter et al. (1994)	0.46	1.67	17	69.6	80.6	13	1.67	73.7	77.5	1.50		64.5	89.3	33*	1.56	70.0	76.9
Depression																	
Bagby et al. (1997)		3.13					3.30			2.75					2.47		
Closed Head Injury (CHI)																	
Berry et al. (1995)																	
No Information		0.43					0.80			0.97					0.68		
Fake CHI		2.46					2.20			2.30					2.39		
Compensation-Seeking CHI		0.90					0.82			1.08					1.01		
Lamb et al. (1994)																	
No Information		1.03					0.90										
Validity and CHI		0.64					0.70										
CHI Information																	
Validity Information																	
Post Traumatic Stress Disorder																	
Lees-Haley (1992)	0.52	2.04	7	98.0	91.3												
Traumatic Brain Injury																	
Greiffenstein et al. (1995)		0.39															

Note. d = effect size, which was computed based on M1 – M2 divided by the pooled standard deviations for the two groups being compared. PPP = positive predictive power. NPP = negative predictive power. PPP and NPP in Total rows have been weighted by sample sizes (i.e., they are not simply averages of the PPP or NPP values).

*Long form of Ds (Gough Dissimulation) scale was used.

cause the person is being evaluated on those dimensions (Schretlen, 1990). The critical issue is the probability that the extent and severity of psychopathology reported by the person is an accurate reflection of his or her history and background. Consequently, clinicians and researchers should not be surprised that measures of overreporting of psychopathology are related positively to measures of psychopathology, while measures of underreporting of psychopathology are related inversely to measures of psychopathology. In evaluating the probability that the person is overreporting, the clinician must evaluate the base rate (prevalence) with which overreporting or underreporting occurs in his or her specific setting in order to have an appropriate estimate of positive predictive power (i.e., the probability that a person said to be overreporting or underreporting is classified accurately).

Three different infrequency scales (F, F_B, $F[p]$) and five other indexes to assess overreporting of psychopathology have been described. It is *not* necessary to use all of these scales and indexes simultaneously since they are correlated highly and consequently are very redundant as was shown in Table 3.20.

It is important that the reader understand that once an MMPI-2 profile has been defined as reflecting the overreporting of psychopathology, it *cannot* be interpreted as a valid profile. The client's specific reasons for overreporting psychopathology should be ascertained by a clinical interview, and the profile can be described as reflecting such a process; however, neither the codetype nor the individual scales can be interpreted.

The reader also should note that in Figure 3.1 (p. 43), once an MMPI-2 is said to be characterized by overreporting of psychopathology, the interpretive process stops. The client could have the MMPI-2 readministered, although such a procedure rarely results in a valid profile. It seems that once a client is motivated for whatever reason to overreport psychopathology, it is very difficult for him or her to endorse the items accurately in this administration. It is not known whether overreporting of psychopathology would persist across treatment settings for a particular client.

Although the codetype from an overreported profile *cannot* be interpreted, it is possible to ascertain whether there are empirical correlates of such profiles in a similar manner to Marks, Seeman, and

Haller's (1974) description of a $K+$ profile, which is described later. Only a few studies have reported explicitly the correlates of overreported profiles. Both Greene (1988b) and Hale, Zimostrad, Duckworth, and Nicholas (1986) found that clients who overreported psychopathology were very likely to terminate treatment within the first few sessions; frequently they did not return after the initial session. This finding that these clients terminate treatment quickly is almost exactly the opposite of what might be anticipated, since these clients are sometimes described as "crying for help" and they would be expected to remain in treatment longer than most clients. Additional research is needed to determine whether there are other correlates of overreported profiles. The relationship between overreporting of psychopathology and treatment outcome has been explored more fully in Greene and Clopton (1999), which can be consulted by the interested reader.

Once these various scales and indexes to identify overreporting of psychopathology have been described, the next step in the implementation of the flowchart in Figure 3.1 can be made. The criteria, summarized in Table 3.24, provide the quantitative data necessary to determine whether the items have been endorsed inaccurately (i.e., to overreport psychopathology). Once it has been determined that the client has overreported psychopathology, the clinician will need to ascertain the reasons for the inaccurate item endorsement by a clinical interview. Table 3.25 provides interpretations of four levels of overreporting of psychopathology.

A summary of the potential causes of overreporting of psychopathology is presented in Table 3.27, as well as some possible solutions for these problems. It remains to be determined whether it is possible to readminister the MMPI-2 to a client who has overreported psychopathology and obtain an accurate pattern of item endorsement. In any event the clinician must remember that neither the codetype nor the individual scales in an overreported profile can be interpreted.

Underreporting of Psychopathology

Underreporting of psychopathology can be assessed by the L (Lie), K (Correction), Other Deception

TABLE 3.27 Potential Causes of and Solutions for Overreporting of Psychopathology

CAUSE	SOLUTION
1. Client is making a "plea for help."	1. Explain to the client that treatment and services will be provided.
2. Client has a phenomenological style to overreact and to be traumatized; frequently seen in Dependent and Histrionic Personality Disorders and Depressive Mood Disorders.	2. May not be any solution short of long-term treatment.
3. Client is trying to look psychopathological because litigation, compensation, or possibility of a disability being confirmed is involved.	3. May not be any solution.

(*ODecp:* Nichols & Greene, 1991), Wiggins' (1959) Social Desirability (*Sd*), Superlative (*S:* Butcher & Han, 1995), and Edwards' (1957) Social Desirability (*So*) scales. These methods for assessing the underreporting of psychopathology will be organized within Paulhus' (1984; 1986) model of social desirability responding that distinguishes between self-deception and impression management. In self-deception clients are conjectured to believe their positive self-reports that they are not experiencing any form of psychopathology, while in impression management clients consciously underreport to create a favorable impression in others. The research on self-deception and impression management will be reviewed more completely once methods for assessing underreporting of psychopathology have been concluded. In contrast to the similarity among the methods for assessing overreporting of psychopathology, the intercorrelations among the methods for assessing underreporting range as low as .54 in psychiatric patients and rarely get higher than .80. These intercorrelations are shown in Table 3.28. The deviant direction for 27 to 100 percent of the items on these scales is "false" (Table 3.21). Any time all of these scales are elevated significantly the possibility of a tendency to endorse the items in the "false" direction should be considered by checking the percentage of items endorsed "false" or the client's score on the True Response Inconsistency (*TRIN*) scale (Table 3.17).

Paulhus' (1984, 1986) two-factor model of socially desirable responding in self-reports of personality provides a framework for understanding how individuals may underreport psychopathology. His model distinguishes between self-deception (in which clients believe their positive self-reports) and impression management (in which clients consciously dissemble to create a favorable impression in others). Paulhus (1986) hypothesized that *self-deception* refers to a motivated unawareness of one of two conflicting cognitions, whereas *impression management* can be conceptualized as a strategic simulation, a motive, or as a skill. Paulhus (1986) suggested that the *K* (Correction) scale and Edwards' (1957) Social Desirability (*So*) scale assessed self-deception on the MMPI, whereas the *L* (Lie), Positive Malingering (*Mp:* Cofer et al., 1949), and Wiggins' (1959) Social Desirability (*Sd*) scales assessed impression management. All of these scales can be scored on the MMPI-2 except that the *Mp* scale has been replaced by the Other Deception (*ODecp:* Nichols & Greene, 1991) scale. Paulhus' concept of impression management corresponds to what Block (1965) identified as the "Alpha" factor on the MMPI, while self-deception corresponds to Wiggins' (1964) "Gamma" factor. The distinction between the MMPI-2 scales measuring impression management (*L, ODecp,* and *Sd*) and self-deception (*K* and *So*) can be seen in their intercorrelations shown in Table 3.28. The Superlative (*S:* Butcher & Han, 1995) scale also would be conceptualized as falling within the self-deception category based on its higher correlations with the *K* and *So* scales than with the *L, ODecp,* and *Sd* scales.

L (Lie) Scale. The *L* (Lie) scale includes 15 items that were selected on a rational basis to identify persons who are deliberately trying to avoid answering

TABLE 3.28 Intercorrelations among Scales Measuring Underreporting of Psychopathology

Normal Individuals (Butcher et al., 1989)

SCALE/INDEX	ODecp	Sd	K	S	So	False
Impression Management						
L	.55	.47	.32	.40	.21	.34
ODecp	–	.85	.29	.37	.36	.15
Sd		–	.08	.16	.16	–.08
Self-Deception						
K			–	.82	.72	.81
S				–	.69	.83
So					–	.71

Psychiatric Patients (Caldwell, 1997a)

SCALE/INDEX	ODecp	Sd	K	S	So	False
Impression Management						
L	.61	.54	.43	.47	.27	.42
ODecp	–	.88	.48	.55	.55	.38
Sd		–	.28	.35	.38	.16
Self-Deception						
K			–	.88	.76	.85
S				–	.77	.86
So					–	.79

Note. L = Lie; *ODecp* = Other Deception (Nichols & Greene, 1991); *Sd* = Wiggins (1959) Social Desirability; *K* = Correction; *S* = Superlative (Butcher & Han, 1995); *So* = Social Desirability (Edwards, 1957); False = percentage of all 567 items endorsed "false."

the MMPI frankly and honestly (Dahlstrom et al., 1972). The scale assesses attitudes and practices that are culturally laudable but actually found only in the most conscientious persons. The content areas within the *L* scale include denial of minor, personal dishonesties and denial of aggression, bad thoughts, and weakness of character. Examples of items on the *L* scale with the deviant answer indicated in parentheses are:

"I do not always tell the truth." (false)

"At times I feel like swearing." (false)

"My table manners are not quite as good at home as when I am out in company." (false)[7]

7. Minnesota Multiphasic Personality Inventory-2 (MMPI-2). Copyright © 1942, 1943 (renewed 1970), 1989 by the Regents of the University of Minnesota. Reproduced by permission of the publisher. "MMPI-2" and "Minnesota Multiphasic Personality Inventory-2" are trademarks owned by the University of Minnesota.

The original Minnesota normative group answered most of the items on the *L* scale in the nondeviant direction; only three items—15, 135, and 165—were answered in the deviant direction by a majority of this sample. In Gravitz's (1970) sample of job applicants, these three items plus two more—45 and 255—were endorsed in the deviant direction by nearly a majority or more of the respondents. A majority of the MMPI-2 normative group also endorsed these same three items (16[15], 123[135], and 153[165]) in the deviant direction.

Gravitz (1970) noted small but consistent gender differences in responding to the items on the *L* scale; this pattern would suggest the need for separate T scores by gender, which were not available on the MMPI. The T scores for the *L* scale as well as the other three Validity scales (*?, F,* and *K*) provided by Hathaway and McKinley (1967) for the MMPI are identical for men and women. Separate T scores by gender are available for all of the Validity scales on the MMPI-2 (Butcher et al., 1989). T scores on the *L* scale tend to vary by only one to three T points between men and women on the MMPI-2, similar to those reported by Gravitz (1970) for the MMPI.

Most adults responded to all items on the *L* scale on the MMPI (Gravitz, 1971); if any items are omitted, they are most likely to be 255 or 285 (Gravitz, 1967). Dahlstrom et al. (1972) have suggested that college students and adolescents are likely to omit a few of the items on the *L* scale (e.g., items 15, 135, 165, and 255) since they may not have had experience with the item content. As yet, no reported research has studied this issue, and similar information is not available for the MMPI-2.

Since "false" is the deviant answer to all items on the *L* scale, the *L* scale is extremely susceptible to unsophisticated deviant test-taking sets, such as the set to answer all items "false." Unusually high (7 or above) raw scores on the *L* scale, particularly in persons for whom such a score is unexpected, should at least raise the suspicion of a deviant test-taking set. The effects of such test-taking attitudes on the various validity indicators and methods of detection of these attitudes will be examined later in this chapter.

More sophisticated deviant response sets may go undetected by the *L* scale. Inspection of the items on the *L* scale reveals that it is readily apparent which responses are the deviant ones. Numerous studies have shown that the *L* scale does not detect sophisticated persons who were given instructions to falsify their answers to the MMPI (Dahlstrom et al., 1972; Vincent, Linsz, & Greene, 1966). These persons apparently realized that it would be unconvincing to give distorted responses to items on the *L* scale.

Thus, the *L* scale can be construed as a measure of psychological sophistication with high scores indicating a lack of such sophistication when the elevation is *not* a reflection of impression management. In this latter circumstance, the *L* scale will be elevated, but the Other Deception (*ODecp*) and Wiggins' Social Desirability (*Sd*) scales will not be elevated. College-educated persons and persons of higher socioeconomic classes rarely score above a raw score of 4. Conversely, persons who are not psychologically minded (including some persons from minority

groups and lower socioeconomic classes) tend to have higher scores. Thus, a person's educational level and socioeconomic class must be kept in mind when interpreting the *L* scale. Persons with a college education who elevate the *L* scale to a T score of 65 or higher are likely to display deficiencies in judgment and lack of insight into their own behavior. Coyle and Heap (1965) have questioned whether such persons might have paranoid trends. Fjordbak (1985) reported that hospitalized male forensic patients who had raw scores greater than 6 on the *L* scale and no Clinical scales elevated had some type of psychotic disorder with prominent paranoid features.

The higher the elevation on the *L* scale, the lower will be the elevation of most Clinical scales. Denial is characteristic of high scores on the *L* scale; denial also results in refusing to acknowledge the presence of any form of psychopathology, thus lowering the elevation of the Clinical scales. The same caveat about impression management needs to be made here, too. Elevations on the *L* scale are occasionally accompanied by elevations on Scales *1* (Hypochondriasis) and *3* (Hysteria), which appear to tap the similar personality dynamics of denial and a lack of psychological mindedness. Elevations on the *L* scale sometimes also are associated with an elevation on Scale *9* (Hypomania) in which the client displays a grandiose self-concept centered around a pervasive denial of psychopathology.

Although few researchers have directly investigated the *L* scale, Burish and Houston (1976) have provided some validational evidence for it. They found that the *L* scale correlated significantly (+.55) with the Denial (*Dn*) scale (Chapter 4, p. 140) and was unrelated to Scale *1* (Hypochondriasis) and Scale *8* (Schizophrenia) in male college students. Hence, the *L* scale was significantly related to a construct (denial) that the *L* scale is intended to measure (convergent validity) and unrelated to two constructs (hypochondriasis and schizophrenia) from which the scale is intended to differ (discriminant validity).

Burish and Houston (1976) also found that students with high scores on the *L* scale performed better in a stressful situation than those with low scores. The students with high scores on the *L* scale appeared to use their defensive strategies across different kinds of potentially threatening situations. Similarly, Matarazzo (1955) found that male medical students with high scores on the *L* scale were less anxious (as measured by the Taylor Manifest Anxiety scale) than those with low scores.

Test-retest reliability coefficients for the *L* scale on the MMPI tend to be slightly lower than those reported for the *F* (Infrequency) and *K* (Correction) scales (Dahlstrom et al., 1975). Reliability coefficients for intervals up to one week range from .70 to .85, and

for intervals of one year or more range from .35 to .60. Test-retest reliability coefficients for the *L* scale on the MMPI-2 are .77 for men and .81 for women over a one-week interval (Butcher et al., 1989).

There are no gender differences on the *L* scale (Table 3.29). There are few age differences on the *L* scale with 18- and 19-year-olds scoring only 2 to 3 T points lower than other age groups whose scores are very consistent. Scores decline systematically with

TABLE 3.29 Effects of Demographic Variables on Scales Measuring Underreporting of Psychopathology in the Caldwell Clinical Dataset

		AGE						
		18–19	*20–29*	*30–39*	*40–49*	*50–59*	*60–69*	*70+*
Scale	N =	*959*	*10,979*	*16,201*	*12,927*	*5,703*	*1,737*	*498*
Impression Management								
L [T]	M =	51.6	55.2	55.5	54.6	54.7	56.1	57.5
L [raw]	M =	3.9	4.7	4.8	4.5	4.6	4.9	5.2
ODecp	M =	11.7	13.2	12.6	12.1	12.2	13.3	14.0
Sd	M =	13.0	13.8	13.3	12.5	12.5	13.6	14.1
Self-Deception								
K [T]	M =	46.1	51.5	52.1	51.5	50.9	51.0	51.2
K [raw]	M =	13.3	15.8	16.1	15.9	15.6	15.6	15.7
S	M =	22.0	27.3	27.4	26.5	25.7	26.0	26.3
So	M =	24.1	27.4	27.1	26.4	25.6	26.2	27.1
		EDUCATION (YEARS)						
		1–8	*9–10*	*11–12*	*13–14*	*15–16*	*17–18*	*19+*
Scale/Index	N =	*1,457*	*2,215*	*14,449*	*10,395*	*9,524*	*4,315*	*3,058*
Impression Management								
L [T]	M =	57.5	55.6	56.2	55.2	53.8	52.5	51.4
L [raw]	M =	5.2	4.8	4.9	4.7	4.4	4.1	3.9
ODecp	M =	13.1	12.4	12.6	12.6	12.5	12.1	12.0
Sd	M =	13.8	13.2	13.3	13.3	13.0	12.5	12.1
Self-Deception								
K [T]	M =	47.5	46.3	49.4	51.8	53.7	54.2	54.6
K [raw]	M =	14.0	13.4	14.8	16.0	16.9	17.1	17.4
S	M =	23.5	22.2	25.1	27.1	28.6	28.8	29.0
So	M =	23.5	23.5	25.4	27.0	28.1	28.6	29.1

Note. All scores are raw scores except as indicated for Scales *L* and *K*.

increasing years of education, although these differences only are about 5 T points when the two extreme levels of education are compared.

Most studies have found that the *L* scale does reasonably well at identifying students who are instructed to underreport psychopathology with the optimal cutting scores ranging from 5 (Lim & Butcher, 1996) to 11 (Austin, 1992). The effect sizes tend to be smaller than those found when students are instructed to overreport psychopathology.

Four levels of elevation of the *L* scale and their interpretation are summarized in Table 3.30.

		GENDER	
		Men	*Women*
Scale/Index	N =	*25,203*	*25,763*
Impression Management			
L [raw]	M =	4.6	4.7
L [T]	M =	54.5	55.5
ODecp	M =	13.5	11.6
Sd	M =	13.6	12.7
Self-Deception			
K [raw]	M =	15.8	15.7
K [T]	M =	51.1	51.4
S	M =	26.7	26.5
So	M =	27.6	25.6

Standard Deviation		N = 50,966
L [T]	SD =	11.4
L [raw]	SD =	2.5
ODecp	SD =	4.9
Sd	SD =	3.9
Self-Deception		
K [T]	SD =	11.3
K [raw]	SD =	5.3
S	SD =	10.3
So	SD =	26.6

K (Correction) Scale. The *K* (Correction) scale consists of 30 items that were empirically selected to assist in identifying persons who displayed significant psychopathology yet had profiles within the normal range. Since the derivation of the *K* scale was described in Chapter 1, it will not be repeated here.

Most of the items on the *K* scale also are scored on other Clinical scales and are fairly equally dispersed across these scales; only five items are unique to the *K* scale. The items usually are scored in the same direction when they appear on another Clinical scale except that eight of the nine items also found on Scale *0* (Social Introversion) are scored in the opposite direction. Item content on the *K* scale is heterogeneous and covers self-control and family and interpersonal relations. Examples of items on the *K* scale with the deviant answer indicated in parentheses are:

> "I certainly feel useless at times." (false)
>
> "People often disappoint me." (false)
>
> "Often I can't understand why I have been so irritable and grouchy." (false)[8]

A *K*-corrected profile is automatically plotted if the standard profile sheet is used (Profile 2.1, p. 33). The *K*-corrected profile was developed by determining the proportion of *K* that, when added to the raw score on the Clinical scale, would maximize the discrimination between the normative groups and the criterion group. McKinley, Hathaway, and Meehl (1948) determined that the discriminations could be improved on five of the Clinical scales by the addition of a proportion of *K.* Thus, Scales *7* (Psychasthenia) and *8* (Schizophrenia) are corrected by the addition of the whole raw score of *K,* whereas Scales *1* (Hypochondriasis), *4* (Psychopathic Deviate), and *9* (Hypomania) are corrected by the addition of a fractional value of *K* (.5, .4, and .2, respectively). They found that the addition of *K* to the other Clinical scales (Scales *2* [Depres-

8. Minnesota Multiphasic Personality Inventory-2 (MMPI-2). Copyright © 1942, 1943 (renewed 1970), 1989 by the Regents of the University of Minnesota. Reproduced by permission of the publisher. "MMPI-2" and "Minnesota Multiphasic Personality Inventory-2" are trademarks owned by the University of Minnesota.

TABLE 3.30   Interpretation of Levels of Elevation on the *L* (Lie) Scale

RAW SCORE	INTERPRETATION
0–2	1. *Low.* A set to endorse all items as "true" is possible. The other validity indicators should be evaluated. Clients may be attempting to create an extremely pathological picture of themselves. Normal persons, who are relatively independent or self-reliant, are generally willing to admit these minor social faults.
3–5	2. *Normal.* These clients are able to achieve an appropriate balance between admitting and denying minor social faults. They may be sophisticated persons who are attempting to create a favorable self-image.
6–7	3. *Moderate.* A random sort may have occurred. The other validity indicators should be evaluated. Normal persons may be slightly more conforming than usual or clients may have a tendency to resort to denial mechanisms.
8+	4. *Marked.* Scores in this range may indicate normal persons who are very self-controlled and who lack insight into their own behavior, persons with very conservative religious and moralistic training or occupations that deny even the most common human faults, unsophisticated persons who are trying to create an unusually favorable impression of themselves as in personnel selection, clients whose dynamics revolve around denial (frequently encountered in histrionic and somatization disorders), or psychiatric inpatients who may be overtly psychotic when all the Clinical scales are *not* elevated above a T score of 60.

sion], *3* [Hysteria], *5* [Masculinity-Femininity], and *6* [Paranoia]) actually reduced their discriminability; so these scales were not *K*-corrected.

The *K*-correction procedure was *not* examined in the restandardization of the MMPI, and the same *K*-weights are added to the same scales on the MMPI-2. Consequently, any critiques of the *K* scale on the MMPI should apply directly to the MMPI-2. Raw scores on the *K* scale are 2–3 points higher on the MMPI-2 than on the MMPI in their respective normative groups so that the effects of the *K* correction will be slightly larger on the MMPI-2 on all five scales that are *K*-corrected. These effects will be less than 5 T points on all five scales.

Despite urgings for investigators to cross-validate these *K*-corrections (Dahlstrom et al., 1972; McKinley et al., 1948; Meehl & Hathaway, 1946), almost no research has been published on the issue. The few published studies on *K*-correction weights (Heilbrun, 1963; Tyler & Michaelis, 1953; Yonge, 1966) found discouraging results.

Heilbrun investigated the *K*-corrections that would maximize the discrimination between normal

college students and maladjusted students who either sought treatment at a university counseling center or were hospitalized. Heilbrun determined that only three scales separated normal from maladjusted college students better when *K*-corrected than when not *K*-corrected. He found that the following weights, different in some cases for men than for women, worked best: Scale *3* (Hysteria), –.7*K* men, –.5*K* women; Scale *7* (Psychasthenia), 1.0*K* men, .8*K* women; and Scale *8* (Schizophrenia), .7*K* men and women. Heilbrun did cross-validate these weights in his student sample. However, no additional research has been conducted in other student samples, so the generalizability of his results remains open to question.

Both Tyler and Michaelis (1953) and Yonge (1966) reported that adding *K* to the five *K*-corrected scales in their college student samples actually reduced the reliability and validity of these scales. Clearly, any clinician using the MMPI-2 in a college setting needs to examine the usage of the traditional *K*-correction procedures. Using Heilbrun's proposed *K*-corrections, determining another more appropriate set of *K*-corrections, or avoiding the use of *K*-corrections altogether might be preferable. The need for additional research in other settings cannot be overemphasized.

Four studies (Archer, Fontaine, & McCrae, 1998; Colby, 1989; Jenkins, 1985; Wooten, 1984) have evaluated the effectiveness of the K-correction procedure in clinical samples with mixed results. Jenkins (1984) found virtually no change in the accuracy of identifying pain patients with Scale *1* (Hypochondriasis) or schizophrenic patients with Scale *8* (Schizophrenia) using K-weights that ranged from –1.0 to +1.5. Essentially, the K-correction procedure had no effect on the accuracy of classifying these groups of patients. Archer et al. (1998) found that the K-correction did not produce higher correlations with external criteria in psychiatric patients, and Colby (1989) found that K-corrected profiles were no better at distinguishing patients from nonpatients than non-K-corrected profiles. However, Wooten found a slight improvement in hit rate using the K-correction in Air Force trainees.

Wooten (1984) also noted that there were frequent changes in codetype when non-K-corrected profiles were compared with the standard K-corrected profile. He concluded that his data favored the use of the K-correction procedure. More than 50 years of using the MMPI and MMPI-2 without investigation of the appropriateness of the K-correction procedure defies explanation. Hopefully, researchers will begin to investigate the K-correction procedure on the MMPI-2.

Researchers have examined other aspects of the K scale than the K-corrections themselves. Several investigators (Heilbrun, 1961; Smith, 1959; Sweetland & Quay, 1953) examined the appropriateness of the scale as a measure of defensiveness and reported that the K scale in a normal population is a measure not of defensiveness but of personality integration and healthy adjustment, with high scores reflecting healthy adjustment.

Similarly, both Tyler and Michaelis (1953) and Yonge (1966) reported that in a normal college student sample the K scale was significantly negatively related to the five K-corrected scales on which high scores do indicate psychopathology. Working with maladjusted college students, Heilbrun (1961) and Nakamura (1960) found, however, that the K scale was a measure of defensiveness. Consequently, it appears that the appropriateness of interpreting K as a measure of defensiveness varies according to the type of client. In a normal population high scores on the K scale do not indicate defensiveness; in a maladjusted population, however, high K scores do suggest defensiveness.

Research on the K scale in other settings also has yielded dismal results. Hunt, Carp, Cass, Winder, and Kantor (1948), Schmidt (1948), and Wooten (1984) reported that the K-correction contributed little to diagnostic efficiency for patients in a military setting. Silver and Sines (1962) also found that the K-correction did not increase the accuracy of predicting diagnostic classification in state hospital patients; the K scale was essentially unrelated to diagnostic classifications. Ruch and Ruch (1967) found that non-K-corrected Clinical scales discriminated better between good and poor salesmen; the K-corrections actually decreased the discriminability of the two groups.

One positive outcome in this area was provided by Ries (1966), who compared state hospital patients who scored higher than a raw score of 15 (T score greater than 55) on the K scale with patients who scored 15 or lower. For patients with raw scores of 16 or higher, 19 of 22 were rated as being unimproved after 60 days of hospitalization and 7 of 19 were rehospitalized within 12 months. For patients scoring 15 or lower, 25 of 31 were rated as being improved after the same time interval, and only 2 of 25 were rehospitalized within 12 months. Another positive outcome, but in the exact opposite direction, was reported by McGrath, Sweeney, O'Malley, and Carlton (1998). They found that chronic pain patients who had higher scores (T scores > 55) on the K scale actually had superior psychological adjustment despite their chronic pain. The discrepancy in the relationship with high scores on the K scale between these two studies may reflect the very different patient samples. Further research is necessary to understand the role of the K scale in treatment outcome.

Little research justifies the continued widespread use of the *K*-correction of the Clinical scales. Hopefully, future research will investigate this area more thoroughly. Meanwhile, clinicians probably need to avoid using *K*-corrections in settings in which normal persons are being evaluated with the MMPI-2. Clinicians still will have to use the *K*-corrections in settings in which psychopathology is suspected because interpretive information virtually is nonexistent for non-*K*-corrected profiles. However, they need to keep in mind the potential inaccuracies that *K*-corrections may introduce.

Another consideration that clinicians need to keep in mind is that clients can achieve a high score on a Clinical scale that is *K*-corrected in different ways. They can either endorse a large number of items in the deviant direction on the Clinical scale or have a large *K*-correction added or any combination of items from the Clinical scale and the *K* scale.

For example, a woman can achieve a total *K*-corrected raw score of 40 (T score of 72) on Scale *8* (Schizophrenia) of the MMPI-2 in a variety of ways, including endorsing 15 Scale *8* items and 25 *K* scale items or 35 Scale *8* items and 5 *K* scale items. The non-*K*-corrected T scores for these two raw scores on Scale *8* are 56 and 78, respectively (Appendix A-2). It should go without saying that in the latter case she is more likely to be endorsing the items like the schizophrenic criterion group than in the former. This is not to suggest that either the *K*-corrected or non-*K*-corrected score is more accurate. The point is that clients achieving such scores will be very different both behaviorally and clinically, and clinicians need to be aware of these differences.

Low scores on the *K* scale (the client consistently admits problems) are accompanied by more frequent elevations of the clinical profile, especially in the psychotic tetrad (Scales *6* [Paranoia], *7* [Psychasthenia], *8* [Schizophrenia], and *9* [Hypomania]). High scores on the *K* scale are associated with lower profile elevations and peaks on the neurotic triad (Scales *1* [Hypochondriasis], *2* [Depression], and *3* [Hysteria]) both in adult psychiatric and in adolescent populations (Dahlstrom et al., 1972).

Clinicians should consider drawing a non-*K*-corrected profile anytime the *K* scale is above a T score of 60 or below a T score of 40. In the former case, there may be too much *K*-correction being added to the profile, while in the latter case, there may not be enough. In both of these instances it is important for the clinician to be very aware of how much of the elevation of the Clinical scale reflects the item content and how much the *K*-correction process. It still will be necessary to interpret the *K*-corrected profile, however, because most, if not all, research has been conducted with *K*-corrected profiles.

The clinician should be sensitive to scores on the *K* scale that are atypical of clients taking the MMPI-2 in a specific setting. For example, in personnel selection very low scores on the *K* scale would be unusual, and clinicians should review such scores closely. Conversely, in psychiatric settings very high scores on the *K* scale would be unusual. When a client with known or suspected psychopathology has a highly elevated score on the *K* scale, the client is likely to be underreporting some form of psychological distress; the cause of the distress may not be discernible from the profile. In this situation it is usually recommended that the client be evaluated carefully for an underlying psychotic process or severe behavior or personality disorders, particularly if the Clinical scales are within the normal range (Normal *K*+ profiles, page 119).

Test-retest reliability coefficients for the *K* scale on the MMPI range from .78 to .92 for an interval up to two weeks and range from .52 to .67 for intervals from eight months to three years (Dahlstrom et al., 1975). Test-retest reliability coefficients for the *K* scale on the MMPI-2 are .84 for men and .81 for women over a one-week interval (Butcher et al., 1989).

There are no gender effects or age effects on the *K* scale except that 18- and 19-year-olds have scores 5 T points lower than patients in their 20s (Table 3.29). Scores on the *K* scale increase 7 T points with more years of education with most of this difference found in patients with less than 15 years of education.

Four levels of elevation on the *K* scale and their interpretation for persons with known or suspected psychopathology are summarized in Table 3.31. Similar information for "normal" persons is summarized in Table 3.32 on page 98.

TABLE 3.31 Interpretation of Levels of Elevation on the K (Correction) Scale for Clients with Suspected or Known Psychopathology

RAW SCORE	INTERPRETATION
<9	1. *Markedly low.* These clients probably have either fabricated or greatly exaggerated their problems to create the impression of a severe emotional disturbance (overreporting). They may be experiencing acute psychotic distress, which may require hospitalization. The clinician should consider plotting a non-K-corrected profile because of the lack of contribution of the K score to those scales that are K-corrected. The prognosis for a psychological intervention is guarded.
9–12	2. *Low.* These clients have limited personal resources and are experiencing severe distress that is being openly acknowledged. They have poor self-concepts and are strongly self-dissatisfied but lack either the interpersonal skills or techniques necessary to alter the situation. These scores also may indicate persons who tend to be excessively open and revealing and who may be masochistic confessors. In lower-class clients this elevation reflects a moderate disturbance, whereas in higher-class clients it reflects low ego strength and more serious distress. The prognosis for a psychological intervention is guarded.
13–17	3. *Normal.* These clients have a proper balance between self-disclosure and self-protection. Such persons have sufficient personal resources to desire and tolerate a psychological intervention. In higher-class clients a moderate level of personal distress would be expected. The prognosis for a psychological intervention is good.
18–22	4. *Moderate.* These clients are being defensive and unwilling to acknowledge psychological distress. This defensiveness may be characterized by denial and hysteroid defenses, particularly in lower-class clients. The clinician should consider plotting a non-K-corrected profile because of the excessive contribution of the high K score to those scales that are K-corrected. The prognosis is guarded.
23+	5. *Marked.* These clients are consistently trying to maintain a facade of adequacy and control and are admitting no problems or weaknesses despite their presence in a mental health setting. Such persons have a serious lack of insight into and understanding of their own behavior. These clients are being extremely defensive about some kind of inadequacy, which may not be directly discernible from the profile. The clinician should examine the reasons that the client might be denying psychopathology and should plot a non-K-corrected profile. The prognosis for any form of psychological intervention is very poor because of the lack of insight into their behavior.

Positive Malingering (Mp) and Other Deception (ODecp) Scales.   The Positive Malingering scale (*Mp:* Cofer et al., 1949) was developed to identify underreporting of psychopathology. Cofer et al. asked groups of college students to endorse the MMPI items like an emotionally disturbed person (overreport) or to make the best possible impression (underreport). They then identified 34 items that were insensitive to overreporting (negative malingering) and yet susceptible to underreporting (positive malingering). They found that a cutting score of 20 or higher correctly identified 96 percent of the accurate MMPIs and 86 percent of the underreported MMPIs. A cutting score of 20 is equivalent to a T score of 69 in men and 73 in women in the original Minnesota normative group. They also noted that scores on the *Mp* scale tended to

TABLE 3.32 Interpretation of Levels of Elevation on the *K* Scale for Normal Individuals

RAW SCORE	INTERPRETATION
0–10	1. *Low.* These clients are acknowledging limited resources for dealing with problems. The clinician should investigate whether the clients actually have some form of psychopathology that they are willing to report.
11–17	2. *Normal.* These clients may be from lower socioeconomic classes or with limited educational levels who have an appropriate balance between self-disclosure and self-protection.
18–22	3. *Moderate.* College-educated and upper-class persons are well adjusted, insightful, self-reliant, and easily capable of dealing with their everyday problems. When under stress, such persons may be unwilling to seek help with their problems.
23+	4. *Marked.* These clients' professed adjustment and self-adequacy are likely to reflect a defensive facade. They probably have little interest in examining the appropriateness of this facade.

be related positively to scores on the Wiener (1948) Subtle scales. Six of the 34 items on the *Mp* scale overlap with the *L* scale.

There has been limited research with the *Mp* scale (Cofer et al., 1949). Otto, Lang, Megargee, and Rosenblatt (1988) reported that the *Mp* scale was able to identify nearly 80 percent of alcoholics who were instructed to hide any problems or shortcomings. Baer, Wetter, and Berry (1992) found in their meta-analysis that the *Mp* scale had one of the largest effect sizes ($d = 1.42$) of MMPI measures of underreporting of psychopathology. The optimal cutting score for the 12 studies that they cited ranged from 16 to 20 with hit rates ranging from 61 to 93 percent.

Nichols and Greene (1991) have updated the *Mp* scale for the MMPI-2 and renamed the scale, Other Deception (*ODecp*). The 33 items on the *ODecp* scale may be found in Appendix B.8. The *ODecp* scale shares 7 items with the *L* (Lie) scale, 24 items (72.7 percent) with Wiggins' Social Desirability (*Sd*) scale, 4 items with the *K* (Correction) scale, 8 items with the Superlative (*S*) scale, and no items with Edwards' Social Desirability (*So*) scale. Given the extensive item overlap between the *ODecp* and *Sd* scales, it seems unnecessary to score both of these scales routinely. Research that investigates the items that are unique to these two scales might be instructive in furthering our understanding of impression management on the MMPI-2. Item content on the *ODecp* scale reflects

confidence in oneself and one's abilities and not having psychological problems, even such minor problems like swearing and not liking everyone. Examples of items on the *ODecp* scale with the deviant answer indicated in parentheses are:

> "I am entirely self-confident." (true)
>
> "I frequently find myself worrying about something." (false)
>
> "I have several times given up doing a thing because I thought too little of my ability." (false)[9]

Women have scores on the *ODecp* scale that are about 5 T points higher than men (see Table 3.29, pp. 92–93). There are minimal effects of age or education on the *ODecp* scale.

Table 3.33 provides the cutting scores that can be used with the *ODecp* scale in the assessment of underreporting of psychopathology in three different settings.

Wiggins' Social Desirability* (Sd) *Scale. Wiggins (1959) developed his Social Desirability (*Sd*) scale to discriminate college students who were instructed to

9. Minnesota Multiphasic Personality Inventory-2 (MMPI-2). Copyright © 1942, 1943 (renewed 1970), 1989 by the Regents of the University of Minnesota. Reproduced by permission of the publisher. "MMPI-2" and "Minnesota Multiphasic Personality Inventory-2" are trademarks owned by the University of Minnesota.

TABLE 3.33   Cutting Scores for Assessing Underreporting of Psychopathology by Setting

						PERCENTILE						
L	*2*	*7*	*16*	*30*	*50*	*70*	*84*	*93*	*98*	*99.2*	*99.7*	*99.9*
Normal[a]		0	1	2	3	4	5	6	9	10	11	12
Clinical[b]	0	1	2	3	4	5	7	8	10	11	12	13
Personnel[c]	0	1	2	4	5	7	9	11	12		13	14

						PERCENTILE						
ODecp	*2*	*7*	*16*	*30*	*50*	*70*	*84*	*93*	*98*	*99.2*	*99.7*	*99.9*
Normal[a]	4	6	7	9	11	13	16	18	21	23	24	26
Clinical[b]	3	5	7	9	12	15	17	20	23	24	26	27
Personnel[c]	7	10	12	15	19	22	24	26	28		29	30

						PERCENTILE						
Sd	*2*	*7*	*16*	*30*	*50*	*70*	*84*	*93*	*98*	*99.2*	*99.7*	*99.9*
Normal[a]	5	7	8	10	12	14	15	17	20	22	24	25
Clinical[b]	5	7	9	10	12	15	17	19	21	23	24	25
Personnel[c]	8	10	12	14	16	19	21	23	25	26	27	28

						PERCENTILE						
K	*2*	*7*	*16*	*30*	*50*	*70*	*84*	*93*	*98*	*99.2*	*99.7*	*99.9*
Normal[a]	5	8	10	12	15	17	19	22	24	25	26	27
Clinical[b]	5	7	9	12	15	19	21	23	25	26	27	28
Personnel[c]	10	13	16	18	21	23	24	25	26		27	28

						PERCENTILE						
S	*2*	*7*	*16*	*30*	*50*	*70*	*84*	*93*	*98*	*99.2*	*99.7*	*99.9*
Normal[a]	8	12	16	20	25	29	34	38	42	44	45	47
Clinical[b]	7	11	15	20	26	32	37	42	46	47	48	49
Personnel[c]	17	23	28	33	38	43	45	47	48	49		50

						PERCENTILE						
So	*2*	*7*	*16*	*30*	*50*	*70*	*84*	*93*	*98*	*99.2*	*99.7*	*99.9*
Normal[a]	16	20	24	27	30	32	34	35	36			37
Clinical[b]	9	13	17	22	27	32	34		36			37
Personnel[c]	25	29	32	34	35		36					37

						PERCENTILE						
False	*2*	*7*	*16*	*30*	*50*	*70*	*84*	*93*	*98*	*99.2*	*99.7*	*99.9*
Normal[a]	44	49	53	57	61	64	67	69	71	72	73	74
Clinical[b]	39	45	50	56	61	65	68	71	73	74	75	76
Personnel[c]	53	58	61	64	67	69	71	73	74	75		76

Notes. All scores are raw scores.
[a]Butcher et al. (1989).
[b]Caldwell (1997a).
[c]Caldwell (1997b).

take the MMPI as people in general would describe as being socially desirable from those who took the test honestly. He identified 40 items that reliably differentiated these two groups of students. A cutting score of 21 on the *Sd* scale identified 74 percent of the dissimulated MMPIs ($N = 250$) and 98 percent of the honest MMPIs ($N = 190$). A cross-validation study using the same cutting score successfully identified 68 percent of the dissimulated MMPIs ($N = 72$) and 100 percent of the honest MMPIs ($N = 50$). Wiggins also noted that the *Mp* scale identified 65 percent of the dissimulated MMPIs and 96 percent of the honest MMPIs, which attests to both the usefulness of the *Mp* scale and their common variance since they share 14 items. The 33 items on the MMPI-2 version of the *Sd* scale can be found in Appendix B-8. Item content on the *Sd* scale reflects self-confidence, good social skills, and being able to make decisions easily. Examples of items on the *Sd* scale with the deviant answer indicated in parentheses are:

> "I am a very sociable person." (true)
>
> "At periods my mind seems to work more slowly than usual." (false)
>
> "I have several times given up doing a thing because I thought too little of my ability." (false)[10]

Baer et al. (1992) found that the *Sd* scale had the largest effect size ($d = 1.60$) of all MMPI measures of underreporting of psychopathology, although it had been used less often than the *L* (Lie), *K* (Correction), or Positive Malingering (*Mp*) scales. The optimal cutting score for the 6 studies that they cited ranged from 21 to 23 with hit rates ranging from 76 to 94 percent.

There are minimal age, education, or gender differences on the *Sd* scale (Table 3.29, pp. 92–93).

Table 3.33 provides the cutting scores that can be used with the *Sd* scale in the assessment of underreporting of psychopathology in three different settings. Four levels of elevation on the *Sd* scale and their interpretation for persons suspected of trying to underreport psychopathology are summarized in Table 3.34.

Superlative (**S**) *Scale.*   Butcher and Han (1995) developed the Superlative (*S*) scale to assess persons who present themselves in a superlative manner that is encountered frequently in individuals who are being screened in personnel settings. The items for the *S* scale were selected by contrasting the MMPI-2 item responses of 274 pilot applicants with the 1,138 men in the MMPI-2 normative group. This analysis produced a set of 52 items with a difference in response frequency of at least 25 percent between the two groups. Further analyses of the homogeneity of the scale removed two items resulting in the current 50 items on the *S* scale. The *S* scale shares 1 item with the *L* (Lie) scale, 8 items with the Other Deception (*ODecp*) scale, 3 items with Wiggins' Social Desirability (*Sd*) scale, 9 items with the *K* (Correction) scale, and no items with Edwards' Social Desirability (*So*) scale. As noted earlier, 88 percent of the items on the *S* scale are false, and it correlates significantly (.82 to .88) with the *K* scale (Table 3.28). Butcher and Han suggested that the 41 items on the *S* scale that do not overlap with the *K* scale appear to operate as a "'virtue-claiming' or problem-denying scale." The items on the *S* scale can be found in Appendix B.8. Item content on the *S* scale reflects general comfort with others who have good intentions, lack of any negative feelings toward others, and not engaging in any type of risk-taking behaviors. Examples of the items on the *S* scale with the deviant answer indicated in parentheses are:

> "I frequently find myself worrying about something." (false)
>
> "People have often misunderstood my intentions when I was trying to put them right and be helpful." (false)
>
> "I easily become impatient with people." (false)[11]

Butcher and Han conducted a component analysis of the *S* scale and identified five factors: Beliefs in Human Goodness; Serenity; Contentment with Life; Patience and Denial of Irritability and Anger; and Denial of Moral Flaws. There is no item overlap among the subscales of the *S* scale and all 50 items are assigned to one of the five factors. Their intercorrelations in the MMPI-2 normative group ranged from .19 to .46.

---

10. Minnesota Multiphasic Personality Inventory-2 (MMPI-2). Copyright © 1942, 1943 (renewed 1970), 1989 by the Regents of the University of Minnesota. Reproduced by permission of the publisher. "MMPI-2" and "Minnesota Multiphasic Personality Inventory-2" are trademarks owned by the University of Minnesota.

11. Ibid.

TABLE 3.34 Interpretation of Levels of Underreporting of Psychopathology

SCALE/INDEX

Sd	S	Interpretation
<11	<21	1. *Low.* These clients are reporting emotional distress and a number of unusual behaviors and symptoms. They clearly have not underreported psychopathology, although they may need to be evaluated as to whether they have overreported psychopathology.
11–15	21–34	2. *Normal.* These clients have endorsed the items accurately. Codetype interpretation may proceed with confidence.
16–20	35–42	3. *Moderate.* These clients may be underreporting the level of emotional distress that they actually are experiencing. Their clinical history and reasons for seeking treatment should be evaluated to assess whether these are commensurate with the level of distress that they are reporting. Even if they are not the "identified" patient, they are not acknowledging the level of emotional distress that might be expected for those who are dealing with psychological problems in another person. If they have engaged in impression management, it may be possible to have them retake the MMPI-2 after discussing with them how they have been overly conservative in describing their problems.
21+	43+	4. *Marked.* These clients are underreporting the extent and severity of their psychopathology. This underreporting may reflect a conscious, intentional distortion of their responses (impression management), a lack of awareness of and insight into their behavior (self-deception), or some combination of both.

Note. Clinicians may prefer to use another scale or index of underreporting from Table 3.33 that can be substituted for the scales in this Table.

High scorers on the *S* scale are described by their spouse as being self-confident, pleasant, relaxed, and cheerful. They also are described as not arguing, not having temper problems, not easily upset or annoyed, not having physical complaints, and not worrying. They present themselves as being well adjusted, responsible, and highly virtuous individuals. Although endorsement of any single item on the *S* scale can represent good adjustment and emotional control, persons who elevate ($T \geq 65$) the *S* scale are claiming more of these virtuous qualities than are encountered in most normal individuals.

There have been only a few studies of the *S* scale (Bagby, Rogers, Nicholson, Buis, Seeman, & Rector, 1997; Butcher, Morfitt, Rouse, & Holden, 1997; Nicholson et al., 1997) given its recent publication. The *S* scale typically was as or more effective than the traditional validity indicators (*L* [Lie], *K* [Correction], and the $F - K$ index) on the MMPI-2 in the detection of underreporting of psychopathology and clearly

should be the focus of further research on this important topic.

There are no gender differences on the *S* scale and few age differences other than 18- and 19-year-olds scoring about 5 T points lower than all other age groups (see Table 3.29, pp. 92–93). Scores on the *S* scale increase with more years of education. Patients with 12 or fewer years of education score 2 to 6 T points lower than patients with more years of education.

Table 3.33 provides the cutting scores that can be used with the *S* scale in the assessment of underreporting of psychopathology in three different settings. Four levels of elevation on the *S* scale and their interpretation for persons suspected of trying to underreport psychopathology are summarized in Table 3.34.

Edwards' Social Desirability* (So) *Scale. Edwards (1957) developed his Social Desirability (*So*) scale by asking 10 judges to give socially desirable responses to 150 MMPI items that he had selected to be heterogeneous in content. These judges had perfect agreement on 79 of these 150 items. These 79 items were later reduced to 39 items by selecting those items that differentiated individuals who had high or low scores on the original scale. He reported that college students had mean scores around 27 to 28 on the 39-item scale. He believed that these items measured the tendency of students to give socially desirable responses to MMPI items regardless of their content. The *So* scale shares 12 items with the *F* (Infrequency) scale and 9 items with the Welsh Anxiety (*A*) scale with the items scored in the opposite direction on the *So* scale (i.e., the socially desirable response is to not endorse the items on the *F* and *A* scales). The 37 items on the MMPI-2 version of the *So* scale can be found in Appendix B.8. Item content on the *So* scale reflects not having any type of psychological problem, good attention and concentration skills, and general comfort with other people. Examples of items on the *So* scale with the deviant answer indicated in parentheses are:

"Life is a strain for me much of the time." (false)

"I sometimes feel that I am about to go to pieces." (false)

"I cannot keep my mind on one thing." (false)[12]

Baer et al. (1992) found that the *So* scale had the smallest effect size ($d = 0.67$) of all MMPI measures of underreporting of psychopathology. The optimal cutting score for the five studies that they cited ranged from 33 to 36 with hit rates ranging from 63 to 79 percent.

There are minimal gender effects on the *So* scale with men having T scores about 3 points higher than women (see Table 3.29, pp. 92–93). There are no age effects on the *So* scale other than 18- and 19-year-olds having T scores 3–4 points lower than all other age groups. There are rather consistent increases in scores on the *So* scale with more years of education; patients with 8 years or less of education have T scores almost

10 points lower than patients with 19 or more years of education.

Table 3.33 provides the cutting scores that can be used with the *So* scale in the assessment of underreporting of psychopathology in three different settings. There is a very limited ceiling for scores on the *So* scale with the average score in all individuals being close to 30 out of a possible 37 items.

F – K *Index (Gough Dissimulation Index).* The *F – K* index (the *raw* score of the *F* scale minus the *raw* score of the *K* scale) also was proposed by Gough (1947, 1950) as an index of underreporting of psychopathology. If the *F – K* index was less than 0, the profile was classified as underreporting (i.e., the client was trying to deny the existence of any form of psychopathology).

Gough's initial reservations about the efficiency of the *F – K* index in detecting underreporting of psychopathology have been corroborated by numerous investigators. Most studies have found extensive overlap in the distributions of the *F – K* index in students who took the MMPI-2 normally and then retook the MMPI-2 to underreport psychopathology. Consequently, clinicians have problems in establishing a consistent cutting score on the *F – K* index that reliably distinguishes normal student profiles from their underreported profiles. The optimal cutting scores on the *F – K* index in college students who were instructed to underreport have ranged from –11 (Bagby, Rogers, Buis, & Kalemba, 1994) to –16 (Baer, Wetter, & Berry, 1995).

One problem with the *F – K* index in identifying underreporting of psychopathology is that anyone who is acknowledging the capability to handle his or her own problems, who is well adjusted (high raw score on the *K* [Correction] scale), and who is not experiencing stress or conflict simultaneously (low raw score on the *F* [Infrequency] scale) will most likely be defined as underreporting rather than normal by this index. Thus, normal persons taking the MMPI-2 often will be inappropriately classified as underreporting on this index.

---

12. Minnesota Multiphasic Personality Inventory-2 (MMPI-2). Copyright © 1942, 1943 (renewed 1970), 1989 by the Regents of the University of Minnesota. Reproduced by permission of the publisher. "MMPI-2" and "Minnesota Multiphasic Personality Inventory-2" are trademarks owned by the University of Minnesota.

Clinical Case 3-5. Bob was a 45-year-old, divorced, white man who had an 11th grade education. He currently was living with one of his ex-wives. His most recent job had been as a cook in a fast-food restaurant. His parole officer had referred him for an outpatient evaluation to determine whether his driver's license should be reinstated.

Bob had used alcohol and marijuana heavily since he was a teenager. He was cited for his first driving-while-intoxicated (DWI) offense at age 18; his most recent DWI, his 13th, occurred 10 months before he took the MMPI-2. At that time his driver's license was revoked. He had been imprisoned on three occasions and had been released about one year ago. His most recent imprisonment had been for stealing television sets at a motel after he found a master key the maid had dropped on the floor of his room. He admitted having murdered a man approximately 15 years earlier in order to prevent being turned in for a crime that he had committed. He was never caught for this murder.

Bob's MMPI-2 profile (Profile 3.8, solid circles) was a Within-Normal-Limit (*WNL*) codetype (i.e., there were no Validity or Clinical scales at or above a T score of 65). Following the flowchart presented in Figure 3.1 (p. 43) for assessing the validity of an MMPI-2, Bob omitted no items and all measures of consistency of item endorsement were well within normal ranges (Table 3.17). (Bob had a raw score of 5 on the Variable Response Inconsistency [*VRIN*] scale, 2 on the $|F - F_B|$ index [absolute difference between the raw score on these two infrequency scales], and 9 on the True Response Inconsistency [*TRIN*] scale.)

The next step in the flowchart is to assess the accuracy of item endorsement. None of the measures of

MMPI-2 PROFILE FOR VALIDITY AND CLINICAL SCALES

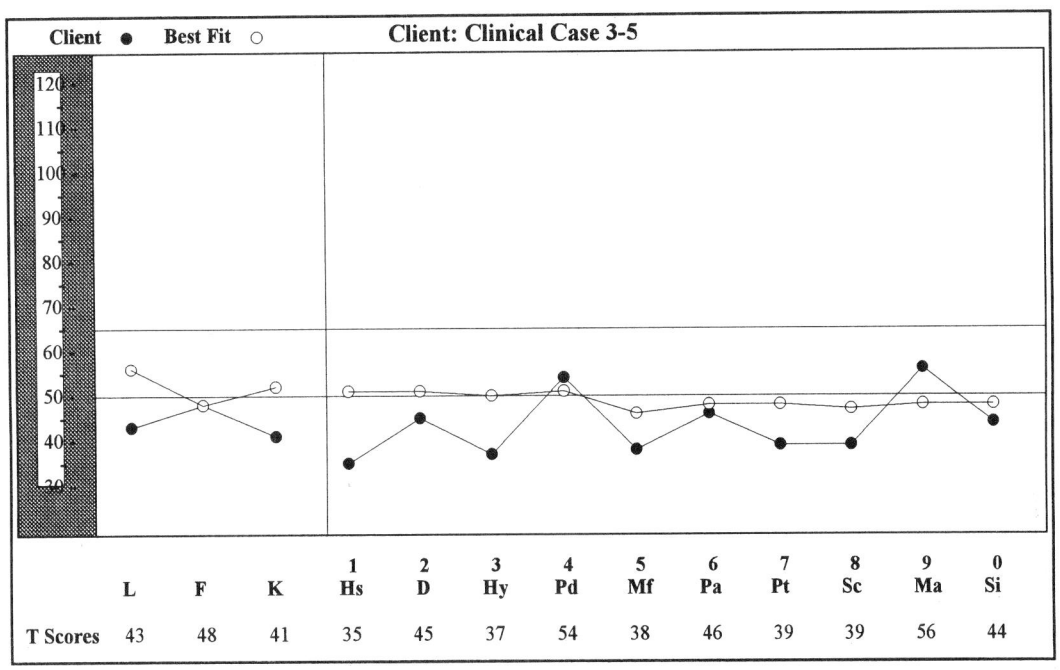

	L	F	K	1 Hs	2 D	3 Hy	4 Pd	5 Mf	6 Pa	7 Pt	8 Sc	9 Ma	0 Si
T Scores	43	48	41	35	45	37	54	38	46	39	39	56	44

PROFILE 3.8

Note. Minnesota Multiphasic Personality Inventory-2 (MMPI-2). Copyright © 1942, 1943 (renewed 1970), 1989 by the Regents of the University of Minnesota. Reproduced by permission of the publisher. "MMPI-2" and "Minnesota Multiphasic Personality Inventory-2" are trademarks owned by the University of Minnesota.

underreporting of psychopathology was above the 84th percentile (Table 3.33). (Bob had raw scores of 2 on the *L* [Lie] scale, 13 on the Other Deception [*ODecp*] scale, 15 on Wiggins' Social Desirability [*Sd*] scale, 11 on the *K* [Correction] scale, 18 on the Superlative [*S*] scale, and 33 on Edwards' Social Desirability [*So*] scale.) Following the flowchart in Figure 3.1, Bob's MMPI-2 is classified as being underreported and the interpretive process would stop.

In this case, the clinician has little temptation to try to interpret the MMPI-2 because no Clinical scales were elevated above a T score of 55. Even though it is obvious that Bob's MMPI-2 profile is underreported because it is *WNL,* it is somewhat surprising that none of these measures of underreporting was elevated. This case illustrates that it is more difficult to assess underreporting than overreporting of psy-

chopathology, and that seriously ingrained, character psychopathology such as Bob's has little impact on most MMPI-2 scales. A content-based interpretation of his MMPI-2 (Profile 3.9), however, did reveal his cynical, antisocial, and substance-abusing qualities (see Nichols & Greene, 1995, pp. 54–64).

Meta-Analyses of Underreporting of Psychopathology

There are only a few reviews of the assessment of underreporting of psychopathology (Greene, 1988a, 1997; Nichols & Greene, 1997) in contrast to the multiple reviews of overreporting of psychopathology that were discussed earlier. Nichols and Greene (1997) have provided a general conceptual framework for understanding the dimensions of underre-

MMPI-2 PROFILE FOR CONTENT SCALES

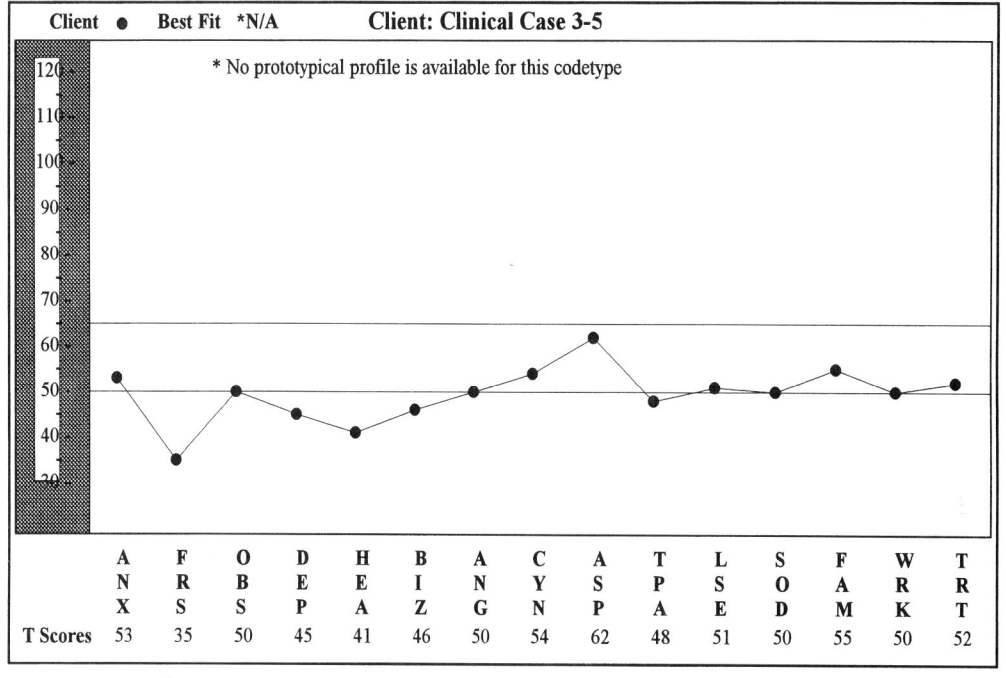

	ANX	FRS	OBS	DEP	HEA	BIZ	ANG	CYN	ASP	TPA	LSE	SOD	FAM	WRK	TRT
T Scores	53	35	50	45	41	46	50	54	62	48	51	50	55	50	52

PROFILE 3.9

Note. Minnesota Multiphasic Personality Inventory-2 (MMPI-2). Copyright © 1942, 1943 (renewed 1970), 1989 by the Regents of the University of Minnesota. Reproduced by permission of the publisher. "MMPI-2" and "Minnesota Multiphasic Personality Inventory-2" are trademarks owned by the University of Minnesota.

porting (deception) in the MMPI-2 that should be consulted by readers interested in this topic. Baer et al. (1992) have conducted the only meta-analysis of underreporting on the MMPI; a similar meta-analysis has not been conducted on the MMPI-2. Baer et al. (1992) found that the largest effect sizes were for scales not scored routinely on the MMPI: Wiggins' Social Desirability (*Sd*) scale and the Positive Malingering (*Mp*) scale, with effect sizes of 1.60 and 1.42, respectively. The effect sizes for the *L* (Lie) and *K* (Correction) scales were 0.94 and 0.90, respectively, while the effect size for the $F - K$ index was 0.71. These effect sizes are about one-half the size that are found in the meta-analyses of the overreporting of psychopathology (Table 3.26). The smaller effect sizes would be expected because there should be less difference between normal behavior and underreported psychopathology than between normal behavior and overreported psychopathology.

Table 3.35 provides a summary of the results of the three most commonly used scales and index on the MMPI-2 to assess underreporting of psychopathology. When college students who are instructed to underreport psychopathology are compared with college students who take the MMPI-2 accurately, all three scales are quite capable of making this discrimination. The effect size is largest for the *L* (Lie) scale ($d = 1.70$), followed by the *K* (Correction) scale ($d = 1.22$), and the $F - K$ index ($d = 1.01$). As noted earlier these effect sizes are smaller than those found in meta-analyses of overreporting of psychopathology (Table 3.26). Although these effects are somewhat smaller, the effect sizes still are very large by Cohen's (1988) standard. Fewer studies have compared college students who are instructed to underreport psychopathology with patients who are presumed to have taken the MMPI-2 accurately. In these studies, the effect sizes are largest for the $F - K$ index ($d = 1.83$), followed by the *K* scale ($d = 1.12$), and the *L* scale ($d = 0.56$). There is sizable range in the optimal cutting scores across these various studies so that it is difficult to reach any definitive conclusions. Cutting scores in the range of 6 to 8 on the *L* scale, 16 to 19 on the *K* scale, and –12 to –16 on the $F - K$ index are fairly typical. The positive and negative predictive power for these scales ranges around 70 percent, which is good. These figures for positive predictive

power are somewhat misleading though because the base rate (prevalence) of underreporting in most of these studies was around 50 percent. If the base rate was decreased to a more likely range, say 10 to 20 percent, the positive predictive power would decrease to around 20 percent, while the negative predictive power would increase to around 95 percent.

Nicholson et al. (1997) used receiver operator characteristic analysis to compare seven different measures of underreporting of psychopathology in college students. They found that all of these measures were reasonably effective at identifying those students who were underreporting, with the Superlative (*S*) scale performing the best and the $F - K$ index performing least well.

There are several general conclusions that can be made about the research on underreporting on the MMPI-2. First, there have been fewer studies in this area compared to the overreporting of psychopathology. This dearth of interest is unwarranted because there are numerous clinical settings in which clients can be assumed to have motivation to underreport psychopathology, such as child custody evaluations as well as in most, if not all, personnel screening settings. Second, virtually all of the extant research has been conducted with college students. Although such analogue research is important to establish the parameters to be investigated, the crux of the issue is how these scales will perform in actual clinical or personnel screening settings. Finally, several scales such as the Superlative (*S*) and the Other Deception (*ODecp*) scale or Wiggins' Social Desirability (*Sd*) scale warrant more serious consideration as potentially useful measures of underreporting of psychopathology rather than the traditional Validity scales of the *L* (Lie) or *K* (Correction) scales, and particularly the $F - K$ index.

Effects of Demographic Variables on Scales Assessing Underreporting of Psychopathology.   There are only a few minor gender differences on these six scales used to assess whether the person is underreporting psychopathology (Table 3.29). Men score 2 to 5 T points higher on the Other Deception (*ODecp*), Wiggins' Social Desirability (*Sd*), and Edwards' Social Desirability (*So*) scales than women. There are no effects of age on any of these scales beyond the age of 20. There is a consistent pattern, however, for the 18-

TABLE 3.35 Effect Sizes and Positive and Negative Predictive Power for Scales and Indexes Assessing Underreporting of Psychopathology

		L				K				F − K			
	Base Rate	Cutting Score	d	PPP	NPP	Cutting Score	d	PPP	NPP	Cutting Score	d	PPP	NPP
Normal Individuals Responding Accurately or Underreporting Psychopathology													
Students													
Austin (1992)	0.55	11	3.07	81.6	74.3	24	1.71	85.7	52.5	−13	1.16	72.0	82.6
Baer et al. (1995)	0.50	6	1.56	82.2	76.4	18	1.73	80.0	80.0	−16	1.90	78.0	78.0
Bagby et al. (1994a)	0.43	8	1.25	86.2	67.2	19	1.39	89.5	72.3	−15	1.27	75.7	83.9
Bagby et al. (1994b)	0.43	6	1.25	78.1	66.4	17	1.43	65.2	68.1	−11	1.31	84.6	96.4
Bagby et al. (1997)	0.50		0.75				1.29				0.82		
Baer et al. (1995)													
Fake Good	0.50	6	2.43	100.0	88.9	17	1.71	76.7	94.4	−12	1.10	70.0	83.3
Fake Good (Low Detail)	0.50	4	0.59	61.5	63.6	13	0.30	53.3	55.6	−9	0.35	50.0	50.0
Fake Good (High Detail)	0.50	3	0.07	48.6	45.5	17	0.04	52.4	66.7	−7	0.16	52.9	57.1
Graham et al. (1991)	0.50	7	1.90	79.4	87.8	16	1.55	76.7	80.8				
Lim & Butcher (1996)													
Deny Problems	0.50	5	1.59	77.2	73.1	16	1.19	64.0	71.4	−14		67.2	70.2
Claim Extreme Virtue	0.50	5	2.06	90.6	83.1	16	1.09	70.4	80.9	−14		68.1	75.5
Timbrook et al. (1993)			2.21										
Mean	0.49	6	1.70	78.6	72.9	17	1.22	70.4	71.5	−12	1.01	70.8	80.0
Personnel Screening													
Butcher (1994)	0.28	7	0.71	10.8	27.2	7	1.73	20.0	32.2				
Normal Individuals Underreporting Psychopathology versus Patients Responding Accurately													
Students													
Bagby et al. (1994a)	0.28	8	0.43	43.1	76.9	6	0.90	54.8	81.5	−15	2.40	58.5	88.0
Bagby et al. (1994b)	0.41	6	0.78	56.8	64.4	5	1.27	68.2	68.6	−11	1.43	74.6	84.6
Bagby et al. (1997)	0.56		0.48				1.19				1.66		
Mean	0.42		0.56	49.0	72.0		1.12	60.4	76.4		1.83	66.0	86.7
Patients Underreporting Psychopathology or Responding Accurately													
Bagby et al. (1997)	0.50		0.86				0.69				0.92		

Note. *d* = effect size, which was computed based on M1 − M2 divided by the pooled standard deviations for the two groups being compared. PPP = positive predictive power. NPP = negative predictive power. PPP and NPP in Total rows have been weighted by sample sizes (i.e., they are not simply averages of the PPP and NPP values).

and 19-year-olds to score about 5 T points higher than the other age groups on all six scales. This pattern of 18- and 19-year-olds scoring more like adolescents than like people in their 20s will be seen repeatedly as the other scales of the MMPI-2 are discussed. The effects of demographic variables will be examined more systematically in Chapter 9, and the performance of adolescents will be discussed in Chapter 10.

There are consistent trends for scores on the three scales assessing impression management (*L* [Lie], Other Deception [*ODecp*], and Wiggins' Social Desirability [*Sd*]) to decrease with more years of education, while scores on the three scales assessing self-deception (*K* [Correction], Superlative [*S*], and Edwards' Social Desirability [*So*] increase. When patients with less than 8 years of education are contrasted with patients with 19 or more years of education, the impression management scales decrease around 2 to 5 T points and the self-deception scales increase 5 to 7 T points. These differences as a function of years of education are approximately one-third to one-half of the size of the differences that were found on the scales and indexes assessing overreporting of psychopathology. This pattern of the substantial effects of education on scores on MMPI-2 scales also will be seen repeatedly and will be examined more fully in Chapter 9.

Summary. Six different scales for assessing the underreporting of psychopathology have been described. After reviewing the relative advantages and disadvantages of each of these scales, the reader should select the scales that are most appropriate for his or her specific clients and treatment setting. The selection of one of these scales of underreporting is more difficult than for overreporting, since they appear to be measuring slightly different aspects of underreporting as indicated by their relatively low intercorrelations (Table 3.28). The $F - K$ index probably is the least likely to be useful given its limited research support. It does seem appropriate to select at least one scale that is assessing impression management and one scale that is assessing self-deception from this set of six scales.

When a client's responses have been identified as being endorsed inaccurately because of underreporting of psychopathology, the MMPI-2 profile is no longer interpretable because it reflects an underreporting response set. The clinician will have little reason to try to interpret such a profile, however, since extreme underreporting results in no Clinical scales being elevated over a T score of 65 and frequently no Clinical scales are above a T score of 60. The clinician should describe the client's style of underreporting psychopathology (impression management, self-deception, or a combination of both), determine the potential causes for this response set, and assess the implications for treatment and intervention. If the clinician can appreciate that an underreported profile is not interpretable because of a response set in which no Clinical scales are elevated, the parallel situation that overreported profiles are equally uninterpretable because of a response set in which most or all Clinical scales are elevated may become more apparent.

Once these scales to identify underreporting of psychopathology have been described, the next step in the implementation of the flowchart in Figure 3.1 (p. 43) can be made. The criteria, summarized in Table 3.33, provide the quantitative data necessary to determine whether the items have been endorsed to underreport psychopathology. Once it has been determined that the client has underreported psychopathology, the clinician will need to ascertain the reasons for the inaccurate item endorsement by a clinical interview.

Four levels of elevation and their interpretation for persons suspected of trying to underreport psychopathology are summarized in Table 3.34. A summary of the potential causes of underreporting of psychopathology as well as some possible solutions for these problems are presented in Table 3.36.

Once clinicians realize that underreporting of psychopathology is encountered frequently in a clinical setting, the empirical correlates of such a response set can be studied. It may be that clients who underreport psychopathology see their problems as less troubling to themselves and, hence, are less motivated to change. Their problems also may be more chronic in nature and, consequently, they may be more difficult to treat if they remain in treatment. Duckworth and Barley (1988) have provided a summary of the correlates of clients who produce such underreported profiles, which should be consulted by the interested

TABLE 3.36 Potential Causes of and Solutions for Underreporting of Psychopathology

CAUSE	SOLUTION
1. Client is not the identified patient (i.e., the client's spouse or another family member is the identified patient) and wants to convince the clinician that he or she does not have any problems.	1. If the client can begin to trust the clinician, it may be possible to readminister the MMPI-2.
2. Client believes that underreporting symptoms is necessary to obtain some desired outcome such as a personnel position, transfer to another agency or institution, and so on.	2. May be no solution.
3. Client believes that he or she does not have any problems, which is encountered frequently in Antisocial and Narcissistic Personality Disorders, Manic Mood Disorders, and many Substance Dependence Disorders.	3. Clients with Substance Dependence Disorders sometimes can be encouraged to be more rigorously honest and have the MMPI-2 readministered.

reader. The reader also should review the discussion of K+ profiles that follows later, which is one form of underreporting psychopathology.

CUTTING SCORES FOR ASSESSING VALIDITY IN *CLINICAL* SETTINGS

In any clinical setting it is presumed that either clients are requesting mental health services because of their own concerns about symptoms and behaviors they are experiencing or someone else has referred them for such concerns. In both circumstances, it is expected that they should be reporting some type of distress that would be reflected by elevations on the MMPI-2 profile. In the former, they are experiencing the distress that served as the motivation for them to seek treatment. In the latter, they would be expected at least to have some concerns that someone has required them to be evaluated, particularly if they have no problems whatsoever. Given that clinicians are warm, empathic, and understanding human beings, it still would be very unusual for clients not to have any affective response to being evaluated when there is nothing wrong with them.

Table 3.37 summarizes the cutting scores that can be used to assess the validity of the MMPI-2 profile in *clinical* settings. This same information is provided for men and women in Profiles 3.10 and 3.11, respectively. The percentiles in Table 3.37 were determined

for every raw score for each scale or index in the Caldwell clinical dataset ($N = 50,966$), which will be described more completely in Chapter 9. This procedure produces equivalent raw scores on each scale or index at the same percentile within the Caldwell clinical dataset and allows the clinician to make direct comparisons among them. The 93rd percentile is equivalent to a T score of 65 and the 98th percentile is equivalent to a T score of 70. Similarly, the 7th percentile is equivalent to a T score of 35 and the 2nd percentile is equivalent to a T score of 30. *Clinicians should be aware that these T scores will not be equivalent to the MMPI-2 profile form because the scores are referenced to a clinical sample rather than the MMPI-2 normative group.* Finally, it will be reiterated one more time that no specific score has been specified as indicating that the client has omitted excessive items, inconsistently endorsed the items, or overreported or underreported psychopathology. Rather the relative frequency with which the scores occur has been provided and the clinician needs to determine whether the client has endorsed the items appropriately at each stage in the process of assessing the validity of this administration of the MMPI-2.

Research is needed to determine whether a specific scale or index of overreporting and underreporting is the most appropriate for a given clinical setting, and whether raising or lowering cutting scores would facilitate the identification of overre-

TABLE 3.37 Cutting Scores for Assessing MMPI-2 Validity in Clinical Settings[a]

Omissions

	PERCENTILE											
	2	7	16	30	50	70	84	93	98	99.2	99.7	99.9
?						0	2	5	12	18	24	27

Consistency of Item Endorsement

	PERCENTILE											
	2	7	16	30	50	70	84	93	98	99.2	99.7	99.9
VRIN	0	1	2	3	5	6	8	9	11	12	13	14
$|F - F_B|$		0		1	2	4	5	7	10	12	14	16
TRIN	6	7	8			9	10	11	12	13	14	15

Accuracy of Item Endorsement
  Overreporting of Psychopathology

	PERCENTILE											
	2	7	16	30	50	70	84	93	98	99.2	99.7	99.9
F		0	1	3	5	8	12	17	24	28	32	35
F_B			0	2	5	9	14	20	24	26	28	
$F(p)$				0	1	2	3	4	7	8	9	10
$F - K$	−24	−22	−19	−16	−11	−5	1	7	15	20	25	28
Ds	1	2	4	7	11	17	22	28	35	39	42	44
K & B	0	1	4	8	16	28	38	47	57	61	65	68
L & W	2	5	8	14	24	37	49	60	73	80	85	89
O − S	−105	−86	−63	−31	19	80	135	186	241	269	291	305
True %	25	27	29	32	37	42	48	53	59	63	66	69

  Underreporting of Psychopathology

	PERCENTILE											
	2	7	16	30	50	70	84	93	98	99.2	99.7	99.9
L	0	1	2	3	4	5	7	8	10	11	12	13
ODecp	3	5	7	9	12	15	17	20	23	24	26	27
Sd	5	7	9	10	12	15	17	19	21	23	24	25
K	5	7	10	12	15	19	21	23	25	26	27	28
S	7	11	15	20	26	32	37	42	46	47	48	49
So	9	13	17	22	27	32	34		36			37
False %	39	45	50	56	61	65	68	71	73	74	75	76

[a]Caldwell (1997a). All scores are raw scores except for $|F - F_B|$, O − S, and $F - K$, which are difference scores.

porting or underreporting. The establishment of the base rates (prevalence) with which overreporting and underreporting are encountered in a specific clinical setting is mandatory in any research that examines these cutting scores. Clinicians need to be aware of the frequency with which overreporting and underreporting occur in their clinical setting and begin to establish the empirical correlates of these response sets so that better assessments, treatments, and interventions can be made.

MMPI-2 Validity Profile for Clinical Settings

Men

Name _____   Age ___

Accuracy of Item Endorsement

Pctl	Inconsistent				Overreporting									Underreporting							Pctl
	?	VRIN	F-FB	TRIN	F	FB	F(p)	F-K	Ds	K&B	L&W	O-S	True%	L	ODecp	Sd	S	K	So	False%	
P		20			39	30		32	46	71	94	330		14	29	27	50	29	37		**P**
e	28	14	19	15	38		10	31		70	92	327	72							76	**e**
r	27		18		37	29		30	45	69	91	324	71								**r**
c	26		17		36	28		28	44	68	90	320	70	13	28	26		28			**c**
e	24		16	14	34	27		27	43	67	87	317	68		27	25	49				**e**
n	23		15		33	26		26	42	65	85	299	67	12			27				**n**
t	21		14		32	25	9	25	40	64	84	294	66			24					**t**
i	19	13	13		30	24		23	39	63	82	285	65		26					75	**i**
l	18			13	29		8	22	38	62	80	280	64		25		48				**l**
e	17		12		28	23		21		61		277	63	11		23					**e**
										60		276									
						22															
												275									
99	16				21			20	37		79	274	62				26				99
	14	12	11		27				36	59	74	264	61		24	22				74	
98	11		10	12	25	20	7	16	34	57	73	249	60				47				98
	9	11	9		22	19	6	14	33	54	70	233	59	10	23	21	46	25		73	
	7				21	17		11	31	53	67	221	57				45				
	6	10	8	11	20	16	5	10	30	51	64	209	56	9	22		44			72	
	5				19	15		9	29	49	62	200	55			20	43	24	36		
93	4				18	14		8	28	48	60	193	54		21					71	93
		9	7		17	13	4	7	27	47	58	185	53	8		19	42				
	3				16	12		6	26	45	57	178	52		20		41	23			
	2		6		14	11	3	4	24	42	52	160	50	7	19	18	40			70	
		8		10	13	9		3	23	39	50	148	49				39	22	35		
84					12			2	22	38	48	137	48							69	84
	1					8		1	21	37	46	132	47	18	17		38	21			
		7	5		11	7		0	20	35	44	123	46	6			37			68	
					9	6	2	-3	18	30	40	97	44		17	16	35	20	34	67	
70	0		4			5		-4	17	29	38	89	43		16		34				70
		6			8			-5	16	27	35	78	42				33	19	33	66	
				9	7	4		-6	15	26	34	71	41	5	15	15	32	18		65	
			3		6	3	1	-8	13	21	29	47	40			14	30		32	64	
		5				2		-9	12	19	27	38	39		14		29	17	31	63	
50					5			-10	11	16	23	22	37	4	13		26		30	62	50
								-11	10	15	22	14				13	26		29		
		4	2		4	1		-12	9	14	20	5	36			25	15	28		61	
								-13		11	18	-7	35		12	12	24	14	27	59	
								-14	8	10	16	-15	34	3	11		23	13	26	58	
30		3		8	3		0	-16	7	7	13	-32	33			11	20		24	57	30
									6		12	-37	32	10			19	12	23	56	
			1					-17		6	11	-44								55	
		2			2			-18	5	5	10	-48	31	2	9	10	18	11	22	54	
								-19	4		8	-62	30				16	16	20	51	
												-66				8	15		19		
16							4		3	7		-69	29				9			50	16
		1		7	1			-20				-73				14	9	18		49	
	1							-21	3	2	6	-78	28	1	7	13		17		48	
		0										-85		1	8		12	8	16	46	
								-22				-88					11		15	45	
									1		4	-91	27	6				7	14	44	
					2							-93				10				43	
								-23				-96	26				9		13	42	
		0								3		-100		5		8		6	12	41	
											5					6			11	40	
2	0			6	0			-24	1	0	2	-108	24	0	4	5	6	5	10	38	2
	?	VRIN	F-FB	TRIN	F	FB	F(p)	F-K	Ds	K&B	L&W	O-S	True%	L	ODecp	Sd	S	K	So	False%	
	Consistent				**Underreporting**									**Overreporting**							

Omissions
? = Cannot Say scale

Consistency of Item Endorsement
VRIN = Variable Response Inconsistency Scale
F-FB = Absolute difference between F (raw) and FB (raw)
TRIN = True Response Inconsistency Scale

Accuracy of Item Endorsement
Overreporting of Psychopathology
F = Infrequency scale
FB = Back Infrequency scale
F(p) = Infrequency - Psychopathology scale
F-K = Raw score of the F scale minus the raw score of the K scale
Ds = Gough Dissimulation scale
K & B = Total number of Koss & Butcher critical items endorsed
L&W = Total number of Lachar & Wrobel critical items endorsed
O-S = Total T score difference for obvious minus subtle subscales
True % = Percentage of Items Endorsed "True"

Underreporting of Psychopathology
Impression Management
L = Lie scale
ODecp = Other Deception scale
Sd = Wiggins Social Desirability scale
Superior Adjustment
S = Superlative Scale
Self-Deception
K = Correction
So = Edwards Social Desirability scale
False % = Percentage of Items Endorsed "False"

10/10/98   Caldwell Clinical Dataset   N = 25,203

PROFILE 3.10

MMPI-2 Validity Profile for Clinical Settings

Women

Name ___   Age ___

	Accuracy of Item Endorsement	
Inconsistent	Overreporting	Underreporting

The chart presents columns for scales: ? (Cannot Say), VRIN, F–FB, TRIN, F, FB, F(p), F–K, Ds, K&B, L&W, O–S, True %, L, ODecp, Sd, S, K, So, False %, with T-score markers (Percentile) ranging across the left and right margins (P e r c e n t i l e) at levels 99, 98, 93, 84, 70, 50, 30, 16, 2.

Bottom axis labels:

	Consistent	Underreporting	Overreporting

Legend (bottom repeat): ? | VRIN F–FB TRIN | F FB F(p) F–K Ds K&B L&W O–S True % | L ODecp Sd S K So False %

Omissions
? = Cannot Say scale

Consistency of Item Endorsement
VRIN = Variable Response Inconsistency Scale
F–FB = Absolute difference between F (raw) and FB (raw)
TRIN = True Response Inconsistency Scale

Accuracy of Item Endorsement

Overreporting of Psychopathology
F = Infrequency scale
FB = Back Infrequency scale
F(p) = Infrequency – Psychopathology scale
F–K = Raw score of the F scale minus the raw score of the K scale
Ds = Gough Dissimulation scale
K & B = Total number of Koss & Butcher critical items endorsed
L&W = Total number of Lachar & Wrobel critical items endorsed
O–S = Total T score difference for obvious minus subtle subscales
True % = Percentage of Items Endorsed "True"

Underreporting of Psychopathology
Impression Management
L = Lie scale
ODecp = Other Deception scale
Sd = Wiggins Social Desirability scale
Superior Adjustment
S = Superlative Scale
Self-Deception
K = Correction
So = Edwards Social Desirability scale
False % = Percentage of Items Endorsed "False"

10/10/98   Caldwell Clinical Dataset   N = 25,763

PROFILE 3.11

Note. Minnesota Multiphasic Personality Inventory-2 (MMPI-2). Copyright © 1942, 1943 (renewed 1970), 1989 by the Regents of the University of Minnesota. Reproduced by permission of the publisher. "MMPI-2" and "Minnesota Multiphasic Personality Inventory-2" are trademarks owned by the University of Minnesota.

FREQUENCY OF INCONSISTENT AND INACCURATE MMPI-2 PROFILES

Table 3.38 provides the frequency with which inconsistent, overreported, and underreported profiles are encountered by codetype on the MMPI-2 in a clinical setting. Table 3.39 provides similar information ranked by the frequency of occurrence for each comparison. A client's profile was defined as being inconsistent in Table 3.38 if the Variable Response Inconsistency (*VRIN*) scale exceeded a raw score of 8 (84th percentile [T score of 60] in the Caldwell clinical dataset).

Some MMPI-2 codetypes could be very likely to reflect inconsistent patterns of item endorsement. For example, 33.8 percent of *6-8/8-6* codetypes could result from inconsistent patterns of item endorsement! In fact, most codetypes that include Scale *8* (Schizophrenia) frequently could result from inconsistent item endorsement. Some codetypes rarely result from inconsistent patterns of item endorsement (i.e., most Spike codetypes and codetypes that include Scale *3* [Hysteria]). Table 3.38 shows that 25 of the 55 codetypes (45.4 percent) could result from inconsistent item endorsement 20 percent or more of the time. Hopefully clinicians realize the importance of assessing the consistency of item endorsement for every MMPI-2 that they administer.

Table 3.38 also indicates the frequency with which overreported and underreported profiles occur by MMPI-2 codetype *once the inconsistent profiles have been removed from the dataset.* A client's profile was defined as reflecting overreporting of psychopathology if the Infrequency-Psychopathology (*F*[*p*]) scale exceeded a raw score of 3, and as underreporting if Wiggins' Social Desirability (*Sd*) or the Superlative (*S*) scale was greater than 17 or 37, respectively. All three of these cutting scores were equivalent to the 84th percentile (T score of 60) in the Caldwell (1997) clinical dataset. Although these cutting scores have been selected somewhat arbitrarily, they do allow comparisons among the codetypes as to the frequency with which overreporting and underreporting psychopathology could occur.

Some MMPI-2 codetypes could be very likely to reflect overreporting of psychopathology with six codetypes (*1-8/8-1, 2-8/8-2, 4-8/8-4, 6-8/8-6, 7-8/8-7,* and *8-9/9-8*) exceeding the cutting score over 25 percent of the time. An additional four codetypes (*3-8/8-3, 4-9/9-4, 8-0/0-8,* and Spike *8*) exceeded the cutting score over 15 percent of the time. Underreporting of psychopathology also occurs frequently with six codetypes (Spike *1*, Spike *3*, *3-5/5-3*, Spike *4*, Spike *5*, and Spike *9*) exceeding the cutting score over 25 percent of the time.

Finally, the frequency with which invalid profiles (i.e., both inconsistent and inaccurate patterns of item endorsement) occur by MMPI-2 codetype can be seen in Tables 3.38 and 3.39. Since the codetypes are ranked by the total percentage of invalid profiles in Table 3.39, it is easily seen that 13 codetypes are invalid by these criteria over 50 percent of the time and 3 codetypes are invalid over 70 percent of the time. The second-lowest ranked codetype (*2-0/0-2*) is still invalid nearly 25 percent of the time. The necessity for checking the consistency and accuracy of item endorsement for all clients should be readily apparent.

Clinicians probably will not be surprised to see that clients with Spike *4* codetypes are among the most likely to underreport psychopathology and *6-8/8-6* codetypes are among the most likely to overreport psychopathology. It is interesting, however, to see how the other codetypes rank relative to each other. For example, it seems somewhat unexpected for *2-4/4-2* codetypes to be ranked so low and for *1-6/6-1* and *1-8/8-1* codetypes to be ranked so high for overreporting of psychopathology. This information on the relative elevation of a number of Validity and Supplementary scales within each codetype will be explored further in Chapter 7 in which prototypic scores for each codetype are discussed.

VALIDITY SCALE CONFIGURATIONS

There are only a small number of Validity scale configurations that occur frequently in most clinical and normal populations. This limited number of common Validity scale configurations is surprising since 27 possible configurations exist if each of the three Validity scales (*L* [Lie], *F* [Infrequency], and *K* [Correction]) is classified as average (T scores of 50 to 59 on *L* and *K* and 50 to 64 on *F*), above average (T scores > 59 on *L* and *K* and > 64 on *F*), or below average (T scores below 50 on *L*, *F*, and *K*). The frequency with

TABLE 3.38 Frequency of Inconsistent and Inaccurate MMPI-2 Profiles by Codetype

Codetype	N	INCONSISTENT[a]		OVERREPORTED[b]		UNDERREPORTED[c]		TOTAL	
		N	%	N	%	N	%	N	%
Spike 1	499	57	11.42	41	8.22	132	26.45	230	46.09
1-2/2-1	1,709	366	21.42	141	8.25	120	7.02	627	36.69
1-3/3-1	5,492	750	13.66	391	7.12	1,094	19.92	2235	40.70
1-4/4-1	233	42	18.03	22	9.44	21	9.01	85	36.48
1-5/5-1	155	31	20.00	18	11.61	23	14.84	72	46.45
1-6/6-1	389	105	26.99	58	14.91	38	9.77	201	51.67
1-7/7-1	211	49	23.22	17	8.06	4	1.90	70	33.18
1-8/8-1	560	195	34.82	152	27.14	25	4.46	372	66.43
1-9/9-1	159	20	12.58	19	11.95	19	11.95	58	36.48
1-0/0-1	65	9	13.85	7	10.77	2	3.08	18	27.69
Spike 2	406	73	17.98	23	5.67	48	11.82	144	35.47
2-3/3-2	2,902	540	18.61	148	5.10	236	8.13	924	31.84
2-4/4-2	860	185	21.51	98	11.40	18	2.09	301	35.00
2-5/5-2	115	27	23.48	11	9.57	9	7.83	47	40.87
2-6/6-2	1,125	262	23.29	143	12.71	37	3.29	442	39.29
2-7/7-2	1,950	335	17.18	149	7.64	48	2.46	532	27.28
2-8/8-2	1,120	259	23.12	371	33.12	13	1.16	643	57.41
2-9/9-2	37	5	13.51	5	13.51	5	13.51	15	40.54
2-0/0-2	669	108	16.14	46	6.88	6	0.90	160	23.92
Spike 3	803	35	4.36	12	1.49	286	35.62	333	41.47
3-4/4-3	774	91	11.76	40	5.17	115	14.86	246	31.78
3-5/5-3	121	14	11.57	9	7.44	44	36.36	67	55.37
3-6/6-3	740	128	17.30	64	8.65	71	9.59	263	35.54
3-7/7-3	446	87	19.51	17	3.81	34	7.62	138	30.94
3-8/8-3	474	149	31.43	102	21.52	15	3.16	266	56.12
3-9/9-3	116	24	20.69	3	2.59	10	8.62	37	31.90
3-0/0-3	14	0	0.00	0	0.00	0	0.00	0	0.00
Spike 4	1,278	109	8.53	31	2.43	358	28.01	498	38.97
4-5/5-4	206	38	18.45	22	10.68	34	16.50	94	45.63
4-6/6-4	1,116	225	20.16	158	14.16	80	7.17	463	41.49
4-7/7-4	449	80	17.82	39	8.69	17	3.79	136	30.29
4-8/8-4	733	203	27.69	214	29.20	25	3.41	442	60.30
4-9/9-4	449	83	18.49	69	15.37	41	9.13	193	42.98
4-0/0-4	72	15	20.83	4	5.56	2	2.78	21	29.17
Spike 5	1,385	96	6.93	66	4.77	572	41.30	734	53.00
5-6/6-5	158	32	20.25	12	7.59	13	8.23	57	36.08
5-7/7-5	69	21	30.43	2	2.90	0	0.00	23	33.33
5-8/8-5	96	54	56.25	12	12.50	4	4.17	70	72.92
5-9/9-5	190	32	16.84	17	8.95	36	18.95	85	44.74
5-0/0-5	42	9	21.43	3	7.14	1	2.38	13	30.95
Spike 6	913	84	9.20	37	4.05	208	22.78	329	36.04
6-7/7-6	496	83	16.73	73	14.72	15	3.02	171	34.48
6-8/8-6	2,442	825	33.78	1,117	45.74	29	1.19	1,971	80.71

(continued)

TABLE 3.38   Frequency of Inconsistent and Inaccurate MMPI-2 Profiles by Codetype (continued)

Codetype	N	INCONSISTENT[a] N	INCONSISTENT[a] %	OVERREPORTED[b] N	OVERREPORTED[b] %	UNDERREPORTED[c] N	UNDERREPORTED[c] %	TOTAL N	TOTAL %
6-9/9-6	368	79	21.47	55	14.95	51	13.86	185	50.27
6-0/0-6	140	18	12.86	18	12.86	2	1.43	38	27.14
Spike 7	185	25	13.51	3	1.62	18	9.73	46	24.86
7-8/8-7	1,344	403	29.99	418	31.10	13	0.97	834	62.05
7-9/9-7	98	22	22.45	11	11.22	4	4.08	37	37.76
7-0/0-7	148	25	16.89	9	6.08	5	3.38	39	26.35
Spike 8	149	38	25.50	24	16.11	14	9.40	76	51.01
8-9/9-8	472	182	38.56	124	26.27	28	5.93	334	70.76
8-0/0-8	97	21	21.65	23	23.71	2	2.06	46	47.42
Spike 9	1,026	95	9.26	41	4.00	287	27.97	423	41.23
9-0/0-9	8	1	12.50	1	12.50	0	0.00	2	25.00
Spike 0	391	63	16.11	16	4.09	24	6.14	103	26.34
Total	36,664	6,907	18.84	4,726	12.89	4,356	11.88	15,989	43.61

[a]Inconsistent profiles were defined as *VRIN* greater than 8.
[b]Overreported profiles were defined as *F(p)* greater than 3.
[c]Underreported profiles were defined as *Sd* greater than 17 or *S* greater than 37.

TABLE 3.39   Inconsistent and Inaccurate MMPI-2 Profiles Ranked by Frequency of Occurrence

INCONSISTENT[a] Codetype	INCONSISTENT[a] %	OVERREPORTED[b] Codetype	OVERREPORTED[b] %	UNDERREPORTED[c] Codetype	UNDERREPORTED[c] %	TOTAL Codetype	TOTAL %
5-8/8-5	56.25	6-8/8-6	45.74	Spike 5	41.30	6-8/8-6	80.71
8-9/9-8	38.56	2-8/8-2	33.12	3-5/5-3	36.36	5-8/8-5	72.92
1-8/8-1	34.82	7-8/8-7	31.10	Spike 3	35.62	8-9/9-8	70.76
6-8/8-6	33.78	4-8/8-4	29.20	Spike 4	28.01	1-8/8-1	66.43
3-8/8-3	31.43	1-8/8-1	27.14	Spike 9	27.97	7-8/8-7	62.05
5-7/7-5	30.43	8-9/9-8	26.27	Spike 1	26.45	4-8/8-4	60.30
7-8/8-7	29.99	8-0/0-8	23.71	Spike 6	22.78	2-8/8-2	57.41
4-8/8-4	27.69	3-8/8-3	21.52	1-3/3-1	19.92	3-8/8-3	56.12
1-6/6-1	26.99	Spike 8	16.11	5-9/9-5	18.95	3-5/5-3	55.37
Spike 8	25.50	4-9/9-4	15.37	4-5/5-4	16.50	Spike 5	53.00
2-5/5-2	23.48	6-9/9-6	14.95	3-4/4-3	14.86	1-6/6-1	51.67
2-6/6-2	23.29	1-6/6-1	14.91	1-5/5-1	14.84	Spike 8	51.01
1-7/7-1	23.22	6-7/7-6	14.72	6-9/9-6	13.86	6-9/9-6	50.27
2-8/8-2	23.12	4-6/6-4	14.16	2-9/9-2	13.51	8-0/0-8	47.42
7-9/9-7	22.45	2-9/9-2	13.51	1-9/9-1	11.95	1-5/5-1	46.45
8-0/0-8	21.65	6-0/0-6	12.86	Spike 2	11.82	Spike 1	46.09
2-4/4-2	21.51	2-6/6-2	12.71	1-6/6-1	9.77	4-5/5-4	45.63
6-9/9-6	21.47	5-8/8-5	12.50	Spike 7	9.73	5-9/9-5	44.74

[a]Inconsistent profiles were defined as *VRIN* greater than 8.
[b]Overreported profiles were defined as *F(p)* greater than 3.
[c]Underreported profiles were defined as *Sd* greater than 17 or *S* greater than 37.

TABLE 3.40   Frequency of Validity Scale Configurations by Sample

	MMPI					
	Clinical Patients				Medical Patients	
	(HEDLUND & WON CHO, 1979)		(GREENE, 1986)		(COLLIGAN & OFFORD, 1986)	
Validity Scale Configuration	N		N		N	
L < 50 F < 51 K < 50	175	1.66	182	1.67	207	1.83
L < 50 F 51–69 K < 50	1,440	13.68	1,471	13.48	976	8.65
L < 50 F > 69 K < 50	1,498	14.23	1,249	11.45	444	3.94
L < 50 F < 51 K < 50–59	199	1.89	279	2.56	464	4.11
L < 50 F 51–69 K < 50–59	616	5.85	847	7.76	937	8.31
L < 50 F > 69 K < 50–59	145	1.38	153	1.40	72	0.64
L < 50 F < 51 K > 59	93	0.88	202	1.85	500	4.43
L < 50 F 51–69 K > 59	145	1.38	230	2.11	359	3.18
L < 50 F > 69 K > 59	14	0.13	17	0.16	10	0.09
L 50–59 F < 51 K < 50	167	1.59	163	1.49	209	1.85
L 50–59 F 51–69 K < 50	1,009	9.59	920	8.43	752	6.67
L 50–59 F > 69 K < 50	826	7.85	611	5.60	242	2.15
L 50–59 F < 51 K 50–59	331	3.15	377	3.46	636	5.64
L 50–59 F 51–69 K 50–59	871	8.28	934	8.56	1,159	10.27
L 50–59 F > 69 K 50–59	213	2.02	275	2.52	72	0.64
L 50–59 F < 51 K > 59	310	2.95	426	3.90	1,212	10.74
L 50–59 F 51–69 K > 59	462	4.39	483	4.43	891	7.90
L 50–59 F > 69 K > 59	36	0.34	66	0.60	18	0.16
L > 59 F < 51 K < 50	30	0.29	20	0.18	43	0.38
L > 59 F 51–69 K < 50	198	1.88	180	1.65	133	1.18
L > 59 F > 69 K < 50	158	1.50	150	1.37	55	0.49
L > 59 F < 51 K 50–59	124	1.18	109	1.00	174	1.54
L > 59 F 51–69 K 50–59	388	3.69	314	2.88	363	3.22
L > 59 F > 69 K 50–59	143	1.36	221	2.03	32	0.28
L > 59 F < 51 K > 59	295	2.80	369	3.38	727	6.44
L > 59 F 51–69 K > 59	547	5.20	448	4.11	578	5.12
L > 59 F > 69 K > 59	91	0.86	215	1.97	16	0.14
Total	10,524		10,911		11,281	

	MMPI-2					
	Clinical Patients		Personnel Applicants		Normal Individuals	
	(CALDWELL, 1997A)		(CALDWELL, 1997B)		(BUTCHER ET AL., 1989)	
Validity Scale Configuration	N		N		N	
L < 50 F < 50 K < 50	1,780	3.49	228	3.65	343	13.19
L < 50 F 50–64 K < 50	3,530	6.93	122	1.95	356	13.69
L < 50 F > 64 K < 50	6,192	12.15	35	0.56	138	5.31
L < 50 F < 50 K < 50–59	2,177	4.27	440	7.04	288	11.08

TABLE 3.40   Frequency of Validity Scale Configurations by Sample (continued)

	MMPI-2					
	Clinical Patients		Personnel Applicants		Normal Individuals	
	(CALDWELL, 1997A)		(CALDWELL, 1997B)		(BUTCHER ET AL., 1989)	
Validity Scale Configuration	N		N		N	
$L < 50\ F\ 50–64\ K < 50–59$	1,623	3.18	71	1.14	109	4.19
$L < 50\ F > 64\ K < 50–59$	648	1.27	6	0.10	12	0.46
$L < 50\ F < 50\ K > 59$	1,707	3.35	406	6.49	142	5.46
$L < 50\ F\ 50–64\ K > 59$	541	1.06	41	0.66	37	1.42
$L < 50\ F > 64\ K > 59$	65	0.13	3	0.05	3	0.12
$L\ 50–59\ F < 50\ K < 50$	1,192	2.34	129	2.06	151	5.81
$L\ 50–59\ F\ 50–64\ K < 50$	2,227	4.37	30	0.48	125	4.81
$L\ 50–59\ F > 65\ K < 50$	3,488	6.84	3	0.05	37	1.42
$L\ 50–59\ F < 50\ K\ 50–59$	2,325	4.56	417	6.67	193	7.42
$L\ 50–59\ F\ 50–64\ K\ 50–59$	1,712	3.36	50	0.80	73	2.81
$L\ 50–59\ F > 65\ K\ 50–59$	749	1.47	4	0.06	9	0.35
$L\ 50–59\ F < 50\ K > 59$	3,158	6.20	736	11.77	133	5.12
$L\ 50–59\ F\ 50–64\ K > 59$	898	1.76	55	0.88	21	0.81
$L\ 50–59\ F > 65\ K > 59$	107	0.21	2	0.03	2	0.08
$L > 59\ F < 50\ K < 50$	740	1.45	78	1.25	68	2.62
$L > 59\ F\ 50–64\ K < 50$	1,411	2.77	28	0.45	42	1.62
$L > 59\ F > 65\ K < 50$	2,288	4.49	5	0.08	20	0.77
$L > 59\ F < 50\ K\ 50–59$	2,038	4.00	530	8.48	101	3.88
$L > 59\ F\ 50–64\ K\ 50–59$	1,865	3.66	64	1.02	38	1.46
$L > 59\ F > 65\ K\ 50–59$	1,076	2.11	24	0.38	15	0.58
$L > 59\ F < 50\ K > 59$	5,354	10.51	2,553	40.84	112	4.31
$L > 59\ F\ 50–64\ K > 59$	1,709	3.35	173	2.77	26	1.00
$L > 59\ F > 65\ K > 59$	366	0.72	18	0.29	6	0.23
Total	50,966		6,251		2,600	

which all 27 configurations occurred in various groups on the MMPI and MMPI-2 is presented in Table 3.40.

The most frequently encountered Validity scale configuration in most clinical settings is illustrated in Figure 3.4. The essential characteristics of this configuration are that the L scale and the K scale are below a T score of 50 and the F scale is at or above a T score of 65 (MMPI-2) or 70 (MMPI). This configuration occurred in 12.15 percent of the psychiatric patients (Caldwell, 1997a) and 5.31 percent of the normal individuals (Butcher et al., 1989) who had taken the MMPI-2, and 14.23 and 11.45 percent of the psychiatric patients (Greene, 1988; Hedlund & Won Cho, 1979) who had taken the MMPI. If scores in the average range on the F scale (T scores of 50 to 64) are included in this configuration, it occurs in 19.08 percent of psychiatric patients (Caldwell, 1997a) and 19.00 percent of normal individuals (Butcher et al., 1989) on the MMPI-2.

Clients with this Validity scale configuration are admitting to personal and emotional difficulties, are requesting assistance with these problems, and are unsure of their own capabilities for dealing with these problems. As the F scale score increases, clients either are experiencing more problems and hence feeling

In an inpatient setting clients with this Validity scale configuration are likely to evidence poorer impulse control and a greater frequency of inappropriate and destructive behavior than clients with other types of Validity scale configurations (Post & Gasparikova-Krasnec, 1979). As the client begins to improve, the *F* scale elevation should decrease and the *K* scale elevation should increase.

Another of the commonly encountered Validity scale configurations is illustrated in Figure 3.5. In this configuration the *L* scale and the *K* scale are elevated at or above a T score of at least 60, and may approach a T score of 65, and the *F* scale is below a T score of 50. This configuration occurred on the MMPI-2 in 10.51 percent of the psychiatric patients (Caldwell, 1997a), 40.84 percent of personnel applicants (Caldwell,

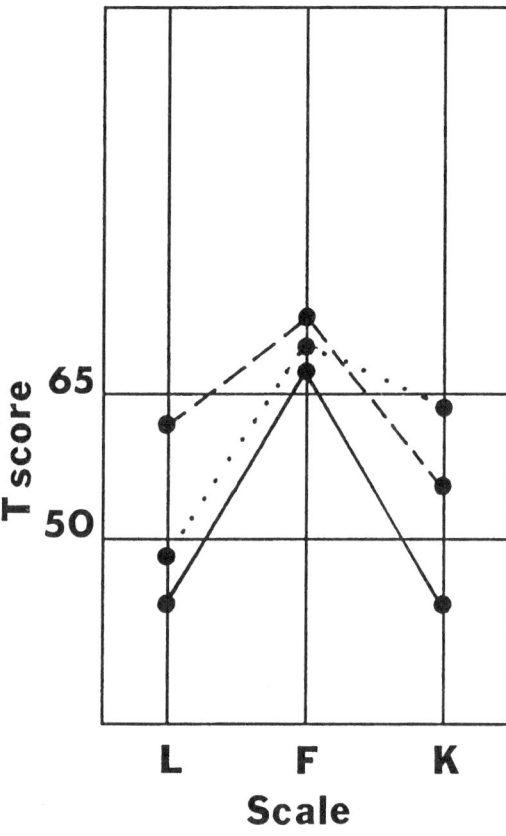

FIGURE 3.4

worse, exaggerating the symptomatology in order to get help sooner, or simulating psychopathology. The clinician can use the other validity indexes described earlier in this chapter to distinguish which of these various causes of the *F* scale elevation is appropriate.

Under most conditions, this Validity scale configuration is most desirable for any form of psychological intervention or treatment. There are two reservations, though: The *F* scale should not be above a T score of 90 to 100, and the *K* scale should not be below a T score of 35. In the former case clients may be experiencing so much stress and conflict that a psychotherapeutic intervention should not be initiated until some of the stress and conflict can be alleviated. In the latter case clients may not have the necessary personal resources for working on their problems.

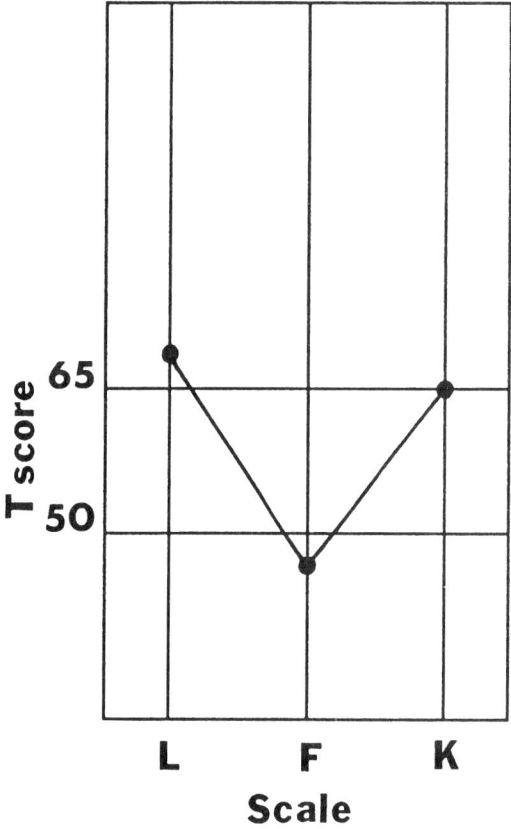

FIGURE 3.5

1997b), and 4.31 percent of normal individuals (Butcher et al., 1989). This configuration occurred less frequently on the MMPI, although it was found in 6.44 percent of medical patients referred for a psychiatric evaluation (Colligan & Offord, 1986). This client is attempting to avoid or deny unacceptable feelings, impulses, and problems. That is, the client is trying to present himself in the best possible light. This client tends to be simplistic and views the world in terms of the extremes of good and bad. The client will have an adequate social adjustment or, at worst, a mild behavioral disturbance (Gross, 1959).

In inpatient settings, clients with this Validity scale configuration are likely to be psychotic, particularly if the Clinical scales also suggest the presence of a psychotic condition (Sines, Baucom, & Gruba, 1979). This Validity scale configuration occurs most frequently among many normal individuals who are underreporting psychopathology (e.g., unsophisticated job applicants) and psychiatric patients with hysteriod or hypochondriacal tendencies. This configuration is often accompanied by elevations on Scales *1* (Hypochondriasis) and *3* (Hysteria) and average scores on the rest of the profile. Deliberate underreporting of psychopathology may be suspected, if there is a legitimate reason for evaluating the client. Typically these clients neither are referred for nor seek treatment. College students instructed to endorse the MMPI items in terms of their "ideal self" produce this Validity scale configuration (Hiner, Ogren, & Baxter, 1969).

A third Validity scale configurations that is encountered frequently is illustrated in Figure 3.6. The essential features of this configuration are that the three Validity scales have a positive slope in which the *L* scale is less than the *F* scale and the *F* scale is less than the *K* scale. Generally, the *L* scale is about a T score of 40, the *F* scale is about a T score of 50 to 55, and the *K* scale is in the T score range of 60 to 70.

This configuration is typical of a normal individual who has the appropriate resources for dealing with problems and who is not experiencing any stress or conflict at the present time. The *K* scale elevation in this configuration will move up or down depending on the person's reference group. For example, a normal college student will score at the upper end of this

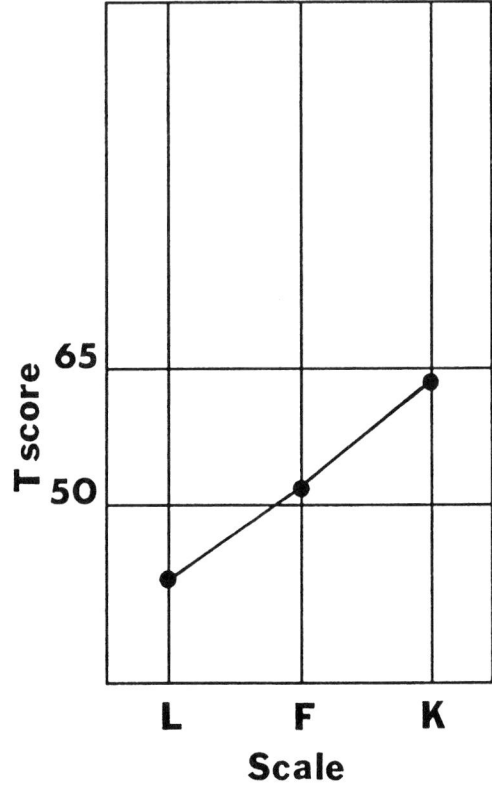

FIGURE 3.6

range, whereas the normal lower-class individual will score at the lower end of this range. A job applicant or a prison inmate who is trying to look "good" may have this Validity scale configuration.

Lanyon and Lutz (1984) found that this Validity scale configuration was characteristic of felony sex offenders who denied any sexual deviant behavior. It is unusual for a self-referred individual in a mental health setting to have this configuration; however, it can occur among (1) "normal" persons involved in marital conflict or (2) upper-class or college-educated persons who show sophisticated defensiveness. In these cases the Clinical scales all will be submerged (within the average range) except for Scale *5* (Masculinity-Femininity) among men.

The last commonly encountered Validity scale configuration is illustrated in Figure 3.7. In this con-

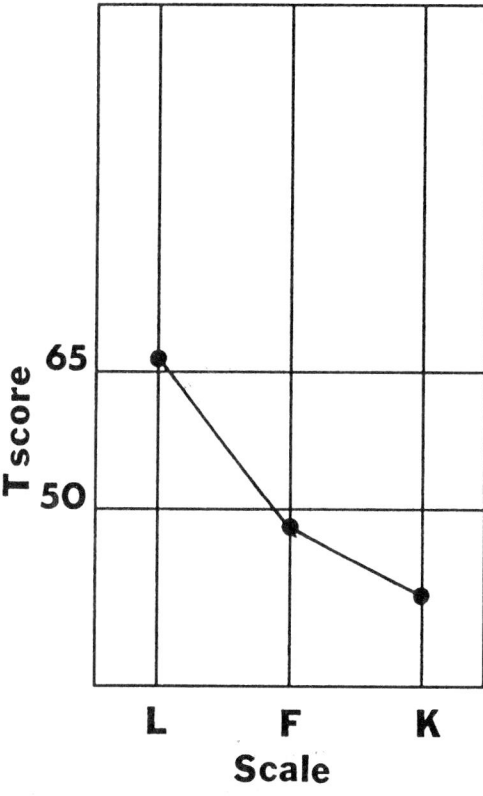

FIGURE 3.7

vention. They are unlikely to admit their problems, and when they do, they lack both the resources for and the interest in psychological interventions. This configuration changes little over time, except that the *F* scale will likely decrease if it is elevated higher than a T score of 50.

NORMAL *K*+ PROFILES

Occasionally a profile will be encountered in which the only significant Validity or Clinical scale elevation is on the *K* scale. Marks and Seeman (1963) identified such a profile as a Normal *K*+ profile. This profile is basically an elaboration of the second commonly encountered Validity scale configuration already described (Figure 3.5). A Normal *K*+ profile (Marks & Seeman, 1963; Marks, Seeman, & Haller, 1974) has the following specific characteristics on the MMPI:

1. Psychiatric inpatients only
2. All Clinical scales below a T score of 70
3. Six or more Clinical scales less than or equal to a T score of 60
4. The *L* (Lie) and *K* (Correction) scales higher than the *F* (Infrequency) scale with the *F* scale below a T score of 60
5. The *K* scale 5 or more T score points higher than the *F* scale

(Clinicians should note that no specific elevation on the *K* scale is specified by these criteria, only the relationship between the *K* scale and the *L* and *F* scales.) Marks and colleagues described these clients as shy, anxious, inhibited, and defensive about admitting that their problems could be psychological. They avoided close interpersonal relationships and were passively resistant. Their personality structure had a schizoid component, their stream of thought was often incoherent, and they frequently appeared perplexed. They also displayed paranoid features: They were suspicious, fearful, and sensitive to anything that might be construed as a demand.

Almost half of the patients with this profile were diagnosed as psychotic, and almost a quarter of them were diagnosed as having a chronic brain syndrome.

figuration the three Validity scales have a negative slope in which the *L* scale is greater than the *F* scale, which is greater than the *K* scale. The *L* scale is elevated to a T score of 65, the *F* scale is about a T score of 50, and the *K* scale is equal to a T score of 40 to 45.

This client is naive and unsophisticated but is trying to look "good." Such clients usually have limited education and come from the lower socioeconomic classes. Their attempt to look good usually is ineffective, and the neurotic triad (Scales *1* [Hypochondriasis], *2* [Depression], and *3* [Hysteria]) generally is elevated. For men, Scale *5* (Masculinity-Femininity) will be low. Even when the *F* scale is elevated, it usually will not exceed a T score of 65; the client is still trying to maintain a facade of looking good despite the admission of some problems. These clients are poor candidates for any form of psychological inter-

As a group, the clients were significantly above average in intelligence, and more than 60 percent were educated beyond the high school level.

A number of investigators have reported the frequency with which the Normal K^+ profile is encountered. Gynther and Brilliant (1968) found that 3.6% of the clients referred for testing at a mental health center met all the preceding criteria for a Normal K^+ profile. Newmark, Gentry, Simpson, and Jones (1978) found that 4.7 percent of an inpatient population who were diagnosed schizophrenic produced a Normal K^+ profile.

Two recent studies (Barley, Sabo, & Greene, 1986; Winters, Newmark, Lumry, Leach, & Weintraub, 1985) reported similar frequency of occurrence of the Normal K^+ profiles. However, Craig (1984) found no Normal K^+ profiles among his male heroin addicts. It appears that the Normal K^+ profile occurs in 3% to 5% of clients in most clinical settings other than possibly substance abuse or dependence.

There has been limited research on the actual correlates of the Normal K^+ profile. It should be remembered that the original correlates of this profile were derived on women psychiatric inpatients (Marks et al., 1974). Gynther and Brilliant (1968) reported no reliable psychological or behavioral differences between the clients with a Normal K^+ profile and other clients. They did find that 45 percent of their patients had psychotic diagnoses.

Barley et al. (1986) found that their patients with a Normal $K+$ profile were less likely to have had chronic illnesses, to have attempted suicide prior to hospitalization, and to have somatic complaints. Their behavior and emotional state were more likely to be overactive, and their current hospitalization was shorter in length. They found that 47 percent of these patients had a psychotic diagnosis, but none had a brain disorder diagnosis.

These studies suggest that clients with a Normal K^+ profile are likely to have a psychotic diagnosis about 50 percent of the time. It is much less clear whether they will have a neuropsychological disorder and what specific behavioral and psychological correlates will be found. Duckworth and Barley (1988) have a comprehensive review of this profile that should be consulted by the interested reader.

SIMULATION AS ROLE PLAYING

The ability to detect clients who are trying to simulate by overreporting or underreporting psychopathology has been mentioned as a benefit of several of the validity indicators. Most investigations of the ability to simulate psychopathology have not provided the individual with an explicit description of the actual behavior to be simulated. The typical instructions vaguely request that the individual answer the items as a "neurotic" or "psychotic" person would. Under these conditions the traditional validity indicators generally are able to detect at least some cases of simulation. When a specific description of the role to be simulated is given to the individual, two consistent results have occurred: (1) The persons are better able to simulate a role than when less specific instructions are provided, and (2) the traditional validity indicators are much less likely to detect this form of simulation.

Lanyon (1967) asked well-adjusted male college students (no Clinical scales greater than a T score of 69) and maladjusted students (at least three Clinical scales greater than a T score of 69 that included at least two scales other than Scales 5 [Masculinity-Femininity] or 9 [Hypomania]) to simulate "very good adjustment" and "psychopathic personality." The students were given a description of a psychopathic personality. Both groups of students could simulate good adjustment, but the well-adjusted students simulated psychopathic personality better than the maladjusted students. When simulating good adjustment, approximately one-third of the students in both groups were able to escape detection by the traditional validity indicators.

In a similar study Wilcox and Dawson (1977) found that college students who were given a description of a paranoid individual while under hypnosis could simulate a paranoid profile without being detected by the traditional Validity scales (L, F, and K). Students who were given the description without being hypnotized, however, produced deviant profiles that were easily detected by the Validity scales. Rather than using an external criterion to assess whether their students actually simulated a paranoid profile, Wilcox and Dawson noted that both groups significantly elevated Scale 6 (Paranoia), which suggests that their manipulation was effective. Their results indicate that some students can simulate deviant profiles without being detected by the Validity scales.

Anthony (1976) asked inpatients, outpatients, and nonprofessional employees of a state hospital to simulate various codetypes on the MMPI when they were given a personality description and case study of that profile type. He rated the degree of similarity between the simulated and criteria profiles. His results, which are difficult to interpret, suggest that ability to simulate a psychopathological role reflects a complex relationship among the client's actual psychopathology, race, gender, and the role to be simulated. He did not find a general negative relationship between psychopathology and the ability to simulate psychopathological roles as he had anticipated. Thus, the hypothesis that psychopathological individuals are generally deficient in role-playing skills could not be supported.

Kroger and Turnbull (1975) asked male college students to take the MMPI either as an Air Force officer or as a creative artist, without providing a more explicit description of these two roles. They found that the students could simulate the profile of Air Force officers, and the traditional validity indicators, including the $F - K$ index, were unable to detect this simulation.

The students produced a simulated profile for the artists that was similar in configuration but more elevated or deviant than the actual artist profile. To investigate this latter result further, they asked two more groups of students to take the MMPI as a creative artist and provided an extensive role description of artists. One group received an accurate role description and the other received an inaccurate one. The students with the accurate role description produced a simulated profile that was nearly identical to the profile of actual artists except for Scale 5 (Masculinity-Femininity); the traditional Validity scales did not detect this simulation.

Thus, students apparently are capable of simulating profiles of both deviant and nondeviant roles without being detected by the traditional Validity scales. Deviant roles appear to be more difficult to simulate. Gough's (1954, 1957) findings that both students and professionals were unable to simulate neurosis also suggest that deviant roles are more dif-

ficult to simulate, particularly if a specific role description is not provided.

Now that these studies have outlined the general framework for the issues that have been examined in this area, the research can be summarized rather quickly into several major categories. The initial studies provided individuals from a variety of normal populations with general or global instructions to overreport psychopathology: students (Austin, 1992; Bagby, Rogers, & Buis, 1994; Graham et al., 1991; Wetter et al., 1992; Worthington & Schlottmann, 1986; Woychyshyn et al., 1992); professionals (Gough, 1954; Lachar & Wrobel, 1979); and community samples (Wetter et al., 1993); as well as in clinical samples: psychiatric patients (Bagby, Rogers, Buis, & Kalemba, 1994; Graham et al., 1991; Rogers et al., 1995); and correctional/forensic patients (Bagby, Rogers, & Buis, 1994; Iverson et al., 1995; Walters, 1988; Walters, White, & Greene, 1988).[13] These studies typically reported that these persons who were instructed to overreport psychopathology could be successfully distinguished from the group taking the test accurately, although the specific scale or index employed and the optimal cutting score tended to vary widely from study to study. As expected, research has demonstrated greater difficulty in distinguishing between the group instructed to overreport psychopathology and actual patients than normal individuals. This line of research has been critiqued because such global instructions have little external validity (Rogers, 1988; Sivec et al., 1994; Wetter et al., 1994). To parallel real-world circumstances, it has been suggested that participants must have or be given specific knowledge of the psychopathology to be overreported or simulated.

The next series of studies made disorder-specific criteria available to the participants who were then instructed to simulate borderline personality disorder (Sivec, Hilsenroth, & Lynn, 1995; Wetter et al., 1993; Wetter et al., 1994); closed head injury (Lamb, Berry, Wetter, & Baer, 1994); paranoia (Sivec et al., 1994); posttraumatic stress disorder (Fairbank, McCaffrey, & Keane, 1985; Wetter et al., 1993); schizophrenia

---

13. These references are intended only to provide examples of the research within each area. They are not an exhaustive listing of all research.

(Rogers et al., 1993; Wetter et al., 1993); and somatoform disorders (Sivec et al., 1994). Two generalizations can be made of this series of studies. First, the traditional Validity scales usually have good success at detecting those disorders such as schizophrenia (Rogers et al., 1993) and borderline personality disorder (Sivec et al., 1995; Wetter et al., 1994) that are characterized by extensive and severe psychopathology. Again, the specific scale or index that is most successful varies by study as does the optimal cutting score. Second, persons who are instructed to overreport a specific disorder that is characterized by circumscribed and less severe psychopathology are able to do so quite readily and are fairly difficult to detect (Lamb et al., 1994; Wetter et al., 1993).

The final series of studies investigated the effects of providing the participants with information about the Validity scales that would be used to detect overreporting or underreporting of psychopathology (Lamb et al., 1994; Rogers et al., 1993), sometimes in combination with information about diagnostic-specific criteria. The more information provided to the participants about the Validity scales, the better they were able to overreport or underreport without being detected (Baer, Wetter, & Berry, 1995; Rogers et al., 1993). Information about the Validity scales was more valuable in avoiding detection of overreporting than was diagnostic-specific criteria (Rogers et al., 1993).

The ethics of providing participants with specific information about the disorders to be assessed as well as the role of Validity scales in assessing overreporting and underreporting of psychopathology have been debated (Ben-Porath, 1994; Berry, Lamb, Wetter, Baer, & Widiger, 1994). These ethical issues are quite complex, and anyone who is contemplating research using such procedures should consult these articles.

DETECTION OF RESPONSE SETS

Another potential problem that the validity indicators attempt to address is detecting any inappropriate response sets that might be utilized by the client. Clients sometimes take the MMPI-2 by using some response set other than accurately endorsing the items. For example, clients with limited but adequate reading ability and intelligence may complete the

MMPI-2 in a half hour or less, which would arouse legitimate concern about the authenticity of the item endorsements. Alternatively, clients may be unable or unwilling to take the MMPI-2, but instead of directly refusing to complete the task, they may endorse all items "true" or "false" or alternate "true" and "false" responses. Finally, a client may try to make himself or herself look better or worse by overreporting or underreporting psychopathology; both of these response sets have been discussed previously.

Clinicians should try to prevent these situations by enlisting the client's full cooperation before starting the test. As mentioned, various validity indicators can help detect these inappropriate response sets when either the profile configuration or other circumstances suggest their possible influence.

The two most blatant of these response sets are "all true" (Profile 3.12) and "all false" (Profile 3.13). Such sets are easy to detect by examining either the answer sheet or the profile sheet. The Validity scale configuration is highly suspect in both instances. In the "all true" response set, the T scores of the L (Lie) and K (Correction) scales are 35 and 30, respectively, and the F scale is greater than a T score of 120. The psychotic tetrad (Scales 6 [Paranoia], 7 [Psychasthenia], 8 [Schizophrenia], and 9 [Hypomania]) is extremely elevated, and the neurotic triad (Scales 1 [Hypochondriasis], 2 [Depression], and 3 [Hysteria]) is around a T score of 50.

In the "all false" response set, all three Validity scales are elevated between T scores of 80 and 90. The elevation of the L (Lie) and K (Correction) scales within this range never occurs in a valid profile. The neurotic triad is extremely elevated along with a moderate elevation on the psychotic tetrad. Most persons using an "all true" or "all false" response set will include a few answers in the other category, and this alters the profile somewhat. Even in these somewhat more sophisticated attempts at simulation, however, a "mostly true" or "mostly false" response set still is readily apparent merely with a casual examination of the Validity scales and indexes.

A response set that is slightly more difficult to detect is a random response set (Profile 3.14). Frequently, this response set is identified as a *random sort*, a term that reflects the early history of the MMPI

PROFILE 3.12

Note. Minnesota Multiphasic Personality Inventory-2 (MMPI-2). Copyright © 1942, 1943 (renewed 1970), 1989 by the Regents of the University of Minnesota. Reproduced by permission of the publisher. "MMPI-2" and "Minnesota Multiphasic Personality Inventory-2" are trademarks owned by the University of Minnesota.

MMPI-2

S.R. Hathaway and J.C. McKinley

Minnesota Multiphasic Personality Inventory-2

Profile for Basic Scales

Minnesota Multiphasic Personality Inventory-2
Copyright © by THE REGENTS OF THE UNIVERSITY OF MINNESOTA
1942, 1943 (renewed 1970), 1989. This Profile Form 1989.
All rights reserved. Distributed exclusively by NATIONAL COMPUTER SYSTEMS, INC.
under license from The University of Minnesota.

"MMPI-2" and "Minnesota Multiphasic Personality Inventory-2" are trademarks owned by
The University of Minnesota. Printed in the United States of America.

Address _____

Occupation _____ Date Tested __/__/__

Education _____ Age _____ Marital Status _____

Referred By _____

MMPI-2 Code _____

Scorer's Initials _____

MALE

"All False" Response Set

	T or Tc	L	F	K	Hs+.5K 1	D 2	Hy 3	Pd+.4K 4	Mf 5	Pa 6	Pt+1K 7	Sc+1K 8	Ma+.2K 9	Si 0	T or Tc
Raw Score		15	19	29	21	37	47	26	31	15	9	19	11	35	
? Raw Score 0															
K to be Added				15			12				29	29	6		
Raw Score with K				36			38					48	17		

NATIONAL
COMPUTER
SYSTEMS

24001

PROFILE 3.13

Note. Minnesota Multiphasic Personality Inventory-2 (MMPI-2). Copyright © 1942, 1943 (renewed 1970),
1989 by the Regents of the University of Minnesota. Reproduced by permission of the publisher. "MMPI-2"
and "Minnesota Multiphasic Personality Inventory-2" are trademarks owned by the University of Minnesota.

PROFILE 3.14

Note. Minnesota Multiphasic Personality Inventory-2 (MMPI-2). Copyright © 1942, 1943 (renewed 1970), 1989 by the Regents of the University of Minnesota. Reproduced by permission of the publisher. "MMPI-2" and "Minnesota Multiphasic Personality Inventory-2" are trademarks owned by the University of Minnesota.

in which each item was printed on a separate card and the client literally sorted the items into "true" and "false" categories.

In random sorts or random response sets, the client endorses the items by randomly marking each item "true" or "false." This set may be suspected when a client completes the MMPI-2 much too quickly. It is important in these cases to confirm that the client has the appropriate intellectual level and reading ability to complete the MMPI-2. Frequently, clients who are deficient in either area are reluctant to acknowledge their deficiency and instead respond randomly. The most apparent aspects of a random sort are the *F* (Infrequency) scale elevation that approaches a T score of 120 and the Scale *8* (Schizophrenia) elevation that approaches a T score of 110. The *L* (Lie) scale also is elevated more highly than would be anticipated with this Clinical scale configuration.

Measures of the consistency of item endorsement can be used to assess whether the client has responded randomly. In addition, a clinical interview will readily identify clients with genuine psychopathology who have profiles that appear similar to a random response set. Such clients will be experiencing an acute personality disorganization if they are not overtly psychotic. Frequently, they are so distressed that they are unable to complete the MMPI-2.

Two other response sets are the "all deviant" and "all nondeviant" response sets (Profile 3.15). These response sets would require the client to answer either all or none of the items like the criterion group for each scale. Both produce theoretical profiles, since each procedure requires that items be answered both "true" and "false" when the item is scored "true" on one scale and "false" on another. This double scoring of items occurs more often than might be expected, since numerous items are scored on more than one scale and occasionally with opposite responses as deviant. Although these two profiles are theoretical, they do illustrate the range in which each scale on the MMPI-2 can vary.

OBVIOUS AND SUBTLE ITEMS

Numerous investigators have examined obvious and subtle items on the MMPI (see review by Dubinsky, Gamble, & Rogers, 1985), and there is a tendency for

each investigator to define *obvious* and *subtle* somewhat differently (cf. Hryckowian & Gynther, 1988; Ward, 1986). Since the Wiener and Harmon (Wiener, 1948) Obvious and Subtle subscales were reviewed earlier, they will not be covered in this section.

Seeman and his colleagues (Vesprani & Seeman, 1974; Wales & Seeman, 1968, 1972) noted that many of the subtle items are also Zero items, items that are scored for abnormality even though a majority of the normative group endorsed the item in the deviant direction. For example, 57.9 percent of the original normative group endorsed the following item as "true": "At times my thoughts have raced ahead faster than I could speak them."[14] Yet a "true" response to this item is scored both on Scales *5* (Masculinity-Femininity) and *9* (Hypomania). Thus, on these scales the deviant response for this item is "true" despite the fact that a majority of the normative group endorsed this item as "true," since a higher proportion of the criterion groups for these scales answered it in the same direction.

There are 84 Zero items that meet this criterion (see Appendix B in Dahlstrom et al., 1972). Seeman and his colleagues further noted that obvious items tended to be X items, which were endorsed by a minority of the original normative group. Consequently, the Zero and X items are roughly comparable to the Wiener and Harmon (Wiener, 1948) Subtle and Obvious items, respectively.

Wales and Seeman (1968) found that subtracting the total number of deviant responses to the X items from the total number of deviant responses to the Zero items provided a useful index for identifying underreporting of psychopathology. Using 84 Zero and 315 X items, they found that college students instructed to underreport could successfully avoid endorsing the X (obvious) items, but they increased their score on the Zero (subtle) items in the direction of increased psychopathology. Wales and Seeman determined that a cutting score of –4 for the Zero minus X difference score correctly identified 100 percent of

---

PROFILE 3.15

Note. Minnesota Multiphasic Personality Inventory-2 (MMPI-2). Copyright © 1942, 1943 (renewed 1970), 1989 by the Regents of the University of Minnesota. Reproduced by permission of the publisher. "MMPI-2" and "Minnesota Multiphasic Personality Inventory-2" are trademarks owned by the University of Minnesota.

the underreported profiles and 70 percent of the real student profiles.

In extending the investigation of Zero and X items to a psychiatric outpatient sample, Vesprani and Seeman (1974) found a similar pattern. When instructed to endorse the items as their "ideal self," the outpatients decreased their scores on the X (obvious) items and increased their scores on the Zero (subtle) items.

A third method of defining obvious and subtle items on the MMPI was devised by Christian et al. (1978). They asked college students to rate on a 5-point scale from very obvious (5) to very subtle (1) how clearly each item indicated a psychological problem. Mean ratings for each item were used to compute obviousness scores for the standard MMPI Validity and Clinical scales, the Zero[15] and X items, and Wiener and Harmon's Obvious and Subtle items. A score of 3 indicated a neutral (neither subtle nor obvious) rating. The mean obviousness ratings for the Validity and Clinical scales, in order from most subtle to most obvious, were:

5	(Masculinity-Femininity)	2.21
K	(Correction)	2.28
L	(Lie)	2.41
0	(Social Introversion)	2.64
3	(Hysteria)	2.81
9	(Hypomania)	2.82
2	(Depression)	2.94
1	(Hypochondriasis)	3.13
4	(Psychopathic Deviate)	3.13
7	(Psychasthenia)	3.47
6	(Paranoia)	3.52
8	(Schizophrenia)	3.64
F	(Infrequency)	3.70

The two surprising ratings are the somewhat subtle mean rating for the L scale, which is routinely described as an obvious scale that does not detect students instructed to underreport psychopathology (Dahlstrom et al., 1972), and the relatively neutral

mean rating of Scale 1 (Hypochondriasis), which has been described as a marker variable for obviousness (cf. Wiener, 1948). It is possible that the students insightfully interpreted the items on the L scale as representing minor social foibles and the items on the Hypochondriasis scale as representing physical or medical problems rather than interpreting any of these items as representing psychological problems.

The mean ratings for the Zero and X items were 2.04 and 3.16, respectively, and the mean ratings for Wiener's (1948) obvious and subtle items were 2.44 and 3.45, respectively. Christian et al. (1978) noted that the mean ratings for both the X items and Wiener's obvious items fall in their neutral category of neither subtle nor obvious. Researchers who are interested in using Christian et al.'s ratings of the obviousness of the MMPI items need to remember that their data are reported by Form R item numbers. A table for converting Form R item numbers to Group Booklet item numbers can be found in Dahlstrom et al. (1972).

Using Christian et al.'s (1978) five categories of subtlety (very subtle, subtle, neutral, obvious, very obvious), Burkhart, Christian, and Gynther (1978) found that when instructed to overreport psychopathology, students endorsed more neutral, obvious, and very obvious items and fewer very subtle items. When instructed to underreport psychopathology, students endorsed fewer neutral, obvious, and very obvious items and more items in the two subtle categories.

These results suggest that obvious and subtle items can help detect overreporting as well as underreporting response sets, as was outlined earlier. The pattern of underreporting students endorsing more subtle items in the pathological direction confirms previous findings by Vesprani and Seeman (1974). Although the cause of this paradox is unclear, Burkhart et al. (1978) conjectured that subtle items may be endorsed more frequently when students are instructed to underreport because such responses are socially desirable.

Using these same five categories of item subtlety (Christian et al., 1978), Gynther, Burkhart, and Hovanitz (1979) examined the relationship between subtle, neutral, and obvious subscales of Scale 4 (Psychopathic Deviate) and scores on a nonconfor-

15. The Zero items used by Christian et al. (1978), which are based on the Zero items found in Dahlstrom et al. (1972), are not the same as the Zero items used by Seeman et al. (cf. Wales & Seeman, 1968).

mity questionnaire. On the nonconformity scale the obvious and subtle subscales were directly related to the scale score for males; for females, only the obvious and neutral subscales were directly related to nonconformity. They concluded that the obvious subscale predicted nonconformity scores better than the subtle or neutral subscales and that the obvious subscale in conjunction with the subtle subscale was a better predictor than either subscale alone. In this situation the subtle subscale apparently enhanced the predictive power of the obvious subscale.

Gynther and his colleagues have extended this same methodology to Scales *2* (Depression: Burkhart, Gynther, & Fromuth, 1980), *3* (Hysteria: Gynther & Burkhart, 1983; Wilson, 1980), and *9* (Hypomania: Hovanitz & Gynther, 1980). They found that subtle items supplied little additional information on Scales *2* and *3,* and they probably could be omitted on these scales. Subtle items seemed to provide information that was not available from the obvious items on Scale *9.* Weed, Ben-Porath, and Butcher (1990) found that the Wiener and Harmon (Wiener, 1948) Subtle subscales actually attenuated validity to the same degree as the addition of a random variable.

Snyter and Graham (1984) using a different definition of item subtlety also found that subtle items may have some utility on Scale *9* (Hypomania). Similar to Gynther et al. (1979), both Snyter and Graham (1984) and Worthington and Schlottmann (1986) found that the subtle items on Scale *4* (Psychopathic Deviate) did not contribute significantly to the prediction of other test scores.

Grossman and Wasyliw (1988; Grossman, Haywood, Ostrov, Wasyliw, & Cavanaugh, 1990; Wasyliw, Grossman, Haywood, & Cavanaugh, 1988) and Posey and Hess (1984, 1985) have investigated the use of the obvious and subtle subscales in forensic settings to assess overreporting of psychopathology. Since Grossman and Wasyliw used the Wiener and Harmon (Wiener, 1948) Obvious and Subtle subscales and Posey and Hess used Christian et al.'s (1978) ratings of obvious and subtle items, their results are not easily integrated. Their research does generally support the use of obvious and subtle subscales to assess overreporting of psychopathology and can provide direction for future work in this area.

There has been a renewed debate in the last decade over the usefulness of obvious and subtle subscales of the MMPI-2. One issue within this debate is whether obvious or subtle subscales are better predictors of external criteria (cf. Dahlstrom, 1991; Jackson, 1971; Weed et al., 1990; Wrobel & Lachar, 1982). The other issue is the usefulness of the obvious and subtle subscales as a measure of overreporting and underreporting of psychopathology with advocates both pro (Brems & Johnson, 1991; Dannenbaum & Lanyon, 1993; Dush, Simons, Platt, Nation, & Ayres, 1994; Greene, 1988; Lees-Haley & Fox, 1990) and con (Schretlen, 1988; Timbrook, Graham, Keiller, & Watts, 1993; Weed et al., 1990).

Hollrah, Schlottmann, Scott, and Brunetti (1995) have provided an overview of the methodological issues that arise in determining the convergent and discriminative validity of the obvious and subtle subscales of the MMPI/MMPI-2. Any researcher who is contemplating work in this area should consult their article. Several conclusions of Hollrah et al. are worthy of noting here: (1) There are pervasive difficulties with the measures used to evaluate the subtle subscales; (2) there is a propensity to validate the obvious subscales with self-report measures comprised only of obvious statements; (3) many studies use nonpsychiatric samples that may restrict the range of scores on these scales; and (4) the decision to use obvious and subtle ratings of general measures of psychopathology to validate specific scales needs to be predicated on the issue being investigated.

CHAPTER 4

Clinical Scales

The clinician will need to become thoroughly familiar with the clinical scales reviewed in this chapter, because this information forms the basis for understanding combinations of scales to be described in Chapter 7. The following areas will be surveyed for each scale: the content areas tapped by the scale; how the scale was developed and the criterion group; general psychometric and clinical information; interpretation and behavioral correlates of high scores in psychiatric and normal populations; interpretations of low scores, usually in a normal population; the effects on scale scores in adults of moderator variables such as age, education, ethnicity, gender, and social class; and a summary table of interpretations for the levels of elevation of the scale.

While interpretation of high-point pairs or codetypes is the primary focus on the MMPI-2, low points on the clinical scales also deserve careful attention even though there has been little systematic research on them. In a clinical setting, for example, low scores (T < 50) on Scales 2 (Depression) and 7 (Psychasthenia) are problematic because the client is *not* reporting any type of emotional distress that might serve as a motivation to change behavior. This neglect of investigation of low points on the MMPI and MMPI-2 in part reflects the emphasis on interpreting the one or two highest clinical scales and frequently ignoring the relative elevation of the other clinical scales. There are a number of alternative interpretations of low points on a given clinical scale (Keiller & Graham, 1993). Low points could represent good adjustment, not psychopathology (Carson, 1969); lesser degrees or amounts of the qualities represented by high scores (e.g., fewer than normal depressive symptoms); or conceptually different qualities than characteristic of higher scores. Graham and his colleagues have begun

to report correlates of low points on MMPI-2 scales (Graham, Ben-Porath, & McNulty, 1997; Keiller & Graham, 1993).

Clinicians should remember that uniform T scores are used for all of the clinical scales except for Scales 5 (Masculinity-Femininity) and 0 (Social Introversion), which still use linear T scores. Clinicians generally emphasize interpretation of the MMPI-2 codetype (the one or two highest clinical scales elevated at or above a T score of 65). Most of them, however, also rely on individual scales to modify and supplement their interpretations. Contrary to widespread assumptions, little actuarial research exists on the behavioral correlates of individual MMPI or MMPI-2 scales. The results of these studies (Boerger, Graham, & Lilly, 1974; Hedlund, 1977; Hovey & Lewis, 1967; Keiller & Graham, 1993; Zelin, 1971) that have examined the correlates of individual MMPI and MMPI-2 scales will be reported throughout this chapter.

SCALE 1: HYPOCHONDRIASIS (*Hs*)

A wide variety of vague and nonspecific concerns about bodily functioning is tapped by the 32 items of Scale 1 (Hypochondriasis). These concerns tend to focus on the abdomen and back, and they persist despite all reassurances and negative medical tests to the contrary. Scale 1 is designed to assess a neurotic concern over bodily functioning (i.e., psychotic concerns about bodily functioning are not found on this Scale).

The criterion group used in developing Scale 1 was a group of hypochondriacs with abnormal, psychoneurotic concern over bodily functioning (McKinley & Hathaway, 1940). (The development of Scale 1 was described in detail in Chapter 1; the reader should review that material if necessary. The reader also should note that the current DSM-IV [American Psychiatric Association, 1994] definition of hypochondriasis emphasizes the fear or belief of the existence of a *serious* disease rather than abnormal concern over bodily functioning, which is the focus of Scale *1*.)

Examples of Scale *1* items with the deviant answer indicated in parentheses are:

"I have few or no pains." (false)

"I feel weak all over much of the time." (true)

"I am about as able to work as I ever was." (false)[1]

There are 7 (21.9%) items unique to Scale *1*. (Unique items are defined here as items that are not found on any other Clinical scale, although these items may overlap with the Validity scales or other MMPI-2 scales. A listing of all of the unique items for each clinical scale can be found in Table 4.31 [pp. 177–178]. The reader should review these items to appreciate what item content is unique to each scale.) A majority of the items (20; 62.5%) overlap with Scale *3* (Hysteria) and 9 (28.1%) items overlap with Scale *2* (Depression). Only 7 of the items overlap with Scales from the psychotic tetrad (Scales *6* [Paranoia], *7* [Psychasthenia], *8* [Schizophrenia], and *9* [Hypomania]), 4 items with Scale *8*, 2 items with Scale *7*, and 1 item with Scale *6*.

The 33-item Tryon, Stein, and Chu (Stein, 1968) Bodily Symptoms scale (see Chapter 5 in Greene [1991]), which was developed by a cluster analysis of all 550 items on the MMPI, contains 23 items from Scale *1*. Wiggins' (1966) Content scales of Organic Symptoms and Poor Health from the MMPI, which were developed on a rational or intuitive basis (see Chapter 5 in Greene [1991]), also overlap substantially with Scale *1*. The 36-item Organic Symptoms scale has 13 items in common with Scale *1* and the 28-item Poor Health scale also contains 13 Scale *1* items. The Content scale of Health Concerns (*HEA*) (Butcher, Graham, Williams, & Ben-Porath, 1990) has 23 of its 36 items in common with Scale *1*. Ben-Porath

and Sherwood (1993) identified three component scales within the *HEA* scale: Gastrointestinal Symptoms (*HEA1*); Neurological Symptoms (*HEA2*); and General Health Concerns (*HEA3*).

Factor analyses of the items on Scale *1* in several different populations have consistently identified two factors, which have been labeled *poor physical health* (Comrey, 1957a; Eichman, 1962; O'Connor & Stefic, 1959; Stein, 1968) and *gastrointestinal difficulties* (Comrey, 1957a; O'Connor & Stefic, 1959). Thus, it seems whether an empirical, rational, or statistical procedure is used, a general dimension of poor physical health and gastrointestinal and neurological symptoms can be identified in the MMPI-2 item pool in a variety of populations.

The deviant response for two-thirds of the items on Scale *1* is "false"; hence, a tendency toward a "false" response set will elevate scores on this Scale. The items on Scale *1* appear to be obvious in content (Dahlstrom et al., 1972), although Christian et al. (1978) found that students rated Scale *1* items as neutral (neither obvious nor subtle) when asked how clearly these items were indicative of a psychological problem.

Table 4.1 lists the 20 scales that have the highest correlations with Scale *1* in the Caldwell (1997a) clinical dataset. There are two primary categories represented within these scales: poor physical health and physical symptoms (Health Concerns; Hysteria, Obvious; Lachar and Wrobel [1979] Somatic Symptoms) and a dimension of general distress, negative emotionality, and pessimism (Koss and Butcher [1973] Acute Anxiety State; Depression, Obvious; the total number of Lachar and Wrobel critical items endorsed). The scales assessing poor physical health and physical symptoms virtually are redundant with Scale *1* as can be seen by the number of correlations greater than .900.

A person who is actually physically ill will obtain only a moderate elevation (T score of 55 to 60) on Scale *1*. Such persons will endorse their legitimate physical symptoms, but they will not endorse the entire gamut of vague physical symptoms tapped by the Scale. Scale *2* (Depression) is more likely to be elevated by actual physical illness than Scale *1*. If a client with actual physical illness obtains a T score of 65 or higher on Scale *1*, there are likely to be

---

TABLE 4.1   Correlations with Scale *1*
(Hypochondriasis) in the Caldwell Clinical Dataset

SCALE *1* (HYPOCHONDRIASIS)

Scale	Abbreviation	r
Health Concerns	HEA	.965
Hysteria, Obvious	Hy-O	.957
Lachar & Wrobel Somatic Symptoms	LWSoma	.953
Somatic Symptoms	Hy_4	.941
Lassitude Malaise	Hy_3	.879
Neurological Symptoms	HEA2	.875
Koss & Butcher Acute Anxiety State	KBAnx	.870
Depression, Obvious	D-O	.857
Total Number of Lachar & Wrobel Critical Items Endorsed	LWSum	.846
Ego Strength	Es	−.842
Depression	D	.818
Physical Malfunctioning	D_3	.816
General Health Concerns	HEA3	.808
College Maladjustment	Mt	.806
Post Traumatic Stress Disorder—Schlenger	PS	.801
Subjective Depression	D_1	.797
Sensorimotor Dissociation	Sc_6	.797
Gastrointestinal Symptoms	HEA1	.796
Hysteria	Hy	.795
Mental Dullness	D_4	.788

Note. All scales that are not described in this chapter are described in Chapters 5 and 6.

hypochondriacal features in addition to the physical condition, and the client is probably trying to manipulate or control significant others in the environment with the hypochondriacal symptoms. Although the client may vehemently argue that the symptoms reflect legitimate physical concerns, the clinician should not ignore the elevation on Scale *1*. The hypochondriacal features in these individuals usually are readily apparent despite their protests to the contrary.

Scale *1* is a crude index of psychological-mindedness or sophistication, with high scorers lacking these attributes. It also is correlated negatively with intelligence (Brower, 1947), which would substantiate the lack of psychological-mindedness in high

scorers. Such persons are uninterested in exploring any psychological reasons for their bodily symptoms. In fact, pity the clinician who directly suggests such a relationship; these clients conclude that the clinician is poorly trained because he or she does not recognize their symptoms as genuine. With disparaging comments about their clinician's lack of training and skills to understand them, these clients trudge off to seek a more favorable second, third, and fourth opinion.

The robustness of these hypochondriacal features often amazes the neophyte clinician, who seemingly can readily recognize the client's motives. Despite, or perhaps because of, the transparency of the motives, any form of psychological intervention is almost surely doomed to fail. Thus, Scale *1* can be understood as a characterological scale (i.e., it reflects a long-term personality style that is stable over time and resistant to change).

High scorers (T scores of 65 or higher) on Scale *1* in any population are characterized by their excessive concern over bodily functions and vague hypochondriacal symptoms, which attests to the construct validity of the scale. In addition, high scorers are described as pessimistic, sour on life, and evidencing long-standing personal inadequacy and ineffectualness. They seem to relish exaggerating the ills of the world and of their own situation. They rarely express hostility overtly; instead, they express their resentment covertly by using physical symptoms to control and manipulate others. Finally, they are unlikely to be diagnosed as being psychotic, although an occasional psychotic individual with somatic delusions may simultaneously elevate Scales *1* and *8* (Schizophrenia).

Low scorers (T scores less than 45) on Scale *1* are a heterogeneous group since their common characteristic is the nonendorsement of hypochondriacal symptoms. They are described as alert, spontaneous, less likely to worry about their health, lack of energy, or to appear worn out, and not unduly concerned about the adverse reactions of others. Good and Brantner (1961) commented that low scorers may be denying hypochondriacal symptoms, but no research has documented this hypothesis. Persons who have worked or lived with hypochondriacs also tend to earn low scores on Scale *1*. Whether the difficulty in working with or relating to hypochondriacs results in a rejection of this personality style or some other factor is involved has not been investigated. Mental health professionals also score in this range.

Test-retest reliability coefficients for Scale *1* are among the largest for any of the MMPI Clinical scales, with correlations ranging from .79 to .86 for up to a two-week interval and .38 to .65 for a one-year interval (Dahlstrom et al., 1975). Test-retest reliability coefficients for Scale *1* on the MMPI-2 for approximately a one-week interval are .85 for men and .85 for women (Butcher et al., 1989).

Women tend to endorse one or two more Scale *1* items than men (Butcher et al., 1989; Caldwell, 1997a; Colligan, Osborne, Swenson, & Offord, 1989; Dahlstrom et al., 1972). Scores on Scale *1* also tend to increase 3 to 4 T points with age in normal individuals (Butcher et al., 1989) and 5 to 6 T points in clinical patients (Caldwell, 1997a). However, medical patients do *not* endorse more Scale *1* items with increasing age (Swenson, Pearson, & Osborne, 1973). Scores on Scale *1* increase 5 to 10 T points as the number of years of education decreases in both normal individuals (Butcher et al., 1989) and clinical patients (Caldwell, 1997a).

A summary of the interpretations for four levels of elevation of Scale *1* is provided in Table 4.2.

SCALE *2:* DEPRESSION (*D*)

The 57 items of Scale *2* (Depression) measure symptomatic depression, which is a general attitude characterized by poor morale, lack of hope in the future, and general dissatisfaction with one's own status (Hathaway & McKinley, 1942). The major content areas within Scale *2* include a lack of interest in activities expressed as general apathy, physical symptoms such as sleep disturbances and gastrointestinal ailments, excessive sensitivity, and lack of sociability (Dahlstrom et al., 1972).

Scale *2* was derived empirically, using an approach identical to that used for Scale *1*. The criterion group used in developing Scale *2* consisted of 50 patients who represented relatively uncomplicated cases of the depressed phase of manic-depressive psychosis. Their responses were contrasted with a normal group to produce a preliminary depression scale.

As with Scale *1* (Hypochondriasis), it was found that some nondepressed clients also scored high on

TABLE 4.2 Interpretation of Levels of Elevation on Scale *1* (Hypochondriasis)

T SCORE	INTERPRETATION
44 and below	1. *Low.* These clients are not reporting any vague physical symptoms. Scores in this range are typical for persons in helping professions and for children of a hypochondriacal parent.
45–57	2. *Normal.* These clients have a typical number of physical symptoms.
58–64	3. *Moderate.* Scores in the lower end of this range are typical for persons with physical disabilities and persons with actual physical illness. These clients have some concern about their bodily functioning and are likely to be seen as immature, stubborn, and lacking drive. Review of Content and/or Supplementary scales may facilitate interpretation in this range.
65 and above	4. *Marked.* These clients are excessively concerned about vague physical symptoms and may use them to manipulate and control others. They are cynical, whiny, demanding of attention, and generally negative and pessimistic. The prognosis for either psychological or physical intervention is guarded. These clients focus on vague bodily symptoms and resist any form of resolution. Conservative interventions reassuring these clients about their physical symptoms are indicated. Review of the Content and/or Supplementary scales may facilitate interpretation at the lower end of this range.

this preliminary depression scale. Consequently, the responses of 50 such nondepressed patients who scored high on this preliminary scale of depression were compared with those of the criterion group, resulting in the identification of 11 correction items that distinguished these two groups of patients. These correction items were scored so that patients who were actually clinically depressed achieved higher scores on the scale. The addition of the 11 correction items resulted in the 60 items that currently appear on Scale 2 of the MMPI. Each of these 60 items was required to meet the following criterion: The frequency of its endorsement had to increase progressively from the normal group through a normal group with depression (normals who achieved high scores on the preliminary depression scale) to the criterion group. The depressed normal group was used to help establish the meaning of intermediate scale values between the normal and criterion groups, which would have been impossible if only the two extreme groups were contrasted. In the restandardization of the MMPI-2, 3 of these 60 items were deleted resulting in the 57 items currently on Scale 2.

Examples of Scale 2 items with the deviant response indicated in parentheses are:

> "I am happy most of the time." (false)
>
> "I find it hard to keep my mind on a task or job." (true)
>
> "I am about as able to work as I ever was." (false)[2]

Scale 2 is thought to measure reactive or exogenous depression rather than "neurotic" or endogenous depression. Accordingly, scores are expected to fluctuate as the clients' moods change. Thus, Scale 2 is an index of how comfortable and secure clients feel about themselves and their environment, with higher scores indicating dissatisfaction. As clients' evaluations of themselves or of the situation changes, scores on Scale 2 should change concomitantly.

It may seem unusual that a psychotic criterion group was used to develop a scale that is part of the neurotic triad (Scales 1 [Hypochondriasis], 2, and 3 [Hysteria]) and is thought to measure reactive depression (Carson, 1969; Dahlstrom et al., 1972). This paradox may be partially explained by Hathaway and McKinley's interest in developing a scale to measure symptomatic depression, which can be a reaction to a variety of causes (such as economic crises, vocational difficulties, or personal problems) and which occurs in a multitude of psychopathological conditions.

Given Hathaway and McKinley's (1942) interest in assessing reactive depression, the specific diagnosis of the criterion group was not important as long as depression was a central feature. Since reactive depression is not a stable trait and will vary markedly over time, using patients in the depressed phase of manic-depressive psychosis as a criterion group ensured that the depressive features were pronounced and central.

There are 13 (22.8%) items unique to Scale 2, and 3 of these are correction items. The overlapping items are relatively evenly distributed among the other Clinical scales: 13 items are shared with Scale 7 (Psychasthenia), 9 items with Scale 8 (Schizophrenia), and 7 items with Scales 4 (Psychopathic Deviant) and 0 (Social Introversion). The deviant response for two-thirds of the items on Scale 2 is "false" so that a tendency to endorse the MMPI-2 items as "false" inflates the scores on Scale 2.

Comrey's (1957b) factor analysis of MMPI items on Scale 2 revealed that 28 of the items loaded on a factor that he labeled *neuroticism;* 12 other items loaded on a factor called *poor physical health.* Only 8 items from Scale 2 are found on Wiggins' (1966) Content scale of Depression, and 10 items are contained within the Tryon, Stein, and Chu (Stein, 1968) Cluster scale of Depression (see Greene [1991], Chapter 5). The Content scale of Depression (*DEP*) from the MMPI-2 (Chapter 5) has only 9 of its 33 items in common with Scale 2. The items found on these depression scales vary dramatically depending on how they were constructed. Moreover, due to the ubiquitous nature of depression, the developers of the various depression scales may have used divergent samples in constructing their measures. Research that investigates the relationships among these different depression scales and their relationship to depressive behaviors is urgently needed.

Wiener and Harmon (Wiener, 1948) judged two-thirds of the items on Scale 2 to be obvious in content. Clients who are severely depressed are more likely to endorse obvious items, whereas mildly depressed persons tend to endorse subtle items (Dahlstrom et al., 1972). Clients are unlikely to endorse items with obvious depressive content until they are significantly depressed (Nelson, 1987). A number of studies (Bence,

Sabourin, Luty, & Thackrey, 1995; Boone, 1994, 1995; Nelson & Cicchetti, 1991; Nelson, Pham, & Uchiyama, 1996; Zalewski, Schatz, Gottesman, & Nichols, 1997) have investigated the Depression, Obvious and Depression, Subtle subscales (Wiener, 1948) and found that the Depression, Obvious subscale was related to other objective measures of depression as well as depressive diagnoses. The Depression, Subtle subscale frequently was unrelated and occasionally inversely related to external measures of depression. (Depression, Obvious correlated .953 with Scale 2 in the Caldwell [1997a] clinical dataset, while Depression, Subtle correlated .073 with Scale 2.) The only caveat that should be mentioned at this point is that researchers have not given adequate attention to considerations of convergent and discriminant validity in the design and interpretation of these studies. The criterion measures have been depression scales or checklists composed of obvious items, so it would be expected that the Depression, Obvious subscale would be more likely to be related to them (convergent validity). In addition, items on any scale including the Depression, Obvious subscale will vary along a dimension of how direct or obvious a measure they are of the construct of interest so that correlations with any external criteria will vary depending upon where each scale lies along this dimension. Conceptually if vegetative or cognitive symptoms are construed to be measures of depression, it would be possible to have correlations with external criteria vary substantially depending upon which set of symptoms was being emphasized in a specific scale even if both sets of symptoms are obvious measures of depression. This issue is very complex and cannot be pursued more fully here, but it is worthy of extensive research.

Table 4.3 lists the 20 scales with the highest correlations with Scale 2 in the Caldwell (1997a) clinical dataset. These scales can be grouped into four categories: symptoms of depression and anxiety (Depression, Obvious; Subjective Depression; Lachar and Wrobel [1979] Depression and Worry; Koss and Butcher [1973] Acute Anxiety State; Anxiety; Psychasthenia), fatigue and lack of energy (Mental Dullness and Lassitude-Malaise), general distress and negative emotionality (College Maladjustment; Psychasthenia; and Ego Strength), and poor physical

TABLE 4.3 Correlations with Scale 2 (Depression) in the Caldwell Clinical Dataset

SCALE 2 (DEPRESSION)		
Scale	Abbreviation	r
Depression, Obvious	D-O	.953
Subjective Depression	D_1	.948
Mental Dullness	D_4	.900
Lassitude-Malaise	Hy_3	.898
Hysteria, Obvious	Hy-O	.870
Lachar & Wrobel Depression and Worry	LWDep	.850
College Maladjustment	Mt	.849
Koss & Butcher Acute Anxiety State	KBAnx	.831
Brooding	D_5	.823
Hypochondriasis	Hs	.818
Ego Strength	Es	−.813
Lack of Ego Mastery, Conative	Sc_4	.805
Psychasthenia	Pt	.804
Koss & Butcher Depressed-Suicidal Ideation	KBDep	.804
Post Traumatic Stress Disorder—Schlenger	PS	.803
Physical Malfunctioning	D_3	.802
Anxiety	ANX	.799
Depression	DEP	.796
Dysphoria	DEP2	.793
Total Number of Koss & Butcher Critical Items Endorsed	KBSum	.779

Note. All scales that are not described in this chapter are described in Chapters 5 and 6.

health and physical symptoms (Hysteria, Obvious; Hypochondriasis; and Physical Malfunctioning).

Interpretation of Scale 2 varies markedly depending on which other Clinical scales are elevated in conjunction with it; consequently, Scale 2 is one of the most difficult Clinical scales to interpret in isolation. An elevated score on Scale 2 reveals that the client is upset and feeling unhappy about something; the precise source of the distress, however, cannot be deduced from Scale 2 alone.

For example, a person in legal custody who is unhappy about being incarcerated and a client in psychotherapy who has low self-esteem and negative self-evaluations may obtain similar raw scores on Scale *2;* their distress, however, clearly emanates from different sources. These sources will be evident from the elevations on the other Clinical scales: Scales *4* (Psychopathic Deviate) and *9* (Hypomania) are likely to be the two highest scales for the person in custody, whereas Scales *2* and *7* (Psychasthenia) will probably be the highest scales for the client in psychotherapy.

When Scale *2* is the only Clinical scale elevated above a T score of 65, a Spike *2* codetype, it has been suggested that a careful evaluation of suicide risk is indicated, particularly if there are no overt behavioral signs of depression (Carson, 1969; Graham, 1987; Greene, 1991). Suicide risk in such clients is generally considered to be greater than when depression is more demonstrable clinically. However, less than 10% of clients with Spike *2* codetypes in the Caldwell (1997a) clinical dataset endorsed MMPI-2 items (150, 303, 506, 520, 524, and 530) that directly inquire about suicidal ideation and attempts (Sepaher, Bongar, & Greene, 1999; also see Chapter 6, pp. 263–267), so the basis for this concern is not apparent from the MMPI-2. The rate of endorsement of these six items in clients with Spike *2* codetypes actually is lower than most other codetypes.

Clinicians are well advised to evaluate all clients carefully with a directive clinical interview if suicide risk is an issue. These six MMPI-2 items (150, 303, 506, 520, 524, and 530) should be reviewed routinely in all clients *regardless of the consistency or accuracy of item endorsement* as a very preliminary means of screening for suicide risk. Other than these six specific items, the MMPI-2 does not assess suicide risk adequately. Even using the MMPI-2 to identify groups of individuals who may be suicide risks is questionable because of the inordinate number of false positives and false negatives that may be generated by any MMPI-2 index used to predict suicide risk. The use of the MMPI-2 in assessing suicide risk will be examined more fully in Chapter 6.

High scorers (T scores of 65 or higher) on Scale *2* have been described in a variety of ways; this variety reflects the fact that depressive features are found as a concomitant to all types of behavior and psychopathology. General descriptions of high scorers indicate that they are depressed, anxious, moody, and inhibited. They display excessive sensitivity to their own decreased level of functioning and usually are withdrawn and isolated. To the extent that these negative attributes represent dissatisfaction with oneself, they will serve as an internal pressure to change and, hence, are a good prognostic sign.

High scorers also frequently report a number of somatic symptoms, sleep difficulties, and a loss of appetite. They are tired and fatigue easily. They frequently have problems with attention and concentration. Moreover, they are rather consistently described as *not* being hyperactive, excited, or belligerent toward others.

Persons with elevated scores on Scale *2* are acknowledging their personal discomfort and dissatisfaction with their current level of functioning. Their subjective distress may represent anxiety and its concomitants, or it may represent a genuine depressive condition. Thus, persons with elevations on Scale *2* will not always be diagnosed as being depressed, since their diagnosis will reflect their prominent symptoms and behaviors. Regardless of their diagnosis, these clients are acknowledging their dissatisfaction with and negative evaluation of their present circumstances.

Persons with moderate elevations (T scores from 57 to 64) on Scale *2* are generally described in similar but less extreme terms. Such persons are seen as shy, prone to worry and depression, and dissatisfied, either with themselves or their personal situation. Bieliauskas and Shekelle (1983) found that normal males with moderate elevations on Scale *2* of the MMPI frequently felt nervous or upset and they spent less time in bed sleeping. They also were more likely to be rated as appearing emotionally tense.

Low scorers (T scores below 45) should be evaluated carefully since some kind of distress or negative mood should be present in most, if not all, clients in clinical settings. Scores in this range suggest that the clients are not affected adversely by the behaviors that led to their referral for an evaluation; that is, *scores in the normal range or below are not appropriate in psychiatric clients.* Low scorers are generally described as active, alert, socially outgoing, and effective in a variety of tasks. They are less likely to have trouble sleeping at night or to worry about their health and more likely to be cheerful and self-confident. Some persons with low scores also are described as undercontrolled; this can be manifested by ostentatiousness, impulsivity, and recklessness (Venn, 1988). For some, their activity, aggressiveness, and tendency to show off interfere with their interpersonal relationships.

It is unclear whether other scales in the profile will help to differentiate among these subtypes of persons with low scores. Very low scores (T scores of approximately 35) seem to represent an inability to tolerate anxiety and a tendency to act out, which could play a role in some of the negative behaviors described earlier. Although this inability to tolerate anxiety makes sense logically, it has not been tested empirically.

Reliability coefficients for Scale 2 on the MMPI are not as low as might be anticipated, given that the Scale is a measure of reactive depression that should vary over time. Generally, reliability coefficients for this Scale are comparable to those for the other Clinical scales. Reliability coefficients of .80 to .90 for intervals up to a month and .40 to .50 for intervals up to a year or more are common for Scale 2 on the MMPI (Dahlstrom et al., 1975). Test-retest reliability coefficients for Scale 2 on the MMPI-2 for approximately a one-week interval are .75 for men and .77 for women (Butcher et al., 1989).

Clinicians have been cautioned about the interpretation of high Scale 2 scores in the aged because of the 3 to 4 T point increase in scores that occurs in normal individuals (cf. Colligan et al., 1983, 1989; Dahlstrom et al., 1975). It has been conjectured that the elderly may be reporting more physical symptoms, which elevates Scale 2. However, neither Dye, Bohm, Anderten, and Won Cho (1983), who studied older psychiatric patients (age 60+), nor Swenson et al. (1973), who studied medical patients, found significant increases in Scale 2 with age. Dye et al. did note that there were subtle qualitative changes in the expression of depression across their three age groups. Scores on Scale 2 do *not* increase with age in psychiatric patients (Caldwell, 1997a; Hedlund & Won Cho, 1979; Schenkenberg, Gottfredson, & Christensen, 1984). Scores on Scale 2 for patients in the Caldwell (1997a) clinical dataset actually decreased from the 50–59 to the 70+ age groups. It appears that age effects on Scale 2 are quite minimal in clinical and medical samples.

Women tend to endorse 2 to 4 more items on Scale 2 than men and older, normal persons tend to endorse 1 or 2 more items than younger, normal persons (Colligan et al., 1983, 1989; Dahlstrom et al., 1972; Leon, Gillum, Gillum, & Gouze, 1979). Scores on Scale 2 decline nearly 10 T points as the level of education increases from grade school to postgraduate work.

The interpretation of Scale 2 at four levels of elevation is summarized in Table 4.4.

TABLE 4.4 Interpretation of Levels of Elevation on Scale 2 (Depression)

T SCORE	INTERPRETATION
44 and below	1. *Low.* These clients tend to be alert, gregarious, and active. Be sure that these behaviors are appropriate for the person's situation and setting (i.e., clients should rarely be scoring in this range).
45–57	2. *Normal.* These clients have a typical number of attitudes and behaviors that reflect symptomatic depression.
58–64	3. *Moderate.* These clients are dissatisfied with something or with themselves, but they may not recognize this state as depression. Their mild degree of dissatisfaction may appropriately represent the situation. Or they may not really be concerned about what is happening to them, or they may have learned to adjust to a chronic depressed existence. Review of the Content and/or Supplementary scales may facilitate interpretation in this range.
65 and above	4. *Marked.* These clients exhibit a general sadness and depressed mood either about life or themselves. The clinician can determine the source of this depressed mood either by asking the client or by examining the Clinical scales. As the scores increase, the pessimism, depression, and hopelessness begin to pervade the client's entire life. These clients tend to be depressed, withdrawn, guilty, and self-deprecating. Review of the Content and/or Supplementary scales may assist the clinician in interpretation at the lower end of this range.

A client can obtain a specific raw score on Scale 2 by endorsing items from any one or various combinations of content areas because of its heterogeneous nature. Knowing which content areas the client is reporting should help the clinician understand the exact nature of each client's distress, especially when clients have identical raw scores. Harris and Lingoes (1955) formed subscales on Scale 2 of the MMPI by subjectively grouping together the items that were either similar in content or seemed to reflect a single attitude or trait. Following this procedure, they identified five groups of items within Scale 2: Subjective Depression (D_1), Psychomotor Retardation (D_2), Physical Malfunctioning (D_3), Mental Dullness (D_4), and Brooding (D_5) (Table 4.5). These Harris and Lingoes subscales were not changed on the MMPI-2.

Harris and Lingoes (1955) did not restrict items to only one subscale; consequently, there is extensive item overlap between some of the subscales. For example, all 10 items on the Brooding (D_5) subscale also appear on the Subjective Depression (D_1) subscale, and 12 of the 15 items on the Mental Dullness subscale are on the Subjective Depression (D_1) subscale. Other subscales, such as the Physical Malfunctioning (D_3) subscale, have few or no items in common with the other subscales.

Miller and Streiner (1985) found that judges who were asked to reproduce the groups of items from the Harris and Lingoes subscales agreed reliably only on 9 of the 28 subscales (Physical Malfunctioning [D_3]; Denial of Social Anxiety [Hy_1]; Need for Affection [Hy_2]; Somatic Complaints [Hy_4]; Family Discord [Pd_1]; Naivete [Pa_3]; Lack of Ego Mastery, Cognitive [Sc_3]; Bizarre Sensory Experiences [Sc_6]; and Amorality [Ma_1]). For 10 of these subscales, the judges did not agree on a single item. Kelch and Wagner (1992) and Davis, Wagner, and Patty (1994) examined the reliabilities of the Harris and Lingoes subscales. They found a number of these scales had very low reliabilities: Physical Malfunctioning (D_3), Inhibition of Aggression (Hy_5), Authority Problems (Pd_2), Amorality (Ma_1), and Ego Inflation (Ma_4). Even though the items on the Physical Malfunctioning (D_3) and Amorality (Ma_1) scales could be identified reliably by judges, they still did not have psychometric reliability. Wrobel (1992), who examined the correlates of the Harris and Lingoes subscales in a sample of psychiatric patients, found

that 12 of these subscales had no reliable correlates. The subscales with the greatest proportion of significant correlations were Subjective Depression (D_1), Brooding (D_5), Social Alienation (Pd_4), and Emotional Alienation (Sc_2). It appears that some subset of these Harris and Lingoes subscales may warrant clinical use and further research, although the exact set of subscales still needs to be determined.

Little research other than Wrobel (1992) has been conducted on the Harris and Lingoes subscales. The research that does exist consists primarily of reporting means and standard deviations for these subscales for various samples of individuals (cf. Gordon & Swart, 1973; Panton, 1959b). McGrath, Powis, and Pogge (1998) have provided descriptive data on all of these subscales for 14 MMPI-2 codetypes. They reported that these data varied as a function of codetype and could be used as a prototype when interpreting a client's MMPI-2 profile. Further discussion of prototypic scores for MMPI-2 codetypes will be deferred until Chapter 7.

Lingoes (1960) identified seven factors in his factor analysis of all 28 of the Harris and Lingoes subscales, which suggests that these subscales are capable of providing information beyond that contained within the standard Clinical scales. However, Bernstein and Garbin (1985) concluded that none of the subscales (Comrey or Harris and Lingoes) could explain the item structure of Scale 2 and they suggested that the entire Scale should be used rather than any set of subscales.

Given all the caveats noted earlier, the Harris and Lingoes subscales may provide helpful interpretive information when Scale 2 is between a T score of 60 and 80. When Scale 2 exceeds a T score of 80, all subscales usually are elevated above a T score of 70, and when there is a T score below 60, none of the subscales will likely be elevated above a T score of 70. A description of high scorers on the Harris and Lingoes subscales for Scale 2 appears in Table 4.5.

These subscales should not be interpreted unless they exceed a T score of 70 because of their restricted variance; on some subscales, endorsing one additional or one fewer item will change the client's score by 2 to 5 T score points. These general guidelines for interpreting the Harris and Lingoes subscales for Scale 2 also apply to the Harris and Lingoes subscales for Scales 3 (Hysteria), 4 (Psychopathic Deviate), 6

TABLE 4.5 Description of High Scorers on the Harris and Lingoes Subscales for Scale *2* (Depression)

SUBSCALE			
Name	*Abbreviation*	*Number of Items*	*Description of High Scorers*
Subjective Depression	D_1	32	These clients are depressed, pessimistic, and have poor morale and low self-esteem. They lack energy for coping with problems. They have problems with attention and concentration. They have difficulties sleeping.
Psychomotor Retardation	D_2	14	These clients avoid social relations and they have difficulty in starting to do things.
Physical Malfunctioning	D_3	11	These clients are generally concerned about their poor health, which has not been as good as their friends for a number of years.
Mental Dullness	D_4	15	These clients have problems with attention, concentration, and their memory. They are apathetic and have difficulty in starting to do things.
Brooding	D_5	10	These clients are depressed, feel useless, and are easily upset by others.

(Paranoia), *8* (Schizophrenia), and *9* (Hypomania). Harris and Lingoes (1955) did not develop subscales for the other Clinical scales.

SCALE *3:* HYSTERIA (*Hy*)

The 60 items of Scale *3* can be classified into two general categories: items reflecting specific somatic symptoms typically in the head, arms, and legs; and items that show that the client considers himself or herself well socialized and well adjusted. Although these two categories of items are either unrelated or negatively correlated in normal individuals, they are closely associated in persons whose personality revolves around histrionic dynamics. Such persons believe that they are well adjusted and only when they are under stress does their proneness to develop conversion-type symptoms as a means of resolving conflict and avoiding responsibility appear. These two categories are contained within the Hysteria, Obvious and Hysteria, Subtle (Wiener, 1948) subscales, respectively, which correlate –.32 in the MMPI-2 normative group (Butcher et al., 1989) and –.44 in the Caldwell (1997a) clinical dataset.

Scale *3* was developed on an empirical basis, using a criterion group composed of 50 patients with either a diagnosis of hysteria or identifiable histrionic personality components. The original Hysteria Scale included numerous somatic symptom items that also appeared on Scale *1* (Hypochondriasis). In an effort to differentiate Scales *1* and *3*, McKinley and Hathaway (1944) eliminated the duplicate items from Scale *3*; this, however, reduced the validity of Scale *3*. Therefore, these items were returned to Scale *3* and deleted from Scale *1* (see the discussion of the construction of Scale *1* in Chapter 1). The result was the current 60 items on Scale *3*.

Examples of the items with the deviant answer indicated in parentheses are:

"I am about as able to work as I ever was." (false)

"I have few or no pains." (false)

"I feel weak all over much of the time." (true)[3]

3. Minnesota Multiphasic Personality Inventory-2 (MMPI-2). Copyright © 1942, 1943 (renewed 1970), 1989 by the Regents of the University of Minnesota. Reproduced by permission of the publisher. "MMPI-2" and "Minnesota Multiphasic Personality Inventory-2" are trademarks owned by the University of Minnesota.

Preliminary use of Scale *3* revealed that many clients tended to get similar scores on Scales *1* (Hypochondriasis) and *3*. Clinical experience, however, demonstrated valid clinical differences in prognosis and treatment for clients who scored relatively higher on Scale *1* or Scale *3*, so McKinley and Hathaway (1944) decided to retain both scales. Clients who scored higher on Scale *1* than Scale *3* tended to have diffuse, vague physical symptoms, and the role of psychological factors in their disability was readily apparent. Clients who scored higher on Scale *3* than Scale *1* were less obviously neurotic; in fact, they appeared normal psychologically except when under stress. Their physical symptoms tended to be specific and were more likely to have psychological components manifested in them.

There are 13 (21.7%) items unique to Scale *3*. One-third (20) of the Scale *3* items overlap with Scale *1* (Hypochondriasis) even after the duplicate somatic symptom items were deleted from Scale *1* and are scored in the same direction. Thus, it stands to reason that these two scales often are simultaneously elevated due to their shared items. The other overlapping Scale *3* items are distributed relatively evenly across the other Clinical scales: 10 items are shared with Scale *4* (Psychopathic Deviate), 8 items with Scales *8* (Schizophrenia) and *0* (Social Introversion), and 7 items with Scale *7* (Psychasthenia). Seven of the 8 items that overlap with Scale *0* are scored in the opposite direction on Scale *3* (i.e., if the item is scored when endorsed "false" on Scale *3*, it is scored when endorsed "true" on Scale *0*). There are 10 items on Scale *3* that overlap with the *K* scale, and they are scored in the same direction. Although Scale *3* is not *K*-corrected, the fact that they share 10 items functionally produces a result similar to a *K*-correction of .33. Consequently, when a non-*K*-corrected profile is constructed (Chapter 2), the contribution of the *K* scale to Scale *3* cannot be removed directly.

As with the other scales in the neurotic triad (Scales *1* [Hypochondriasis], *2* [Depression], and *3*), "false" is the deviant response for 47 (78 percent) of the items on Scale *3*. The profile for an "all false" response set in Chapter 3 (p. 124) illustrates the emphasis on "false" as the deviant response on these scales in the neurotic triad. Wiener and Harmon (Wiener, 1948) judged the items on Scale *3* to be almost evenly split between obvious and subtle items. As noted earlier, the Hysteria, Obvious subscale consists of items assessing specific somatic symptoms, while the Hysteria, Subtle subscale consists of items showing that the person considers himself or herself well socialized and well adjusted.

Studies of the associations among individual items on Scale *3* have yielded generally convergent results. Using factor analysis, Comrey (1957c) identified five factors: *poor physical health, shyness, cynicism, headaches,* and *neuroticism.* Through cluster analysis Little and Fisher (1958) identified two relatively independent clusters of items: *admission of physiologic symptoms* and *denial.* These two clusters were used to develop the Admission (*Ad*) and Denial (*Dn*) Scales. The *Ad* scale correlates positively (~.90) with Scale *1* (Hypochondriasis), which is logical since the two scales have 18 items in common. The *Dn* scale correlates positively (~.80) with *K*, with which it has 9 items in common. Clients who have high scores on the *Ad* scale report a number of somatic symptoms and have poor interpersonal relationships. High scorers on the *Dn* scale are described as lacking insight into their own behavior and morally virtuous. Little and Fisher (1958) believe that when both of these scales are elevated, the person should have conversion reaction dynamics. The Hysteria, Obvious (*Hy-O*) and Subtle (*Hy-S*) subscales can be used interchangeably with the *Ad* and *Dn* scales, respectively. The *Hy-O* scale shares 30 of its 32 items with the *Ad* scale and all 26 items on the *Dn* scale are contained within the 28 items on the *Hy-S* scale.

The *Dn* scale (Little & Fisher, 1958) has been used in many studies of defensive styles and their effects on behavior (cf. Weinstein, Averill, Opton, & Lazarus, 1968). The *Dn* scale also shares 19 of its 26 items with Byrne, Barry, and Nelson's (1963) Repression-Sensitization Scale, which has been extensively investigated as a measure of personality. The clinician who is interested in pursuing this line of research should consult Dahlstrom et al. (1975) for a review.

Table 4.6 lists the 20 scales with the highest correlations with Scale *3* in the Caldwell (1997a) clinical dataset. There are two primary categories represented within these scales: physical symptoms and general

TABLE 4.6 Correlations with Scale *3* (Hysteria) in the Caldwell Clinical Dataset

SCALE *3* (HYSTERIA)

Scale	Abbreviation	r
Hysteria, Obvious	Hy-O	.809
Hypochondriasis	Hs	.795
Somatic Symptoms	Hy_4	.778
Lassitude-Malaise	Hy_3	.763
Health Concerns	HEA	.751
Lachar & Wrobel Somatic Symptoms	LWSoma	.743
Depression	D	.724
Physical Malfunctioning	D3	.699
Koss & Butcher Acute Anxiety State	KBAnx	.682
General Health Concerns	HEA3	.675
Neurological Symptoms	HEA2	.671
Depression, Obvious	D-O	.668
Subjective Depression	D_1	.632
Mental Dullness	D_4	.625
Ego Strength	Es	−.616
Gastrointestinal Symptoms	HEA1	.592
Lachar & Wrobel Depression and Worry	LWDep	.584
Total Number of Lachar & Wrobel Critical Items Endorsed	LWSum	.567
College Maladjustment	Mt	.558
Sensorimotor Dissociation	Sc_6	.545

Note. All scales that are not described in this chapter are described in Chapters 5 and 6.

distress that is characterized by depression, anxiety, and worry. Virtually the same scales are correlated with Scale *3* that were correlated with Scale *1* (Hypochondriasis) (Table 4.1). The correlations with Scale *3* are somewhat lower than those with Scale *1,* because Scale *3* also contains items that characterize the client as considering himself or herself well socialized and well adjusted.

High scorers on Scale *3* (T scores of 65 or higher) are described as self-centered, immature, and infantile. They are demanding of attention and manipulative in interpersonal relationships. They tend to be uninhibited and outgoing in their social relationships, although they relate with others on a superficial and immature level. As their T score on Scale *0* (Social Introversion) approaches 30, the superficiality and lack of real intimacy in their interpersonal relationships become even more apparent.

Their insensitivity to others and lack of empathy reflect their egocentric involvement. Their primary defenses are denial and repression, and they generally appear to be defensive and overcontrolled. They tend to be emotionally immature and labile. A profound fear of pain, both emotional and physical, may characterize high scorers. When under stress, high scorers are likely to display specific physical complaints such as headaches, chest pains, or tachycardia. At these times they also display transient depressive features and anxiety. High scorers on Scale *3* are rarely psychotic, although their symptomatology may be quite dramatic during periods of stress.

Because of their strong need to be liked and their desire to make a good initial impression on others, high scorers appear to be good candidates for psychological interventions since they will respond positively to the clinician. Their desire for attention and support further suggests that they will enjoy interacting with the clinician. They are, however, generally intolerant of analysis of their personality dynamics and frequently place inordinate demands on their clinician. Their histrionic style usually is so deeply ingrained that they are unaware of it. When the clinician points out the realities of their situation, they frequently cannot see their role in it and claim that the clinician does not understand them. Thus, despite the positive initial impression, any form of psychological intervention will be a trying task for the clinician.

Low scorers on Scale *3* (T scores less than 45) are described as socially isolated, shy, conforming, and relatively unadventurous. They are likely to have limited interests. They tend to feel that life is tough, are sarcastic and caustic, and feel worn out. They are seen as having few defenses to protect them from the external environment and consequently are vulnerable to a harsh and overwhelming environment.

Elevated scores on Scale *3* can be interpreted relatively successfully in isolation from the other Clinical scales because the behavioral and clinical correlates of Scale *3* are usually stable regardless of scores on the other Clinical scales. The clinician should be sure, however, that the client has endorsed both sets of items within Scale *3*—specific somatic symptoms (*Hy-O*) and denial of psychological problems (*Hy-S*)—before interpreting it in isolation; that is, both subscales should be elevated above a T score of 70. When only the *Hy-O* or *Hy-S* subscale is elevated, the interpretation will reflect whichever item content the client has endorsed.

However, McGrath and O'Malley (1986) found that the *K* (Correction) scale and Scales *1* (Hypochondriasis) and *3* needed to be elevated to ensure that both denial of problems and specific somatic complaints were present. The statement is sometimes made (Duckworth & Anderson, 1986) that the client will see and acknowledge behaviors indicated by Clinical scales whose elevations are higher than Scale *3* but deny and fail to see behaviors indicated by scales whose elevations are lower than Scale *3*. Thus, if Scales *2* (Depression) and *3* are at T scores of 80 and 70, respectively, the client is reputed to see and acknowledge the depressive features. If these T scores are reversed, however, the client purportedly will deny the depressive features. Since no research has investigated this hypothesized relationship, the clinician is cautioned against a noncritical use of such interpretations.

Test-retest reliability coefficients for Scale *3* on the MMPI range from .63 to .84 for intervals up to two weeks and from .36 to .72 for intervals up to one year (Dahlstrom et al., 1975). Test-retest reliability coefficients for Scale *3* on the MMPI-2 for approximately a one-week interval are .72 for men and .76 for women (Butcher et al., 1989).

Women endorse 2 or 3 more Scale *3* items than men. Age has little impact on Scale *3* in normal individuals (Butcher et al., 1989; Colligan et al., 1983, 1989), medical patients (Swenson et al., 1973), or psychiatric patients (Caldwell, 1997a; Hedlund & Won Cho, 1979). Although education has limited impact on Scale *3* scores, scores *increase* 3 to 4 T points in normal individuals as years of education increase (Butcher et al., 1989), while scores *decrease* 3 to 4 T points in psychiatric patients as years of education increase (Caldwell, 1997a).

The interpretation of Scale *3* at four levels of elevation is summarized in Table 4.7.

Harris and Lingoes (1955) identified five subscales within Scale *3:* Denial of Social Anxiety (*Hy₁*), Need for Affection (*Hy₂*), Lassitude-Malaise (*Hy₃*), Somatic Symptoms (Complaints) (*Hy₄*), and Inhibition of Aggression (*Hy₅*) (Table 4.8). Two of these subscales overlap substantially with the *Ad* scale: Lassitude-Malaise (*Hy₃*) has 14 of its 15 items in common

TABLE 4.7 Interpretation of Levels of Elevation on Scale *3* (Hysteria)

T SCORE	INTERPRETATION
44 and below	1. *Low.* These clients tend to be caustic, sarcastic, and socially isolated. They have few defenses. They are seen as having narrow interests and being socially conforming.
45–57	2. *Normal.* These clients have a typical number of concerns about their physical functioning and the motives of other people.
58–64	3. *Moderate.* These clients are likely to be exhibitionistic, extroverted, and superficial. They are naive, self-centered, and deny any problems. They prefer to look on the optimistic side of life and avoid unpleasant issues. Review of the Content and/or Supplementary scales may facilitate interpretation in this range.
65 and above	4. *Marked.* These clients are naive, suggestible, lack insight into their own and others' behavior, and deny any psychological problems. Under stress, specific physical symptoms will appear. Despite the initial positive impression they make on the clinician, any form of psychological intervention will be difficult. They look for simplistic, concrete solutions to their problems, solutions that do not require self-examination. Review of the Content and/or Supplementary scales may facilitate interpretation at the lower end of this range.

TABLE 4.8 Description of High Scorers on the Harris and Lingoes Subscales for Scale *3* (Hysteria)

SUBSCALE			
Name	Abbreviation	Number of Items	Description of High Scorers
Denial of Social Anxiety	Hy_1	6	These clients relate easily to others and are socially extroverted.
Need for Affection	Hy_2	12	These clients believe that others can be trusted and that they have their best interests at heart. They are optimistic. They do not analyze the motives of others.
Lassitude-Malaise	Hy_3	15	These clients are depressed and have sleep difficulties. They are tired and fatigue easily. They are not in good physical health.
Somatic Symptoms (Somatic Complaints)	Hy_4	17	These clients report a number of physical symptoms that are localized in their head, arms, and legs.
Inhibition of Aggression	Hy_5	7	These clients dislike crime and violence. They do not get angry or swear.

with the *Ad* scale, and Somatic Symptoms (Hy_4) (Complaints) has 16 of its 17 items in common with the *Ad* scale. The other three subscales—Denial of Social Anxiety (Hy_1), Need for Affection (Hy_2), and Inhibition of Aggression (Hy_5)—overlap completely with the *Dn* scale, except that Inhibition of Aggression (Hy_5) has one item that does not appear on the *Dn* scale. Because of this almost complete overlap among the *Ad* and *Dn* scales, the *Hy-O* and *Hy-S* subscales, and the Harris and Lingoes subscales for Scale *3*, it is unnecessary to score all of these scales.

The names for several of the Harris and Lingoes subscales have been retitled here to reflect their item content more accurately. Somatic Complaints (Hy_4) is more appropriately titled as Somatic Symptoms, Persecutory Ideas (Pa_1) as Ideas of External Influence, and Bizarre Sensory Experiences (Sc_6) as Sensorimotor Dissociation. The actual title will be indicated parenthetically so that the reader is aware of these changes.

Two of Wiggins' (1966) content scales share items with the subscales for Scale *3:* the Organic Symptoms scale has 11 items, and the Poor Health scale has 3 items in common with the Somatic Symptoms (Complaints) subscale. Prokop (1986) has shown how the Harris and Lingoes subscales for Scale *3* can be useful in the treatment of low-back-pain patients, and Miller and Streiner (1985) found that the items on three of these five subscales (Denial of Social Anxiety [Hy_1]; Need for Affection [Hy_2]; Somatic Symptoms (Complaints) [Hy_4];) could be replicated by judges. The caveat that the Harris and Lingoes scales should only be interpreted when they exceed a T score of 70 is not viable for Hy_1 (Denial of Social Anxiety) because the highest possible T score is 61 in men and women. In this instance, clinicians should consider a T score of 56 on Hy_1 as being significant because the client has endorsed five of the six items on this scale. The subscales for Scale *3* seem to be assessing similar functions in a variety of populations, and they appear to warrant continued clinical use and experimental investigation.

NEUROTIC TRIAD CONFIGURATIONS

Four configurations encompass the most frequently encountered relationships among the three scales in the neurotic triad—Scales *1* (Hypochondriasis), *2* (Depression), and *3* (Hysteria). Since these configurations will be described in more detail in Chapter 7 under their respective codetypes, the review here will be brief.

One general statement needs to be made about the relative elevation of these neurotic triad configurations. The overall elevation of the MMPI-2 profile typically reflects the acuteness of the specific psychiatric disorder that the client is experiencing. As the client becomes more adjusted to the disorder as it becomes more chronic, the elevation of the profile decreases until all Clinical scales frequently may be below a T score of 65. In the neurotic triad configurations, however, the elevation of these scales *increases* as the disorder becomes more chronic, while more acute disorders actually will produce lower relative elevations. The factors that affect the elevation of the MMPI-2 profile will be explored more fully in Chapter 8.

The first configuration is a conversion "V" (Figure 4.1). A client with this configuration is converting personally distressing troubles into more rational or socially acceptable problems; that is, the person is converting psychological problems into physical symptoms. The overall elevation of this configuration reflects the amount and chronicity of psychological distress that the client is experiencing.

As Scales *1* and *3* both approach a T score of 90, the tenuousness of these defenses, which are quite chronic in nature, becomes readily apparent to everyone except the client. The relative elevation of Scale *2* compared to Scales *1* and *3* also reflects the adequacy of the "conversion defenses." The greater the relative elevation of Scales *1* and *3* compared to Scale *2,* the more severe, long-standing, and resistant to change are the client's defenses against facing the actual source of distress in his or her life.

The other important characteristic of this configuration is the relative elevation of Scales *1* and *3*. When Scale *3* is higher than Scale *1,* the client tends to be optimistic about physical symptoms, which are specific and usually focused in the head and the extremities. In contrast, the client with Scale *1* higher than Scale *3* tends to be bitter and pessimistic about vague and general physical symptoms.

The emphasis on physical symptoms along with the denial of any psychological basis for them makes clients with this configuration poor candidates for any form of psychological treatment. It is common for this neurotic triad configuration to be accompanied

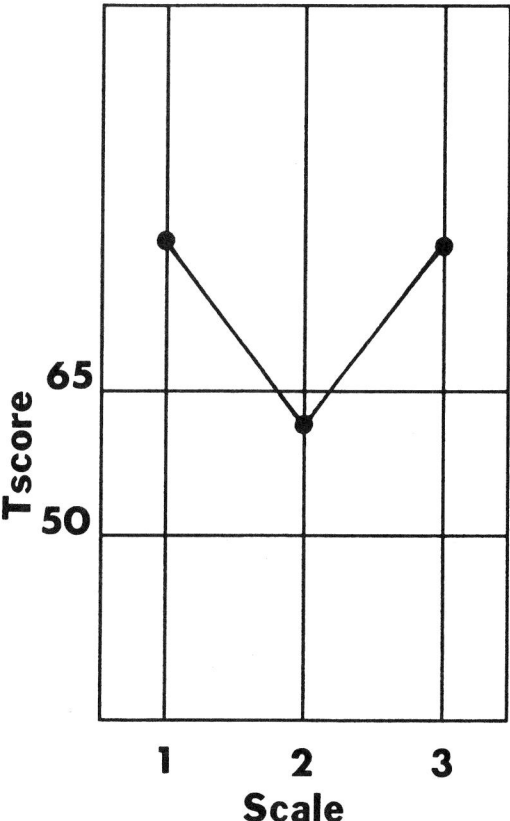

FIGURE 4.1

by a similar Validity scale configuration (see Figure 3.5, p. 117).

Another common neurotic triad configuration is the descending pattern (Figure 4.2). The essential feature of this pattern is that all three scales are elevated above a T score of 65, with Scale *1* being the highest, followed by Scales *2* and *3* in descending order. Clients with this configuration have a long-standing hypersensitivity to even the most minor physical dysfunction, and they have constant physical symptoms without adequate physical pathology. Their physical symptoms often include nausea, dizziness, insomnia, and headaches. These clients typically have stable work records and marital relations. As would be expected, they see little if any correlation between their physical symptoms and any psychological problems. Prognosis is poor for any short-term psychological in-

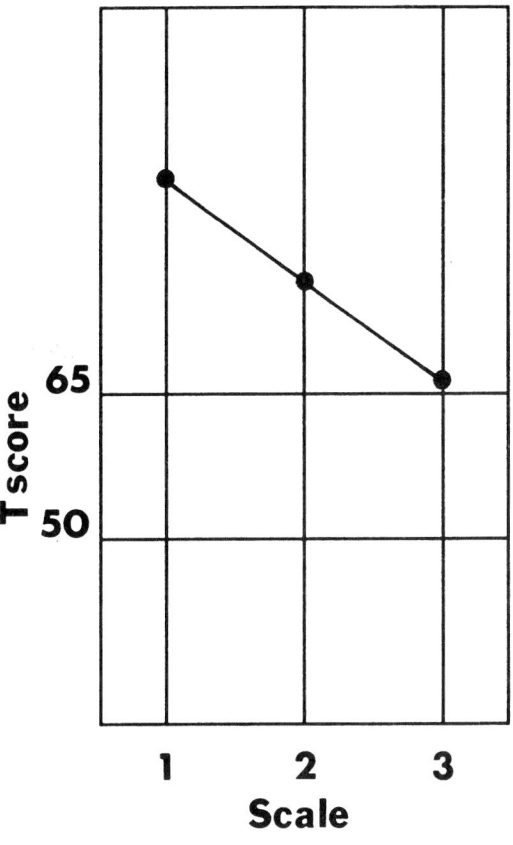

FIGURE 4.2

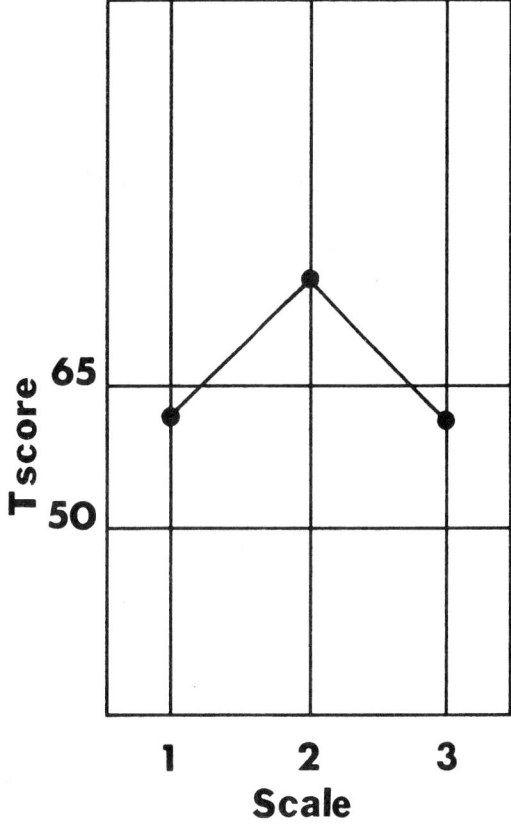

FIGURE 4.3

tervention. This configuration is frequently found in men over the age of 35 who feel "over the hill."

Figure 4.3 illustrates a third common neurotic triad configuration. Its main feature is the elevation of Scale *2;* although all three Scales are elevated, Scale *2* is higher than Scales *1* and *3*. These clients have rather chronic problems with mixed symptomatology. Multiple physical symptoms, depression, and hysteroid features are typical, particularly as this configuration increases in overall elevation. When Scale *1* is below a T score of 65 and Scales *2* and *3* are above a T score of 70, the clients frequently are overcontrolled emotionally and report feeling "bottled up."

These clients usually are fatigued, anxious, and filled with self-doubts, which prevent them from doing anything. They are described as dependent and immature. Such persons often have learned to tolerate great unhappiness and a high level of discomfort; consequently, they may have poor motivation for treatment. They seem to operate at low levels of efficiency for extended periods of time.

The fourth common neurotic triad configuration is the ascending pattern (Figure 4.4). In this configuration all three scales are greater than a T score of 65 and each succeeding scale is higher than the previous one. This pattern typically is found in women who have a history of gynecological complaints. (Duckworth and Anderson [1986] call this the "hysterectomy" profile.) The women report many marital problems, including sexual complaints such as frigidity and a lifelong history of ill health. Men with this configuration are likely to be in chronic states of anxiety and exhibit the physical effects of prolonged tension and worrying, such as gastric distress and ulcers.

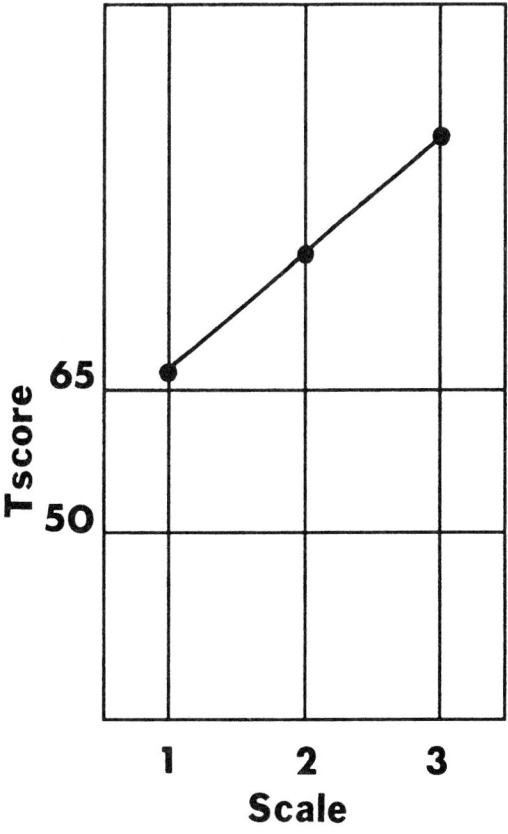

FIGURE 4.4

In both men and women this configuration reflects a mixture of depressive features with numerous physical symptoms. A high level of anxiety with insomnia and anorexia usually accompanies the clinical picture. Lack of psychological insight and resistance to psychological interpretation of behavior are typical of clients with this configuration.

SCALE *4:* PSYCHOPATHIC DEVIATE *(Pd)*

General social maladjustment and the absence of strongly pleasant experiences are assessed by the 50 items of Scale *4* (McKinley & Hathaway, 1944). The major content areas of the items are diverse and in some cases seem contradictory. The items tap concerns about family and authority figures in general, self- and social alienation, and boredom. Other items assess the

denial of social shyness and the assertion of social poise and confidence. As with Scale *3* (Hysteria), the simultaneous endorsement of apparently contradictory groups of items was particularly characteristic of the criterion group used to construct Scale *4.*

Scale *4* was constructed empirically using a criterion group of young persons primarily between the ages of 17 and 22 diagnosed as psychopathic personalities, asocial and amoral types, who were referred for testing by the courts because of their delinquent activities. None of the criterion cases was a major criminal type; most were characterized by a long history of minor delinquency. When they engaged in delinquent behavior, they generally did so without planning or forethought and with little effort to avoid being caught.

All members of the criterion group, which included more women than men, were involved in legal proceedings, and many were incarcerated. Hence, their emotional responses of depression and boredom could have reflected their current circumstances rather than any real, inherent characteristics. The responses of this criterion group were contrasted with those of a sample of the married members of the original Minnesota normative group and a sample of college applicants. This procedure resulted in the 50 items currently on Scale *4.*

Examples of this scale's items with the deviant response in parentheses are:

> "I am happy most of the time." (false)
>
> "No one seems to understand me." (true)
>
> "I wish I could be as happy as others seem to be." (true)[4]

McKinley and Hathaway (1944) also cross-validated Scale *4* by examining two other groups' total score on the scale. These two groups were a sample of psychiatric inpatients and a group of prison inmates, all diagnosed as psychopathic personalities. A T score of 70 or above on Scale *4* was achieved by

---

4. Minnesota Multiphasic Personality Inventory-2 (MMPI-2). Copyright © 1942, 1943 (renewed 1970), 1989 by the Regents of the University of Minnesota. Reproduced by permission of the publisher. "MMPI-2" and "Minnesota Multiphasic Personality Inventory-2" are trademarks owned by the University of Minnesota.

59 percent of the prisoners and 45 percent of the inpatients. McKinley and Hathaway called Scale *4 Psychopathic Deviate* to indicate that it was not expected to differentiate all cases of psychopathic personality. Rather Scale *4* could identify about one-half or more of those clients diagnosed as psychopathic personalities.

There are 15 (30.0%) items unique to Scale *4*. It shares 5 to 11 items with all Clinical scales except Scales *1* (Hypochondriasis) and *5* (Masculinity-Femininity), and it shares 4 and 7 items with the *F* (Infrequency) and *K* (Correction) scales, respectively. Scale *4* has almost an equal number of "true" and "false" deviant responses, and it has slightly more obvious than subtle items (Wiener, 1948).

Factor analyses of the items have yielded similar results in a variety of populations. Generally five factors are identified: *shyness, hypersensitivity, delinquency, impulse control,* and *neuroticism* (Astin, 1959, 1961; Comrey, 1958a). Comrey (1958a) also identified a family dissension factor in his mixed sample of normals and psychiatric patients, but Astin (1959) did not in his sample of adult male narcotic addicts. Monroe, Miller, and Lyle (1964) extended Astin's factor analytic scales to assist in screening adult addict patients.

Table 4.9 lists the 20 scales with the highest correlations with Scale *4* in the Caldwell (1997a) clinical sample. There are three primary categories represented within these scales: alienation (Self-Alienation; Social Alienation); general distress and negative emotionality (total number of Koss and Butcher [1973] and Lachar and Wrobel [1979] critical items endorsed; Post Traumatic Stress Disorder; Depression; Self-Deprecation); and family/marital problems (Marital Distress; Familial Discord; Family Problems; Lachar and Wrobel [1979] Family Conflict). It is somewhat surprising that scales reflecting problems with authority figures and antisocial attitudes and behavior are not among these 20 scales. It is likely that these latter categories would be more prominent in groups with larger proportions of persons with psychopathic qualities such as prisoners.

High scorers on Scale *4* (T scores of 65 or higher) usually are described in unfavorable terms: angry, impulsive, emotionally shallow, and unpredictable. They are socially nonconforming, disregarding

TABLE 4.9 Correlations with Scale *4* (Psychopathic Deviate) in the Caldwell Clinical Dataset

SCALE *4* (PSYCHOPATHIC DEVIATE)

Scale	Abbreviation	r
Psychopathic Deviate, Obvious	Pd-O	.921
Self-Alienation	Pd$_5$	.833
Marital Distress	MDS	.813
Social Alienation	Pd$_4$	.801
Total Number of Koss & Butcher Critical Items Endorsed	KBSum	.790
Post Traumatic Stress Disorder—Keane	PK	.781
Total Number of Lachar & Wrobel Critical Items Endorsed	LWSum	.767
Depression	DEP	.764
Schizophrenia	Sc	.763
Post Traumatic Stress Disorder—Schlenger	PS	.760
Gough Dissimulation Scale	Ds	.756
Koss & Butcher Depressed Suicidal Ideation	KBDep	.753
Social Alienation	Sc$_1$	.750
Self-Deprecation	DEP3	.741
Familial Discord	Pd$_1$	.731
Family Problems	FAM	.728
College Maladjustment	Mt	.728
Psychasthenia	Pt	.725
Welsh Anxiety	A	.721
Lachar & Wrobel Family Conflict	LWFam	.712

Note. All scales that are not described in this chapter are described in Chapters 5 and 6.

social rules and conventions in general and authority figures in particular. They harbor a brooding resentment and hostility toward authority figures, which may or may not be overtly displayed. In the absence of an antisocial history, this hostility may have been directed inwardly toward the self. Thus, a marked elevation on Scale *4* indicates the presence of antisocial attitudes and behaviors, *but it does not necessarily mean that these behaviors will be expressed overtly.*

Other Clinical scales, especially Scale 9 (Hypomania), usually are elevated if these antisocial behaviors are overtly expressed. High scorers have a perfectionistic and narcissistic conception of themselves, and they use these personal standards as a rationalization for ignoring social conventions. This perfectionistic self-concept is illustrated by the typical profile for a high scorer: Scale 4 is the only Clinical scale elevated above a T score of 65 (a Spike 4 codetype). Rather than representing conscious avoidance of deviant responses, this codetype seems to reflect their perfectionistic conception of themselves. The corresponding low scores on Scales 2 (Depression) and 7 (Psychasthenia) indicate that their behavior is not causing them any type of distress or concern.

High scorers (T scores of 65 or higher) are socially outgoing, energetic, and socially facile; thus, they make a good initial impression on others. Longer exposure to them soon reveals, however, their irresponsibility, unreliability, moodiness, and resentment. Novice clinicians frequently are awed by this initial impression and then dismayed when their underlying qualities begin to emerge. The clinician should be aware of the favorable initial impression typical of high scorers and not be overly influenced by it.

Depression, when evident in high scorers, usually consists of depressive thoughts and feelings but not actually psychomotor retardation or the other vegetative signs of depression. The depression most often represents dissatisfaction about the current limits being placed on the client's behavior rather than any actual concern or guilt about their behavior. Frequently, high scorers will not elevate Scale 2 (Depression) at all even when external constraints are being placed on their behavior. In these circumstances, a successful psychotherapeutic intervention is highly unlikely because the clients are not concerned about their behavior and they expect others to change to meet their demands. For most high scorers on Scale 4, personal maturation rather than some other form of intervention is usually most effective in changing their behavior.

High scorers on Scale 4 are very likely to be diagnosed as having some form of personality disorder; they are unlikely to receive a psychotic diagnosis. They often have a long history of inadequate familial and social relations, which seems to reflect a characterological adjustment.

Elevations on Scale 4 are correlated positively with the frequency of delinquent and criminal behaviors and recidivism rates (Forgac, Cassel, & Michaels, 1984; Gearing, 1979; Holland & Levi, 1983). Hare's (1985) finding of little agreement between clinical judgments or behavioral measures and self-report measures for assessing psychopathy should be noted by clinicians who are interested in researching this area and trying to integrate the information.

Heilbrun (1979) found that an index of psychopathy based in part on the raw score on Scale 4 was directly related to the frequency of violent crimes in a sample of white prisoners, but only in those prisoners with IQs less than 95. Since violent crimes tend to be impulsive, Heilbrun speculated that the relationship between violent crime and lower levels of intelligence may reflect a limit on or lack of temporary cognitive restraints.

Gearing (1979) provides a comprehensive review of the use of the MMPI in prison settings. Walters (1985) reported that prisoners with behavioral diagnoses of Antisocial Personality Disorder scored higher on Scale 4 than prisoners without such behavioral diagnoses. However, Rogers, Gillis, and Dickens (1989) found that forensic patients with diagnoses of Antisocial Personality Disorder were no more likely to have Scale 4 as one of their two highest Clinical scales than forensic patients with diagnoses of Schizophrenic Disorder, Affective Disorder, Substance Abuse Disorder, or Other Personality Disorders. The forensic patients with diagnoses of Antisocial Personality Disorder were most likely to have a Spike 4 codetype and least likely to have a 4-9/9-4 codetype among the seven codetypes containing Scale 4 that they reported.

Normal persons who achieve high scores on Scale 4 (T scores of 65 or higher) are described in fairly similar and unflattering terms: rebellious, immature, exhibitionistic, unconventional, and nonconforming. Such persons may display a generalized deviancy from societal standards and conventions, although they are not displaying psychopathic behaviors per se.

Nearly 10 percent of college students obtain T scores greater than 70 on Scale 4 of the MMPI, and the possibility of developing separate norms for college populations has been discussed (Forsyth, 1967; Goodstein, 1954; Murray, Munley, & Gilbart, 1965).

King and Kelley (1977a), however, found that college students requesting counseling who elevated Scale *4* above a T score of 70 had a history of legal, academic, and criminal difficulties. These students also were likely to be diagnosed as having a personality disorder. Thus, at least in this sample, elevation of Scale *4* seemed to reflect significant psychopathology. Whether similar psychopathology accompanies elevations of Scale *4* among college students who are not seeking psychological services remains to be examined.

Butcher, Graham, Dahlstrom, and Bowman (1990) reported that normal college students had similar scores on Scale *4* and the other Validity and Clinical scales of the MMPI-2 as the MMPI-2 normative group. They concluded that the MMPI-2 norms were appropriate for college students so separate norms would not be needed.

Low scorers on Scale *4* (T scores less than 45) are generally described as conventional, conforming, and submissive. They are less likely to be moody, get angry, or to act stubbornly. These persons are socially constricted, rigid, and have narrow interests. Men are frequently described as being uninterested in sexual activity, particularly when Scale *4* is the low point in the profile.

Scores on Scale *4* on the MMPI tend to be fairly stable with test-retest reliability coefficients of .59 to .84 for intervals up to one month and coefficients of .49 to .61 for intervals up to a year (Dahlstrom et al., 1975). Test-retest reliability coefficients for Scale *4* on the MMPI-2 for approximately a one-week interval are .81 for men and .79 for women (Butcher et al., 1989).

There are few gender differences in the distribution of raw scores on Scale *4*. In fact, the T score equivalents of each raw score are identical on the standard MMPI profile sheet, and they are generally within 1 or 2 T points on the MMPI-2. Scores on Scale *4* tend to decrease 10 to 12 T points with age in normal, medical, and psychiatric populations (Butcher et al., 1989; Caldwell, 1997a; Colligan et al., 1983, 1989; Hedlund & Won Cho, 1979; Swenson et al., 1973); this pattern is thought to reflect the slow maturational changes that occur in persons with elevated scores. Several normal groups score in the high-normal and low-moderate range on Scale *4:* social activists,

adolescents, and mental health professionals. Scores on Scale *4* are unrelated to years of education in normal individuals (Butcher et al., 1989), and decrease 3 to 5 T points in psychiatric patients with increasing years of education (Caldwell, 1997a).

The interpretation of Scale *4* at four levels of elevation is summarized in Table 4.10.

Harris and Lingoes (1955) identified four subscales within Scale *4:* Familial Discord (Pd_1), Authority Conflict (Pd_2), Social Imperturbability (Pd_3), and Alienation (Table 4.11). They further subdivided their Alienation scale into Social Alienation (Pd_4) and Self-Alienation (Pd_5). In constructing these MMPI subscales, Harris and Lingoes added to each subscale two to six items not found on Scale *4*. They did not provide a rationale for adding these items, nor did they add items to the subscales for any of the other Clinical scales. In the restandardization of the MMPI-2, it was noted that Harris and Lingoes had used a preliminary version of Scale *4,* which included items that were not on the final version (Butcher et al., 1989, p. 29). These additional items were excluded from the Harris and Lingoes subscales within Scale *4* on the MMPI-2 so that these subscales now have a similar format to the other Harris and Lingoes subscales.

Several of Harris and Lingoes' subscales overlap substantially with the factors identified by factor analysis that were described previously: Social Alienation (Pd_4) overlaps with hypersensitivity, Self-Alienation (Pd_5) with neuroticism, and Social Imperturbability (Pd_3) with shyness. Furthermore, the Familial Discord (Pd_1) subscale shares 8 of its 11 items with Wiggins' (1966) Family Problems scale, and the Authority Conflict (Pd_2) subscale shares 3 of its 11 items with Wiggins' Authority Conflict scale. Thus, it appears that regardless of the method used to construct subscales within Scale *4,* four or five factors are frequently identified in most populations. Bloomquist and Dossa (1988) reviewed the family functioning items on the MMPI and found that the Familial Discord (Pd_1) scale was correlated positively with family dysfunction.

The MMPI-2 Content scales (Butcher et al., 1990) share few items with Scale *4*. Family Problems (*FAM*) shares 6 items with Scale *4,* all of which are within the Familial Discord (Pd_1) subscale. Antisocial Practices (*ASP*) shares only 3 items with Scale *4,*

TABLE 4.10 Interpretation of Levels of Elevation on Scale *4* (Psychopathic Deviate)

T SCORE	INTERPRETATION
44 and below	1. *Low.* These clients tend to be rigid and conventional. They usually are able to tolerate much mediocrity and boredom. Men may lack interest in heterosexual activity, particularly if this scale is the low point.
45–57	2. *Normal.* These clients have a typical number of concerns about their family members and authority figures. They are comfortable with themselves and others.
58–64	3. *Moderate.* These clients may be genuinely concerned about social problems and issues; they may be responding to situational conflicts, or they may have adjusted to a habitual level of interpersonal and social conflict. If the conflict is situational, the score should return to the normal range as the conflict is resolved. Review of the Content and/or Supplementary scales may facilitate interpretation of scores in this range.
65 and above	4. *Marked.* These clients are fighting against something, which is usually some form of conflict with members of their family or with authority figures. These conflicts may *not* necessarily be acted out overtly; the rebelliousness and anger toward others are readily apparent even in these cases. They are likely to be unreliable, egocentric, and irresponsible. They may be unable to learn from experience or to plan ahead. These clients have a good social facade and make a good initial impression, but the psychopathic features will surface in longer interactions or under stress. Psychological interventions are less effective than maturation in achieving change. Review of the Content and/or Supplementary scales may be helpful at the lower end of this range.

TABLE 4.11 Description of High Scorers on the Harris and Lingoes Subscales for Scale *4* (Psychopathic Deviate)

SUBSCALE			
Name	*Abbreviation*	*Number of Items*	*Description of High Scorers*
Familial Discord	Pd_1	9	These clients quarrel with their family members and their home life is generally unpleasant.
Authority Conflict	Pd_2	8	These clients report that they had behavioral problems during their school years and may have been in trouble with the law.
Social Imperturbability	Pd_3	6	These clients are very comfortable in social situations because they are unconcerned about what others think about them.
Social Alienation	Pd_4	13	These clients believe that no one understands them. They are unhappy and regret the things that they have done. They believe that others talk about them and have it in for them.
Self-Alienation	Pd_5	12	These clients are depressed and regret the things that they have done. They are pessimistic and may use alcohol excessively.

and none of these items is within the Authority Conflict (Pd_2) subscale. Cynicism (*CYN*) shares only 1 item and Anger (*ANG*) shares no items with Scale *4.*

SCALE 5: MASCULINITY-FEMININITY (*MF*)

The 56 items comprising Scale *5* (Masculinity-Femininity) are very heterogeneous in content. The major content areas include interests in vocations and hobbies, aesthetic preferences, activity-passivity, and personal sensitivity.

Scale *5* was developed in a slightly different manner than the other Clinical scales. Hathaway and McKinley (Hathaway, 1956) had intended to use a large sample of homosexual men and women in empirically developing a scale of masculinity-femininity, but they quickly discovered that samples of homosexual individuals were too heterogeneous to use as a single criterion group. They identified at least three subgroups of homosexuals within their samples, each with an apparently different source or cause of homosexuality.

Because of their difficulty in obtaining a large number of cases within each subgroup, they decided to restrict their criterion sample to one subgroup—male homosexual inverts. Such persons were thought to engage in homoerotic behavior as a part of their feminine (i.e., inverted) personality characteristics; many such men, however, are too inhibited or conflicted to express their homosexuality overtly (Dahlstrom et al., 1972). The primary criterion group then consisted of 13 homosexual invert men who were selected for their freedom from any form of psychopathology.

Since most of the items used to identify sexual inversion were added to the item pool after the data had already been collected from the original Minnesota normative sample, separate groups of normals had to be gathered to contrast with the criterion group. These normal groups consisted of 54 male soldiers and 67 female airline employees. The initial item selection for Scale *5* resulted from contrasting the normal men with the criterion group (Dahlstrom et al., 1972). Items selected on this basis were then checked to ensure that they separated the "normal" men from the "normal" women.

Finally, a group of feminine men was defined by the Attitude-Interest Analysis Test of Terman and Miles (1938), and the responses of these feminine men were contrasted with those of the "normal" men. The 60 items that contrasted the groups in all three comparisons became Scale *5* on the MMPI. Four of these 60 items were deleted in the restandardization of the MMPI-2 resulting in the current 56 items on Scale *5.*

Hathaway and McKinley (Hathaway, 1956) were unsuccessful in their attempt to develop a separate scale (*Fm*) to identify female homosexual inversion. They found that their *Fm* scale correlated positively with Scale *5*, so they abandoned it in favor of a single scale of Masculinity-Femininity.

Examples of items on Scale *5* with the deviant response in parentheses are:

> "There was no time in my life when I liked to play with dolls." (false)
>
> "I like mechanics magazines." (false)
>
> "I enjoy reading love stories." (true)[5]

The items on Scale *5* have not been investigated as extensively as the other Clinical scales. Part of this lack of research is because the scale was not routinely scored in the early years of the MMPI. In fact, some clinicians still refer to the Clinical scales excluding Scales *5* and *0* (Social Introversion), which reflects the early tradition of MMPI usage.

The same 56 items are used to assess masculinity-femininity for men and women. Responses to these items are scored as deviant when they reflect femininity in men and masculinity in women. Thus, high T scores result when a client endorses the items like a person of the opposite gender. For 4 of the items (121, 166, 209, and 268), which deal with the admission of sexually deviant behaviors, the same response is considered deviant for both men and women. For the other 52 items, the scoring for a deviant response is reversed for the genders (i.e., if "true" is the deviant response to a specific item for men reflecting femi-

5. Minnesota Multiphasic Personality Inventory-2 (MMPI-2). Copyright © 1942, 1943 (renewed 1970), 1989 by the Regents of the University of Minnesota. Reproduced by permission of the publisher. "MMPI-2" and "Minnesota Multiphasic Personality Inventory-2" are trademarks owned by the University of Minnesota.

ninity, "false" is the deviant response for women reflecting masculinity). This reversal in scoring of the deviant responses is not evident at the item level (Appendix B.1) because the scoring key suggests that the items are scored in the same manner for men and women except for the foregoing 4 items. The reversal in scoring is produced by inverting the total raw score for the scale in women (Profile 1.4 [p. 19] and Profile 2.1 [p. 33]) so that low raw scores reflecting masculinity produce elevated T scores.

This procedure was intended to provide a basis of uniform interpretations of elevated scores since these scores would indicate that the person was endorsing the items like a person of the opposite gender. Immense differences exist, however, between the behavioral correlates of men and women at various elevations on Scale 5; thus, separate interpretations for men and women must be used.

Hathaway and McKinley (Hathaway, 1956) apparently assumed that masculinity-femininity was a bipolar dimension with masculinity at one end and femininity at the other. Numerous investigators (cf. Aaronson, 1959; Gonen & Lansky, 1968; Sines, 1977) have suggested that Scale 5 is not bipolar and that it is more likely to be multidimensional. Both factor analytic (Graham, Schroeder, & Lilly, 1971) and rational (Martin, 1993; Pepper & Strong, 1958) subscales formed with Scale 5 items also support its multidimensional nature.

Constantinople (1973) provided an excellent review questioning whether masculinity-femininity is a bipolar dimension that can be adequately measured by a single score. Baucom (1976) empirically demonstrated that independent measures of masculinity and femininity can be developed from the California Psychological Inventory (Gough, 1957), and Peterson (Peterson & Dahlstrom, 1992) developed independent scales of masculinity and femininity for the MMPI-2: the Supplementary scales for Gender Role—Masculine and Gender Role—Feminine that will be reviewed in Chapter 6.

There are 33 (58.9%) items unique to Scale 5, which is the largest percentage of unique items for any of the Clinical scales. It shares no more than 4 items with any Clinical scale other than Scale 0 (Social Introversion) with which it shares 9 items. Wiener and Harmon (Wiener, 1948) did not develop

obvious and subtle subscales for Scale 5. Dahlstrom et al. (1972) stated that most of the items are psychologically obvious, which supports the contention that homosexuals can conceal their sexual orientation without being detected by this Scale (Bieliauskas, 1965). There are approximately the same number of "true" and "false" deviant responses to scale 5 items, which means that either an "all true" or "all false" response set will not appreciably affect raw scores on this scale.

Table 4.12 lists the 20 scales with the highest correlations with Scale 5 in the Caldwell (1997a) clinical sample. There are three primary categories represented within these scales: femininity (Feminine Gender Identity, Gender Role—Feminine, Stereotypical Feminine Interests); fears, anxiety, and negative mood (Hypersensitivity/Anxiety, Multiple Fears, Fears, Dysphoria); and inhibition (Constraint, MacAndrew Alcoholism—Revised, Aggressiveness).

There are a paucity of data on the behavioral correlates of Scale 5 in various populations, again reflecting the early history of the MMPI in which this scale was not routinely scored or described in most research. What research has been done discusses men and women separately because of the very different correlates of specific T scores for the two genders.

High-scoring men (T scores of 65 or higher) in psychiatric populations are described as passive, socially sensitive and perceptive, having a wide range of aesthetic and social interests, and inner-directed. They also are seen as being dependent and insecure regarding their masculine role; often they tend to identify with a feminine role. Depression, anxiety, tension, and guilt frequently are reported (Ward & Dillon, 1990). If men are homosexual or have homosexual concerns and are willing to acknowledge these behaviors or concerns openly, they will achieve high scores on Scale 5 (Aaronson & Grumpelt, 1961; Dean & Richardson, 1964; Friberg, 1967; Manosevitz, 1971; Singer, 1970). If they do not acknowledge these behaviors, they will not elevate the scale at all since item content on Scale 5 is psychologically obvious (Wong, 1984).

The fact that a variety of factors, such as education and vocational interests, tends to be associated with elevated scores on Scale 5 of the MMPI in men further reduces the usefulness of this scale in diagnosing homosexuality (Burton, 1947; Friberg, 1967),

TABLE 4.12 Correlations with Scale 5 (Masculinity-Femininity) in the Caldwell Clinical Dataset

SCALE 5 (MASCULINITY-FEMININITY)

Scale	Abbreviation	r
Feminine Gender Identity	Mf_6	.708
Gender Role—Feminine	GF	.699
Augmented Feminine Interests	Mf_9	.646
Augmented Masculine Interests	Mf_8	−.582
Stereotypical Feminine Interests	Mf_3	.580
Stereotypical Masculine Interests	Mf_1	−.549
Gender Role—Masculine	GM	−.519
Other Deception	ODecp	−.434
Hypersensitivity/Anxiety	Mf_2	.430
Aesthetic Interests	Mf_5	.388
Multiple Fears	FRS2	.343
Constraint	CON	.318
Wiggins' Social Desirability	Sd	−.309
MacAndrew Alcoholism—Revised	MAC-R	−.300
Fears	FRS	.288
Aggressiveness	AGG	−.285
Ego Strength	Es	−.278
Lachar & Wrobel Antisocial Attitude	LWAnti	−.264
Dysphoria	DEP2	.259
Hysteria	Hy	.253
Depression	D	.253
Restraint	Mf_7	−.251

Note. All scales that are not described in this chapter are described in Chapters 5 and 6.

since the elevation on the scale may reflect these factors rather than homosexual behaviors or concerns. Raw scores on Scale 5 are positively correlated with level of education, particularly in the T score range of 55 to 65. Education per se, however, is insufficient to elevate scores much above a T score of 65 on the MMPI (Dean & Richardson, 1964; Manosevitz, 1971). Consequently, high scores in men cannot simply be dismissed as reflecting their humanistic and liberal arts oriented college education.

The interpretation of Scale 5 on the MMPI-2 may be problematic because of the relatively high educational level of the normative sample (Chapter 1). It is apparent that scores on Scale 5 tend to be about 10 T points lower in men and 2 to 3 T points higher in women on the MMPI-2 than on the original MMPI. Research clearly is needed to determine whether the MMPI correlates of Scale 5 that are described later can be applied directly to the MMPI-2. Long and Graham (1991) found no significant correlates of scores on Scale 5 in the men in the MMPI-2 normative group and they questioned the usefulness of Scale 5. Clinicians should recall that linear T scores are used on Scales 5 and 0 of the MMPI-2 rather than uniform T scores that are used on the other Clinical scales.

When only Scale 5 is elevated without accompanying elevations on other Clinical scales, clients are likely to be seen as not having a psychiatric disorder even in a psychiatric setting (King & Kelley, 1977b; Rosen, 1974). High-scoring normal men are generally described in positive terms: curious, socially perceptive, peaceable, tolerant, and psychologically complex. They also are described as passive and prone to worry. They have wide philosophical and aesthetic interests.

High-scoring women (T scores of 65 or higher) in psychiatric populations are seen as being aggressive, unfriendly, suspicious, dominating, and competitive or manipulative in interpersonal relations (Blais, 1995). In an inpatient psychiatric setting high-scoring women may have features of a psychotic thought disorder (Boerger et al., 1974). They have difficulty remembering, are slow moving and sluggish, and report hallucinations, thinking disturbances, and psychomotor withdrawal-retardation.

High-scoring normal women (T scores of 65 or higher) are seen as being bold, unsympathetic, and adventurous (Todd & Gynther, 1988). Somewhat surprisingly, no one has reported that they have masculine interests or that they do not have feminine interests. The lack of additional correlates of high scores in normal women reflects the infrequency with which such scores occurred on the MMPI.

Low-scoring men (T scores less than 40) are easygoing, adventurous, and coarse. They may display an almost compulsive masculinity and will emphasize their masculine interests. They tend to lack individuality and originality.

Low-scoring women (T scores less than 40) are passive, submissive, yielding, and demure. They strongly identify with a traditional feminine role. Extremely low-scoring women (T scores below 35) are likely to be constricted, self-pitying, faultfinding, and self-deprecating. They frequently display almost a caricature of an extreme feminine role. They appear helpless and utterly dependent on significant others to take care of them. This behavior often is manipulative but can occasionally represent genuine helplessness.

Test-retest reliability coefficients for Scale 5 of the MMPI range from .72 to .91 for intervals up to two weeks, with very similar coefficients for men and women. Reliability coefficients range from .34 to .63 for intervals up to one year, again with little difference between men and women (Dahlstrom et al., 1975). Test-retest reliability coefficients for Scale 5 on the MMPI-2 for approximately a one-week interval are .82 for men and .73 for women (Butcher et al., 1989).

Education has a predominant influence on raw scores on Scale 5 in men and somewhat less influence on raw scores in women on the MMPI. T scores for men can be expected to be in the range of 55 to 70 as a result of a college education and the vocational interests and training that are part of the educational process. A man who has a liberal arts education can be expected to score at the upper end of this range, whereas a man who has an engineering or basic sciences oriented degree will score at the lower end of this range. Men with education below the college level also can be expected to score at the lower end of this range or below. Consequently, either a low T score in a male liberal arts major or a high T score in a male high school graduate should be investigated by the clinician because of the unusualness of such scores. To the extent that social class will affect a man's vocational interests and his conceptions of what behaviors are appropriate within a masculine role, social class affects Scale 5 T scores, as does education.

Graham and Tisdale (1983) reported a number of differences between female graduate and undergraduate students on Scale 5 on the MMPI. The graduate students described themselves and were described as being more conscientious, insightful, reflective, unaffected, and unconventional than the undergraduates. The graduate students also described themselves and were described as being less formal, mild, opportunistic, and silent than the undergraduates. It appears that women with low scores on Scale 5 may be described in a variety of different terms depending upon their level of education.

There are obvious gender differences in the distribution of raw scores on Scale 5 on both the MMPI and MMPI-2, which have been described earlier. Scores on Scale 5 on the MMPI-2 are not affected by age in normal, medical, and psychiatric populations (Butcher et al., 1989; Caldwell, 1997a; Colligan et al., 1983, 1989; Hedlund & Won Cho, 1979; Swenson et al., 1973). Scores on Scale 5 on the MMPI-2 also are unrelated to years of education in normal individuals (Butcher et al., 1989) and psychiatric patients (Caldwell, 1997a). The existence of substantial effects of education on Scale 5 on the MMPI, while there are virtually no effects of education on the MMPI-2, warrants further investigation into the reasons for these differences. These differences may reflect the differences in the educational level of the MMPI and MMPI-2 normative groups, changes in society across 50 years, or some other factor.

The interpretation of four levels of scores on Scale 5 is provided for men in Table 4.13 and for women in Table 4.14.

Harris and Lingoes (1955) did not develop subscales for Scale 5. Pepper and Strong (1958) rationally identified five subgroups of items within Scale 5: Personal and Emotional Sensitivity, Sexual Identification, Altruism, Feminine Occupational Identification, and Denial of Masculine Occupations. Serkownek (1975) developed six subscales within Scale 5 based on the factor analysis carried out by Graham et al. (1971): Narcissism-Hypersensitivity; Stereotypic Feminine Interests; Denial of Stereotypic Masculine Interests; Heterosexual Discomfort-Passivity; Introspective-Critical; and Socially Retiring. Martin (1993) also used factor analysis to identify seven subscales within Scale 5 of the MMPI-2 normative group (Table 4.15): Denial of Stereotypical Masculine Interests (Mf_1); Hypersensitivity/Anxiety (Mf_2); Stereotypical Feminine Interests (Mf_3); Low Cynicism (Mf_4); Aesthetic Interests (Mf_5); Feminine Gen-

TABLE 4.13 Interpretation of Levels of Elevation for Men on Scale 5 (Masculinity-Femininity)

T SCORE	INTERPRETATION
44 and below	1. *Low.* These men identify very strongly with the traditional masculine role, and they may be compulsive and inflexible about their masculinity.
45–57	2. *Normal.* These men are interested in traditional masculine interests and activities.
58–64	3. *Moderate.* These men tend toward aesthetic interests such as art, music, and literature. They may be rather passive and prefer to work through problems in a covert and indirect manner.
65 and above	4. *Marked.* These men are passive, inner-directed, and have aesthetic interests and activities. They do not identify with the traditional masculine role. Self-proclaimed homosexuals and persons willing to admit overtly their homosexual concerns will score in this range. Homosexual behavior and/or concerns, however, can be easily concealed without elevating Scale 5 or the Validity scales. Be very cautious about diagnosing a client as homosexual solely on the basis of a score in this range.

TABLE 4.14 Interpretation of Levels of Elevation for Women on Scale 5 (Masculinity-Femininity)

T SCORE	INTERPRETATION
40 and below	1. *Low.* These women tend to be coy, seductive, and appear helpless. They overidentify with the feminine role and at times are almost a caricature of it. This behavior may be subtly manipulative or they may conceive of themselves as actually helpless. These clients should elevate the Supplementary scale of Gender Role—Feminine (*GF*).
41–57	2. *Normal.* These women are genuinely interested in traditional feminine interests and activities.
58–64	3. *Moderate.* These women are less traditionally oriented toward a feminine role than women who score low, and they have an interest in masculine activities as well.
65 and above	4. *Marked.* These women may or may not have actual masculine interests, but they are definitely *not* interested in appearing or behaving according to a traditional feminine role. They may become anxious if they are expected to limit their behavior to what is prescribed by a traditional feminine role. Aggressive behavior is likely to be seen, while homosexual behavior is unlikely to be seen.

der Identity (Mf_6); and Restraint (Mf_7). The three subscales of Denial of Stereotypical Masculine Interests (Mf_1), Stereotypical Feminine Interests (Mf_3), and Feminine Gender Identity (Mf_6) were thought to be related to the construct of masculinity and femininity and were combined into a single bipolar scale named Composite Femininity-Masculinity (Mf_{10}). The items for these ten subscales may be found in Appendix B.13.

SCALE 6: PARANOIA (*Pa*)

Interpersonal sensitivity, moral self-righteousness, and suspiciousness are assessed by the 40 items that make up Scale 6 (Paranoia). The content of some items is clearly psychotic, acknowledging the exist-

ence of delusions and paranoid thought processes. Hathaway and McKinley (Hathaway, 1956) never described the criterion group of paranoid patients used to develop Scale 6 empirically. They considered Scale 6 to be a weak preliminary scale, although they were unable to develop a better scale.

In any case, the exact number and composition of patients in the paranoid criterion group are not known. These patients were judged to have paranoid symptoms, although few of them were classified as "only" paranoid. Most were diagnosed as having a paranoid state, paranoid condition, or paranoid schizophrenia. It can be assumed that Scale 6 was empirically derived by contrasting the item endorsements of this

TABLE 4.15   Description of High Scorers on the Martin (1993) Subscales
for Scale *5* (Masculinity-Femininity)

| SUBSCALE | | | |
Name	Abbreviation	Number of Items	Description of High Scorers
Denial of Stereotypical Masculine Interests	Mf_1	11	These clients lack interest in activities thought to be typical of most men.
Hypersensitivity/Anxiety	Mf_2	13	These clients are worried, anxious, and very sensitive to how others react to them.
Stereotypical Feminine Interests	Mf_3	6	These clients have interests thought to be typical of most women.
Low Cynicism	Mf_4	6	These clients are not cynical or suspicious of others' motivation.
Aesthetic Interests	Mf_5	5	These clients have interests in the arts and written expression such as poetry.
Feminine Gender Identity	Mf_6	5	These clients have and are comfortable with a feminine gender identity.
Restraint	Mf_7	6	These clients are not interested in loud and aggressive activities.
Composite Femininity-Masculinity	Mf_{10}	22	These clients have interests thought to be typical of women and have a feminine gender identity.

unspecified paranoid criterion group with the original Minnesota normative group.

Examples of items on Scale *6* with the deviant response indicated in parentheses are:

> "I have certainly had more than my share of things to worry about." (true)

> "I have no enemies who really wish to harm me." (false)

> "I believe I am being plotted against." (true)[6]

There has been only limited study of the individual items on Scale *6*. Comrey's (1958b) factor analysis of the items revealed four factors of *paranoia—actual persecution, imagined persecution, delusion,* and *hopelessness, guilt-ridden*—as well as several other factors that are not clearly related to paranoia-neuroticism, cynicism, hysteria, and rigidity. Ward, Kersh, and Waxmonsky (1998) identified three factors in male substance abusers: *paranoia, low morale, and naivete.* Their three factors overlapped meaningfully with Comrey's factors and the three Harris and Lingoes subscales for Scale *6* that will be described shortly. Wiggins' (1966) Psychoticism scale overlaps with 19 of the 40 items on Scale *6* and shares numerous items with Comrey's four paranoid factors. The Tryon, Stein, and Chu (Stein, 1968) subscale of Suspicion and Mistrust shares only one item with Scale *6*. The MMPI-2 Content scale (Butcher et al., 1990) of Bizarre Mentation (Chapter 5) overlaps with only 8 of the 40 items on Scale *6*. This limited commonality among these scales thought to be measuring aspects of paranoia probably reflects the heterogeneity of the patients in the criterion group.

There are 12 (30.0%) items unique to Scale *6*. It shares 13 items with Scale *8* (Schizophrenia), 9 items with the *F* (Infrequency) scale, and 8 items with Scale

4 (Psychopathic Deviate). Wiener and Harmon (Wiener, 1948) felt that more Scale *6* items were obvious (23) than subtle (17). There are slightly more "true" (24) than "false" (16) deviant responses to Scale *6* items. As the "all true" profile (p. 123) illustrates, Scale *6* and the succeeding Scales have an increasingly larger proportion of "true" responses as deviant. Thus, "all true" response sets can be identified by the extreme elevations on the psychotic tetrad (Scales *6*, *7* [Psychasthenia], *8* [Schizophrenia], and *9* [Hypomania]).

Table 4.16 lists the 20 scales with the highest correlations with Scale *6* in the Caldwell (1997a) clinical dataset. There are three primary categories represented within these scales: paranoia and psychotic behavior (Paranoia; Ideas of External Influence; Persecutory Ideas; Schizophrenia); general distress and negative emotionality (total number of Koss and Butcher [1973] and Lachar and Wrobel [1979] critical items endorsed; Post Traumatic Stress Disorder; Depression); and social alienation (Social Alienation).

High scorers on Scale *6* are generally described as being suspicious, hostile, guarded, overly sensitive, argumentative, and prone to blame others. They often express their hostility overtly and rationalize it as a result of what others have done to them. In addition, an egocentric self-righteousness seems to permeate their behavior. Although they may not actually evidence a psychotic thought disorder, usually the paranoid character structure is evident.

Dahlstrom et al. (1972) observed that Scale *6* is quite sensitive to fluctuations in the degree and intensity of delusional material in psychiatric cases; the research support for this statement, however, is limited at best. Vestre and Watson (1972) could not identify a linear or a curvilinear relationship between Scale *6* scores and paranoid symptomatology, and Endicott, Jortner, and Abramoff (1969) actually found an inverse relationship between Scale *6* scores and clinical ratings of suspiciousness.

It also is commonly reported that Scale *6* on the MMPI has few false positives (nonparanoid persons scoring above a T score of 70), presumably because of the rather obvious nature of the scale items (cf. Carson, 1969). Vestre and Watson (1972) found, however, that 9 of 22 patients with T scores greater than 75 on Scale *6* had no rated paranoid symptoma-

tology. Consequently, high scorers are likely to show a paranoid character structure if not a psychotic thought disorder, but there are more exceptions to this statement than was formerly thought. Because of the rigidity and suspiciousness of high scorers, interpersonal contact is difficult.

TABLE 4.16 Correlations with Scale *6* (Paranoia) in the Caldwell Clinical Dataset

SCALE 6 (PARANOIA)

Scale	Abbreviation	r
Paranoia, Obvious	Pa-O	.861
Ideas of External Influence	Pa_1	.807
Total Number of Koss & Butcher Critical Items Endorsed	KBSum	.767
Total Number of Lachar & Wrobel Critical Items Endorsed	LWSum	.759
Schizophrenia	Sc	.749
Koss & Butcher Persecutory Ideas	KBPers	.749
Lachar & Wrobel Deviant Beliefs	LWDBlf	.741
Post Traumatic Stress Disorder—Keane	PK	.737
Poignancy	Pa_2	.734
Post Traumatic Stress Disorder—Schlenger	PS	.724
Infrequency	F	.714
Social Alienation	Sc_1	.711
Social Alienation	Pd_4	.706
Psychopathic Deviate, Obvious	Pd-O	.704
Depression	DEP	.703
Back Infrequency	F_B	.696
Psychasthenia	Pt	.696
Koss & Butcher Depressed Suicidal Ideation	KBDep	.689
Lachar & Wrobel Depression and Worry	LWDep	.684
Edwards' Social Desirability	So	−.679

Note. All scales that are not described in this chapter are described in Chapters 5 and 6.

Numerous investigators have found that Scale 6 does not reliably separate groups of paranoid clients from other diagnostic groups (Harris, Wittner, Koppell, & Hilf, 1970; Scagnelli, 1975; Tarter & Perley, 1975). Scagnelli (1975) reported that the Dependency (Dy) scale (see Chapter 5 in Greene [1991]) reliably separated female paranoid patients from other diagnostic groups, with the paranoid patients scoring lower on the Dy scale. Further research on the Dy scale seems warranted to determine whether it can reliably separate paranoid groups from other diagnostic groups.

Normal individuals who score in the moderate range (T scores of 58 to 64) on Scale 6 are described very differently from high scorers in psychiatric populations; this appears to reflect the shift in behavioral correlates in moving from moderate to marked scores as well as the population differences. High-scoring normals are described as being interpersonally sensitive, emotional, rational, and clear thinking. To the extent that sensitivity to others and empathy reflect some of the same underlying dynamics as suspiciousness and projection, this shift in correlates from moderate to marked scores is logical.

Clients who score in the normal range on Scale 6 (T scores of 45 to 57) fall into two major categories: clients without any paranoid symptomatology, and clients whose paranoid symptomatology is well ingrained and who have sufficient reality testing to avoid endorsing the obvious items on Scale 6. The latter group would be expected to elevate the subtle subscale of Scale 6 (Wiener, 1948), but no research has addressed this issue. This group also provides ample evidence for the statement that scores in the normal range on a scale may not reflect normality.

It is sometimes stated that extremely paranoid patients will get scores in the low range (T scores less than 40) (Carson, 1969; Good & Brantner, 1961), but the available research indicates that their scores are more likely to fall above the low range (Endicott et al., 1969; Vestre & Watson, 1972).

Low-scoring individuals (T scores less than 45) in a psychiatric population are frequently described as stubborn, evasive, and overly cautious. As previously discussed, there seems to be little evidence that they are paranoid. Low-scoring normals are described in generally positive terms: socially competent, having narrow interests, trusting, balanced, and conventional. They sometimes are characterized as being overly trusting and unaware of or insensitive to the motives of others; they frequently appear gullible as a result. Anderson (1956) found that low-scoring college students generally were in academic difficulty due to underachievement and reported difficulties with their parents. He conjectured that repressed or denied hostility may interfere with academic success.

Scores on Scale 6 tend to be less stable over time than scores on the other Clinical scales. Test-retest reliability coefficients for Scale 6 of the MMPI for intervals up to two weeks range from .49 to .89, and for intervals of one year from .32 to .65 (Dahlstrom et al., 1975). Test-retest reliability coefficients for Scale 6 on the MMPI-2 for approximately a one-week interval are .67 for men and .58 for women (Butcher et al., 1989).

There are no gender differences on Scale 6 of the MMPI since the same T scores are used for men and women; raw scores also are very similar in men and women on the MMPI-2. Scores tend to decrease 3 to 6 T points with age in normal and medical populations (Butcher et al., 1989; Colligan et al., 1983, 1989; Swenson et al., 1973) and 6 to 10 T points in psychiatric samples (Caldwell, 1997a; Hedlund & Won Cho, 1979). Education has minimal impact on Scale 6 in normal individuals (Butcher et al., 1989), while T scores decline 5 to 7 T points in psychiatric samples (Caldwell, 1997a) with increasing years of education.

A summary of the interpretations of four levels of elevation on Scale 6 is presented in Table 4.17.

Harris and Lingoes (1955) developed three subscales within Scale 6: Ideas of External Influence (Persecutory Ideas) (Pa_1), Poignancy (Pa_2), and Naivete (Pa_3) (Table 4.18). There is nearly complete overlap between Comrey's (1958b) paranoid, neuroticism, and cynicism factors and Harris and Lingoes' (1955) three subscales of Ideas of External Influence (Persecutory Ideas) (Pa_1), Poignancy (Pa_2), and Naivete (Pa_3), respectively. Ward et al. (1998) also found overlap between their three factors and the Harris and Lingoes subscales. However, they found that neither the Poignancy (Pa_2) or the Naivete (Pa_3) subscale had adequate internal consistency. They suggested that some items among these subscales might be reassigned to improve their validity.

TABLE 4.17 Interpretation of Levels of Elevation on Scale 6 (Paranoia)

T SCORE	INTERPRETATION
44 and below	1. *Low.* These clients have narrow interests and tend to be insensitive to and unaware of the motives of other people. Students are frequently underachievers.
45–57	2. *Normal.* These clients are interpersonally sensitive and think clearly and rationally.
58–64	3. *Moderate.* Mental health workers who are interpersonally sensitive and empathic with others frequently score in this range. These clients may be overly sensitive to criticism and personalize the action of others toward themselves. Review of the Content and/or Supplementary scales may facilitate interpretation of scores in this range.
65 and above	4. *Marked.* These clients are likely to be suspicious, hostile, and overly sensitive and usually overtly verbalize these qualities. A delusional or thought disorder may be readily apparent. Review of the Content and/or Supplementary scales may be helpful at the lower end of this range.

Since Endicott et al. (1969) reported only small positive correlations between clinical ratings of suspiciousness and Scale 6 scores, it may be that Scale 6 is an inadequate measure of the construct of suspiciousness, which is a central feature of paranoid behavior. Nevertheless, it appears that regardless of the method used to develop subscales within Scale 6, three factors are identified, and these can be adequately assessed by the Harris and Lingoes' (1955) subscales. However, as noted by Ward et al. (1998), it may be possible to improve upon the Poignancy (Pa_2) and the Naivete (Pa_3) subscales.

SCALE *4-5-6* CONFIGURATIONS

One configuration of Scales *4*, *5*, and *6* is seen frequently in women on the MMPI. Given the changes noted earlier on Scale *5* of the MMPI-2 in both men and women, it is not clear whether similar correlates with this configuration actually will be found on the MMPI-2. Consequently, the following information should be considered to be relevant only to the MMPI until research documents its applicability to the MMPI-2.

Scales *4* and *6* are above a T score of 70, and Scale *5* is below a T score of 35 (Figure 4.5, p. 160).

TABLE 4.18 Description of High Scorers on the Harris and Lingoes Subscales for Scale 6 (Paranoia)

	SUBSCALE		
Name	*Abbreviation*	*Number of Items*	*Description of High Scorers*
Ideas of External Influence (Persecutory Ideas)	Pa_1	17	These clients have ideas of external influence; they externalize blame for their problems, frustrations, and failures; in the extreme degree, they have persecutory ideas; they also project responsibility for their negative feelings.
Poignancy	Pa_2	9	These clients consider themselves something special and different from other people; they are high-strung and "thin-skinned;" they cherish sensitive feelings; they are overly subjective.
Naivete	Pa_3	9	These clients affirm moral virtue; they are excessively generous about the motives of others; they are righteous about ethical matters; they display an obtuse naivete; they deny distrust and hostility.

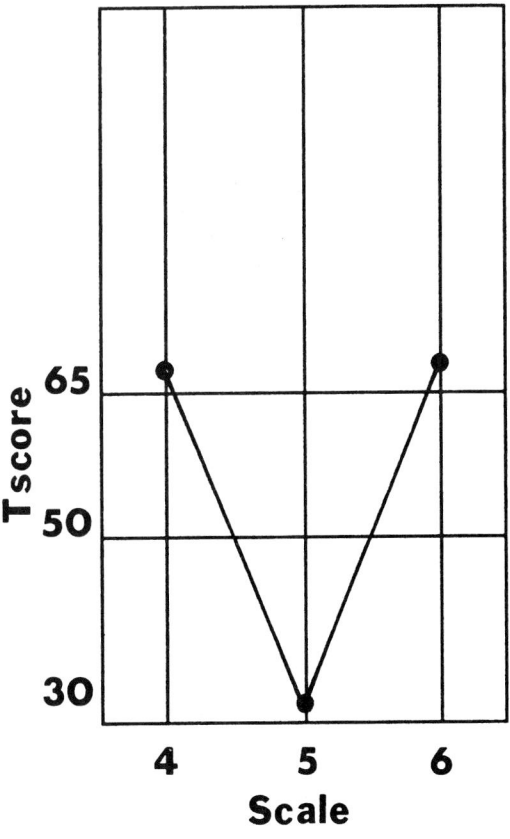

FIGURE 4.5

It is not necessary that Scales *4* and *6* be the high points in the MMPI profile, but it is mandatory that the T scores be in the indicated ranges since Scale *5* will be 10 to 20 T points lower than Scales *4* and *6* in most women.

These women are hostile and angry but unable to express these feelings directly. They resort to irritating other people into attacking them, and then seem to revel over how badly they are mistreated. They are excessively demanding, dependent, and have an almost inordinate need for affection (Walters & Solomon, 1982). Unfortunately, their behaviors only serve to alienate significant others, and this decreases the likelihood that their needs will be met. As would be expected, marital difficulties, familial problems, and sexual dysfunctions are common. These women are very adept at getting clinicians to aggress against them, which makes therapeutic intervention very difficult.

Pendleton, Tisdale, Moll, and Marler (1990) evaluated whether bulimic women were more likely to have a *4-5-6* configuration on the MMPI than other psychiatric patients or normal women, because these personality characteristics frequently are ascribed to them. They found no significant differences between these three groups in the frequency with which a *4-5-6* configuration occurred.

When Scale *3* is elevated higher than this configuration, women will be superficially sociable and deny the existence of any hostile feelings toward others. These women are particularly adept at enraging others without any real understanding of their involvement in the process. Their demanding, manipulative, and hostile qualities are readily apparent to everyone but themselves. This pattern of behavior represents a chronic means of manipulating and controlling others, which is difficult to alter through psychological intervention.

SCALE *7:* PSYCHASTHENIA (*Pt*)

The 48 items of Scale *7* (Psychasthenia) are designed to assess the neurotic syndrome of psychasthenia, which is characterized by the person's inability to resist specific actions or thoughts regardless of their maladaptive nature. This diagnostic label is no longer used, and such persons are now diagnosed as having obsessive-compulsive disorders. In addition to obsessive-compulsive features, Scale *7* taps abnormal fears, self-criticism, difficulties in concentration, and guilt feelings. The item content does not reflect specific obsessions or compulsive rituals; instead a characterologic basis for a wide variety of psychasthenic symptoms is tapped (Dahlstrom et al., 1972). The anxiety assessed by Scale *7* is of a long-term nature or trait anxiety, although the scale is somewhat responsive to situational stress as well.

McKinley and Hathaway (1942) developed Scale *7* empirically by contrasting a criterion group of 20 patients whose final diagnosis was psychasthenia with a subgroup of the original Minnesota normative sample and the college normative sample. At least one and possibly two of the criterion group patients were diagnosed incorrectly.

Since many patients with psychasthenia are not so disabled as to require hospitalization, McKinley and Hathaway (1942) were limited in the number of criterion cases available. They were reluctant to use outpatient cases because of the difficulty of studying such patients in depth to confirm their diagnosis. Once items were selected by contrasting the criterion group with the two normative samples, additional items were chosen that correlated with the total score on this preliminary scale in a sample of 100 normal persons. An analogous procedure was followed in a sample of 100 randomly selected psychiatric patients, and a few more items were added that correlated with the total score on the preliminary scale. As a result of all these procedures, 48 items were selected for Scale 7.

Examples of items on Scale 7 with the deviant response indicated in parentheses are:

> "I feel anxiety about something or someone almost all the time." (true)

> "I have a habit of counting things that are not important such as bulbs on electric signs, and so forth." (true)

> "Bad words, often terrible words, come into my mind and I cannot get rid of them." (true)[7]

There have been limited studies of the items on Scale 7. Comrey (1958c) identified seven principal factors: *neuroticism, anxiety, withdrawal, poor concentration, agitation, psychotic tendencies,* and *poor physical health.* None of these factors could be labeled *psychasthenia,* although some of the features of this syndrome can be seen in the factor names.

There are only 10 (20.8%) items unique to Scale 7. It shares 17 items with Scale 8 (Schizophrenia), 13 items with Scale 2 (Depression), and from 2 to 9 items with the other Clinical scales. Consequently, Scale 7 can be expected to covary directly with the other Clinical scales because of the extensive item overlap. Given the large number of items overlapping with the Clinical scales, it is somewhat unexpected that Scale 7 only shares 1 item with the *F* (Infrequency) scale and 2 items with the *K* (Correc-

tion) scale that are scored in the opposite direction. Wiener and Harmon (Wiener, 1948) were unable to develop subtle and obvious subscales for Scale 7 since almost all of the items were obvious in nature. The deviant response to most of the Scale 7 items is "true" (39 of 48).

There is limited overlap between the items on Scale 7 and Wiggins' (1966) Content scales or the Tryon, Stein, and Chu (Stein, 1968) Cluster scales. Scale 7 has 5 items in common with Wiggins' Phobia scale, 6 items with Wiggins' Poor Morale scale, and 9 items with Wiggins' Depression scale. It has 11 items in common with Tryon, Stein, and Chu's Tension, Worry, and Fear scale, 8 items with their Depression and Apathy scale, and 7 items with their Autism and Disruptive Thought scale. Scale 7 has 9 items in common with the MMPI-2 Content scale of Depression (*DEP*), 6 items with the Anxiety (*ANX*) scale, 5 items with the Obsessions (*OBS*) scale, and 4 items with the Low Self-Esteem (*LSE*) scale. Scale 7 appears to be a composite of a number of different items reflecting generalized distress and discomfort that is common to most MMPI-2 scales.

Table 4.19 lists the 20 scales with the highest correlations with Scale 7 in the Caldwell (1997a) clinical dataset. There is only one category represented within these scales: general distress and negative emotionality. Again, Scale 7 is a composite measure of general distress and discomfort that permeates the MMPI-2 item pool.

High scorers on Scale 7 (T scores of 65 or higher) are usually described as being anxious, tense, indecisive, and unable to concentrate. They frequently display obsessive thoughts and ruminations, self-doubt, and associated depressive features. Although specific phobias or compulsive behaviors may be seen in high scorers, they are not characteristically seen. In fact, many rigidly compulsive clients may not elevate Scale 7 at all, since their intellectual defenses are sufficient to control their anxieties, feelings of insecurity, and so on.

Basically, high scorers are clients whose characteristic defenses of intellectualization, rationalization, and undoing are no longer capable of controlling their anxiety and tension. High scorers display an extreme concern over their physical functioning; their physical symptoms typically center around the cardiovascular

7. Minnesota Multiphasic Personality Inventory-2 (MMPI-2). Copyright © 1942, 1943 (renewed 1970), 1989 by the Regents of the University of Minnesota. Reproduced by permission of the publisher. "MMPI-2" and "Minnesota Multiphasic Personality Inventory-2" are trademarks owned by the University of Minnesota.

TABLE 4.19 Correlations with Scale 7 (Psychasthenia) in the Caldwell Clinical Dataset

SCALE 7 (PSYCHASTHENIA)		
Scale	Abbreviation	r
Post Traumatic Stress Disorder—Schlenger	PS	.962
Welsh Anxiety	A	.951
Post Traumatic Stress Disorder—Keane	PK	.948
College Maladjustment	Mt	.946
Edwards' Social Desirability	So	−.937
Total Number of Koss & Butcher Critical Items Endorsed	KBSum	.937
Schizophrenia	Sc	.925
Total Number of Lachar & Wrobel Critical Items Endorsed	LWSum	.922
Work Interference	WRK	.917
Total T Score Difference of Obvious and Subtle Subscales	O - S	.916
Lachar & Wrobel Depression and Worry	LWDep	.913
Depression	DEP	.913
Anxiety	ANX	.912
Depression, Obvious	D-O	.911
Koss & Butcher Depressed Suicidal Ideation	KBDep	.900
Subjective Depression	D_1	.895
Brooding	D_5	.893
Mental Dullness	D_4	.884
Lack of Ego Mastery, Conative	Sc_4	.881
Negative Emotional Experience	NEN	.879

Note. All scales that are not described in this chapter are described in Chapters 5 and 6.

system, although gastrointestinal symptoms are common. Their physical symptoms generally reflect their high anxiety levels and the effects of anxiety on their physical functioning. Symptomatic treatment of their anxiety frequently is necessary before initiating any other form of therapeutic intervention.

High-scoring normals (T scores of 65 or higher) are generally described in positive terms although some of them, particularly women, display neurotic features to some degree. High-scoring men are described as being sentimental, responsible, conscientious, verbal, formal, unemotional, and idealistic. High-scoring women, however, are described as being prone to worry, emotional, high strung, and generally dissatisfied with themselves.

Griffith, Upshaw, and Fowler (1958) found that high scorers on Scale 7 were more doubtful than high scorers on Scale 9 (Hypomania) in their judgments in a psychophysiological weight discrimination task. Griffith and Fowler (1960) found that high scorers on Scale 7 were more compliant with an administrator's request to participate in an experiment than high scorers on Scale 4 (Psychopathic Deviate).

Low scorers on Scale 7 (T scores less than 45) are described in generally positive terms. They are seen as being responsible, cheerful, easygoing, capable, and efficient. They also are seen as relaxed and not anxious, fearful, or prone to worry.

Test-retest reliability coefficients for Scale 7 on the MMPI tend to be higher for intervals up to two weeks than for the other Clinical scales, with correlations ranging from .74 to .93. For intervals up to one year, test-retest correlations are much lower, ranging from .37 to .58 (Dahlstrom et al., 1975). Test-retest reliability coefficients for Scale 7 on the MMPI-2 for approximately a one-week interval are .89 for men and .88 for women (Butcher et al., 1989).

Women endorse 2 to 3 more Scale 7 items than men. There is little change in scores on Scale 7 with increasing age in normal samples (Butcher et al., 1989; Colligan et al., 1983, 1989); however, scores in medical patients (Swenson et al., 1973) and psychiatric patients (Caldwell, 1997a; Hedlund & Won Cho, 1979) tend to decline 3 to 6 T points with age. Education has minimal impact on Scale 7 in normal individuals (Butcher et al., 1989), while scores decline 6 to 8 T points in psychiatric patients (Caldwell, 1997a) with increasing years of education.

A summary of the interpretations of four levels of elevations on Scale 7 is presented in Table 4.20.

Harris and Lingoes (1955) found that the Scale 7 items did not lend themselves to subclassification; hence, they were unable to identify any subscales.

TABLE 4.20 Interpretation of Levels of Elevation on Scale 7 (Psychasthenia)

T SCORE	INTERPRETATION
44 and below	1. *Low.* These clients are secure and comfortable with themselves and are emotionally stable. They are success oriented, persistent, and capable. There is an absence of worries and a relaxed attitude toward responsibilities. Be sure that these behaviors are appropriate for the person's situation and setting (i.e., clients should rarely be scoring in this range).
45–57	2. *Normal.* These clients can handle work and personal responsibilities without undue worry or anxiety.
58–64	3. *Moderate.* These clients are generally punctual in meeting their obligations and may worry if unable to do so. They do not see themselves as anxious nor do others see them as anxious. Review of the Content and/or Supplemental scales may facilitate interpretation in this range.
65–89	4. *Marked.* These clients are worried, tense, and indecisive. Agitation may develop and overt anxiety is usually apparent both to themselves and to others.
90 and above	5. *Extreme.* These clients usually have agitated ruminations and obsessions that no longer control anxiety. Disabling guilt feelings may be present. Psychopharmacological treatment of the anxiety may be necessary before other forms of therapeutic interventions are instituted.

Thus, it appears that the use of an internal consistency approach in selecting items for Scale 7 resulted in the selection of a wide variety of heterogeneous items that tap general distress and negative emotionality; these items cannot be separated meaningfully into subscales.

SCALE 8: SCHIZOPHRENIA (*Sc*)

Scale 8 (Schizophrenia) consists of 78 items, which is 25 to 125 percent more items than in the other Clinical scales. The items assess a wide variety of content areas, including bizarre thought processes and peculiar perceptions, social alienation, poor familial relationships, difficulties in concentration and impulse control, lack of deep interests, disturbing questions of self-worth and self-identity, and sexual difficulties.

Scale 8 was developed empirically by contrasting the item endorsements of the original Minnesota normative group with the responses of two partly overlapping groups of 50 patients who had been diagnosed as schizophrenic (Hathaway, 1956). The criterion group included assorted subtypes of schizophrenia and included slightly more women (60 percent) than men (40 percent).

Hathaway (1956) reported that four separate preliminary schizophrenia scales were derived in an attempt to improve the ratio of true to false positive cases identified. Each of the preliminary scales adequately separated schizophrenics from normals, but they also identified a number of other diagnostic groups as schizophrenic.

Hathaway and McKinley (Hathaway, 1956) also attempted to develop scales to identify each of the major subtypes of schizophrenia without success. They finally selected the fourth of the preliminary scales as being the best, despite its problem of identifying other diagnostic groups as schizophrenic. Using the *K*-correction procedure (Chapters 1 and 3) reduced the number of false positives on this 78-item scale.

Examples of items on Scale 8 with the deviant response in parentheses are:

> "I dislike having people around me." (true)

> "I often feel as if things are not real." (true)

> "I hear strange things when I am alone." (true)[8]

There are 26 (33.3%) items unique to Scale 8. The overlapping items are distributed among a number of the other Clinical scales: 17 items are shared with Scale 7 (Psychasthenia), 13 items with Scale 6 (Paranoia), and 11 items with Scale 9 (Hypomania). It also shares 15 items with the *F* (Infrequency) scale. Scale *8* shares from 4 to 10 items with the rest of the Clinical scales. Wiener and Harmon (Wiener, 1948) were unable to develop subtle and obvious scales within the scale since most of the items were obvious in content. The deviant response to almost three-fourths (59/78) of the items is "true."

Scale *8* overlaps somewhat with Wiggins' (1966) Content scales of Psychoticism (17/48), Organic Symptoms (13/36), and Depression (9/33). The rather substantial overlap with the Organic Symptoms scale and the limited overlap with the Psychoticism scale illustrate both the heterogeneity of the Scale *8* items and the differences in the processes of rational and empirical item selection. Scale *8* overlaps minimally with the Tryon, Stein, and Chu (Stein, 1968) Cluster scales, sharing some items with the Autism and Disruptive Thought (8/23), Depression (8/28), and Tension, Worry, and Fear (7/36) scales. Scale *8* also shares items with a number of the MMPI-2 (Butcher et al., 1990) Content scales: Bizarre Mentation (8/23), Depression (7/33), Health Concerns (6/36), and Family Problems (6/16).

There have been few investigations of the individual items on Scale *8*. Comrey's (Comrey & Marggraff, 1958) factor analysis of this scale included only 58 items because of limited computer capacity available at that time. (He omitted the 17 items that overlap with Scale *7* and 3 additional items.) Comrey identified seven major factors: *paranoia, poor concentration, poor physical health, psychotic tendencies, rejection, withdrawal,* and *sex concern.* It is surprising that in spite of the increased computer capacity now available, no one has factor analyzed all 78 items on Scale *8* in the three decades since Comrey reported his analysis.

Again, it is apparent that the method of item selection produces different items to measure similar content areas. Further research is needed to establish the empirical correlates of these various groupings of items.

Table 4.21 lists the 20 scales with the highest correlations with Scale *8* in the Caldwell (1997a) clinical dataset. There is only one category represented within these scales as was found with Scale *7* (Psychasthenia): general distress and negative emotionality. It is somewhat surprising that no scale with

TABLE 4.21   Correlations with Scale *8* (Schizophrenia) in the Caldwell Clinical Dataset

SCALE *8* (SCHIZOPHRENIA)		
Scale	*Abbreviation*	*r*
Total Number of Lachar & Wrobel Critical Items Endorsed	LWSum	.953
Post Traumatic Stress Disorder—Schlenger	PS	.953
Total Number of Koss & Butcher Critical Items Endorsed	KBSum	.945
Post Traumatic Stress Disorder—Keane	PK	.944
Total T Score Difference of Obvious and Subtle Subscales	O - S	.929
Psychasthenia	Pt	.925
Gough Dissimulation Scale	Ds	.923
Edwards' Social Desirability	So	−.911
Gough Dissimulation Index	F - K	.904
Welsh Anxiety	A	.895
Social Alienation	Sc_1	.893
Depression	DEP	.888
Lack of Ego Mastery, Cognitive	Sc_3	.888
College Maladjustment	Mt	.881
Koss & Butcher Mental Confusion	KBMent	.881
Lack of Ego Mastery, Conative	Sc_4	.879
Work Interference	WRK	.878
Koss & Butcher Depressed Suicidal Ideation	KBDep	.875
Lachar & Wrobel Depression and Worry	LWDep	.875
Infrequency	F	.869

Note. All scales that are not described in this chapter are described in Chapters 5 and 6.

specific psychotic or paranoid content is among the top 20 scales. Scale *8* also is a composite measure of general distress and negative emotionality that permeates the MMPI-2 item pool.

Scale *8* is probably the single most difficult scale to interpret in isolation because of the variety of factors that can result in an elevated score. Since the total number of the items on the *K* (Correction) scale endorsed in the deviant direction is added to the raw score on Scale *8* to plot a *K*-corrected profile, approximately 20 Scale *8* items endorsed in the deviant direction are sufficient to produce a T score greater than 65 when the client has an average score on the *K* scale. Consequently, a client can endorse any combination of 20 or more of the 78 items on Scale *8* to obtain a T score greater than 65. It also is important to know the combination of items from the *K* scale and Scale *8* that the client is endorsing to produce a specific T score. For example, men can obtain a T score of 74 by endorsing any combination of 40 items from the *K* scale and Scale *8*. A man who endorsed 30 items on the *K* scale and 10 items on Scale *8* will be very different from a man who endorsed 5 items on the *K* scale and 35 items on Scale *8*. The former individual has a non-*K*-corrected T score of 49 on Scale *8,* while the latter individual has a non-*K*-corrected T score of 80 (Appendix A.2, pp. 511–512). The latter individual would be expected to be much more similar to the criterion group for Scale *8* than the former individual. Similar considerations must be kept in mind when interpreting the other *K*-corrected Scales: *1* (Hypochondriasis), *4* (Psychopathic Deviate), *7* (Psychasthenia), and *9* (Hypomania). The clinician is strongly encouraged to construct a non-*K*-corrected profile (Chapter 3, p. 96) anytime the *K* scale is greater than a raw score of 18 (T score of 56) or less than a raw score of 11 (T score of 41) in order to have an appreciation of the relative contributions of the *K* scale and the item content of the *K*-corrected scales in the standard *K*-corrected profile.

Several attempts have been made to develop subscales using item analysis within Scale *8* to distinguish between actual cases of schizophrenia and other diagnostic groups (Benarick, Guthrie, & Snyder, 1951; Harding, Holz, & Kawakami, 1958). These studies, however, have not been successfully replicated (Quay & Rowell, 1955; Rubin, 1954). Virtually none of the items selected by Benarick et al. (1951) or Harding et al. (1958) overlap with either Wiggins' (1966) Psychoticism scale or the Tryon, Stein, and Chu (Stein, 1968) Autism and Disruptive Thought scale. This finding suggests that research is warranted

with these latter two scales on differentiating schizophrenics from other diagnostic groups, although the scales are more likely to be sensitive to psychotic behaviors in general than to schizophrenia per se.

Newmark et al. (1978) developed four criteria that were successful in identifying 72 percent of hospitalized patients with an admitting diagnosis of schizophrenia. Their MMPI criteria were as follows:

1. Scale *8* is in the T score range of 80 to 100, inclusive.
2. The total raw score on Scale *8* with the K-correction includes 35 percent or fewer items from the *K* scale.[9]
3. The *F* (Infrequency) scale is in the T score range of 75 to 95, inclusive.
4. Scale *8* is greater than or equal to Scale *7* (Psychasthenia).

Newmark et al. found that only 5.5 percent of patients in other diagnostic categories were labeled schizophrenic (false positives) using their criteria. They also reported that the Harris and Lingoes subscales for Scale *8* did not accurately identify the schizophrenic patients. The fact that Newmark et al. had to include both the *F* (Infrequency) scale and Scale *7* (Psychasthenia) to identify 72 percent of their sample correctly further demonstrates the futility of trying to diagnose schizophrenia on the basis of Scale *8* alone.

This latter point is supported by Walters' (1984) finding that Scale *8* produced a 61 percent classification accuracy in distinguishing between schizophrenic and schizophrenia-spectrum and general psychiatric patients. However, Walters and Greece (1988) found that codetypes containing Scale *8* were more likely (64.4 percent) in schizophrenic patients than bipolar disorder, manic patients (35.5 percent).

High scorers on Scale *8* (T scores of 65 or higher) are described as cold, apathetic, alienated, misunderstood, and having difficulties in thinking and communication, which may reflect an actual psychotic thought disorder. These individuals feel that they are lacking something essential to be a real person. They tend to prefer daydreaming and fantasy to interper-

---

9. This second criterion can be stated more simply as follows: The raw score on Scale *8* *without* the *K*-correction should be twice the raw score on the *K* scale.

sonal relationships. They feel isolated, inferior, and self-dissatisfied.

As Scale *8* approaches and exceeds a T score of 75, particularly when these T scores are the result of a small *K*-correction (T < 41), peculiarities in logic and thinking become more apparent or actual schizoid or schizophrenic thought processes may even be evident. High scorers may appear confused and disoriented and may exercise poor judgment. They frequently display associated depressive features and psychomotor retardation. All of these behaviors may be the result of a schizophrenic process, a schizoid adjustment, or severe and prolonged stress.

Extremely high scorers (T scores > 100) usually are characterized by suffering from severe and prolonged stress, accompanied by an acute decompensation, if the items have been endorsed consistently and accurately (Chapter 3). These characteristics will be readily apparent in the clinical interview. These persons typically are not schizophrenic; they are more likely to be undergoing acute psychotic reactions. For example, an adolescent going through an identity crisis will frequently score in this extreme range.

Normals who achieve high scores on Scale *8* (T scores of 65 or higher) are described in a variety of terms that seem to reflect the changing correlates of the scale as elevations increase. Normals who achieve T scores of 75 or higher, which are the result of small *K*-corrections (T < 41), are generally described in a similar manner as high scorers in psychiatric populations. Anderson and Kunce (1984) found that their university counseling center clients, whose highest Clinical scale was Scale *8* (*M* = 91), were more difficult to treat than other clients and shared a number of characteristics such as feeling socially isolated, relationship difficulties, stressful home life, and so on. However, these clients did not display the severe symptoms that might be expected with such a high T score on Scale *8*.

Normals with less extreme elevations (T scores of 57 to 64) are described as self-dissatisfied, irritable, having wide interests, and immature. They are unlikely to be perceived as being deviant or withdrawn and may be seen as creative, individualistic, and imaginative. They like theoretical and abstract philosophical issues.

Low scorers (T scores less than 45) are seen as being compliant, submissive, and overly accepting of authority. They tend to have very practical interests with little concern about theoretical or philosophical issues. They also have difficulty understanding persons who approach issues in a theoretical or philosophical manner.

Test-retest reliability coefficients for Scale *8* on the MMPI for intervals up to two weeks range from .74 to .95, and for intervals up to one year from .37 to .64 (Dahlstrom et al., 1975). Test-retest reliability coefficients for Scale *8* on the MMPI-2 for approximately a one-week interval are .87 for men and .80 for women (Butcher et al., 1989).

There are small gender differences on Scale *8* with women likely to endorse about one more item than men. Scores tend to decrease 5 to 10 T points with age in normal individuals (Butcher et al., 1989; Colligan et al., 1983, 1989), 5 to 6 T points in medical patients (Swenson et al., 1973), and 6 to 10 T points in psychiatric patients (Caldwell, 1997a; Hedlund & Won Cho, 1979). Education has minimal impact on Scale *8* scores in normal individuals (Butcher et al., 1989), while scores decline nearly 12 T points in psychiatric patients (Caldwell, 1997a) with increasing years of education. Marital status appears to be unrelated to Scale *8* scores (Caldwell, 1997a; Lacks, Rothenberg, & Unger, 1970).

A summary of the interpretations of five levels of elevation on Scale *8* is presented in Table 4.22.

Harris and Lingoes (1955) identified three subscales within the items on Scale *8* and divided these first two subscales into two and three smaller subscales, respectively (Table 4.23, p. 168) for a total of six subscales. Thus, the Object Loss subscale is divided into Social Alienation (Sc_1) and Emotional Alienation (Sc_2) subscales. The Lack of Ego Mastery, Intrapsychic Autonomy subscale is divided into Lack of Ego Mastery, Cognitive (Sc_3); Lack of Ego Mastery, Conative (Sc_4); and Lack of Ego Mastery, Defective Inhibition subscales (Sc_5). The sixth subscale is Sensorimotor Dissociation (Bizarre Sensory Experiences) (Sc_6). Since Comrey (Comrey & Marggraff, 1958) omitted 20 items in his factor analysis of Scale *8,* there is no meaningful way to compare his factors with the Harris and Lingoes (1955) subscales.

There has been only limited research reported on the Harris and Lingoes subscales. Wrobel (1992) found significant correlates with the Emotional Alienation (Sc_2), Lack of Ego Mastery, Conative (Sc_4), and

TABLE 4.22 Interpretation of Levels of Elevation on Scale 8 (Schizophrenia)

T SCORE	INTERPRETATION
44 and below	1. *Low.* These clients are conventional, realistic, and uninterested in theoretical or philosophical issues. They are unimaginative and concrete and may have difficulty with persons who perceive the world differently than they do.
45–57	2. *Normal.* Chronic schizophrenics who have adjusted to their psychotic process may score in this range. Otherwise, clients report a typical number of concerns about themselves and how they relate to others.
58–64	3. *Moderate.* These clients think differently from others, though this may reflect creativity, an avant-garde attitude, or actual schizoid-like processes. These clients tend to avoid reality through fantasy and daydreams. Review of the Content and/or Supplementary scales may help to differentiate among these alternatives; the clinician also should examine what other Clinical scales are elevated.
65–89	4. *Marked.* These clients feel alienated and remote from their environment, which may reflect an actual psychotic process or situational or personal distress. Review of the Content and/or Supplementary scales may be helpful at the lower end of this range. Difficulties in logic and concentration and poor judgment become apparent as scores move higher in this range. As scores approach a T score of 80, the presence of a thought disorder is likely. Therapeutic interventions should be directive and supportive and frequently require psychotropic medications.
90 and above	5. *Extreme.* These clients are under acute, severe situational stress. Clients going through an identity crisis will score in this range. These clients typically are *not* schizophrenic, although they may have a brief psychotic episode.

Sensorimotor Dissociation (Sc_6) in psychiatric patients, and McFall, Moore, Kivlahan, and Capestany (1988) found that the Lack of Ego Mastery, Conative (Sc_4) and Sensorimotor Dissociation (Sc_6) reliably differentiated psychotic and nonpsychotic patients. Finally, Bornstein and Kozora (1990) found that both seizure disorder and neurological disorder patients produced significant elevations on the the Lack of Ego Mastery, Cognitive (Sc_3) and Sensorimotor Dissociation (Sc_6) subscales indicating that these subscales are not specific to schizophrenic disorders.

SCALE 6-7-8 CONFIGURATIONS

One configuration of Scales 6 (Paranoia), 7 (Psychasthenia), and 8 (Schizophrenia) is seen frequently. It consists of Scales 6 and 8 being above a T score of 80, and Scale 7 being above a T score of 65 (Figure 4.6, p. 169). Scales 6 and 8 will be the high-point pair of this configuration. This configuration is sometimes called the paranoid valley or a psychotic "V."

Clients exhibiting this configuration are likely to be emotionally withdrawn, socially isolated, suspicious, hostile, and lacking insight into their own behavior. They also may have thought disorders, delusions, and hallucinations. They usually are labeled as being psychotic with the most frequent diagnosis being paranoid schizophrenia. (The clinician should examine the description of a 6-8/8-6 codetype in Chapter 7 for more information on this configuration.)

This configuration probably occurs most frequently in invalid profiles. It is characteristic of an "all true" response set (p. 123) and random item endorsement (p. 125) so the clinician needs to examine measures of the consistency of item endorsement. It also occurs frequently when clients are overreporting psychopathology; the clinician should examine measures of the accuracy of item endorsement.

If the clinician has determined that this 6-7-8 configuration is valid (i.e., measures of the consistency and accuracy of item endorsement are in the appropriate ranges), Scales 2 (Depression) and 0 (Social Introversion) may be helpful in distinguishing between clients with a thought disorder and clients with a mood disorder with psychotic features (Post, Clopton, Keefer, Rosenberg, Blyth, & Stein, 1986). Walters and Greene (1988) also found similar results on Scales 2 and 0 between groups of inpatients with thought and mood disorders, but they could not identify any decision rule to discriminate the individual patients accurately. Consequently, clinicians should consider the following decision rule to be tentative: Scales 2 and 0 usually are above a T score of 60 in

TABLE 4.23 Description of High Scorers on the Harris and Lingoes Subscales for Scale *8* (Schizophrenia)

SUBSCALE			
Name	Abbreviation	Number of Items	Description of High Scorers
Social Alienation	Sc_1	21	These clients feel a lack of rapport with other people; they withdraw from meaningful relationships with others.
Emotional Alienation	Sc_2	11	These clients feel a lack of rapport with themselves; they experience the self as strange and alien; they display flattened or distorted affect and apathy.
Lack of Ego Mastery, Cognitive	Sc_3	10	These clients admit autonomous thought processes; they have strange and puzzling ideas.
Lack of Ego Mastery, Conative	Sc_4	14	These clients have feelings of "psychological weakness;" they show abulia, inertia, massive inhibition, and regression.
Lack of Ego Mastery, Defective Inhibition	Sc_5	11	These clients have feelings of not being in control of their impulses; they experience their emotions as strange and alien; they are at the mercy of their impulses and feelings and may show dissociation of affect.
Sensorimotor Dissociation (Bizarre Sensory Experience)	Sc_6	20	These clients have feelings of change in the perception of themselves and their body image; they experience feelings of depersonalization and estrangement.

clients with thought disorders and below a T score of 55 in clients with a manic mood disorder. Wiggins' (1966) Psychoticism scale and the MMPI-2 Content scale (Butcher et al., 1989) of Bizarre Mentation will *not* distinguish between these two disorders since they are general measures of psychoticism. However, Wiggins' Hypomania scale will be higher in clients with a manic mood disorder.

SCALE *9:* HYPOMANIA (*Ma*)

The milder degrees of manic excitement, characterized by an elated but unstable mood, psychomotor excitement, and flight of ideas are covered by the 46 items comprising Scale *9* (Hypomania: McKinley & Hathaway, 1944). The items range over a wide variety of content areas including overactivity, both behaviorally and cognitively, grandiosity, egocentricity, and irritability.

The criterion group for Scale *9* consisted of 24 manic patients of moderate or mild severity since more severe cases would not cooperate with testing.

The item endorsements of this criterion group were contrasted with those of the original Minnesota normative group to develop Scale *9* empirically, resulting in the 46 items currently on Scale *9*.

The clinician needs to understand that the label of *hypomania* refers to elevated scores, not T scores below 50 as the prefix *hypo* might suggest. A normal activity level is indicated by T scores in the normal range (45 to 57), and more elevated scores indicate increasing levels of mania. Hence, elevated scores indicate hypomania, and increasingly higher scores reflect mania and ultimately hypermania. Since actual cases of mania and hypermania are readily identified behaviorally, it is the more moderate cases that need to be identified by Scale *9*.

Examples of items on Scale *9* with the deviant response in parentheses are:

"When I get bored I like to stir up some excitement." (true)

"I am an important person." (true)

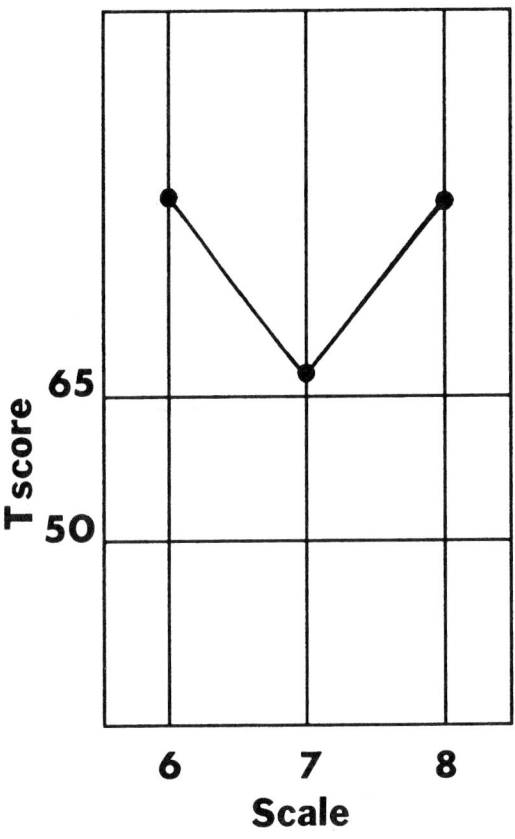

FIGURE 4.6

"I don't blame people for trying to grab everything they can get in this world." (true)[10]

There are 16 (34.8%) items unique to Scale 9. It shares 11 items with Scale 8 (Schizophrenia), but only from 1 to 7 items with the rest of the Validity and Clinical scales. Wiener and Harmon (Wiener, 1948) found that the scale had an equal number of obvious and subtle items. Again, the preponderance of deviant responses are "true" (35/46), as with the other scales in the psychotic tetrad.

10. Minnesota Multiphasic Personality Inventory-2 (MMPI-2). Copyright © 1942, 1943 (renewed 1970), 1989 by the Regents of the University of Minnesota. Reproduced by permission of the publisher. "MMPI-2" and "Minnesota Multiphasic Personality Inventory-2" are trademarks owned by the University of Minnesota.

Scale 9 also shares few items with any of Wiggins' (1966) Content scales; even with Wiggins' Hypomania scale the overlap is minimal (7/25). There is even less overlap with any of the Tryon, Stein, and Chu (Stein, 1968) Cluster scales; Scale 9 has no more than 4 items in common with any of these scales. Finally, Scale 9 shares few items with the MMPI-2 Content scales (Butcher et al., 1990). As with Scale 8 (Schizophrenia), it appears that different methods of grouping items into scales produce quite different results, and the correlates of these scales need to be empirically investigated.

Comrey (1958d) found that Scale 9 had the most diversified factor content of any of the Clinical scales and that most of the factor content was unique to this scale. He identified 11 major sources of variance: *shyness, bitterness, acceptance of taboos, poor reality contact, thrill seeking, social dependency, psychopathic personality, high water consumption, hypomania, agitation,* and *defensiveness.*

Table 4.24 lists the 20 scales with the highest correlations with Scale 9 in the Caldwell (1997a) clinical dataset. There are four categories represented within these scales: hypomania (Hypomania, Obvious; Psychomotor Acceleration; Ego Inflation; Hypomania, Subtle); psychotic symptoms (Bizarre Mentation; Lachar and Wrobel [1979] Deviant Thinking; Psychoticism; Schizophrenia); disregard for societal norms (Antisocial Practices; Social Responsibility); and cynicism (Cynicism; Interpersonal Suspiciousness).

Scale 9 also is difficult to interpret in isolation. It can be conceptualized as providing energy to activate the qualities identified by other elevated Clinical scales. Thus, a client who elevates Scale 4 (Psychopathic Deviate) along with Scale 9 will display very different behaviors than a client who simultaneously elevates Scales 8 (Schizophrenia) and 9 (see the description of 4-9/9-4 and 8-9/9-8 codetypes in Chapter 7).

Scale 9 often is described as being elevated in persons with brain damage (cf. Carson, 1969). Although some brain-damaged persons may display hyperactive and impulsive behaviors, virtually any type of emotional response may occur in brain-damaged persons, particularly depression. The MMPI-2 is an excellent instrument to assess the response of a person to brain damage, but there is not a typical score on

TABLE 4.24 Correlations with Scale 9 (Hypomania) in the Caldwell Clinical Dataset

SCALE 9 (HYPOMANIA)

Scale	Abbreviation	r
Hypomania, Obvious	Ma-O	.839
Psychomotor Acceleration	Ma_2	.747
Ego Inflation	Ma_4	.715
Hypomania, Subtle	Ma-S	.667
Lack of Ego Mastery, Defective Inhibition	Sc_5	.631
Depression, Subtle	D-S	−.604
Antisocial Practices	ASP	.598
Bizarre Mentation	BIZ	.587
Lachar & Wrobel Deviant Thinking	LWDThk	.581
Psychoticism	PSY	.578
Schizotypal Characteristics	BIZ2	.577
Superlative	S	−.576
Antisocial Attitudes	ASP1	.573
Social Responsibility	Re	−.572
Gough Dissimulation Scale	Ds	.572
Cynicism	CYN	.569
Gough Dissimulation Index	F - K	.567
Interpersonal Suspiciousness	CYN2	.566
Schizophrenia	Sc	.557
Total Number of Lachar & Wrobel Critical Items Endorsed	LWSum	.556

Note. All scales that are not described in this chapter are described in Chapters 5 and 6.

Scale *9* or a typical clinical profile for brain-damaged persons. Some persons may respond to brain damage by becoming depressed; others may become apathetic, withdrawn, and display psychotic features; still others may be virtually unaffected. Farr and Martin (1988) have reviewed the performance of neuropsychological samples on a number of MMPI scales and indexes.

Post et al. (1986) found that bipolar disorder, manic patients had higher scores on Scale *9* than other psychotic psychiatric patients and general psy-

chiatric patients. They found that discriminant analysis, with Scales *2* (Depression), *9*, and *0* (Social Introversion) as predictors, correctly classified 82.5 percent of the patients in their derivation sample and 74.2 percent in the cross-validation sample. However, Walters and Greene (1988) found that Scale *9* did not discriminate between bipolar disorder, manic patients and schizophrenic patients. Similar to Post et al. (1986), they found that Scale *0* did discriminate between these two groups of patients with schizophrenics earning higher scores.

High scorers on Scale *9* (T scores of 65 or higher) are described as being impulsive, competitive, talkative, narcissistic, amoral, extroverted, and superficial in social relationships. They typically have problems in controlling their behavior and display hostile, irritable qualities (Graham et al., 1997). They are *not* described as depressed. They may display actual manic features: flight of ideas, lability of mood, delusions of grandeur, impulsivity, and hyperactivity.

High-scoring normals (T scores of 65 or higher) are described in generally positive terms: friendly, sociable, energetic, talkative, and enthusiastic. Basically they have a pleasant, outgoing temperament. If scores become elevated over a T score of 75, other features become apparent—hyperactivity, impulsivity, and irritability. There may even be acting out of conflicts in such persons.

Low scorers (T scores less than 45) also are described in positive terms. They are considered dependable, reliable, mature, and conscientious. They frequently participate very little in social activities. They are unlikely to stir up excitement, swear, or talk too much.

Extremely low scores (T scores below 38 in most groups; discussed later) are described as apathetic, having little energy, and listless. Such persons usually are significantly depressed regardless of their score on Scale *2* (Depression). The possibility of serious depression should be considered when Scale *9* is in this range even if the rest of the profile is within normal limits. In fact, low scores on Scale *9* are generally better indicators of the presence of significant depression than high scores on Scale 2. The clinician should evaluate suicide potential in these clients, particularly if the client seems to be getting more energized.

Test-retest reliability coefficients for Scale 9 on the MMPI for intervals up to two weeks range from .63 to .96; for intervals up to one year they range from .43 to .64 (Dahlstrom et al., 1975). Test-retest reliability coefficients for Scale 9 on the MMPI-2 for approximately a one-week interval are .83 for men and .68 for women (Butcher et al., 1989).

There are no gender differences on Scale 9; in fact, identical T score conversions are used for both men and women in the standard MMPI profile, and their raw scores are very similar on the MMPI-2. Scores on Scale 9 decrease significantly with increasing age. Normal individuals (Butcher et al., 1989; Colligan et al., 1983), medical patients (Swenson et al., 1973), and psychiatric patients (Caldwell, 1997a) under the age of 20 have average T scores of nearly 60, while normal individuals and psychiatric patients 70 years of age and older average around 45. Thus, interpretations of high and low scores on Scale 9 must take into account these normal variations as a function of age. Clients whose scores on Scale 9 are 10 or more T points higher or lower than these expected ranges should be evaluated for the presence of a mood disorder. Education has no impact on Scale 9 in normal individuals or psychiatric patients except that psychiatric patients with less than an 11th grade education elevate Scale 9 3 to 4 T points.

A summary of the interpretations of four levels of elevation of Scale 9 is presented in Table 4.25.

Harris and Lingoes (1955) identified four subscales within Scale 9: Amorality (*Ma₁*), Psychomotor Acceleration (*Ma₂*), Imperturbability (*Ma₃*), and Ego Inflation (*Ma₄*) (Table 4.26, p. 172). There is little overlap between Comrey's factors and the Harris and Lingoes subscales. The Psychomotor Acceleration (*Ma₂*) subscale shares some items with thrill seeking and agitation, and Imperturbability (*Ma₃*) shares a few items with shyness.

SCALE 0: SOCIAL INTROVERSION (*Si*)

The 69 items in Scale 0 (Social Introversion) were selected to assess the social introversion-extroversion dimension with high scores reflecting social introversion. The social introvert is uncomfortable in social interactions and typically withdraws from such inter-

TABLE 4.25 Interpretation of Levels of Elevation on Scale 9 (Hypomania)

T SCORE	INTERPRETATION
44 and below	1. *Low.* These clients have a low energy and activity level that may reflect situational circumstances such as fatigue or actual depression. Extremely low scores ($T < 35$) indicate depression irrespective of the elevation on Scale 2. Normal persons over the age of 60 frequently score in the upper end of this range.
45–57	2. *Normal.* Normal college students and adolescents score in the upper end of this range or even slightly higher. These clients have a normal activity level.
58–64	3. *Moderate.* These clients are active, outgoing, and energetic. External restrictions on their activity level may result in agitation and overtly expressed dissatisfaction. Review of the Content and/or Supplementary scales may facilitate interpretation in this range.
65 and above	4. *Marked.* These clients are overactive, emotionally labile, and may experience flight of ideas. Although the client's mood is typically euphoric, outbursts of temper may occur. These clients are impulsive and may have an inability to delay gratification. Manic features become increasingly pronounced with more elevated scores. The narcissistic and grandiose features also become more apparent. Review of the Content and/or Supplementary scales may facilitate interpretation at the lower end of this range.

actions when possible. This individual may have limited social skills or simply prefer to be alone or with a small group of friends. The social extrovert is socially outgoing, gregarious, and seeks social interactions. Item content on Scale 0 reflects personal discomfort in social situations, isolation, general maladjustment, and self-deprecation.

Scale 0 was not based on a psychiatric syndrome; rather it was developed by using a psychological test—the Minnesota T-S-E Inventory (Evans & McConnell,

TABLE 4.26 Description of High Scorers on the Harris and Lingoes Subscales for Scale 9 (Hypomania)

| | SUBSCALE | | |
Name	Abbreviation	Number of Items	Description of High Scorers
Amorality	Ma_1	6	These clients have a callousness about their own motives and goals and those of other people; they are disarmingly frank; they deny guilt.
Psychomotor Acceleration	Ma_2	11	These clients are hyperactive and labile; they show flight from "inner life" and anxiety, and pressure for action.
Imperturbability	Ma_3	8	These clients are confident in social situations; they deny sensitivity; they proclaim independence from the opinions of other persons.
Ego Inflation	Ma_4	9	These clients feel self-important to the point of unrealistic grandiosity.

1941)—to form criterion groups. The Minnesota T-S-E Inventory assesses introversion-extroversion in three areas: thinking (T), social (S), and emotional (E).

Drake (1946) limited his investigation of introversion-extroversion to the social area as assessed by the Minnesota T-S-E Inventory. He selected items for Scale *0* by contrasting groups of students in the guidance program at the University of Wisconsin. Two groups were formed: 50 female students scoring above the 65th percentile on the social introversion-extroversion subscale of the Minnesota T-S-E Inventory, and 50 female students scoring below the 35th percentile. After those items were eliminated that had a very high or very low frequency of endorsement in either or both groups, 70 items were selected that discriminated these two groups. One of these items was deleted in the restandardization of the MMPI-2 resulting in the current 69 items on Scale *0*.

Drake (1946) later tested male students on Scale *0* and computed separate norms for men and women. The distributions of the total raw score for these two groups were so similar that Drake combined them into a single group to establish the norms on the MMPI.

Examples of items on Scale *0* with the deviant response in parentheses are:

"At parties I am more likely to sit by myself or with just one other person than to join in with the crowd." (true)

"Whenever possible I avoid being in a crowd." (true)

"If given the chance I would make a good leader of people." (false)[11]

There are 27 (39.1%) items unique to Scale *0*. It shares 8 items with Scale *7* (Psychasthenia) and 7 items with Scale *2* (Depression) that are scored in the same direction, and 8 items with the *K* (Correction) scale, 7 items with Scale *3* (Hysteria), 6 items with Scale *4* (Psychopathic Deviate), and 5 items with Scale *9* (Hypomania) that are scored in the opposite direction. Wiener and Harmon (Wiener, 1948) did not develop subtle and obvious subscales for Scale *0*. Christian et al. (1978) found that students rated Scale *0* items as being neutral, neither subtle nor obvious. There are almost exactly the same number of "true" (34) as "false" (35) deviant responses to Scale *0* items.

11. Minnesota Multiphasic Personality Inventory-2 (MMPI-2). Copyright © 1942, 1943 (renewed 1970), 1989 by the Regents of the University of Minnesota. Reproduced by permission of the publisher. "MMPI-2" and "Minnesota Multiphasic Personality Inventory-2" are trademarks owned by the University of Minnesota.

Scale *0* overlaps significantly with Wiggins' (1966) Social Maladjustment scale (21/27), which Wiggins characterized as corresponding roughly to an introversion-extroversion dimension. Scale *0* also has substantial item overlap with the Tryon, Stein, and Chu (Stein, 1968) Social Introversion scale (20/26). Regardless of the method of item grouping, a dimension of social introversion-extroversion appears to permeate the MMPI items.

Table 4.27 lists the 20 scales with the highest correlations with Scale *0* in the Caldwell (1997a) clinical sample. There are three categories represented within these scales: introversion (Shyness/Self-Consciousness; Introversion); social alienation (Social Discomfort; Alienation—Self and Others; Social Imperturbability); and general distress and negative emotionality (Welsh Anxiety; Subjective Depression; Work Interference; Psychasthenia; Low Self-Esteem; Total T Score Difference of Obvious and Subtle subscales; Post Traumatic Stress Disorder; Negative Treatment Indicators; College Maladjustment; Depression).

High scorers on Scale *0* (T scores of 65 or higher) in both psychiatric and normal populations are described similarly. They are seen as socially introverted, shy, and withdrawn. Patients also are described as insecure, pessimistic, self-deprecating, and anxious in their interactions with others (Graham et al., 1997). Scale *0* scores tend to be unrelated to psychopathology since elevations may reflect a schizoid withdrawal from interpersonal relationships, neurotic withdrawal, and self-deprecation as a function of personal distress, or merely an introverted orientation. In other words, the exact interpretation of Scale *0* will depend on the client's situation and the other Clinical scales that are elevated.

Low scorers (T scores less than 45) are essentially described as being extroverted. They are sociable, outgoing, and versatile in their interactions with others. They participate in many social activities. They may be unable to delay gratification and be undercontrolled emotionally.

Extremely low scorers (T scores below 35) are described as being flighty, superficial in their relationships with others, and lacking any real intimacy. These characteristics are especially likely if the client

TABLE 4.27 Correlations with Scale *0* (Social Introversion) in the Caldwell Clinical Dataset

SCALE *0* (SOCIAL INTROVERSION)		
Scale	*Abbreviation*	r
Social Discomfort	SOD	.892
Shyness/ Self-Consciousness	Si_1	.856
Edwards' Social Desirability	So	−.825
Introversion	SOD1	.825
Welsh Anxiety	A	.804
Subjective Depression	D1	.803
Work Interference	WRK	.800
Psychasthenia	Pt	.798
Low Self-Esteem	LSE	.791
Total T Score Difference of Obvious and Subtle Subscales	O - S	.788
Shyness	SOD2	.785
Postive Emotional Experience	PEE	−.785
Depression, Obvious	D-O	.782
Post Traumatic Stress Disorder—Keane	PK	.778
Negative Treatment Indicators	TRT	.777
College Maladjustment	Mt	.777
Post Traumatic Stress Disorder—Schlenger	PS	.776
Alienation—Self and Others	Si_3	.774
Social Imperturbability	Pd_3	−.769
Depression	DEP	.763

Note. All scales that are not described in this chapter are described in Chapters 5 and 6.

simultaneously elevates Scale *3* (Hysteria) or *4* (Psychopathic Deviate).

Elevation of Scale *0* typically suppresses the acting out seen with elevations of Scales *4* (Psychopathic Deviate) and *9* (Hypomania), whereas it may accentuate the ruminating behaviors seen with elevations on Scales *2* (Depression) or *7* (Psychasthenia) and especially Scale *8* (Schizophrenia).

Linear T scores are used on Scale *0* for the MMPI-2 as was the case on the MMPI. T scores on Scale *0* seldom get very high or very low. It is one of the few MMPI-2 scales on which linear T scores closely represent the frequency with which a score will be obtained (i.e., a T score of 65 or higher will occur two to three times in 100 cases). Consequently, clinicians can begin to interpret Scale *0* on the MMPI-2 when T scores reach 60 or higher and 40 or lower.

Test-retest reliability coefficients for Scale *0* on the MMPI usually are higher than for the other Clinical scales. Correlations for intervals up to two weeks range from .80 to .96 and for intervals up to one year from .54 to .76 (Dahlstrom et al., 1975). Test-retest reliability coefficients for Scale *0* on the MMPI-2 for approximately a one-week interval are .92 for men and .91 for women (Butcher et al., 1989).

Although there were no gender differences on Scale *0* on the MMPI as noted earlier, women endorse 2 more items than men on the MMPI-2. These gender differences will not affect the interpretation of Scale *0*, however, which is based on T scores by gender. Scores on Scale *0* seemingly are unaffected by age in normal samples (Butcher et al., 1989; Colligan et al., 1983, 1989), medical patients (Swenson et al., 1973), or psychiatric patients (Caldwell, 1997a; Hedlund & Won Cho, 1979). Scores on Scale *0* decrease 5 to 6 T points in normal individuals (Butcher et al., 1989) and psychiatric patients (Caldwell, 1997a) with increasing years of education. Scale *0* appears to have an important role in marital relationships. Couples with T scores on Scale *0* that differ by 20 points or more will frequently report marital conflicts over their social relationships. One partner prefers to be alone or with small groups of friends while the other prefers larger social functions. This difference in social orientation may have appealed to them initially, but it can become a source of marital conflict.

A summary of the interpretations of four levels of elevation of Scale *0* is given in Table 4.28.

Comrey (1957a) did not factor analyze the items on Scale *0*. Ward and Perry (1998) identified three factors on Scale *0* in a group of psychiatric patients and substance abusers: *insecurity, low assertion,* and *social inhibition.* Harris and Lingoes (1955) did not attempt to create subscales for this scale. Serkownek (1975) used the results of Graham et al.'s (1971) factor analysis to create six subscales for Scale *0:* Inferiority and Discomfort, Affiliation, Social Excitement, Sensi-

TABLE 4.28 Interpretation of Levels of Elevation on Scale *0* (Social Introversion)

T SCORE	INTERPRETATION
44 and below	1. *Low.* These clients are socially extroverted, gregarious, and socially poised. A person with an extremely low score ($T < 35$) may have very superficial social relationships without any real depth. The clinician should be very cautious of labeling these clients schizophrenic.
45–57	2. *Normal.* These clients report a balance between socially extroverted and introverted attitudes and behaviors.
58–64	3. *Moderate.* These clients prefer to be alone or with a small group of friends. They have the ability to interact with others, but generally prefer not to. Review of the Content and/or Supplementary scales may facilitate interpretation in this range.
65 and above	4. *Marked.* These clients are introverted, shy, and socially insecure. In addition, they withdraw from and avoid significant others, which serves to exacerbate their problems since others might be able to help them. The likelihood of acting out is decreased and ruminative behavior is increased. Intervention should specifically address the client's tendency to withdraw. Review of the Content and/or Supplementary scales may facilitate interpretation at the lower end of this range.

tivity, Interpersonal Trust, and Physical-Somatic Concerns. Williams (1983) found that Serkownek's subscales were in the acceptable ranges of reliability in college students and provided preliminary interpretive information for men and women.

Ben-Porath, Hostetler, Butcher, and Graham (1989) developed new content-homogeneous subscales for Scale *0* as an alternative to the Serkownek (1975) subscales. Ben-Porath et al. identified three subscales in college students: Shyness/Self-Consciousness (Si_1), Social Avoidance (Si_2), and Alienation—Self and Others (Si_3) (Table 4.29). These three subscales accounted for nearly 90 percent of the variance in Scale

0 scores. Based on their factor analyses of the items on Scale *0,* Ward and Perry (1998) concluded that the Shyness/Self-Consciousness (Si_1) and Social Avoidance (Si_2) subscales are related to the construct of social introversion, while the Alienation—Self and Others (Si_3) scale is a measure of negative emotionality. Sieber and Meyers (1992) examined the correlates of these subscales in college students and found that high scorers on the Shyness/Self-Consciousness (Si_1) subscale were more alienated, less social, and had self-esteem. High scorers on the Social Avoidance (Si_2) subscale actively attempted to escape social events and tended to be shy. Finally, high scorers on the Alienation—Self and Others (Si_3) subscale had lowered self-esteem, were more publicly self-conscious, and less social.

ITEM OVERLAP AMONG MMPI-2 SCALES

Table 4.30 summarizes the item overlap and intercorrelations among the MMPI-2 Clinical scales. The information on item overlap already has been presented individually for each scale. Table 4.30 (p. 176) allows the reader to appreciate the impact of item overlap among all of the Clinical scales at one time. It is readily apparent that among the Validity scales, the *L* (Lie) scale shares items with few scales, the *F* (Infrequency) scale primarily shares items with Scales *6*

(Paranoia) and *8* (Schizophrenia), while the *K* (Correction) scale shares items with Scales *2* (Depression), *3* (Hysteria), and *4* (Psychopathic Deviate). Higher scores on the *F* scale and lower scores on the *K* scale reflect more problems or symptoms, which produce the negative correlation between them (–.57). Both the *F* and *K* scales have substantial correlations (positive and negative, respectively) with most of the Clinical scales except for Scale *5* (Masculinity-Femininity), even those scales with which they share minimal item overlap.

Most of the Clinical scales except for Scale *5* (Masculinity-Femininity) also have substantial correlations (> .50) regardless of the number of items that are shared. The magnitude of the correlation is not a simple function of the number of shared items. For example, Scale *1* (Hypochondriasis) correlates .795 with Scale *3* (Hysteria) with which it shares 20 items, and .770 with Scale *7* (Psychasthenia) with which it only shares 2 items. Scale *9* (Hypomania) tends to have the lowest correlations among the Clinical scales. The substantial correlations among the MMPI-2 Validity and Clinical scales mean that they are not independent measures, which is a frequent assumption of statistical tests.

Table 4.31 (pp. 177–178) presents the unique items for each of the Clinical scales. These items provide insight into the item content that is unique to each of the Clinical scales.

TABLE 4.29 Description of High Scorers on the Ben-Porath et al. Subscales for Scale *0* (Social Introversion)

SUBSCALE			
Name	*Abbreviation*	*Number of Items*	*Description of High Scorers*
Shyness/Self-Consciousness	Si_1	14	These clients are shy around others and easily embarrassed. They are uncomfortable in social and new situations, and avoid contact with people.
Social Avoidance	Si_2	8	These clients dislike and avoid group activities of all types, and act to keep people at a distance.
Alienation—Self and Others	Si_3	17	These clients have low self-esteem and lack self-confidence. They question their own judgment. They are nervous, fearful, and indecisive. They lack interest in things.

TABLE 4.30 Item Overlap and Intercorrelations among the MMPI-2 Validity and Clinical Scales in the Caldwell Clinical Dataset

	L S	L O	F S	F O	K S	K O	1(Hs) S	1(Hs) O	2(D) S	2(D) O	3(Hy) S	3(Hy) O	4(Pd) S	4(Pd) O	5(Mff) S	5(Mff) O	5(Mfm) S	5(Mfm) O	6(Pa) S	6(Pa) O	7(Pt) S	7(Pt) O	8(Sc) S	8(Sc) O	9(Ma) S	9(Ma) O	0(Si) S	0(Si) O
L	—	—	1	0	0	0	0	0	2	0	0	0	0	0	1	0	1	0	0	0	0	0	0	0	2	0	0	0
F	-.154		—	—	0	0	1	0	2	0	1	0	4	0	2	0	2	0	9	0	1	0	15	0	1	0	0	0
K	.427		-.570		—	—	0	0	6	2	10	0	7	1	1	2	1	2	2	0	0	2	1	0	4	0	1	8
1(Hs)	-.075		.624		-.508		—	—	9	1	20	0	1	0	0	0	0	0	1	0	2	0	4	0	0	0	0	0
2(D)	-.045		.584		-.431		.818		—	—	13	0	7	0	2	0	2	0	2	0	13	0	9	0	1	4	1	1
3(Hy)	.081		.363		-.072		.795		.724		—	—	10	0	3	1	3	1	4	0	7	0	8	0	4	2	7	1
4(Pd)	-.307		.695		-.537		.538		.587		.387		—	—	2	1	1	2	8	0	6	0	10	0	6	1	5	6
5(Mff)	-.079		-.042		-.022		.133		.217		.237		.067		—	—	52	4	2	0	1	0	1	3	3	0	6	3
5(Mfm)	-.182		.086		-.159		.208		.272		.259		.196		.935		—	—	2	0	1	0	3	1	3	0	5	4
6(Pa)	-.144		.714		-.426		.586		.594		.479		.663		.124		.221		—	—	1	0	3	1	4	2	5	4
7(Pt)	-.313		.752		-.755		.770		.804		.499		.725		.146		.277		.696		—	—	13	0	4	2	4	4
8(Sc)	-.270		.869		-.720		.767		.731		.481		.763		.049		.202		.749		.925		—	—	11	0	1	1
9(Ma)	-.235		.488		-.522		.331		.125		.079		.469		-.121		.008		.386		.457		.557		—	—	1	5
0(Si)	-.149		.638		-.641		.617		.731		.313		.539		.140		.207		.511		.798		.743		.141		—	—

Note. "S" indicates that the deviant response for the item is the same on both scales; "O" indicates that the deviant response is "true" on one scale and "false" on the other scale.

TABLE 4.31 Unique Items on MMPI-2 Clinical Scales

1 (Hs)   Total: 7 Items

TRUE					**FALSE**				
28	53	59	97	111	57				
149									

2 (D)   Total: 13 Items

TRUE					**FALSE**				
5					37	43	75	118	134
					142	178	188	223	245
					260	330			

3 (Hy)   Total: 13 Items

TRUE					**FALSE**				
40	172	230			7	14	58	115	116
					124	151	159	213	241

4 (Pd)   Total: 15 Items

TRUE					**FALSE**				
52	54	71	105	195	83	160	171	214	217
202	225	264	288		261				

5 (Mf)   Total: 33 Items

TRUE					**FALSE**				
1	19	27	63	69	4	62	64	67	74
103	120	132	133	163	80	119	121	128	137
184	194	197	199	201	187	191	236		
235	239	254	257	272					

6 (Pa)   Total: 12 Items

TRUE					**FALSE**				
24	144	162	305	334	283	286	297	314	315
336	361								

7 (Pt)   Total: 10 Items

TRUE					**FALSE**				
301	304	309	310	313	174	293			
317	327	331							

8 (Sc)   Total: 26 Items

TRUE					**FALSE**				
48	180	252	274	279	6	90	192	210	276
281	287	291	292	298	278	290	295	343	
299	303	311	319	322					
323	332								

(continued)

TABLE 4.31 Unique Items on MMPI-2 Clinical Scales (continued)

9 (Ma)									Total: 16 Items
TRUE					**FALSE**				
50	61	87	155	169	88	93	136	154	
200	206	211	220	227					
250	269								

0 (Si)									Total: 27 Items
TRUE					**FALSE**				
337	338	347	348	351	262	335	340	342	344
352	357	364	367	368	345	350	353	354	358
369					359	360	362	363	366
					370				

Table 4.32 provides the correlations among the demographic variables of age, education, and gender and the Clinical scales in the MMPI-2 normative group (Butcher et al., 1989) and the Caldwell (1997a) clinical dataset. (Chapter 9 will be devoted entirely to the examination of the effects of demographic variables on MMPI-2 performance so this discussion will be brief.) Scales *4* (Psychopathic Deviate) and *9* (Hypomania) have the largest correlations with age in normal individuals. Individuals 70 years of age and older in the MMPI-2 normative group had a mean T score of 44.8 and 46.6 on these two scales, respectively, while individuals 20 to 29 years old had a mean T score of 51.5 and 53.1, respectively (Table 9.3). Thus, age will modify any Clinical scale less than 7 or 8 T points at the most, and less than 5 T points more

TABLE 4.32 Effects of Demographic Variables on the MMPI-2 Clinical Scales

	CORRELATION					
	Age		*Gender*[a]		*Education*	
	NORMALS[b]	PATIENTS[c]	NORMALS[b]	PATIENTS[c]	NORMALS[b]	PATIENTS[c]
1(Hs)	0.085	0.164	0.117	0.166	−0.254	−0.199
2(D)	0.129	0.149	0.185	0.183	−0.124	−0.146
3(Hy)	0.086	0.185	0.126	0.196	0.067	−0.066
4(Pd)	−0.227	−0.052	−0.039	−0.017	−0.102	−0.159
5(Mff)	0.024	0.056	0.691	0.659	0.131	0.117
5(Mfm)	−0.088	0.032	0.640	0.598	0.137	0.102
6(Pa)	−0.161	0.005	0.022	0.047	0.028	−0.113
7(Pt)	−0.110	0.036	0.103	0.105	−0.187	−0.192
8(Sc)	−0.141	0.027	0.002	0.047	−0.182	−0.213
9(Ma)	−0.213	−0.101	−0.089	−0.080	−0.097	−0.156
0(Si)	0.064	0.086	0.116	0.103	−0.169	−0.181

[a]Positive correlations reflect that women have higher scores on the indicated scale.
[b]Butcher et al., 1989.
[c]Caldwell, 1997a.

typically. The correlations with age are smaller in the psychiatric patients than in the normal individuals. The largest correlations in the psychiatric patients were on Scales *1* (Hypochondriasis), *2* (Depression), and *3* (Hysteria). There were approximately 5 to 8 T points differences between patients 70 years of age and older and patients 20 to 29 years old.

The correlations of the Clinical scales with gender tend to be similar in normal individuals and psychiatric patients. (A positive correlation with gender in Table 4.32 reflects that women have higher scores on the scale.) The largest correlations are with Scale *5* (Masculinity-Femininity) as would be expected. Women tend to have raw scores that are two to three points higher than men's (Table 9.9). Since all of the Clinical scales are expressed as T scores, these differences in raw scores will not affect their interpretation.

The correlations of the Clinical scales with education also are very similar in normal individuals and psychiatric patients. The largest correlations are with Scale *1* (Hypochondriasis). Normal individuals and psychiatric patients with less than a 9th grade education have a mean T score of 54.8 and 66.1 on Scale *1*, respectively, while normal individuals and psychiatric patients with 19 or more years of education have a mean T score of 49.0 and 56.9, respectively (Table 9.15). This difference of almost 10 T points in psychiatric patients illustrates how aware clinicians need to be of the effects of education on MMPI-2 interpretation.

Table 4.33 provides the percentage of items on each Clinical scale for which "true" and "false" are the deviant responses. As noted earlier, Scales *1* (Hypochondriasis), *2* (Depression), and *3* (Hysteria) typically have "false" as the deviant response, while Scales *6* (Paranoia), *7* (Psychasthenia), *8* (Schizophrenia), and *9* (Hypomania) typically have "true" as the deviant response. The clinician should note the percentage of items that the client has endorsed "true" and "false" *before* beginning to interpret the MMPI-2 profile to ascertain whether a response set is a major

TABLE 4.33 True and False Composition and Obviousness Ratings of the MMPI-2 Clinical Scales

	PERCENTAGE		
	True	*False*	*Obviousness*[a]
1(Hs)	34.4	65.6	3.14
2(D)	35.1	64.9	2.95
3(Hy)	22.7	78.3	2.85
4(Pd)	48.0	52.0	3.13
5(Mff)	44.6	55.4	2.17
5(Mfm)	41.1	58.9	2.23
6(Pa)	62.5	37.5	3.52
7(Pt)	81.2	18.8	3.48
8(Sc)	75.6	24.4	3.67
9(Ma)	76.1	23.9	2.88
0(Si)	52.2	47.8	2.68

[a]Ratings by a college sample of the degree of obviousness of the content of each item (Christian, Burkhart, & Gynther, 1978).

contributor to the elevation of either set of scales. Profiles 3.12 and 3.13 (pp. 123–124) illustrated the effects of endorsing all of the items "true" or "false" on each of the MMPI-2 Clinical scales, respectively.

Table 4.33 also provides the mean rating of the obviousness of the content of the items on each of the Clinical scales. These ratings are based on the research of Christian et al. (1978) who asked college students to rate how clearly the content of each MMPI item was indicative of a psychological problem when it was endorsed "true" and when it was endorsed "false." Very obvious items were assigned a rating of 5, obvious a rating of 4, neither obvious nor subtle a rating of 3, subtle a rating of 2, and very subtle a rating of 1. Most of the Clinical scales are rated as being neither obvious nor subtle with mean scores around 3.00. Scales *7* (Psychasthenia) and *8* (Schizophrenia) have the highest ratings for obviousness of content and Scale *5* (Masculinity-Femininity) has the lowest mean rating.

CHAPTER 5

Content Scales, Content Component Scales, and the MMPI-2 Structural Summary

MMPI

The content of individual items basically was ignored in the development of the original MMPI scales because at that time methods of item selection that relied extensively on item content had fallen into disfavor. Since these issues were reviewed in Chapter 1, they will not be reiterated here. Numerous investigators (cf. Jackson, 1971), however, believed that item content should not be ignored in test construction or interpretation.

Wiggins' (1966) Content scales represent a systematic attempt to develop a means of examining the client's responses to the content of individual MMPI items, and the Butcher et al. (1990) Content scales reflect a similar approach on the MMPI-2. Since Wiggins' Content scales were developed prior to Butcher et al.'s Content scales on the MMPI-2, Wiggins' scales will be reviewed first. Clinicians' interest in critical items, discussed in Chapter 6, reflect a similar interest in item content.

The first two levels of Leary's multilevel interpersonal circumplex (1956, 1957) are helpful in understanding the relationship between the Content and Clinical scales on the MMPI-2. Leary categorizes Level I data as those which are concerned with how a person is described by others. The data at Level I are objective and public, and may or may not agree with the person's own view of himself or herself or circumstances. It is this level that is reflected in the MMPI-2 Clinical scales. By contrast, Level II data are conscious descriptions of the person's phenomenological experience of his or her behavior, symptoms, traits, and relations with others. Content scales are especially sensitive to data at this level. Again, the person's self-report may well not coincide with how

others see him or her. These levels and their corresponding sets of scales reflect points of view and should not be considered to be mutually exclusive.

Wiggins (1966) began by grouping the MMPI items into the 26-item content categories (Table 1.2, p. 5), originally proposed by Hathaway and McKinley (1940). He then applied both psychometric and intuitive procedures to produce 13 substantive dimensions of item content. He developed his Content scales on normal college students and validated them on additional normal populations and a psychiatric sample.

Wiggins selected the items for the Content scales so that they did not share common items with one another and so that scale homogeneity was maximized; each Content scale was constructed to be a homogeneous measure of its substantive dimension that did not overlap with other scales. The name and abbreviation of each of these 13 scales appear in Table 5.1.

Research on the Wiggins Content scales has consistently supported their validity and generalizability to new populations. Wiggins, Goldberg, and Appelbaum (1971), Jarnecke and Chambers (1977), and Mezzich, Damarin, and Erickson (1974) found that the Content scales demonstrated the expected relationships to other test measures and behaviors. For example, clients who elevated the Wiggins Depression scale were more likely to exhibit depressive behaviors and to elevate other tests that measured depression than clients who did not elevate this scale.

Jarnecke and Chambers (1977), Lachar and Alexander (1978), and Mezzich et al. (1974) found that the Content scales were generalizable to psychiatric inpatients and Air Force personnel. Payne and Wiggins (1972) reported that hospitalized patients with the same codetype, as defined by the Gilberstadt and

TABLE 5.1   Items from the Wiggins' Content Scales Retained on the MMPI-2

WIGGINS' CONTENT SCALE	ITEMS ON MMPI SCALE	NUMBER OF ITEMS RETAINED ON MMPI-2	
Poor Health	28	19	(67.9%)
Depression	33	33	(100.0%)
Organic Symptoms	36	32	(88.9%)
Family Problems	16	16	(100.0%)
Authority Conflict	20	20	(100.0%)
Feminine Interests	30	23	(76.7%)
Religious Fundamentalism	12	1	(8.3%)
Manifest Hostility	27	25	(92.6%)
Poor Morale	23	22	(95.7%)
Phobias	27	26	(96.3%)
Psychoticism	48	45	(93.8%)
Hypomania	25	23	(92.0%)
Social Maladjustment	27	26	(96.3%)

Duker (1965) profile classification system, tended to produce similar scores on the Content scales, and these scores were consistent with the established correlates of the codetype. Consequently, it seems that the Wiggins Content scales adequately assess their respective dimensions, and they can be generalized to new populations with little, if any, loss in predictive power.

Nichols (1987) has provided an excellent overview of the Wiggins Content scales and their relationship with their respective Clinical scales as well as illustrative cases. Nichols' monograph should be consulted by every clinician who is interested in learning more about these scales. Greene (1991, pp. 195–199) provides a briefer overview of the Wiggins Content scales that can be consulted by the interested reader.

Most of the items on the Wiggins content scales have been retained on the MMPI-2 (Table 5.1 and Kohutek, 1992a). Kohutek (1992b) found that the deleted items did not statistically alter scores on the Wiggins Content scales in psychiatric patients, so clinicians can continue to use these scales if desired. All the items on the Religious Fundamentalism scale

have been eliminated except for a single item that precludes its use on the MMPI-2.

MMPI-2

Butcher et al. (1990) followed procedures similar to those of Wiggins in developing new content scales for the MMPI-2. Butcher began to develop the MMPI-2 Content scales by sorting the 704 items of the AX booklet (the original 550 items from the MMPI plus 154 additional new items that were under consideration for inclusion in the MMPI-2) into 22 provisional categories. These content categories were developed from an examination of Hathaway and McKinley's original categories, the results of a large-scale replicated item factor analysis of the MMPI (Johnson, Null, Butcher, & Johnson, 1984), and a review of the newly written items for the MMPI-2. He then produced definitions for each category and, with the assistance of Graham and Williams, assigned items to them. Provisional content scales were established from sets of items agreed to by at least two of these three authors. They then discussed the composition of each of the provisional scales, item by item, until consensus was reached. Twenty-one revised provisional scales remained after one was dropped because of an insufficient number of items. Four of the revised provisional scales were found to have unacceptably low internal consistencies and were dropped from further development. At this stage, however, a new provisional scale, Cynicism, was added bringing the number of scales for continuing investigation to 18. Computation of the correlations between the purified scales and each of the remaining items in the MMPI-AX item pool was undertaken to add new items that strengthened the internal consistency of these scales, but that had not heretofore been identified as belonging to the content domain of the scale. These purified and augmented scales then were subjected to a rational review to determine if the provisional name and definition of the scale needed refinement, and to identify and eliminate any items having an insufficient content affinity for the scale even though their statistical association was strong. At this stage, two scales were combined and two others were dropped, leaving 15 scales. In the next step, items were identified that were more highly correlated with other scales and they either were eliminated or reassigned. In this stage, overlapping items were permitted so long as the scales sharing items were related conceptually. In the final step, uniform T scores were created and rational descriptions based upon each scale's final item content were composed. Caldwell (1991) and Nichols (1992) have provided reviews of Butcher et al. (1990) that can be consulted by the interested reader.

Ben-Porath and Sherwood (1993) have developed subscales for most of the Content scales that they called Content Component scales. These Content Component scales will be described within their respective Content scale. It is important to realize that there are a number of these Content Component scales for which the maximum possible T score is less than 75 and occasionally less than 70 (Appendix A.8). In men these scales and the highest possible T score are: Irritability (*ANG2*), 72; Interpersonal Suspiciousness (*CYN2*), 71; and Impatience (*TPA1*), 68. In women these scales are: Multiple Fears (*FRS2*), 69; Irritability (*ANG2*), 72; Interpersonal Suspiciousness (*CYN2*), 73; Impatience (*TPA1*), 70; and Shyness (*SOD2*), 69.

The final MMPI-2 Content scales and their respective Content Component scales and abbreviations are listed in Table 5.2. An easy means of beginning to understand each Content scale is to review the actual items on each scale (see Appendix B.6 for the item numbers or Butcher et al. [1990, pp. 192–199] for a listing of the Content scale items and Appendix B.7 or Ben-Porath and Sherwood [1993, pp. 43–48] for the Content Component scale items). As can be seen in Table 5.2, most of the items on the MMPI-2 Content scales are from the original MMPI item pool except for the Low Self-Esteem (*LSE*), Work Interference (*WRK*), and Negative Treatment Indicators (*TRT*) scales. That is, the MMPI-2 Content scales are not composed primarily of new items.

Before describing the MMPI-2 Content scales in detail, it may be helpful to compare the Wiggins and MMPI-2 Content scales. Table 5.3 (p. 184) presents the item overlap and intercorrelations between the MMPI-2 Content scales and the Wiggins Content scales. Despite having similar names, differences often appear upon closer examination. Only two Content scales (Fears [*FRS*] and Phobias; Bizarre

Mentation [*BIZ*] and Psychoticism) have substantial item overlap. The Wiggins Depression scale and the MMPI-2 Content scale of Depression (*DEP*) have only 16 of their 33 items in common, and both of these scales have few items in common with Scale 2 (Depression). Six (18%) of the original Wiggins Depression items now appear on the MMPI-2 Content scale of Anxiety (*ANX*). Eight (24%) of the items on the *DEP* scale are from the 107 newly written items for the MMPI-2, including three of the four new items with suicidal content. Whether these three "Depression" scales are measuring different facets of depressive phenomenology or different types of depression remains to be determined.

Similarly, the Wiggins Family Problems scale and the MMPI-2 Content scale of Family Problems (*FAM*) have only 10 items in common. Eight of the 27 items on the Wiggins Hostility scale now appear on the MMPI-2 Anger (*ANG*) scale, and 9 appear on the MMPI-2 Type A Behavior (*TPA*) scale. Thirteen of the 36 items on the MMPI-2 Health Concerns (*HEA*) scale formerly were on the Wiggins Poor Health scale, but 20, more than half of the items on the MMPI-2 *HEA* scale, were taken from the Wiggins Organic Symptoms scale. Nine items, including four with genitourinary and three with bowel content, were among those dropped in the MMPI-2 item pool that were formerly on the Wiggins Poor Health scale.

The changes just described, while unsuspected from the names of the scales, are apt to have significant consequences for the interpretation of the MMPI-2 Content scales and their empirical correlates. In the case of the MMPI-2 Content scale of Depression (*DEP*), the loss of its "anxiety" content and the addition of items denoting suicidal ideation should strengthen its performance as a measure of depressive symptomatology. Although not necessarily a superior measure of somatic preoccupation or overconcern than its Wiggins predecessor, the MMPI-2 Health Concerns (*HEA*) scale, with its shift toward symptoms localized to the head and musculature and away from lower gastrointestinal and genitourinary content, should show a corresponding shift in its empirical correlates. As a result of these and other differences between the Wiggins and MMPI-2 Content scales to be described further later, clinicians familiar with the

TABLE 5.2   Source of Items on the MMPI-2 Content and Content Component Scales

CONTENT AND COMPONENT SCALES	ABBREVIATION	NUMBER OF ITEMS	MMPI ITEMS	NEW ITEMS
Anxiety	ANX	23	20	3
Fears	FRS	23	22	1
Generalized Fearfulness	FRS1	12	11	1
Multiple Fears	FRS2	10	10	0
Obsessions	OBS	16	10	6
Depression	DEP	33	25	8
Lack of Drive	DEP1	12	8	4
Dysphoria	DEP2	6	6	0
Self-Deprecation	DEP3	7	6	1
Suicidal Ideation	DEP4	5	2	3
Health Concerns	HEA	36	36	0
Gastrointestinal Symptoms	HEA1	5	5	0
Neurological Symptoms	HEA2	12	12	0
General Health Concerns	HEA3	6	6	0
Bizarre Mentation	BIZ	23	19	4
Psychotic Symptomatology	BIZ1	11	9	2
Schizotypal Characteristics	BIZ2	9	8	1
Anger	ANG	16	10	6
Explosive Behavior	ANG1	7	4	3
Irritability	ANG2	7	4	3
Cynicism	CYN	23	21	2
Misanthropic Beliefs	CYN1	15	13	2
Interpersonal Suspiciousness	CYN2	8	8	0
Antisocial Practices	ASP	22	21	1
Antisocial Attitudes	ASP1	16	15	1
Antisocial Behavior	ASP2	5	5	0
Type A	TPA	19	12	7
Impatience	TPA1	6	3	3
Competitive Drive	TPA2	9	6	3
Low Self-Esteem	LSE	24	13	11
Self-Doubt	LSE1	11	8	3
Submissiveness	LSE2	6	4	2
Social Discomfort	SOD	24	21	3
Introversion	SOD1	16	14	2
Shyness	SOD2	7	6	0
Family Problems	FAM	25	16	9
Family Discord	FAM1	12	8	4
Familial Alienation	FAM2	5	3	2
Work Interference	WRK	33	22	11
Negative Treatment Indicators	TRT	26	8	18
Low Motivation	TRT1	11	3	8
Inability to Disclose	TRT2	5	2	3

Note. Scale names, abbreviations, and items are from Butcher et al. (1990) for the Content scales and from Ben-Porath and Sherwood (1993) for the Content Component scales.

TABLE 5.3 Item Overlap and Intercorrelations between the MMPI-2 and Wiggins Content Scales

	ITEMS			
MMPI-2	N	*Overlap*[a]	r	*Wiggins*
Anxiety (*ANX*)	23	6 (26.1%)	.894	Depression
Fears (*FRS*)	23	19 (82.6%)	.948	Phobias
Obsessions (*OBS*)	16			None
Depression (*DEP*)	33	16 (48.5%)	.959	Depression
Health Concerns (*HEA*)	36	13 (36.1%)	.916	Poor Health
Health Concerns (*HEA*)	36	20 (55.5%)	.941	Organic Symptoms
Bizarre Mentation (*BIZ*)	23	19 (82.6%)	.920	Psychoticism
Anger (*ANG*)	16	8 (50.0%)	.867	Hostility
Cynicism (*CYN*)	23	12 (52.2%)	.885	Authority Conflict
Antisocial Practices (*ASP*)	22	12 (54.5%)	.903	Authority Conflict
Type A (*TPA*)	19	9 (47.4%)	.865	Hostility
Low Self-Esteem (*LSE*)	24	6 (25.0%)	.894	Poor Morale
Social Discomfort (*SOD*)	24	16 (66.7%)	.943	Social Maladjustment
Family Problems (*FAM*)	25	10 (40.0%)	.908	Family Problems
Work Interference (*WRK*)	33			None
Negative Treatment Indicators (*TRT*)	26			None

[a]The percentages indicate the number of items on the Wiggins Content scale that are also on the corresponding MMPI-2 Content scale.

Wiggins Content scales cannot assume that their knowledge of the former set of scales can be transferred directly to the MMPI-2 Content scales.

There is a substantial degree of item overlap within the MMPI-2 Content scales (Table 5.4) unlike the Wiggins (1966) Content scales that have no overlapping items. Only three scales (Fears [*FRS*], Health Concerns [*HEA*], and Social Discomfort [*SOD*]) have no items in common with the other Content scales. Four scales (Obsessions [*OBS*], Cynicism [*CYN*], Work Interference [*WRK*], and Negative Treatment Indicators [*TRT*]) have almost one-half of their items in common with the other Content scales. There also is a substantial degree of correlation or shared variance among most of these scales (Table 5.4). Only the *FRS* and *HEA* scales have correlations that tend to be below .600 with the other Content scales.

The MMPI-2 Content scales are organized around four themes: internal symptoms, external or aggressive tendencies, a devalued view of the self,

and general problem areas. The internal symptoms cluster, the Anxiety (*ANX*), Fears (*FRS*), Obsessions (*OBS*), Depression (*DEP*), Health Concerns (*HEA*), and Bizarre Mentation (*BIZ*) scales, is oriented toward Axis I disorders. The external or aggressive tendencies cluster, the Anger (*ANG*), Cynicism (*CYN*), Antisocial Practices (*ASP*), and Type A (*TPA*) scales, is directed toward the Axis II disorders. The devalued view of the self category contains only one scale: the Low Self-Esteem (*LSE*) scale. The general problem areas assessed include the Social Discomfort (*SOD*), Family Problems (*FAM*), Work Interference (*WRK*), and Negative Treatment Indicators (*TRT*) scales. Although these themes may appear conceptually distinct, they are not independent in a statistical sense as was seen in their relatively high positive intercorrelations (Table 5.4).

Several precautionary statements need to be made about the MMPI-2 Content scales before beginning to discuss the interpretation of each individual

TABLE 5.4 Item Overlap and Intercorrelations among the MMPI-2 Content Scales in the Caldwell Clinical Dataset

	ANX	FRS	OBS	DEP	HEA	BIZ	ANG	CYN	ASP	TPA	LSE	SOD	FAM	WRK	TRT
ANX	–	0	2	0	0	0	0	0	0	0	0	0	0	5	0
FRS	.530	–	0	0	0	0	0	0	0	0	0	0	0	0	0
OBS	.808	.517	–	0	0	0	0	0	0	0	0	0	0	4	3
DEP	.854	.485	.786	–	0	0	0	1	0	0	2	0	0	1	6
HEA	.737	.537	.599	.683	–	0	0	0	0	0	0	0	0	0	0
BIZ	.580	.495	.639	.623	.552	–	0	0	0	0	0	0	1	0	0
ANG	.685	.385	.689	.679	.529	.574	–	0	0	3	0	0	0	1	0
CYN	.557	.399	.630	.582	.455	.613	.614	–	7	1	0	0	0	1	1
ASP	.415	.242	.518	.468	.298	.534	.585	.791	–	1	0	0	0	0	0
TPA	.608	.373	.652	.574	.443	.552	.773	.675	.612	–	0	0	0	2	0
LSE	.758	.496	.806	.847	.587	.589	.612	.561	.455	.541	–	0	0	1	2
SOD	.570	.372	.552	.633	.461	.386	.432	.403	.290	.385	.642	–	0	0	0
FAM	.596	.376	.642	.652	.441	.592	.649	.585	.545	.588	.635	.433	–	1	0
WRK	.878	.528	.869	.885	.692	.625	.703	.623	.493	.645	.864	.644	.655	–	4
TRT	.788	.511	.818	.891	.625	.638	.667	.642	.527	.608	.865	.648	.645	.881	–

Content scale. First, since the MMPI-2 Content scales are obvious measures of symptomatology, it is possible for the client to present an inaccurate self-description. High scores (T scores of 65 or higher) may be the result of the client's accurate description of the presence of these symptoms or the client's overreporting of them. Similarly, low scores (T scores less than 45) on the MMPI-2 Content scales could represent the client's accurate description of the absence of these symptoms or the client's refusal to acknowledge the presence of such symptoms.

Second, the deviant response for a majority of the items on the MMPI-2 Content scales is "true," so a score on the True Response Inconsistency (TRIN) scale of 12 or higher would be expected to increase elevations on most of these scales, while a score on the TRIN scale of 6 or lower would be expected to lower elevations.

Third, a number of the items on these scales are clustered in the last 100 items so any waning of the client's motivation toward the end of the test could adversely affect these scales.

The procedures described in Chapter 3 for assessing the accuracy of item endorsement should be followed routinely and particularly when the clinician is interested in interpreting the MMPI-2 Content scales. It will be assumed in the following description of each MMPI-2 Content scale that the client has endorsed the items accurately so that the focus can be placed on interpreting the content of the client's responses.

Each Content scale will be described in turn in the following sections. In this discussion, high scores or elevated scores will denote T scores of 65 or higher on the scale in question, while low scores will denote T scores of 45 or lower unless indicated otherwise. When one Content scale is said to be higher than another, a difference of at least 10 T points is required because of the large amount of generalized distress and negative emotionality or first-factor variance that produces similar elevations and positive intercorrelations (Table 5.4) among all of these scales.

Anxiety (ANX)

The Anxiety (ANX) scale contains 23 items of which 18 have "true" as the deviant response. The ANX scale has the highest correlations with Scales 7 (Psychasthenia: .912) and 8 (Schizophrenia: .833), and with the Welsh Anxiety (A: .902), College Maladjustment (Mt: .930), Post Traumatic Stress Disorder—Keane

(*PK*: .893), and Post Traumatic Stress Disorder—Schlenger (*PS*: .913) scales. The primary theme in the *ANX* scale is generalized distress and negative emotionality that has an anxious flavor. Specifically anxious features will dominate the clinical presentation only when the *ANX* scale is elevated clearly above other first-factor measures of generalized distress and negative emotionality (*A, Mt, PK,* and *PS*).

Ben-Porath and Sherwood (1993) did not identify Content Component scales within the *ANX* scale. Ward (1997) identified two factors within the *ANX* scale in male substance abusers: *ANX*-Trait and *ANX*-Worry. The first factor consisted of items descriptive of proclivities to anxiety and symptoms or subjective feelings of anxiety. The second factor consisted of items pertaining to worrying or obsessional thinking.

The *ANX* scale is a major source of variance in predicting scores on a number of scales on the Symptom Checklist-90-Revised (SCL-90-R: Derogatis, 1983) and the Brief Psychiatric Rating Scale (BPRS: Overall & Gorham, 1962) in psychiatric patients (Archer, Aiduk, Griffin, & Elkins, 1996) and college students (Ben-Porath, McCully, & Almagor, 1993). Interestingly enough, none of the same MMPI-2 Content scales was found to be the best predictor of the same SCL-90-R scale by both Archer et al., and Ben-Porath et al., and frequently an entirely different set of Content scales predicted the same SCL-90-R scale. One reason for this lack of congruence in results may reflect that Archer et al. used psychiatric patients while Ben-Porath used college students. For example, Archer et al. found that the Phobic Anxiety scale on the SCL-90-R was predicted by the *ANX,* Social Discomfort (*SOD*), Fears (*FRS*), and Health Concerns (*HEA*) scales in male psychiatric patients, while Ben-Porath et al. found that the Phobic Anxiety scale was predicted by the Bizarre Mentation (*BIZ*) and Negative Treatment Indicators (*TRT*) scales in male college students. Archer et al. did find that the *ANX* scale was the best predictor of the Anxiety scale on the SCL-90-R in both male and female psychiatric patients. Ben-Porath found that the *ANX* scale was the best predictor of the Trait Anxiety scale on the State-Trait Anxiety Inventory (STAI: Spielberger, Gorsuch, Lushene, Vagg, & Jacobs, 1984) in female college students, but the *FRS,* Depression (*DEP*), and Work

Interference (*WRK*) scales were the best predictors of this scale in male college students.

There are two general conclusions that can be drawn from these two studies. First, the relationship between any MMPI-2 Content scale and external criteria may not be as straightforward as clinicians would like to think. Given the nature of the items on the *ANX* scale, it is more likely to be related to external criteria that assess the cognitive and affective aspects of anxiety rather than the behavioral and physiological aspects in patients who emphasize the former aspects of anxiety in their clinical presentation. Second, there is a large component of shared variance among the MMPI-2 Content scales because of their common theme of generalized distress and negative emotionality, which will affect the discriminative ability of any Content scale (Fraboni, Jackson, & Helmes, 1993; Jackson, Fraboni, & Helmes, 1997). The clinician must appreciate the relative contribution of negative mood states in a patient before trying to assess the existence of a specific mood state such as anxiety or depression. As noted earlier, the *ANX* scale should be elevated at least 10 T points higher than the other measures of generalized distress and negative emotionality, such as the *DEP,* Low Self-Esteem (*LSE*), *TRT,* and *WRK* scales, before the clinician concludes that this particular patient is reporting anxiety.

Graham et al. (1997) have provided empirical correlates of the MMPI-2 Content scales for psychiatric outpatients who were classified as having high scores (T > 64), normal scores (T = 41–64), or low scores (T < 41) on each Content scale. These correlates will be included in the description of the high and low scorers, but not included in the overall discussion of research on each Content scale.

High scorers on the *ANX* scale are characterized by excessive worry against a backdrop of nervous tension, disturbed sleep, and problems with attention and concentration. Their subjective stress levels already are so high that decisions and disappointments are felt to carry the risk of total mental fragmentation and collapse; hence, the anxiety in question is close to panic. They feel "stressed out" and carry a strong sense both of dread and of vulnerability to upset from almost any quarter. The anxiety also is generalized; any and all events are seen as potentially disastrous and devastating. They constantly worry that a sudden unanticipated event will cause them to "go to pieces." Since the symptoms of anxiety pervade their conscious experience, they generally have neither the means nor the inclination to conceal these symptoms. The *ANX* scale has only a single item reporting somatic manifestations of anxiety, heart pounding and shortness of breath. Two of the items denote financial concerns.

Low scorers on the *ANX* scale have an absence of normal worry, tension, and anxiety that may be found in psychopathic individuals (high scores on Scales *4* [Psychopathic Deviate] and/or *9* [Hypomania] and the Antisocial Practices [*ASP*] scale) or clients whose rigid defenses are preventing any awareness of such symptoms.

Elevations on other scales in the presence of high scores on the *ANX* scale provide a basis for inferring the object of the client's anxiety. For example, a concurrent elevation on the Bizarre Mentation (*BIZ*) scale may reflect particular concern about strange experiences and psychotic disintegration, while a concurrent elevation on the Low Self-Esteem (*LSE*) scale suggests particular apprehensions around self-devaluation, narcissistic injuries, and the imminent withdrawal of dependency supports. A concurrent elevation on the Depression (*DEP*) scale may suggest fears of a worsening of depressive experience, falling into despair, and a collapse into helplessness and hopelessness.

Fears (*FRS*)

The Fears (*FRS*) scale contains 23 items of which 16 have "true" as the deviant response. The *FRS* scale has the highest correlations with Scales *7* (Psychasthenia: .563) and *8* (Schizophrenia: .551), and with the Welsh Anxiety (*A*: .533), Ego Strength (*Es*: −.664), College Maladjustment (*Mt*: .507), Gender Role—Masculine (*GM*: −.752), Post Traumatic Stress Disorder—Keane (*PK*: .529), and Post Traumatic Stress Disorder—Schlenger (*PS*: .546) scales. The correlations with these scales are reflecting the general level of distress seen in clients with high scores on the *FRS* scale rather than any specific fears.

The *FRS* scale has no counterpart among the standard Clinical scales of the MMPI-2 and shares few items with them or any of the other Content or Supplementary scales. As a result, the presence or absence of fears has to be assessed directly by the *FRS* scale. The word *fear* and its cognates (*afraid, dread, frightened*) appear in more than three-quarters of the items. The several groups of items include (1) specific fears of a classically phobic type (darkness, heights, open and closed spaces); (2) loss of physical integrity, especially through germs and tissue damage; and (3) admissions of general neurotic fearfulness and a low threshold for feeling fearful that is likely to be incapacitating; (4) animals such as mice, snakes, and spiders; and (5) natural phenomena such as earthquakes, lightning and storms, and fire and water.

Ben-Porath and Sherwood (1993) identified two Content Component scales within the *FRS* scale: Generalized Fearfulness (*FRS1*) and Multiple Fears (*FRS2*). The *FRS1* scale encompasses most of the items in groups 1, 2, and 3 listed previously, while most of the items contained in the *FRS2* scale are from groups 4 and 5. The *FRS1* scale has a broadly apprehensive tone in the client's approach to daily life. This tone places an emphasis upon the dangers or potential harmfulness of objects and circumstances in the environment. The *FRS2* scale is simply an enumeration of relatively common phobic objects and circumstances. The *FRS2* scale will need to be interpreted at T scores around 60 in women because the highest possible T score is 69.

There virtually has been no research on the *FRS* scale. Archer et al. (1996) found that the *FRS* scale was one of the predictors of Phobic Anxiety on the SCL-90-R and Somatic Concerns on the BPRS, but only in male psychiatric patients. Ben-Porath et al. (1993) found that the *FRS* scale was the best predictor of Trait Anxiety on the STAI in male college students. However, the *FRS* scale was not a significant predictor of Trait Anxiety in female college students. It remains to see whether these gender differences reflect substantive variance related to the *FRS* scale or simply are an artifact of some other unknown variable.

High scorers on the *FRS* scale have excessive fearfulness (*FRS1*) of objects and circumstances in their environment. They generally are apprehensive, anxious, and easily frightened. They also may have more specific phobic concerns (*FRS2*) and somatic symptoms. These phobic concerns are multiple in nature when the *FRS2* scale is elevated, because men have to endorse 6 and women 8 of the 10 items to get a T score of 60.

Low scorers on the *FRS* scale are fearless and disregard or are oblivious to the consequences of behavior or punishment. These behaviors may be found in clients with maniclike features that include euphoria, fearlessness, and poor judgment (high scores on Scale *9* [Hypomania]; low scores on Scale *0* [Social Introversion] and the Social Discomfort [*SOD*] scale), or psychopathic recklessness (high scores on Scale *4* [Psychopathic Deviate] and the Family Problems [*FAM*] and Antisocial Practices [*ASP*] scales). Low-scoring men also may have rigid attitudes regarding sex role requirements (low scores on Scale *5* [Masculinity-Femininity]; high scores on the Gender Role—Masculine [*GM*] scale). They are achievement oriented.

Both the *ANX* and *FRS* scales tap phenomena of apprehension. In the case of the *ANX* scale, the apprehension is trepidation over the unpredictability of external and internal events that are feared to lead to disorganization and chaos. The defense against this feared breakdown is active in the sense of involving preparation to contend with or absorb the threatened event. Through obsessive worry, the client has a means of anticipating catastrophe in time to avert or avoid it. In the *FRS* scale, however, the apprehension is condensed onto a particular object or situation. The focus is on the avoidance of injury and harm, and the defense against these dangers is fundamentally passive. The client seeks not to contend with the feared object or situation, but to avoid it. The condensation of apprehension onto known objects and situations enables developmentally more advanced mechanisms to be brought to bear in the management of anxiety based on repression and displacement. These mechanisms restore a sense of freedom from fear in those areas of life and functioning that do not risk exposure to the feared object or situation. When both the *ANX* and *FRS* scales are elevated, but the *FRS* scale is higher, the effort to utilize more mature defensive measures against external and internal threats is suggested, while the reverse pattern would suggest a reliance on more primitive defenses. The items on the *FRS* scale are more socially desirable and less negativistic than the *ANX* scale, another indication that the *FRS* scale is associated with more mature modes of defensive functioning. These differences may explain, in part, why the correlation (.530) between the *FRS* and *ANX* scales is not greater.

In some clients experiencing generalized and incapacitating fear or anxiety, an elevated score on the *FRS* scale may be operating to mask more serious psychopathology. This outcome is analogous to the familiar relationship between Scales *7* (Psychasthenia) and *8* (Schizophrenia) in which the degree to which Scale *7* exceeds Scale *8,* given the elevation of both scales, reflects the extent of the client's ongoing struggle to contain psychotic symptoms.

Obsessions (*OBS*)

The Obsessions (*OBS*) scale contains 16 items, all of which have "true" as the deviant response. The *OBS* scale has the highest correlations with Scales *K* (Correction: −.761), *7* (Psychasthenia: .860), *8* (Schizophrenia: .806), and *0* (Social Introversion: .708), and with the Welsh Anxiety (*A*: .891), College Maladjustment (*Mt*: .808), Post Traumatic Stress Disorder—Keane (*PK*: .829), and Post Traumatic Stress Disorder—Schlenger (*PS*: .837) scales. The primary theme within the *OBS* scale is the rumination about the never-ending possibilities to be considered in any situation or circumstance and the resulting indecisiveness when decisions are to be made. These specific features only will dominate the clinical presentation when the *OBS* scale is elevated clearly above other first-factor measures of generalized distress and negative emotionality (*A, Mt, PK,* and *PS*).

Ben-Porath and Sherwood (1993) did not identify Content Component scales within the *OBS* scale.

There has been virtually no research on the *OBS* scale. Archer et al. (1996) found that the Obsessive-Compulsive scale on the SCL-90-R was predicted by the Work Interference (*WRK*) and Health Concerns (*HEA*) scales in both male and female psychiatric patients. The *OBS* scale was not a significant predictor of the Obsessive-Compulsive scale or any other scale on the SCL-90-R or BPRS in these psychiatric patients. Ben-Porath et al. (1993) did find that the Anxiety

(*ANX*) and *OBS* scales were predictors of the Obsessive-Compulsive scale on the SCL-90-R in both male and female college students. However, the *ANX* scale loaded before the *OBS* scale in the regression analysis (i.e., the *ANX* scale was a better predictor of the Obsessive-Compulsive scale than the *OBS* scale).

High scorers on the *OBS* scale have overly busy but massively inefficient cognitive processes. Their decision-making processes become bogged down in detail, but this indecisiveness seems to occur against a backdrop of timidity, if not dread, when faced with the necessity of taking practical action. They are insecure, anxious, and depressed. The significant correlations with measures of anger and hostility, such as the Wiggins Manifest Hostility (.696) scale and the MMPI-2 Content scales of Anger (*ANG*: .689) and Type A (*TPA*: .652), suggest that clients with high scores on the *OBS* scale may have passive-aggressive tendencies. They may be using their indecisiveness, obsessions, and preoccupation with detail as a means of coping with the "unfair" demands and expectations of others.

Low scorers on the *OBS* scale make decisions with self-confidence and dispatch. This ease in decision making may reflect a histrionic personality style (high scores on Scale *3* [Hysteria]) in which little attention is paid to details. Very low scores (T scores of 37 or lower) may imply overconfidence and a hasty and incautious approach to decision making that frequently is seen in clients with manic (high scores on Scale *9* [Hypomania] in conjunction with low scores on Scale *2* [Depression]) or psychopathic features (high scores on Scale *4* [Psychopathic Deviate] and/or *9*, and the Antisocial Practices [*ASP*] scale). The negative implications of low scores on the *OBS* scale are likely to be negligible, or at least not readily apparent, unless a low score on the *OBS* scale is accompanied by a low, and preferably lower, score on the *FRS* scale.

It is unclear what relation, if any, would be expected between the *OBS* scale and the diagnoses of Obsessive-Compulsive Disorder or Obsessive-Compulsive Personality Disorder. An appropriate scale for the identification of these disorders would need to include items having content related to such things as symmetry, checking, perfectionism, concerns about contamination, restriction of affect, stinginess, preoccupation with details, and forbidden aggressive, sexual, or sacrilegious thoughts and actions, as well as with indecision. The MMPI-2 item pool does not include a sufficient number or variety of items with such content that may preclude the detection of Obsessive Disorders. In order to have any relevance for the diagnosis of obsessional personality styles, it is important that the *OBS* scale exceed both the *ANX* and *FRS* scales by a margin of at least 10 T points to ensure that the *OBS* scale is not being elevated by the generalized distress and negative emotionality that is common to all Content scales.

It is rather unusual to have concurrent elevations with the *OBS* scale that reflect an accurate endorsement of the items, because the other Content and Content Component scales do not have substantial groups of items that would be the focus of the client's obsessions. Concurrent elevations on the *ANX* and *FRS* scales along with the *OBS* scale would be expected in clients who are trying to cope rather unsuccessfully with massive amounts of anxiety and stress (high scores on Scales *F* [Infrequency], *2* [Depression], *7* [Psychasthenia], and *0* [Social Introversion]). Their misery is readily apparent to themselves and others.

Depression (*DEP*)

The Depression (*DEP*) scale contains 33 items of which 28 have "true" as the deviant response. The *DEP* scale has the highest correlations with Scales *7* (Psychasthenia: .913) and *8* (Schizophrenia: .888), and with the Welsh Anxiety (*A*: .915), College Maladjustment (*Mt*: .912), Post Traumatic Stress Disorder—Keane (*PK*: .934), and Post Traumatic Stress Disorder—Schlenger (*PS*: .931) scales. There clearly is a large degree of generalized distress and negative emotionality that is common to all of these scales.

Six of the items scored on the Wiggins Depression scale now appear on the MMPI-2 Anxiety (*ANX*) scale. Although the MMPI-2 and Wiggins Depression scales correlate .959, the improved separation between the anxious and depressive content in the *DEP* scale suggests that it is likely to have somewhat greater specificity and discriminant validity than its predecessor among the Wiggins scales. The *DEP* scale overlaps Scale *2* (Depression) by only nine items, indicating that the two scales are likely to have significantly different empirical correlates. All of the overlapping items are found on the Subjective Depression (D_1) scale, and eight of the nine appear on the Brooding (D_5) scale. Descriptions of being worthless and impotent, along with a view of the self as inadequate or inferior, are primary in the *DEP* scale, but secondary in Scale *2*. Conversely, the syndromal characteristics of depression such as psychomotor retardation, the inhibition of aggression, vegetative symptoms such as sleep disturbance, anorexia, and weight loss making up an important part of Scale *2,* are largely absent from the *DEP* scale. The relative elevations of the *DEP* scale and Scale *2* are helpful in determining both the type and severity of depressive phenomena. When the *DEP* scale exceeds Scale *2* by at least 10 T points, a chronic condition with predominantly characterological features is suggested; when Scale *2* exceeds the *DEP* scale, vegetative symptoms and a less complicated symptom picture are characteristic (Streit, Greene, Cogan, & Davis, 1993).

Ben-Porath and Sherwood (1993) identified four Content Component scales within the *DEP* scale: Lack of Drive (*DEP1*), Dysphoria (*DEP2*), Self-Deprecation (*DEP3*), and Suicidal Ideation (*DEP4*). The *DEP1* scale indicates despair and a loss of pleasure and interest in and motivation for life. High scores reflect apathy, anhedonia, an inability to accomplish even the routine tasks of daily life, and a sense of resignation. The *DEP2* scale reflects dysphoric mood in the form of subjective unhappiness, especially a sense of brooding and feeling blue, and of being subject to moody spells. Four of the six items overlap with the Brooding (D_5) scale. The *DEP3* scale reflects self-dissatisfaction, guilt and a sense of moral failure, and a negative self-concept. High scorers admit to ideas of guilt, helplessness, hopelessness, regret and remorse, uselessness, and worthlessness. The *DEP4* scale assesses a pessimism about the future that is so dire as to support a wish to die and thoughts of suicide. High scores raise the question of suicide potential, the need for its assessment, and the probable wisdom of initial precautions against suicidal acts or gestures. A raw score of zero on the *DEP4* scale, however, does *not* absolve the clinician

from needing to evaluate the client for suicidal ideation or attempts because all of the items with suicidal content within the MMPI-2 item pool are not found on the *DEP4* scale (e.g., items 150, 524, 530). As Ben-Porath and Sherwood (1993) pointed out, the *DEP1, DEP2,* and *DEP3* scales assess characteristics that are similar to the diagnostic criteria for a major depressive disorder. Ward (1997) identified only three factors within the *DEP* scale in male substance abusers. His factor of *DEP*—Trait contained all but one of the items from *DEP2* plus six additional items. His factor of *DEP*—Hopelessness essentially was a composite of *DEP1* and *DEP4*. Finally, his factor of *DEP*—Self-Deprecation contained all of the items from *DEP3* plus two additional items.

In contrast to the other MMPI-2 Content scales, there has been a fair amount of research on the *DEP* scale. Archer et al. (1996) found that the *DEP* scale was the best predictor of the Depression scale on the SCL-90-R and the Depressive Mood scale of the BPRS in male and female psychiatric patients. The lack of discriminative validity for the *DEP* scale in these patients can be seen in that the *DEP* scale also was the best predictor of Psychoticism on the SCL-90-R. Ben-Porath et al. (1993) found that the *DEP* scale was the best predictor of the Beck Depression Inventory (BDI: Beck, 1987) in male college students, but the *ANX* and *DEP* scales were the best predictors in female college students. Again, the lack of discriminative validity can be seen in that the *ANX* scale actually loaded before the *DEP* scale in the regression analysis. Ben-Porath et al. also found the *DEP* scale was the best predictor of the Paranoid Ideation and Psychoticism scales on the SCL-90-R, which are additional evidence for the lack of discriminative validity of the *DEP* scale. The finding that the *DEP* scale was the best predictor of psychotic criteria in both studies may suggest that the *DEP* scale is assessing the negative emotionality that is associated with more severe forms of psychopathology rather than depressive mood per se. However, Wetzler, Khadivi, and Moser (1998) found that the Bizarre Mentation (*BIZ*) scale was a better predictor of psychotic diagnoses than the *DEP* scale.

Two studies (Ben-Porath, Butcher, & Graham, 1991; Munley, Busby, & Jaynes, 1997) have shown that the *DEP* scale can better differentiate between groups of patients with diagnoses of schizophrenia and major depression than Scale *2* (Depression). However, Wetzler et al. (1998) found that the positive predictive power for the *DEP* scale and Scale *2* was virtually identical (.66 and .68, respectively). In all three studies, the *DEP* scale had the highest elevation of all of the Content scales in the patients with diagnoses of major depression.

The *DEP* scale had a higher correlation with the Beck Depression Inventory (Boone, 1994) and the Michill Adjective Rating Scale of Unhappiness (Quereshi & Kleman, 1996) and identified more patients with depressive diagnoses (Bence et al., 1995) than Scale *2* (Depression). The *DEP* scale also had a higher correlation with the Beck (1988) Hopelessness scale than Scale *2* (Boone, 1994; Thackston-Hawkins, Compton, & Kelly, 1994). The latter finding would be expected because the *DEP* scale contains items (*DEP4*) that directly assess suicidal behaviors.

High scorers on the *DEP* scale report despair and a loss of interest, and feelings of fatigue, apathy, and exhaustion (*DEP1*). They are unhappy, blue, and quick to cry (*DEP2*). They show a collapse in self-efficacy and self-regard to the point that they feel guilt-ridden, useless, unpardonably sinful, and condemned (*DEP3*). They feel hopeless and contemplate suicide (*DEP4*).

Low scorers on the *DEP* scale more clearly indicate the absence (or denial) of depressiveness than the presence of elated or expansive mood. Some low scorers will be seen as defensive, euphoric, irritable, or overactive (high scores on Scales *4* [Psychopathic Deviate] and/or *9* [Hypomania]).

Elevations on other scales in the presence of high scores on the *DEP* scale provide a basis for inferring the source of the client's depression. Concurrent elevations on the Bizarre Mentation (*BIZ*), Family Problems (*FAM*), or Health Concerns (*HEA*) scales will reflect the client's concerns about these particular areas of their life.

Health Concerns (*HEA*)

The Health Concerns (*HEA*) scale contains 36 items of which 14 have "true" as the deviant response. The *HEA* scale has the highest correlations with Scales *1* (Hypochondriasis: .965), with which it shares 23 items, *8* (Schizophrenia: 769), and *2* (Depression: .761) and with the Ego Strength (*Es*: −.832), Post Traumatic Stress Disorder—Schlenger (*PS*: .780), and College Maladjustment (*Mt*: .763) scales. Twenty of the *HEA* items appeared on the Wiggins Organic Symptoms scale and 13 appeared on the Wiggins Poor Health (*HEA*) scale. The MMPI-2 *HEA* scale contains many items denoting symptoms in and about the head, sensory and motor problems, and a few items reporting losses of consciousness.

The characterological features associated with Scale *1* (Hypochondriasis) are even more apparent in the *HEA* scale, because of the absence of any "dampening" effect of the *K* correction in the *HEA* scale. The *K* correction to the raw score on Scale *1* tends to attenuate its association with measures of dependency, hostility, and other trait measures. The correlates of these two scales are much more similar when the *HEA* scale is compared with the non-*K*-corrected version of Scale *1*.

Ben-Porath and Sherwood (1993) identified three Content Component scales within the *HEA* scale: Gastrointestinal Symptoms (*HEA1*), Neurological Symptoms (*HEA2*), and General Health Concerns (*HEA3*). The *HEA1* scale primarily assesses upper-gastrointestinal functions through symptoms such as nausea, vomiting, stomach pain and discomfort, and constipation. The *HEA2* scale assesses sensory and motor problems, losses of consciousness, and pains localized in the head. The *HEA3* scale indicates poor health and health worries and preoccupations.

There has been a limited amount of research on the *HEA* scale. Both Archer et al. (1996) and Ben-Porath et al. (1993) found that the *HEA* scale was the best predictor of the Somatization scale of the SCL-90-R in men and women. Archer et al. also found that the *HEA* scale was the best predictor of the BPRS scale of Somatic Concern. Similar to Scale *1* (Hypochondriasis), the *HEA* scale is a robust measure of somatic symptoms and has good external validity. The essential interchangeability of Scale *1* and the *HEA* scale can be seen in the fact that neither scale demonstrated incremental validity over the other scale in predicting the Somatization scale of the SCL-90-R in male or female psychiatric patients (Archer et al., 1996). The *HEA* scale shares 23 of its 36 items and correlates .965 with Scale *1*, which is a major determinant of the similarity in these results (see Table 5.6, p. 206).

High scorers on the *HEA* scale are reporting a number of gastrointestinal symptoms (*HEA1*) and neurological symptoms (*HEA2*). The clinician should determine how frequently clients have these symptoms and whether they have been evaluated recently by a physician. A medical or neurological evaluation is warranted particularly when the elevation on the *HEA* scale is primarily the result of the elevation of the *HEA2* scale. Such clients are in poor health and they worry about their health and catching diseases (*HEA3*).

Low scorers on the *HEA* scale are indicating the lack of any type of concern about their health. This lack of concern only becomes problematic if they have some bonafide disease, because they may not realize the importance of complying with the treatment regime.

Elevations on other Content scales in conjunction with an elevation on the *HEA* scale is helpful in understanding clients' health concerns. The simultaneous elevation, or lack thereof, of the Anxiety (*ANX*) or Depression (*DEP*) scales indicates whether clients are experiencing negative affect with these physical symptoms. The predominant focus of clients on physical symptoms and exclusion of the possibility of any type of psychological problems may be particularly apparent when the *ANX* and *DEP* scales are not elevated. When the Bizarre Mentation (*BIZ*) scale is elevated along with the *HEA* scale, clients may have somatic delusions.

Bizarre Mentation (*BIZ*)

The Bizarre Mentation (*BIZ*) scale contains 24 items, all of which but one have "true" as the deviant response. The *BIZ* scale has the highest correlations with Scales *F* (Infrequency: .794), *8* (Schizophrenia: .782), and *6* (Paranoia: .679) and the Back Infrequency (F_B: .766), Post Traumatic Stress Disorder—Keane (*PK*: .717), and Post Traumatic Stress Disorder—Schlenger (*PS*: .704) scales. The *BIZ* scale is an overt measure of psychotic thought processes and, accordingly, it is the

content analogue of the *6-8/8-6* codetype (see Chapter 7, p. 352).

Ben-Porath and Sherwood (1993) divided the *BIZ* scale into two Content Component scales: Psychotic Symptomatology (*BIZ1*) and Schizotypal Characteristics (*BIZ2*). The *BIZ1* scale has overtly psychotic content reflecting positive symptoms such as hallucinations and delusions of persecution and control characteristic of schizophrenia and other psychotic conditions. Nearly half of these items refer to paranoid symptomatology. The *BIZ2* scale has less obviously psychotic content than the *BIZ1* scale. The *BIZ2* scale reflects unusual, odd, peculiar, and eccentric thoughts and experiences. These intrusive thoughts and uncanny sensory experiences are sometimes seen in prodromal or residual phases of schizophrenia, dissociative conditions, and mood disorders with psychotic features. The client only has to endorse three items on either the *BIZ1* or *BIZ2* scale to have a T score of 60. Clients should not be diagnosed with some form of psychotic disorder solely on the basis of a moderate elevation even on the *BIZ1* scale because of the limited number of items needed to produce a significant elevation that can be the result of endorsing relatively benign items.

One of the more important uses of the *BIZ* scale is as an index of the degree to which psychotic content has contributed to elevations on Scales *F* (Infrequency), *6* (Paranoia), and *8* (Schizophrenia). Both Scales *6* and *8* have substantial item content that emphasizes negative emotionality and both may easily be elevated in depressive conditions as well as in psychotic conditions. Alienation and lowered self-esteem also may elevate Scale *8* in many different conditions. The *BIZ* scale can provide valuable guidance in the interpretation of Scales *F*, *6*, and *8* by emphasizing the importance of psychotic content when supported by elevation on the *BIZ* scale (especially the *BIZ1* scale), and by avoiding such emphasis when it cannot, thereby averting excessively pathological interpretations of Scale *8*.

The *BIZ* scale is the other MMPI-2 Content scale besides the *DEP* scale that has been researched to any degree. Both Archer et al. (1996) and Ben-Porath et al. (1993) found that the *DEP* scale rather than the *BIZ* scale was the best predictor of Paranoid Ideation and Psychoticism on the SCL-90-R. Typically the

BIZ scale was the next best predictor after the *DEP* scale. Archer et al. did find that the *BIZ* scale was the best predictor of the Hallucinatory Behavior and Unusual Thought Content scales of the BPRS, although the correlations were about one-half of the magnitude of those that were found with the MMPI-2 Content scales.

Ben-Porath et al. (1991), Munley et al. (1997), and Wetzler et al. (1998) found that neither the *BIZ* scale nor Scale *8* (Schizophrenia) differentiated between groups of patients with diagnoses of Schizophrenia and Major Depression. The *BIZ* scale always was higher in the patients with Schizophrenia than the patients with Major Depression, while Scale *8* actually was higher in the patients with Major Depression in several of the comparisons. Wetzler et al. found that the positive predictive power for the *BIZ* scale was higher than for Scale *8* (.54 and .37, respectively) and was an improvement over the prevalence rate (.36).

High scorers on the *BIZ* scale are reporting a variety of overtly psychotic symptoms (*BIZ1*). These psychotic symptoms should be readily apparent on even casual interactions with the client and they are very likely to be the reason that the client is being seen for treatment. High scorers on the *BIZ* scale, especially when this elevation is primarily the result of the elevation of the *BIZ1* scale, have impaired insight, an inability to enter into collaborative relationships, and a grandiose sense of having been selected or appointed for a secret and lofty mission or endowed with special powers. They also report strange, puzzling ideas and experiences (*BIZ2*) that are not overtly psychotic in and of themselves.

Low scorers on the *BIZ* scale are not reporting any type of psychotic content or even unusual or atypical ideas. These low scores frequently are seen in conjunction with elevations on Scales *1* (Hypochondriasis) and/or *3* (Hysteria) in which the clients want to avoid any possible suggestion that they might have psychological problems, particularly serious ones.

The relative elevations of the *BIZ* and Low Self-Esteem (*LSE*) scales also can provide a useful index of the relative contributions of psychotic content and impaired self-esteem to high scores on Scale *8* (Schizophrenia). The *LSE* scale is very sensitive to the kinds of fixed, negative self-attitudes that often result in high Scale *8* scores, which are encountered in a number of nonpsychotic conditions such as depressive mood disorders.

Anger (*ANG*)

The Anger (*ANG*) scale contains 16 items, all of which but one have "true" as the deviant response. Inexplicably, the *ANG* scale does *not* include item 372 "I am not easily angered."[1] The *ANG* scale has the highest correlations with the *K* (Correction: –.769) scale and Scales *7* (Psychasthenia: .722) and *8* (Schizophrenia: .715), and with the Superlative (*S*: –.803), Post Traumatic Stress Disorder—Schlenger (*PS*: .754), and Post Traumatic Stress Disorder—Keane (*PK*: .743) scales. The *ANG* scale has a higher correlation with Scale *4* (Psychopathic Deviate: .621) than it does with Scale *6* (Paranoia: .494), which suggests that the *ANG* scale reflects as much, if not more, the lack of concern about social convention as the actual expression of anger.

Ben-Porath and Sherwood (1993) divided the *ANG* scale into two Content Component scales: Explosive Behavior (*ANG1*) and Irritability (*ANG2*). The *ANG1* scale assesses explosive and violent episodes that have been directed toward both persons and property, and are likely to have resulted in injury and damage. These behaviors are reminiscent of the criteria for Intermittent Explosive Disorder. The *ANG2* scale indicates a great deal of anger and irritability accompanied by a sense of distress and perplexity that may to some degree inhibit the behavioral outbursts. This combination of anger and inhibition themes in the *ANG2* scale suggests that it may reflect anger that is emitted within a context of self-justification such as argumentativeness, disagreeableness, and passive-aggressive behaviors. There is a very limited ceiling on the *ANG2* scale in men and women so clinicians will need to begin to consider it elevated at T scores around 65.

Ben-Porath et al. (1993) found that the *ANG* scale was the best predictor of the Trait Anger scale of the State-Trait Anger Expression Inventory (Spielberger,

---

1. Minnesota Multiphasic Personality Inventory-2 (MMPI-2). Copyright © 1942, 1943 (renewed 1970), 1989 by the Regents of the University of Minnesota. Reproduced by permission of the publisher. "MMPI-2" and "Minnesota Multiphasic Personality Inventory-2" are trademarks owned by the University of Minnesota.

1987) in male and female college students. Archer et al. (1996) found that the *ANG* scale was the best predictor of the Hostility scale of the SCL-90-R in both male and female psychiatric patients. The *ANG* scale also was the best predictor of the Hostility scale of the BPRS in male psychiatric patients. Equally important, the *ANG* scale was not a significant predictor of almost all of the other SCL-90-R scales or BPRS scales in men or women. It would appear that the *ANG* scale may have some degree of discriminant validity relative to the other MMPI-2 Content scales. Kawachi, Sparrow, Spiro, Vokonas, and Weiss (1996) found that normal men with elevated scores on the *ANG* scale had increased risks of coronary heart disease. This topic will be reviewed further when the Hostility (*Ho*) scale is discussed in Chapter 6.

Clark (1994) found that the *ANG* scale was related to the externalization of anger in male pain patients and was not related to current anger or anger turned inward. That is, the *ANG* scale was an index of a trait of anger and the externalization of anger. Schill and Wang (1990) and O'Laughlin and Schill (1994) also found the *ANG* scale was related to the externalization of anger and lack of control of anger in male and female college students.

High scorers on the *ANG* scale have poorly controlled anger. They are irritable, volatile, and intolerant of frustration. They are prone to angry tirades and destructive outbursts that have the potential to hurt others and damage property (*ANG1*). If constrained by external circumstances, they also express their anger in more controlled ways through frequent nagging, teasing, demanding, and being stubborn. High scorers frequently will report being a helpless spectator to their angry outbursts. They disapprove of their own destructiveness, yet feel unable to stop themselves (*ANG2*). Any gratification that they might report is in the release of anger, not in the damage occasioned by such release. As with the Anxiety (*ANX*) scale, high scorers on the *ANG* scale have a high urgency to express what they are experiencing. They also are described as being depressed, histrionic, and as having family problems.

Low scorers on the *ANG* scale are capable of feeling angry yet control its overt expression, or they may be denying the presence of any type of angry feelings.

Elevations on other Content scales help the clinician to understand clients' reaction to their anger. The simultaneous elevation, or lack thereof, of the Anxiety (*ANX*) or Depression (*DEP*) scales indicates whether the client is experiencing negative emotionality associated with the expression of anger. Low scores on the *ANX* and *DEP* scales in conjunction with high scores on the *ANG* scale that primarily reflect the *ANG1* scale are a particularly pathological combination, in contrast to high scores on the *ANX* and *DEP* scales in conjunction with high scores on the *ANG* scale that primarily reflect the *ANG2* scale. The former combination of scales only becomes more serious when accompanied by an elevation on the Bizarre Mentation (*BIZ*) or Antisocial Practices (*ASP*) scales.

Cynicism (*CYN*)

The Cynicism (*CYN*) scale contains 23 items, all of which have "true" as the deviant response. Seventeen items overlap with the Cook and Medley (1954) Hostility scale (*Ho*), which will be described in Chapter 6. The *CYN* scale has the highest correlations with the *K* (Correction: −.780) scale and Scale *8* (Schizophrenia: .642), and with the Welsh Anxiety (*A*: .644), Post Traumatic Stress Disorder—Keane (*PK*: .641), and Post Traumatic Stress Disorder—Schlenger (*PS*: .629) scales. The *CYN* scale models a dimension that covers a broad range of sentiments from an obtuse absence of skepticism regarding the motives of others (low scores), through normal prudent regard for one's vulnerability to the actions of others (normal scores), to the unqualified misanthropic conviction that others are dishonorable, unprincipled, and corrupt (high scores).

Ben-Porath and Sherwood (1993) identified two Component scales within the *CYN* scale: Misanthropic Beliefs (*CYN1*) and Interpersonal Suspiciousness (*CYN2*). The *CYN1* scale emphasizes a view of others as deceitful, selfish, untrustworthy, manipulative, unsympathetic, and disloyal. The *CYN2* scale emphasizes similar sentiments but includes a theme of being a target of others' hostile or exploitive actions that leads to suspicious and guarded reactions. They feel vulnerable to others, especially superiors, who are stingy with recognition and understanding, and who are trying to put them at a disadvantage. The *CYN2* scale has a more dysphoric tone than the *CYN1* scale. Both the *CYN1* and *CYN2* scales have a very limited ceiling in men and women. Clinicians will need to consider both of these scales to be elevated at T scores around 65.

Both Archer et al. (1996) and Ben-Porath et al. (1993) found that the *CYN* scale was one of the significant predictors of the Paranoid Ideation scale of the SCL-90-R. In all cases, the *DEP* scale accounted for more variance than the *CYN* scale. The *CYN* scale appears to contribute some unique variance in predicting several of the more serious symptoms (anger, paranoid ideation, psychoticism) of psychopathology on the SCL-90-R.

Clark (1994) found the *CYN* scale was related to depression and sensitivity to criticism in male pain patients. He cautioned that the *CYN* scale may be valuable only as a measure of the client's opinions of the motives of others.

High scorers on the *CYN* scale assert that others are to be distrusted because they act only in self-interest, resort to honesty only to avoid detection, and act friendly only because it makes others easier to exploit (*CYN1*). They see life as a jungle in which they must be constantly on the lookout for any competitive advantage, because others will use any means at their disposal to claim such advantage for themselves if they are given the opportunity. They have no qualms about resorting to deception, hypocrisy, and manipulation to get away with whatever they can. They justify their exploitive behaviors with the rationalization that others are equally selfish, dishonest, and amoral (*CYN2*).

Low scorers on the *CYN* scale do not have even a normal level of skepticism regarding the goodwill of others. They maintain that they and others are completely trustworthy and driven solely by prosocial and altruistic motivations. They portray themselves as enjoying consummately harmonious relationships, in which conflict and ill will are not to be found. Such characterizations frequently are seen in consort with elevations on Scale *3* (Hysteria). Low scores on the *CYN* scale also can indicate an unusual aversion to giving offense to others for fear that to do so might risk rejection or the loss of dependency supports.

The *CYN* scale is most likely to be elevated with the Antisocial Practices (*ASP*) and Bizarre Mentation (*BIZ*) scales. The combination of either of these scales with the *CYN* scale only makes its correlates more pathological.

Antisocial Practices (*ASP*)

The Antisocial Practices (*ASP*) scale contains 22 items with all but one having "true" as the deviant response. The *ASP* scale has the highest correlations with the *K* (Correction: –.663) and Scale *9* (Hypomania: .598), and with the Social Responsibility (Re: –.748) scale. The *ASP* scale correlates only .512 with Scale *4* (Psychopathic Deviate). Other researchers (Butcher et al., 1990; Lilienfeld, 1996) have reported correlations in the range of .26 to .45 for the *ASP* scale with Scale *4*.

Ben-Porath and Sherwood (1993) identified two Component scales within the *ASP* scale: Antisocial Attitudes (*ASP1*) and Antisocial Behavior (*ASP2*). The *ASP1* scale reflects a disdain for rules and laws, a willingness to steal given the opportunity, and a cynical view of the motives of others. There is a strong implicit theme of defective empathy as well as a generalized disregard of others. The *ASP2* scale consists of admissions of delinquencies in the past, including theft, truancy, school suspensions, and conflict with school and legal authorities. There is only one item (266) on the *ASP2* scale that even has the potential to reflect current antisocial behavior and it is written in the past tense; the remaining items reflect behaviors that occurred during school years. The imbalance in the length of the two *ASP* Component scales is such that the full scale name is something of a misnomer, since those items dealing with actual misbehavior (*ASP2*) comprise slightly less than one-quarter of the full *ASP* scale. Moreover, the *ASP2* scale is only weakly correlated (.343) with the *ASP1* scale, a further indication that the relation of the *ASP1* scale to actual antisocial behavior is tenuous.

There has been virtually no research on the *ASP* scale. Neither Archer et al. (1996) nor Ben-Porath et al. (1993) found the *ASP* scale to be a predictor of any of the SCL-90-R or BPRS scales that they reported. Lilienfeld (1996) found only moderate (.26 to .45) correlations between the *ASP* scale and Scale *4* (Psychopathic Deviate) in three samples of college students. The *ASP* scale was more highly related to measures of aggression, lack of trustworthiness, and externalization of blame than Scale *4,* while Scale *4* was more related to measures of depression and alienation than the *ASP* scale.

High scorers on the *ASP* scale are reporting a disregard for rules and social conventions coupled with a cynical perspective on the motives of others (*ASP1*). They have little concern or empathy for others. They are prone to abuse substances and to engage in other risky behaviors. They may have a history of antisocial behaviors while they were in school (*ASP2*).

Low scorers on the *ASP* scale see themselves as conventional individuals who abide by the rules and trust the motives of others. If they are experiencing emotional distress, it is being turned inward toward themselves rather than being acted out toward others.

The simultaneous elevation, or lack thereof, of the Anxiety (*ANX*) or Depression (*DEP*) scales indicates whether the client is experiencing negative emotionality associated with the presence of antisocial attitudes or behaviors. It is particularly pathological when the *ASP* scale as well as the *CYN* scale are elevated and both the *ANX* and *DEP* scales are not elevated. In this pattern of low scores on the *ANX* and *DEP* scales, when the *ASP* scale is more elevated than the *CYN* scale, the client is more likely to have psychopathic features; when the *CYN* scale is more elevated than the *ASP* scale, the client is more likely to have paranoid features.

Type A (*TPA*)

The Type A (*TPA*) scale contains 19 items, all of which have "true" as the deviant response. The *TPA* scale has the highest correlations with the *K* scale (Correction: −.751) and Scales *7* (Psychasthenia: .635) and *8* (Schizophrenia: .631), and with the Superlative (*S:* −.807), Welsh Anxiety (*A:* .665), Post Traumatic Stress Disorder—Schlenger (*PS:* .643) and Post Traumatic Stress Disorder—Keane (*PK:* .638) scales.

The concept of the Type A or coronary-prone personality as operationalized in the Jenkins Activity Survey (Jenkins, Rosenman, & Friedman, 1967) included three components: Speed and Impatience, Job Involvement, and Hard Driving. The first component focused on time urgency, the second component with the person's determination to meet or exceed occupational demands, and the third component with a serious, competitive, and hard driving self-concept. The items on the *TPA* scale fail to cover these components adequately. The Job Involvement component is insufficiently represented with, at most, two items (507, 531). The Hard Driving component is biased so heavily toward hostility that the themes of competitiveness and self-imposed demands for performance tend to recede into the background.

Ben-Porath and Sherwood (1993) divided the *TPA* scale into two Component scales: Impatience (*TPA1*) and Competitiveness (*TPA2*). The *TPA1* scale conveys a sense of time urgency along with irritability at having to wait in line or to be interrupted. The *TPA2* scale conveys less a spirit of competitiveness than of resentment and vengefulness. They want to get even with people who oppose them and they relish the misfortunes of people whom they dislike. Although both the *TPA1* and *TPA2* scales convey themes of anger, the *TPA1* scale is closer to the irritable-angry emotionality of the *ANG* scale, while the *TPA2* scale is more controlled, hostile, and vengeful than the *ANG* scale. Since the *TPA2* scale contains half again as many items as the *TPA1* scale, the quality of the *TPA2* scale is imparted to the full *TPA* scale. Type A behavior is more strongly suggested when scores on the *TPA1* scale exceed those on the *TPA2* scale than when the reverse pattern is seen. There is a very limited ceiling on the *TPA1* scale in men and women. Clinicians will need to consider this scale to be elevated at T scores around 60.

There has been only limited research on the *TPA* scale. Neither Archer et al. (1996) nor Ben-Porath et al. (1993) found the *TPA* scale to be a predictor of any of the SCL-90-R or BPRS scales that they reported. Kawachi, Sparrow, Kubzansky, Spiro, Vokonas, and Weiss (1998) found that men with raw scores greater than 11 (T score of 56) on the *TPA* scale had a significantly increased risk of coronary heart disease.

High scorers on the *TPA* scale have a pressured urgency to get things done and they become irritated when having to wait in line or are interrupted at their work (*TPA1*). They want to get even with people who oppose or have wronged them, and they are pleased when these people get into trouble (*TPA2*). They also are described as being depressed and having family problems.

Low scorers on the *TPA* scale are more relaxed about carrying out their activities and are not concerned when they are interrupted by others, or they may have a dysphoric mood that makes them less able to get things done.

There is a more urgent press for the expression of anger involved in the *ANG* scale than in the *TPA* scale. The high scorer on the *TPA* scale is better controlled and more deliberate than the high scorer on the *ANG* scale at comparable elevations. The high scorer on the *TPA* scale also is less dysphoric and anhedonic and less inclined to avoid or deny evidence of personal errors or shortcomings than the high scorer on the *ANG* scale. That is, the *TPA* scale is thematically more grandiose and narcissistic than the *ANG* scale. The content of the *TPA* scale also is more cynical and suspicious than the *ANG* scale. While the high scorer on the *ANG* scale is more irritable, angry, and volatile than the high scorer on the *TPA* scale, there is less determination to control and inflict emotional injury on others. The greater control inherent in the *TPA* scale is sufficient to create an impression of assertiveness at times when a comparable score on the *ANG* scale would create an impression of excessive anger. A concurrent elevation on the Cynicism (*CYN*) scale supports the inference of Type A dynamics when the *CYN* scale exceeds the Antisocial Practices (*ASP*) scale and when the Misanthropic Beliefs (*CYN1*) scale exceeds the Interpersonal Suspiciousness (*CYN2*) scale. Scores on the *CYN* and *CYN1* scales exceeding the *TPA2* scale also may have incremental value in identifying the Type A pattern.

Low Self-Esteem (*LSE*)

The Low Self-Esteem (*LSE*) scale contains 24 items with all but 3 having "true" as the deviant response. The *LSE* scale has the highest correlations with Scales *7* (Psychasthenia: .851), *8* (Schizophrenia: .812), and *0* (Social Introversion: .791), and with the Welsh Anxiety (*A*: .870), Post Traumatic Stress Disorder—Schlenger (*PS*: .832), Post Traumatic

Stress Disorder—Keane (*PK*: .821), and College Maladjustment (*Mt*: .810) scales. The *LSE* scale is composed of items admitting personal and interpersonal shortcomings that are found in a wide variety of MMPI-2 scales.

Ben-Porath and Sherwood (1993) divided the *LSE* scale into two Component scales: Self-Doubt (*LSE1*) and Submissiveness (*LSE2*). The *LSE1* scale reflects very negative self-attributions that are mostly phrased in such a way as to convey not self-doubt per se, but the *conviction* of personal inferiority and inadequacy. That is, these negative self-attributions are relatively fixed and sum to an overall negative or devalued identity. The *LSE2* scale reflects passivity, a subservient obedience to others and, by implication, an avoidance of responsibility. When both the *LSE1* and *LSE2* scales are elevated, these clients are compliant with requests but they have little expectation of being competent to carry them out successfully. Others may describe such behaviors as passive-aggressive or self-defeating.

There has been only very limited research on the *LSE* scale. Neither Archer et al. (1996) nor Ben-Porath et al. (1993) found the *LSE* scale to be a predictor of any of the SCL-90-R or BPRS scales that they reported. Brems and Lloyd (1995) identified three factors within the *LSE* scale in college students: Ineptitude, Low Self-Value, and Negative Comparison to Others. The last two factors are essentially contained within the *LSE1* scale, while the first factor is a mixture of items from the entire *LSE* scale. They also obtained a correlation of −.69 between the *LSE* scale and Rosenberg's (1965) Self-Esteem scale.

High scorers on the *LSE* scale feel less capable, less attractive, less self-confident, and generally less adequate than others (*LSE1*). They feel so overwhelmingly incompetent and inferior to others that the independent management of their lives seems out of the question (*LSE2*). They are anxious, pessimistic, insecure, and depressed. The *LSE* scale is the Content scale, and particularly the *LSE2* scale, that is most sensitive to ego-syntonic pathological dependency.

Low scorers on the *LSE* scale see themselves as very capable to meet the demands of their environment. There may be a grandiose or narcissistic flavor to this evaluation of their abilities and competence that does not match their actual circumstances. Elevations on Scales *4* (Psychopathic Deviate) and *9* (Hypomania) are common in such clients who have unrealistic evaluations of themselves.

The *LSE* scale may be contrasted with the Depression (*DEP*) scale in terms of locus of control, with the *LSE* scale being more "external" than the *DEP* scale. Whereas clients with elevated scores on the *DEP* scales see themselves as worthless, demanding, and relatively extrapunitive, clients with elevated scores on the *LSE* scale see themselves as helpless, passive, dependent, and intropunitive. The *LSE* scale is highly intercorrelated with the Obsessions (*OBS*), *DEP*, Work Interference (*WRK*), and Negative Treatment Indicators (*TRT*) scales. An underlying theme in each of these scales is an inability to perform: The *OBS* scale stresses the inability to make decisions and act on them; the *DEP* scale stresses the inability to mobilize sufficient personal resources to engage life; the *WRK* scale stresses the inability to perform or produce on the job; and the *TRT* scale stresses the inability to rise above helplessness and despair in order to grapple with personal problems. Together, these scales form a quintet for which the theme of motivational inertia may be almost as significant as their common core of negative emotionality. That is, clients showing peaks on these scales are reporting feeling depleted, immobilized, blocked, and helpless.

Social Discomfort (*SOD*)

The Social Discomfort (*SOD*) scale contains 24 items of which 13 have "true" as the deviant response. Eighteen (75%) of these *SOD* items overlap with Scale *0* (Social Introversion), and most of the nonoverlapping items express a preference for being alone. Hence, the theme of interpersonal isolation is a good deal stronger in the *SOD* scale than in Scale *0*. Like Scale *0*, the *SOD* scale is bipolar with high scores connoting introversion and low scores connoting extroversion. The *SOD* scale has the highest correlations with Scales *0* (.892), *7* (Psychasthenia: .651), *8* (Schizophrenia: .620), and *2* (Depression: .614), and with the Post Traumatic Stress Disorder—Keane (*PK*: .652), Welsh Anxiety (*A*: .644), Post Traumatic Stress Disorder—Schlenger (*PS*: .640), and College Maladjustment (*Mt*: .621) scales. The *SOD* scale, like Scale *0*, is not a pure measure of extroversion-introversion. Instead introversion is permeated with generalized distress and negative emotionality.

Ben-Porath and Sherwood (1993) divided the *SOD* scale into two Component scales: Introversion (*SOD1*) and Shyness (*SOD2*). The *SOD1* scale emphasizes the avoidance of group and social situations, an aversion for interpersonal interaction, and a preference for being alone. The *SOD1* scale contains all of the items of the Social Avoidance (Si_2) scale and is the more "behavioral" of these two scales. The *SOD2* scale conveys a sense of inhibition and fear of embarrassment that pervades interactions with others, especially strangers, and in group situations. They believe that they lack social skills and are likely to be seen as reticent and standoffish. All of the items of the *SOD2* scale are contained within the Shyness/Self-Consciousness (Si_1) scale. Ben-Porath and Sherwood (1993) suggested that a low score on the *SOD1* scale coupled with a high score on the *SOD2* scale may reflect an aspiration to be more socially involved and a desire for an increased sense of personal comfort and control in interaction. This pattern is somewhat akin to stage fright, in which others are not rigidly avoided but simply approached with a sense of anxious trepidation. Very low scores on both of the *SOD1* and *SOD2* scales suggest a superficial interactional style that frequently is encountered in clients with manic/hypomanic features (high scores on Scale *9* [Hypomania]). There is a very limited ceiling on the *SOD2* scale in men and women. Clinicians will need to consider this scale to be elevated at T scores around 65.

There has been little research on the *SOD* scale. Neither Archer et al. (1996) nor Ben-Porath et al. (1993) found the *SOD* scale to be a predictor of any of the SCL-90-R scales that they reported. Archer et al. did find that the *SOD* scale was the best predictor of Emotional Withdrawal on the BPRS in male psychiatric patients.

High scorers on the *SOD* scale seek to stay away from other people, whether individuals or groups, because they feel uneasy and awkward in such situations, and because they are happier being alone (*SOD1*). They do not report feeling lonely. They see themselves as lacking social skills and being socially inept (*SOD2*). They are described as being insecure, anxious, depressed, and pessimistic.

Low scorers on the *SOD* scale have a gregarious, outgoing style and they enjoy social interactions either individually or in groups. They evidence a high level of social comfort and confidence by being friendly, fun loving, talkative, and flexible.

Elevations on the *SOD* scale may reflect the kinds of anergic withdrawal and social anhedonia seen in depressive syndromes (high scores on Scale *2* [Depression] and the Depression [*DEP*] scale, and low scores on Scale *9* [Hypomania]), or the interpersonal aversiveness and social withdrawal seen in schizophrenic processes (high scores on Scales *F* [Infrequency], *6* [Paranoia], *8* [Schizophrenia], and the Bizarre Mentation [*BIZ*] scale). Low scores in which the *SOD1* scale exceeds the *SOD2* scale are consistent with narcissistic, psychopathic, and manic/hypomanic states (high scores on Scales *4* [Psychopathic Deviate], *9* [Hypomania], and the Antisocial Practices [*ASP*] scale).

Family Problems (*FAM*)

The Family Problems (*FAM*) scale contains 25 items of which 20 have "true" as the deviant response. The *FAM* scale has the highest correlations with Scales *4* (Psychopathic Deviate: .728), *8* (Schizophrenia: .714), *K* (Correction: −.665), and *F* (Infrequency: .657) and with the Superlative (*S*: −.716), Post Traumatic Stress Disorder—Keane (*PK*: .684), Welsh Anxiety (*A*: .683), and Post Traumatic Stress Disorder—Schlenger (*PS*: .675) scales.

The items on the *FAM* scale refer to current family and family of origin in about equal measure, while reference to the parental home more clearly dominates the items on the Familial Discord (*Pd₁*) scale. The *Pd₁* scale shows a relatively greater emphasis on the parents as restricting freedom, independence, and efforts toward emancipation. The *FAM* scale conveys a relatively greater sense of family turbulence, pathology, and estrangement. As a result, scores on the *FAM* scale exceeding those on the *Pd₁* scale may be a reflection of current family distress, while the reverse pattern suggests that family strife may be largely con-

fined to the parental home. The client's age, family history, and current family circumstance, of course, must be considered in the interpretations of *Pd₁* and *FAM* and its component scales.

Ben-Porath and Sherwood (1993) identified two Component scales within the *FAM* scale: Family Discord (*FAM1*) and Familial Alienation (*FAM2*). The *FAM1* scale stresses intrafamilial conflict and animosity, with family members being seen as quarrelsome, disagreeable, and ill-tempered. Their family is an unpleasant, noxious environment from which they would like to escape. Less than half the length of the *FAM1* scale, the *FAM2* scale stresses an emotional detachment from family. They have severed ties with their family in order to cut their losses for their inability or disinclination to provide emotional support. Ben-Porath and Sherwood (1993) suggested that high scores on the *FAM2* scale when the *FAM1* scale is low indicate disengagement from family. This pattern also would seem to suggest a much greater sense of indifference, perhaps with some feeling of sorrow about the shortcomings of family as a source of emotional provisions. The opposite pattern suggests the persistence of attachment despite the familial turmoil and discord. When both the *FAM1* and *FAM2* scales are elevated, a state of resentful alienation is suggested in which physical ties have been severed but unresolved emotional attachments continue to exist.

There has been virtually no research on the *FAM* scale. Neither Archer et al. (1996) nor Ben-Porath et al. (1993) found the *FAM* scale to be a predictor of any of the SCL-90-R scales that they reported. Archer et al. did find that the *FAM* scale was one of the predictors of the Emotional Withdrawal and Grandiosity scales of the BPRS in female psychiatric patients. Given the limited research, it is unclear whether the *FAM* scale may contribute some unique variance in women or if this relationship was an artifact of some other variable.

Ben-Porath and Sherwood (1993) found that men in a forensic diagnostic sample who had high scores on the *FAM* scale had a history of poor relationships with their fathers, siblings, family, spouses, and friends, had more frequently lost physical and legal custody of their children, and had been arrested while previously on probation.

High scorers on the *FAM* scale not only feel deprived and mistreated by their family (*FAM1*), but appear to have acquired or augmented a set of dispositions that maintains more generalized antagonism toward others into adulthood. They are emotionally detached and alienated from family members (*FAM2*). They are apt to be seen by others as immature and overreactive people who harbor grave doubts about and deeply negative attitudes toward themselves, but who are equally mistrustful and disparaging of others. This pattern of correlates is reminiscent of the pattern of traits seen in Borderline Personality Disorder and Substance Dependence Disorders.

Low scorers on the *FAM* scale see their family as being free of discord and turmoil and supportive of them. It is important to determine whether this positive characterization of their family accurately reflects their environment. This positive construal of the family frequently is seen in clients with histrionic features (high scores on Scale *3* [Hysteria]).

Concurrent elevations on other Content scales can indicate whether clients' dissatisfaction with their family extends to others. A concurrent elevation on the Cynicism (*CYN*) scale implies distrust and dissatisfaction that have apparently generalized to others. This distrust and dissatisfaction may reach paranoid proportions when the Bizarre Mentation (*BIZ*) scale also is elevated. A concurrent elevation on the Antisocial Practices (*ASP*) scale when the *ASP* scale exceeds the Cynicism (*CYN*) scale and the Social Discomfort (*SOD*) scale is low is the Content scale equivalent of the psychopathic *4-9/9-4* codetype type (see Chapter 7, pp. 345–346). Clinically, this codetype is associated with immaturity and substance abuse, and with assaultiveness and destructiveness.

Work Interference (*WRK*)

The Work Interference (*WRK*) scale contains 33 items, all of which but 5 have "true" as the deviant response. Almost 40% of the items contain the word *work* or one of its cognates. The *WRK* scale has the highest correlations with Scales *7* (Psychasthenia: .917), *8* (Schizophrenia: .878), and *0* (Social Introversion: .800), and with the Welsh Anxiety (*A*: .936), Post Traumatic Stress Disorder—Schlenger (*PS*:

.918), College Maladjustment (*Mt*: .917), and Post Traumatic Stress Disorder—Keane (*PK*: .899) scales. The *WRK* scale is a measure of generalized distress and negative emotionality that has been trimmed to the context of work, emphasizing the kinds of problems that would be expected to have adverse effects on productivity. The interferences covered in the *WRK* scale include both interpersonal difficulties and the kinds of attitudes and symptoms that impair efficiency and impede output. Nevertheless, it still is necessary to verify that these qualities actually are interfering with the client's work behavior.

Ben-Porath and Sherwood (1993) did not identify Component scales within the *WRK* scale.

There has been little research on the *WRK* scale. Ben-Porath et al. (1993) found that the *WRK* scale did not predict any of the SCL-90-R scales in their college students. Archer et al. (1996) found that the *WRK* scale was the best predictor of the Obsessive-Compulsive and Interpersonal Sensitivity scales in male and female psychiatric patients. The discriminative validity of the *WRK* scale is very tenuous when it is the best predictor of such disparate constructs.

High scorers on the *WRK* scale are experiencing a wide variety of problems that interfere with their abilities to carry out their work responsibilities. They find it hard to concentrate on tasks and they give up easily in the face of adversity. There is a dysphoric quality that permeates their life and interferes with their work.

Low scorers on the *WRK* scale have adequate energy and the capability to marshal their abilities to carry out their work responsibilities. They have the capacity for cooperative interactions with fellow employees and an ability to limit the influence of personal problems and symptoms on job performance.

Because of its extensive shared variance with the first factor of generalized distress and negative emotionality, the interpretive implications of the *WRK* scale are most likely to be realized when it is more elevated than the Welsh Anxiety (*A*) scale. Although problems that may interfere with functioning in employment are suggested by elevations on the *WRK* scale alone, such elevations cannot be taken to indicate occupational malfunctioning *specifically*. The requirement that the *WRK* scale exceeds the *A* scale strengthens the implication of specific work interferences to the extent of this difference. The elevation on the *WRK* scale should be compared with the elevations on the Obsessions (*OBS*), Depression (*DEP*), Low Self-Esteem (*LSE*), and Negative Treatment Indicators (*TRT*) scales as means of gaining additional insight into the kinds of problems that may most threaten work performance.

Negative Treatment Indicators (*TRT*)

The Negative Treatment Indicators (*TRT*) scale contains 26 items with all but 4 having "true" as the deviant response. The *TRT* scale has the highest correlations with Scales *8* (Schizophrenia: .854), *7* (Psychasthenia: .851), and *0* (Social Introversion: .777), and with the Post Traumatic Stress Disorder—Schlenger (*PS*: .873), Post Traumatic Stress Disorder—Keane (*PK*: .873), Welsh Anxiety (*A*: .873), and College Maladjustment (*Mt*: .828) scales. As a whole, the *TRT* scale reflects a depressive state in which apathy, despair, and helplessness reach such a level of severity as to result in immobilization.

Ben-Porath and Sherwood (1993) divided the *TRT* scale into two Component scales: Low Motivation (*TRT1*) and Inability to Disclose (*TRT2*). The *TRT1* scale connotes apathy, an external locus of control, and a tendency to give up quickly in the face of obstacles because of a lack of personal resources. They feel helpless and motivationally destitute to the point that any kind of struggle against problems and adversity is futile and pointless. The *TRT2* scale is less than half the length of the *TRT1* scale, and extends the theme of futility to the realm of verbal interactions. The *TRT2* scale reflects a disinclination to volunteer personal information and significant discomfort when they are asked to do so by others. They do not wish to reveal information about their personal problems. When the *TRT1* scale also is elevated, their reasoning appears to be that confiding in others not only increases personal discomfort, but does so without offering any countervailing benefits.

Since both the item content and the empirical correlates of the *TRT* scale are so heavily biased toward depression, it is most improbable that scores on the *TRT* scale or its components have much to contribute to estimates of prognosis for psychotherapeutic treatments. The *TRT* scale may serve as a better predictor and description of the *severity* of depressive symptoms than as a specific and reliable indicator of negative prognostic factors for the psychotherapy of depression or any other similar disorders. The interpretation of low scores on the *TRT* scale and its components is equally problematic. Since low scorers on the *TRT* scale are adequately motivated, self-confident, planful, and persistent, they are likely to be less distressed and, therefore, less motivated for psychotherapy. The mere capacity to disclose personal information also affords no guarantee that the material revealed can be discussed productively, reflectively, or insightfully. For these reasons, both the positive and the negative predictive power of the *TRT* scale is highly suspect. Until evidence of the validity of the *TRT* scale for its intended purpose is forthcoming, this scale should be interpreted conservatively and with due caution.

There has been only limited research on the *TRT* scale. Neither Archer et al. (1996) nor Ben-Porath et al. (1993) found the *TRT* scale to be a predictor of any of the SCL-90-R or BPRS scales that they reported. Clark (1996), Haller, Knisely, Elswick, Dawson, and Schnoll (1997), and Munley and Busby (1994) reported that the *TRT* scale did not predict dropout from treatment in male pain patients, female perinatal substance abusers, or psychiatric inpatients, respectively. Clark also reported that the *TRT* scale could predict either a positive or negative response to treatment depending upon the outcome measure used. Thackston-Hawkins et al. (1994) found that the Subjective Depression (D_1) and *TRT* scales were significant predictors ($R^2 = .41$) of the Beck (1988) Hopelessness scale in college students. Chisholm, Crowther, and Ben-Porath (1997) found that the *TRT* scale predicted clients' global improvement in psychopathology as a result of psychotherapy even after controlling for the influence of generalized distress and negative emotionality and the clients' initial level of psychopathology. This outcome is the exact opposite of what would be expected. These findings of positive, negative, and no relationship with treatment exemplify the complex and seemingly contradictory nature of the *TRT* scale that was discussed earlier.

High scorers on the *TRT* scale are helpless and hopeless in the face of their seemingly overwhelming problems (*TRT1*). They are apathetic, depressive, and impotent. They do not like to talk about their personal problems and are uncomfortable when they have to do so (*TRT2*). As noted previously, it is imperative that the clinician ascertain whether these qualities are manifestations of depression and, consequently, more treatable, or if they reflect more characterological aspects of the client.

Low scorers on the *TRT* scale have confidence in their abilities to deal with their problems. They are willing to talk about their problems, which they are likely to attribute to what others are doing to them. They are not experiencing emotional distress to any significant degree that limits their motivation for any type of intervention. There may be a grandiose or narcissistic flavor to this evaluation of their abilities and competence that does not match their actual circumstances. Elevations on Scales *4* (Psychopathic Deviate) and *9* (Hypomania) are common in such clients who have unrealistic evaluations of themselves.

Concurrent elevations of other Content scales with the *TRT* scale are most likely the result of the generalized distress and negative emotionality that are common to all of them.

A summary of the interpretations of all of the MMPI-2 Content scales is given in Table 5.5.

GENERAL PRINCIPLES FOR THE INTERPRETATION OF CONTENT SCALES

The Content scales encourage a shared frame of reference between clients and the clinician that, if seized by both, defines the assessment process as a collaborative enterprise. Such collaboration can lead to a clear sense that the client is speaking, the clinician is listening, and the two are in a state of communication (cf. Finn, 1996; Fischer, 1994). However, the MMPI-2 Content scales are highly vulnerable to any variations in the accuracy of item endorsement. The strong thematic character of these scales, combined with the general obviousness or face validity of the items comprising them, makes it very easy for clients to distort their responses in whatever manner is desired. This feature is both an asset and a liability for the assessment process. It is an asset in the sense that the homo-geneity and obviousness of these scales facilitate communication between clients and the clinician. Content scales allow clients to reveal the kinds of symptoms, concerns, and attitudes that are most salient and problematic to them. Clients can report the kinds of difficulties creating concern, rank order their severity, and contrast them with problem areas that are not of concern. Presumably those areas experienced by clients as being conflict free are well within their abilities or resources to manage. Uniform T scores are used with the MMPI-2 Content scales so the T scores are equivalent across them (see Chapter 2). Thus, the Content scales can be ranked from high to low to provide a relative index of their importance and severity for clients. The highest-ranked Content scales reflect their most important concerns and will need to be the initial focus of any treatment or intervention. The lowest-ranked Content scales reflect areas of less concern and they can be deferred until later in the treatment process, if they are a focus of treatment at all.

The obvious, homogeneous character of the Content scales is a liability in the sense that clients who wish to provide an inaccurate endorsement of the items will find few obstacles for doing so. This potential liability once again emphasizes the importance of properly preparing the clients for the assessment process and its purposes, and seeking their cooperation as collaborators rather than subjects (cf. Finn, 1996; Fischer, 1994). Clinicians must explore ways that the assessment process will help to answer questions of significance to clients and provide prompt and detailed feedback. The risks of inaccurate item endorsement are greatest when clients feel deprived of a stake in a collaborative relationship with the clinician and the outcome of the assessment.

Clients wishing to present a distorted picture of their adjustment may choose to overreport or underreport all of their problems, or they may selectively emphasize some areas of difficulty and deemphasize others. Some clients, typically among the most disturbed, will intentionally overreport or underreport some kinds of symptoms, but inadvertently report or fail to report other symptoms. Such patterns of item endorsement can enormously confound and frustrate efforts at a content-based interpretation of the MMPI-2.

TABLE 5.5 Description of the MMPI-2 Content Scales

	CLINICAL AREA	
Abbreviation	*Name*	*Description*

Internal Symptomatic Behaviors

ANX	Anxiety	These clients report general symptoms of anxiety, nervousness, worries, and sleep and concentration difficulties. They have difficulty making decisions. They fear losing their minds and are afraid that they are about to go to pieces. They find life a strain and work under a great deal of tension and stress.
FRS	Fears	These clients are generally fearful and afraid (*FRS1*). They also report a large number of specific fears (*FRS2*): animals (snakes, mice, spiders); events in nature (dirt, earthquakes, fire, lightning, windstorms, water); darkness, blood, money, high places, and so on.
OBS	Obsessions	These clients have great difficulty making decisions, ruminate excessively, worry excessively, and have intrusive thoughts. They dislike change. They count and save unimportant things.
DEP	Depression	These clients are unable to get going and get things done in their lives (*DEP1*). They have depressive mood and thoughts, feel blue and unhappy, and are likely to brood (*DEP2*). They are uncertain about their future and find their lives empty and meaningless. They cry easily. They are self-critical and guilty (*DEP3*). They may report suicidal ideation or attempts (*DEP4*).
HEA	Health Concerns	These clients report specific gastrointestinal symptoms such as nausea and vomiting (*HEA1*). They report a number of neurological symptoms: pains in the chest, neck, and head; their muscles may be paralyzed or twitch and jump; and they have fainting and dizzy spells (*HEA2*). They worry about their health and catching disease. They believe that they are experiencing poor health (*HEA3*).
BIZ	Bizarre Mentation	These clients report strange thoughts, paranoid ideation, and hallucinations; in short, they report psychotic thought processes (*BIZ1*). They also report strange and unusual experiences and thoughts and ideas of reference (*BIZ2*).

External Aggressive Tendencies

ANG	Anger	These clients report that they may swear or lose control and smash objects, pick fights, and hurt someone in a fight (*ANG1*). They also describe themselves as being irritable, grouchy, impatient, hotheaded, annoyed, and stubborn (*ANG2*).
CYN	Cynicism	These clients expect other people to be interested in their own welfare and see others as unwilling to help or support them (*CYN1*). People use each other and are friendly only for selfish reasons. They do not trust others and are suspicious of their motives (*CYN2*).
ASP	Antisocial Practices	These clients have attitudes similar to individuals who break the law, even if not actually engaging in antisocial behavior. They expect other people to lie (*ASP1*). They report stealing things, other problem behaviors, and antisocial practices *during their school years* (*ASP2*).
TPA	Type A	These clients do not like to wait or be interrupted, and frequently become impatient, grouchy, irritable, and annoyed (*TPA1*). They are hard-driving, fast-moving, and work-oriented individuals, who are seen as willing to do anything needed to succeed (*TPA2*).

(continued)

TABLE 5.5   Description of the MMPI-2 Content Scales (continued)

	CLINICAL AREA	
Abbreviation	*Name*	*Description*

Negative Self-Views

LSE	Low Self-Esteem	These clients have very low opinions of themselves, and they are uncomfortable if people say nice things about them. They believe that they are unattractive, awkward and clumsy, useless, and a burden to others, who do not like them. They lack self-confidence (*LSE1*). They are passive and obedient individuals who show little initiative. They are prone to give up too easily (*LSE2*).

General Problem Areas: Social, Familial, Work, and Treatment

SOD	Social Discomfort	These clients are very uneasy around others and are happier by themselves. They avoid interpersonal contact whenever possible (*SOD1*). They see themselves as shy. They dislike parties and other group events, because they do not like meeting people and find it hard to talk (*SOD2*).
FAM	Family Problems	These clients report considerable familial discord and strife. Their families are lacking love, support, and companionship, and these clients wanted to leave home (*FAM1*). They are alienated from and unattached to their family. They do not see their family as a source of support (*FAM2*).
WRK	Work Interference	These clients report that they are not as able to work as they once were and that they work under a great deal of tension. They are tired, lack energy, and are sick of what they have to do. They dislike making decisions and lack self-confidence. They give up easily and shrink from facing a crisis or problem. Clinicians need to check explicitly that these behaviors and symptoms actually are interfering with the clients' work performance.
TRT	Negative Treatment Indicators	These clients give up quickly and do not care about what is happening to them, since nothing can be done about their problems. They may be viewed as apathetic and lacking in self-confidence (*TRT1*). They dislike going to doctors and they believe that they should not discuss their personal problems with others. They do not believe that anyone understands or cares about them (*TRT2*).

Note. Adapted from Ben-Porath and Sherwood (1993), *The MMPI-2 content component scales.* Minneapolis: University of Minnesota Press; Butcher et al. (1989), *Manual for administration and scoring of the MMPI-2.* Minneapolis: University of Minnesota Press; and Butcher et al. (1990), *Development and use of the MMPI-2 content scales.* Minneapolis: University of Minnesota Press.

The Content scales share extensive first-factor variance or generalized distress and negative emotionality (Table 5.4; Endler, Parker, & Butcher, 1993). A substantial elevation on a specific Content scale is required before the shared variance can be assumed to have been exhausted and unique variance begins to appear. The Welsh Anxiety (*A*) scale can be used as the baseline for first-factor variance and deviations from this baseline used to determine whether there is any unique variance in the elevation of a specific Content scale. If a client has a T score of 75 on the *A* scale, a T score of 85 on the Anxiety (*ANX*) or Depression (*DEP*) scale begins to reflect the unique variance of each of these Content scales beyond the generalized distress that is common to both of them. Similarly, a T score of 65 on the Low Self-Esteem (*LSE*) or Family Problems (*FAM*) scale reflects that generalized distress is *not* impacting the client's functioning in these areas.

Similar considerations apply to low scores on the Content scales. In a number of cases, such low scores result from an underreporting of psychopathology on the MMPI-2. It is still important to evaluate the overall success of the client's efforts to underreport psychopathology, and, where a failure to do so is indicated, to identify the possible causes for such failure. For example, consider a client who has all of the Content scales below T scores of 60 and all scales except the Anger (*ANG* = 53) and Type A (*TPA* = 58) scales are below T scores of 50. Although these low T scores suggest that the underreporting of psychopathology has occurred, the avoidance of items reflecting angry or hostile content was relatively less successful. It may be that the client is comfortable endorsing a few of the *ANG* and *TPA* items out of a feeling that his anger, when present, is never less than fully justified.

A NOTE ON INCREMENTAL VALIDITY

Butcher and his colleagues (Ben-Porath et al., 1991; Ben-Porath et al., 1993; Butcher et al., 1995) have suggested that incremental validity should be one of the criteria used in evaluating new MMPI-2 scales. Incremental validity indicates whether the new MMPI-2 scale adds significant variance to the relationship with a criterion beyond that provided by the original scale. Incremental validity seems particularly appropriate for many of the MMPI-2 Content scales because of the existence of a Clinical scale with which there is some degree of conceptual or theoretical similarity. Hierarchical multiple regression analyses typically are used to address this issue of incremental validity. Numerous studies (Archer et al., 1996; Ben-Porath et al., 1991; Ben-Porath et al., 1993; Lilienfeld, 1996) have demonstrated that several of the MMPI-2 Content (Bizarre Mentation [*BIZ*], Depression [*DEP*], and Antisocial Practices [*ASP*]) scales have modest incremental validity over their corresponding Clinical scale, while the Clinical scales rarely provide incremental validity over their

corresponding Content scale. There is one major caveat, however, that must be kept in mind when evaluating all of these studies. In every study the criterion used to determine incremental validity was very specific and homogeneous, so it would be expected that a more specific and homogeneous Content scale would be a better predictor of that criterion than a general and heterogeneous Clinical scale. In this regard, it would seem that some of the longer Content Component (Ben-Porath & Sherwood, 1993) scales might perform even better than the parent Component scale in these comparisons because they are even more homogeneous measures. The existence of subscales within many of the MMPI-2 Clinical scales attests to their heterogeneous composition, which was described in detail in Chapter 4. It seems imperative in these studies of incremental validity that researchers give serious consideration to the nature of the criterion being used to evaluate the scales. Many of the issues that were raised in Chapter 3 in the discussion of obvious and subtle subscales also are germane here and should be reviewed before undertaking research on this topic.

PSYCHOMETRIC CHARACTERISTICS

Table 5.4 (p. 185) provided the item overlap and intercorrelations among all of the MMPI-2 Content scales. That information will not be repeated here other than to comment that several of the MMPI-2 Content scales have substantial item overlap and most of these scales tend to be significantly intercorrelated.

The top half of Table 5.6 (p. 206) shows the item overlap among the Content scales and the standard Validity and Clinical scales. Two columns are included for each scale. The numbers in the column labeled "S" indicate how many items the two scales share that are scored in the same direction. The Anxiety (*ANX*) scale shares six items with Scale 2 (Depression) that are scored in the same direction (i.e., the deviant response is either "true" or "false" on both scales). In this specific example, all six items are scored as "true" on the *ANX* scale and Scale 2. The column labeled "O" indicates how many items the two scales share that are scored in the opposite direction. The *ANX* scale and the *K* (Correction) scale share three items that are scored in the opposite direction

TABLE 5.6 Item Overlap and Intercorrelations between the MMPI-2 Validity and Clinical Scales and the Content Scales in the Caldwell Clinical Dataset

	L		F		K		1(Hs)		2(D)		3(Hy)		4(Pd)		5(Mff)		5(Mfm)		6(Pa)		7(Pt)		8(Sc)		9(Ma)		0(Si)	
	S	O	S	O	S	O	S	O	S	O	S	O	S	O	S	O	S	O	S	O	S	O	S	O	S	O	S	O
ANX	0	0	1	0	0	3	2	0	6	0	3	0	1	0	1	0	1	0	1	0	6	0	4	1	1	0	1	0
FRS	0	0	1	0	0	0	0	0	0	0	1	0	0	0	1	0	1	0	1	0	2	0	2	0	0	1	0	0
OBS	0	0	0	0	0	1	0	0	0	1	0	1	0	0	1	0	1	0	0	0	5	0	0	0	2	0	2	0
DEP	0	0	3	0	0	1	1	0	9	0	4	0	6	0	0	0	0	0	4	0	9	0	7	0	0	0	2	0
HEA	0	0	3	0	0	0	23	0	8	2	16	0	0	0	0	0	0	0	1	0	3	0	6	0	0	0	2	0
BIZ	0	0	10	0	0	0	0	0	0	0	0	0	2	0	0	0	0	0	8	0	0	1	8	0	0	0	0	1
ANG	0	1	0	0	0	3	0	0	0	3	0	2	1	0	0	0	0	0	0	0	0	0	0	0	0	0	1	0
CYN	0	0	0	0	0	5	0	0	0	1	0	6	0	1	3	0	3	0	0	7	0	0	0	0	0	0	5	0
ASP	0	1	3	0	0	2	0	0	0	1	0	3	3	0	0	3	0	3	1	5	0	0	1	0	4	0	3	0
TPA	0	0	0	0	0	1	0	0	0	1	0	1	0	0	0	0	0	0	0	0	1	0	0	0	0	1	2	0
LSE	0	0	1	0	0	2	0	0	3	0	0	0	0	1	1	0	1	0	0	0	4	0	3	0	0	0	3	0
SOD	0	0	1	0	0	1	0	0	2	0	0	3	0	3	1	0	1	0	0	0	2	0	6	0	0	2	18	0
FAM	0	0	2	0	0	2	0	0	0	0	1	0	6	0	2	0	2	0	1	0	0	0	4	0	4	0	6	0
WRK	0	0	3	0	0	2	1	0	5	0	2	3	3	1	0	0	0	0	1	1	3	0	4	0	2	1	6	0
TRT	0	0	1	0	0	0	0	0	1	0	0	0	1	0	0	0	0	0	1	0	0	0	3	0	0	0	2	0

	L	F	K	1(Hs)	2(D)	3(Hy)	4(Pd)	5(Mff)	5(Mfm)	6(Pa)	7(Pt)	8(Sc)	9(Ma)	0(Si)
ANX	-.291	.660	-.718	.768	.799	.542	.686	.121	.324	.663	.912	.833	.410	.720
FRS	-.067	.487	-.434	.525	.478	.337	.335	.026	.208	.411	.563	.551	.215	.503
OBS	-.355	.662	-.761	.600	.597	.277	.625	.073	.279	.565	.860	.806	.490	.708
DEP	-.261	.764	-.686	.713	.796	.479	.764	.043	.294	.703	.913	.888	.403	.763
HEA	-.085	.640	-.510	.965	.761	.751	.529	.009	.206	.589	.751	.769	.366	.593
BIZ	-.185	.792	-.588	.517	.398	.230	.577	-.110	.168	.679	.665	.782	.587	.484
ANG	-.425	.600	-.769	.527	.436	.205	.621	-.002	.185	.494	.722	.715	.533	.536
CYN	-.225	.567	-.780	.447	.338	-.004	.501	-.190	.003	.306	.606	.642	.569	.546
ASP	-.363	.533	-.653	.279	.170	-.117	.512	-.237	-.014	.226	.481	.543	.598	.379
TPA	-.411	.530	-.751	.434	.338	.078	.500	-.044	.133	.395	.635	.631	.530	.486
LSE	-.266	.713	-.677	.601	.676	.315	.638	.040	.254	.584	.851	.812	.342	.791
SOD	-.139	.552	-.516	.485	.614	.229	.424	.066	.250	.445	.651	.620	.050	.892
FAM	-.352	.657	-.665	.426	.391	.152	.728	.061	.302	.494	.649	.714	.519	.528
WRK	-.307	.739	-.744	.717	.763	.425	.699	.052	.287	.632	.917	.878	.423	.800
TRT	-.247	.761	-.699	.642	.686	.338	.674	-.028	.198	.621	.851	.854	.403	.777

Note. "S" indicates that the deviant response for the item is the same on both scales; "O" indicates that the deviant response is "true" on one scale and "false" on the other scale.

(i.e., the deviant response is "true" on one scale and "false" on the other). In this specific example, all three items are scored as "true" on the *ANX* scale and as "false" on the *K* scale. Scale 8 (Schizophrenia) shares five items with the *ANX* scale: four items that are scored in the same direction on both scales and one item that is scored in the opposite direction.

The bottom half of Table 5.6 provides the correlations among the Content scales and the standard Validity and Clinical scales. The Anxiety (*ANX*) scale correlates –.291 with the *L* (Lie) scale, while the Fears (*FRS*) scale correlates –.067 with the *L* scale. The reader should note the high correlations among the *ANX,* Depression (*DEP*), Low Self-Esteem (*LSE*), Work Interference (*WRK*), and Negative Treatment Indicators (*TRT*) scales and most of the standard Validity and Clinical scales. That is, there is a substantial common variance among all of these scales that reflects generalized distress and negative emotionality with little specificity to any particular disorder.

Some of the standard Validity and Clinical scales that share items with the MMPI-2 Content scales make good intuitive sense: the Health Concerns (*HEA*) scale with Scales *1* (Hypochondriasis: 23 items) and *3* (Hysteria: 16 items, 15 of which are scored on Hysteria, Obvious); the Bizarre Mentation (*BIZ*) scale with Scale *8* (Schizophrenia: 8 items); and the Social Discomfort (*SOD*) scale with Scale *0* (Social Introversion: 18 items). However, other relationships, and particularly the lack thereof, among these scales are more puzzling. The Depression (*DEP*) scale has only nine items in common with Scale *2* (Depression) and shares items with most of the other Clinical scales. The Antisocial Practices (*ASP*), Cynicism (*CYN*), and Anger (*ANG*) scales have few items in common with Scale *4* (Psychopathic Deviate). The *CYN* and *ANG* scales share few items with any of the standard Validity and Clinical scales, while the Anxiety (*ANX*) scale shares items with all of the standard Validity and Clinical scales except for the *L* (Lie) scale.

The same pattern of overlapping items is seen among the MMPI-2 Supplementary and Content scales (Table 5.7). The Anxiety (*ANX*), Depression (*DEP*), and Work Interference (*WRK*) scales share a number of items with the Supplementary scales reflecting first-factor variance or generalized distress and negative emotionality: the Welsh Anxiety (*A*: 7

items) scale, the College Maladjustment (*Mt*: 10 items) scale, and the two Post Traumatic Stress Disorder (*PK*: 8 items, *PS*: 11 items) scales and their intercorrelations exceed 0.890. The Cynicism (*CYN*) scale shares 17 items with the Hostility (*Ho*) scale.

Table 5.8 provides the correlations among the demographic variables of age, education, and gender with the Content scales in the MMPI-2 normative group (Butcher et al., 1989) and psychiatric patients (Caldwell, 1997a). (Chapter 9 will be devoted entirely to the examination of the effects of demographic variables on MMPI-2 performance, so this discussion will be relatively brief.) The Anger (*ANG*) scale among the Content scales had the largest correlation (–.160) with age in normal individuals. Individuals 70 years of age and older in the MMPI-2 normative group had a mean T score of 47.4 on the *ANG* scale, while individuals 20 to 29 years old had a mean T score of 51.7 (Table 9.6, pp. 440–441). Thus, age will modify any Content scale in normal individuals by less than 5 T points at the most. The Health Concerns (*HEA*) scale among the Content scales had the largest correlation (.151) with age in psychiatric patients. Patients 20 to 29 years of age had a mean T score of 55.4 on the *HEA* scale, while patients 70 years of age and older had a mean T score of 61.6 (Table 9.6). The correlations with age are typically even smaller in psychiatric patients than are seen in normal individuals. Age will modify any of the Content scales in psychiatric patients by less than 6 T points.

The correlations among the Content scales with gender tend to be similar in normal individuals and psychiatric patients. (A positive correlation with gender in Table 5.8 reflects that women have higher scores on the scale.) The largest correlations are with the Fears (*FRS*) scale: .383 in normal individuals and .313 in psychiatric patients. Women endorse two to three more of the *FRS* items than men (Table 9.12, p. 449). These differences do not affect the interpretation of the *FRS* scale because the T scores are provided by gender.

The correlations among the Content scales with education also tend to be similar in normal individuals and psychiatric patients. The largest correlations are with the Cynicism (*CYN*) and Antisocial Practices (*ASP*) scales: –.334 and –.248 in normal individuals and –.271 and –.256 in psychiatric patients,

TABLE 5.7 Item Overlap and Intercorrelations between the MMPI-2 Content and Supplementary Scales in the Caldwell Clinical Dataset

	A		R		Es		MAC-R		O-H		Do		Re		Mt		GM		GF		PK		PS		AAS		APS		MDS		Ho		CAL-R	
	S	O	S	O	S	O	S	O	S	O	S	O	S	O	S	O	S	O	S	O	S	O	S	O	S	O	S	O	S	O	S	O	S	O
ANX	7	0	0	0	0	4	0	1	1	1	0	1	0	0	10	0	0	2	0	0	8	0	11	0	0	0	2	0	0	0	0	0	0	0
FRS	0	0	0	0	0	5	0	1	1	0	0	0	0	1	0	0	0	10	0	0	0	0	1	0	0	0	0	0	0	0	0	0	1	0
OBS	5	0	0	0	0	4	0	0	0	0	0	1	0	0	0	0	0	1	0	0	4	0	2	0	0	0	1	0	0	1	0	0	0	1
DEP	9	0	0	0	0	3	3	0	0	1	1	1	0	0	10	0	0	3	0	0	11	0	11	0	0	0	1	1	1	0	1	0	2	0
HEA	0	0	4	0	0	8	2	1	1	0	0	0	1	0	2	0	0	4	0	0	2	0	4	0	0	0	0	0	0	0	0	0	2	0
BIZ	1	0	0	0	0	3	1	0	0	0	0	0	0	0	0	0	0	0	0	0	3	0	4	0	0	0	0	0	0	0	0	0	1	5
ANG	0	0	0	3	0	0	0	1	0	2	0	1	0	1	1	0	0	0	0	1	2	0	3	0	0	0	2	0	0	0	2	0	1	0
CYN	0	0	0	1	0	0	1	0	1	0	0	2	0	2	2	0	0	0	0	0	0	0	0	0	0	1	0	2	0	0	17	0	0	1
ASP	0	0	0	1	0	1	4	0	0	0	0	2	0	5	0	0	0	0	0	0	0	0	0	0	1	0	0	1	0	0	7	0	0	1
TPA	0	0	0	2	0	0	1	0	0	1	0	2	0	3	0	0	0	0	0	2	1	0	0	0	0	0	1	0	0	0	6	0	0	1
LSE	2	0	0	0	0	1	0	1	0	0	2	0	0	0	3	0	0	3	0	0	0	0	1	0	0	0	0	0	0	0	0	0	0	1
SOD	0	0	3	0	0	0	0	2	0	0	0	1	0	1	1	0	0	1	0	1	0	0	3	0	0	0	0	1	0	0	2	0	0	0
FAM	0	0	0	2	0	0	1	2	0	0	0	0	0	0	1	0	0	0	0	0	3	0	2	0	0	0	0	1	6	0	3	0	1	0
WRK	8	0	1	0	1	3	2	0	2	0	3	0	0	0	9	0	0	3	0	0	5	0	5	0	0	0	0	0	1	0	1	0	0	1
TRT	1	0	0	0	0	1	1	0	0	0	0	1	0	0	0	0	0	1	0	0	3	0	3	0	1	0	1	4	3	0	1	0	0	0

	A	R	Es	MAC-R	O-H	Do	Re	Mt	GM	GF	PK	PS	AAS	APS	MDS	Ho	CAL-R
ANX	.902	.022	-.830	.125	-.404	-.640	-.462	.930	-.776	-.229	.893	.913	.369	.374	.719	.642	.018
FRS	.533	.114	-.664	.049	-.108	-.463	-.284	.507	-.752	-.102	.529	.546	.166	.085	.395	.430	.015
OBS	.891	-.110	-.753	.225	-.473	-.659	-.549	.808	-.747	-.273	.829	.837	.425	.348	.715	.715	.101
DEP	.915	.047	-.806	.183	-.421	-.685	-.492	.912	-.773	-.323	.934	.931	.430	.253	.803	.667	.108
HEA	.682	.168	-.832	.122	-.210	-.539	-.317	.763	-.722	-.238	.741	.780	.270	.178	.556	.491	-.117
BIZ	.653	-.154	-.646	.385	-.293	-.542	-.558	.585	-.639	-.408	.717	.704	.439	.160	.586	.689	.178
ANG	.728	-.292	-.577	.369	-.543	-.522	-.646	.713	-.576	-.391	.743	.754	.498	.406	.652	.727	.117
CYN	.644	-.264	-.540	.421	-.383	-.598	-.611	.602	-.542	-.361	.641	.629	.396	.118	.576	.921	.081
ASP	.517	-.362	-.346	.557	-.439	-.518	-.748	.470	-.423	-.507	.525	.503	.566	.223	.498	.781	.206
TPA	.665	-.357	-.493	.371	-.561	-.450	-.611	.621	-.527	-.345	.638	.643	.417	.362	.565	.791	.080
LSE	.870	.041	-.739	.141	-.420	-.708	-.495	.810	-.772	-.274	.821	.832	.404	.215	.731	.651	.126
SOD	.644	.300	-.579	-.086	-.321	-.543	-.297	.621	-.585	-.221	.652	.640	.253	.031	.554	.477	.004
FAM	.683	-.225	-.518	.295	-.413	-.509	-.596	.628	-.586	-.374	.684	.675	.518	.262	.812	.693	.228
WRK	.936	.024	-.814	.149	-.464	-.719	-.523	.917	-.797	-.289	.899	.918	.418	.291	.771	.709	.063
TRT	.873	.021	-.767	.209	-.440	-.703	-.519	.828	-.747	-.342	.873	.873	.435	.161	.776	.714	.107

Note. "S" indicates that the deviant response for the item is the same on both scales; "O" indicates that the deviant response is "true" on one scale and "false" on the other scale.

208

TABLE 5.8   Effects of Demographic Variables on the MMPI-2 Content Scales

| | CORRELATION | | | | | |
| | Age | | Gender[a] | | Education | |
	NORMALS[b]	PATIENTS[c]	NORMALS[b]	PATIENTS[c]	NORMALS[b]	PATIENTS[c]
ANX	−.128	.063	.114	.126	−.118	−.148
FRS	.129	.113	.383	.313	−.265	−.199
OBS	.042	.043	.088	.074	−.179	−.176
DEP	−.075	.047	.109	.081	−.195	−.180
HEA	.064	.151	.101	.151	−.209	−.196
BIZ	−.131	−.053	−.019	−.010	−.233	−.215
ANG	−.160	−.027	.009	.001	−.185	−.174
CYN	.033	−.013	−.072	−.055	−.334	−.271
ASP	−.146	−.105	−.215	−.187	−.248	−.256
TPA	.016	.050	−.095	−.067	−.092	−.095
LSE	.092	.040	.111	.103	−.233	−.195
SOD	.001	.085	−.012	.015	−.066	−.118
FAM	−.147	−.040	.110	.072	−.154	−.147
WRK	−.026	.053	.113	.108	−.200	−.186
TRT	.079	.052	.042	.049	−.239	−.211

[a]Positive correlations reflect that women have higher scores on the indicated scale.
[b]Butcher et al., 1989.
[c]Caldwell, 1997a.

respectively. Normal individuals and psychiatric patients with less than 9 years of education had mean T scores of 56.8 and 56.1 on the *ANG* scale, respectively, while normal individual and psychiatric patients with more than 18 years of education had mean T scores of 46.1 and 47.6, respectively (Table 9.18, pp. 458–459). There are nearly 10 T points difference between normal individuals and psychiatric patients with less than 9 years of education and more than 18 years of education on the Depression (*DEP*), Bizarre Mentation (*BIZ*), Anger (*ANG*), Antisocial Practices (*ASP*), Low Self-Esteem (*LSE*), Family Problems (*FAM*), Work Interference (*WRK*), and Negative Treatment Indicators (*TRT*) scales. Clinicians need to be more aware of the potential effects of education on most of the Content scales because of the large differences that are found.

Table 5.9 reports the percentage of items on each Content scale for which "true" and "false" are the deviant response. Almost all of the Content scales ex-

cept for the Health Concerns (*HEA*) and Social Discomfort (*SOD*) scales have "true" as the deviant response for three-fourths or more of the items. Clients who have a propensity to endorse the items in either the "true" or "false" direction will raise or lower all of these Content scales in unison. The clinician should note the percentage of items that clients have endorsed "true" and "false" *before* beginning to interpret any of these scales to ascertain whether a response set is a major contributor to their elevation. Profile 5.1 illustrates the effects of endorsing all of the items "true" or "false" on each of the MMPI-2 Content scales.

Table 5.9 also provides the mean rating of the obviousness of the content of the items on each of the Content scales (Christian et al., 1978). The Anxiety (*ANX*) scale has a mean rating of 3.53 that indicates its items are slightly obvious in content. The items on most of the Content scales are rated as being neither obvious nor subtle with mean ratings around 3.00.

TABLE 5.9 True and False Composition of the MMPI-2 Content Scales

	Number of Items	PERCENTAGE		OBVIOUSNESS[a]	
		True	False	Mean	Items
ANX	23	78.3	21.7	3.53	20
FRS	23	69.6	30.4	3.15	22
OBS	16	100.0	0.0	3.24	10
DEP	33	84.8	15.2	3.66	25
HEA	36	38.9	61.1	3.16	36
BIZ	23	95.7	4.3	4.03	19
ANG	16	93.8	6.2	2.91	10
CYN	23	100.0	0.0	3.01	21
ASP	22	95.5	4.5	3.10	21
TPA	19	100.0	0.0	3.03	12
LSE	24	87.5	12.5	3.38	13
SOD	24	54.2	45.8	2.82	21
FAM	25	80.0	20.0	3.17	16
WRK	33	84.8	15.2	3.11	22
TRT	26	88.5	11.5	3.43	8

[a]These ratings are based on Christian et al. (1978).

The Bizarre Mentation (*BIZ*) scale has the highest mean (4.03) rating for obviousness among the content scales, while the Social Discomfort (*SOD*) scale has the lowest rating (2.82).

MMPI-2 STRUCTURAL SUMMARY

Clinicians trying to learn the interrelationships among only the basic Validity and Clinical scales on the MMPI-2 are faced by a daunting information processing task (cf. Faust, 1984). Trying to keep track of the dozens of additional scales makes this task virtually impossible. (At the time of writing this text, the National Computer Systems' Extended Score Report provides scores on 129 different MMPI-2 scales. This number would be even higher if the Personality Disorder scales [Morey, Waugh, & Blashfield, 1985], Personality Psychopathology Five [Harkness, McNulty, & Ben-Porath, 1995] scales, Obvious and Subtle subscales [Wiener, 1948], and Wiggins Content [1966] scales were included.) If clinicians are unfazed by the sheer number of scales on the MMPI-2,

there are a number of associated problems to consider. First, the name of an MMPI-2 scale may be a very misleading guide to its suitability as a measure of a specific construct. Similarly named scales such as Scale *2* (Depression) and the MMPI-2 Content scale of Depression (*DEP*) may have quite different clinical correlates (cf. Nichols, 1987, 1988; Streit et al., 1993). Conversely, scales with different names may have very similar clinical correlates. For example, Scale *7* (Psychasthenia) and the Welsh Anxiety (*A*), College Maladjustment (*Mt*), Post Traumatic Stress Disorder—Keane (*PK*), and Post Traumatic Stress Disorder—Schlenger (*PS*) scales are all measures of generalized distress and negative emotionality that are highly intercorrelated, with pairwise coefficients greater than .90 (see Table 6.12, pp. 238–239). Second, some scales are used in ways that their names may not suggest. For example, despite its name, the MacAndrew Alcoholism (MAC: MacAndrew, 1965) scale is widely seen as a general addiction scale, not limited to alcohol addiction, and is a more general measure of risk-taking behaviors. Third, items assessing the same content may be displaced unevenly across a number of disparate scales. The large group of items reflecting cynicism and mistrustful attitudes toward others can be found on scales with names as diverse as the Cynicism (*CYN*), Wiggins (1966) Authority Conflict (*AUT*), Hostility (*Ho*: Cook & Medley, 1954), and Antisocial Practices (*ASP*) scales, and, scored in the opposite direction, the Need for Affection (Hy_2) and Moral Virtue (Pa_3) scales.

The standard format for reporting MMPI-2 scores is organized in clusters or groups that emphasize the types or origins of particular scales or sets of scales rather than their interpretive meanings. This standard format makes it time-consuming and burdensome to compare scores on scales from different sets that have similar interpretive implications. The clinician must move back and forth through the many groups of scores in order to ascertain areas of significant redundancy among scores. In this format, the standard Validity and Clinical scales appear first, and they are followed by the Supplementary scales, the MMPI-2 Content scales, and the Harris and Lingoes subscales. The greatest virtue of the standard format is that it encourages the recognition of configural pat-

PROFILE 5.1

Note. Minnesota Multiphasic Personality Inventory-2 (MMPI-2). Copyright © 1942, 1943 (renewed 1970), 1989 by the Regents of the University of Minnesota. Reproduced by permission of the publisher. "MMPI-2" and "Minnesota Multiphasic Personality Inventory-2" are trademarks owned by the University of Minnesota.

terns within each set of scales. However, this format makes it very difficult to recognize similarities or differences between sets of scales.

The MMPI-2 Structural Summary (Greene & Nichols, 1995; Nichols & Greene, 1995) is a template for organizing in a logical and coherent manner the multitude of scales and indices that are scored on the MMPI-2. The Structural Summary facilitates the efficient review of MMPI-2 findings by providing a set of clinically relevant categories into which scales of disparate names, types, and origins have been sorted. This organization maximizes the extraction of interpretive information, while minimizing the amount of time required to do so. The Structural Summary achieves these goals by enabling the most salient factors in test performance to stand out, allowing a rapid appraisal of consistency and robustness of trends in MMPI-2 data, and by following a sequence of topics that facilitates the preparation of interpretive reports. The advantages that the Structural Summary brings to the analysis of the MMPI-2 are not limited to profiles of any particular configuration. Regardless of whether profiles are well or poorly defined, typical or atypical, elevated or unelevated, the Structural Summary will highlight trends in the MMPI-2 profile that are of clinical importance. If anything, the Structural Summary may demonstrate its greatest utility in the interpretation of uncommon and atypical profiles, as well as profiles having low or marginal elevations, simply because, for these kinds of cases, the standard interpretive literature is least adequate.

Since the Rorschach technique was recast by Exner into the Comprehensive System (Exner, 1993), the Rorschach Structural Summary has become the central point of departure for its interpretation. The MMPI-2 Structural Summary does *not* intend to play such a role in the MMPI-2 environment, in which the fundamental standard for interpretation remains the standard Validity and Clinical scales and the resulting codetype analysis. The role of the MMPI-2 Structural Summary is similar to that of its Rorschach counterpart, however, in that it organizes a great variety of apparently disparate observations into a coherent format, reducing the risk that important scores and configural features will be overlooked. Organizing scales with similar meanings and implications into mean-

ingful categories supports an improved calibration of interpretive inferences. When all of a group of related scales are elevated, the characteristic in question is likely to be potent or pervasive, or both. When some scales are elevated but others in the group are not, the characteristic, depending upon the pattern, may be weak, inconsistent, or strong, but it is likely to be more narrow and specific.

The structural relationships among scales served as the basis for empirical ordering among and within the Structural Summary categories. Various statistical procedures were used to derive MMPI-2 Structural Summary categories, including studies of item overlap, examination of scale internal consistencies, and the confirmation of patterns of covariation among measures using correlational and factor analytic techniques. Within each block of scores, scales are arranged in descending order of adequacy as measures of the concept given in the category or subcategory name. Several considerations entered into decisions concerning how scales were ranked within each category: (a) item content, (b) item overlap (positive and negative, with high positive and low negative overlap favoring higher rank), (c) magnitude of loadings attained on factors related to the concept embodied in the category, (d) magnitude of loadings on certain other factors to which the scales should not be related, (e) length of the scales (longer scales favored), and (f) internal consistencies and variances (with higher values favoring higher rank). Given the number of features available to contribute to decisions involving the assignment of scales to categories and the order of scales within each of the categories, the experience and judgment of the authors played an important role in setting the form of the MMPI-2 Structural Summary.

The MMPI-2 Structural Summary is divided into six major sections: Test-Taking Attitudes, Factor Scales, Moods, Cognitions, Interpersonal Relations, and Other Problem Areas. Each section contains from 2 to 12 subsections, with some subsections containing further subdivisions. Table 5.10 presents an overview of the arrangement of the MMPI-2 Structural Summary. The scores on the MMPI-2 Structural Summary are presented in one or more blocks within each substantive category. For example, for the category Second-Factor Scales (Overcontrol vs. Undercontrol),

TABLE 5.10 Categories and Subcategories for the MMPI-2 Structural Summary

Test-Taking Attitudes

1. Omissions
2. Consistency
3. Accuracy
   A. Self—Unfavorable
   B. Self—Favorable

Factor Scales

1. First-Factor Scales (General Distress)
2. Second-Factor Scales (Overcontrol vs. Undercontrol)
   A. Emotional Overcontrol
   B. Behavioral Overcontrol

Moods

1. Depression
   A. Depressed Mood/Dysphoria
   B. Depressed Ideation/Attitudes
   C. Mental Insufficiency
   D. Vegetative Signs
2. Anhedonia
3. Elation
4. Anxiety
5. Guilt
6. Fears
7. Emotional Alienation (Hopelessness)
8. Anger/Hostility
9. Denial of Anger/Hostility

Cognitions

1. Unconventional Thought
2. Psychotic Thought Processes
3. Grandiose Thought Processes
4. Paranoid Thought Processes
5. Obsessions/Ruminations

Cognitions (continued)

6. Cynicism
7. Memory, Attention, and Concentration
8. Defense Mechanisms
   A. Repression
   B. Denial
   C. Somatization
   D. Rationalization/Intellectualization
   E. Externalization
   F. Projection
   G. Acting Out
   H. Fantasy

Interpersonal Relations

1. Extroversion/Introversion
   A. Extroversion
   B. Introversion
2. Social Alienation
3. Self-Alienation
4. Masculinity/Femininity
5. Family Alienation
6. Delinquency/Antisocial Practices
7. Authority Conflict/Antisocial Attitudes
8. Passive/Aggressive Struggles
9. Passivity/Submissiveness
10. Dependency
11. Dominance/Assertiveness
12. Narcissism

Other Problem Areas

1. Substance Abuse
2. Suicidal Ideation
3. Sleep Disturbances
4. Sexual Difficulties

two blocks of scales have been identified that are associated with specific aspects of this dimension, scales that address emotional overcontrol and scales that address behavioral overcontrol (Table 5.11). Within the first block, scores are further separated into two subgroups: Scores for the Welsh Repression (R) scale are separated from scores for the Psychomotor Retardation (D_2), Depression-Subtle (D-S), Type A (TPA), Anger (ANG), and Inhibition of Aggression (Hy_5) scales to indicate that the R scale is a superior measure of the emotional overcontrol dimension. The other scales, from D_2 to Hy_5, although strongly re-

TABLE 5.11 MMPI-2 Structural Summary, Page Two

TEST-TAKING ATTITUDES

1. Omissions

    __3__ ? (Cannot Say)

2. Consistency

    __9__ VRIN (Variable Response) [raw]

    __65__ VRIN (Variable Response) [T]

    __10__ TRIN (True Response) [raw]

    __57T__ TRIN (True Response) [T]

3. Accuracy

  A. Self—Unfavorable

    __12__ F (Infrequency) [raw]

    __73__ F (Infrequency) [T]

    __5__ F_B (Infrequency Back) [raw]

    __63__ F_B (Infrequency Back) [T]

__34__ $O - S$ (Total T Score Differences on Obvious-Subtle Scales)

__-1__ $F - K$ [raw scores]

__20__ $K - B$ (Total Critical Items Endorsed)

__28__ L&W (Total Critical Items Endorsed)

__44__ True % (Percent True)

B. Self—Favorable

    __6__ L (Lie) [raw]

    __61__ L (Lie) [T]

    __13__ K (Correction) [raw]

    __45__ K (Correction) [T]

    __55__ False % (Percent FALSE)

FACTOR SCALES

1. First Factor Scales (General Distress)

    __53__ A (Welsh Anxiety)

    __*47__ Pt (Psychasthenia)

    __54__ PS (PTSD—Schlenger)

    __52__ PK (PTSD—Keane)

    __54__ Mt (College Maladjustment)

    __50__ WRK (Work Interference)

    __45__ ANX (Anxiety)

    __64__ TRT (Negative Treatment)

    __62__ LSE (Low Self-Esteem)

    __66__ DEP (Depression)

    [45] K (Correction) [low]

    [54] Es (Ego Strength) [low]

2. Second Factor Scales (Overcontrol vs. Undercontrol)

  A. Emotional Overcontrol

    __56__ R (Repression)

    __59__ D_2 (Psychomotor Retardation)

__48__ D-S (Depression, Subtle)

[68] TPA (Type A) [low]

[50] ANG (Anger) [low]

__48__ Hy_5 (Inhibition of Aggression)

B. Behavioral Overcontrol

[68] Pd_2 (Authority Conflict) [low]

__34__ Re (Social Responsibility)

__37__ GF (Gender Role—Feminine)

[69] MAC-R (MacAndrew Alcoholism) [low]

[55] ASP (Antisocial Practices) [low]

[68] Pd-O (Psychopathic Deviate, Obvious) [low]

__35__ O-H (Overcontrolled-Hostility)

Note. From the MMPI-2 Structural Summary by R. L. Greene and D. S. Nichols, Copyright © 1995 by Psychological Assessment Resources, Inc., Odessa, FL. Reproduced with permission of the publisher.
*Non-K-corrected T scores are entered for clinical scales *Hs, Pd, Pt, Sc,* and *Ma.*

lated to this dimension, evidence various biases that render them less appropriate as comprehensive summaries of the dimension.

An exception to this rule of the scales being ordered from most to least salient is the location of the Koss and Butcher (1973) and Lachar and Wrobel (1979) sets of critical items. These sets of critical items are positioned at the bottom of those categories in which they are found because they have not been scaled. Instead, it is indicated how many items occur in the set and how many of these items the client has endorsed. In Table 5.12, under B. Depressed Ideation/Attitudes, there are 22 items in the Koss and Butcher (K-B) critical item set of Depression-Suicidal Ideation, and the client has endorsed 13 of them. There are 16 items in the Lachar and Wrobel (L&W) critical item set of Depression and Worry, and the client has endorsed 9 of them. Nichols and Greene (1995, Table 3, p. 16) have provided suggested cutting scores for these critical item sets for clinical settings.

When one of the K-corrected Clinical scales of the MMPI-2 (i.e., Scales 1 [Hypochondriasis], 4 [Psychopathic Deviate], 7 [Psychasthenia], 8 (Schizophrenia], and 9 [Hypomania]) appears in the Structural Summary, it is presented in its non-K-corrected T score form that is noted by an "*". (Scale 7 [Psychasthenia] under First-Factor Scales in Table 5.11 is an example of this procedure.) These scales are *not* K-corrected because the emphasis in the MMPI-2 Structural Summary is on content, and the K scale taps very different content than these Clinical scales. The K scale consists of items that reflect the denial of psychological symptoms and the absence of interpersonal conflict, while the MMPI-2 Clinical scales are marked by the presence of a variety of psychological symptoms and all types of interpersonal conflict. Using the K-corrected versions of these five Clinical scales has the potential effect of combining disparate groups of items into a single measure that would confuse rather than enhance a structural interpretation of the MMPI-2. Consequently, to avoid this potential problem, it is extremely important, particularly when completing the MMPI-2 Structural Summary by hand, to utilize the non-K-corrected versions of these five Clinical scales.

Clinicians using the MMPI-2 Structural Summary for the first time may be surprised when a specific scale is not found within a particular category. The best example of such an omission is the Welsh Anxiety (A) scale, which does not appear among the scales given under the 4. Anxiety category (Table 5.12), even though its name suggests that it would belong in it. When the Anxiety category is defined in terms of item content, the A scale has slightly lower correlations with the Anxiety content scale (ANX: .902) than with the MMPI-2 Depression content scale (DEP: .915). By examining the correlations of other scales with the A scale, some of which will be summarized in Table 6.1 (p. 221), it can be seen that this scale is sensitive not only to anxiety, but also to several other sources of distress as well, including depression, confusion, negative self-concept, and psychoticism, among others. The value of the A scale as a specific indicator of anxiety is so compromised as to render it misleading for this purpose. On the other hand, the A scale is an excellent index of a client's overall level of generalized distress and negative emotionality, whereas the ANX scale, like the DEP, Low Self-Esteem (LSE), and other scales, tends to be biased toward one or another of the specific forms that generalized distress and negative emotionality can take.

Because of differences in the way scales are keyed, some blocks of scores contain scales that reflect a given characteristic when their scores are low, which is indicated by brackets after the scale name ([low]). These scales have an inverse relation to the trait or characteristic being assessed. For example, the Gender Role—Masculine (GM) [low] scale appears below the Fears (FRS) scale in the 6. Fears category (Table 5.12). Almost half of the FRS items, 10 of 23, appear on the GM scale but are scored in the opposite direction; i.e., if the deviant response is "true" on the FRS scale, the deviant response is "false" on the GM scale, and vice versa. Thus, low scores on the GM scale are consistent with higher levels of fears and fearfulness. In some cases, most of the scales for a given block are presented as measures for a category when scores are low as in Second-Factor Scales (Overcontrol vs. Undercontrol), B. Behavioral Overcontrol (Table 5.11). In this case, the best measures

TABLE 5.12 MMPI-2 Structural Summary, Page Three

<table>
<tr><th colspan="2" style="text-align:center">MOODS</th></tr>
<tr><td>

1. Depression

  A. Depressed Mood/Dysphoria

84	D_1	(Subjective Depression)
68	D_5	(Brooding)
59	Pa_2	(Poignancy)

  B. Depressed Ideation/Attitudes

77	DEP	(Depression)
49	Sc_2	(Emotional Alienation)
13/22	K-B	(Depression-Suicidal Ideation)
9/16	L&W	(Depression and Worry)
3/5	Items	150, 303, 506, 520, 524 endorsed "true"

  C. Mental Insufficiency

84	D_4	(Mental Dullness)
67	Sc_3	(Lack of Ego Mastery, Cognitive)
65	Sc_4	(Lack of Ego Mastery, Conative)
84	D_2	(Psychomotor Retardation)

  D. Vegetative Signs

78	D_3	(Physical Malfunctioning)
43	Hy_3	(Lassitude-Malaise)
84	D_2	(Psychomotor Retardation)
61	HEA	(Health Concerns)
2/6	L&W	(Sexual Concern and Deviation)
3/6	L&W	(Sleep Disturbance)
[40]	Ma_2	(Psychomotor Acceleration) [low]

2. Anhedonia

68	D_5	(Brooding)
77	DEP	(Depression)
84	D_4	(Mental Dullness)
65	Sc_4	(Lack of Ego Mastery, Conative)
49	Sc_2	(Emotional Alienation)

</td><td>

84	D_2	(Psychomotor Retardation)
82	Pd_5	(Self Alienation)

3. Elation

*51	Ma	(Hypomania)
[92]	D	(Depression) [low]
56	Ma_4	(Ego Inflation)
[68]	LSE	(Low Self-Esteem) [low]
[46]	FRS	(Fears) [low]
[77]	DEP	(Depression) [low]

4. Anxiety

69	ANX	(Anxiety)
*71	Pt	(Psychasthenia)
8/17	K-B	(Acute Anxiety State)
4/11	L&W	(Anxiety & Tension)

5. Guilt

82	Pd_5	(Self-Alienation)
68	D_5	(Brooding)

6. Fears

46	FRS	(Fears)
[32]	GM	(Gender Role—Masculine) [low]
[30]	Es	(Ego Strength) [low]
*71	Pt	(Psychasthenia)
*67	Sc	(Schizophrenia)
59	Sc_5	(Lack of Ego Matery, Defective Inhibition)

7. Emotional Alienation (Hopelessness)

49	Sc_2	(Emotional Alienation)
82	Pd_5	(Self-Alienation)
69	Sc_1	(Social Alienation)

</td></tr>
</table>

* Non-*K*-corrected T scores are entered for clinical scales *Hs, Pd, Pt, Sc,* and *Ma.*

for the dimension are Block's (1965) Ego-Control scale and the Constraint (*CON*: Harkness et al., 1995) scale in which overcontrol is associated with high scores. Unfortunately, neither hand nor computer scoring is readily available for either of these scales.

Scores may be most conveniently transposed onto the Structural Summary form using The MMPI-2 Structural Summary software (Greene & Nichols, 1995), which prepares a Structural Summary report from MMPI-2 scores entered by the clinician or by accepting the output file from the National Computer System's Extended Score Report and its variants. The MMPI-2 Structural Summary also may be prepared by hand scoring the MMPI-2 or transcribing from the National Computer System's Extended Score Reports onto the MMPI-2 Structural Summary form.

Nichols and Greene (1995, Chapter 4) have delineated the interpretive process for the MMPI-2 Structural Summary. The use of the MMPI-2 Structural Summary will be illustrated in Chapter 8 when two MMPI-2 profiles are interpreted.

CHAPTER 6

Supplementary Scales, Critical Items, and Short Forms

The popularity of the MMPI quickly led to the proliferation of additional means of garnering information from the item pool. The apparent ease with which investigators can identify a criterion group and contrast their responses to all 550 items on the MMPI with a normal group has resulted in more than 450 special scales (Dahlstrom et al., 1975).

A large number of these MMPI scales are too limited or specialized for widespread use and few of them are cross-validated. Consequently, only some of the more widely used Supplementary scales will be considered here. It is necessary to administer all 567 MMPI-2 items if all the Supplementary and Content scales and critical items are to be evaluated. The client can stop after answering the first 370 items of the MMPI-2 (see Chapter 2) and the clinician still can score the standard Validity and Clinical scales and plot the standard profile.

The clinician must realize, however, that most of the Supplementary scales and critical item lists that will be discussed in this chapter also require scoring many of the last 200 items. Consequently, these additional sources of information about the client must be sacrificed if only the first 370 items are administered. In most circumstances, if it is appropriate to administer the first 370 items on the MMPI-2, there is limited rationale for not administering the last 200 items.

The discussion of the MMPI-2 Supplementary scales will be organized into two groups. The four Supplementary scales (Welsh Anxiety [A], Welsh Repression [R], Ego Strength [Es], and MacAndrew Alcohol—Revised [MAC-R]) that are scored by most clinicians who use the MMPI-2 will be discussed first. Then the remaining Supplementary scales will be discussed. Finally, the MMPI-2 Personality Disorder (Morey et al., 1985) scales and the Personality Psychopathology Five (Harkness et al., 1995) scales that are not scored routinely will be discussed briefly.

Next, certain items within the MMPI-2 have been identified as "critical" or "stop" items because by endorsing any one of these items, the client is acknowledging the existence of behavior or psychopathology that may demand immediate attention. This chapter will review various lists of critical items and the problems of identifying what and how many items are actually critical. Another set of MMPI-2 items has been identified as "correction" items that should be removed when scoring the MMPI-2 because the patient is conjectured to be endorsing these items due to the presence of a physical disease or brain injury rather than psychopathology. These various sets of correction items will be reviewed along with suggestions about how to evaluate such procedures when interpreting the MMPI-2. Finally, this chapter will review the research on MMPI short forms (i.e., abbreviated versions of the MMPI that attempt to predict the scores on the Validity and Clinical scales from a limited number of items), and will conclude with the reasons why they are not recommended for use in clinical practice.

SUPPLEMENTARY SCALES

Before undertaking the development of a new scale on the MMPI-2, the clinician is strongly encouraged to review Clopton's (1974, 1978b, 1979a, 1982; Clopton & Neuringer, 1977a; Levitt, 1978) description of the methodology for the development of scales and the description of the common methodological problems in MMPI (Butcher & Tellegen, 1978) and

MMPI-2 (Butcher et al., 1995; Greene, Gwin, & Staal, 1997) research. The use of logistic regression rather than other statistical procedures such as chi square to select items also is recommended, because logistic regression ensures that each item contributes unique variance to the scale. Davis and Offord (1997) have outlined in general terms the use of logistic regression in scale development, and Davis, Offord, Colligan, and Morse (1991) used logistic regression in developing the Common Alcoholism Logistic (*CAL*) scale that will be reviewed later.

The associated issue of whether these new scales generate redundant information already provided by the standard Validity and Clinical scales has not been investigated widely. Clopton and Klein (1978) found that three Supplementary scales (Prejudice, Ego Strength, and MacAndrew Alcoholism) were highly related to the scores on the standard Validity and Clinical scales. They found, however, that a client's individual scores on these three scales could not be predicted accurately. Archer, Elkins, Aiduk, and Griffin (1997) examined the incremental validity of the Supplementary scales in a large sample of psychiatric patients. They found that the Supplementary scales only marginally increased the correlations with external criteria. This issue of the possible redundancy of the Supplementary scales with the standard Validity and Clinical scales needs further investigation.

The interest in the Supplementary scales of the MMPI has increased in the last decade as evidenced by three recent texts (Caldwell, 1988; Levitt, 1989; Levitt & Gotts, 1995). Caldwell has provided interpretive information on 104 different Supplementary scales and Levitt on 68. Both Caldwell and Levitt reviewed the Harris and Lingoes (1955) subscales, Wiggins' (1966) Content scales, and the Tryon, Stein, and Chu Cluster scales (Stein, 1968). The interpretive information in both books reflects the authors' clinical experience in using the various scales with little empirical data presented.

Levitt (1989; Levitt & Gotts, 1995) also included a list of Supplementary scales that are not recommended for clinical use. The rationale for including a specific scale in this list was not made explicit other than a general statement about lack of experimental evaluation. No doubt some clinicians will be concerned that their favorite scale is on Levitt's "hit" list. Levitt also recommended the use of several scales in his text that would seem to reflect the same lack of experimental validation such as the Tryon, Stein, and Chu Cluster scales (Stein, 1968), Overcontrolled Hostility (Megargee et al., 1967), and the Wiener and Harmon (Wiener, 1948) Depression-Subtle subscale.

Colligan et al. (1989) have provided percentile ranks from their contemporary normative sample by gender for many of the scales reviewed in this chapter.

Welsh Anxiety (*A*) and Repression (*R*) Scales

Factor-analytic studies of the MMPI *clinical scales* have consistently identified two factors that are variously labeled and interpreted. (Factor-analytic studies of the MMPI *items* have identified as many as 21 factors [e.g., Johnson, Null, Butcher, & Johnson, 1984].) Welsh (1956) constructed his Anxiety (*A*) and Repression (*R*) scales to measure these two factors. The first factor has been interpreted in several different ways, and investigators debated for nearly ten years over which interpretation was most appropriate.

Welsh found that the first factor has high positive correlations with Scales *7* (Psychasthenia: .951) and *8* (Schizophrenia: 895) and high negative correlations with the *K* (Correction: −.792) scale.[1] The first factor has been identified as reflecting a personality factor labeled anxiety (Welsh, 1956), lack of ego resiliency (Block, 1965), and general maladjustment (Tyler, 1951). This factor also has been identified as reflecting a response bias factor labeled social desirability (Edwards & Diers, 1962) or the deviation hypothesis (Berg, 1955, 1957). In the deviation hypothesis, the actual item content and personality characteristics are deemed to be unimportant since a general response tendency is the primary determinant of whether or not the client endorses a specific item.

After a decade of debate, Block (1965) demonstrated that the factor structure of the MMPI was virtually unchanged when the potential of response bias, particularly social desirability and acquiescence, was controlled. Although Jackson (1967) questioned

---

1. These correlations are for the psychiatric patients in the Caldwell (1997a) clinical dataset.

Block's research on several methodological issues, Block's findings convinced most investigators that the first factor should be interpreted as a personality factor rather than a response bias factor. More recently, Shweder (1977a, 1977b) renewed the debate when he posited that the first factor reflects a conceptual linkage among test items that is not a personality factor.

The reader is encouraged to examine Shweder's (1977a) proposed interpretation, Block's (1977) and Edwards' (1977) response to Shweder, and Shweder's (1977b) reply to Block and Edwards for further information on this heated debate. Dahlstrom et al. (1975) provided an in-depth analysis of the major sources of variance in the MMPI, which is also pertinent to this debate. Most MMPI researchers concur with Block's position; however, the informed reader can decide for himself or herself which interpretation of the first factor of the MMPI seems most appropriate.

Unlike the first factor, the interpretation of the second factor of the MMPI has not been controversial. Welsh (1956) reported that the second factor has moderately positive correlations with Scales *2* (Depression: .384), *3* (Hysteria: 390), *5* (Masculinity-Femininity: .165), and *6* (Paranoia: .073), and a moderate negative correlation with Scale *9* (Hypomania: −.449).[2] He identified the second factor as reflecting a personality factor, which he labeled repression. The correlations between the second factor and the Clinical scales are much more modest than those found with the first factor, and the correlations with Scales *5* and *6* in the Caldwell (Caldwell, 1997a) dataset are substantially lower than what Welsh (1956) found.

To develop the *A* and *R* scales, Welsh selected male Veterans Administration (VA) patients who scored at or beyond the upper and lower 10 percent of a preliminary scale designed to assess each factor; he then contrasted the responses of these extreme groups on all 550 MMPI items. The *A* scale consists of 39 items that showed at least a 75 percent separation between high and low scores in two separate VA sam-

ples. The *R* scale consists of 37 items (40 items on the MMPI) that showed at least a 60 percent separation of high and low scorers in the same two samples. The items on the *A* and *R* scales are provided in Appendix B.5 for the MMPI-2.

The major content areas in the *A* scale are:

1. Problems in attention and concentration
2. Negative emotional tone and dysphoria
3. Lack of energy and pessimism
4. Negative self-evaluation and hypersensitivity
5. Obsessions and ruminations

The *A* scale has substantial item overlap and is correlated significantly with a number of the standard Clinical scales (See Table 6.13, pp. 240–241). It shares 13 items with Scale *7* (Psychasthenia), 11 items with Scale *0* (Social Introversion), 8 items with Scale *8* (Schizophrenia), and 6 items with Scale *2* (Depression). Given the large number of items overlapping with the Clinical scales, it is somewhat unexpected that the *A* scale shares no items with the *F* (Infrequency) scale and 5 items with the *K* (Correction) scale that are scored in the opposite direction. (When these 5 items are endorsed "true," they are scored on the *A* scale; when they are endorsed "false," they are scored on the *K* scale.) The *A* scale also shares items with a number of the other Supplementary scales (see Table 6.12, pp. 238–239): 14 items with the Post Traumatic Stress Disorder—Schlenger (*PS*) scale, 12 items with the College Maladjustment (*Mt*) scale, 9 items with the Post Traumatic Stress Disorder—Keane (*PK*) scale, and 9 items with Ego Strength (*Es*) scales that are scored in the opposite direction. Finally, Scale *A* has 9 items in common with the MMPI-2 Content scale of Depression (*DEP*), 8 items with the Work Interference (*WRK*) scale, and 7 items with the Anxiety (*ANX*) scale (Table 5.7). The *A* scale is a composite of a number of different items reflecting generalized distress and discomfort and negative emotionality that are common to most MMPI-2 scales.

All of these scales that share items with the *A* scale can be conceptualized as first-factor scales (i.e., measures of generalized distress and negative emotionality). Since these scales are redundant measures of the first factor, it is not clear what additional infor-

---

2. These correlations are for the psychiatric patients in the Caldwell (1997a) clinical dataset.

TABLE 6.1 Correlations with the Welsh Anxiety (*A*) Scale in the Caldwell
Clinical Dataset

WELSH ANXIETY (A) SCALE		
Scale	*Abbreviation*	r
Psychasthenia	*Pt*	.951
Post Traumatic Stress Disorder—Schlenger	*PS*	.941
Edwards' Social Desirability	*So*	−.937
Work Interference	*WRK*	.936
College Maladjustment	*Mt*	.930
Post Traumatic Stress Disorder—Keane	*PK*	.927
Total Number of Koss & Butcher Critical Items Endorsed	KBSum	.920
Depression	*DEP*	.915
Koss & Butcher Depressed-Suicidal Ideation	*KBDep*	.904
Anxiety	*ANX*	.902
Total T Score Difference of Obvious and Subtle Subscales	O - S	.900
Schizophrenia	*Sc*	.895
Alienation—Self and Others	Si_3	.895
Lachar & Wrobel Depression and Worry	LWDep	.892
Negative Emotional Experience	*NEN*	.891
Obsessions	*OBS*	.891
Brooding	D_5	.889
Total Number of Lachar & Wrobel Critical Items Endorsed	LWSum	.886
Negative Treatment Indicators	*TRT*	.873
Low Self-Esteem	*LSE*	.870
Gough Dissimulation Scale	*Ds*	.869

mation is gained by scoring all of these Supplementary scales beyond the *A* scale. Research that demonstrates the discriminant or incremental validity for each of these first-factor scales is needed if all of these scales are to be scored routinely.

The deviant response is "true" for all but one of the *A* scale items and "false" for all of the *R* scale items, which means that either a "true" or "false" response set will substantially affect scores on both of these scales. The True Response Inconsistency (*TRIN*) scale scores above 9 would be expected with high scores on the *A* scale and below 9 with high scores on the *R* scale (see Chapter 3, pp. 53–54). The items on the *A* and *R* scales have a mean rating of 3.17 and 2.32 for the obviousness of content, respectively (Christian et al., 1978).[3] The *A* scale is a slightly obvious and the *R* scale is a subtle measure of psycho-logical problems. (Christian et al. had college students evaluate how clearly each MMPI item was indicative of a psychological problem. They were to assign ratings of 5 to any MMPI items with very obvious content, 4 to any items with obvious content, 3 to any items with neither obvious nor subtle content, 2 to any items with subtle content, and 1 to any items with very subtle content.)

Table 6.1 lists the 20 scales with the highest correlations with the *A* scale in the Caldwell (1997a)

3. Christian et al. (1978) reported their ratings of the obviousness of MMPI items using Form R item numbers. The MMPI Form R item number has to be transformed to the MMPI Group Booklet item number before transforming it into the corresponding MMPI-2 item number. Butcher et al. (1989, Appendix I) also provide these ratings of the obviousness of the MMPI-2 items.

clinical dataset. There is only one category represented within all of these scales: generalized distress and negative emotionality. Again, the *A* scale is a composite measure of generalized distress and negative emotionality that permeates the MMPI-2 item pool.

High scorers (T scores of 65 or higher) on the *A* scale are described as generally emotionally distressed, anxious, and lacking confidence in their own abilities. They are characterized as reacting to situational stress or personal distress. The elevation of Scale *A* reflects their level of discomfort that usually motivates them to enter into psychological treatment. The general negative emotionality being assessed by the *A* scale is more likely to reflect situational stress rather than long-term characterologic distress, which is assessed by Scale *7* (Psychasthenia).

Low scorers (T scores of 44 or lower) on the *A* scale usually are described as well adjusted and not overtly anxious. They may be impulsive and display behavioral problems, although these behaviors are not upsetting to them. They also are described as verbally fluent and competent in social situations. Low scores on the *A* scale are *not* expected in clinical settings, because clients should be experiencing some level of generalized distress and negative emotionality either because they are seeking or someone referred them for psychological treatment.

Age does not affect scores on the *A* scale beyond age 20. However, both normal individuals (Butcher et al., 1989) and psychiatric patients (Caldwell, 1997a) under age 20 score about 5 T points higher than persons 20 and older. Women tend to endorse about 2 more items than men (Butcher et al., 1989; Caldwell, 1997a). (Gender differences will *not* affect the interpretation of any MMPI-2 scale that is interpreted in T scores because the T scores are provided separately for men and women, which "corrects" for these differences in raw scores.) Scores increase substantially as the number of years of education decreases. Both normal individuals (Butcher et al., 1989) and psychiatric patients (Caldwell, 1997a) with less than a 9th grade education have scores 6 to 8 T points higher than their counterparts with more than 18 years of education.

A summary of the interpretations of five levels of elevation of the *A* scale is provided in Table 6.2.

TABLE 6.2 Interpretations of Levels of Elevation on the Welsh Anxiety (*A*) Scale

T SCORE	INTERPRETATION
44 and below	1. *Low.* These clients are not overtly expressing any form of generalized distress or negative emotionality. They are extroverted, verbally fluent, and confident in their own abilities. They may be impulsive. Such low scores in clients in clinical settings would *not* be expected. Be sure that a score in this range is appropriate for the client.
45–57	2. *Normal.* These clients have a normal level of generalized distress and negative emotionality.
58–64	3. *Moderate.* These clients are reporting a significant degree of generalized distress and negative emotionality that should be readily apparent. They usually are motivated to seek treatment because of their level of distress.
65–79	4. *Marked.* These clients are reporting an ever-increasing level of generalized distress and negative emotionality that may be totally debilitating. They frequently are seen as maladjusted and emotionally upset, which may reflect a situational crisis or a more chronic problem.
80 and above	5. *Extreme.* These clients are likely to be overreporting psychopathology (see Chapter 3).

The major content areas in the *R* scale are the denial and suppression of and/or constriction and inhibition of interests *either positive or negative* in:

1. Health and physical symptoms
2. Emotionality, violence, and activity
3. Family and relationship problems
4. Social dominance and social participation
5. Personal and vocational pursuits

The *R* scale shares fewer items with other scales than the *A* scale. It has 10 items in common with Scale *2* (Depression), 8 items with Scale *5* (Masculinity-

Femininity), 3 of which are scored in the opposite direction, and 8 items with Scale *0* (Social Introversion) (Table 6.13). The *R* scale has even less overlap with the other Supplementary scales. It shares 7 items with the Gender Role—Feminine (*GF*) scale, 4 of which are scored in the opposite direction, 6 items with the MacAndrew Alcoholism—Revised (*MAC-R*) scale, all of which are scored in the opposite direction, and 4 items with the Social Responsibility (*Re*) (Table 6.12). The *R* scale shares 4 items with the MMPI-2 Content scale of Health Concerns (*HEA*) and 3 items with the Social Discomfort (*SOD*) scale. It also shares 3 items with the Anger (*ANG*) scale that are scored in the opposite direction (Table 5.7). The *R* scale is a collection of a number of heterogeneous items that is somewhat unexpected as a marker for the second factor of the MMPI-2 (i.e., there is much more variability in the items marking the second factor than the first factor).

Table 6.3 lists the 20 scales with the highest correlations with the *R* scale in the Caldwell (1997a) clinical dataset. There are a number of categories represented within these scales: inhibition of aggression in particular and any activity generally (Aggression, MacAndrew Alcoholism—Revised, Psychomotor Retardation, Depression, Subtle); lack of participation in social activities (Social Avoidance); and following social conventions (Constraint, Social Responsibility, Antisocial Practices). These correlations with the *R* scale are much lower and more diverse than what were found with the *A* scale.

High scorers (T scores of 58 or higher) on the *R* scale are seen as being unwilling to discuss their problems, which may reflect conscious suppression, constriction, and inhibition of interests in events around them, or actual repression and denial. In the latter situation they also will typically elevate the *K* (Correction) scale and Scale *3* (Hysteria), which would substantiate their repressive nature. These persons appear constricted, inhibited, and overcontrolled, and lack insight into their own behavior. They are unwilling to discuss any form of psychopathology even though it may be apparent to everyone but themselves.

Low scorers (T scores of 44 or lower) on the *R* scale are willing to discuss what problems they are experiencing. They see no reason to try to suppress or inhibit their awareness of these problems, which re-

TABLE 6.3 Correlations with the Welsh Repression (*R*) Scale in the Caldwell Clinical Dataset

WELSH REPRESSION (*R*) SCALE		
Scale	*Abbreviation*	r
Aggression	*AGG*	−.531
MacAndrew Alcoholism—Revised	*MAC-R*	−.523
Psychomotor Retardation	D_2	.519
Positive Emotional Experience	*PEE*	−.511
Depression, Subtle	*D-S*	.490
Constraint	*CON*	.464
Hypomania	*Ma*	−.449
Social Avoidance	Si_2	.438
Hypomania, Subtle	*Ma-S*	−.435
Psychomotor Acceleration	Ma_2	−.420
Hysteria	*Hy*	.390
Inhibition of Aggression	Hy_5	.386
Depression	*D*	.384
Social Responsibility	*Re*	.377
Competitive Drive	TPT_2	−.367
Antisocial Practices	*ASP*	−.362
Addiction Potential Scale	*APS*	−.359
Type A	*TPA*	−.357
Ego Inflation	Ma_4	−.355
Lie	*L*	.354

flects their attributions that others are responsible for their problems. They tend to be socially extroverted and outgoing in their relationships with others.

Scores on the *R* scale increase 7 to 8 T points with age in both normal individuals (Butcher et al., 1989) and psychiatric patients (Caldwell, 1997a). Women endorse about one more item than men (Butcher et al., 1989; Caldwell, 1997a). Education has negligible effects on scores.

A summary of the interpretations of four levels of elevation of the *R* scale is given in Table 6.4.

Welsh (1965) provided a summary of interpretations of the *A* and *R* scales when both scales are employed conjointly. (This summary table also appears in Dahlstrom et al. [1972], pp. 238–239.) Welsh cautioned clinicians against making cookbook interpretations of these descriptions; rather he suggested that

TABLE 6.4 Interpretations of Levels of Elevation on the Welsh Repression (R) Scale

T SCORE	INTERPRETATION
44 and below	1. *Low.* These clients either do not have problems or are willing to discuss the problems that they perceive themselves as having. They see no need to inhibit or suppress awareness of any problems that they may be experiencing.
45–57	2. *Normal.* These clients show an appropriate level of willingness to discuss their behavior and problems.
58–64	3. *Moderate.* These clients are using their personal resources in an attempt to control, inhibit, suppress, and cope with the problems that they are experiencing. They are trying to inhibit or suppress the overt expression of any emotions, particularly anger.
65 and above	4. *Marked.* These clients are likely to be underreporting any problems they may have. They may be merely suppressing this material because of the setting, such as personnel screening or a child custody evaluation, or repressing and denying that any problems exist. The *K* (Correction) scale and Scales *3* (Hysteria) and *Hy-S* (Hysteria, Subtle) usually are elevated in this latter situation. These clients typically lack insight into their own behavior.

the interpretations be considered as tentative hypotheses for further investigation. Duckworth and Anderson (1986) reported that Welsh's system was not accurate for college students except for the high *A* and high *R* description. They furnished a more limited summary of the joint elevations of the *A* and *R* scales, which they found useful in college students. Sprock and Bienek (1998) found little consistency (51 percent agreement) in the category of Welsh's system into which their college students were assigned who took the MMPI and MMPI-2 over a one-week inter-

val. Both of these studies indicate that Welsh's conjoint interpretations of the *A* and *R* scales should not be applied directly to the MMPI-2.

Despite these caveats, it is important to consider the relative elevations of the *A* and *R* scales in the interpretation of any MMPI-2 profile. It could be argued that these two scales should be interpreted before the MMPI-2 codetype, because they represent the major sources of variance among the scales. Regardless of the order of interpretation, the *A* and *R* scales should be evaluated routinely.

A summary of the potential conjoint interpretations of the *A* and *R* scales is given in Table 6.5.

Ego Strength (*Es*) Scale

Barron (1953) developed the Ego Strength (*Es*) scale by correlating the MMPI item responses of 33 neurotic clients at two separate test administrations. Each client completed all 550 items on the MMPI before psychotherapy was initiated and then again after six months of psychotherapy. The clients were divided into two groups: 17 of them were judged to have clearly improved after six months of psychotherapy, and the other 16 were judged to be unimproved after the same interval.

Barron identified 68 items (only 52 items remain on the MMPI-2) that significantly correlated with rated improvement in these 33 clients. He concluded that these items measured a general capacity for personality integration, or ego strength—hence, the name of the scale. He believed that the *Es* scale assessed the latent ego strength of the person and that this would be an important determinant of response to psychotherapy.

Although all the clients were seeking psychotherapy for some sort of psychological difficulty, a high score on the *Es* scale, which indicates good ego strength, suggested that the person had resources that would emerge as therapy progressed. Since the *Es* scale has a moderate to very high negative correlation with all Validity and Clinical scales except one (it has a high positive correlation with the *K* [Correction] scale), Barron hypothesized that clients with high scores on the *Es* scale were more likely to be facing situational stresses whereas clients with low scores on

TABLE 6.5 Conjoint Interpretation of the Welsh Anxiety (*A*) and Repression (*R*) Scales in Clinical Settings

Welsh Anxiety (A)	WELSH REPRESSION (R)		
	58 and above	*45–57*	*44 and below*
65 and above	These clients are reporting a moderate to severe level of emotional distress despite their best attempts to inhibit or suppress any awareness of their problems. They see themselves as being responsible for their problems and are very motivated to work on finding relief from them. They feel like their problems are overwhelming them.	These clients are reporting a moderate to severe level of emotional distress. They are trying to cope with their problems, although they are not sure that they have adequate resources to do so.	These clients are reporting a moderate to severe level of emotional distress. They see themselves as having few resources for coping with or handling this distress. They are likely to be overreporting psychopathology.
51–64	These clients are reporting a mild level of emotional distress even though they are trying to inhibit or suppress any awareness of their problems. This pattern may reflect an acute problem in clients with adequate coping skills or more chronic problems in clients who are defensive and guarded.	These clients are reporting a mild level of emotional distress and adequate resources for coping with their problems. They are likely to externalize their problems, particularly as the T score on *R* goes below 50.	These clients are reporting a mild level of emotional distress that is likely to reflect an acute stressor. They have little motivation to examine their own behavior once the stressor is removed.
50 and below	These clients are not reporting any emotional distress, which reflects their significant attempts to inhibit or suppress any awareness of their problems. They are likely to be underreporting psychopathology.	These clients are not reporting any emotional distress, which reflects their attempt to inhibit or suppress any awareness of their current problems. Others may see them as somewhat guarded or defensive.	These clients are not reporting any emotional distress nor are they trying to inhibit or suppress any awareness of problems that they may be experiencing. Their behaviors and symptoms are chronic and ego syntonic. They blame others for their problems.

the *Es* scale were more likely to be experiencing chronic, characterologic problems.

The *Es* scale has substantial item overlap with a number of the standard Clinical scales with the items being scored in the opposite direction on the *Es* scale (Table 6.13). The *Es* scale shares 10 items with Scales *2* (Depression) and *3* (Hysteria); 9 items with Scales *7* (Psychasthenia) and *8* (Schizophrenia); and 7 items

with Scale *1* (Hypochondriasis). The *Es* scale also has substantial item overlap with several of the other Supplementary scales (Table 6.12), and again the items are scored in the opposite direction: 10 items with the Post Traumatic Stress Disorder—Keane (*PK*) and Post Traumatic Stress Disorder—Schlenger (*PS*) scales; 9 items with the Welsh Anxiety (*A*) scale; and 6 items with the College Maladjustment (*Mt*) scale.

Finally, the *Es* scale shares some items again scored in the opposite direction with a number of the MMPI-2 Content scales: 8 items with the Health Concerns (*HEA*) scale, 5 items with the Fears (*FRS*) scale, and 4 items with the Anxiety (*ANX*) and Obsessions (*OBS*) scales (Table 5.7). The *Es* scale is a composite of a number of items reflecting the *absence* of generalized distress and negative emotionality similar to the *A* scale that reflects the *presence* of generalized distress and negative emotionality. The *Es* and *A* scales are correlated negatively (–0.831), as would be expected.

The deviant response is "false" for 32 (61.5%) of the 52 items on the *Es* scale. This relative balance between "true" and "false" deviant responses means that neither a "true" nor a "false" response set will have much effect on the *Es* scale. The items on the *Es* scale have a mean rating of 2.20 for the obviousness of content that indicates its items are a subtle measure of psychological problems.

Table 6.6 lists the 20 scales with the highest correlations with the *Es* scale in the Caldwell (1997a) clinical dataset. There are only two categories represented within these scales: absence of general negative emotionality and depression and anxiety more specifically (Post Traumatic Stress Disorder, Depression, Obvious, Psychasthenia); and absence of somatic symptoms (Hysteria, Obvious, Hypochondriasis, Health Concerns). These correlations are nearly as large, although negative, as were seen with the Welsh Anxiety (*A*) scale in Table 6.1. Thus, the *Es* scale could be conceptualized as a negative marker for the first factor rather than as a measure of ego strength. That is, high scorers on the *Es* scale are saying that they are not generally maladjusted or emotionally distressed, which would seem to make them poor candidates for psychotherapy.

Probably no other Supplementary scale has generated as much research with contradictory results as the *Es* scale; various studies have reported positive, no, and inverse relationships between the *Es* scale and outcome in psychotherapy. Dahlstrom et al. (1975) have provided a comprehensive review of these studies. They also pointed out the paradoxical relationship between psychotherapy outcome and *Es* scores as reported by Barron (1953) (i.e., patients reporting

TABLE 6.6 Correlations with the Ego Strength (*Es*) Scale in the Caldwell Clinical Dataset

EGO STRENGTH (*Es*) SCALE		
Scale	Abbreviation	r
Hysteria, Obvious	Hy-O	–.876
Post Traumatic Stress Disorder—Schlenger	PS	–.875
Depression, Obvious	D-O	–.874
Total Number of Lachar & Wrobel Critical Items Endorsed	LWSum	–.873
Psychasthenia	Pt	–.865
Post Traumatic Stress Disorder—Keane	PK	–.855
Edwards' Social Desirability	So	.855
Schizophrenia	Sc	–.849
Total Number of Koss & Butcher Critical Items Endorsed	KBSum	–.847
College Maladjustment	Mt	–.847
Hypochondriasis	Hs	–.842
Total T Score Difference of Obvious and Subtle Subscales	O - S	–.842
Subjective Depression	D_1	–.840
Lachar & Wrobel Somatic Symptoms	LWSoma	–.835
Koss & Butcher Acute Anxiety State	KBAnx	–.834
Health Concerns	HEA	–.832
Welsh Anxiety	A	–.831
Lassitude-Malaise	Hy_3	–.831
Anxiety	ANX	–.830
Lachar & Wrobel Depression and Worry	LWDep	–.827

less emotional distress having better outcomes in psychotherapy rather than vice versa).

Clients with high scores on the *Es* scale would be expected to have relatively normal MMPI-2 profiles because of the negative correlations between the *Es* scale and the Clinical scales. Normal profiles would suggest that either these clients have no problems or they are unwilling to admit any problems; yet they are requesting psychological treatment. Psychological intervention may be unnecessary in the former instance and very difficult in the latter because of defensiveness and resistance. Clients with high scores on the *Es* scale and an elevated MMPI-2 profile may be indicating that they have the appropriate resources for dealing with their problems, which probably are of recent origin. As a consequence of these different profiles that could be obtained with high scores on the *Es* scale, sampling differences could produce the variety of relationships to psychotherapy outcome described previously.

The plethora of studies reporting no relationship between the *Es* scale and psychotherapy outcome indicates that the *Es* scale is of little usefulness in routinely predicting the response of a given client to psychotherapy. If further research on the *Es* scale is deemed necessary, it should try to identify those subgroups of clients in whom positive or negative psychotherapy outcome is expected.

There is virtually no research on the *Es* scale on the MMPI-2. The inconsistent findings in the earlier research may have dissuaded most researchers from investigating the scale. Given that almost one-fourth of the items were deleted from the *Es* scale on the MMPI-2, it is very likely that its correlates have been changed, although Sprock and Bienek (1998) found moderately high agreement ($r = .75$) in scores on the *Es* scale between the MMPI and MMPI-2 in their college students. Schuldberg (1992) reported that the *Es* scale on the MMPI-2 actually had higher correlations with measures of psychological health and well-being than the original scale. It is imperative that any research on the *Es* scale demonstrate its discriminative or incremental validity from other measures of first-factor distress.

High scorers (T scores of 65 or higher) on the *Es* scale describe themselves as experiencing little emotional distress and having few physical symptoms. They have good attention and concentration skills and they can focus on what they need to be doing. They would seem to have little motivation to engage in a psychotherapeutic process, because of the absence of any emotional distress.

Low scorers (T scores of 44 or lower) on the *Es* scale are experiencing significant emotional distress. As T scores approach 35 or lower, they may be feeling overwhelmed by their problems and see themselves as having inadequate coping skills. There is some question of whether they may be overreporting psychopathology (Lees-Haley, 1992).

Scores on the *Es* scale decrease 4 to 5 T points with age in both normal individuals (Butcher et al., 1989) and psychiatric patients (Caldwell, 1997a). Men endorse about 3 to 5 more items than women (Butcher et al., 1989; Caldwell, 1997a). Scores decrease nearly 6 T points in normal individuals and 10 T points in psychiatric patients as the number of years of education increases.

A summary of the interpretations of four levels of elevation of the *Es* scale is given in Table 6.7.

TABLE 6.7 Interpretations of Levels of Elevation on the Ego Strength (*Es*) Scale

T SCORE	INTERPRETATION
44 and below	1. *Low.* These clients are reporting a significant degree of generalized distress and negative emotionality. They may see themselves as having few personal resources or coping skills for dealing with their problems. Overreporting of psychopathology may occur at T scores of 35 or lower.
45–57	2. *Normal.* These clients are reporting a normal level of generalized distress and negative emotionality.
58–64	3. *Moderate.* These clients are reporting less generalized distress and emotional distress than typical for a clinical setting. They may be experiencing relatively minor problems and/or believe that they have adequate personal resources for coping with their problems.
65 and above	4. *Marked.* These clients are not reporting any type of generalized distress, negative emotionality, or physical symptoms. They can concentrate on and attend to events happening around them.

MacAndrew Alcoholism—Revised (*MAC-R*) Scale

Several early investigators (Hampton, 1953; Holmes, 1953; Hoyt & Sedlacek, 1958) attempted to develop MMPI scales to detect alcoholism with limited success (cf. Clopton, 1978a; MacAndrew & Geertsma, 1964). MacAndrew (1965) was more successful in developing his Alcoholism (*MAC*) scale. He selected items that differentiated alcoholic outpatients from nonalcoholic, psychiatric outpatients. All patients were men, and most were white. MacAndrew identified 51 MMPI items that reliably separated these groups. Two of these 51 MMPI items (215 and 460) actually refer to alcohol use, and most investigators eliminate these two items, leaving 49 items on the *MAC* scale.

In the original sample, a raw score of 24 items or more to identify a patient as alcoholic correctly classified 81.8 percent of the patients. In a cross-validation sample this same cutting score correctly classified 81.5 percent of the patients, which is an unusually small loss of accuracy in classification. Through a factor analysis of the *MAC* scale, Schwartz and Graham (1979) found that the scale taps several discrete dimensions of personality and behavior, including impulsivity, high energy levels, interpersonal shallowness, and general psychological maladjustment, but not general antisociality.

Although MacAndrew (1965) developed the *MAC* scale on men and intended it to be used only with men, researchers quickly extended its use to women (cf. Rich & Davis, 1969; Schwartz & Graham, 1979). In fact, popular usage of the *MAC* scale does not recognize that the scale was developed originally for men; consequently, the use of the *MAC* scale in men and women will be reviewed here.

Recently MacAndrew has developed substance abuse scales specifically for use with young men (Substance Abuse Proclivity scale [*SAP*]: MacAndrew, 1986) and women (MacAndrew, 1988). Research on these two scales has been very limited. MacAndrew (1987) reported that the *SAP* scale was correlated negatively with age, which suggested that it was "tapping something more fundamental than the accumulated consequences of chronic substance abuse" (p. 145).

MacAndrew also found that the detection rates with the *SAP* and *MAC* scales were almost identical in these young adults. The very similar detection rates for the two scales are somewhat surprising since they share only nine items in common. If other studies reveal that the *SAP* and *MAC* scales produce similar results, it would appear unnecessary to score both scales.

Four MMPI items (58, 378, 483, and 488) on the *MAC* scale were deleted in developing the MMPI-2. The rationale for dropping these items is apparent because they either have religious content or a sexist bias. Item 460, "I have used alcohol moderately (or not at all),"[4] also was deleted, which along with item 215, is found on the 51-item version of the *MAC* scale. The deletion of item 460, since item 215 was retained, is not clear because Colligan, Davis, Morse, and Offord (1988) found that this item, after item 215, provided better classification rates than any of the alcoholism scales in their medical patients. The deletion of item 460 may not be a problem, however, because items 215 and 460 are deleted frequently from the *MAC* scale to create a 49-item, subtle measure of substance abuse.

Since interpretation of the *MAC* scale traditionally is based on raw scores instead of T scores, four items were added to the *MAC-R* scale on the MMPI-2 by contrasting the item responses of a group of male alcoholics with male psychiatric patients. Clinicians should note that item 387 on the MMPI-2, "I can express my true feelings only when I drink,"[5] is included on the *MAC-R* with "true" as the deviant response.

There have been only three reported studies of the comparability of the *MAC* and *MAC-R* scales with mixed results (Greene, Arredondo, & Davis, 1990; Mundt, 1992; Sawrie, Kabat, Dietz, Greene, Arre-dondo, & Mann, 1996). Greene et al. compared scores for both scales in alcoholic and psychiatric in-

---

4. Minnesota Multiphasic Personality Inventory-2 (MMPI-2). Copyright © 1942, 1943 (renewed 1970), 1989 by the Regents of the University of Minnesota. Reproduced by permission of the publisher. "MMPI-2" and "Minnesota Multiphasic Personality Inventory-2" are trademarks owned by the University of Minnesota.
5. Ibid.

patients by gender from the same treatment settings who had taken either the *MAC* or *MAC-R* scale. The only notable difference was for male alcoholics to endorse on the average one more item on the *MAC-R* scale than on the *MAC* scale (Table 6.7 in Greene [1991]). Mundt administered both scales to prisoners and he found that the *MAC-R* scale was significantly lower than the *MAC* scale. Sawrie et al. (1996) determined that the factor structure of the *MAC-R* scale was very similar to the factor structure of the *MAC* scale (Schwartz & Graham, 1979). Although additional research on the comparability of the two scales is warranted, given that 45 of the 49 items on the *MAC-R* scale are unchanged from the *MAC* scale, there is little reason to expect substantial differences.

The *MAC-R* scale has substantial item overlap with a number of the standard Clinical scales (Table 6.13). The *MAC-R* scale shares 8 items with Scale *4* (Psychopathic Deviate), one of which is scored in the opposite direction, and 5 items with Scales *F* (Infrequency) and *9* (Hypomania). It also shares 6 items with Scale *5* (Masculinity-Femininity) in women and 5 items with Scales *5* (Masculinity-Femininity) in men, *8* (Schizophrenia), and *0* (Social Introversion), all of which are scored in the opposite direction. The *MAC-R* scale also has substantial item overlap with several of the other Supplementary scales (Table 6.12): 9 items with the Addiction Potential (*APS*) scale that are scored in the same direction. It also shares 9 items with the Social Responsibility (*Re*) scale and 6 items with the Welsh Repression (*R*) and Dominance (*Do*) scales, all of which are scored in the opposite direction. Finally, *MAC-R* shares few items with the MMPI-2 Content scales: 4 items with the Antisocial Practices (*ASP*) scale and 3 items with the Depression scale (*DEP*) (Table 5.7). The *MAC-R* scale consists of a heterogeneous set of items covering a wide range of behaviors and symptoms that is typical for an empirically derived scale.

The deviant response for 38 (77.6%) of the 49 items on the *MAC-R* scale is "true"; hence, a tendency toward a "true" response set will elevate scores on the *MAC-R* scale. The items on the *MAC-R* scale have a mean rating of 2.66 for the obviousness of content

that indicates its items are somewhat subtle as a measure of psychological problems.

Table 6.8 lists the 20 scales with the highest correlations with the *MAC-R* scale in the Caldwell (1997a) clinical dataset. There is a variety of categories represented within these scales: antisocial behavior and attitudes (Lachar and Wrobel Antisocial Attitude, Antisocial Behavior, Antisocial Practices); lack of inhibition, constraint, and control (Constraint, Welsh Repression); aggressiveness and anger (Aggressiveness, Explosive Behavior); substance abuse (Addiction Admission); and cynicism (Cynicism, Interpersonal Suspiciousness).

TABLE 6.8 Correlations with the MacAndrew Alcoholism—Revised (*MAC-R*) Scale in the Caldwell Clinical Dataset

MACANDREW ALCOHOLISM—REVISED (*MAC-R*) SCALE

Scale	Abbreviation	r
Social Responsibility	Re	−.601
Lachar & Wrobel Antisocial Attitude	LWAnti	.589
Antisocial Behavior	ASP2	.573
Antisocial Practices	ASP	.557
Hypomania	Ma	.550
Constraint	CON	−.549
Welsh Repression	R	−.523
Aggressiveness	AGG	.502
Addiction Admission	AAS	.484
Gender Role—Feminine	GF	−.481
Hypomania, Obvious	Ma-O	.451
Depression, Subtle	D-S	−.447
Antisocial Attitudes	ASP1	.434
Explosive Behavior	ANG1	.431
Koss & Butcher Situational Stress Due to Alcoholism	KBSub	.428
Cynicism	CYN	.421
Interpersonal Suspiciousness	CYN2	.403
Authority Problems	Pd_2	.390
Bizarre Mentation	BIZ	.385
Inhibition of Aggression	Hy_5	−.384

Probably no single MMPI scale has generated more research than the *MAC* scale, and numerous reviews are available (cf. Allen, 1991; Apfeldorf, 1978; Gottesman & Prescott, 1989; Greene & Garvin, 1988; MacAndrew, 1981; Megargee, 1985). In the interests of brevity only a summary of the prolific research on the *MAC* scale will be provided here. This summary will draw heavily on the review by Greene and Garvin (1988). The interested reader should consult that review or any of the other reviews cited previously for more specific information and references on the *MAC* scale. Table 6.9 provides a summary of the performance on the *MAC* scale as a function of sample, age, gender, and ethnicity (Greene & Garvin, 1988).

The weighted (by sample size) mean score on the *MAC* scale in normal, white, adult male samples is 23.1 ($SD = 4.3$), which is only slightly below MacAndrew's traditional cutting score of 24. Gender differences in these normal, white, adult and adolescent samples are very consistent with men scoring approximately two raw-score points higher than women ($M = 20.3$; $SD = 3.8$). Normal, white adults and adolescents seem to have similar means and standard deviations; this finding is consistent with the report by Colligan and Offord (1987b) of no age differences on the *MAC* scale in their contemporary normative sample. Essentially no data exist on the *MAC* scale in normal samples of nonwhite ethnic groups. Hit rates in these normal samples ranged around 80 percent with approximately 20 percent false positives (normal individuals classified as alcoholic).

Both white, adult male ($M = 23.3$; $SD = 4.6$) and female ($M = 21.7$; $SD = 4.8$) psychiatric samples score slightly higher than their normal counterparts (male: $M = 23.1$; $SD = 4.3$) (female: $M = 20.3$; $SD = 3.8$). Again, men score approximately two raw-score points higher than women. Both male and female psychiatric patients are more variable in their performance on the *MAC* scale with slightly larger standard deviations.

In contrast to the adult samples, both male and female adolescent psychiatric samples have lower weighted mean scores on the *MAC* scale than their normal counterparts. The adolescent psychiatric samples also are extremely variable in their performance with standard deviations that are almost twice as large as those found in their normal counterparts. This increase in variability in both adult and adolescent

psychiatric samples implies that hit rates and classification accuracy will decrease when alcoholics are contrasted with psychiatric patients rather than normal individuals.

Hit rates in these white psychiatric samples ranged around 75 percent, with approximately 35 percent false positives. (The reader should note that these percentages do not add to 100 since they are weighted by sample size.) Both the hit rate and the false positive percentage decreased about 5 percentage points in the adult samples as compared with normal samples; however, the false positive percentage more than doubled in the adolescent samples.

Black, male adult psychiatric patients have a weighted mean score of 26.3 ($SD = 4.9$) on the *MAC* scale that is significantly higher than MacAndrew's (1965) recommended cutting score of 24. These black patients had a mean score that was five raw-score points higher than their normal colleagues. Both the hit rate and the false positive percentage were nearly 60 percent in these black patients. Although the sample size in these black patients was significantly smaller than any of the other samples, which may limit the generalizability of the results, clinicians should be very cautious in using the *MAC* scale in nonwhite ethnic groups.

This caution about the use of the *MAC* scale with blacks has been noted by several authors (cf. Graham & Mayo, 1985; Walters, Greene, Jeffrey, Kruzich, & Haskin, 1983). Again, there is almost a total lack of data on the *MAC* scale in nonwhite ethnic groups of psychiatric samples.

There has been only limited data on the *MAC* scale in medical patients, which is somewhat surprising since nearly 90 percent of the individuals who misuse alcohol are seen by their physician in a year (Kamerow, Pincus, & Macdonald, 1986). Davis, Colligan, Morse, and Offord (1987) reported that their white, male medical patients had an average of 37.3 percent false positives, and their female patients averaged 20.3 percent false positives. These false positive percentages in medical patients are comparable with those reported in psychiatric patients, so it would be expected that hit rates also would be comparable.

Colligan et al. (1988) found that none of seven alcoholism scales, one of which was the *MAC* scale, could be recommended for use in a medical setting

TABLE 6.9 Summary Table of the Performance on the MacAndrew Alcoholism (*MAC*) Scale as a Function of Age, Gender, and Ethnicity

Sample	N	Age	M	SD	False Positives	Hit Rate
			MAC (RAW SCORE)			
Normal Individuals						
White						
Male adults	2,975	34.5	23.1	4.3	26.5	76.2
Male adolescents	352	17.0	22.7	3.7	19.2	77.8
Female adults	1,460	40.6	20.3	3.8	19.0	80.4
Female adolescents	213	15.8	20.9	4.0	7.4	86.6
Black						
Male adults	19	23.3	21.3	3.3	–	–
Psychiatric Patients						
White						
Male adults	2,285	37.2	23.3	4.6	31.4	72.3
Male adolescents	749	16.7	19.8	7.8	42.3	68.0
Female adults	485	36.8	21.7	4.8	21.7	77.4
Female adolescents	444	16.4	20.4	6.9	37.0	74.0
Black						
Male adults	128	23.3	26.3	4.9	59.5	60.0
Medical Patients						
White						
Male adults	5,353	49.0	–	–	37.3	–
Female adults	6,737	48.8	–	–	20.3	–
Alcoholics						
White						
Male adults	6,512	40.8	28.4	5.5	20.4	73.1
Male adolescents	409	17.6	27.1	4.0	18.4	77.6
Female adults	1,045	40.8	25.3	4.3	46.5	76.4
Female adolescents	163	15.8	26.2	4.6	11.5	87.9
Black						
Male adults	297	29.3	27.4	4.7	21.6	60.5
Polydrug Patients						
White						
Male adults	952	26.9	27.7	4.1	37.6	–
Female adults	127	41.5	–	–	72.5	
Black						
Male adults	607	27.9	28.0	5.8	20.8	–

Note. From "Substance abuse/dependence" by R. L. Greene & R. D. Garvin in R. L. Greene (Ed.), *The MMPI: Use with specific populations*, 1988, p. 181. All rights reserved. Reprinted by permission of Allyn & Bacon.

because of the unsatisfactory classification rates. They did find that MMPI item 215 (MMPI-2 item 264), "I have used alcohol excessively,"[6] provided better classification rates for their medical patients than any of the alcoholism scales they reviewed. The need for additional research on how to detect substance abuse and dependence in medical patients, particularly in other ethnic groups, should be evident.

White, adult, male alcoholics had weighted mean scores significantly higher ($M = 28.4$; $SD = 5.5$) than their female counterparts ($M = 25.3$; $SD = 4.3$), and both samples were substantially above MacAndrew's (1965) suggested cutting score of 24. The pattern already noted in normal individuals and psychiatric patients for men to score about two raw-score points higher than women also was apparent, and even larger in alcoholic samples.

Male and female, white adolescent alcoholics had weighted mean scores that were somewhat comparable to those for adults. Hit rates and false negative (alcoholics classified as being nonalcoholic) percentages were very comparable for white, male adult and adolescent alcoholics. However, the false negative percentage was significantly higher in adult female alcoholics and significantly lower in adolescent female alcoholics. Black, male alcoholics had a weighted mean score of 27.4 ($SD = 4.7$) that is only one raw-score point higher than their psychiatric counterparts.

These small differences in mean scores between black alcoholic and psychiatric patients make it nearly impossible for the *MAC* scale to discriminate between these two groups, hence the caution about using the *MAC* scale with nonwhite ethnic groups that was noted earlier. As expected because of the small mean differences between groups, hit rates in black, male alcoholics averaged only 60 percent. There are limited data on the use of the *MAC* scale in black, female alcoholics and essentially no data for other eth-

nic groups. Again, the need for research on the *MAC* scale in all nonwhite ethnic groups should be evident.

White, adult male polydrug abusers had a weighted mean score of 27.7 ($SD = 4.1$); black, adult male polydrug abusers had a weighted mean score of 28.0 ($SD = 5.8$). The false negative percentage in white polydrug abusers was nearly double (37.6 percent) that seen in their alcoholic counterparts (20.4 percent), while it was nearly identical in black polydrug abusers (20.8 percent) and alcoholics (21.6 percent). It is evident that the *MAC* scale is not simply an alcoholism scale; rather it is a more general measure of substance abuse that includes alcohol as well as other drugs. The only data reported on white, adult female polydrug abusers revealed 72.5 percent false negatives.

Higher scores on the *MAC* scale sometimes are interpreted as suggesting that the client is more likely to be a substance abuser or to have more serious problems with substance abuse. Actually, higher scores on the *MAC* scale simply indicate that the client is more likely to remain above whatever cutting score is being used despite any psychometric error that may be associated with the scale. The interested reader is referred to Wiggins (1973) for an in-depth review of this issue.

A number of general conclusions can be drawn after this rather lengthy summary on the use of the *MAC* scale in a variety of samples:

1. Men score about two raw-score points higher than women across most samples, which indicates that different cutting scores will be necessary by gender.
2. There is not a single, optimal cutting score with scores anywhere from 24 to 29 being used in different studies.
3. Cutting scores appear to be influenced by a number of factors; clinicians need to begin to determine empirically the best cutting score for their specific treatment facility to optimize the percentage of patients correctly classified as substance abusers.
4. Clinicians need to be very cautious in using the *MAC* scale in nonwhite ethnic groups.
5. Hit rates and classification accuracy decrease when clinicians are trying to discriminate

6. Minnesota Multiphasic Personality Inventory-2 (MMPI-2). Copyright © 1942, 1943 (renewed 1970), 1989 by the Regents of the University of Minnesota. Reproduced by permission of the publisher. "MMPI-2" and "Minnesota Multiphasic Personality Inventory-2" are trademarks owned by the University of Minnesota.

between substance abusers and nonsubstance-abusing, psychiatric patients, which is a frequent differential diagnosis.

6. Hit rates and classification accuracy may be unacceptably low in medical samples.
7. The *MAC* scale is a general measure of substance abuse that is not specific to alcoholism.

One group of investigators (Hoffmann, Loper, & Kammeier, 1974; Kammeier, Hoffmann, & Loper, 1973; Loper, Kammeier, & Hoffmann, 1973) examined the MMPI scores of male college students who were later treated for alcoholism. An average of 13 years elapsed between college admission and entrance into an alcoholism treatment program for these men. These investigators compared the alcoholics' scores on the *MAC* scale upon admission to college and at entrance into treatment with the scores of a control group of students who were admitted to college at the same time. The alcoholics had higher scores on the *MAC* scale both at college admission and at entrance into treatment than the control group of students. Using a cutting score of 26, the *MAC* scale correctly classified 72 percent of the alcoholic sample both at college admission and at entrance into treatment. The consistency of classification by the *MAC* scale across such an extensive time interval suggests that the *MAC* scale is tapping a dimension of behavior that is resistant to change. This conclusion also is supported by the finding that scores on the *MAC* scale in alcoholics remain elevated after treatment (Huber & Danahy, 1975; Gallucci, Kay, & Thornby, 1989; Rohan, Tatro, & Rotman, 1969).

In addition to the general conclusions that were drawn earlier about the use of the *MAC* and *MAC-R* scales, there is one overriding issue that cannot be disregarded and that is the base rate of substance abuse for the setting in which the *MAC-R* scale is being used. For example, a hit rate of 75 percent and a false positive percentage of 20 percent with the *MAC-R* scale is very respectable in a setting in which the prevalence or base rate for alcoholism is 50 percent. The prevalence rates for alcoholism are much lower than 50 percent, however, in most settings.

It has been estimated that the lifetime prevalence rate for alcoholism is approximately 8 percent and approximately 20 percent of medical patients have substance abuse or substance-related problems (Robins et al., 1984). Consequently, the hit rates and classification accuracies for the *MAC-R* scale that have been reported previously will be of limited usefulness in most real-life settings, such as personnel selection or screening medical patients, in which there is a very low prevalence rate, or treatment settings in which there is a very high prevalence rate (Gripshover & Dacey, 1994). Gottesman and Prescott (1989) have presented a cogent review of this issue that should be read by all clinicians.

A number of studies have reported limited success using the *MAC* or *MAC-R* scale in normal groups. Levenson et al. (1990) specifically examined the meaning of false positives (nonalcoholics who would be classified as being alcoholic) on the *MAC* scale. They found that nearly three-fourths (71%) of their normal men with scores on the *MAC* scale above 27, which is nearly one standard deviation above the typical cutting score of 24, had no legal or drinking problems. They concluded that the *MAC* scale is not an alcoholism scale per se. Instead it is a measure of general personality traits that may be related to problem drinking. Murray, Barnes, and Patton (1994) found that the *MAC* scale identified only 29.9 percent of their entire community sample who met DSM-III-R criteria for substance abuse or dependence. The sensitivity of the *MAC* scale also varied significantly based upon the age and gender of these individuals. Svanum and his colleagues (Svanum & Ehrmann, 1993; Svanum, McGrew, & Ehrmann, 1994) also found that the *MAC* and *MAC-R* scales had limited specificity in the identification of college students who have substance use disorders. Finally, Lapham et al. (1995) found that less than one-half (48%) of the participants in their first driving while intoxicated screening program, who met DSM-III-R criteria for a diagnosis of alcohol abuse or dependence, had scores on the *MAC* scale of 28 or higher. In these studies, the prevalence rates ranged from approximately 10 to 40 percent, which illustrates the effects of low prevalence rates on the accuracy of prediction with any scale. All of these results confirm the cautions suggested by Gottesman and Prescott about the limited utility of the *MAC* scale to identify substance abuse or dependence in settings in which there is a low preva-lence rate.

High scorers (T scores of 65 or higher) on the *MAC-R* scale are described as being impulsive, risk-taking, sensation-seeking individuals, who frequently have a propensity to abuse alcohol and/or stimulating drugs. They are uninhibited, sociable individuals who appear to use repression and religion in an attempt to control their rebellious, delinquent impulses. They also are described as having a high energy level, hav-ing shallow interpersonal relationships, and being generally psychologically maladjusted.

Low scorers (T scores less than 45) on the *MAC-R* scale are described as being depressed, inhibited, overcontrolled individuals, who also may abuse sub-stances, but in a different manner. If they abuse sub-stances, they will prefer alcohol or sedating drugs.

MacAndrew (1981) has suggested one possible interpretation of low scores on the *MAC* scale. MacAndrew conjectured that the *MAC* scale taps a fundamental bipolar dimension of personality with high scorers (raw scores of 24 or higher) being de-scribed as "moving (with 'boldness') into the world, albeit in a sometimes rancorous and ill-considered fashion, with little regard for future consequences" (p. 618), whereas low scorers (raw scores of 23 or lower) "give every appearance of being 'neurotics-who-also-happen-to-drink-too-much'" (p. 620).

MacAndrew suggested that high scorers on the *MAC* scale could be identified as primary alcoholics, and low scorers as being reactive or secondary alco-holics. In support of this formulation, both Svanum and Ehrmann (1992) and Ward and Jackson (1990) found that primary alcoholics had higher scores on the *MAC* scale than secondary alcoholics, and Knowles and Schroeder (1990) found that college students with a positive family history for alcoholism had higher scores on the *MAC* scale than students with a negative family history. In this formulation of the *MAC* scale, substance abuse cannot be predicted since both high and low scorers can abuse substances. Rather the *MAC* scale is assessing a fundamental di-mension of personality that will affect how the client will manifest his or her substance abuse. If this for-mulation by MacAndrew is accurate, clinicians would need to avoid using the *MAC* scale to predict whether a client will abuse substances, which has

been the standard use of the *MAC* scale since it was first developed. Allen (1991) has suggested that these differences between high and low scorers on the *MAC* scale may assist in matching alcoholics to treatment. Cognitive-behavioral psychotherapy for depression might be very useful for low scorers, while more be-havioral treatments oriented toward reducing impul-sivity and sensation seeking could be useful for high scorers. Sawrie et al. (1996) also suggested that clini-cians might consider different treatment interventions for patients who elevated different components of the *MAC-R* scale. Readers interested in treatment match-ing for alcoholics should see (Project MATCH Re-search Group, 1993).

Greene (1990) reported that mean scores on the *MAC* scale varied significantly by MMPI codetype, which would appear to support MacAndrew's con-ceptualization of his scale as a measure of a dimen-sion of personality rather than as a measure of substance abuse per se. Some codetypes (*6-9/9-6, 4-9/9-4*) in men and women rarely had *MAC* scores less than 24 and it would seem inappropriate to as-sume that all of these psychiatric patients abused sub-stances, whereas other codetypes (*2-7/7-2, 2-8/8-2*) rarely had scores above the cutting score of 24, partic-ularly in women. Wolf, Schubert, Patterson, Grande, and Pendleton (1990) reported that patients with a di-agnosis of only Antisocial Personality Disorder had higher scores on the *MAC* than patients with only di-agnoses of Alcohol or Drug Dependence or both di-agnoses, which also supports the contention that all patients with elevated scores on the *MAC* scale do not abuse substances.

Table 6.10 provides the mean scores on the *MAC-R* scale by MMPI-2 codetype for male and female psy-chiatric patients (Caldwell, 1997a) as well as the per-centage of each codetype that has a score of 24 or higher. Clinicians should see the apparent danger of identifying a client as a potential substance abuser or not based on the *MAC-R* scale without considering the prototypic score for the codetype. For example, clients with *2-7/7-2* codetypes, who are likely to be "neurotic" and risk avoiders, would be unlikely to have elevated scores on the *MAC-R* scale regardless of whether they abuse substances, whereas clients with *6-9/9-6* code-types, who are likely to act out, be impulsive, and be risk takers, would be very likely to have elevated

TABLE 6.10   Raw Scores on the MacAndrew Alcoholism—Revised (*MAC-R*) Scale by Codetype and Gender in the Caldwell Clinical Dataset

	MEN				WOMEN			
Codetype	N	M	SD	% > 23	N	M	SD	% > 23
Spike 1	268	21.98	3.94	36.94	215	18.59	3.09	6.51
1-2/2-1	671	20.56	4.23	24.89	1,005	17.78	3.70	7.06
1-3/3-1	2,035	20.31	4.20	21.13	3,188	18.42	3.60	8.03
1-4/4-1	97	23.21	4.19	46.39	127	21.55	4.34	30.71
1-5/5-1	19	21.37	3.98	36.84	126	20.11	3.60	19.05
1-6/6-1	188	22.91	4.27	40.96	195	20.47	3.73	17.95
1-7/7-1	113	22.08	4.85	34.51	89	19.40	3.96	13.48
1-8/8-1	272	23.90	4.75	50.00	236	21.55	4.27	34.32
1-9/9-1	77	25.97	3.92	76.62	81	22.35	3.43	37.04
1-0/0-1	33	20.88	4.11	24.24	32	16.81	4.15	6.25
Spike 2	212	19.52	3.58	12.74	190	17.31	3.34	2.63
2-3/3-2	909	18.29	4.15	10.34	1,932	16.43	3.71	3.73
2-4/4-2	313	21.85	4.43	36.74	542	18.87	4.34	15.13
2-5/5-2	49	17.14	3.48	4.08	64	19.27	2.82	7.81
2-6/6-2	399	20.03	4.41	21.80	705	17.90	3.76	7.52
2-7/7-2	888	18.87	4.42	14.64	1,046	16.89	3.76	4.88
2-8/8-2	358	20.73	5.07	29.05	717	18.92	3.99	12.83
2-9/9-2	12	24.83	4.47	50.00	24	20.37	3.03	16.67
2-0/0-2	339	17.83	4.21	8.85	326	15.48	3.64	1.53
Spike 3	372	19.08	3.29	8.33	412	17.29	2.86	2.18
3-4/4-3	298	20.85	4.53	26.85	454	18.83	3.73	11.89
3-5/5-3	42	19.88	4.61	21.43	72	19.11	3.55	8.33
3-6/6-3	311	21.03	4.28	27.65	423	18.89	3.89	11.35
3-7/7-3	239	19.52	4.43	18.83	203	17.58	3.62	3.94
3-8/8-3	222	21.72	4.65	32.88	217	19.89	3.90	17.51
3-9/9-3	38	23.32	4.25	42.11	78	20.64	4.22	20.51
3-0/0-3	7	19.57	4.31	28.57	7	15.14	2.27	0.00
Spike 4	685	22.69	4.07	39.56	583	19.55	3.65	14.24
4-5/5-4	79	20.85	4.34	27.85	125	22.08	4.13	34.40
4-6/6-4	565	23.99	4.40	51.68	539	21.63	4.06	31.73
4-7/7-4	236	23.15	4.66	45.34	210	20.15	4.18	20.00
4-8/8-4	339	24.00	4.77	55.46	353	21.68	4.33	31.73
4-9/9-4	237	26.51	4.55	71.73	203	24.02	3.72	55.67
4-0/0-4	41	21.41	4.51	31.71	29	19.76	4.36	17.24
Spike 5	294	18.78	3.47	8.84	1,071	19.69	3.18	10.92
5-6/6-5	84	19.77	3.25	10.71	70	21.06	4.00	24.29
5-7/7-5	51	18.67	4.41	13.73	17	18.94	3.31	0.00
5-8/8-5	23	19.13	3.27	13.04	53	21.91	4.73	33.96
5-9/9-5	44	22.16	3.54	36.36	143	23.51	4.01	55.24
5-0/0-5	27	15.15	3.45	0.00	15	18.87	4.73	26.67
Spike 6	494	21.68	3.83	29.35	415	18.98	3.23	8.67
6-7/7-6	315	22.01	4.63	36.51	178	19.40	4.73	23.03
6-8/8-6	1,087	24.91	4.80	60.99	842	22.41	4.62	38.48

(continued)

TABLE 6.10 Raw Scores on the MacAndrew Alcoholism—Revised (*MAC-R*) Scale by Codetype and Gender in the Caldwell Clinical Dataset (continued)

Codetype	MEN				WOMEN			
	N	M	SD	% > 23	N	M	SD	% > 23
6-9/9-6	207	26.05	4.20	74.40	149	22.62	3.95	37.58
6-0/0-6	89	21.04	4.52	28.09	50	16.84	3.50	2.00
Spike 7	119	20.60	4.14	22.69	66	17.71	3.38	4.55
7-8/8-7	858	22.42	4.98	39.98	405	20.65	4.51	25.19
7-9/9-7	58	24.97	5.32	58.62	40	21.77	3.42	27.50
7-0/0-7	108	18.98	4.51	17.59	39	14.46	2.85	0.00
Spike 8	87	21.80	4.24	39.08	58	18.52	3.94	6.90
8-9/9-8	256	26.39	4.42	73.44	168	23.08	4.52	47.02
8-0/0-8	65	19.91	5.18	21.54	31	17.97	4.48	6.45
Spike 9	590	24.06	3.78	52.88	435	21.37	3.34	25.06
9-0/0-9	6	24.33	5.72	50.00	2	17.00	4.24	0.00
Spike 0	240	18.78	4.43	15.00	148	16.73	3.92	6.08
Total	16,065	21.49	4.34	36.08	19,143	18.97	3.79	14.07
Minimum		15.15	3.25	0.00		14.46	2.27	0.00
Maximum		26.51	5.72	76.62		24.02	4.73	55.67

scores on the *MAC-R* scale again regardless of whether they abuse substances. As can be seen in Table 6.10, the mean score on the *MAC-R* scale for a *2-7/7-2* codetype is a raw score of 18.87 in men and 16.89 in women, while in *6-9/9-6* codetypes it is a raw score of 26.05 in men and 22.62 in women. This difference of 7.18 points in men and 5.73 points in women in the mean score on the *MAC-R* scale between these two codetypes is more than 1.5 standard deviations, which is a huge effect size by whatever standard is used. There is a difference of almost 10 *raw*-score points between the codetype with the lowest and the highest mean score in men and women. There are similar variations by codetype in the percentage of patients who have raw scores of 24 or higher.

The gender differences that were noted previously on the *MAC* scale also are very apparent on the *MAC-R* scale (Table 6.10). For example, over one-third (36.94%) of the male patients with Spike *1* codetypes had raw scores on the *MAC-R* scale of 24 or higher, while less than one-tenth (6.51%) of the female patients with Spike *1* codetypes had raw scores

of 24 or higher. The mean for all male patients in Table 6.10 is 21.49 as compared to 18.97 for all female patients, a difference of almost exactly 2.5 raw-score points. These mean raw scores on the *MAC-R* scale in patients are very similar to the MMPI-2 normative group (Butcher et al., 1989): men = 20.81 and women = 18.85. Slightly over one-third (36.08%) of the male psychiatric patients had raw scores of 24 or higher, while only 14.07 percent of the female psychiatric patients had such scores. These gender differences would be negated on the *MAC-R* scale if T scores were interpreted instead of raw scores. The tradition of interpreting raw scores on the *MAC-R* scale requires clinicians to use different cutting scores for men and women. A single cutting score of 24 simply is not appropriate for both men and women.

Scores on the *MAC-R* scale essentially are unrelated to age in both normal individuals (Butcher et al., 1989) and psychiatric patients (Caldwell, 1997a). Men endorse 2 to 3 more items than women (Butcher et al., 1989; Caldwell, 1997a). Scores decrease 14 T points in normal individuals and 10 T points in psychiatric patients as the number of years of education increases.

A summary of the interpretations of four levels of elevation of the *MAC-R* scale is given in Table 6.11.

Psychometric Characteristics

Table 6.12 (pp. 238–239) provides the item overlap and intercorrelations among all of the MMPI-2 Supplementary scales that will be reviewed in this Chapter. Table 6.12 merely summarizes all of this information into one convenient source in which the reader can examine simultaneously whatever scales are of interest. Tables 6.13 (pp. 240–241) and 5.7 provide the item overlap and intercorrelations among the the Supplementary scales and the standard Validity and Clinical scales and the Content scales, respectively. The rest of the Supplementary scales that are listed in Tables 6.12, 6.13, and 5.7, which have not been described yet, will be reviewed later in this Chapter because they are not used as frequently by clinicians.

The top half of Table 6.12 shows the item overlap among the the Supplementary scales. Two columns

are included for each scale. The numbers in the column labeled "S" indicate how many items the two scales share that are scored in the same direction. The Welsh Anxiety (*A*) scale shares 12 items with the College Maladjustment (*Mt*) scale that are scored in the same direction (i.e., the deviant response is either "true" or "false" on both scales). In this specific example, all 12 items are scored as "true" on the *A* and *Mt* scales. The column labeled "O" indicates how many items the two scales share that are scored in the opposite direction. The *A* and the Ego Strength (*Es*) scales share 9 items that are scored in the opposite direction (i.e., the deviant response is "true" on one scale and "false" on the other). In this specific example, all 9 items are scored as "true" on the *A* scale and as "false" on the *Es* scale. The MacAndrew Alcoholism—Revised (*MAC-R*) scale shares 3 items with the *A* scale: 1 item that is scored in the same direction on both scales and 2 items that are scored in the opposite direction.

The bottom half of Table 6.12 provides the correlations among the Supplementary scales. The Welsh Anxiety (*A*) scale correlates –.041 with the the Welsh Repression (*R*) scale and –.831 with the Ego Strength (*Es*) scale. The reader should use the *A* scale as a

TABLE 6.11   Interpretations of Levels of Elevation on the MacAndrew Alcoholism—Revised (*MAC-R*) Scale

	RAW SCORE		
T Score	*Men*	*Women*	*Interpretation*
44 and below	18 and below	16 and below	1. *Low.* These clients are risk avoiders who have depressive features. They tend to be introverted and avoid social interactions. If they abuse substances, they will prefer alcohol or sedatives and they are more likely to be secondary alcoholics.
45–57	19–24	17–21	2. *Normal.* These clients have a balance between risk avoiding and risk taking.
58–64	25–27	22–24	3. *Moderate.* These clients are extraverted and have a high energy level. They like to be socially engaged and are not overly concerned about how others perceive them. If they abuse substances, they will prefer alcohol or stimulants.
65 and above	28 and above	25 and above	4. *Marked.* These clients are extraverted risk takers, who are impulsive and sensation seeking. If they abuse substances, they will prefer alcohol or stimulants and they are more likely to be primary alcoholics.

TABLE 6.12   Item Overlap and Intercorrelations among the MMPI-2 Supplementary Scales

	A		R		ES		MAC-R		O-H		DO		RE		MT	
	S	O	S	O	S	O	S	O	S	O	S	O	S	O	S	O
A	–	–	0	0	0	9	1	2	0	2	0	5	0	0	12	0
R	−.041		–	–	1	3	0	6	2	0	0	0	4	1	1	1
Es	−.831		−.172		–	–	0	4	0	3	4	0	2	1	0	6
MAC-R	.181		−.523		−.108		–	–	1	2	2	6	0	9	1	3
O-H	−.493		.333		.243		−.272		–	–	1	0	2	1	0	1
Do	−.722		−.035		.677		−.264		.310		–	–	5	0	0	4
Re	−.548		.377		.377		−.601		.466		.549		–	–	0	0
Mt	.930		.052		−.847		.119		−.439		−.689		−.484		–	–
GM	−.749		−.159		.804		.028		.199		.600		.335		−.740	
GF	−.124		.294		−.038		−.481		.308		.162		.466		−.097	
PK	.927		−.001		−.855		.222		−.431		−.713		−.554		.923	
PS	.941		.014		−.875		.193		−.434		−.709		−.541		.946	
AAS	.443		−.256		−.296		.484		−.362		−.390		−.616		.390	
APS	.342		−.359		−.165		.294		−.409		−.103		−.403		.340	
MDS	.791		−.050		−.652		.200		−.407		−.582		−.531		.763	
Ho	.742		−.314		−.582		.429		−.481		−.615		−.686		.678	
CAL-R	.090		−.194		.014		.315		−.139		−.137		−.259		.012	

Note. "S" indicates that the deviant response for the item is the same on both scales; "O" indicates that the deviant response is "true" on one scale and "false" on the other scale.

marker for the first factor in Tables 6.12, 6.13, and 5.7 to understand how much generalized distress and negative emotionality will elevate a specific scale. The correlations of .951 on the A scale with Scale 7 (Psychasthenia) and .895 with Scale 8 (Schizophrenia) (Table 6.13) indicate that all three of these scales are elevated to a significant degree by generalized distress and negative emotionality. Scales 7 and 8 may be better measures that clients are generally distressed and unhappy rather than that they have the specific characteristics of the individual scale. The reader is reminded that elevations on a Clinical scale indicate that the client endorses the items *like* the criterion group, *not* that the client is a member of that criterion group. The patients who served as the criterion groups for Scales 7 and 8 obviously were generally distressed and unhappy as well as possessing the more specific symptoms that would be expected given their diagnoses. Consequently, clinicians need to ascertain how much of a client's scores on Scales 7 and 8 reflect generalized distress and negative emo-

tionality before making any specific interpretations of these two scales. This same caveat holds for all scales that have substantial correlations with the A scale.

Table 6.14 (p. 242) provides the correlations among the demographic variables of age, education, and gender and the Supplementary scales in the MMPI-2 normative group (Butcher et al., 1989) and psychiatric patients (Caldwell, 1997a). (Chapter 9 will be devoted entirely to the examination of the effects of demographic variables on MMPI-2 performance so this discussion will be relatively brief.) The Addiction Admission Scale (*AAS*) among the Supplementary scales has the largest correlation (−.300) with age in normal individuals. Individuals 70 years of age and older in the MMPI-2 normative group had a mean T score of 44.9 on *AAS*, while individuals 20 to 29 years old had a mean score of 53.8 (Table 9.7, p. 442–443). Thus, age will modify any Supplementary scale in normal individuals by less than 10 T points at the most, and 5 T points or less more typically. The Social Responsibility (*Re*) scale among the

	GM		GF		PK		PS		AAS		APS		MDS		HO		CAL-R	
	S	O	S	O	S	O	S	O	S	O	S	O	S	O	S	O	S	O
	0	3	0	0	9	0	14	0	0	0	1	0	1	0	3	0	0	1
	0	2	3	4	0	2	1	2	0	0	0	5	0	0	0	3	1	2
	7	1	0	3	0	10	0	10	0	0	1	1	0	0	2	2	3	1
	3	0	4	5	3	1	1	3	3	0	9	0	0	0	2	1	3	0
	0	2	2	1	1	0	2	2	0	0	1	3	0	0	2	1	0	2
	2	0	2	1	0	3	1	2	0	1	1	0	0	0	1	2	0	2
	3	1	6	1	0	1	0	2	0	1	0	4	0	0	0	4	1	1
	1	4	1	0	10	0	13	0	0	0	1	0	1	0	3	0	1	3
	–	–	0	0	0	1	0	3	0	0	2	1	0	0	0	0	1	1
		.045	–	–	0	0	0	0	0	4	2	0	0	0	0	2	1	1
	-.794		-.274		–	–	26	0	0	0	2	1	4	0	1	0	3	0
	-.809		-.250		.972		–	–	0	0	2	0	4	0	3	0	1	1
	-.225		-.450		.458		.442		–	–	0	0	0	0	0	0	1	0
	-.187		-.074		.281		.298		.341		–	–	0	0	0	4	3	0
	-.576		-.196		.820		.807		.471		.254		–	–	0	0	1	0
	-.501		-.333		.732		.721		.466		.212		.665		–	–	2	1
	.004		-.212		.109		.070		.463		.206		.179		.130		–	–

Supplementary scales had the largest correlation (.137) with age in psychiatric patients. Patients 20 to 29 years of age had a mean score of 47.4 on the *Re* scale, while patients 70 years of age and older had a mean score of 52.7 (Table 9.7). The correlations with age are even smaller in psychiatric patients than are seen in normal individuals. Age will modify any of the Supplementary scales in psychiatric patients by less than 5 T points.

The correlations among the Supplementary scales with gender tend to be similar in normal individuals and psychiatric patients. (A positive correlation with gender in Table 6.14 reflects that women have higher scores on the scale.) The largest correlations are with the gender scales (Gender Role—Feminine [*GF*] and Gender Role—Masculine [*GM*]) as would be expected. Both normal men and male psychiatric patients have higher scores on the Ego Strength (*Es*), MacAndrew Alcoholism—Revised (*MAC-R*), and Addiction Admission (*AAS*) scales than women. Men have scores two to four raw-score points higher on all

of these scales than women (Table 9.13, p. 450). Since all of the Supplementary scales except for the *MAC-R* scale are interpreted as T scores, these differences in raw scores will not affect the interpretation of these scales. As noted repeatedly earlier, if the *MAC-R* scale is interpreted in raw scores, as it is traditionally, the cutting scores must be adjusted for these differences between men and women.

The correlations among the Supplementary scales with education also tend to be similar in normal individuals and psychiatric patients. The largest correlations are with the Dominance (*Do*) and Social Responsibility (*Re*) scales: .406 and .314 in normal individuals and .362 and .279 in psychiatric patients, respectively. Normal individuals and psychiatric patients with less than 9 years of education had mean scores of 36.8 and 39.9 on the *Do* scale, respectively, while normal individual and psychiatric patients with more than 18 years of education had mean scores of 56.3 and 52.4, respectively (Table 9.19, pp. 459–460). These mean differences on the *Do* scale average

TABLE 6.13　Item Overlap and Intercorrelations between the MMPI-2 Clinical and Supplementary Scales in the Caldwell (1997a) Dataset

	A		R		Es		MAC-R		O-H		Do	
	S	O	S	O	S	O	S	O	S	O	S	O
L	0	0	0	0	0	0	1	0	3	0	0	1
F	0	0	2	1	0	3	5	0	0	0	0	0
K	0	5	4	0	1	1	0	0	3	0	1	1
Hs	0	0	3	0	0	7	1	1	1	0	0	0
D	6	0	10	0	1	10	0	4	1	2	0	4
Hy	2	2	4	0	1	10	1	4	4	0	1	2
Pd	3	1	0	0	1	5	7	1	2	2	2	4
Mf-f	1	0	5	3	1	6	3	5	3	1	2	0
Mf-m	1	0	5	3	2	5	2	6	3	1	2	0
Pa	1	0	2	0	0	3	3	0	2	1	1	0
Pt	13	0	0	0	0	9	1	2	1	1	0	6
Sc	8	0	2	1	1	9	2	5	0	0	0	2
Ma	0	1	0	2	2	3	5	0	0	3	2	3
Si	11	0	8	0	0	7	0	5	1	2	0	5

	A	R	Es	MAC-R	O-H	Do
L	−.343	.354	.114	−.161	.519	.082
F	.726	.027	−.703	.307	−.326	−.613
K	−.792	.303	.613	−.321	.557	.612
1(Hs)	.700	.206	−.842	.077	−.211	−.553
2(D)	.746	.384	−.813	−.118	−.212	−.583
3(Hy)	.397	.390	−.616	−.154	.049	−.257
4(Pd)	.721	−.060	−.608	.311	−.364	−.539
5(Mf-f)	.145	.200	−.225	−.337	.127	.024
5(Mf-m)	.279	.112	−.304	−.256	.020	−.067
6(Pa)	.654	.073	−.664	.188	−.211	−.457
7(Pt)	.951	.018	−.865	.159	−.447	−.732
8(Sc)	.895	−.014	−.849	.247	−.414	−.702
9(Ma)	.451	−.449	−.369	.550	−.361	−.363
0(Si)	.804	.284	−.735	−.061	−.355	−.681

Note. "S" indicates that the deviant response for the item is the same on both scales; "O" indicates that the deviant response is "true" on one scale and "false" on the other scale.
[a]Men only.
[b]Women only.

nearly 20 T points (i.e., nearly two standard deviations). There are nearly 10 T points difference between normal individuals and psychiatric patients with less than 9 years of education and more than 18 years of education on the Ego Strength (*Es*), MacAndrew Alcoholism—Revised (*MAC-R*), the Post Traumatic Stress Disorder—Keane (*PK*), and Post Traumatic Stress Disorder—Schlenger (*PS*) scales. Clinicians need to be more aware of the potential effects of education on the interpretation of a number of these Supplementary scales, because of the large differences that are found.

Table 6.15 (p. 243) reports the percentage of items on each Supplementary scale for which "true"

	Re		Mt		GM		GF		PK		PS		AAS		APS		MDS		Ho		CAL-R	
	S	O	S	O	S	O	S	O	S	O	S	O	S	O	S	O	S	O	S	O	S	O
	1	0	0	1	0	0	1	1	0	1	0	0	0	0	0	4	0	0	0	0	1	0
	0	1	0	0	0	0	0	2	5	0	4	0	2	0	1	4	1	1	1	0	3	1
	1	0	1	3	0	0	0	0	0	3	0	2	0	0	2	4	0	1	0	7	0	2
	1	0	6	0	0	5	0	0	5	0	5	0	0	0	0	0	0	0	0	0	1	5
	1	0	16	0	0	4	2	0	11	2	11	2	0	0	2	4	1	0	1	2	3	2
	3	0	9	2	0	5	0	1	9	1	10	2	1	0	2	2	2	1	0	8	2	5
	0	5	5	0	1	2	1	4	11	0	9	0	3	0	3	2	8	0	4	1	4	1
	4	1	0	0	0	9	16	0	1	0	0	0	0	0	4	4	1	0	2	5	1	0
	4	1	0	0	0	9	15	1	1	0	0	0	0	0	4	4	1	0	2	5	0	1
	0	3	2	2	1	2	0	1	7	0	6	0	1	0	2	0	2	0	3	5	4	0
	0	1	14	0	0	5	0	0	17	0	17	0	0	0	3	0	0	0	0	0	0	1
	0	2	9	0	0	2	0	1	19	0	27	0	0	0	2	0	3	0	2	0	2	0
	0	3	3	1	1	1	0	5	3	0	5	0	0	0	3	1	1	0	5	1	4	1
	2	2	6	0	0	8	2	1	8	1	5	1	0	1	0	5	1	0	9	0	0	1

Re	Mt	GM[a]	GF[b]	PK	PS	AAS	APS	MDS	Ho	CAL-R
.410	-.295	.175	.090	-.292	-.280	-.341	-.600	-.303	-.325	-.133
-.553	.698	-.697	-.491	.812	.797	.513	.093	.715	.655	.206
.626	-.733	.629	.313	-.748	-.745	-.443	-.369	-.669	-.836	-.113
-.294	.806	-.724	-.218	.763	.801	.240	.174	.564	.480	-.145
-.205	.849	-.706	-.125	.775	.803	.180	.140	.603	.389	-.077
.032	.558	-.448	-.048	.482	.528	.043	.119	.325	.028	-.182
-.596	.728	-.597	-.383	.781	.760	.569	.329	.813	.595	.278
.187	.148	-.240	.463	.084	.107	-.098	.122	.096	-.132	-.042
.039	.267	-.387	.302	.219	.238	.036	.229	.236	.009	.012
-.392	.645	-.613	-.289	.737	.724	.365	.211	.617	.447	.153
-.533	.946	-.829	-.301	.948	.962	.427	.346	.769	.699	.069
-.573	.881	-.801	-.419	.944	.953	.483	.254	.803	.735	.131
-.572	.414	-.363	-.438	.496	.493	.429	.294	.441	.618	.213
-.357	.777	-.738	-.192	.778	.776	.273	.056	.658	.606	.002

and "false" are the deviant response. Almost all (97.4%) of the items on the Welsh Anxiety (A) scale have "true" as the deviant response, while all of the items on the Welsh Repression (R) scale have "false" as the deviant response. Several of the other Supplementary scales have "true" as the deviant response for a preponderance of their items (MacAndrew Alcoholism—Revised [MAC-R], Post Traumatic Stress Disorder—Keane [PK], Post Traumatic Stress Disorder—Schlenger [PS], Addiction Admission [AAS], and Hostility [Ho]). Several other Supplementary scales have "false" as the deviant response for a preponderance of their items (Overcontrolled-Hostility [O-H], Dominance [Do], and Social Responsibility

TABLE 6.14 Effects of Demographic Variables on the MMPI-2 Supplementary Scales

	CORRELATION					
	Age		Gender[a]		Education	
	NORMALS[b]	PATIENTS[c]	NORMALS[b]	PATIENTS[c]	NORMALS[b]	PATIENTS[c]
A	−.038	.038	.106	.092	−.193	−.174
R	.162	.136	.137	.192	.039	−.013
Es	−.101	−.115	−.299	−.232	.263	.229
MAC-R	−.003	−.070	−.236	−.265	−.281	−.224
O-H	.002	−.070	.177	.155	.022	.025
Do	.065	.064	−.059	−.062	.406	.362
Re	.209	.137	.128	.143	.314	.279
Mt	−.043	.079	.074	.106	−.191	−.177
GM	−.017	−.080	−.609	−.474	.239	.192
GF	.134	.098	.750	.706	.034	.108
PK	−.161	.003	.039	.065	−.197	−.205
PS	−.132	.035	.077	.091	−.208	−.203
AAS	−.300	−.124	−.223	−.154	−.076	−.149
APS	−.177	.030	−.032	−.041	.070	.057
MDS	−.110	.001	.024	.033	−.103	−.150
Ho	−.049	−.043	−.079	−.061	−.294	−.236
CAL-R	−.109	−.077	−.033	−.050	−.068	−.031

[a]Positive correlations reflect that women have higher scores on the indicated scale.
[b]Butcher et al., 1989.
[c]Caldwell, 1997a.

[Re]). A client who has a propensity to endorse the items in either the "true" or "false" direction will raise or lower all of these scales in unison. The clinician should note the percentage of items that the client has endorsed "true" and "false" *before* beginning to interpret any of these scales to ascertain whether a response set is a major contributor to the elevation of these scales. Profiles 6.1 (p. 244) and 6.2 (p. 245) illustrate the effects of endorsing all of the items "true" or "false" on each of the MMPI-2 Supplementary scales, respectively.

Table 6.15 also provides the mean rating of the obviousness of the content of the items on each of the Supplementary scales. These ratings are based on the research of Christian et al. (1978) who asked college students to rate how clearly the content of each MMPI item was indicative of a psychological prob-

lem when it was endorsed "true" and when it was endorsed "false." Very obvious items were assigned a rating of 5, obvious a rating of 4, neither obvious nor subtle a rating of 3, subtle a rating of 2, and very subtle a rating of 1. The mean rating for each Supplementary scale was obtained by summing the ratings of the obviousness of each item as it was keyed "true" or "false" on the scale. Since Christian et al. obtained their ratings on the original MMPI items, these mean ratings are based on the number of MMPI items that were retained on the MMPI-2 version of the scale. The Welsh Anxiety (A) scale has a mean rating of 3.07 that indicates its items are neither obvious nor subtle in content, while the Welsh Repression (R) scale has a mean rating of 2.32 that indicates its items are subtle. The Post Traumatic Stress Disorder— Schlenger (PS) scale has the highest mean (3.67) rat-

TABLE 6.15 True and False Composition of the MMPI-2 Supplementary Scales

	Number of Items	PERCENTAGE		OBVIOUSNESS[a]	
		True	False	Mean	Items
A	39	97.4	2.6	3.17	39
R	37	0.0	100.0	2.32	37
Es	52	38.5	61.5	2.20	52
MAC-R	49	77.6	22.4	2.66	45
O-H	28	25.0	75.0	2.41	28
Do	25	24.0	76.0	2.21	25
Re	30	20.0	80.0	2.05	30
Mt	41	68.3	31.7	3.29	41
GM	47	40.4	59.6	1.96	42
GF	46	32.6	67.4	2.01	37
PK	46	82.6	17.4	3.67	46
PS	60	78.3	21.7	3.61	53
AAS	13	76.9	23.1	3.49	6
APS	39	59.0	41.0	2.53	31
MDS	14	57.1	42.9	3.44	9
Ho	50	94.0	6.0	2.98	50
CAL-R	27	55.6	44.4	2.66	27

[a]These ratings are based on Christian et al. (1978).

ing for obviousness among the supplementary scales, while the Gender Role—Masculine (*GM*) scale has the lowest rating (1.96).

A scale usually is a more direct measure of the construct being assessed as its items become more obvious, and the easier it is for clients to distort their responses if they are so motivated. An item that reads "I am depressed" would have a high rating of obviousness and be related directly to obvious measures of depression such as the Beck Depression Inventory (Beck, 1987). Clients who wished to either present themselves as depressed or not would know to endorse this item "true" or "false" accordingly. The ratings of the obviousness of the items on the Supplementary scales provide the clinician with an index of how directly each scale is a measure of psychopathology and how easy it is for clients to distort their responses to the items if they wanted to do so.

The reader also should note that these items are being rated as to their obviousness as being indicative

of a psychological problem. If another criterion were used, such as whether the items are indicative of socially appropriate behaviors, the Social Responsibility (*Re*) scale would have the highest rating for obviousness among the Supplementary scales.

ADDITIONAL MMPI-2 SUPPLEMENTARY SCALES[7]

Overcontrolled-Hostility (*O-H*) Scale

Megargee and Mendelsohn (1962) attempted to cross-validate 12 MMPI indexes of hostility by contrasting groups of male criminals who were classified as extremely assaultive, moderately assaultive, and nonassaultive. None of these 12 scales correctly identified the extremely assaultive groups of criminals. In fact, Megargee and Mendelsohn found that the extremely assaultive criminals were more likely to score significantly lower on these scales (i.e., the extremely assaultive criminals demonstrated lower hostility scores and better impulse control than the other groups). In a similar study of 21 MMPI scales and indexes of hostility Deiker (1974) also reported that his extremely assaultive group scored significantly lower than other assaultive groups on 13 of 17 scales that were significantly different.

In light of these paradoxical results, Megargee et al. (1967) developed a new scale to assist in the identification of assaultive individuals. They began by distinguishing between undercontrolled and overcontrolled assaultive individuals because they believed that different factors led to assaultive outbursts in these two groups. They believed that undercontrolled individuals have failed to learn to control their aggressive impulses, and their aggressive behaviors occur in response to some external form of provocation. Overcontrolled individuals, however, rigidly defend against any expression of aggressive impulses irrespective of the provocation until finally some provocation or other factor results in their acting out, frequently in an extremely destructive fashion.

---

7. The scales within this section are discussed in the order that they appear on the MMPI-2 profile sheet for Supplementary scales.

MMPI-2

S R Hathaway and J C McKinley
Minnesota Multiphasic
Personality Inventory -2

Profile for Supplementary Scales

Minnesota Multiphasic Personality Inventory-2
Copyright © by THE REGENTS OF THE UNIVERSITY OF MINNESOTA
1942, 1943 (renewed 1970), 1989. This Profile Form 1989.
All rights reserved. Distributed exclusively by NATIONAL COMPUTER SYSTEMS, INC.
under license from The University of Minnesota.

"MMPI-2" and "Minnesota Multiphasic Personality Inventory-2" are trademarks owned by
The University of Minnesota. Printed in the United States of America.

Name	Profile 6-1	
Address		
Occupation		Date Tested
Education	Age	Marital Status
Referred by		
Scorer's Initials		

FEMALE

All "True" Responses

Raw Score	38	0	20	38	7	6	6	28	19	15	38	47	8	2	17	37	5	19

NATIONAL COMPUTER SYSTEMS
24004

PROFILE 6.1

Note. Minnesota Multiphasic Personality Inventory-2 (MMPI-2). Copyright © 1942, 1943 (renewed 1970), 1989 by the Regents of the University of Minnesota. Reproduced by permission of the publisher. "MMPI-2" and "Minnesota Multiphasic Personality Inventory-2" are trademarks owned by the University of Minnesota.

PROFILE 6.2

Note. Minnesota Multiphasic Personality Inventory-2 (MMPI-2). Copyright © 1942, 1943 (renewed 1970), 1989 by the Regents of the University of Minnesota. Reproduced by permission of the publisher. "MMPI-2" and "Minnesota Multiphasic Personality Inventory-2" are trademarks owned by the University of Minnesota.

Megargee et al. (1967) felt that the latter group was more important to identify since their assaultive behaviors occur unexpectedly and frequently very violently. They contrasted the item responses of four groups of men: 14 extremely assaultive prisoners, 25 moderately assaultive prisoners, 25 nonassaultive prisoners, and 46 normals. The 55 items that differentiated between the assaultive and nonassaultive prisoners then were cross-validated in new groups of extremely assaultive, moderately assaultive, and nonassaultive prisoners. They eliminated items that did not differentiate among these new groups of assaultive and nonassaultive prisoners, and the 31 (28 items on the MMPI-2) remaining items became the Overcontrolled-Hostility (*O-H*) Scale.

Megargee et al. (1967) did not suggest a specific cutting score to be used on this scale. Instead, they recommended that investigators determine the most appropriate cutting score in their own treatment setting based on which errors are more tolerable—false positives (identifying a person as overcontrolled and hostile who is not) or false negatives (identifying a person as not being overcontrolled and hostile who actually is).

The *O-H* scale shares only a few items with the standard Clinical scales (Table 6.13). The *O-H* scale shares four items with Scale *3* (Hysteria) and three items with Scales *L* (Lie), *K* (Correction), and *5* (Masculinity-Femininity). It also shares three items with Scale *9* (Hypomania) that are scored in the opposite direction. The *O-H* scale also has minimal item overlap with the other Supplementary scales (Table 6.12). It shares 3 items with the Ego Strength (*Es*) and Addiction Potential (*APS*) scales that are scored in the opposite direction. Finally, the *O-H* scale shares no more than two items with any of the MMPI-2 Content scales (Table 5.7). The *O-H* scale is one of the few Supplementary scales that appears to have the potential for assessing unique content because it shares so few items with the other scales.

The deviant response for three-fourths of the items on the *O-H* scale is "false"; hence, a tendency toward a "false" response set will elevate scores on the *O-H* scale. The items on the *O-H* scale have a mean rating of 2.41 for the obviousness of content that indicates its items are somewhat subtle as a measure of psychological problems.

Research on the *O-H* scale has been very mixed. Prisoners whose crimes were judged to reflect overcontrolled hostility scored higher on the *O-H* scale than prisoners whose crimes were judged to reflect undercontrolled hostility (Megargee et al., 1967). Deiker (1974) found that the *O-H* scale was one of the few MMPI scales that could accurately identify male prisoners who were extremely assaultive. He questioned whether a negative response bias might account for the obtained results since two-thirds of the items on the *O-H* scale have "false" as the deviant response.

Megargee and Cook (1975) demonstrated, however, that *O-H* scales balanced for "naysaying" (equivalent numbers of "true" and "false" deviant responses) yielded similar if not better results than the original *O-H* scale, which indicated that a negative response bias cannot explain the results obtained with the *O-H* scale. Both Lane and Kling (1979) and White and Heilbrun (1995) found that the *O-H* scale reliably discriminated between overcontrolled, assaultive, forensic psychiatric patients and undercontrolled assaultive patients.

Quinsey, Maguire, and Varney (1983) reported that murderers who scored high on the *O-H* scale were less assertive than murderers who scored low on this scale. They suggested that assertiveness training may be beneficial with persons who have high scores on the *O-H* scale. Henderson (1983) also found that overcontrolled violent offenders were less aggressive and less assertive than undercontrolled violent offenders.

Several studies found that the *O-H* scale does not discriminate between violent and nonviolent criminals (Hoppe & Singer, 1976; Mallory & Walker, 1972; Truscott, 1990). The first two of these studies administered the *O-H* scale out of context of the entire MMPI, but it is not clear if this factor would be sufficient to invalidate the results. Gudjonsson, Petursson, Sigurdardottir, and Skulason (1991) found that other-deception and self-deception accounted for almost one-half of the variance in scores on the *O-H* scale, which suggests that different levels of deception in the various samples of patients might account for the varying outcomes.

Werner, Becker, and Yesavage (1983) found that the *O-H* scale was not correlated with assaultiveness in psychotic, male psychiatric inpatients. Most investigators, including Megargee et al. (1967) and Deiker

(1974), found only small mean differences (two items) between assaultive and nonassaultive groups, so it is possible that even minor variations in procedure may be sufficient to obscure these differences. Investigators also have been inconsistent in whether or not they distinguish between overcontrolled and undercontrolled hostility in their assaultive groups; this inconsistency may further obscure the reported results.

Hutton, Miner, Blades, and Langfeldt (1992) found that the only predictor of the *O-H* scale in forensic psychiatric inpatients was ethnicity, with blacks scoring higher than whites. Almost one-half (43%) of the blacks had T scores of 70 or higher. They also found that none of the descriptors of the overcontrolled individual was related to scores on the *O-H* scale. Both Leonard (1977) and Lester and Clopton (1979) reported that the *O-H* scale did not reliably distinguish between psychiatric patients who completed suicide and nonsuicidal psychiatric patients.

Additional research on the *O-H* scale clearly is needed. The apparent finding that even minor procedural changes, such as administering the *O-H* scale in isolation, may alter the effectiveness of the *O-H* scale suggests that it should be used cautiously in identifying specific individuals as overcontrolled and hostile. Investigators also will need to determine the most efficient cutting score for the *O-H* scale in their treatment setting, as Megargee et al. (1967) recommended. The low prevalence rates for overcontrolled hostility also mean that there is little likelihood that the *O-H* scale will have adequate positive predictive power in any setting.

Finally, Gearing (1979) pointed out the similarity between the behaviors characteristic of persons with *4-3* codetypes (Davis & Sines, 1971; Persons & Marks, 1971) and the behaviors expected of a high scorer on the *O-H* scale. Research is needed to determine whether similar behaviors are being assessed in these two instances.

High scorers (T scores of 65 or higher) on the *O-H* scale are described as displaying excessive control of their hostile impulses and as being socially alienated. They are reluctant to admit any form of psychological symptoms, even though they are sometimes diagnosed as being psychotic. They are seen as being rigid and not displaying anxiety overtly. They may be candidates for assertiveness training. The fun-damental question in these clients is whether this self-description is accurate or a facade. The clinician needs to evaluate measures of underreporting, particularly self-deception.

Low scorers (T scores less than 45) on the *O-H* scale are able to acknowledge that they are nervous and they worry about what happens around them. They are aware of being angry and irritable.

Scores on the *O-H* scale are not affected by age in either normal individuals (Butcher et al., 1989) or psychiatric patients (Caldwell, 1997a). Women endorse one more item than men (Butcher et al., 1989; Caldwell, 1997a). Education also has minimal effects on scores on the *O-H* scale with increases of less than 4 T points in normal individuals and 2 T points in psychiatric patients from the lowest to the highest ranges.

Dominance (*Do*) Scale

Gough, McClosky, and Meehl (1951) developed the Dominance (*Do*) scale by contrasting the item responses of both high school and college students who were judged by their peers to be most and least dominant. Their intent in the development of the *Do* scale was to identify strong, dominant, influential persons who were able to take initiative and exercise leadership.

Gough et al. (1951) identified 60 items that differentiated subgroups of male and female students who were most and least dominant. Only 28 of these items are found on the MMPI, and they comprise the MMPI *Do* scale. These 28 items (25 items remain on the MMPI-2) are keyed so that high scores indicate more dominant behaviors. The total of 60 items identified by Gough et al. make up the Dominance scale on the California Psychological Inventory (Gough, 1957). Gough et al. noted that since their items were validated in normal student populations, additional research would be necessary to validate the use of the MMPI *Do* scale with adults and in psychopathological groups.

The *Do* scale has limited item overlap with the standard Clinical scales (Table 6.13). The *Do* scale shares 6 items with Scale *7* (Psychasthenia); 5 items with Scale *0* (Social Introversion); and 4 items with Scales *2* (Depression) and *4* (Psychopathic Deviate), all of which are scored in the opposite direction. The *Do* scale also has limited item overlap with the other Supplementary scales (Table 6.12): 5 items with the Social Responsibility (*Re*) scale and 4 items with the Ego Strength (*Es*) scale. It also shares 6 items with the MacAndrew Alcoholism—Revised (*MAC-R*) scale and 4 items with College Maladjustment (*Mt*) that are scored in the opposite direction. Finally, the *Do* scale shares no more than three items with any of the MMPI-2 Content scales (Table 5.7), all of which are scored in the opposite direction. The *Do* scale, like the *O-H* scale, is another of the few Supplementary scales that appears to have the potential for assessing unique variance on the MMPI-2 because it shares so few items with the other scales.

The deviant response for three-fourths of the items on the *Do* scale is "false"; hence, a tendency toward a "false" response set will elevate scores on the *Do* scale. The items on the *Do* scale have a mean rating of 2.21 for the obviousness of content, which indicates its items are a subtle measure of psychological problems.

Research on the MMPI *Do* scale has been exceedingly sparse. Olmsted and Monachesi's (1956) finding that firefighters achieved only slightly higher scores on the *Do* scale than students suggests that student norms could be generalized to adult samples. Olmsted and Monachesi also found that firefighters with the rank of captain did not have higher *Do* scores than regular firefighters; this finding led them to question the validity of the *Do* scale. On the other hand, Knapp (1960) found that military officers achieved higher *Do* scores than enlisted men, and Knapp questioned whether dominance played the same role in firefighters as in military personnel. Duckworth and Anderson (1986) reported that college students have an average T score of 60 on the *Do* scale (i.e., current college students score somewhat higher on *Do* than the students on which Gough et al. [1951] developed the scale). Hedayat and Kelly (1991) found a correlation of 0.86 between staff's ratings of the dominance of psychiatric patients and scores on the *Do* scale. Men with higher scores on the *Do* scale were more likely to be living in an apartment than a group home or with their family.

The lack of further research on the *Do* scale makes conclusions difficult to draw. The Dominance scale on the California Psychological Inventory (Gough, 1957), which shares 28 of 60 items with the MMPI *Do* scale, is one of the better validated scales (Megargee, 1972). There also has been no research on the *Do* scale on the MMPI-2. Research is needed to determine whether it is an adequate measure of interpersonal dominance and to document the generalization of student norms and test correlates to adult samples.

High scorers (T scores of 65 or higher) on the *Do* scale are described as being able to take charge of and responsibility for their lives. They are poised, self-assured, and confident of their own abilities. They address problems in a realistic, task-oriented fashion and feel adequate in their ability to overcome any obstacles that they may encounter. They have good attention and concentration and make decisions easily.

Low scorers (T scores less than 45) on the *Do* scale have not been investigated adequately. These persons prefer to have others take responsibility for their lives. They frequently have high scores on the MMPI Dependency (*Dy*) scale (see Greene [1991], p. 213), which further substantiates their reliance on others to meet their needs. Since the Dependency scale is not scored routinely on the MMPI-2, even though 48 of its 57 items have been retained, research is needed to determine the correlates of low scores on the *Do* scale.

Scores on the *Do* scale are unaffected by age or gender in both normal individuals (Butcher et al., 1989) and psychiatric patients (Caldwell, 1997a). Education has substantial effects on scores on the *Do* scale with increases of nearly 15 T points in normal individuals and psychiatric patients from the lowest to the highest ranges. Normal individuals and psychiatric patients with less than 9 years of education have mean T scores of 36.8 and 39.9, while normal individuals and psychiatric patients with more than 18 years of education have mean T scores of 56.3 and 52.4, respectively (Table 9.19).

Social Responsibility (*Re*) Scale

Gough et al. (1952) developed the Social Responsibility (*Re*) scale by contrasting the item responses of both high school and college students who were judged by their peers to be most and least responsible members, ignoring such considerations as friendliness, popularity, and so on. The responsible person was defined as "one who shows a ready willingness to accept the consequences of his own behavior, dependability, trustworthiness, and a sense of obligation to the group" (Gough et al., 1952, p. 74). Such a person would have a sense of commitment to the group and others, is dependable, and possesses integrity. They identified 56 items that reliably distinguished between students who were the most and least socially responsible. These 56 items comprise the Social Responsibility scale on the California Psychological Inventory (Gough, 1957). Only 32 of these items are found on the MMPI, and these 32 items (30 items on the MMPI-2) comprise the MMPI *Re* scale.

Gough et al. (1952) described high scorers on the *Re* scale as showing greater concern for social and moral issues, disapproving of favoritism, emphasizing carrying one's own share of duties and burdens, having a sense of trust and confidence in the world, and being poised and self-assured. They did not describe low scorers on the *Re* scale. They noted that since their items were validated in normal student populations, additional research would be necessary to validate the use of the MMPI *Re* scale with adults and in clinical settings.

The *Re* scale has limited item overlap with the standard Clinical scales (Table 6.13). The *Re* scale shares 5 items with Scale *5* (Masculinity-Femininity) and 3 items with Scale *3* (Hysteria). It also shares 5 items with Scale *4* (Psychopathic Deviate) and 3 items with Scales *6* (Paranoia) and *9* (Hypomania) that are scored in the opposite direction. The *Re* scale also has limited item overlap with the other Supplementary scales (Table 6.12): 9 items with the MacAndrew Alcoholism—Revised (*MAC-R*) scale and 4 items with the Addiction Potential (*APS*) and Hostility (*Ho*) scales, all of which are scored in the opposite direction. It also shares 6 items with the Gender Role—Feminine (*GF*) scale; 5 items with the Dominance (*Do*) scale, and 4 items with the Welsh Repression (*R*) scale. Finally, the *Re* scale shares few items with any of the MMPI-2 Content scales (Table 5.7): 5 items with the Antisocial Practices (*ASP*) scale and 3 items with the Type A (*TPA*) scale that are scored in the opposite direction. The *Re* scale, like the *Do* scale, is one of the few MMPI-2 scales that has positive attributes.

The deviant response for four-fifths of the items on the *Re* scale is "false"; hence, a tendency toward a "false" response set will elevate scores on the *Re* scale. The items on the *Re* scale have a mean rating of 2.05 for the obviousness of content, which indicates its items are a subtle measure of psychological problems.

There has been virtually no research on the *Re* scale. Knapp (1960) reported that Marine Corps officers had higher scores than enlisted men, and Olmstead and Monachesi (1956) found that fire captains had higher scores than firefighters, although these differences were not statistically reliable. Duckworth and Anderson (1986) suggested that high scorers on the *Re* scale are accepting of a previously held value system, whereas low scorers are changing away from such a value system. They also provide suggested interpretations of ranges of scores on the *Re* scale. Such interpretations should be used cautiously until empirical research is available to validate them.

High scorers (T scores of 65 or higher) on the *Re* scale behave in a socially appropriate manner. They are very conventional individuals who interact easily with others.

Low scorers (T scores less than 45) on the *Re* scale had a variety of behavior problems while they were in school. They have antisocial attitudes.

Scores on the *Re* scale increase 4 to 5 T points with age in both normal individuals (Butcher et al., 1989) and psychiatric patients (Caldwell, 1997a). There are no gender differences on the *Re* scale in normal individuals (Butcher et al., 1989) or psychiatric patients (Caldwell, 1997a). Education has substantial effects on the *Re* scale with increases of 10 to 12 T points in normal individuals and in psychiatric patients from the lowest to the highest ranges. Normal individuals and psychiatric patients with less than 9 years of education have mean T scores of 43.8 and 45.0, while normal individuals and psychiatric patients with more than 18 years of education have mean T scores of 55.9 and 54.2, respectively (Table 9.19).

College Maladjustment (*Mt*) Scale

Kleinmuntz (1960, 1961a) developed the College Maladjustment (*Mt*) scale by contrasting the item responses of 40 students who were referred to a university mental hygiene clinic for routine mental health screening required by their teacher's college with 40 students who were referred for treatment and who had remained in psychotherapy for at least three sessions. He excluded Scale 5 (Masculinity-Femininity) items since they were selected to differentiate between men and women. He identified 43 items (41 items on the MMPI-2) that reliably differentiated these two groups of students. The maladjusted student, who was defined by a score of 15 or higher, was an ineffectual, pessimistic, procrastinating, anxious, and worried person who tended to somatize and who found life to be a strain much of the time.

Kleinmuntz (1961b) found that his *Mt* scale did not accurately separate college students with potential maladjustment from those students who made a satisfactory adjustment during their first year of college. Subsequently, Kleinmuntz (1963) developed a computerized system based in part on the *Mt* scale to differentiate maladjusted and well-adjusted students. His use of the *Mt* scale and the MMPI in general quickly evolved into the issue of automated versus clinical judgment in the identification of maladjusted college students. The interested clinician should see Wiggins (1973) and Faust (1984) for an overview of this topic.

The *Mt* scale has substantial item overlap with a number of the standard Clinical scales (Table 6.13). The *Mt* scale shares 16 items with Scale 2 (Depression), 14 items with Scale 7 (Psychasthenia), and 9 items with Scale 8 (Schizophrenia). The *Mt* scale also has substantial item overlap with several of the other Supplementary scales (Table 6.12): 13 items with the Post Traumatic Stress Disorder—Schlenger (*PS*) scale; 12 items with the Welsh Anxiety (*A*) scale; and 10 items with the Post Traumatic Stress Disorder—Keane (*PK*) scale. Finally, the *Mt* scale has substantial item overlap with a number of the MMPI-2 Content scales (Table 5.7): 10 items with the Anxiety (*ANX*) and Depression (*DEP*) scales and 9 items with the Work Interference (*WRK*) scale. The *Mt* scale is a composite of a number of items reflecting generalized distress and negative emotionality and as such is another marker for the first factor along with the *A, PK,* and *PS* scales.

The deviant response for two-thirds of the items on the *Mt* scale is "true"; hence, a tendency toward a "true" response set will elevate scores on the *Mt* scale.

The items on the *Mt* scale have a mean rating of 3.29 for the obviousness of content, which indicates its items are a somewhat obvious measure of psychological problems.

Research on the *Mt* scale is almost nonexistent. Phillips and McCord (1998) found that the *Mt* scale significantly differentiated those college students who sought counseling from those who did not. They also found that adding a fraction (0.20) of the *K* (Correction) scale to the *Mt* scale enhanced the differentiation of these two groups of students.

High scorers (T scores of 65 or higher) on the *Mt* scale are described as generally emotionally distressed, anxious, and lacking confidence in their own abilities. They are characterized as reacting to situational stress or personal distress and the elevation of the *Mt* scale reflects their level of discomfort. Because of this discomfort, they are usually motivated to enter into psychological treatment.

Low scorers (T scores of 44 or lower) on the *Mt* scale are usually described as well adjusted and not overtly anxious. They may be impulsive and display behavioral problems, although these behaviors are not upsetting to them. Low scores on the *Mt* scale are not expected in clinical settings, because clients should be experiencing some level of generalized distress either because they are seeking or someone referred them for psychological treatment.

Scores on the *Mt* scale are unaffected by age in both normal individuals (Butcher et al., 1989) and psychiatric patients (Caldwell, 1997a). Women endorse about 1 to 2 more items than men (Butcher et al., 1989; Caldwell, 1997a). Education has substantial effects on the *Mt* scale, with decreases of 6 T points in normal individuals and nearly 10 T points in psychiatric patients from the lowest to the highest ranges. Normal individuals and psychiatric patients with less than 9 years of education have mean scores of 52.8 and 62.0, while normal individuals and psychiatric patients with more than 18 years of education have mean scores of 46.8 and 52.8, respectively (Table 9.19).

Gender Role Scales

Peterson and Dahlstrom (1992) developed separate gender role scales for men (Gender Role—Masculine

[*GM*]) and women (Gender Role—Feminine [*GF*]) on the MMPI-2. They included an item on one of the gender scales if it was endorsed by a majority of one gender and by at least 10 percent fewer of the opposite gender. The availability of separate gender role scales for men and women avoids some of the pitfalls of the bipolar Scale *5* (see Chapter 4) and allows for the determination of the client's score separately on each scale. A quick perusal of the items on the *GM* and *GF* scales (see Appendix B-5) will reveal that a very stereotypic characterization of each gender has been produced by this method of selecting the items for each scale. The items on each scale are so stereotypic for each gender that it does not seem likely that a person would score high on both scales and be classified as androgynous.

Gender Role—Masculine. The Gender Role— Masculine (*GM*) scale has substantial item overlap with a number of the standard Clinical scales (Table 6.13). The *GM* scale shares 9 items with Scale *5* (Masculinity-Femininity), 8 items with Scale *0* (Social Introversion), and 5 items with Scales *1* (Hypochondriasis), *3* (Hysteria), and *7* (Psychasthenia), all of which are scored in the opposite direction. The *GM* scale has substantial item overlap with only one of the Supplementary scales (Table 6.12): 7 items with the Ego Strength (*Es*) scale. Finally, the *GM* scale shares a substantial number of items with only one of the MMPI-2 content scales (Table 5.7): 10 items with the Fears (*FRS*) scale, all of which are scored in the opposite direction. The *GM* scale is a composite of a number of items reflecting very stereotypic masculine behavior and the absence of negative emotionality and particularly fear.

The deviant response for about 60 percent of the items on the *GM* scale is "false"; hence, a tendency toward a "true" or "false" response set will not elevate scores on the *GM* scale. The items on the *GM* scale have a mean rating of 1.96 for the obviousness of content, which indicates its items are a subtle measure of psychological problems.

Research on the *GM* scale has supported that the *GM* scale is a measure of well-being (Castlebury & Durham, 1997) and personal strength (Johnson, Jones, & Brems, 1996), but it has little relationship

with other measures of sex roles (Johnson et al., 1996).

High scorers (T scores of 65 or higher) on the *GM* scale are self-confident and they make decisions easily. They have few fears and experience little emotional distress. They have very stereotypic masculine interests and engage in stereotypic masculine activities.

Low scorers (T scores less than 45) on the *GM* scale are fearful individuals who are experiencing a significant degree of emotional distress. They have little interest in typical masculine activities. They are socially introverted and tend to have a cynical outlook on life.

Scores on the *GM* scale are unaffected by age in both normal individuals (Butcher et al., 1989) and psychiatric patients (Caldwell, 1997a). Men endorse about 7 to 8 more items than women (Butcher et al., 1989; Caldwell, 1997a). Education has moderate effects on scores on the *GM* scale with increases of nearly 6 T points in normal individuals and psychiatric patients from the lowest to the highest ranges. Normal individuals and psychiatric patients with less than 9 years of education have mean T scores of 46.6 and 42.2, while normal individuals and psychiatric patients with more than 18 years of education have mean T scores of 53.1 and 49.5, respectively (Table 9.19).

Gender Role—Feminine. The Gender Role— Feminine (*GF*) scale has substantial item overlap with only one of the standard Clinical scales (Table 6.13). The *GF* scale shares 16 items with Scale *5* (Masculinity-Femininity). The *GF* scale also shares 5 items with Scale *9* (Hypomania) and 4 items with Scale *4* (Psychopathic Deviate), all of which are scored in the opposite direction. The *GF* scale also has substantial item overlap with several of the other Supplementary scales (Table 6.12): 6 items with the Social Responsibility (*Re*) scale; 9 items with the MacAndrew Alcoholism—Revised (*MAC-R*) scale, 5 of which are scored in the opposite direction; and 7 items with the Welsh Repression (*R*) scale, 4 of which are scored in the opposite direction. Finally, the *GF* scale shares some items with only one of the MMPI-2 content scales (Table 5.7): 5 items with the

Antisocial Practices (*ASP*) scale, all of which are scored in the opposite direction. The *GF* scale is a composite of a number of items reflecting very stereotypic feminine behavior.

The deviant response for about two-thirds of the items on the *GF* scale is "false"; hence, a tendency toward a "false" response set will elevate scores on the *GF* scale. The items on the *GM* scale have a mean rating of 2.01 for the obviousness of content, which indicates its items are a subtle measure of psychological problems.

Research on the *GF* scale has shown that it is correlated with measures of interpersonal affiliation (Johnson et al., 1996) and possibly with measures of psychological well-being (Castlebury & Durham, 1997).

High scorers (T scores of 65 or higher) on the *GF* scale have very stereotypic feminine interests and they engage in stereotypic feminine activities. They are very socially responsible and they interact easily with others. They do not abuse substances.

Low scorers (T scores less than 45) on the *GF* scale have little interest in typical feminine activities. They may abuse substances.

Scores on the *GF* scale increase 8 to 10 T points with age in both normal individuals (Butcher et al., 1989) and psychiatric patients (Caldwell, 1997a). Women endorse about 10 more items than men (Butcher et al., 1989; Caldwell, 1997a). Education has moderate effects on scores on the *GF* scale, with increases of nearly 5 T points in normal individuals and psychiatric patients from the lowest to the highest ranges. Normal individuals and psychiatric patients with less than 9 years of education have mean scores of 50.3 and 46.2, while normal individuals and psychiatric patients with more than 18 years of education have mean scores of 55.0 and 52.5, respectively (Table 9.19).

McGrath, Sapareto, and Pogge (1998) have developed a Masculine-Feminine Pathology scale to identify symptoms and behaviors of psychopathology that are more reflective of men or women. They keyed the 54 items so that higher scores were associated with femininity. High scorers on the scale were characterized by anxious distress, somatic symptoms, hypersensitivity, and interpersonal sensitivity.

Post Traumatic Stress Disorder Scales

Keane, Malloy, and Fairbank (1984) developed their Post Traumatic Stress Disorder (*PK*) scale by contrasting the item responses of 100 male veterans who had Post Traumatic Stress Disorder with 100 male veterans who had psychiatric diagnoses other than Post Traumatic Stress Disorder. They identified 49 items from the first 400 items of Form R of the MMPI that differentiated the two groups at the .001 level. They found that a cutting score of 30 was optimal for separating the two groups with a hit rate of 82 percent. The MMPI-2 retains 46 of these 49 items.

Hit rates in cross-validation studies of the *PK* scale have ranged from 38 percent (Gayton, Burchstead, & Matthews, 1986) to 80 percent (Schlenger & Kulka, 1987) and averaged in the 70 to 75 percent range (Penk, Keane, Robinowitz, Fowler, Bell, & Finkelstein, 1988). Denny, Robinowitz, and Penk (1987) and Penk et al. (1988) have provided reviews of the research on various PTSD scales.

The *PK* scale has substantial item overlap with a number of the standard Clinical scales (Table 6.13). *PK* shares 19 items with Scale *8* (Schizophrenia), 17 items with Scale *7* (Psychasthenia), and 11 items with Scales *2* (Depression) and *4* (Psychopathic Deviate). *PK* also has substantial item overlap with several of the other Supplementary scales (Table 6.12): 26 items with the Post Traumatic Stress Disorder—Schlenger (*PS*) scale; 10 items with the College Maladjustment (*Mt*) scale; 9 items with the Welsh Anxiety (*A*) scale; and 10 items with the Ego Strength (*Es*) scale, all of which are scored in the opposite direction. Finally, *PK* shares items with a number of the MMPI-2 Content scales (Table 5.7): 11 items with the Depression (*DEP*) scale and 9 items with the Anxiety (*ANX*) scale. *PK* is a composite of a number of items reflecting generalized distress and as such is another marker for the first factor like *A, Mt,* and *PS*.

The deviant response for four-fifths of the items on the *PK* scale is "true"; hence, a tendency toward a "true" response set will elevate scores on this Scale. The items on the *PK* scale have a mean rating of 3.67 for the obviousness of content, which indicates its items are an obvious measure of psychological problems.

High scorers (T scores of 65 or higher) on the *PK* scale are described as generally emotionally distressed, anxious, and lacking confidence in their own abilities. They are characterized as reacting to situational stress or personal distress and the elevation of *PK* reflects their level of discomfort. Because of this discomfort, they are usually motivated to enter into psychological treatment.

Low scorers (T scores of 44 or lower) on the *PK* scale are usually described as well adjusted and not overtly anxious. They may be impulsive and display behavioral problems, although these behaviors are not upsetting to them. Low scores on the *PK* are *not* expected in clinical settings, because clients should be experiencing some level of generalized distress either because they are seeking or someone referred them for psychological treatment.

Scores on the *PK* scale decrease 10 to 12 T points with age in both normal individuals (Butcher et al., 1989) and psychiatric patients (Caldwell, 1997a). Women endorse about 1 to 2 more items than men (Butcher et al., 1989; Caldwell, 1997a). Education has substantial effects on scores on the *PK* scale with decreases of nearly 6 T points in normal individuals and 12 T points in psychiatric patients from the lowest to the highest ranges. Normal individuals and psychiatric patients with less than 9 years of education have mean scores of 52.5 and 64.5, while normal individuals and psychiatric patients with more than 18 years of education have mean scores of 46.6 and 52.1, respectively (Table 9.19).

Schlenger and Kulka (1987) developed their Post Traumatic Stress Disorder (*PS*) scale by contrasting the item responses of healthy Vietnam-era veterans with veterans with Post Traumatic Stress Disorder who did not have any other psychiatric diagnosis. Their scale consists of 60 items on the MMPI-2.

The *PS* scale has substantial item overlap with a number of the standard Clinical scales (Table 6.13). *PS* shares 27 items with Scale *8* (Schizophrenia), 17 items with Scale *7* (Psychasthenia), 11 items with Scale *2* (Depression), 10 items with Scale *3* (Hysteria), and 9 items with Scale *4* (Psychopathic Deviate). *PS* also has substantial item overlap with several of the other Supplementary scales (Table 6.12): 26 items with the Post Traumatic Stress Disorder—Keane

(*PK*) scale; 14 items with the Welsh Anxiety (*A*) scale; 13 items with the College Maladjustment (*Mt*) scale; and 10 items with the Ego Strength (*Es*) scale, all of which are scored in the opposite direction. Finally, *PS* shares items with a number of the MMPI-2 Content scales (Table 5.7): 11 items with the Depression (*DEP*) and Anxiety (*ANX*) scales. *PS*, like *PK*, is a composite of a number of items reflecting generalized distress and as such is another marker for the first factor like *A* and *Mt*.

The deviant response for four-fifths of the items on the *PS* scale is "true"; hence, a tendency toward a "true" response set will elevate scores on *PS*. The items on the *PS* scale have a mean rating of 3.61 for the obviousness of content that indicates, which items are an obvious measure of psychological problems.

In contrast to the other Supplementary scales, there is a wealth of research on the *PK* and *PS* scales. The only issue that will be addressed here is whether these scales have any discriminant validity. The correlations reported in Table 6.12 and other studies such as (Miller, Goldberg, and Streiner [1995]) demonstrate that the *PK* and *PS* scales are measures of general distress with little specificity for Post Traumatic Stress Disorder. Clinicians should be very cautious of diagnosing clients as having Post Traumatic Stress Disorder based on their scores on these two scales because of the significant amount of first-factor variance in both scales. Research is needed that outlines the relative advantages and disadvantages of the *PK* and *PS* scales. This research would need to demonstrate the discriminative validity of these scales as compared to all of the other first-factor scales. That is, the *PK* and *PS* scales may be *sensitive* to the distress that is seen in clients with Post Traumatic Stress Disorder, but these scales are *not specific* to that disorder because they will be elevated in any form of psychopathology in which clients are experiencing generalized distress and negative emotionality. In the interim little is to be gained by scoring and using both of these scales because they are so redundant and saturated with first-factor variance.

Issues also have been raised as to whether the *PK* and *PS* scales can be applied to civilian trauma and acute stress disorders (Gaston, Brunet, Koszycki, & Bradwejn, 1996; McCaffrey, Hickling, & Marrazo,

1989). In response to these concerns, Gaston, Brunet, Koszycki, and Bradwejn (1998) developed new MMPI scales for Acute and Chronic Post Traumatic Stress Disorder in civilians. Their preliminary research suggested that the new scales had hit rates around 80 percent.

High scorers (T scores of 65 or higher) and low scorers (T scores less than 45) on the *PS* scale are described in a nearly identical manner to the same scores on the *PK* scale and these descriptions will not be repeated here.

Scores on the *PS* scale decrease 8 to 10 T points with age in both normal individuals (Butcher et al., 1989) and psychiatric patients (Caldwell, 1997a). Women endorse about 1 to 3 more items than men (Butcher et al., 1989; Caldwell, 1997a). Education has substantial effects on scores on the *PS* scale with decreases of nearly 7 T points in normal individuals and 12 T points in psychiatric patients from the lowest to the highest ranges. Normal individuals and psychiatric patients with less than 9 years of education have mean scores of 52.9 and 65.0, while normal individuals and psychiatric patients with more than 18 years of education have mean scores of 46.3 and 52.6, respectively (Table 9.19).

Addiction Admission Scale (*AAS*)

Weed, Butcher, McKenna, and Ben-Porath (1992) developed the Addiction Admission[8] Scale (*AAS*) by identifying 14 items on the basis of their obvious content relation to substance abuse within the MMPI-2 item pool. Three items were deleted from these original 14 items because they did not contribute to the internal consistency of the preliminary scale, and two items were added because of their high correlation with the total score. This process resulted in the 13 items on the *AAS*.

The *AAS* has minimal item overlap with any of the standard Clinical scales (Table 6.13). The *AAS* shares 3 items with Scale *4* (Psychopathic Deviate). The *AAS* also has limited item overlap with the other

Supplementary scales (Table 6.12): 3 items with the MacAndrew Alcoholism—Revised (*MAC-R*) scale; and 4 items with the Gender Role—Feminine (*GF*) scale, all of which are scored in the opposite direction. Finally, the *AAS* shares virtually no items with any of the MMPI-2 Content scales (Table 5.7). The *AAS* is a very homogeneous set of items directly assessing substance use and abuse.

The deviant response for three-fourths of the items on the *AAS* is "true"; hence, a tendency toward a "true" response set will elevate scores on the *AAS*. The items on the *AAS* have a mean rating of 3.49 for the obviousness of content, which indicates its items are a somewhat obvious measure of psychological problems.

A number of studies (Aaronson, Dent, & Kline, 1996; Greene, Weed, Butcher, Arredondo, & Davis, 1992; Svanum et al., 1994) have documented the usefulness of the *AAS* to identify substance abuse. These studies routinely report that the *AAS* performs better at identifying individuals who are abusing substances than less direct measures such as the Addiction Potential Scale (*APS*) and the MacAndrew Alcoholism—Revised (*MAC-R*) scale. Weed, Butcher, and Ben-Porath (1995) have provided a thorough review of all MMPI-2 measures of substance abuse.

High scorers (T scores of 65 or higher) on the *AAS* are acknowledging their widespread use and probable abuse of substances. Since a number of these items are written in the past tense, it is important to determine whether the use or abuse of substances is ongoing or reflects earlier behavior patterns. Two items (489: "I have a drug or alcohol problem" and 511: "Once a week or more I get high or drunk")[9] should be explored with clients whenever they are endorsed as being "true." They are likely to have legal problems and problems in controlling the expression of their anger.

Low scorers (T scores less than 45) on the *AAS* are not reporting any type of substance use or abuse.

---

8. This scale initially was called the Addiction Acknowledgement scale, but subsequently has become known as the Addiction Admission scale.

9. Minnesota Multiphasic Personality Inventory-2 (MMPI-2). Copyright © 1942, 1943 (renewed 1970), 1989 by the Regents of the University of Minnesota. Reproduced by permission of the publisher. "MMPI-2" and "Minnesota Multiphasic Personality Inventory-2" are trademarks owned by the University of Minnesota.

It is important to ascertain whether this self-description is consistent with others' views of their use of substances.

Scores on the *AAS* decrease 8 to 9 T points with age in both normal individuals (Butcher et al., 1989) and psychiatric patients (Caldwell, 1997a). Men endorse about one more item than women (Butcher et al., 1989; Caldwell, 1997a). Education has moderate effects on scores on the *AAS* with decreases of nearly 5 T points in normal individuals and psychiatric patients from the lowest to the highest ranges. Normal individuals and psychiatric patients with less than 9 years of education have mean scores of 52.7 and 52.0, while normal individuals and psychiatric patients with more than 18 years of education have mean scores of 47.3 and 47.1, respectively (Table 9.19).

Addiction Potential Scale (*APS*)

Weed et al. (1992) developed the Addiction Potential Scale (*APS*) by identifying 180 MMPI-2 items that substance abusers endorsed more or less frequently than both normal individuals and psychiatric patients. These 180 items were contrasted by gender between the substance abuse patients and normal individuals and psychiatric patients, and 51 items were selected that discriminated strongly in at least three of these four comparisons. An additional 10 items were retained from the 78 items that discriminated strongly in two of these four comparisons, because they were on the MacAndrew Alcoholism (*MAC*) scale. The frequency of endorsement by gender of these 61 items was examined, and 15 items were dropped because the frequency of endorsement of the substance abuse patients fell between that of the normal individuals and the psychiatric patients. In order to avoid reliance on obvious item content and to distinguish the *APS* from the Addiction Admission Scale (*AAS*), four items with obvious reference to alcohol abuse were dropped. Finally, three items were dropped from the preliminary scale because of negative item-total correlations. The remaining 39 items comprise the Addiction Potential Scale.

The *APS* has some item overlap with most of the standard Clinical scales (Table 6.13). The *APS* shares 8 items with Scale *5* (Masculinity-Femininity), 4 of

which are scored in the opposite direction, and 3 items with Scales *4* (Psychopathic Deviate) and *7* (Psychasthenia). The *APS* scale also shares 4 items with Scales *L* (Lie), *F* (Infrequency), *K* (Correction), and *2* (Depression), all of which are scored in the opposite direction. The *APS* also has substantial item overlap with several of the other Supplementary scales (Table 6.12): 9 items with the MacAndrew Alcoholism—Revised (*MAC-R*) scale, 5 items with the Welsh Repression (*R*) scale, and 4 items with the Social Responsibility (*Re*) and Hostility (*Ho*) scales, all of which are scored in the opposite direction on the last three scales. Finally, the *APS* shares few items with any of the MMPI-2 Content scales (Table 5.7). The most overlap is 4 items with the Negative Treatment Indicators (*TRT*) scale. The *APS* is a composite of a heterogeneous group of items reflecting the varied consequences of substance abuse that have less of a flavor of resentment and antisocial qualities than might be expected.

The heterogeneity among the *APS* items was confirmed through factor analysis by Sawrie et al. (1996). They identified five factors among alcoholic and psychiatric inpatients: *Satisfaction with Self, Lack of Self-Efficacy, Antisocial Acting Out, Surgency,* and *Risk Taking.* They also illustrated how scores on these factors can be used to differentiate among patients who are abusing substances.

The deviant response for almost 60 percent of the items on the *APS* is "true"; hence, a tendency toward a "true" or "false" response set will not elevate scores on the *APS*. The items on the *APS* have a mean rating of 2.53 for the obviousness of content, which indicates its items are a somewhat subtle measure of psychological problems.

The *APS* appears to be more accurate at discriminating between substance abuse patients and psychiatric patients than the MacAndrew Alcoholism—Revised (*MAC-R*) scale (Greene et al., 1992; Weed et al., 1992). Weed et al. (1995) have provided a thorough review of all MMPI-2 measures of substance abuse.

High scorers (T scores of 65 or higher) on the *APS* are generally distressed and upset as well as angry and resentful. They describe themselves in negative terms and they are concerned about what others think of them. They are prone to abuse substances.

Low scorers (T scores less than 45) on the *APS* describe themselves in relatively positive terms. They are not distressed or angry. If they are abusing substances, they either are not experiencing or not reporting any negative consequences.

Scores on the *APS* decrease 8 to 10 T points with age in both normal individuals (Butcher et al., 1989) and psychiatric patients (Caldwell, 1997a). There are no gender differences in normal individuals (Butcher et al., 1989) or psychiatric patients (Caldwell, 1997a). Education has small to moderate effects on scores on the *APS* with increases of 4 T points in normal individuals and 3 T points in psychiatric patients from the lowest to the highest ranges. Normal individuals and psychiatric patients with less than 9 years of education have mean T scores of 44.6 and 47.4, while normal individuals and psychiatric patients with more than 18 years of education have mean T scores of 49.0 and 49.8, respectively (Table 9.19).

Marital Distress Scale (*MDS*)

Hjemboe, Butcher, and Almagor (1992) started the development of the Marital Distress Scale (*MDS*) by selecting 17 items from the MMPI-2 that correlated with the Dyadic Adjustment Scale (*DAS*) in 150 heterosexual couples in marital counseling. These 17 items were correlated with the *DAS* in a cross-validation sample of 384 couples from the MMPI-2 restandardization sample and 2 items were eliminated. All of the MMPI-2 items then were correlated with the provisional 15-item scale. Subsequent analyses revealed that 3 of these additional items improved the correlation of the scale with the *DAS*. Four of these items were eliminated on the basis of extraneous content, which resulted in the 14 items on the *MDS*. They also created uniform T scores for the *MDS*; it is the only Supplementary scale on the MMPI-2 that uses uniform T scores. The *MDS* had a positive predictive power of 40.6 using a T score greater than 60 (raw score of 6 or more) as a cutoff with a base rate of .147 in their sample of normal and distressed couples.

The *MDS* has substantial item overlap with only one of the standard Clinical scales (Table 6.13). The *MDS* shares 8 items with Scale *4* (Psychopathic Deviate). The *MDS* has limited item overlap with only two of the other Supplementary scales (Table 6.12): 4 items with the Post Traumatic Stress Disorder—Keane (*PK*) and the Post Traumatic Stress Disorder—Schlenger (*PS*) scales. Finally, the *MDS* shares items with only one of the MMPI-2 Content scales (Table 5.7): 6 items with the Family Problems (*FAM*) scale. The *MDS* is a very homogeneous set of items reflecting marital and family problems.

The deviant response for almost 60 percent of the items on the *MDS* is "true"; hence, a tendency toward a "true" or "false" response set will not elevate scores on the *MDS*. The items on the *MDS* have a mean rating of 3.44 for the obviousness of content, which indicates its items are neither an obvious nor subtle measure of psychological problems.

There has been no additional research on the *MDS*. As noted earlier, the *MDS* shares six items with the Content scale of Family Problems (*FAM*), and the Wiggins' Family Problems scale and the *FAM* scale share few items. A topic that needs to be pursued on the MMPI-2 is the nature of the many items relating to family problems and familial discord and whether they pertain to the current familial circumstances or the family of origin.

High scorers (T scores of 65 or higher) on the *MDS* are experiencing significant distress in their marital relationships. They are alienated from others and generally distressed.

Low scorers (T scores less than 45) on the *MDS* are reporting an absence of general distress and marital distress in particular.

Scores on the *MDS* decrease almost 10 T points with age in both normal individuals (Butcher et al., 1989) and psychiatric patients (Caldwell, 1997a). There are no gender differences in normal individuals (Butcher et al., 1989) or psychiatric patients (Caldwell, 1997a). Education has moderate effects on scores on the *MDS* with decreases of nearly 7 T points in normal individuals and 8 T points in psychiatric patients from the lowest to the highest ranges. Normal individuals and psychiatric patients with less than 9 years of education have mean scores of 57.1 and 60.3, respectively, while normal individuals and psychiatric patients with more than 18 years of education have mean scores of 50.5 and 52.9, respectively (Table 9.19).

Hostility (*Ho*) Scale

Cook and Medley (1954) developed the Hostility (*Ho*) scale by contrasting two groups of teachers who scored at the two extremes of the Minnesota Teacher Attitude Inventory. Teachers who had low scores on the inventory described themselves as hostile and their students as dishonest, insincere, untrustworthy, and lazy. Cook and Medley identified 77 items that differentiated the two groups. Five clinical psychologists then reviewed the items and eliminated 27 items, resulting in the 50 items on the *Ho* scale.

The *Ho* scale has substantial item overlap with a number of the standard Clinical scales (Table 6.13). *Ho* shares 9 items with Scale *0* (Social Introversion); 8 items with Scale *3* (Hysteria) that are scored in the opposite direction; 7 items with the *K* (Correction) scale that are scored in the opposite direction; 8 items with Scale *6* (Paranoia), 5 of which are scored in the opposite direction; and 7 items with Scale *5* (Masculinity-Femininity), 5 of which are scored in the opposite direction. The *Ho* scale has minimal item overlap with the other Supplementary scales (Table 6.12): 4 items with the Social Responsibility (*Re*) scale and 4 items with the Addiction Potential Scale (*APS*), all of which are scored in the opposite direction. Finally, the *Ho* scale has substantial item overlap with a number of the MMPI-2 Content scales (Table 5.7): 17 items with Cynicism (*CYN*), 7 items with Antisocial Practices (*ASP*), and 6 items with the Type A (*TPA*) scales.

The deviant response for nearly all (94.0%) of the items on the *Ho* scale is "true"; hence, a tendency toward a "true" response set will elevate scores on the *Ho* scale. The items on the *Ho* scale have a mean rating of 2.98 for the obviousness of content, which indicates its items are neither an obvious nor a subtle measure of psychological problems.

Han, Weed, Calhoun, and Butcher (1995) identified four factors within the *Ho* scale in a large sample of normal individuals and psychiatric patients: *Cynicism, Hypersensitivity, Aggressive Responding,* and *Social Avoidance.* All of these factors except *Aggressive Responding* are very similar to the categories that are represented in the scales correlated with the *Ho* scale.

Research on the *Ho* scale has been extremely prolific primarily because of an early study that found the *Ho* scale to be a significant risk factor for coronary heart disease (Williams, Haney, Lee, Kong, Blumenthal, & Whalen, 1980). Subsequent research has been more equivocal with four studies finding similar results (Almada et al., 1991; Barefoot, Dahlstrom, & Williams, 1983; Barefoot, Dodge, Peterson, Dahlstrom, & Williams, 1989; Shekelle, Gale, Ostfeld, & Paul, 1983) and four studies that did not (Friedman & Booth-Kewley, 1987; Hearn, Murray, & Luepker, 1989; Leon, Finn, Murray, & Bailey, 1988; McCranie, Watkins, Brandsma, & Sisson, 1986). Colligan and Offord (1988) further complicated this topic by demonstrating that there was significant overlap in the distribution of scores on the *Ho* scale in normal individuals, general medical patients, substance abuse patients, and psychiatric patients. They also found that a majority of their normal individuals age 39 and younger had elevated scores on the *Ho* scale. Finally, Barefoot, Peterson, Dahlstrom, Siegler, Anderson, and Williams (1991) found that scores on the *Ho* scale were associated significantly with race, education, gender, occupation, and income, and Leiker and Hailey (1988) found that high scorers on the *Ho* scale had poorer health habits. There appear to be enough issues associated with the *Ho* scale and health to keep researchers busy for years.

Men with high scores (T scores of 65 or higher) on the *Ho* scale are rated as being hotheaded, bossy, demanding, and argumentative, while women are rated as being nervous, fearful, depressed, and having paranoid tendencies. They also are generally distressed and experiencing negative emotionality.

Low scorers (T scores less than 45) on the *Ho* scale are conventional individuals who relate easily to others. They describe themselves in relatively positive terms. They are trusting of others and their motivation. They may be naive.

Scores on the *Ho* scale are unaffected by age in both normal individuals (Butcher et al., 1989) and psychiatric patients (Caldwell, 1997a). Men endorse about 1 more item than women (Butcher et al., 1989; Caldwell, 1997a). Education has rather substantial effects on scores on the *Ho* scale with decreases of nearly 10 T points in normal individuals and psychiatric patients from the lowest to the highest ranges. Normal individuals and psychiatric patients with less than 9 years of education have mean scores of 55.0 and 54.7, respectively, while normal individuals and psychiatric patients with more than 18 years of education have mean scores of 44.5 and 45.3, respectively (Table 9.19).

Common Alcohol Logistic—Revised (*CAL-R*) Scale

Davis et al. (1991) developed the Common Alcohol Logistic (*CAL*) scale because of their concern that existing MMPI alcohol scales lacked adequate positive predictive power given the low base rate or prevalence of alcohol-related problems in general medical settings. Gottesman and Prescott (1989) raised similar concerns about the MacAndrew Alcoholism (*MAC*) scale in psychiatric patients that were discussed earlier. Davis et al. used a number of noteworthy procedures in developing the *CAL* scale that should be followed by any clinician who is thinking about developing a new MMPI-2 scale. First, they used logistic regression to identify MMPI items that provided unique variance when added to the new scale, rather than using univariate chi-square analyses that can and do identify items that are highly intercorrelated and essentially redundant to one another. Second, they used large samples of patients to validate and cross-validate their new scale. Only Weed et al. (1992) in developing the Addiction Admission Scale (*AAS*) and Addiction Potential Scale (*APS*) had comparable sample sizes to those used by Davis et al. Third, they used receiver operating characteristic (ROC) curves that allow the simultaneous comparison of two scales (*MAC* vs. *CAL*) at all levels of sensitivity and specificity. Most investigators report only the sensitivity and specificity of their new scale at whatever cutting score they have identified. Finally, they reported the positive and negative predictive power of the *CAL* scale at various prevalence rates so that clinicians can appreciate how well the scale will identify alcoholics.

Davis et al. (1991) created derivation and cross-validation samples of alcoholic patients and a contrast group composed of normal individuals, medical patients who took the MMPI at the request of their phy-

sicians, and medical patients who volunteered to take the MMPI. The 33 items for the *CAL* scale were identified and the item weights were assigned by using logistic regression from the total pool of 566 MMPI items. Given the large sample sizes, there was virtually no shrinkage upon cross-validation of the *CAL* scale. The positive predictive power of the *CAL* scale at a prevalence of 0.10 was 58.8 in men and 69.0 in women in contrast to 13.7 in men and 12.5 in women for the *MAC* scale. Davis et al. found that a normalized T score of 61 or higher in men and 63 or higher in women resulted in a sensitivity of approximately 90 percent (i.e., 90 percent of the medical patients were identified as *not* being alcoholics at these cutting scores).

Scoring the *CAL* scale by hand is somewhat involved. The clinician must sum the item weights for the *CAL* items that were endorsed in the deviant direction. This weighted raw score then is converted to a normalized T score by gender through a table of weighted raw scores (Table 4, Davis et al., 1991, pp. 639–641).

Malinchoc, Offord, Colligan, and Morse (1994) revised the *CAL* scale for the MMPI-2 by dropping the six items on the *CAL* scale that were not retained on the MMPI-2. They recomputed the item weights using logistic regression on similar groups of patients and the resulting 27 items became the *CAL-R* scale that is appropriate for use with either the MMPI or MMPI-2. They did *not* use the MMPI-2 item pool in this revision so it remains to be seen whether any of the new MMPI-2 items, particularly the items asking about alcohol and drug abuse, would have been selected for inclusion on the scale. They provided formulas for calculating the normalized T scores for the *CAL* and *CAL-R* scales that may be easier for clinicians than looking up the T scores in tables.

The *CAL-R* scale has moderate item overlap with a number of the standard Clinical scales (Table 6.13). The *CAL-R* scale shares 7 items with Scale *3* (Hysteria), 5 of which are scored in the opposite direction; 6 items with Scale *1* (Hypochondriasis), 5 of which are scored in the opposite direction; and 5 items with Scales *4* (Psychopathic Deviate) and *9* (Hypomania), 1 of which is scored in the opposite direction on both scales. The *CAL-R* scale shares 1 to 4 items with most of the other Supplementary scales (Table 6.12). The

CAL-R scale shares 3 items with the MacAndrew Alcoholism—Revised (*MAC-R*) scale. Finally, the *CAL-R* scale shares few items with any of the MMPI-2 Content scales (Table 5.7). It does share 6 items with the Health Concerns (*HEA*) scale, 5 of which are scored in the opposite direction. It is somewhat unexpected that the absence of physical symptoms is a significant component of a scale assessing substance abuse.

The deviant response for slightly over one-half of the items on the *CAL-R* scale is "true"; hence, a tendency toward a "true" or "false" response set will not elevate scores on the *CAL-R* scale. The items on the *CAL-R* scale have a mean rating of 2.66 for the obviousness of content, which indicates its items are a somewhat subtle measure of psychological problems.

Despite the excellent results on the preliminary research with the *CAL* and *CAL-R* scales, these scales virtually have been ignored. Durham (1994) found that the *CAL-R* scale performed slightly better than the MacAndrew Alcoholism—Revised (*MAC-R*) scale at identifying female alcoholics, but the *CAL-R* scale did not identify male cocaine abusers. Hays and Revetto (1992) found in screening for alcohol disorders that the *CAL* scale had lower positive predictive power (23.6, 41.0, and 68.8) at prevalence rates of 0.10, 0.20, and 0.44 than the *MAC* scale (56.2, 74.3, and 90.2), respectively. Hays and Revetto used psychiatric patients as one of their contrast groups, while Davis et al. (1991) and Malinchoc et al. (1994) used medical patients, which may account for the differences in their results.

High scorers (T scores of 65 or higher) on the *CAL-R* scale have used alcohol excessively and they feel alienated from others and members of their family. They do not report physical symptoms as a consequence of their use of alcohol.

Low scorers (T scores less than 45) on the *CAL-R* scale do not abuse alcohol. Clinicians will have to determine from other sources whether this statement is an accurate description of the client.

Scores on the *CAL-R* scale decrease 2 to 3 T points with age in both normal individuals (Butcher et al., 1989) and psychiatric patients (Caldwell, 1997a). Men endorse about 1 more item than women (Butcher et al., 1989; Caldwell, 1997a). Education has only moderate effects on scores on the *CAL-R* scale, with

decreases of 7 T points from the lowest to the highest ranges in normal individuals and no changes at all in psychiatric patients. Normal individuals with less than 9 years of education have a mean T score of 55.7, while normal individuals with more than 18 years of education have a mean T score of 48.6 (Table 9.19).

PERSONALITY DISORDER SCALES

Morey et al. (1985) developed separate MMPI Personality Disorder scales for each of the 11 *DSM-III* (American Psychiatric Association, 1980) personality disorders: Histrionic; Narcissistic; Borderline; Antisocial; Dependency; Compulsive; Passive-Aggressive; Paranoid; Schizotypal; Avoidant; and Schizoid. Morey et al. developed their Personality Disorder scales in a similar manner as Wiggins (1966) devised his Content scales, so their methodology will not be described here. The Personality Disorder scales are virtually intact on the MMPI-2. No scale has lost more than two items and eight of the nonoverlapping scales and six of the overlapping scales have lost no items.

Since many items were common to more than one scale, Morey et al. (1985) developed both a complete and a nonoverlapping version of these scales. They created the nonoverlapping version of each scale by assigning overlapping items to the one scale with which these items had their highest correlation. "As a result, two sets of scales were developed: a complete set and a nonoverlapping set, which contained the same total number of items as the complete set but which eliminated item overlap" (p. 247). A comprehensive review of these scales can be found in Morey and Smith (1988).

Colligan, Morey, and Offord (1994, 1995) have provided normative tables for both the MMPI and MMPI-2 versions of the Personality Disorder scales based on their adult (Colligan et al., 1983, 1989) and adolescent (Colligan & Offord, 1992) contemporary normative samples.[10]

Research on the Personality Disorder scales primarily has consisted of convergent validity studies with the Millon Clinical Multiaxial Inventory (MCMI:

---

10. One item was listed incorrectly in Colligan et al. (1994). The correction can be found in Colligan et al. (1995).

Millon, 1983, 1987) and diagnostic efficiency studies with Personality Disorder diagnoses as the criterion. Table 6.16 summarizes the studies that have reported the convergent validity of these two sets of scales. Most of these coefficients are in the range of 0.40 to 0.70 except for the Compulsive scale, which actually is correlated negatively with the corresponding MCMI scale. Millon's theoretical conceptualization of personality disorders, which is used as the model for the MCMI, does not correspond exactly with the *DSM* classifications of personality disorders (cf. Widiger & Corbitt, 1993), which limits how well these scales can be correlated with each other.

Table 6.17 provides the results of the studies that have reported diagnostic efficiency statistics for the Personality Disorder scales. The negative predictive power (NPP) for all of these scales is quite good and typically is in the range of .80 to .95. NPP indicates how well T scores less than 70 on the specific Personality Disorder scale predict that the patient does *not* have that specific Personality Disorder diagnosis. Thus, the Personality Disorder scales are better at stating that the patient does *not* have a specific personality disorder diagnosis than they are at suggesting what diagnosis the patient should have. The positive predic-

tive power (PPP) is quite variable for all of the Personality Disorder scales, frequently ranging from 0.00 to 1.00. Only the Avoidant Personality Disorder scale and possibly the Borderline Personality Disorder scale have reasonably consistent and adequate PPP. The clinician should remember that NPP being better than PPP with the Personality Disorder scales is not specific to these scales. Rather it reflects the likely outcome of any scale that is assessing disorders with low prevalence rates (cf. Baldesserini et al., 1983).

It is difficult to draw any firm conclusions based on the extant research on the Morey et al. (1985) Personality Disorder scales. They do seem very worthy of further exploration, particularly to better establish their diagnostic efficiency. Clinicians can use the scores from these scales in conjunction with the other data from the MMPI-2 in order to assess patients with personality disorders.

There has been significant interest in Narcissistic Personality Disorder on the MMPI and MMPI-2 that is relatively independent of the work of Morey et al. (1985). Ashby, Lee, and Duke (1979), Raskin and Novacek (1989), and Wink and Gough (1990) have created specific MMPI Narcissism scales. Chatham, Tibbals, and Harrington (1993) have reported the

TABLE 6.16   Convergent Validity between the MMPI-2 and MCMI-II Personality Disorder Scales

	N	CLUSTER A			CLUSTER B				CLUSTER C		
		PAR	SZD	STY	ANT	BDL	HST	NAR	AVD	DEP	CPS
MMPI and MCMI											
Chatham et al. (1993)	70							.66			
Dubro & Wetzler (1989)	56	.44	.35	.51	.14	.28	.66	.55	.65	.68	−.42
McCann (1989)	47	.08	.67	.74	.15	.42	.68	.78	.82	.50	−.30
Morey & Le Vine (1988)	76	.69	.68	.78	.25	.54	.71	.55	.76	.68	−.31
Schuler et al. (1994)	104	.32	.74	.53	.25	.37	.69	.73	.79	.67	−.27
Streiner & Miller (1988)	74	.33	.64	.41	.30	.55	.61	.66	.62	.52	−.38
Wise (1996)		.27	.62	.48	.09	.46	.63	.66	.76	.53	−.13
MMPI and MCMI-II											
McCann (1991)	80	.50	.73	.86	.57	.68	.74	.65	.87	.56	−.04
MMPI-2 and MCMI-II											
Bollinger (1997)	107	.64	.67	.49	.62	.41	.63	.48	.65	.46	−.13
Wise (1996)	72	.52	.66	.68	.46	.68	.57	.68	.76	.63	−.10

TABLE 6.17 Diagnostic Efficiency Statistics for the MMPI Personality Disorder Scales

Cluster A

PARANOID PD	CRITERION	PR	SEN	SPE	PPP	NPP
Guthrie & Mobley (1994)	SCID-II	.20	.64	.86	.54	.90
Hills (1995)	SCID-II		.33	.75	.15	.89
Miller et al. (1992)	SIDP	.09	.83	.79	.98	.29
SCHIZOID PD	**CRITERION**	**PR**	**SEN**	**SPE**	**PPP**	**NPP**
Guthrie & Mobley (1994)	SCID-II	.11	1.00	.82	.40	1.00
Hills (1995)	SCID-II		.43	.90	.20	.96
Miller et al. (1992)	SIDP	.04	1.00	.97	1.00	.60
SCHIZOTYPAL PD	**CRITERION**	**PR**	**SEN**	**SPE**	**PPP**	**NPP**
Guthrie & Mobley (1994)	SCID-II	.18	.60	.87	.50	.91
Hills (1995)	SCID-II		1.00	.78	.16	1.00
Miller et al. (1992)	SIDP	.03	1.00	.94	.37	1.00

Cluster B

ANTISOCIAL PD	CRITERION	PR	SEN	SPE	PPP	NPP
Castlebury et al. (1997)[a]	DSM-IV	.60	.87	.95	.93	.90
Guthrie & Mobley (1994)	SCID-II	.04	1.00	.75	.13	1.00
Hills (1995)	SCID-II		.46	.76	.33	.84
Miller et al. (1992)	SIDP	.05	.83	.96	.51	.99
BORDERLINE PD	**CRITERION**	**PR**	**SEN**	**SPE**	**PPP**	**NPP**
Castlebury et al. (1997)[a]	DSM-IV	.80	.63	.90	.86	.71
Dubro et al. (1988)	SIDP	.18	.10	.89	.15	.83
Guthrie & Mobley (1994)	SCID-II	.20	.36	.82	.33	.84
Hills (1995)	SCID-II		.41	.85	.54	.77
Miller et al. (1992)	SIDP	.14	.27	.94	.89	.42
Trull (1991)	DSM-III-R	.20	.25	.83	.27	.91
HISTRIONIC PD	**CRITERION**	**PR**	**SEN**	**SPE**	**PPP**	**NPP**
Dubro et al. (1988)	SIDP	.14	.00	1.00	.00	.86
Guthrie & Mobley (1994)	SCID-II	.04	.50	1.00	1.00	.98
Hills (1995)	SCID-II		.14	.99	.50	.95
Miller et al. (1992)	SIDP	.07	.22	.96	.31	.94
Schotte et al. (1993)[b]	SCID-II	.30	.74	.92	.85	.85
NARCISSISTIC PD	**CRITERION**	**PR**	**SEN**	**SPE**	**PPP**	**NPP**
Castlebury et al. (1997)[a]	DSM-IV	.52	1.00	1.00	.72	.77
Chatham et al. (1993)[b]	NPI	.50	.94	.94	.94	.94
Dubro et al. (1988)	SIDP	.14	.00	1.00	.00	.86
Guthrie & Mobley (1994)	SCID-II	.07	.00	.98	.00	.93
Hills (1995)	SCID-II		.00	.96	.00	.93
Miller et al. (1992)	SIDP	.17	.33	.99	.87	.94

(continued)

TABLE 6.17 Diagnostic Efficiency Statistics for the MMPI Personality Disorder Scales (continued)

Cluster C

AVOIDANT PD	CRITERION	PR	SEN	SPE	PPP	NPP
Dubro et al. (1988)	SIDP	.07	.78	.91	.66	.96
Guthrie & Mobley (1994)	SCID-II	.33	.67	.97	.92	.86
Hills (1995)	SCID-II		.64	.84	.47	.92
Miller et al. (1992)	SIDP	.35	.72	1.00	1.00	.87
DEPENDENT PD	**CRITERION**	**PR**	**SEN**	**SPE**	**PPP**	**NPP**
Dubro et al. (1988)	SIDP	.04	.44	.83	.34	.88
Guthrie & Mobley (1994)	SCID-II	.11	.33	.88	.25	.91
Hills (1995)	SCID-II		.50	.89	.45	.90
Miller et al. (1992)	SIDP	.38	.83	1.00	1.00	.78
COMPULSIVE PD	**CRITERION**	**PR**	**SEN**	**SPE**	**PPP**	**NPP**
Guthrie & Mobley (1994)	SCID-II	.13	.00	1.00	.00	.87
Hills (1995)	SCID-II		.00	1.00	.00	.90
Miller et al. (1992)	SIDP	.61	.13	1.00	1.00	.42

[a]MMPI-2 Personality Disorder scales were used.
[b]These values were estimated from the means and standard deviations for the two groups of patients.

item overlap and intercorrelations among all of these Narcissism scales, which includes the Morey et al. Narcissism scale. There appears to be significant convergence among all of the scales except for the Ashby et al. scale. Hilsenroth, Handler, and Blais (1996) have provided a comprehensive review of the assessment procedures that have been used in the study of Narcissistic Personality Disorder that should be consulted by the interested reader.

PERSONALITY PSYCHOPATHOLOGY FIVE (*PSY-5*) SCALES

Harkness and McNulty (Harkness & McNulty, 1994; Harkness et al., 1995) created a five-factor model called the Personality Psychopathology Five (*PSY-5*) to aid in the description of normal personality and to complement the diagnosis of personality disorders. Using replicated rational selection, Harkness and McNulty (1994) identified five factors within 60 descriptors of normal and abnormal human behavior: Aggressiveness (*AGG*), Psychoticism (*PSY*), Con-

straint (*CON*), Negative Emotionality/Neuroticism (*NEN*), and Positive Emotionality/Extroversion (*PEE*). The *AGG* construct assesses offensive aggression and possibly the enjoyment of dominating, frightening, and controlling others. The *PSY* construct assesses the cognitive ability of the individual to model the external, objective world in an accurate manner. Persons who are low on the *PSY* construct can realize that their model is not working and accommodate or revise the model to fit their environment. The *CON* construct assesses a dimension from rule following versus rule breaking and criminality. The *NEN* construct assesses a broad affective disposition to experience negative emotions focusing on anxiety and nervousness. The *PEE* construct assesses a broad disposition to experience positive affects and to seek out and to enjoy social experiences.

Harkness et al. (1995) developed MMPI-2 scales and McNulty, Harkness, Ben-Porath, and Williams (1997) developed MMPI-A scales to measure the *PSY-5* factors. Appendix B.9 provides the item composition and scoring information for these scales.

There has been only limited research with the *PSY-5* scales because of their recent development. Trull, Useda, Costa, and McCrae (1995) compared the *PSY-5* scales with the NEO Personality Inventory (Costa & McCrae, 1985). The *PEE* and *NEN* scales resembled the NEO-PI dimensions of Extroversion and Neuroticism, respectively. The other *PSY-5* scales were related to specific NEO-PI facet scales rather than NEO-PI dimensions. None of the *PSY-5* scales was related consistently to Openness on the NEO-PI. They concluded that the two instruments assess overlapping but not identical sets of constructs.

Table 6.18 (p. 264–265) provides the correlations between the *PSY-5* scales and the MMPI-2 Validity and Clinical scales, Supplementary scales, and Content scales. The *AGG* scale correlates with only Scale 9 (Hypomania: .527) among the Validity and Clinical scales, the Welsh Repression (*R*: –.531), MacAndrew Alcoholism—Revised (MAC-R: .502), and Hostility (*Ho*: .481) scales among the Supplementary scales, and the Type A (*TPA*: .501), Cynicism (*CYN*: .450), Antisocial Practices (*ASP*: .438), and Anger (*ANG*: .422) scales among the Content scales. This pattern of intercorrelations would suggest that the *AGG* scale is measuring anger, hostility, and the lack of regard for social rules and conventions. The *PSY* scale appears to be measuring a general distress factor, much like the *NEN* scale, because of its sizable correlations with most of the other MMPI-2 scales. The *PSY* scale does have its largest correlations with Scale 8 (Schizophrenia: .800) and the *F* (Infrequency: .807) and Bizarre Mentation (*BIZ*: .923) scales. The *CON* scale is not correlated to most of the other MMPI-2 scales and, thus, would appear to have the potential to contribute additional information when interpreting the MMPI-2. The largest correlations of the *CON* scale are with Scale 9 (Hypomania: –.402) and the MacAndrew Alcoholism—Revised (*MAC-R*: –.549), Addiction Admission (*AAS*: –.526), and Antisocial Practices (*ASP*: –.580) scales. The *NEN* scale is another of the numerous markers for the first factor of general distress and negative emotionality on the MMPI-2. Finally, the *PEE* scale generally has its largest (negative) correlations with MMPI-2 markers for the first factor.

The *PSY-5* scales are another potential source of information for the clinician in interpreting the MMPI-2 profile. Research that demonstrates their

usefulness in patients with personality disorder diagnoses is needed. Until such information is available clinicians are cautioned to interpret them very conservatively.

SUICIDE SCALES

Numerous attempts have been made to use the MMPI to predict the occurrence of suicide and/or suicide threats through scales such as the Suicide Threat scale (Farberow & Devries, 1967), profile analysis (cf. Clopton, Pallis, & Birtchnell, 1979; Leonard, 1977), and clinical judgment (Clopton & Baucom, 1979). Clopton (1979b) and Eyman and Eyman (1991, 1992) have provided a comprehensive review of the use of the MMPI in predicting suicide, a review that the interested reader should consult.

The initial hurdle faced in predicting suicide with the MMPI-2 or any other assessment device is the extremely low frequency with which suicide occurs in most populations. Even if a test were 75 percent accurate in predicting suicide, which would be unusually high for most tests, a more accurate prediction can be made by simply stating that all patients will be nonsuicidal because the frequency of suicide is less than 25 percent in any group. Consequently, any index of suicide will yield a large number of false positives (clients identified as suicidal who are nonsuicidal) because of this low frequency of occurrence.

Although it would seem that false positives are of less concern than false negatives (clients who are identified as nonsuicidal who commit suicide), the ethical and practical implications of falsely identifying a client as suicidal also must be considered (Rosen, 1954).

The clinical literature on the MMPI is replete with references to specific scales or codetypes that are frequently associated with suicide. For example, significant elevations (T scores > 70) on Scales 2 (Depression) and/or 7 (Psychasthenia) are described as increasing the likelihood of suicide attempts (cf. Carson, 1969; Dahlstrom et al., 1972; Graham, 1987).

Dahlstrom et al. (1972) also noted that when the client has a Spike 2 profile (Scale 2 [Depression] is the only clinical scale elevated above a T score of 70) but denies depressive thoughts and feelings, the risk of suicide is increased. On the other hand, numerous

TABLE 6.18   Intercorrelations among the Personality Psychopathology Five (PSY-5) Scales and the Clinical, Supplementary, and Content Scales in the Caldwell Clinical Dataset

SCALE	PERSONALITY PSYCHOPATHOLOGY FIVE (PSY-5)				
Clinical	*AGG*	*PSY*	*CON*	*NEN*	*PEE*
L	−.155	−.204	.385	−.374	.027
F	.207	.807	−.149	.673	−.546
K	−.322	−.653	.199	−.810	.290
Hs	.084	.548	.126	.652	−.557
D	−.129	.454	.228	.644	−.772
Hy	−.096	.220	.241	.338	−.489
Pd	.191	.607	−.280	.699	−.498
Mf-f	−.323	−.039	.365	.145	−.143
Mf-m	−.241	.086	.218	.291	−.170
Pa	.109	.673	−.027	.615	−.483
Pt	.095	.708	−.019	.879	−.620
Sc	.199	.800	−.104	.820	−.589
Ma	.527	.578	−.402	.472	.076
Si	−.119	.562	.163	.709	−.785
Supplementary	*AGG*	*PSY*	*CON*	*NEN*	*PEE*
A	.105	.709	−.043	.891	−.585
R	−.531	−.146	.464	−.120	−.511
Es	−.032	−.665	−.174	−.759	.594
MAC-R	.502	.375	−.549	.243	.221
O-H	−.226	−.336	.332	−.492	.176
Do	−.032	−.583	.032	−.656	.452
Re	−.400	−.570	.581	−.586	.135
Mt	.095	.649	−.009	.858	−.646
GM	.121	−.546	−.266	−.733	.477
GF	−.427	−.259	.625	−.117	.030
PK	.174	.758	−.073	.866	−.632
PS	.159	.744	−.047	.878	−.632
AAS	.244	.436	−.526	.459	−.159
APS	.138	.157	−.348	.399	.047
MDS	.153	.630	−.149	.746	−.527
Ho	.481	.772	−.253	.740	−.279
CAL-R	.103	.162	−.310	.111	.052
Content	*AGG*	*PSY*	*CON*	*NEN*	*PEE*
ANX	.097	.637	.017	.887	−.567
FRS	.011	.503	.260	.578	−.318
OBS	.121	.680	−.048	.832	−.452
DEP	.091	.679	−.040	.821	−.664
HEA	.112	.572	.092	.648	−.508
BIZ	.319	.923	−.161	.627	−.291
ANG	.422	.610	−.272	.829	−.331
CYN	.450	.712	−.219	.636	−.227
ASP	.438	.595	−.580	.530	−.120

Content	AGG	PSY	CON	NEN	PEE
TPA	.501	.603	−.247	.712	−.212
LSE	−.061	.640	−.009	.774	−.594
SOD	−.122	.451	.090	.558	−.781
FAM	.243	.600	−.242	.692	−.324
WRK	.059	.689	−.019	.844	−.619
TRT	.094	.699	−.036	.797	−.600

studies have found no difference in Scale 2 scores of suicidal and nonsuicidal individuals (Clopton & Jones, 1975; Farberow, 1956; Simon & Gilberstadt, 1958). Suicidal and nonsuicidal persons also do not differ consistently on any of the other standard MMPI scales (Clopton, 1979b; Clopton, Post, & Larde, 1983; Spirito, Faust, Myers, & Bechtel, 1988; Watson, Klett, Walters, & Vassar, 1984).

Table 6.19 (pp. 266–267) provides the frequency with which the MMPI-2 item "520. Lately I have thought a lot about killing myself"[11] is endorsed as "true" in the Caldwell (1997a) clinical dataset. Neither men nor women who have Spike 2 (Depression) codetypes are very likely to endorse this item. In fact, patients with Spike 2 codetypes have among the lowest frequency of endorsement of this item of any of the 55 codetypes. If this item can be assumed to be related to suicide attempts, it would appear that the conjectures that patients with Spike 2 codetypes have an increased likelihood of attempting suicide will need to be reexamined. In contrast to Spike 2, almost 50 percent of patients with 6-8/8-6 codetypes are likely to endorse Item 520. Sepaher, Bongar, and Greene (1999) have explored the frequency of endorsement of a number of MMPI-2 items that may be related to suicide attempts within all 55 codetypes, which can be consulted by the interested reader.

Both Leonard (1977) and Clopton et al. (1979) found that multivariate statistical procedures, which simultaneously consider scores from a number of the Clinical scales, could reliably distinguish female suicidal groups from control groups but not male suicidal groups from control groups. Leonard (1977) did not cross-validate her results; Clopton et al. (1979) found upon cross-validation that the percentage of female patients correctly classified decreased from 36 to 28 percent.

Clopton et al. (1979) reported the following relationship between Scales 1 (Hypochondriasis) and 2 (Depression) in their study, which deserves further investigation. Among clients with 7-8/8-7 codetypes, the relative elevation of Scales 1 and 2 was significantly associated with whether the client had attempted suicide. Scale 1 was greater than Scale 2 in 60 percent of the nonsuicidal clients, whereas Scale 2 was greater than Scale 1 in 64 percent of the suicidal clients.

Clopton et al. (1983) did find that discriminant analysis could reliably distinguish between patients who recently attempted suicide and nonsuicidal patients, which held up on cross-validation. However, neither the original results (58.8 percent for females; 63.3 percent for males) nor the cross-validation results (53.9 percent for females; 58.6 percent for males) were particularly impressive.

Clopton and Baucom (1979) presented six psychologists who had extensive experience in MMPI interpretation with the profiles of male suicidal and nonsuicidal clients. None of the psychologists could reliably identify the clients in each group. The psychologists' ratings of eight variables thought to be related to suicide risk also did not differ for the suicidal and nonsuicidal clients.

Thus, any method using the MMPI-2—whether it involves single scales, profile analysis, Supplementary

11. Minnesota Multiphasic Personality Inventory-2 (MMPI-2). Copyright © 1942, 1943 (renewed 1970), 1989 by the Regents of the University of Minnesota. Reproduced by permission of the publisher. "MMPI-2" and "Minnesota Multiphasic Personality Inventory-2" are trademarks owned by the University of Minnesota.

TABLE 6.19 Frequency of a "True" Response to MMPI-2 Item 520 by Codetype in the Caldwell Clinical Dataset

	FREQUENCY OF A "TRUE" RESPONSE					
	Men		Women		Total	
CODETYPE	N	%	N	%	N	%
Spike 1	268	2.61	215	1.86	483	2.28
1-2/2-1	671	10.43	1,005	13.73	1,676	12.41
1-3/3-1	2,035	9.14	3,188	6.02	5,223	7.24
1-4/4-1	97	4.12	127	9.45	224	7.14
1-5/5-1	19	5.26	126	3.17	145	3.45
1-6/6-1	188	10.64	195	8.72	383	9.66
1-7/7-1	113	14.16	89	6.74	202	10.89
1-8/8-1	272	23.53	236	30.08	508	26.57
1-9/9-1	77	5.19	81	6.17	158	5.70
1-0/0-1	33	12.12	32	9.38	65	10.77
Spike 2	212	6.13	190	4.74	402	5.47
2-3/3-2	909	15.51	1,932	16.98	2,841	16.51
2-4/4-2	313	18.85	542	21.03	855	20.23
2-5/5-2	49	10.20	64	4.69	113	7.08
2-6/6-2	399	20.55	705	24.11	1,104	22.83
2-7/7-2	888	22.30	1,046	20.75	1,934	21.46
2-8/8-2	358	38.55	717	41.28	1,075	40.37
2-9/9-2	12	0.00	24	8.33	36	5.56
2-0/0-2	339	12.98	326	12.27	665	12.63
Spike 3	372	0.00	412	1.21	784	0.64
3-4/4-3	298	9.06	454	8.37	752	8.64
3-5/5-3	42	4.76	72	0.00	114	1.75
3-6/6-3	311	18.33	423	15.84	734	16.89
3-7/7-3	239	17.15	203	9.85	442	13.80
3-8/8-3	222	33.33	217	31.34	439	32.35
3-9/9-3	38	2.63	78	5.13	116	4.31
3-0/0-3	7	0.00	7	0.00	14	0.00
Spike 4	685	1.61	583	0.86	1,268	1.26
4-5/5-4	79	3.80	125	4.00	204	3.92
4-6/6-4	565	14.69	539	15.77	1,104	15.22
4-7/7-4	236	19.49	210	16.19	446	17.94
4-8/8-4	339	26.84	353	30.59	692	28.76
4-9/9-4	237	7.59	203	7.88	440	7.73
4-0/0-4	41	7.32	29	13.79	70	10.00
Spike 5	294	2.72	1,071	0.75	1,365	1.17
5-6/6-5	84	1.19	70	2.86	154	1.95
5-7/7-5	51	11.76	17	0.00	68	8.82
5-8/8-5	23	13.04	53	11.32	76	11.84
5-9/9-5	44	0.00	143	2.80	187	2.14
5-0/0-5	27	3.70	15	6.67	42	4.76
Spike 6	494	3.24	415	3.37	909	3.30
6-7/7-6	315	19.37	178	16.85	493	18.46

| | FREQUENCY OF A "TRUE" RESPONSE | | | | | |
| | Men | | Women | | Total | |
CODETYPE	N	%	N	%	N	%
6-8/8-6	1,087	46.09	842	44.66	1,929	45.46
6-9/9-6	207	10.63	149	5.37	356	8.43
6-0/0-6	89	6.74	50	4.00	139	5.76
Spike 7	119	3.36	66	4.55	185	3.78
7-8/8-7	858	33.92	405	31.85	1,263	33.25
7-9/9-7	58	5.17	40	10.00	98	7.14
7-0/0-7	108	8.33	39	7.69	147	8.16
Spike 8	87	4.60	58	6.90	145	5.52
8-9/9-8	256	19.53	168	19.05	424	19.34
8-0/0-8	65	23.08	31	12.90	96	19.79
Spike 9	590	0.85	435	0.92	1,025	0.88
9-0/0-9	6	16.67	2	0.00	8	12.50
Spike 0	240	4.58	148	4.05	388	4.38
Total	16,065	15.75	19,143	14.26	35,208	14.94

scales, or item analysis—appears disappointing in the prediction of suicide. In fact, Eyman and Eyman (1991) concluded "no MMPI item, scale, or profile configuration has been found to differentiate consistently between suicidal and nonsuicidal individuals" (p. 47).

As Clopton (1979b) pointed out, the research question of greater interest is whether the MMPI can increase the accuracy of identifying suicidal clients, not whether the MMPI by itself is sufficient to predict suicide. Some investigators appear to assume that both suicide gestures or attempts and actual suicides result from a single cause without fully appreciating the multitude of factors that lead the client to attempt or commit suicide. Future research should discriminate among the various causes and types of suicide to determine whether specific scale patterns can assist in successfully identifying some subgroups of suicidal clients.

PSYCHOTIC-NEUROTIC INDEXES

Numerous MMPI indexes, those that involve combining various Validity and/or Clinical scales in a linear or a configural pattern, have been proposed as an additional means of determining how a client should be diagnosed. Peterson (1954) developed six diagnostic signs that he found were characteristic of psychotic (schizophrenic) MMPI patterns:

1. Four or more Clinical scales are greater than a T score of 70.
2. The *F* (Infrequency) scale is greater than a T score of 64.
3. Scales *6* (Paranoia), *8* (Schizophrenia), and *9* (Hypomania) are greater than Scales *1* (Hypochondriasis), *2* (Depression), and *3* (Hysteria).
4. Scale *2* is greater than Scales *1* and *3*.
5. Scale *8* is greater than Scale *7* (Psychasthenia).
6. Scale *6* or *9* is greater than a T score of 70.

The presence of three or more of these signs was characteristic of a psychotic profile pattern.

Taulbee and Sisson (1957) developed 16 signs, which involve comparison of one Clinical scale with another Clinical scale, as an index of whether the profile suggests a neurotic or a psychotic disorder (Table 6.20, p. 268). Each of these signs is scored as being present or absent. The presence of 13 or more of

TABLE 6.20 Taulbee-Sisson Signs for Neurotic Patterns[a]

SIGN	SIGN
Scale *1* > Scale *3*	Scale *2* > Scale *6*
Scale *1* > Scale *4*	Scale *3* > Scale *4*
Scale *1* > Scale *5*	Scale *3* > Scale *5*
Scale *1* > Scale *6*	Scale *3* > Scale *6*
Scale *1* > Scale *7*	Scale *3* > Scale *9*
Scale *1* > Scale *8*	Scale *7* > Scale *5*
Scale *1* > Scale *9*	Scale *7* > Scale *6*
Scale *2* > Scale *4*	Scale *7* > Scale *8*

Note. The signs are from Taulbee and Sisson (1957).

[a]Each sign is scored as present or absent. Scores from 13 to 16 are indicative of a neurotic pattern; scores from 0 to 6 are indicative of a psychotic pattern.

these signs suggests a neurotic pattern, whereas the presence of 6 or fewer signs suggests a schizophrenic pattern.

Meehl and Dahlstrom (1960) developed a set of complex configural rules (Meehl-Dahlstrom rules) to classify an MMPI profile as neurotic, psychotic, or indeterminate. (These rules are found in Dahlstrom et al. [1972].) Henrichs (1964, 1966) expanded the Meehl-Dahlstrom rules to include another category, character or behavior disorders.

Three studies are particularly relevant to the use of linear or configural indexes to make decisions about MMPI profile patterns. In a task examining linear and configural models of clinical judgment, Wiggins and Hoffman (1968) asked experienced clinicians to sort MMPI profiles on a distribution from neurotic through normal to psychotic. Slightly more than half of their clinicians (16/29) appeared to use configural cues in making their judgments, but a linear model could accurately estimate their judgments.

In two similar studies Goldberg (1965, 1969) found that a linear model accounted for most of the variance in clinicians' judgments of whether an MMPI profile should be classified as neurotic or psychotic, and a linear model was superior to all other models in estimating these judgments. Goldberg suggested a linear index [(Scale *L* + Scale *6* + Scale *8*) − (Scale *3* + Scale *7*)] as being one of the most accurate

in making this distinction between neurotic and psychotic profiles.[12]

Of course, these findings that a linear model can accurately estimate a clinician's judgments of whether an MMPI profile is neurotic or psychotic does not necessarily imply that the clinician makes decisions in this manner; they do suggest that the clinician should give greater considerations to such models in making judgments. Wiggins (1973) provided an extensive examination of the issues involved in clinical prediction, which the interested clinician is urged to read.

Little research has been conducted to validate these indexes to discriminate between neurotic and psychotic MMPI profiles. Meehl (1959) found that both the Meehl-Dahlstrom rules and the Taulbee-Sisson signs were better than individual clinicians in determining whether an MMPI profile should be classified as neurotic or psychotic. Winter and Stortroen (1963) reported that the Peterson signs were more accurate than the Meehl-Dahlstrom rules or the Taulbee-Sisson signs in discriminating among MMPI profiles from normals, patients with physical illness, and hospitalized schizophrenics.

Since neither the Meehl-Dahlstrom rules nor the Taulbee-Sisson signs were designed to identify normal profiles or profiles of patients with physical illness, it is unclear what meaning to assign to the superiority of the Peterson signs in their study.

Giannetti, Johnson, Klingler, and Williams (1978) found that the Goldberg index was superior to the Meehl-Dahlstrom rules, the Taulbee-Sisson signs, and the Peterson signs in discriminating neurotic from psychotic MMPI profiles. They also found that the Meehl-Dahlstrom rules and the Taulbee-Sisson signs achieved less than chance accuracy in making this discrimination.

The paucity of research in this area makes it difficult to draw definitive conclusions. It does appear that the Goldberg index may be superior to the other indexes in discriminating neurotic from psychotic MMPI profiles, although additional research is needed to investigate their utility thoroughly.

12. These scales are all *K*-corrected T scores. A score greater than 45 on the Goldberg index indicates a psychotic profile pattern, and a score of 44 or below indicates a neurotic profile pattern.

CRITICAL ITEMS

Despite the inherent difficulties in understanding responses to individual MMPI items (difficulties that provided the original impetus for the empirical selection of items on the MMPI), clinicians have been unwilling to ignore the information that might be contained in those responses. The original set of individual items, which were thought to require careful scrutiny if answered in the deviant direction, was rationally or intuitively selected by Grayson (1951). These 38 MMPI items were selected as being highly indicative of severe psychopathology and have accordingly been considered *stop* or *critical* items.

Caldwell (1969) developed on a rational basis a more comprehensive set of 66 MMPI items to identify severe, generally psychotic symptomatology. The content areas of his MMPI-2 items appear in Table 6.21. Caldwell has added a number of new MMPI-2 items to his list of critical items.

Koss and Butcher (1973) and Koss, Butcher, and Hoffmann (1976) examined the MMPI items endorsed by patients in crisis situations. They obtained MMPI responses from 723 male Veterans Administration hospital patients in six separate crisis situa-

TABLE 6.21 Content Areas for Caldwell MMPI-2 Critical Items

NUMBER OF ITEMS		CONTENT AREA
MMPI	*MMPI-2*	
11	12	Distress and Depression
5	11	Suicidal Thoughts
10	11	Ideas of Reference, Persecution, and Delusions
9	9	Peculiar Experiences and Hallucinations
6	6	Sexual Difficulties
5	6	Authority Problems and Poor Control
3	8	Alcohol and Drugs
7	7	Family Discord
10	11	Somatic Concerns
0	5	Aggressive Impulses

Note. The content area names are from Caldwell (1969).

tions: acute anxiety, depressed-suicidal ideation, threatened assault, situational stress due to alcoholism, mental confusion, and persecutory ideas.

The number of items that significantly discriminated each crisis group from a noncrisis control group ranged from 10 items in the threatened assault group to 89 items in the depressed-suicidal ideation group. Examination of these items reveals that the item content generally relates directly to the crisis situations. Thus, it appears that these patients were both willing and able to reveal accurate information about themselves.

Koss and Butcher (1973) also asked eight clinical judges to select those MMPI items that would be relevant (face valid) to the six crisis groups. This procedure resulted in 96 items that four of the eight judges agreed would be relevant. When Koss and Butcher checked the responses of the patients to these items, they found that 67 items actually discriminated a crisis group from the control group. More importantly, Koss and Butcher (1973) could not find any apparent differences between face-valid items that were empirically related to a crisis situation and those face-valid items that were not. Koss et al. (1976) indicated that the Grayson (1951) and Caldwell (1969) critical items are inadequate samples of behavior of potential interest to the clinician and that better critical items could be identified.

All but five of the original Koss and Butcher (1973) critical items have been retained on the MMPI-2 and nine items have been added. These item changes can be seen in Table 6.22 (p. 270). The rationale for these changes has not been provided other than to state that empirical criteria were used to add items to content areas of Depressed-Suicidal Ideation and Situational Stress Due to Alcoholism (Butcher et al., 1989, p. 48).

A question that needs to be addressed, however, is the frequency with which these items are endorsed by normal individuals. Even though clients in a crisis may endorse a particular item, it may still be true that normal individuals endorse the items more often than not. For example, perhaps 75 percent of a crisis group endorsed a specific item, whereas 60 percent of a normal group endorsed the same item. This difference could be statistically significant; if an individual endorsed the item, however, that would not necessar-

TABLE 6.22   Changes in Items on the Koss and Butcher Critical Items

	NUMBER OF ITEMS		
Crisis Situation	*MMPI*	*Deleted*	*MMPI-2*
Acute Anxiety	18	1	17
Depressed—Suicidal Ideation	17	0	22
Threatened Assault	5	0	5
Situational Stress Due to Alcoholism	3	1	7
Mental Confusion	12	1	11
Persecutory Ideas	18	2	16
Total	73	5	78

Note. Names and number of items are from Koss and Butcher (1973) and Butcher, Dahlstrom, Graham, Tellegen, and Kaemmer (1989).

ily indicate that the individual is in a crisis because 60 percent of a normal sample also endorse that item. The frequency with which normal individuals endorse critical items will be discussed after the development of the Lachar and Wrobel (1979) critical items has been described.

Lachar and Wrobel (1979) developed a set of critical items designed to be face-valid descriptors of psychological concerns. They first identified 14 categories of symptoms that summarized problems that motivate people to seek psychological treatment and that help the clinician make diagnostic decisions. Then 14 clinical psychologists read each MMPI item and nominated items that would be face-valid indicators of psychopathology in one of these 14 categories. Items nominated by at least 6 of the 14 clinicians, together with the Grayson (1951) and Caldwell (1969) critical items, were empirically validated by contrasting item response frequencies for normals and psychiatric samples matched for gender and race.

Lachar and Wrobel were able to validate 130 of the 177 items nominated. After eliminating 19 items that were highly duplicative of item content in other items on the list, they arrived at a final list of 111 critical items. Lachar and Wrobel reported that 80 percent of the 111 items reliably differentiated normal from psychiatric samples for adult men, women, blacks, and whites. They concluded that responses to these critical items could serve as accurate representations of the client's psychological concerns. All but

four of the Lachar and Wrobel (1979) critical items have been retained on the MMPI-2 (see Appendix C). Two items were dropped from the Sexual Concern and Deviation group, and one item from Deviant Thinking and Experience and Substance Abuse. The content areas for these items appear in Table 6.23.

TABLE 6.23   Content Areas for the Lachar and Wrobel MMPI-2 Critical Items

NUMBER OF ITEMS	CONTENT AREA
	Psychological Discomfort
11	Anxiety and Tension
16	Depression and Worry
6	Sleep Disturbance
	Bodily Distortions
15	Deviant Beliefs
10	Deviant Thinking and Experience
	Characterologic Adjustment
3	Substance Abuse
9	Antisocial Attitude
4	Family Conflict
4	Problematic Anger
6	Sexual Concern and Deviation
23	Somatic Symptoms

Note. The content area names are from Lachar and Wrobel (1979).

Although critical item lists are widely employed in both automated and individual clinical interpretations of the MMPI-2, there is little information on what meaning or clinical importance to assign to a deviant response to a specific critical item. Most clinicians seem to assume that any deviant response is worthy of further investigation, even without any information on the base rate (frequency) with which a given critical item is endorsed by normal or pathological samples. In addition, until recently, the individual critical items had not been validated to determine whether deviant responses were empirically related to the actual behavior of the individual.

Saunders and Gravitz (1974) found that normal women were more likely to endorse the Grayson (1951) critical items reflecting internal conflict or stress, whereas normal men were more likely to endorse the items reflecting acting-out behaviors. Newton (1968) reported that psychiatric samples endorsed on the average about 9 of the 38 Grayson critical items. Gravitz (1968) reported that normal adults infrequently endorse any of these items, although 5 of the 38 items were endorsed by more than 10 percent of his sample. The frequency of endorsement of these items ranged from 0.5 percent to 12.5 percent in men and from 0.9 percent to 29.3 percent in women. These results certainly question the appropriateness of considering these items critical in an absolute sense.

Similarly, the university students described in Greene (1980), who can be assumed to be relatively normal, endorsed an average of six of the Grayson critical items. Only 36.4 percent of this student sample endorsed three or fewer items. Again, it seems that the high frequency of endorsement of the Grayson critical items by normal samples seriously questions how "critical" these items actually are. In addition, none of the preceding studies provides any empirical validation of the Grayson critical items.

In comparing the responses of their six crisis groups with the normal group, Koss et al. (1976) found substantial overlap between the distributions of the total number of their deviant responses to the Grayson critical items. Consequently, they could not identify any cutting score that accurately classified normal and crisis samples. Thus, there is little evidence that the Grayson critical items are useful either in identifying behaviors that need attention or in classifying clients as normal or psychopathological.

No research has been published on the Caldwell (1969) critical items. Caldwell used procedures similar to Grayson's in constructing his critical items; therefore, it seems likely that the foregoing reservations about the Grayson critical items also would apply to the Caldwell critical items.

There has been very little research with either the Koss and Butcher (1973) or Lachar and Wrobel (1979) critical items. Evans (1984b) found that his sample of normal adults endorsed more critical items than groups of psychiatric patients and alcoholics in the Koss and Butcher content areas of Acute Anxiety and Situational Stress Due to Alcoholism. His normal adults also endorsed more items than patients in the Lachar and Wrobel content area of Problematic Anger. These normal adults endorsed an average of 16 of the Koss and Butcher critical items and 12 of the Lachar and Wrobel critical items. Holmes, Sabalis, Chestnut, and Khoury (1984) reported that parents of children referred for outpatient psychiatric services significantly increased the number of critical items that they endorsed from the period of 1970 to 1974 to 1976 to 1979. Aaronson, Dent, Webb, and Kline (1996) found that the frequency of endorsement of both the Koss and Butcher and Lachar and Wrobel critical items decreased significantly with age in veterans entering a domiciliary. They suggested that endorsement of these critical items would have more clinical significance with increasing age because of the lowered likelihood of endorsement.

The frequency with which the Koss and Butcher (1973) critical items were endorsed by men and women in three different samples are presented in Tables 6.24 (p. 272) and 6.25 (p. 273), respectively. Several general comments can be made about the mean number of critical items endorsed by each sample. First, the personnel screening applicants endorsed fewer of these items than the MMPI-2 normative group, who endorsed fewer items than the psychiatric patients. Second, women irrespective of the sample are more likely to endorse items within the Acute Anxiety and Depressed-Suicidal Ideation areas than men. Third, the MMPI-2 normative group endorsed as many items in the Situational Stress Due to Alcoholism and Threatened Assault areas as the

TABLE 6.24   Frequency of Endorsement of Critical Items by Sample for Men

Koss and Butcher Crisis Situation	Number of Items	PERSONNEL APPLICANTS (CALDWELL, 1997C) (N = 4,122)		NORMAL INDIVIDUALS (BUTCHER ET AL., 1989) (N = 1,138)		PSYCHIATRIC PATIENTS (CALDWELL, 1997A) (N = 25,203)	
		M	SD	M	SD	M	SD
Acute Anxiety	17	1.43	1.35	3.19	2.48	5.61	4.58
Depressed—Suicidal Ideation	22	0.97	1.39	3.26	3.22	5.90	5.70
Mental Confusion	11	0.36	0.76	1.17	1.54	2.22	2.53
Persecutory Ideas	16	0.55	1.04	1.47	1.84	2.75	3.28
Situational Stress Due to Alcoholism	7	0.33	0.69	1.71	1.52	1.79	1.76
Threatened Assault	5	0.28	0.68	1.31	1.31	1.35	1.46
Total	78	3.92	4.14	12.11	8.63	19.62	16.18

Lachar and Wrobel Content Area	Items	M	SD	M	SD	M	SD
Antisocial Attitude	9	1.84	1.46	2.51	1.81	2.88	1.95
Anxiety and Tension	11	0.89	0.97	2.01	1.73	3.35	2.82
Depression and Worry	16	0.57	1.07	2.40	2.34	4.64	4.42
Deviant Beliefs	15	0.41	0.84	1.13	1.37	2.03	2.55
Deviant Thinking and Experience	10	0.94	1.18	1.75	1.40	2.13	1.97
Family Conflict	4	0.27	0.58	0.74	0.90	1.11	1.20
Problematic Anger	4	0.18	0.51	0.92	1.03	0.97	1.15
Sexual Concern and Deviation	6	0.27	0.61	1.23	1.22	1.44	1.40
Sleep Disturbance	6	0.73	0.74	1.12	1.10	1.95	1.77
Somatic Symptoms	23	1.04	1.43	2.93	2.65	5.61	5.45
Substance Abuse	3	0.24	0.52	0.83	0.82	0.82	0.88
Total	107	7.36	6.06	17.58	10.03	26.91	19.38

psychiatric patients; thus, the items in these two categories may be influenced by some extraneous variables, such as the willingness to report problem behaviors or the interpretation that is being made of the item content. Finally, even normal individuals endorse a moderate percentage of critical items within any area, which suggests that exploring every critical item endorsed by a client may likely be a very time-consuming process.

The frequency of endorsement of the Lachar and Wrobel (1979) MMPI-2 critical items in the same three samples of men and women is presented in Ta-

bles 6.24 and 6.25, respectively. Again, some general conclusions can be drawn with the same pattern of results emerging as was seen with the Koss and Butcher (1973) critical items. First, the personnel screening applicants endorsed fewer of these items than the MMPI-2 normative group, who endorsed fewer items than the psychiatric patients. Second, women irrespective of the sample were more likely than men to endorse items in the Anxiety and Tension, Depression and Worry, and Sleep Disturbance areas. Third, men irrespective of the sample were more likely than women to endorse items in the Antisocial Attitude area. Fourth, the nor-

TABLE 6.25   Frequency of Endorsement of Critical Items by Sample for Women

		PERSONNEL APPLICANTS (CALDWELL, 1997C) (N = 1,788)		NORMAL INDIVIDUALS (BUTCHER ET AL., 1989) (N = 1,462)		PSYCHIATRIC PATIENTS (CALDWELL, 1997A) (N = 25,763)	
Koss and Butcher *Crisis Situation*	*Number of Items*	M	SD	M	SD	M	SD
Acute Anxiety	17	1.97	1.69	3.65	2.77	6.94	4.71
Depressed—Suicidal Ideation	22	1.46	1.85	3.88	3.55	6.88	5.85
Mental Confusion	11	0.35	0.79	0.98	1.42	2.33	2.48
Persecutory Ideas	16	0.63	1.17	1.27	1.71	2.69	3.10
Situational Stress Due to Alcoholism	7	0.45	0.79	1.14	1.26	1.35	1.50
Threatened Assault	5	0.47	0.85	1.20	1.20	1.23	1.34
Total	78	5.33	5.23	12.12	8.90	21.41	15.78
Lachar and Wrobel *Content Area*	*Items*	M	SD	M	SD	M	SD
Antisocial Attitude	9	1.49	1.30	1.53	1.43	1.80	1.58
Anxiety and Tension	11	1.22	1.23	2.19	1.81	3.93	2.93
Depression and Worry	16	0.99	1.41	2.72	2.59	5.52	4.48
Deviant Beliefs	15	0.51	0.98	0.98	1.25	1.92	2.39
Deviant Thinking and Experience	10	1.09	1.13	1.67	1.30	2.12	1.87
Family Conflict	4	0.53	0.82	0.89	1.04	1.22	1.25
Problematic Anger	4	0.33	0.65	0.82	0.94	0.86	1.05
Sexual Concern and Deviation	6	0.70	0.92	1.21	1.20	1.51	1.37
Sleep Disturbance	6	0.94	0.87	1.49	1.29	2.53	1.86
Somatic Symptoms	23	1.64	0.87	3.68	3.21	7.47	5.80
Substance Abuse	3	0.32	0.59	0.56	0.76	0.62	0.81
Total	107	9.75	7.57	17.74	10.71	29.51	19.04

mal individuals endorsed nearly the same number of items in the Deviant Thinking and Experience, Problematic Anger, Sexual Concern and Deviation, and Substance Abuse as the psychiatric patients, which would cause one to question how critical the items are within these four areas. Finally, even the MMPI-2 normative group, who are supposedly normal, endorsed an average of 16.8 percent of these critical items.

Table 6.26 (p. 274) provides the frequency with which the Koss and Butcher (1973) and Lachar and Wrobel (1979) critical items were endorsed by age in the Caldwell (1997a) clinical dataset. The 18- and 19-

year-old psychiatric patients endorsed substantially more of these critical items than patients age 20 and above. (This difference between 18- and 19-year-old psychiatric patients and patients age 20 and above occurs frequently and will be explored in more depth in Chapter 9.) The total number of critical items endorsed increased three or four items from 20 to 60 years of age and then declined thereafter. This pattern of endorsing more critical items with age is exactly the opposite of the pattern reported by Aaronson et al. (1996). It is unclear what factor(s) produces these diametrically opposed results.

TABLE 6.26   Frequency of Endorsement of Critical Items by Age in the Caldwell Clinical Dataset

			AGE					
	18–19	*20–29*	*30–39*	*40–49*	*50–59*	*60–69*	*70+*	
Koss and Butcher								
Crisis Situation N =	959	10,979	16,201	12,927	5,703	1,737	498	*Correlation*
Acute Anxiety	6.54	5.43	6.13	6.65	7.27	6.74	5.94	0.102
Depressed—Suicidal Ideation	7.99	5.81	6.07	6.68	7.05	6.33	5.49	0.043
Mental Confusion	3.49	2.18	2.14	2.24	2.41	2.13	1.58	−0.011
Persecutory Ideas	3.92	2.63	2.66	2.64	2.65	2.35	1.87	−0.031
Situational Stress Due to Alcoholism	2.13	1.57	1.60	1.58	1.33	1.18	0.94	−0.072
Threatened Assault	2.08	1.32	1.21	1.24	1.19	1.07	0.91	−0.059
Total	26.17	18.94	19.80	21.03	21.89	19.80	16.73	0.025

			AGE					
	18–19	*20–29*	*30–39*	*40–49*	*50–59*	*60–69*	*70+*	
Lachar and Wrobel								
Content Area N =	959	10,979	16,201	12,927	5,703	1,737	498	*Correlation*
Antisocial Attitude	3.28	2.57	2.35	2.15	1.93	1.69	1.39	−0.156
Anxiety and Tension	4.38	3.37	3.55	3.73	3.96	3.50	2.84	0.028
Depression and Worry	5.97	4.43	4.83	5.38	5.83	5.28	4.81	0.077
Deviant Beliefs	2.76	1.78	1.92	1.99	2.06	1.86	1.52	0.009
Deviant Thinking and Experience	3.21	2.21	2.06	2.02	1.98	1.88	1.65	−0.070
Family Conflict	1.84	1.17	1.11	1.15	1.04	0.90	0.68	−0.068
Problematic Anger	1.54	0.95	0.85	0.87	0.84	0.79	0.72	−0.058
Sexual Concern and Deviation	1.75	1.38	1.48	1.52	1.50	1.42	1.31	0.012
Sleep Disturbance	2.40	2.07	2.21	2.28	2.48	2.40	2.05	0.051
Somatic Symptoms	6.78	5.45	6.29	6.67	7.94	7.52	6.69	0.122
Substance Abuse	0.93	0.75	0.73	0.71	0.61	0.52	0.43	−0.072
Total	34.84	26.14	27.38	28.78	30.18	27.76	24.10	0.033

There are consistent trends for a number of the individual sets of critical items to decrease with age even though the correlations are quite small. The Koss and Butcher Situational Stress Due to Alcoholism and Threatened Assault critical items and the Lachar and Wrobel Antisocial Attitude, Deviant Thinking and Experience, Family Conflict, Problematic Anger, and Substance Abuse critical items decrease consistently with age. Ladd (1996) also found that the Lachar and Wrobel Antisocial Attitude critical items declined with age in his chemically dependent inpatients. However, he did not find any age-related changes in the other sets of critical items. Aaronson et al. (1996) did not report data for the individual sets of critical items. None of the individual sets of critical items increases consistently with age.

The Koss and Butcher Acute Anxiety and Depressed-Suicidal Ideation critical items and the Lachar and Wrobel Somatic Symptoms critical items generally increase up to the age of 60 and decline thereafter.

If the clinician intends to pursue every critical item endorsed by the client, there is the potential of expending a large amount of time because of the frequency of endorsement of these items even by normal individuals. The sheer number (107) of the Lachar and Wrobel (1979) critical items, which includes 97 items scored on the standard Validity and Clinical scales, would make routine inspection of all these items even more laborious in a clinical sample. If the clinician could review with the client each critical item that had been endorsed in one minute, 20 to 30 minutes would be spent reviewing the Koss and Butcher critical items and another 20 to 30 minutes reviewing the Lachar and Wrobel critical items. It is instructive for clinicians who are learning the MMPI-2 to pursue clients' reasons for endorsing each of the critical items to gain an appreciation for the wide variety of explanations that are offered for the meaning of individual items. Clinicians quickly will realize the hazards of assigning too much weight to the endorsement of a single item, no matter how "critical" it may seem, because of the variety of interpretations given to the content of the item.

Both the Koss and Butcher (1973) and Lachar and Wrobel (1979) critical item sets warrant further research to determine how well these items identify critical areas of psychological concern in a variety of settings and populations. For example, no criteria have been established to determine how many items within a given area can be answered before the clinician should investigate further; research is needed to establish such criteria, although it violates the initial assumption that any item endorsed was deemed to be critical. Tables 6.24 and 6.25 provided the frequency with which these items were endorsed in three different samples, which can be used as a starting point for deciding what number of critical items is "critical" within a given content area. Ladd (1996) found that the endorsement of the Koss and Butcher and Lachar and Wrobel critical items was not related to other clinical criteria in his chemically dependent inpatients, which suggests that pursuing these critical items as they are constituted presently may not be worthwhile. Items need to be identified that do not discriminate effectively among groups so that the number of items can be reduced to a manageable size. A number of items seem to be likely candidates for deletion within the Koss and Butcher areas of Situational Stress Due to Alcoholism and Threatened Assault and the Lachar and Wrobel areas of Deviant Thinking and Experience, Problematic Anger, Sexual Concern and Deviation, and Substance Abuse because normal individuals were as likely to endorse items within these areas as the psychiatric patients. Finally, the influence of a client's tendency to overreport or underreport psychopathology on the endorsement of these critical items needs to be investigated, since the fact that a client endorses a specific critical item does not mean that he or she is providing an accurate self-report.

Clinicians need to realize that they *cannot* rely on any listing of critical items to be exhaustive of all of the items on the MMPI-2 within a specific content area. There is little item overlap within similar content areas on the Koss and Butcher and Lachar and Wrobel critical items, which suggests that a different meaning of the word *critical* is being used by these investigators. These differences in the items identified within the same content area reflect a number of different factors. First, each set of critical items was developed following a different methodology. Koss and Butcher identified items that were critical for specific crisis groups, while Lachar and Wrobel identified items that were face-valid descriptors of psychological concerns. Second, the author(s) may be trying to identify different nuances within the same content area or have different conceptualizations of the same content area. Finally, the Lachar and Wrobel (1979) critical items were identified within the MMPI item pool and only the item numbers have been changed to match the MMPI-2. This set of critical items has not been updated to include any of the new items on the MMPI-2.

Items within the general content area of depression can be used as an example of the differences among the sets of critical items that have been selected. Koss and Butcher (1973) identified 22 items within the content area of Depressed-Suicidal Ideation, Lachar and Wrobel (1979) identified 16 items within Depression and Worry, and Caldwell (1969) identified 12 items within Distress and Depression.

Only one item (130) is included on all three of these lists of critical items for depression. There are 19 (52.8%) items that are unique to one of these lists out of a total of 36 items. Some of these differences in the items selected may be reflected in the titles. Koss and Butcher have added "suicidal ideation," Lachar and Wrobel have added "worry," and Caldwell has added "distress" to the content area of depression. The reader could review the MMPI-2 item pool to see how many items he or she would select as having depressive content and how many items overlap with these three sets of critical items.

Four of the six items (150, 303, 506, 520, 524, 530) that have been identified repeatedly throughout this text as reflecting suicidal ideation are included by Koss and Butcher (150 and 530 are not included), while Lachar and Wrobel and Caldwell only included the first two of these six items. This latter list of critical items was developed within the MMPI item pool and only the item numbers have been changed to be consistent with the MMPI-2, so it is not possible for them to include the new items within the MMPI-2. Clinicians who relied solely on any set of critical items to assess for suicidal ideation or attempts have the distinct possibility of overlooking items that have been endorsed by the client.

CORRECTION ITEMS

A number of investigators over the last few decades have suggested that some MMPI/MMPI-2 items ("correction" items) should be removed when assessing patients with specific neurological or physical disabilities because these patients would endorse the selected items because of their bona fide disability rather than the presence of psychopathology. These "correction" items have been selected both rationally and empirically for patients with cerebrovascular accidents (Gass, 1992, 1996; Gass & Lawhorn, 1991); multiple sclerosis (Baldwin, 1952; Marsh, Hirsch, & Leung, 1982; Meyerink, Reitan, & Selz, 1988; Mueller & Grace, 1988); head injury (Alfano, Finlayson, Stearns, & Neilson, 1990; Alfano, Neilson, Paniak, & Finlayson, 1992; Artzy, 1994; Cripe, Maxwell, & Hill, 1995; Dunn & Lees-Haley, 1995; Gass, 1991; Gass & Russell, 1991; Hamilton, Finlayson, & Alfano, 1995; Van Balen, Van Limbeek, & De Mey,

1997); rheumatoid arthritis (Pincus, Callahan, Bradley, Vaughn, & Wolfe, 1986); and spinal cord injury (Rodevich & Wanlass, 1995; Taylor, 1970).

The usual paradigm in these studies in which the items are selected rationally is to ask a panel of two to ten experts to review the item pool to identify those items that would be answered in the deviant direction based on the presence of the specific neurological or physical disability in question. The items identified by a majority of these experts are then deleted, the MMPI/MMPI-2 is rescored, and *T scores are computed in the usual manner* (i.e., no attempt is made to correct for the items that have been deleted from any scale). Not surprisingly, the standard profile is lower once these items have been deleted, and those scales from which the largest number of items are deleted are affected the most. Based on these decreases in scale elevation, researchers conclude that the MMPI/MMPI-2 is biased against the neurological or physical disability being investigated and their correction should be used.

Before evaluating the assumptions that are being made in these correction procedures, the actual items identified in these studies will be reviewed. Both empirical (Alfano et al., 1992; Artzy, 1994; Dunn & Lees-Haley, 1995; Gass, 1991) and rational (Gass & Russell, 1991; Van Balen et al., 1997) methodologies have been used to identify items that are reflective of the bona fide symptoms of head injury. Table 6.27 provides the MMPI-2 items that were selected by these two methodologies. The total number of items identified as being symptoms of head injury varied from 14 (Gass, 1991) to 48 (Van Balen et al., 1997). Empirical procedures identified about one-third to one-half of the number of items that were identified rationally, which suggests that head-injured patients do not exhibit all of the symptoms that are expected of them. Dunn and Lees-Haley (1995) were able to replicate only 5 of the 14 items identified empirically by Gass (1991). Gass and Russell (1991) rationally selected only 10 of the 14 items that Gass (1991) had selected empirically, even though they had identified a total of 42 items (40 items on the MMPI-2) that were neurologically related. Conversely, only 10 of their 42 rationally selected items were validated empirically. Only five MMPI-2 items (31, 106, 147, 180, and 325) were selected in all five studies (excluding

TABLE 6.27 MMPI-2 Correction Items for Head Injury

	EMPIRICAL				RATIONAL		
Item	Alfano et al. (1992)	Artzy (1994)	Gass (1991)	Dunn & Lees-Haley (1995)	Gass & Russell (1991)	Van Balen et al. (1997)	Total
3					F	F	2
5					T		1
8					T		1
10	F				F	F	3
12	F				F		2
18						T	1
20					T		1
23						T	1
31	T	T	T		T	T	5
33					T		1
35		T					1
38	T					T	2
39						T	1
40					T	T	2
45					F	F	2
47					T		1
53		T			T	T	3
57						F	1
69		T					1
90					T		1
91		F				F	2
101			T		T	T	3
106	F	F	F		F	F	5
119		T					1
137		T					1
141						F	1
143					T		1
146		T				T	2
147	T	T	T		T	T	5
148					T		1
149			T			T	2
152					F	F	2
164					F	F	2
165			F		F	F	3
166					T		1
168		T				T	2
170			T				1
172			T				1
173					F	F	2
175			T		T		2
176					F	F	2
177	F				F	F	3

(continued)

TABLE 6.27 MMPI-2 Correction Items for Head Injury (continued)

| | EMPIRICAL | | | | RATIONAL | | |
Item	Alfano et al. (1992)	Artzy (1994)	Gass (1991)	Dunn & Lees-Haley (1995)	Gass & Russell (1991)	Van Balen et al. (1997)	Total
179	F		F		F	F	4
180	T	T	T		T	T	5
182						T	1
204				T	T		2
208					T		1
224					F	F	2
229		T				T	2
247	T		T	T		T	4
249					F	F	3
252					T	T	2
253					T		1
255					F	F	2
258					T		1
266		F					1
295	F			F	F	F	4
298				T			1
299	T	T			T	T	4
308		T				T	2
309		T				T	2
325	T	T	T		T	T	5
341						T	1
372				T			1
404						F	1
464						T	1
472						T	1
475						T	1
476						T	1
525				T		T	2
541					T		1
561						F	1
565						T	1
Total	13	18	14	5	40	48	

Dunn & Lees-Haley [1995] who were replicating Gass [1991]). These results would suggest that specific sample characteristics in addition to head injury are impacting which items are identified and that rational methods of selecting neurologically related items drastically overestimate the actual number of such items. Both of these results would suggest some caution in their use as correction items.

The top half of Table 6.28 provides the intercorrelations in psychiatric patients among these five correction scales. Despite the limited item overlap among these five scales, they still are highly intercorrelated.

A number of issues are raised when using these correction procedures when evaluating head-injured patients that must be considered. Similar issues could be raised in other medical and physical conditions.

TABLE 6.28   Intercorrelations among Sets of Correction Items in the Caldwell Clinical Dataset

| | HEAD INJURY | | | | |
| | Empirical | | | Rational | |
HEAD INJURY SCALE	ALFANO ET AL. (1993)	ARTZY (1994)	GASS (1991)	GASS & RUSSELL (1991)	VAN BALEN ET AL. (1997)
Alfano et al. (1992)	–				
Artzy (1993)	.870	–			
Gass (1991)	.944	.870	–		
Gass & Russell (1991)	.921	.838	.918	–	
Van Balen et al. (1997)	.935	.891	.943	.967	–

| | HEAD INJURY | | | | |
| | Empirical | | | Rational | |
CHRONIC BRAIN DISEASE OR OTHER PHYSICAL DISEASE/INJURY SCALE	ALFANO ET AL. (1993)	ARTZY (1994)	GASS (1991)	GASS & RUSSELL (1991)	VAN BALEN ET AL. (1997)
Cerebrovascular Disease					
Gass (1992)	.908	.832	.910	.956	.955
Multiple Sclerosis					
Mueller & Grace (1988)	.895	.802	.898	.931	.933
Meyerink et al. (1988)	.932	.844	.929	.968	.968
Rheumatoid Arthritis					
Pincus et al. (1986)	.821	.702	.790	.908	.880
Spinal Cord Injury					
Rodevich & Wanlass (1995)	.889	.785	.865	.960	.932
Taylor (1970)	.848	.714	.822	.883	.861

First, it is assumed that head-injured patients have no prior psychiatric or medical history that could affect their endorsement of these items. However, head-injured patients are likely to have extensive histories that could provide a number of reasons for endorsing these items that have no relationship at all to their current neurological impairment. Second, it is assumed that head-injured patients are not experiencing some form of psychopathology as a response to their head injury that might be producing the symptoms rather than the head injury per se. It would seem natural enough for head-injured patients to have rather extensive depressive symptoms as a result of a head injury that reflect how significantly their lives have been changed. Any reported memory deficits could reflect their depressive symptoms as well as or instead of their head injury. Finally, the psychometric procedure of deleting items alters the psychometric characteristics of the MMPI-2 scale so that it cannot be interpreted in the usual manner. Rather it would be necessary to determine the correlates of the MMPI-2 scale with external criteria after these items have been deleted, and, more importantly, to demonstrate that the shortened scale is a better predictor of these criteria than the original scale.

Table 6.29 lists the 46 correction items that have been identified for patients with chronic brain diseases (cerebrovascular disease and multiple sclerosis)

TABLE 6.29 Correction Items for Chronic Brain Disease and Other Physical Diseases and Injuries

	CHRONIC BRAIN DISEASES			PHYSICAL DISEASES/INJURIES			
Item	Gass (1991)	Mueller & Grace (1988)	Meyerink et al. (1988)	Pincus et al. (1986)	Rodevich & Wanlass (1995)	Taylor (1970)	Total
3				F	F		2
8					F		1
10	F		F	F	F	F	5
12		F			F		2
20			F		F		2
23		T					1
31	T		T				2
32			T				1
33				F	F		2
38			T	T	T		3
39			T				1
43			F				1
44					T		1
45	F		F	F	F	F	5
47	F						1
53	T	T	T		T	T	5
57			F	F	F		3
91		F	F		F	F	4
106	F	F	F				3
141	F			F			2
143					F	F	2
147	T		T				2
148	F		F	F	F	F	5
152	F	F	F	F	F		5
159			F		F		2
164	F	F	F		F		4
165			F				1
166					T		1
168	T						1
172	T	T	T				3
173	F	F	F				3
175	T	T	T	T	T		5
177	F	F	F		F	F	5
179		F	F		F	F	4
182	T	T	T				3
218					T		1
224	F		F	F	F		4
229	T						1
247	T	T	T		T	T	5
249	F	F	F				3
253					T		1

	CHRONIC BRAIN DISEASES			PHYSICAL DISEASES/INJURIES			
Item	Gass (1991)	Mueller & Grace (1988)	Meyerink et al. (1988)	Pincus et al. (1986)	Rodevich & Wanlass (1995)	Taylor (1970)	Total
268					T		1
295		F	F		F	F	4
296			T				1
325			T				1
464		T			T		2
Total	21	17	30	11	28	10	

and medical disabilities (rheumatoid arthritis and spinal cord injury). Only 3 of the 17 items on Mueller and Grace's (1988) multiple sclerosis scale were not identified by Meyerink et al. (1988), and all 10 of the items on Taylor's (1970) spinal cord injury scale are contained within Rodevich and Wanlass' (1995) scale. Despite the disparate nature of the diseases and disabilities that are being compared in these six studies, eight items (10, 45, 53, 148, 152, 175, 177, and 247) are common to five of the six studies. The items that have been identified in these studies tend not to be specific to any single disease or disability, but are common to a number of them. The lack of specificity of these various sets of items can be seen in Table 6.30, which illustrates the extremely high degree of intercorrelation among all of them. These sets of correction items also are highly intercorrelated with the sets of correction items for head injury (see the bottom half of Table 6.28). There are 39 (50.0%) items out of a total of 78 items that are common to these correction items presented in Tables 6.27 and 6.29, which again speaks to the lack of specificity of any single set of correction items.

This analysis of the commonality among the correction items across groups of patients with acute or chronic brain injury and physical disabilities or injuries leads to several conclusions. First, there are few items that are able to be cross-validated across groups of patients with diverse neurological and physical disabilities and, as the cause(s) of the neurological or

TABLE 6.30 Intercorrelations among Sets of Correction Items for Chronic Brain Disease and Other Physical Diseases and Injuries in the Caldwell Clinical Dataset

	CHRONIC BRAIN DISEASES			PHYSICAL DISEASES/INJURIES	
Correction Scale	Gass (1991)	Mueller & Grace (1988)	Meyerink et al. (1988)	Pincus et al. (1986)	Rodevich & Wanlass (1995)
Gass (1991)	–				
Mueller & Grace (1988)	.949	–			
Meyerink et al. (1988)	.973	.952	–		
Pincus et al. (1986)	.900	.833	.903	–	
Rodevich & Wanlass (1995)	.932	.931	.955	.930	–
Taylor (1970)	.896	.896	.907	.848	.918

physical disabilities gets more disparate, there are fewer items in common. Second, a large number of these items are sensitive to disability in general rather than to any specific form of disability. This point becomes very evident when the intercorrelations among these correction scales are examined (Table 6.28), which range from .702 to .968 in the Caldwell (1997a) clinical dataset. Cripe et al. (1995) found that the Cripe neurological symptom scales did not differentiate among groups of neurological, chronic pain, and psychiatric patients, which also supports that although these scales may be measures of neurological symptoms, they are not specific to patients with neurological disabilities or any other disability. Thus, it appears safe to conclude that there is not a specific set of items that appears to be common to any group of patients with a disability and that will identify the patients as members of that group. Cripe (1996, 1997) has outlined the issues to be considered when using the MMPI-2 to evaluate patients with neurological impairment.

The complexity of the issues raised in the evaluation of patients with medical or neurological disabilities is exemplified by the results of Youngjohn, Davis, and Wolf (1997) who found that patients with moderate to severe head injuries had lower scores on the MMPI-2 than patients with mild head injuries. They also found that the patients who were involved in litigation elevated MMPI-2 scores even more. Berry and Butcher (1998) and Youngjohn, Burrows, and Erdal (1995) have discussed how to evaluate head-injured patients for the possibility of overreporting of symptoms when litigation or compensation is involved. Finally, Brulot, Strauss, and Spellacy (1997) found no relationship between three sets of correction items for head injury (Alfano et al., 1993; Artzy, 1994; Gass, 1991) and duration of loss of consciousness, posttraumatic amnesia, or any tests of memory or attention in patients with mild head injuries. They did find significant correlations ($r > .507$) between these correction scales and the MMPI-2 Content scale of Depression (*DEP*).

Cripe et al.'s (1995) neurological-symptom MMPI-2 items (Appendix B.12) could be used as a means whereby patients provide the clinician with an indication of the specific categories in which they are experiencing symptoms. The clinician then can ex-

plore whether these specific symptoms are the result of the neurological impairment, the reaction to living with the impairment, prior or comorbid psychiatric problems, or more likely some combination of all of these factors. Profile 6.3 provides the frequency with which Cripe et al.'s items were endorsed in the Caldwell (1997a) clinical dataset. These psychiatric patients endorsed a number of these items, which illustrates how the symptoms are not specific to neurological impairments. A similar profile could be created based on a large sample of neurologically impaired patients or specific groups of such patients to understand how this particular patient's symptoms differ from similar patients'.

Research that examines whether patients with a specific neurological impairment have different empirical correlates when any correction items are removed is needed. Clinicians should be very hesitant to use any of these sets of correction items with MMPI-2 profiles until they have been validated empirically across several settings. There are a number of excellent overviews of the issues involved in the use of the MMPI-2 with patients with medical or neurological impairments that should be consulted by the interested reader (Berry & Butcher, 1998; Cripe, 1997, 1999; Reitan & Wolfson, 1997).

SHORT FORMS

The extensive number of items in the MMPI-2 (567) and MMPI (566) and the length of time required to complete the test (an hour for most clients and ranging upward to several hours for a few individuals) has led to numerous proposals to shorten or reduce the number of items on the test. Three of the more commonly used short forms of the MMPI will be reviewed here—Kincannon's (1968) Mini-Mult, Faschingbauer's Abbreviated MMPI (FAM: 1974), and Overall and Gomez-Mont's (1974) MMPI-168.

The clinician who desires more in-depth analysis of these short forms of the MMPI or other less frequently used short forms should consult Faschingbauer and Newmark (1978). Stevens and Reilley (1980) have provided another recent review of the literature on short forms. The interested reader also should consult Greene's (1982) response to the review by Stevens and Reilley. Butcher and Hostetler (1990)

MMPI-2 Neuropsychology Profile for Clinical Settings

Name _____   Age ____   Gender _____   DATE __/__/__

Normalized T	AM	BB	EB	FE	GC	HD	HE	ME	MT	PN	SB	SD	SE	SL	SO	VN	VO	Normalized T
						Cripe's Neurological Symptom Scales												
80	7	5	20	5	9	6	4	5	6	2	5	5	10	3	5	3	2	80
75			19						5			4	9					75
70		4	18		8	5			4			3	8		4	2		70
														2				
65	6		17	4	7	4		4	3		2	4	7				1	65
	5	3	14		5	3	3		2				6		3	1		
55	4		13	3	4	2		3	1	1	1	3	5	1				55
	3	2	10	2	3	1	2	2					4		2	0		
50	2	1	8	1	2			1	0	0	0	2	3	0			0	50
	1		6		1	0	1	0				1	2		1			
45			4	0									1					45
		0	3		0		0					0						
40	0		2										0					40
															0			
35																		35
			1															
30			0															30
	AM	BB	EB	FE	GC	HD	HE	ME	MT	PN	SB	SD	SE	SL	SO	VN	VO	

— — — — — — — — — — —

AM = Attention/Mental Control
BB = Biobehavioral
EB = Emotional/Behavioral Control
FE = Fatigue/Energy
GC = General Cogntive
HD = Headaches
HE = Health
ME = Memory
MT = Motor

PN = Pain
SB = Seizures/Blank Episodes
SD = Sleep Disturbance
SE = Sensory
SL = Speech/Language
SO = Social
VN = Vertigo/Nausea
VO = Vocational

Caldwell Dataset (1997a)
N = 50, 966

PROFILE 6.3

have reviewed the research on the use of short forms on the MMPI with suggestions for how these issues might be addressed on the MMPI-2. Any clinician who is contemplating research on short forms on the MMPI-2 should consult this article before starting.

Kincannon's (1968) short form of the MMPI was developed based on Comrey's factor analyses of the validity and clinical scales (cf. Comrey, 1957a). Kincannon selected items to represent each cluster within each scale. He chose items that were scored on the greatest number of scales (i.e., items with the most overlap across scales, and most of his items are scored on three to five different scales).

Following this procedure, he identified 71 items, which he called the Mini-Mult. Kincannon also reworded these 71 items because he intended that they be used in an interrogative fashion in an interview format. The Mini-Mult yields an estimate of all the Validity and Clinical scales except Scales *5* (Masculinity-Femininity) and *0* (Social Introversion). Graham and Schroeder (1972) provided items that can be added to the Mini-Mult so that Scales *5* and *0* can be scored. The actual items on the Mini-Mult, the procedures for transforming raw scores on the shortened scales into estimates of the raw scores on the original scales, and the instructions for administration can be found in Kincannon's (1968) original article.

Faschingbauer's (1974) short form of the MMPI, the FAM, also was developed based on Comrey's factor analyses of the standard Validity and Clinical scales (cf. Comrey, 1957a). In addition, Faschingbauer used Graham, Schroeder, and Lilly's (1971) factor analyses of Scales *5* and *0,* which were not factored by Comrey, and the results of research on deficiencies in Kincannon's (1968) Mini-Mult.

One-third of the items were selected on the basis of the greatest amount of overlap with other scales, one-third for the least amount of overlap, and one-third for the greatest number of intercorrelations greater than 0.29 with the other items. This procedure yielded preliminary short-form scales, which then were correlated with their corresponding original scales in a sample of 100 college males. For the FAM scales that did not correlate greater than 0.84 with their corresponding scale, items were added and de-

leted until this criterion was met. This final step yielded the 166 items in the FAM, which estimates all the standard Validity and Clinical scales.

Faschingbauer (1974) reported that when the FAM and MMPI were administered as two separate tests in a psychiatric sample, 60 percent of the profiles had an identical high-point scale and 28 percent had the same two high-point scales in any order. The FAM was more accurate in predicting high-point scales in the standard profile and detecting invalid profiles than other short forms.

The MMPI-168 was developed by Overall and Gomez-Mont (1974) because of their need for a brief screening test in view of the disappointing results that they obtained from evaluation of the validity of the Mini-Mult in their psychiatric setting. They selected the first 168 items of the MMPI as a screening test largely because item 168 appears as the last item at the bottom of page 7 of the Form R test booklet, providing a convenient stopping point for the client. Of course, if the group booklet form is used, item 168 will have to be marked as the last item to be answered since it is in the middle of the fourth page.

One advantage of the MMPI-168 is that the regular scoring templates can be used, and Overall and Gomez-Mont (1974) provide regression equations for estimating the scores on all the Validity and Clinical scales from the obtained raw scores. They believe that most of the information in the standard profile is well represented in the first 168 items of the MMPI.

Research on the frequency with which short forms can predict the standard MMPI codetype has yielded mixed results. Hoffmann and Butcher (1975) found that the Mini-Mult, FAM, and MMPI-168 were comparable in their ability to predict specific codetypes with hit rates ranging from 0.0 percent to 65 percent, 13.0 percent to 74.0 percent, and 6.8 percent to 74.0 percent, respectively. Hedlund, Won Cho, and Powell (1975) found that the Mini-Mult and MMPI-168 concurred with the standard MMPI high-point pair in 33 percent and 45 percent of their clients, respectively.

Evans (1984b) reported an average concordance rate of 35 percent for codetypes between the MMPI-168 and the standard MMPI in a sample of alcoholic patients. Concordance rates for specific codetypes ranged from 78 percent for a *2-4/4-2* codetype to 15 percent for a *7-8/8-7* codetype. In all of these studies the short forms were not independently administered; rather each short form was extracted from the standard MMPI, which would inflate the relationship between the short form and standard MMPI.

Hoffmann and Butcher (1975) concluded that there was insufficient evidence to advocate the clinical use of any of the short forms. They particularly cautioned against trying to use a short form with existing interpretive systems based on the standard MMPI because of the low frequency of concordance between the two tests in terms of high-point pairs. Graham (1987) voiced the same caution.

A virtual flood of studies has reported comparisons between a specific short form and the standard MMPI to document subject or setting characteristics. Almost all these studies have focused exclusively on how well the short form can predict the standard MMPI without considering the direct validity of the short form. Since the MMPI is an imperfect predictor of an external criterion, using a short form with questionable validity to predict the standard MMPI only seems to compound the potential for error. As Hoffmann and Butcher (1975) suggested, it would make more sense to use direct predictive approaches with short-form tests whereby a specific criterion is predicted.

Vincent et al. (1984) devised an actuarial system for use with the MMPI-168 (Overall & Gomez-Mont, 1974) that can be seen as one attempt to determine the specific correlates of a short-form test. Their actuarial system is very preliminary since it is based on a sample of 400 patients referred to a private psychiatric clinic. This approach is one that should be followed in using a short-form test (i.e., it needs to be construed as a new test that must be validated directly). However, if the clinician is going to devote the time and effort to validate a short form as a new test, it would make more sense to begin with a new item pool and not be limited by any inherent shortcomings of the MMPI item pool and scales (Streiner & Miller, 1986).

Only a few studies have directly compared the utility of short forms and the standard MMPI in predicting an external criterion. Poythress and Blaney (1978) compared psychologists' Q-sort ratings of the

FAM, Mini-Mult, and the standard MMPI in 36 patients with a wide variety of psychopathology. The standard MMPI yielded moderately higher but not statistically significant Q-sort ratings than the FAM, and the standard MMPI was significantly better than the Mini-Mult.

Using a similar procedure, Rand (1979) also found that Q-sorts produced by psychologists from the standard MMPI were significantly different from the Mini-Mult for 10 college students. Newmark, Ziff, Finch, and Kendall (1978) reported that the correlations of the FAM, MMPI-168, and standard MMPI with direct measures of psychopathology seemed comparable. Butcher, Kendall, and Hoffman (1980) pointed out that Newmark et al.'s (1978) results appear to represent an atypical sample and they questioned whether these results can be generalized to other settings. Moreland (1984) found that neither the FAM nor the MMPI-168 could be substituted for the standard MMPI in predicting ratings of psychiatric patients.

Until further research has been conducted on the FAM, Mini-Mult, and MMPI-168, clinicians should be extremely cautious in using any short form routinely. Clinicians should be particularly wary of trying to use a short form to predict the standard MMPI profile and then follow existing interpretive systems based on the standard MMPI since concordance between codetypes is generally limited.

The research on the Mini-Mult (Kincannon, 1968) has yielded consistently negative results, which should cause the clinician to question its appropriateness in most situations. The fact that the MMPI-168 (Overall & Gomez-Mont, 1974) seems to yield comparable results to the FAM is interesting because of the more elaborate statistical procedures that Faschingbauer (1974) used in developing the FAM. If future comparisons of the FAM and MMPI-168 with external validity criteria continue to produce similar results, the MMPI-168 would have some inherent advantages because the standard booklets and scoring templates can be retained.

There seems to be little justification for the use of short forms of the MMPI on a psychometric basis (McLaughlin, Helmes, & Howe, 1983; Streiner & Miller, 1986), from a clinical perspective (Edinger,

1981), based on their clinical utility (Helmes & McLaughlin, 1983), or based on their concordance with the standard MMPI (Evans, 1984b; Hedlund et al., 1975; Hoffmann & Butcher, 1975). Consequently, short forms of the MMPI should not be used as a pre-dictor of or substitute for the standard MMPI, and cli-nicians who continue to use them will have to demonstrate their usefulness empirically for whatever purpose they have in mind. It also would seem that these same caveats should hold for MMPI-2.

CHAPTER 7

Codetypes

The correlates of MMPI-2 codetypes (specific combinations of the 10 Clinical scales) will be considered in this chapter. These codetypes typically have been studied according to high-point pairs, that is, the two scales with the highest elevation at or above a T score of 65 on the MMPI-2.

A codetype is referred to by writing the numbers of the two scales involved with the more elevated one first. For example, if a client's two highest scores on the MMPI-2 are on Scales *2* (Depression) and *7* (Psychasthenia), and both are above a T score of 65 but Scale *7* is higher than Scale *2,* then the client's codetype would be *7-2.* If the two highest Clinical scales have identical T scores, they are listed in numerical order. In this example, if both Scales *2* and *7* had identical T scores of 75, the client's codetype would be *2-7.* There are 90 possible codetypes on the MMPI-2 and MMPI following this procedure.

The order of the scales within the codetype will *not* be differentiated unless empirical data indicate that the correlates of the codetype do change depending on which scale is more highly elevated. For example, *1-2/2-1* codetypes will not be distinguished from each other. When scale order within a codetype does produce different correlates, these will be noted explicitly.

The amount of material presented on a codetype is a rough index of the frequency with which the codetype is encountered. Some codetypes occur frequently, such as *2-4/4-2, 4-9/9-4,* and *6-8/8-6;* other codetypes are rarely encountered in any setting, such as *2-9/9-2, 3-0/0-3,* and *9-0/0-9.* The actual frequency with which codetypes are encountered in psychiatric and medical settings will be provided later.

Generally, the relationships among any of the Validity scales are not discussed because the Validity scales serve primarily to establish whether a specific MMPI-2 profile can be interpreted. When an important relationship does exist between a Validity scale and a codetype, this relationship will be mentioned.

The correlates of profiles in which only one Clinical scale is elevated at or above a T score of 65 on the MMPI-2 (Spike profiles) also will be discussed. Finally, the correlates of high-point triads (three most highly elevated Clinical scales) will be examined when the addition of a third scale significantly modifies the interpretation of the codetype.

This chapter will provide only the general correlates of each codetype. The clinician is strongly encouraged to become familiar with the available references providing more detailed information on profile interpretations that have been developed within a specific population, and to know under what circumstances each source might be most useful.

MMPI COOKBOOK INTERPRETIVE SYSTEMS

Gilberstadt (Gilberstadt, 1970; Gilberstadt & Duker, 1965) and Marks and Seeman (Marks & Seeman, 1963; Marks, Seeman, & Haller, 1974) have developed the most widely known actuarial cookbooks for the MMPI. Gilberstadt developed his interpretive system on male inpatients at a Veterans Administration hospital. He used five criteria for including a client in his preliminary analysis: (1) MMPI administered within 21 days before or after admission; (2) age range from 20 to 60; (3) primary diagnosis not brain damage; (4) L (Lie) ≤ 60, F (Infrequency) ≤ 85, and K (Correction) ≤ 70; and (5) Shipley Institute of Living Scale IQ estimate ≥ 105. Gilberstadt cautioned the clinician about applying his cookbook when any of these criteria is not met. He identified 19 codetypes among these clients, for which he provided the following data:

1. the most probable diagnosis
2. the list of complaints, traits, and symptoms associated with the specific codetype

3. the cardinal features of the client as a summary description

4. descriptive clinical information about the client

Gilberstadt also provided actuarial rules for identifying each codetype. For example, the rules for specifying a *1-2-3* codetype are:

> Scales *1* (Hypochondriasis), *2* (Depression), and *3* (Hysteria) ≥ 70
> Scale *1* > Scale *2* $\geq$ Scale *3*
> No other Clinical scale greater than 70
> Scales *L* (Lie) ≤ 65, *F* (Infrequency) ≤ 85, and *K* (Correction) ≤ 70

Clopton (1975) has developed a computerized version of the Gilberstadt and Duker (1965) system.

Marks and Seeman (1963; Marks et al., 1974) developed their MMPI interpretive system on hospitalized psychiatric clients seen in a university medical center, two-thirds of whom were women. These clients were literate, over 18 years of age, and voluntarily seeking treatment for problems of personal adjustment.

Marks and Seeman (1963) identified 9 preliminary codetypes in an original sample; in new samples they revised and refined these 9 codetypes and identified 11 additional codetypes. Before including a codetype within their system, Marks and Seeman insisted on studying at least 20 clients with that codetype; Gilberstadt and Duker (1965), on the other hand, used as few as 6 clients in some of their codetypes. In their system Marks and Seeman determined the actual correlates of each codetype for women only. When they were able to examine differences between men and women within a codetype, they found no significant differences.

Marks and Seeman (1963) originally defined their codetypes by complex configural rules; later they modified their classification procedure (Marks et al., 1974) in view of Gynther, Altman, and Sletten's (1973) demonstration that codetypes were more useful than their original configural rules. For example, Marks and Seeman (1963) originally defined a *2-7* codetype by the following criteria:

> Scales *2* (Depression) and *7* (Psychasthenia) ≥ 70
> Scale *2* minus Scale *8* (Schizophrenia) ≥ 15 points

> Scale *7* > Scales *1* (Hypochondriasis) and *3* (Hysteria)
> Scale *7* minus Scale *4* (Psychopathic Deviate) $\geq$ 10 points
> Scale *7* minus Scale *6* (Paranoia) ≥ 10 points
> Scale *7* minus Scale *8* ≥ 10 points
> Scale *9* (Hypomania) ≤ 60
> Scales *L* (Lie), *F* (Infrequency), and *K* (Correction) ≤ 70

In their revised classification procedure (Marks et al., 1974), a *2-7* codetype is simply that: Scales *2* (Depression) and *7* (Psychasthenia) are the two highest Clinical scales at or above a T score of 70. Thus, 12 of their 16 current codetypes are defined simply by the two highest Clinical scales. The other 4 codetypes are defined by the more complex configural rules as in their original system. They also developed 29 codetypes for adolescents, which will be discussed in Chapter 10.

Marks and Seeman did not report the percentage of profiles that could be classified in their revised system, although they did report that nearly 75 percent of their profiles could be classified in their original system. It would be expected that even more profiles should be classifiable in their revised system. Whether the simplified criteria for classifying profiles within codetypes significantly alters the applicability of the system will need to be determined empirically.

Although these two profile interpretation systems are specific and rather extensive, some interpretive problems remain. When either Gilberstadt's (Gilberstadt & Duker, 1965) or Marks and Seeman's (1963) original system is used, surprising variation occurs among the Clinical scales obtained by clients within a specific codetype (cf. Sines, 1966). For example, a client with a *2-7* codetype may have Scale *1* (Hypochondriasis) at a T score of 75 or 40 or Scale *8* (Schizophrenia) at a T score of 80 or 50. The relative elevation of these other Clinical scales can have significant impact on the interpretation of the codetype.

Moreover, it is commonly reported that only 15 to 35 percent of codetypes from a given clinical setting will fit into any of the codetypes (Fowler & Coyle, 1968a; Meikle & Gerritse, 1970; Shultz, Gibeau, & Barry, 1968). Even when some of the configural rules for codetypes are relaxed, the number of profiles that can be interpreted with either system does not increase appreciably (Pauker, 1966).

Two additional MMPI profile interpretation systems have been developed, one by Gynther and his colleagues (Gynther et al., 1973) and the other by Lachar (1974). Gynther et al. developed replicated correlates of 14 MMPI codetypes that occurred at least 30 or more times in a sample of 3,400 inpatients in public mental health facilities. They reported that 55 to 60 percent of MMPIs for white clients could be classified into one of these codetypes.

They also produced other interesting findings: No evidence could be found that the correlates of a high-point triad differed significantly from the two-point codetype; absolute elevation of the codetype above a T score of 70 did not affect the obtained correlates; gender may have affected the correlates within a given codetype; and similar codetypes obtained from blacks and whites required different interpretations.

The only rule required for classifying a profile within Gynther et al.'s system is that the raw score on the *F* (Infrequency) scale be less than 26. Gynther et al. (1973) also provided a separate interpretation of profiles in which the raw score on the *F* scale equals or exceeds 26. As Gynther acknowledged, the interpretive narratives generated by this system are exceedingly brief compared to other systems.

For example, the complete narrative for a *1-3/3-1* codetype is:

> *This type of client may display an unusual amount of bodily concern, often in the form of multiple somatic complaints, that sometimes reach the proportions of hypochondriasis. However, it should be noted that sometimes real physical problems are the cause of the client's concerns. (Gynther et al., 1973, p. 273)*

The very limited number of replicated correlates in the Gynther system for specific MMPI codetypes should be kept in mind when interpretation of profiles is discussed in Chapter 8 so that one can appreciate the amount of nonvalidated material that may be included.

Lachar (1974) developed an automated MMPI interpretive system in a manner very different from the three systems examined. The system was developed predominantly with a young, male, military sample, and each paragraph in this system was evaluated by having clinicians familiar with the client rate

its accuracy. In the description of Lachar's (1974) system, the clinician can readily see what rules were used to select a specific statement and how frequently clinicians judged the paragraph to be accurate.

For example, if only Scale *9* (Hypomania) on the MMPI exceeds a T score of 69 in the client's profile, the following paragraph will be used:

> *Similar individuals are often seen as talkative, distractible, and restless. A low frustration tolerance and an insufficient capacity for delay is often accompanied by irritability and maladaptive hyperactivity of thought and action [1/19]. (Lachar, 1974, p. 119)*

The numbers in brackets indicate that this paragraph was used in 19 of 1,472 clients and was judged inaccurate once.

Lachar's system has the unique advantage of providing some statement or paragraph for all MMPI profiles, and it provides correlates of 28 codetypes. It also attempts to provide at least rudimentary validation of the common interpretations made about individual scales and codetypes. Unfortunately, Lachar's instructions to his clinicians to judge the accuracy of each paragraph may have biased his system toward overgeneralized (high base rate) statements that are accurate but also not discriminating in describing clients. The reader interested in this area of research should consult Meehl (1956) or Greene (1977, 1978b).

King and Kelley (1977a, 1977b; Kelley & King, 1978, 1979a, 1979b, 1979c) reported the behavioral correlates of specific MMPI codetypes in a college student outpatient sample. The students were almost exclusively white, predominantly single, and mostly self-referred. King and Kelley required a minimum of five students within each codetype, and they analyzed for gender differences within a codetype if there were five or more men and women. Since they have not summarized their research into a single source, it is necessary to consult each of the original articles for the behavioral correlates of that codetype. The codetypes for which behavioral correlates have been reported by King and Kelley as well as the original article to be consulted will be indicated following the descriptions of the respective codetypes.

So far, MMPI cookbooks have not been the panacea that was originally thought. Increasing the specificity of a particular codetype helps by enhancing the homogeneity of the group and increasing the probability of finding reliable empirical correlates; however, it also substantially reduces the number of profiles that could be classified within a codetype.

If the rules for defining codetypes are relaxed so that more profiles can be classified, the probability of finding reliable correlates decreases because of the heterogeneity of profiles within the codetype. Furthermore, when correlates of a codetype are being assessed, it is difficult to identify sufficient numbers of profiles while controlling for significant demographic variables. MMPI cookbooks, nevertheless, can assist clinicians who are working in certain settings and with certain sample characteristics.

It should be emphasized that the correlates of a specific codetype found in one population or setting may not be found in a new population or setting. Hence, the generalization of the correlates of a codetype to new groups or environmental settings needs to be made cautiously until the necessary research has been conducted. Confident application of these interpretive systems to other populations and settings requires empirical research, which is virtually nonexistent.

In the interim the clinician needs to be familiar with MMPI codetypes in order to (1) understand and validate cookbooks when they are available for use, (2) modify and adapt the cookbook descriptions to fit the specific client in question, and (3) interpret meaningfully those profiles that do not fit into any interpretive system.

In a nutshell, if there is an empirically derived cookbook that is appropriate for a specific client and setting, the clinician should use it. In the absence of such information, the clinician will need to do the best job possible with whatever information is available. The clinician currently is in no real danger of being replaced by a cookbook or even a computer, but discussion of this topic will be reserved for the next chapter.

FREQUENCIES OF CODETYPES

The clinician needs to be aware of the relative frequency with which MMPI-2 and MMPI codetypes are encountered in specific settings. Each codetype does not occur equally often for several reasons. First, the specific forms of psychopathology that are associated with each Clinical scale have different base rates

(prevalence). Second, the specific setting in which the MMPI-2 is administered affects which codetypes are likely to be seen. It should not come as a surprise that codetypes emphasizing Scales *1* (Hypochondriasis), *2* (Depression), and *3* (Hysteria) occur frequently in medical settings, while Scales *4* (Psychopathic Deviate), *8* (Schizophrenia), and *9* (Hypomania) occur frequently in psychiatric settings.

Finally, the linear T scores that were used with the original Minnesota normative group are not equivalent from scale to scale, as was discussed in Chapter 2. The transition to uniform T scores on the MMPI-2 also has changed the relationships among the Clinical scales, as will be seen later.

The information on the frequency of MMPI codetypes will be reported first, followed by similar information on the MMPI-2.

MMPI

Table 7.1 (pp. 292–293) provides the frequency with which each MMPI codetype occurred in two large samples of psychiatric patients. Hedlund and Won Cho (1979) collected a large sample ($N \cong 21,000$) of psychiatric inpatients and outpatients in the 1970s. Approximately 7,500 of these patients were administered the 399-item Form R and they were excluded from further analyses because of interest in the entire MMPI item pool. Using criteria specified by Nichols, Greene, and Schmolck (1989) to assess consistency of item endorsement, an additional 1,874 patients were excluded because of inconsistent item endorsement and 1,014 patients were excluded because they omitted more than 30 items, which resulted in a final sample of 10,524 patients.

The careful reader might note that the number of men and women in Hedlund and Won Cho's (1979) sample of psychiatric patients in Table 7.1 are 6,145 and 2,575, respectively, or a total of 8,720 patients—and wonder what happened to the other 1,804 patients. These 1,804 (17.1 percent) patients had no MMPI Clinical scale greater than a T score of 69 and, consequently, are not classifiable in a specific codetype. Thus, the most frequent codetype in Table 7.1 is a Within-Normal-Limit (*WNL*) codetype, which occurred in 17.1 percent of these patients. Duckworth and Barley (1988) have provided a comprehensive analysis of *WNL* codetypes that should be reviewed by clinicians.

Greene (1989) collected a large sample of psychiatric inpatients and outpatients in the 1980s. Using similar criteria as specified previously to exclude patients because of inconsistent item endorsement or because they omitted more than 30 items resulted in a final sample of 10,888 patients. The most frequent codetype in this psychiatric sample also was *WNL*, which occurred in 17.9 percent of the patients.

Several conclusions can be drawn quickly even from a cursory review of Table 7.1. First, it is apparent that all MMPI codetypes did not occur equally often. Some codetypes are very common (*1-3/3-1, 2-7/7-2,* Spike *4, 4-8/8-4, 6-8/8-6,* Spike *9,* etc.), whereas other codetypes are very rare (*1-0/0-1, 2-9/9-2, 3-0/0-3, 5-0/0-5, 9-0/0-9,* etc.).

Second, the frequency of the various codetypes tends to correspond to the amount of clinical literature that is available. For example, little interpretive information is available on *1-0/0-1, 3-0/0-3,* and *9-0/0-9* codetypes, as will be seen later, which occurred infrequently in either men or women. Conversely, *1-3/3-1, 2-7/7-2,* and Spike *4* codetypes occur frequently in both men and women and have a large body of interpretive information.

Third, there is surprisingly little variation in the frequency with which the codetypes occur between these two large samples, although there are some differences as a function of gender. Several codetypes occur about twice as often in men (*1-2/2-1, 1-8/8-1,* Spike *2*), while others occur about twice as often in women (*1-3/3-1, 2-3/3-2,* Spike *3, 4-6/6-4,* Spike *6*).

Finally, *WNL* profiles are the most common codetype in both men and women in both of these samples.

It would be instructive for every clinician to construct tables such as these in his or her own setting so that frequent codetypes can be identified. Such frequent codetypes could be examined more closely to determine whether specific subgroups are apparent that could enhance treatment interventions and outcomes. These subgroups within frequent codetypes will not be reported here because of limited space.

The clinician also needs to be aware that the setting in which the MMPI is administered will affect the frequency with which specific codetypes are

found. Table 7.2 provides the frequency with which each MMPI codetype occurred in a large sample of male and female medical clients who were referred for psychiatric evaluations at the Mayo Clinic (Colligan & Offord, 1986). It must be noted that these clients are a subset of general medical clients since their physicians referred them for psychiatric evaluation.

It is readily apparent that Scales *1* (Hypochondriasis), *2* (Depression), and *3* (Hysteria) are much more likely to be elevated in these clients than in psychiatric clients. Approximately 70 percent (men, 69.5; women, 72.7) of the profiles in these medical clients referred for psychiatric evaluations had their highest MMPI Clinical scale among the neurotic triad (Scales *1, 2,* and *3*) compared to approximately 25 percent (men, 27.1; women, 25.2) of the profiles of Hedlund and Won Cho's (1979) psychiatric clients. *WNL* codetypes occurred in 23.0 percent of the male and 27.1 percent of the female medical patients.

The most frequent codetypes in these female medical clients were *1-3/3-1* (28.03 percent), Spike *3* (8.44 percent), and *2-3/3-2* (8.38 percent), whereas the most frequent codetypes in Hedlund and Won Cho's (1979) female psychiatric clients were *6-8/8-6* (9.51 percent), *4-8/8-4* (8.62 percent), Spike *4* (7.46 percent), and *4-6/6-4* (6.49 percent). The most frequent codetypes in male medical clients were *1-3/3-1* (17.95 percent), *1-2/2-1* (14.64 percent), and *2-7/7-2* (9.36 percent), whereas the most frequent codetypes in male psychiatric clients were Spike *4* (9.16 percent), *4-8/8-4* (7.34 percent), *6-8/8-6* (7.31 percent), and *4-9/9-4* (6.31 percent).

It is evident both that there is no overlap in the most frequent codetypes between these two settings and that gender has only minimal impact within a setting. When gender differences were found in these medical patients, they were similar to what was found in psychiatric patients. Several codetypes occurred in these medical patients about twice as often in men (*1-2/2-1, 2-7/7-2*), while others occurred more often in women (*1-3/3-1, 2-3/3-2,* Spike *3*). These data should help the clinician realize the potential effect of the setting in which the MMPI is administered on the frequency with which the various codetypes are encountered.

Clinicians also need to be aware of the frequency with which low points among the Clinical scales are

TABLE 7.1 Frequency of MMPI Codetypes in Psychiatric Inpatients and Outpatients

| | HEDLUND & WON CHO (1979) | | | | | | GREENE (1989) | | | | | |
| | Men | | Women | | Total | | Men | | Women | | Total | |
CODETYPE	N	%	N	%	N	%	N	%	N	%	N	%
Spike 1	62	1.01	12	0.47	74	0.85	65	1.43	25	0.57	90	1.01
1-2/2-1	300	4.88	49	1.90	349	4.00	273	5.99	91	2.08	364	4.07
1-3/3-1	141	2.29	97	3.77	238	2.73	172	3.77	314	7.18	486	5.44
1-4/4-1	112	1.82	24	0.93	136	1.56	43	0.94	35	0.80	78	0.87
1-5/5-1	10	0.16	3	0.12	13	0.15	18	0.39	2	0.05	20	0.22
1-6/6-1	15	0.24	10	0.39	25	0.29	11	0.24	18	0.41	29	0.32
1-7/7-1	24	0.39	2	0.08	26	0.30	28	0.61	9	0.21	37	0.41
1-8/8-1	163	2.65	29	1.13	192	2.20	142	3.12	78	1.78	220	2.46
1-9/9-1	40	0.65	8	0.31	48	0.55	33	0.72	9	0.21	42	0.47
1-0/0-1	3	0.05	1	0.04	4	0.05	2	0.04	5	0.11	7	0.08
Spike 2	187	3.04	46	1.79	233	2.67	167	3.66	78	1.78	245	2.74
2-3/3-2	92	1.50	75	2.91	167	1.92	83	1.82	203	4.64	286	3.20
2-4/4-2	468	7.62	140	5.44	608	6.97	265	5.81	220	5.03	485	5.43
2-5/5-2	38	0.62	3	0.12	41	0.47	74	1.62	2	0.05	76	0.85
2-6/6-2	55	0.90	27	1.05	82	0.94	39	0.86	83	1.90	122	1.37
2-7/7-2	301	4.90	104	4.04	405	4.64	280	6.14	209	4.78	489	5.47
2-8/8-2	355	5.78	128	4.97	483	5.54	309	6.78	217	4.96	526	5.89
2-9/9-2	13	0.21	6	0.23	19	0.22	11	0.24	7	0.16	18	0.20
2-0/0-2	54	0.88	55	2.14	109	1.25	25	0.55	95	2.17	120	1.34
Spike 3	18	0.29	27	1.05	45	0.52	17	0.37	101	2.31	118	1.32
3-4/4-3	88	1.43	80	3.11	168	1.93	52	1.14	142	3.24	194	2.17
3-5/5-3	11	0.18	1	0.04	12	0.14	17	0.37	6	0.14	23	0.26
3-6/6-3	7	0.11	13	0.50	20	0.23	2	0.04	25	0.57	27	0.30
3-7/7-3	3	0.05	12	0.47	15	0.17	14	0.31	34	0.78	48	0.54
3-8/8-3	13	0.21	27	1.05	40	0.46	16	0.35	38	0.87	54	0.60
3-9/9-3	11	0.18	9	0.35	20	0.23	22	0.48	17	0.39	39	0.44
3-0/0-3	0	0.00	4	0.16	4	0.05	0	0.00	5	0.11	5	0.06

Codetype	N	%	N	%	N	%	N	%	N	%	N	%
Spike 4	563	9.16	192	7.46	755	8.66	240	5.27	240	5.48	480	5.37
4-5/5-4	99	1.61	15	0.58	114	1.31	85	1.86	10	0.23	95	1.06
4-6/6-4	189	3.08	167	6.49	356	4.08	87	1.91	195	4.46	282	3.16
4-7/7-4	131	2.13	19	0.74	150	1.72	100	2.19	85	1.94	185	2.07
4-8/8-4	451	7.34	222	8.62	673	7.72	258	5.66	403	9.21	661	7.40
4-9/9-4	388	6.31	126	4.89	514	5.89	183	4.01	160	3.66	343	3.84
4-0/0-4	14	0.23	17	0.66	31	0.36	4	0.09	27	0.62	31	0.35
Spike 5	72	1.17	41	1.59	113	1.30	117	2.57	42	0.96	159	1.78
5-6/6-5	19	0.31	3	0.12	22	0.25	27	0.59	9	0.21	36	0.40
5-7/7-5	14	0.23	1	0.04	15	0.17	44	0.97	1	0.02	45	0.50
5-8/8-5	37	0.60	5	0.19	42	0.48	42	0.92	11	0.25	53	0.59
5-9/9-5	50	0.81	10	0.39	60	0.69	39	0.86	8	0.18	47	0.53
5-0/0-5	2	0.03	2	0.08	4	0.05	4	0.09	1	0.02	5	0.06
Spike 6	52	0.85	54	2.10	106	1.22	36	0.79	67	1.53	103	1.15
6-7/7-6	24	0.39	11	0.43	35	0.40	15	0.33	21	0.48	36	0.40
6-8/8-6	449	7.31	245	9.51	694	7.96	302	6.63	322	7.36	624	6.98
6-9/9-6	70	1.14	65	2.52	135	1.55	39	0.86	64	1.46	103	1.15
6-0/0-6	3	0.05	10	0.39	13	0.15	3	0.07	9	0.21	12	0.13
Spike 7	27	0.44	9	0.35	36	0.41	18	0.39	13	0.30	31	0.35
7-8/8-7	329	5.35	107	4.16	436	5.00	318	6.98	175	4.00	493	5.52
7-9/9-7	36	0.59	6	0.23	42	0.48	31	0.68	5	0.11	36	0.40
7-0/0-7	10	0.16	6	0.23	16	0.18	11	0.24	19	0.43	30	0.34
Spike 8	26	0.42	17	0.66	43	0.49	37	0.81	23	0.53	60	0.67
8-9/9-8	222	3.61	86	3.34	308	3.53	145	3.18	128	2.93	273	3.06
8-0/0-8	6	0.10	19	0.74	25	0.29	3	0.07	23	0.53	26	0.29
Spike 9	254	4.13	93	3.61	347	3.98	180	3.95	177	4.04	358	4.01
9-0/0-9	2	0.03	1	0.04	3	0.03	0	0.00	1	0.02	1	0.01
Spike 0	22	0.36	34	1.32	56	0.64	10	0.22	69	1.58	79	0.88
Any Codetype	6,145	83.5	2,575	81.3	8,720	82.9	4,558	84.7	4,376	79.4	8,935	82.1
WNL	1,211	16.5	593	18.7	1,804	17.1	821	15.3	1,133	20.6	1,954	17.9
Total	7,356	100.0	3,168	100.0	10,524	100.0	5,379	100.0	5,509	100.0	10,888	100.0

TABLE 7.2   Frequency of MMPI Codetypes in Medical Outpatient Referrals at the Mayo Clinic (Colligan & Offord, 1986)

Codetype	MEN N	MEN %	WOMEN N	WOMEN %	TOTAL N	TOTAL %
Spike 1	133	3.67	136	2.83	269	3.20
1-2/2-1	530	14.64	291	6.07	821	9.75
1-3/3-1	650	17.95	1,345	28.03	1,995	23.70
1-4/4-1	37	1.02	35	0.73	72	0.86
1-5/5-1	23	0.64	7	0.15	30	0.36
1-6/6-1	8	0.22	14	0.29	22	0.26
1-7/7-1	38	1.05	9	0.19	47	0.56
1-8/8-1	59	1.63	46	0.96	105	1.25
1-9/9-1	25	0.69	33	0.69	58	0.69
1-0/0-1	5	0.14	19	0.40	24	0.29
Spike 2	172	4.75	157	3.27	329	3.91
2-3/3-2	191	5.27	402	8.38	593	7.04
2-4/4-2	123	3.40	153	3.19	276	3.28
2-5/5-2	69	1.91	3	0.06	72	0.86
2-6/6-2	37	1.02	76	1.58	113	1.34
2-7/7-2	339	9.36	242	5.04	581	6.90
2-8/8-2	150	4.14	145	3.02	295	3.50
2-9/9-2	10	0.28	9	0.19	19	0.23
2-0/0-2	46	1.27	131	2.73	177	2.10
Spike 3	76	2.10	405	8.44	481	5.71
3-4/4-3	48	1.33	110	2.29	158	1.88
3-5/5-3	26	0.72	3	0.06	29	0.34
3-6/6-3	3	0.08	44	0.92	47	0.56
3-7/7-3	15	0.41	31	0.65	46	0.55
3-8/8-3	12	0.33	41	0.85	53	0.63
3-9/9-3	11	0.30	40	0.83	51	0.61
3-0/0-3	0	0.00	3	0.06	3	0.04
Spike 4	90	2.49	107	2.23	197	2.34
4-5/5-4	35	0.97	2	0.04	37	0.44
4-6/6-4	22	0.61	73	1.52	95	1.13
4-7/7-4	27	0.75	26	0.54	53	0.63
4-8/8-4	60	1.66	95	1.98	155	1.84
4-9/9-4	43	1.19	52	1.08	95	1.13
4-0/0-4	1	0.03	10	0.21	11	0.13
Spike 5	95	2.62	18	0.38	113	1.34
5-6/6-5	14	0.39	1	0.02	15	0.18
5-7/7-5	12	0.33	1	0.02	13	0.15
5-8/8-5	15	0.41	1	0.02	16	0.19
5-9/9-5	16	0.44	6	0.13	22	0.26
5-0/0-5	1	0.03	1	0.02	2	0.02
Spike 6	24	0.66	51	1.06	75	0.89
6-7/7-6	6	0.17	11	0.23	17	0.20
6-8/8-6	49	1.35	68	1.42	117	1.39
6-9/9-6	8	0.22	24	0.50	32	0.38
6-0/0-6	0	0.00	10	0.21	10	0.12

	MEN		WOMEN		TOTAL	
Codetype	*N*	*%*	*N*	*%*	*N*	*%*
Spike *7*	20	0.55	13	0.27	33	0.39
7-8/8-7	90	2.49	77	1.60	167	1.98
7-9/9-7	7	0.19	1	0.02	8	0.10
7-0/0-7	4	0.11	12	0.25	16	0.19
Spike *8*	14	0.39	11	0.23	25	0.30
8-9/9-8	47	1.30	33	0.69	80	0.95
8-0/0-8	2	0.06	3	0.06	5	0.06
Spike *9*	74	2.04	95	1.98	169	2.01
9-0/0-9	0	0.00	2	0.04	2	0.02
Spike *0*	9	0.25	64	1.33	73	0.87
Any Codetype	3,621	77.0	4,798	72.9	8,419	74.6
WNL	1,079	23.0	1,783	27.1	2,862	25.4
Total	4,700	100.0	6,581	100.0	11,281	100.0

encountered in frequently occurring codetypes. Codetype interpretation of the MMPI-2 or the MMPI emphasizes the high point(s) among the Clinical scales and, consequently, less attention is paid to low-point scales. Since the low-point scale already is available in the standard profile, clinicians can make use of this information without any additional work.

For example, a low point on Scale *9* (Hypomania) in conjunction with a high point on Scale *2* (Depression) should alert the clinician to the presence of significant depressive symptoms. Hathaway and Meehl (1951, pp. xxvii–xxix) provided data on the frequency with which low points occur with each high-point scale, but they did not report low points for specific codetypes.

Table 7.3 (pp. 296–299) provides the frequency of low points on the MMPI clinical scales for all codetypes in the Hedlund and Won Cho (1979) sample of psychiatric patients. Scale *9* (Hypomania) is a common low point when either Scale *1* (Hypochondriasis) or *2* (Depression) is the highest clinical scale in both men and women. However, Scale *9* is much less often the low point when Scale *4* (Psychopathic Deviate) is the highest Clinical scale; instead Scale *0* (Social Introversion) is a frequent low point. As might be expected, Scale *5* (Masculinity-Femininity)

is the most common low point in women, while Scale *0* is the most common low point in men. It also is interesting to note that Scales *4* (Psychopathic Deviate), *7* (Psychasthenia), and *8* (Schizophrenia) are rarely a low point with any codetype in either men or women. The clinician could consult Table 7.3 with every profile to determine whether the person's low-point scale is one that occurs commonly, and incorporate that information into the profile interpretation.

As the clinician amasses data in his or her specific setting, it is highly recommended that codetype frequency and low-point frequency tables be constructed so that the effects of this specific setting can be ascertained. Sample sizes as small as several hundred clients are sufficient to start providing reasonable estimates of the relative frequencies of the codetypes.

MMPI-2

Table 7.4 (pp. 300–301) provides the frequency with which each MMPI-2 codetype occurs in the Caldwell (1997a) clinical dataset, which is described more fully in Chapter 9. Similar conclusions can be drawn from Table 7.4 on the frequency of MMPI-2 codetypes as were drawn from Table 7.1 on the frequency

TABLE 7.3 Frequency of Low-Point Scales for MMPI Codetypes by Gender
in Psychiatric Patients (Hedlund & Won Cho, 1979)

CODETYPE	1(Hs)	2(D)	3(Hy)	4(Pd)	5(Mf)	6(Pa)	7(Pt)	8(Sc)	9(Ma)	0(Si)
Spike *1*										
Men	0.00	3.23	1.61	1.61	24.19	11.29	11.29	11.29	9.68	25.81
Women	0.00	8.33	0.00	0.00	33.33	16.67	8.33	8.33	8.33	16.67
1-2/2-1										
Men	0.00	0.00	1.00	4.67	27.00	11.67	2.00	6.00	33.00	14.67
Women	0.00	0.00	0.00	4.08	40.82	8.16	4.08	0.00	42.86	0.00
1-3/3-1										
Men	0.00	2.13	0.00	0.71	18.44	6.38	2.84	2.84	16.31	50.35
Women	0.00	1.03	0.00	6.19	51.55	5.15	2.06	0.00	23.71	10.31
1-4/4-1										
Men	0.00	2.68	0.00	0.00	27.68	8.93	4.46	1.79	16.96	37.50
Women	0.00	0.00	0.00	0.00	54.17	4.17	0.00	0.00	20.83	20.83
1-5/5-1										
Men	0.00	10.00	0.00	0.00	0.00	0.00	10.00	10.00	10.00	60.00
Women	0.00	0.00	0.00	33.33	0.00	0.00	33.33	0.00	0.00	33.33
1-6/6-1										
Men	0.00	0.00	0.00	6.67	33.33	0.00	20.00	0.00	26.67	13.33
Women	0.00	0.00	0.00	0.00	80.00	0.00	0.00	0.00	20.00	0.00
1-7/7-1										
Men	0.00	0.00	0.00	4.17	37.50	8.33	0.00	0.00	20.83	29.17
Women	0.00	0.00	0.00	0.00	100.00	0.00	0.00	0.00	0.00	0.00
1-8/8-1										
Men	0.00	0.61	0.00	1.23	46.01	4.91	0.61	0.00	11.04	35.58
Women	0.00	0.00	0.00	3.45	75.86	3.45	0.00	0.00	3.45	13.79
1-9/9-1										
Men	0.00	7.50	0.00	2.50	22.50	0.00	0.00	0.00	0.00	67.50
Women	0.00	0.00	0.00	0.00	50.00	0.00	0.00	0.00	0.00	50.00
1-0/0-1										
Men	0.00	0.00	0.00	33.33	0.00	33.33	0.00	33.33	0.00	0.00
Women	0.00	0.00	0.00	100.00	0.00	0.00	0.00	0.00	0.00	0.00
Spike *2*										
Men	10.70	0.00	2.67	4.28	17.11	17.65	2.14	13.90	25.67	5.88
Women	6.52	0.00	2.17	10.87	36.96	8.70	0.00	2.17	32.61	0.00
2-3/3-2										
Men	0.00	0.00	0.00	1.09	15.22	3.26	1.09	4.35	44.57	30.43
Women	0.00	0.00	0.00	0.00	64.00	0.00	0.00	0.00	34.67	1.33
2-4/4-2										
Men	17.95	0.00	2.56	0.00	18.80	6.84	1.28	5.13	23.29	24.15
Women	6.43	0.00	0.71	0.00	65.00	2.86	1.43	0.00	18.57	5.00
2-5/5-2										
Men	15.79	0.00	5.26	7.89	0.00	7.89	2.63	2.63	42.11	15.79
Women	0.00	0.00	33.33	0.00	0.00	0.00	0.00	0.00	66.67	0.00
2-6/6-2										
Men	25.45	0.00	9.09	1.82	14.55	0.00	0.00	5.45	36.36	7.27
Women	7.41	0.00	3.70	3.70	74.07	0.00	0.00	0.00	11.11	0.00

CODETYPE	1(Hs)	2(D)	3(Hy)	4(Pd)	5(Mf)	6(Pa)	7(Pt)	8(Sc)	9(Ma)	0(Si)
2-7/7-2										
Men	10.96	0.00	3.99	2.99	19.27	7.31	0.00	1.00	48.17	6.31
Women	0.00	0.00	0.96	1.92	64.42	1.92	0.00	0.00	30.77	0.00
2-8/8-2										
Men	9.58	0.00	7.89	1.69	32.39	4.23	0.56	0.00	34.65	9.01
Women	5.47	0.00	2.34	0.78	69.53	1.56	0.00	0.00	19.53	0.78
2-9/9-2										
Men	7.69	0.00	0.00	0.00	23.08	15.38	0.00	0.00	0.00	53.85
Women	16.67	0.00	0.00	0.00	66.67	0.00	0.00	0.00	0.00	16.67
2-0/0-2										
Men	18.52	0.00	5.56	1.85	9.26	3.70	1.85	5.56	53.70	0.00
Women	5.45	0.00	1.82	5.45	41.82	7.27	0.00	0.00	38.18	0.00
Spike 3										
Men	0.00	0.00	0.00	0.00	11.11	22.22	11.11	5.56	22.22	27.78
Women	0.00	0.00	0.00	3.70	33.33	11.11	14.81	3.70	14.81	18.52
3-4/4-3										
Men	0.00	0.00	0.00	0.00	7.95	4.55	2.27	1.14	14.77	69.32
Women	1.25	1.25	0.00	0.00	58.75	1.25	3.75	0.00	5.00	28.75
3-5/5-3										
Men	0.00	0.00	0.00	0.00	0.00	18.18	0.00	0.00	0.00	81.82
Women	0.00	0.00	0.00	0.00	0.00	0.00	0.00	0.00	100.00	0.00
3-6/6-3										
Men	0.00	0.00	0.00	0.00	0.00	0.00	0.00	14.29	14.29	71.43
Women	0.00	7.69	0.00	0.00	69.23	0.00	0.00	0.00	15.38	7.69
3-7/7-3										
Men	0.00	0.00	0.00	0.00	0.00	33.33	0.00	0.00	0.00	66.67
Women	0.00	0.00	0.00	0.00	66.67	0.00	0.00	0.00	25.00	8.33
3-8/8-3										
Men	0.00	0.00	0.00	0.00	30.77	7.69	0.00	0.00	15.38	46.15
Women	0.00	3.70	0.00	3.70	74.07	3.70	0.00	0.00	0.00	14.81
3-9/9-3										
Men	0.00	0.00	0.00	0.00	9.09	9.09	9.09	0.00	0.00	72.73
Women	11.11	11.11	0.00	0.00	33.33	11.11	0.00	0.00	0.00	33.33
3-0/0-3										
Men	0.00	0.00	0.00	0.00	0.00	0.00	0.00	0.00	0.00	0.00
Women	0.00	0.00	0.00	0.00	50.00	0.00	0.00	0.00	50.00	0.00
Spike 4										
Men	11.90	3.02	3.20	0.00	19.18	9.06	4.80	4.80	7.46	36.59
Women	14.06	6.25	4.17	0.00	36.46	6.25	4.69	1.56	6.25	20.31
4-5/5-4										
Men	19.19	5.05	1.01	0.00	0.00	5.05	2.02	4.04	6.06	57.58
Women	20.00	13.33	0.00	0.00	0.00	13.33	0.00	6.67	13.33	33.33
4-6/6-4										
Men	28.57	4.23	4.76	0.00	15.34	0.00	4.76	1.06	4.23	37.04
Women	15.57	4.79	4.79	0.00	54.49	0.00	5.99	0.00	5.99	8.38

(continued)

TABLE 7.3 Frequency of Low-Point Scales for MMPI Codetypes by Gender in Psychiatric Patients (Hedlund & Won Cho, 1979) (continued)

CODETYPE	1(Hs)	2(D)	3(Hy)	4(Pd)	5(Mf)	6(Pa)	7(Pt)	8(Sc)	9(Ma)	0(Si)
4-7/7-4										
Men	30.53	1.53	4.58	0.00	20.61	3.82	0.00	1.53	9.92	27.48
Women	21.05	0.00	0.00	0.00	47.37	5.26	0.00	0.00	15.79	10.53
4-8/8-4										
Men	18.18	1.55	10.64	0.00	22.62	2.66	0.89	0.00	7.76	35.70
Women	11.71	3.60	2.70	0.00	62.61	0.45	0.45	0.00	6.76	11.71
4-9/9-4										
Men	16.24	9.28	6.44	0.00	9.28	3.61	2.84	0.00	0.00	52.32
Women	10.32	11.90	5.56	0.00	31.75	0.79	3.17	0.00	0.00	36.51
4-0/0-4										
Men	42.86	0.00	7.14	0.00	14.29	7.14	0.00	7.14	21.43	0.00
Women	11.76	5.88	11.76	0.00	64.71	5.88	0.00	0.00	0.00	0.00
Spike 5										
Men	20.83	2.78	1.39	1.39	0.00	2.78	5.56	5.56	9.72	50.00
Women	12.20	7.32	9.76	4.88	0.00	26.83	19.51	2.44	4.88	12.20
5-6/6-5										
Men	10.53	10.53	5.26	5.26	0.00	0.00	0.00	10.53	10.53	47.37
Women	0.00	66.67	33.33	0.00	0.00	0.00	0.00	0.00	0.00	0.00
5-7/7-5										
Men	14.29	7.14	21.43	14.29	0.00	7.14	0.00	0.00	21.43	14.29
Women	0.00	0.00	0.00	0.00	0.00	100.00	0.00	0.00	0.00	0.00
5-8/8-5										
Men	35.14	8.11	10.81	0.00	0.00	2.70	0.00	0.00	0.00	43.24
Women	20.00	40.00	20.00	0.00	0.00	0.00	0.00	0.00	20.00	0.00
5-9/9-5										
Men	26.00	14.00	0.00	4.00	0.00	0.00	2.00	0.00	0.00	54.00
Women	0.00	20.00	30.00	0.00	0.00	0.00	0.00	0.00	0.00	50.00
5-0/0-5										
Men	50.00	0.00	50.00	0.00	0.00	0.00	0.00	0.00	0.00	0.00
Women	50.00	0.00	0.00	0.00	0.00	50.00	0.00	0.00	0.00	0.00
Spike 6										
Men	38.46	7.69	11.54	0.00	11.54	0.00	5.77	1.92	5.77	17.31
Women	18.52	1.85	16.67	1.85	37.04	0.00	3.70	3.70	7.41	9.26
6-7/7-6										
Men	29.17	0.00	16.67	4.17	20.83	0.00	0.00	0.00	8.33	20.83
Women	9.09	0.00	0.00	0.00	90.91	0.00	0.00	0.00	0.00	0.00
6-8/8-6										
Men	15.59	3.12	13.59	0.89	32.74	0.00	1.11	0.00	6.68	26.28
Women	8.57	4.49	12.65	3.67	63.27	0.00	0.41	0.00	1.22	5.71
6-9/9-6										
Men	27.14	18.57	14.29	1.43	2.86	0.00	4.29	0.00	0.00	31.43
Women	13.85	24.62	15.38	1.54	24.62	0.00	3.08	0.00	0.00	16.92
6-0/0-6										
Men	100.00	0.00	0.00	0.00	0.00	0.00	0.00	0.00	0.00	0.00
Women	10.00	0.00	0.00	10.00	50.00	0.00	0.00	0.00	30.00	0.00

CODETYPE	1(Hs)	2(D)	3(Hy)	4(Pd)	5(Mf)	6(Pa)	7(Pt)	8(Sc)	9(Ma)	0(Si)
Spike 7										
Men	40.74	3.70	11.11	3.70	11.11	3.70	0.00	3.70	11.11	11.11
Women	11.11	0.00	0.00	0.00	55.56	0.00	0.00	0.00	22.22	11.11
7-8/8-7										
Men	16.11	2.74	9.12	3.34	30.40	3.04	0.00	0.00	15.20	20.06
Women	7.48	0.00	4.67	0.93	75.70	0.00	0.00	0.00	9.35	1.87
7-9/9-7										
Men	36.11	8.33	5.56	0.00	22.22	0.00	0.00	0.00	0.00	27.78
Women	16.67	16.67	33.33	0.00	16.67	16.67	0.00	0.00	0.00	0.00
7-0/0-7										
Men	40.00	0.00	30.00	0.00	0.00	10.00	0.00	0.00	20.00	0.00
Women	0.00	0.00	16.67	0.00	50.00	16.67	0.00	0.00	16.67	0.00
Spike 8										
Men	3.85	7.69	11.54	0.00	23.08	7.69	3.85	0.00	3.85	38.46
Women	11.76	17.65	11.76	0.00	23.53	5.88	5.88	0.00	5.88	17.65
8-9/9-8										
Men	13.06	12.61	17.57	0.00	14.86	3.15	0.00	0.00	0.00	38.74
Women	13.95	23.26	10.47	3.49	37.21	0.00	0.00	0.00	0.00	11.63
8-0/0-8										
Men	33.33	0.00	16.67	16.67	0.00	0.00	0.00	0.00	33.33	0.00
Women	15.79	5.26	31.58	5.26	42.11	0.00	0.00	0.00	0.00	0.00
Spike 9										
Men	21.65	14.17	11.02	1.57	10.24	5.91	2.76	1.97	0.00	30.71
Women	22.58	24.73	10.75	0.00	17.20	4.30	3.23	1.08	0.00	16.13
9-0/0-9										
Men	50.00	0.00	50.00	0.00	0.00	0.00	0.00	0.00	0.00	0.00
Women	0.00	0.00	0.00	0.00	100.00	0.00	0.00	0.00	0.00	0.00
Spike 0										
Men	22.73	4.55	13.64	4.55	0.00	4.55	0.00	31.82	18.18	0.00
Women	14.71	2.94	5.88	5.88	32.35	2.94	0.00	2.94	32.35	0.00
Total										
Men	14.19	3.48	6.23	1.32	19.98	5.31	2.02	2.54	15.33	29.60
Women	8.93	5.36	5.28	1.79	50.80	2.87	2.17	0.47	11.61	10.72

of MMPI codetypes. First, all MMPI-2 codetypes did not occur equally often. Some codetypes are very common (1-3/3-1, 2-3/3-2, 2-7/7-2, and 6-8/8-6), whereas other codetypes are very rare (1-0/0-1, 2-9/9-2, 3-0/0-3, 5-0/0-5, 9-0/0-9, etc.).

Second, there is surprisingly little variation in the frequency with which the codetypes occurred as a function of gender. Several codetypes occurred about twice as often in men (1-2/2-1, 7-8/8-7), while others occurred about twice as often in women (2-3/3-2, Spike 5). There appear to be fewer gender differ-ences in the frequency of MMPI-2 codetypes than MMPI codetypes. Some codetypes that occurred more frequently in women on the MMPI (Spike 3, 4-6/6-4, Spike 6), actually were more frequent in men on the MMPI-2. In a similar reversal in the frequency of occurrence, 1-2/2-1 codetypes were more common in men on the MMPI and in women on the MMPI-2.

Finally, WNL profiles are the most common codetype in both men (36.26 percent) and women (25.70 percent).

TABLE 7.4   Frequency of MMPI-2 Codetypes in Psychiatric Inpatients and Outpatients (Caldwell, 1997a)

Codetype	MEN		WOMEN		TOTAL	
	N	%	N	%	N	%
Spike *1*	268	1.67	215	1.12	483	1.37
1-2/2-1	671	4.18	1,005	5.25	1,676	4.76
1-3/3-1	2,035	12.67	3,188	16.65	5,223	14.83
1-4/4-1	97	0.60	127	0.66	224	0.64
1-5/5-1	19	0.12	126	0.66	145	0.41
1-6/6-1	188	1.17	195	1.02	383	1.09
1-7/7-1	113	0.70	89	0.46	202	0.57
1-8/8-1	272	1.69	236	1.23	508	1.44
1-9/9-1	77	0.48	81	0.42	158	0.45
1-0/0-1	33	0.21	32	0.17	65	0.18
Spike *2*	212	1.32	190	0.99	402	1.14
2-3/3-2	909	5.66	1,932	10.09	2,841	8.07
2-4/4-2	313	1.95	542	2.83	855	2.43
2-5/5-2	49	0.31	64	0.33	113	0.32
2-6/6-2	399	2.48	705	3.68	1,104	3.14
2-7/7-2	888	5.53	1,046	5.46	1,934	5.49
2-8/8-2	358	2.23	717	3.75	1,075	3.05
2-9/9-2	12	0.07	24	0.13	36	0.10
2-0/0-2	339	2.11	326	1.70	665	1.89
Spike *3*	372	2.32	412	2.15	784	2.23
3-4/4-3	298	1.85	454	2.37	752	2.14
3-5/5-3	42	0.26	72	0.38	114	0.32
3-6/6-3	311	1.94	423	2.21	734	2.08
3-7/7-3	239	1.49	203	1.06	442	1.26
3-8/8-3	222	1.38	217	1.13	439	1.25
3-9/9-3	38	0.24	78	0.41	116	0.33
3-0/0-3	7	0.04	7	0.04	14	0.04
Spike *4*	685	4.26	583	3.05	1,268	3.60
4-5/5-4	79	0.49	125	0.65	204	0.58
4-6/6-4	565	3.52	539	2.82	1,104	3.14
4-7/7-4	236	1.47	210	1.10	446	1.27
4-8/8-4	339	2.11	353	1.84	692	1.97
4-9/9-4	237	1.48	203	1.06	440	1.25
4-0/0-4	41	0.26	29	0.15	70	0.20
Spike *5*	294	1.83	1,071	5.59	1,365	3.88
5-6/6-5	84	0.52	70	0.37	154	0.44
5-7/7-5	51	0.32	17	0.09	68	0.19
5-8/8-5	23	0.14	53	0.28	76	0.22
5-9/9-5	44	0.27	143	0.75	187	0.53
5-0/0-5	27	0.17	15	0.08	42	0.12
Spike *6*	494	3.08	415	2.17	909	2.58
6-7/7-6	315	1.96	178	0.93	493	1.40
6-8/8-6	1,087	6.77	842	4.40	1,929	5.48

Codetype	MEN		WOMEN		TOTAL	
	N	%	N	%	N	%
6-9/9-6	207	1.29	149	0.78	356	1.01
6-0/0-6	89	0.55	50	0.26	139	0.39
Spike 7	119	0.74	66	0.34	185	0.53
7-8/8-7	858	5.34	405	2.12	1,263	3.59
7-9/9-7	58	0.36	40	0.21	98	0.28
7-0/0-7	108	0.67	39	0.20	147	0.42
Spike 8	87	0.54	58	0.30	145	0.41
8-9/9-8	256	1.59	168	0.88	424	1.20
8-0/0-8	65	0.40	31	0.16	96	0.27
Spike 9	590	3.67	435	2.27	1,025	2.91
9-0/0-9	6	0.04	2	0.01	8	0.02
Spike 0	240	1.49	148	0.77	388	1.10
Any Codetype	16,065	63.74	19,143	74.30	35,208	69.08
WNL	9,138	36.26	6,620	25.70	15,758	30.92
Total	25,203	100.00	25,763	100.00	50,966	100.00

A simple rule that describes the changes on the MMPI-2 is that codetypes involving Scales *3* (Hysteria) and *6* (Paranoia) have increased in frequency and codetypes involving Scales *4* (Psychopathic Deviate) and *8* (Schizophrenia) have decreased in frequency. These Clinical scales are the ones in which the change from linear T scores on the MMPI to uniform T scores on the MMPI-2 were the largest, which produced the resulting changes in the frequency with which specific codetypes occur.

Table 7.5 provides the frequency of low points on the MMPI-2 Clinical scales for the Caldwell (1997a) clinical dataset. There are three major differences between the frequency of low points on the MMPI (Table 7.3) and the MMPI-2 (Table 7.5): (1) Scale *5* (Masculinity-Femininity) is much less likely to be a low point on the MMPI-2 in women; (2) Scale *5* is almost as twice as likely to be a low point on the MMPI-2 in men; and (3) Scale *0* (Social Introversion) is much less likely to be a low point on the MMPI-2 in men and more likely in women. Low points on Scale *5* of the MMPI-2 now occur almost equally often in men and women, whereas low points on Scale *5* of the MMPI occurred over twice as often

in women. Other than these three changes, it appears that the same low points on the MMPI-2 tend to be associated with specific codetypes as were found on the MMPI. Again, clinicians are encouraged to consult Table 7.5 for every profile to determine whether a person's low-point scale is one that occurs commonly, and incorporate that information into the profile interpretation.

CONCORDANCE BETWEEN MMPI-2 AND MMPI CODETYPES

One of the critical issues with the advent of the MMPI-2 is the concordance between the MMPI-2 and MMPI codetypes (i.e., how frequently the MMPI-2 and MMPI codetype would be similar or identical for a specific client). Two general comments need to be made about codetype concordance before examining the data on this issue. First, if the rationale for revising the MMPI is valid in that the items and norms on the MMPI do not accurately reflect our contemporary society (see Chapter 1), then it makes little sense to expect the MMPI-2 and the MMPI to have perfect concordance. In fact, perfect concordance

TABLE 7.5 Frequency of Low-Point Scales for MMPI-2 Codetypes by Gender in Psychiatric Inpatients and Outpatients (Caldwell, 1997a)

CODETYPE	1(Hs)	2(D)	3(Hy)	4(Pd)	5(Mf)	6(Pa)	7(Pt)	8(Sc)	9(Ma)	0(Si)
Spike 1										
Men	0.00	1.80	0.72	7.19	37.41	10.43	5.04	2.88	14.39	20.14
Women	0.00	3.62	0.90	9.95	13.57	20.81	8.60	1.81	17.65	23.08
1-2/2-1										
Men	0.00	0.00	0.44	7.71	41.48	7.86	1.31	0.87	36.97	3.35
Women	0.00	0.00	0.20	10.27	33.95	8.51	0.68	1.17	41.10	4.11
1-3/3-1										
Men	0.00	0.18	0.00	4.64	32.46	5.51	1.01	1.01	28.24	26.95
Women	0.00	0.39	0.00	6.43	26.52	7.48	1.63	0.84	22.69	34.01
1-4/4-1										
Men	0.00	0.00	0.99	0.00	40.59	10.89	3.96	1.98	16.83	24.75
Women	0.00	0.76	0.76	0.00	25.76	11.36	1.52	0.76	19.70	39.39
1-5/5-1										
Men	0.00	0.00	0.00	5.26	0.00	26.32	5.26	10.53	26.32	26.32
Women	0.00	2.21	1.47	11.03	0.00	32.35	9.56	2.21	14.71	26.47
1-6/6-1										
Men	0.00	2.63	0.00	8.42	38.42	0.00	5.79	0.53	21.58	22.63
Women	0.00	2.01	1.01	11.56	35.68	0.00	3.52	1.01	18.09	27.14
1-7/7-1										
Men	0.00	0.00	0.83	9.17	46.67	5.83	0.00	0.83	29.17	7.50
Women	0.00	1.10	1.10	15.38	52.75	7.69	0.00	0.00	12.09	9.89
1-8/8-1										
Men	0.00	0.00	0.33	7.89	59.54	5.92	0.66	0.00	15.79	9.87
Women	0.00	1.95	0.39	11.33	48.83	5.08	0.39	0.00	12.11	19.92
1-9/9-1										
Men	0.00	1.30	0.00	5.19	49.35	11.69	3.90	0.00	0.00	28.57
Women	0.00	4.88	0.00	8.54	14.63	14.63	1.22	0.00	0.00	56.10
1-0/0-1										
Men	0.00	3.03	0.00	9.09	27.27	12.12	3.03	3.03	42.42	0.00
Women	0.00	0.00	0.00	9.38	28.13	15.63	0.00	0.00	46.88	0.00
Spike 2										
Men	5.58	0.00	4.19	5.12	22.79	9.77	2.79	8.37	37.21	4.19
Women	6.28	0.00	6.28	7.85	23.04	7.85	1.57	3.66	37.70	5.76
2-3/3-2										
Men	0.00	0.00	0.00	3.10	23.02	4.07	0.43	1.39	56.21	11.78
Women	0.00	0.00	0.00	2.85	38.57	3.00	0.10	0.66	43.55	11.28
2-4/4-2										
Men	11.99	0.00	3.79	0.00	23.03	2.84	0.32	1.89	46.37	9.78
Women	4.05	0.00	3.31	0.00	50.64	2.95	0.37	0.37	32.78	5.52
2-5/5-2										
Men	12.24	0.00	6.12	2.04	0.00	8.16	0.00	4.08	57.14	10.20
Women	10.61	0.00	9.09	10.61	0.00	22.73	0.00	4.55	30.30	12.12
2-6/6-2										
Men	7.33	0.00	3.91	3.18	29.58	0.00	0.24	2.44	48.66	4.65
Women	3.35	0.00	2.37	3.35	43.58	0.00	0.14	0.28	41.76	5.17

CODETYPE	1(Hs)	2(D)	3(Hy)	4(Pd)	5(Mf)	6(Pa)	7(Pt)	8(Sc)	9(Ma)	0(Si)
2-7/7-2										
Men	3.69	0.00	2.13	2.68	22.26	2.24	0.00	0.56	63.65	2.80
Women	1.04	0.00	1.52	4.17	43.28	2.84	0.00	0.09	44.79	2.27
2-8/8-2										
Men	2.65	0.00	5.03	2.38	42.59	3.70	0.00	0.00	42.33	1.32
Women	1.21	0.00	2.83	2.56	53.10	1.89	0.13	0.00	33.96	4.31
2-9/9-2										
Men	0.00	0.00	0.00	8.33	58.33	8.33	0.00	0.00	0.00	25.00
Women	0.00	0.00	12.00	12.00	20.00	16.00	4.00	0.00	0.00	36.00
2-0/0-2										
Men	7.89	0.00	6.73	3.80	11.40	4.68	0.58	1.17	63.74	0.00
Women	4.28	0.00	7.95	4.89	24.46	3.67	0.00	0.92	53.82	0.00
Spike *3*										
Men	0.78	2.61	0.00	1.57	12.53	6.53	3.13	8.09	24.54	40.21
Women	0.71	2.86	0.00	2.86	17.14	5.71	4.76	6.19	17.62	42.14
3-4/4-3										
Men	0.33	1.63	0.00	0.00	16.99	4.90	0.98	1.63	30.07	43.46
Women	0.21	0.64	0.00	0.00	38.68	2.56	1.50	0.85	20.09	35.47
3-5/5-3										
Men	0.00	4.76	0.00	0.00	0.00	4.76	4.76	7.14	23.81	54.76
Women	0.00	2.53	0.00	2.53	0.00	24.05	3.80	1.27	13.92	51.90
3-6/6-3										
Men	0.96	0.96	0.00	0.64	23.64	0.00	1.28	1.60	27.80	43.13
Women	0.23	0.47	0.00	3.04	43.09	0.00	1.17	1.41	13.58	37.00
3-7/7-3										
Men	0.41	0.00	0.00	2.89	24.79	2.48	0.00	1.24	44.63	23.55
Women	0.00	0.49	0.00	2.45	54.90	2.45	0.00	0.00	20.59	19.12
3-8/8-3										
Men	0.00	0.80	0.00	2.79	43.43	3.98	0.40	0.00	23.90	24.70
Women	0.00	0.00	0.00	1.79	49.33	4.93	0.00	0.00	17.49	26.46
3-9/9-3										
Men	2.63	7.89	0.00	0.00	15.79	10.53	2.63	0.00	0.00	60.53
Women	0.00	2.56	0.00	5.13	25.64	5.13	2.56	0.00	0.00	58.97
3-0/0-3										
Men	0.00	0.00	0.00	0.00	28.57	14.29	0.00	0.00	57.14	0.00
Women	0.00	0.00	0.00	0.00	71.43	0.00	0.00	0.00	28.57	0.00
Spike *4*										
Men	10.76	5.96	3.63	0.00	18.75	3.63	2.91	1.16	13.37	39.83
Women	9.49	5.42	4.07	0.00	17.97	5.76	6.10	3.56	12.54	35.08
4-5/5-4										
Men	17.72	2.53	5.06	0.00	0.00	7.59	2.53	1.27	25.32	37.97
Women	9.45	6.30	12.60	0.00	0.00	7.09	8.66	0.79	8.66	46.46
4-6/6-4										
Men	19.76	1.75	7.69	0.00	20.98	0.00	1.92	0.87	20.45	26.57
Women	10.48	2.02	6.99	0.00	42.10	0.00	2.02	0.55	10.11	25.74

(continued)

TABLE 7.5 Frequency of Low-Point Scales for MMPI-2 Codetypes by Gender in Psychiatric Inpatients and Outpatients (Caldwell, 1997a) (continued)

CODETYPE	1(Hs)	2(D)	3(Hy)	4(Pd)	5(Mf)	6(Pa)	7(Pt)	8(Sc)	9(Ma)	0(Si)
4-7/7-4										
Men	18.49	1.26	6.30	0.00	24.37	1.68	0.00	0.00	26.47	21.43
Women	8.06	0.95	7.58	0.00	51.66	1.42	0.00	0.00	14.69	15.64
4-8/8-4										
Men	15.07	2.74	8.49	0.00	38.08	1.37	0.00	0.00	15.34	18.90
Women	8.15	2.17	10.87	0.00	36.41	2.99	0.27	0.00	13.32	25.82
4-9/9-4										
Men	11.48	9.43	6.97	0.00	27.87	3.28	2.87	0.41	0.00	37.70
Women	15.61	10.73	11.71	0.00	16.59	0.00	0.98	0.00	0.00	44.39
4-0/0-4										
Men	11.63	2.33	25.58	0.00	20.93	2.33	2.33	0.00	34.88	0.00
Women	20.69	0.00	41.38	0.00	24.14	0.00	0.00	0.00	13.79	0.00
Spike 5										
Men	17.63	12.88	4.07	4.75	0.00	6.44	4.07	4.07	19.32	26.78
Women	4.77	9.63	10.46	3.39	0.00	15.50	11.19	4.59	8.26	32.20
5-6/6-5										
Men	30.95	8.33	4.76	0.00	0.00	0.00	3.57	2.38	19.05	30.95
Women	9.46	5.41	31.08	8.11	0.00	0.00	6.76	2.70	12.16	24.32
5-7/7-5										
Men	33.33	1.96	9.80	5.88	0.00	5.88	0.00	1.96	29.41	11.76
Women	0.00	5.56	27.78	11.11	0.00	27.78	0.00	0.00	11.11	16.67
5-8/8-5										
Men	30.43	4.35	13.04	4.35	0.00	4.35	0.00	0.00	13.04	30.43
Women	4.11	17.81	35.62	9.59	0.00	6.85	1.37	0.00	8.22	16.44
5-9/9-5										
Men	15.91	22.73	2.27	0.00	0.00	4.55	2.27	2.27	0.00	50.00
Women	4.79	19.86	30.82	7.53	0.00	10.27	4.11	0.00	0.00	22.60
5-0/0-5										
Men	44.44	0.00	11.11	0.00	0.00	3.70	0.00	3.70	37.04	0.00
Women	20.00	0.00	46.67	0.00	0.00	13.33	0.00	6.67	13.33	0.00
Spike 6										
Men	13.91	8.06	6.25	3.43	10.89	0.00	3.83	7.06	15.93	30.65
Women	11.75	4.32	7.67	3.84	24.22	0.00	4.32	3.84	11.99	28.06
6-7/7-6										
Men	12.58	1.26	5.97	4.40	29.87	0.00	0.00	0.31	31.76	13.84
Women	2.81	1.69	6.74	5.06	56.18	0.00	0.00	0.00	19.10	8.43
6-8/8-6										
Men	4.84	1.33	10.51	2.31	58.44	0.00	0.35	0.00	15.14	7.08
Women	3.74	2.86	10.15	3.74	48.47	0.00	0.49	0.00	16.55	13.99
6-9/9-6										
Men	12.26	12.26	15.09	0.94	20.75	0.00	3.30	0.47	0.00	34.91
Women	10.90	10.26	17.31	3.85	12.82	0.00	1.92	0.00	0.00	42.95
6-0/0-6										
Men	28.89	0.00	16.67	3.33	13.33	0.00	0.00	1.11	36.67	0.00
Women	18.00	0.00	16.00	4.00	34.00	0.00	6.00	0.00	22.00	0.00

CODETYPE	1(Hs)	2(D)	3(Hy)	4(Pd)	5(Mf)	6(Pa)	7(Pt)	8(Sc)	9(Ma)	0(Si)
Spike 7										
Men	10.08	1.68	14.29	4.20	19.33	5.88	0.00	5.88	26.05	12.61
Women	18.18	1.52	10.61	4.55	31.82	6.06	0.00	0.00	19.70	7.58
7-8/8-7										
Men	5.30	0.76	9.51	3.89	44.11	2.92	0.00	0.00	27.35	6.16
Women	1.67	0.72	9.31	4.77	52.27	2.86	0.00	0.00	18.14	10.26
7-9/9-7										
Men	13.79	6.90	20.69	1.72	17.24	6.90	0.00	0.00	0.00	32.76
Women	7.50	0.00	15.00	5.00	30.00	0.00	0.00	0.00	0.00	42.50
7-0/0-7										
Men	12.84	1.83	16.51	3.67	7.34	5.50	0.00	0.00	52.29	0.00
Women	12.82	0.00	17.95	7.69	30.77	2.56	0.00	0.00	28.21	0.00
Spike 8										
Men	8.99	8.99	15.73	3.37	25.84	10.11	3.37	0.00	6.74	16.85
Women	11.67	8.33	26.67	8.33	15.00	8.33	0.00	0.00	11.67	10.00
8-9/9-8										
Men	6.23	8.65	20.76	2.42	42.56	3.81	0.35	0.00	0.00	15.22
Women	4.37	10.38	24.59	6.56	12.02	2.73	2.73	0.00	0.00	36.61
8-0/0-8										
Men	13.64	0.00	22.73	3.03	18.18	4.55	0.00	0.00	37.88	0.00
Women	0.00	0.00	38.71	0.00	22.58	3.23	0.00	0.00	35.48	0.00
Spike 9										
Men	6.61	17.29	8.14	1.02	19.83	7.63	3.56	1.86	0.00	34.07
Women	11.01	10.32	10.09	2.52	8.49	5.50	5.50	1.61	0.00	44.95
9-0/0-9										
Men	33.33	0.00	33.33	0.00	16.67	16.67	0.00	0.00	0.00	0.00
Women	50.00	0.00	0.00	0.00	0.00	50.00	0.00	0.00	0.00	0.00
Spike 0										
Men	12.45	0.83	17.84	7.47	11.20	8.71	2.90	6.64	31.95	0.00
Women	9.33	0.67	25.33	5.33	17.33	7.33	2.67	6.67	25.33	0.00
Total										
Men	6.41	2.58	4.82	3.09	28.63	3.99	1.38	1.56	28.40	19.13
Women	3.12	2.16	4.53	4.27	32.12	5.22	2.09	1.19	23.73	21.57

would suggest that there was little reason to revise the MMPI.

Second, it is not clear whether the MMPI or the MMPI-2 should serve as the "gold" standard against which the other test is evaluated. That is, if the MMPI-2 and MMPI codetype do not agree for a specific client, is the MMPI-2 or the MMPI inaccurate? It is typically assumed that the MMPI should serve as the standard, but it is equally plausible that the MMPI-2 could be the standard.

There are two different methods for developing data that can be used for assessing concordance between the MMPI-2 and the MMPI. First, MMPI data can be quickly transformed to simulate the MMPI-2 by dropping the 13 items that were not retained on the MMPI-2 and converting the raw scores into the appropriate T scores. This procedure assumes that the changes made at the item level on the MMPI-2 will not have a systematic effect on the data. It also is possible to score both the MMPI-2 and the MMPI if

Form AX, the form used to collect the restandardization data, was administered since it contains all of the items on the MMPI and the MMPI-2.

Second, the MMPI and the MMPI-2 can be administered to the same clients with some interval of time between the two test administrations (cf. Harrell, Honaker, & Parnell, 1992). This latter method has been used infrequently, because it requires a significant amount of time and effort on the part of the clinician. It also tends to confound test-retest reliability changes with the differences between the MMPI and the MMPI-2.

Table 7.6 provides the concordance between specific MMPI-2 and MMPI codetypes in the sample of psychiatric inpatients and outpatients collected by Hedlund and Won Cho (1979). These MMPI data were transformed to simulate the MMPI-2 by dropping the 13 items that were not retained on the MMPI-2 and converting the raw scores into the appropriate T scores. The left-hand column indicates the specific MMPI-2 codetype and the next columns report the concordance rates on the MMPI by gender and then for the entire sample. For instance, there were 92 men with Spike *1* codetypes on the MMPI-2 in this sample of psychiatric patients, and 64.1 percent of them also had a Spike *1* codetype on the MMPI.

The concordance rate within each gender is reported twice for each codetype: first with the requirement that the two highest Clinical scales be in the same order, and second allowing the two highest Clinical scales to be in either order. For example, there were 218 men with *1-2/2-1* codetypes on the MMPI-2. When it was required that these men have the same codetype on the MMPI-2 and the MMPI (i.e., if the man had a *1-2* codetype on the MMPI-2, then he had to have a *1-2* codetype on the MMPI), the concordance rate was 67.0 percent. When Scales *1* and *2* were allowed to be in either order as the two highest Clinical scales, the concordance rate in these men was 81.7 percent.

The average concordance rate across all MMPI-2 codetypes was around 50 percent when the two highest Clinical scales had to be in the same order, and around 65 percent when the two highest Clinical scales could be in either order. Several codetypes (*2-4/4-2, 2-8/8-2, 4-8/8-4,* and *4-9/9-4*) had very high concordance rates in men, whereas a different set of codetypes (Spike *2,* Spike *3,* Spike *4, 4-8/8-4, 4-9/9-4,* Spike *7,* and Spike *0*) had very high concordance rates in women. There also were a number of codetypes that had very low concordance rates: *1-6/6-1* and *2-6/6-2* codetypes in men and women, and *2-0/0-2, 4-0/0-4,* and *6-9/9-6* codetypes in men.

Butcher et al. (1989) provided information on the concordance between the MMPI-2 and the MMPI using Form AX in a sample of 423 psychiatric patients (Table G.4, p. 110). They reported concordance rates for specific codetypes that were very similar to those seen in Table 7.6, which would suggest that the simulation of MMPI-2 data provided in Table 7.6 is reasonably accurate. Thus, clinicians could use the data in Table 7.6 as a good approximation of the concordance to be expected between the MMPI-2 and the MMPI in psychiatric samples.

Table 7.7 (p. 308) provides similar information as Table 7.6 on the concordance between simulated MMPI-2 and actual MMPI codetypes in the sample of psychiatric inpatients and outpatients collected by Hedlund and Won Cho (1979), except that now MMPI codetypes are reported in the left-hand column and the concordance rates are reported for the MMPI-2. A quick perusal of Tables 7.6 and 7.7 will reveal that concordance rates for specific codetypes can vary drastically depending on whether the MMPI-2 or the MMPI is used as the criterion.

For example, *4-8/8-4* codetypes on the MMPI have a concordance rate of 35 percent on the MMPI-2 in men and women (Table 7.7), whereas *4-8/8-4* codetypes on the MMPI-2 have a concordance rate over 90 percent on the MMPI in men and women (Table 7.6). Thus, *4-8/8-4* codetypes on the MMPI-2 should be a very homogeneous subset of *4-8/8-4* codetypes on the MMPI, and it would be expected that *4-8/8-4* codetypes on the MMPI-2 should have more reliable correlates since the codetype is more homogeneous.

The opposite pattern for concordance rates between the MMPI-2 and the MMPI also can be found. For example, *1-3/3-1* codetypes on the MMPI have a concordance rate over 90 percent on the MMPI-2 in men and women (Table 7.7), whereas *1-3/3-1* codetypes on the MMPI-2 have a concordance rate around 50 percent on the MMPI in men and women (Table 7.6). Thus, *1-3/3-1* codetypes on the MMPI-2 are a more heterogeneous subset of *1-3/3-1* codetypes

TABLE 7.6   Concordance between MMPI-2 and MMPI Codetypes

		MMPI CODETYPE						
		Men			Women		Total	
		TWO HIGHEST SCALES			TWO HIGHEST SCALES		TWO HIGHEST SCALES	
MMPI-2 Codetype	N	Same Order	Either Order	N	Same Order	Either Order	Same Order	Either Order
Spike 1	92	64.1%	–	20	60.0%	–	63.4%	–
1-2/2-1	218	67.0	81.7%	93	50.6	50.6%	62.1	72.4%
1-3/3-1	295	34.2	47.8	163	48.5	57.7	39.3	51.3
1-4/4-1	71	49.3	64.8	28	21.4	53.6	41.4	61.6
1-6/6-1	60	20.0	26.7	37	21.6	21.6	20.6	24.8
1-8/8-1	83	50.6	84.3	36	38.9	50.0	47.1	73.9
Spike 2	128	53.1	–	38	81.6	–	59.6	–
2-3/3-2	134	28.4	53.7	130	50.8	56.9	39.4	55.3
2-4/4-2	228	81.6	92.1	115	47.8	61.7	70.3	81.9
2-6/6-2	107	21.5	43.9	86	31.4	32.6	25.9	38.9
2-7/7-2	242	63.2	78.9	177	46.9	52.0	56.3	67.5
2-8/8-2	116	85.3	94.8	103	38.8	63.1	63.4	79.9
2-0/0-2	210	11.9	21.9	86	40.7	51.2	20.3	30.4
Spike 3	37	48.7	–	29	82.8	–	63.7	–
3-4/4-3	107	34.6	56.1	67	35.8	67.2	35.1	60.4
Spike 4	416	68.5	–	88	100.0	–	74.0	–
4-6/6-4	278	30.9	56.5	133	60.2	85.7	40.4	65.9
4-7/7-4	84	65.5	76.2	19	36.8	42.1	60.2	69.9
4-8/8-4	159	83.6	97.5	81	92.6	98.8	86.6	97.9
4-9/9-4	232	75.0	89.7	87	75.9	96.6	75.2	91.6
4-0/0-4	51	2.0	15.7	16	37.5	56.3	10.5	25.4
Spike 5	47	53.2	–	75	73.3	–	65.6	–
Spike 6	80	50.0	–	36	75.0	–	57.8	–
6-8/8-6	654	23.7	58.0	224	52.2	82.6	31.0	64.3
6-9/9-6	174	29.9	37.9	87	54.0	66.7	37.9	47.5
Spike 7	11	45.8	–	12	100.0	–	74.1	–
7-8/8-7	221	58.8	81.4	105	54.3	74.3	57.4	79.1
Spike 8	22	36.4	–	28	46.4	–	42.0	–
8-9/9-8	149	60.4	83.9	65	75.4	87.7	65.0	85.1
Spike 9	256	63.7	–	70	70.7	–	65.2	–
Spike 0	97	48.5	–	25	92.6	–	57.5	–
Mean		48.7	64.0		57.9	62.3	51.9	63.1
Weighted Mean		49.2	65.1		55.6	65.7	51.4	65.4
N		5,059	3,873		2,359	1,938	7,418	5,811

TABLE 7.7   Concordance between MMPI and MMPI-2 Codetypes

MMPI Codetype		MMPI-2 CODETYPE							
		Men			Women			Total	
		TWO HIGHEST SCALES			TWO HIGHEST SCALES			TWO HIGHEST SCALES	
	N	Same Order	Either Order	N	Same Order	Either Order		Same Order	Either Order
Spike *1*	66	89.4%	–	23	52.2%	–		79.8%	–
1-2/2-1	299	48.8	59.5%	50	78.0	82.0%		53.0	62.7%
1-3/3-1	144	70.1	97.9	97	81.4	96.9		74.6	97.5
1-4/4-1	112	31.3	41.1	28	21.4	53.6		29.3	43.6
1-6/6-1	16	75.0	100.0	10	80.0	80.0		76.9	92.3
1-8/8-1	160	26.3	43.8	28	50.0	64.3		29.8	46.9
Spike *2*	141	48.2	–	76	40.8	–		45.6	–
2-3/3-2	93	40.9	77.4	79	83.5	93.7		60.5	84.9
2-4/4-2	458	40.6	45.9	134	33.6	53.0		39.0	47.5
2-6/6-2	100	23.0	71.0	60	45.0	48.3		31.3	62.5
2-7/7-2	292	52.4	65.4	98	84.7	93.9		60.5	72.6
2-8/8-2	338	29.3	32.5	122	32.8	53.3		30.2	38.0
2-0/0-2	56	44.6	82.1	55	63.6	80.0		54.0	81.1
Spike *3*	37	48.7	–	29	82.8	–		63.7	–
3-4/4-3	88	42.0	65.9	80	30.0	56.3		36.3	61.3
Spike *4*	315	90.5	–	172	51.2	–		76.6	–
4-6/6-4	192	44.8	81.8	166	48.7	62.7		46.6	72.9
4-7/7-4	134	41.0	47.8	21	33.3	38.1		40.0	46.5
4-8/8-4	438	30.4	35.4	226	33.2	35.4		31.4	35.4
4-9/9-4	373	46.6	55.8	130	50.8	64.6		47.7	58.1
4-0/0-4	14	35.7	85.7	18	33.3	50.0		34.4	65.6
Spike *5*	30	83.3	–	72	76.4	–		78.4	–
Spike *6*	49	81.6	–	55	49.1	–		64.4	–
6-8/8 6	440	35.2	86.1	246	47.6	75.2		39.6	82.2
6-9/9-6	69	75.4	95.7	63	74.6	92.1		75.0	94.0
Spike *7*	18	61.1	–	19	63.2	–		62.2	–
7-8/8-7	341	38.1	53.1	109	52.3	71.6		41.5	57.6
Spike *8*	12	66.7	–	28	46.4	–		52.5	–
8-9/9-8	216	41.7	57.9	90	54.4	63.3		45.4	59.5
Spike *9*	177	92.1	–	99	70.7	–		84.4	–
Spike *0*	47	100.0	–	50	50.0	–		74.2	–
Mean		54.0	65.8		54.7	67.1		53.5	64.9
Weighted Mean		47.5	58.4		52.4	65.9		49.1	60.7
N		5,265	4,373		2,533	1,910		7,798	6,283

on the MMPI, and it would be expected that *1-3/3-1* codetypes on the MMPI-2 should have less reliable correlates since the codetype is more heterogeneous.

Despite these differences in concordance rates between specific codetypes depending upon whether the MMPI-2 or the MMPI is used as the criterion, the average concordance rate is around 50 percent if the two highest Clinical scales are required to be in the same order, and around 60 percent if the two highest Clinical scales can be in either order.

Another way of examining the concordance between the MMPI-2 and the MMPI is to require that the specific codetype be "well defined," that is, that there be at least a 5 T point difference between the scales in the codetype and the next highest Clinical scale. Such a requirement is thought to produce a codetype that would be relatively stable over time if the client were to retake the MMPI-2 or the MMPI.

Table 7.8 provides the concordance rates for "well defined" codetypes when the MMPI-2 is used

TABLE 7.8 Concordance between MMPI-2 and MMPI Codetypes for Well Defined Codetypes

		MMPI CODETYPE						
		Men			Women		Total	
		TWO HIGHEST SCALES			TWO HIGHEST SCALES		TWO HIGHEST SCALES	
MMPI-2 Codetype	N	Same Order	Either Order	N	Same Order	Either Order	Same Order	Either Order
Spike *1*	20	80.0%	–	1	100.0%	–	81.0%	–
1-2/2-1	24	100.0	100.0%	8	75.0	75.0%	93.8	93.8%
1-3/3-1	24	83.3	91.7	17	94.1	94.1	87.8	92.7
Spike *2*	53	71.7	–	27	100.0	–	81.3	–
2-3/3-2	6	66.7	83.3	14	92.9	92.9	85.0	90.0
2-4/4-2	36	100.0	100.0	10	90.0	90.0	97.8	97.8
2-7/7-2	34	100.0	100.0	25	76.0	76.0	89.8	89.8
2-0/0-2	70	21.4	21.4	29	93.1	93.1	42.4	42.4
Spike *3*	5	100.0	–	10	100.0	–	100.0	–
3-4/4-3	5	80.0	100.0	5	60.0	80.0	70.0	90.0
Spike *4*	200	70.0	–	56	100.0	–	76.5	–
4-6/6-4	20	80.0	90.0	14	100.0	100.0	88.2	94.1
4-8/8-4	19	100.0	100.0	12	100.0	100.0	100.0	100.0
4-9/9-4	49	93.9	93.9	20	100.0	100.0	95.7	95.7
4-0/0-4	13	7.7	7.7	7	85.7	85.7	35.0	35.0
Spike *5*	20	70.0	–	36	100.0	–	89.3	–
Spike *6*	23	78.3	–	22	90.9	–	84.4	–
6-8/8-6	111	25.2	86.5	35	80.0	94.3	38.4	88.4
6-9/9-6	18	72.2	72.2	10	100.0	100.0	82.1	82.1
Spike *7*	5	80.0	–	5	100.0	–	90.0	–
7-8/8-7	26	100.0	100.0	14	92.7	92.7	97.4	97.4
8-9/9-8	21	95.2	100.0	12	100.0	100.0	97.0	100.0
Spike *9*	130	81.5	–	51	94.1	–	85.1	–
Mean		76.4	83.1		92.4	91.6	82.1	86.0
Weighted Mean		69.4	80.0		93.4	92.2	77.1	84.0
N		932	476		440	232	1,372	708

as the criterion, and Table 7.9 provides similar information when the MMPI is used as the criterion. Two conclusions are apparent when Tables 7.8 and 7.9 are contrasted with Tables 7.6 and 7.7, respectively: (1) Concordance rates have increased dramatically and now average around 80 percent in men and over 90 percent in women, and (2) almost three-fourths of the profiles do not meet this criterion.

Graham (1990a) reported similar concordance rates for well defined codetypes in the Butcher et al. (1989) sample of psychiatric patients: 82 percent for male psychiatric patients and 97 percent for the female patients. Graham did not indicate how many profiles did not meet the criterion of being well defined. Again, it seems that the simulation of MMPI-2 data based on the MMPIs collected by Hedlund and

TABLE 7.9   Concordance between MMPI and MMPI-2 Codetypes for Well Defined Codetypes

		MMPI-2 CODETYPE							
		Men			Women			Total	
		TWO HIGHEST SCALES			TWO HIGHEST SCALES			TWO HIGHEST SCALES	
MMPI Codetype	N	Same Order	Either Order	N	Same Order	Either Order		Same Order	Either Order
Spike *1*	19	84.2%	–	3	33.3%	–		77.3%	–
1-2/2-1	28	85.7		5	100.0			87.9	87.9%
			85.7%			100.0%			
1-3/3-1	22	90.9	100.0	16	100.0	100.0		94.7	100.0
Spike *2*	64	59.4	–	30	90.0	–		69.1	–
2-3/3-2	6	66.7	66.7	13	100.0	100.0		89.5	89.5
2-4/4-2	63	30.2	30.2	9	100.0	100.0		38.9	38.9
2-7/7-2	53	64.2	64.2	19	100.0	100.0		73.6	73.6
2-8/8-2	29	24.1	24.1	3	33.3	33.3		25.0	25.0
2-0/0-2	15	100.0	100.0	34	79.4	79.4		85.7	85.7
Spike *3*	5	100.0	–	11	90.9	–		93.8	–
3-4/4-3	6	66.7	66.7	4	75.0	75.0		70.0	70.0
Spike *4*	145	96.6	–	63	88.9	–		94.2	–
4-6/6-4	20	80.0	90.0	16	87.5	87.5		83.3	88.9
4-8/8-4	38	50.0	50.0	13	92.3	92.3		60.8	60.8
4-9/9-4	92	50.0	50.0	23	87.0	87.0		57.4	57.4
Spike *5*	15	93.3	–	38	94.7	–		94.3	–
Spike *6*	21	85.7	–	24	83.3	–		84.4	–
6-8/8-6	105	26.7	91.4	34	82.4	97.1		40.3	92.8
6-9/9-6	13	100.0	100.0	10	100.0	100.0		100.0	100.0
Spike *7*	4	100.0	–	6	83.3	–		90.0	–
7-8/8-7	31	83.9	83.9	13	100.0	100.0		88.6	88.7
Spike *8*	1	100.0	–	3	66.7	–		75.0	–
8-9/9-8	27	63.0	77.8	12	100.0	100.0		74.4	84.6
Spike *9*	107	99.1	–	49	98.0	–		98.7	–
Mean		75.0	72.0		86.1	90.1		77.0	76.3
Weighted Mean		68.2	67.2		90.2	92.4		75.4	74.2
N		929	548		451	224		1,380	772

Won Cho (1979) in their psychiatric patients is reasonably accurate.

Although very little was changed in terms of item composition between the standard Validity and Clinical scales of the MMPI and MMPI-2, research on codetype comparability has been very popular with over 40 published studies since 1990. At least four factors will increase the overall level of concordance as reported in these studies: (1) using only "well defined" codetypes as demonstrated earlier in Tables 7.6 and 7.8; (2) eliminating within-normal-limits (*WNL*) profiles before calculating concordance; (3) using clinical samples rather than college students or the MMPI-2 restandardization sample; and (4) administering only Form AX (containing all of the MMPI and MMPI-2 items in a single instrument) rather than separate administrations of the MMPI and MMPI-2. Consequently, there is a wide range of opinions on the degree of codetype comparability between the MMPI and MMPI-2, ranging from 50% to 90% using well-defined codetypes, and 40% to 70% for nonrestrictive codetypes (cf. Dahlstrom, 1992; Edwards, Morrison, & Weissman, 1993a, 1993b; Graham, Timbrook, Ben-Porath, & Butcher, 1991; Morrison, Edwards, Weissman, Allen, & DeLaCruz, 1995). Rarely do these researchers report whether the degree of concordance varies as a function of specific codetype, although it does, as was demonstrated previously.

Research is needed that reports the empirical correlates of specific MMPI-2 codetypes regardless of the concordance between the MMPI-2 and the MMPI. In fact, clinicians should be discouraged from reporting information on the concordance rates between the MMPI-2 and the MMPI, because it impedes the investigation of the empirical correlates of specific MMPI-2 codetypes. Until such research is available, clinicians can use concordance rates as another piece of information in evaluating how to interpret an MMPI-2 codetype.

Researchers should ascertain the specific empirical correlates of well-defined MMPI-2 codetypes and then investigate whether these relationships change when nonrestrictive codetypes are included. Researchers also should consider replotting the MMPI-2 as an MMPI using Appendix K from the *MMPI-2 Manual* (Butcher et al., 1989) to assess whether the correlates provide a better fit to the MMPI or the MMPI-2 codetype. Such a procedure also will be necessary so that the results can be compared to the existing literature on the correlates of MMPI codetypes.

Clinical impressions suggest that well-defined MMPI codetypes are very similar on the MMPI-2. In the time since the debut of the MMPI-2 only one study has reported the empirical correlates of specific MMPI-2 codetypes (Archer, Griffin, & Aiduk, 1995) despite repeated calls for such research (Dahlstrom, 1992; Harrell et al., 1992; Morrison et al., 1995). Archer et al. found that the descriptors for ten frequently occurring MMPI-2 codetypes were similar to those on the MMPI, which is reassuring. Until additional empirical data are available, clinicians will need to use the correlates of MMPI codetypes carefully in the interpretation of the MMPI-2.

CODETYPE STABILITY

There are few empirical data that indicate how consistently clients will obtain the same codetype on two successive administrations of the MMPI or the MMPI-2. The research on the stability of the MMPI historically focused either upon the individual Validity and Clinical scales (these coefficients were reported in Chapters 3 and 4, respectively) or group mean profiles (cf. Lichenstein & Bryan, 1966; Pauker, 1966; Warman & Hannum, 1965), which leaves unanswered whether individual clients' codetypes have remained unchanged. Clearly, there would be at least some cause for concern if a client obtained a *4-9/9-4* codetype on one occasion and upon a second administration of the MMPI-2 a few months later in another setting obtained a *2-7/7-2* codetype.

Graham, Smith, and Schwartz (1986) have provided empirical data on the stability of MMPI codetypes for 405 psychiatric inpatients. They reported 42.7%, 44.0%, and 27.7% agreement across an average interval of approximately three months for high-point, low-point, and two-point codetypes, respectively. Only seven specific codetypes (*2-3/3-2, 2-4/4-2, 4-8/8-4, 4-9/9-4, 6-8/8-6, 7-8/8-7,* and *8-9/9-8*) occurred frequently enough to assess their stability; the agreement for these seven codetypes ranged from 26.4 percent (*6-8/8-6*) to 41.4 percent (*4-9/9-4*). If the patients were classified into the categories of neurotic, psychotic, and characterologic, 58.1 percent remained in the same category when retested.

Greene et al. (1993) provided similar data on 454 alcoholic inpatients who had taken the MMPI during two different hospitalizations separated by at least six months. Approximately 40 percent of the men and 32 percent of the women had the same high-point scale on the two successive administrations of the MMPI. However, they had the same codetype only 12 and 13 percent of the time, respectively. It is even more interesting that almost 30 percent of these men and women had two totally different high-point scales when they took the MMPI on their second admission.

These data on codetype stability suggest several important conclusions. First, clinicians should be cautious about making long-term predictions from a single administration of the MMPI-2. Second, it is not clear whether the shifts that do occur in codetypes across time reflect meaningful changes in the patients' behaviors, psychometric instability of the MMPI-2, or some combination of both of these factors. Finally, research is needed to provide additional information on this issue.

RELATIONSHIP BETWEEN CODETYPES AND PSYCHIATRIC DIAGNOSES

Clinicians may be prone to believe that specific diagnoses are associated with certain codetypes. Unfortunately, there is more heterogeneity in psychiatric diagnoses within a given codetype than clinicians might expect. For example, Marks et al. (1974) reported that 68 percent of adult patients with a 6-8/8-6 codetype were diagnosed as being psychotic (schizophrenic or paranoid were the most frequent diagnoses), 18 percent as personality disordered (paranoid), and 14 percent as chronic organic brain syndrome.

Gilberstadt and Duker (1965) reported that the diagnosis for their 8-6 codetype was paranoid schizophrenia; since they reported prototypic codetypes, they did not provide information on the frequency with which 8-6 codetypes were diagnosed as being schizophrenic. Hathaway and Meehl (1951) found that 16 (46 percent) of their 35 patients with 6-8/8-6 codetypes had some form of schizophrenic diagnosis. Their patients also were twice as likely to be diagnosed as schizophrenic when they had an 8-6 code-

type as compared with a 6-8 codetype. It appears that patients with a 6-8/8-6 codetype have a significant probability of receiving a schizophrenic diagnosis, although a number of other diagnoses also can be encountered.

Similar data can be provided for 8-9/9-8 codetypes so that the clinician can see that heterogeneity in psychiatric diagnoses is characteristic of all codetypes. Marks et al. (1974) found that 70 percent of adult patients with an 8-9/9-8 codetype were diagnosed as being psychotic (schizophrenic or mixed were the most common diagnoses), 17 percent as neurotic (depression), and 9 percent as acute organic brain syndrome.

Gilberstadt and Duker (1965) reported that the diagnosis for their prototypic 8-9 codetype was schizophrenic reaction, catatonic type with alternative diagnoses of "schizo-manic" psychosis and paranoid schizophrenia. Hathaway and Meehl found that 3 (37.5%) of their 8 patients with 9-8 codetypes were diagnosed as manic-depressive, manic type. Only 5 patients had 8-9 codetypes and none was diagnosed as manic-depressive, manic type. Thus, it appears that bipolar disorder, manic diagnoses may be common in 8-9/9-8 codetypes but such diagnoses occur less than one-half the time at the most and probably closer to one-quarter.

Greene (1988a) has summarized the frequency with which various codetypes were found in specific diagnostic groups, and he found the expected relationship between codetypes and diagnostic groups. For example, 2-7/7-2 codetypes occurred frequently in depressed patients, 6-8/8-6 codetypes in schizophrenic patients, 6-9/9-6 codetypes in manic patients, and so on. However, the most frequent codetypes in these groups occurred less than 20% of the time. It also appeared that as the sample sizes increased, the variability in performance within a specific diagnostic group increased rather than decreased.

The clinician should consult the individual chapters in Greene (1988b) to review MMPI performance within specific diagnostic groups, namely, chronic pain (Prokop, 1988), schizophrenia (Walters, 1988b), mood disorders (Nichols, 1988), personality disorders (Morey & Smith, 1988), substance abuse/dependence (Greene & Garvin, 1988), Post Traumatic Stress Disorder (Penk et al., 1988), neuropsychological dysfunction (Farr & Martin, 1988), and child abuse and sexual abuse (Friedrich, 1988).

PROTOTYPIC SCORES FOR CODETYPES

Although the primary focus of this chapter will be on the correlates of each codetype, it is important for the clinician to realize that the relative elevation of the other Clinical scales as well as the elevation of a number of the Supplementary scales can drastically alter the potential interpretation.

Profiles 7.1 and 7.2 provide examples of two individuals, both of whom have a *4-9/9-4* codetype. Even a quick perusal of the two profiles reveals that these individuals would behave very differently in a clinical interview and they would have different reasons for being referred for treatment. The first individual (Profile 7.1) is very likely to have been referred for behavioral difficulties and/or criminal activities, whereas the other individual (Profile 7.2) is more likely to have interpersonal difficulties, probably with a spouse or another family member.

Profiles 7.1 (p. 314) and 7.2 (p. 315) illustrate the importance of assessing how well the obtained profile matches the "prototypic" scores for that specific codetype. Appendix D contains tables with the prototypic scores for every codetype discussed in this chapter based on the Caldwell (1997a) clinical dataset. Each table in Appendix D provides the prototypic scores for all of the MMPI-2 Validity and Clinical scales as well as all of the Content, Content Component, and Supplementary scales that are scored commonly. Examples of these tables are provided in this chapter for five frequently occurring codetypes: Spike *1, 2-4/4-2, 2-7/7-2, 4-9/9-4,* and *6-8/8-6.* The use of prototypic scores also will be illustrated in Chapter 8 when specific MMPI-2 profiles are interpreted.

There are few data to address the issue of whether prototypic scores for specific MMPI-2 codetypes would be similar in different psychiatric settings even if their frequency of occurrence is not the same. Profiles 7.3 (p. 316) and 7.4 (p. 317) indicate the similarities between *2-4/4-2* and *6-8/8-6* codetypes in psychiatric patients (Hedlund & Won Cho, 1976) and medical patients referred for a psychiatric evaluation (Colligan & Offord, 1986). Despite the different frequencies with which these two codetypes are encoun-

tered in these settings (see Tables 7.1 and 7.2), their scores on the MMPI standard Validity and Clinical scales are very similar. In fact, the prototypic scores for the same codetype in these two settings are virtually identical.

Persons who are being screened for personnel selection would be expected to have very different patterns of scores on the MMPI-2 Validity and Clinical scales, and are generally unlikely to elevate most scales. Research is needed to determine whether prototypic scores for a specific codetype in a personnel setting are similar to those in a psychiatric setting despite the relative differences in elevation that would be expected.

Since persons in a personnel setting would be expected to minimize or underreport any type of psychological problem if they are trying to qualify for a position, they generally will not elevate any Clinical scale on the MMPI-2 to a T score of 65 or higher. In those rare instances in which they do produce a standard codetype, it would be interesting to determine whether the pattern of scores on the standard Validity and Clinical scales is similar to that found in psychiatric settings.

Broughton (1984) and Horowitz, Wright, Lowenstein, and Parad (1981) have described the use of prototypes as a means of assessing personality or psychopathological constructs. These references can provide a starting point for the clinician who is interested in a more conceptual understanding of this approach to the assessment of psychopathology.

Several general comments need to be made about these prototypic scores that are provided for each codetype: All scores are reported as T scores with the appropriate Clinical scales *K*-corrected. Raw scores are provided for the following scales: Cannot Say (*?*), total T score difference on the Wiener and Harmon (Wiener, 1948) Obvious and Subtle subscales, and the total number of Koss and Butcher (1973) and Lachar and Wrobel (1979) critical items endorsed.

As a clinical rule of thumb, any score that varies by more than one standard deviation (approximately 10 T points) from the prototypic score for that scale should be evaluated as to whether and how it might modify the standard interpretation of that codetype. For example, the prototypic T scores on Scales *2* (Depression) and *0* (Social Introversion) for an MMPI-2

PROFILE 7.1

MMPI-2
S.R. Hathaway and J.C. McKinley
Minnesota Multiphasic Personality Inventory -2™

Name __Profile 7-2__

Address _____

Occupation _____ Date Tested __ / __ / __

Education _____ Age _____ Marital Status _____

Referred By _____

MMPI-2 Code _____

Scorer's Initials _____

FEMALE

Non-prototypic Scores for

4-9/9-4 Codetypes

Raw Score ___

? Raw Score ___   K to be Added ___

Raw Score with K ___

PROFILE 7.2

Note. Minnesota Multiphasic Personality Inventory-2 (MMPI-2). Copyright © 1942, 1943 (renewed 1970), 1989 by the Regents of the University of Minnesota. Reproduced by permission of the publisher. "MMPI-2" and "Minnesota Multiphasic Personality Inventory-2" are trademarks owned by the University of Minnesota.

MMPI-2™
S.R. Hathaway and J.C. McKinley
Minnesota Multiphasic Personality Inventory -2™

Profile for Basic Scales

Minnesota Multiphasic Personality Inventory-2
Copyright © by THE REGENTS OF THE UNIVERSITY OF MINNESOTA
1942, 1943 (renewed 1970), 1989. This Profile Form 1989.
All rights reserved. Distributed exclusively by NATIONAL COMPUTER SYSTEMS, INC.
under license from The University of Minnesota.

"MMPI-2" and "Minnesota Multiphasic Personality Inventory-2" are trademarks owned by
The University of Minnesota. Printed in the United States of America.

Name _Profile 7-3_

Address ___

Occupation ___ Date Tested _/ /_

Education ___ Age ___ Marital Status ___

Referred By ___

MMPI-2 Code ___

Scorer's Initials ___

Prototypic Scores for 2-4/4-2 Codetypes

Medical Outpatient Referrals

(Colligan & Offord, 1986)

▲——▲

Psychiatric Patients

(Hedlund & Won Cho, 1979)

●——●

MALE

Raw Score ___

? Raw Score ___

K to be Added ___

Raw Score with K ___

NATIONAL
COMPUTER
SYSTEMS

24001

PROFILE 7.3

Note. Minnesota Multiphasic Personality Inventory-2 (MMPI-2). Copyright © 1942, 1943 (renewed 1970), 1989 by the Regents of the University of Minnesota. Reproduced by permission of the publisher. "MMPI-2" and "Minnesota Multiphasic Personality Inventory-2" are trademarks owned by the University of Minnesota.

Profile for Basic Scales

Minnesota Multiphasic Personality Inventory-2
Copyright © by THE REGENTS OF THE UNIVERSITY OF MINNESOTA
1942, 1943 (renewed 1970), 1989. This Profile Form 1989.
All rights reserved. Distributed exclusively by NATIONAL COMPUTER SYSTEMS, INC.
under license from The University of Minnesota.

"MMPI-2" and "Minnesota Multiphasic Personality Inventory-2" are trademarks owned by
The University of Minnesota. Printed in the United States of America.

Name __Profile 7-4__

Prototypic Scores for 6-8/8-6 Codetypes

Medical Outpatient Referrals

(Colligan & Offord, 1986)

Psychiatric Patients

(Hedlund & Won Cho, 1979)

PROFILE 7.4

Note. Minnesota Multiphasic Personality Inventory-2 (MMPI-2). Copyright © 1942, 1943 (renewed 1970), 1989 by the Regents of the University of Minnesota. Reproduced by permission of the publisher. "MMPI-2" and "Minnesota Multiphasic Personality Inventory-2" are trademarks owned by the University of Minnesota.

4-9/9-4 codetype are 52.4 and 45.1 (see Table 7.13), respectively. If a client has T scores of 65 and 60 for these two scales, the client is less likely to act out and is reporting more emotional distress as a consequence of his or her behavior.

An intriguing research question that has not even been addressed yet is whether clients who deviate significantly from the prototypic scores for a codetype are less likely to manifest its correlates. It also would be interesting to see if profiles that deviate from the prototype for the codetype are more similar to the pattern of scores for another codetype.

Greene and Brown (1998) have developed a computer interpretive program for the MMPI-2 that provides quantitative indexes of how well a client's scores on the standard Validity and Clinical scales match his or her codetype and 295 prototypic codetypes. McGrath et al. (1998) have reported the descriptive statistics for the Harris and Lingoes subscales for 14 MMPI-2 codetypes that also can be used as prototypes.

Finally, it would be very appropriate for clinicians to develop their own prototypic scores for codetypes that occur frequently in their setting. Once these prototypes have been identified within a specific setting, the clinician also could begin to see if subgroups of profiles were occurring within the codetype, and determine whether they were clinical correlates for these subgroups.

CODETYPES[1]

Any correlate of a codetype discussed in this chapter or in any interpretive system is a probabilistic statement that may or may not apply to a specific client. Each statement should be understood as applying to most clients or typical of clients with such a codetype. Consequently, most of these qualifiers have been omitted in the following pages.

It also will be assumed that the clinician has assessed the consistency and accuracy of item endorsement (Chapter 3), so disclaimers will not be pre-

sented with each codetype as appropriate. For example, the clinician might recall that 33.78 percent of *6-8/8-6* codetypes on the MMPI-2 are a result of inconsistent patterns of item endorsement and 45.74 percent are the result of overreporting of psychopathology (Table 3.39, p. 114).

A number of the codetypes occur infrequently and, consequently, there is little information available for interpretation, as was noted earlier. In such situations it is frequently helpful to note the third highest Clinical scale, particularly when Scales *5* (Masculinity-Femininity) and/or *0* (Social Introversion) are among the two highest scales. Anytime Scales *5* and/ or *0* are among the two highest Clinical scales, it probably would be a good idea to examine which Clinical scale(s) are next highest and to consider how the interpretation of the codetype might be changed by considering these scales. For example, if a client has a *1-5/5-1* codetype and Scale *3* (Hysteria) is the third highest scale, it probably would be instructive to consider that the client has a *1-3/3-1* codetype with a high Scale *5*. Research is needed to determine when the third highest Clinical scale can and should be substituted for one of the two highest scales to improve the accuracy of the interpretation of the MMPI-2 profile.

The description of each codetype initially started with the generic interpretations that are available in any of the standard MMPI-2 references (Butcher & Williams, 1992; Graham, 1993; Greene, 1991). These interpretations are a compilation of the empirical data and clinical lore that have been accumulated over the 50 years of usage of the MMPI and MMPI-2. Each statement contained in these interpretations was placed into one of the categories (Moods, Cognitions, Interpersonal Relations, Other Problem Areas) that were used in the development of the MMPI-2 Structural Summary (Greene & Nichols, 1995; Nichols & Greene, 1995). Three additional sources of information were added to complete the interpretation for each codetype: an MMPI-2 Structural Summary, the Content Component scales (Ben-Porath & Sherwood, 1993), and item analyses.

The prototypic MMPI-2 Structural Summary (Greene & Nichols, 1995; Nichols & Greene, 1995) was produced for each codetype that provides the typical content that is associated with it. The Content

---

1. The gender for the pronouns within each codetype is determined by whether the codetype was more frequent in men or women (see Table 7.4) in the Caldwell (1997a) clinical dataset.

Component scales (Ben-Porath & Sherwood, 1993) were scored and ranked from high to low to indicate their relative importance within each codetype. This procedure provided another indication of which content areas were most or least likely to be associated with each prototypic codetype. The frequency of endorsement for all 567 items of the MMPI-2 for a large sample of patients was computed as well as the frequency of endorsement of each codetype. The difference in the frequency of endorsement of each item was computed between the entire sample and the patients with each codetype. These differences in the frequency of endorsement then were ranked to identify those items that were most characteristic of patients within each codetype. Items that were endorsed at a difference of 10% or larger were used in developing the interpretive text.

Thus, the description of each codetype is based on an extensive and empirical analysis of its characteristic pattern of scores on all of the MMPI-2 scales and the items that are most likely to be endorsed. In addition, these descriptions were supplemented by any empirical correlates that have been reported in the literature.

Within-Normal-Limit (*WNL*) (30.92%)[2]

Clients who do not elevate any Clinical scale at or above a T score of 65 on the MMPI-2 are quite common in psychiatric settings. In fact, a *WNL* codetype is the most frequently occurring codetype in most, if not all, psychiatric settings as was noted earlier.

The client describes himself as being happy, healthy, and contented. He sees his relationships as being satisfying. It is very important to determine whether this self-description is consistent with the reason(s) for which he is being evaluated. He is not reporting any type of emotional distress either as a result of the behaviors or symptoms that led him to be evaluated or of the process of being evaluated.

His problems tend to be chronically ingrained and he has become adjusted to them. He may be psychotic or manifest a severe characterologic disorder. He has little motivation to consider change.

Archer et al. (1995), Duckworth and Barley (1988), and Kelley and King (1978) provide interpretive information on *WNL* codetypes.

Spike *1* (1.37%)[3]

Moods: The client is not experiencing any type of emotional distress despite his physical symptoms. He is calm, happy, and interested in his daily life. His feelings are not easily hurt.

Cognitions: He has good attention and concentration skills. He is self-confident. He invests little effort in understanding the psychological reactions of himself or others, and he believes that his psychological functioning is quite good. He has difficulty seeing how his physical complaints could be related to his psychological functioning.

Interpersonal Relations: He is extroverted and relates easily with others. He sees others as understanding him and getting along with him. His home life was pleasant and he did not want to leave home. His physical symptoms may be used to control and manipulate others.

Other Problem Areas: His physical health is not as good as that of his friends. He is less able to work now than he was in the past. He has a long history of vague physical symptoms and ailments. His exaggerated concern about these symptoms primarily reflects a somatization process even if they also have some objective basis. His history and background should be reviewed to determine whether a medical or neuropsychological evaluation is warranted.

There is a slight possibility of suicidal ideation that should be evaluated. He may abuse prescribed medications.

Treatment: His prognosis is guarded. He is experiencing little emotional distress to serve as motivation

---

2. This percentage reflects the frequency with which *WNL* codetypes occurred in the total (*N* = 50,966) Caldwell (1997a) clinical dataset.

3. This percentage reflects the frequency with which this codetype occurred in the Caldwell (1997a) clinical sample after *WNL* codetypes had been excluded (*N* = 35,208).

for any intervention, and he prefers to emphasize his physical symptoms rather than psychological processes. This pattern represents a stable, chronic mode of adjustment that is difficult to modify. Conservative treatment that provides symptomatic relief may become the basis for more long-term interventions.

Tables 7.10 and D.1 provide the prototypic scores for Spike *1* codetypes.

1-2/2-1 (4.76%)

Moods: The client is experiencing a mild to moderate level of emotional distress characterized by tension, anxiety, and dysphoria. She reports physical symptoms that are reflective of anxiety. She is grouchy, easily frustrated, and irritable. It is rather unusual for her to report that she is depressed despite how she may appear to others. Criticism or scolding hurts her terribly. She feels unable to get going and get things done in her life.

Cognitions: She has concentration difficulties. She tends to think in a very concrete manner and to focus on her physical ailments. She believes her judgment is not as good as it was in the past. She lacks insight into her somatic symptoms and behavior, often refusing to acknowledge that her symptoms are related to emotional conflict and are used as a means of avoiding her psychological problems.

Interpersonal Relations: She is introverted and finds it hard to talk when she meets new people. She is shy and reserved around other people. Her family did not find fault with her or object to her friends.

Other Problem Areas: Her physical health is not as good as that of her friends, and she worries about her health. She reports a variety of physical and neurological symptoms and some general pain. She often reports nausea, vomiting, weakness, insomnia, and fatigue rather than classical depressive features. Dizziness, chest and back pains, and tachycardia may be reported. The somatic symptoms are focused around the alimentary system, particularly on abdominal pain and backaches. Her symptoms are vague, nonspecific, and difficult to isolate medically. Even when

or if she has real physical symptoms, she exaggerates their severity. She will return to her physician(s) repeatedly with limited change in her physical condition. Her history and background should be reviewed to determine whether a medical or neuropsychological evaluation is warranted.

She does not sleep well or wake up fresh and rested most mornings. She feels tired a good deal of the time, has little energy, and tires quickly. Abuse of prescribed medications is possible, and suicidal ideation should be evaluated carefully.

Treatment: Her prognosis is poor for any form of traditional psychotherapy because of her difficulty in understanding that her problems might have a psychological component. She will seek another medical opinion when a physician suggests that her problems could reflect psychological factors. Conservative medical treatment is recommended because her physical ailments are difficult to document. Short-term interventions focused on providing symptomatic relief from her physical ailments may be beneficial and can provide the foundation for more traditional psychotherapy.

Gynther et al. (1973) reported that these clients were frequently alcoholics, but no other researcher has found this codetype to be characteristic of alcoholics (cf. Clopton, 1978; Greene & Garvin, 1988). Gilberstadt and Duker (1965), Gynther et al. (1973), and Marks et al. (1974) provide additional interpretive information on *1-2/2-1* codetypes, and Table D.2 provides the prototypic scores.

1-3/3-1 (14.83%)

Clients with *1-3/3-1* codetypes are found frequently in both normal and psychiatric populations. When Scales *1* (Hypochondriasis) and *3* (Hysteria) are at or greater than a T score of 65 on the MMPI-2 and Scales *1* and *3* are greater than Scale *2* (Depression) by 10 T points, this profile is a classic conversion "V" (Chapter 4, p. 144). In general, the higher the elevation of the conversion "V," the more rigid are her defenses. A conversion "V" above a T score of 80 suggests that many of her efforts are ineffectively directed toward trying to

Table 7-10

Prototypic Scores for Spike 1 Codetypes (N = 483)

Demographics

Demographics		M	SD	Marital Status	%
Age		41.4	14.6	Never Married	29.3
Education		11.6	5.6	Married	50.0
Gender		%		Separated	2.1
	Men	54.5		Divorced	16.4
	Women	44.5		Widowed	2.1

Test-Taking Scales

Omissions		M	SD	Consistency		M	SD
	?	1.2	3.3	VRIN		50.1	9.9
				|F - FB|		2.7	1.9
				TRIN		49.7	9.7

Accuracy of Item Endorsement

Underreporting		M	SD	Overreporting		M	SD
	False %	63.5	6.0		True %	35.3	6.0
Impression	L	58.5	12.0	Infrequency	F	49.8	7.8
Management	ODecp	57.5	10.2		FB	49.1	8.4
	Sd	57.2	10.3		F[p]	51.8	11.1
Superlative	S	53.7	8.8	Critical Items	K & B	12.2	6.4
Adjustment					L & W	21.3	8.0
Self-Deception	K	54.5	9.0	Dissimulation	F - K	-13.2	5.5
	So	51.5	7.8		Ds	49.5	8.3
					O - S	5.5	47.2

Scales

Validity and Clinical			Supplementary			Morey et al. Overlapping Personality Disorder		
Scale	M	SD	Scale	M	SD	Scale	M	SD
?	1.2	3.3	A	45.6	7.0	PAR	48.8	9.1
L	58.5	12.0	R	55.1	9.3	SZD	48.9	9.4
F	49.8	7.8	Es	46.5	8.8	STY	47.0	8.7
K	54.5	9.0	TRIN	49.7	9.7	ANT	46.7	8.8
1(Hs)	68.3	3.5	VRIN	50.1	9.9	BDL	46.1	8.5
2(D)	55.6	6.1	O-H	56.6	10.9	HST	48.7	9.3
3(Hy)	58.6	4.6	Do	48.1	9.3	NAR	51.9	8.5
4(Pd)	50.9	7.0	Re	50.8	9.4	AVD	46.1	7.7
5(Mf)	47.9	8.8	GM	47.8	9.1	DEP	46.6	7.9
6(Pa)	49.6	8.3	GF	49.7	8.5	CPS	46.0	9.1
7(Pt)	51.0	6.9	Mt	50.1	7.3	Personality		
8(Sc)	51.8	6.4	PK	48.2	7.2	Psychopathology Five		
9(Ma)	49.4	7.1	PS	49.2	7.1	Scale	M	SD
0(Si)	48.3	7.7	MAC-R	50.6	8.9	AGG	50.0	8.3
			APS	45.6	11.3	PSY	48.5	9.0
			AAS	46.3	8.6	CON	52.2	9.2
			MDS	46.9	7.5	NEN	47.6	8.2
			Ho	48.3	8.4	PEE	50.1	7.9
			CAL-R	45.4	10.3			

Content			Content Component					
Scale	M	SD	Scale	M	SD	Scale	M	SD
ANX	51.8	8.0	FRS1	50.7	12.3	ASP1	49.1	9.2
FRS	50.6	10.9	FRS2	49.8	10.4	ASP2	49.5	10.4
OBS	45.7	8.1	DEP1	49.5	7.4	TPA1	45.8	9.5
DEP	48.7	7.2	DEP2	48.1	8.5	TPA2	47.1	9.9
HEA	63.3	6.6	DEP3	46.4	7.4	LSE1	45.0	6.6
BIZ	48.8	8.1	DEP4	47.6	8.2	LSE2	46.7	7.9
ANG	46.8	8.3	HEA1	60.6	13.2	SOD1	48.1	8.3
CYN	50.7	9.4	HEA2	60.2	11.4	SOD2	47.7	9.1
ASP	49.5	8.8	HEA3	61.1	10.4	FAM1	44.7	8.3
TPA	46.4	9.3	BIZ1	47.7	7.6	FAM2	48.6	9.1
LSE	46.2	7.4	BIZ2	47.0	7.3	TRT1	47.5	7.5
SOD	48.0	8.2	ANG1	47.2	8.0	TRT2	46.3	8.5
FAM	46.2	7.9	ANG2	46.9	8.9			
WRK	48.1	7.5	CYN1	50.7	9.8			
TRT	47.5	7.8	CYN2	49.4	9.9			

Note: All scores are T scores except: Cannot Say, K & B and L & W critical items which are raw scores; True % and False % which are the percentage of items endorsed "true" or "false;" and |F - FB|, F - K, and O - S which are difference scores.

ward off anxiety, particularly if the *F* (Infrequency) scale also is significantly elevated.

The absolute elevation of the conversion "V" is not related to whether a psychological or an organic diagnosis is likely to be made (Schwartz & Krupp, 1971), although persons above age 40 are more likely to receive an organic diagnosis and younger women are more likely to receive a psychological diagnosis (Schwartz, Osborne, & Krupp, 1972). Hence, elevations on Scales *1* and *3* cannot be used reliably to distinguish functional disorders from actual physical disease. In either case she is using somatic symptoms to avoid thinking or dealing with psychological problems.

Clients with a *1-3* codetype are more likely to show more somatization features than the hysterical features characteristic of clients with a *3-1* codetype. Her physical symptoms are usually more nonspecific and vague and likely to involve backaches, gastrointestinal symptoms, and so on. She also is more pessimistic and concerned about her physical symptoms.

Clients with a *1-3-9* profile have been described as having a chronic brain syndrome with trauma and personality disorder (Gilberstadt & Duker, 1965). Neither Schwartz (1969) nor Golden, Sweet, and Osmon (1979) were able to replicate this codetype as being characteristic of brain-damaged persons.

Moods: The client is experiencing very mild emotional distress characterized by tension. She frequently worries about something. She also experiences a very mild level of dysphoria. Her dysphoria and worry are not overtly expressed, no matter how concerned she is about her poor physical functioning. Her daily life is full of things that keep her interested. She describes herself as being tired, inefficient, and lethargic, and as being treated unfairly by life.

Cognitions: She tends to think in a very concrete manner and to focus on her physical ailments. She values being seen as logical and without psychological problems. Her concentration and memory are adequate. Her judgment is better than it ever was. She finds it easy to make decisions. She is self-confident. She believes that most people are honest and can be trusted. She does not analyze the reasons for her or

others' behavior. She strongly defends her own opinions, and she likes to let people know where she stands on issues.

She lacks insight into her own behavior and is very resistant to interpretations that there could be psychological involvement in the physical symptoms. Even when her symptoms seem bizarre, she is unlikely to be psychotic. Others are likely to experience her physical symptoms as being used in a manipulative or passive-aggressive manner.

Interpersonal Relations: She is extroverted and makes friends quickly. She finds it easy to talk when she meets new people. She is very conventional and conforming to societal standards. Her family did not object to her friends, and she did not want to leave home.

Other Problem Areas: Her physical health is not as good as that of her friends, and she worries about her health. She reports a wide variety of physical and neurological symptoms such as gastrointestinal difficulties, chest and neck pains, hay fever and/or asthma, and balance and coordination difficulties. She tires quickly and feels tired a good deal of the time. She has sleep difficulties. Her history and background should be reviewed to determine whether a medical or neuropsychological evaluation is warranted.

She may abuse substances, usually prescribed medications. She is unlikely to have been in trouble with the law. She is less able to work now than she was in the past. Although suicidal ideation is quite unusual, the possibility of suicidal ideation should be evaluated carefully.

Treatment: Her prognosis is generally poor because she has little motivation for any type of psychological intervention. She prefers to focus on her physical symptoms rather than on any form of psychological process. She is not naturally introspective, which will complicate the implementation of any therapeutic intervention. Conservative medical treatment is recommended because her physical ailments are difficult to document. Short-term interventions focused on providing symptomatic relief from her physical ailments may be beneficial and can provide the foundation for more traditional psychotherapy.

Gilberstadt and Duker (1965), Gynther et al. (1973), Marks et al. (1974), and Prokop (1988) provide additional interpretive information on *1-3/3-1* codetypes, and Table D.3 provides the prototypic scores.

1-4/4-1 (0.64%)

Moods: The client is experiencing minimal emotional distress in that she describes herself as being happy most of the time. She is usually calm and not easily upset, yet she believes that she has not lived the "right kind of life." Others see her as pessimistic, whiny, and nagging.

Cognitions: She has good concentration and memory. Her judgment is better now than it ever was. She is self-confident. She makes decisions easily. She believes that others are only interested in themselves.

Interpersonal Relations: She is extroverted and sees herself as relating easily with others, while others see her as having poor social skills. Her parents often objected to her friends. She quarrels with her family members, and she very much wanted to leave home. Her interpersonal and familial relationships are characterized by turmoil and chronic complaining.

Other Problem Areas: She reports general pain and discomfort with few specific physical symptoms. She is likely to abuse substances and to have been in trouble with the law. She is less able to work now than she was in the past.

Treatment: Her prognosis is generally poor. Her problems are chronic and characterologic, and there is limited emotional distress that might serve as motivation for an intervention. Short-term behavioral interventions that focus on her reasons for entering treatment will be most effective. Her focus on somatic symptoms is essentially chronic in nature and, consequently, quite resistant to change or intervention.

Gynther et al. (1973) provide further interpretive information on *1-4/4-1* codetypes, and Table D.4 provides the prototypic scores.

1-5/5-1 (0.41%)

Moods: The client is not experiencing any emotional distress in that she is happy most of the time and her daily life is full of things that keep her interested. She has few fears. She focuses her dissatisfaction with life on her physical problems and symptoms. In response to stress, she will exhibit an increase in the frequency and/or severity of her physical symptoms, and become irritable and easily annoyed.

Cognitions: She has good concentration and memory. She is self-confident and can make up her mind easily. She has strong opinions. She believes that it takes a lot of effort to convince most people of the truth.

Interpersonal Relations: She is extroverted. She believes that she would make a good leader of people and that she relates easily to others. Others are more aware of her fussy, complaining attitude about almost everything. Her home life was pleasant, and she has few quarrels with her family. She is not bothered by what others think of her. Her worries disappear when she gets into a crowd of lively friends. Her vague physical symptoms are used to avoid personal responsibilities.

Other Problem Areas: Her physical health is not as good as that of her friends. She has a few gastrointestinal symptoms and general pain. She has sleep difficulties. She is not likely to abuse substances or to have suicidal ideation. She is less able to work now than she was in the past. She is very conventional and unlikely to have behavioral problems.

Treatment: Her prognosis is guarded. She is experiencing no emotional distress that might serve as motivation for an intervention. She will prefer to focus on physical symptoms rather than on psychological process, which will complicate any intervention. Short-term behavioral interventions that focus on her reasons for entering treatment will be most effective.

Tanner (1990) provides further interpretive information on *1-5/5-1* codetypes, and Table D.5 provides the prototypic scores.

1-6/6-1 (1.09%)

Moods: The client is experiencing mild emotional distress characterized by brooding, resentment, negativism, and anhedonia. He is irritable, grouchy, and stubborn at best, and often feels anger that he will express directly. He does not understand why he is so irritable and grouchy. He is unaware of these angry characteristics or will attribute them to the way others treat him. He is more sensitive and feels emotions more intensely than others. He finds it hard to "get going" and has little hope of success if he does manage to get something started.

Cognitions: His memory is good, and he believes that his judgment is better now than it ever was. He is sensitive to any form of criticism, assumes others are against him, and anticipates being rejected. He is sure that he is being talked about, that someone "has it in" for him, and that he has enemies who really wish to harm him. He often thinks of things that are too bad to talk about. Despite these thoughts, he does not think that there is something wrong with his mind. He has limited insight into his problems.

He reports a number of symptoms that may reflect a psychotic process or a very long-term characterologic condition. His presenting problems, background, and history should be reviewed with this possibility in mind.

Interpersonal Relations: He is slightly introverted and socially alienated. His interpersonal relations are usually characterized by conflict, and he blames others for his present circumstances and problems. He believes that he would make a good leader of people. He thinks that people often misunderstand his intentions when he is trying to be helpful. The only place that he feels relaxed is at home.

Other Problem Areas: His physical health is not as good as that of his friends. He reports a wide variety of physical and neurologic symptoms. He tires quickly and feels weak all over much of the time. His sleep is fitful and disturbed. His history and background should be reviewed to determine whether a medical or neuropsychological evaluation is warranted.

He may abuse substances. He may have suicidal ideation that should be evaluated carefully.

Treatment: His prognosis is generally poor. His problems are chronic and characterologic in nature, which make any intervention more difficult. It may be difficult to get him to focus on psychological rather than on physical factors as the causes of his present problems. His irritability and negativism also make it more difficult to establish a therapeutic alliance with him. Short-term behavioral interventions that focus on his reasons for entering treatment will be most beneficial and may facilitate the establishment of a therapeutic alliance. Cognitive-behavioral interventions that focus on his dysphoria, anger, and anhedonia will be helpful if he will engage in the therapeutic process.

Table D.6 provides the prototypic scores for *1-6/6-1* codetypes.

1-7/7-1 (0.57%)

Moods: The client is experiencing moderate emotional distress characterized by general apprehensiveness, worrying, and anxiety. He is a chronic worrier who broods and ruminates about himself, his problems, and his physical well-being. He exhibits a wide variety of physical symptoms that reflect constant tension and anxiety as well as general pain and discomfort. He may have depressive features and often feels insecure, inhibited, inferior, and guilty. He is more sensitive than most people, and he is easily embarrassed. Life is a strain for him much of the time. He wishes that he could be as happy as others seem to be. He regrets things that he has done. He feels disappointments so keenly that he cannot put them out of his mind. Although he is irritable, impatient, and grouchy, he is unlikely to express anger overtly or to be aggressive toward others.

Cognitions: He has problems with concentration, and he immediately forgets what people tell him. He is bothered by repetitive thoughts and is concerned that he may be "losing his mind." He dreams and thinks about things that are best kept to himself. Intellectualization is quite common.

Interpersonal Relations: He is somewhat intro-verted, shy, and bashful. He has trouble thinking of the right things to say when he is with others. He worries about his interpersonal skills or lack thereof. He is not assertive and not likely to speak to others unless they speak first. His home life was pleasant.

Other Problem Areas: He is concerned about his physical health and has a wide variety of physical symptoms as well as general pain and discomfort. He feels weak all over and tired much of the time. He has sleep difficulties. He often exhibits an increase in the frequency and severity of his physical symptoms in response to stress and anxiety. His history and background should be reviewed to determine whether a medical evaluation is warranted.

He may abuse substances in the sedative/hypnotic class. He is unlikely to get into behavioral problems. Suicidal ideation should be monitored carefully.

Treatment: His prognosis is poor. His problems are characterologic and strongly resistant to change. He prefers to focus on physical symptoms rather than on psychological processes. Psychopharmacologic interventions may be considered to reduce his level of anxiety and to help him sleep. However, such an intervention is likely to increase his focus on the physical rather than the psychological aspects of his problems. Cognitive-behavioral interventions that help him reduce his level of anxiety are frequently beneficial. His somatization features are resistant to intervention or change.

Table D.7 provides the prototypic scores for *1-7/ 7-1* codetypes.

1-8/8-1 (1.44%)

Moods: The client is experiencing moderate emotional distress characterized by dysphoria, agitation, and anhedonia. He finds it difficult to "get going" and has little hope of success if he does manage to start something. He is generally apprehensive and easily frightened. He wishes that he could be as happy as others seem to be. He is irritable, stubborn, and grouchy.

Cognitions: He has concentration and memory difficulties, and he is easily distracted and confused. His

judgment is not as good now as it was in the past. He lacks self-confidence. He often feels as if things are not real. He is bothered by strangers looking at him critically, and he is sure that others are talking about him. He dreams about things that are best kept to himself. He hears strange things when he is alone. He is bothered by thoughts about sex. He may have physical symptoms of a bizarre nature that actually may be delusional. These physical symptoms also may represent defenses against the emergence of actual psychotic material. He is cynical and believes that most people are only interested in their own welfare.

He reports a number of symptoms that may reflect a psychotic process or a very long-term characterologic condition. His presenting problems, background, and history should be reviewed with this possibility in mind.

Interpersonal Relations: He is introverted and socially alienated. He finds it hard to talk when he meets new people. His home life was as pleasant as that of most people he knows. His family and relatives got along quite well. His way of doing things is apt to be misunderstood by others. He distrusts others and feels alienated, isolated, and different from other people. Other people see him as odd, strange, or bizarre.

Other Problem Areas: He experiences pain in a number of areas of his body and physical and neurological symptoms. These symptoms may be atypical and might even border on being delusional. He has a great deal of difficulty handling stress and may exhibit an increase in symptoms in response to stress. He feels weak all over much of the time. His history and background should be reviewed to determine whether a medical or neuropsychological evaluation is warranted.

His sleep is fitful and disturbed. He may have suicidal ideation that should be evaluated carefully. He may abuse substances.

Treatment: His prognosis is generally poor given the characterologic nature of his problems. Establishing a therapeutic alliance is very challenging because of the serious character pathology that is present. He may prefer to focus on his physical symptoms rather than on any psychological problems. Psychopharmacologic interventions may be necessary to deal with his dysphoria and agitation. The probability of meaningful long-term change is low. Short-term behavioral interventions that focus on his reasons for entering treatment will be most effective.

Gilberstadt and Duker (1965) provide additional interpretive information on *1-8/8-1* codetypes, and Table D.8 provides the prototypic scores.

1-9/9-1 (0.45%)

Moods: The client is experiencing minimal emotional distress. He describes himself as happy, carefree, and self-reliant regardless of what others think. He is described as stubborn, oppositional, and often said to be hotheaded. He has few fears compared to most people. His daily life is full of things that keep him interested. When he gets bored, he likes to stir up excitement. Something exciting will almost always make him feel better when he is feeling low.

Cognitions: His concentration and memory are adequate. He is self-confident, and he makes up his mind easily. He believes that others are only interested in their own welfare.

Interpersonal Relations: He is extroverted and mixes easily with others. He likes to go to loud parties and social events. His home life was pleasant. He believes that if given the chance, he would make a good leader of people. His way of doing things is apt to be misundcrstood by others. IIe finds it easy to ask for help from his friends.

Other Problem Areas: His physical health is not as good as that of his friends. He has a number of physical and neuropsychological symptoms; his history and background should be reviewed to determine whether a medical or neuropsychological evaluation is warranted.

He may abuse substances. There is a slight possibility of suicidal ideation.

Treatment: His prognosis is guarded. His problems are very characterologic in nature and do not produce enough emotional distress to motivate him to engage in treatment. He may prefer to focus on his physical symptoms rather than on psychological processes. Short-term behavioral interventions that focus on his reasons for entering treatment will be most appropriate. He has little interest in or motivation for long-term treatment.

Table D.9 provides the prototypic scores for *1-9/9-1* codetypes.

1-0/0-1 (0.18%)

Moods: The client is experiencing moderate emotional distress characterized by dysphoria and anxiety, yet he states that he is happy most of the time. He is easily embarrassed.

Cognitions: His concentration and memory are adequate and his judgment is better now than it ever was. He is greatly bothered by forgetting where he put things. He tends to be mildly obsessive and ruminative. He is not assertive and finds it hard to defend his rights. He is easily defeated in an argument.

Interpersonal Relations: He is very shy, introverted, and socially withdrawn. He finds it difficult to talk when he meets new people. Whenever possible he will avoid being in a crowd. He is a very conventional, law-abiding individual primarily out of fear of being caught. He has ordinary interest patterns. He is bothered when people compliment him or say nice things about him.

Other Problem Areas: He reports a number of gastrointestinal and neurologic symptoms. He tires quickly. He has a number of physical and neuropsychological symptoms; his history and background should be reviewed to determine whether a medical or neuropsychological evaluation is warranted.

He is unlikely to abuse substances or have suicidal ideation.

Treatment: Prognosis is guarded because he is experiencing little emotional distress that would motivate him for treatment. His problems are characterologic in nature, which complicate any therapeutic intervention. Short-term behavioral interventions that focus on his reasons for entering treatment will be beneficial. Assertiveness or social-skill training may also be helpful.

Table D.10 provides the prototypic scores for *1-0/0-1* codetypes.

Spike 2 (1.14%)

Clients who elevate only Scale 2 (Depression) are likely to be experiencing a mild reactive depression even if they do not report depressive feelings. If Scale 9 (Hypomania) is below a T score of 45, particularly in persons under the age of 30, the probability of significant depression is even higher. Suicidal ideation and plans should be routinely evaluated, although they are very unlikely to endorse the items on the MMPI-2 that have specific suicidal content (Chapter 6).

Moods: The client is experiencing a minimal level of emotional distress characterized by depression and an even milder level of anxiety. He cannot understand why he is so impatient and grouchy. He wishes that he could be as happy as others seem to be. He feels useless at times. He feels inadequate, lacks self-confidence, is pessimistic about the future, and has strong guilt feelings. He feels unable to "get going" and to get things done when he does manage to start something. He may have a low level of anhedonia.

Cognitions: His concentration and memory are adequate. His judgment is not as good now as it was in the past. He lacks self-confidence. His thought processes are very common with no unusual ideas or experiences and he is unlikely to be psychotic.

Interpersonal Relations: He is socially reserved and introverted. He is passive, dependent, and tends to withdraw in the face of conflict or stress, which serves to exacerbate his depressive symptomatology. His family demonstrated love and companionship toward him, and his parents approved of his friends.

Other Problem Areas: He is in good physical health. Although he is less able to work now than he was in the past, he has enough energy to do his work. He does not have sleep problems. He is very conventional and does not get into trouble over his behavior. There is a slight possibility of suicidal ideation that should be evaluated. He is unlikely to abuse substances.

Treatment: His prognosis is fair. There is limited motivation for any kind of long-term intervention because he is experiencing minimal distress. Short-term behavioral interventions focused on his reasons for entering treatment will be important initially and he will show significant improvement within a relatively short period of time. If he becomes engaged in the treatment process, cognitive-behavioral therapy focusing on his depressive cognitions will be beneficial.

Kelley and King (1979a) provide additional interpretive information on Spike 2 codetypes, and Table D.11 provides the prototypic scores.

2-3/3-2 (8.07%)

Moods: The client is experiencing a mild to moderate level of emotional distress characterized by dysphoria, worrying, and anhedonia. She frequently worries about something. She feels inadequate, helpless, and insecure. She is easily hurt by criticism or scolding and has difficulty expressing her feelings. She is overcontrolled and fearful of losing control. She is likely to experience increases in depression, fatigue, and physical symptoms in response to stress. She is unlikely to express her anger overtly.

Cognitions: She has concentration difficulties and memory problems. She has low self-esteem, lacks self-confidence, and is self-doubting. Her judgment is not as good now as it was in the past. She sometimes thinks that she is about to "go to pieces." She does not analyze the reasons for her or others' behavior.

Interpersonal Relations: She is somewhat introverted and does not like loud parties or social events. She feels socially inadequate, avoids social involvements, and presents herself as helpless, immature, and dependent. She gets along well with members of her family.

Other Problem Areas: She has a number of mild physical ailments, and her physical health is not as good as that of her friends. She tires quickly. She has sleep difficulties and she does not wake up fresh and rested most mornings. Her poor health interferes with her ability to work. She may be sexually dysfunctional, which may represent her control of sexual feelings or an expression of her unhappiness with her spouse. She has a number of physical and neurologic symptoms; her history and background should be reviewed to determine whether a medical or neuropsychological evaluation is warranted.

She is a very conventional individual who is unlikely to have behavioral problems. She is not likely to abuse substances. There is some possibility of suicidal ideation that needs to be evaluated.

Treatment: Her prognosis is generally poor because she lacks insight into her own behavior and sees little chance for significant change in her life. She has grown accustomed to her chronic problems, and she continues to function at a lowered level of efficiency for prolonged periods of time. Short-term behavioral therapy that focuses on her reasons for entering treatment may be beneficial and may allow for the development of a therapeutic alliance that would be necessary for long-term therapy. She will prefer to discuss her physical symptoms rather than her psychological processes. She is not naturally introspective, which will complicate the therapeutic process.

Archer et al. (1995) and Gynther et al. (1973) furnish additional interpretive information on *2-3/3-2* codetypes, and Table D.12 provides the prototypic scores.

2-4/4-2 (2.43%)

Clients may achieve *2-4/4-2* codetypes for a myriad of reasons and as a result it is a difficult codetype to interpret. One critical factor, which should be assessed through an interview with her or knowledge of her reason(s) for taking the MMPI-2, is whether Scale *2* (Depression) is being elevated by internal (intrapsychic) and/or external (situational) causes. Examples of the latter are psychopathic individuals who have been caught in some illicit or illegal activity and who are being evaluated as a consequence of their behavior. The depression in these persons represents the constraints being placed on their behavior; their depression, or possibly frustration and boredom at being

externally constrained, will alleviate itself quickly once they manage to extricate themselves from their present situation. The presence of even this situational depression in these persons suggests a better prognosis than persons in similar circumstances who achieve a Spike *4* or a *4-9/9-4* codetype.

These psychopathic clients with a *2-4/4-2* codetype can be understood best by examining the correlates of a Spike *4* codetype. She will display excellent intellectual insight into her behavior, make a positive impression of her earnestness on the clinician, and vehemently protest that she will change her behavior. Despite her "sincere" intentions, recurrences of acting out are very likely, followed by the same protestations to do better when caught again.

Another subgroup of clients with *2-4/4-2* codetypes is more likely to be chronically depressed and unhappy without evidence of antisocial acting out. She will be displaying hostility and resentment, which often result from marital conflict, familial difficulties, or similar situations that make her feel trapped and hopeless.

She is immature, dependent, and egocentric and often vacillates between pitying herself and blaming others for her difficulties. These behaviors are chronic in nature and difficult to resolve through psychological interventions. Involvement of the other members of the family or the spouse in the therapeutic interaction is important if meaningful behavior change is to occur.

Clients with *2-4/4-2* codetypes are frequently identified as alcoholics (cf. Archer et al., 1995; Clopton, 1978a; Graham & Strenger, 1988; Greene & Garvin, 1988). Hodo and Fowler (1976) reported that 21 percent of 1,009 white male alcoholics had this codetype and that this was the most frequent codetype among these men. Greene and Garvin (1988) in their summary of MMPI research on substance abuse samples found that 15.3% of male and 14.8% of female alcoholics had a *2-4/4-2* codetype. Gynther et al. (1973) also found that alcoholism was a replicated correlate of this codetype in their psychiatric sample. These clients will evidence depressive features, familial conflict, and vocational problems characteristic of alcoholics.

In determining which of the foregoing descriptions fits a specific client, useful information can be obtained by analyzing the Content scales; a number of the Supplementary scales such as Dominance, MacAndrew Alcoholism, and so on (Chapters 5 and 6); the reasons why the client is taking the MMPI-2; and the other Clinical scales.

Moods: The client is experiencing a moderate level of emotional distress characterized by dysphoria, resentment, agitation, and anhedonia. These moods often arise in response to some external problem or difficulty. While she may express guilt and remorse, and may promise to change her behavior, her expressions typically are not sincere. She is grouchy, irritable, and stubborn. She feels that she has not lived the "right kind of life," and she regrets many things that she has done. She wishes that she could be as happy as others seem to be.

Cognitions: Her memory is good, but her judgment is not as good now as it was in the past. She lacks self-confidence. She sometimes thinks that she is about to "go to pieces." She is dubious of the motivation of other people and believes that they are interested only in their own welfare. A theme of cynicism permeates her interactions. She knows who is responsible for most of her troubles.

Interpersonal Relations: She is slightly introverted. Her home life is not as pleasant as that of most people. She quarrels with members of her family and feels alienated from them. She very much wanted to leave home.

Other Problem Areas: She is in good health. Her sleep is disturbed by her thoughts and ideas. She is likely to abuse substances and to have been in trouble with the law. She may have suicidal ideation that needs to be monitored carefully because of her potential for substance abuse.

Treatment: Her prognosis is generally poor for traditional methods of individual psychotherapy unless a mood disorder is the primary diagnosis. In the latter instance, cognitive-behavioral psychotherapy focused on the depressive cognitions will be beneficial. Evaluation for antidepressant medication may be in-dicated in cases of more severe depression. Group therapy with individuals with similar behaviors may be effective when a mood disorder is not the primary diagnosis.

Archer et al. (1995), Gynther et al. (1973), and Kelley and King (1979a) provide additional interpretive information on *2-4/4-2* codetypes, and Tables 7.11 and D.13 provide the prototypic scores.

2-5/5-2 (0.32%)

There are almost no published data on *2-5/5-2* codetypes. King and Kelley (1977b) found that male college students who were psychiatric outpatients with this codetype were anxious, disoriented, and withdrawn. These students dated infrequently, had somatic symptoms, and had a physical history for their symptoms and difficulties.

Moods: The client is experiencing mild emotional distress characterized by dysphoria. Her depressive symptomatology tends to be chronic in nature. Criticism or scolding hurts her terribly. She feels useless at times.

Cognitions: She lacks self-confidence and is bothered by thoughts about sex. She believes that others are primarily interested in their own welfare.

Interpersonal Relations: She is passive, dependent, shy, and introverted, although she has adequate social skills. She tends to be satisfied with her familial and interpersonal relations. She is very conventional and is unlikely to get into trouble because of her behavior. She has wide interests.

Other Problem Areas: She is in good physical health and sleeps well, but she is easily awakened by noise.

Treatment: Her prognosis is fair. She generally responds well to short-term therapy that focuses on her dysphoria even though it may be relatively mild. There is very limited motivation for any type of long-term psychotherapy.

King and Kelley (1977b) and Tanner (1990) provide additional interpretive information on *2-5/5-2*

Table 7-11

Prototypic Scores for 2-4/4-2 Codetypes (N = 855)

Demographics

Demographics			M	SD	Marital Status		%
	Age		36.0	11.4		Never Married	41.1
	Education		12.5	4.8		Married	35.0
	Gender		%			Separated	6.4
		Men	36.6			Divorced	16.5
		Women	63.4			Widowed	1.0

Test-Taking Scales

Omissions		M	SD	Consistency		M	SD
	?	0.9	2.5		VRIN	54.4	9.8
					|F - FB|	4.1	2.8
					TRIN	47.3	10.6

Accuracy of Item Endorsement

Underreporting		M	SD	Overreporting		M	SD
	False %	57.3	6.5		True %	41.6	6.5
Impression	L	50.4	9.4	Infrequency	F	69.3	15.0
Management	ODecp	41.5	8.4		FB	67.7	18.1
	Sd	44.4	9.7		F[p]	55.7	12.6
Superior	S	43.6	8.5	Critical Items	K & B	31.8	10.5
Adjustment					L & W	37.2	12.2
Self-Deception	K	31.1	6.4	Dissimulation	F - K	-3.4	7.2
	So	34.3	10.7		Ds	65.0	12.3
					O - S	79.4	59.9

Scales

Validity and Clinical			Supplementary			Morey et al. Overlapping Personality Disorder		
Scale	M	SD	Scale	M	SD	Scale	M	SD
?	0.9	2.5	A	63.6	8.9	PAR	59.2	10.8
L	50.4	9.4	R	57.1	10.5	SZD	56.4	12.1
F	69.3	15.0	Es	36.3	10.8	STY	61.1	10.8
K	45.8	8.8	TRIN	47.3	10.6	ANT	57.4	10.5
1(Hs)	61.9	10.5	VRIN	54.4	9.8	BDL	56.9	10.0
2(D)	80.4	9.7	O-H	48.5	10.4	HST	43.6	10.8
3(Hy)	64.5	10.3	Do	37.4	10.6	NAR	41.5	10.2
4(Pd)	80.5	8.9	Re	41.2	10.9	AVD	60.8	9.8
5(Mf)	50.2	9.7	GM	41.3	8.6	DEP	63.1	10.9
6(Pa)	64.9	10.6	GF	46.2	10.4	CPS	54.0	8.6
7(Pt)	69.2	9.5	Mt	70.4	9.0	Personality Psychopathology Five		
8(Sc)	67.2	10.5	PK	69.8	11.0			
9(Ma)	49.9	8.6	PS	69.3	11.1	Scale	M	SD
0(Si)	61.0	9.4	MAC-R	50.4	11.3	AGG	47.0	10.2
			APS	53.2	10.1	PSY	55.5	10.8
			AAS	57.7	12.1	CON	46.8	10.1
			MDS	71.7	11.0	NEN	61.8	9.4
			Ho	55.5	9.3	PEE	30.9	11.7
			CAL-R	57.0	10.7			

Content			Content Component					
Scale	M	SD	Scale	M	SD	Scale	M	SD
ANX	68.4	10.2	FRS1	53.1	12.4	ASP1	51.8	9.4
FRS	50.6	10.3	FRS2	48.6	9.8	ASP2	58.6	13.2
OBS	57.0	10.3	DEP1	72.2	14.4	TPA1	53.0	10.7
DEP	72.1	10.3	DEP2	71.6	9.6	TPA2	51.2	10.1
HEA	60.5	10.0	DEP3	67.9	10.6	LSE1	64.6	12.2
BIZ	53.5	9.2	DEP4	66.9	26.3	LSE2	54.1	11.0
ANG	56.4	11.7	HEA1	57.8	13.4	SOD1	59.0	12.0
CYN	54.0	9.4	HEA2	53.5	11.5	SOD2	53.0	9.9
ASP	54.6	10.3	HEA3	65.1	12.6	FAM1	60.1	11.4
TPA	52.1	10.8	BIZ1	49.1	10.0	FAM2	64.0	14.5
LSE	62.8	11.3	BIZ2	53.6	10.5	TRT1	65.8	13.9
SOD	58.4	11.7	ANG1	54.3	11.4	TRT2	53.7	11.2
FAM	64.3	11.7	ANG2	56.2	10.6			
WRK	66.0	11.5	CYN1	53.8	9.5			
TRT	64.4	12.0	CYN2	53.0	9.8			

Note. All scores are T scores except: Cannot Say, K & B and L & W critical items which are raw scores; True % and False % which are the percentage of items endorsed "true" or "false;" and |F - FB|, F - K, and O - S which are difference scores.

codetypes, and Table D.14 provides the prototypic scores.

2-6/6-2 (3.14%)

Moods: The client is experiencing a moderate level of emotional distress that is characterized by brooding, dysphoria, anger, and anhedonia. Most of the time she feels depressed and worried about something. She generally feels angry with both herself and others. She is openly hostile and resentful toward others. She is more sensitive and feels emotions more intensely than others, and her feelings are easily hurt. She feels disappointments so keenly that she cannot put them out of her mind. She wishes that she could be as happy as others seem to be. The future seems hopeless to her. She is unable to "get going" and to get things done in her life.

Cognitions: She finds it hard to concentrate on a task or job, and her judgment is not as good now as it was in the past. She lacks self-confidence. She is sensitive to any form of criticism and prone to overinterpret the most innocuous comments. She assumes others are against her, and anticipates being rejected. She thinks that she is about to "go to pieces" and to "lose her mind." She is sure that she is being talked about and that strangers are looking at her critically. She thinks that she is no good at all.

She reports a number of symptoms that may reflect a psychotic process. Her presenting problems, background, and history should be reviewed carefully with this characteristic in mind.

Interpersonal Relations: She is shy and introverted, and she finds it hard to talk to strangers. She feels lonely even when she is with people. She dislikes being around people and spends most of her spare time by herself. She believes that no one seems to understand her. Her behavior generally invites others to reject and avoid her.

Other Problem Areas: She is concerned about her health but does not report any specific physical symptoms. She feels tired a good deal of the time. Her sleep is frequently disturbed by thoughts or ideas running through her mind. Suicidal ideation is likely and should be evaluated carefully. She may abuse substances.

Treatment: Her prognosis is guarded because her behavior reflects a chronic pattern of adjustment that is difficult to alter. Her anger and brooding resentment make it very difficult to develop a therapeutic alliance. Short-term behavioral interventions that focus on her reasons for entering treatment will be most beneficial. Cognitive-behavioral therapy that focuses on her dysphoria and anger also may be appropriate. Evaluation for antidepressant medication may be indicated in cases of more severe depression.

Kelley and King (1979a) provide additional interpretive information on *2-6/6-2* codetypes, and Table D.15 provides the prototypic scores.

2-7/7-2 (5.49%)

Clients with *2-7/7-2* codetypes are very common in most types of psychiatric settings. Suicidal ideation and plans should be assessed carefully. Clinicians should routinely evaluate the client's responses to items 150, 303, 506, 520, 524, and 530 on the MMPI-2 in all clients, and particularly in this codetype, since the item content reflects suicidal ideation and/or suicide attempts.

If Scale *7* (Psychasthenia) is extremely elevated (T score > 85) and particularly if Scale *7* also is higher than Scale *2* (Depression), clients may be so agitated and worried that these symptoms should be addressed through methods such as psychopharmacologic treatment or situational intervention before treatment is initiated.

Since these codetypes occur so frequently, it often is possible to examine the third highest Clinical scale to augment the interpretation. Three scales (3 [Hysteria], 4 [Psychopathic Deviate], and 8 [Schizophrenia]) often are elevated with Scales *2* (Depression) and *7* (Psychasthenia), thus producing three high-point triads: *2-7/7-2-(3), 2-7/7-2-(4),* and *2-7/7-2-(8).*

A client with a *2-7/7-2-(3)* codetype, which is the least frequent of the three triads, is likely to be a docile, passive individual who is most comfortable in very dependent interpersonal relationships. She is adept at inspiring others to take care of her and to protect her from her cruel fate. She may even persuade the clinician to try to save her. That is, she is very successful at tapping any tendency a clinician may have toward rescuing or saving a client. Intervention into this chronic behavior pattern is fraught with problems even for the experienced clinician, who must provide appropriate support and empathy while inducing significant behavior change by confronting or interpreting the client's behavior.

A client with a *2-7/7-2-(4)* codetype is characterized by chronic, deeply ingrained depressive features in conjunction with extensive feelings of inadequacy and guilt. She is self-deprecating and tries to make others feel superior by focusing on her weaknesses and inadequacies. She refuses to recognize her extensive dependency on others. The clinical extreme of the behavior shown by these clients is a psychotic depressive reaction, although few clients with this codetype are diagnosed as such.

She reports financial difficulties, marital problems, and problems with alcohol. Because of the chronic, deep-seated nature of her problems and her reluctance to expose herself to anxiety, prognosis for significant behavior change is poor. Treatment aimed at alleviating the depressive features may be most beneficial for short-term goals.

A client with a *2-7/7-2-(8)* codetype often appears in psychiatric settings. She will have multiple neurotic symptoms that are of a chronic nature. Her major symptoms include depression, nervousness, and obsessions. She is ruminatively introspective and evidences excessive indecision, doubts, and worry. She complains of difficulties in concentration and thinking. There is a real question of whether these multiple neurotic symptoms actually mask a thought disorder. Hence, careful evaluation for a thought disorder is indicated.

She may have suicidal ruminations; these need to be evaluated carefully. Again, clinicians are reminded to review the client's responses to items 150, 303, 506, 520, 524, and 530 on the MMPI-2. She is withdrawn and socially introverted, and these characteristics exacerbate her obsessive and ruminative behaviors. Psychopharmacologic intervention is indicated frequently. Psychotherapeutic interventions should initially be directed toward solving her immediate problems and should avoid any introspective type of self-analysis.

Moods: The client is experiencing a moderate to severe level of emotional distress characterized by dysphoria, guilt, and anxiety. She views herself as being irritable and grouchy, although others are more aware of her dysphoria. She experiences little pleasure from life, and life in general is a strain for her. She is a chronic worrier who broods and ruminates about herself and her problems, which are readily apparent to her and others. She is likely to overreact to minor stress with agitation, guilt, and self-punishment. She lacks self-confidence and feels insecure, inadequate, and inferior. She is unlikely to express anger overtly or to be aggressive toward others.

Cognitions: She is obsessed with her perceived personal deficiencies and views herself as useless and no good at all despite frequent evidence of her personal achievements. She has a hard time concentrating and finds it difficult to keep her mind on a task or job. She believes that her judgment is poor and that she has memory problems. She is reluctant to start a task, and she gives up quickly when things go wrong. Her inertia and lack of drive reflect her depressive cognitions and negative expectations. Making any type of decision is very difficult for her, and making important decisions is nearly impossible. She is pessimistic and hopeless about the possibility of any substantial change in her circumstances. She feels guilty when her high standards and expectations are not met.

Interpersonal Relations: She is shy and introverted. She is easily embarrassed and generally uncomfortable around others. She finds it difficult to talk with people whom she does not know and will avoid people if given the opportunity. She is alienated from others and herself. She is passive and dependent in her relationships with others, and she is unlikely to be assertive.

Other Problem Areas: She often will report cardiovascular symptoms that reflect her chronic state of tension and anxiety, insomnia, and decreased appetite. Suicidal thoughts and attempts are fairly likely and should be evaluated carefully. Substance abuse may exist secondary to an underlying mood disorder. She is likely to prefer drugs in the sedative/hypnotic class if she uses them. She finds it difficult to sleep because of her ruminating and worrying. Sleep medications should be prescribed cautiously, if at all, because of the potential for suicide.

Treatment: Her prognosis is generally quite good. She sees herself as being responsible for her difficulties and is willing to examine her behavior, even at great length. She has a natural introspective orientation as well as the motivation to change, which augurs well for any psychotherapeutic intervention. Cognitive-behavioral psychotherapy focusing on her depressive cognitions will be very beneficial to her. Evaluation for antidepressant medication may be indicated in cases of more severe depression.

Archer et al. (1995), Gilberstadt and Duker (1965), Gynther et al. (1973), Kelley and King (1979c, 1980), and Marks et al. (1974) provide additional interpretive information on *2-7/7-2* codetypes and their triads. Tables 7.12 and D.16 provide the prototypic scores.

2-8/8-2 (3.05%)

There are a number of differences in the observed correlates of *2-8* and *8-2* codetypes, which will be described briefly before discussing *2-8/8-2* codetypes more generally. A client with a *2-8* codetype is experiencing severe depression with associated anxiety and agitation. She frequently fears loss of control. Her depression and agitation are usually sufficient to produce confusion, forgetfulness, and difficulties in concentration and attention. She often displays obsessive ruminations. Evaluation for a thought disorder may be appropriate. Somatic symptoms are common, such as difficulty in sleeping or fatigue. She tends to withdraw and isolate herself from interpersonal relationships and activities, which will exacerbate her symptomatology.

Suicidal ideation is a prominent feature and suicide attempts are quite frequent; suicide potential should be evaluated carefully as well as the client's

responses to items 150, 303, 506, 520, 524, and 530. This codetype represents a chronic level of adjustment of marginal quality, so prognosis for intervention and change is poor.

A client with an *8-2* codetype is more likely to evidence actual schizophrenic features in addition to the behaviors just described. Auditory and/or visual hallucinations and systematized delusions may be present. A careful evaluation for a thought disorder should be made. Somatic symptoms of a bizarre nature may be seen.

She also is depressed, isolated, and withdrawn. Suicidal ruminations and suicide attempts are quite frequent; suicide potential should be evaluated carefully as well as the client's responses to items 150, 303, 506, 520, 524, and 530. This is a chronic pattern of adjustment that usually results in psychiatric hospitalization.

Moods: The client is experiencing severe emotional distress that is characterized by dysphoria and anhedonia. She is depressed, agitated, anxious, and guilty. She also is impatient, irritable, and angry. She does not seem to care what happens to her. She has difficulty starting to do things and she has little hope of success if she does get started. She has lost her desire to work out her problems.

Cognitions: She has difficulty with concentration, forgetfulness, and memory problems. Her judgment is not as good now as it was in the past. She lacks self-confidence. She is worried that there is something wrong with her mind, that she may be "losing her mind," and that she is about to "go to pieces." Much of the time she thinks that she has done something wrong or evil. She thinks that strangers are looking at her critically. She generally feels worthless and inadequate. She avoids facing a crisis or difficulty. She gives up quickly when things go wrong. She believes that others are only interested in themselves and care little about her.

She reports a number of symptoms that may reflect a psychotic process or a very long-term characterologic condition. Her presenting problems, background, and history should be reviewed with this possibility in mind.

Table 7-12

Prototypic Scores for 2-7/7-2 Codetypes (N = 1,934)

Demographics

Demographics		M	SD	Marital Status	%
Age		38.6	13.0	Never Married	32.6
Education		12.5	5.1	Married	48.0
Gender		%		Separated	3.6
	Men	45.9		Divorced	14.2
	Women	54.1		Widowed	1.5

Test-Taking Scales

Omissions		M	SD	Consistency		M	SD
	?	1.3	3.5		VRIN	53.9	9.7
					|F - FB|	3.4	2.6
					TRIN	51.0	10.7

Accuracy of Item Endorsement

Underreporting		M	SD	Overreporting		M	SD
	False %	55.7	6.5		True %	43.1	6.5
Impression	L	51.6	10.1	Infrequency	F	67.1	14.1
Management	ODecp	40.5	8.3		FB	72.1	19.6
	Sd	43.5	9.7		F[p]	54.4	11.6
Superior	S	44.6	8.4	Critical Items	K & B	33.7	9.7
Adjustment					L & W	40.0	12.0
Self-Deception	K	31.1	6.4	Dissimulation	F - K	-3.8	6.7
	So	28.6	10.0		Ds	64.6	12.1
					O - S	103.5	58.7

Scales

Validity and Clinical			Supplementary			Morey et al. Overlapping Personality Disorder		
Scale	M	SD	Scale	M	SD	Scale	M	SD
?	1.3	3.5	A	69.4	8.4	PAR	57.5	10.9
L	51.6	10.1	R	60.9	10.7	SZD	60.9	11.5
F	67.1	14.1	Es	28.3	12.1	STY	65.3	10.7
K	45.6	8.3	TRIN	51.0	10.7	ANT	50.6	10.2
1(Hs)	67.3	11.1	VRIN	53.9	9.7	BDL	55.3	9.1
2(D)	85.7	10.5	O-H	48.1	10.3	HST	36.8	10.3
3(Hy)	68.4	11.3	Do	33.0	9.9	NAR	34.5	10.3
4(Pd)	64.0	10.4	Re	45.9	10.0	AVD	67.6	9.3
5(Mf)	51.0	9.5	GM	35.3	9.7	DEP	68.7	11.1
6(Pa)	66.0	11.0	GF	50.0	9.0	CPS	57.1	8.5
7(Pt)	82.8	9.4	Mt	74.9	8.1	Personality Psychopathology Five		
8(Sc)	72.0	11.0	PK	73.5	11.6	Scale	M	SD
9(Ma)	47.4	8.5	PS	75.3	11.2	AGG	41.3	10.2
0(Si)	67.5	9.3	MAC-R	44.6	10.2	PSY	56.8	11.6
			APS	52.4	9.4	CON	55.0	10.1
			AAS	51.3	11.1	NEN	63.9	9.1
			MDS	63.8	11.6	PEE	27.5	12.3
			Ho	54.0	9.4			
			CAL-R	50.3	11.3			

Content			Content Component					
Scale	M	SD	Scale	M	SD	Scale	M	SD
ANX	74.5	9.5	FRS1	61.3	17.3	ASP1	50.2	9.6
FRS	56.8	12.4	FRS2	52.5	10.4	ASP2	50.2	11.1
OBS	63.5	10.1	DEP1	75.0	14.3	TPA1	55.2	10.2
DEP	73.7	9.9	DEP2	73.8	9.6	TPA2	50.0	9.7
HEA	64.8	11.0	DEP3	66.4	9.8	LSE1	68.6	11.3
BIZ	54.7	10.2	DEP4	69.8	26.0	LSE2	60.1	11.8
ANG	55.5	11.1	HEA1	60.8	15.1	SOD1	63.7	11.7
CYN	52.6	9.9	HEA2	59.2	14.1	SOD2	60.3	9.2
ASP	50.7	9.6	HEA3	67.5	13.0	FAM1	52.4	11.1
TPA	51.9	10.2	BIZ1	50.9	11.4	FAM2	53.9	12.7
LSE	68.7	11.6	BIZ2	54.9	11.3	TRT1	71.8	15.0
SOD	65.1	11.9	ANG1	52.1	10.9	TRT2	55.7	10.7
FAM	55.1	11.2	ANG2	57.3	10.4			
WRK	70.9	10.3	CYN1	52.4	10.2			
TRT	68.8	12.4	CYN2	51.4	9.6			

Note. All scores are T scores except: Cannot Say, K & B and L & W critical items which are raw scores; True % and False % which are the percentage of items endorsed "true" or "false;" and |F - FB|, F - K, and O - S which are difference scores.

Interpersonal Relations: She is very introverted, and withdraws from and keeps others at a distance. She dislikes having people around her and spends most of her spare time by herself. She feels lonely even when she is with people. Her withdrawal and isolation only serve to exacerbate her symptoms. She believes that no one seems to understand her. Her family is critical of her, and she feels alienated from them.

Other Problem Areas: She reports a number of physical symptoms associated with neurological functioning. Her history and background should be reviewed carefully to determine whether physical or neuropsychological factors may be contributing to her present condition, and whether a medical or neuropsychological evaluation is needed.

Suicidal ideation is very likely and suicide potential should be evaluated carefully and monitored regularly. She is likely to abuse substances. She has sleep difficulties. At times she has a strong urge to do something shocking or harmful that warrants investigation.

Treatment: Her prognosis is generally poor. Her problems are chronic, and hospitalization may be required to stabilize her condition. Psychopharmacologic interventions may be necessary to deal with her concerns that she may be "losing her mind," to help her sleep, and to elevate her mood. The probability of meaningful long-term change is low. Short-term behavioral interventions that focus on her reasons for entering treatment will be most beneficial.

Archer et al. (1995), Gilberstadt and Duker (1965), Gynther et al. (1973), Kelley and King (1979b, 1980), and Marks et al. (1974) provide additional interpretive information on *2-8/8-2* codetypes. Table D.17 provides the prototypic scores.

2-9/9-2 (0.10%)

Clients with *2-9/9-2* codetypes demonstrate an interesting example of a Clinical scale configuration that might not be anticipated: clients who simultaneously evidence significant depression and hypomanic tendencies. It is frequently stated that *2-9/9-2* codetypes are characteristic of brain-damaged individuals (cf. Lachar, 1974), but subsequent research has not been able to replicate these findings (see Farr and Martin [1988] for a review of this research).

Moods: The client is experiencing mild emotional distress that is characterized by agitation, brooding, and worrying. She frequently worries about something, and she has more than her share of things to worry about. Her feelings are easily hurt. She wishes that she could be as happy as others seem to be. She is stubborn, impatient, and grouchy. She has a high activity level and may exhibit an agitated depression. When she gets bored, she likes to stir up excitement, and if she is feeling low, something exciting will always make her feel better. In response to stress, she often exhibits an increase in the expression of somatic symptoms, becomes agitated, or abuses substances.

Cognitions: She lacks self-confidence. Her judgment is not as good now as it was in the past. She believes in telling only that portion of the truth that does not hurt her, particularly if she finds herself in trouble. She also believes that others will lie to avoid being caught. She strongly defends her own opinions. She has a daydream life about which she does not tell others.

Interpersonal Relations: She is extroverted and relates easily to others. She likes parties and social events. People have misunderstood her intentions when she has tried to be helpful. She very much wanted to leave home.

Other Problem Areas: Although she worries about her health, she does not report any specific physical symptoms. She is very likely to abuse substances. At times she has a strong urge to do something shocking or harmful that warrants investigation. She is likely to have suicidal ideation that should be reviewed carefully because of her proneness to engage in risky behaviors, impulsivity, and substance abuse.

Treatment: Her prognosis is generally guarded. The possibility of an underlying mood disorder should be evaluated carefully. If a bipolar disorder is identified, psychopharmacologic intervention is indicated. Otherwise, psychological intervention is probably best directed toward the depressive features. Short-term behavioral interventions that focus on her reasons for entering treatment will be most beneficial.

Table D.18 provides the prototypic scores for *2-9/9-2* codetypes.

2-0/0-2 (1.89%)

Moods: The client is experiencing very mild emotional distress characterized by chronic brooding, dysphoria, and anhedonia. Criticism or scolding hurts him terribly. He feels disappointments so keenly that he cannot put them out of his mind. He feels useless at times. He cannot understand why he so easily becomes impatient and grouchy with others. He is not happy with himself the way he is. He feels unable to "get going" and to make changes in his life.

Cognitions: He lacks self-confidence and finds it hard to be assertive because he is so reserved. He avoids crises and difficulties and is easily defeated in an argument. He gives up quickly when things go wrong, when others criticize him, or when he thinks that he is unable to do something.

Interpersonal Relations: He is very shy, bashful, and conventional. He avoids interactions with others. He finds it hard to talk when he meets new people. He sees himself as socially inept and awkward; others are more likely to describe him as shy and reserved. He feels lonely even when he is with people. He is very sensitive to the reactions of others and is easily embarrassed in social situations. He finds it difficult to confide in others about himself, and he becomes nervous when people ask him personal questions.

Other Problem Areas: He is unlikely to abuse substances. He is very unlikely to get into trouble because of his behavior. Suicidal ideation is possible and should be monitored.

Treatment: His prognosis is fair. He is very accustomed to his characterologic problems, and he is reluctant to think of making changes in his life. Essentially he has adjusted to his depressive state, and engaging him in psychotherapeutic endeavors may be difficult. His difficulty in self-disclosing complicates

the development of a therapeutic alliance. Social skills and assertiveness training frequently are beneficial. He responds well to structured treatment approaches that prescribe what he is to do. Cognitive-behavioral approaches that focus on his depressive cognitions also will be beneficial. Group psychotherapy will be helpful in providing a social perspective for his problems and in dealing directly with his avoidant behaviors.

Kelley and King (1979a) provide additional interpretive information on *2-0/0-2* codetypes, and Table D.19 provides the prototypic scores.

Spike 3 (2.23%)

Moods: The client is not experiencing any type of emotional distress. He is happy and finds his daily life interesting and pleasurable. He sees himself as bright, cheerful, and optimistic. He uses repression and denial to maintain his cheerful outlook on life. He is unwilling to express any type of feelings of anger.

Cognitions: He believes that he thinks clearly and logically, but others perceive him to be flighty and unfocused. He is typically immature and egocentric, and displays other hysteroid features. When under stress, he will develop physical symptoms that have obvious secondary gain characteristics. He can make up his mind easily and he believes that his judgment is better than it ever was. He does not analyze the reasons for his behavior or the behavior of others. He believes that others can be trusted and that they have his best interests at heart. He is self-confident.

Interpersonal Relations: He interacts easily with others and likes to be in social situations. He is a very conventional individual who is unlikely to get into trouble because of his behavior. His parents had reasonable expectations of him, and he did not want to leave home. He sees his relations with other people as being harmonious and he expresses an almost unassailable optimism. Even when faced with overwhelming failure in his life, he will maintain that everything is going fine.

Other Problem Areas: Although his physical health is not as good as that of his friends, he only reports a few mild physical symptoms. He is unlikely to abuse substances or to report suicidal ideation.

Treatment: His prognosis is guarded for any type of intervention because he is experiencing little personal distress. He is very comfortable with himself, which decreases motivation to change his behavior. He is extremely resistant to entertaining the idea that psychological factors could in any way be involved in his current problems. Short-term behavioral interventions that focus on his reasons for entering treatment will be most beneficial. Prognosis for significant behavior change is unlikely unless he can be involved in long-term psychotherapy. Generally, he will terminate any professional contact once he has weathered his current crisis.

Table D.20 provides the prototypic scores for Spike *3* codetypes.

3-4/4-3 (2.14%)

Clients with *3-4* codetypes display different correlates than clients with *4-3* codetypes, so each of these will be described in turn before describing *3-4/4-3* codetypes in more general terms. The relationship between Scales *3* and *4* serves as an index of whether persons will control and inhibit their socially unacceptable impulses, particularly aggression and hostility. A client with a *3-4* codetype is an immature, egocentric individual who discharges her hostile feelings indirectly. Overtly, she appears to be quiet and conforming. She may become involved with acting-out individuals and satisfy her own hostile tendencies in a vicarious fashion.

A man may express fears of being homosexual, if Scale *5* also is elevated, but he is unlikely to have overtly acted out his homosexual impulses. He reports marital or family problems with little understanding of his role in them. He generally has chronic problems that are difficult to change.

A client with a *4-3* codetype is characterized by poorly controlled anger and hostility that is expressed in a cyclic fashion. Often he is eventually incarcerated for his violent acts. The presence of violent, acting out behavior in these persons has been replicated in several studies (Davis & Sines, 1971; Persons & Marks, 1971). However, Buck and Graham (1978)

and O'Sullivan and Jemelka (1993) failed to replicate this finding. In fact, O'Sullivan and Jemelka found few significant differences between male felon offenders with *3-4* codetypes and *4-3* codetypes.

He is a quiet, withdrawn individual, and his sudden outbursts come as a surprise to others. He displays poor judgment under stress, but his emotional or violent outbursts may be only minimally related to external stress or provocation. His outbursts are not illogical or irrational unless Scale *8* (Schizophrenia) also is elevated. The cyclic pattern of violent outbursts with intermittent periods of appropriate behavior represents a chronic and stable personality disorder that is extremely difficult to change. Davis and Sines (1971) could not find any lasting effects of any form of psychological intervention or incarceration.

Moods: The client reports a very mild level of emotional distress that is characterized by a general dissatisfaction with life rather than by any specific mood. She frequently worries about something. She reports that she has not lived the "right kind of life," her daily life is not full of things that keep her interested, and she is not happy most of the time. She sometimes feels that difficulties are piling up so high that she cannot overcome them. She will use indirect, passive means of expressing her anger.

Cognitions: She sees herself as quite capable and able to make decisions easily. Her memory and concentration skills are good. She tends to be defensive, guarded, and unwilling to acknowledge psychological problems even when they are readily apparent to others. She does not analyze the sources and consequences of her own or others' feelings and behavior. She believes that it is safe to trust others and they are willing to help. She is very direct and comfortable in stating her opinions to others.

Interpersonal Relations: She is an extroverted and very sociable person who finds it easy to relate and talk to others. She is not concerned about what others think of her. Her home life was not pleasant and she often quarrels with members of her family. She very much wanted to leave home. She works out things for herself rather asking others for help.

Other Problem Areas: Although she is concerned about her health, she does not report any specific symptoms other than dizzy spells. She is likely to abuse substances and to have been in trouble with the law. She does not wake up fresh and rested most mornings.

Treatment: Her prognosis is very poor because her problems are characterologic and not readily amenable to change. She is experiencing minimal emotional distress and has little concern about her behavior, limiting her motivation for treatment. Her tendency not to analyze her or others' behavior complicates most interventions. Short-term behavioral interventions that focus on her reasons for entering treatment will be most effective.

Gilberstadt and Duker (1965) and Kelley and King (1979a) provide additional interpretive information on *3-4/4-3* codetypes, and Table D.21 provides the prototypic scores.

3-5/5-3 (0.32%)

Moods: The client is experiencing minimal emotional distress. She describes herself as happy, calm, and self-confident. Her daily life is full of things that keep her interested.

Cognitions: She has good concentration and memory skills. She can make decisions easily and is self-confident. She has little interest in examining the motives or behaviors of others. She is very direct in expressing her opinions to others. She does not think of things that are too bad to talk about.

Interpersonal Relations: She is extroverted and relates easily to others. She finds it easy to talk when she meets new people. Others see her as manipulative, crafty, immature, and demanding. She has few quarrels with members of her family.

Other Problem Areas: She does not report having behavioral problems or getting into trouble because of her behavior. She is unlikely to abuse substances. She feels tired a good deal of the time.

Treatment: Her prognosis is guarded for any type of intervention because she is experiencing little emo-

tional distress. Short-term behavioral interventions that focus on her reasons for entering treatment will be most effective.

Tanner (1990) provides additional interpretive information on *3-5/5-3* codetypes, and Table D.22 provides the prototypic scores.

3-6/6-3 (2.08%)

Moods: The client is reporting a mild to moderate level of emotional distress characterized by dysphoria and tension. She feels anxiety about something or someone almost all of the time, and frequently worries about something. She is fearful and generally apprehensive about what is happening around her. She is more sensitive and feels emotions more intensely than most people. Life is a strain for her much of the time. Others may see her as an angry, hostile individual who strongly denies these readily apparent feelings even though these attributes are apparent to everyone but herself. She usually expresses her anger in indirect, passive ways. She feels unable to "get going" and to get things done in her life. She may be anhedonic.

Cognitions: She makes decisions easily and feels confident of her own abilities, and yet she believes that her difficulties are piling up so high that she cannot overcome them. She often will deny and resent any kind of psychological interpretation of her problems. She sometimes thinks that she is about to "go to pieces." She is sure that she is being talked about and that someone may have it in for her. She does not analyze the motivation for others' behavior, and she believes that they can be trusted to do what they say.

The possibility of paranoid or psychotic features should be evaluated, even though these features are relatively unusual.

Interpersonal Relations: She is slightly introverted and somewhat uncomfortable in social situations. She feels lonely even when she is with people. Her parents did not object to her friends, and her home life was as pleasant as that of most families. She perceives her relations in positive terms and has difficulty understanding why others react to her the way they do. The hostility, egocentricity, and uncooperativeness become readily apparent in any relationship of more than a casual nature.

Other Problem Areas: She reports a number of physical symptoms such as her heart pounding, headaches, fainting spells, dizzy spells, and so on. She feels tired a good deal of the time and has sleep problems. These physical symptoms warrant careful review and possible referral for a medical or neuropsychological evaluation.

She is likely to have suicidal ideation that should be evaluated carefully. Her use of sleep medications needs to be monitored, particularly if she has suicidal ideation. She is unlikely to have been in trouble because of her behavior.

Treatment: Her prognosis is generally guarded to poor because of the characterologic nature of her problems. Her tendency not to analyze her or others' behavior complicates most interventions. Short-term behavioral interventions that focus on her reasons for entering treatment will be most beneficial. The prognosis for significant behavior change is poor.

Table D.23 provides the prototypic scores for *3-6/6-3* codetypes.

3-7/7-3 (1.26%)

Moods: The client is experiencing moderate distress characterized by worry, tension, agitation, and dysphoria. He feels anxiety about something almost all of the time, and he will develop chronic physical ailments in the head or the extremities resulting from psychological stress and conflicts. He is fearful and frequently phobic. He is more sensitive than others and inclined to take things hard. His feelings are easily hurt. Life is a strain for him much of the time. He feels unable to "get going" and to get things done in his life. He may be anhedonic.

Cognitions: He has problems concentrating and keeping his mind on a task or job. He sometimes thinks that he is about to "go to pieces." He tends to highly ruminative and obsessive. Despite the overt behavioral evidence of tension and anxiety, he will deny the existence of psychological problems and be unconcerned about his physical ailments. He lacks self-

confidence and thinks that he is useless. He gives up on a task quickly if others criticize him or if he thinks that he cannot do something. He does not analyze the motives of others or the reasons for their behavior.

Interpersonal Relations: He is slightly introverted. He feels lonely even when he is with people. His family and friends do not find fault with him. He does not feel alienated from them or from most people. He is passive and dependent in his relations with others and very concerned over what others think of him.

Other Problem Areas: He worries about his health. He is unlikely to abuse any kind of substance or to get into trouble because of his behavior. He has problems sleeping and feels tired most of the time. He is likely to have suicidal ideation that should be evaluated carefully.

Treatment: His prognosis is generally guarded to poor because of the chronic nature of his problems. His lack of insight into his hysteroid mechanisms makes psychological intervention slow and arduous at best. Psychopharmacologic interventions may be necessary to decrease his level of anxiety and agitation. Short-term behavioral interventions that focus on his reasons for entering treatment will be most effective and will facilitate the development of a therapeutic alliance. Long-term therapy will be beneficial if he can be motivated to participate.

Table D.24 provides the prototypic scores for *3-7/7-3* codetypes.

3-8/8-3 (1.25%)

Moods: The client is experiencing moderate to severe emotional distress characterized by apathy, fearfulness, hopelessness, and dysphoria. He often is emotionally inappropriate and apathetic. Life is a strain for him, and he sees little opportunity for any improvement. He feels unable to "get going" and to get things accomplished in his life. He is anhedonic.

Cognitions: He finds it hard to concentrate on a task or job, and he has memory problems. He is likely to be experiencing significant psychological distress despite his attempts to deny and repress problems. He is concerned that his mind is not working appropriately and that he may be "losing his mind" or about to "go to pieces." He has had very strange and peculiar experiences and dreams and thoughts that are best kept to himself. He is concerned that strangers are looking at him critically, and he tends to be hypervigilant.

He may actually be psychotic, and the possibility of a thought disorder should be evaluated carefully. When psychotic reactions are seen, there are infantile, narcissistic qualities accompanied by behavioral regression.

Interpersonal Relations: Although he is somewhat introverted, he likes parties and social events. He has adequate social skills, but he is so focused on his personal problems that he has little energy to devote to others. He is significantly alienated from others and himself, but he also says that he enjoys social gatherings just to be with people. His home life is not pleasant. His relations are marked by immaturity, egocentricity, and dependency.

Other Problem Areas: He reports a wide variety of physical symptoms. Psychological stress is converted into physical symptoms, which may consist of headaches, insomnia, fatigue, or bizarre symptoms. He has nightmares every few nights. He has fainting and blank spells that warrant careful review and possible referral for a medical or neuropsychological evaluation. He has strong urges to do something shocking or harmful that need to be evaluated to ascertain whether they involve a danger to himself or others. He is likely to have suicidal ideation. His sense of futility and hopelessness increases the probability of suicidal behavior.

Treatment: His prognosis is very guarded. Once medical or neuropsychological factors and risk management issues have been addressed, if necessary, a reality-focused, behavioral intervention should be implemented so that he feels less overwhelmed by his problems. Psychopharmacologic interventions may be necessary to deal with his dysphoria, concerns that he may be "losing his mind," and sleeping problems.

Supportive procedures that bolster the hysteroid defenses are frequently sufficient to weather the current crisis. Any form of insight-oriented psychotherapy should be considered carefully because of the possibility of an underlying psychotic process.

Marks et al. (1974) provide additional interpretive information on *3-8/8-3* codetypes, and Table D.25 provides the prototypic scores.

3-9/9-3 (0.33%)

Moods: The client is experiencing a very minimal level of emotional distress or problems. In fact, she describes herself as being happy most of the time, and she frequently becomes excited. When she gets bored, she likes to stir up excitement. If she is feeling low, something exciting will almost always make her feel better. Others describe her as stubborn, emotionally labile, irritable, and angry.

Cognitions: She can make decisions quickly. At times her thoughts have come faster than she could speak them. She is sure of her opinions and is not easily defeated in an argument. She spends little time analyzing the reasons others have for their behavior or actions.

Interpersonal Relations: She is gregarious, outgoing, and sociable even though her interpersonal relations may be superficial. She makes friends quickly and likes to be around people. She readily makes her presence known in any social setting. Her problems disappear when she is in a crowd of lively friends.

Other Problem Areas: She is prone to abuse substances. She may report acute attacks of physical symptoms, such as chest pains, cardiovascular problems, and headaches. These symptoms improve rapidly with medical intervention only to recur at a later date. She also may report fainting and blank spells that warrant a careful review and a possible referral for a medical or neuropsychological evaluation. She sometimes does not need sleep because she has so much energy.

Treatment: Her prognosis is guarded. She has a very stable, characterologic pattern to her relations that produces little emotional distress for her, limiting motivation for any type of treatment. She is unwilling to examine psychological factors in her behavior and will forgo treatment once her physical symptoms abate. Short-term behavioral interventions focused on her reasons for entering treatment will be most effective. She will be very verbal and demanding of the therapist.

Kelley and King (1979a) provide additional interpretive information on *3-9/9-3* codetypes, and Table D.26 provides the prototypic scores.

3-0/0-3 (0.04%)

There is little information on *3-0/0-3* codetypes. The underlying processes tapped by these two scales should be antithetical, and the infrequent occurrence of this codetype seems to support this contention. The rarity of occurrence of *3-0/0-3* codetypes is all the more remarkable since other codetypes that supposedly tap antithetical processes are not frequently seen, such as *4-7/7-4*.

Moods: The client is experiencing a moderate level of emotional distress. He is fearful and frequently phobic. He is easily embarrassed, and his feelings are hurt easily. He often has "spells of the blues" and is rarely happy. He experiences little pleasure in life and may be anhedonic.

Cognitions: He is very unsure of his own abilities and will give up on a task or job if others criticize him. He lacks confidence and is very self-conscious.

Interpersonal Relations: He is very shy, withdrawn, and socially reserved. He tends to isolate himself and to avoid interacting with others. His home life was unpleasant, and his family was critical of him. He describes himself as being very conventional and law-abiding; he has not been in trouble because of his behavior.

Other Problem Areas: He is unlikely to abuse substances. He reports a few vague physical ailments.

Treatment: His prognosis is guarded. The very chronic and characterologic nature of his problems makes any intervention more difficult. He also is unable to confide in others about himself, which makes the establishment of a therapeutic alliance very difficult. Short-term behavioral interventions focused on his reasons for entering treatment will be most effective initially. Once a stable therapeutic relationship can be established, more long-term psychotherapies may be warranted to address the characterologic issues.

Table D.27 provides the prototypic scores for *3-0/0-3* codetypes.

Spike *4* (3.60%)

Several investigators have reported that Spike *4* codetypes occur frequently in college students and have questioned whether new norms are needed (cf. Goodstein, 1954). King and Kelley (1977a) found in their college student sample that Spike *4* codetypes were indicative of significant psychopathology, and they concluded that new norms were not needed in their psychiatric outpatient clinic.

Moods: The client is very comfortable with himself and his behavior, and he reports minimal emotional distress. Although life is not a strain for him and he is happy most of the time, he wishes that he could be as happy as others seem to be, and he thinks that he has not lived the "right kind of life." That is, there are undercurrents of a chronic dysphoria that go unrecognized. He has a low tolerance for frustration, and this quality combined with poorly controlled anger and poor self-control often results in outbursts of physical aggression.

Cognitions: He thinks clearly and rationally and reports good insight into his own behavior. Memory and concentration are very good. His confidence and assurance in his abilities may be a facade for underlying feelings of insecurity, inadequacy, and dependency. He tends to be egocentric and lacks insight into his own behavior.

Interpersonal Relations: He is extroverted and makes a good first impression on others, but this impression does not last long. His interpersonal relations are often shallow and superficial. He has difficulty in more intimate interpersonal relationships. These qualities become more pathognomonic as Scale *0* (Social Introversion) approaches a T score of 30. These relations typically are not reciprocal and are marked by distrust, a lack of empathy, and irresponsibility. His family is critical of him, and he is alienated from them. He wanted to leave home. He may show impulsive behavior, rebelliousness, and poor relationships with authority figures.

Other Problem Areas: He is likely to abuse substances. He is very likely to have engaged in antisocial behaviors during his school years and to continue to engage in reckless behaviors that may or may not be explicitly illegal. He is in good physical health. He is as able to work as he ever was. He sleeps well and wakes up fresh and rested.

Treatment: His prognosis is guarded unless treatment begins early in his life. He is experiencing little personal distress, and he expects others to change to meet his expectations. He conceives of himself as being better than other people, externalizes blame for his problems onto others, and has little insight into his own behavior. He is unlikely to be self-referred; rather a social agency usually refers him. As soon as the social agency no longer requires treatment he will discontinue therapy. His psychopathic qualities make him a poor candidate for psychotherapy. These psychopathic qualities tend to be alleviated by age; maturation is often seen as a viable though long-term treatment alternative. If they do not change with age, some form of vocational counseling and career guidance that draws on his "skills and talents" may be useful. Scores below a T score of 50 on Scale *2* (Depression) in combination with a Spike *4* codetype of even moderate elevation indicates an especially low probability of behavior change. Because he is not inclined to undertake any serious examination of his own behavior, short-term behavioral interventions focused on his reasons for entering treatment will be most effective.

Gilberstadt and Duker (1965) and King and Kelley (1977a) provide additional interpretive information on Spike *4* codetypes, and Table D.28 provides the prototypic scores.

4-5/5-4 (0.58%)

Clients with a *4-5/5-4* codetype may be concerned about homoerotic impulses, and a subset of persons with this codetype will be actively homosexual. These active homosexuals display this codetype only if they want to acknowledge openly their homosexual status. If they so desire, they can deny the presence of homosexual impulses or behaviors without being detected by any Validity or Clinical scale configuration. Hence, the detection of homosexual behavior in *4-5/5-4* codetypes is best accomplished when the clinician directly asks the client about such activity. Erickson, Luxenberg, Walbek, and Seely (1987) reported that a *4-5/5-4* codetype was among the most frequent in their sample of sex offenders.

Male college students with *4-5/5-4* codetypes are described as experiencing general interpersonal difficulties of a transient nature with only slight indications of a significant personality disorder (King & Kelley, 1977b). Although these students are passive and experiencing heterosexual adjustment problems, homosexuality is not characteristic of them.

Moods: The client is reporting minimal emotional distress or concern about her behavior or present circumstances. It is not clear whether this lack of distress reflects defensiveness, her character structure, or an accurate self-description. Regardless, she indicates that she is happy and calm most of the time.

Cognitions: She thinks clearly and rationally and reports good insight into her behavior. Others see her as being very defensive and guarded about revealing herself. Her concentration and memory are good, and she believes that her judgment is good. She believes that others are interested only in their own welfare.

Interpersonal Relations: She is comfortable in social situations and likes parties and dances. She is likely to be nonconforming to social standards and norms. She is likely to act on these impulses in passive or indirect ways rather than through direct behavioral expression. Her parents objected to her friends. She frequently quarrels with her parents, and she has wanted to leave home.

Other Problem Areas: She is in good physical health and has few physical symptoms. She is as capable of working as she ever was. She does not have sleep difficulties. Substance abuse is likely and should be reviewed carefully.

Treatment: Her prognosis is generally guarded to poor due to the characterologic nature of her problems. She is experiencing little emotional distress, so there is limited motivation for her to change her behavior. Short-term behavioral interventions focused on her reasons for entering treatment will be most effective.

King and Kelley (1977b) and Tanner (1990) provide additional interpretive information on *4-5/5-4* codetypes, and Table D.29 provides the prototypic scores.

4-6/6-4 (3.14%)

Moods: The client is experiencing mild to moderate emotional distress that is characterized by brooding, dysphoria, and anhedonia. He is generally stubborn, argumentative, and angry. He is usually able to control the expression of his anger, but he does exhibit episodic angry outbursts, particularly in response to stress. He will externalize blame for his anger. He broods and worries constantly over what is happening to him. He wishes that he could be as happy as others seem to be. He feels unable to "get going" and to get things done.

Cognitions: He has good concentration skills and a good memory. He remembers very well, and for a long time, anything that people say or do to him. He is very sensitive to and resentful of any demands being placed on him. He is sure that he is being talked about. He believes that someone has it in for him and that people say insulting and vulgar things about him. He is suspicious of the motives of others and knows that he would have been more successful if people had not had it in for him. He knows who is responsible for most of his troubles.

When Scale *8* (Schizophrenia) also is elevated, he will be even more evasive and defensive about admitting any form of psychological problem, and difficulties in logic and judgment begin to appear. He seethes with anger, which in conjunction with his sensitivity to criticism and suspiciousness can lead to unpredictable and irrational violent outbursts. He is likely to be openly defiant and hostile. His solution for behavioral change is to have others change to meet his expectations.

He reports a number of symptoms that may reflect a psychotic process. His presenting problems, background, and history should be reviewed carefully with this possibility in mind.

Interpersonal Relations: He is likely to have a long history of very poor interpersonal relations and severe social maladjustment with a poor work history. His relations are characterized often by resentment, anger, and suspiciousness. He sees his family as extremely uncaring and critical and his home life as very unpleasant. He very much wanted to leave home. He is alienated and detached from his family and society. He believes that no one understands him and his way of doing things.

Other Problem Areas: He is as able to work as he ever was despite his poor work history. He is in good physical health. He is likely to abuse substances. Suicidal ideation is possible and needs to be evaluated carefully. He is apathetic and hopeless, and he broods over his problems, which increases the probability of his acting out either toward himself or others if they provoke him.

Treatment: His prognosis is generally quite poor due to his denial of personal responsibility for his problems that are very chronic and characterologic. He will be very demanding and will engage in frequent testing of the therapist. Short-term behavioral interventions that are presented in a direct and explicit manner will be most effective.

Archer et al. (1995) and Marks et al. (1974) provide additional interpretive information on *4-6/6-4* codetypes, and Table D.30 provides the prototypic scores.

4-7/7-4 (1.27%)

Clients with *4-7/7-4* codetypes are an example of the apparently paradoxical elevation of two antithetical scales. Since Scale *4* (Psychopathic Deviate) assesses persons' insensitivity to and disregard of the social consequences of their behavior, and Scale *7* (Psychasthenia) assesses persons' excessive concern about and analysis of their own behavior, it does not seem likely that simultaneous elevations on these two scales should occur. Nevertheless, they do.

The primary characteristic of these clients is cyclic behavior between these two extremes. It is as if Scale *4* characteristics become dominant for a period of time and the clients act out impulsively with little regard for social conventions and the needs and wishes of other people. Following these periods of acting out, the Scale *7* characteristics become dominant, and the clients will feel guilty, remorseful, and self-deprecating about having exhibited such behaviors. They appear to be overcontrolled during this phase, but these controls are not sufficient to prevent recurrences of acting out.

The clinician will encounter these clients during their guilty, remorseful phase, and the clinician is likely to believe that significant therapeutic progress is being made. All too often, however, these individuals will again act out impulsively and return feeling guiltier, and so on. Successfully intervening in this behavior cycle is very difficult without a long-term therapeutic relationship.

Moods: The client is experiencing a mild to moderate level of emotional distress characterized by anxiety and agitation. He worries about possible misfortunes and becomes agitated and upset easily. He feels anxiety about someone or something most of the time. He is easily angered and frequently impatient with others. He is unmotivated and feels unable to do much to help himself at this time.

Cognitions: He exhibits a cyclical pattern of acting out followed by excessive concern, regret, and remorse over his behavior. However, his remorse does not inhibit the repetition of this behavior and further episodes of acting out. He thinks that he is "no good at all," and he gives up quickly when things go wrong. He lacks self-confidence, has difficulty making decisions, and lets others make decisions for him when problems occur. He sees others as being interested only in themselves and unlikely to be of assis-

tance to him. An undercurrent of cynicism permeates his interactions.

Interpersonal Relations: His interpersonal relations are marked by conflict and are often disrupted by episodic acting out. He is not particularly sensitive or responsive to the needs of others, except after something has happened. He sees his family as uncaring and critical. His home life was very unpleasant, and he wanted to leave home.

Other Problem Areas: He is in good health and has no sleep problems. Sexual acting out and substance abuse are likely. Suicidal ideation should be evaluated carefully.

Treatment: His prognosis is generally poor for short-term psychotherapy and guarded for long-term intensive psychotherapy. His remorse and guilt over acting out may give the impression of more insight and motivation to change than are actually present. Once his remorse and guilt have dissipated, his motivation will disappear quickly. Helping him to recognize his cyclic patterns and then to understand their dynamics is a primary goal in treatment.

Kelley and King (1979a) provide interpretive information on *4-7/7-4* codetypes, and Table D.31 provides the prototypic scores.

4-8/8-4 (1.97%)

A client with *4-8/8-4* codetypes is typically characterized by a chronic marginal schizoid adjustment, if he is not actually schizophrenic. His behavior is typically unpredictable and nonconforming at best. He frequently gets into social and legal difficulties because of his poor judgment and his problems in logic and thinking. A history of criminal activity with numerous arrests is common. His crimes often are poorly planned and executed and may involve bizarre or violent behaviors. This is a frequent codetype among child molesters (Hall, Mauiro, Vitaliano, & Proctor, 1986; McCreary, 1975), rapists (Armentrout & Hauer, 1978), rapists and exposers (Rader, 1977), sex offenders (Erickson et al., 1987), and unwed mothers who choose to keep their baby rather than place it for adoption (Horn & Turner, 1976). He is chronically maladjusted, which indicates that any form of psychological intervention will be of limited benefit.

Moods: The client is experiencing a moderate to severe level of emotional distress that is characterized by dysphoria, agitation, and anhedonia. He often feels resentful and angry, and has difficulty controlling or expressing his anger appropriately. In response to stress, he is likely to either withdraw completely or to act out his angry impulses. He feels insecure, isolated, rejected, and unwanted. He is threatened by a world that he views as hostile and dangerous. He finds it very difficult to get things done in his life and has little hope of being successful if he could get motivated at something.

Cognitions: He has difficulty concentrating and focusing on tasks. He exhibits poor judgment and is often unpredictable and impulsive. He thinks and dreams about things that he knows are best kept to himself. He is suspicious of the motives of others and hypervigilant.

He reports a number of symptoms that may reflect a psychotic process. His presenting problems, background, and history should be reviewed carefully with this possibility in mind.

Interpersonal Relations: He is introverted and has difficulty with close, emotional relations. He lacks basic social skills and tends to be socially withdrawn and isolated. He is emotionally distant, feels lonely, and knows that no one understands him and his problems. His tendency to feel rejected by others often leads to hostility and conflict, which only exacerbate his feelings of being alienated from others. He sees his family as extremely uncaring and critical and his home life as very unpleasant.

Other Problem Areas: He is likely to have a history of suicidal behavior so suicide ideation should be evaluated carefully. His isolation, hopelessness, and proneness to act out impulsively toward himself or others increase the potential for suicide. He is very likely to abuse substances. He has problems sleeping, which exacerbate all of his problems.

If he commits a crime, it is likely to be poorly planned and executed and may involve bizarre or violent behavior. His problems frequently involve inappropriate sexual behavior.

Treatment: His prognosis is generally very poor because of the characterologic nature of his problems. Psychopharmacologic interventions, other than possibly antidepressants, also are unlikely to be very effective because of the characterologic problems involved. Interventions focused on specific behavioral objectives may be useful. His difficulties in forming an emotional relationship and his reluctance to self-disclose make the establishment of a therapeutic alliance problematic at best. Any form of insight-oriented therapy is contraindicated.

Archer et al. (1995), Gynther et al. (1973), and Marks et al. (1974) provide additional interpretive information on *4-8/8-4* codetypes, and Table D.32 provides the prototypic scores.

4-9/9-4 (1.25%)

Clients with *4-9/9-4* codetypes are likely to display some form of acting out behavior. The hypomania seemingly energizes or activates the behaviors assessed by Scale *4* (Psychopathic Deviate). This codetype is common in clients with marital problems, illegitimate pregnancies, child abuse (Paulson, Afifi, Thomason, & Chaleff, 1974), alcohol or drug abuse (Greene & Garvin, 1988; Hodo & Fowler, 1976; Loper et al., 1973), delinquency, repeated crimes of indecent exposure (McCreary, 1975), and sex offenses (Erickson et al., 1987; Hall et al., 1986). Sheppard, Smith, and Rosenbaum (1988) found that 50 percent of their patients within a *4-9/9-4* cluster type did not complete a 30-day alcohol treatment program.

Huesmann, Lefkowitz, and Eron (1978) reported that the sum of the T scores on Scales *F* (Infrequency), *4*, and *9* was a valid predictor of aggression in older adolescents. Normal males ($M = 183.3$) and females ($M = 178.9$) scored significantly lower than delinquent males ($M = 217.4$) and females ($M = 237.7$) on this index. Huesmann et al. did not report standard deviations by group or sex; they stated that the composite standard deviation was about 25. Since there is substantial overlap in these distributions, it remains to be seen how useful this index will be for predicting aggression in individual clients. O'Laughlin and Schill (1994) reported that the composite score on this index was correlated positively (0.26) with self-monitored aggression in male college students.

Moods: The client is experiencing minimal emotional distress or concern about his behavior or present circumstances. He dislikes being bored and inactive and will stir up excitement if he gets bored. He frequently has intense feelings of anger and hostility that result in episodic outbursts of anger. He is likely to exhibit increased anger and hostility in response to stress. He is oppositional when he is not overtly angry.

Cognitions: His concentration and memory are good. He exhibits very poor judgment, often acts out without considering the consequences of his actions, and has difficulty learning from experience. He is unwilling to accept responsibility for his own behavior, and he exhibits a persistent tendency to get into trouble. He is cynical.

Acting out is his primary defense mechanism, although rationalization also plays an important role. When Scales 6 (Paranoia) and 8 (Schizophrenia) also are elevated and with higher elevations on Scale 9, there is an increased probability of acting out episodes that may be quite intense and violent.

Interpersonal Relations: He mixes easily with others, and he likes parties and loud social events. He is very socially facile, and he makes a good first impression. More long-term contact will reveal that his interpersonal relations are superficial and marked by impulsivity, distrust, a lack of empathy, and egocentricity. He has numerous long-standing problems with his family and persons in positions of authority. He exhibits an enduring tendency to get into trouble, usually only in a way that damages his own or his family's reputation, although antisocial and criminal acts are not uncommon.

Other Problem Areas: He is in good physical health and does not tire easily. Suicidal behavior is likely and should be evaluated carefully because of his impulsive, risk-taking behavior and propensity to abuse substances. He is likely to have a history of legal and school problems and acting out, even if he is not in legal trouble at the present time.

Treatment: His prognosis is guarded unless treatment begins early in his life. This characterologic process tends to result in fixed behavior patterns that are difficult to change. He is experiencing little emotional distress that might serve as motivation to change his behavior. Behavioral or short-term interventions that focus on the specific behaviors that led him to treatment or group therapies with similar individuals will be most effective.

Archer et al. (1995), Gilberstadt and Duker (1965), Gynther et al. (1973), King and Kelley (1977a), and Marks et al. (1974) provide additional interpretive information on *4-9/9-4* codetypes. Tables 7.13 and D.33 provide the prototypic scores.

4-0/0-4 (0.20%)

Clients with *4-0/0-4* codetypes are statistically rare (Tables 7.1, 7.2, and 7.4). In fact, this codetype is so unusual that it is not listed in any of the major MMPI references. Theoretically, this infrequency of occurrence makes sense because psychopathic persons who typically elevate Scale *4* (Psychopathic Deviate) are unconcerned and lack anxiety about interpersonal relationships and, consequently, should score low on Scale *0* (Social Introversion). Hence, at a theoretical level, no specific classification of psychopathology would be expected to show this particular codetype.

Moods: The client is experiencing a mild level of emotional distress characterized by dysphoria and anhedonia. He wishes that he could be as happy as others seem to be. He frequently regrets the things that he has done, and he is generally displeased with his life. He lacks drive and motivation.

Cognitions: His memory and concentration are good. He is dubious of the motivations of others and believes that they will lie if necessary to get out of trouble. He lacks self-confidence, and he lets others

Table 7-13

Prototypic Scores for 4-9/9-4 Codetypes (N = 440)

Demographics

Demographics		M	SD	Marital Status		%
Age		28.3	10.5	Never Married		58.4
Education		11.2	5.0	Married		20.2
Gender		%		Separated		7.9
	Men	53.9		Divorced		12.3
	Women	46.1		Widowed		1.3

Test-Taking Scales

Omissions		M	SD	Consistency	M	SD
	?	0.9	2.5	VRIN	52.7	10.4
				|F - FB|	4.2	3.1
				TRIN	50.5	10.3

Accuracy of Item Endorsement

Underreporting		M	SD	Overreporting		M	SD
	False %	54.4	7.2		True %	44.4	7.2
Impression	L	49.0	9.9	Infrequency	F	63.8	14.8
Management	ODecp	50.4	8.6		FB	60.3	14.8
	Sd	53.6	9.0		F[p]	57.5	14.7
Superior	S	43.2	9.0	Critical Items	K & B	23.6	10.3
Adjustment					L & W	31.4	11.6
Self-Deception	K	47.0	9.2	Dissimulation	F - K	-5.4	7.8
	So	45.0	10.7		Ds	61.9	11.5
					O - S	39.7	61.7

Scales

Validity and Clinical			Supplementary			Morey et al. Overlapping Personality Disorder		
Scale	M	SD	Scale	M	SD	Scale	M	SD
?	0.9	2.5	A	54.6	9.9	PAR	60.0	12.0
L	49.0	9.9	R	42.6	8.7	SZD	43.3	8.0
F	63.8	14.8	Es	46.2	10.1	STY	50.5	8.9
K	47.0	9.2	TRIN	50.5	10.3	ANT	64.1	10.8
1(Hs)	51.6	9.0	VRIN	52.7	10.4	BDL	59.8	10.4
2(D)	52.4	9.1	O-H	48.1	10.1	HST	58.4	7.2
3(Hy)	52.6	9.0	Do	41.2	11.5	NAR	59.2	7.7
4(Pd)	75.4	8.1	Re	34.6	11.4	AVD	45.6	6.9
5(Mf)	50.4	10.3	GM	48.6	8.7	DEP	52.1	9.6
6(Pa)	59.2	9.8	GF	37.6	11.0	CPS	53.5	9.4
7(Pt)	56.7	9.1	Mt	57.9	10.3	Personality Psychopathology Five		
8(Sc)	61.9	9.1	PK	60.8	11.7			
9(Ma)	75.2	7.9	PS	60.1	11.2	Scale	M	SD
0(Si)	45.1	7.6	MAC-R	63.0	10.3	AGG	59.5	10.1
			APS	56.2	10.5	PSY	58.9	12.5
			AAS	61.1	11.9	CON	36.0	10.2
			MDS	63.4	10.9	NEN	56.6	10.2
			Ho	58.1	9.9	PEE	52.9	7.9
			CAL-R	59.9	10.2			

Content			Content Component					
Scale	M	SD	Scale	M	SD	Scale	M	SD
ANX	57.9	10.1	FRS1	51.0	10.2	ASP1	58.7	10.8
FRS	47.3	9.5	FRS2	45.5	9.9	ASP2	64.4	12.7
OBS	54.3	10.3	DEP1	58.9	12.4	TPA1	50.7	10.4
DEP	59.2	9.8	DEP2	56.5	11.2	TPA2	55.9	11.2
HEA	53.7	9.0	DEP3	59.1	11.6	LSE1	51.4	9.6
BIZ	58.8	10.3	DEP4	52.8	15.9	LSE2	49.9	9.5
ANG	58.9	12.2	HEA1	52.4	11.6	SOD1	44.5	7.3
CYN	58.0	10.9	HEA2	51.6	10.1	SOD2	42.3	7.0
ASP	63.6	12.8	HEA3	53.3	9.9	FAM1	62.5	11.0
TPA	54.8	11.7	BIZ1	54.2	13.0	FAM2	60.5	14.0
LSE	52.0	9.0	BIZ2	58.0	12.0	TRT1	54.5	12.1
SOD	43.6	7.1	ANG1	59.6	12.9	TRT2	50.6	10.3
FAM	64.4	11.6	ANG2	55.3	10.2			
WRK	56.1	10.2	CYN1	56.9	10.1			
TRT	55.4	11.7	CYN2	56.3	9.8			

Note: All scores are T scores except: Cannot Say, K & B and L & W critical items which are raw scores; True % and False % which are the percentage of items endorsed "true" or "false;" and \|F - FB\|, F - K, and O - S which are difference scores.

take charge when problems arise. Others misunderstand his way of doing things.

Interpersonal Relations: He is a shy, retiring individual who actively avoids social interactions. He reports numerous quarrels with family members and problems interacting with persons in positions of authority. He sees his home life as being unpleasant and having little love or companionship. He wanted to leave home as a consequence of these strained familial relations.

Other Problem Areas: He does not have sleep difficulties. He is in good physical health and is as able to work as he ever was. He should be evaluated carefully for suicidal ideation; he is hopeless and sees little likelihood of any change in his circumstances. He is likely to abuse substances. He tends to be very conventional and does not get into trouble because of his behavior.

Treatment: His prognosis is guarded because of the characterologic nature of his problems. Interventions focused on social skills or assertiveness training are frequently beneficial. He has little motivation for any long-term intervention.

  Table D.34 provides the prototypic scores for *4-0/0-4* codetypes.

Spike 5 (3.88%)

There is little information on the empirical correlates of elevations on Scale *5* (Masculinity-Femininity). The paucity of data reflects the fact that Scale *5* was not among the original Clinical scales and, thus, it was not included in the early clinical research on the MMPI. Only King and Kelley (1977b) and Tanner (1990) have examined the behavioral correlates of codetypes in which Scale *5* is one of the high-point scales. Scale *5* is the least well-developed and standardized scale of the individual scales on the MMPI, which also has contributed to its lack of attention. It remains to be seen whether Scale *5* will fare any better on the MMPI-2.

  King and Kelley (1977b) found that student outpatients at a university mental health center with Spike *5* codetypes were generally normal students with no significant psychopathology despite their seeking treatment.

Moods: The client is experiencing no emotional distress; she is very comfortable with herself and her behavior. She describes herself as self-confident, easygoing, and assured. She is happy most of the time.

Cognitions: She believes that she has good judgment. She can concentrate very well on tasks, and her memory is fine. She is not troubled by recurring thoughts or dreams.

Interpersonal Relations: She relates easily to others and makes a good impression on them. She believes that her home life is pleasant. She did report a few problems in school as a youngster.

Other Problem Areas: She is in good physical health and sleeps well. She is not likely to abuse substances.

Treatment: Her prognosis is guarded because she is experiencing little emotional distress, limiting her motivation to engage in any type of therapeutic intervention. She also is reluctant to discuss personal issues with others, including therapists. Short-term therapies focusing on the behaviors that led her to treatment will be the most beneficial.

  King and Kelley (1977b) provide additional information on Spike *5* codetypes, and Table D.35 provides the prototypic scores.

5-6/6-5 (0.44%)

Moods: The client is not experiencing any type of emotional distress; he describes himself as being happy and self-confident. He reports that he has never felt better than he does now. He is often described as being aloof, impulsive, abrasive, irritable, and easily angered.

Cognitions: He has strong religious and political beliefs that he is quite willing to express to others in a very direct and sometimes forceful manner. He thinks that he has good judgment. He believes that he would have been more successful if others had not had "it in for him," and he knows who is responsible for his troubles.

Interpersonal Relations: He is uncomfortable in social situations and avoids people if possible because he is uncertain of their motivations for any interaction. He is most comfortable when he is alone. He is not concerned about what others think of him.

Other Problem Areas: He is in good physical health and is as able to work as he ever was. He is not likely to abuse substances. His worries about sexual matters should be explored with him. He does not have sleep difficulties. He is likely to have suicidal ideation that should be evaluated.

Treatment: His prognosis is guarded because of his reluctance to consider that he may play a role in his current problems. He is reluctant to open up to others, and he is frequently described as being guarded and resistant. Short-term behavioral interventions that focus on his reasons for entering treatment will be most effective.

Tanner (1990) provides additional interpretive information on *5-6/6-5* codetypes, and Table D.36 provides the prototypic scores.

5-7/7-5 (0.19%)

Moods: The client is experiencing mild to moderate emotional distress characterized by rather chronic anxiety and mild depressive symptoms. He feels anxiety about something most of the time. He is generally fearful and apprehensive. He is easily agitated, and sometimes he gets so agitated that he finds it hard to sleep. He is more sensitive than most people and his feelings are easily hurt.

Cognitions: He is bothered by recurring thoughts and ideas, and sometimes thinks of things that are too bad to talk about. He lacks self-confidence.

Interpersonal Relations: He is shy, bashful, and easily embarrassed. He is more sensitive than most people, and his feelings are easily hurt. He describes his home and family life as being very pleasant.

Other Problem Areas: He is in good physical health and is as able to work as he ever was. He is not likely to abuse substances. His concern about sexual issues should be explored. He does not have problems with the law.

Treatment: His prognosis is good for long-term therapy if he has the motivation to engage in the process. He will respond very positively to supportive therapies that provide reassurance about his symptomatology.

King and Kelley (1977b) and Tanner (1990) provide additional interpretive information on *5-7/7-5* codetypes, and Table D.37 provides the prototypic scores.

5-8/8-5 (0.22%)

A client with a *5-8/8-5* codetype is likely to have a family history of alcohol abuse, mental illness, and physical abuse. She frequently has a long psychiatric history that began in childhood. She reports reactive depression, paresthesia, and religious preoccupations but has intact thought processes. She can be described as an odd, eccentric individual who has difficulty making emotional contact with others. She reports numerous conflicts over sexuality both in herself and in her relationships with others.

Moods: The client is experiencing mild emotional distress characterized by a mild dysphoria and anhedonia. She does not report any sustained moods although she can become excited and full of energy for seemingly no reason at all. She is generally fearful and apprehensive of her environment.

Cognitions: She has problems with concentration. She has strange thoughts and hears strange things when she is alone. She also experiences dreams and ideas that are best kept to herself. She often feels as if things are not real. She is dubious and suspicious of the motivation of others who she believes are interested only in their own welfare. She believes that she should take advantage of others if given the opportunity.

She reports a number of symptoms that may reflect a psychotic process. Her presenting problems, background, and history should be reviewed carefully with this possibility in mind.

Interpersonal Relations: She is shy and reserved, and she avoids others if possible. She is never happier than when she is alone. She can be described as odd and eccentric, and she has difficulty making emotional contact with others. Her interpersonal relations are strained at best. Although her relations with her family are conflictual and unpleasant, she believes that her home life is as pleasant as that of most people she knows.

Other Problem Areas: She is in good physical health and is as able to work as she ever was. She has sleep difficulties. She reports numerous concerns about her sexuality and her sexual relationships that should be explored carefully. The possibility of suicidal ideation should be evaluated.

Treatment: Her prognosis is guarded because of the characterologic nature of her difficulties. Long-term therapy frequently is necessary to produce significant changes in her behavior. Short-term therapies focusing on the behaviors that led her to treatment will be most beneficial until she is more willing to engage in the therapeutic process.
    King and Kelley (1977b) and Tanner (1990) provide additional interpretive information on *5-8/8-5* codetypes, and Table D.38 provides the prototypic scores.

5-9/9-5 (0.53%)

Moods: The client is experiencing little emotional distress; she is very comfortable with herself and her own behavior. She is happy most of the time, and she has never felt better than she does right now. She likes to keep active and becomes bored easily. When she becomes bored, she likes to stir up excitement.

Cognitions: Her memory and concentration are good. She believes that her judgment is better than it ever has been. She is dubious and suspicious of the motivations of others who she believes are interested only in their own welfare. She believes that she should take advantage of others if given the opportunity.

Interpersonal Relations: She is self-confident, easygoing, and assured. She relates easily to others and makes a good impression on them even though she is not concerned about what others think of her. She prefers to be a leader of groups. There is a considerable degree of stress and conflict in her family.

Other Problem Areas: She is in good physical health and is as able to work as she ever was. She does not tire easily. She is likely to abuse substances to reduce anxiety with a relatively high incidence of violence when drinking.

Treatment: Her prognosis is very guarded at best. She is experiencing little emotional distress, limiting her motivation to engage in any type of therapeutic intervention. Short-term therapies focusing on the behaviors that led her to treatment will be most beneficial.
    Tanner (1990) provides additional interpretive information on *5-9/9-5* codetypes, and Table D.39 provides the prototypic scores.

5-0/0-5 (0.12%)

Moods: The client is experiencing minimal emotional distress. He is not depressed or anxious, but he is irritable and grouchy, and he frequently becomes impatient with others. He does not appear to be defensive or guarded. He describes himself as happy and content with his life.

Cognitions: He gives up quickly when things go wrong for him, and he is easily defeated in an argument. He lacks self-confidence.

Interpersonal Relations: He is very socially introverted and tends to withdraw from and avoid social contact. He is easily embarrassed in social situations. He rarely gets into trouble because of his behavior.

Other Problem Areas: He is not likely to abuse substances.

Treatment: His prognosis is guarded because he sees himself as having few psychological problems, so there is little motivation for any therapeutic intervention. Short-term behavioral interventions that focus on his reasons for entering treatment will be most effective.

Table D.40 provides the prototypic scores for *5-0/0-5* codetypes.

Spike 6 (2.58%)

Clients who elevate only Scale 6 (Paranoia) are relatively rare. Since the item content on Scale 6 is obvious, the paranoid symptomatology is usually evident in clients with Spike 6 profiles. The possibility of a paranoid process should be evaluated.

Moods: The client is not experiencing any emotional distress; he is calm, happy, and well adjusted. Although he has many things to worry about, he is satisfied with himself the way he is. He reports a mild degree of dysphoria and anhedonia, of which he has limited awareness.

Cognitions: He believes that he thinks clearly and has good judgment and memory. He finds it easy to focus on a task and has good concentration skills. He is confident in his abilities. He is very vigilant of what goes on around him. He believes that he is more sensitive than others and that they may be talking about him. He is suspicious, distrustful, and projects blame for his problems onto others.

He reports a few symptoms that may reflect an underlying psychotic process; his history and background should be reviewed carefully with this possibility in mind.

Interpersonal Relations: He appears to be comfortable around others, which actually reflects his aloofness from and lack of genuine involvement with others. Others see him as being defensive and guarded. He does not report any problems with members of his family or other behavioral problems.

Other Problem Areas: He is in good physical health and he sleeps well. He is as able to work as well as he ever was. He is not likely to abuse substances.

Treatment: His prognosis is guarded because of his lack of emotional distress and consequent reluctance to consider that he might have any psychological problems. Forging a therapeutic alliance is difficult because of his propensity to distance himself emotionally from others. The discrepancy between how he perceives himself and how others perceive him and his behavior also complicates establishing an alliance with him. Behavioral or cognitive-behavioral interventions that do not require insight are most likely to be successful with him.

Table D.41 provides the prototypic scores for Spike 6 codetypes.

6-7/7-6 (1.40%)

Moods: The client is experiencing mild to moderate emotional distress characterized by brooding, anxiety, and worrying. He is depressed and he broods and ruminates about his problems and resentments. He expresses anger indirectly. He is also rigid, hypersensitive, and stubborn. Life is a strain for him much of the time, and he has little hope of it changing for the better. He is easily embarrassed, his feelings are easily hurt, and he is more sensitive than most people.

Cognitions: He has problems concentrating on a task and difficulty making up his mind because of his ruminations. He frequently projects his problems onto others. He lacks self-confidence and thinks that he is no good at all. He is sure that others talk about him and look at him critically. He thinks of things that are too bad to talk about, and he is concerned that he has done something wrong or evil. He is afraid of "losing his mind" or "going to pieces."

He reports a number of symptoms that may reflect a psychotic process; his background and history should be reviewed carefully with this possibility in mind.

Interpersonal Relations: He is extremely uncomfortable in interpersonal situations. He tends to keep people at a distance and often exercises poor social judgment. He feels lonely even when he is around people. He becomes nervous when people ask him personal questions, and he finds it difficult to confide in others about himself. His hypersensitivity and tendency to misinterpret the statements and behaviors of others often lead to volatile and distant relationships.

Other Problem Areas: He has problems sleeping because of his ruminations, and he feels tired a good deal of the time. He is likely to abuse substances. Suicidal ideation should be monitored carefully. He is unlikely to have a history of behavioral or legal problems.

He reports a number of neurologic symptoms; his history and background should be reviewed to determine whether a medical or neuropsychological evaluation is warranted.

Treatment: His prognosis is generally guarded because his problems tend to be chronic and characterologic. His concerns about self-disclosure and his interpersonal discomfort further complicate the development of a therapeutic alliance. Psychopharmacologic interventions may be necessary to alleviate his excessive worrying and ruminations. Short-term behavioral interventions that focus on his reasons for entering treatment will be most effective.

Kelley and King (1979a) provide additional interpretive information on *6-7/7-6* codetypes, and Table D.42 provides the prototypic scores.

6-8/8-6 (5.48%)

Moods: The client is experiencing severe emotional distress characterized by dysphoria, agitation, worrying, and anhedonia. He is very fearful, easily frightened, and generally apprehensive, and he dreads what might happen to him. His affect is likely to be blunted or inappropriate. He sees little opportunity of improving his circumstances, further dampening his mood.

Cognitions: He has concentration and attention difficulties, memory deficits, and poor judgment. He lacks self-confidence and feels inferior and insecure. In addition, he often feels guilty. He feels as if things are not real and he worries that there is something wrong with his mind. He may be preoccupied about and ruminate over abstract, theoretical issues, religion, and sexual themes. He thinks that people say vulgar and insulting things about him, that they have it in for him, and that they are trying to influence his mind. He believes that his dreams and thoughts are best kept to himself rather than shared with others. Behavioral regression, autistic thought processes, in-

appropriate affect, and bizarre associations may be seen.

He reports a number of symptoms that may reflect a psychotic process. His presenting problems, background, and history should be reviewed carefully with this possibility in mind.

Interpersonal Relations: He is extremely introverted and very uncomfortable around others. His behavior is likely to be unpredictable and inappropriate, also making others uneasy around him. He is suspicious and distrustful of others, and he avoids serious emotional relationships. He is resentful of any demands made on him by others. He has poor social skills. He generally feels apathetic, socially isolated and withdrawn, and he believes that no one understands him. He is lonely most of the time even when he is around people.

Other Problem Areas: He is likely to have suicidal ideation. He feels hopeless and is generally apathetic, so his potential for suicide should be monitored carefully. He has sleep difficulties that exacerbate all of his problems. He is very likely to abuse substances.

Treatment: His prognosis is generally poor. His problems are chronic and severe although his ability to work may not be severely impaired as long as the job does not involve any appreciable amount of contact with people. Some type of psychopharmacologic intervention may be necessary to stabilize his thought processes and mood and to help him sleep. Short-term behavioral interventions are warranted rather than any form of insight-oriented psychotherapy.

Archer et al. (1995), Gilberstadt and Duker (1965), Gynther et al. (1973), and Marks et al. (1974) provide further interpretive information on *6-8/8-6* codetypes. Tables 7.14 and D-43 provide the prototypic scores.

6-9/9-6 (1.01%)

Moods: The client is experiencing a mild to moderate level of emotional distress characterized by agitation, tension, and excitement. When he gets bored, he likes to stir up excitement. He frequently feels

Table 7-14

Prototypic Scores for 6-8/8-6 Codetypes (N = 1,929)

Demographics

Demographics		M	SD	Marital Status	%
Age		34.0	12.4	Never Married	47.5
Education		11.0	4.9	Married	33.2
Gender		%		Separated	5.2
	Men	56.4		Divorced	13.1
	Women	43.6		Widowed	1.0

Test-Taking Scales

Omissions		M	SD	Consistency		M	SD
	?	1.6	3.7	VRIN		55.8	11.5
				|F - FB|		5.6	4.2
				TRIN		56.2	13.0

Accuracy of Item Endorsement

Underreporting		M	SD	Overreporting		M	SD
	False %	44.1	8.0	True %		54.6	8.0
Impression	L	50.5	10.0	Infrequency	F	99.0	19.3
Management	ODecp	44.6	9.7		FB	105.4	27.5
	Sd	48.5	10.7		F[p]	78.4	20.0
Superior	S	37.1	8.3	Critical Items	K & B	49.4	12.6
Adjustment					L & W	63.6	16.5
Self-Deception	K	31.1	6.4	Dissimulation	F - K	11.4	9.7
	So	19.5	12.5		Ds	85.5	14.8
					O - S	195.9	71.5

Scales

Validity and Clinical			Supplementary			Morey et al. Overlapping Personality Disorder		
Scale	M	SD	Scale	M	SD	Scale	M	SD
?	1.6	3.7	A	74.0	9.4	PAR	78.2	11.6
L	50.5	10.0	R	51.5	11.4	SZD	61.8	12.5
F	99.0	19.3	Es	17.2	13.9	STY	78.7	12.6
K	37.7	7.5	TRIN	56.2	13.0	ANT	61.5	11.8
1(Hs)	73.6	15.2	VRIN	55.8	11.5	BDL	63.8	9.7
2(D)	77.3	14.0	O-H	47.2	10.3	HST	40.5	11.6
3(Hy)	70.8	15.8	Do	29.2	11.0	NAR	42.7	11.5
4(Pd)	73.9	12.1	Re	34.0	11.6	AVD	66.7	10.6
5(Mf)	54.1	9.4	GM	29.9	12.3	DEP	66.7	12.5
6(Pa)	96.5	13.4	GF	40.0	11.6	CPS	62.1	8.6
7(Pt)	80.9	12.9	Mt	76.7	9.7	Personality Psychopathology Five		
8(Sc)	95.0	13.9	PK	88.0	13.6			
9(Ma)	64.4	11.4	PS	87.9	12.9	Scale	M	SD
0(Si)	66.1	10.7	MAC-R	59.0	11.7	AGG	55.8	11.3
			APS	53.1	10.5	PSY	89.3	18.2
			AAS	60.8	14.4	CON	47.4	12.1
			MDS	76.3	12.3	NEN	70.7	9.6
			Ho	67.1	9.0	PEE	33.0	14.3
			CAL-R	56.7	11.1			

Content			Content Component					
Scale	M	SD	Scale	M	SD	Scale	M	SD
ANX	77.5	10.3	FRS1	78.1	23.1	ASP1	58.5	9.9
FRS	65.2	15.4	FRS2	54.3	10.8	ASP2	59.2	13.4
OBS	69.9	11.2	DEP1	81.7	15.0	TPA1	59.0	9.3
DEP	80.4	11.6	DEP2	74.1	10.8	TPA2	60.9	11.3
HEA	77.9	14.6	DEP3	73.6	12.2	LSE1	70.4	13.4
BIZ	84.4	15.7	DEP4	90.0	30.2	LSE2	61.8	11.8
ANG	66.7	11.8	HEA1	71.6	18.6	SOD1	64.3	12.5
CYN	64.9	10.8	HEA2	81.3	18.6	SOD2	57.8	9.8
ASP	61.6	12.3	HEA3	69.1	13.4	FAM1	65.8	12.2
TPA	62.6	12.7	BIZ1	91.3	27.3	FAM2	62.3	14.6
LSE	72.3	13.1	BIZ2	80.4	12.8	TRT1	78.4	16.3
SOD	65.0	12.9	ANG1	65.3	12.5	TRT2	62.5	10.2
FAM	70.8	13.3	ANG2	62.7	8.7			
WRK	76.0	11.6	CYN1	61.6	9.0			
TRT	77.9	13.3	CYN2	62.4	8.5			

Note. All scores are T scores except: Cannot Say, K & B and L & W critical items which are raw scores; True % and False % which are the percentage of items endorsed "true" or "false;" and \|F - FB\|, F - K, and O - S which are difference scores.

unusually cheerful and happy without any demonstrable cause. In addition, he reports mild dysphoria and general anhedonia. He has difficulty expressing his feelings appropriately and may vacillate between overcontrolling and undercontrolling his emotions. He easily becomes impatient with others, and they will perceive him as irritable, grouchy, and hotheaded.

Cognitions: Sometimes he becomes so agitated and excited that he may have difficulty in concentrating and thinking. He often exercises poor judgment, although he thinks that his judgment is very good. He has strange and unusual thoughts and dreams that he believes are best kept to himself. He often believes that he is being punished without cause. He is grandiose, egocentric, and cynical of the abilities of others.

He reports symptoms that may reflect a psychotic process that is more likely to reflect a mood disorder than a thought disorder or a very long-term characterologic condition. His presenting problems, background, and history should be reviewed with this possibility in mind.

Interpersonal Relations: He is very active, energetic, and outgoing socially, and he believes that he would make a good leader of people. Others are apt to misunderstand his intentions even when he is trying to be helpful. He is unconcerned about others' evaluations of him and is socially alienated.

Other Problem Areas: He frequently finds that sleep is not necessary because he is so full of energy. He clearly has enough energy to do his work. He is in good physical health. He is very prone to abuse substances. Suicidal ideation should be monitored carefully because of his impulsive tendencies.

Treatment: His prognosis is generally poor because of his limited concerns about his own behavior. Psychopharmacologic interventions are frequently warranted because of the agitation and excitement. Short-term behavioral interventions that focus on his reasons for entering treatment will be most effective.

Gynther et al. (1973) and Marks et al. (1974) provide additional interpretive information on *6-9/9-6*.

codetypes, and Table D.44 provides the prototypic scores.

6-0/0-6 (0.39%)

Moods: The client is experiencing a moderate level of distress, and he worries about possible misfortunes. He has recurring dysphoric moods from which he is slow to recover. He gets little pleasure from life and may actually be anhedonic. Others view him as moody, impatient, and grouchy. His feelings are easily hurt, and he is very sensitive to criticism or scolding.

Cognitions: He believes that he thinks clearly and has good judgment and memory. He thinks that other people are talking about him and looking at him critically, and that they are interested only in themselves and have little real concern for him. He lacks self-confidence and is swayed easily by the opinions of others.

Interpersonal Relations: He is very shy and bashful and is easily embarrassed in social situations. He is not assertive and is unwilling to confront others. He feels lonely much of the time even when he is around people. He finds it very difficult to confide in others about himself. He has pleasant relations with his family and is most comfortable when he is home.

Other Problem Areas: He is in good physical health now and has been for the past few years. He has problems sleeping. He may abuse substances.

Treatment: His prognosis is fair. He is likely to benefit from assertiveness or social-skill training. He finds it difficult to open up and share with others, making the establishment of a therapeutic alliance very difficult. His problems are chronic in nature, and long-term therapy is warranted once a therapeutic relationship is established.

Table D.45 provides the prototypic scores for *6-0/0-6* codetypes.

Spike 7 (0.53%)

Clients who elevate only Scale 7 (Psychasthenia) are relatively uncommon because of the extensive item overlap between Scale 7 and the other Clinical scales, especially Scales 2 (Depression) and 8 (Schizophrenia).

Moods: The client is experiencing a very mild level of emotional distress characterized by anxiety. He is happy most of the time, and he generally feels cheerful. Despite describing himself as being happy, he experiences a mild to moderate level of anxiety, and he is easily frightened and often phobic. He is impatient with others and becomes annoyed over even minor mishaps.

Cognitions: He lacks self-confidence and is prone to give up easily because he underestimates his own ability. He obsesses and ruminates over what is happening to him and around him.

Interpersonal Relations: He is a very shy, reserved individual who becomes embarrassed easily. He is very dependent upon others and easily influenced by them. His social isolation and fear of social interaction keep him out of behavioral problems. He describes his home life as pleasant with very few quarrels.

Other Problem Areas: He is in good physical health and as able to work as he ever was. He experiences few pains or physical symptoms. He has minor sleep difficulties, but these are not particularly upsetting to him. He is unlikely to have suicidal ideation or to abuse substances.

Treatment: His prognosis is good for long-term therapy. He has a very stable personality structure, which requires long-term psychological treatment to produce significant behavioral change. He is unlikely to require hospitalization, although his symptoms may seriously interfere with his job and general interpersonal relations. Social-skill training or assertiveness training frequently is beneficial and will facilitate the establishment of a therapeutic alliance.

Table D.46 provides the prototypic scores for Spike 7 codetypes.

7-8/8-7 (3.59%)

Clients with 7-8/8-7 codetypes share numerous clinical features in common, but scale order is important in understanding their behavior. When Scale 7 (Psychasthenia) is higher than Scale 8 (Schizophrenia), clients still are resisting the establishment of serious thought and behavior disorders. That is, the thoughts and behaviors that they are experiencing are still upsetting and distressing to them, which is a positive clinical sign. When Scale 8 is higher than Scale 7, clients may be adapting to the presence of serious psychopathology, which makes intervention more difficult.

Hall et al. (1986) found this codetype to occur frequently in men who sexually assaulted children.

Moods: The client is experiencing a moderate level of emotional distress characterized by dysphoria, brooding, and agitation. He is chronically stressed, and he becomes more agitated or withdrawn as his level of stress increases. He is generally apprehensive and fearful of his environment. He obtains little pleasure from life and has little motivation to try to change his circumstances. Anhedonia may be present.

Cognitions: He has difficulty thinking, and his concentration is poor. He lacks self-confidence and he gives up quickly when things go wrong. He reports strange and peculiar thoughts that he believes are best not to share with others. He thinks that there is something wrong with his mind. He obsesses and ruminates about his feelings and problems and believes that he has done something wrong or evil. He often engages in sexual fantasies, and his sexual adjustment is likely to be poor. He is cynical and suspicious of the motives of other people.

He reports a number of symptoms that may reflect a psychotic process or a very long-term characterologic condition. His presenting problems, background, and history should be reviewed with this possibility in mind.

Interpersonal Relations: He is extremely introverted and socially uncomfortable and has poor social skills and judgment. He has difficulty forming close, personal relationships. He is very alienated. He is indecisive and passive in his relationships with others and often feels isolated and lonely even when he is around people.

Other Problem Areas: Sleep difficulties are common. He is likely to have suicidal ideation that should be monitored carefully. He has a number of neurologic symptoms; his history should be reviewed to determine whether a medical or neuropsychological evaluation is warranted. He is likely to abuse substances.

Treatment: His prognosis is generally poor given the characterologic nature of his problems and his diminished motivation to work. Establishing a therapeutic alliance is very challenging because of the serious character pathology that is present and because of his difficulty in forming interpersonal relations. Psychopharmacologic intervention may be necessary to decrease his level of agitation and to help him sleep. Cognitive-behavioral interventions focused on his depressive and anxious cognitive processes will be beneficial.

Archer et al. (1995), Gilberstadt and Duker (1965), Gynther et al. (1973), and Kelley and King (1980) provide additional interpretive information on *7-8/8-7* codetypes. Table D.47 provides the prototypic scores.

7-9/9-7 (0.28%)

Moods: The client is experiencing a moderate level of emotional distress characterized by dysphoria, worrying, agitation, and anhedonia. Frequently he becomes agitated and excited. He will stir up excitement when he gets bored. He can become impatient and grouchy with others.

Cognitions: He finds it difficult to relax and interrupt his obsessive ruminations about his fears and problems. He may experience periods of impulsive and inconsiderate behavior followed by guilt feelings and self-criticism. His thinking may be tangential or disconnected. He may exhibit poor judgment. In response to stress he may become more agitated and ruminative. He doubts that others have his best interests at heart, and he questions their motives if they try to help him. He has thoughts that he is reluctant to share with others and some problems that he will never disclose. The possibility of manic or hypomanic features should be investigated.

Interpersonal Relations: He is immature and self-centered. His inconsiderate and impulsive behavior causes difficulty in establishing personal contacts on more than a superficial level. He experiences a considerable level of strife and conflict with his family. He is alienated from his family and others. He wanted to leave home as a result of this conflict and alienation.

Other Problem Areas: His excitement and agitation frequently make it difficult for him to sleep. He is very likely to abuse substances. He reports a number of neurologic symptoms; his history should be reviewed to determine their cause. Suicidal ideation should be monitored carefully because of his impulsivity and potential for substance abuse.

Treatment: His prognosis is guarded because of the chronic nature of his problems, the difficulty he has in establishing close relationships, and his belief that his problems should be kept to himself. Psychopharmacologic intervention may be indicated to assist in decreasing his anxiety, agitation, and excitement. Short-term behavioral interventions that focus on his reasons for entering treatment will be most effective.

Kelley and King (1979a) provide additional interpretive information on *7-9/9-7* codetypes, and Table D.48 provides the prototypic scores.

7-0/0-7 (0.42%)

Moods: The client is experiencing a moderate level of emotional distress characterized by dysphoria, worrying, and guilt. He gets little pleasure from life and may be anhedonic. He frequently becomes impatient with others, who may view him as apathetic because of his perceived inability to better his circumstances.

Cognitions: He thinks little of his own ability and gives up easily when things go wrong. He ruminates and obsesses over what he has done and what he needs to do. He has problems with concentration.

Interpersonal Relations: He is a very shy, reserved individual who becomes embarrassed easily. He lacks self-confidence and is easily threatened or intimidated by others. He tends to give up when things go wrong or others express opposition. His social isolation and fear of social interaction keep him out of behavioral problems. He has trouble knowing what to talk about when in a group of people.

Other Problem Areas: He is not likely to abuse substances. He is as able to work as he ever was. He is in good physical health. Suicidal ideation is very likely and should be evaluated carefully.

Treatment: His prognosis is good for long-term therapy. Social-skill training or assertiveness training may be beneficial. He finds it difficult to tell others about himself, which will make establishing a therapeutic alliance difficult.

Table D.49 provides the prototypic scores for *7-0/0-7* codetypes.

Spike 8 (0.41%)

Moods: The client is not experiencing any type of emotional distress; he describes himself in positive terms such as being happy most of the time, not worrying, and being no more nervous than other people. He is calm and not easily upset, and he does not tire quickly. However, he acknowledges a mild, general level of dissatisfaction and fearfulness that borders on anhedonia. His anger and irritability are readily apparent to others. He can be argumentative and confrontational sometimes with little apparent provocation.

Cognitions: He believes that his memory, concentration, and judgment are good. He has dreams and fantasies that he is reluctant to share with others. He is somewhat cynical and dubious about the motives of people around him. Some original, unusual, or eccentric qualities may be present in his thinking. At best, he has abstract theoretical or philosophical interests and a tendency not to conform. He may be psychotic, with feelings of unreality, memory difficulties, and confused or bizarre thoughts or beliefs. Hallucinations, psychomotor retardation, and withdrawal are possible. A history of psychiatric hospitalizations is possible.

Interpersonal Relations: He is seen as being confident in social situations. His confidence reflects lack of concern about what others think of him rather than actual social skills and presence. He is not self-conscious, and his feelings are not easily hurt. He tends to be aloof and socially alienated from others, which decreases the probability of his getting into behavioral difficulties even though he tends to be undercontrolled.

Other Problem Areas: He does not have sleep difficulties. He is likely to abuse substances. He is in good physical health and as able to work as he ever was. He does not worry about his health and is not experiencing pain. There is a slight possibility of suicidal ideation.

Treatment: His prognosis is guarded. He sees himself as being well adjusted, so there is little motivation for any intervention. Short-term behavioral interventions that focus on his reasons for entering treatment will be most effective.

Table D.50 provides the prototypic scores for Spike 8 codetypes.

8-9/9-8 (1.20%)

Clients with *8-9/9-8* codetypes evidence serious psychopathology, even when these scales are only slightly elevated above a T score of 65 on the MMPI-2.

Moods: The client is experiencing moderate to severe emotional distress characterized by agitation and excitement. He often is seen initially in an acute state of hyperactivity, excitement, confusion, and disorientation. He is likely to be emotionally labile, demanding, hostile, irritable, evasive, suspicious, and distrustful. He is unpredictable and prone to act out unexpectedly.

Cognitions: He may have difficulty concentrating and thinking clearly. His judgment and reality testing may be quite poor. In response to stress, he is likely to become more disorganized and agitated or to engage in more daydreaming and fantasy.

He reports a number of symptoms that may reflect a psychotic process or a very long-term characterologic condition. His presenting problems, background, and history should be reviewed with this possibility in mind.

Interpersonal Relations: His behavior may be unpredictable, and he may act out unexpectedly. He is fearful of relating to others; consequently, close relations are usually lacking. When present, they are often marked by distrust, suspicion, and anger. He is boastful, emotionally labile, and egocentric.

Other Problem Areas: He has poor sexual adjustment. He is very likely to abuse substances. Suicidal ideation is likely and should be monitored carefully because of his impulsivity and potential for substance abuse.

Treatment: His prognosis is generally poor. Psychopharmacologic intervention may be helpful in reducing his agitation. The difficulties he experiences in focusing on specific issues and his fear of relating to others often preclude good therapeutic contact and outcome. Short-term behavioral interventions that focus on his reasons for entering treatment will be most effective.

Gilberstadt and Duker (1965), Gynther et al. (1973), and Marks et al. (1974) provide additional interpretive information on *8-9/9-8* codetypes. Table D.51 provides the prototypic scores.

8-0/0-8 (0.27%)

Moods: The client is experiencing mild emotional distress characterized by dysphoria, anxiety, and guilt. He gets little pleasure from life. He is easily frightened and frequently phobic. He is irritable, impatient, and grouchy. He gives up easily and avoids conflict whenever possible.

Cognitions: He has trouble making decisions and worries about what others will think of decisions that he has made. He gives up quickly when things go wrong for him and avoids conflict whenever possible. He thinks that he is "no good at all," lacks self-confidence, and believes that no one understands him. He sees others as being interested only in themselves and unlikely to be of assistance to him. He also is suspicious of their motives if they do offer to help him. An undercurrent of cynicism permeates his interactions.

Interpersonal Relations: He is extremely introverted, shy, and bashful. He is easily embarrassed and intimidated in social situations. He finds it hard to talk when he meets new people. He is withdrawn, socially isolated, and avoids interpersonal relations. He reports that his family life was conflictual and unsatisfying and that he very much wanted to leave home. He feels lonely even when he is with people. He may have schizoid features.

Other Problem Areas: He is not likely to abuse substances. He is in good physical health and does not report sleep difficulties.

Treatment: His prognosis is good for short-term behavioral interventions that focus on his reasons for entering treatment. Assertiveness or social-skill training may be beneficial. He generally is nonverbal, which complicates the development of a therapeutic alliance that is needed for long-term psychotherapy.

Table D.52 provides the prototypic scores for *8-0/0-8* codetypes.

Spike 9 (2.91%)

Moods: The client is not experiencing any emotional distress. He definitely is not depressed, anxious, or fearful, and he reports almost no distress of any kind. His mood is easily elevated by doing something exciting if he should happen to feel depressed. He is grandiose, hyperactive, and talkative. He is rebellious and hostile, and he has difficulty controlling his impulses.

Cognitions: He has good memory and concentration, and he believes that his judgment is better than it ever has been. He finds it easy to make decisions and to focus on what needs to be done. He believes that his goals are within easy reach. He sees others as being interested only in themselves and unlikely to be of assistance to him. He is suspicious of their motives if they do offer to help him. An undercurrent of cynicism permeates his interactions.

He may evidence manic features, which should be carefully investigated. His thought processes may become bizarre during acute hypomanic phases, and he may become extremely belligerent if his grandiose plans are interrupted.

Interpersonal Relations: He is extroverted and he believes that he relates easily to others, although his relations have no real depth or intimacy. He is very self-confident and prefers to be a leader of the group. He expresses his ideas and behaviors directly with little thought or concern about the reactions of others. Others see him as an overactive, angry, and difficult individual who is defensive and guarded. He is frequently in conflict with members of his family and persons in positions of authority. He is not particularly concerned about these negative evaluations, and he is likely to attribute them to the failure of others to appreciate his ideas and skills.

Other Problem Areas: He does not experience sleep difficulties. He is in good physical health and does not tire easily. He is as capable of working as he ever was. He is very likely to abuse substances. He is prone to impulsive acting out and may have a history of criminal and interpersonal problems.

Treatment: His prognosis is poor because he is experiencing little emotional distress, limiting his motivation for any intervention. Short-term behavioral interventions that focus on his reasons for entering treatment may be effective. If manic features are evident, a psychopharmacologic intervention is indicated.

Gilberstadt and Duker (1965) provide additional interpretive information on Spike *9* codetypes, and Table D.53 provides the prototypic scores.

9-0/0-9 (0.02%)

Moods: Although the client is experiencing a moderate level of emotional distress, he describes himself as being happy and well adjusted. His mood is easily elevated by doing something exciting if he should happen to feel low.

Cognitions: He believes that he thinks clearly and has good judgment. He is skeptical of the motives of others to the point of being cynical. He frequently manipulates other people. He is egocentric, self-confident, and occasionally grandiose.

Interpersonal Relations: He tends to be socially introverted even though he has adequate social skills. He feels alienated from his family, and they are critical of him and his friends. He is prone to bend the rules as long as he thinks that he will not be caught.

Other Problem Areas: He is as able to work as he ever was. He is in good physical health and experiences few pains or physical symptoms. He is unlikely to abuse substances or get into behavioral difficulties.

Treatment: His prognosis is fair. Short-term behavioral interventions that focus on his specific reasons for seeking treatment are frequently beneficial. There is little motivation for long-term therapy.

Table D.54 provides the prototypic scores for *9-0/0-9* codetypes.

Spike *0* (1.10%)

Moods: The client is experiencing only a mild level of distress that tends to be chronic in nature. He believes that he is happy most of the time even though he reports a mild level of dysphoric mood and anhedonia. He is easily frightened and may actually be phobic.

Cognitions: He is not concerned about his psychological functioning. His memory is good. He tends to ruminate over what is going on around him, and he finds it difficult to make up his mind. He is cynical and questions the motives of other people.

Interpersonal Relations: He is very shy, bashful, and introverted, and he is easily embarrassed in social situations. He lacks self-confidence and is easily overwhelmed by others. He is uncomfortable speaking to others and reluctant to make his opinions known to them. His introversion and isolation help to keep him from getting into behavioral problems. He feels alienated from others including his family. Whether this interpersonal discomfort represents a schizoid adjustment, a neurotic reaction, or simply a lifestyle preference will have to be determined by understanding his history and his reason(s) for taking the MMPI-2.

Other Problem Areas: He is in good physical health, and he reports few or no physical pains. He is not likely to abuse substances. He does not get into trouble because of his behavior.

Treatment: His prognosis is guarded. His minimal level of distress and chronic problems preclude long-term treatment goals. His difficulty in trusting and opening up to others makes the establishment of a therapeutic alliance a slow process. Assertiveness or social-skill training may be beneficial if he can be engaged in the therapeutic process.

King and Kelley (1977a) provide additional interpretive information on Spike *0* codetypes. Table D.55 provides the prototypic scores.

CHAPTER 8

Interpreting the MMPI-2 Profile

The preceding chapters have reviewed the common interpretive statements made about specific elevations on the individual Validity and Clinical scales, the Supplementary scales, and the Content scales, and have explored the various relationships among these sets of scales. All of these sources of information provide the database used in profile interpretation of the MMPI-2. Consequently, the reader should be thoroughly familiar with the preceding Chapters and refer back to specific sections when appropriate and necessary in interpreting individual MMPI-2 profiles.

The task of this chapter will be to analyze the interpretive process for MMPI-2 profiles. In addition to a discussion of issues in profile interpretation, two profiles are presented to serve as examples of the interpretive process. Each profile will be interpreted by an individual clinician. This interpretation will then be compared and contrasted with interpretations produced by three computer-based interpretive systems.

COMPARISON GROUPS

There are many different groups with which an MMPI-2 profile can be compared, and the interpretation that will be made will vary as a function of which comparison group is used. The most general interpretation compares the client with all persons in a given group. In the standard MMPI-2 profile, the client is being compared with all men or women in the MMPI-2 normative group (Butcher et al., 1989). The client also can be compared to all psychiatric patients (Caldwell, 1997a), personnel screening applicants (Caldwell, 1997b; Cord, Sajwaj, Tolliver, & Ford, 1997), child custody litigants (Bathurst, Gottfried, & Gottfried, 1997), prison inmates (Megargee, Mercer, & Carbonell, 1999), personal injury plaintiffs (Lees-Haley, 1997), pain patients (Caldwell, 1998b), and so on. Table 8.1

(p. 362) illustrates how the client's T score on the *F* (Infrequency) and *K* (Correction) scales will have different interpretations depending on which of the samples is being used as a comparison group. A client with a T score of 60 on the *F* scale is 15 points higher than the mean of the child custody litigants (Bathurst et al., 1997) and personnel screening applicants (Caldwell, 1997b; Cord et al., 1997), and slightly lower than the mean of the psychiatric patients (Caldwell, 1997a) and personal injury plaintiffs (Lees-Haley, 1997). In the former group, a T score of 60 is relatively unusual, whereas in the latter two groups it is very common. Tables 3.17 (p. 63) and 3.24 (pp. 75–76) provide the cutting scores for assessing the consistency and accuracy of item endorsement in clinical patients (Caldwell, 1997a), the MMPI-2 normative group (Butcher et al., 1989), and personnel screening applicants (Caldwell, 1997b), which will illustrate how the same scale will have different interpretations depending on which group is used for a comparison.

Another group with which the MMPI-2 can be compared in the interpretive process is some subgrouping of the entire group that has been considered previously. The most common subgrouping of the MMPI-2 is based on codetype analysis. Although the frequency with which a specific codetype occurs in a group will vary rather drastically, as was discussed in Chapter 7, the prototypic MMPI-2 profile for individual codetypes appears to be relatively invariant across groups. Table 8.1 also provides the mean scores on the *F* (Infrequency) and *K* (Correction) scales for nine different MMPI-2 codetypes. The mean T score on the *F* scale varies from 46.8 in Spike *3* codetypes to 99.0 in *6-8/8-6* codetypes, and the *K* scale varies from 37.3 in *8-0/0-8* codetypes to 59.0 in Spike *3* codetypes. A client with a T score of 60 on the *F* scale is almost 15 points higher than the mean for Spike *3* codetypes,

TABLE 8.1   Effects of Setting and Codetype on MMPI-2 Scale Interpretation

| | MMPI-2 SCALE | | | |
| | F (Infrequency) | | K (Correction) | |
SETTING/AUTHOR(S)	M	SD	M	SD
Civilian Personnel Screening (Caldwell, 1997b)	44.0	5.8	61.4	8.8
Nuclear Power Plant Personnel Screening (Cord et al., 1997)	44.2		56.9	
Child Custody Litigants (Bathurst et al., 1997)	44.7	6.8	58.7	8.6
Normal Individuals (Butcher et al., 1989)	50.0	10.0	50.0	10.0
Pain Patients (Caldwell, 1998b)	57.2	17.0	51.2	10.3
Prison Inmates (Megargee et al., 1999)	58.0	14.9	49.0	10.0
Personal Injury Plaintiffs (Lees-Haley, 1997)	62.0	20.3	50.0	10.8
Psychiatric Patients (Caldwell, 1997a)	60.4	21.5	51.3	11.6

| | MMPI-2 SCALE | | | |
| | F (Infrequency) | | K (Correction) | |
CODETYPE	M	SD	M	SD
6/8-8-6	99.0	19.3	37.7	7.5
7-8/8-7	84.6	18.3	40.8	8.2
8-0/0-8	76.0	13.1	37.3	7.4
2-4/4-2	69.3	15.0	45.8	8.8
2-7/7-2	67.1	14.1	45.6	8.3
6-9/9-6	64.3	16.6	44.3	9.3
4-9/9-4	63.8	14.8	47.0	9.2
1-3/3-1	57.2	12.4	54.5	9.6
Spike 3	46.8	6.4	59.0	8.5

and nearly 40 points lower than the mean for *6-8/8-6* codetypes. A T score of 60 is unusual in both of these codetypes; in the former it is higher than expected and in the latter it is much lower than expected.

A codetype analysis can be further refined by considering additional Clinical scales to create three- and four-point codetypes. There are a number of two-point codetypes that have frequent three-point variants that should be considered in the interpretation of the MMPI-2. These three-point codetypes, such as variants of *2-4/4-2* and *2-7/7-2* codetypes, were noted in Chapter 7, when the parent two-point codetype was discussed. Again, the interpretation of a client's score

on a given scale will change as the prototypic score changes in the three-point codetypes within a particular group.

The final "group" with which the MMPI-2 can be compared in the interpretive process is the individual client him- or herself (i.e., an idiographic interpretation). In this comparison the relative elevations of the scales become important because they indicate which content domains are more or less important for this particular client. A client who has T scores of 75 and 60 on the Content scales of Depression (*DEP*) and Anxiety (*ANX*), respectively, is saying that symptoms of depression are more of a problem than symptoms of anxiety. The MMPI-2 Content (Butcher et al., 1990) and Content Component (Ben-Porath & Sherwood, 1993) scales and the MMPI-2 Structural Summary (Greene & Nichols, 1995; Nichols & Greene, 1995) are excellent means of developing such an idiographic interpretation of a client's MMPI-2 profile, because the various content domains can be juxtaposed so that the clinician can compare them directly.

The clinician should compare the client's MMPI-2 profile with all of the appropriate groups in order to extract the maximal amount of information for the interpretive process.

EFFECTS OF DEMOGRAPHIC VARIABLES

Basic demographic data on the client whose MMPI-2 profile is being interpreted are needed in order to help the clinician determine which comparison group to use. At a minimum, the clinician needs to know the client's age, gender, educational level, social class, ethnic group, and setting in which the MMPI-2 was administered; any of these variables can drastically alter the interpretation of particular scales or the entire profile. For example, a T score of 60 on Scale *9* (Hypomania) may be typical for an 18-year-old and extremely unusual for a 60-year-old. Thus, only after the basic demographic data are known is the clinician ready to start interpreting the MMPI-2 profile.

The effects of demographic variables on MMPI-2 performance will be reviewed in Chapter 9. Further discussion of this topic will be deferred until that chapter.

PRELIMINARY ISSUES IN PROFILE INTERPRETATION

Several issues should be discussed prior to undertaking an analysis of the process of MMPI-2 interpretation. First, the interpretive process in this chapter will be "blind," that is, done without any additional sources of data about the client. This is not to suggest that the clinician in actual practice should follow such a procedure, but it is necessary here in order to limit the interpretation to a finite, known database. Such a procedure ensures that readers will know what data are used in making the interpretation and that they will become aware of what information can and cannot be obtained from the MMPI-2. There are obviously questions that the clinician cannot answer from the MMPI-2 alone, and this blind analysis should sensitize the clinician to the additional data that are needed to answer these particular questions.

Second, MMPI-2 data, like most clinical data, are amenable to more than one interpretation. Thus, the clinician's task, and the task in the examples provided, is not to find the one and only "correct" interpretation. It is, rather, to find an interpretation of the profile that is internally and theoretically consistent as well as empirically testable.

The focus of this chapter, then, is to explore how interpretations are made rather than to decide which alternative interpretation is "better." The reader should keep this in mind when it appears that only one "correct" interpretation is being made of each profile in this chapter. It is possible that each profile may have an alternative interpretation, and once the reader understands the procedure explained in this chapter, he or she may discover a "better" interpretation. This process of becoming an informed skeptic when interpreting MMPI-2 profiles is strongly encouraged.

Finally, even though the description of the process of analysis is being limited to the MMPI-2, the same general skills and procedures are involved in the interpretation of any clinical material, including the Rorschach, an interview, or dreams. Hopefully, the empirical nature of the MMPI-2 will make understanding of this basic process of interpretation easier. (The interested reader should consult Levy's [1963] text, *Psychological Interpretation,* for a more abstract discussion of this issue.)

GENERAL ISSUES IN THE INTERPRETIVE PROCESS

There are a number of general issues that need to be raised that occur in the interpretive process for any psychological test. These issues will be raised here and then not discussed further in the interests of space. The clinician needs to understand, however, that each of these issues still applies throughout the description of the interpretive process for every MMPI-2 profile.

Clinicians must have a clear understanding and awareness of the base rates (prevalence) with which specific symptoms, behaviors, and diagnoses occur in general, and in their setting in particular (cf. Finn & Kamphuis, 1995). If the lifetime prevalence for Major Depressive Disorder is from 10 to 25 percent in women and from 5 to 12 percent in men, while lifetime prevalence for Schizophrenia is from 0.5 to 1 percent (American Psychiatric Association, 1994), the clinician should realize that the former diagnosis is much more likely than the latter. The probability that an elevation on Scale 8 (Schizophrenia) is the result of schizophrenia is quite low when the prevalence is around 1 percent. However, if 75 percent of the clients in a specific setting are schizophrenic, any hypothesis stating that the client is not schizophrenic is going against the base rates regardless of the elevation on Scale 8. The *Diagnostic and Statistical Manual of Mental Disorders* (American Psychiatric Association, 1994) provides the clinician with invaluable information on prevalence rates as well as the impact of demographic variables on each diagnosis.

Clinicians also must be wary of making "Barnum"-type statements (Meehl, 1956), which are accurate for virtually everyone in the reference group and, hence, are meaningless in describing a specific client. Thus, to hypothesize that an acutely psychotic patient is having heterosexual difficulties is neither particularly brilliant nor insightful. On the other hand, the accuracy of such statements should not be ignored, and they should be tailored to make them more specific for the individual.

All too often, once clinicians are familiar with base rates and Barnum-type statements, they avoid any statement that could be even vaguely labeled as such. Unfortunately, such a reaction is much like "throwing the baby out with the bath water." The clinician is afraid to make any base rate statement even when it may provide the most accurate appraisal of the situation. For example, if an elevated score on Scale 3 (Hysteria) virtually excludes the possibility of the client having a psychotic diagnosis, the clinician should not ignore the data simply because of the base rate. The clinician is advised to use Barnum-type statements that have virtually 0 percent or 100 percent applicability only when they provide important information about the client that otherwise might be overlooked.

Clinicians should use a disconfirmatory rather than a confirmatory strategy when integrating various sources of information during the interpretive process. Clinicians, like all humans, are prone to search for information that confirms their hypothesis or hunch once it has been made rather than searching for information that would disconfirm it. Given the robustness of this confirmatory bias (cf. Dawes, 1994; Faust, 1984), clinicians should be alert for any information that is directly contradictory to their hypothesis. For example, if Scale 8 (Schizophrenia) is elevated to a T score of 80, which could suggest the presence of psychotic symptoms in the client, the clinician should look for any information that would contradict this hypothesis. A T score of 50 or lower on the Bizarre Mentation (*BIZ*) scale would disconfirm the potentially psychotic interpretation of Scale 8 and indicate that some other interpretation must be considered.

The role of shared items or item overlap and shared variance must be considered when noting that two or more scales are elevated. There are many examples of scales that share a large percentage of items within the MMPI-2. Scale 1 (Hypochondriasis, 32 items) and Health Concerns (*HEA*, 36 items) share 23 (71.9%) items so it is not surprising that their correlation is 0.965. The Hostility (*Ho*, 50 items) and Cynicism (*CYN*, 23 items) scales share 17 (73.9%) items and their correlation is 0.921. The Post Traumatic Stress Disorder—Keane (*PK*, 46 items) scale and Post Traumatic Stress Disorder—Schlenger (*PS*, 60 items) scale share 26 (56.5%) items and their correlation is 0.972. Tables 4.30, 5.6, 5.7, 6.12, and 6.13 that reported item overlap among the various sets of scales need to be consulted before emphasizing the fact that a client has elevated two specific scales.

MMPI-2 scales can be correlated substantially even though they share no items because of common variance, usually first-factor (generalized distress and negative emotionality) variance. The Welsh Anxiety (*A*) scale correlates 0.873 and 0.870 with the Negative Treatment Indicators (*TRT*) and Low Self-Esteem (*LSE*) scales, respectively, even though they share few items. The *F* (Infrequency) scale correlates 0.859

with the F_B scale, which share no items. The Social Alienation (Sc_1) scale correlates 0.774 with the Alienation—Self and Others (Si_3) scale, which share no items.

MMPI-2 scales also can be correlated substantially because of both shared items and shared variance. The Welsh Anxiety (A, 39 items) scale and the Content scale of Anxiety (ANX, 23 items) correlate 0.902, even though they share only 7 (30.4%) items. The Social Responsibility (Re, 30 items) scale and the Content scale of Antisocial Practices (ASP, 22 items) correlate –0.748 and they share 5 (22.7%) items that are scored in the opposite direction (i.e., "true" on one scale and "false" on the other or vice versa). The K (Correction, 30 items) scale correlates 0.819 with the Hysteria, Subtle ($Hy-S$, 28 items) scale, which share 10 (33.3%) items.

Finally, the clinician must give appropriate consideration to positive predictive (PPP) and negative predictive power (NPP) when interpreting any scale. PPP is the probability that a client with a score above the cutoff on a scale actually has the disorder in question, while NPP is the probability that a client with a score below the cutoff does not have the disorder. PPP and NPP rather than sensitivity and specificity should be used in making these decisions, because PPP and NPP take the base rate (prevalence) of the behavior or diagnosis into consideration, while sensitivity and specificity do not. Most studies artificially create a base rate of 50 percent because equal sample sizes are used to facilitate statistical analyses. If PPP and NPP are computed in these studies, which they should be, the clinician may not realize that these values of PPP and NPP will change drastically when the base rate is adjusted to reflect more accurately the frequency with which most diagnostic conditions occur in clinical settings. Baldessarini et al. (1983) have provided an excellent overview of the use of PPP and NPP that should be a standard reference for all clinicians. Gottesman and Prescott (1989) used the MacAndrew Alcoholism (MAC: MacAndrew, 1965) scale to illustrate the abuses that can occur in the use of a scale to classify individuals when clinicians are not aware of PPP and NPP.

Table 8.2 illustrates the difference between sensitivity and specificity and PPP and NPP in a study in which Scale 2 (Depression) is being used to predict a diagnosis of depression. In this hypothetical example, sensitivity and specificity were set at 70 and 80 percent, respectively, and the optimal cutting score has been set at a T score of 65. In the initial study, in which equal sample sizes were used, both the PPP (77.8 percent) and NPP (72.7 percent) are quite good and they show a significant improvement over the base rate of 50 percent. The sensitivity and specificity are unchanged in these three examples in which the base rate (prevalence) decreases from 50 to 10 to 1 percent. PPP decreases and NPP increases dramatically with these reductions in base rate. At a base rate of 1 percent, the PPP is 3.4 percent, which means that slightly over 3 clients out of 100 will be identified accurately by Scale 2, or conversely, nearly 97 out of 100 clients will be misidentified. Given that the base rates with which most behaviors, symptoms, and diagnoses occur in any clinical setting are much closer to 10 percent than 50 percent, NPP always will be substantially higher than PPP. This fact should encourage clinicians to give more consideration to low scores in the MMPI-2 profile because they can make more accurate predictions from low scores rather than elevated scores. For example, when Scale 2 is below a T score of 65, or even lower, the NPP that the client is not depressed is quite high, as can be seen in Table 8.2 (p. 366), which has significant implications for potential diagnoses and treatments.

Now that these general issues in the interpretive process have been considered, attention can be turned to the specific process of interpreting an MMPI-2 profile.

THE INTERPRETIVE PROCESS

Figure 8.1 (p. 367) illustrates the many steps in the pathway between an external criterion, such as determining readiness for treatment, a specific diagnostic category, or whatever variables are of interest to the clinician, and the MMPI-2 profile. The number of intermediate steps between any external criterion and the MMPI-2 profile should help clinicians appreciate why there are not stronger relationships with MMPI-2 variables. The general issue of making a diagnosis of some mental disorder such as Dysthymic Disorder

TABLE 8.2   Effects of Prevalence on Positive and Negative Predictive Power

Prevalence (Base Rate) = 50%

Scale 2 (D)	Depressed Yes	No	Total
T >=65	350	100	450
T < 65	150	400	550
Total	500	500	1000

PPP = 350/450 = 77.8%
NPP = 400/550 = 72.7%
Sensitivity = 350/500 = 70.0%
Specificity = 400/500 = 80.0%

Prevalence (Base Rate) = 10%

Scale 2 (D)	Depressed Yes	No	Total
T >=65	70	180	250
T < 65	30	720	750
Total	100	900	1000

PPP = 70/250 = 28.0%
NPP = 720/750 = 96.0%
Sensitivity = 70/100 = 70.0%
Specificity = 720/900 = 80.0%

Prevalence (Base Rate) = 1%

Scale 2 (D)	Depressed Yes	No	Total
T >=65	7	198	205
T < 65	3	792	795
Total	10	990	1000

PPP = 7/205 = 3.4%
NPP = 792/795 = 99.6%
Sensitivity = 7/10 = 70.0%
Specificity = 792/990 = 80.0%

will be used in illustrating this process, although any other variable would work equally as well.

An initial issue is whether monothetic or polythetic criteria are to be used in making the diagnosis of a mental disorder. Monothetic criteria detail the necessary and sufficient features in order to make the diagnosis; that is, the client must meet *all* of the criteria in order to be diagnosed. Polythetic criteria require only that a minimal number of the features be present; that is, the client must meet some subset of all of the criteria, such as four of seven criteria, in order to be diagnosed, but which of the seven criteria the client must meet are *not* specified. Consequently,

polythetic criteria are likely to recognize a number of diverse features, which are thought to overlap in the disorder, but they are not mutually exclusive. It is possible in a disorder defined by polythetic criteria to have two patients who share few, if any, features. It has been suggested (Livesley, 1986) that in disorders defined by polythetic criteria not all patients are equally good representations of the disorder and that prototypic behaviors and/or patients could be identified that would facilitate establishing more agreement among clinicians in making the diagnosis of the disorder. Livesley (1986) has provided examples of the prototypic behaviors that are seen in personality dis-

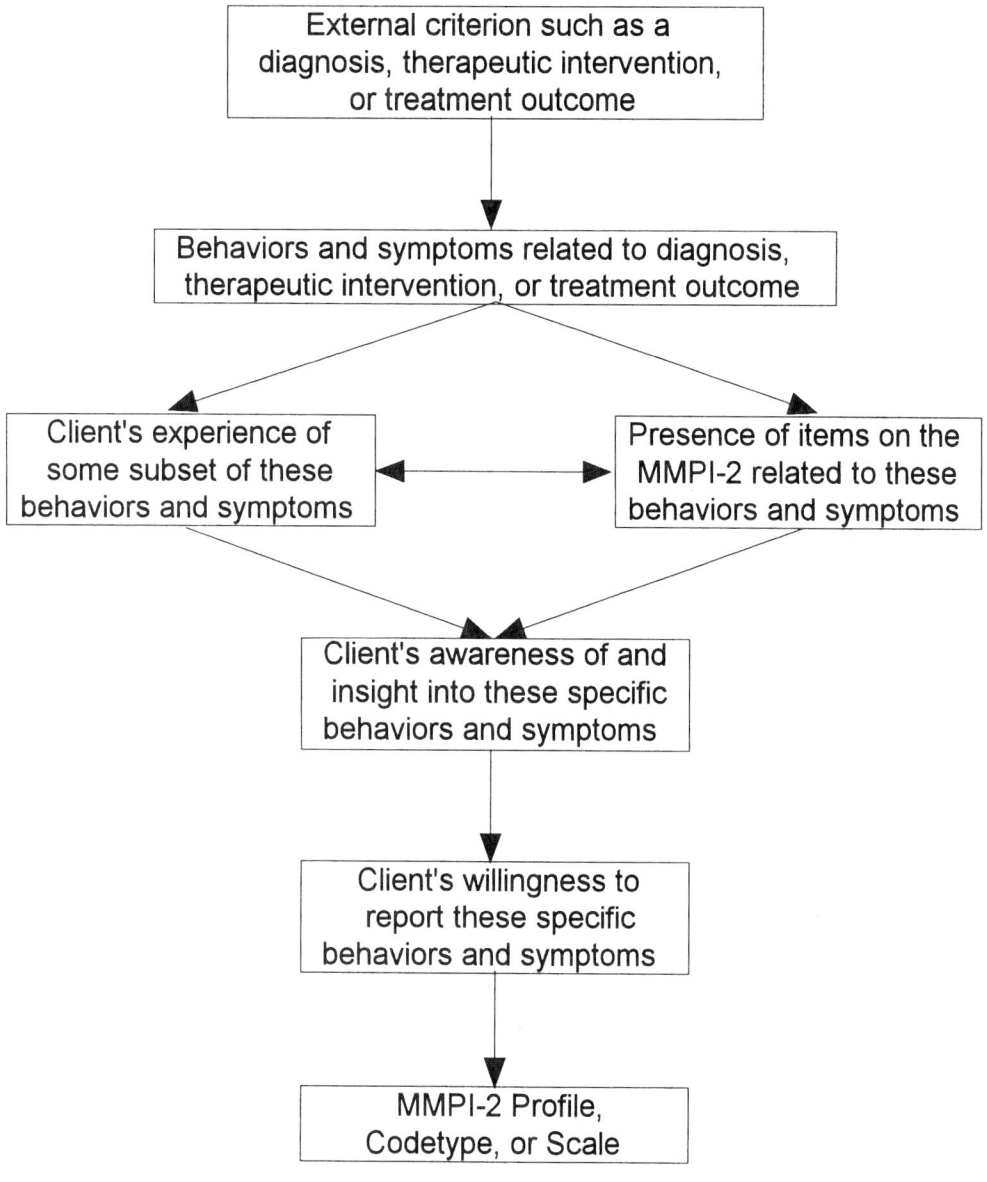

FIGURE 8.1   Steps between an External Criterion and a Client's MMPI-2 Profile

orders, which could serve as a basis for identifying such characteristics. Polythetic criteria do reflect the overlap among various diagnostic categories with few firm boundaries that are seen clinically, although such criteria also result in more heterogeneous diagnostic categories. The more variability in the number of criteria for a diagnosis of a specific mental disorder should lower the probability of finding common codetypes and produce larger variances on the content and supplemental scales. Each ensuing edition of the *Diagnostic and Statistical Manual of Mental Disorders* (American Psychiatric Association, 1980, 1987, 1994) tends to emphasize polythetic criteria more than monothetic criteria, so clinicians need to be aware that different criteria may be used for diagnoses when comparing MMPI-2 studies.

Once it is realized that clients may experience different subsets of symptoms and behaviors within a specific diagnostic category, the associated issue can be considered of whether the MMPI-2 contains items that allow clients to report these symptoms and behaviors. If the items are not on the MMPI-2, there obviously is no way for clients to report them. The adequacy of the MMPI item pool was mentioned in Chapter 1 when the number of items in the different categories were described (p. 5). Some categories such as physical symptoms are well represented in the MMPI item pool, while other areas such as the traits and behaviors expected in the Personality Disorders are less well represented.

The next step is to consider the client's level of awareness of and insight into their symptoms of Dysthymic Disorder. The more awareness that clients have of their symptoms, the better they will be able to report them. Obviously, if clients are not aware of specific symptom(s), they cannot report them on the MMPI-2. It also seems reasonable to assume that clients would *not* have the same degree of insight into and awareness of all of their symptoms. Some clients may have more insight into their interpersonal functioning than into their emotions and vice versa. Clients also would *not* be expected to experience the same subset of symptoms in the same manner. Some clients may focus on the cognitive features of their symptoms, while other clients may focus on their affective or interpersonal features. If a specific diagnostic category emphasizes cognitive features, for example, a client who has more insight into and prefers to focus on cognitive features will be more likely to report them.

If clients are aware of their symptoms, their willingness to report these symptoms becomes the next step in the pathway between a diagnosis of Dysthymic Disorder and the MMPI-2 profile. The setting in which the MMPI-2 is administered will have an immense impact on how or whether symptoms will be reported. The same person taking the MMPI-2 as part of a child custody evaluation or a workers' compensation evaluation has very different motivation whether to report symptoms, and the resulting profiles will be very different. There also is a natural propensity for people to differ in their willingness to report and discuss their symptoms, which is independent of the setting in which the MMPI-2 is administered. For some people the glass always is "half full," while for others it always is "half empty." Depending on their cognitive or motivational perspective, a different number of symptoms of varying severity will be reported, even if the clients have similar insight into and willingness to report their symptoms of Dysthymic Disorder. The importance of cognitive variables on MMPI-2 profiles has not been investigated and they clearly are worthy of study. For example, do patients with depressive diagnoses who have a sharpening (sensitizing) cognitive style versus a leveling (repressing) cognitive style report different symptoms of varying levels of severity that impact treatment outcomes?

Once clinicians are aware of these many steps that lead to the MMPI-2 profile, they are in a better position to understand the many factors that can affect the interpretation and that need to be considered.

Empirically Based Interpretation

Figure 8.2 illustrates the steps in the interpretation of the MMPI-2 profile. It will be assumed that the validity of this specific administration of the MMPI-2 has been assessed following the flow chart (p. 43) in Chapter 3. Once it has been ascertained that the client has endorsed the items consistently and accurately, the clinician must decide whether an empirically based and/or content-based interpretation of the MMPI-2 is to be used. Traditionally, the interpretation of the MMPI-2 has been empirically based with an almost total disregard of content, although in recent years there is more and more emphasis being placed on content-based interpretation of the MMPI-2 (cf. Butcher et al., 1990). The optimal solution is to use both approaches and to integrate them into a single, coherent interpretation. As illustrated in

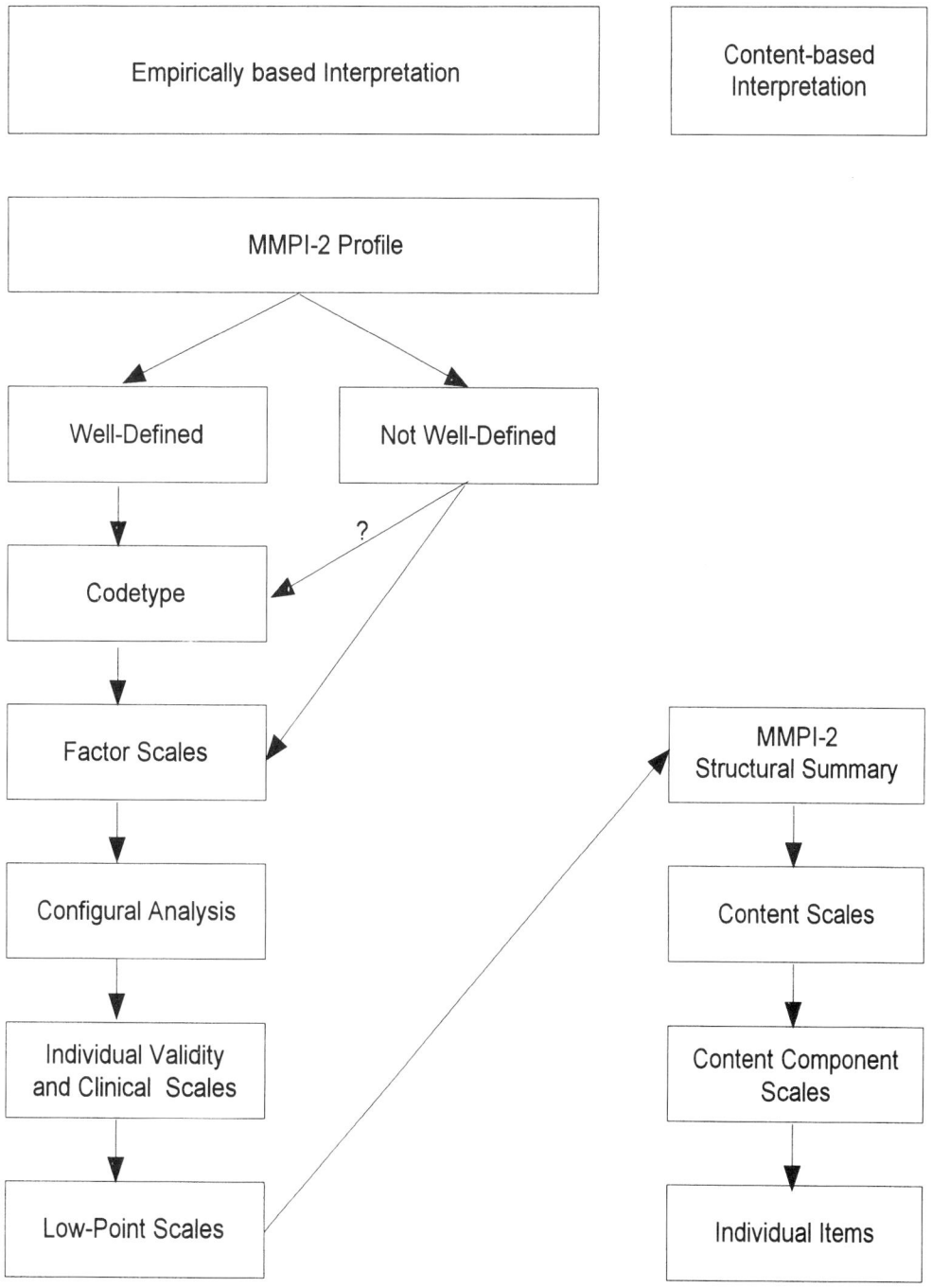

FIGURE 8.2 Flow Chart for Interpreting the MMPI-2

Figure 8.2, an empirically based interpretation will be made initially of the MMPI-2 profile and then it can be supplemented by a content-based interpretation if desired.

Well-Defined versus Not Well-Defined Codetypes. The first step is for the clinician to determine the MMPI-2 codetype, the single (Spike codetype) or two highest Clinical scales (two-point codetype) at or above a T score of 65, and whether or not it is well defined. Well-defined MMPI-2 codetypes are those in which the two highest Clinical scales are at least 5 T points above the remaining scales in the profile (Profile 8.1), while codetypes that are not well de-

fined have the three, or more, highest Clinical scales within a range of 5 T points (Profile 8.2). In the former instance, the clinician readily knows what codetype to interpret because the profile is well defined. In the latter instance, however, the clinician is faced with the sometimes daunting task of trying to determine which MMPI-2 codetype should be interpreted. If the codetype is well defined, as illustrated in Profile 8.1, the clinician should look up the codetype interpretation in Chapter 7. The codetype interpretation serves as the general framework within which the other scales will be interpreted.

If the codetype is not well defined, as illustrated in Profile 8.2, which will occur in two-thirds to three-

MMPI-2 PROFILE FOR VALIDITY AND CLINICAL SCALES

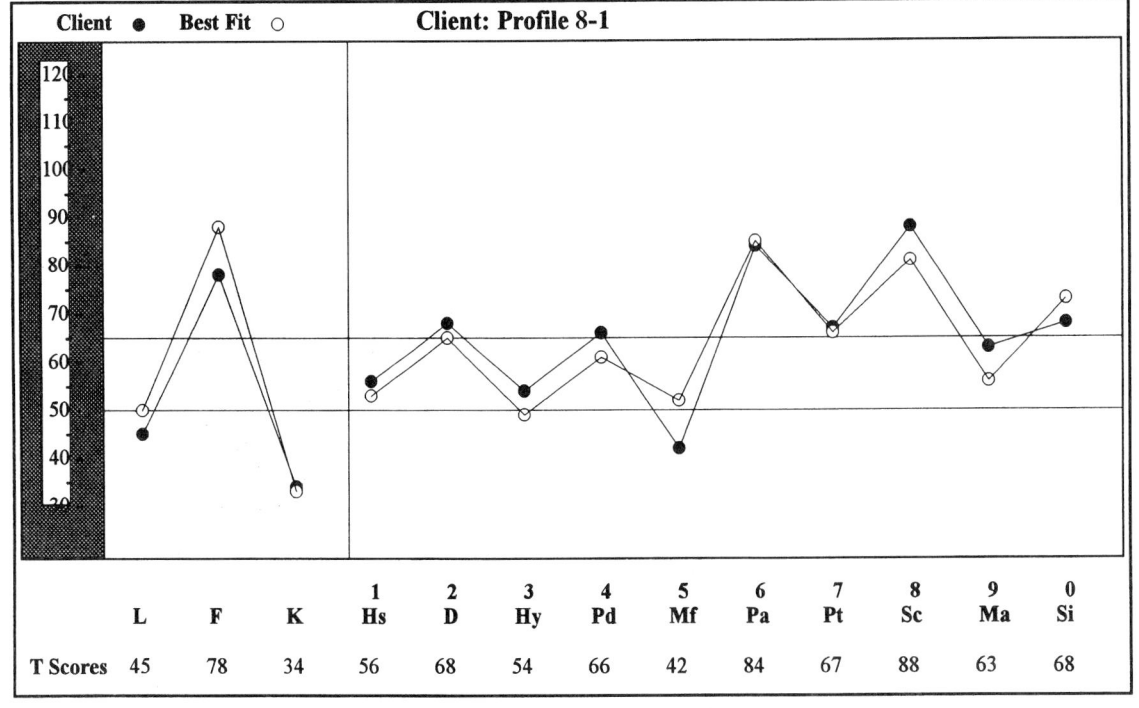

PROFILE 8.1

Note. Minnesota Multiphasic Personality Inventory-2 (MMPI-2). Copyright © 1942, 1943 (renewed 1970), 1989 by the Regents of the University of Minnesota. Reproduced by permission of the publisher. "MMPI-2" and "Minnesota Multiphasic Personality Inventory-2" are trademarks owned by the University of Minnesota.

MMPI-2 PROFILE FOR VALIDITY AND CLINICAL SCALES

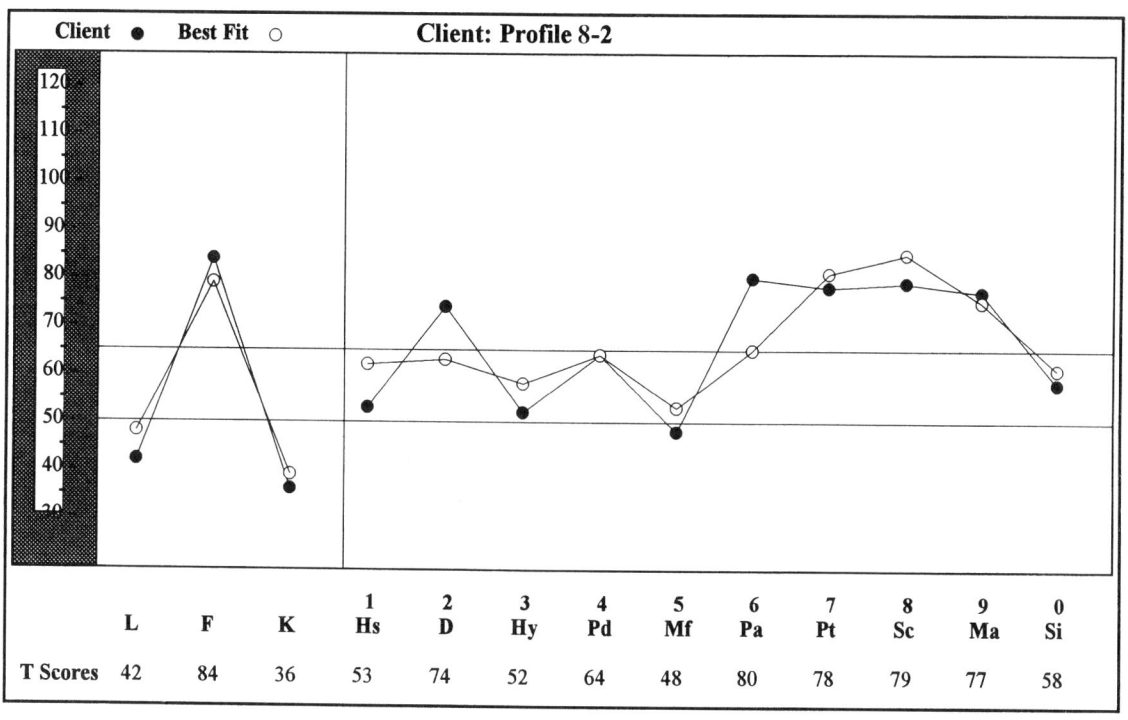

	L	F	K	1 Hs	2 D	3 Hy	4 Pd	5 Mf	6 Pa	7 Pt	8 Sc	9 Ma	0 Si
T Scores	42	84	36	53	74	52	64	48	80	78	79	77	58

PROFILE 8.2

Note. Minnesota Multiphasic Personality Inventory-2 (MMPI-2). Copyright © 1942, 1943 (renewed 1970), 1989 by the Regents of the University of Minnesota. Reproduced by permission of the publisher. "MMPI-2" and "Minnesota Multiphasic Personality Inventory-2" are trademarks owned by the University of Minnesota.

fourths of MMPI-2 profiles (Table 7.8, p. 309) that are administered, the clinician is faced with the dilemma of determining which codetype to use as the general framework for the interpretation. There are three potential solutions to this dilemma and no empirical data to suggest which solution is best. First, Caldwell (1985) has suggested that his "A-B-C-D" paradigm can be used with profiles that are not well defined, which involves considering all possible two-point combinations of the highest scales. Table 8.3 illustrates the use of this "A-B-C-D" paradigm with Profile 8.2. Although Profile 8.2 is literally a *6-8/8-6* codetype because these are the two highest Clinical scales, the clinician has potentially six different code-

types that can be interpreted and little basis for deciding which one to select. Clinicians who are less familiar with the MMPI-2 and the frequency with which codetypes occur that are not well defined are easily overwhelmed by such profiles, because they do not have the clinical experience to draw upon in deciding which codetype to use for interpretation. There also is no empirical basis for deciding which codetype should be selected for interpretation. This latter point is well worth clinical investigation because of the frequency with which MMPI-2 profiles occur that are not well defined. Using Profile 8.2 and the six different codetypes that can potentially be used for its interpretation as an example, it would be instructive

TABLE 8.3 Caldwell's "A-B-C-D" Paradigm with Profile 8.2

A	B	C	D
Scale 6 = 80	Scale 7 = 78	Scale 8 = 79	Scale 9 = 77

POTENTIAL TWO-POINT CODETYPES
6-7/7-6
6-8/8-6
6-9/9-6
7-8/8-7
7-9/9-7
8-9/9-8

to have research that demonstrated both the viability of Caldwell's "A-B-C-D" paradigm and indicated which of the potential codetype(s) was most appropriate for interpreting this specific MMPI-2 profile.

Second, the MMPI-2 Adult Interpretive System (Greene & Brown, 1998; Greene, Brown, & Kovan, 1998) provides an index of the "goodness-of-fit" between every MMPI-2 profile and its prototype, which gives the clinician an empirical basis for deciding which codetype to interpret for profiles that are not well defined. (This goodness-of-fit will be illustrated for the two MMPI-2s that are interpreted later in this chapter.) These measures of the goodness-of-fit of Profile 8.2 to a prototype also could become one quick index of the viability of Caldwell's "A-B-C-D" paradigm by assessing which of these six codetypes had the best fit.

Third, the clinician could forgo trying to determine the specific codetype and proceed to the next step. This third procedure obviously is very conservative, but at the price of the loss of the general framework for the interpretation that is provided by the codetype. Figure 8.2 illustrates the choice that the clinician must make if the MMPI-2 profile is not well defined.

Codetype Description. The codetype is the basis of any MMPI-2 interpretation. In fact, many MMPI-2

interpretive systems look no farther than the codetype for any profile (i.e., no other scales or configurations are interpreted). For a codetype analysis it is only necessary that two Clinical scales or a single Clinical scale (a Spike profile) be elevated at or above a T score of 65 on the MMPI-2. Once the codetype for the profile has been determined, interpretation begins by selecting the description of this particular codetype (Chapter 7).

In selecting the description of the codetype, there are several issues to consider. The first issue is whether the order of the two scales in the codetype makes a difference in interpretation and whether the reference source being used discriminates order within this codetype. (Codetypes in which scale order is important have been noted explicitly in Chapter 7.)

Although order of scales within codetypes seems basic to any interpretive system, a little simple arithmetic will show how difficult it is to implement such a system. A codetype system based on all 10 Clinical scales in any combination involves 45 ($[10 \times 9]/2 = 45$) possible codetypes. Controlling for gender (male, female), age (late adolescent, adult, aged), and education (high school or less, some college, college graduate), with a minimum of 10 persons per group, requires a sample of more than 8,000 ($2 \times 3 \times 3 \times 10 \times 45 = 8,100$) persons. Controlling for the order of the scales would double the number of persons required. Obviously, if finer discriminations in any of these groups are of interest, or if other variables such as ethnic group or reason for referral are of interest, the number of persons required for an interpretive system quickly becomes astronomical.

Consequently, the clinician should be aware of how each interpretive system was developed and must work within the limitations of the data each provides. A prime example of the importance of scale order can be seen in *1-3/3-1* codetypes. It is important to know which scale is higher in this codetype for accurate interpretation, since they represent two very different groups of individuals; interpretive systems that do not discriminate between these two codetypes will usually contain a single description filled with seemingly contradictory data.

A second issue in interpreting MMPI-2 codetypes involves the criterion group on which the interpretive system is based. Possible criterion groups on which interpretive systems have been developed include male veterans (Gilberstadt, 1970; Gilberstadt & Duker, 1965), psychiatric inpatients (Gynther et al., 1973; Lachar, 1974; Marks et al., 1974), a wide variety of diagnostic and pathological groups (Lanyon, 1968), and college students (Drake & Oetting, 1959; Kelley & King, 1978, 1979a, 1979b, 1979c, 1980; King & Kelley, 1977a, 1977b).

Several references in addition to this text also provide general interpretive data on codetypes: Archer (1987), Butcher and Williams (1992), Dahlstrom et al. (1972), Duckworth and Anderson (1986), Friedman, Webb, and Lewak (1989), Good and Brantner (1961, 1974), Graham (1987, 1990, 1993), and Lachar (1974).

When the client whose profile is being interpreted matches one of the preceding criterion groups, the clinician should consult the appropriate source. An even greater improvement, however, is when such information is available from the clinician's own institution or setting. It is unlikely that this goal will ever be reached for many discrete settings, but a serious student of the MMPI-2 should collect as much information as possible on local clientele. Since most clinicians will never have access to a sufficient number of clients to evolve a local interpretive system, the best that can be hoped for is the appropriate modifications of the most applicable system.

A third issue in interpreting codetypes involves profile elevation. Although there are some notable exceptions (e.g., Gilberstadt & Duker, 1965), most interpretive systems do not discriminate among scale elevations above a T score of 70 on the MMPI, the cutoff for inclusion as a codetype. This is not to say that the developers of such systems believe that distinguishing among scale elevations above a T score of 70 on the MMPI is unimportant. Rather, the problem is again one of how many variables it is feasible to incorporate into a system and still have it remain in manageable proportions.

The clinician, then, is faced with the need to take into consideration the degree of elevation of the MMPI-2 codetype and has little empirical direction on how to do so. For some codetypes (e.g., *4-9/9-4*) a

difference of 10 to 20 T score points seemingly has little clinical import, whereas for other pairs (e.g., *7-8/8-7*) such a difference cannot be ignored. To a certain extent, the higher the elevation of the codetype, the more distress the client is experiencing or reporting and the more ego alien or ego dystonic is the psychopathology. For personality disorders, the higher elevations indicate that the pathology is more ingrained and resistant to change.

Beyond these simple statements it seems that the importance of the degree of elevation of a codetype is a question that still needs to be researched. The degree of elevation of the entire profile has been researched more extensively, probably because it is easier to investigate. (This issue will be taken up when interpretation of the entire profile is discussed in the third step.) Finally, it is being assumed that a T score of 65 on the MMPI-2 is equivalent to a T score of 70 on the MMPI. This assumption is probably fairly safe since elevation does not appear to have any systematic effects on profile interpretation of the MMPI, but at a minimum clinicians need to be aware that this assumption is being made with the MMPI-2.

Once the description of the codetype has been selected, the clinician can start generating hypotheses about the type of client who would produce such a description. The statements drawn from the description of the codetype will be compared with the other interpretations for consistencies and inconsistencies at the following stages of the interpretive process. Redundant interpretations serve to highlight the important characteristics of the client, whereas inconsistent features represent areas that need to be examined more carefully.

There is a tendency for clinicians using the MMPI-2 to discuss high-point triads in addition to spike or two-point codetypes (cf. Duckworth & Anderson, 1986; Friedman et al., 1989). This approach recognizes the amount of information not being used by a codetype system and the increased specificity offered by discriminating among subgroups within any particular codetype. The increase in specificity, however, is offset by the difficulty of obtaining a large enough sample of profiles to make such a system feasible. This approach to the analysis of high-point triads is not an analysis of scale configuration; rather, it simply follows the rationale for a high-point pair system with an additional scale.

Therefore, all of the foregoing discussion of the procedures and problems of high-point pair analysis is equally applicable to high-point triads. Some investigators (cf. Gynther et al., 1973) have been unable to find replicable correlates of high-point triads that differ from those of the respective codetype. For example, Gynther et al. found that the correlates of a 2-1-3 high-point triad did not differ from those for a 2-1 codetype.

Factor Scales. The second step in the process of interpreting the MMPI-2 profile is to examine the relative elevation of the Welsh Anxiety (*A*) and Repression (*R*) scales as markers of the first and second factors and their conjoint interpretation (Table 6.5, p. 225). These two scales are a measure of how much emotional distress the client is experiencing (*A*) and what resources or coping skills the client has for coping with this distress (*R*). It cannot be stressed enough that low scores on Scale *A* must be weighted heavily because the client is saying that he or she is *not* experiencing any emotional distress. Even if the client is not the "identified" patient, the client is saying that there is no distress as a result of living with the patient, bringing the patient to treatment, and so on, which also is unusual. Scales *A* and *R* are another general framework, in addition to the codetype, within which the other scales can be interpreted.

Configural Analysis. The third step in the interpretation of the MMPI-2 profile involves configural analysis of subsets of the Validity and Clinical scales. At this level of analysis, groups of scales, typically triads, are examined at the same time. The best example of such configural analysis involves the Validity Scales (*L* [Lie], *F* [Infrequency], and *K* [Correction]), the neurotic triad (Scales *1* [Hypochondriasis], *2* [Depression], and *3* [Hysteria]), or the psychotic tetrad (Scales *6* [Paranoia], *7* [Psychasthenia], *8* [Schizophrenia], and *9* [Hypomania]).

The complexity increases appreciably in a configural analysis because the degree of relative elevation of each scale within the triad or tetrad must be

considered as well as its overall elevation. The initial step in this analysis is a close examination of the behavioral and clinical correlates of the specific elevation for each scale within the configuration. This information then must be combined and integrated with that for the configuration as a whole. In carrying out this third step, it is necessary to match the configuration as closely as possible to the various examples provided. Obviously, the closer the configuration being analyzed fits one of the examples, the better or more accurately the empirical and clinical correlates should describe the client in question.

The entire MMPI-2 profile also can be subjected to a configural analysis. This level of analysis typically is limited to the Clinical scales, because the Validity scales lend themselves more readily to a triad configural analysis as described previously. It is clearly the most complex level of analysis and frequently it is given only passing consideration in interpreting the MMPI-2. The primary reason for its neglect is the difficulty involved in attempting to match an entire profile for configuration. The MMPI-2 Adult Interpretive System (Greene & Brown, 1998; Greene et al., 1998), which was discussed earlier, matches the entire MMPI-2 profile including the Validity scales for configuration to a potential pool of 295 prototypes. The specific MMPI-2 codetype to be interpreted is selected based on the best configural match to the prototype. This process will be illustrated for the two clinical cases that follow.

Even though there is not an entire interpretive system at this level of configural analysis, there are characteristic profiles for specific diagnostic groups and subgroups. Lanyon's (1968) text on group profiles provides the most readily available data, but he does not furnish any information other than simply a mean profile for various diagnostic groups. That is, he does not give any empirical or clinical correlates for each profile. If the clinician can determine how closely the profile being interpreted matches one of Lanyon's diagnostic groups, this source may be of some help in interpretation.

The primary features in interpreting the configuration of the MMPI-2 profile are its elevation, slope, and phasicity. Each of these features will be examined in turn.

The overall elevation of the Clinical scales gives a fairly accurate representation of how much distress the client is experiencing and how ego alien or ego dystonic is the symptomatology that the client is acknowledging. It is important to remember that *it is not the presence of the behaviors or symptoms per se that produces the elevation of the MMPI-2 profile, but whether the client finds these behaviors or symptoms to be distressing.* The higher the elevation of the Clinical scales, the more the client is saying that he or she is distressed by these behaviors or symptoms. Sometimes, in their "cry for help," clients will even overemphasize their symptomatology in order to ensure that they will receive assistance sooner. (A careful examination of the scales to assess overreporting of psychopathology that were discussed in Chapter 3 will be helpful in these circumstances.) In general, however, the higher the overall elevation of the Clinical scales, the more distress the client is experiencing and the more likely the client is to resemble those individuals on whom the scales were constructed. Conversely, the lower the overall elevation of the Clinical scales when the client has serious behavioral problems or severe psychopathology, the less distress the client is experiencing. This circumstance frequently is seen in patients with severe personality disorders or chronic psychotic conditions.

If sequential MMPI-2s are examined for the same client and that client is either neurotic or psychotic, there is a characteristic pattern in the overall elevation of the Clinical scales. In psychotic disorders there is a gradual or sudden increase in the elevation of the entire profile that corresponds to the onset of the symptomatology. If the condition becomes chronic, there will be a gradual decrease, first in the neurotic triad (Scales *1* [Hypochondriasis], *2* [Depression], and *3* [Hysteria]), while the psychotic tetrad (Scales *6* [Paranoia], *7* [Psychasthenia], *8* [Schizophrenia], and *9* [Hypomania]) remains elevated. Finally, as the psychotic symptomatology becomes integrated into the client's personality, the psychotic tetrad also decreases in elevation and none of the Clinical scales is elevated.

Thus, without additional information it is difficult to discriminate the profile of a client with a chronic psychotic condition from the profile of a normal person. Confirmation of this point can be easily obtained by using the Meehl-Dahlstrom (1960) rules for profile classification, which were intended for use with hospitalized patients, on a normal person's MMPI. These rules will classify a normal profile as psychotic most of the time. (This fact should also be a reminder to use the appropriate criterion group for interpreting any MMPI-2 profile.) The interested reader also could compare the mean MMPI profiles for chronic schizophrenics and normals in Lanyon's (1968) text; there are virtually no differences between the two profiles!

In neurotic disorders there is an elevation in the neurotic triad corresponding to the onset of the symptomatology. As the neurosis becomes more disturbing and upsetting to the client, there will be a concomitant increase in the elevation of the psychotic tetrad, although these scales rarely get much over a T score of 75. As the neurotic symptomatology subsides, there will be a gradual reversal of this sequence until a within-normal-limits (*WNL*) profile is achieved.

The interpretation of the slope of the MMPI-2 profile is based largely upon the relationship between the neurotic triad (Scales *1* [Hypochondriasis], *2* [Depression], and *3* [Hysteria]) and the psychotic tetrad (Scales *6* [Paranoia], *7* [Psychasthenia], *8* [Schizophrenia], and *9* [Hypomania]). Positive slope reflects the fact that the psychotic tetrad is elevated more highly than the neurotic triad, and negative slope indicates the reverse relationship between these two groups of scales. Positive slope is generally related to psychological disorders in which the client is experiencing limited impulse control, poor contact with reality, or even disorientation and confusion. In short, positive slope is generally related to psychotic disorders, particularly when elevation is considered in conjunction with slope.

Negative slope is more characteristic of acute psychological upsets involving anxiety, depression, poor morale, and physical symptoms without psychotic distortions. The height of the general elevation in the profile with a negative or positive slope corresponds to the magnitude of the discomfort and distress the client is experiencing. At lower elevations, profiles with zero slope (flat profiles) typically are found in normal individuals, clients with a chronic psychotic condition, or clients with severe, ingrained behavior or personality disorders. At higher elevations, profiles with zero slope are characteristic of clients with quite diverse forms of psychopathology such as Borderline Personality Disorder or Post Traumatic Stress Disorder. In these diagnostic classifications, many psychotic symptoms can be detected, although actual psychotic disorders are not readily discerned.

Phasicity, which is a measure of the number of peaks in the profile, is the least commonly used index in profile interpretation. Primarily, this disinterest reflects the fact that this index is so confounded with elevation and slope of codetypes that there is little to be gained by considering it. Since most interpretive systems are based on codetypes, it seems that most profiles are best classified as being biphasic. There are only two additional comments that need to be made about phasicity.

First, the flatter the profile, the more likely the person is to be well adjusted, particularly at lower elevations, or the person has the characteristics discussed earlier for profiles with zero slope. Second, a "saw-toothed" profile in which Scales 2 (Depression), 4 (Psychopathic Deviate), 6 (Paranoia), and 8 (Schizophrenia) are significantly elevated above the other Clinical scales is a particularly malignant profile. Clients with this saw-toothed profile are likely to be experiencing a very serious psychotic disorder. The clinician should note that the flat and the saw-toothed profiles represent the extremes of phasicity; most profiles, which are biphasic, fall between these two extremes.

Again, the inferences garnered from the configurations should be examined for consistencies and inconsistencies with all the previous information. At this point redundant inferences, all representing cardinal features of the client, should be appearing. Also, any glaring discrepancies with these inferences should be carefully noted, since they will need to be dealt with when all the material is finally integrated into one report.

Individual Validity and Clinical Scales. In the fourth step, the clinician should examine the client's scores on each of the individual Validity and Clinical scales. For each scale, the clinician needs to decide whether this score is in the normal or deviant range for this particular client. (This procedure will be illus-

trated for the two sample profile interpretations later in this chapter.)

At this point the clinician should note what a score in this range for each scale means by referring back to the earlier sections of this text. It is important to remember that a score in the normal range on any scale may be as deviant as a score in the deviant range. For example, if the client has recently committed some heinous or bizarre crime and yet the MMPI-2 does not indicate the presence of any guilt, remorse, or depression, these "normal" scores should provide valuable information about the client's personality and potential for significant behavior change.

Each scale should be analyzed sequentially with the notes made on what each score means and any hypotheses recorded that occur to the clinician while proceeding through this process. Once familiar with all of the individual Validity and Clinical scales, the clinician should make predictions about ensuing scales on the basis of the score on a particular scale.

At this step of the interpretive process the clinician should be willing to entertain virtually any hypothesis that fits the data. No hypothesis should be summarily dismissed unless there are absolutely no data to support it. This does not mean that great inferential leaps can be made from the data, but it is wise to acknowledge even tenuous hypotheses at this step.

The neophyte clinician tends to alternate between the two extremes: refusing to make any inferences whatsoever from the data or making such great inferential leaps that virtually no one would give credence to his or her hypothesis. Hopefully, by being aware of these extremes, the clinician can learn to follow a more moderate course and cautiously assert hypotheses about the meaning of scores on particular scales.

It is extremely important, at any level of MMPI-2 interpretation, for the clinician to be wary of focusing exclusively on any one feature and consequently ignoring, biasing, or misinterpreting the rest of the data. The clinician always has to be willing to entertain alternate hypotheses or inferences from the test data. All too often a novice clinician selects one characteristic or feature as being important and then cannot get away from this perceptual set in interpreting the test data. Instead, the clinician should acknowledge inconsistencies with the inference being made and consider other inferences that might be better able to fit the data. But even after the clinician feels that the best inferences have been selected from those available and all alternative inferences have been carefully rejected, he or she should come back to the data at a later time with an open mind. The precautions about using a disconfirmatory rather than a confirmatory strategy in interpreting the MMPI-2 was noted earlier.

Low-Point Scales.   The last step in the empirically based interpretation of the MMPI-2 profile is to note the low-point Clinical scales, which are essentially the converse of the high-point scales. Frequently, clinicians who are learning to interpret the MMPI-2 focus solely on the analysis of the codetype or some other feature of the profile and miss other significant data, usually the low points in the profile. This is unfortunate since there are several scales for which low points are particularly significant (Chapter 4). Some interpreters of the MMPI even argue that focusing on low points is a means of determining the kinds of behavior the client is defending against and does not want to reveal (cf. Duckworth & Anderson, 1986). There is no known research to support the tenability of this inference.

On several Clinical scales, moreover, low points do not represent the opposite end of the dimension measured by high points. At any rate, the clinician should note low points in the profile, keeping in mind that low-point interpretation is generally based on absolute rather than relative elevation of the low-point scale. For example, a low point on Scale *3* (Hysteria) at a T score of 47 does not indicate the same potential problem areas for the client as a low point at a T score of 31 on this scale. The latter score is much more unusual and, hence, clinically more important. The reader also should recall that Table 7.5 (pp. 302–305) provided the frequency with which low points are found in all MMPI-2 codetypes. Again, the importance of realizing the very substantial NPP of low scores cannot be emphasized too much.

If the clinician is only going to make an empirically based interpretation of the MMPI-2, the interpretive process concludes by integrating all of this information into a coherent report on the client. Clini-

cians are encouraged to make a content-based interpretation of the MMPI-2 routinely because there is little reason to ignore this valuable information that is readily available at minimal cost.

Content-Based Interpretation

The steps in a content-based interpretation of the MMPI-2 also are illustrated in Figure 8.2. A content-based interpretation of an MMPI-2 profile literally analyzes the content of the client's responses collated into the MMPI-2 Structural Summary (Greene & Nichols, 1995; Nichols & Greene, 1995), Content scales (Butcher et al., 1990), Content Component scales (Ben-Porath & Sherwood, 1993), or as individual items (Koss & Butcher, 1973; Lachar & Wrobel, 1979). It is very important to verify the accuracy of item endorsement as described in Chapter 3 before undertaking a content-based interpretation of the MMPI-2, because the client must have both the awareness of the item content *and* the willingness to report it. If either of these assumptions is not valid, an empirically based interpretation of the MMPI-2 should be more meaningful. The client obviously cannot report item content if he or she is not aware of it, and there frequently are situational factors such as forensic evaluations or personnel screenings in which the client may not desire to report the item content even if he or she is aware of it. If both of these assumptions are valid, the item content provides an excellent means of amplifying and refining the empirically based interpretation.

The progression in the steps from a specific section of the MMPI-2 Structural Summary (Greene & Nichols, 1995; Nichols & Greene, 1995), to a Content (Butcher, Graham, Williams, & Ben-Porath, 1990) scale, to a Content Component (Ben-Porath & Sherwood, 1993) scale, to an individual item can be conceptualized as moving from a global overview of a content domain within the MMPI-2 item pool to a specific item within that domain. At each step the interpretation of the content is refined and sharpened based on the additional information that is available.

Each of these steps will be described in order and then a clinical example will illustrate how the interpretation of the MMPI-2 can change based on the additional information that is available at each ensuing step.

MMPI-2 Structural Summary. The first step in a content-based interpretation of the MMPI-2 is to construct a Structural Summary (Greene & Nichols, 1995; Nichols & Greene, 1995), which was described in Chapter 5. The MMPI-2 Structural Summary facilitates the interpretation of the MMPI-2 by providing a set of clinically relevant categories into which scales of disparate names, types, and origins can be sorted. This organization maximizes the extraction of test information by making the most salient factors stand out, allowing a rapid appraisal of the robustness of trends in MMPI-2 data, and by following a sequence of topics that facilitates the preparation of an interpretive report. When all of a group of related scales are elevated within a specific category on the MMPI-2 Structural Summary, the content domain in question is likely to be potent or pervasive, or both. When some scales are elevated within the category, but others in the group are not, the content domain, depending upon the pattern, may be weak, inconsistent, or strong, but it is likely to be narrower and more specific. In this latter instance, the ensuing steps will facilitate understanding these changes in nuances within the domain.

The MMPI-2 Structural Summary serves several purposes in the interpretation of the MMPI-2. First, it functions as a mnemonic for MMPI-2 scores, arranging them in categories that maximize the likelihood that their interpretive significance, when present, will be noticed. Second, the Structural Summary can be used with well-defined MMPI-2 profiles to call attention to aspects of the MMPI-2 that have not been included in the usual codetype description. Finally, the information provided in the Structural Summary may serve as the primary basis for interpretation for codetypes that occur infrequently, whose empirical correlates have not been established, or are not well defined.

The use of the MMPI-2 Structural Summary in the interpretation of an MMPI-2 profile will be illustrated in the two clinical cases that are presented later in this chapter.

Content Scales. The second step in a content-based interpretation of the MMPI-2 evaluates the client's scores on the MMPI-2 Content (Butcher et al., 1990) scales. The Content scales provide an assessment of the client's functioning in 15 different domains of homogeneous content.[1] Some of the Content scales overlap rather directly with the standard Clinical scales, such as Health Concerns (*HEA*) with Scale *1* (Hypochondriasis), and provide little additional interpretive information. Other Content scales provide useful information when used in conjunction with the Clinical scales. For example, Bizarre Mentation (*BIZ*) is very valuable in understanding how to interpret an elevation on Scale *8* (Schizophrenia). A client who elevates both Scale *8* and *BIZ* is very likely to be psychotic, while a client who elevates Scale *8* without elevating *BIZ* is more likely to be alienated and estranged from others without actually being psychotic. Finally, several Content scales such as Anger (*ANG*) and Cynicism (*CYN*) provide interpretive information that is not found within the standard Clinical scales of the MMPI-2.

The relative importance of these content domains to the client can be determined directly by ranking the 15 Content scales by T score. This ranking provides an index of which domains are most to least important in describing this particular client. For example, a client, who has T scores of 52 and 77 on the Content scales of Bizarre Mentation (*BIZ*) and Health Concerns (*HEA*), respectively, is very different from a client who has similar T scores on the Content scales of Low Self-Esteem (*LSE*) and Antisocial Practices (*ASP*).

Although low scores on the MMPI-2 Content scales do not have interpretive significance (Butcher et al., 1990) as noted in Chapter 5, they do indicate content domains that are of less importance to the client, and as such should not be overlooked. A client who has T scores of 50 or lower on the Content scales of Anxiety (*ANX*) and Depression (*DEP*) is stating that he or she is not experiencing any negative emotions as a result of the behaviors or symptoms that led to the administration of the MMPI-2.

1. Wiggins' (1966) Content scales can be used in a similar manner.

Content Component Scales. The third step in a content-based interpretation of the MMPI-2 is to examine the Content Component (Ben-Porath & Sherwood, 1993) scales. The Content Component scales represent clusters of meaningful groups of items within each Content (Butcher et al., 1990) scale. These Component scales are meant to highlight the salience of the various content domains within the parent Content scale. For example, the Content scale of Depression (*DEP*) has four Component scales: Lack of Drive (*DEP1*); Dysphoria (*DEP2*); Self-Deprecation (*DEP3*); and Suicidal Ideation (*DEP4*). A client who has an elevated T score on *DEP* may achieve that score by endorsing any combination of these four Component scales. Since the client would have a different clinical picture and treatment issues depending upon which set of Component scales is elevated, examination of the Component scales will facilitate the interpretation of the elevation on *DEP*.

Although Ben-Porath and Sherwood (1993) recommended that the Content Component scales only should be interpreted if the parent Content scale is elevated to a T score of 60 or higher, their focus is on augmenting the interpretation of the parent Content scale. In a content-based interpretation, the focus is on meaningful groups of items that can be represented very appropriately by a Content Component scale regardless of the elevation of the parent Content scale. There also are MMPI-2s in which one Component scale within the parent Content scale is very high and the other Component scale is very low, which produces only an average elevation on the parent Content scale. In such circumstances, the interpretation of the Content Component scale greatly enhances the interpretation of the MMPI-2 profile, even though the parent Content scale is not elevated. A clear example of this circumstance occurs when a male client has a T score of 77 on Explosive Behavior (*ANG1*) and a T score of 41 on Irritability (*ANG2*) that results in a T score of 53 on the parent scale of Anger (*ANG*). The failure to note and interpret the significant elevation on *ANG2* could create serious problems in the treatment process for him and the clinician. Similarly, a female client could have a T score of 120 on Suicidal Ideation (*DEP4*) without elevating the parent scale of Depression (*DEP*) to a T score of

60. Finally, the clinician should recall that a number of the Content Component scales have a very limited ceiling on the maximum possible T score as was noted in Chapter 5.

In a content-based interpretation of the MMPI-2, the clinician should examine the scores on all of the Content Component scales regardless of the elevation of the parent Content scale. It is an excellent idea to examine these Component scales anytime that the MMPI-2 is administered regardless of the approach that is to be taken to interpretation.

The relative importance of these content domains to the client can be determined directly by ranking the Content Component scales by T score in a similar manner as ranking the parent Content scales. The T scores used with the Content Component scales are linear T scores rather than uniform T scores that are used with the parent Content scales. Consequently, the T scores on the Content Component scales are *not* equivalent across all of these scales. This difference in T scores must be kept in mind when examining the relative rankings of the Content Component scales. The ranking of the Content Component scales provides another index of which domains are most to least important in describing this particular client. These rankings will be illustrated when the two clinical cases are interpreted later in this chapter.

Individual Items. The last step in a content-based interpretation is to examine the client's responses to individual MMPI-2 items. The specific items within a content area can be used to confirm, disconfirm, or refine an interpretation that has been suggested in the earlier steps. In this step the items are used to provide the final specificity to a content domain.

A clinician has a variety of ways of investigating the client's response to individual MMPI-2 items. One natural starting point is the actual items that the client has endorsed on a Content (Butcher et al., 1990) scale or a Content Component (Ben-Porath & Sherwood, 1993) scale. Items on scales with similar content and the Koss and Butcher (1973) and Lachar and Wrobel (1979) critical items can be explored next to supplement the description provided by the items endorsed on the Content and Content Component scales. Finally, Dahlstrom (1993) has provided an alphabetical listing of the key words for all MMPI-2 items that can be used to look for individual items with similar content.

The importance of reviewing the individual items that inquire about suicidal behavior (150, 303, 506, 520, 524, and 530) has been repeated several times. There are a number of other items that are equally important to consider in evaluating any client such as: "Someone has been trying to poison me," "I have a drug or alcohol problem," "Once a week or more I get high or drunk," "Sometimes I cut or injure myself on purpose without knowing why,"[2] and so on. The clinician in reviewing the MMPI-2 item pool may identify other items that he or she believes are important to review routinely regardless of the content domain in which they are found.

There are many caveats that must be kept in mind when interpreting individual MMPI-2 items so that the clinician is not overinterpreting them. First, there is an unreliability of any single item that can be the result of momentary lapses of attention in marking the item on the answer sheet, hurriedly reading the item, misunderstanding some key word in the item, and so on. It is not unusual when querying clients about a response to a specific item that they will say that they do not remember responding to the item in that manner or they do not know why they responded in the manner that they did. Second, the referent for key words in items may be ambiguous and allow for multiple interpretations. For example, the MMPI-2 item "I am a good mixer"[3] can be endorsed in the "true" direction because the person is a good baker, bartender, painter, chemist, pharmacist, disc jockey, light technician, and so on. This inherent ambiguity in items was one of the rationales for the original emphasis on selecting items empirically for the MMPI scales. Third, there is the tyranny of adverbs that affects the content-based understanding of many MMPI-2 items. Two clients may endorse the MMPI-2 item "I have very few headaches"[4] in the "true" direction, one client because he only has one headache

a year and another because she only has one headache a day. In an empirically based interpretation, the important issue is whether clients believe that they have few headaches rather than the actual number of headaches experienced in a given time period. In a content-based interpretation, it would be easy for the clinician to conclude that this client has few headaches, because it is exactly her interpretation of the item. However, the clinician may be missing that an important physical symptom is occurring quite frequently in the client's life. Finally, there is ambiguity of the time period that the client is using as a referent for responding to an item. This point can be made salient by considering the MMPI-2 item "Lately I have thought a lot about killing myself."[5] Clients could endorse this item in the "false" direction because the frequency of such thoughts has decreased over some time period, even though the thoughts still are occurring daily, hourly, and so on.

Summary

Table 8.4 provides an example of how a content-based interpretation of the MMPI-2 can enhance the understanding of two clients with similar scores on the MMPI-2 Content (Butcher et al., 1990) scales of Anger (*ANG*) and Type A (*TPA*) as measures of the content domain of anger and hostility. The section of the MMPI-2 Structural Summary (Greene & Nichols, 1995; Nichols & Greene, 1995) on Anger and Hostility, which contains the *ANG, TPA,* and Lack of Ego Mastery, Defective Inhibition (*Sc5*) scales, is identical in these two male clients. The Structural Summary indicates that they have endorsed different numbers of the Koss and Butcher's (1973) Threatened Assault critical items and items among 150, 540, 542, and 548, but it does not indicate whether these differences have any importance clinically. The Content Component (Ben-Porath & Sherwood, 1993) scales start to illustrate that these two men are endorsing different aspects of the content domain of anger and hostility. Further refinement of these differences is apparent in looking at the specific items that each of them has endorsed. Mr. Smith is reporting that he is angry, impa-

---

2. Minnesota Multiphasic Personality Inventory-2 (MMPI-2). Copyright © 1942, 1943 (renewed 1970), 1989 by the Regents of the University of Minnesota. Reproduced by permission of the publisher. "MMPI-2" and "Minnesota Multiphasic Personality Inventory-2" are trademarks owned by the University of Minnesota.
3. Ibid.

4. Ibid.
5. Ibid.

TABLE 8.4 Examples of Content-Based Interpretation

STEP	MR. SMITH	MR. JONES
1. MMPI-2 Structural Summary		
8. Anger/Hostility		
ANG (Anger)	70	70
TPA (Type A)	68	68
SC$_5$ (Defective Inhibition)	75	75
K-B (Threatened Assault)	2/5	4/5
4 Items (150, 540, 542, 548)	1/4	3/4
2. Content Scales		
Anger (*ANG*)	70	70
Type A (*TPA*)	68	68
3. Content Component Scales		
Explosive Behavior (*ANG1*)	58	77
Irritability (*ANG2*)	72	67
Impatience (*TPA1*)	68	68
Competitive Drive (*TPA2*)	56	71
4. Individual Items[a]		
134. "At times I feel like picking a fight with someone."	False	True
389. "I am often said to be hotheaded."	False	True
548. "I've been so angry at times that I've hurt someone in a physical fight."	False	True

[a]Minnesota Multiphasic Personality Inventory-2 (MMPI-2). Copyright © 1942, 1943 (renewed 1970), 1989 by the Regents of the University of Minnesota. Reproduced by permission of the publisher. "MMPI-2" and "Minnesota Multiphasic Personality Inventory-2" are trademarks owned by the University of Minnesota.

tient, and irritable, but he does not express his anger overtly, while Mr. Jones acknowledges these same moods as well as reporting that he has and is likely to express his anger physically. Treatment of Mr. Jones would focus first on helping him to control and inhibit the overt expression of his anger, while the treatment of Mr. Smith could begin with the examination of the causes of his anger. These differences in the treatment process for these two men could easily be overlooked if the clinician only examined the Content scales.

EXAMPLES OF PROFILE INTERPRETATION

The procedure for interpreting the MMPI-2 profile, which was described earlier, will be illustrated for two clients. Each of these profiles was interpreted by an individual clinician and also by three computerized scoring services. For each client, background information and the MMPI-2 profiles are presented. Then the clinician's analysis of the consistency and accuracy of item endorsement following the steps in Figure 3.1, and the interpretation of the codetype, factor scales, individual Validity and Clinical scales, and Content scales are given. This sequence reflects the steps in Figure 8.2 that the clinician followed in gathering information to interpret the profile.

This information is followed by the clinician's integration of all these sources of information into a profile interpretation. Next, the three computer interpretations are provided. Finally, some general comments are made about the four interpretations of each profile. In addition to the MMPI-2 profiles, the clinician was provided only the basic demographic data on each client, so the clinician and the computer-scoring systems had similar information on which to make the profile interpretation.

The two examples for profile interpretation were selected so that one example matched the prototype for the codetype rather closely; the second example had a number of the Clinical and Supplementary scales different from the prototype for the codetype. Readers can see these differences for themselves by comparing Profile 8.5 for the first example with Profile 8.9 for the second, which also have the prototypic scores plotted for the standard Validity and Clinical scales. It would be expected that the computer interpretations would be much more accurate when the profile matches the codetype than when it does not. The clinician may or may not be able to realize that the second profile varies in significant ways from the prototype and incorporate that information into the interpretation.

Interpreting the MMPI-2: Example 1

The client is a 41-year-old, separated, white man who was admitted for the second time to the state hospital. His previous hospitalization occurred two years ago following a separation from his wife, and resulted from his increasing agitation over trying to maintain his relationship with his wife. He had been telephoning her as many as 75 times a day, driving by her residence repeatedly, and physically abused her once. At that point the wife obtained a restraining order because the patient was "obsessed with keeping the family together."

He believes that he is in the state hospital because the judge and police are fabricating evidence against him. His wife reported continued harassment and he recently chased his son home from school. He states that it is God's will for him and his family to be reunited, and he insists that they were never actually separated. He believes that his family wants him to return home but he cannot because of constant interference from the police and the judge.

There is no history of alcohol or drug use.

The client believes that there is no reason for him to be in the state hospital and he has filed suit to be released immediately. The MMPI-2 (Profiles 8.3, 8.4, and 8.5) was administered approximately one week after he entered the hospital. The prototypic scores for *6-9/9-6* codetypes can be found in Table 8.5.

Clinician's Interpretation

Validity (Chapter 3 and Validity Profile 8.6).
Item Omissions.

$? = 3$ He endorsed all of the items except three. None of these three items is omitted by most clients (Table 3.3, p. 46). Item omissions are not a problem for profile interpretation. The content of these items is 88: "I believe women ought to have as much sexual freedom as men"; 258: "I can sleep during the day but not at night"; and 259: "I am sure I am being talked about."[6] There does not appear to be any theme to these omitted items.

Consistency of Item Endorsement.

$VRIN = 9$
$|F - F_B| = 7$ The score on *VRIN* and the absolute difference between F and F_B are approaching a T score of 70 or the 98th percentile in clinical patients, but the profile still is in the interpretable range. The fact that the raw score of 12 on the F scale is higher than the raw score of 5 on the F_B scale suggests that this difference may be due to the content of the items on the two scales rather than inconsistent endorsement.

Accuracy of Item Endorsement.

$F(p) = 2$
$F - K = -1$ Both scales and indexes for assessing overreporting of psychopathology are well within the expected range for clinical patients. (Because he has two Clinical scales elevated above a T score of 65, there is little reason to be concerned about underreporting of psychopathology, although these scales also are within the expected range for patients.) When his scores are compared to the prototype for a *6-9/9-6* codetype (Table 8.5), he is reporting somewhat less distress than most clients with this codetype. Profile interpretation may proceed since the client has endorsed the items accurately.

Validity Scales.

$L = 61$ He may have a tendency to resort to denial mechanisms or be trying to create a favorable impression of himself.

PROFILE 8.3

Note. Minnesota Multiphasic Personality Inventory-2 (MMPI-2). Copyright © 1942, 1943 (renewed 1970), 1989 by the Regents of the University of Minnesota. Reproduced by permission of the publisher. "MMPI-2" and "Minnesota Multiphasic Personality Inventory-2" are trademarks owned by the University of Minnesota.

Profile for Content Scales
Butcher, Graham, Williams and Ben-Porath (1989)

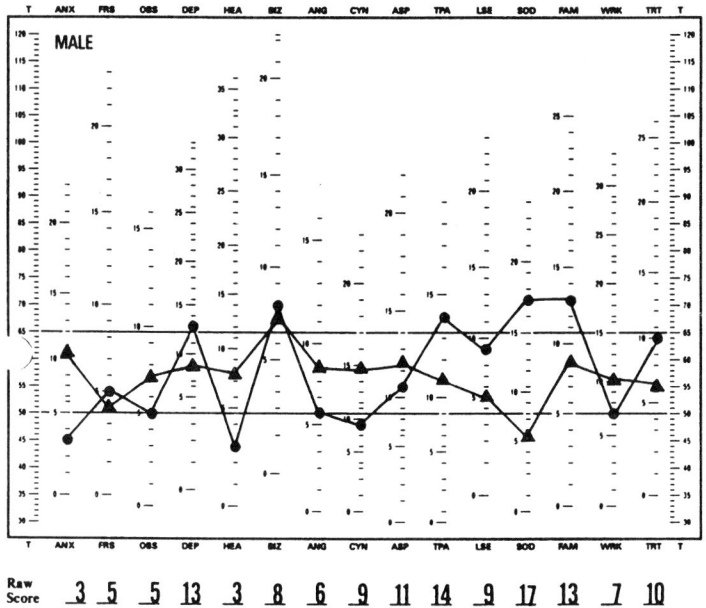

Raw Score	ANX	FRS	OBS	DEP	HEA	BIZ	ANG	CYN	ASP	TPA	LSE	SOD	FAM	WRK	TRT
	3	5	5	13	3	8	6	9	11	14	9	17	13	7	10

PROFILE 8.4

Note. Minnesota Multiphasic Personality Inventory-2 (MMPI-2). Copyright © 1942, 1943 (renewed 1970), 1989 by the Regents of the University of Minnesota. Reproduced by permission of the publisher. "MMPI-2" and "Minnesota Multiphasic Personality Inventory-2" are trademarks owned by the University of Minnesota.

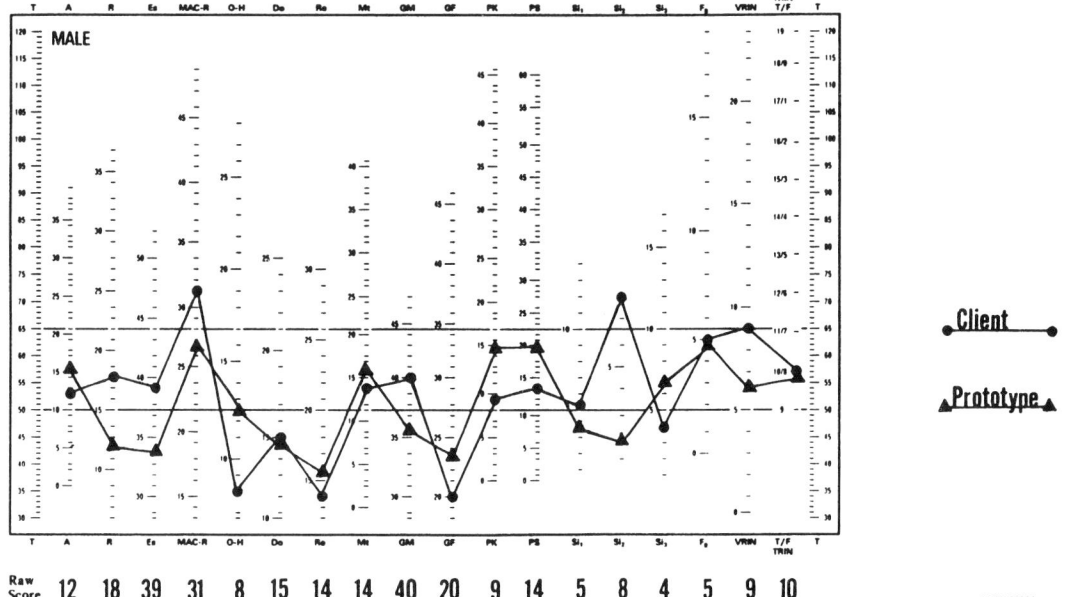

PROFILE 8.5

Note. Minnesota Multiphasic Personality Inventory-2 (MMPI-2). Copyright © 1942, 1943 (renewed 1970), 1989 by the Regents of the University of Minnesota. Reproduced by permission of the publisher. "MMPI-2" and "Minnesota Multiphasic Personality Inventory-2" are trademarks owned by the University of Minnesota.

Table 8-5

Prototypic Scores for 6-9/9-6 Codetypes (N = 356)

Demographics

Demographics		M	SD	Marital Status	%
Age		32.1	11.9	Never Married	52.7
Education		11.6	5.3	Married	28.1
Gender		%		Separated	7.6
	Men	58.1		Divorced	11.7
	Women	41.9		Widowed	0.0

Test-Taking Scales

Omissions		M	SD	Consistency		M	SD
	?	0.9	2.6	VRIN		52.8	11.8
				|F - FB|		4.2	3.3
				TRIN		55.6	12.2

Accuracy of Item Endorsement

Underreporting		M	SD	Overreporting		M	SD
	False %	52.0	8.0	True %		46.8	8.0
Impression	L	50.5	10.4	Infrequency	F	64.3	16.6
Management	ODecp	53.9	9.2		FB	62.3	17.9
	Sd	57.5	9.3		F[p]	60.0	15.6
Superior	S	43.7	9.2	Critical Items	K & B	25.3	10.7
Adjustment					L & W	34.3	13.0
Self-Deception	K	31.1	6.4	Dissimulation	F - K	-3.8	8.6
	So	42.6	11.1		Ds	61.4	12.0
					O - S	60.3	66.9

Scales

Validity and Clinical			Supplementary			Morey et al. Overlapping Personality Disorder		
Scale	M	SD	Scale	M	SD	Scale	M	SD
?	0.9	2.6	A	56.5	10.4	PAR	65.7	12.6
L	50.5	10.4	R	43.0	8.6	SZD	45.3	8.6
F	64.3	16.6	Es	42.3	11.0	STY	56.0	10.1
K	44.3	9.3	TRIN	55.6	12.2	ANT	57.7	11.3
1(Hs)	52.5	10.6	VRIN	52.8	11.8	BDL	60.5	10.4
2(D)	50.7	9.4	O-H	49.4	10.4	HST	56.7	7.8
3(Hy)	51.6	10.3	Do	43.5	12.2	NAR	58.6	7.3
4(Pd)	59.7	9.0	Re	37.8	10.7	AVD	47.8	8.0
5(Mf)	50.7	9.1	GM	46.0	9.4	DEP	52.1	10.1
6(Pa)	75.3	8.0	GF	41.3	11.0	CPS	55.6	9.4
7(Pt)	57.0	9.2	Mt	57.2	10.4	Personality Psychopathology Five		
8(Sc)	62.3	9.7	PK	60.9	11.4	Scale	M	SD
9(Ma)	75.4	8.0	PS	60.9	11.6	AGG	59.0	9.7
0(Si)	45.8	8.5	MAC-R	60.8	10.1	PSY	67.5	15.6
			APS	55.1	10.2	CON	41.7	10.1
			AAS	55.6	11.3	NEN	58.1	10.2
			MDS	57.2	10.7	PEE	56.3	7.1
			Ho	59.4	10.2			
			CAL-R	55.5	10.2			

Content			Content Component					
Scale	M	SD	Scale	M	SD	Scale	M	SD
ANX	60.7	10.2	FRS1	54.8	14.1	ASP1	56.2	11.0
FRS	50.4	10.5	FRS2	47.3	9.6	ASP2	57.7	12.0
OBS	56.2	11.0	DEP1	56.9	12.4	TPA1	51.3	10.3
DEP	58.4	10.4	DEP2	57.0	11.5	TPA2	57.8	11.4
HEA	56.9	10.3	DEP3	56.4	12.0	LSE1	50.7	9.4
BIZ	66.6	12.6	DEP4	53.6	15.8	LSE2	52.0	10.9
ANG	58.4	12.2	HEA1	53.9	12.3	SOD1	45.8	8.1
CYN	58.1	11.8	HEA2	56.9	13.3	SOD2	45.2	8.4
ASP	59.0	12.5	HEA3	54.3	10.8	FAM1	57.1	11.4
TPA	56.3	12.0	BIZ1	66.0	19.0	FAM2	52.8	12.7
LSE	52.9	10.1	BIZ2	64.2	12.8	TRT1	54.5	12.9
SOD	45.5	8.1	ANG1	57.9	12.5	TRT2	51.4	10.3
FAM	59.0	11.5	ANG2	55.9	10.4			
WRK	55.9	10.6	CYN1	55.6	10.9			
TRT	55.3	11.6	CYN2	57.9	9.5			

Note. All scores are T scores except: Cannot Say, K & B and L & W critical items which are raw scores; True % and False % which are the percentage of items endorsed "true" or "false;" and |F - FB|, F - K, and O - S which are difference scores.

MMPI-2 Validity Profile for Clinical Settings

Men

Name   Example 1   Age   41

	Inconsistent			Accuracy of Item Endorsement												
				Overreporting									Underreporting			

(MMPI-2 validity profile chart plotting T-scores from 85 to 30 across scales: ? , VRIN, F-FB, TRIN, F, FB, F(p), F-K, Ds, K&B, L&W, O-S, True %, L, ODecp, Sd, S, K, So, False %. Bottom labels: Consistent / Underreporting / Overreporting with raw scores: 3, 9, 7, 10, 12, 5, 2, -1, 13, 20, 28, 33, 44, 6, 17, 13, 25, 13, 29, 55)

Omissions
  ? = Cannot Say scale

Consistency
  VRIN = Variable Response Inconsistency Scale
  F-FB = Absolute difference between F (raw) and FB (raw)
  TRIN = True Response Inconsistency Scale

Overreporting of Psychopathology
  F = Infrequency scale
  FB = Back Infrequency scale
  F(p) = Infrequency - Psychopathology scale
  F-K = Raw score of the F scale minus the raw score of the K scale
  Ds = Gough Dissimulation scale
  K & B = Total number of Koss & Butcher critical items endorsed
  L&W = Total number of Lachar & Wrobel critical items endorsed
  O-S = Total T score difference for obvious minus subtle subscales
  True % = Percentage of Items Endorsed "True"

Underreporting of Psychopathology
  Impression Management
    L = Lie scale
    ODecp = Other Deception scale
    Sd = Wiggins Social Desirability scale
  Superior Adjustment
    S = Superlative Scale
  Self-Deception
    K = Correction
    So = Edwards Social Desirability scale
    False % = Percentage of Items Endorsed "False"

1/10/98   Caldwell Clinical Sample   N = 25,203

PROFILE 8.6

Note. Minnesota Multiphasic Personality Inventory-2 (MMPI-2). Copyright © 1942, 1943 (renewed 1970), 1989 by the Regents of the University of Minnesota. Reproduced by permission of the publisher. "MMPI-2" and "Minnesota Multiphasic Personality Inventory-2" are trademarks owned by the University of Minnesota.

$F = 73$ He is acknowledging the unusual experiences represented in this scale more than the typical individual.

$K = 45$ He describes himself as having adequate personal resources for coping with his problems. He has a proper balance between self-disclosure and self-protection.

Validity Scale Configuration.

(Figure 3.4 dashed line) He is admitting to personal and emotional difficulties, and simultaneously trying to defend himself against these problems in an unsophisticated manner. This pattern of ineffective defenses with the simultaneous admission of fairly severe problems is typical of chronically maladjusted clients. He is not an optimal client for any type of psychological intervention.

Codetype Description.

(Chapter 7) A client with a *6-9/9-6* codetype is usually encountered only in inpatient settings.

Moods. He is experiencing a mild to moderate level of emotional distress characterized by agitation, tension, and excitement. When he gets bored, he likes to stir up excitement. He frequently feels unusually cheerful and happy without any demonstrable cause. In addition, he reports mild dysphoria and general anhedonia. He has difficulty expressing his feelings appropriately and may vacillate between overcontrolling and undercontrolling his emotions. He easily becomes impatient with others, and they will perceive him as irritable, grouchy, and hotheaded.

Cognitions. Sometimes he becomes so agitated and excited that he may have difficulty in concentrating and thinking. He often exercises poor judgment, although he thinks that his judgment is very good. He has strange and unusual thoughts and dreams that he believes are best kept to himself. He often believes that he is being punished without cause. He is grandiose, egocentric, and cynical of the abilities of others.

He reports symptoms that may reflect a psychotic process that is more likely to reflect a mood disorder than a thought disorder or a very long-term, characterologic condition. His presenting problems, background, and history should be reviewed with this possibility in mind.

Interpersonal Relations. He is very active, energetic, and outgoing socially, and he believes that he would make a good leader of people. Others are apt to misunderstand his intentions even when he is trying to be helpful. He is unconcerned about others' evaluations of him and is socially alienated.

Other Problem Areas. He frequently finds that sleep is not necessary because he is so full of energy. He clearly has enough energy to do his work. He is in good physical health. He is very prone to abuse substances. Suicidal ideation should be monitored carefully because of his impulsive tendencies.

Treatment. His prognosis is generally poor because of his limited concerns about his own behavior. Psychopharmacologic interventions are frequently warranted because of the agitation and excitement. Short-term behavioral interventions that focus on his reasons for entering treatment will be most effective.

Prototypic Scores.

(Table 8.5)　The client was approximately one standard deviation above the mean on the *L* (Lie), *F* (Infrequency), *0* (Social Introversion), and Social Discomfort (*SOD*) scales, and one standard deviation below the mean on Scales *1* (Hypochondriasis), *3* (Hysteria), and *7* (Psychasthenia), and the Content scales of Anxiety (*ANX*) and Health Concerns (*HEA*). It will be important to ensure that these atypical scores for the prototype are accounted for in the interpretation.

Factor Scales.

(Chapter 6)

A = 53　He is experiencing a normal amount of emotional distress, which is very unusual given that he is hospitalized. Note the low scores on other first-factor scales (Scales *7* [Psychasthenia] = 41; College Maladjustment [*Mt*] = 54; PTSD— Keane [*PK*] = 52; and PTSD— Schlenger [*PS*] = 54).

R = 56　He shows an appropriate willingness to discuss his behavior and problems.

Clinical Scales.

(Chapter 4)

1(Hs) = 42　He is not reporting any health-related problems or vague physical symptoms.

2(D) = 47　He reports a typical number of attitudes and behaviors that reflect symptomatic depression. Neither his presence in the state hospital (even though he believes that he is being confined unjustly) nor his problems with the judge and police that led him to be sent to the hospital are seen as being upsetting or distressful. His normal score is *not* normal!

3(Hy) = 43　He tends to be caustic, sarcastic, and socially isolated. He has few defenses. He has narrow interests and is socially conforming.

4(Pd) = 64　He has adjusted to a habitual level of interpersonal and social conflict.

Pd₁ = 65　He quarrels with members of his family and his home life is generally unpleasant.

Pd₂ = 68　He had behavioral problems during his school years and may have been in trouble with the law.

5(Mf) = 46　He has traditional masculine interests and activities.

6(Pa) = 79　He is likely to be suspicious, hostile, and overly sensitive and overtly verbalizes these qualities. A delusional or thought disorder may be readily apparent.

Pa₁ = 82　He has ideas of external influence. He externalizes blame for his problems, frustrations, and failures. He may have persecutory ideas. He projects responsibility for his negative feelings.

Pa₂ = 62　He may consider himself as special and different from other people. He is very sensitive to what others say and do.

7(Pt) = 41　He is secure and comfortable with himself and is emotionally stable. He is success oriented, persistent, and capable. There is an absence of worries and a relaxed attitude toward responsibilities. Again, similar to Scale *2* (Depression), he is not reporting any type of anxiety or distress.

8(Sc) = 60　He thinks differently than others. He tends to avoid reality through fantasy and daydreams.

Sc₁ = 72　He feels alienated from himself. He has flattened or distorted affect.

Sc₆ = 70　He is experiencing a number of unusual sensorimotor symptoms.

$9(Ma) = 69$ He is overactive, emotionally labile, and may experience flight of ideas. Although his mood is typically euphoric, outbursts of temper may occur. He is impulsive and may have an inability to delay gratification. Manic, narcissistic, and grandiose features may be seen.

$Ma_1 = 74$ He is callous about his motives and the motives of others.

$0(Si) = 56$ He reports a balance between socially extroverted and introverted attitudes and behaviors.

$Si_2 = 71$ He dislikes and avoids group activities. He keeps other people at a distance from himself.

MMPI-2 Structural Summary (Table 8.6).

The MMPI-2 Structural Summary highlights a number of significant issues. First, he is *not* experiencing any sort of negative mood either as a result of his presence in the hospital or the behaviors and symptoms that led him to be hospitalized. Second, there are clear indications of paranoid and psychotic thought processes. Third, he uses projection and acting out as his primary defense mechanisms. Fourth, he is alienated from his family and other people. Finally, he is not suicidal nor does he report abusing substances.

Content Scales.

(Chapter 5)

$ANX = 45$ He does not report general symptoms of anxiety as has been noted several times previously.

$FRS = 54$ He has a typical number of specific fears.

$OBS = 50$ He does not report obsessional thoughts.

$DEP = 66$ He has depressive mood and thoughts. He feels blue, unhappy, and is likely to brood. He is uncertain about his future and finds his life empty and meaningless. He is self-critical, guilty, and lonely. He may report suicidal ideation or attempts.

$DEP1 = 68$ He feels like he is unable to get going and get things done in his life. He is experiencing a general lack of drive and motivation. He may be anhedonic.

$HEA = 44$ He does not report any concerns about his health.

$BIZ = 70$ He reports strange thoughts and experiences, paranoid ideation, and hallucinations.

$BIZ1 = 91$ He reports a number of overtly psychotic symptoms that suggest the presence of delusions and hallucinations associated with some form of psychotic disorder.

$ANG = 50$ He does not see himself as being angry, moody, or irritable.

$CYN = 48$ He is not cynical.

$ASP = 55$ He did not engage in problematic behaviors while in school. He does not have beliefs and attitudes of an antisocial nature.

$TPA = 68$ He is hard driving, fast moving, and work oriented. He frequently becomes impatient, grouchy, irritable, and annoyed. He does not like to wait, be interrupted, or believe that someone has gotten the best of him.

$LSE = 62$ He has a low opinion of himself, and he is uncomfortable if others say nice things about him. He believes that he is unattractive, awkward, and clumsy. He lacks self-confidence and sees himself as not as good or capable as others.

$LSE1 = 70$ He has a very low opinion of himself. He believes that he is disliked and not respected by others.

TABLE 8.6 MMPI-2 Structural Summary, Example 1

<table>
<tr><td colspan="2" align="center">**TEST-TAKING ATTITUDES**</td></tr>
</table>

1. Omissions

   __3__   ? (Cannot Say)

2. Consistency

   __9__   VRIN (Variable Response) [raw]

  __65__ VRIN (Variable Response) [T]

  __10__ TRIN (True Response) [raw]

  __57T__ TRIN (True Response) [T]

3. Accuracy

  A. Self—Unfavorable

    __12__ F (Infrequency) [raw]

    __73__ F (Infrequency) [T]

    __5__ F_B (Infrequency Back) [raw]

    __63__ F_B (Infrequency Back) [T]

  __34__ $O - S$ (Total T Score Differences on Obvious-Subtle Scales)

  __-1__ $F - K$ [raw scores]

  __20__ $K - B$ (Total Critical Items Endorsed)

  __28__ L&W (Total Critical Items Endorsed)

  __44__ True % (Percent True)

B. Self—Favorable

    __6__ L (Lie) [raw]

    __61__ L (Lie) [T]

    __13__ K (Correction) [raw]

    __45__ K (Correction) [T]

    __55__ False % (Percent FALSE)

<table>
<tr><td colspan="2" align="center">**FACTOR SCALES**</td></tr>
</table>

1. First Factor Scales (General Distress)

  __53__ A (Welsh Anxiety)

  __*47__ Pt (Psychasthenia)

  __54__ PS (PTSD—Schlenger)

  __52__ PK (PTSD—Keane)

  __54__ Mt (College Maladjustment)

  __50__ WRK (Work Interference)

  __45__ ANX (Anxiety)

  __64__ TRT (Negative Treatment)

  __62__ LSE (Low Self-Esteem)

  __66__ DEP (Depression)

  [45] K (Correction) [low]

  [54] Es (Ego Strength) [low]

2. Second Factor Scales
   (Overcontrol vs. Undercontrol)

  A. Emotional Overcontrol

    __56__ R   (Repression)

    __59__ D_2 (Psychomotor Retardation)

  __48__ D-S   (Depression, Subtle)

  [68] TPA (Type A) [low]

  [50] ANG (Anger) [low]

  __48__ Hy_5 (Inhibition of Aggression)

B. Behavioral Overcontrol

  [68] Pd_2 (Authority Conflict) [low]

  __34__ Re   (Social Responsibility)

  __37__ GF   (Gender Role—Feminine)

  [69] MAC-R (MacAndrew Alcoholism) [low]

  [55] ASP (Antisocial Practices) [low]

  [68] Pd-O (Psychopathic Deviate, Obvious) [low]

  __35__ O-H (Overcontrolled-Hostility)

(continued)

TABLE 8.6 MMPI-2 Structural Summary, Example 1 (continued)

MOODS

1. Depression

   A. Depressed Mood/Dysphoria

     56   D_1 (Subjective Depression)

     51   D_5 (Brooding)

     62   Pa_2 (Poignancy)

   B. Depressed Ideation/Attitudes

     66   DEP   Depression

     59   Sc_2 (Emotional Alienation)

     6/22   K-B   (Depression-Suicidal Ideation)

     4/16   L&W (Depression & Worry)

     0/5   Items 150, 303, 506, 520, 524 endorsed "true"

   C. Mental Insufficiency

     53   D_4 (Mental Dullness)

     48   Sc_3 (Lack of Ego Mastery, Cognitive)

     49   Sc_4 (Lack of Ego Mastery, Conative)

     59   D_2 (Psychomotor Retardation)

   D. Vegetative Signs

     43   D_3 (Physical Malfunctioning)

     52   Hy_3 (Lassitude-Malaise)

     59   D_2 (Psychomotor Retardation)

     44   HEA (Health Concerns)

     2/6   L&W (Sexual Concern & Deviation)

     0/6   L&W (Sleep Disturbance)

     [58] Ma_2 (Psychomotor Acceleration) [low]]

2. Anhedonia

     51   D_5 (Brooding)

     66   DEP (Depression)

     53   D_4 (Mental Dullness)

     49   Sc_4 (Lack of Ego Mastery, Conative)

     59   Sc_2 (Emotional Alienation)

     59   D_2 (Psychomotor Retardation)

     63   Pd_5 (Self-Alienation)

3. Elation

     *67   Ma   (Hypomania)

     [47]   D   (Depression) [low]

     63   Ma_4 (Ego Inflation)

     [62]   LSE (Low Self-Esteem) [low]

     [54]   FRS (Fears) [low]

     [66]   DEP (Depression) [low]

4. Anxiety

     45   ANX (Anxiety)

     *47   Pt   (Psychasthenia)

     1/17   K-B   (Acute Anxiety State)

     0/11   L&W (Anxiety and Tension)

5. Guilt

     63   Pd_5 (Self-Alienation)

     51   D_5 (Brooding)

6. Fears

     54   FRS   (Fears)

     [53]   GM   (Gender Role—Masculine) [low]

     [54]   Es   (Ego Strength) [low]

     *47   Pt   (Psychasthenia)

     *61   Sc   (Schizophrenia)

     54   Sc_5 (Lack of Ego Mastery, Defective Inhibition)

7. Emotional Alienation (Hopelessness)

     49   Sc_2 (Emotional Alienation)

     82   Pd_5 (Self-Alienation)

     69   Sc_1 (Social Alienation)

8. Anger/Hostility

     50   ANG (Anger)

     68   TPA (Type A)

     54   Sc_5 (Lack of Ego Mastery, Defective Inhibition)

     1/5   K-B   (Threatened Assault)

     0/4   Items 150, 540, 542, 548 endorsed "true"

9. Denial of Anger/Hostility

     [50]   ANG (Anger) [low]

     35   O-H (Overcontrolled-Hostility)

     [68]   TPA (Type A) [low]

     [54] Sc_5 (Lack of Ego Mastery, Defective Inhibitions) [low]

     48   Hy_5 (Inhibition of Aggression)

(continued)

TABLE 8.6 MMPI-2 Structural Summary, Example 1 (continued)

COGNITIONS

1. Unconventional Thought Processes
   - 59 Sc_2 (Emotional Alienation)
   - 58 Ma_2 (Psychomotor Acceleration)
   - 73   F   (Infrequency)

2. Psychotic Thought Processes
   - 70   BIZ   (Bizarre Mentation)
   - 61   Sc   (Schizophrenia)
   - 48 Sc_3 (Lack of Ego Mastery, Cognitive)
   - 70 Sc_6 (Sensorimotor Dissociation)
   - 73   F   (Infrequency)
   - 53 D_4 (Mental Dullness)
   - 2/11   K-B   (Mental Confusion)
   - 4/10   L&W   (Deviant Thinking and Experience)

3. Grandiosity
   - 63 Ma_4 (Ego Inflation)
   - [62]   LSE   (Low Self-Esteem) [low]

4. Paranoid Thought Processes
   - 82 Pa_1 (Ideas of External Influence)
   - 80   Pa-O   (Paranoia, Obvious)
   - 70   BIZ   (Bizarre Mentation)
   - 79   Pa   (Paranoia)
   - 72 Sc_1 (Social Alienation)
   - 62 Pd_4 (Social Alienation)
   - 7/16   K-B   (Persecutory Ideas)
   - 7/15   L&W   (Deviant Beliefs)

5. Obsessions/Ruminations
   - 50   OBS   (Obsessions)
   - *47   Pt   (Psychasthenia)
   - [54]   Es   (Ego Strength) [low]

6. Cynicism
   - 48   CYN   (Cynicism)
   - [46] Pa_3 (Moral Virtue) [low]
   - [43] Hy_2 (Need for Affection) [low]
   - 55   ASP   (Antisocial Practices)
   - [47]   Hy-S   (Hysteria, Subtle) [low]
   - 74 Ma_1 (Amorality)

7. Memory, Attention, and Concentration
   - 53 D_4 (Mental Dullness)
   - 48 Sc_3 (Lack of Ego Mastery, Cognitive)
   - 49 Sc_4 (Lack of Ego Mastery, Conative)
   - 2/11   K-B   (Mental Confusion)

8. Defense Mechanisms

   A. Repression
   - 47   Hy-S   (Hysteria, Subtle)
   - 43   Hy   (Hysteria)
   - 56   R   (Repression)
   - 45   K   (Correction)
   - 48   D-S   (Depression, Subtle)

   B. Denial
   - 61   L   (Lie)
   - 45   K   (Correction)
   - 55   FALSE %   (Percent FALSE)
   - 57T   TRIN   (True Response Inconsistency) [False]

   C. Somatization
   - 44   HEA   (Health Concerns)
   - *46   Hs   (Hypochondriasis)
   - 43 Hy_4 (Somatic Complaints)
   - 45   Hy-O   (Hysteria, Obvious)
   - 70 Sc_6 (Sensorimotor Dissociation)
   - 43 D_3 (Physical Malfunctioning)
   - 3/23   L&W   (Somatic Symptoms)

   D. Rationalization/Intellectualism
   - 79   Pa   (Paranoia)
   - 46   Mf   (Masculinity-Femininity)
   - 66   Pd   (Psychopathic Deviate)
   - *47   Pt   (Psychasthenia)

   E. Externalization
   - 43   Hy   (Hysteria)
   - *66   Pd   (Psychopathic Deviate)
   - 79   Pa   (Paranoia)
   - *67   Ma   (Hypomania)

(continued)

TABLE 8.6 MMPI-2 Structural Summary, Example 1 (continued)

COGNITIONS (CONTINUED)

F. Projection

79	Pa	(Paranoia)
80	Pa-O	(Paranoia, Obvious)
82	Pa$_1$	(Ideas of External Influence)
62	Pd$_4$	(Social Alienation)

G. Acting Out

*67	Ma	(Hypomania)
69	MAC-R	(MacAndrew Alcoholism—Revised)
*66	Pd	(Psychopathic Deviate)

55	ASP	(Antisocial Practices)
68	Pd$_2$	(Authority Conflict)
54	Sc$_5$	(Lack of Ego Mastery, Defective Inhibition)
70	Sc$_6$	(Sensorimotor Dissociation)

H. Fantasy

*61	Sc	(Schizophrenia)
49	Sc$_4$	(Lack of Ego Mastery, Conative)
70	BIZ	(Bizarre Mentation)
[48]	Hy$_5$	(Inhibition of Aggression) [low]

INTERPERSONAL RELATIONS

1. Extroversion/Introversion

   A. Extroversion

52	Pd$_3$	(Social Imperturbability)
51	Hy$_1$	(Denial of Social Anxiety)
41	Ma$_3$	(Imperturbability)
47	Hy-S	(Hysteria, Subtle)
[71]	SOD	(Social Discomfort) [low]
[56]	Si	(Social Introversion) [low]
43	Hy	(Hysteria)

   B. Introversion

71	SOD	(Social Discomfort)
56	Si	(Social Introversion)
51	Si$_1$	(Shyness/Self-Consciousness)
71	Si$_2$	(Social Avoidance)
[52]	Pd$_3$	(Social Imperturbability) [low]
[51]	Hy$_1$	(Denial of Social Anxiety) [low]
[47]	Hy-S	(Hysteria, Subtle) [low]

2. Social-Alienation

72	Sc$_1$	(Social Alienation)
62	Pd$_4$	(Social Alienation)
*61	Sc	(Schizophrenia)
47	Si$_3$	(Alienation—Self and Others)
66	Pd	(Psychopathic Deviate)
71	Si$_2$	(Social Avoidance)

3. Self-Alienation

62	LSE	(Low Self-Esteem)
63	Pd$_5$	(Self-Alienation)
59	Sc$_2$	(Emotional Alienation)
[63]	Ma$_4$	(Ego Inflation) [low]

4. Masculinity/Femininity

46	Mf	(Masculinity-Femininity)
37	GF	(Gender Role—Feminine)
53	GM	(Gender Role—Masculine)
63	Ma$_4$	(Ego Inflation) [low=Feminine; high=Masculine]

5. Family Alienation

71	FAM	(Family Problems)
65	Pd$_1$	(Familial Discord)
72	Sc$_1$	(Social Alienation)
73	F	(Infrequency)
3/4	L&W	(Family Conflict)

6. Delinquency/Antisocial Practices

68	Pd$_2$	(Authority Conflict)
3/9	L&W	(Antisocial Attitude)
[34]	Re	(Social Responsibility) [low]
55	ASP	(Antisocial Practices)
[37]	GF	(Gender Role—Feminine) [low]

(continued)

TABLE 8.6   MMPI-2 Structural Summary, Example 1 (continued)

INTERPERSONAL RELATIONS (CONTINUED)

7. Authority Conflict/Antisocial Attitudes

55	ASP	(Antisocial Practices)
48	CYN	(Cynicism)
3/9	L&W	(Antisocial Attitude)
[34]	Re	(Social Responsibility) [low]
[37]	GF	(Gender Role—Feminine) [low]

8. Passive/Aggressive Struggles

63	Ma_4	(Ego Inflation)
49	Sc_4	(Lack of Ego Mastery, Conative)
68	TPA	(Type A)

9. Passivity/Submissiveness

43	Hy_2	(Need for Affection)
59	D_2	(Psychomotor Retardation)
[63]	Ma_4	(Ego Inflation) [low]
[68]	Pd_2	(Authority Conflict) [low]
62	LSE	(Low Self-Esteem)
46	Mf	(Masculine-Femininity)
[68]	TPA	(Type A) [low]

10. Dependency

47	Si_3	(Alienation—Self and Others)
62	LSE	(Low Self-Esteem)

50	WRK	(Work Interference)
[53]	GM	(Gender Role—Masculine) [low]
[51]	Hy_1	(Denial of Social Anxiety)
[52]	Pd_3	(Social Imperturbability) [low]

11. Dominance/Assertiveness

45	Do	(Dominance)
[62]	LSE	(Low Self-Esteem) [low]
52	Pd_3	(Social Imperturbability)
[51]	Si_1	(Shyness/Self-Consciousness) [low]
[56]	Si	(Social Introversion) [low]
53	GM	(Gender Role—Masculine)
[35]	O-H	(Overcontrolled-Hostility) [low]

12. Narcissism

52	Pd_3	(Social Imperturbability)
[51]	Si_1	(Shyness/Self-Consciousness) [low]
1[71]	SOD	(Social Discomfort) [low]
[62]	LSE	(Low Self-Esteem) [low]
68	TPA	(Type A)

OTHER PROBLEM AREAS

1. Substance Abuse

60	AAS	(Addiction Admission)
41	APS	(Addiction Potential)
69	MAC-R	(MacAndrew Alcoholism—Revised)
63	Pd_5	(Self-Alienation)
3/7	K-B	(Situational Stress Due to Alcoholism)
1/3	L&W	(Substance Abuse)

2. Suicidal Ideation

59	Sc_2	(Emotional Alienation)
66	DEP	(Depression)
49	Sc_4	(Lack of Ego Mastery, Conative)

51	D_5	(Brooding)
0/5		Items 150, 303, 506, 520, 524 endorsed "true"

3. Sleep Disturbances

45	ANX	(Anxiety)
*47	Pt	(Psychasthenia)
56	D_1	(Subjective Depression)
48	D-O	(Depression, Obvious)
45	Hy-O	(Hysteria, Obvious)
*61	Sc	(Schizophrenia)
0/6	L&W	(Sleep Disturbance)

4. Sexual Difficulties

*61	Sc	(Schizophrenia)
2/6	L&W	(Sexual Concern and Deviation)

Note. From the MMPI-2 Structural Summary by R. L. Greene and D. S. Nichols, Copyright © 1995 by Psychological Assessment Resources, Inc., Odessa, FL. Reprinted with permission of the publisher.
*Non-K-corrected T scores are entered for scales *Hs, Pd, Pt, Sc,* and *Ma.*

$SOD = 71$ — He is very uneasy around others and is happier by himself. He sees himself as being shy. He dislikes parties and other group events.

$SOD1 = 76$ — He dislikes the company of others to the point that he avoids interpersonal contact. He keeps other people at a distance.

$FAM = 71$ — He reports considerable familial discord. His family was lacking love, support, and companionship. Members of his family are nervous and have quick tempers, and they are to be avoided.

$FAM1 = 70$ — He has or is currently experiencing a considerable degree of strife and discord in his family. His family life is full of conflict.

$FAM2 = 76$ — He feels alienated from and unattached to his family. He does not feel emotionally supported by his family.

$WRK = 50$ — He is as able to work as he ever was, and his current problems are not interfering with his ability to work.

$TRT = 64$ — He dislikes going to doctors and he believes that he should not discuss his personal problems with others. He does not believe that anyone understands or cares about him.

Rankings of Content Component Scales.

Table 8.7 contains the rankings of all of the Content Component scales for this patient as well as for the prototypic 6-9/9-6 codetype. He is significantly more introverted ($SOD1$) than typical and he is experiencing more familial discord ($FAM1$) and alienation ($FAM2$). He has less explosive behavior ($ANG1$) and anxiety (ANX) than the prototypic patient.

Supplementary Scales.

(Chapter 6)

$MAC\text{-}R = 31$ (raw score) — He has a significant probability of abusing alcohol or drugs. He is likely to be impulsive, have a high energy level, have shallow interpersonal relationships, and be psychologically maladjusted.

$APS = 41$ — He describes himself in positive terms. He is neither distressed nor angry.

$AAS = 60$ — He uses alcohol and/or other substances more than most people.

$Do = 45$ — He has a normal range of dominant and assertive behaviors.

$Es = 54$ — He is reporting a normal level of generalized distress and negative emotionality.

$GM = 53$ — He has a normal range of interests in masculine activities.

$GF = 37$ — He has little interest in feminine activities. He is experiencing a significant amount of emotional distress and may abuse substances.

$MDS = 60$ — He is dissatisfied with his marital relations.

$O\text{-}H = 35$ — He is able to acknowledge that he is nervous and worries about what happens around him. He is aware of being angry.

$Re = 34$ — He is unconcerned about social conventions and may have antisocial characteristics.

Profile Interpretation[7]

Test-Taking Behaviors. The client endorsed the items consistently ($VRIN$, $|F - F_B|$) and accurately ($F - K$; $F[p]$), although he is reporting less distress than most clients with this codetype on the MMPI-2. He is admitting to personal and emotional difficulties, and simultaneously trying to defend himself against

---

7. The parenthetical references to specific scales or indexes are provided so clinicians can see the source(s) for the statements in the interpretation. These parenthetical references would be deleted in an actual report.

TABLE 8.7   Ranking of Content Components for Example 1

Content Components for MMPI-2 Codetypes		
Example 1		
	Scale	T Score
BIZ1	Psychotic Symptomatology	91
FAM2	Familial Alienation	76
SOD1	Introversion	76
FAM1	Family Discord	70
LSE1	Self-Doubt	70
DEP1	Lack of Drive	68
TRT2	Inability to Disclose	68
DEP3	Self-Depreciation	62
TPA2	Competitive Drive	61
ASP2	Antisocial Behavior	59
DEP2	Dysphoria	59
TPA1	Impatience	57
ANG2	Irritability	56
ASP1	Antisocial Attitudes	55
LSE2	Submissiveness	55
BIZ2	Schizotypal Characteristics	54
TRT1	Low Motivation	54
CYN2	Interpersonal Suspiciousness	53
FRS1	Generalized Fearfulness	53
FRS2	Multiple Fears	52
OBS	Obsessiveness	50
WRK	Work Interference	50
HEA2	Neurological Symptoms	47
SOD2	Shyness	47
CYN1	Misanthropic Beliefs	46
ANG1	Explosive Behavior	45
ANX	Anxiety	45
DEP4	Suicidal Ideation	45
HEA1	Gastrointestinal Symptoms	44
HEA3	General Health Concerns	40

Content Components for MMPI-2 Codetypes		
Prototypic 6-9/9-6		
	Scale	T Score
BIZ1	Psychotic Symptomatology	66
BIZ2	Schizotypal Characteristics	64
ANX	Anxiety	61
CYN2	Interpersonal Suspiciousness	58
ANG1	Explosive Behavior	58
TPA2	Competitive Drive	58
ASP2	Antisocial Behavior	58
FAM1	Family Discord	57
DEP2	Dysphoria	57
HEA2	Neurological Symptoms	57
DEP1	Lack of Drive	57
DEP3	Self-Depreciation	56
ASP1	Antisocial Attitudes	56
OBS	Obsessiveness	56
WRK	Work Interference	56
ANG2	Irritability	56
CYN1	Misanthropic Beliefs	56
FRS1	Generalized Fearfulness	55
TRT1	Low Motivation	54
HEA3	General Health Concerns	54
HEA1	Gastrointestinal Symptoms	54
DEP4	Suicidal Ideation	54
FAM2	Familial Alienation	53
LSE2	Submissiveness	52
TRT2	Inability to Disclose	51
TPA1	Impatience	51
LSE1	Self-Doubt	51
FRS2	Multiple Fears	47
SOD1	Introversion	46
SOD2	Shyness	45

these problems in an unsophisticated manner (Validity scale configuration). This pattern of ineffective defenses with the simultaneous admission of fairly severe problems is typical of chronically maladjusted clients (Validity scale configuration).

Moods.   The client did not describe himself as being depressed (Scale *2*), anxious (Scale *7*), or emotionally distressed (*A, Mt, PK, PS, ANX*) despite his presence in the state hospital. Neither his being hospitalized nor the behaviors that led him to being hospitalized are creating any emotional distress. He does not see

himself as being angry (*ANG*) or cynical (*CYN*). Others are likely to see him as angry and hostile (*6-9/9-6* codetype; *TPA*) and blaming them for his problems (*Pa₁, DEP*). Outbursts of temper (Scale *9; TPA*) or physical acting out may occur (Scale *6*).

Cognitions.   He has difficulty thinking and concentrating, and may exercise poor judgment (*6-9/9-6* codetype). He thinks differently than other people (Scale *8*), and he reports strange thoughts and experiences (*BIZ*). There is a strong likelihood of a potentially psychotic process that needs to be evaluated carefully (*6-9/9-6* codetype; *BIZ*). A review of his background and reasons for coming to the state hospital may be sufficient to document the presence of a psychotic process.

Interpersonal Relations.   The client reports a balance between socially extroverted and introverted attitudes and behaviors (Scale *0*). He has traditional masculine interests and activities (Scale *5*). He is very uneasy around others and is happier by himself (*SOD*). The client sees himself as shy and he avoids others when given the opportunity (*SOD*). He has shallow interpersonal relationships (*MAC-R*) and considerable familial discord (*FAM*).

Other Problem Areas.   He does not report suicidal ideation or any history of suicide attempts. He is not concerned about his health (Scale *1; HEA*). He is likely to abuse substances (*MAC-R*).

Treatment.   The client is a poor candidate for most forms of psychological interventions for a variety of reasons. He is experiencing little internalized distress (Scales *2, 7, A, Mt, PK, PS, ANX*), and he is prone to blame others for his problems (Scale *6, Pa₁*) and to expect them to change to meet his needs. His problems are chronic in nature (Validity scale configuration), and he sees little hope of changing (*TRT*). He dislikes going to doctors and he believes that he should not discuss his personal problems with anyone (*TRT*). He also may be prone to abuse alcohol or other drugs (*MAC-R*), which will only exacerbate all of the problems described previously.

Therapy will proceed slowly at best and should focus on his relationships with members of his family (*FAM*). It will be important for the therapist not to place any unusual demands on the client until some trust in the relationship is developed (Scale *6*). Despite all of his problems, he does not see his work as being affected by his problems (*WRK*). If his statement about his work is accurate, it could be used as a point of strength from which to address other issues.

Diagnostic Impression

Axis I   296.44   Rule out Bipolar Disorder, Manic Type, with Mood-Congruent Psychotic Features

301.13   Rule out Cyclothymia

Axis II   301.00   Rule out Paranoid Personality Disorder

Computer Interpretation: The Minnesota Report[8]

Profile Validity.   The client has endorsed a number of psychological symptoms in a generally frank and open manner. His profile is likely to be problem oriented rather than defensive. His MMPI-2 Clinical and Content scale profiles are likely to be a valid indication of his present personality functioning.

Symptomatic Patterns.   The behavioral correlates included in the narrative report are likely to provide a good description of the client's current personality functioning. The clinical scale prototype used in the report, which incorporates correlates of *Pa* and *Ma*, is based on scores with high profile definition. This MMPI-2 clinical profile suggests that the client may not view his problems as extreme or unmanageable at this time because problem denial and externalization of blame are characteristic of his adjustment. He may present the view that he is rather fun-loving, extroverted, and enthusiastic, but he may become so involved in activities that he ignores some important aspects of life. He may become easily bored or frustrated and may feel the need to move on to other things even if some projects are left unfinished. He may also behave impulsively and may occasionally appear irresponsible, although he will tend to deny this. This MMPI-2 pattern reflects some maladaptive personality features that are likely to persist. In general, he tends to deny problems rather than confront them. Some individuals with this profile have an obsessional and "driven" quality to their behavior.

In addition, the following description is suggested by the content of the client's item responses. He has endorsed a number of items suggesting that he is experiencing low morale and a depressed mood. He views the world as a threatening place, sees himself as having been unjustly blamed for others' problems, and feels that he is getting a raw deal out of life.

8. Adult Clinical System-Revised. Copyright © 1989, 1993 by the Regents of the University of Minnesota. All rights reserved.

He endorsed a number of extreme and bizarre thoughts, suggesting the presence of delusions or hallucinations. He apparently believes that he has special mystical powers or a special "mission" in life that others do not understand or accept. He considers himself to be in good health and does not complain of somatic difficulties.

Profile Frequency. Profile interpretation can be greatly facilitated by examining the relative frequency of clinical scale patterns in various settings. The client's high-point clinical scale score (*Pa*) occurs in 9.6% of the MMPI-2 normative sample of men. However, only 3% of the sample have *Pa* as the peak score at or above a T score of 65, and only 2.2% have well-defined *Pa* spikes. This elevated MMPI-2 profile type (*6-9/9-6*) is very rare in samples of normals, occurring in less than 1% of the MMPI-2 normative sample of men.

The frequency of this MMPI-2 high-point *Pa* score is relatively high in various inpatient settings. In the Graham and Butcher (1988) sample of psychiatric inpatients, this profile peak is the second most frequent peak score (15.7%) for males, with 12.6% of the cases scoring in the clinically significant range (8.2% are well defined). In the large NCS inpatient sample, this high-point clinical scale score (*Pa*) is the third most frequent peak score, occurring in 14.3% of the men. Moreover, 12.1% of the males in the inpatient sample have this high-point scale spike at or over a T score of 65, and 7.5% are well defined in that range. Male inpatients in a Veterans Administration setting (Arbisi & Ben-Porath, 1993) produce this high-point peak score with 10.1% frequency; 9.1% of the cases have *Pa* elevated above a T score of 65, and 6.1% of the cases are well defined.

This elevated MMPI-2 profile type (*6-9/9-6*) is found in 4.4% of the males in the Graham and Butcher (1988) sample, in 1.7% of the males in the NCS inpatient sample, and in 1.3% of the men in a Veterans Administration inpatient sample (Arbisi & Ben-Porath, 1993).

The client scored relatively highly on *MAC-R,* suggesting the possibility of a drug- or alcohol-abuse problem. The base rate data on his profile type among residents in alcohol and drug programs should also be evaluated. His high-point MMPI-2 score, *Pa,* is the third highest peak score among alcohol- and drug-abusing populations. Over 14.5% of the men in sub-stance-abuse treatment programs have this pattern, perhaps reflecting guardedness about their problems (McKenna & Butcher, 1987).

Profile Stability. The relative scale elevation of the highest scales in the client's clinical profile reflects high profile definition. If he is retested at a later date, the peak scores on this test are likely to retain their relative salience in his retest profile pattern. His high-point score on *Pa* is likely to show moderate test-retest stability. Short-term test-retest studies have shown a correlation of 0.67 for this high-point score. Spiro, Butcher, Levenson, Aldwin, and Bosse (1993) reported a moderate test-retest stability of 0.55 in a large study of normals over a five-year test-retest period.

Interpersonal Relations. Individuals with this MMPI-2 clinical profile can make a good initial impression because they typically possess a high degree of interpersonal awareness. They are also generally effective at persuading others. However, the client's relationships often become strained because of his need to control others and because of his interpersonal rigidity. He may be viewed by others as blunt and overbearing in relationships. The client may be experiencing some social alienation at this time. He may feel that others do not understand him, and he may tend to blame them for his problems. He may also have some difficulty with emotional control and, under stress, may have emotional outbursts. Some individuals with this profile have problems forming intimate relationships because of their suspiciousness and aggressiveness.

The content of this client's MMPI-2 responses suggests the following additional information concerning his interpersonal relations. He views his home situation as unpleasant and lacking in love and understanding. His social relationships are likely to be viewed by others as problematic. He may be visibly uneasy around others, sits alone in group situations, and dislikes engaging in group activities.

Diagnostic Considerations. The client's characteristic mistrust and moodiness should be considered in any diagnostic formulation. His unusual thinking and bizarre ideas need to be taken into consideration in any diagnostic formulation.

His extremely high scores on the addiction proneness indicators suggest the possible development of an addictive disorder. Further evaluation of substance use or abuse problems is strongly recommended. In his responses to the MMPI-2, he has acknowledged some problems with excessive use or abuse of addictive substances.

Treatment Considerations.   When clients are brought into psychotherapy at the insistence of others, they may at first be agreeable and may seem to enjoy treatment. Often, however, they become bored or are diverted from treatment by other activities. The client may be experiencing some social alienation at this time. He may feel that others do not understand him and he may tend to blame them for his problems. He may also have some difficulty with emotional control and, under stress, may have emotional outbursts.

If psychological treatment is being considered, it may be profitable for the therapist to explore the client's treatment motivation early in therapy. The item content he endorsed includes some feelings and attitudes that could be unproductive in psychological treatment and in implementing change.

Examination of item content reveals a considerable number of problems with his home life. He feels extremely unhappy and alienated from his family. He reports that his home life is unpleasant and that he does not expect it to improve. Any psychological intervention will need to focus on his negative family feelings if progress is to be made.

His acknowledged problems with alcohol or drug use should be addressed in therapy.

Computer Interpretation: MMPI-2 Adult Interpretive System[9]

Profile matches and scores for the client are provided in Table 8.8. The algorithms for profile matching determined that the client is best matched to a *4-6/6-4-(9)* codetype rather than a *6-9/9-6* codetype, which is the client's actual codetype. Accordingly, the computer interpretation is provided for a *4-6/6-4-(9)* co-

detype. The MMPI-2 Adult Interpretive System allows the clinician to request the interpretation of a *6-9/9-6* codetype, if desired, but it is not presented here to save space.

Configural Interpretation.
Codetype: 4-6/6-4-(9).
Clinical Presentation.
Moods.   The client is reporting minimal emotional distress or concern about his behavior or present circumstances. He is oppositional and stubborn when he is not overtly angry. He becomes impatient with others easily, and they will perceive him as irritable, grouchy, and hotheaded. He frequently has intense feelings of anger and hostility that result in episodic outbursts of anger. He is likely to exhibit increased anger and hostility in response to stress. He often is agitated and excited. He dislikes being bored and inactive and will stir up excitement if he gets bored.

Cognitions.   The client exhibits very poor judgment, often acts out without considering the consequences of his actions, and has difficulty learning from experience. He is unwilling to accept responsibility for his own behavior and exhibits a persistent tendency to get into trouble. He externalizes his feelings and attributes his problems to others, and he often believes that he is being punished without cause. He is grandiose, egocentric, and cynical of the abilities of others. He is sure that he is being talked about. He believes that people say insulting and vulgar things about him. He is suspicious of the motives of others and knows that he would have been more successful if people had not had "it in for him." He knows who is responsible for most of his troubles.

Interpersonal Relations.   The client is very active, energetic, and socially outgoing, and he likes parties and loud social events. However, his suspiciousness, hypersensitivity, and fear of emotional involvement often result in unsatisfying and volatile interpersonal relations. These characteristics also make it likely that others will misunderstand his intentions even when he is trying to be helpful. He has numerous long-standing problems with his family and persons in positions of authority. He sees his family as extremely uncaring and critical and his home life as very unpleasant. His family disliked his friends, and he felt like leaving home.

---

9. From the MMPI-2 Adult Interpretive System, Copyright © 1998 by Psychological Assessment Resources, Inc., Odessa, FL. Reproduced with permission of the publisher.

TABLE 8.8 Profile Matches and Scores for Standard Validity and Clinical Scales

Best Three Matches with Client's Profile:

DISCRIMINANT FUNCTION			COHEN'S INDEX			DEVIATION SQUARED		
Codetype	*Score*	*Probability*	*Codetype*	*rc*	*Percentile*	*Codetype*	*D²*	*Percentile*
6-9/9-6	155.130	.750	Spike 6-(8)	0.870	97%	*4-6/6-4-(9)*	752	87%
4-6/6-4	153.320	.123	Spike 6-(9)	0.823	94%	*6-9/9-6-(4)*	741	86%
Spike 6	153.014	.090	Spike 6-(4)	0.804	91%	*6-9/9-6*	889	76%

	Scale	Client's Profile 6-9/9-6	Best Fit Prototype Profile 4-6/6-4-(9)
Codetype:		6-9/9-6	4-6/6-4-(9)
rc:		0.847	0.849
D2:		889	752
	L	61	52
	F	73	70
	K	45	42
1	*Hs*	42	50
2	*D*	47	54
3	*Hy*	43	52
4	*Pd*	64 –	77
5	*Mf*	46	48
6	*Pa*	79	78
7	*Pt*	41 –	56
8	*Sc*	60	62
9	*Ma*	69	70
0	*Si*	56	47
Mean Clinical Elevation:		56	58
Scatter:		12	13
Client Age:		41	29
Men (Percent):		X	61%
Women (Percent):			39%

Note. From the MMPI-2 Adult Interpretive System, Copyright © 1998 by Psychological Assessment Resources, Inc., Odessa, FL. Reprinted with permission of the publisher.

Other Problem Areas. The client believes that he is as able to work now as he was in the past and that he is in good physical health. He frequently finds that sleep is not necessary because he is so full of energy. He clearly has enough energy to do his work. He is very likely to abuse substances. Marital problems, sexual acting out, delinquent behaviors, academic underachievement, and legal difficulties are very likely. He is likely to have suicidal ideation that should be evaluated carefully because of his impulsive, risk-taking behavior and propensity to abuse substances.

Treatment. The client's prognosis is guarded unless treatment begins early in his life. This characterologic process tends to result in fixed behavior patterns that are difficult to change. He is experiencing little emotional distress that might serve as motivation to change his behavior. Behavioral or short-term interventions that focus on the specific behaviors that led him to treatment and group therapies with similar individuals will be most effective. Psychopharmacologic interventions are warranted if it can be ascertained that he has a mood disorder. Because of his propensity for suicide and substance abuse, medications should be carefully monitored.

Possible Diagnoses

Axis I   Rule out Mood Disorders
292.84   Substance-Induced Mood Disorder
296.xx   Bipolar I Disorder, Hypomanic
296.89   Bipolar II Disorder, Hypomanic
301.13   Cyclothymic Disorder

Rule out Adjustment Disorders
309.3   Adjustment Disorder with Disturbance of Conduct

Rule out Substance-Related Disorders
305.00   Alcohol Abuse
305.60   Cocaine Abuse
305.70   Amphetamine Abuse

Axis II   Rule out Personality Disorders
301.70   Antisocial Personality Disorder
301.81   Narcissistic Personality Disorder
301.83   Borderline Personality Disorder

Computer Interpretation: Caldwell Report[10]

Test-Taking Attitude.

Attention and Comprehension.   The client's score on the Variable Response Inconsistency scale (*VRIN*) was mildly elevated but within the normal range. This indicates that he was able to read and comprehend most if not all of the test items, that he was rarely if at any time inattentive in considering his responses, and that

10. The permission of Dr. Alex B. Caldwell, Caldwell Report, Los Angeles, California, to reproduce this report is gratefully acknowledged.

he adequately matched the item numbers in the booklet to the corresponding numbers on the answer sheet. He does not appear to have had any serious difficulties in understanding the content or in responding to the format of the inventory.

Attitude and Approach.   He made a few atypical responses to the inventory. Otherwise, his approach was straightforward and not unduly defensive. The profile appears valid by the usual criteria for scales *L, F,* and *K*.

He made a few atypical and rarely given responses to the items occurring in the second half of the inventory (scale F_B). This was a somewhat unusual shift from having made proportionately many more atypical responses to the earlier MMPI-2 items (scale *F*). During the latter part of the inventory, his attention to the meaning of the items may have improved, he may have had a "change of mind" during the latter part of the inventory toward not overstating his level of disturbance, or he may have avoided early careless errors; but which of these alternatives applies cannot be determined from these two *F* scores alone.

Sociocultural Influences vs. Conscious Distortion. The supplemental Validity scales indicate that he was trying to "look good" on the MMPI. He showed a moderate level of conscious defensiveness, responding "too positively" to many of the MMPI items. Despite this, he showed little elevation on scale *K*, suggesting a rather uneven to limited level of verbal sophistication. His below average score on the scale measuring his level of currently attained, recently experienced, or self-perceived socioeconomic status (*Ss*) is consistent with his having obtained a relatively unsophisticated *K* score, despite this tendency to "fake good." Some of his Clinical scales are apt to be under-elevated, and the following report may understate his level of disturbance (as with scale *L*, we cannot tell from the *Mp* and *Sd* scales which of his scales are most under-elevated).

There were no indications on the *Ds* scale of any attempt to malinger or exaggerate his level of disturbance. The scattered atypical and rarely given responses shown in his elevation on scale *F* appear, in the absence of any *Ds* elevation, to reflect the valid reporting of some unusual experiences and attitudes on the MMPI. The elevation on *F* also suggests an internally driven person who may be described as dissatisfied, restless, changeable, or complex and possibly as moody, talkative, opinionated, or curious (his *F* score was not at all due to exaggeration or overstatement). Despite the mildly elevated *F* score, his clinical scale scores are not likely to be overelevated; the *F* score does not appear to reflect any consciously self-critical distortion or biasing of his responses. These scores suggest a person who is defensive in some areas but willing to report somewhat atypical reactions in other areas. The extent of distress that he did report indeed does appear genuine.

Symptoms and Personality Characteristics. The profile suggests intense and abruptly angry reactions, which he is not able to express in adaptive and satisfactory ways. He is apt to misinterpret the intentions of others and to overreact to anything he perceives or suspects to be a threat to his security. He would be quick to feel poorly treated and unfairly dealt with. When he feels "wronged," he would be quite slow to forgive and forget. Such projections, evasiveness when challenged, a circumstantial stream of thought, and breakdowns of his reality testing would reflect pervasive paranoid characteristics. These distortions could prove to be delusional. Difficulties with drugs or with alcohol would readily aggravate these problems. Nevertheless, his ego strength tests as well above average, which predicts organized functioning and immediate, practical self-sufficiency in many areas.

His profile indicates a general pattern of hypomanic excitability and overactivity. His plans and expectations could be seen by others as unrealistically optimistic. He is likely to take on multiple activities or commitments, as if needing to distract himself as well as to prove his self-worth. He could be particularly conflicted around the importance of taking advantage of all the opportunities that he does get lest he "lose out" on an important experience. He may also be seen as stubborn about doing things "my own way," as if demanding validation that his way is "the right way."

Talkative and expansive when things are going well for him, he is apt to become abruptly emotional when under pressure. He tests as irritable and demanding when crossed, and personal setbacks could easily break down his controls over his aggressive impulses. Confused and high strung, he appears capable of sharp temper outbursts if not physical assaultiveness. These outbursts could be the adult equivalent of temper tantrums in his childhood. The profile would not rule out a potential for dangerous violence.

He tests as notably impulsive and as lacking in tolerance for frustrations. His chronic anger may be expressed through repeated resentments and defiance of authority figures. Needs for attention and approval are likely to conflict with his fears of being hurt and his underlying ambivalences about emotional closeness and vulnerability. This could focus specifically on sexual behavior and approach-avoidance conflicts about involvement with women. That is, his positive needs for sexual gratification could particularly conflict with his difficulties around emotional closeness. Wanting of female company, he is vulnerable to problems around his sexual impulsiveness. The ego gratifications around his sexual activities could have become overemphasized and, thus, they could distort the giving and receiving of love. However, he would be quickly resentful of external controls and especially of what he would see as "meddling" by friends or family members. His overall balance of masculine and feminine interests is within the normal range for his age and education.

In many cases this pattern has been associated with past feelings of having been mistreated, which led to an adult style of overprotecting against being victimized by anyone. During childhood siblings and other family members of such clients had been openly favored because of physical or various other handicaps. Unreleased resentments accumulated around the child's efforts to deal with feelings of not being appreciated along with increasingly fixed projections that served to explain why "they never treated me right." In many cases one of the parents had been away from the home or had been an otherwise unavailable figure with whom to identify. Frequently the patient as a child had been particularly demanding of the mother's attention with a lack of substantial emotional gratifications. This led to a conflict between wanting affection and hating domination. Chronic patterns of blame and targets of resentments and unforgiving anger accumulated in these family interactions. As adults these feelings of being unappreciated and of seeing others as unfairly favored over them repeatedly led to resentments and projections as well as a defensive pride. Often these feelings had erupted in their marriages as acute mother-in-law conflicts along with overreactions to other outside interventions in their marriages. Despite these interpersonal problems, past periods of good work adjustment are likely, although these clients could have repeatedly overreacted to threats to their careers and especially to any clear or imminent job failures.

Diagnostic Impression. The typical diagnoses are of paranoid and schizo-affective schizophrenia and bipolar manic-depressive illness, manic type. Some of these patients were seen as borderline schizophrenic without a definitely psychotic decompensation. Secondary personality disorder diagnoses such as narcissistic personality and passive-aggressive personality, aggressive type, are fairly common in these cases. A secondary diagnosis reflecting chronic abuse of or dependence on alcohol, drugs, or other chemical agents may also be indicated. It should be re-emphasized that the client's general understatement of his problems and his mildly idealized self-presentation make his profile more ambiguous than most.

Treatment Considerations. The pattern indicates a major risk of a "paranoid explosion" if the client felt trapped and cornered. Similar patients have often benefitted from antimanic agents. In some cases lithium was combined with an initial use of a nonsedating phenothiazine, and the latter was gradually tapered off and discontinued over a period of weeks. While the calming effects usually were desirable if not urgent, some of these patients reacted against such medications in part because of their secret fears of being poisoned. Others resisted such medications because of their fears of becoming depressed and their dislike of being "drugged." The client's re-

sponses suggest a careful evaluation of his use of alcohol. He tests as severely addiction prone.

His makeup is often associated with histories of alcoholism or related forms of chronic chemical abuse and dependence. His responses suggest asking if he has been in trouble with the law. If currently involved, the stress of this could have precipitated or aggravated his symptoms or otherwise have led him to make professional contact. His responses also suggest a careful review of his sexual history as to any repetitive pattern involving (1) increasing sexual tension, (2) hasty or ill-judged sexual encounters, and (3) subsequent struggles over his self-justifications that block out his negative self-judgments. If not already expressed in the interview, the therapist may wish to follow up the patient's "true" responses to the following items:

> "Someone has it in for me."
>
> "There are persons who are trying to steal my thoughts and ideas."
>
> "Someone has control over my mind."[11]

Long-standing paranoid features and any fixed and defended projections of his anger would predict a relatively gradual recovery from the current episode. Previous breakdowns or emotional upheavals would be prognostically unfavorable, even if of a different nature from his current adjustment. The family histories of similar patients usually suggest genetic contributions, especially where these involve histories of major mood swings in family members.

His guardedness and defensiveness suggest a great reluctance to open up in psychotherapy, to expose himself psychologically, and to risk his precarious pride. Projecting anger onto the therapist, he would be vigilantly sensitive to what he would perceive to be "hostile interpretations" by the therapist,

---

11. Minnesota Multiphasic Personality Inventory-2 (MMPI-2). Copyright © 1942, 1943 (renewed 1970), 1989 by the Regents of the University of Minnesota. Reproduced by permission of the publisher. "MMPI-2" and "Minnesota Multiphasic Personality Inventory-2" are trademarks owned by the University of Minnesota.

and he could even try to provoke such interpretations as a way of testing the therapist. His strong needs to keep control over himself could help him to regain his previous level of practical functioning. However, these controls could also put a "tight lid" on exploring his emotional feelings. The low level of expressed anxiety and depression would also tend to limit his involvement in treatment. Contacts with family members and other informants could add considerable perspective to the situational variations of his behavior and the related current stresses.

The indications from the consciousness defensiveness scales—that he tended to bias many of his responses in a self-favorable direction—recommend a consideration of how he expected the test results to be used. That is, he may have been concerned lest the results of the inventory reflect poorly on him, perhaps be used against him, or otherwise somehow end up being hurtful to his self-interests. How to respond to his needs to minimize his problems and to understate his discomforts depends, of course, on the context and circumstances of the testing.

The treatment of many similar cases has begun with reality confrontations around current frustrations, including what the patient is doing and what he is running around or away from facing. He would benefit from supportive reality testing when life becomes threatening and acutely disturbing to him. Accepting and then managing his many resentments of family members and of his ex-wife could be central, even if he were slow and roundabout in letting go of his denial. Interviews are likely to focus on helping him to recognize and verbalize the immediate hurt-anger sequences in these interactions. This could involve a careful balance between enabling him to express his intensely angry feelings while also cultivating social ease and more mutually satisfying interpersonal roles. He may be slow to accept his own anger as a normal and sometimes desirable reaction lest his anger go out of control. The channeling and directing of his intense energies and needs for excitement and stimulation can be beneficial; vigorous physical activities were reported as a positive compensation for many patients with similar profiles. Ways in which he felt superior to his peers as a child or now feels emotionally unique

and different could lead to an exploration of his interpersonal ambivalences. A related assertion of personal beliefs, of elaborated explanations of ongoing events, and of unchallengeable values and self-justifications may overprotect against painful criticism and threats to his self-esteem. A very gradual acceptance of the intensity and directions of his own angry feelings could help him to express them more appropriately and lead to an eventual relaxing and freeing up of his controls.

General Comments

All four interpretations for this first example are in general agreement about the profile's primary features: The client blames others for his problems, which are chronic in nature; he is angry, hostile, and may become physically assaultive, although he describes himself as not being angry; he has strange and unusual experiences that may reflect a psychotic process; he has significant familial problems; he is not motivated for treatment and will be difficult to treat; he has difficulties with substance abuse; and he has a paranoid disorder or bipolar disorder, manic type.

All four interpretations were incorrect as to the presence of substance abuse, according to all available information, since the client did not use alcohol or other substances and he had no history of such use. As noted in Chapter 6, the MacAndrew Alcoholism (*MAC*) scale typically is elevated in *6-9/9-6* codetypes regardless of substance use, which would indicate that the *MAC-R* was a false positive in this client.

The client was released from the hospital after a stay of approximately two weeks because of the threatened litigation. He was referred for outpatient treatment at his local mental health clinic. Once he was released from the hospital, he filed suit against all of the people and agencies that he believed were involved in his hospitalization. He did not keep any of his appointments at the mental health clinic.

The reader has probably already noticed the different types of interpretations provided by the three computer-based interpretive systems. Both The Minnesota Report™ and Caldwell Report are like the evaluations that the individual clinician would write, whereas the MMPI-2 Adult Interpretive System provides a briefer narrative that the clinician would have to integrate with other material.

Both the Caldwell Report and the MMPI-2 Adult Interpretive System use a configural approach to profile interpretation, and the MMPI-2 Adult Interpretive System provides a quantitative estimate of how well the client's profile matches prototypic codetypes. The Caldwell Report provides the most detailed and dynamic interpretation of the client's profile and it suggests a number of issues that might be explored in treatment. The interested reader also can take each statement in these interpretations and try to deduce the scales and indexes that were used as the basis for making the statement.

Interpreting the MMPI-2: Example 2

The client is a 32-year-old, married, white woman, who was admitted to the hospital as a result of an overdose of medication and her verbalized statements of further suicidal attempts. She reported four previous suicidal gestures by overdose; the most recent attempt was due to her depression over her husband's physical disabilities. She also is addicted to heroin and needed to be withdrawn from it while she was hospitalized.

The client has been married for five years to an alcoholic, who is physically disabled. It was the second marriage for both of them. She had a five-year relationship prior to her present marriage that was very chaotic. That man committed suicide several years after the termination of their relationship.

She feels trapped in her dysfunctional marital relationship, but her dependency needs are so great that she cannot bring herself to terminate the relationship, even though she has good skills for employment and some insight into the unhealthiness of their relationship. She was not seriously depressed but rather chronically dysthymic and fearful of making changes in her life.

The MMPI-2 (Profiles 8.7 to 8.9) was administered approximately one week after she entered the hospital. The prototypic scores for *2-4/4-2* codetypes can be found in Table 8.9.

Clinician's Interpretation

Validity (Chapter 3 and Validity Profile 8.10).
Item Omissions.
$? = 0$ She endorsed all of the items.

Consistency of Item Endorsement.
$VRIN = 4$ She endorsed the items consistently.
$|F - F_B| = 4$ The profile may be interpreted for accuracy of item endorsement.

Accuracy of Item Endorsement.
$F(p) = 0$ Both scales and indexes for assessing overreporting of psychopathology are well within the expected range for clinical patients. (Because she has five Clinical scales elevated above a T score of 65, there is little reason to be concerned about underreporting of psychopathology, although these scales also are within the expected range for patients.) When her scores are compared to the prototype for a *2-4/4-2* codetype (Table 8.9), she is reporting somewhat less distress than most clients with this codetype. Profile interpretation may proceed since the client has endorsed the items accurately.
$F - K = -1$

Validity Scales.
$L = 38$ She is relatively independent or self-reliant and generally willing to admit to minor social faults.
$F = 72$ She is acknowledging the unusual experiences represented in this scale more than the typical individual.
$K = 41$ She describes herself as having limited personal resources for coping with her problems. She is experiencing severe distress that is acknowledged openly. She has a poor self-concept and is strongly

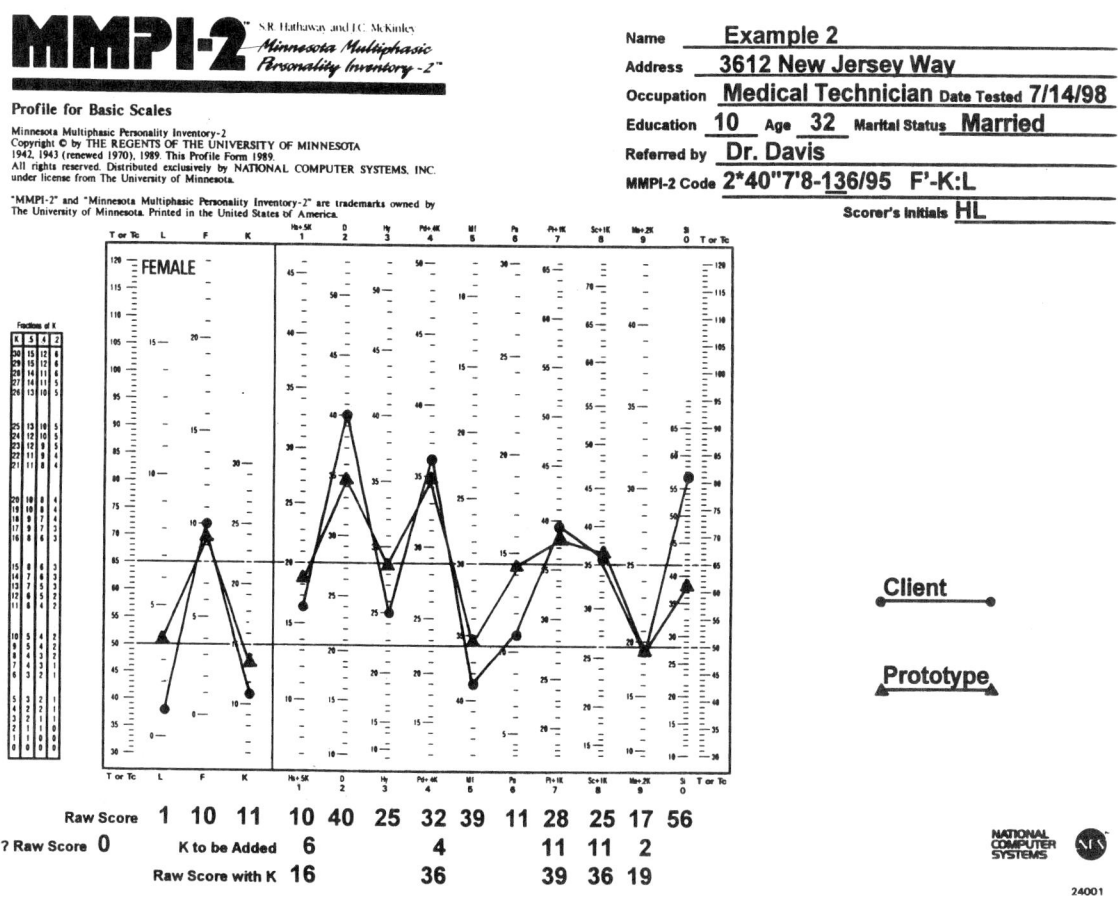

PROFILE 8.7

Note. Minnesota Multiphasic Personality Inventory-2 (MMPI-2). Copyright © 1942, 1943 (renewed 1970), 1989 by the Regents of the University of Minnesota. Reproduced by permission of the publisher. "MMPI-2" and "Minnesota Multiphasic Personality Inventory-2" are trademarks owned by the University of Minnesota.

MMPI-2™

S.R. Hathaway and J.C. McKinley
Minnesota Multiphasic Personality Inventory - 2™

Profile for Content Scales
Butcher, Graham, Williams and Ben-Porath (1989)

Minnesota Multiphasic Personality Inventory-2
Copyright © by THE REGENTS OF THE UNIVERSITY OF MINNESOTA
1942, 1943 (renewed 1970), 1989. This Profile Form 1989.
All rights reserved. Distributed exclusively by NATIONAL COMPUTER SYSTEMS, INC.
under license from The University of Minnesota.
"MMPI-2" and "Minnesota Multiphasic Personality Inventory-2" are trademarks owned by
The University of Minnesota. Printed in the United States of America.

Name	Example 2
Address	3612 New Jersey Way
Occupation	Medical Technician **Date Tested** 7/14/98
Education 10 Age 32 Marital Status	Married
Referred by	Dr. Davis
Scorer's Initials	HL

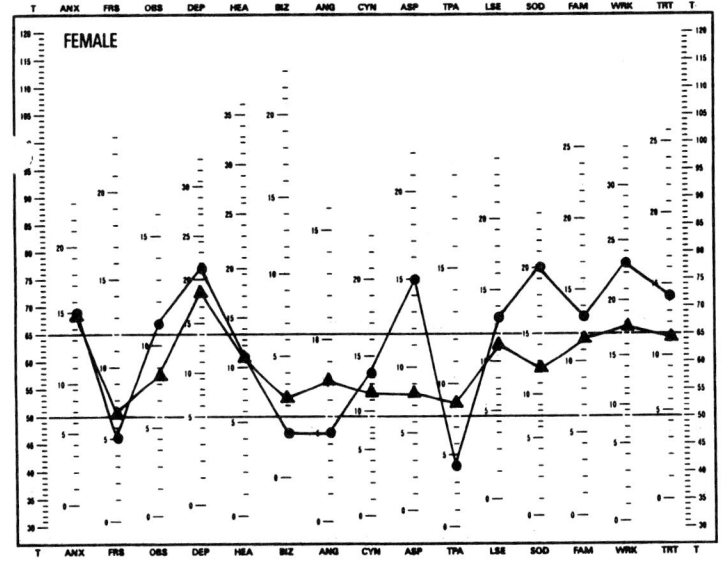

FEMALE

Client

Prototype

Raw Score	15	5	11	21	11	1	5	14	15	4	13	20	13	23	14

NATIONAL COMPUTER SYSTEMS

PROFILE 8.8

Note. Minnesota Multiphasic Personality Inventory-2 (MMPI-2). Copyright © 1942, 1943 (renewed 1970), 1989 by the Regents of the University of Minnesota. Reproduced by permission of the publisher. "MMPI-2" and "Minnesota Multiphasic Personality Inventory-2" are trademarks owned by the University of Minnesota.

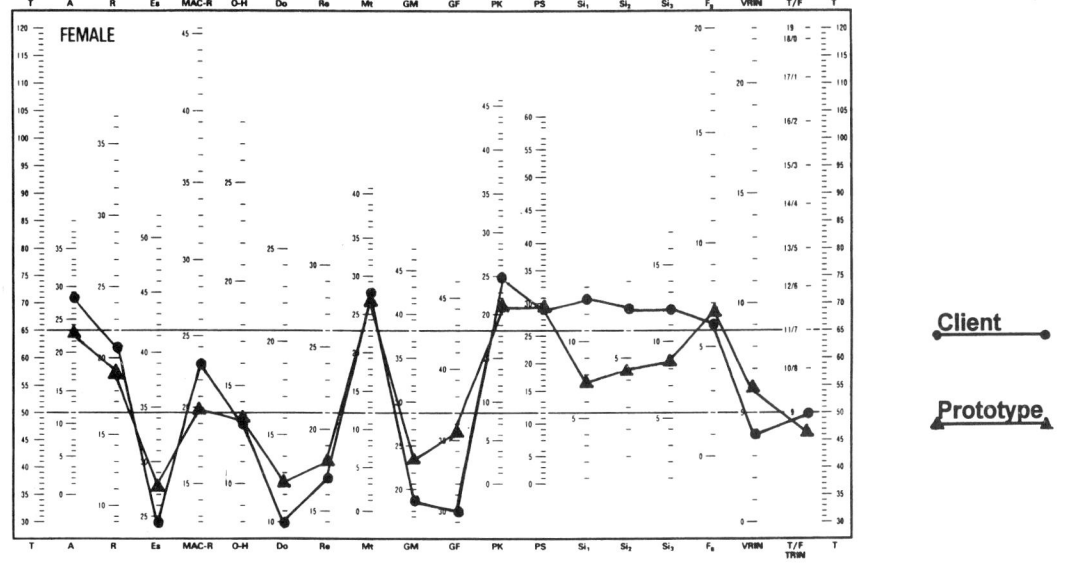

PROFILE 8.9

Note. Minnesota Multiphasic Personality Inventory-2 (MMPI-2). Copyright © 1942, 1943 (renewed 1970), 1989 by the Regents of the University of Minnesota. Reproduced by permission of the publisher. "MMPI-2" and "Minnesota Multiphasic Personality Inventory-2" are trademarks owned by the University of Minnesota.

Table 8-9
Prototypic Scores for 2-4/4-2 Codetypes (N = 855)

Demographics

Demographics		M	SD	Marital Status	%
Age		36.0	11.4	Never Married	41.1
Education		12.5	4.8	Married	35.0
Gender		%		Separated	6.4
	Men	36.6		Divorced	16.5
	Women	63.4		Widowed	1.0

Test-Taking Scales

Omissions		M	SD	Consistency		M	SD
	?	0.9	2.5	VRIN		54.4	9.8
				|F - FB|		4.1	2.8
				TRIN		47.3	10.6

Accuracy of Item Endorsement

Underreporting		M	SD	Overreporting		M	SD
	False %	57.3	6.5		True %	41.6	6.5
Impression	L	50.4	9.4	Infrequency	F	69.3	15.0
Management	ODecp	41.5	8.4		FB	67.7	18.1
	Sd	44.4	9.7		F[p]	55.7	12.6
Superior	S	43.6	8.5	Critical Items	K & B	31.8	10.5
Adjustment					L & W	37.2	12.2
Self-Deception	K	31.1	6.4	Dissimulation	F - K	-3.4	7.2
	So	34.3	10.7		Ds	65.0	12.3
					O - S	79.4	59.9

Scales

Validity and Clinical			Supplementary			Morey et al. Overlapping Personality Disorder		
Scale	M	SD	Scale	M	SD	Scale	M	SD
?	0.9	2.5	A	63.6	8.9	PAR	59.2	10.8
L	50.4	9.4	R	57.1	10.5	SZD	56.4	12.1
F	69.3	15.0	Es	36.3	10.8	STY	61.1	10.8
K	45.8	8.8	TRIN	47.3	10.6	ANT	57.4	10.5
1(Hs)	61.9	10.5	VRIN	54.4	9.8	BDL	56.9	10.0
2(D)	80.4	9.7	O-H	48.5	10.4	HST	43.6	10.8
3(Hy)	64.5	10.3	Do	37.4	10.6	NAR	41.5	10.2
4(Pd)	80.5	8.9	Re	41.2	10.9	AVD	60.8	9.8
5(Mf)	50.2	9.7	GM	41.3	8.6	DEP	63.1	10.9
6(Pa)	64.9	10.6	GF	46.2	10.4	CPS	54.0	8.6
7(Pt)	69.2	9.5	Mt	70.4	9.0	Personality Psychopathology Five		
8(Sc)	67.2	10.5	PK	69.8	11.0	Scale	M	SD
9(Ma)	49.9	8.6	PS	69.3	11.1	AGG	47.0	10.2
0(Si)	61.0	9.4	MAC-R	50.4	11.3	PSY	55.5	10.8
			APS	53.2	10.1	CON	46.8	10.1
			AAS	57.7	12.1	NEN	61.8	9.4
			MDS	71.7	11.0	PEE	30.9	11.7
			Ho	55.5	9.3			
			CAL-R	57.0	10.7			

Content			Content Component					
Scale	M	SD	Scale	M	SD	Scale	M	SD
ANX	68.4	10.2	FRS1	53.1	12.4	ASP1	51.8	9.4
FRS	50.6	10.3	FRS2	48.6	9.8	ASP2	58.6	13.2
OBS	57.0	10.3	DEP1	72.2	14.4	TPA1	53.0	10.7
DEP	72.1	10.3	DEP2	71.6	9.6	TPA2	51.2	10.1
HEA	60.5	10.0	DEP3	67.9	10.6	LSE1	64.6	12.2
BIZ	53.5	9.2	DEP4	66.9	26.3	LSE2	54.1	11.0
ANG	56.4	11.7	HEA1	57.8	13.4	SOD1	59.0	12.0
CYN	54.0	9.4	HEA2	53.5	11.5	SOD2	53.0	9.9
ASP	54.6	10.3	HEA3	65.1	12.6	FAM1	60.1	11.4
TPA	52.1	10.8	BIZ1	49.1	10.0	FAM2	64.0	14.5
LSE	62.8	11.3	BIZ2	53.6	10.5	TRT1	65.8	13.9
SOD	58.4	11.7	ANG1	54.3	11.4	TRT2	53.7	11.2
FAM	64.3	11.7	ANG2	56.2	10.6			
WRK	66.0	11.5	CYN1	53.8	9.5			
TRT	64.4	12.0	CYN2	53.0	9.8			

Note. All scores are T scores except: Cannot Say, K & B and L & W critical items which are raw scores; True % and False % which are the percentage of items endorsed "true" or "false;" and |F - FB|, F - K, and O - S which are difference scores.

MMPI-2 Validity Profile for Clinical Settings

Women

Name   Example 2   Age   32

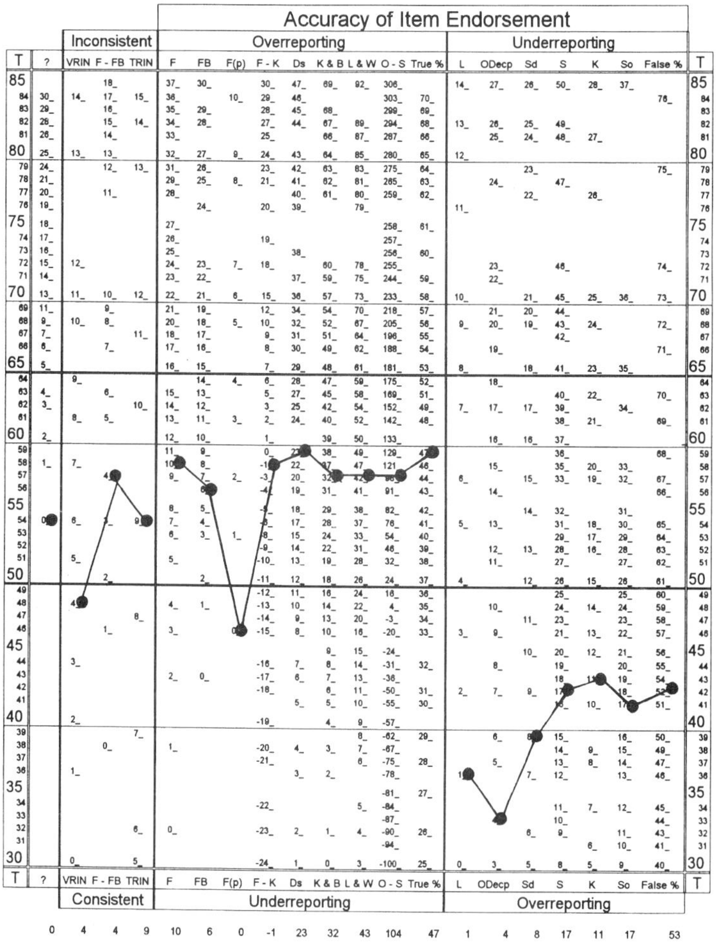

Accuracy of Item Endorsement chart with the following column groupings:

- **Inconsistent** — ? , VRIN, F - FB, TRIN
- **Overreporting** — F, FB, F(p), F - K, Ds, K & B, L & W, O - S, True %
- **Underreporting** — L, ODecp, Sd, S, K, So, False %

(Top axis labeled; bottom reversed: **Consistent**, **Underreporting**, **Overreporting**)

Bottom reference values:

?	VRIN	F - FB	TRIN	F	FB	F(p)	F - K	Ds	K & B	L & W	O - S	True %	L	ODecp	Sd	S	K	So	False %
0	4	4	9	10	6	0	-1	23	32	43	104	47	1	4	8	17	11	17	53

Omissions
? = Cannot Say scale

Consistency
VRIN = Variable Response Inconsistency Scale
F-FB = Absolute difference between F (raw) and FB (raw)
TRIN = True Response Inconsistency Scale

Overreporting of Psychopathology
F = Infrequency scale
FB = Back Infrequency scale
F(p) = Infrequency - Psychopathology scale
F-K = Raw score of the F scale minus the raw score of the K scale
Ds = Gough Dissimulation scale
K & B = Total number of Koss & Butcher critical items endorsed
L&W = Total number of Lachar & Wrobel critical items endorsed
O-S = Total T score difference for obvious minus subtle subscales
True % = Percentage of Items Endorsed "True"

Underreporting of Psychopathology
Impression Management
L = Lie scale
ODecp = Other Deception scale
Sd = Wiggins Social Desirability scale
Superior Adjustment
S = Superlative Scale
Self-Deception
K = Correction
So = Edwards Social Desirability scale
False % = Percentage of Items Endorsed "False"

1/10/98   Caldwell Clinical Sample   N = 25,763

PROFILE 8.10

Note. Minnesota Multiphasic Personality Inventory-2 (MMPI-2). Copyright © 1942, 1943 (renewed 1970), 1989 by the Regents of the University of Minnesota. Reproduced by permission of the publisher. "MMPI-2" and "Minnesota Multiphasic Personality Inventory-2" are trademarks owned by the University of Minnesota.

dissatisfied, but she lacks either the interpersonal skills or techniques necessary to alter her situation.

Validity Scale Configuration.

(Figure 3.3, solid line) She is admitting to personal and emotional problems, and she is requesting assistance in dealing with them. She is unsure of her own capabilities for dealing with these problems.

Codetype Description.

(Chapter 7) Clients may achieve *2-4/4-2* codetypes for a myriad of reasons and, as a result, it is a difficult codetype to interpret. One critical factor, which should be assessed through an interview with her or knowledge of her reason(s) for taking the MMPI-2, is whether Scale *2* (Depression) is being elevated by internal (intrapsychic) and/or external (situational) causes.

Moods. She is experiencing a moderate level of emotional distress characterized by dysphoria, resentment, agitation, and anhedonia. These moods often arise in response to some external problem or difficulty. While she may express guilt and remorse, and may promise to change her behavior, her expressions typically are not sincere. She is grouchy, irritable, and stubborn. She feels that she has not lived the "right kind of life," and she regrets many things that she has done. She wishes that she could be as happy as others seem to be.

Cognitions. Her memory is good, but her judgment is not as good now as it was in the past. She lacks self-confidence. She sometimes thinks that she is about to "go to pieces." She is dubi-

ous of the motivation of other people and believes that they are interested only in their own welfare. A theme of cynicism permeates her interactions. She knows who is responsible for most of her troubles.

Interpersonal Relations. She is slightly introverted. Her home life is not as pleasant as that of most people. She quarrels with members of her family and feels alienated from them. She very much wanted to leave home.

Other Problem Areas. She is in good health. Her sleep is disturbed by her thoughts and ideas. She is likely to abuse substances and to have been in trouble with the law. She may have suicidal ideation that needs to be monitored carefully because of her potential for substance abuse.

Treatment. Her prognosis is generally poor for traditional methods of individual psychotherapy unless a mood disorder is the primary diagnosis. In the latter instance, cognitive-behavioral psychotherapy focused on the depressive cognitions will be beneficial. Evaluation for anti-depressant medication may be indicated in cases of more severe depression. Group therapy with individuals with similar behaviors may be effective when a mood disorder is not the primary diagnosis.

Prototypic Scores.

(Table 8.9)

Factor Scales.

(Chapter 6)

$A = 71$ She has a mild to moderate level of anxiety and distress. She is maladjusted and emotionally upset, which may reflect a situational crisis or a more chronic problem. Note that other first-factor scales (College Maladjustment [*Mt*] = 72, PTSD—Keane [*PK*] = 75, PTSD—Schlenger [*PS*] = 69) are in the same range as *A*.

R = 62 | She is reluctant to discuss her behavior and any problems she may have. She may be merely suppressing this material or repressing and denying that any problems exist. She may lack insight into her own behavior.

Clinical Scales.
(Chapter 4)

$1(Hs) = 57$ — She has a typical number of physical ailments.

$2(D) = 92$ — She exhibits a general sadness and depressed mood either about life or herself. Pessimism, depression, and hopelessness are pervading her life. She is depressed, withdrawn, guilty, and self-deprecating.

$D_1 = 84$ — She is depressed, pessimistic, and has poor morale and self-esteem. She lacks energy for coping with her problems. She has problems with attention and concentration and difficulties sleeping.

$D_2 = 84$ — She avoids social relations and has difficulty starting to do things.

$D_3 = 78$ — She is generally concerned about her poor health, which is not as good as her friends.

$D_4 = 84$ — She has problems with attention, concentration, and memory. She is apathetic and has difficulty starting to do things.

$D_5 = 68$ — She is depressed, feels useless, and is easily upset by others.

$3(Hy) = 56$ — She has a typical number of attitudes and behaviors that relate to hysteric dynamics.

$4(Pd) = 84$ — She is fighting against something, which is usually some form of conflict with authority figures. These conflicts may not necessarily be acted out overtly; the rebelliousness and hostility toward authority figures are readily apparent even in these cases. She is likely to be unreliable, egocentric, and irresponsible. She may be unable to learn from experience or to plan ahead. She has a good social facade and makes a good initial impression, but the psychopathic features will surface in longer interactions or under stress. Psychological interventions are less effective than maturation in achieving change.

$Pd_1 = 80$ — She quarrels with members of her family and her home life is generally unpleasant.

$Pd_2 = 62$ — She does not report that she had behavioral problems during her school years or that she has been in trouble with the law. Her problems may involve more of the familial aspects of Scale *4* (Psychopathic Deviate) rather than the authority conflict seen in sociopathic individuals.

$Pd_4 = 71$ — She believes that no one understands her. She is unhappy and regrets the things that she has done. She believes that others talk about her and have it in for her.

$Pd_5 = 82$ — She is depressed and regrets the things that she has done. She is pessimistic and may use alcohol excessively.

$5(Mf) = 43$ — She is genuinely interested in traditional feminine interests and activities. She may be passive in this role.

$6(Pa) = 52$ — She may be very sensitive and suspicious, yet able to avoid endorsing the obvious items on this scale. She

7(Pt) = 72   She is worried, tense, and indecisive. Agitation may develop and overt anxiety is usually apparent both to her and to others. Disabling guilt feelings may be present.

8(Sc) = 66   She feels alienated and remote from her environment. Therapeutic interventions should be directive and supportive.

9(Ma) = 49   She has a normal activity level.

0(Si) = 81   She is introverted, shy, and socially insecure. In addition, she withdraws from and avoids significant others, which serves to exacerbate her problems since others might be able to help her. The likelihood of acting out is decreased and ruminative behavior is increased.

Si_1 = 71   She is shy around others and easily embarrassed. She is uncomfortable in social and new situations, and she avoids contact with people.

Si_2 = 69   She dislikes and avoids group activities of all types, and she keeps people at a distance.

Si_3 = 69   She has low self-esteem and lacks self-confidence. She questions her own judgment. She is nervous, fearful, and indecisive. She lacks interest in things.

MMPI-2 Structural Summary (Table 8.10).

The MMPI-2 Structural Summary highlights a number of significant issues. First, she is experiencing a generally negative mood state characterized by depression, anxiety, guilt, and possibly anhedonia. Second, she is not psychotic. She obsesses and ruminates over her problems and she is cynical. Third, she is very introverted and alienated from others, herself, and her family. Finally, she has significant problems with the abuse of substances. She is suicidal and has sleep difficulties.

Content Scales.
(Chapter 5)

ANX = 69   She reported general symptoms of anxiety, nervousness, worries, and sleep and concentration difficulties. She has difficulty making decisions. She finds life a strain and works under a great deal of tension and stress.

FRS = 46   She has a typical number of specific fears.

OBS = 67   She has great difficulty making decisions, ruminates excessively, worries excessively, and has intrusive thoughts. She dislikes change. She counts and saves unimportant things.

DEP = 77   She has depressive mood and thoughts. She feels blue and unhappy, and is likely to brood. She is uncertain about her future and finds her life empty and meaningless. She cries easily. She is self-critical, guilty, and lonely. She may report suicidal ideation or attempts.

DEP1 = 80   She feels like she is unable to get going and get things done in her life. She is experiencing a general lack of drive and motivation. She may be anhedonic.

DEP2 = 72   She is depressed and she experiences recurring spells of depression from which she is slow to recover. Others see her as being moody.

DEP3 = 75   She has a negative self-concept. She feels useless and helpless, and has a negative, unrealistic perception of her own abilities. She has a low self-confidence.

DEP4 = 93   She is currently contemplating and may already have attempted

TABLE 8.10 MMPI-2 Structural Summary, Example 2

TEST-TAKING ATTITUDES

1. Omissions

    _0_   ? (Cannot Say)

2. Consistency

    _4_   VRIN (Variable Response) [raw]

    _46_   VRIN (Variable Response) [T]

    _9_   TRIN (True Response) [raw]

    _50_   TRIN (True Response) [T]

3. Accuracy

  A. Self—Unfavorable

    _10_ F (Infrequency) [raw]

    _72_ F (Infrequency) [T]

    _6_ F_B (Infrequency Back) [raw]

    _66_ F_B (Infrequency Back) [T]

    _103_ $O - S$ (Total T Score Differences on Obvious-Subtle Scales)

    _−1_ $F - K$ [raw scores]

    _32_ $K - B$ (Total Critical Items Endorsed)

    _43_ $L\&W$ (Total Critical Items Endorsed)

    _47_   True % (Percent True)

  B. Self—Favorable

    _1_ L (Lie) [raw]

    _38_ L (Lie) [T]

    _11_ K (Correction) [raw]

    _41_ K (Correction) [T]

    _53_   False % (Percent FALSE)

FACTOR SCALES

1. First Factor Scales (General Distress)

    _71_ A (Welsh Anxiety)

    _*71_ Pt (Psychasthenia)

    _69_ PS (PTSD—Schlenger)

    _75_ PK (PTSD—Keane)

    _72_ Mt (College Maladjustment)

    _78_ WRK (Work Interference)

    _69_ ANX (Anxiety)

    _72_ TRT (Negative Treatment)

    _68_ LSE (Low Self-Esteem)

    _77_ DEP (Depression)

    _[41]_ K (Correction) [low]

    _[30]_ Es (Ego Strength) [low]

2. Second Factor Scales (Overcontrol vs. Undercontrol)

  A. Emotional Overcontrol

    _62_   R   (Repression)

    _84_ D_2 (Psychomotor Retardation)

    _65_ D-S (Depression, Subtle)

    _[41]_ TPA (Type A) [low]

    _[47]_ ANG (Anger) [low]

    _31_ Hy_5 (Inhibition of Aggression)

  B. Behavioral Overcontrol

    _[62]_ Pd_2 (Authority Conflict) [low]

    _38_ Re (Social Responsibility)

    _35_ GF (Gender Role—Feminine)

    _[56]_ MAC-R (MacAndrew Alcoholism—Revised) [low]

    _[75]_ ASP (Antisocial Practices) [low]

    _[87]_ Pd-O (Psychopathic Deviate, Obvious) [low]

    _48_ O-H (Overcontrolled-Hostility)

(continued)

TABLE 8.10 MMPI-2 Structural Summary, Example 2 (continued)

MOODS

1. Depression

   A. Depressed Mood/Dysphoria
   - 84 D_1 (Subjective Depression)
   - 68 D_5 (Brooding)
   - 59 Pa_2 (Poignancy)

   B. Depressed Ideation/Attitudes
   - 77   DEP   Depression
   - 49 Sc_2 (Emotional Alienation)
   - 13/22   K-B   (Depression-Suicidal Ideation)
   - 9/16   L&W   (Depression & Worry)
   - 3/5   Items 150, 303, 506, 520, 524 endorsed "true"

   C. Mental Insufficiency
   - 84 D_4 (Mental Dullness)
   - 67 Sc_3 (Lack of Ego Mastery, Cognitive)
   - 65 Sc_4 (Lack of Ego Mastery, Conative)
   - 84 D_2 (Psychomotor Retardation)

   D. Vegetative Signs
   - 78 D_3 (Physical Malfunctioning)
   - 43 Hy_3 (Lassitude-Malaise)
   - 84 D_2 (Psychomotor Retardation)
   - 61   HEA   (Health Concerns)
   - 2/6   L&W   (Sexual Concern & Deviation)
   - 3/6   L&W   (Sleep Disturbance)
   - [40] Ma_2 (Psychomotor Acceleration) [low]

2. Anhedonia
   - 68 D_5 (Brooding)
   - 77   DEP   (Depression)
   - 84 D_4 (Mental Dullness)
   - 65 Sc_4 (Lack of Ego Mastery, Conative)
   - 49 Sc_2 (Emotional Alienation)
   - 84 D_2 (Psychomotor Retardation)
   - 82 Pd_5 (Self-Alienation)

3. Elation
   - *51   Ma   (Hypomania)
   - [92]   D   (Depression) [low]
   - 56 Ma_4 (Ego Inflation)
   - [68]   LSE   (Low Self-Esteem) [low]

   - [46]   FRS   (Fears) [low]
   - [77]   DEP   (Depression) [low]

4. Anxiety
   - 69   ANX   (Anxiety)
   - *71   Pt   (Psychasthenia)
   - 8/17   K-B   (Acute Anxiety State)
   - 4/11   L&W   (Anxiety and Tension)

5. Guilt
   - 82 Pd_5 (Self-Alienation)
   - 68 D_5 (Brooding)

6. Fears
   - 46   FRS   (Fears)
   - [32]   GM   (Gender Role—Masculine) [low]
   - [30]   Es   (Ego Strength) [low]
   - *71   Pt   (Psychasthenia)
   - *67   Sc   (Schizophrenia)
   - 59 Sc_5 (Lack of Ego Mastery, Defective Inhibition)

7. Emotional Alienation (Hopelessness)
   - 49 Sc_2 (Emotional Alienation)
   - 82 Pd_5 (Self-Alienation)
   - 69 Sc_1 (Social Alienation)

8. Anger/Hostility
   - 47   ANG   (Anger)
   - 41   TPA   (Type A)
   - 59 Sc_5 (Lack of Ego Mastery, Defective Inhibition)
   - 1/5   K-B   (Threatened Assault)
   - 2/4   Items 150, 540, 542, 548 endorsed "true"

9. Denial of Anger/Hostility
   - [47]   ANG   (Anger) [low]
   - 48   O-H   (Overcontrolled-Hostility)
   - [41]   TPA   (Type A) [low]
   - [59] Sc_5 (Lack of Ego Mastery, Defective Inhibitions) [low]
   - 31 Hy_5 (Inhibition of Aggression)

(continued)

TABLE 8.10 MMPI-2 Structural Summary, Example 2 (continued)

COGNITIONS

1. Unconventional Thought Processes
   - __49__ Sc_2 (Emotional Alienation)
   - __40__ Ma_2 (Psychomotor Acceleration)
   - __72__ F (Infrequency)

2. Psychotic Thought Processes
   - __47__ BIZ (Bizarre Mentation)
   - __67__ Sc (Schizophrenia)
   - __67__ Sc_3 (Lack of Ego Mastery, Cognitive)
   - __59__ Sc_6 (Sensorimotor Dissociation)
   - __72__ F (Infrequency)
   - __84__ D_4 (Mental Dullness)
   - __2/11__ K-B (Mental Confusion)
   - __1/10__ L&W (Deviant Thinking and Experience)

3. Grandiosity
   - __56__ Ma_4 (Ego Inflation)
   - __[68]__ LSE (Low Self-Esteem) [low]

4. Paranoid Thought Processes
   - __51__ Pa_1 (Ideas of External Influence)
   - __68__ Pa-O (Paranoia, Obvious)
   - __47__ BIZ (Bizarre Mentation)
   - __52__ Pa (Paranoia)
   - __69__ Sc_1 (Social Alienation)
   - __71__ Pd_4 (Social Alienation)
   - __1/16__ K-B (Persecutory Ideas)
   - __1/15__ L&W (Deviant Beliefs)

5. Obsessions/Ruminations
   - __67__ OBS (Obsessions)
   - __*71__ Pt (Psychasthenia)
   - __[30]__ Es (Ego Strength) [low]

6. Cynicism
   - __58__ CYN (Cynicism)
   - __[41]__ Pa_3 (Moral Virtue) [low]
   - __[42]__ Hy_2 (Need for Affection) [low]
   - __75__ ASP (Antisocial Practices)
   - __[39]__ Hy-S (Hysteria, Subtle) [low]
   - __62__ Ma1 (Amorality)

7. Memory, Attention, and Concentration
   - __84__ D_4 (Mental Dullness)
   - __67__ Sc_3 (Lack of Ego Mastery, Cognitive)
   - __65__ Sc_4 (Lack of Ego Mastery, Conative)
   - __2/11__ K-B (Mental Confusion)

8. Defense Mechanisms

   A. Repression
   - __39__ Hy-S (Hysteria, Subtle)
   - __56__ Hy (Hysteria)
   - __62__ R (Repression)
   - __41__ K (Correction)
   - __65__ D-S (Depression, Subtle)

   B. Denial
   - __38__ L (Lie)
   - __41__ K (Correction)
   - __53__ FALSE % (Percent FALSE)
   - __50__ TRIN (True Response Inconsistency) [False]

   C. Somatization
   - __61__ HEA (Health Concerns)
   - __*59__ Hs (Hypochondriasis)
   - __57__ Hy_4 (Somatic Complaints)
   - __67__ Hy-O (Hysteria, Obvious)
   - __59__ Sc_6 (Sensorimotor Dissociation)
   - __78__ D_3 (Physical Malfunctioning)
   - __11/23__ L&W (Somatic Symptoms)

   D. Rationalization/Intellectualization
   - __52__ Pa (Paranoia)
   - __43__ Mf (Masculinity-Femininity)
   - __85__ Pd (Psychopathic Deviate)
   - __*71__ Pt (Psychasthenia)

   E. Externalization
   - __56__ Hy (Hysteria)
   - __*85__ Pd (Psychopathic Deviate)
   - __52__ Pa (Paranoia)
   - __*51__ Ma (Hypomania)

(continued)

TABLE 8.10 MMPI-2 Structural Summary, Example 2 (continued)

COGNITIONS (CONTINUED)

F. Projection

52	Pa	(Paranoia)
68	Pa-O	(Paranoia, Obvious)
51	Pa1	(Ideas of External Influence)
71	Pd4	(Social Alienation)

75	ASP	(Antisocial Practices)
62	Pd2	(Authority Conflict)
59	Sc5	(Lack of Ego Mastery, Defective Inhibition)
59	Sc6	(Sensorimotor Dissociation)

G. Acting Out

*51	Ma	(Hypomania)
56	MAC-R	(MacAndrew Alcoholism—Revised)
*85	Pd	(Psychopathic Deviate)

H. Fantasy

*67	Sc	(Schizophrenia)
65	Sc4	(Lack of Ego Mastery, Conative)
47	BIZ	(Bizarre Mentation)
[31]	Hy5	(Inhibition of Aggression) [low]

INTERPERSONAL RELATIONS

1. Extroversion/Introversion

   A. Extroversion

36	Pd3	(Social Imperturbability)
40	Hy1	(Denial of Social Anxiety)
37	Ma3	(Imperturbability)
39	Hy-S	(Hysteria, Subtle)
[77]	SOD	(Social Discomfort) [low]
[78]	Si	(Social Introversion) [low]
56	Hy	(Hysteria)

   B. Introversion

77	SOD	(Social Discomfort)
78	Si	(Social Introversion)
71	Si1	(Shyness/Self-Consciousness)
69	Si2	(Social Avoidance)
[36]	Pd3	(Social Imperturbability) [low]
[40]	Hy1	(Denial of Social Anxiety) [low]
[39]	Hy-S	(Hysteria, Subtle) [low]

2. Social Alienation

69	Sc1	(Social Alienation)
71	Pd4	(Social Alienation)
*67	Sc	(Schizophrenia)
69	Si3	(Alienation—Self and Others)
*85	Pd	(Psychopathic Deviate)
69	Si2	(Social Avoidance)

3. Self-Alienation

68	LSE	(Low Self-Esteem)
82	Pd5	(Self-Alienation)
49	Sc2	(Emotional Alienation)
[56]	Ma4	(Ego Inflation) [low]

4. Masculinity/Femininity

43	Mf	(Masculinity-Femininity)
35	GF	(Gender Role—Feminine)
32	GM	(Gender Role—Masculine)
[56]	Ma4	(Ego Inflation)z [low=Feminine; high=Masculine]

5. Family Alienation

68	FAM	(Family Problems)
80	Pd1	(Familial Discord)
69	Sc1	(Social Alienation)
72	F	(Infrequency)
4/4	L&W	(Family Conflict)

6. Delinquency/Antisocial Practices

62	Pd2	(Authority Conflict)
4/9	L&W	(Antisocial Attitude)
[38]	Re	(Social Responsibility) [low]
75	ASP	(Antisocial Practices)
[35]	GF	(Gender Role—Feminine) [low]

(continued)

TABLE 8.6 MMPI-2 Structural Summary, Example 2 (continued)

INTERPERSONAL RELATIONS (CONTINUED)

7. Authority Conflict/Antisocial Attitudes
    - 75 ASP (Antisocial Practices)
    - 58 CYN (Cynicism)
    - 4/9 L&W (Antisocial Attitude)
    - [38] Re (Social Responsibility) [low]
    - [35] GF (Gender Role—Feminine) [low]

8. Passive/Aggressive Struggles
    - 56 Ma_4 (Ego Inflation)
    - 65 Sc_4 (Lack of Ego Mastery, Conative)
    - 41 TPA (Type A)

9. Passivity/Submissiveness
    - 42 Hy_2 (Need for Affection)
    - 84 D_2 (Psychomotor Retardation)
    - [56] Ma_4 (Ego Inflation) [low]
    - [62] Pd_2 (Authority Conflict) [low]
    - 68 LSE (Low Self-Esteem)
    - 43 Mf (Masculinity-Femininity)
    - [41] TPA (Type A) [low]

10. Dependency
    - 69 Si_3 (Alienation—Self and Others)
    - 68 LSE (Low Self-Esteem)

- 78 WRK (Work Interference)
- [32] GM (Gender Role—Masculine) [low]
- 40 Hy_1 (Denial of Social Anxiety)
- [36] Pd_3 (Social Imperturbability) [low]

11. Dominance/Assertiveness
    - 30 Do (Dominance)
    - [68] LSE (Low Self-Esteem) [low]
    - 36 Pd_3 (Social Imperturbability)
    - [71] Si_1 (Shyness/Self-Consciousness) [low]
    - [78] Si (Social Introversion) [low]
    - 32 GM (Gender Role—Masculine)
    - [48] O-H (Overcontrolled-Hostility) [low]

12. Narcissism
    - 36 Pd_3 (Social Imperturbability)
    - [71] Si_1 (Shyness/Self-Consciousness) [low]
    - [77] SOD (Social Discomfort) [low]
    - [68] LSE (Low Self-Esteem) [low]
    - 41 TPA (Type A)

OTHER PROBLEM AREAS

1. Substance Abuse
    - 84 AAS (Addiction Admission)
    - 54 APS (Addiction Potential)
    - 56 MAC-R (MacAndrew Alcoholism—Revised)
    - 82 Pd_5 (Self-Alienation)
    - 7/7 K-B (Situational Stress Due to Alcoholism)
    - 3/3 L&W (Substance Abuse)

2. Suicidal Ideation
    - 49 Sc_2 (Emotional Alienation)
    - 77 DEP (Depression)
    - 65 Sc_4 (Lack of Ego Mastery, Conative)

- 68 D_5 (Brooding)
- 3/5 Items 150, 303, 506, 520, 524 endorsed "true"

3. Sleep Disturbances
    - 69 ANX (Anxiety)
    - *71 Pt (Psychasthenia)
    - 84 D_1 (Subjective Depression)
    - 83 D-O (Depression, Obvious)
    - 67 Hy-O (Hysteria, Obvious)
    - *67 Sc (Schizophrenia)
    - 3/6 L&W (Sleep Disturbance)

4. Sexual Difficulties
    - *67 Sc (Schizophrenia)
    - 2/6 L&W (Sexual Concern and Deviation)

Note. From the MMPI-2 Structural Summary by R. L. Greene and D. S. Nichols, Copyright © 1995 by Psychological Assessment Resources, Inc., Odessa, FL. Reprinted with permission of the publisher.
*Non-K-corrected T scores are entered for clinical scales *Hs, Pd, Pt, Sc,* and *Ma.*

suicide. She should be assessed for the potential for suicide.

HEA = 61   She has an usual number of concerns about her health.

BIZ = 41   She does not report strange thoughts or experiences.

ANG = 47   She is not moody, irritable, or angry.

CYN = 58   She is not cynical.

ASP = 75   She reported stealing things, other problem behaviors, and antisocial practices during her school years. She has attitudes similar to individuals who break the law, even if she is not engaging in antisocial behavior.

ASP1 = 70   She has beliefs and attitudes of an antisocial nature. She has little respect for the law, and does not see a need to maintain an orderly society. She views crime and criminals with a forgiving, almost admiring attitude. She is less likely to attend religious services and functions.

ASP2 = 71   She has a history of antisocial behaviors and problems in school, and may have been in trouble with the law. She may abuse drugs or engage in other reckless and illegal behavior.

TPA = 41   She is not a hard-driving, fast-moving, work-oriented person.

LSE = 68   She has a very low opinion of herself and is uncomfortable if people say nice things about her. She believes that she is unattractive, awkward and clumsy, useless, and a burden to others, who do not like her. She sees herself as not as good or capable as others, and she cannot do anything well.

LSE2 = 75   She tends to give in to others very easily, is readily downed in an argument, and is generally prone to follow the advice and lead of others, showing little or no initiative. She is viewed as being passive and obedient, and being prone to give up too easily.

SOD = 77   She is very uneasy around others and is happier by herself. She sees herself as shy. She dislikes parties and other group events.

SOD1 = 73   She is prone to dislike the company of others to the point of avoiding interpersonal contact. She does not like attending parties or other social events where she will have to interact with others. She is viewed by others as keeping people at a distance.

SOD2 = 69   She is shy and uncomfortable in social situations. She may wish that she were not so shy and were more comfortable around people. She finds it particularly difficult to interact with new people or people whom she does not know fairly well.

FAM = 68   She reports considerable familial discord. Her family lacks love, support, and companionship, and she wanted to leave home. Family members are nervous and have quick tempers. They are to be avoided and may be hated.

FAM2 = 77   She reports feeling alienated and unattached to her family. She does not view her family as a source of emotional support and she does not have strong emotional ties to her family.

WRK = 78   She is not as able to work as she once was and she works under a great deal of tension. She is tired, lacks energy, and is sick of what she has to do. She dislikes making decisions and lacks self-confidence. She gives up easily and shrinks from facing a crisis or problem.

$TRT = 72$ She dislikes going to doctors and she believes that she should not discuss her personal problems with others. She prefers to take drugs or medicine, since talking about problems does not help. She does not believe that anyone understands or cares about her. She gives up quickly and does not care about what is happening to her, since nothing can be done about her problems.

$TRT1 = 76$ She is unmotivated or may feel unable to do much to help herself at this time. She may be viewed as apathetic, having given up on her chances for improving her situation. Others view her as being prone to give up too easily and lacking in self-confidence.

$TRT2 = 75$ She feels that she is unable to open up to others, including members of the helping professions. She is very uncomfortable in discussing personal information and believes that others are unable to understand her.

Rankings of Content Component Scales.

Table 8.11 contains the rankings of all of the Content Component scales for this patient as well as for the prototypic *2-4/4-2* codetype. She is experiencing more familial alienation (*FAM2*) and is more submissive (*LSE2*) than most patients. She has less explosive behavior (*ANG1*), gastrointestinal symptoms (*HEA1*), and general health concerns (*HEA3*) than the prototypic patient.

Supplementary Scales.
(Chapter 6)

$MAC-R = 23$
(raw score) She has a normal balance between risk-taking and risk-avoiding behaviors.

$APS = 54$ She has a normal score.

$AAS = 84$ She is acknowledging her widespread use and probable abuse of alcohol or other substances. She is likely to have legal problems and problems in controlling her anger.

$Do = 30$ She is reluctant to take charge of her own life. She is reporting a significant degree of generalized distress and negative emotionality.

$Es = 30$ She is reporting a significant degree of generalized distress and negative emotionality.

$GM = 32$ She is socially introverted and has a cynical outlook on life. She is reporting a significant degree of generalized distress and negative emotionality.

$GF = 35$ She has little interest in typical feminine activities. She is experiencing a significant amount of emotional distress and may abuse substances.

$MDS = 79$ She is reporting significant distress in her marital relations. She is alienated from others and generally distressed.

$O-H = 48$ She has a normal degree of anger and awareness of her problems.

$Re = 38$ She is unconcerned about social conventions and may have antisocial characteristics.

Profile Interpretation[12]

Test-Taking Behaviors. The client endorsed the items consistently (*VRIN*, $|F - F_B|$) and accurately ($F - K$; $F[p]$). She is experiencing a mild to moderate degree of emotional distress (*F* scale). She is admitting to personal and emotional problems, is requesting assistance with these problems, and is unsure of her own capabilities for dealing with these problems (Validity scale configuration).

---

12. The parenthetical references to specific scales or indexes are provided so clinicians can see the source(s) for the statements in the interpretation. These parenthetical references would be deleted in an actual report.

TABLE 8.11 Ranking of Content Components for Example 2

Content Components for MMPI-2 Codetypes		
Profile Example 2		
	Scale	T Score
DEP4	Suicidal Ideation	93
DEP1	Lack of Drive	80
WRK	Work Interference	78
FAM2	Familial Alienation	77
TRT1	Low Motivation	76
DEP3	Self-Depreciation	75
LSE2	Submissiveness	75
TRT2	Inability to Disclose	75
SOD1	Introversion	73
DEP2	Dysphoria	72
ANX	Anxiety	71
ASP2	Antisocial Behavior	71
ASP1	Antisocial Attitudes	70
SOD2	Shyness	69
HEA2	Neurological Symptoms	67
OBS	Obsessiveness	67
CYN1	Misanthropic Beliefs	62
FAM1	Family Discord	62
LSE1	Self-Doubt	62
HEA3	General Health Concerns	56
ANG2	Irritability	54
CYN2	Interpersonal Suspiciousness	54
BIZ2	Schizotypal Characteristics	47
TPA1	Impatience	46
BIZ1	Psychotic Symptomatology	44
FRS2	Multiple Fears	43
HEA1	Gastrointestinal Symptoms	43
FRS1	Generalized Fearfulness	42
ANG1	Explosive Behavior	39
TPA2	Competitive Drive	36

Content Components for MMPI-2 Codetypes		
Prototypic 2-4/4-2		
	Scale	T Score
DEP1	Lack of Drive	72
DEP2	Dysphoria	72
ANX	Anxiety	68
DEP3	Self-Depreciation	68
DEP4	Suicidal Ideation	67
WRK	Work Interference	66
TRT1	Low Motivation	66
HEA3	General Health Concerns	65
LSE1	Self-Doubt	65
FAM2	Familial Alienation	64
FAM1	Family Discord	60
SOD1	Introversion	59
ASP2	Antisocial Behavior	59
HEA1	Gastrointestinal Symptoms	58
OBS	Obsessiveness	57
ANG2	Irritability	56
ANG1	Explosive Behavior	54
LSE2	Submissiveness	54
CYN1	Misanthropic Beliefs	54
TRT2	Inability to Disclose	54
BIZ2	Schizotypal Characteristics	54
HEA2	Neurological Symptoms	54
FRS1	Generalized Fearfulness	53
SOD2	Shyness	53
CYN2	Interpersonal Suspiciousness	53
TPA1	Impatience	53
ASP1	Antisocial Attitudes	52
TPA2	Competitive Drive	51
BIZ1	Psychotic Symptomatology	49
FRS2	Multiple Fears	49

Moods. The client is depressed, guilty, withdrawn, and self-deprecating (Scale *2*). Pessimism, depression, and hopelessness are pervading her life (Scale *2*). She is uncertain about her future and finds her life empty and meaningless (*DEP*). She reports suicidal ideation that should be evaluated carefully (*DEP*). She has a very low opinion of herself, and believes that she is unattractive, awkward and clumsy, useless, and a burden to others who do not like her (*LSE*). She is tired, lacks energy, and is sick of what she has to do (*WRK*). She does not believe that anyone understands or cares about her (*TRT*).

She also is worried, tense, and indecisive (Scales *7, A, ANX*). Her agitation and anxiety are readily apparent to her and to others (Scale *7*).

She does not describe herself as being angry or having problems in controlling her anger (*ANG*).

Cognitious. The client has great difficulty making decisions, ruminates excessively, and has intrusive thoughts (*OBS*). She vacillates between pitying herself and blaming others for her difficulties (*2-4/4-2* codetype). She did not report any strange thoughts or unusual experiences (*BIZ*). She has concentration and memory difficulties because of her extensive depressive symptomatology and does not trust her judgment (Scale 2).

Interpersonal Relations.   The client is significantly more introverted than her peers (Scale 0). She is shy and socially insecure (SOD). She withdraws from and avoids significant others, which serves to exacerbate her problems since others might be able to help her (Scale 0). She is very uncomfortable around others and is happier by herself (SOD).

She has traditional feminine interests and activities (Scale 5).

She has considerable familial discord (Pd_1, FAM). Her family lacks love, support, and companionship. Her family members are nervous and have quick tempers.

Treatment.   The client's significant depressive symptomatology and general hopelessness about her life must be directly addressed (Scale 2, DEP). Her suicidal ideation needs to be evaluated carefully and monitored on an ongoing basis, particularly as her mood begins to improve (DEP). Depending on the severity of her depression and the sources of distress in her current situation, antidepressant medication may be appropriate (Scale 2).

Her family is a significant part of her current distress and should be an initial focus in therapy (Pd_1, FAM). Involvement of her spouse and other members of the family is important if meaningful behavior change is to occur (2-4/4-2 codetype).

Therapeutic interventions should be directive and supportive (Scale 8). Group therapy would be very beneficial since it would directly counteract her tendency to isolate herself and avoid other people (Scale 0), and it would help her realize that other people have similar problems. Neither individual nor group therapy should be confrontive until a good therapeutic relationship has been established (LSE).

She reports a history of antisocial behaviors that needs to be reviewed to determine whether such behaviors are still being expressed (ASP). These antisocial behaviors may reflect issues around her family or more general antisocial behavior.

Diagnostic Impression.

Axis I   300.40   Rule out Dysthymia
Axis II   301.82   Rule out Avoidant Personality
                    Disorder
          301.60   Rule out Dependent Personality
                    Disorder

Computer Interpretation: The Minnesota Report[13]

Profile Validity.   This is a valid MMPI-2 clinical profile. The client has cooperated in the evaluation, admitting to a number of psychological problems in a frank and open manner. Individuals with this profile tend to be blunt and may openly complain to others about their psychological problems. The client tends to be quite self-critical and may appear to have inadequate psychological defense mechanisms. She may be seeking psychological help at this time because she feels that things are out of control and unmanageable.

Symptomatic Patterns.   The personality and behavioral descriptions provided by this MMPI-2 profile code incorporated correlates of D, Pt, and Pd. These descriptions are likely to be a good match with the empirical literature because of the client's well-defined profile type. Individuals with this MMPI-2 clinical profile tend to exhibit a pattern of chronic psychological maladjustment. The client appears to be quite anxious and depressed at this time. She may be feeling some tension and somatic distress along with her psychological problems and may want relief from situational pressures. Individuals with this profile tend to have long-standing personality problems and are presently experiencing situational distress. Although they might express a desire to change and may feel remorse over past behavior, they tend to change only temporarily, eventually drifting back into the old pattern.

Apparently quite immature and hedonistic, she may have a recent history of impulsive, acting-out behavior and substance abuse that resulted in considerable situational stress. She exhibits a pattern of

13. Adult Clinical System-Revised. Copyright © 1989, 1993 by the Regents of the University of Minnesota. All rights reserved.

superficial guilt or remorse about her behavior, but she does not accept much responsibility for her actions. She may avoid confrontation and deny problems.

In addition, the following description is suggested by the content of the client's item responses. She has endorsed a number of items suggesting that she is experiencing low morale and a depressed mood. She reports a preoccupation with feeling guilty and unworthy. She feels that she deserves to be punished for wrongs she has committed. She feels regretful and unhappy about life, and she seems plagued by anxiety and worry about the future. She feels hopeless at times and feels that she is a condemned person. She has difficulty managing routine affairs, and the items she endorsed suggest a poor memory, concentration problems, and an inability to make decisions. She appears to be immobilized and withdrawn and has no energy for life. She views her physical health as failing and reports numerous somatic concerns. She feels that life is no longer worthwhile and that she is losing control of her thought processes.

According to her response content, there is a strong possibility that she has seriously contemplated suicide. She endorsed items suggesting a history of suicidal ideation. It is important to perform a suicide assessment and, if necessary, take appropriate precautions. She has acknowledged having suicidal thoughts recently. Although she denies suicidal attempts in the past, given her current mood, an evaluation of suicidal potential appears to be indicated. The client's recent thinking is likely to be characterized by obsessiveness and indecision. She feels somewhat self-alienated and expresses some personal misgivings or a vague sense of remorse about past acts. She feels that life is unrewarding and dull, and she finds it hard to settle down. She reports some antisocial beliefs and attitudes, admits to rule violations, and acknowledges antisocial behavior in the past.

Profile Frequency.   Profile interpretation can be greatly facilitated by examining the relative frequency of clinical scale patterns in various settings. The client's high-point clinical scale score (D) occurs in 7% of the MMPI-2 normative sample of women. However, only 4.4% of the women have D scale peak scores at or above a T score of 65, and only 2.1% have well-defined D spikes. This elevated MMPI-2 profile configuration (2-4/4-2) is very rare in samples of normals, occurring in less than 1% of the MMPI-2 normative sample of women.

This high-point MMPI-2 score is very frequent among various inpatient women. In the Graham and Butcher (1988) sample, the D scale occurs as the high point in 12.2% of the females (12.2% of the cased are at or above a T score of 65, and 8.4% are well defined in that range). In the NCS inpatient sample, the high-point clinical scale score on D occurs in 25.4% of the women. Moreover, 24.3% have the D scale spike at or over a T score of 65, and 13.8% produce well-defined D scale peak scores in that range.

This elevated MMPI-2 profile configuration (2-4/4-2) is found in 3.1% of the females in the Graham and Butcher (1988) sample and in 5.9% of the females in the NCS inpatient sample.

The client scored relatively highly on *AAS,* suggesting the possibility of a drug- or alcohol-abuse problem. The base rate data on her profile type among residents in alcohol and drug programs should also be evaluated. Her high-point MMPI-2 score, *D,* is the second highest peak score among women in alcohol- and drug-abusing populations. Over 20.1% of the women in substance-abuse treatment programs have this peak scale elevation in their profile pattern (McKenna & Butcher, 1987).

Profile Stability.   The relative scale elevation of the highest scales in her clinical profile reflects high profile definition. If she is retested at a later date, the peak scores on this test are likely to retain their relative salience in her retest profile pattern. Her high-point score on D is likely to remain stable over time. Short-term test-retest studies have shown a correlation of 0.77 for this high-point score.

Interpersonal Relations.   The client is probably experiencing disturbed interpersonal relationships, possibly owing to her acting-out behavior.

The content of this client's MMPI-2 responses suggests the following additional information concerning her interpersonal relations. Her social relationships are likely to be viewed by others as problematic. She may be visibly uneasy around others, sits alone in group situations, and dislikes engaging in group activities.

Diagnostic Considerations. Individuals with this profile are often diagnosed as having a personality disorder (dependent or passive-aggressive type) with a substance use disorder. Her response content is consistent with the antisocial features in her history. These factors should be taken into consideration in arriving at a clinical diagnosis. The alcohol or drug problems she has acknowledged in her responses should be taken into consideration in any diagnostic evaluation. Her self-reported tendency toward experiencing depressed mood should be taken into consideration in any diagnostic formulation.

Treatment Considerations. Individuals with this profile code type may seek psychological therapy in an effort to reduce the current situational distress they are experiencing. The sincerity of their motivation to change their behavior should be carefully evaluated. They may verbalize a great need for help and may show early gains, but as frustration mounts, they may terminate early. Acting-out behavior is a possibility once the clients' anxiety and depression about their current problems diminish. They are probably experiencing multiple problems that make it difficult to focus treatment. Long-term behavioral change may be difficult to obtain.

Individuals with this profile are often predisposed to substance use or abuse disorders. Any treatment program involving medication should be carefully monitored. Some individuals with this profile attempt to manipulate others through suicidal gestures. Thus, the possibility that clients might use prescription medication for that purpose should also be taken into consideration.

The client endorsed item content that seems to indicate low potential for change. She may feel that her problems are not addressable through therapy and that she is not likely to benefit much from psychological treatment at this time. Her apparently negative treatment attitudes may need to be explored early in therapy if treatment is to be successful.

Her item content suggests some family conflicts that are causing her considerable concern at this time. She feels unhappy about her life and resents having an unpleasant home life. Psychological intervention could profitably focus, in part, on clarifying her feelings about her family.

In any intervention or psychological evaluation program involving occupational adjustment, her negative work attitudes could become an important problem to overcome. She has a number of attitudes and feelings that could interfere with work adjustment.

Her acknowledged problems with alcohol or drug use should be addressed in therapy.

Computer Interpretation: MMPI-2 Adult Interpretive System[14]

Profile matches and scores for the client are provided in Table 8.12.

Configural Interpretation.
Codetype: 2-7/7-2-(4).
Clinical Presentation:
Moods. The client is experiencing a moderate level of emotional distress characterized by dysphoria, brooding, and agitation. She also is irritable and grouchy. She experiences little pleasure from life, and life in general is a strain for her. She is likely to overreact to minor stress with agitation, guilt, self-reproach, and self-punishment. She lacks self-confidence and feels insecure, inadequate, and inferior. She is unlikely to express anger overtly or to be aggressive toward others.

Cognitions. The client is well aware of her personal deficiencies and views herself as useless and "no good at all." She has a hard time concentrating and finds it difficult to keep her mind on a task or job. She believes that her judgment is poor and that she has memory problems. She is reluctant to start a task, and she gives up quickly when things go

---

14. From the MMPI-2 Adult Interpretive System, Copyright © 1998 by Psychological Assessment Resources, Inc., Odessa, FL. Reproduced with permission of the publisher.

TABLE 8.12 Profile Matches and Scores for Standard Validity and Clinical Scales

Best Three Matches with Client's Profile:

DISCRIMINANT FUNCTION			COHEN'S INDEX			DEVIATION SQUARED		
Codetype	*Score*	*Probability*	*Codetype*	*rc*	*Percentile*	*Codetype*	*D²*	*Percentile*
2-4/4-2	165.930	.790	*2-4/4-2-(0)*	0.966	99%	*2-8/8-2-(0)*	1,222	64%
2-0/0-2	164.307	.156	*2-0/0-2-(4)*	0.927	95%	*2-7/7-2-(4)*	1,001	62%
4-0/0-4	162.641	.029	Spike 2-(4)	0.831	94%	*2-4/4-2-(7)*	980	56%

	Scale	Client's Profile *2-4/4-2-(0)*	Best Fit Prototype Profile *2-7/7-2-(4)*
Codetype:		*2-4/4-2-(0)*	*2-7/7-2-(4)*
rc:		0.966	0.913
D²:		1,016	1,001
	L	38–	48
	F	72	64
	K	41	47
1	*Hs*	57	60
2	*D*	92+	81
3	*Hy*	56	61
4	*Pd*	84+	73
5	*Mf*	43	48
6	*Pa*	52	60
7	*Pt*	72	80
8	*Sc*	66	67
9	*Ma*	49	48
0	*Si*	81+	62
Mean Clinical Elevation:		62	61
Scatter:		17	13
Client Age:		32	38
Men (Percent):			45%
Women (Percent):		X	55%

Note. From the MMPI-2 Adult Interpretive System, Copyright © 1998 by Psychological Assessment Resources, Inc., Odessa, FL. Reproduced with permission of the publisher.

wrong. Her inertia and lack of drive reflect her depressive cognitions and negative expectations. Making any type of decision is very difficult for her, and making important decisions is nearly impossible. She is pessimistic and hopeless about the possibility of any substantial change in her circumstances. She feels guilty when her high standards and expectations are not met.

Interpersonal Relations. The client is very shy and introverted. She is easily embarrassed and generally uncomfortable around others. She finds it difficult to talk with people whom she does not know and will avoid people if given the opportunity. She is alienated from others and herself. She is passive and dependent in her relationships with others.

Other Problem Areas.   The client is likely to have suicidal ideation that should be evaluated carefully. She may abuse substances secondary to an underlying mood disorder. She is likely to prefer drugs in the sedative/hypnotic class if she uses them. She finds it difficult to sleep. Sleep medications should be prescribed cautiously, if at all, because of the potential for suicide.

Treatment.   The client's prognosis is good. She sees herself as being responsible for her difficulties and is willing to examine her behavior. Cognitive-behavioral psychotherapy focusing on her depressive cognitions will be very beneficial to her. Evaluation for antidepressant medication may be indicated in cases of more severe depression.

Possible Diagnoses.
Axis I   Rule out Mood Disorders
292.84   Substance-Induced Mood Disorder
296.xx   Major Depressive Disorder
296.xx   Bipolar I Disorder, Depressed
296.89   Bipolar II Disorder, Depressed
300.4   Dysthymic Disorder

Rule out Substance-Related Disorders
305.00   Alcohol Abuse
305.20   Cannabis Abuse
305.40   Sedative, Hypnotic, and Anxiolytic Abuse
305.50   Opioid Abuse

Rule out Adjustment Disorders
309.0   Adjustment Disorder with Depressed Mood
309.28   Adjustment Disorder with Mixed Anxiety and Depressed Mood

Rule out Anxiety Disorders
300.02   Generalized Anxiety Disorder
Axis II   Rule out Personality Disorders
301.6   Dependent Personality Disorder
301.82   Avoidant Personality Disorder

Computer Interpretation: Caldwell Report[15]

Test-Taking Attitude.

Attention and Comprehension.   The client's score on the Variable Response Inconsistency scale (*VRIN*) was unelevated; her item responses were self-consistent throughout the inventory. This suggests that she was clearly able to read and comprehend the test items, that she was attentive in considering her responses, and that she consistently matched the item numbers in the booklet to the corresponding numbers on the answer sheet. She does not appear to have had any difficulties in understanding the content or responding to the format of the inventory.

Attitude and Approach.   Considering scales *L, F,* and *K,* the client was open and mildly self-critical in her approach to the inventory. The profile appears valid by the usual criteria for these scales.

She made a few atypical and rarely given responses to the items occurring in the last half of the inventory (scale F_B). These were not notably disproportionate to her frequency of atypical responses to the earlier MMPI-2 items (scale *F*). The profile does not appear to be of questionable validity because of atypical responding.

Sociocultural Influences vs. Conscious Distortion. The supplemental Validity scales show that the client obtained a somewhat elevated score on the "fake bad" scale (*Ds*), although her score on the *F* (rare answer) scale was not exceptionally elevated. This most likely indicates an overemphasis on if not a mild exaggeration of her distresses in responding to the items. It should be noted that some confused and marginally or overtly psychotic patients have shown this degree of willingness to admit a variety of peculiar but genuinely experienced symptoms without conscious exaggeration. Her score on the *K* scale is in the average range, and her score on the scale measuring her currently attained, recently experienced, or self-perceived socioeconomic status (*Ss*) is at or above average. These scores suggest a person of

15. The permission of Dr. Alex B. Caldwell, Caldwell Report, Los Angeles, California, to reproduce this report is gratefully acknowledged.

about average to above average socioeconomic status identification who appears openly willing to admit to psychological symptoms and distresses, if not somewhat overstating them.

Symptoms and Personality Characteristics. The profile shows a severe level of anxiety and depression. The pattern suggests extremely low moods and complaints of nervousness, worry, fears, self-doubts, feelings of inferiority, and loss of initiative. The client appears prone to overreact with excessive anxiety and poorly regulated emotions to minor matters or even fancied threats. She is apt to become quite tense and ruminative and to have chronic difficulties in getting to sleep. The current level of her day-to-day coping and immediate practical self-sufficiency tests as partially disorganized in a variety of areas.

The profile indicates a severe passive-aggressive or related personality disorder. She is likely to get many secondary gains from her symptoms, even though her undercontrol of her impulses and lapses of judgment are self-defeating in the long run. Her ability to conform socially tests as poor. Repeated difficulties and conflicts over limits on her behavior are suggested. She appears quite immature and insecure with indications of repeated misunderstandings and long-standing resentments in her close personal relationships. She tests as vulnerable to increasing difficulties with alcohol.

Persisting problems in regulating her expressions of anger are indicated along with chronic, underlying resentments over dependency frustrations. Fears of confirming her self-dislike would lead to a self-protective interpersonal distancing. These fears would, however, repeatedly block self-assertive expressions of anger.

The client's profile is related to the dependency-manipulative, "Daddy's girl" lifestyle pattern. She would play a daughter-to-father role toward her husband, relating in dependent and immature ways to him as well as to other males in her life. She is likely to be seen as clutching onto men in masochistic or even self-destructive relationships and as becoming symptomatic when she was threatened with losing such quasi-paternal supports. The husbands of patients with this pattern have a notably high frequency of psychological breakdowns. This pattern is typi-

cally associated with histories of almost no premarital dating. She tests as severely introverted and socially shy. She appears mildly to moderately withdrawn. Her balance of masculine and feminine interests is within the normal range for women.

Diagnostic Impression. The diagnoses most commonly associated with this profile are of depressive and anxiety neuroses. Secondary diagnoses such as the passive-dependent type of personality trait disturbance are also typical. A few of these patients showed secondary schizoid trends.

Treatment Considerations. The profile suggests a mild suicide risk; this could become serious if the client's situation grew worse and her depression became more intense. In some similar cases the use of alcohol effectively became a slow form of suicide. Antidepressants and energizers have been of limited benefit with patients who obtained similar profiles. Her responses suggest a serious risk of chronic alcoholism, if not a self-destructive use of alcohol. Her responses suggest asking if she has been in trouble with the law. If currently involved, the stress of this could have precipitated or aggravated her symptoms or otherwise have led her to make professional contact. The profile emphasizes the importance of contacts with her relatives or other informants. The clarification of all the precipitating circumstances would be particularly indicated including possible adjustments to them that she may fail to mention.

The family can be of specific benefit in minimizing the secondary gains. Treatment motivation is apt to decline as soon as her situation begins to improve and external stresses are reduced. Many patients with this pattern have terminated treatment before the therapist felt it to be complete, some against therapeutic advice. The client tests as very prone to manipulate treatment, and the character problems strongly warn against involvement in her manipulations. She is apt to be outwardly obliging because of her needs for attention and affection, which would obscure her underlying resentments and passive-aggressive tendencies. The treatment relationship may develop slowly because of her fears of being hurt and her emotional distortions. In general her emotional constrictions and her tendency to declare certain topics "off limits" could necessitate careful handling and patience in therapy. If she is currently going through an intense life crisis, then she may show fairly rapid and extensive emotional changes. Subsequent retesting is apt to be more than usually informative for reevaluating such shifts and for updating treatment directions and goals.

The expected response to short-term treatment is fair to good. The client tests as prone to focus in interviews on her fears, worries, and shortcomings. She could benefit from a greater awareness of the ways in which she sacrifices long-term goals for immediate gratifications and relief of anxiety. She could also benefit from an increased awareness of the manipulations and countermanipulations of guilt around her victim role. New activities in which she has to exert initiative with a risk of failure are apt to require repeated encouragement and reassurances. These could include projects to develop new activities and interests as well as initiative in dealing with current personal dilemmas.

General Comments

All four interpretations are in general agreement about the primary features of this client's profile: mild to moderate depression and anxiety with associated guilt; difficulties with interpersonal relations, particularly with members of her family; significant social introversion and avoidance of social interaction; history of antisocial behavior; presence of suicidal ideation; and obsessive and ruminative thoughts.

The four interpretations did not concur whether the client was angry and hostile; antidepressant medications would be appropriate; acting out will occur; substance use or abuse is a problem; and the client should have a personality disorder diagnosis. It is apparent that the computer-based test interpretations were having a hard time deciding whether the *2-4/4-2* codetype reflected a personality disorder, some form of depressive disorder, and/or a substance use disorder. This confusion is real since all three diagnoses were appropriate for the client given her history. Her discharge diagnoses from the hospital were Heroin Dependence; Alcohol Dependence, in Remission; Dysthymia; and Dependent Personality Disorder.

It is interesting to note that all four interpretations only discussed suicidal ideation since the client did not report any suicide attempts despite her history and reasons for being hospitalized. In this specific instance, all four interpretations were incorrect because the client did not provide accurate information. All four interpretations did stress the importance of evaluating her suicidal ideation carefully.

The client made satisfactory progress while hospitalized and was discharged with a significant improvement in her mood. Although she verbalized insight into her familial problems and the changes that she needed to make in her life, she chose to return to live with her disabled spouse. Subsequent follow-up interviews as an outpatient did not reveal any significant changes in her life circumstances.

CHAPTER 9

Effects of Demographic Variables and Setting

Clinicians generally are aware that a number of demographic variables such as age, gender, education, and ethnicity may have a potential effect on the interpretation of the MMPI-2. However, there is little systematic research that has investigated the influence of any single demographic variable on specific MMPI or MMPI-2 scales or codetypes, let alone combinations of these variables. Only the variables of age in the comparison of adolescents and adults and ethnic group membership in the comparison of blacks and whites have been explored in any real depth.

The setting in which the MMPI-2 is administered also has a substantial effect on MMPI-2 scores. The MMPI-2 is used routinely to screen police officers, firefighters, airflight crew members as well as many other groups for the presence of psychopathology. In these personnel-screening situations, persons realize that acknowledging the presence of any type of psychopathology decreases substantially the probability of their selection; consequently, they minimize reporting any symptoms of psychopathology and significantly lower the overall elevation of their MMPI-2 profiles. The MMPI-2 also is used frequently in forensic evaluations in which there may be motivation *to acknowledge* (criminal cases in which the person pleads not guilty by reason of insanity; workers' compensation cases) or *not to acknowledge* (child custody evaluations; parole evaluations) psychopathology, which elevates or lowers the resulting MMPI-2 profile, respectively. The reader should recall that deviant responses, responses like the criterion group, are scored on the MMPI-2 scales so that acknowledging the presence of psychopathology serves to increase scale scores and to elevate the MMPI-2 profile and vice versa.

This chapter will begin with an overview of the effects of a single demographic variable on MMPI-2

performance. (Greene [1991] and Gynther [1983] have summarized the research on the effects of demographic variables on MMPI performance.) In analyzing the effects of demographic variables, a criterion of a difference of at least one-half of a standard deviation (5 T points) will be used to denote significance. This criterion reflects that differences less than one-half of a standard deviation or an effect size of .50 (Cohen, 1988) are within the standard error of measurement for most MMPI-2 scales and are unlikely to have any clinical significance. Next, the effects of combinations of demographic variables will be reviewed briefly. The chapter will conclude with a discussion of the effects of the setting in which the MMPI-2 is administered and the resulting impact on scores.

CALDWELL CLINICAL DATASET

Before starting the overview of the effects of demographic variables on MMPI-2 performance, it is necessary to describe the Caldwell (1997a) clinical dataset that will be the primary data source for most of the analyses in this chapter and that has been used repeatedly in the earlier chapters. The Caldwell clinical dataset consists of 52,543 MMPI-2s from psychiatric inpatients and outpatients that were sent to the Caldwell Report for scoring and/or interpretation. This sample actually is a subset of a still larger sample that is being accumulated that was not completed when these analyzes were made. Given the size of the current Caldwell clinical dataset, the loss of the additional MMPI-2s did not seem to be a serious problem.

The first step in analyzing the Caldwell (1997a) clinical dataset was to run frequency distributions on a number of scales used to assess the validity of an MMPI-2 profile. Descriptions of these scales were provided in Chapter 3. Outliers were defined as cases that approached or exceeded the 99th percentile in the frequency distribution of each scale. Table 9.1 lists each scale, the criterion used to define an outlier, and the number of cases that were deleted by the criterion. The same exclusionary criteria were applied to both the Caldwell clinical dataset and the MMPI-2 normative group so that any comparisons between these two groups would be comparable on these variables. A total of 1,577 (3.0%) cases were excluded from the Caldwell clinical dataset and 11 (0.4%) cases from the MMPI-2 normative group, which resulted in sample sizes of 50,966 and 2,589, respectively. The demographic characteristics of the Caldwell clinical dataset and this subset of the entire MMPI-2 normative group are presented in Table 9.2.

AGE

Specific norms are not provided by age on the MMPI-2, even though it is well known that there are substantial effects of age below the age of 20. These age effects are reflected in the development of separate sets of adolescent norms for the original MMPI (Marks & Briggs, 1972), and the restandardization of a different form of the MMPI for adolescents (MMPI-A: Butcher et al., 1992). The performance of adolescents

on the MMPI and MMPI-A will be reviewed in Chapter 10.

Table 9.3 (pp. 433–435) provides the mean scores for the MMPI-2 Validity and Clinical scales by age in ten-year ranges for normal individuals (Butcher et al., 1989; Butcher et al., 1991) and the Caldwell (1997a) clinical dataset. The large sample sizes in all of these groups suggest that any age effects that are found should be stable and generalize to other groups. Given that these age comparisons involve different cohorts being tested in each range of years (i.e., a cross-sectional comparison), it is not possible to know for sure whether these effects actually reflect the influence of age or some other difference between the cohorts.

There appear to be minimal age effects on any of the MMPI-2 Validity scales in these three samples with the exception that T scores on the *L* (Lie) scale increased 6 to 7 points across the six ten-year ranges in the MMPI-2 normative group (Table 9.3). There also were minimal age effects in these three samples on any of the Clinical scales except for Scales *4* (Psychopathic Deviate), *6* (Paranoia), and *9* (Hypomania). There were decreases of nearly 10 T points on Scale *4, 6,* and *9* across the six ten-year ranges. There were increases of almost 10 T points from the 20 to 29 to

TABLE 9.1   Validity Measures and Exclusionary Criteria

	CLINICAL[a]	NORMAL[b]
Total Number of MMPI-2s	*52,543*	*2,600*
VALIDITY MEASURE AND CRITERION	NUMBER OF CASES EXCLUDED	NUMBER OF CASES EXCLUDED
Omissions (?) > 30 items	266	1
Variable Response Inconsistency (*VRIN*) scale > 14	416	1
True Response Inconsistency (*TRIN*) scale > 15	56	2
True Response Inconsistency (*TRIN*) scale < 4	55	3
Infrequency-Psychopathology (*F[p]*) scale > 10	555	0
Percent of True Responses > 74%	54	0
Percent of False Responses > 76%	419	7
Total Number of Cases Excluded[c]	1,577 (3.0%)	11 (0.4%)

[a]Caldwell (1997a).

[b]Butcher et al. (1989).

[c]Some cases met more than one exclusionary criterion so that the total number of cases excluded does not equal the sum of the cases excluded by each criterion.

TABLE 9.2 Demographic Characteristics of the Caldwell Clinical
Dataset and the MMPI-2 Normative Group

Variable	CLINICAL[a]		NORMAL[b]	
	N	Percentage	N	Percentage
Age				
18–19	959	1.9%	48	1.9%
20–29	10,979	21.5	638	24.6
30–39	16,201	31.8	768	29.7
40–49	12,927	25.4	398	15.4
50–59	5,703	11.2	320	12.4
60–69	1,737	3.4	277	10.7
70+	498	1.0	140	5.4
Missing	1,962	3.8	0	0.0
M	37.3		41.0	
SD	12.4		15.3	
Gender				
Men	25,203	49.5%	1,131	43.7%
Women	25,763	50.5	1,458	56.3
Education				
1– 8 Years	1,457	2.9%	21	0.8%
9–10 Years	2,215	4.3	50	1.9
11–12 Years	14,449	28.4	691	26.7
13–14 Years	10,395	20.4	465	18.0
15–16 Years	9,524	18.7	882	34.1
17–18 Years	4,315	8.5	317	12.2
19+ Years	3,058	6.0	163	6.3
Missing	5,553	10.9	0	0.0
M	12.5		14.7	
SD	5.2		2.6	
Marital Status				
Never Married	15,256	29.9%	516	19.9%
Married	19,567	38.4	1,709	66.0
Separated	3,161	6.2	55	2.1
Divorced	7,614	14.9	220	8.5
Widowed	655	1.3	89	3.4
Missing	4,713	9.2	0	0.0

[a]Caldwell (1997a).
[b]Butcher et al. (1989).

TABLE 9.3 Age Effects on MMPI-2 Validity and Clinical Scales

| | AGE RANGE | | | | | | | |
	18–19	*20–29*	*30–39*	*40–49*	*50–59*	*60–69*	*70+*	*Correlation*
L (Lie)								
Normal[a]	48.2	48.9	48.7	49.4	51.2	52.9	54.9	.171
Normal[b]	47.3							
Normal[c]	52.9							
Normal[d]				53.6	54.5	56.2	56.9	
Clinical[e]	51.6	55.2	55.5	54.6	54.7	56.1	57.5	.006
F (Infrequency)								
Normal[a]	57.5	51.3	49.4	49.0	49.1	48.4	49.8	−.095
Normal[b]	53.5							
Normal[c]	57.0							
Normal[d]				48.7	47.4	47.3	47.4	
Clinical[e]	65.9	57.6	57.8	59.0	59.8	57.7	55.3	.007
K (Correction)								
Normal[a]	45.6	48.9	50.6	49.9	50.7	50.8	50.1	.064
Normal[b]	47.7							
Normal[c]	46.6							
Normal[d]				52.5	54.1	54.0	53.0	
Clinical[e]	46.1	51.5	52.1	51.5	50.9	51.0	51.2	.000
Scale *1* (Hypochondriasis)								
Normal[a]	50.8	49.0	48.6	50.4	51.1	52.1	53.4	.085
Normal[b]	51.6							
Normal[c]	51.5							
Normal[d]				50.7	49.8	50.8	52.4	
Clinical[e]	58.7	57.4	61.0	63.9	67.4	66.3	64.9	.164
Scale *2* (Depression)								
Normal[a]	47.5	48.3	49.3	50.1	51.1	51.7	53.8	.129
Normal[b]	48.3							
Normal[c]	49.5							
Normal[d]				49.4	50.4	51.7	53.7	
Clinical[e]	61.4	58.8	62.1	64.8	68.1	66.1	64.2	.149
Scale *3* (Hysteria)								
Normal[a]	48.7	49.0	49.4	50.7	51.7	50.4	51.8	.086
Normal[b]	49.7							
Normal[c]	47.7							
Normal[d]				52.7	52.0	51.3	50.7	
Clinical[e]	58.5	58.4	63.0	66.1	69.0	66.6	63.4	.185

(continued)

TABLE 9.3   Age Effects on MMPI-2 Validity and Clinical Scales (continued)

| | AGE RANGE | | | | | | | |
	18–19	20–29	30–39	40–49	50–59	60–69	70+	Correlation
Scale 4 (Psychopathic Deviate)								
Normal[a]	54.4	51.5	50.9	50.3	48.8	46.9	44.8	–.227
Normal[b]	53.1							
Normal[c]	54.6							
Normal[d]				50.1	47.3	46.1	43.9	
Clinical[e]	63.9	59.5	60.1	60.0	59.0	56.0	51.7	–.052
Scale 5 (Masculinity-Femininity)								
Normal[a]	50.9	51.2	50.5	49.0	49.2	49.2	49.1	–.039
Normal[b]	48.1							
Normal[c]	43.7							
Normal[d]				44.6	44.7	43.5	44.8	
Clinical[e]	52.1	50.8	51.0	50.9	50.7	50.5	50.8	.048
Scale 6 (Paranoia)								
Normal[a]	50.6	51.8	50.4	49.7	49.6	47.8	45.9	–.161
Normal[b]	52.9							
Normal[c]	53.1							
Normal[d]				48.2	46.2	45.5	44.3	
Clinical[e]	64.3	58.9	61.2	61.7	61.3	58.1	53.3	.005
Scale 7 (Psychasthenia)								
Normal[a]	54.2	51.4	50.2	48.7	49.3	49.2	49.6	–.110
Normal[b]	54.9							
Normal[c]	54.1							
Normal[d]				46.3	45.5	45.7	46.5	
Clinical[e]	64.4	59.0	60.3	61.8	63.1	60.7	57.2	.036
Scale 8 (Schizophrenia)								
Normal[a]	57.3	51.6	49.9	48.6	49.5	48.5	48.2	–.141
Normal[b]	55.5							
Normal[c]	56.4							
Normal[d]				46.5	44.6	45.4	45.9	
Clinical[e]	67.1	59.5	60.3	62.0	63.2	61.2	56.8	.027
Scale 9 (Hypomania)								
Normal[a]	61.1	53.1	49.5	49.1	48.9	47.1	46.6	–.213
Normal[b]	56.7							
Normal[c]	58.6							
Normal[d]				47.9	46.7	44.8	44.0	
Clinical[e]	59.4	53.2	51.6	51.2	50.7	50.2	48.1	–.101

	AGE RANGE							
	18–19	*20–29*	*30–39*	*40–49*	*50–59*	*60–69*	*70+*	*Correlation*
Scale *0* (Social Introversion)								
Normal[a]	48.3	48.7	50.2	50.3	50.3	51.0	51.1	.064
Normal[b]	48.1							
Normal[c]	49.7							
Normal[d]				48.6	48.5	49.7	51.7	
Clinical[e]	54.1	50.6	51.8	53.4	54.6	53.9	52.9	.086

[a]Butcher et al. (1989). [b]Butcher et al. (1990a). [c]Butcher et al. (1991). [d]Butcher et al. (1990b).
[e]Caldwell (1997a).

the 50 to 59 age range in the Caldwell (1997a) clinical dataset on Scales *1* (Hypochondriasis), *2* (Depression), and *3* (Hysteria), and then decreases of nearly 5 T points in the next two age ranges. This pattern of changes with age was not seen in either sample of normal individuals on these three scales except that scores on Scale *2* increased slightly over 5 points in the MMPI-2 normative group (Table 9.3).

There are five conclusions that can be drawn from this analysis of age effects on the MMPI-2 Validity and Clinical scales. First and probably most important, age effects were very similar in normal individuals and psychiatric patients across most of these scales. Second, T scores on Scales *4* (Psychopathic Deviate), *6* (Paranoia), and *9* (Hypomania) decreased about 10 T points with age. Third, the increases in T scores on Scales *1* (Hypochondriasis), *2* (Depression), and *3* (Hysteria) in psychiatric patients appeared to reach their peak in the 50–59 age range and start decreasing thereafter, which is not seen in the normal individuals. Fourth, these age effects typically did not exceed 10 T points and were more likely to be in the range of 5 to 7 T points on those scales that were impacted by age, which is only somewhat larger than the standard error of measurement. Finally, persons under the age of 20 generally had the highest scores and persons over the age of 70 had the lowest scores on the Validity and Clinical scales so that age effects were maximized when these two extreme age groups were compared. In the age range of 21 to 69, however, there were minimal age effects.

Given that there were age differences on some of the MMPI-2 Clinical scales, the next logical question to ask is whether age impacts the frequency with which MMPI-2 codetypes occurred in the Caldwell (1997a) clinical dataset. It seems logical to assume that if Scales *1* (Hypochondriasis), *2* (Depression), and *3* (Hysteria) increased with age in psychiatric patients, then codetypes composed of these three scales should increase in frequency with age, too. Similarly, if Scales *4* (Psychopathic Deviate) and *9* (Hypomania) decreased with age, then codetypes composed of these two scales should decrease in frequency with age. Table 9.4 provides the frequency with which all of the spike and two-point MMPI-2 codetypes occurred in the same age ranges used in the previous analysis. Spike *1*, *1-2/2-1*, and *1-3/3-1* codetypes consistently increased in frequency across these six age ranges and these three codetypes were two or three times more frequent in the 70+ age range than in the 20–29 age range. Not only were these three codetypes more frequent in the older age ranges, they also comprised over 40 percent of all codetypes found in the 70+ age range and under 13 percent in the 20–29 age range. Patients with these three codetypes frequently have a diagnosis within the category of Somatoform Disorders, so the next question is whether the diagnosis of Somatoform Disorders varies with age. Studies of the lifetime prevalence of DSM-III (Robins et al., 1984) and DSM-III-R (Kessler et al., 1994) diagnoses have found that most psychiatric diagnoses decline with age and higher socioeconomic status. Somatoform Disorders diagnoses were relatively uncommon at all

TABLE 9.4 Frequency of MMPI-2 Codetypes in the Caldwell Clinical Dataset within Specific Age Ranges

| | AGE RANGE | | | | | | | | | | | | | | Total | |
| | 18–19 | | 20–29 | | 30–39 | | 40–49 | | 50–59 | | 60–69 | | 70+ | | | |
CODETYPE	N	%	N	%	N	%	N	%	N	%	N	%	N	%	N	%
Spike 1	8	1.0	69	1.0	145	1.3	123	1.3	69	1.6	36	2.8	21	5.7	471	1.4
1-2/2-1	12	1.6	184	2.7	479	4.4	496	5.4	310	7.1	109	8.4	47	12.8	1,637	4.9
1-3/3-1	31	4.0	594	8.8	1,516	14.0	1,606	17.5	974	22.2	292	22.5	88	24.0	5,101	15.2
1-4/4-1	3	0.4	49	0.7	75	0.7	53	0.6	29	0.7	5	0.4	0	0.0	214	0.6
1-5/5-1	3	0.4	31	0.5	41	0.4	35	0.4	19	0.4	11	0.8	3	0.8	143	0.4
1-6/6-1	2	0.3	49	0.7	143	1.3	102	1.1	52	1.2	23	1.8	3	0.8	374	1.1
1-7/7-1	2	0.3	52	0.8	59	0.5	42	0.5	28	0.6	13	1.0	4	1.1	200	0.6
1-8/8-1	8	1.0	75	1.1	146	1.3	131	1.4	76	1.7	34	2.6	8	2.2	478	1.4
1-9/9-1	5	0.6	29	0.4	50	0.5	35	0.4	17	0.4	7	0.5	2	0.5	145	0.4
1-0/0-1	1	0.1	6	0.1	20	0.2	22	0.2	8	0.2	5	0.4	0	0.0	62	0.2
Spike 2	7	0.9	53	0.8	134	1.2	95	1.0	60	1.4	23	1.8	16	4.4	388	1.2
2-3/3-2	17	2.2	346	5.1	808	7.4	925	10.1	519	11.8	133	10.2	39	10.6	2,787	8.3
2-4/4-2	16	2.1	209	3.1	287	2.6	208	2.3	83	1.9	17	1.3	4	1.1	824	2.5
2-5/5-2	1	0.1	25	0.4	33	0.3	36	0.4	11	0.3	4	0.3	2	0.5	112	0.3
2-6/6-2	15	1.9	198	2.9	383	3.5	301	3.3	133	3.0	40	3.1	7	1.9	1,077	3.2
2-7/7-2	38	4.9	372	5.5	554	5.1	518	5.7	293	6.7	78	6.0	18	4.9	1,871	5.6
2-8/8-2	20	2.6	197	2.9	303	2.8	278	3.0	173	3.9	48	3.7	11	3.0	1,030	3.1
2-9/9-2	0	0.0	11	0.2	11	0.1	9	0.1	3	0.1	0	0.0	0	0.0	34	0.1
2-0/0-2	14	1.8	88	1.3	196	1.8	217	2.4	94	2.1	26	2.0	10	2.7	645	1.9
Spike 3	5	0.6	101	1.5	249	2.3	255	2.8	105	2.4	44	3.4	13	3.5	772	2.3
3-4/4-3	11	1.4	140	2.1	262	2.4	213	2.3	83	1.9	19	1.5	4	1.1	732	2.2
3-5/5-3	2	0.3	21	0.3	31	0.3	36	0.4	18	0.4	4	0.3	0	0.0	112	0.3
3-6/6-3	10	1.3	93	1.4	286	2.6	212	2.3	92	2.1	22	1.7	1	0.3	716	2.1
3-7/7-3	10	1.3	73	1.1	147	1.4	125	1.4	54	1.2	22	1.7	2	0.5	433	1.3
3-8/8-3	9	1.2	72	1.1	135	1.2	120	1.3	64	1.5	15	1.2	3	0.8	418	1.2
3-9/9-3	1	0.1	16	0.2	37	0.3	42	0.5	10	0.2	3	0.2	0	0.0	109	0.3
3-0/0-3	0	0.0	3	0.0	5	0.0	3	0.0	2	0.0	1	0.1	0	0.0	14	0.0
Spike 4	37	4.8	286	4.2	474	4.4	304	3.3	84	1.9	13	1.0	2	0.5	1,200	3.6
4-5/5-4	6	0.8	57	0.8	72	0.7	34	0.4	16	0.4	5	0.4	0	0.0	190	0.6

	N	%	N	%	N	%	N	%	N	%	N	%	N	%	N	%
4-6/6-4	42	5.4	287	4.3	369	3.4	238	2.6	84	1.9	11	0.8	0	0.0	1,031	3.1
4-7/7-4	20	2.6	154	2.3	136	1.3	77	0.8	23	0.5	6	0.5	0	0.0	416	1.2
4-8/8-4	32	4.1	187	2.8	199	1.8	132	1.4	37	0.8	12	0.9	1	0.3	600	1.8
4-9/9-4	34	4.4	128	1.9	120	1.1	58	0.6	12	0.3	1	0.1	0	0.0	353	1.1
4-0/0-4	2	0.3	15	0.2	21	0.2	18	0.2	7	0.2	2	0.2	0	0.0	65	0.2
Spike 5	20	2.6	453	6.7	465	4.3	257	2.8	92	2.1	31	2.4	10	2.7	1,328	4.0
5-6/6-5	6	0.8	37	0.5	47	0.4	38	0.4	12	0.3	7	0.5	1	0.3	148	0.4
5-7/7-5	3	0.4	16	0.2	28	0.3	12	0.1	5	0.1	0	0.0	2	0.5	66	0.2
5-8/8-5	3	0.4	26	0.4	19	0.2	12	0.1	5	0.1	4	0.3	2	0.5	71	0.2
5-9/9-5	6	0.8	71	1.1	45	0.4	27	0.3	13	0.3	5	0.4	2	0.5	169	0.5
5-0/0-5	2	0.3	9	0.1	16	0.1	11	0.1	3	0.1	1	0.1	0	0.0	42	0.1
Spike 6	9	1.2	142	2.1	379	3.5	251	2.7	86	2.0	14	1.1	6	1.6	887	2.6
6-7/7-6	20	2.6	129	1.9	172	1.6	92	1.0	45	1.0	6	0.5	1	0.3	465	1.4
6-8/8-6	72	9.3	463	6.9	585	5.4	431	4.7	159	3.6	38	2.9	4	1.1	1,752	5.2
6-9/9-6	20	2.6	94	1.4	103	0.9	69	0.8	20	0.5	4	0.3	1	0.3	311	0.9
6-0/0-6	4	0.5	25	0.4	47	0.4	46	0.5	10	0.2	3	0.2	1	0.3	136	0.4
Spike 7	6	0.8	54	0.8	59	0.5	41	0.4	12	0.3	3	0.2	3	0.8	178	0.5
7-8/8-7	56	7.2	297	4.4	358	3.3	318	3.5	102	2.3	38	2.9	6	1.6	1,175	3.5
7-9/9-7	8	1.0	36	0.5	21	0.2	18	0.2	5	0.1	2	0.2	0	0.0	90	0.3
7-0/0-7	5	0.6	32	0.5	55	0.5	32	0.3	13	0.3	3	0.2	1	0.3	141	0.4
Spike 8	8	1.0	48	0.7	26	0.2	30	0.3	11	0.3	5	0.4	2	0.5	130	0.4
8-9/9-8	39	5.0	125	1.9	81	0.7	47	0.5	16	0.4	7	0.5	4	1.1	319	1.0
8-0/0-8	3	0.4	25	0.4	29	0.3	27	0.3	4	0.1	1	0.1	0	0.0	89	0.3
Spike 9	47	6.1	311	4.6	289	2.7	190	2.1	68	1.6	24	1.8	7	1.9	936	2.8
9-0/0-9	1	0.1	4	0.1	2	0.0	1	0.0	0	0.0	0	0.0	0	0.0	8	0.0
Spike 0	12	1.6	69	1.0	106	1.0	111	1.2	57	1.3	18	1.4	5	1.4	378	1.1
Subtotal	774	80.7	6,736	61.4	10,858	67.0	9,160	70.9	4380	76.8	1,298	74.7	367	73.7	33,573	64.5
WNL	185	19.3	4,243	38.6	5,343	33.0	3,767	29.1	1,323	23.2	439	25.3	131	26.3	17,393	35.5
Total	959	100.0	10,979	100.0	16,201	100.0	12,927	100.0	5,703	100.0	1737	100.0	498	100.0	49,004	100.0

Note. The percentages for specific codetypes are reported as a function of the number of codetypes represented in the subtotal row because they represent the actual number of clinical patients who produced a clinical elevation on the scale(s).

ages, but particularly so over age 65. The decrease in prevalence for these Disorders with age obviously cannot account for the increase in the frequency of Spike *1*, *1-2/2-1*, and *1-3/3-1* codetypes with age. Thus, the age effects, which were seen on Scales *1*, *2*, and *3* when these scales were considered individually, persisted when they were combined into codetypes.

Spike *4* and *4-9/9-4* codetypes demonstrated a consistent decrease in frequency across these same age ranges and comprised less than 1 percent of all codetypes in the 70+ age range, while they comprised nearly 6 percent in the 20–29 age range. Patients with these codetypes frequently have a diagnosis of Antisocial Personality Disorder, which is much more common in men and also declines with age (Kessler et al., 1994; Robins et al., 1984). The decline in the frequency of Spike *4* and *4-9/9-4* codetypes followed the same pattern as the lifetime prevalence of the diagnosis of Antisocial Personality Disorder.

Table 9.5 lists the 20 most frequently occurring MMPI-2 codetypes within these seven age ranges. The *1-3/3-1* codetypes were the most frequent codetypes in all age ranges (8.9 to 24.0%) except 18- to 19-year-olds (4.0%) and the frequency of this codetype increased with age as noted earlier. The *6-8/8-6* codetypes also occurred frequently, particularly in the younger age ranges (1.1 to 9.3%) and they decreased in frequency with age. The *2-7/7-2* codetypes were common in all age ranges and did not change in frequency (4.9 to 6.7%).

There were virtually no age effects on the MMPI-2 Content scales (Butcher et al., 1990) in any of these three samples, except that the 18- to 19-year-olds had T scores on a number of the Content scales (Depression [*DEP*], Bizarre Mentation [*BIZ*], Anger [*ANG*], Cynicism [*CYN*], and Antisocial Practices [*ASP*]) that were 5 to 8 T points higher than the 20- to 29-year-olds (Table 9.6, pp. 440–441). There also were only five Content scales (Anxiety [*ANX*], Depression [*DEP*], Health Concerns [*HEA*], Work Interference [*WRK*], and Negative Treatment Indicators [*TRT*]) on which the clinical sample consistently had higher scores than the normal samples. The same pattern of T scores increasing about 5 to 8 T points from age 20 to 59 and declining thereafter was seen on the Content scales of *HEA* and *DEP* as was found on

Scales *1* (Hypochondriasis) and *2* (Depression). Given the similarity between these pairs of Clinical and Content scales, it is important to note that Scale *4* (Psychopathic Deviate) and the *ASP* scale did not demonstrate the same pattern between them. The *ASP* scale showed little change after age 30 while Scale *4* continued to decline consistently across the age span.

There also were virtually no age effects on the MMPI-2 Supplementary scales (Butcher et al., 1989) in any of these three samples, except that again the 18- to 19-year-olds had T scores on several of the scales (Welsh Anxiety [*A*], Back Infrequency [F_B], Post Traumatic Stress Disorder—Keane [*PK*], Post Traumatic Stress Disorder—Schlenger [*PS*]) that were 5 to 8 T points higher than 20- to 29-year-olds (Table 9.7, pp. 442–443). Again, the pattern of few differences between the normal sample and the clinical sample was found in all age ranges except for the Welsh Repression (*R*), Ego Strength (*Es*), F_B, College Maladjustment (*Mt*), *PK*, and *PS* scales. All of these scales except the *R* scale are measures of generalized distress and negative emotionality and should be higher in clinical samples. It is remarkable that these scales are not more elevated relative to the MMPI-2 normative group.

Finally, the effects of age on specific MMPI-2 items selected because of their content can be examined (Table 9.8, pp. 444–445). (No attempt was made to identify those items that demonstrated the largest changes with age.) The frequency of endorsement of items addressing substance use (264, 489, and 511), anger (389 and 548), and suicide (303, 506, and 524) declined consistently with age in both normal and clinical samples. There were several items, however, that did not demonstrate the differences in the frequency of endorsement between clinical and normal samples that might be expected. For example, normal individuals were as likely to endorse items reflecting excessive use of alcohol (Item 264), trouble with the law (Item 266), being hotheaded (Item 389), getting high or drunk (Item 511), and hurting someone in a physical fight (Item 548) as clinical patients. This finding that normal individuals were as, or more, likely to endorse specific items needs to be kept in mind when the MMPI-2 is interpreted at the item level. This issue was explored in Chapter 6 when "critical" items were discussed.

TABLE 9.5 Ranking of the Frequency of MMPI-2 Codetypes in the Caldwell Clinical Dataset within Specific Age Ranges

AGE RANGE

18–19		20–29		30–39		40–49		50–59		60–69		70+		Total	
CODETYPE	%	CODETYPE	%	CODETYPE	%	CODETYPE	%	CODETYPE	%	CODETYPE	%	CODETYPE	%	CODETYPE	%
6-8/8-6	9.3	1-3/3-1	8.8	1-3/3-1	14.0	1-3/3-1	17.5	1-3/3-1	22.2	1-3/3-1	22.5	1-3/3-1	24.0	1-3/3-1	15.2
7-8/8-7	7.2	6-8/8-6	6.9	2-3/3-2	7.4	2-3/3-2	10.1	2-3/3-2	11.8	2-3/3-2	10.2	1-2/2-1	12.8	2-3/3-2	8.3
Spike 9	6.1	Spike 5	6.7	6-8/8-6	5.4	2-7/7-2	5.7	1-2/2-1	7.1	1-2/2-1	8.4	2-3/3-2	10.6	2-7/7-2	5.6
4-6/6-4	5.4	2-7/7-2	5.5	2-7/7-2	5.1	1-2/2-1	5.4	2-7/7-2	6.7	2-7/7-2	6.0	Spike 1	5.7	6-8/8-6	5.2
8-9/9-8	5.0	2-3/3-2	5.1	Spike 4	4.4	6-8/8-6	4.7	2-8/8-2	3.9	2-8/8-2	3.7	2-7/7-2	4.9	1-2/2-1	4.9
2-7/7-2	4.9	Spike 9	4.6	1-2/2-1	4.4	7-8/8-7	3.5	6-8/8-6	3.6	Spike 3	3.4	Spike 2	4.4	Spike 5	4.0
Spike 4	4.8	7-8/8-7	4.4	Spike 5	4.3	2-6/6-2	3.3	2-6/6-2	3.0	2-6/6-2	3.1	Spike 3	3.5	Spike 4	3.6
4-9/9-4	4.4	4-6/6-4	4.3	Spike 6	3.5	Spike 4	3.3	Spike 3	2.4	6-8/8-6	2.9	2-8/8-2	3.0	7-8/8-7	3.5
4-8/8-4	4.1	Spike 4	4.2	2-6/6-2	3.5	2-8/8-2	3.0	7-8/8-7	2.3	7-8/8-7	2.9	2-0/0-2	2.7	2-6/6-2	3.2
1-3/3-1	4.0	2-4/4-2	3.1	4-6/6-4	3.4	Spike 3	2.8	2-0/0-2	2.1	Spike 1	2.8	Spike 5	2.7	2-8/8-2	3.1
2-8/8-2	2.6	2-6/6-2	2.9	7-8/8-7	3.3	Spike 5	2.8	3-6/6-3	2.1	1-8/8-1	2.6	1-8/8-1	2.2	4-6/6-4	3.1
4-7/7-4	2.6	2-8/8-2	2.9	2-8/8-2	2.8	Spike 6	2.7	Spike 5	2.1	Spike 5	2.4	2-6/6-2	1.9	Spike 9	2.8
6-7/7-6	2.6	4-8/8-4	2.8	Spike 9	2.7	4-6/6-4	2.6	Spike 6	2.0	2-0/0-2	2.0	Spike 9	1.9	Spike 6	2.6
6-9/9-6	2.6	1-2/2-1	2.7	3-6/6-3	2.6	2-0/0-2	2.4	2-4/4-2	1.9	1-6/6-1	1.8	7-8/8-7	1.6	2-4/4-2	2.5
Spike 5	2.6	4-7/7-4	2.3	2-4/4-2	2.6	2-4/4-2	2.3	3-4/4-3	1.9	Spike 2	1.8	Spike 6	1.6	Spike 3	2.3
2-3/3-2	2.2	3-4/4-3	2.1	3-4/4-3	2.4	3-4/4-3	2.3	4-6/6-4	1.9	Spike 9	1.8	Spike 0	1.4	3-4/4-3	2.2
2-4/4-2	2.1	Spike 6	2.1	Spike 3	2.3	3-6/6-3	2.3	Spike 4	1.9	3-6/6-3	1.7	1-7/7-1	1.1	3-6/6-3	2.1
2-6/6-2	1.9	4-9/9-4	1.9	4-8/8-4	1.8	Spike 9	2.1	1-8/8-1	1.7	3-7/7-3	1.7	2-4/4-2	1.1	2-0/0-2	1.9
2-0/0-2	1.8	6-7/7-6	1.9	2-0/0-2	1.8	1-8/8-1	1.8	Spike 1	1.6	3-4/4-3	1.5	3-4/4-3	1.1	4-8/8-4	1.8
1-2/2-1	1.6	8-9/9-8	1.9	6-7/7-6	1.6	3-7/7-3	1.4	Spike 9	1.6	Spike 0	1.4	6-8/8-6	1.1	1-8/8-1	1.4

TABLE 9.6 Age Effects on MMPI-2 Content Scales

	AGE RANGE							
	18–19	*20–29*	*30–39*	*40–49*	*50–59*	*60–69*	*70+*	*Correlation*
Anxiety (*ANX*)								
Normal[a]	52.1	51.0	50.5	49.9	48.9	47.5	48.1	−.128
Normal[b]				48.3	46.8	45.5	45.4	
Clinical[c]	61.7	56.6	58.3	59.8	61.1	58.8	55.9	.063
Fears (*FRS*)								
Normal[a]	50.6	48.7	48.6	50.1	51.2	53.2	53.4	.129
Normal[b]				46.1	49.0	49.1	50.3	
Clinical[c]	51.6	50.0	50.6	51.8	54.0	55.6	55.6	.113
Obsessions (*OBS*)								
Normal[a]	54.5	50.0	48.9	49.7	49.6	51.3	52.5	.042
Normal[b]				45.6	46.5	47.5	49.3	
Clinical[c]	56.8	50.3	50.1	51.2	52.7	52.6	52.9	.043
Depression (*DEP*)								
Normal[a]	54.9	51.2	49.6	49.7	49.3	49.0	50.3	−.075
Normal[b]				48.0	46.7	46.9	47.1	
Clinical[c]	62.4	55.4	56.2	58.1	59.3	57.8	56.3	.047
Health Concerns (*HEA*)								
Normal[a]	53.0	49.7	48.6	50.4	50.7	50.9	52.6	.064
Normal[b]				50.6	49.4	49.8	50.8	
Clinical[c]	59.6	55.4	58.0	60.8	64.1	63.0	61.6	.151
Bizarre Mentation (*BIZ*)								
Normal[a]	57.8	52.2	49.4	49.2	49.0	49.5	48.3	−.131
Normal[b]				46.0	46.1	46.2	46.3	
Clinical[c]	61.2	53.7	53.1	52.9	53.0	52.3	51.0	−.053
Anger (*ANG*)								
Normal[a]	56.7	51.7	50.0	50.2	48.4	47.5	47.4	−.160
Normal[b]				49.8	47.6	46.5	46.0	
Clinical[c]	55.8	50.6	50.2	50.6	50.4	49.1	47.6	−.027
Cynicism (*CYN*)								
Normal[a]	57.4	50.3	48.5	50.0	49.8	51.2	52.4	.033
Normal[b]				49.1	48.6	50.1	50.7	
Clinical[c]	55.3	50.6	49.2	49.4	50.5	51.4	51.6	−.013
Antisocial Practices (*ASP*)								
Normal[a]	59.5	52.2	49.1	49.8	48.7	47.5	48.6	−.146
Normal[b]				49.3	48.6	48.0	47.9	
Clinical[c]	56.7	50.8	48.7	48.1	48.0	47.8	47.7	−.105

	AGE RANGE							
	18–19	*20–29*	*30–39*	*40–49*	*50–59*	*60–69*	*70+*	*Correlation*
Type A (*TPA*)								
Normal[a]	54.6	49.8	49.1	50.5	50.4	49.9	50.3	.016
Normal[b]				49.5	48.4	48.5	48.2	
Clinical[c]	52.8	47.7	47.6	48.7	49.6	49.2	49.3	.050
Low Self-Esteem (*LSE*)								
Normal[a]	51.9	49.2	49.1	50.2	50.3	51.7	53.5	.092
Normal[b]				46.7	47.7	49.4	51.0	
Clinical[c]	57.9	51.6	51.9	53.2	54.4	53.8	53.6	.040
Social Discomfort (*SOD*)								
Normal[a]	47.8	49.1	50.9	50.4	50.0	49.4	49.3	.001
Normal[b]				48.3	47.9	47.7	49.0	
Clinical[c]	52.1	49.9	51.7	53.3	53.8	52.3	50.5	.085
Family Problems (*FAM*)								
Normal[a]	55.3	51.5	49.9	50.6	48.6	48.0	46.9	−.147
Normal[b]				50.3	47.0	46.6	46.1	
Clinical[c]	58.1	51.9	51.3	51.8	51.2	50.7	49.5	−.040
Work Interference (*WRK*)								
Normal[a]	53.6	50.4	49.8	49.5	49.2	50.1	50.9	−.026
Normal[b]				46.8	45.8	46.5	47.7	
Clinical[c]	60.2	52.9	53.6	55.2	56.9	55.2	54.0	.053
Negative Treatment Indicators (*TRT*)								
Normal[a]	53.7	49.7	48.6	49.7	50.8	51.4	53.8	−.026
Normal[b]				48.1	47.7	48.9	50.8	
Clinical[c]	58.9	52.6	52.9	54.5	56.0	55.7	55.5	.052

[a]Butcher et al. (1989).
[b]Butcher et al. (1991).
[c]Caldwell (1997a).

In summary, scales assessing physical symptoms (Scale *1* [Hypochondriasis], Scale *3* [Hysteria], and Health Concerns [*HEA*]) and depression (Scale *2* [Depression] and Depression [*DEP*]) increased 5 to 8 T points up to age 60, as did the frequency of code-types composed of these Clinical scales. These changes did not seem to reflect that the underlying psychopathology has increased in frequency because studies of the lifetime prevalence of DSM-III (Robins et al., 1984) and DSM-III-R (Kessler et al., 1994) diagnoses have found that most psychiatric diagnoses decline with age. Scales *4* (Psychopathic Deviate), *6* (Paranoia), and *9* (Hypomania) decreased 5 to 10 T points with age, but this decrease was not accompanied by a similar decrease in the Content scale of Antisocial Practices (*ASP*) because many of its items are

TABLE 9.7   Age Effects on MMPI-2 Supplementary Scales

| | AGE RANGE | | | | | | | |
	18–19	*20–29*	*30–39*	*40–49*	*50–59*	*60–69*	*70+*	*Correlation*
Welsh Anxiety (*A*)								
Normal[a]	55.1	50.6	49.6	49.6	49.5	49.7	50.9	−.038
Clinical[b]	59.2	52.2	52.5	53.9	55.0	54.0	52.7	.038
Welsh Repression (*R*)								
Normal[a]	44.9	47.8	49.9	50.1	51.5	51.7	53.9	.161
Clinical[b]	50.6	53.1	54.9	55.8	57.3	57.4	57.3	.136
Ego Strength (*Es*)								
Normal[a]	46.3	50.7	51.5	51.0	48.9	48.0	46.2	−.101
Clinical[b]	41.8	46.7	45.3	44.0	41.8	41.4	41.0	−.115
MacAndrew Alcoholism—Revised (*MAC-R*)								
Normal[a]	51.7	48.8	46.3	48.0	48.4	47.9	48.2	−.003
Clinical[b]	52.1	50.7	49.9	48.9	48.9	48.8	48.5	−.070
Overcontrolled-Hostility (*O-H*)								
Normal[a]	49.8	50.0	50.0	49.4	50.0	50.6	50.3	−.002
Clinical[b]	51.8	55.5	54.7	53.5	52.6	53.7	53.4	−.070
Dominance (*Do*)								
Normal[a]	43.3	48.7	51.2	51.1	51.3	50.8	48.3	.065
Clinical[b]	40.0	44.4	45.4	46.2	45.4	45.5	45.7	.064
Social Responsibility (*Re*)								
Normal[a]	42.1	47.4	50.5	50.7	52.3	52.6	53.4	.209
Clinical[b]	42.7	47.4	49.1	50.1	50.5	51.4	52.7	.137
College Maladjustment (*Mt*)								
Normal[a]	55.1	50.7	49.7	49.5	49.3	49.5	51.2	−.043
Clinical[b]	61.8	54.9	56.1	58.1	60.1	58.4	56.7	.079
Gender Role—Masculine (*GM*)								
Normal[a]	47.5	50.4	51.1	50.7	49.8	48.7	48.8	−.017
Clinical[b]	43.9	47.9	47.2	46.1	44.6	44.1	45.0	−.080
Gender Role—Feminine (*GF*)								
Normal[a]	45.1	48.8	51.9	52.5	54.1	55.2	56.2	.134
Clinical[b]	45.5	47.3	48.5	49.5	50.5	52.0	53.2	.098
Post Traumatic Stress Disorder—Keane (*PK*)								
Normal[a]	58.0	52.2	49.9	49.0	48.6	48.0	48.4	−.161
Clinical[b]	65.3	56.8	57.1	58.1	58.9	56.8	53.4	.003
Post Traumatic Stress Disorder—Schlenger (*PS*)								
Normal[a]	57.3	51.6	49.8	49.3	48.7	48.0	49.0	−.132
Clinical[b]	65.2	56.7	57.3	59.0	60.5	58.4	55.3	.035

	AGE RANGE							
	18–19	*20–29*	*30–39*	*40–49*	*50–59*	*60–69*	*70+*	*Correlation*
Addiction Admission (*AAS*)								
Normal[a]	52.9	53.8	51.4	49.0	45.9	45.4	44.9	−.300
Clinical[b]	54.1	50.7	50.1	49.3	47.3	46.0	44.9	−.124
Addiction Potential (*APS*)								
Normal[a]	51.9	50.8	50.0	49.7	48.8	47.0	45.5	−.177
Clinical[b]	51.4	47.9	48.5	49.4	49.6	48.6	47.6	.030
Marital Distress (*MDS*)								
Normal[a]	57.9	53.0	52.1	52.1	51.2	50.7	49.1	−.110
Clinical[b]	60.8	54.5	54.7	56.0	55.8	54.1	51.8	.001
Hostility (*Ho*)								
Normal[a]	57.5	50.7	48.5	49.4	48.6	49.5	50.2	−.049
Clinical[b]	56.1	50.5	49.2	49.2	49.6	49.7	49.2	−.043
Common Alcohol Logistic—Revised (*CAL-R*)								
Normal[a]	52.2	52.9	51.3	51.0	50.2	49.8	49.6	−.109
Clinical[b]	52.1	52.0	51.2	50.6	49.7	49.5	48.7	−.077

[a]Butcher et al. (1989).
[b]Caldwell (1997a).

written in the past tense and relate to school-age behaviors. It also appears that persons who were 18 to 19 years old elevated the MMPI-2 more like their younger brethren (Gumbiner, 1997; Pancoast & Archer, 1992) than persons who were 20 to 29 years old. (An analysis of the Clinical scales in one-year increments between the ages of 18 and 25 demonstrated that most of these age effects had occurred by the age of 20 or 21 depending on the specific scale being examined.) It is possible that adolescent norms may need to be extended to include 18- to 19-year-olds, although this issue will need to be resolved empirically. At a minimum, clinicians should realize that 18- to 19-year-olds tended to elevate a number of the MMPI-2 scales 5 to 10 T points higher than persons 20 to 29 years old. Finally, it should be mentioned again that these effects actually may reflect cohort differences rather than age differences because different groups of individuals were being compared.

GENDER

Hathaway and McKinley (1983) were aware of the effects of gender on MMPI profiles because they developed separate norms for all of the Clinical scales except Scales 6 (Paranoia), 9 (Hypomania), and 0 (Social Introversion). They did not develop separate norms for any of the Validity scales, although men scored slightly higher on the *F* (Infrequency) and *K* (Correction) scales, and lower on the *L* (Lie) scale.

All of the data in the tables in this section examining the effects of gender on the MMPI-2 scales will be expressed as *raw* scores. Because separate T score norms and profile sheets are used for men and women, gender cannot have any appreciable effect on MMPI-2 profiles when the data are analyzed or profiled as T scores. In fact, if gender did affect MMPI-2 profiles when expressed in T scores, that would be one basis for arguing that the T score conversions are somehow

TABLE 9.8   Age Effects on Specific MMPI-2 Items

Item	AGE RANGE (PERCENT TRUE RESPONSES)						
	18–19	*20–29*	*30–39*	*40–49*	*50–59*	*60–69*	*70+*
95 (I am happy most of the time.[a])							
Normal[b]	89.6	90.4	87.5	90.2	88.7	91.0	92.1
Clinical[c]	57.7	69.0	64.2	59.5	57.3	63.3	73.3
162 (Someone has been trying to poison me.[a])							
Normal[b]	0.0	0.8	0.4	0.3	0.6	0.7	0.7
Clinical[c]	2.3	0.9	1.6	1.6	1.9	1.7	0.8
165 (My memory seems to be all right.[a])							
Normal[b]	93.8	93.7	92.1	91.2	88.4	87.0	76.4
Clinical[c]	74.6	78.2	71.8	63.1	55.0	59.0	60.2
216 (Someone has been trying to rob me.[a])							
Normal[b]	4.2	1.4	2.0	2.8	2.8	1.8	3.6
Clinical[c]	5.4	3.3	4.2	4.7	5.5	5.8	6.6
224 (I have few or no pains.[a])							
Normal[b]	77.1	85.7	85.0	78.9	80.9	72.2	74.3
Clinical[c]	63.1	68.8	59.1	52.2	43.2	42.4	38.8
264 (I have used alcohol excessively.[a])							
Normal[b]	27.1	39.5	35.0	34.2	25.6	24.5	15.0
Clinical[c]	29.4	29.1	29.7	29.2	25.1	22.3	15.5
266 (I have never been in trouble with the law.[a])							
Normal[b]	77.1	67.7	71.5	69.6	83.1	80.5	83.6
Clinical[c]	59.5	63.0	62.5	66.8	72.0	75.3	81.1
303 (Most of the time I wish I were dead.[a])							
Normal[b]	2.1	2.4	2.2	4.0	2.8	2.5	1.4
Clinical[c]	16.4	10.2	9.4	11.3	11.4	9.4	5.8
389 (I am often said to be hotheaded.[a])							
Normal[b]	33.3	18.7	13.8	17.8	14.7	13.0	16.4
Clinical[c]	29.5	21.2	19.3	18.1	16.4	16.8	16.5
489 (I have a drug or alcohol problem.[a])							
Normal[b]	8.3	5.2	5.2	5.5	4.1	4.3	3.6
Clinical[c]	10.7	9.4	11.1	10.1	8.2	8.3	3.8
499 (I hate going to doctors even when I'm sick.[a])							
Normal[b]	37.5	29.8	31.3	37.4	36.3	30.7	34.3
Clinical[c]	38.2	39.6	41.0	41.7	44.1	44.2	38.8
506 (I recently have considered killing myself.[a])							
Normal[b]	10.4	6.1	4.2	3.3	3.4	1.4	2.9
Clinical[c]	24.2	14.5	15.7	18.0	17.4	13.9	9.2

Item	AGE RANGE (PERCENT TRUE RESPONSES)						
	18–19	*20–29*	*30–39*	*40–49*	*50–59*	*60–69*	*70+*
511 (Once a week or more I get high or drunk.[a])							
Normal[b]	20.8	24.1	15.8	9.8	6.3	5.1	1.4
Clinical[c]	17.2	10.3	8.3	6.6	5.3	3.7	2.2
520 (Lately I have thought a lot about killing myself.[a])							
Normal[b]	8.3	2.7	2.2	1.3	1.9	0.4	0.7
Clinical[c]	16.5	9.3	10.3	11.8	12.2	10.7	8.0
548 (I've been so angry at times that I've hurt someone in a physical fight.[a])							
Normal[b]	33.3	18.2	12.2	15.3	10.0	6.9	7.9
Clinical[c]	27.3	16.1	12.2	11.0	8.9	5.9	3.8

[a]Minnesota Multiphasic Personality Inventory-2 (MMPI-2). Copyright © 1942, 1943 (renewed 1970), 1989 by the Regents of the University of Minnesota. Reproduced by permission of the publisher. "MMPI-2" and "Minnesota Multiphasic Personality Inventory-2" are trademarks owned by the University of Minnesota.
[b]Butcher et al. (1989).
[c]Caldwell (1997a).

inappropriate. Raw scores are preferable for analyzing data when *only* men or women are being studied (Butcher & Tellegen, 1978), and is absolutely necessary if gender differences are to be examined.

Table 9.9 provides the mean scores for the MMPI-2 Validity and Clinical scales by gender for normal individuals (Butcher et al., 1989; Butcher et al., 1990) and the Caldwell (1997a) clinical dataset. There were minimal effects on any of the MMPI-2 Validity scales in these three samples. There were somewhat larger effects of gender on the Clinical scales with women consistently endorsing more items on Scales *1* (Hypochondriasis), *2* (Depression), *3* (Hysteria), *7* (Psychasthenia), and *0* (Social Introversion), while men endorsed more items only on Scale *9* (Hypomania). It goes without saying that there were huge effects of gender on Scale *5* (Masculinity-Femininity). These differences in the frequency of endorsement of the items were never more than two to three items across all of the Clinical scales except for Scale *5*.

There are two conclusions that can be drawn from this analysis of gender effects on the MMPI-2 Validity and Clinical scales. First, women were more willing to report negative symptoms and behaviors than men, which produced higher raw scores on a number of the Clinical scales. Second, any gender differences tended to be rather small, which should be accommodated easily through separate T score norms. Unigender norms for the MMPI-2 have been discussed (Tellegen, 1992). If unigender norms were used, they would have limited impact on the interpretation of the MMPI-2 because of these relatively small differences in raw scores between men and women.

Table 9.10 (pp. 447–448) provides the frequency with which all MMPI-2 codetypes occurred by gender and Table 9.11 (p. 448) ranks the 20 most frequently occurring MMPI-2 codetypes by gender in the Caldwell (1997a) clinical dataset. Codetypes containing Scale *8* (Schizophrenia: *6-8/8-6* and *7-8/8-7*) occurred about twice as often in men as in women, and Spike-*5* and *2-3/3-2* codetypes occurred about twice as often in women as in men. Most of the codetypes, however, occurred about equally often in men and women.

Table 9.12 (p. 449) provides the mean scores for the MMPI-2 Content (Butcher et al., 1990) scales by gender for normal individuals (Butcher et al., 1989)

TABLE 9.9 Gender Effects on MMPI-2 Validity and Clinical Scales (Raw Scores)

	MEN	WOMEN	CORRELATION[d]		MEN	WOMEN	CORRELATION[d]
L (Lie)				Scale *5* (Masculinity-Femininity)			
Normal[a]	3.5	3.6	.007	Normal[a]	26.0	36.0	.735
Normal[b]	3.3	2.8		Normal[b]	25.4	34.9	
Clinical[c]	4.6	4.7	.027	Clinical[c]	25.9	35.2	.711
F (Infrequency)				Scale *6* (Paranoia)			
Normal[a]	4.5	3.6	–.140	Normal[a]	10.1	10.2	.022
Normal[b]	5.3	4.9		Normal[b]	10.9	11.1	
Clinical[c]	7.0	6.8	–.015	Clinical[c]	13.0	13.4	.047
K (Correction)				Scale *7* (Psychasthenia)			
Normal[a]	15.3	15.0	–.029	Normal[a]	11.2	12.7	.103
Normal[b]	14.4	13.8		Normal[b]	14.1	16.5	
Clinical[c]	15.8	15.7	–.018	Clinical[c]	15.6	18.0	.105
Scale *1* (Hypochondriasis)				Scale *8* (Schizophrenia)			
Normal[a]	4.9	5.9	.117	Normal[a]	11.1	11.2	.002
Normal[b]	5.1	6.9		Normal[b]	15.0	15.5	
Clinical[c]	8.8	11.5	.166	Clinical[c]	16.7	18.2	.047
Scale *2* (Depression)				Scale *9* (Hypomania)			
Normal[a]	18.3	20.1	.185	Normal[a]	16.9	16.1	–.089
Normal[b]	17.0	19.6		Normal[b]	20.4	18.8	
Clinical[c]	23.9	27.1	.183	Clinical[c]	17.6	16.9	–.080
Scale *3* (Hysteria)				Scale *0* (Social Introversion)			
Normal[a]	20.8	22.1	.126	Normal[a]	25.8	28.0	.116
Normal[b]	20.4	22.2		Normal[b]	23.7	26.7	
Clinical[c]	25.8	28.7	.196	Clinical[c]	28.0	30.3	.103
Scale *4* (Psychopathic Deviate)							
Normal[a]	16.5	16.2	–.039				
Normal[b]	17.8	17.8					
Clinical[c]	20.5	20.3	–.017				

[a]Butcher et al. (1989).
[b]Butcher et al. (1990).
[c]Caldwell (1997a).
[d]Positive correlations reflect that women have higher scores on the scale.

and the Caldwell (1997a) clinical dataset. There were rather consistent effects of gender on the MMPI-2 Content scales in these two samples. Women were more likely to report negative symptoms and behaviors than men, which produced slightly higher raw scores on most of the Content scales: Anxiety (*ANX*); Fears (*FRS*); Obsessions (*OBS*); Depression (*DEP*); Health Concerns (*HEA*); Low Self-Esteem (*LSE*); Family Problems (*FAM*); Work Interference (*WRK*); and Negative Treatment Indicators (*TRT*). These differences typically were only one to two items. Men had higher raw scores on several of the Content scales: Cynicism (*CYN*); Antisocial Practices (*ASP*); and Type A (*TPA*). Somewhat surprisingly, there were no gender differences on the Anger (*ANG*) scale.

TABLE 9.10 Gender Effects on MMPI-2 Codetypes in the Caldwell Clinical Dataset

	MEN		WOMEN		TOTAL	
Codetype	N	%	N	%	N	%
Spike 1	268	1.7	215	1.1	483	1.4
1-2/2-1	671	4.2	1,005	5.2	1,676	4.8
1-3/3-1	2,035	12.7	3,188	16.7	5,223	14.8
1-4/4-1	97	0.6	127	0.7	224	0.6
1-5/5-1	19	0.1	126	0.7	145	0.4
1-6/6-1	188	1.2	195	1.0	383	1.1
1-7/7-1	113	0.7	89	0.5	202	0.6
1-8/8-1	272	1.7	236	1.2	508	1.4
1-9/9-1	77	0.5	81	0.4	158	0.4
1-0/0-1	33	0.2	32	0.2	65	0.2
Spike 2	212	1.3	190	1.0	402	1.1
2-3/3-2	909	5.7	1,932	10.1	2,841	8.1
2-4/4-2	313	1.9	542	2.8	855	2.4
2-5/5-2	49	0.3	64	0.3	113	0.3
2-6/6-2	399	2.5	705	3.7	1,104	3.1
2-7/7-2	888	5.5	1,046	5.5	1,934	5.5
2-8/8-2	358	2.2	717	3.7	1,075	3.1
2-9/9-2	12	0.1	24	0.1	36	0.1
2-0/0-2	339	2.1	326	1.7	665	1.9
Spike 3	372	2.3	412	2.2	784	2.2
3-4/4-3	298	1.9	454	2.4	752	2.1
3-5/5-3	42	0.3	72	0.4	114	0.3
3-6/6-3	311	1.9	423	2.2	734	2.1
3-7/7-3	239	1.5	203	1.1	442	1.3
3-8/8-3	222	1.4	217	1.1	439	1.2
3-9/9-3	38	0.2	78	0.4	116	0.3
3-0/0-3	7	0.0	7	0.0	14	0.0
Spike 4	685	4.3	583	3.0	1,268	3.6
4-5/5-4	79	0.5	125	0.7	204	0.6
4-6/6-4	565	3.5	539	2.8	1,104	3.1
4-7/7-4	236	1.5	210	1.1	446	1.3
4-8/8-4	339	2.1	353	1.8	692	2.0
4-9/9-4	237	1.5	203	1.1	440	1.2
4-0/0-4	41	0.3	29	0.2	70	0.2
Spike 5	294	1.8	1,071	5.6	1,365	3.9
5-6/6-5	84	0.5	70	0.4	154	0.4
5-7/7-5	51	0.3	17	0.1	68	0.2
5-8/8-5	23	0.1	53	0.3	76	0.2
5-9/9-5	44	0.3	143	0.7	187	0.5
5-0/0-5	27	0.2	15	0.1	42	0.1
Spike 6	494	3.1	415	2.2	909	2.6
6-7/7-6	315	2.0	178	0.9	493	1.4
6-8/8-6	1,087	6.8	842	4.4	1,929	5.5
6-9/9-6	207	1.3	149	0.8	356	1.0
6-0/0-6	89	0.6	50	0.3	139	0.4

(continued)

TABLE 9.10   Gender Effects on MMPI-2 Codetypes in the Caldwell Clinical Dataset (continued)

Codetype	MEN		WOMEN		TOTAL	
	N	%	N	%	N	%
Spike 7	119	0.7	66	0.3	185	0.5
7-8/8-7	858	5.3	405	2.1	1,263	3.6
7-9/9-7	58	0.4	40	0.2	98	0.3
7-0/0-7	108	0.7	39	0.2	147	0.4
Spike 8	87	0.5	58	0.3	145	0.4
8-9/9-8	256	1.6	168	0.9	424	1.2
8-0/0-8	65	0.4	31	0.2	96	0.3
Spike 9	590	3.7	435	2.3	1,025	2.9
9-0/0-9	6	0.0	2	0.0	8	0.0
Spike 0	240	1.5	148	0.8	388	1.1
Subtotal	16,065	63.7	19,143	74.3	35,208	69.1
WNL	9,138	36.3	6,620	25.7	15,758	30.9
Total	25,203	100.0	25,763	100.0	50,966	100.0

Note. The percentages for specific codetypes are reported as a function of the number of codetypes represented in the subtotal row because they represent the actual number of clinical patients who produced a clinical elevation on the scale(s).

TABLE 9.11   Ranking of the Frequency of MMPI-2 Codetypes within Gender in the Caldwell Clinical Dataset

MEN		WOMEN		TOTAL	
Codetype	%	Codetype	%	Codetype	%
1-3/3-1	12.7	1-3/3-1	16.7	1-3/3-1	14.8
6-8/8-6	6.8	2-3/3-2	10.1	2-3/3-2	8.1
2-3/3-2	5.7	Spike 5	5.6	2-7/7-2	5.5
2-7/7-2	5.5	2-7/7-2	5.5	6-8/8-6	5.5
7-8/8-7	5.3	1-2/2-1	5.2	1-2/2-1	4.8
Spike 4	4.3	6-8/8-6	4.4	Spike 5	3.9
1-2/2-1	4.2	2-6/6-2	3.7	7-8/8-7	3.6
Spike 9	3.7	2-8/8-2	3.7	Spike 4	3.6
4-6/6-4	3.5	Spike 4	3.0	2-6/6-2	3.1
Spike 6	3.1	2-4/4-2	2.8	2-8/8-2	3.1
2-6/6-2	2.5	4-6/6-4	2.8	4-6/6-4	3.1
Spike 3	2.3	3-4/4-3	2.4	Spike 9	2.9
2-8/8-2	2.2	Spike 9	2.3	Spike 6	2.6
2-0/0-2	2.1	3-6/6-3	2.2	2-4/4-2	2.4
4-8/8-4	2.1	Spike 3	2.2	Spike 3	2.2
6-7/7-6	2.0	Spike 6	2.2	3-4/4-3	2.1
2-4/4-2	1.9	7-8/8-7	2.1	3-6/6-3	2.1
3-4/4-3	1.9	4-8/8-4	1.8	4-8/8-4	2.0
3-6/6-3	1.9	2-0/0-2	1.7	2-0/0-2	1.9
Spike 5	1.8	1-8/8-1	1.2	1-8/8-1	1.4

TABLE 9.12   Gender Effects on MMPI-2 Content Scales (Raw Scores)

	MEN	WOMEN	CORRELATION[c]		MEN	WOMEN	CORRELATION[c]
Anxiety (*ANX*)				Antisocial Practices (*ASP*)			
Normal[a]	5.5	6.5	.114	Normal[a]	7.9	6.2	−.215
Clinical[b]	9.0	10.7	.126	Clinical[b]	7.6	6.0	−.187
Fears (*FRS*)				Type A (*TPA*)			
Normal[a]	3.8	6.6	.383	Normal[a]	8.1	7.4	−.095
Clinical[b]	4.3	6.9	.313	Clinical[b]	7.4	6.8	−.067
Obsessions (*OBS*)				Low Self-Esteem (*LSE*)			
Normal[a]	4.9	5.5	.088	Normal[a]	4.2	5.2	.111
Clinical[b]	5.3	5.9	.074	Clinical[b]	5.4	6.6	.103
Depression (*DEP*)				Social Discomfort (*SOD*)			
Normal[a]	4.8	5.9	.109	Normal[a]	7.6	7.5	−.012
Clinical[b]	8.8	10.1	.081	Clinical[b]	8.4	8.6	.015
Health Concerns (*HEA*)				Family Problems (*FAM*)			
Normal[a]	5.2	6.1	.101	Normal[a]	5.3	6.1	.110
Clinical[b]	9.0	11.4	.151	Clinical[b]	6.2	6.9	.072
Bizarre Mentation (*BIZ*)				Work Interference (*WRK*)			
Normal[a]	2.3	2.2	−.019	Normal[a]	7.3	8.5	.113
Clinical[b]	2.3	3.2	−.010	Clinical[b]	9.7	11.4	.108
Anger (*ANG*)				Negative Treatment Indicators (*TRT*)			
Normal[a]	5.6	5.7	.009	Normal[a]	4.7	5.0	.042
Clinical[b]	5.8	5.8	.001	Clinical[b]	6.3	6.9	.049
Cynicism (*CYN*)							
Normal[a]	9.5	8.7	−.072				
Clinical[b]	9.4	8.8	−.055				

[a]Butcher et al. (1989).
[b]Caldwell (1997a).
[c]Positive correlations reflect that women have higher scores on the scale.

Table 9.13 (p. 450) provides the mean scores for the MMPI-2 Supplementary scales by gender for normal individuals (Butcher et al., 1989) and the Caldwell (1997a) clinical dataset. There were several patterns of the effects of gender on the MMPI-2 Supplementary scales (Butcher et al., 1989) in these two samples. Again, women were more likely to report negative symptoms and behaviors than men, which produced slightly higher raw scores on a number of the Supplementary scales: Anxiety (*A*); College Maladjustment (*Mt*); Post Traumatic Stress Disorder—Keane (*PK*); and Post Traumatic Stress Disorder—Schlenger (*PS*), and lower raw scores on the Ego Strength (*Es*) scale. Men had slightly higher raw scores on all of the alcohol and drug scales than women: MacAndrew Alcoholism—Revised (*MAC-R*); Addiction Admission (*AAS*); Addiction Potential (*APS*); and Common Alcohol Logistic—Revised (*CAL-R*). Women had higher raw scores on the Overcontrolled-Hostility (*O-H*) scale, while men had higher raw scores on the Hostility (*Ho*)

TABLE 9.13 Gender Effects on MMPI-2 Supplementary Scales (Raw Scores)

	MEN	WOMEN	CORRELATION[c]		MEN	WOMEN	CORRELATION[c]
Welsh Anxiety (A)				Gender Role—Feminine (GF)			
Normal[a]	10.0	11.6	.106	Normal[a]	27.9	37.7	.750
Clinical[b]	12.9	14.8	.092	Clinical[b]	28.1	36.7	.706
Welsh Repression (R)				Post Traumatic Stress Disorder—Keane (PK)			
Normal[a]	15.1	16.3	.137	Normal[a]	8.0	8.5	.039
Clinical[b]	17.1	18.8	.192	Clinical[b]	12.8	14.3	.065
Ego Strength (Es)				Post Traumatic Stress Disorder—Schlenger (PS)			
Normal[a]	37.4	34.4	−.299	Normal[a]	10.5	11.8	.077
Clinical[b]	34.0	30.3	−.232	Clinical[b]	17.4	20.1	.091
MacAndrew Alcoholism—Revised (MAC-R)				Addiction Admission (AAS)			
Normal[a]	20.8	18.9	−.236	Normal[a]	2.9	2.0	−.223
Clinical[b]	21.1	18.8	−.265	Clinical[b]	2.8	2.1	−.154
Overcontrolled-Hostility (O-H)				Addiction Potential (APS)			
Normal[a]	12.5	13.5	.177	Normal[a]	23.2	22.8	−.032
Clinical[b]	13.8	14.8	.155	Clinical[b]	23.1	22.7	−.041
Dominance (Do)				Marital Distress (MDS)			
Normal[a]	16.6	16.3	−.059	Normal[a]	2.8	2.9	.024
Clinical[b]	15.1	14.6	−.062	Clinical[b]	4.1	4.3	.033
Social Responsibility (Re)				Hostility (Ho)			
Normal[a]	20.1	21.0	.128	Normal[a]	18.3	17.0	−.079
Clinical[b]	19.6	20.8	.143	Clinical[b]	18.8	17.5	−.061
College Maladjustment (Mt)				Common Alcohol Logistic—Revised (CAL-R[d])			
Normal[a]	11.3	12.3	.074	Normal[a]	126.3	117.6	−.033
Clinical[b]	15.9	18.1	.106	Clinical[b]	126.6	117.0	−.050
Gender Role—Masculine (GM)							
Normal[a]	37.5	28.8	−.609				
Clinical[b]	35.1	27.4	−.474				

[a]Butcher et al. (1989).
[b]Caldwell (1997a).
[c]Positive correlations reflect that women have higher scores on the scale.
[d]This scale is scored by adding the logistic weights for each item; this difference is slightly more than one item.

scale. The two gender role scales (Gender Role—Masculine [GM] and Gender Role—Feminine [GF]) had substantial gender differences, as would be expected. Finally, those few scales measuring positive attributes on the MMPI-2 had no appreciable gender differences: Dominance (Do) and Social Responsibility (Re).

The effects of gender on specific MMPI-2 items are provided in Table 9.14. Both normal men and men in the Caldwell (1997a) clinical dataset were more likely to endorse items reflecting excessive use of alcohol (264), trouble with the law (266), having a drug or alcohol problem (489), getting high or drunk (511), and hurting someone in a physical fight (548) than

TABLE 9.14   Gender Effects on Specific MMPI-2 Items

	PERCENTAGE OF TRUE RESPONSES			PERCENTAGE OF TRUE RESPONSES	
Item	Men	Women	*Item*	Men	Women
95 (I am happy most of the time.[a])			389 (I am often said to be hotheaded.[a])		
Normal[b]	89.8	89.2	Normal[b]	16.8	15.6
Clinical[c]	66.0	59.9	Clinical[c]	21.1	18.2
162 (Someone has been trying to poison me.[a])			489 (I have a drug or alcohol problem.[a])		
Normal[b]	0.8	0.3	Normal[b]	6.9	3.5
Clinical[c]	1.7	1.3	Clinical[c]	12.4	7.6
165 (My memory seems to be all right.[a])			499 (I hate going to doctors even when I'm sick.[a])		
Normal[b]	90.5	90.5	Normal[b]	32.7	32.6
Clinical[c]	72.6	64.7	Clinical[c]	40.2	42.6
216 (Someone has been trying to rob me.[a])			506 (I recently have considered killing myself.[a])		
Normal[b]	2.7	1.8	Normal[b]	4.6	3.8
Clinical[c]	5.0	3.9	Clinical[c]	16.0	17.0
224 (I have few or no pains.[a])			511 (Once a week or more I get high or drunk.[a])		
Normal[b]	82.1	81.3	Normal[b]	19.7	9.4
Clinical[c]	62.5	51.4	Clinical[c]	11.0	5.3
264 (I have used alcohol excessively.[a])			520 (Lately I have thought a lot about killing myself.[a])		
Normal[b]	44.6	23.0	Normal[b]	1.9	2.1
Clinical[c]	35.0	21.7	Clinical[c]	10.6	11.3
266 (I have never been in trouble with the law.[a])			548 (I've been so angry at times that I've hurt someone in a physical fight.[a])		
Normal[b]	59.5	84.2	Normal[b]	19.7	8.4
Clinical[c]	51.4	78.7	Clinical[c]	17.3	8.9
303 (Most of the time I wish I were dead.[a])					
Normal[b]	1.6	3.4			
Clinical[c]	9.2	12.2			

[a]Minnesota Multiphasic Personality Inventory-2 (MMPI-2). Copyright © 1942, 1943 (renewed 1970), 1989 by the Regents of the University of Minnesota. Reproduced by permission of the publisher. "MMPI-2" and "Minnesota Multiphasic Personality Inventory-2" are trademarks owned by the University of Minnesota.
[b]Butcher et al. (1989).
[c]Caldwell (1997a).

women. Women were somewhat more likely to endorse items reflecting suicidal ideation (303, 506, 520) than men. These differences in the endorsement of the items by gender are similar to what were found for the Clinical, Content, and Supplementary scales.

In summary, women generally were more willing to report negative symptoms and behaviors than men,

which produced higher raw scores on a number of the Clinical, Content, and Supplementary scales. Men were more likely to have higher raw scores on the alcohol and drug, antisocial, and hostility scales. These differences were similar in both normal individuals (Butcher et al., 1989) and the Caldwell (1997a) clinical dataset, and typically were in the range of two to three items. The use of separate T scores by gender eliminates even these minimal effects. Consequently, gender will have virtually no effect on the interpretation of the MMPI-2 except for the MacAndrew Alcoholism—Revised (*MAC-R*) scale because it is the only MMPI-2 scale that is interpreted routinely in raw scores.

EDUCATION

As noted in Chapter 1, the MMPI-2 normative group averaged nearly 15 years of education (Butcher et al., 1989), while the original MMPI normative group averaged around 8 years of education (Dahlstrom et al., 1972). This difference in level of education between the MMPI and the MMPI-2 has been a source of concern (cf. Caldwell, 1990). Butcher (1990) categorized the MMPI-2 normative group into five groups based on years of education and concluded that the MMPI-2 T scores showed minimal impact from education. Most of the mean scale scores for all five levels of education fell at or very near a T score of 50. Only the *K* (Correction) scale in men and women and Scale *5* (Masculinity-Femininity) in men were significantly correlated with years of education. Butcher did suggest that the interpretation of scores on Scale *5* in men with less than a high school education or with postgraduate training should be adjusted slightly to account for the small effects of education.

When the men and women in the MMPI-2 normative group with less than a high school education were contrasted with men and women with postgraduate education (Dahlstrom & Tellegen, 1993, pp. 58–59), the differences on the following scales exceeded 5 T points: *L* (Lie: women only), *F* (Infrequency), *K* (Correction), *5* (Masculinity-Femininity), and *0* (Social Introversion). Men and women with less than a high school education had higher scores in all of these comparisons except for the *K* scale and Scale *5*.

Table 9.15 provides the mean scores for the MMPI-2 Validity and Clinical scales by years of education in seven categories for normal individuals (Butcher et al., 1989) and the Caldwell (1997a) clinical dataset. There appear to be substantial effects of education on the MMPI-2 Validity and Clinical scales in both normal individuals (Butcher et al., 1989) and the Caldwell (1997a) clinical dataset. In

contrast to the findings of few differences between normal and clinical samples in the effects of age or gender, the effects of education on MMPI-2 performance did vary occasionally between these two samples. The most remarkable finding is that Scale *5* (Masculinity-Femininity) was *not* affected by years of education, because Scale *5* on the MMPI had significant education effects, particularly in men. Since there were only four items dropped on Scale *5* from the MMPI to the MMPI-2, it appears that the T scores based on the MMPI-2 normative group have eliminated the effects of education on Scale *5*. The general pattern in both normal and clinical samples was for the scores on all of the Validity and Clinical scales to decrease with increasing years of education except for the *K* (Correction) scale on which scores increased. These decreases usually were slightly larger in the clinical sample than in the normal sample and were the largest when persons with 10 years or less of education were contrasted with persons with 11 years or more of education. The complexity of the effects of education can be seen on Scale *3* (Hysteria) in which scores increased slightly in the normal sample and decreased slightly in the clinical sample with more years of education, and Scale *8* (Schizophrenia) in which scores essentially were constant in the normal sample and decreased nearly 15 T points in the clinical sample.

There are five conclusions that can be drawn from this analysis of the effects of education on the MMPI-2 Validity and Clinical scales. First, Scale *5* (Masculinity-Femininity) on the MMPI-2 was *not* affected by years of education, unlike on the MMPI. Second, the effects of education were larger than those found for age or gender. Third, T scores on most of the Validity and Clinical scales decreased 5 to 10 T points with increasing years of education in both normal and clinical samples. Fourth, these decreases tended to be slightly larger in the clinical sample than in the normal sample. Finally, the largest differences as a function of level of education were found when persons with less than 10 years of education were contrasted with persons with 11 or more years of education. It appears that clinicians need to be aware of the substantial impact of education on the interpretation of the MMPI-2, particularly in clients with 10 or fewer years of education. It is especially important to check the consistency of item

TABLE 9.15 Education Effects on MMPI-2 Validity and Clinical Scales

	EDUCATION RANGE (YEARS)							
	1–8	*9–10*	*11–12*	*13–14*	*15–16*	*17–18*	*19+*	*Correlation*
L (Lie)								
Normal[a]	58.9	53.2	51.6	49.8	48.9	49.2	48.0	–.144
Clinical[b]	57.5	55.6	56.2	55.2	53.8	52.5	51.4	–.128
F (Infrequency)								
Normal[a]	54.9	54.9	51.6	50.6	48.8	48.1	46.9	–.180
Clinical[b]	68.9	69.4	61.8	57.7	54.8	53.4	52.2	–.229
K (Correction)								
Normal[a]	45.0	42.6	47.5	48.8	51.2	53.3	53.6	.236
Clinical[b]	47.5	46.3	49.4	51.8	53.7	54.2	54.6	.196
Scale *1* (Hypochondriasis)								
Normal[a]	54.8	53.3	51.2	50.5	49.0	48.9	49.0	–.254
Clinical[b]	66.1	64.3	64.0	62.0	59.3	58.2	56.9	–.199
Scale *2* (Depression)								
Normal[a]	54.9	53.3	51.1	49.9	49.1	48.8	49.1	–.124
Clinical[b]	66.9	66.4	65.5	62.7	60.1	59.0	58.5	–.146
Scale *3* (Hysteria)								
Normal[a]	48.1	49.0	49.3	49.7	49.9	51.4	52.0	.067
Clinical[b]	65.2	63.8	64.6	63.8	62.1	61.7	61.1	–.066
Scale *4* (Psychopathic Deviate)								
Normal[a]	49.7	50.9	50.0	50.0	49.9	50.7	48.8	–.102
Clinical[b]	62.2	64.8	61.0	59.4	58.3	58.2	57.9	–.159
Scale *5* (Masculinity-Femininity)								
Normal[a]	47.7	49.0	49.4	49.5	50.2	50.5	53.3	.100
Clinical[b]	52.0	51.4	50.5	50.4	50.6	51.2	52.5	.091
Scale *6* (Paranoia)								
Normal[a]	48.1	53.0	49.4	49.5	50.3	50.6	50.4	.028
Clinical[b]	64.8	65.6	62.4	60.3	59.0	58.7	58.3	–.113
Scale *7* (Psychasthenia)								
Normal[a]	50.9	51.1	50.2	50.0	50.2	50.1	49.0	–.187
Clinical[b]	65.0	64.9	62.8	60.6	58.8	57.9	57.4	–.192
Scale *8* (Schizophrenia)								
Normal[a]	49.5	53.0	50.0	50.3	49.6	50.2	48.8	–.182
Clinical[b]	68.4	68.4	63.4	60.7	58.5	57.5	56.4	–.213
Scale *9* (Hypomania)								
Normal[a]	47.3	52.0	50.3	51.0	50.0	49.6	47.6	–.097
Clinical[b]	55.5	56.2	52.8	51.9	50.9	50.4	49.6	–.156
Scale *0* (Social Introversion)								
Normal[a]	55.6	54.1	51.8	50.0	48.9	48.3	48.9	–.169
Clinical[b]	56.2	56.5	54.7	51.7	50.1	49.6	49.5	–.181

[a]Butcher et al. (1989).
[b]Caldwell (1997a).

TABLE 9.16 Education Effects on MMPI-2 Codetypes in the Caldwell Clinical Dataset

EDUCATION RANGE (YEARS)

CODETYPE	1–8 N	1–8 %	9–10 N	9–10 %	11–12 N	11–12 %	13–14 N	13–14 %	15–16 N	15–16 %	17–18 N	17–18 %	19+ N	19+ %	Total N	Total %
Spike 1	15	1.3	15	0.8	141	1.3	106	1.5	74	1.3	40	1.5	19	1.1	410	1.3
1-2/2-1	82	6.9	83	4.5	572	5.3	383	5.5	217	3.7	89	3.4	39	2.2	1,465	4.7
1-3/3-1	174	14.6	215	11.6	1,576	14.6	1,165	16.8	878	14.9	374	14.1	221	12.3	4,603	14.8
1-4/4-1	7	0.6	17	0.9	79	0.7	44	0.6	24	0.4	12	0.5	9	0.5	192	0.6
1-5/5-1	6	0.5	9	0.5	44	0.4	30	0.4	16	0.3	10	0.4	4	0.2	119	0.4
1-6/6-1	15	1.3	22	1.2	118	1.1	98	1.4	50	0.9	27	1.0	7	0.4	337	1.1
1-7/7-1	7	0.6	10	0.5	86	0.8	40	0.6	24	0.4	10	0.4	8	0.4	185	0.6
1-8/8-1	31	2.6	45	2.4	163	1.5	103	1.5	47	0.8	13	0.5	10	0.6	412	1.3
1-9/9-1	0	0.0	8	0.4	62	0.6	27	0.4	19	0.3	8	0.3	9	0.5	133	0.4
1-0/0-1	4	0.3	4	0.2	25	0.2	14	0.2	10	0.2	0	0.0	1	0.1	58	0.2
Spike 2	10	0.8	22	1.2	116	1.1	71	1.0	76	1.3	29	1.1	31	1.7	355	0.1
2-3/3-2	63	5.3	102	5.5	953	8.9	596	8.6	482	8.2	228	8.6	149	8.3	2,573	8.3
2-4/4-2	29	2.4	37	2.0	248	2.3	189	2.7	165	2.8	70	2.6	40	2.2	778	2.5
2-5/5-2	6	0.5	5	0.3	23	0.2	14	0.2	34	0.6	8	0.3	7	0.4	97	0.3
2-6/6-2	38	3.2	44	2.4	325	3.0	207	3.0	198	3.4	98	3.7	53	2.9	963	3.1
2-7/7-2	31	2.6	93	5.0	610	5.7	406	5.9	337	5.7	140	5.3	113	6.3	1,730	5.6
2-8/8-2	49	4.1	69	3.7	391	3.6	214	3.1	124	2.1	48	1.8	46	2.6	941	3.0
2-9/9-2	1	0.1	0	0.0	16	0.1	4	0.1	5	0.1	1	0.0	1	0.1	28	0.1
2-0/0-2	9	0.8	23	1.2	219	2.0	124	1.8	106	1.8	65	2.5	42	2.3	588	1.9
Spike 3	13	1.1	15	0.8	178	1.7	153	2.2	172	2.9	96	3.6	83	4.6	710	2.3
3-4/4-3	11	0.9	30	1.6	193	1.8	143	2.1	154	2.6	89	3.4	62	3.4	682	2.2
3-5/5-3	3	0.3	2	0.1	23	0.2	25	0.4	15	0.3	15	0.6	14	0.8	97	0.3
3-6/6-3	17	1.4	25	1.4	180	1.7	150	2.2	155	2.6	83	3.1	40	2.2	650	2.1
3-7/7-3	10	0.8	11	0.6	125	1.2	77	1.1	102	1.7	35	1.3	33	1.8	393	1.3
3-8/8-3	21	1.8	20	1.1	141	1.3	87	1.3	79	1.3	28	1.1	17	0.9	393	1.3
3-9/9-3	4	0.3	6	0.3	28	0.3	17	0.2	31	0.5	13	0.5	6	0.3	105	0.3
3-0/0-3	0	0.0	0	0.0	4	0.0	4	0.1	2	0.0	1	0.0	1	0.1	12	0.0
Spike 4	26	2.2	74	4.0	355	3.3	226	3.3	228	3.9	129	4.9	97	5.4	1,135	3.7
4-5/5-4	7	0.6	14	0.8	50	0.5	29	0.4	30	0.5	17	0.6	21	1.2	168	0.5
4-6/6-4	37	3.1	79	4.3	382	3.5	204	2.9	165	2.8	73	2.8	48	2.7	988	3.2

Codetype	N	%	N	%	N	%	N	%	N	%	N	%	N	%	N	%
4-7/7-4	13	1.1	26	1.4	125	1.2	86	1.2	103	1.8	30	1.1	23	1.3	406	1.3
4-8/8-4	26	2.2	61	3.3	231	2.1	113	1.6	115	2.0	35	1.3	30	1.7	611	2.0
4-9/9-4	18	1.5	49	2.7	142	1.3	81	1.2	55	0.9	30	1.1	10	0.6	385	1.2
4-0/0-4	2	0.2	4	0.2	23	0.2	17	0.2	4	0.1	3	0.1	6	0.3	59	0.2
Spike 5	41	3.4	36	1.9	335	3.1	239	3.5	287	4.9	144	5.4	108	6.0	1,190	3.8
5-6/6-5	1	0.1	9	0.5	41	0.4	17	0.2	33	0.6	8	0.3	24	1.3	133	0.4
5-7/7-5	3	0.3	0	0.0	9	0.1	19	0.3	12	0.2	11	0.4	7	0.4	61	0.2
5-8/8-5	7	0.6	4	0.2	16	0.1	10	0.1	14	0.2	3	0.1	3	0.2	57	0.2
5-9/9-5	7	0.6	15	0.8	41	0.4	28	0.4	36	0.6	12	0.5	11	0.6	150	0.5
5-0/0-5	1	0.1	2	0.1	10	0.1	7	0.1	5	0.1	8	0.3	6	0.3	39	0.1
Spike 6	21	1.8	34	1.8	226	2.1	163	2.4	194	3.3	97	3.7	92	5.1	827	2.7
6-7/7-6	13	1.1	32	1.7	146	1.4	106	1.5	83	1.4	35	1.3	24	1.3	439	1.4
6-8/8-6	123	10.3	194	10.5	717	6.7	322	4.6	234	4.0	71	2.7	38	2.1	1,699	5.5
6-9/9-6	18	1.5	26	1.4	107	1.0	70	1.0	46	0.8	29	1.1	15	0.8	311	1.0
6-0/0-6	3	0.3	6	0.3	52	0.5	30	0.4	20	0.3	11	0.4	8	0.4	130	0.4
Spike 7	7	0.6	2	0.1	43	0.4	29	0.4	43	0.7	17	0.6	18	1.0	159	0.5
7-8/8-7	68	5.7	115	6.2	405	3.8	206	3.0	194	3.3	79	3.0	36	2.0	1,103	3.6
7-9/9-7	3	0.3	1	0.1	28	0.3	25	0.4	13	0.2	7	0.3	6	0.3	83	0.3
7-0/0-7	2	0.2	7	0.4	43	0.4	27	0.4	25	0.4	17	0.6	16	0.9	137	0.4
Spike 8	8	0.7	8	0.4	42	0.4	24	0.3	16	0.3	11	0.4	7	0.4	116	0.4
8-9/9-8	39	3.3	50	2.7	131	1.2	64	0.9	44	0.7	9	0.3	8	0.4	345	1.1
8-0/0-8	4	0.3	5	0.3	37	0.3	12	0.2	18	0.3	8	0.3	3	0.2	87	0.3
Spike 9	34	2.8	44	2.4	265	2.5	200	2.9	199	3.4	91	3.4	51	2.8	884	2.8
9-0/0-9	0	0.0	1	0.1	3	0.0	1	0.0	0	0.0	2	0.1	0	0.0	7	0.0
Spike 0	7	0.6	18	1.0	117	1.1	80	1.2	62	1.1	36	1.4	22	1.2	342	1.1
Subtotal	1,195	82.0	1,848	83.4	10,761	74.5	6,926	66.6	5,874	61.7	2,653	61.5	1,803	59.0	31,060	68.4
WNL	262	18.0	367	16.6	3,688	25.5	3,469	33.4	3,650	38.3	1,662	38.5	1,255	41.0	14,353	31.6
Total	1,457	100.0	2,215	100.0	14,449	100.0	10,395	100.0	9,524	100.0	4,315	100.0	3,058	100.0	45,413	100.0

Note. The percentages for specific codetypes are reported as a function of the number of codetypes represented in the subtotal row because they represent the actual number of clinical patients who produced a clinical elevation on the scale(s).

endorsement in these clients because they may not have adequate reading skills given the eighth grade reading level of the MMPI-2.

Table 9.16 (p. 454–455) provides the frequency with which all MMPI-2 codetypes occurred by levels of education and Table 9.17 ranks the 20 most frequently occurring MMPI-2 codetypes by levels of education in the Caldwell (1997a) clinical dataset. There does not appear to be any easy generalization that captures the relationship between levels of education and the frequency with which MMPI-2 codetypes occurred. The *1-3/3-1* codetypes were the most common across all levels of education and their frequency of occurrence did not change, ranging from 11.6 to 16.8 percent. There is a pattern for the frequency of at least some of the codetypes to change between 10 years or less and 11 years or more of education. For example, the *2-3/3-2* codetypes averaged around 5.4 percent in persons with 10 years or less of education and increased to around 8.5 percent in the higher levels of education. Conversely, the *6-8/8-6* codetypes averaged around 10.4 percent in the two lowest levels of education and then decreased with each increasing level of education. The *7-8/8-7* codetypes averaged around 6.0 percent in the two lowest levels of education and then stabilized around 3.2 percent in the higher levels of education.

There were consistent declines in the T scores on all of the MMPI-2 Content scales (Butcher et al., 1990) in these both normal and clinical samples with increasing levels of education (Table 9.18, pp. 458–459). Unlike the Clinical scales, there were few differences between the normal and clinical samples on most of the Content scales. These differences as a function of the level of education approached 10 T points on a number of the Content scales: Fears (*FRS*); Depression (*DEP*); Health Concerns (*HEA*); Bizarre Mentation (*BIZ*); Anger (*ANG*); Cynicism (*CYN*); Antisocial Practices (*ASP*); Low Self-Esteem (*LSE*); Work Interference (*WRK*); and Negative Treatment Indicators (*TRT*). Only the Type A (TPA) scale and the Social Discomfort (*SOD*) scale did not demonstrate any consistent changes with increases in years of education. The effects of education were slightly larger on the Content scales than on the Clinical scales.

There also were significant effects of the level of education on the MMPI-2 Supplementary scales in the normal and clinical samples (Table 9.19, pp. 459–460). The Supplementary scales can be divided into three groups with T scores increasing in the one group (Ego Strength [*Es*]; Dominance [*Do*]; Social Responsibility [*Re*]; Gender Role—Masculine [*GM*]; Gender Role—Feminine [*GF*];), decreasing in the second group (Welsh Anxiety [*A*]; MacAndrew Alcoholism—Revised [*MAC-R*]; College Maladjustment [*Mt*]; Post Traumatic Stress Disorder—Keane [*PK*]; Post Traumatic Stress Disorder—Schlenger [*PS*]; Marital Distress [*MDS*]; and Hostility [*Ho*]), and being unchanged in the third group (Welsh Repression [*R*]; Overcontrolled-Hostility [*O-H*]; Addiction Admission [*AAS*]; Addiction Potential [*APS*]; and Common Alcohol Logistic—Revised [*CAL-R*]) with increases in the years of education. The first two groups reflect that both normal individuals and patients reported fewer symptoms of psychopathology and more positive attributes with increasing years of education. Scales assessing alcohol and drug abuse were less likely to decrease with increasing years of education. The *MAC-R* scale is a more general measure of the propensity to display risk-taking behaviors that would be expected to show substantial declines with increasing years of education.

Finally, the effects of the years of education on specific MMPI-2 items is presented in Table 9.20 (pp. 461–462). As the years of education increased, both normal individuals and patients were more likely to be happy all of the time (95), be satisfied with their memory (165), and have few pains (224), and less likely to have suicidal ideation (303, 506, 520), be hotheaded (389), have a drug or alcohol problem (489), and hurt someone in a physical fight (548). There were smaller effects of education on the excessive use of alcohol (264), trouble with the law (266), and getting drunk or high (511) than might be expected in both normal and clinical samples.

In summary, education had a larger impact on the interpretation of the MMPI-2 than age or gender. Persons with 10 years of education or less in both normal and clinical samples had substantially higher T scores on a number of the MMPI-2 Clinical, Content, and Supplementary scales than persons with 11 or more years of education. Generally there were limited differences between persons with more than 11 years of education on any of the Clinical scales except for the F (Infrequency) scale and Scales *1* (Hypochondriasis)

TABLE 9.17 Ranking of the Frequency of MMPI-2 Codetypes by Level of Education in the Caldwell Clinical Dataset

EDUCATION RANGE (YEARS)

1–8		9–10		11–12		13–14		15–16		17–18		19+		Total	
CODETYPE	%	CODETYPE	%	CODETYPE	%	CODETYPE	%	CODETYPE	%	CODETYPE	%	CODETYPE	%	CODETYPE	%
1-3/3-1	14.6	1-3/3-1	11.6	1-3/3-1	14.6	1-3/3-1	16.8	1-3/3-1	14.9	1-3/3-1	14.1	1-3/3-1	12.3	1-3/3-1	14.8
6-8/8-6	10.3	6-8/8-6	10.5	2-3/3-2	8.9	2-3/3-2	8.6	2-3/3-2	8.2	2-3/3-2	8.6	2-3/3-2	8.3	2-3/3-2	8.3
1-2/2-1	6.9	7-8/8-7	6.2	6-8/8-6	6.7	2-7/7-2	5.9	2-7/7-2	5.7	Spike 5	5.4	2-7/7-2	6.3	2-7/7-2	5.6
7-8/8-7	5.7	2-3/3-2	5.5	2-7/7-2	5.7	1-2/2-1	5.5	Spike 5	4.9	2-7/7-2	5.3	Spike 5	6.0	6-8/8-6	5.5
2-3/3-2	5.3	2-7/7-2	5.0	1-2/2-1	5.3	6-8/8-6	4.6	6-8/8-6	4.0	Spike 4	4.9	Spike 4	5.4	1-2/2-1	4.7
2-8/8-2	4.1	1-2/2-1	4.5	7-8/8-7	3.8	Spike 5	3.5	Spike 4	3.9	2-6/6-2	3.7	Spike 6	5.1	Spike 5	3.8
Spike 5	3.4	4-6/6-4	4.3	2-8/8-2	3.6	Spike 4	3.3	1-2/2-1	3.7	Spike 6	3.7	Spike 3	4.6	Spike 4	3.7
8-9/9-8	3.3	Spike 4	4.0	4-6/6-4	3.5	2-8/8-2	3.1	2-6/6-2	3.4	Spike 3	3.6	3-4/4-3	3.4	7-8/8-7	3.6
2-6/6-2	3.2	2-8/8-2	3.7	Spike 4	3.3	2-6/6-2	3.0	Spike 9	3.4	1-2/2-1	3.4	2-6/6-2	2.9	4-6/6-4	3.2
4-6/6-4	3.1	4-8/8-4	3.3	Spike 5	3.1	7-8/8-7	3.0	7-8/8-7	3.3	3-4/4-3	3.4	Spike 9	2.8	2-6/6-2	3.1
Spike 9	2.8	4-9/9-4	2.7	2-6/6-2	3.0	4-6/6-4	2.9	Spike 6	3.3	Spike 9	3.4	4-6/6-4	2.7	2-8/8-2	3.0
1-8/8-1	2.6	8-9/9-8	2.7	Spike 9	2.5	Spike 9	2.9	Spike 3	2.9	3-6/6-3	3.1	2-8/8-2	2.6	Spike 9	2.8
2-7/7-2	2.6	1-8/8-1	2.4	2-4/4-2	2.3	2-4/4-2	2.7	2-4/4-2	2.8	7-8/8-7	3.0	2-0/0-2	2.3	Spike 6	2.7
2-4/4-2	2.4	2-6/6-2	2.4	4-8/8-4	2.1	Spike 6	2.4	4-6/6-4	2.8	4-6/6-4	2.8	1-2/2-1	2.2	2-4/4-2	2.5
4-8/8-4	2.2	Spike 9	2.4	Spike 6	2.1	3-6/6-3	2.2	3-4/4-3	2.6	6-8/8-6	2.7	2-4/4-2	2.2	Spike 3	2.3
Spike 4	2.2	2-4/4-2	2.0	2-0/0-2	2.0	Spike 3	2.2	3-6/6-3	2.6	2-4/4-2	2.6	3-6/6-3	2.2	3-4/4-3	2.2
3-8/8-3	1.8	Spike 5	1.9	3-4/4-3	1.8	3-4/4-3	2.1	2-8/8-2	2.1	2-0/0-2	2.5	6-8/8-6	2.1	3-6/6-3	2.1
Spike 6	1.8	Spike 6	1.8	3-6/6-3	1.7	2-0/0-2	1.8	4-8/8-4	2.0	2-8/8-2	1.8	7-8/8-7	2.0	4-8/8-4	2.0
4-9/9-4	1.5	6-7/7-6	1.7	Spike 3	1.7	4-8/8-4	1.6	2-0/0-2	1.8	Spike 1	1.5	3-7/7-3	1.8	2-0/0-2	1.9
6-9/9-6	1.5	3-4/4-3	1.6	1-8/8-1	1.5	1-8/8-1	1.5	4-7/7-4	1.8	Spike 0	1.4	4-8/8-4	1.7	6-7/7-6	1.4

TABLE 9.18 Education Effects on MMPI-2 Content Scales

Scale	EDUCATION RANGE (YEARS)							Correlation
	1–8	9–10	11–12	13–14	15–16	17–18	19+	
Anxiety (*ANX*)								
Normal[a]	51.2	55.0	51.0	50.2	49.3	48.8	48.2	–.118
Clinical[b]	62.3	62.8	60.9	58.4	56.4	55.7	55.5	–.148
Fears (*FRS*)								
Normal[a]	55.2	58.1	52.9	50.5	48.4	47.1	47.1	–.265
Clinical[b]	57.9	55.4	53.2	50.7	49.2	48.3	48.2	–.199
Obsessions (*OBS*)								
Normal[a]	52.8	56.5	51.8	50.5	48.8	48.1	47.5	–.179
Clinical[b]	55.7	56.4	53.1	50.5	48.6	48.3	48.1	–.176
Depression (*DEP*)								
Normal[a]	54.0	57.0	52.1	50.7	49.0	48.0	46.6	–.195
Clinical[b]	62.9	63.7	59.9	56.4	54.1	53.4	53.0	–.180
Health Concerns (*HEA*)								
Normal[a]	57.1	57.5	51.9	50.6	48.7	47.7	47.7	–.209
Clinical[b]	65.3	64.2	62.0	58.9	55.7	54.8	53.5	–.196
Bizarre Mentation (*BIZ*)								
Normal[a]	57.5	57.3	52.3	51.2	49.0	47.4	45.7	–.233
Clinical[b]	60.0	60.3	55.8	52.9	50.9	49.7	48.6	–.215
Anger (*ANG*)								
Normal[a]	49.4	56.8	51.8	51.0	49.1	47.6	46.1	–.185
Clinical[b]	54.1	56.1	52.6	50.2	48.5	47.9	47.6	–.174
Cynicism (*CYN*)								
Normal[a]	58.3	59.7	53.7	51.5	48.0	45.7	45.3	–.334
Clinical[b]	55.7	56.5	52.7	49.6	47.0	45.9	45.1	–.271
Antisocial Practices (*ASP*)								
Normal[a]	54.4	57.6	52.9	51.4	48.4	46.2	45.6	–.248
Clinical[b]	54.4	57.0	51.5	48.6	46.5	45.6	44.8	–.256
Type A (*TPA*)								
Normal[a]	49.0	54.2	50.8	50.6	49.6	47.9	47.9	–.092
Clinical[b]	51.5	52.0	49.2	47.9	47.2	47.2	47.4	–.095
Low Self-Esteem (*LSE*)								
Normal[a]	56.7	57.1	52.4	51.0	48.5	47.3	47.3	–.233
Clinical[b]	58.3	58.7	55.3	52.1	49.9	49.3	48.9	–.195
Social Discomfort (*SOD*)								
Normal[a]	52.6	53.2	51.0	49.7	49.2	49.3	50.1	–.066
Clinical[b]	54.1	54.6	53.7	51.4	50.1	49.9	50.0	–.118

Scale	EDUCATION RANGE (YEARS)							Correlation
	1–8	*9–10*	*11–12*	*13–14*	*15–16*	*17–18*	*19+*	
Family Problems (*FAM*)								
Normal[a]	54.0	55.4	51.2	50.7	49.2	48.5	47.6	–.154
Clinical[b]	56.1	58.6	53.3	51.1	49.8	49.9	49.7	–.147
Work Interference (*WRK*)								
Normal[a]	55.5	56.7	51.9	50.4	49.1	48.0	46.6	–.200
Clinical[b]	60.1	60.8	57.0	54.0	51.8	51.1	50.4	–.186
Negative Treatment Indicators (*TRT*)								
Normal[a]	56.6	57.6	52.8	50.6	48.6	46.6	47.6	–.239
Clinical[b]	60.5	61.2	56.9	53.1	50.8	49.6	49.1	–.211

[a]Butcher et al. (1989).
[b]Caldwell (1997a).

TABLE 9.19   Education Effects on MMPI-2 Supplementary Scales

Scale	EDUCATION RANGE (YEARS)							Correlation
	1–8	*9–10*	*11–12*	*13–14*	*15–16*	*17–18*	*19+*	
Welsh Anxiety (*A*)								
Normal[a]	53.0	57.1	51.9	50.8	49.1	48.1	46.6	–.193
Clinical[b]	58.1	58.9	55.5	52.8	51.0	50.3	50.0	–.174
Welsh Repression (*R*)								
Normal[a]	54.5	47.8	49.7	49.0	49.9	50.1	53.3	.039
Clinical[b]	55.7	54.2	55.3	54.6	54.7	54.5	54.9	–.013
Ego Strength (*Es*)								
Normal[a]	42.4	43.2	47.4	49.4	51.9	52.6	52.7	.263
Clinical[b]	39.7	39.7	42.1	44.9	47.3	48.2	49.0	.229
MacAndrew Alcoholism—Revised (*MAC-R*)								
Normal[a]	56.1	56.6	50.8	49.7	46.0	44.2	42.5	–.281
Clinical[b]	52.7	55.2	52.0	49.7	47.4	46.1	45.1	–.224
Overcontrolled-Hostility (*O-H*)								
Normal[a]	53.9	47.8	49.8	49.3	50.0	50.6	51.8	.022
Clinical[b]	53.5	52.6	53.7	54.4	54.4	54.1	54.6	.025
Dominance (*Do*)								
Normal[a]	36.8	41.3	46.0	49.1	52.3	54.6	56.3	.406
Clinical[b]	39.9	38.4	41.5	45.3	48.8	50.7	52.4	.362

(continued)

TABLE 9.19 Education Effects on MMPI-2 Supplementary Scales (continued)

Scale	1–8	9–10	11–12	13–14	15–16	17–18	19+	Correlation
			EDUCATION RANGE (YEARS)					
Social Responsibility (*Re*)								
Normal[a]	43.8	41.5	46.9	48.9	51.7	54.2	55.9	.314
Clinical[b]	45.0	41.8	46.3	49.2	51.7	52.9	54.2	.279
College Maladjustment (*Mt*)								
Normal[a]	52.8	55.8	52.0	50.8	49.0	47.9	46.8	−.191
Clinical[b]	62.0	62.8	59.7	56.7	54.3	53.4	52.8	−.177
Gender Role—Masculine (*GM*)								
Normal[a]	46.6	43.7	47.4	49.8	51.7	53.1	53.1	.239
Clinical[b]	42.2	42.5	44.5	47.1	48.8	49.5	49.5	.192
Gender Role—Feminine (*GF*)								
Normal[a]	50.3	47.9	50.6	51.3	52.5	53.4	55.0	.034
Clinical[b]	46.2	44.9	47.3	48.8	50.2	51.4	52.5	.108
Post Traumatic Stress Disorder—Keane (*PK*)								
Normal[a]	52.5	55.9	51.9	51.2	49.0	47.5	46.6	−.197
Clinical[b]	64.5	65.6	61.0	57.2	54.4	53.2	52.1	−.205
Post Traumatic Stress Disorder—Schlenger (*PS*)								
Normal[a]	52.9	57.1	52.0	50.8	48.8	47.7	46.3	−.208
Clinical[b]	65.0	66.1	61.5	57.8	54.9	53.7	52.6	−.203
Addiction Admission (*AAS*)								
Normal[a]	52.7	53.1	50.4	50.8	50.0	48.4	47.3	−.076
Clinical[b]	52.0	54.8	51.2	49.1	48.0	47.3	47.1	−.149
Addiction Potential (*APS*)								
Normal[a]	44.6	51.4	48.9	49.9	49.7	49.7	49.0	.070
Clinical[b]	47.4	49.3	49.0	48.8	48.7	49.3	49.8	.057
Marital Distress (*MDS*)								
Normal[a]	57.1	56.2	52.9	52.4	51.3	51.2	50.5	−.103
Clinical[b]	60.3	61.6	57.0	54.6	53.2	53.1	52.9	−.150
Hostility (*Ho*)								
Normal[a]	55.0	58.5	52.8	50.9	48.0	45.5	44.5	−.294
Clinical[b]	54.7	55.8	52.2	49.5	47.2	46.2	45.3	−.236
Common Alcohol Logistic—Revised (*CAL-R*)								
Normal[a]	55.7	54.5	51.5	50.7	51.9	50.4	48.6	−.068
Clinical[b]	51.1	52.6	51.3	50.6	50.7	50.4	50.5	−.031

[a]Butcher et al. (1989).
[b]Caldwell (1997a).

TABLE 9.20 Education Effects on Specific MMPI-2 Items

	EDUCATION RANGE (YEARS)						
	1–8	*9–10*	*11–12*	*13–14*	*15–16*	*17–18*	*19+*
95 (I am happy most of the time.[a])							
Normal[b]	81.0	94.0	89.6	89.0	90.5	86.8	89.6
Clinical[c]	56.0	55.3	59.6	64.0	66.5	67.6	66.8
162 (Someone has been trying to poison me.[a])							
Normal[b]	4.8	0.0	0.6	0.6	0.3	0.9	0.0
Clinical[c]	3.3	3.0	1.9	1.2	1.0	1.0	0.5
165 (My memory seems to be all right.[a])							
Normal[b]	85.7	84.0	89.0	91.0	91.3	90.9	93.9
Clinical[c]	62.0	60.6	64.3	68.0	73.8	74.9	78.3
216 (Someone has been trying to rob me.[a])							
Normal[b]	4.8	8.0	2.3	2.2	1.7	2.5	1.2
Clinical[c]	7.9	6.7	5.1	4.1	3.4	3.1	2.7
224 (I have few or no pains.[a])							
Normal[b]	71.4	72.0	78.6	81.7	83.0	85.8	83.4
Clinical[c]	49.0	48.8	50.8	56.6	63.5	65.4	69.0
264 (I have used alcohol excessively.[a])							
Normal[b]	42.9	40.0	31.3	29.7	35.9	30.0	28.2
Clinical[c]	27.0	32.2	29.5	27.0	26.9	26.7	27.9
266 (I have never been in trouble with the law.[a])							
Normal[b]	71.4	50.0	71.9	68.4	76.2	78.5	76.7
Clinical[c]	59.2	46.5	59.0	66.7	72.2	75.2	74.7
303 (Most of the time I wish I were dead.[a])							
Normal[b]	4.8	2.0	2.9	4.1	2.4	1.6	0.0
Clinical[c]	18.4	19.8	13.5	9.7	7.1	6.0	5.5
389 (I am often said to be hotheaded.[a])							
Normal[b]	28.6	44.0	21.3	18.3	13.7	8.5	6.1
Clinical[c]	32.7	33.8	23.9	17.5	13.7	12.2	12.4
489 (I have a drug or alcohol problem.[a])							
Normal[b]	14.3	12.0	5.6	6.7	3.9	3.5	3.1
Clinical[c]	13.3	17.0	12.8	8.1	6.9	5.6	7.4
499 (I hate going to doctors even when I'm sick.[a])							
Normal[b]	47.6	66.0	40.1	33.5	28.2	23.0	29.4
Clinical[c]	46.9	52.6	49.0	40.5	34.7	30.2	27.8
506 (I recently have considered killing myself.[a])							
Normal[b]	9.5	2.0	3.6	4.7	5.0	2.8	3.1
Clinical[c]	19.9	24.4	18.3	15.8	13.8	13.4	14.0

TABLE 9.20 Education Effects on Specific MMPI-2 Items (continued)

	EDUCATION RANGE (YEARS)						
	1–8	*9–10*	*11–12*	*13–14*	*15–16*	*17–18*	*19+*
511 (Once a week or more I get high or drunk.[a])							
Normal[b]	19.0	18.0	14.6	15.5	13.9	9.8	12.3
Clinical[c]	9.3	14.0	10.3	6.7	5.9	4.4	4.7
520 (Lately I have thought a lot about killing myself.[a])							
Normal[b]	0.0	2.0	2.7	2.6	1.7	1.3	0.0
Clinical[c]	16.5	17.3	12.7	10.1	8.5	7.6	7.9
548 (I've been so angry at times that I've hurt someone in a physical fight.[a])							
Normal[b]	19.0	30.0	19.2	14.8	9.8	8.5	9.2
Clinical[c]	19.3	27.1	16.5	11.9	8.5	6.7	6.5

[a]Minnesota Multiphasic Personality Inventory-2 (MMPI-2). Copyright © 1942, 1943 (renewed 1970), 1989 by the Regents of the University of Minnesota. Reprinted by permission of the publisher. "MMPI-2" and "Minnesota Multiphasic Inventory-2" are trademarks owned by the University of Minnesota.
[b]Butcher et al. (1989).
[c]Caldwell (1997a).

and *8* (Schizophrenia). However, T scores on the Content scales demonstrated a steady decrease with increasing years of education. Both normal individuals and patients reported fewer symptoms of psychopathology and more positive attributes with increasing years of education. Clinicians need to be much more aware of the potential effects of education on the interpretation of the MMPI-2, particularly in clients with 10 or fewer years of education.

MARITAL STATUS

There is virtually no published research on the effects of marital status on MMPI or MMPI-2 performance. None of the standard references to the MMPI or MMPI-2 (Butcher & Williams, 1992; Dahlstrom et al., 1972, 1975; Graham, 1993; Greene, 1991) include marital status in the subject index. The extant research typically has found no relationship between MMPI (Brown & Dunbar, 1978; Swain-Holcomb & Thorne, 1984) or MMPI-2 performance and marital status, but given the limited power of most of these studies it is unclear whether marital status has no effect whatsoever or its effects are simply minimal.

Table 9.21 provides the mean scores for the MMPI-2 Validity and Clinical scales for five classifications of marital status for normal individuals (Butcher et al., 1989) and the Caldwell (1997a) clinical dataset. Marital status had virtually no effect on the Validity or Clinical scales in either sample. Widowed patients had higher scores on Scales *1* (Hypochondriasis), *2* (Depression), and *3* (Hysteria) than the other four categories of marital status. These widowed patients also were older than the other categories, which may partially account for these differences.

Table 9.22 (pp. 464–465) provides the frequency with which all MMPI-2 codetypes occurred in these five classifications of marital status and Table 9.23 (p. 466) ranks the 20 most frequently occurring MMPI-2 codetypes for these same five classifications in the Caldwell (1997a) clinical dataset. There are few generalizations that can be made: The *6-8/8-6* codetypes occurred almost twice as often among never married patients as in the other four classifications of marital status; Spike *4* codetypes occurred more than twice as often among separated patients; and the *7-8/8-7* codetypes occurred one and one-half times as often among never married patients.

TABLE 9.21 Marital Status Effects on MMPI-2 Validity and Clinical Scales

Scale	MARITAL STATUS				
	Never Married	Married	Separated	Divorced	Widowed
L (Lie)					
Normal[a]	49.2	50.0	51.0	49.0	54.3
Clinical[b]	53.9	55.3	55.7	55.2	57.3
F (Infrequency)					
Normal[a]	52.7	48.6	52.7	51.2	50.9
Clinical[b]	61.1	57.3	55.1	58.4	61.9
K (Correction)					
Normal[a]	49.4	50.2	48.9	50.5	49.4
Clinical[b]	50.3	51.6	54.5	52.1	50.5
Scale 1 (Hypochondriasis)					
Normal[a]	49.1	50.1	50.6	50.4	51.6
Clinical[b]	60.2	63.1	57.5	62.5	68.1
Scale 2 (Depression)					
Normal[a]	49.4	49.9	52.9	49.5	51.7
Clinical[b]	62.2	63.9	57.9	62.9	68.4
Scale 3 (Hysteria)					
Normal[a]	49.1	50.0	49.9	51.9	50.4
Clinical[b]	61.3	64.9	60.8	64.6	68.4
Scale 4 (Psychopathic Deviate)					
Normal[a]	53.2	48.7	56.9	51.9	46.3
Clinical[b]	61.6	58.3	59.9	60.0	58.2
Scale 5 (Masculinity-Femininity)					
Normal[a]	52.5	49.1	53.0	49.6	53.4
Clinical[b]	51.9	50.0	50.7	50.8	51.8
Scale 6 (Paranoia)					
Normal[a]	52.0	49.3	52.1	51.0	46.9
Clinical[b]	61.8	59.8	60.4	61.6	60.2
Scale 7 (Psychasthenia)					
Normal[a]	52.0	49.6	51.4	49.6	48.0
Clinical[b]	61.9	60.9	56.9	60.1	63.2
Scale 8 (Schizophrenia)					
Normal[a]	53.0	48.8	53.6	50.9	48.6
Clinical[b]	63.2	60.4	57.3	60.5	64.0
Scale 9 (Hypomania)					
Normal[a]	53.6	48.8	53.7	51.4	48.0
Clinical[b]	54.3	50.6	51.2	51.5	52.1
Scale 0 (Social Introversion)					
Normal[a]	49.4	50.3	49.6	48.2	50.9
Clinical[b]	52.5	53.0	49.1	51.7	54.6

[a]Butcher et al. (1989).
[b]Caldwell (1997a).

TABLE 9.22 Frequency of MMPI-2 Codetypes by Marital Status in the Caldwell Clinical Dataset

| | MARITAL STATUS | | | | | | | | | | | |
| | Never Married | | Married | | Separated | | Divorced | | Widowed | | Total | |
CODETYPE	N	%	N	%	N	%	N	%	N	%	N	%
Spike 1	125	1.1	213	1.6	9	0.5	70	1.4	9	1.7	426	1.3
1-2/2-1	340	3.1	802	6.0	58	3.1	268	5.2	45	8.4	1,513	4.8
1-3/3-1	1,147	10.5	2,445	18.3	196	10.6	850	16.6	108	20.1	4,746	15.0
1-4/4-1	62	0.6	78	0.6	12	0.6	37	0.7	4	0.7	193	0.6
1-5/5-1	43	0.4	53	0.4	1	0.1	19	0.4	5	0.9	121	0.4
1-6/6-1	93	0.9	172	1.3	14	0.8	71	1.4	8	1.5	358	1.1
1-7/7-1	61	0.6	83	0.6	6	0.3	29	0.6	6	1.1	185	0.6
1-8/8-1	160	1.5	195	1.5	19	1.0	51	1.0	13	2.4	438	1.4
1-9/9-1	63	0.6	48	0.4	5	0.3	19	0.4	1	0.2	136	0.4
1-0/0-1	12	0.1	31	0.2	2	0.1	10	0.2	3	0.6	58	0.2
Spike 2	95	0.9	207	1.6	14	0.8	35	0.7	8	1.5	359	1.1
2-3/3-2	625	5.7	1,308	9.8	111	6.0	485	9.5	68	12.7	2,597	8.2
2-4/4-2	326	3.0	278	2.1	51	2.8	131	2.6	8	1.5	794	2.5
2-5/5-2	41	0.4	32	0.2	7	0.4	15	0.3	1	0.2	96	0.3
2-6/6-2	325	3.0	411	3.1	59	3.2	196	3.8	16	3.0	1,007	3.2
2-7/7-2	581	5.3	857	6.4	65	3.5	254	5.0	27	5.0	1,784	5.6
2-8/8-2	332	3.1	395	3.0	30	1.6	181	3.5	27	5.0	965	3.0
2-9/9-2	11	0.1	18	0.1	2	0.1	3	0.1	0	0.0	34	0.1
2-0/0-2	180	1.7	297	2.2	21	1.1	90	1.8	10	1.9	598	1.9
Spike 3	158	1.5	339	2.5	81	4.4	126	2.5	16	3.0	720	2.3
3-4/4-3	218	2.0	269	2.0	78	4.2	121	2.4	13	2.4	699	2.2
3-5/5-3	40	0.4	45	0.3	6	0.3	8	0.2	0	0.0	99	0.3
3-6/6-3	153	1.4	300	2.3	67	3.6	130	2.5	7	1.3	657	2.1
3-7/7-3	136	1.3	190	1.4	12	0.6	65	1.3	4	0.7	407	1.3
3-8/8-3	140	1.3	177	1.3	17	0.9	58	1.1	9	1.7	401	1.3
3-9/9-3	28	0.3	56	0.4	7	0.4	12	0.2	3	0.6	106	0.3
3-0/0-3	1	0.0	10	0.1	0	0.0	1	0.0	0	0.0	12	0.0
Spike 4	415	3.8	388	2.9	139	7.5	198	3.9	6	1.1	1,146	3.6
4-5/5-4	87	0.8	46	0.3	12	0.6	28	0.5	0	0.0	173	0.5
4-6/6-4	400	3.7	307	2.3	89	4.8	182	3.5	9	1.7	987	3.1
4-7/7-4	203	1.9	123	0.9	24	1.3	53	1.0	3	0.6	406	1.3
4-8/8-4	326	3.0	183	1.4	37	2.0	69	1.3	6	1.1	621	2.0
4-9/9-4	223	2.1	77	0.6	30	1.6	47	0.9	5	0.9	382	1.2
4-0/0-4	24	0.2	21	0.2	5	0.3	9	0.2	0	0.0	59	0.2
Spike 5	487	4.5	418	3.1	86	4.7	202	3.9	13	2.4	1,206	3.8
5-6/6-5	53	0.5	39	0.3	14	0.8	29	0.6	2	0.4	137	0.4
5-7/7-5	39	0.4	15	0.1	0	0.0	7	0.1	1	0.2	62	0.2
5-8/8-5	30	0.3	20	0.2	2	0.1	8	0.2	0	0.0	60	0.2
5-9/9-5	73	0.7	46	0.3	8	0.4	23	0.4	3	0.6	153	0.5
5-0/0-5	17	0.2	17	0.1	3	0.2	2	0.0	1	0.2	40	0.1
Spike 6	227	2.1	284	2.1	126	6.8	185	3.6	4	0.7	826	2.6
6-7/7-6	207	1.9	163	1.2	22	1.2	56	1.1	1	0.2	449	1.4

| | MARITAL STATUS | | | | | | | | | | | | |
| | Never Married | | Married | | Separated | | Divorced | | Widowed | | Total | |
CODETYPE	N	%	N	%	N	%	N	%	N	%	N	%
6-8/8-6	816	7.5	570	4.3	89	4.8	225	4.4	18	3.4	1,718	5.4
6-9/9-6	167	1.5	89	0.7	24	1.3	37	0.7	0	0.0	317	1.0
6-0/0-6	35	0.3	62	0.5	10	0.5	17	0.3	1	0.2	125	0.4
Spike 7	74	0.7	69	0.5	5	0.3	23	0.4	1	0.2	172	0.5
7-8/8-7	508	4.7	403	3.0	56	3.0	134	2.6	16	3.0	1,117	3.5
7-9/9-7	51	0.5	18	0.1	3	0.2	15	0.3	3	0.6	90	0.3
7-0/0-7	53	0.5	73	0.5	4	0.2	11	0.2	1	0.2	142	0.4
Spike 8	80	0.7	29	0.2	2	0.1	8	0.2	3	0.6	122	0.4
8-9/9-8	243	2.2	64	0.5	14	0.8	28	0.5	6	1.1	355	1.1
8-0/0-8	46	0.4	29	0.2	3	0.2	9	0.2	1	0.2	88	0.3
Spike 9	411	3.8	275	2.1	64	3.5	142	2.8	12	2.2	904	2.8
9-0/0-9	5	0.0	2	0.0	0	0.0	0	0.0	0	0.0	7	0.0
Spike 0	82	0.8	192	1.4	26	1.4	48	0.9	2	0.4	350	1.1
Subtotal	10,878	71.3	13,331	68.1	1,847	58.4	5,130	67.4	537	82.0	31,723	68.6
WNL	4,378	28.7	6,236	31.9	1,314	41.6	2,484	32.6	118	18.0	14,530	31.4
Total	15,256	100.0	19,567	100.0	3,161	100.0	7,614	100.0	655	100.0	46,253	100.0

Note. The percentages for specific codetypes are reported as a function of the number of codetypes represented in the subtotal row because they represent the actual number of clinical patients who produced a clinical elevation on the scale(s).

There were few effects of marital status on the MMPI-2 Content scales (Butcher et al., 1990) in these two samples with most mean T scores in the range of 48 to 54 on all scales (Table 9.24 pp. 467–468). Widowed patients elevated the Depression (*DEP*) and Health Concerns (*HEA*) scales about 5 T points higher than the other four classifications of marital status. These findings are similar to the findings on the Clinical scales except the elevations were not quite as high.

There also were minimal effects of marital status on the MMPI-2 Supplementary scales in these two samples (Table 9.25, pp. 468–469). Separated patients had T scores nearly 5 T points lower on those scales measuring general distress and negative emotionality (Welsh Anxiety [*A*]; College Maladjustment [*Mt*]; Post Traumatic Stress Disorder—Keane [*PK*]; Post Traumatic Stress Disorder—Schlenger [*PS*]) than the other four classifications of marital status.

Otherwise it is remarkable how little difference there is either within or between these two samples as a function of these five classifications of marital status.

Finally, the effects of marital status on specific MMPI-2 items selected are provided in Table 9.26 (pp. 470–471). The only item that had distinct differences among these five classifications of marital status relates to whether normal individuals get high or drunk on a regular basis (511): Separated (30.9%); Never Married (23.1%); Divorced (15.9%); Married (10.7%); and Widowed (6.7%). The patients in all five classifications were much less likely to endorse this item and there were minimal differences among four of the five classifications on it.

In summary, marital status had virtually no effect on any of the MMPI-2 Validity, Clinical, Content, or Supplementary scales, or individual items. It appears that clinicians do not need to be concerned about the

TABLE 9.23 Ranking of the Frequency of MMPI-2 Codetypes by Marital Status in the Caldwell Clinical Dataset

MARITAL STATUS

Never Married		Married		Separated		Divorced		Widowed		Total	
CODETYPE	%	CODETYPE	%	CODETYPE	%	CODETYPE	%	CODETYPE	%	CODETYPE	%
1-3/3-1	10.5	1-3/3-1	18.3	1-3/3-1	10.6	1-3/3-1	16.6	1-3/3-1	20.1	1-3/3-1	15.0
6-8/8-6	7.5	2-3/3-2	9.8	Spike 4	7.5	2-3/3-2	9.5	2-3/3-2	12.7	2-3/3-2	8.2
2-3/3-2	5.7	2-7/7-2	6.4	Spike 6	6.8	1-2/2-1	5.2	1-2/2-1	8.4	2-7/7-2	5.6
2-7/7-2	5.3	1-2/2-1	6.0	2-3/3-2	6.0	2-7/7-2	5.0	2-7/7-2	5.0	6-8/8-6	5.4
7-8/8-7	4.7	6-8/8-6	4.3	4-6/6-4	4.8	6-8/8-6	4.4	2-8/8-2	5.0	1-2/2-1	4.8
Spike 5	4.5	Spike 5	3.1	6-8/8-6	4.8	Spike 5	3.9	6-8/8-6	3.4	Spike 5	3.8
Spike 4	3.8	2-6/6-2	3.1	Spike 5	4.7	Spike 4	3.9	2-6/6-2	3.0	Spike 4	3.6
Spike 9	3.8	7-8/8-7	3.0	Spike 3	4.4	2-6/6-2	3.8	7-8/8-7	3.0	7-8/8-7	3.5
4-6/6-4	3.7	2-8/8-2	3.0	3-4/4-3	4.2	Spike 6	3.6	Spike 3	3.0	2-6/6-2	3.2
1-2/2-1	3.1	Spike 4	2.9	3-6/6-3	3.6	4-6/6-4	3.5	1-8/8-1	2.4	4-6/6-4	3.1
2-8/8-2	3.1	Spike 3	2.5	2-7/7-2	3.5	2-8/8-2	3.5	3-4/4-3	2.4	2-8/8-2	3.0
2-4/4-2	3.0	4-6/6-4	2.3	Spike 9	3.5	Spike 9	2.8	Spike 5	2.4	Spike 9	2.8
4-8/8-4	3.0	3-6/6-3	2.3	2-6/6-2	3.2	7-8/8-7	2.6	Spike 9	2.2	Spike 6	2.6
2-6/6-2	3.0	2-0/0-2	2.2	1-2/2-1	3.1	2-4/4-2	2.6	2-0/0-2	1.9	2-4/4-2	2.5
8-9/9-8	2.2	Spike 6	2.1	7-8/8-7	3.0	3-6/6-3	2.5	3-8/8-3	1.7	Spike 3	2.3
Spike 6	2.1	2-4/4-2	2.1	2-4/4-2	2.8	Spike 3	2.5	4-6/6-4	1.7	3-4/4-3	2.2
4-9/9-4	2.1	Spike 9	2.1	4-8/8-4	2.0	3-4/4-3	2.4	Spike 1	1.7	3-6/6-3	2.1
3-4/4-3	2.0	3-4/4-3	2.0	2-8/8-2	1.6	2-0/0-2	1.8	1-6/6-1	1.5	4-8/8-4	2.0
6-7/7-6	1.9	Spike 1	1.6	4-9/9-4	1.6	1-6/6-1	1.4	2-4/4-2	1.5	2-0/0-2	1.9
4-7/7-4	1.9	Spike 2	1.6	Spike 0	1.4	Spike 1	1.4	Spike 2	1.5	6-7/7-6	1.4

TABLE 9.24 Marital Status Effects on MMPI-2 Content Scales

	MARITAL STATUS				
Scale	Never Married	Married	Separated	Divorced	Widowed
Anxiety (*ANX*)					
Normal[a]	51.1	49.4	53.0	50.9	47.8
Clinical[b]	59.1	58.9	55.4	58.7	60.9
Fears (*FRS*)					
Normal[a]	48.1	50.3	53.2	49.8	52.9
Clinical[b]	51.0	51.8	49.4	51.0	55.0
Obsessions (*OBS*)					
Normal[a]	50.1	49.7	49.9	50.5	51.3
Clinical[b]	52.3	50.8	47.8	50.2	54.1
Depression (*DEP*)					
Normal[a]	52.0	49.3	54.0	50.6	50.3
Clinical[b]	58.7	56.7	52.7	56.6	61.3
Health Concerns (*HEA*)					
Normal[a]	49.8	49.8	51.2	50.2	50.9
Clinical[b]	58.5	59.8	54.1	59.5	64.6
Bizarre Mentation (*BIZ*)					
Normal[a]	52.1	49.3	54.1	50.7	49.6
Clinical[b]	55.6	52.1	51.7	52.8	54.3
Anger (*ANG*)					
Normal[a]	51.3	49.7	50.4	50.0	47.7
Clinical[b]	51.9	50.7	47.5	49.3	50.2
Cynicism (*CYN*)					
Normal[a]	50.6	49.4	55.2	50.6	53.7
Clinical[b]	51.6	49.2	47.1	49.7	52.2
Antisocial Practices (*ASP*)					
Normal[a]	52.2	49.1	53.0	50.6	49.5
Clinical[b]	51.4	47.9	46.9	48.5	49.0
Type A (*TPA*)					
Normal[a]	49.9	49.9	49.3	49.6	49.8
Clinical[b]	49.4	48.3	45.5	47.6	49.5
Low Self-Esteem (*LSE*)					
Normal[a]	49.3	50.1	49.7	49.5	52.1
Clinical[b]	53.7	52.7	49.5	51.7	55.5
Social Discomfort (*SOD*)					
Normal[a]	50.3	49.8	50.3	49.8	51.2
Clinical[b]	52.1	52.2	49.1	51.9	54.0

(continued)

TABLE 9.24 Marital Status Effects on MMPI-2 Content Scales (continued)

	MARITAL STATUS				
Scale	Never Married	Married	Separated	Divorced	Widowed
Family Problems (*FAM*)					
Normal[a]	52.2	49.1	56.1	50.9	48.1
Clinical[b]	54.0	50.8	50.2	51.0	51.2
Work Interference (*WRK*)					
Normal[a]	50.9	49.6	52.0	50.5	50.1
Clinical[b]	56.0	54.3	50.1	53.9	57.6
Negative Treatment Indicators (*TRT*)					
Normal[a]	50.3	49.6	52.3	49.6	54.2
Clinical[b]	55.2	53.9	49.6	52.9	58.2

[a]Butcher et al. (1989).
[b]Caldwell (1997a).

TABLE 9.25 Marital Status Effects on MMPI-2 Supplementary Scales

	MARITAL STATUS				
Scale	Never Married	Married	Separated	Divorced	Widowed
Welsh Anxiety (*A*)					
Normal[a]	51.1	49.6	51.8	50.5	50.2
Clinical[b]	54.9	53.1	49.3	52.6	55.9
Welsh Repression (*R*)					
Normal[a]	48.9	50.2	49.0	49.5	53.0
Clinical[b]	53.7	55.7	54.7	55.4	57.6
Ego Strength (*Es*)					
Normal[a]	50.5	50.2	46.9	50.3	47.3
Clinical[b]	44.4	44.3	48.3	44.9	40.1
MacAndrew Alcoholism—Revised (*MAC-R*)					
Normal[a]	48.4	47.0	54.2	49.9	49.1
Clinical[b]	50.3	48.5	49.7	50.4	50.9
Overcontrolled-Hostility (*O-H*)					
Normal[a]	50.4	49.8	50.8	50.3	50.3
Clinical[b]	53.9	53.6	56.4	54.9	53.7
Dominance (*Do*)					
Normal[a]	49.0	50.6	45.7	51.8	48.6
Clinical[b]	44.1	45.6	47.9	46.0	43.7

| | MARITAL STATUS | | | | |
Scale	Never Married	Married	Separated	Divorced	Widowed
Social Responsibility (*Re*)					
Normal[a]	48.3	50.8	46.6	50.8	52.1
Clinical[b]	47.0	50.1	51.0	49.6	49.7
Gender Role—Masculine (*GM*)					
Normal[a]	50.9	50.0	49.8	50.8	50.2
Clinical[b]	46.3	46.2	48.9	47.4	44.7
Gender Role—Feminine (*GF*)					
Normal[a]	49.4	53.0	47.7	50.6	53.4
Clinical[b]	47.7	49.5	50.1	49.0	49.2
College Maladjustment (*Mt*)					
Normal[a]	51.2	49.6	52.5	50.1	50.1
Clinical[b]	58.1	57.3	51.9	56.4	60.3
Post Traumatic Stress Disorder—Keane (*PK*)					
Normal[a]	52.6	49.1	54.4	50.1	49.3
Clinical[b]	59.9	57.2	53.1	56.8	60.3
Post Traumatic Stress Disorder—Schlenger (*PS*)					
Normal[a]	52.3	49.1	53.1	50.5	49.4
Clinical[b]	60.2	58.0	53.0	57.4	61.4
Addiction Admission (*AAS*)					
Normal[a]	53.2	48.8	54.9	51.9	46.3
Clinical[b]	51.4	48.0	48.8	49.5	48.7
Addiction Potential (*APS*)					
Normal[a]	50.8	49.0	50.6	51.5	45.4
Clinical[b]	49.3	48.4	48.4	49.1	48.4
Marital Distress (*MDS*)					
Normal[a]	55.5	50.3	60.4	55.0	50.9
Clinical[b]	57.4	53.8	54.9	55.6	55.9
Hostility (*Ho*)					
Normal[a]	48.2	50.1	45.9	49.6	48.1
Clinical[b]	47.3	50.0	52.3	49.8	48.5
Common Alcohol Logistic—Revised (*CAL-R*)					
Normal[a]	53.0	50.4	55.6	52.5	50.7
Clinical[b]	51.8	49.4	53.2	51.5	50.1

[a]Butcher et al. (1989).
[b]Caldwell (1997a).

TABLE 9.26 Marital Status Effects on Specific MMPI-2 Items

Item	Never Married	Married	Separated	Divorced	Widowed
			MARITAL STATUS		
95 (I am happy most of the time.[a])					
Normal[b]	86.2	91.0	80.0	85.5	93.3
Clinical[c]	60.8	62.8	72.5	62.9	57.3
162 (Someone has been trying to poison me.[a])					
Normal[b]	0.2	0.6	1.8	0.5	1.1
Clinical[c]	1.7	1.3	1.1	1.5	2.4
165 (My memory seems to be all right.[a])					
Normal[b]	92.6	90.5	89.1	90.5	79.8
Clinical[c]	72.1	65.5	78.1	67.1	56.6
216 (Someone has been trying to rob me.[a])					
Normal[b]	2.3	1.6	5.5	4.1	4.5
Clinical[c]	4.9	3.7	4.6	4.8	7.0
224 (I have few or no pains.[a])					
Normal[b]	86.4	80.9	74.5	80.5	75.3
Clinical[c]	60.4	53.4	69.9	55.5	39.5
264 (I have used alcohol excessively.[a])					
Normal[b]	36.2	31.5	40.0	35.9	15.7
Clinical[c]	30.1	25.2	27.7	28.6	22.3
266 (I have never been in trouble with the law.[a])					
Normal[b]	68.8	74.7	63.6	73.2	83.1
Clinical[c]	61.8	70.3	63.7	64.3	74.8
303 (Most of the time I wish I were dead.[a])					
Normal[b]	4.1	1.8	1.8	3.6	6.7
Clinical[c]	12.5	9.4	7.6	10.5	17.1
389 (I am often said to be hotheaded.[a])					
Normal[b]	19.8	15.3	20.0	14.5	13.5
Clinical[c]	21.7	19.1	14.6	16.4	17.7
489 (I have a drug or alcohol problem.[a])					
Normal[b]	6.2	4.0	9.1	8.6	4.5
Clinical[c]	11.3	7.1	10.1	9.3	8.4
499 (I hate going to doctors even when I'm sick.[a])					
Normal[b]	30.2	34.3	21.8	27.7	33.7
Clinical[c]	39.9	42.1	35.2	41.6	51.9
506 (I recently have considered killing myself.[a])					
Normal[b]	8.5	2.8	12.7	3.6	1.1
Clinical[c]	18.2	15.3	13.3	16.1	20.6

Item	MARITAL STATUS				
	Never Married	Married	Separated	Divorced	Widowed
511 (Once a week or more I get high or drunk.[a])					
Normal[b]	23.1	10.7	30.9	15.9	6.7
Clinical[c]	11.2	5.6	5.3	5.4	4.6
520 (Lately I have thought a lot about killing myself.[a])					
Normal[b]	4.8	0.9	1.8	3.6	2.2
Clinical[c]	12.2	10.0	8.4	10.8	16.5
548 (I've been so angry at times that I've hurt someone in a physical fight.[a])					
Normal[b]	17.1	11.8	25.5	15.0	14.6
Clinical[c]	16.2	10.8	11.8	10.6	8.9

[a]Minnesota Multiphasic Personality Inventory-2 (MMPI-2). Copyright © 1942, 1943 (renewed 1970), 1989 by the Regents of the University of Minnesota. Reproduced by permission of the publisher. "MMPI-2" and "Minnesota Multiphasic Personality Inventory-2" are trademarks owned by the University of Minnesota.
[b]Butcher et al. (1989).
[c]Caldwell (1997a).

effects of marital status on the interpretation of the MMPI-2. The absence of research on the effects of marital status on MMPI and MMPI-2 interpretation, which was noted earlier, may simply reflect that there is nothing to be found and, consequently, nothing to publish.

OCCUPATION AND INCOME

There do not appear to be any systematic effects of occupation or income within the MMPI-2 normative group (Dahlstrom & Tellegen, 1993; Long, Graham, & Timbrook, 1994). There have been no studies of the effects of these two factors in clinical samples. To the extent that these two factors reflect socioeconomic status, it would be expected that they would demonstrate similar effects as education because education and occupation are the two factors most often used to measure social class.

ETHNIC GROUP MEMBERSHIP

There have been several reviews of the influence of ethnic group membership on MMPI performance. Dahlstrom, Lachar, and Dahlstrom (1986) have pro-

vided a thorough, in-depth analysis of the influence of ethnic group membership on MMPI performance that should be read by everyone who is interested in this topic, and Dana (1990, 1993, 1995, 1998) has provided a general overview of multiethnic assessment. There have been a number of other recent reviews that should be consulted for a variety of perspectives on this topic (Costello, Tiffany, & Gier, 1972; Greene, 1987; Greene, 1991, Chapter 8; Gynther, 1972, 1979, 1989; Gynther & Green, 1980; Moreland, 1996; Pritchard & Rosenblatt, 1980a, 1980b; Zalewski & Greene, 1996). This MMPI research will be summarized rather briefly and then it will be followed by an in-depth examination of the influence of ethnic group membership on MMPI-2 performance.

The MMPI and the MMPI-2 have been translated into a number of different languages for use around the world (cf. Butcher, 1985, 1996; Butcher & Clark, 1979; Butcher & Pancheri, 1976; Lucio, Reyes-Lagunes, & Scott, 1994), which allows for the investigation of the effects of cultural factors on MMPI and MMPI-2 performance from an international perspective. The reader who is interested in this perspective should contact these resources for additional information.

A number of the general issues that must be considered in conducting research on the effects of ethnic group membership on MMPI-2 performance will be raised in the overview of the MMPI. These issues will not be reiterated when the MMPI-2 is discussed.

MMPI[1]

Most research on the effects of ethnic group membership on MMPI performance has focused on blacks, although there has been some research with Hispanics,[2] Asian Americans, and Native Americans. The first issue, of course, is whether ethnic group membership influences MMPI results when other potentially confounding factors such as socioeconomic status and educational level are controlled. If ethnic group membership does affect MMPI scale scores when these factors are controlled, the critical issue becomes whether MMPI interpretations based on white norms or some other ethnic group are more valid. Each of these issues will be examined in turn.

The prototypic investigation of the effects of ethnic group membership on MMPI performance consists of obtaining a sample of individuals from some specific ethnic group and then plotting the obtained profile against the original normative group or another ethnic group. If differences occur between the two groups on any scale, the typical conclusion is that the MMPI as a whole or some subset of scales is affected by membership in that ethnic group.

Rarely do such prototypic studies determine whether these obtained differences are of sufficient magnitude to affect clinical interpretation and, more importantly, they virtually never determine whether these different scores actually affect the empirical correlates of the scale. A number of issues must be considered before the conclusion is justified that the observed results reflect the effects of ethnic group membership. Greene (1987) has summarized a number of methodological issues that need to be considered that can potentially affect the interpretation of any ethnic differences that are found.

Researchers tend to be very casual about reporting the criteria used to specify membership within the

ethnic group whose MMPI performance is being evaluated. Most often, the persons are self-described as black, Hispanic, Asian American, and so on, with little consideration of the heterogeneity that exists within any ethnic group. For example, Okazaki (1998) noted that Asian and Pacific Islander Americans "can trace their roots to 28 countries of origin or ethnic group or to 25 identified Pacific Island cultures" (p. 56), and Allen (1998) stated that there are "510 federally recognized Native entities, including American Indian tribes and Alaska Native Villages" (p. 18). Similar heterogeneity occurs among blacks (Lindsey, 1998) and Hispanics (Cuellar, 1998).

Sometimes Hispanic subjects, and even less frequently, Asian American subjects, will be classified on the basis of their surname, which at least assures that at some point in their family heritage they had membership in the ethnic group. However, a surname does not determine whether persons actually are members of the ethnic group, or more important, whether they have any identification with that group. In an attempt to address this problem, some researchers have used the Acculturation scale for Mexican Americans (Cuellar, Harris, & Jasso, 1980; Cuellar, Arnold, & Maldonado, 1995) as a moderator variable in examining MMPI performance in Hispanic individuals (e.g., Montgomery & Orozco, 1985; Canul & Cross, 1994). In a similar vein, Costello (1977) proposed a scale that can be used to assess "functional" identification with black culture, although it has not yet been used in any reported study. Suinn and his colleagues (Suinn, Ahuna, & Khoo, 1992; Suinn, Khoo, & Ahuna, 1995; Suinn, Rikard-Figueroa, Lew, & Vigil, 1987) have developed a scale to measure acculturation in Asian Americans, which has seen only limited use with the MMPI-2.

Clearly, researchers need to become more sophisticated in assessing membership in and identification with a specific ethnic group when they are interested in examining MMPI performance, because the cultural factors that are so important in determining how psychopathology will be manifested in a person may be only loosely related to ethnic group membership. The utilization of the extant acculturation scales or some other explicit measure of identification with the ethnic group under study is mandatory in this research area. It simply is not acceptable for researchers to la-

---

1. This section has drawn substantially on Greene's (1987) review of ethnicity and MMPI performance.

bel their participants as members of an ethnic group based on skin color, surname, or self-description.

Black-White Comparisons.   The early research of black-white differences on the MMPI compared scores on the Validity and Clinical scales. The general procedure for these studies was to administer the MMPI to a group of blacks and whites and then to compare their mean scores on the Validity and Clinical scales. Even a cursory review of this literature suggests that there is no consistent pattern to black-white differences on the MMPI. Clearly, a statement that blacks or whites routinely had higher scores on any specific Validity or Clinical scale is *not* warranted across this entire range of studies. Even within specific populations, there are few generalizations that can be made in a reliable manner.

For example, in normal populations it has been stated that blacks frequently had higher scores on the *F* (Infrequency) scale and Scales *8* (Schizophrenia) and *9* (Hypomania) than whites. However, a majority of the 27 comparisons within normal samples in Table 9.27 found no reliable differences on these three scales, although when differences did occur, blacks had higher scores than whites. In fact, there was no scale that was consistently higher either in blacks or whites in a majority of the studies. Consequently, it appears inappropriate to conclude that blacks routinely had higher scores than whites on any of the Validity or Clinical scales in any sample.

It is possible that the black samples in these studies may have differed in their identification with a black culture, which would tend to obscure any real black-white differences. Harrison and Kass (1968), for example, found that northern blacks scored between southern blacks and whites on the *?* (Cannot Say) and *F* (Infrequency) scales and Scales *9* (Hypomania) and *0* (Social Introversion), which led them to conjecture that northern blacks may be acquiring white culture. Moreover, Erdberg (1975) found that black-white differences were less in urban than in rural settings.

2. A multitude of terms have been used to describe persons within a specific ethnic group such as *Chicano, Hispanic, Mexican, Mexican American,* and so on. In order to provide consistency throughout this chapter, the terms *Asian American, Hispanic,* and *Native American* will be used.

The three studies (Erdberg, 1975; McDonald & Gynther, 1962, 1963) that reported the preponderance of significant black-white differences on the MMPI in normal individuals were conducted in the South, which lends some credence to Harrison and Kass's (1968) hypothesis. Ball (1960) and Baughman and Dahlstrom (1968), however, also conducted their research in the South, and these investigators found few black-white differences.

Thus, some factor(s) other than ethnicity—perhaps identification with a black culture independent of geographic location—may be contributing to whether black-white differences are found. Costello (1977) has developed an index to help control for this factor in studying black-white differences on the MMPI, but it has not been utilized in any study.

In response to the finding that blacks usually had higher scores on the MMPI *F* (Infrequency) scale, Gynther, Lachar, and Dahlstrom (1978) developed a new *F* (Infrequency) scale for blacks. They identified 33 items that were endorsed by less than 10 percent of a combined normal male and female black sample. Only 22 of these 33 items (66.7 percent) are on the standard *F* scale. Blacks and whites, however, responded quite similarly to the 33 items on the new *F* scale for blacks; 28 of these 33 items also were endorsed by less than 10 percent of a white sample. Gynther et al. (1978) suggested that raw scores of 3, 7, and 11 on the new *F* scale for blacks should be considered equivalent to T scores of 50, 60, and 70 on the MMPI, respectively. This new *F* scale for blacks can be used as a measure of a black client's endorsement of items that were endorsed infrequently by normal black individuals, in a fashion similar to the standard *F* scale. It remains to be seen, however, whether black clients who elevate the new *F* scale for blacks will demonstrate the same behavioral correlates as are found in white clients who elevate the standard *F* scale.

The specific population that is being examined also appears to be an important factor as to whether black-white differences will be found. Thus, in substance abuse samples, whites rather frequently had higher scores than blacks on those scales for which reliable differences were found, whereas in psychiatric samples there did not appear to be any reliable pattern to the black-white comparisons.

TABLE 9.27 Black-White Differences on the MMPI Validity and Clinical Scales

Study	VALIDITY SCALES			CLINICAL SCALES									
	L	F	K	1	2	3	4	5	6	7	8	9	0
Normal Samples													
Ball (1960)													
Men				B									
Women		B	W			W					B		B
Butcher, Ball, & Ray (1964)													
Men	B		B					W	W	W		B	W
Women	B							B	W				
Erdberg (1975)													
Rural women	W	B	W			W	B	W	B		B	B	
Rural men	W	B	W	B			B		B	B	B	B	
Urban women	W		W	W	W	W						B	W
Urban men													
Gynther, Fowler, & Erdberg (1971)													
Men		B	W		B		B	B	B	B	B	B	B
Women		B	W				B	B	B	B	B	B	B
Harrison & Kass (1967)													
King, Carroll, & Fuller (1977)													
Kirk & Zucker (1979)[a]													
McDonald & Gynther (1962)													
Men	B				B								
Women					B								
McDonald & Gynther (1963)[b]													
Men, social class 1–2	B											B	
Men, social class 3	B			B									
Men, social class 4	B			B							B	B	
Women, social class 1–2	B							B					
Women, social class 3													
Women, social class 4													
Moore & Handal (1980)													
Men		B							B	B	B	B	
Women									B				
Muller & Bruno (1988)													
Muller & Bruno (1990)													
Sutker & Kilpatrick (1973)													
Men													
Women							B						
Walters, Greene, & Jeffrey (1984)													
Forensic Samples													
Caldwell (1953)								B				B	
Cooke, Pogany, & Johnston (1974)							W		B				
Costello, Fine, & Blau (1973)													
Elion & Megargee (1975)[c]							B						
Flanagan & Lewis (1969)												B	
Fry (1949)												B	
Holcomb & Adams (1982)												B	

Study	VALIDITY SCALES			CLINICAL SCALES									
	L	F	K	1	2	3	4	5	6	7	8	9	0
Forensic Samples													
Holcomb, Adams, & Ponder (1984)			B										W
Ingram et al. (1985)													
Recidivist		B											
Nonrecidivist	B												
McCreary & Padilla (1977)			B			W						B	
Murphree, Karabelas, & Bryan (1962)[d]													
Panton (1959a)		B				W					B		
Rosenblatt & Pritchard (1978)				B		W					B	B	
Stanton (1956)													
Walters (1986)													
Control									W				
Index		B					W		B				
Substance Abuse Samples													
Hill, Haertzen, & Glaser (1960)					W							B	
Patalano (1978)													
Men		B						W					W
Women					W			B		W			W
Patterson et al. (1981)													
Penk et al. (1981)													
Penk et al. (1982)													
Penk et al. (1978)		W											W
Sutker, Archer, & Allain (1978)		W			W				W	W			
Sutker, Archer, & Allain (1980)[e]													
Men (Fetter)					W	W					B		W
Women (Fetter)		W		W	W	W	W	B	W	W	W		W
Men (NARA)													
Women (NARA)		W		W	W	W	W	B		W	W	W	
Walters, Greene, & Jeffrey (1984)													
Weiss & Russakoff (1977)					W				W				
Medical/Welfare Samples													
Hokanson & Calden (1960)					W	B			B	B			
McGill (1980)													
Nelson et al. (1996)													
Men		B							B	B	B	B	
Women		B					B		B	B	B		
Psychiatric Samples													
Bertelson, Marks, & May (1982)		B						B			B		
Butcher, Braswell, & Raney (1983)													
Men													
Women		B									B		
Costello et al. (1973)													
Men		B											
Women		B	W				B		B		B	B	

(continued)

TABLE 9.27   Black-White Differences on the MMPI Validity and Clinical Scales (continued)

Study	VALIDITY SCALES			CLINICAL SCALES									
	L	F	K	1	2	3	4	5	6	7	8	9	0
Psychiatric Samples													
Davis (1975)													
Schizophrenic													
Nonschizophrenic													
Davis, Beck, & Ryan (1973)													
High education			B	B	W			W	W	W			
Low education		W			W	W			W	W	W		
Davis & Jones (1974)													
High education schizophrenic												W	
High education nonschizophrenic									W				
Low education schizophrenic								B	B		B	B	
Low education nonschizophrenic				B			W	W			B	B	
Genthner & Graham (1976)	B										B		
Kirk & Zucker (1979)					B								
Klinge & Strauss (1976)													
Liske & McCormick (1976)													
Miller, Knapp, & Daniels (1968)				B				W			B		
Miller, Wertz, & Counts (1961)				B				W					
Peteroy & Pirrello (1982)[f]													
Smith & Graham (1981)[g]													

Adapted from "Ethnicity and MMPI Performance: A Review" by Roger L. Greene, 1989, *Journal of Consulting and Clinical Psychology,* 55, pp. 500–502. Copyright 1989 by the American Psychological Association. Reprinted by permission.

Note B = Blacks scored higher than whites; W = Whites scored higher than blacks. Differences less than 5 T points between two groups were not charted, regardless of statistical significance. When a study reported multiple comparisons between two groups, only the results of the most rigorous comparisons were charted.

[a]Compared only Scale *2.*

[b]Social classes 1 and 2 = independent or dependent occupations involving skill and the supervision of others; Social class 3 = dependent occupations involving skill but little supervision of others; Social class 4 = dependent occupations involving little skill and little supervision of others.

[c]Compared only Scale *4.*

[d]Compared only Scales *K* and *4.*

[e]NARA = Narcotic Addict Rehabilitation Act Program, Tulane University School of Medicine; Fetter = Franklin C. Fetter Drug Abuse Program, Charleston, SC.

[f]Compared only Scales *F, 8,* and *9.*

[g]Compared only Scale *F.*

It has been conjectured (cf. Penk, Robinowitz, Roberts, Dolan, & Atkins, 1981) that whites who became substance abusers were more disturbed than blacks, which would account for the higher elevations in the former group. Since groups of substance abusers have not been matched for type or severity of psychopathology and then examined for black-white differences, there are no data to address this issue directly. However, when psychiatric patients were matched on education and for type of psychopathology (Davis,

Beck, & Ryan, 1973), no black-white differences were found. Again, it seems that any simple explanation of the pattern of black-white differences within and between populations is not readily apparent without giving adequate consideration to the multitude of moderator variables that may affect performance.

One final comment about black-white differences on the Validity and Clinical scales seems warranted. The more rigorously that moderator variables and profile validity issues were controlled by an investigator, the less likely it was that black-white differences were found. For example, Costello et al. (1972) reported that no black-white differences were found if invalid profiles were excluded. Similarly, Penk and his colleagues (Penk et al., 1981; Penk, Roberts, Robinowitz, Dolan, Atkins, & Woodward, 1982) found no black-white differences in substance abuse patients when age, education, socioeconomic status, and intelligence were controlled statistically.

Thus, it appears that moderator variables, such as socioeconomic status, education, and intelligence, as well as profile validity issues, are important factors to be controlled in any MMPI research and particularly when the potential effect of ethnic group membership is being examined. Rather than discussing the fact that normal individuals within a specific ethnic group tend to have more elevated scores on the Validity and Clinical scales than whites, it seems much more important to consider the role of the moderator variables listed previously such as socioeconomic status, education, and intelligence. As stated by Pritchard and Rosenblatt (1980a), it seems premature to conclude that new norms for blacks are needed. However, it does appear necessary for clinicians and researchers to become more aware of the multitude of potential factors that can affect MMPI performance.

The paucity of studies that have examined directly whether there are distinct empirical correlates of the obtained black-white differences is amazing, particularly when it is realized that this issue has been investigated for nearly 40 years on the MMPI. Investigators seem content to report small black-white differences in performance on a specific scale without considering whether these differences have any clinical correlates or relevance. Gynther, Altman, and Warbin (1973b) were unable to replicate any of the correlates of raw scores greater than 25 (T score of 98) on the standard *F* (Infrequency) scale in black psychi-

atric patients; they were, however, successful in replicating these correlates in white patients. Gynther et al.'s findings suggest that the meaning of high *F* scale scores in blacks remains unclear. In one of the few additional validity studies, Elion and Megargee (1975) tested the validity of Scale *4* (Psychopathic Deviate) in blacks and concluded that there was no need to derive a new Scale *4* to assess antisocial behavior patterns among blacks. They did suggest that 5 T points should be subtracted from Scale *4* after *K*-correction in black clients to offset the tendency that they found for blacks to have slightly higher scores than whites on this scale. Finally, Marks et al. (1974) found few black-white differences in the correlates of their adolescent codetypes, although they only had a small sample of 61 black adolescents.

Only three studies (Elion & Megargee, 1975; Genthner & Graham, 1976; Smith & Graham, 1981) have examined the empirical correlates of the black-white differences that were found, and two of the three studies (Elion & Megargee, 1975; Genthner & Graham, 1976) concluded that there were no differences in the external correlates of the MMPI.

Four studies have examined the correlates of specific codetypes and scale elevations (Clark & Miller, 1971; Gynther, Altman, & Warbin, 1973a, 1973b; Strauss, Gynther, & Wallhermfechtel, 1974). In none of these four studies were the black correlates identical to the white correlates, although Clark & Miller (1971) reported that the cardinal features of their *8-6* profiles were remarkably similar. Shore (1976) reviewed the statistical analysis of the data reported by Strauss et al. (1974) and concluded that there was no clear evidence for greater misdiagnosis among blacks than whites.

Thus, at least three of these seven studies have found different correlates for blacks and whites on the MMPI. The interested reader should consult Pritchard and Rosenblatt's (1980a, 1980b) criticisms of these studies, however, before assuming that these correlates are reliable. Clearly, additional research is needed to investigate the clinical correlates of black-white differences in MMPI performance when the potential influence of moderator variables has been controlled adequately.

Only a few studies have investigated whether there are differences in the discriminability of blacks and whites within and between diagnostic groups using the MMPI. Both Cowan, Watkins, and Davis

(1975) and Davis (1975) examined black-white differences in matched groups of schizophrenics and nonschizophrenics and found no significant differences for ethnic group membership. Cowan et al. did find that blacks with less than 12 years of education were more likely to be misclassified than blacks with 12 years or more of education or whites. Their results appear to be compatible with Rosenblatt and Pritchard (1978), who found differences for ethnic group membership only in patients with IQs below 94.

Strauss et al. (1974) examined black-white differences between groups of patients diagnosed as exhibiting behavior disorders and psychoses. Using a discriminant function analysis, they reported that black patients with behavior disorders were misclassified more than any of the other groups of patients. But Shore (1976) indicated that this result reflected a computational error and concluded that there were no significant black-white differences in the Strauss et al.'s (1974) study.

Because of the limited amount of research, it is difficult to conclude whether there are black-white differences between various diagnostic groups as assessed by the MMPI. There does appear to be a tendency for blacks with limited education and IQs below average to score differently than whites on the MMPI, and the clinician should consider whether these variables are relevant when interpreting a black client's MMPI.

There has been very little research on black-white differences for the numerous MMPI Supplementary scales. The limited research appears to show that few reliable black-white differences were found with fewer significant results than on the Validity and Clinical scales. Even given the fact that moderator variables generally were not controlled in most of these studies, few reliable differences were found. It is interesting to note that black and white substance abusers seemed to score in the same range on the MacAndrew Alcoholism (*MAC*) scale, yet normal blacks had higher scores than whites. Since the *MAC* scale is used so widely, more research on the potential effects of ethnic group membership, particularly in interaction with the type of setting, is needed.

A number of investigators have reported black-white differences at the item level on the MMPI (Costello, 1973, 1977; Gynther & Witt, 1976; Harri-

son & Kass, 1967, 1968; Jones, 1978; Miller, Knapp, & Daniels, 1968; Witt & Gynther, 1975). Although from 58 to 213 items have been found to differentiate blacks from whites in a given study, there has been limited overlap among these items across the various studies. In reviewing six studies of item-level differences among blacks and whites, Costello (1977) reported that "three items differentiated [blacks and whites] six of six times, seven items discriminated five of six times, and 22 items discriminated four of six times" (p. 515). Nine of the 32 items that Costello identified to differentiate blacks and whites on the MMPI have been dropped from the MMPI-2, which suggests that there should be even fewer black-white differences at the item level on the MMPI-2.

Again, the need to control for the potential effect of moderator variables must be underscored in these studies. Consequently, there does not appear to be any real conclusion that can be drawn from these findings other than that item-level endorsement frequencies may vary in different samples with a very small number of items consistently differentiating blacks and whites.

Hispanic-White Comparisons[3]. There are a number of general articles that have addressed issues in the culturally competent assessment of Hispanics (Cuellar, 1998; Dana, 1995; Geisinger, 1992; Velasquez, 1992, 1995). These articles, and particularly the edited book by Geisinger, should be consulted before undertaking research with this ethnic group.

There has been very little research that has examined Hispanic-white differences on the Validity and Clinical scales of the MMPI. Consequently, conclusions are even more difficult to make than in black samples. There does not appear to be any pattern to these comparisons and there are few data to support the contention that Hispanics frequently had higher scores on the *L* (Lie) scale and lower scores on Scale 5 (Masculinity-Femininity; cf. Greene, 1980), although when differences are found they tended to be in that direction. There does appear to be a tendency

---

3. Given the limited number of studies on the MMPI in Asian American, Hispanic, and Native American samples, these data have been incorporated into the respective MMPI-2 tables that will be summarized later in this chapter.

for fewer Hispanic-white differences to be found than when black-white comparisons are made.

Velasquez and his colleagues (Velasquez, 1984, 1992; Velasquez & Callahan, 1990a, 1990b; Velasquez, Callahan, & Carrillo, 1989; Velasquez, Callahan, & Young, 1993; Velasquez & Gimenez, 1987) have provided the most systematic research on the use of the MMPI in Hispanics. There is not a simple generalization that summarizes their research, although their results tended to be similar to what has been reported by others. Velasquez and Gimenez (1987) did not find any relationship between DSM-III diagnosis and the Validity and Clinical scales on the MMPI in Hispanic inpatients; this failure to find a specific relationship between the MMPI and DSM-III diagnoses has been reported frequently (cf. Greene, 1988).

Velasquez and Callahan (1990a) found that Hispanic alcoholics had lower scores on the MMPI than white alcoholics similar to the relationship found in black-white comparisons in alcoholics. This latter finding that Hispanic alcoholics, like black alcoholics, had lower scores on the MMPI when differences were found requires that any study of ethnic differences on the MMPI include the setting in which the test is administered as a potential confounding factor. Finally, it must be noted that Velasquez, like many other investigators in this area of research, did not report how ethnicity is defined in any of his studies.

There have been only three studies (Dolan, Roberts, Penk, Robinowitz, & Atkins, 1983; McCreary & Padilla, 1977; Page & Bozlee, 1982) that have reported Hispanic-white differences on any of the Supplementary scales, with almost no overlap in the scales reported. McCreary and Padilla (1977) found no differences between Hispanic and white prisoners, and Page and Bozlee (1982) found no differences between Hispanic and white substance abusers on the MacAndrew Alcoholism (*MAC*) scale. McCreary and Padilla reported that Hispanics had higher scores on the Overcontrolled-Hostility (*O-H*) scale, and Dolan et al. (1983) found no differences larger than 5 T points on any of the Wiggins (1966) Content scales.

There have been no studies of Hispanic-white differences at the item level.

Black-Hispanic Comparisons. Only five studies have investigated black-Hispanic differences on the Validity and Clinical scales (Holland, 1979; McCreary & Padilla, 1977; McGill, 1980; Penk et al., 1981; Velasquez & Callahan, 1990b). Holland's (1979) sample of Hispanic prisoners had lower scores on Scales 5 (Masculinity-Femininity) and 8 (Schizophrenia) than blacks, whereas McCreary and Padilla's (1977) Hispanic prisoners had higher scores on the *K* (Correction) scale and Scales 1 (Hypochondriasis), 2 (Depression), and 3 (Hysteria). McGill (1980) found that Hispanic women welfare recipients had higher scores on the *L* (Lie) and *K* (Correction) scales and lower scores on Scale 9 (Hypomania) than blacks. Penk et al. (1981) reported that Hispanic male substance abusers had higher scores on Scale 2 and lower scores on Scale 5 than blacks. Finally, Velasquez and Callahan (1990b) did not find any differences between black and Hispanic schizophrenics. It should be evident that there is no clear pattern to be found in these black-Hispanic comparisons.

McCreary and Padilla (1977) are the only investigators to report black-Hispanic comparisons on any of the MMPI Supplementary scales. They found that Hispanic prisoners had lower scores on the Mac-Andrew Alcoholism (*MAC*) scale than blacks.

Native American-White Comparisons. There are fewer general articles that have addressed issues in the culturally competent assessment of Native Americans (Allen, 1998). This article should be consulted before undertaking research with this ethnic group.

For the first time in the comparison of the MMPI performance of two ethnic groups, there appears to be a clear pattern for normal Indians to have higher scores on most of the Clinical scales than their white counterparts, even though there were no differences on the Validity scales. This conclusion must be tempered by the fact that only two studies have been conducted, especially because similar trends were not evident in psychiatric and substance abuse samples. In these latter two samples, much as in black-white and Hispanic-white comparisons, there was no consistent pattern at all.

Only one study (Uecker, Boutilier, & Richardson, 1980) has investigated the performance of Native American samples on any of the MMPI Supplementary scales. Uecker et al. found no differences between Native American and white substance abusers on the

MacAndrew Alcoholism (*MAC*) scale. Uecker et al. did not report data from a Native American sample who were not substance abusers, so it is not known whether they also would have elevated the *MAC* scale as seen in normal blacks as mentioned earlier.

There have been no studies of Native American-white differences at the item level, although Arthur (1944) discussed the various interpretations that her Native American students gave to some of the items. For example, one Native American student answered "true" to the items, "I worry about my wife," and "My children worry me," because he worried about them even though he was not married and had no children.

Asian American-White Comparisons.   There are a number of general articles that have addressed issues in the culturally competent assessment of Asian Americans (Kwan, 1994; Okazaki, 1998; Okazaki & Sue, 1995a, 1995b). These articles should be consulted before undertaking research with this ethnic group.

There have been almost no studies of the performance of Asian Americans on the MMPI. Since Sue and Sue (1974) found a number of differences between their samples, it appears clear that more research is need in this ethnic group. It is particularly important for the study by Sue and Sue to be replicated, since in the other ethnic groups that were reviewed previously, there was a tendency toward fewer differences between groups in psychiatric samples than in normal samples.

There have been no studies that have examined Asian American-white performance on any of the MMPI Supplementary scales. There also have been no studies of the differences in the pattern of item endorsements between Asian Americans and whites.

Summary.   After reviewing the effects of ethnic group membership on MMPI performance, there appear to be a number of comments that can be made about the research being conducted in this area. First, the failure to find any consistent pattern of scale differences between any two ethnic groups in any population would suggest that it is very premature to begin to develop new norms for various ethnic groups. It appears that moderator variables, such as socioeconomic status, education, and intelligence, as well as profile validity, are more important determinants of

MMPI performance than ethnic group membership. Definitely, research is needed that examines the role of identified cultural factors on MMPI performance when appropriate controls are instituted for the multitude of factors that can affect the results.

Second, the frequent failure to assess in any manner the persons' identifications with their ethnic group is quite notable. It seems very questionable to be making statements about the effects of ethnic group membership on MMPI performance without some means of ensuring that the persons actually identify with and belong to the ethnic group. Thus, investigations of the effects of ethnic group membership on MMPI performance need to give more serious consideration to the role of cultural factors and stop assuming that identity with the ethnic group is determined by the person's skin color, surname, or self-description. Some reliable and valid means of assessing persons' degrees of identification with their culture would greatly enhance research on this topic, such as the acculturation scale for Mexican Americans (Cuellar et al., 1980, 1995) and Asian Americans (Suinn et al., 1987, 1992, 1995).

Third, researchers need to stop reporting small mean differences between two groups, which are frequently poorly defined, and begin to assess the empirical correlates of any differences that are found. The fact that fewer than 10 studies actually have examined the empirical correlates of ethnic group membership and MMPI performance should indicate the direction for future research.

Finally, there is a real dearth of studies on the multitude of MMPI Supplementary scales in any ethnic group. Since a number of these Supplementary scales are scored routinely, research is needed to examine the effects of ethnic group membership on performance on these scales. It should go without saying that the previously stated guidelines for research on the MMPI Validity and Clinical scales also apply to research on these Supplementary scales.

MMPI-2

Black-White Comparisons.   There have been only a few studies of black-white differences on the MMPI-2 in contrast to the large number of studies on the MMPI. Only two of the comparisons of the Validity and Clinical scales in either normal men or women were significant between blacks and whites (Table 9.28). Black male students had higher scores on Scale *8* (Schizophrenia) than white male students (Goldman, Cooke, & Dahlstrom, 1995). Timbrook and Graham (1994) screened their subjects on several criteria for validity and matched them on age, years of education, and family income. The largest difference they found was 4 T points on Scale *8* in adult men and Scale *5* (Masculinity-Femininity) in adult women. There appear to be very few black-white differences on the Validity and Clinical scales of the MMPI-2 in normal samples. This finding of few black-white differences in normal samples on the MMPI-2 is somewhat unexpected because most of the black-white differences on the MMPI were found in normal samples.

Research on black-white differences in psychiatric samples is somewhat more common than in other settings (Table 9.28). The only comparison that was clinically significant more than once was for blacks to have higher scores on Scales *6* (Paranoia) and *8* (Schizophrenia) than whites, which occurred in two of the five comparisons that were made (Arbisi, Ben-Porath, & McNulty, 1998; Frueh, Smith, & Libet, 1996). In the other three comparisons there were no black-white differences on Scales *6* and *8*, so it would be hard to conclude that there actually are black-white differences on these two scales. None of these studies matched their subjects on any potentially confounding variables. However, both Arbisi et al. and McNulty et al. screened their MMPI-2s on several validity criteria before making any comparisons.

TABLE 9.28   Black-White Differences on the MMPI-2 Validity and Clinical Scales

Study	VALIDITY SCALES			CLINICAL SCALES									
	L	F	K	1	2	3	4	5	6	7	8	9	0
Normal Samples													
Goldman et al. (1995)													
Men											B		
Women													
Kornfield (1995)				W									
Timbrook & Graham (1994)													
Men													
Women													
Forensic Samples													
Ben-Porath et al. (1995)													W
Frank et al. (1997)	B						B				B		
Psychiatric Samples													
Arbisi et al. (1998)		B					B		B		B	B	
Frueh et al. (1996)[a]									B		B		
Freuh et al. (1997)													
Ganellen & Harlem (1997)										W			
McNulty et al. (1997)													
Men	B												
Women													

Note. B = Blacks scored higher than whites; W = Whites scored higher than blacks. Differences less than 5 T points between two groups were not charted, regardless of statistical significance.
[a]Reported only Scales *2, 4, 6, 7, 8,* and *9.*

There have been only two studies of black-white differences in forensic settings and no studies in substance abuse settings on the MMPI-2 Validity and Clinical scales. It would be interesting to see whether the reversal of the pattern of black-white differences in substance abuse settings occurs on the MMPI-2 as was found on the MMPI.

The MMPI-2 Content (Butcher et al., 1990) and Supplementary scales have received scant attention in looking for black-white differences similar to the inattention that was found with the MMPI (Table 9.29). There have been no studies of the Content or Supplementary scales in normal samples. Neither of the two studies with psychiatric samples nor forensic samples found black-white differences on the same Content scale. Thus, there does not appear to be any consistent pattern for black-white differences on the Content scales, although more research is warranted. The only consistent finding on the Supplementary scales was for blacks to have higher scores on the Overcontrolled-Hostility (*O-H*) scale than whites (Frank, Velasquez, Reimann, & Salazar, 1997; Ganellen & Harlam, 1997; Hutton et al., 1992). The lack of black-white differences on the MacAndrew Alcoholism—Revised (*MAC-R*) scale is unexpected, because such differences were encountered frequently on the MMPI (Table 6.9, p. 231).

The most important advance in the study of black-white differences on the MMPI-2 has been made by Arbisi et al. (1998), McNulty, Graham, Ben-Porath, and Stein (1997), and Timbrook and Graham (1994), who have examined the empirical correlates as well as the mean differences between the two groups. Timbrook and Graham used regression equations to predict partners' ratings of their subjects. The only significant difference they found was for scores on Scale *7* (Psychasthenia) to *underpredict* ratings of anxiety for black women. This outcome is interesting because the primary concern with the MMPI has been that the test may *overpathologize* blacks. Both Arbisi et al. and McNulty et al. found no black-white differences in the correlations between the MMPI-2 Validity, Clinical, and Content scales and record review forms and therapists' ratings of the patients, respectively. In all three of these studies, the most striking finding was the high degree of similarity between the blacks and whites on these external criteria.

It seems safe to conclude that there are no viable black-white differences on the MMPI-2 even given the limited number of studies. The substantial sample sizes, careful attention to profile validity, and matching of subjects on a number of potential confounding variables greatly reduce the concern about such factors impacting the results. More importantly, however, the examination for and the finding of no differences in the external correlates between blacks and whites make this conclusion very straightforward.

Hispanic-White Comparisons. There have been several comparisons of Hispanic-white differences on the MMPI-2 in normal samples (Table 9.30). There were almost no significant differences found in any of these comparisons on the MMPI-2 Validity and Clinical scales. Most of the differences that were found on any of the forms of the MMPI occurred in two studies. Whitworth (1988) found that Mexican American students who were given the MMPI in Spanish had higher scores on most of the Validity and Clinical scales than Anglo-American students. Gumbiner (1998) found that Hispanic adolescent boys had higher scores on most of the Validity and Clinical scales of the MMPI-A than the MMPI-A normative group. Given that all of the MMPI-2 studies have been conducted with college students, it seems premature to conclude that there are no Hispanic-white differences without further research on normal adult samples. It does appear, however, that there are fewer Hispanic-white differences on the MMPI-2 than on the MMPI in normal samples similar to the pattern that was found with blacks.

There has been only one study of Hispanic-white differences on the MMPI-2 in psychiatric samples, one study in forensic samples, and no studies in substance abuse samples on the Validity and Clinical scales (Table 9.30). The limited number of studies precludes any conclusion other than that more research is needed in this area.

There have been no studies of Hispanic-white differences on the MMPI-2 Content scales and limited research on the Supplementary scales (Table 9.31). Essentially no Hispanic-white differences were found in any of the comparisons of any of the Supplementary scales.

Native American-White Comparisons. Three separate studies (Butcher et al., 1989; Pace, Choney, Blair, Hill, & Lacey, 1997; Robin, Greene, Albaugh, & Caldwell, 1999) have reported the performance of normal

TABLE 9.29 Black-White Differences on the MMPI-2 Content and Supplementary Scales

						CONTENT SCALES									
Study	ANX	FRS	OBS	DEP	HEA	BIZ	ANG	CYN	ASP	TPA	LSE	SOD	FAM	WRK	TRT
							Psychiatric Samples								
Arbisi et al. (1998)				B		B	B	B	B				B		B
Freuh et al. (1997)															
McNulty et al. (1997)															
Men	W	B													
Women											W				
							Forensic Samples								
Ben-Porath et al. (1995)						B		B	B						
Frank et al. (1997)[a]								B	B			B			

				SUPPLEMENTARY SCALES			
Study	A	R	Es	MAC-R	O-H	AAS	APS
			Psychiatric Samples				
Ganellen & Harlem (1997)					B		
			Forensic Samples				
Ben-Porath et al. (1995)[b]				B			
Frank et al. (1997)							
Hutton et al. (1992)[c]					B		
Rowell (1992)[d]							
Non-problem drinkers				B			
Problem drinkers							

Note. B = Blacks scored higher than whites; W = Whites scored higher than blacks. Differences less than 5 T points between two groups were not charted, regardless of statistical significance.

[a]Reported only the *SOD* scale.
[b]Compared only the *MAC-R, APS,* and *AAS* scales.
[c]Compared only the *O-H* scale.
[d]Compared only the *MAC-R* scale.

TABLE 9.30 Hispanic-White Differences on the MMPI and MMPI-2 Validity and Clinical Scales

| Study | VALIDITY SCALES | | | CLINICAL SCALES | | | | | | | | | |
	L	F	K	1	2	3	4	5	6	7	8	9	0
Normal Samples													
MMPI													
Montgomery & Orozco (1985)		H									H		
Padilla et al. (1982)[a]													
N-L factor	H			H				W					
SES factor	W		W				H						
Reilley & Knight (1970)													
Whitworth (1988)													
Mexican American in English													
Mexican American in Spanish	H	H		H	H		H	H	H	H	H		H
MMPI-2													
Canul & Cross (1994)[b]													
High acculturation													
Anglo-oriented bicultural													
Mexican-oriented bicultural	H												
Kornfield (1995)				W									
Whitworth & McBlaine (1993)													
Whitworth & Unterbrink (1994)											H		
MMPI-A													
Gumbiner (1998) [adolescents]													
Boys	H	H		H	H	H	H		H	H	H		H
Girls					H			H					
Negy et al. (1997) [adolescents]													
Psychiatric Samples													
MMPI													
Hibbs et al. (1979)													
Men							W						
Women				H					H				
Lawson et al. (1982)	H												
Plemons (1977)	H		H				W	W		W		W	
Velasquez & Callahan (1990b)	H			H	H				H	H	H	H	
Velasquez et al. (1993)		H		H	H	H		H		H	H		
MMPI-2													
Ganellen & Harlem (1997)	H				W	W							
Haskell (1996)	H			H	H				H	H		W	

Study	VALIDITY SCALES			CLINICAL SCALES									
	L	F	K	1	2	3	4	5	6	7	8	9	0
Forensic Samples													
MMPI													
Holland (1979)								W					
McCreary & Padilla (1977)			H										
MMPI-2													
Frank et al. (1997)	H	H											
Substance Abuse Samples													
MMPI													
Page & Bozlee (1982)					H								
Penk et al. (1981)								W					
Velasquez & Callahan (1990a)					W		W	W	W	W	W		W
Medical Sample													
MMPI													
Nelson et al. (1996)													
Men	H			H				W					
Women	H							H					
Welfare Sample													
MMPI													
McGill (1980)								H				W	

Note. H = Hispanics scored higher than whites; W = Whites scored higher than Hispanics.
Differences less than 5 T points between two groups were not charted, regardless of statistical significance.

[a]N-L factor = Normality-Language factor; SES factor = socioeconomic status.

[b]Studied only the *L* and *K* scales and Scale *5.*

samples of Native Americans on the MMPI-2 (Table 9.32). In all of these studies, the MMPI-2 normative sample served as the comparison group. These studies rather consistently found that Native Americans have higher scores on the *F* (Infrequency) scale and Scales 8 (Schizophrenia) and 9 (Hypomania) as well as several other Clinical scales. The large number of differences between Native Americans and whites on the MMPI-2 in normal samples is similar to what was found on the MMPI. However, there is virtually no overlap in the scales that were different between the two groups on the MMPI and MMPI-2. It seems safe to conclude that Native Americans will have higher scores on the MMPI-2 than whites, although less confidence can be placed in exactly which of the Validity and Clinical scales will demonstrate these differences.

Robin et al. (1999) also compared their two tribes when they had been divided into four groups based on socioeconomic status. There tended to be fewer differences between either tribe and the MMPI-2 normative group in the highest socioeconomic status. Even in this group, however, the *L* (Lie) scale in both men and

TABLE 9.31   Hispanic-White Differences on the MMPI-2 Supplementary Scales

	SUPPLEMENTARY SCALES				
Study	A	R	Es	MAC-R	O-H
			Psychiatric Samples		
Ganellen & Harlem (1997)					H
			Forensic Samples		
Frank et al. (1997)					
Rowell (1992)a					
Non-problem drinkers					
Problem drinkers					
			Substance Abuse Samples		
Lapham et al. (1995)[a]				H	

Note. H = Hispanics scored higher than whites; W = Whites scored higher than Hispanics. Differences less than 5 T points between two groups were not charted, regardless of statistical significance.

[a]Compared only the *MAC-R* scale.

women, and Scales *4* (Psychopathic Deviate) in men and *5* (Masculinity-Femininity) in women were still more than 5 T points higher than the MMPI-2 normative group in both tribes. The group with the lower socioeconomic status tended to be at least 5 T points higher on all of the scales except the *K* (Correction) scale and Scale *3* (Hysteria) on which they were 5 T points lower than the MMPI-2 normative group. It appears that the differences between Native Americans and whites are not attenuated fully when groups are matched on socioeconomic status.

There have been no studies of the MMPI-2 in any other setting that has compared Native Americans and whites or any study that has reported the results on the Content and Supplementary scales.

Asian American-White Comparisons. There have been only two studies of Asian American-white differences in normal samples on the MMPI-2, both of which were carried out in college students (Table 9.33, p. 488). Sue, Keefe, Enomoto, Durvasula, and Chao (1996) found that less acculturated Asian American students showed more differences from whites than highly acculturated Asian American students. They also found that Asian American

women students showed more differences from whites than men students. Both Sue et al. and Stevens, Kwan, and Graybill (1993) controlled for the effects of demographic variables so it is unclear why the results of these two studies are so discrepant.

There have been no studies of the MMPI-2 in any other setting that has compared Asian Americans and whites or any study that has reported the results on the Content and Supplementary scales.

Summary. After reviewing the effects of ethnic group membership on MMPI-2 performance, there appear to be a number of similar comments that could be made about this research that would be redundant with the comments about the MMPI research, so they will not be repeated here. Although increasing attention is being paid to whether the participants actually identify with their ethnic group, there still are a number of studies that give this topic only passing consideration at best. Even if researchers are sensitive to the issues of identification with and acculturation to the specific ethnic group, there is little apparent awareness of the heterogeneity that exists within any ethnic group. The reliance on college students as the primary source of subjects for this research is unlikely to address

TABLE 9.32 Native American–White Differences on the MMPI and MMPI-2 Validity and Clinical Scales

Study	VALIDITY SCALES			CLINICAL SCALES									
	L	F	K	1	2	3	4	5	6	7	8	9	0
						Normal Samples							
MMPI													
Arthur (1944)[a]													
Men				I									
Women				I		I	I						
Herreid & Herreid (1966)													
Men native				I					I	I			
Women native			I	I		I			I	I	I		
Men nonnative									I				
Women nonnative											I		
MMPI-2													
Butcher et al. (1989)		I											
Pace et al. (1997)													
Eastern Woodland Oklahoma		I		I					I		I	I	
Southwest Oklahoma	I	I		I				I	I		I	I	
Robin et al. (1999)													
Plains	I	I		I				I			I	I	
Southwest	I	I						I			I	I	
						Psychiatric Samples							
MMPI													
Butcher et al. (1983)													
Men									W	W			
Women	W									W			
Pollack & Shore (1980)[b]	I		I	I	I	I		I	I	I	I	I	
						Substance Abuse Samples							
MMPI													
Kline et al. (1973)										I			
Page & Bozlee (1982)													
Uecker et al. (1980)						W	W						

Note. I = Native Americans scored higher than whites; W = Whites scored higher than Native Americans. Differences less than 5 T points between two groups were not charted, regardless of statistical significance.

[a]Reported data only for Scales *1–4.*

[b]Compared their Native American *psychiatric* patients with the original Minnesota normative sample, which produced the larger number of significant results.

TABLE 9.33 Asian American-White Differences on the MMPI and MMPI-2 Validity and Clinical Scales

Study	VALIDITY SCALES			CLINICAL SCALES									
	L	F	K	1	2	3	4	5	6	7	8	9	0
Normal Samples													
MMPI													
Marsella et al. (1975)[a]													
Chinese men													
Chinese women					A								
Japanese men					A								
Japanese women													
MMPI-2													
Stevens et al. (1993)													
Chinese men													A
Chinese women	A												
Sue et al. (1996)													
Highly acculturated men	A	A											
Less acculturated men	A	A		A	A				A	A	A		A
Highly acculturated women		A			A		A		A	A	A		
Less acculturated women	A	A	W	A	A		A		A	A	A	A	A
Psychiatric Samples													
MMPI													
Sue & Sue (1974)													
Men	A	A		A	A		A		A	A	A		A
Women	A	A											A
Tsushima & Onorato (1982)													
Men							W						
Women													

Note: A = Asian Americans scored higher than whites; W = Whites scored higher than Asian Americans. Differences less than 5 T points between two groups were not charted, regardless of statistical significance.
[a]Compared only Scale 2.

adequately the effects of ethnic group membership on MMPI-2 performance because its effects are likely to be minimized in students.

Researchers infrequently give appropriate attention to the multitude of demographic variables that can potentially impact MMPI-2 performance. It almost unheard of for research in this area to consider simultaneously whether: (1) the participants identify with their ethnic group; (2) the MMPI-2 profiles are valid; (3) differences on demographic variables such as education and socioeconomic status have impacted the MMPI-2 scales; and (4) there are empirical correlates of any differences that are found. The fact that only three studies actually have examined the empirical correlates of ethnic group membership and MMPI-2 performance should indicate the direction for future research.

Finally, there is a real dearth of studies on the multitude of MMPI-2 Content and Supplementary scales in any ethnic group. Since this information is readily available if the entire MMPI-2 has been administered, it is unclear why researchers only are reporting the Validity and Clinical scales.

MULTIPLE DEMOGRAPHIC VARIABLES

Multivariate regressions of age, education, gender, ethnicity, and occupation on the Validity and Clinical scales in the MMPI-2 normative group (Dahlstrom & Tellegen, 1993) and psychiatric patients (Caldwell, 1997a [age, education, and gender only]; Schinka, LaLone, & Greene, 1998) have shown that the percentage of variance accounted for by any of these variables does not exceed 10 percent for any MMPI-2 scale. The only exception to this generalization is Scale 5 (Masculinity-Femininity) in which slightly over 50 percent of the variance is accounted for by gender. The correlations of age, gender, and education with the various MMPI-2 scales in both the MMPI-2 normative group and the Caldwell clinical dataset that were reported in the tables earlier in this chapter account for similar percentages of variance.

The potential effects of examining several demographic variables simultaneously can be illustrated within the Caldwell (1997a) clinical dataset. All possible combinations of age, gender, education, and marital status for all of the sets of MMPI-2 scales will not be explored because it would expand significantly the number of tables and pages in this chapter. Instead one example that considers three demographic variables simultaneously will be discussed. Table 9.34 presents the means and standard deviations for the MMPI-2 Validity and Clinical scales in the Caldwell (1997a) clinical dataset for seven age ranges within three levels of education for men and women.

There are several generalizations that are readily apparent in examining the data presented in Table 9.34. First, scores tend to increase 5 to 10 T points on a majority of the Clinical scales as the number of years of education decreases. Second, gender has almost no impact whatsoever because T scores are being compared rather than raw scores. Finally, any age effects tend to be smaller in patients with 17 or more years of education as compared to patients with 12 or fewer years of education. However, it still must be kept in mind that these variables of age, education, and gender account for no more than 8 percent of the variance in any of the Validity and Clinical scales of the MMPI-2, and more typically account for only 3 to 4 percent of the variance.

SUMMARY

It is clear that demographic variables have significant effects on MMPI-2 codetypes, scales, and items. However, there is not a simple, direct relationship between any single demographic variable and scores on a given scale. It also appears that the more data that are available on a single variable, the more complex are the relationships that are identified. Research in this area still is in the preliminary stages in which single variables are examined at a time. Research that looks at the potential interaction of two or more of these variables simply is nonexistent. It also is necessary for researchers to progress beyond merely reporting mean T scores as a function of some demographic variable and begin to examine whether the correlates of a given MMPI-2 scale and codetype change as a function of the demographic variable. Stated simply, the question is whether a man with an eighth grade education and an IQ of 90 will have the same correlates of a *2-7/7-2* codetype as a woman with a college degree and an IQ of 120. It is time to begin to look for empirical answers to basic questions such as these.

It does appear that demographic variables will have minimal impact on the MMPI-2 profile in most individuals, if the client is 20 years of age or older and has at least 12 years of education. It may be important to monitor the validity of the MMPI-2 profile more closely in persons with limited education and lower socioeconomic occupations. A major reason that demographic effects are seen in these persons may simply reflect that the reading level of the MMPI-2 is the eighth grade.

SETTING

The setting in which the MMPI-2 is administered can have significant impact on whether the scales will or will not be elevated. The MMPI-2 is used routinely to screen police officers, firefighters, clergy, and airflight crew members as well as many other groups for the presence of psychopathology. In these personnel-screening situations, persons realize that acknowledging the presence of any type of psychopathology decreases substantially the probability of their selection; consequently, they minimize reporting any symptoms of psychopathology and significantly lower the overall

TABLE 9.34 Effects of Age, Gender, and Education on the MMPI-2 Validity and Clinical Scales in the Caldwell Clinical Dataset

L *(Lie) –* R-*square = .023*

Education Gender	AGE RANGE						
	18–19	*20–29*	*30–39*	*40–49*	*50–59*	*60–69*	*70+*
1–12 Years							
Men	52.5	56.7	56.4	55.5	55.0	56.3	55.0
Women	52.5	57.2	57.9	57.4	57.0	59.3	58.9
13–16 Years							
Men	49.5	55.1	54.5	53.7	53.8	54.7	55.4
Women	49.6	53.6	55.3	54.9	54.6	56.8	57.7
17+ Years							
Men	–	51.2	52.0	51.9	51.6	51.3	54.2
Women	–	51.6	52.0	52.2	52.9	55.7	58.8

F *(Infrequency) –* R-*square = .047*

Education Gender	AGE RANGE						
	18–19	*20–29*	*30–39*	*40–49*	*50–59*	*60–69*	*70+*
1–12 Years							
Men	66.9	60.3	60.5	63.3	64.2	59.9	59.3
Women	69.6	63.0	62.9	64.8	64.9	60.3	57.5
13–16 Years							
Men	56.2	51.9	53.5	56.5	56.6	55.0	53.9
Women	63.7	56.7	57.5	59.8	59.9	57.8	53.9
17+ Years							
Men	–	51.4	50.9	51.5	53.0	53.6	48.2
Women	–	52.6	53.9	54.6	57.1	55.8	53.4

K *(Correction) –* R-*square = .032*

Education Gender	AGE RANGE						
	18–19	*20–29*	*30–39*	*40–49*	*50–59*	*60–69*	*70+*
1–12 Years							
Men	45.7	49.2	49.6	48.2	47.3	47.9	46.9
Women	45.9	49.3	50.5	49.4	49.2	49.5	50.1
13–16 Years							
Men	47.9	54.5	53.3	51.9	51.4	51.4	52.7
Women	46.1	52.3	53.4	52.2	51.8	52.7	53.0
17+ Years							
Men	–	53.9	54.6	54.1	53.1	53.3	54.3
Women	–	54.1	55.0	55.4	54.2	54.7	54.5

Hs *(Hypochondriasis) –* R-*square = .079*

Education Gender	AGE RANGE						
	18–19	*20–29*	*30–39*	*40–49*	*50–59*	*60–69*	*70+*
1–12 Years							
Men	57.5	58.6	62.2	67.2	71.9	68.8	64.3
Women	61.0	60.7	64.9	70.0	72.2	69.8	69.4

Hs *(Hypochondriasis)* – R-*square* = .079

| Education | AGE RANGE | | | | | | |
Gender	18–19	20–29	30–39	40–49	50–59	60–69	70+
13–16 Years							
Men	55.0	53.8	57.8	61.4	64.2	65.2	66.6
Women	60.7	58.1	61.4	65.7	68.5	66.3	64.4
17+ Years							
Men	–	53.8	54.8	56.6	59.1	60.3	56.7
Women	–	54.1	58.3	59.3	65.0	64.8	63.2

D *(Depression)* – R-*square* = .061

| Education | AGE RANGE | | | | | | |
Gender	18–19	20–29	30–39	40–49	50–59	60–69	70+
1–12 Years							
Men	59.6	60.6	63.5	67.8	72.2	69.0	66.7
Women	63.4	63.0	66.3	71.7	73.6	70.3	68.2
13–16 Years							
Men	59.3	54.3	58.7	62.2	65.2	63.6	66.6
Women	63.7	59.4	61.9	66.6	68.8	66.0	62.4
17+ Years							
Men	–	54.8	57.2	57.9	60.8	61.3	56.6
Women	–	54.9	59.2	59.5	65.3	63.5	58.3

Hy *(Hysteria)* – R-*square* = .056

| Education | AGE RANGE | | | | | | |
Gender	18–19	20–29	30–39	40–49	50–59	60–69	70+
1–12 Years							
Men	56.2	58.1	62.7	67.4	71.5	67.2	62.3
Women	60.7	61.3	66.3	71.1	73.0	69.3	67.3
13–16 Years							
Men	56.1	55.7	60.3	63.7	66.3	66.7	67.1
Women	61.8	60.2	63.9	68.4	70.7	67.2	62.5
17+ Years							
Men	–	57.1	59.6	60.7	62.9	62.6	60.1
Women	–	57.4	62.3	62.9	67.7	68.4	61.8

Pd *(Psychopathic Deviate)* – R-*square* = .011

| Education | AGE RANGE | | | | | | |
Gender	18–19	20–29	30–39	40–49	50–59	60–69	70+
1–12 Years							
Men	65.4	60.8	61.4	61.9	60.8	55.6	54.9
Women	64.9	62.0	61.5	61.5	59.9	55.5	50.2
13–16 Years							
Men	58.9	57.3	58.5	59.8	58.3	55.2	54.5
Women	61.2	59.1	59.7	60.0	58.9	56.4	50.9

(continued)

TABLE 9.34 Effects of Age, Gender, and Education on the MMPI-2 Validity and Clinical Scales in the Caldwell Clinical Dataset (continued)

Pd *(Psychopathic Deviate)* – R-*square* = .011

Education	AGE RANGE						
Gender	18–19	20–29	30–39	40–49	50–59	60–69	70+
17+ Years							
Men	–	56.8	58.2	57.9	57.9	56.6	50.7
Women	–	57.1	59.4	58.5	58.6	57.3	49.7

Mf *(Masculinity-Femininity)* – R-*square* = .007

Education	AGE RANGE						
Gender	18–19	20–29	30–39	40–49	50–59	60–69	70+
1–12 Years							
Men	50.1	47.0	48.2	49.3	48.3	47.8	48.3
Women	55.1	54.4	53.1	52.5	51.9	52.0	52.8
13–16 Years							
Men	52.9	48.4	50.5	51.2	50.3	50.0	50.6
Women	51.5	52.1	51.2	49.7	49.9	49.4	51.1
17+ Years							
Men	–	52.9	54.1	53.5	53.7	52.8	51.4
Women	–	51.6	49.6	48.5	49.1	48.2	49.9

Pa *(Paranoia)* – R-*square* = .011

Education	AGE RANGE						
Gender	18–19	20–29	30–39	40–49	50–59	60–69	70+
1–12 Years							
Men	66.0	61.0	63.1	64.6	64.2	58.5	57.4
Women	64.4	61.6	63.2	64.0	62.9	58.3	54.0
13–16 Years							
Men	58.0	55.4	59.8	61.2	60.6	57.3	56.7
Women	64.0	58.9	60.6	61.7	60.2	58.1	48.5
17+ Years							
Men	–	56.1	58.6	59.1	59.2	57.2	51.5
Women	–	56.5	59.3	58.4	60.2	58.9	53.1

Pt *(Psychasthenia)* – R-*square* = .023

Education	AGE RANGE						
Gender	18–19	20–29	30–39	40–49	50–59	60–69	70+
1–12 Years							
Men	65.0	60.7	61.9	65.3	67.6	62.7	60.3
Women	64.7	60.7	62.5	66.0	66.7	62.7	59.3
13–16 Years							
Men	62.6	56.4	58.5	60.6	61.7	59.6	60.1
Women	63.5	58.7	59.5	62.4	63.0	60.6	55.3
17+ Years							
Men	–	57.8	58.4	57.2	57.9	58.2	50.5
Women	–	56.1	58.0	57.2	59.5	58.9	53.8

Sc *(Schizophrenia)* – R-*square = .028*

Education	AGE RANGE						
Gender	*18–19*	*20–29*	*30–39*	*40–49*	*50–59*	*60–69*	*70+*
1–12 Years							
Men	68.8	62.1	62.4	65.8	67.6	63.6	59.6
Women	67.6	62.1	63.3	66.6	67.0	62.2	58.3
13–16 Years							
Men	62.6	56.3	57.8	60.1	60.9	59.8	58.8
Women	65.0	58.7	59.7	62.8	63.2	61.3	55.1
17+ Years							
Men	–	56.7	56.5	56.1	57.3	58.7	50.9
Women	–	55.4	57.3	57.6	60.6	59.4	54.6

Ma *(Hypomania)* – R-*square = .018*

Education	AGE RANGE						
Gender	*18–19*	*20–29*	*30–39*	*40–49*	*50–59*	*60–69*	*70+*
1–12 Years							
Men	61.4	54.7	52.5	52.2	51.2	49.3	48.1
Women	59.8	53.4	51.8	52.2	51.4	50.8	48.0
13–16 Years							
Men	56.5	52.0	51.1	50.5	49.9	50.1	48.3
Women	56.5	52.7	51.4	51.7	51.1	50.2	47.0
17+ Years							
Men	–	51.2	50.0	49.5	49.2	49.5	46.7
Women	–	51.7	50.8	49.9	50.3	50.5	51.6

Si *(Social Introversion)* – R-*square = .042*

Education	AGE RANGE						
Gender	*18–19*	*20–29*	*30–39*	*40–49*	*50–59*	*60–69*	*70+*
1–12 Years							
Men	54.9	53.0	54.2	57.1	58.7	56.6	56.5
Women	54.4	53.4	54.3	56.8	57.5	56.0	54.9
13–16 Years							
Men	51.9	47.5	49.8	52.8	53.6	51.8	51.9
Women	53.5	49.4	50.6	52.7	53.6	53.1	51.9
17+ Years							
Men	–	48.7	49.6	49.9	51.2	51.6	48.1
Women	–	46.9	48.5	49.3	51.2	50.5	49.7

elevation of their MMPI-2 profiles. This point is readily apparent in Table 9.35 in which the highest mean Clinical scale in the three personnel-screening samples is at a T score of 54 on Scale *5* (Masculinity-Femininity). A majority of these mean T scores on the Clinical scales are below a T score of 50 (i.e., they are reporting fewer symptoms and distress than the average person in the MMPI-2 normative group).

The MMPI-2 also is used frequently in forensic evaluations in which there may be motivation *to*

TABLE 9.35   Effects of Setting on the MMPI-2 Validity and Clinical Scales

SETTING/STUDY	L	F	K	1(Hs)	2(D)	3(Hy)	4(Pd)	5(Mf)	6(Pa)	7(Pt)	8(Sc)	9(Ma)	0(Si)
Personnel Screening													
Civilians													
(Caldwell, 1997b)	62	44	61	48	46	49	51	47	47	47	48	50	40
Clergy													
(Putnam et al., 1996)	51	43	56	51	49	53	50	54	53	51	50	49	47
Nuclear Power Plant													
(Cord et al., 1997)	56	44	49	47	47	49	50	45	47	47	46	48	46
Forensic													
Child Custody Litigants													
(Bathurst et al., 1997)	56	45	59	48	47	52	51	51	52	47	47	48	43
Personal Injury Plaintiffs													
(Lees-Haley, 1997)	57	62	50	69	70	71	58	51	61	66	65	51	55
Normal Individuals													
(Butcher et al., 1989)	50	50	50	50	50	50	50	50	50	50	50	50	50
Prison													
Inmates													
(Megargee et al., 1999)	57	58	49	54	56	53	64	52	59	56	57	57	52
Psychiatric													
Pain Patients													
(Caldwell, 1998b)	54	58	51	73	70	75	59	50	59	62	62	51	51
Psychiatric Patients													
(Caldwell, 1997a)	55	60	51	62	63	64	60	51	61	61	62	52	53

acknowledge (criminal cases in which the person pleads not guilty by reason of insanity; workers' compensation cases) or *not to acknowledge* (child custody evaluations; parole evaluations) psychopathology, which elevates or lowers the resulting MMPI-2 profile, respectively. The results of these differences in motivation, which approach two standard deviations on some Clinical scales, can be seen by comparing the sample of child custody litigants with the personal injury plaintiffs in Table 9.35. There also are differences of one to two standard deviations on most of the Clinical scales between the personal injury plaintiffs and all of the personnel-screening samples.

Finally, patients in medical settings tend to elevate Scales *1* (Hypochondriasis), *2* (Depression), and *3* (Hysteria) relative to the other Clinical scales. This point was made earlier in Chapter 7 when the frequencies of codetypes in psychiatric patients (Table 7.1) were compared to medical patients referred for a psychiatric evaluation (Table 7.2). Nearly 50 percent of the MMPI codetypes in the medical patients were contained within combinations of Scales *1, 2,* and *3*, while less than 25 percent of the codetypes in psychiatric patients were among these scales. The pain patients in Table 9.35 have mean T scores on Scales *1, 2,* and *3* that are one standard deviation higher than the psychiatric patients.

Clinicians would be well served to determine the mean profile for their specific setting as well as the frequency of MMPI-2 codetypes. This information will facilitate the interpretation of the MMPI-2 because the scales can be very sensitive to the effects of the setting in which it is administered.

CHAPTER 10

Adolescents and Elderly Adults

The original standardization sample of the MMPI consisted of white Minnesota adults, primarily between the ages of 16 and 55 (Hathaway & McKinley, 1940). Numerous investigators questioned whether the interpretation of the MMPI for individuals who were outside this age range might be improved by using a different set of norms. This chapter will begin by reviewing the use of the MMPI with adolescents. Next, the MMPI-A (Butcher et al., 1992) will be discussed, which has been developed specifically for use with adolescents. The MMPI-2 is *not* intended for use with anyone under 18 years of age (Butcher et al., 1989). Finally, the use of the MMPI and MMPI-2 in elderly adults, individuals who are 60 years of age and older, will be reviewed. All of the issues that have been raised in the previous Chapters about the interpretation of the MMPI-2 are germane for the interpretation of the MMPI and MMPI-A in adolescents and the MMPI and MMPI-2 in elderly adults and they will not be repeated here.

ADOLESCENTS

MMPI

Hathaway and Monachesi (1963), in an extensive study of the MMPI performance of adolescents, administered the MMPI to 3,971 ninth graders (mean age about 15) in the Minneapolis public school system during the 1947–1948 school year. They also microfilmed each student's school record at the time of testing. Two and four years later, they determined how many of these students had records with the local juvenile division of the police department or probation office. During the spring of 1954 these researchers tested 11,329 additional ninth graders who represented a sample of the entire state of Minnesota. They again microfilmed each student's school record, had each student com-

plete a personal data sheet, and obtained the teacher's prediction of which students were likely to have legal or emotional difficulties. Three years later they determined how many of these students had records by examining local community police and court files.

In 1957, when most of this second set of ninth graders were now twelfth graders (mean age about 18), Hathaway and Monachesi readministered the MMPI to 3,976 students. Hathaway and Monachesi obviously have a wealth of data, only part of which is relevant to the issue of how adolescents differ from adults in terms of their MMPI performance. (The reader who is interested in the use of the MMPI to predict delinquency in adolescents, which was the main thrust of Hathaway and Monachesi's research project, should consult their book.)

Relevant to the current topic of MMPI norms, Hathaway and Monachesi found that ninth graders had mean scores with K-corrections on Scales *4* (Psychopathic Deviate), *8* (Schizophrenia), and *9* (Hypomania), which were approximately 10 T points higher than the original Minnesota normative sample of adults. On the rest of the Validity and Clinical scales, the ninth graders scored very similarly to the adult sample. Thus, these adolescents were more likely to have elevations on Scales *4, 8,* and *9* if adult MMPI norms were used. They also were less likely to have profiles in which all Clinical scales were below a T score of 70 than were the normal adults.

The issue that Hathaway and Monachesi did not directly address is whether these MMPI scale elevations in normal adolescents reflected some form of psychological distress and maladjustment that was characteristic of the turmoil of adolescence or whether these elevations reflected mere differences in the frequency of item endorsement that may not have psychopathologic implications.

Hathaway and Monachesi seemed to favor the former interpretation since they did not advocate the use of special adolescent norms with the MMPI. Instead, they suggested that both the standard adult profile and an adolescent-normed profile should be plotted so that the clinician can understand the contrast between adolescents and adults. The clinician, however, when provided with the potentially divergent and contradictory information from two profiles on the same adolescent, needs to know which source of information is more accurate, and Hathaway and Monachesi (1963) did not answer this question.

The students who were retested with the MMPI in the twelfth grade provided some interesting information on profile stability. Test-retest reliability coefficients were highest for the *K* (Correction) scale—.52 for males and .56 for females—and Scale *0* (Social Introversion)—.54 for males and .61 for females. By contrast, Scales *4* (Psychopathic Deviate)—.36 for males and .38 for females—and *6* (Paranoia)—.32 for males and .36 for females—had the lowest reliability coefficients.

As might be expected, profile stability as defined by the single high-point scale was highest when that scale was a T score of 70 or higher. For example, more than half of the adolescents, both male and female, with Scale *4* (Psychopathic Deviate) greater than a T score of 69 on initial testing, had Scale *4* as one of the two highest scales when retested. This relationship, however, did not hold for all scales. Scale *5* (Masculinity-Femininity), for example, was likely to shift from a high-point scale to one of the three lowest Clinical scales across this three-year interval.

Hathaway and Monachesi wondered whether there may be an active differentiation of sex roles during this time span that results in Scale *5* (Masculinity-Femininity) scores changing so dramatically. Whatever the reason, Scale *5* scores did change drastically in some adolescents during this time interval.

Following the lead of Hathaway and Monachesi, Ball (1962) also examined the relationship of personality to social deviancy among Kentucky adolescents. Only the data on the nondelinquent adolescents will be reviewed here since they are germane to the issue of how normal adolescents differ from the original Minnesota normative sample on the MMPI. Both

male and female adolescents achieved mean T scores near 60 on the *F* (Infrequency) scale and Scales *4* (Psychopathic Deviate), *7* (Psychasthenia), *8* (Schizophrenia), and *9* (Hypomania), with the other Clinical scales averaging near a mean T score of 50. This pattern of scores is very similar to what Hathaway and Monachesi (1963) reported for their Minnesota adolescents who were tested nearly 10 years earlier.

In a comprehensive study of black-white differences on a variety of intellectual, academic, and personality factors, Baughman and Dahlstrom (1968) reported the MMPI performance of eighth graders. Only discussion of the data on white adolescents will be reviewed in this section. Again, a similar pattern of MMPI scale scores was found in the white eighth graders. The *F* (Infrequency) scale and Scales *4* (Psychopathic Deviate), *7* (Psychasthenia), *8* (Schizophrenia), and *9* (Hypomania) were elevated to a mean T score of nearly 60 in both girls and boys, with Scales *8* and *9* elevated almost to a mean T score of 70 in boys.

It appears that normal adolescents display significant elevation on a number of the standard MMPI Validity and Clinical scales when the adult norms from the original Minnesota normative sample are used. If the clinician is interested in knowing how an adolescent client compares with normal adolescents rather than with the original, adult normative group on the MMPI, an adolescent norm profile, described in the next section, should be constructed.

Marks, Seeman, and Haller (1974) have done the most extensive MMPI research on emotional disturbance in adolescents. They also have described how the adolescent norms for the MMPI were derived, primarily crediting Peter F. Briggs. Briggs selected 100 boys and 100 girls aged 14, 15, and 16 years, and 80 boys and 40 girls aged 17 years from the students studied by Hathaway and Monachesi (1963).

In order to obtain a larger and more nationally representative sample, Marks et al. collected 1,046 additional MMPI profiles in 1964 and 1965 from both rural and urban, public and private school students residing in Alabama, California, Kansas, Missouri, North Carolina, and Ohio. All of these students were presumed to be white and at the time of testing were neither institutionalized nor being treated for emotional disturbance (Marks et al., 1974).

By combining these two groups of students, the adolescent norms for the standard Validity and Clinical scales for boys and girls in four age groups (14 and below, 15, 16, and 17 and 18) were constructed (see Appendix H, Tables 6 to 9, Dahlstrom et al., 1972). Only if adolescents were still living with their parents were 18-year-olds included in the oldest group. If an 18-year-old was not living with his or her parents, it was deemed more appropriate to use adult norms, although there has not been any research to demonstrate which set of norms is better.

Although Marks et al. (1974) advocated that emotional disturbance in adolescents needs to be established against adolescent norms, they did concur with Hathaway and Monachesi (1963) that adolescent scores on the MMPI also should be compared to adult norms. Thus, Marks et al. recommended that both an adult- and an adolescent-normed profile should be constructed for adolescents.

The clinician who desires to construct a profile from adolescent norms must locate the correct table for the age and sex of the adolescent in Appendix H of Dahlstrom et al. (1972) and determine the T score equivalent of the raw score on each scale; these tables are *not K*-corrected. These T scores then are plotted directly on the standard profile sheet. The clinician should indicate on the profile sheet that the profile was plotted using adolescent norms; this procedure will prevent another clinician who uses the profile from assuming that the profile has been misplotted, since the adolescent and adult T scores for each raw score will not be the same. Adolescent profile sheets are available so that clinicians can plot the T score equivalents of the raw scores directly without consulting Appendix H.

In addition to describing the development of adolescent norms, Marks et al. (1974) assessed the empirical correlates of MMPI codetypes in a sample of 834 white boys and girls between the ages of 12 and 18 who were not mentally retarded but who had adjustment problems causing them to seek or be referred for professional services. Each of these teenagers completed a personal data sheet, and for each teenager a therapist completed a case data schedule, an adjective checklist, and a *Q*-sort after a minimum of 10 hours of therapy. All of the therapist's ratings were made independent of the MMPI.

Each of the descriptors from the information provided by the teenager and the therapist was evaluated for gender differences and deleted if significant. Marks et al. also eliminated descriptors with exceedingly high (≥ 90 percent) or low (< 10 percent) frequencies of occurrence. This procedure resulted in a pool of 1,265 descriptors, which were related to the codetypes on the MMPI based on adolescent norms.

When ties occurred among the high-point scales, the profile was classified into a codetype on the basis of the scale with the lowest number. For example, if Scales *1, 2,* and *3* were the three highest scales and had equivalent T scores, the profile was classified as a *1-2/2-1* codetype. Similarly, if Scale *2* was the highest and Scales *3, 4,* and *7* were tied for the second highest scale, the profile was classified as a *2-3/3-2* codetype.

Marks et al. were able to identify 29 codetypes, irrespective of scale order, with a minimum of at least 10 cases per high-point pair. They then developed an actuarial description based on the descriptors that were significantly associated with each of these 29 codetypes. The narrative description for each of these codetypes is approximately two pages long, and the clinician will need to consult Marks et al.'s (1974) book to use their interpretive system. For profiles that do not fit into one of these 29 codetypes, Marks et al. recommended that the second highest scale should be disregarded and that the profile should be reclassified using the first and third highest scales. If the profile was still not classifiable using the first and third highest scales, the profile was considered to be unclassifiable, and their interpretive system cannot be used.

Only one study (Williams & Butcher, 1989b) has attempted to validate the correlates of any of the codetypes developed by Marks et al. in another sample of adolescents; this study will be reviewed later.

Marks et al. (1974) dealt with the problem of testing adolescents with the MMPI by using adolescent norms, which sometimes lead to codetypes different from those that would be derived if the adult norms were used. In addition, they used an adolescent population to develop a set of behavioral correlates, or narrative descriptions, for these codetypes. Marks et al.'s narrative descriptions have not been cross-validated in another adolescent population, and the research in this area has yielded mixed results. Ehrenworth and

Archer (1985) found that interpretations based on the descriptions by Marks et al. were rated as being less accurate than other interpretations in a sample of adolescent inpatients, whereas Archer, Gordon, Giannetti, and Singles (1988) reported that the clinical correlates of single Clinical scales in adolescent inpatients were similar to those of Marks et al. Consequently, clinicians should use the Marks et al. descriptions cautiously.

There has been an almost geometric increase in research on the use of the MMPI with adolescents in recent years. This increase in research has been spearheaded by the work of Archer (cf. Archer, 1984, 1987, 1988) and Williams (cf. Williams, 1986; Williams & Butcher, 1989a, 1989b). Their contributions should be reviewed by any clinician who is using the MMPI with adolescents. Archer (1987) provides a single, comprehensive overview of this entire area.

Several issues arise when the MMPI is used with adolescents. The first issue is whether adult norms, adolescent norms, or both sets of norms should be used with adolescents. As noted earlier, Hathaway and Monachesi (1963) and Marks et al. (1974) recommended that adult- and adolescent-normed profiles should be constructed for adolescents. However, Archer (1984, 1987) advocated that adolescent norms should be used exclusively with adolescents, and he presented a cogent rationale for their use that should be read by clinicians. Williams (1986) also indicated that adolescent norms were the most appropriate for adolescents, but she suggested that both profiles should be plotted for adolescents.

Once it has been decided that adolescent norms will be used, the next issue is whether T scores of 70 and above should continue to be the criterion for defining a significant elevation on the scales. Since adolescent norms produce a general lowering of the entire profile, Archer (1984, 1987; Ehrenworth & Archer, 1985) has recommended that T scores of 65 and above be used to define significant clinical elevations similar to the procedure now being used on the MMPI-2.

Additional empirical research that assesses whether a T score of 65 or 70 facilitates the interpretation of adolescent MMPIs is needed. In the interim, clinicians would seem to be well advised to follow Archer's (1984, 1987) suggestion and use adolescent norms for adolescents and interpret their profiles at T scores of 65 and above.

A final issue is whether the adolescent or the adult correlates provide a more accurate interpretation once adolescent norms serve as the base to derive a codetype. Using adolescent and adult norms, Lachar, Klinge, and Grisell (1976) obtained valid profiles on 100 adolescents, most of whom were hospitalized. Interpretations of the two profiles for each adolescent were generated using Lachar's (1974) automated interpretive system for adults. Clinicians then were asked to rate these interpretations for accuracy.

The interpretations of profiles generated from adolescent norms, in comparison to interpretations of profiles generated from adult norms, were rated more accurate 61 times, as accurate 13 times, and less accurate 26 times. Only 10 percent of the adolescent norm interpretations were judged to be inaccurate, and 20 percent of the adult norm interpretations were judged to be inaccurate. Wimbish (1984) reported similar findings in a sample of inpatient adolescent substance abusers.

Hence, it appears that even when an interpretive system (Lachar's) based on adults is used, profiles based on adolescent norms provide a more accurate description of adolescents than do profiles based on adult norms. It remains to be seen, however, whether other adult interpretive systems and individual clinicians will demonstrate the same improvement in accuracy with the use of adolescent norms.

Once the decision has been made to use adolescent norms, the clinician now has three different sets of norms from which to choose: (1) Marks et al. (1974), which have been described previously and which have served as the standard for adolescent MMPIs since they were published originally; (2) Gottesman, Hanson, Kroeker, and Briggs (1987); and (3) Colligan and Offord (1989).

Gottesman et al. developed their norms by using the MMPI responses of 12,953 15-year-olds and 3,492 18-year-olds, who composed the entire sample of adolescents studied by Hathaway and Monachesi (1963). Instead of using linear T scores as traditionally had been done with the MMPI, Gottesman et al. used a normalizing procedure based on power transformations of the raw scores to produce T scores that had equivalent percentile ranks across the scales.

Colligan and Offord (1989) developed their norms by collecting a sample of adolescents in the Mayo Clinic catchment area in a similar manner as they had collected their adult data (Chapter 1). Colligan and Offord also used normalized T scores in their adolescent sample as they had in their adult sample (Chapter 2). Since the same issues of codetype concordance are raised among these various sets of adolescent norms as were discussed in Chapter 7 about codetype concordance between the MMPI and the MMPI-2, they will not be reiterated here.

Archer, Pancoast, and Klinefelter (1989) reported the codetype concordance among these three sets of adolescent norms to range from 22 to 31 percent for an adolescent sample of 100 inpatients, 100 outpatients, and 100 normals. They did not find the two newer sets of norms to have higher hit rates in classifying adolescents as normal or psychologically distressed, but they did substantiate higher sensitivity rates using a T score of 65 rather than a T score of 70 to classify an adolescent as psychologically distressed. They cautioned clinicians about using these newer sets of adolescent norms to produce a codetype that would be interpreted based on the existing MMPI research because of the limited concordance rates.

Williams and Butcher reported the empirical correlates of the MMPI standard Validity and Clinical scales (1989a) and codetypes (1989b) in a large, inpatient, adolescent sample. These adolescents had similar descriptors associated to the individual MMPI scales that had been found in adults. Williams and Butcher (1989a) concluded that their results supported the use of adult descriptors for adolescent MMPI interpretations as suggested previously by Archer (1987) and Williams (1986). Archer and his colleagues (Archer, Gordon, Anderson, & Giannetti, 1989; Archer, Gordon, Giannetti, & Singles, 1988) reported the correlates of individual MMPI clinical and supplementary scales in adolescent inpatients. They also found that the correlates were similar to those found with adults on the MMPI.

Although Williams and Butcher (1989b) found that the relative frequency of the various codetypes in their sample was very comparable to those reported by Marks et al. (1974), they were unable to replicate the correlates of specific codetypes found in Marks et al. or the adult codetype literature. This latter finding suggests that the validity of traditional MMPI codetypes in adolescents may be limited.

Since the development of an adolescent interpretive system for the MMPI is still in its infancy, one solution may be to use adolescent norms and empirical correlates of individual Validity and Clinical scales based on adolescents when testing this population. An alternative procedure, which can be followed while an adolescent interpretive system such as Marks et al. (1974) is being cross-validated, is to use adolescent norms to generate the profile and then to use an adult interpretive system.

This procedure, as Lachar et al. (1976) and Wimbish (1984) demonstrated, provides some improvement over utilizing both adult norms and adult correlates of a codetype to interpret an adolescent's MMPI. However, it must be noted that Williams and Butcher (1989b) were unable to replicate the correlates of specific adolescent codetypes, which suggests that clinicians should be cautious in using this procedure.

MMPI-A

The MMPI-A (Butcher et al., 1992) represents the restandardization of the MMPI to create a version that is specifically adapted for adolescents. Restandardization of the MMPI was needed to provide item content that was more appropriate for adolescents, develop scales to assess symptoms and behaviors more common to adolescents, and create current norms for the inventory. Continuity between the MMPI and the MMPI-A was maintained as much as possible, although it was recognized that some changes would be necessary to adapt the MMPI for adolescents. Thus, the items on the Validity and Clinical scales of the MMPI are basically unchanged on the MMPI-A (Table 10.1) except for the F (Infrequency) scale and Scale 5 (Masculinity-Femininity), which lost 27 and 16 items, respectively. The MMPI-A still retains 12 of the 31 items that were dropped from the F scale.

In the development of the MMPI-A, the Restandardization Committee (Butcher et al., 1992) started

TABLE 10.1 Items Dropped from the Validity and Clinical Scales on the MMPI-A

| | | ITEMS | |
SCALE	MMPI	DROPPED	MMPI-A
L (Lie)	15	1	14
F (Infrequency)	64	27	66[a]
K (Correction)	30	0	30
1 (Hypochondriasis)	33	1	32
2 (Depression)	60	3	57
3 (Hysteria)	60	0	60
4 (Psychopathic Deviate)	50	1	49
5 (Masculinity-Femininity)	60	16	44
6 (Paranoia)	40	0	40
7 (Psychasthenia)	48	0	48
8 (Schizophrenia)	78	1	77
9 (Hypomania)	46	0	46
0 (Social Introversion)	70	8	62

[a]The F scale on the MMPI-A has 29 additional items that are not found on the F scale on the original MMPI.

TABLE 10.2 Changes in Items from the MMPI to the MMPI-A

	NUMBER OF ITEMS
MMPI	*566*
Drop 16 repeated items	−16
Drop 58 items from the standard Validity and Clinical scales	−58
Drop 121 additional items	−121
Total	367
Add 121 items from Form TX	+121
MMPI-A	*478*

changes that were made in the transition from the 566 items on the MMPI to the 478 items on the MMPI-A.

The MMPI-A was standardized on a sample of 1,610 adolescents who resided in eight different states (California, Minnesota, New York, North Carolina, Ohio, Pennsylvania, Virginia, and Washington). These adolescents "were derived from samples of generally limited representativeness in terms of ethnicity, geographical region, and rural-urban residence" (Butcher et al., 1989, p. 10). The demographic characteristics of this sample can be seen in Table 10.3. Similar to the MMPI-2, the MMPI-A normative sample is predominantly white and the adolescents' parents tended to be well educated and to be in professional and managerial occupations.

The MMPI-A is intended to be used with adolescents in the age range of 14 to 18. The Restandardization Committee thought that the validity of the data for 13-year-olds was too questionable to warrant inclusion in the normative sample. It is possible, however, that bright, mature 12- and 13-year-olds might be able to take the MMPI-A appropriately, but research is needed to document this position. The Restandardization Committee also suggested that the MMPI-A be used for 18-year-olds who are in high school and the MMPI-2 be used for those who are in college and living an independent lifestyle. Shaevel and Archer (1996) have suggested that a conservative approach would be to plot both the MMPI-A profile and the MMPI-2 profile for 18-year-olds when the clinician cannot decide which form of the test is more appropri-

with the 550 items on the original MMPI (i.e., they first deleted the 16 repeated items). They reworded 82 of these 550 items to eliminate outdated and sexist language and to make these items more easily understood. Williams, Ben-Porath, and Hevern (1994) determined that the psychometric properties of 20 of these reworded items were the same or better than the original items. They also included 58 items from Form AX that was used to collect the normative data for the MMPI-2. The Restandardization Committee then added 96 provisional items "to assess problems, behaviors, and attitudes of adolescents in areas related to identity formation, negative peer-group influence, school and teachers, relationships with parents and families, and sexuality" (Butcher et al., 1992 p. 5). Thus, Form TX had a total of 704 items and was used to collect the normative data for the MMPI-A.

When finalizing the items to be included on the MMPI-A, the Restandardization Committee deleted 121 items from the original MMPI in addition to the 58 items deleted from the standard Validity and Clinical scales and the 16 repeated items. The rationale for including and dropping items from Form TX that resulted in the 478 items on the MMPI-A has not been made explicit to date. Table 10.2 illustrates the

TABLE 10.3 Demographic Variables for the MMPI-A Normative Sample

VARIABLE	N	%	VARIABLE	N	%
Gender			*Father's Education*		
Girls	815	50.3%	Grade School	32	2.0%
Boys	805	49.7	Some High School	147	9.1
Ethnicity			High School Graduate	364	22.5
White	1,235	76.2%	Some College	222	13.7
Black	200	12.3	College Graduate	534	33.0
Native American	47	2.9	Graduate School	274	16.9
Hispanic	34	2.1	Missing	47	2.9
Asian American	46	2.8	*Mother's Education*		
Other	41	2.5	Grade School	20	1.2%
Age			Some High School	92	5.7
14	367	22.7%	High School Graduate	480	29.6
15	438	27.0	Some College	328	20.2
16	430	26.5	College Graduate	504	31.1
17	298	18.4	Graduate School	159	9.8
18	87	5.4	Missing	37	2.3
Current Living Situation					
Mother and Father	1,075	66.4%			
Mother Only	420	25.9			
Father Only	62	3.8			
Other	63	3.9			
Grade					
7th	8	0.5%			
8th	121	7.5			
9th	416	25.7			
10th	473	29.2			
11th	390	24.1			
12th	211	13.0			
Missing	1	0.1			

Note. Adapted from Butcher et al. (1992).

ate. The data on age effects on the MMPI-2 that were reviewed in the previous chapter would suggest that all 18-year-olds should be given the MMPI-A, but research is needed to answer this question definitively.

It is suggested that the adolescent should have at least a seventh-grade reading level in order to take the MMPI-A (Butcher et al., 1992). Krakauer, Archer, and Gordon (1993) have developed the Items-Easy and Items-Difficult scales for the MMPI-A. These scales consist of items equivalent in frequency of endorsement but differing in their level of reading difficulty, which can be used to identify adolescents who are having reading difficulties. The clinician must check measures of consistency (Baer, Ballenger, Berry, & Wetter, 1997) and accuracy of item endorsement very carefully with adolescents because of the higher probability that they will be noncooperative or noncompliant with the assessment process, in addition to the potential problems of reading comprehension.

The *K*-correction procedure, which was described in detail in Chapters 2 and 3, is *not* used with the MMPI-A unlike the original MMPI and MMPI-2.

Adolescent MMPIs had not been *K*-corrected in traditional practice so there is more continuity on the MMPI-A in not using the *K*-correction process. Alperin, Archer, and Coates (1996) investigated whether the use of *K* weights developed specifically in adolescents would facilitate the discrimination between normal and clinical samples. They found that the adoption of a *K*-correction procedure did not improve the discrimination between these two groups, which supports not using the *K*-correction procedure in adolescents. Uniform T scores were used for all Clinical scales except Scales *5* (Masculinity-Femininity) and *0* (Social Introversion) and the new Content scales on the MMPI-A similar to the process on the MMPI-2.

The Harris and Lingoes subscales for the Clinical scales are unchanged on the MMPI-A except for the few changes at the item level that were made on the MMPI-2 and carried over to the MMPI-A. The same subscales are used for Scale *0* (Social Introversion) on the MMPI-A that are used on the MMPI-2 (Ben-Porath et al., 1989).

Several Supplementary scales are available to assist the clinician in interpreting the Validity and Clinical scales on the MMPI-A. These Supplementary scales will be familiar to the clinician who has used the MMPI or MMPI-2: MacAndrew Alcoholism—Revised (*MAC-R*) scale and Welsh Anxiety (*A*) and Repression (*R*) scales. These scales have had a few minor changes made in them at the item level. Three new scales are represented in the Supplementary scales on the MMPI-A: Alcohol/Drug Problem Acknowledgment (*ACK:* Weed, Butcher, & Williams, 1994); Alcohol/Drug Proneness (*PRO:* Weed et al., 1994); and Immaturity (*IMM:* Archer, Pancoast, & Gordon, 1994); and four new Validity scales: F_1 and F_2 (Subscales of the [*F*] scale); True Response Inconsistency *TRIN*; and Variable Response Inconsistency *VRIN*. The *F* (Infrequency) scale on the MMPI-A has been divided into two 33-item subscales. The items on the F_1 scale are found in the first half of the test and the items on the F_2 scale are found in the second half of the test. The raw scores on the F_1 and F_2 scales can be compared in a similar manner to the *F* (Infrequency) and F_B (Back Infrequency) scales on the MMPI-2 to assess whether the adolescent has endorsed more or less of these infrequently endorsed

items on the second half of the test. The Alcohol/Drug Problem Acknowledgment (*ACK*) and Alcohol/Drug Proneness (*PRO*) scales were developed in the same manner as the Addiction Admission (*AAS*) and Addiction Potential (*APS*) scales on the MMPI-2. Gallucci (1997) examined the ability of the MMPI-A clinical and alcohol scales to classify adolescent substance abusers into groups characterized by behavioral undercontrol, behavioral overcontrol, or both. A discriminant function based on seven scales (MacAndrew Alcoholism—Revised, Scale *2* [Depression], Scale *4* [Psychopathic Deviate], Scale *9* [Hypomania], Alcohol/Drug Problem Proneness, and Alcohol/Drug Problem Acknowledgment) correctly classified 79.4 percent of these adolescents into the correct group.

A total of 15 new Content scales have been developed for the MMPI-A (Williams, Butcher, Ben-Porath, & Graham, 1992). These scales are Anxiety, Obsessions, Depression, Health Concerns, Alienation, Bizarre Mentation, Anger, Cynicism, Conduct Problems, Low Self-Esteem, Low Aspirations, Social Discomfort, Family Problems, School Problems, and Negative Treatment Indicators. These scales were developed in a similar manner to the MMPI-2 Content (Butcher et al., 1990) scales. The stages in the development of the MMPI-A Content scales are outlined in Butcher et al. (1992, p. 61) and explained more fully in Williams et al. (1992). Arita and Baer (1998) examined the convergent and discriminant validity of the Content scales of Anxiety, Depression, Health Concerns, Alienation, Anger, Conduct Problems, and Social Discomfort in adolescent inpatients. Neither the Anxiety nor the Depression scale discriminated among the various other measures and appear to be more general measures of nonspecific distress. The other Content scales that they studied demonstrated reasonable convergent and discriminant validity.

The MMPI-A Structural Summary (Archer & Krishnamurthy, 1994) has been created to provide a conceptual framework for the eight factors that have been identified in the MMPI-A item pool (Archer, Belevich, & Elkins, 1994; Archer & Krishnamurthy, 1997). The MMPI-A Structural Summary organizes all of the MMPI-A scales and subscales within each of these factors based on their degree of correlation with each factor. Archer, Krishnamurthy, and Jacob-

chasthenia), *8* (Schizophrenia), and *9* (Hypomania) than the younger men. He concluded that within the age ranges (20 to 55) of his study, the T scores derived from the original Minnesota normative sample were valid. Brozek also provided a detailed analysis of items that separated the older and younger age groups. The reader who is interested in this information should consult Brozek's (1955) article.

Leon et al. (1979) have reported 30-year follow-up data on the MMPI performance of the healthy professional men described by Brozek. These researchers were able to obtain MMPI data on 71 of these men who had completed the MMPI at four different times (1947, 1953, 1960, and 1977). The mean age of the 71 men in 1977 was 77 years. When the scale scores from 1947 were contrasted with those in 1977, these men achieved significantly higher scores on all Validity and Clinical scales except the *L* (Lie) scale, although all scale scores were still below a mean T score of 62. When scale scores from 1960 were compared with those in 1977, these men achieved significantly higher scores on Scales *L* (Lie), *2* (Depression), *7* (Psychasthenia), *8* (Schizophrenia), and *0* (Social Introversion). The largest difference in scale scores between 1960 and 1977, however, was only 5 T points on Scale *2*. There was striking stability of scores over this 30-year interval for Scales *5* (Masculinity-Femininity), *9* (Hypomania), and *0* (Social Introversion), and 23.9 percent of these men had the same codetype. Leon et al. (1979) suggested that the elevations on Scales *2* and *3* (Hysteria) in an aging sample may reflect realistic somatic concerns rather than the usual depressive and hysteroid correlates found in younger adults.

Swenson (1961) asked 210 persons aged 60 years or more who had completed a brief attitude questionnaire to take the MMPI. Only 95 (45.1 percent) of these persons completed the MMPI: 31 men and 64 women with a median age of 71.4 years. None had a known mental disorder sufficient to warrant a psychiatric diagnosis. It is possible that the large percentage of older individuals who did not complete the MMPI may somehow bias the representativeness of this sample, but the nature of these biases is unknown.

The scores of these 95 persons served as the basis for constructing the T score norms for the aged (Appendix H, Table 4, Dahlstrom et al., 1972). They scored from 6 to 9 T points higher on Scales *1* (Hypochondriasis), *2* (Depression), *3* (Hysteria), and *5* (Masculinity-Femininity) and 3 T points lower on Scale *9* (Hypomania) than the original Minnesota normative sample. Scales *1, 2, 3,* and *0* (Social Introversion) were the most frequently occurring high-point scales in both sexes. The median profiles for this aged sample were commonly of a neurotic pattern (elevations on Scales *1, 2,* and *3*) and only rarely gave evidence of a psychotic or a behavior disorder pattern.

Fillenbaum and Pfeiffer (1976) collected the Mini-Mult (Kincannon, 1968) as a portion of a broad questionnaire administered to a 10 percent random sample of noninstitutionalized persons 65 years and older living in a southern community. The Mini-Mult was read to the person by a trained interviewer, and responses were obtained to all 71 items on the Mini-Mult from 249 men (171 white, 78 black) and 391 women (250 white, 141 black). An additional 298 persons answered some of the items, and 59 answered none of the items; their responses were not analyzed.

Fillenbaum and Pfeiffer found only one item (25) that was endorsed differently as a function of gender or ethnic group. The mean T scores in both sexes and ethnic group for the eight Clinical scales measured by the Mini-Mult (which excludes Scales *5* [Masculinity-Femininity] and *0* [Social Introversion]) were approximately 60, except for Scale *9* (Hypomania), which was approximately 50. If this sample can be considered to be relatively normal, it appears that the Mini-Mult overestimates the amount of psychopathology in an aged sample and, hence, will have limited usefulness. Clinicians should review the discussion of short forms of the MMPI in Chapter 6 before using them with any clients.

Taylor, Strassberg, and Turner (1989) provided MMPI data on a community sample between the ages of 60 to 90. These elderly adults scored 5 to 10 T points above the MMPI normative group on most of the Validity and Clinical scales.

Colligan and Offord (1992) summarized the MMPI scores of their adult (Colligan et al., 1983) and adolescent (Colligan & Offord, 1989) normative samples that covered an age span of 85 years. When the adults in the 60 to 69 age range and 70 and over were compared with the 50 to 59 age group, several scales increased slightly in the former two groups (*L* [Lie], *F* [Infrequency], *1* [Hypochondriasis], *2* [Depression], *3* [Hysteria], and *0* [Social Introversion]) and other scales decreased slightly (*4* [Psychopathic Deviate], *7* [Psychasthenia], *8* [Schizophrenia], and *9* [Hypomania]). The largest increases were seen on the *L* scale, which approached 5 T points, while the largest decreases were seen on Scale *4*, which approached 3 T points.

The limited amount of research on MMPI performance in normal samples of elderly adults allows for only a few general conclusions. It appears that elderly adults may elevate Scales *1* (Hypochondriasis), *2* (Depression), and *3* (Hysteria) about 5 to 10 T points, elevate Scale *0* (Social Introversion) about 5 T points, and lower Scale *9* (Hypomania) about 3 T points compared to the original Minnesota normative sample. It must be remembered, however, that most groups of normal individuals regardless of age elevated most of the Validity and Clinical scales on the MMPI about 5 to 8 T points (see Chapter 1), so it is difficult to know whether these differences seen in normal elderly adults are a function of their age or simply reflect some artifact of the original Minnesota normative group.

Using norms for elderly adults (Appendix H, Table 4, Dahlstrom et al., 1972; Appendix O, Colligan et al., 1983) in constructing a profile for a person 70 years or older will allow the clinician to compare the person's scores to others of similar age. There is no published research, however, on how to interpret an MMPI profile constructed on these norms.

Again, research is needed to determine whether correlates of profiles constructed on the original Minnesota normative sample will apply in a similar fashion to elderly adults. It might be best for the clinician to plot two profiles for an elderly client: the standard profile and an elderly adult–normed profile. By examining the latter profile, the clinician could determine how the client compares on the various scales with persons in his or her age range. The clinician, however, probably should interpret the standard profile and use the elderly adult–normed profile only to supplement the interpretation.

Swenson et al. (1973) provided MMPI data on 1,733 male and 1,471 female outpatients 70 years of age and older who were seen at the Mayo Clinic between 1962 and 1965. They excluded any patient referred primarily for psychiatric evaluation and treatment. Both male and female patients scored about a T score of 60 on Scales *1* (Hypochondriasis), *2* (Depression), and *3* (Hysteria), a T score of 55 on Scale *0* (Social Introversion), and a T score of 48 on Scale *9* (Hypomania). This pattern of scores is very similar to what Swenson (1961) reported. Swenson et al. (1973), however, reported similar elevations on Scales *1*, *2*, and *3* in medical patients aged 16 to 69. Thus, it is not possible to conclude whether the elevations on Scales *1*, *2*, and *3* in patients 70 years of age and older reflect age per se or some other factor.

Fow, Sittig, Dorris, Breisinger, and Anthony (1994) examined age and gender effects on the MMPI in patients with chronic pain. The most common pattern was for scores to decrease on most of the Validity and Clinical scales for patients in the age ranges of 60 to 69 and 70 to 90. They also found comparable elevations on Scales *1* (Hypochondriasis), *2* (Depression, and *3* (Hysteria) across the entire age range from 30 to 60 similar to what Swenson et al. (1973) had found in psychiatric outpatients.

It appears that elderly psychiatric patients and chronic pain patients produce very similar elevations on the MMPI as comparable patients who are a decade or two younger.

MMPI-2

Even though the MMPI-2 has been in existence for almost a decade, there is only limited research available on normal elderly adults. Despite the limited number of studies (Bolla-Wilson & Bleecker, 1989; Butcher et al., 1991; Priest & Meunier, 1993; Strassberg, Clutton, & Korboot, 1991), the MMPI-2 performance has been very consistent in normal elderly adults. The most remarkable finding is that these normal elderly adults are *not* showing the elevations on Scales *1* (Hypochondriasis), *2* (Depression), and *3* (Hysteria) that had been seen on the MMPI. Only Strassberg et al. (1991) found their normal men to have a T score of 56 on Scale *1* and 59 on Scale *2*. Otherwise all of these elderly adults had T scores of approximately 50 on these three scales. These normal elderly adults did show slight declines on Scales *4* (Psychopathic Deviate) and *9* (Hypomania) similar to what had been seen on the MMPI.

There have been no studies that have examined the MMPI-2 performance of elderly clinical samples and such research clearly is needed. The fact that there were few differences between elderly and younger patients on the MMPI suggests that there are unlikely to be any differences on the MMPI-2. It will be important for researchers to publish the fact that they find no differences between these age groups on the MMPI-2 so that clinicians are aware that the research actually has been conducted.

Given the increased longevity that is characteristic of all people today, there will be more need to use the MMPI-2 in the elderly. Here is an area that needs to have lots of attention for the foreseeable future.

Appendix A

T Score Tables

TABLE A.1 Uniform and Linear T Score Conversions for Basic Scales with K Corrections

Females

L*	F*	K*	Hs +.5K	D	Hy	Pd +.4K	Mf*	Pa	Pt +1K	Sc +1K	Ma +.2K	Si*	RAW SCORE
													73
													72
													71
													70
												95	69
												93	68
												92	67
									120	120		91	66
									119	119		90	65
									117	118		89	64
									116	116		88	63
									114	115		87	62
									112	114		86	61
									110	112		85	60
									108	111		84	59
									106	109		83	58
									105	108		82	57
									103	106		81	56
									101	105		80	55
									99	103		79	54
				120					97	102		78	53
				118	120				95	100		77	52
				116	118				94	99		75	51
				114	115	120			92	97		74	50
				112	113	118			90	96		73	49
				109	111	115			88	94		72	48
				107	108	113			86	93		71	47
			120	105	106	110			84	91		70	46
			117	103	104	107			83	90		69	45
			115	101	101	105	30		81	88	120	68	44
			113	99	99	102	33		79	87	118	67	43
			111	96	96	100	35		77	85	115	66	42
			109	94	94	97	38		75	84	112	65	41
			107	92	92	94	40		73	82	109	64	40
			105	90	89	92	43		72	81	106	63	39
			103	88	87	89	45		70	79	103	62	38
			101	86	84	87	47		68	78	100	61	37
			99	83	82	84	50		66	76	97	60	36
			97	81	80	81	52		64	75	94	59	35

RAW SCORE / K-FRACTION

Males

L*	F*	K*	Hs +.5K	D	Hy	Pd +.4K	Mf*	Pa	Pt +1K	Sc +1K	Ma +.2K	Si*
												100
												99
												98
										120		97
										119		96
										117		94
										115		93
										113		92
										112		91
										110		90
										108		89
									120	106		88
									118	105		86
									115	103		85
							109		113	101		84
				120			107		111	100		83
				119			105		109	98		82
				117			103		107	96		81
				115			101		105	94		80
				114		120	99		102	93		79
				112	120	117	97		100	91		77
				110	119	115	95		98	89		76
				108	116	112	93		96	87		75
				106	114	110	91		94	86		74
				104	111	107	89		92	84		73
				102	109	105	87		89	82		72
			120	100	106	102	85		87	81		71
			119	98	104	100	83		85	79	120	70
			116	97	101	97	81		83	77	117	69
			114	95	99	95	79		81	75	114	68
			112	93	96	92	78		79	74	110	67
			110	91	94	90	76		77	72	107	66
			108	89	91	87	74		74	70	104	65
			105	87	89	84	72		72	68	101	64
			103	85	86	82	70		70	67	98	63
			101	83	84	79	68		68	65	94	62

RAW SCORE / K-FRACTION

Females

L*	F*	K*	Hs +.5K	D	Hy	Pd +.4K	Mf*	Pa	Pt +1K	Sc +1K	Ma +.2K	Si*

(continued)

509

TABLE A.1 Uniform and Linear T Score Conversions for Basic Scales with K Corrections (continued)

Females

RAW SCORE	L* K-FRACTION	F* K-FRACTION	K* K-FRACTION	Hs +.5K	D	Hy	Pd +.4K	Mf*	Pa	Pt +1K	Sc +1K	Ma +.2K	Si*
34				94	79	77	79	55		62	63	91	58
33				92	77	75	76	57		61	62	88	56
32				90	75	73	73	60		59	60	85	55
31				88	72	70	71	62		57	59	82	54
30				86	70	68	68	65		55	57	79	53
29				84	68	65	66	67		53	55	76	52
28		120	83	82	66	63	63	69		51	53	74	51
27		116	81	80	64	61	60	72	120	50	52	71	50
26		113	78	78	62	58	58	74	118	48	50	68	49
25		109	76	76	59	56	55	77	111	47	48	65	48
24		106	74	73	57	54	53	79	107	44	46	62	47
23		103	72	71	55	51	51	82	103	42	44	59	46
22		99	70	69	53	49	49	84	100	40	42	56	45
21		96	67	67	51	47	47	87	96	38	41	53	44
20		92	65	65	49	45	45	89	92	37	40	51	43
19		89	63	63	47	43	43	92	89	35	39	49	42
18		85	61	61	46	41	41	94	85	33	37	47	41
17		82	59	59	44	39	39	96	81	32	36	45	40
16		79	56	56	42	38	37	99	78	31	34	43	38
15	105	75	54	54	40	36	36	101	74	30	33	41	37
14	100	72	52	51	38	35	34	104	70		32	39	36
13	95	68	50	49	36	34	32	106	67		31	37	35
12	90	65	48	46	34	32	30	109	63		30	35	34
11	86	61	46	43	32	31		111	59			33	33
10	81	58	43	40	30	30		114	56			31	32
9	76	55	41	38				116	52			30	31
8	71	51	39	35				118	49				30
7	66	48	37	33				120	45				
6	62	44	35	30					42				
5	57	41	32						39				
4	52	37	30						37				
3	47								34				
2	42								32				
1	38								31				
0	33								30				

Males

RAW SCORE	L* K-FRACTION	F* K-FRACTION	K* K-FRACTION	Hs +.5K	D	Hy	Pd +.4K	Mf*	Pa	Pt +1K	Sc +1K	Ma +.2K	Si*
34				99	81	81	77	66		66	63	91	60
33				97	80	79	74	64		64	62	88	59
32				94	78	76	72	62		61	60	85	58
31				92	76	74	69	60		59	58	81	57
30				90	74	71	67	58		57	56	78	56
29				88	72	69	64	56		55	54	75	55
28		120	81	86	70	66	62	54	120	53	53	72	54
27		119	79	84	68	64	59	52	119	51	51	69	53
26		116	77	81	66	61	57	50	116	49	49	65	51
25		113	75	79	64	59	54	48	112	47	47	62	50
24		110	72	77	62	57	52	46	108	45	45	59	49
23		107	70	75	61	54	50	44	105	43	44	56	48
22		104	68	73	59	52	48	42	101	41	42	53	46
21		101	66	70	57	50	46	40	97	39	40	51	45
20		98	64	68	54	47	44	38	94	37	39	49	44
19		95	62	66	52	45	42	36	90	35	37	47	42
18		92	60	64	50	43	40	34	86	33	36	45	41
17		89	58	62	47	42	38	32	83	32	34	43	40
16		85	56	59	45	40	37	30	79	30	33	41	39
15	100	82	54	57	42	38	35		75		32	39	38
14	96	79	51	54	40	37	34		72		31	38	37
13	92	76	49	51	38	35	32		68		30	36	36
12	87	73	47	48	36	34	31		64			35	34
11	83	70	45	45	34	33	30		61			33	33
10	78	67	43	42	32	32			57			31	32
9	74	64	41	39	30	31			53			30	31
8	70	61	39	37		30			49				30
7	65	58	37	34					46				
6	61	55	35	33					42				
5	56	51	33	31					39				
4	52	48	30	30					37				
3	48	45							34				
2	45	42							32				
1	42	39							31				
0	39	36							30				

*Linear T scores.

510

TABLE A.2 Uniform and Linear T Score Conversions for Basic Scales without K Corrections

Females

RAW SCORE	L*	F*	K*	Hs	D	Hy	Pd	Mf*	Pa	Pt	Sc	Ma	Si*
72													
71											120		
70											118		
69											117		95
68											116		93
67											115		92
66											114		91
65											113		90
64											112		89
63											111		88
62											109		87
61											108		86
60											107		85
59											106		84
58											105		83
57											104		82
56											103		81
55											102		80
54											100		79
53					120						99		78
52					118	120					98		77
51					116	118					97		75
50					114	115					96		74
49					112	113					95		73
48					109	111				98	94		72
47					107	108	120			97	93		71
46					105	106	118			95	92		70
45					103	104	116			94	90		69
44					101	101	113	30		93	89		68
43					99	99	111	33		91	88	120	67
42					96	96	109	35		90	87	119	66
41					94	94	106	38		89	86	116	65
40					92	92	104	40		87	84	114	64
39					90	89	102	43		86	83	111	63
38					88	87	99	45		84	81	108	62
37					86	84	97	47		83	80	105	61
36					83	82	95	50		82	79	102	60

Males

RAW SCORE	L*	F*	K*	Hs	D	Hy	Pd	Mf*	Pa	Pt	Sc	Ma	Si*
72													
71													
70													
69													100
68											120		99
67											119		98
66											117		97
65											116		96
64											115		94
63											114		93
62											113		92
61											111		91
60											110		90
59											109		89
58											108		88
57											107		86
56								109			105		85
55					120			107			104		84
54					119			105			103		83
53					117			103			102		82
52					115			101			100		81
51					114			99			99		80
50					112	120		97			98		79
49					110	119		95			97		77
48					108	116	120	93		104	96		76
47					106	114	117	91		103	94		75
46					104	111	115	89		101	93		74
45					102	109	113	87		100	92		73
44					100	106	111	85		98	91		72
43					98	104	109	83		97	90		71
42					97	101	106	81		95	88	120	70
41					95	99	104	79		94	87	118	68
40					93	96	102	78		92	86	115	67
39					91	94	100	76		91	85	112	66
38					89	91	97	74		89	84	109	65
37					87	89	95	72		88	82	106	64
36					85	86	93	70		86	81	103	63

(continued)

TABLE A.2 Uniform and Linear T Score Conversions for Basic Scales without K Corrections (continued)

Females

RAW SCORE	L*	F*	K*	Hs	D	Hy	Pd	Mf*	Pa	Pt	Sc	Ma	Si*	RAW SCORE
35					81	80	92	52		80	78	100	59	35
34					79	77	90	55		79	77	97	58	34
33					77	75	88	57		78	76	94	56	33
32				100	75	73	85	60		76	75	91	55	32
31				98	72	70	83	62		75	74	89	54	31
30				97	70	68	81	65		73	72	86	53	30
29			83	95	68	65	78	67		72	71	83	52	29
28			81	93	66	63	76	69	120	71	70	80	51	28
27			78	91	64	61	74	72	118	69	69	77	50	27
26			76	89	62	58	72	74	114	68	68	75	49	26
25			74	87	59	56	69	77	111	67	67	72	48	25
24		120	72	85	57	54	67	79	107	65	66	69	47	24
23		116	70	83	55	51	65	82	103	64	65	66	46	23
22		113	67	82	53	49	62	84	100	62	63	64	45	22
21		109	65	80	51	47	60	87	96	61	62	61	44	21
20		106	63	78	49	45	58	89	92	60	61	58	43	20
19		103	61	76	47	43	55	92	89	58	60	55	42	19
18		99	59	74	46	41	53	94	85	57	59	53	41	18
17		96	56	72	44	39	51	96	81	56	58	51	40	17
16		92	54	70	42	38	49	99	78	55	57	49	38	16
15	105	89	52	69	40	36	47	101	74	53	56	47	37	15
14	100	85	50	67	38	35	45	104	70	52	55	45	36	14
13	95	82	48	65	36	34	43	106	67	51	53	43	35	13
12	90	79	46	63	34	32	41	109	63	50	52	41	34	12
11	86	75	43	61	32	31	39	111	59	48	51	40	33	11
10	81	72	41	59	30	30	37	114	56	47	50	38	32	10
9	76	68	39	57			35	116	52	46	48	36	31	9
8	71	65	37	56			33	118	49	44	47	34	30	8
7	66	61	35	54			31	120	45	43	45	32		7
6	62	58	32	52			30		42	41	43	30		6
5	57	55	30	49					39	39	42			5
4	52	51		47					37	37	39			4
3	47	48		44					34	35	37			3
2	42	44		41					32	33	35			2
1	38	41		37					31	31	32			1
0	33	37		33					30	30	30			0

Males

RAW SCORE	L*	F*	K*	Hs	D	Hy	Pd	Mf*	Pa	Pt	Sc	Ma	Si*	RAW SCORE
35					83	84	91	68		85	80	100	62	35
34					81	81	89	66		83	79	97	60	34
33					80	79	86	64		82	78	94	59	33
32					78	76	84	62		80	76	91	58	32
31					76	74	82	60		79	75	88	57	31
30					74	71	80	58		78	74	85	56	30
29			81	101	72	69	77	56		76	73	82	55	29
28			79	99	70	66	75	54	120	75	72	79	54	28
27			77	97	68	64	73	52	119	73	70	76	53	27
26			75	95	66	61	71	50	116	72	69	73	51	26
25			72	93	64	59	68	48	112	70	68	70	50	25
24		110	70	91	62	57	66	46	108	69	67	67	49	24
23		107	68	89	61	54	64	44	105	67	66	64	48	23
22		104	66	87	59	52	62	42	101	66	64	61	47	22
21		101	64	85	57	50	60	40	97	64	63	58	46	21
20		98	62	83	54	47	57	38	94	63	62	56	45	20
19		95	60	81	52	45	55	36	90	61	61	53	44	19
18		92	58	79	50	43	53	34	86	60	60	51	42	18
17		89	56	77	47	42	51	32	83	58	58	49	41	17
16		85	54	75	45	40	49	30	79	57	57	47	40	16
15	100	82	51	73	42	38	46		75	56	56	45	39	15
14	96	79	49	71	40	37	44		72	54	55	43	38	14
13	92	76	47	69	38	35	42		68	53	54	42	37	13
12	87	73	45	67	36	34	40		64	52	52	40	36	12
11	83	70	43	65	34	33	38		61	50	51	38	34	11
10	78	67	41	63	32	32	36		57	49	49	37	33	10
9	74	64	39	61	30	31	34		53	47	48	35	32	9
8	70	61	37	59		30	33		49	46	46	33	31	8
7	65	58	35	57			31		46	44	45	31	30	7
6	61	55	33	54			30		42	42	43	30		6
5	56	51	30	52					39	41	41			5
4	52	48		49					37	39	39			4
3	48	45		46					34	37	37			3
2	43	42		42					32	34	35			2
1	39	39		38					31	32	32			1
0	35	36		34					30	30	30			0

*Linear T scores.

512

TABLE A.3 Linear T Score Conversions for Harris-Lingoes Subscales

Males

RAW SCORE	D_1	D_2	D_3	D_4	D_5	Hy_1	Hy_2	Hy_3	Hy_4	Hy_5	Pd_1	Pd_2	Pd_3	Pd_4	Pd_5	Pa_1	Pa_2	Pa_3	Sc_1	Sc_2	Sc_3	Sc_4	Sc_5	Sc_6	Ma_1	Ma_2	Ma_3	Ma_4	RAW SCORE
32	116																												32
31	114																													31
30	111																													30
29	108																													29
28	106																													28
27	103																													27
26	100																													26
25	98																													25
24	95																													24
23	93																													23
22	90																													22
21	87																													21
20	85																			120										20
19	82																		117										19
18	79																		113										18
17	77								120										109					120					17
16	74								116										105					119					16
15	71			110				106	111										101			114		114					15
14	69	98		105				102	106							120			97			109		109					14
13	66	92		101				97	101					98		118			92			103		104					13
12	64	87		96				93	96					92	91	112			88			103	117	99					12
11	61	81	116	91			71	88	91					87	87	106			84			98	117	95					11
10	58	76	108	86	96		67	84	86					82	82	100			80		103	92	110	90		78			10
9	56	70	100	82	91		63	79	82		98			77	77	94	96	70	76	120	96	87	103	85		73		89	9
8	53	65	91	77	85		59	75	77		91	80		71	72	88	89	65	72	117	90	82	96	80		68	77	82	8
7	50	59	83	72	79		55	70	72	78	84	73		66	67	82	82	60	68	107	84	76	89	75	81	63	71	76	7
6	48	54	75	67	74	61	51	66	67	71	78	67	63	61	63	76	75	56	64	98	78	71	82	70	74	58	65	69	6
5	45	48	67	62	68	56	47	61	62	63	71	60	57	56	58	70	68	51	59	88	72	65	75	65	66	53	59	63	5
4	42	43	59	58	62	51	43	57	57	55	65	53	51	50	53	64	62	46	55	78	66	60	68	60	58	49	53	56	4
3	40	37	51	53	57	45	40	52	52	48	58	47	45	45	48	58	55	41	51	69	60	55	61	55	50	44	47	50	3
2	37	32	43	48	51	40	36	48	48	40	51	40	39	40	43	52	48	36	47	59	54	49	54	51	42	39	41	43	2
1	35	30	35	43	45	34	32	43	43	33	45	33	33	35	38	46	41	32	43	50	48	44	47	46	35	34	35	37	1
0	32		30	38	40	30	30	38	38	30	38	30	30	30	34	40	34	30	39	40	42	39	40	41		30	30	30	0

Males

RAW SCORE	D_1	D_2	D_3	D_4	D_5	Hy_1	Hy_2	Hy_3	Hy_4	Hy_5	Pd_1	Pd_2	Pd_3	Pd_4	Pd_5	Pa_1	Pa_2	Pa_3	Sc_1	Sc_2	Sc_3	Sc_4	Sc_5	Sc_6	Ma_1	Ma_2	Ma_3	Ma_4	RAW SCORE

(continued)

TABLE A.3 Linear T Score Conversions for Harris-Lingoes Subscales (continued)

Females

RAW SCORE	D1	D2	D3	D4	D5	Hy1	Hy2	Hy3	Hy4	Hy5	Pd1	Pd2	Pd3	Pd4	Pd5	Pa1	Pa2	Pa3	Sc1	Sc2	Sc3	Sc4	Sc5	Sc6	Ma1	Ma2	Ma3	Ma4	RAW SCORE
32	108																												32
31	105																												31
30	103																												30
29	101																												29
28	98																												28
27	96																												27
26	94																												26
25	91																												25
24	89																												24
23	86																												23
22	84																												22
21	82																		119										21
20	79																		115										20
19	77																		111										19
18	75																		108					120					18
17	72								105										104					118					17
16	70								101										100					113					16
15	67			106				99	97										96					109					15
14	65	95		102				95	93							120			92			111		104					14
13	63	90		97				91	89							117			88			106		100					13
12	60	84		93				87	85							111			84			100		95					12
11	58	79	107	88				83	81							105			81			95	110	91					11
10	56	73	100	84	89		71	79	77					81	82	99			77		104	90	104	86		80			10
9	53	68	93	79	83		67	75	73		92	92		75	77	93	91	69	73	120	98	85	97	81		75		86	9
8	51	62	85	75	78		63	71	69		86	84		70	72	87	84	65	69	113	92	80	91	77		70	82	80	8
7	48	57	78	70	73		59	67	65	77	80	77		65	68	81	78	60	65	104	86	75	85	72		65	75	74	7
6	46	51	70	66	68	61	55	63	61	70	74	69	64	60	63	75	72	55	61	95	80	70	78	68	87	60	69	68	6
5	44	46	63	61	63	56	50	59	57	62	68	61	58	54	58	69	65	50	57	86	74	65	72	63	79	55	62	62	5
4	41	41	56	57	58	51	46	55	53	54	62	53	52	49	53	63	59	45	53	76	67	59	65	59	70	50	56	56	4
3	39	35	48	52	53	45	42	51	49	46	56	46	47	44	48	57	53	41	50	67	61	54	59	54	62	45	50	49	3
2	37	30	41	48	47	40	38	47	45	39	50	46	41	38	43	51	46	36	46	58	55	49	53	50	54	40	43	43	2
1	34		34	43	42	35	34	43	41	30	44	38	35	33	39	45	40	31	42	49	49	44	46	45	45	35	37	37	1
0	32		30	38	37	30	30	39	37		38	30	30	30	34	39	34	30	38	40	43	39	40	41	37	30	30	31	0

Females

RAW SCORE	D1	D2	D3	D4	D5	Hy1	Hy2	Hy3	Hy4	Hy5	Pd1	Pd2	Pd3	Pd4	Pd5	Pa1	Pa2	Pa3	Sc1	Sc2	Sc3	Sc4	Sc5	Sc6	Ma1	Ma2	Ma3	Ma4	RAW SCORE

TABLE A.4 Linear T Score Conversions for Wiener-Harmon Subtle-Obvious Subscales

Males

RAW SCORE	D-O	D-S	Hy-O	Hy-S	Pd-O	Pd-S	Pa-O	Pa-S	Ma-O	Ma-S
39										
38	120									
37	118									
36	116									
35	114									
34	111									
33	109									
32	107		120							
31	104		117							
30	102		114							
29	100		111							
28	97		109		108					
27	95		106		106					
26	93		103		103					
25	90		100		100					
24	88		98		98					
23	86		95		95				105	98
22	83		92		92				101	95
21	81		90		90				98	91
20	79		89		87				95	87
19	76		87	78	84				91	83
18	74		84	75	82		116	90	88	80
17	72		82	73	79		112	86	84	76
16	69		81	71	76	95	107	82	81	72
15	67		78	68	74	91	102	77	78	69
14	65		76	66	71	87	98	73	74	65
13	62		73	64	68	83	93	69	71	61
12	60	78	70	61	66	79	89	65	67	57
11	58	75	67	59	63	76	84	60	64	54
10	55	71	64	57	60	72	80	56	61	50
9	53	67	62	52	58	68	75	52	57	46
8	51	63	59	50	55	64	70	48	54	42
7	48	59	56	47	52	60	66	43	51	39
6	46	55	53	45	50	56	61	39	47	35
5	44	52	51	43	47	52	57	35	44	31
4	41	48	48	41	44	48	52	31	40	
3	39	44	45	38	42	45	47		37	
2	37	40	42	36	39	41	43		34	
1	34	36	40	34	36	37	38		30	
0	32	32	37	31	34	33				

RAW SCORE	D-O	D-S	Hy-O	Hy-S	Pd-O	Pd-S	Pa-O	Pa-S	Ma-O	Ma-S

Females

RAW SCORE	D-O	D-S	Hy-O	Hy-S	Pd-O	Pd-S	Pa-O	Pa-S	Ma-O	Ma-S
39	112									
38	110									
37	108									
36	106									
35	104									
34	102									
33	100									
32	98		112							
31	96		110							
30	94		108							
29	92		105							
28	89		103		111					
27	87		101		108					
26	85		98		105					
25	83		96		103					
24	81		93		100					
23	79		91		97					
22	77		89		95				106	
21	75		86		92				103	
20	73		84		89				99	
19	71		82	78	87		120		96	
18	69		79	76	84		115		92	101
17	67		77	73	81		111		89	97
16	65		75	71	79	95	107		86	93
15	63		72	69	76	91	103		82	90
14	61		70	66	73	87	98	91	79	86
13	59		67	64	70	83	94	87	76	82
12	57		65	61	68	79	90	82	72	78
11	55	77	63	59	65	75	85	78	69	74
10	53	73	60	56	62	71	81	74	66	70
9	51	69	58	54	60	67	77	69	62	67
8	48	65	56	51	57	63	72	65	59	63
7	46	61	53	49	54	59	68	61	55	59
6	44	57	51	47	52	55	64	57	52	55
5	42	53	48	44	49	51	60	52	49	51
4	40	48	46	42	46	47	55	48	45	47
3	38	44	44	39	44	43	51	44	42	44
2	36	40	41	37	41	39	47	39	39	40
1	34	36	39	34	38	35	42	35	35	36
0	32	32	37	32	35	31	38	31	32	32

RAW SCORE	D-O	D-S	Hy-O	Hy-S	Pd-O	Pd-S	Pa-O	Pa-S	Ma-O	Ma-S

TABLE A.5 Linear T Score Conversions for *Si* Subscales

RAW SCORE	Males			Females		
	Si_1	Si_2	Si_3	Si_1	Si_2	Si_3
17			86			83
16			83			80
15			80			77
14	77		77	74		74
13	74		74	71		72
12	71		71	68		69
11	68		68	65		66
10	65		65	63		63
9	62		62	60		61
8	59	71	59	57	74	58
7	56	67	56	55	69	55
6	54	62	53	52	65	52
5	51	58	50	49	60	49
4	48	54	47	46	56	47
3	45	49	44	44	51	44
2	42	45	41	41	47	41
1	39	41	38	38	42	38
0	36	37	35	36	37	35
RAW SCORE	Males			Females		
	Si_1	Si_2	Si_3	Si_1	Si_2	Si_3

TABLE A.6　Linear T Score Conversions for Supplementary Scales

Males

RAW SCORE	A	R	Es	MAC-R	F_B	TRIN	VRIN	O-H	Do	Re	Mt	GM	GF	PK	PS	MDS	APS	AAS	RAW SCORE
60															112				60
59															111				59
58															109				58
57															108				57
56															107				56
55															106				55
54															104				54
53															103				53
52			83												102				52
51			81												101				51
50			78												99				50
49			76	114											98				49
48			74	112											97				48
47			72	110											96				47
46			69	108								69	88	113	94				46
45			67	105								67	86	112	93				45
44			65	103								65	84	110	92				44
43			63	101								63	82	108	91				43
42			60	98								61	80	107	89				42
41			58	96							96	58	78	105	88				41
40			56	94							95	56	76	103	87				40
39	91		54	92							93	54	73	102	86		92		39
38	89	98	51	89							91	52	71	100	84		90		38
37	88	96	49	87							90	50	69	98	83		87		37
36	87	94	47	85							88	48	67	97	82		84		36
35	85	92	45	82							87	46	65	95	81		82		35
34	84	89	43	80							85	44	63	93	79		79		34
33	82	87	40	78							84	42	61	92	78		76		33
32	81	85	38	76							82	40	59	90	77		73		32
31	80	83	36	73							81	38	57	88	76		71		31
30	78		34	71						76	79	34	54	87	74		68		30
RAW SCORE	A	R	Es	MAC-R	F_B	TRIN	VRIN	O-H	Do	Re	Mt	GM	GF	PK	PS	MDS	APS	AAS	RAW SCORE

Males

(continued)

517

TABLE A.6 Linear T Score Conversions for Supplementary Scales (continued)

Males

RAW SCORE	A	R	Es	MAC-R	F_B	TRIN	VRIN	O-H	Do	Re	Mt	GM	GF	PK	PS	MDS	APS	AAS	RAW SCORE
29	77	81	31	69						73	77	32	52	85	73		65		29
28	75	78	30	66						70	76	30	50	83	72		63		28
27	74	76		64						68	74		48	82	71		60		27
26	73	74		62				103		65	73		46	80	69		57		26
25	71	72		60				99		63	71		44	78	68		54		25
24	70	69		57			120	96	78	60	70		42	77	67		52		24
23	68	67		55			118	93	75	57	68		40	75	66		49		23
22	67	65		53			115	89	72	55	67		37	73	64		46		22
21	65	63		50			111	86	68	52	65		35	72	63		44		21
20	64	61		48			107	82	65	50	64		33	70	62		41		20
19	63	58		46	120	120T	103	79	61	47	62		31	68	61		38		19
18	61	56		44	116	114T	99	76	58	45	60		30	67	59		35		18
17	60	54		41	112	107T	96	72	55	42	59			65	58		33		17
16	58	52		39	108	100T	92	69	51	39	57			63	57		30		16
15	57	50		37	104	93T	88	65	48	37	56			62	56				15
14	56	47		34	100	86T	84	62	45	34	54			60	54	102			14
13	54	45		32	96	79T	80	58	41	32	53			58	53	97		100	13
12	53	43		30	92	72T	76	55	38	30	51			57	52	92		95	12
11	51	41			87	65T	73	52	34		50			55	51	88		90	11
10	50	39			83	57T	69	48	31		48			53	49	83		85	10
9	49	36			79	50	65	45	30		46			52	48	79		80	9
8	47	34			75	57F	61	41			45			50	47	74		75	8
7	46	32			71	64F	57	38			43			48	46	69		70	7
6	44	30			67	71F	54	35			42			47	44	65		65	6
5	43				63	78F	50	31			40			45	43	60		60	5
4	42				59	85F	46	30			39			43	42	56		56	4
3	40				55	92F	42				37			42	41	51		51	3
2	39				51	99F	38				36			40	39	46		46	2
1	37				46	107F	34				34			38	38	42		41	1
0	36				42	114F	31				32			37	37	37		36	0
RAW SCORE	A	R	Es	MAC-R	F_B	TRIN	VRIN	O-H	Do	Re	Mt	GM	GF	PK	PS	MDS	APS	AAS	RAW SCORE

Males

Females

RAW SCORE	A	R	Es	MAC-R	F_B	TRIN	VRIN	O-H	Do	Re	Mt	GM	GF	PK	PS	MDS	APS	AAS
60															104			
59															103			
58															102			
57															100			
56															99			
55															98			
54															97			
53															96			
52			86												95			
51			84												94			
50			82												93			
49			80												92			
48			78												90			
47			76									78			89			
46			74									76	71	107	88			
45			72	120								75	69	106	87			
44			70	118								73	66	104	86			
43			68	115								72	64	103	85			
42			66	113								70	61	101	84			
41			64	110							91	69	59	99	83			
40			61	107							90	67	56	98	81			
39	85		59	105							88	66	53	96	80		93	
38	83		57	102							87	64	51	95	79		90	
37	82	104	55	99							85	63	48	93	78		87	
36	81	102	53	96							84	61	46	92	77		85	
35	80	99	51	94							82	59	43	90	76		82	
34	78	96	49	91							81	58	40	89	75		79	
33	77	94	47	88							80	56	38	87	74		77	
32	76	91	45	86							78	55	35	86	73		74	
31	74	88	43	83							77	53	33	84	71		71	
30	73	86	41	80						77	75	52	30	83	70		69	

Females

RAW SCORE	A	R	Es	MAC-R	F_B	TRIN	VRIN	O-H	Do	Re	Mt	GM	GF	PK	PS	MDS	APS	AAS

(continued)

TABLE A.6 Linear T Score Conversions for Supplementary Scales (continued)

Females

RAW SCORE	A	R	Es	MAC-R	F_B	TRIN	VRIN	O-H	Do	Re	Mt	GM	GF	PK	PS	MDS	APS	AAS	RAW SCORE
29	72	83	39	78						74	74	50		81	69		66		29
28	71	81	37	75				103		71	72	49		80	68		63		28
27	69	78	35	72				99		68	71	47		78	67		60		27
26	68	75	33	69				96		65	70	46		77	66		58		26
25	67	73	31	67				92	80	62	68	44		75	65		55		25
24	66	70	30	64				88	77	59	67	43		74	64		52		24
23	64	67		61			120	85	73	56	65	41		72	62		50		23
22	63	65		59			118	81	70	53	64	40		71	61		47		22
21	62	62		56			114	77	66	50	62	38		69	60		44		21
20	61	60		53	120		110	74	63	47	61	36		67	59		42		20
19	59	57		50	116	120T	106	70	59	44	60	35		66	58		39		19
18	58	54		48	112	118T	102	66	56	41	58	33		64	57		36		18
17	57	52		45	108	111T	98	63	53	38	57	32		63	56		33		17
16	56	49		42	105	103T	94	59	49	35	55	30		61	55		31		16
15	54	46		40	101	95T	90	55	46	32	54			60	54		30		15
14	53	44		37	97	88T	86	52	42	30	52			58	52	98			14
13	52	41		34	93	80T	82	48	39		51			57	51	93		113	13
12	50	39		31	89	73T	78	44	35		50			55	50	89		107	12
11	49	36		30	85	65T	74	41	32		48			54	49	85		101	11
10	48	33			81	58T	70	37	30		47			52	48	80		95	10
9	47	31			77	50	66	33			45			51	47	76		90	9
8	45	30			74	58F	62	30			44			49	46	72		84	8
7	44				70	65F	58				42			48	45	68		78	7
6	43				66	73F	54				41			46	43	63		73	6
5	42				62	80F	50				40			45	42	59		67	5
4	40				58	88F	46				38			43	41	55		61	4
3	39				54	95F	42				37			42	40	50		56	3
2	38				50	103F	38				35			40	39	46		50	2
1	37				46	111F	34				34			39	38	42		44	1
0	35				42	118F	30				32			37	37	38		39	0
RAW SCORE	A	R	Es	MAC-R	F_B	TRIN	VRIN	O-H	Do	Re	Mt	GM	GF	PK	PS	MDS	APS	AAS	RAW SCORE

Females

TABLE A.7 Uniform T Score Conversions for Content Scales

Males

RAW SCORE	ANX	FRS	OBS	DEP	HEA	BIZ	ANG	CYN	ASP	TPA	LSE	SOD	FAM	WRK	TRT
36					112										
35					110										
34					108										
33				100	106									98	
32				99	105									96	
31				97	103									94	
30				95	101									92	
29				94	99									90	
28				92	97									89	
27				90	95									87	
26				88	93							105		85	104
25				87	91							102	105	83	101
24		113		85	89	120					101	99	102	81	99
23	92	110		83	87	119		94			98	89	99	79	96
22	90	107		82	85	115		90	89		96	86	97	78	94
21	87	103		80	83	112		87	85		93	84	94	76	91
20	85	100		78	81	108		83	81		91	81	91	74	89
19	82	97		77	80	105		79	77	85	88	78	88	72	86
18	80	93		75	78	101		76	72	81	85	76	85	70	84
17	77	90		73	76	98		72	68	77	83	73	82	68	81
16	75	87	87	71	74	94	86	69	64	72	80	71	80	67	79
15	72	84	84	70	72	91	82	65	60	68	77	68	77	65	76
14	70	80	80	68	70	88	80	62	56	64	75	65	74	63	74
13	67	77	77	66	68	84	77	59	53	60	72	63	71	61	71
12	65	73	73	65	66	81	74	56	50	57	70	60	68	59	69
11	62	70	70	63	64	78	70	54	48	53	67	58	66	57	66
10	60	67	66	61	62	74	67	52	46	50	64	55	63	56	64
9	57	64	63	60	60	70	63	51	44	48	62	54	61	54	61
8	55	60	59	58	58	67	60	49	43	46	59	52	59	52	59
7	53	57	56	56	56	63	56	47	41	44	57	50	57	50	56
6	52	54	53	55	53	60	53	46	40	43	55	49	55	48	54
5	50	51	50	53	51	57	50	44	38	41	53	47	52	46	52
4	47	48	47	51	48	54	46	43	36	40	51	45	50	44	49
3	45	45	44	48	44	51	43	41	34	38	48	43	47	41	47
2	42	41	41	45	41	48	40	40	32	36	45	41	44	39	43
1	39	39	37	41	37	44	36	38	31	33	41	37	41	36	39
0	35	35	33	36	33	41	32	34	30	30	35	35	33	33	35

Females

RAW SCORE	ANX	FRS	OBS	DEP	HEA	BIZ	ANG	CYN	ASP	TPA	LSE	SOD	FAM	WRK	TRT
36					107										
35					105										
34					103										
33				97	101									99	
32				95	100									97	
31				93	98									95	
30				92	96									92	
29				90	94									90	
28				88	92									88	
27				87	90									86	
26				85	89							87		84	102
25				83	87							85	99	82	100
24				82	85	113					97	84	96	80	97
23	89	101		80	83	110		83			94	82	94	78	95
22	86	98		78	81	108		80	98		92	80	91	76	92
21	84	94		77	79	105		77	94		89	78	89	73	89
20	81	91		75	77	102		75	91		86	75	86	71	87
19	79	88		73	76	99		72	88	94	84	72	83	69	84
18	76	85		72	74	96		69	85	90	81	70	81	67	82
17	74	81		70	73	93		67	82	86	78	68	78	65	79
16	71	78	87	68	72	90	88	64	79	81	76	65	75	63	77
15	69	75	83	67	70	87	84	61	75	77	73	63	73	61	74
14	66	72	79	65	68	84	80	58	72	73	70	60	70	59	72
13	64	68	75	63	66	81	76	56	69	69	68	58	68	57	69
12	61	65	71	62	64	79	72	53	66	64	65	56	65	55	67
11	59	62	67	61	63	76	68	51	63	60	62	54	62	53	64
10	56	59	63	59	61	72	64	50	59	56	60	52	60	51	61
9	55	56	59	58	59	68	60	48	56	53	57	50	57	50	59
8	53	53	56	57	57	64	56	46	54	50	55	49	55	48	57
7	51	51	53	55	55	60	53	44	52	48	54	47	52	46	55
6	49	48	50	53	53	56	50	42	49	45	52	44	50	45	53
5	47	46	47	51	51	52	47	40	47	43	51	41	47	43	51
4	45	44	44	49	49	47	45	39	45	41	49	39	45	40	49
3	43	41	41	46	46	42	42	38	42	38	47	36	42	37	46
2	41	38	38	43	43	39	39	36	39	36	44	35	39	34	43
1	37	35	35	39	40	36	36	35	35	33	40	32	36	31	39
0	34	31	32	34	32	31	31	33	33	30	35	32	32	31	35

TABLE A.8 Linear T Score Conversions for Content Component Scales

Males

Raw Score	FRS1	FRS2	DEP1	DEP2	DEP3	DEP4	HEA1	HEA2	HEA3	BIZ1	BIZ2	ANG1	ANG2	CYN1	CYN2	ASP1	ASP2	TPA1	TPA2	LSE1	LSE2	SOD1	SOD2	FAM1	FAM2	TRT1	TRT2	Raw Score
16																78						82						16
15														74		75						79						15
14														71		72						76						14
13														68		69						73						13
12			106					120						65		66						71		95				12
11			100					114						63		63				95		68		90		107		11
10		81	95					107						60		60				90		65		85		101		10
9	120	76	89					100			99			57		57			76	85		62		80		95		9
8	116	71	84					94			93			55	71	55			71	80		59		75		89		8
7	107	66	79		91			87		120	86	83	72	52	66	52			66	75	83	56	74	70		83		7
6	98	61	73	93	83			80	89	114	80	77	67	49	62	49		68	61	70	76	53	68	65		77		6
5	89	56	68	85	76	120	109	74	81	102	73	71	61	46	57	46	74	63	56	64	76	50	63	60	84	71	75	5
4	80	52	62	76	69	112	96	67	72	91	67	64	56	44	53	43	67	57	50	59	69	47	58	55	76	66	68	4
3	71	47	57	68	62	95	83	60	64	79	60	58	51	41	48	40	59	51	45	54	62	45	52	50	67	60	60	3
2	62	42	51	59	55	79	70	54	56	67	54	52	46	38	43	37	52	45	40	49	55	42	47	45	58	54	52	2
1	53	37	46	51	48	62	57	47	48	55	47	45	41	35	39	35	45	39	35	44	48	39	41	40	49	48	45	1
0	44	32	40	42	41	45	44	40	40	44	41	39	35	33	34	32	38	34	30	39	41	36	36	35	40	42	37	0

Raw Score	FRS1	FRS2	DEP1	DEP2	DEP3	DEP4	HEA1	HEA2	HEA3	BIZ1	BIZ2	ANG1	ANG2	CYN1	CYN2	ASP1	ASP2	TPA1	TPA2	LSE1	LSE2	SOD1	SOD2	FAM1	FAM2	TRT1	TRT2	Raw Score

Females

Raw Score	FRS1	FRS2	DEP1	DEP2	DEP3	DEP4	HEA1	HEA2	HEA3	BIZ1	BIZ2	ANG1	ANG2	CYN1	CYN2	ASP1	ASP2	TPA1	TPA2	LSE1	LSE2	SOD1	SOD2	FAM1	FAM2	TRT1	TRT2	Raw Score
16																82						85						16
15														76		79						82						15
14														73		76						79						14
13														70		73						76						13
12	120		100					105						67		70						73		91				12
11	114		95					99						64		67				89		70		86		96		11
10	107		90					94						62		64				85		67		81		91		10
9	101	69	85					89			97			59		61			82	80		64		76		86		9
8	94	65	80					83			91			56	73	58			76	75		61		71		81		8
7	88	60	75		89			78			85	91	70	53	68	55			70	71	75	58	69	67		76		7
6	81	56	70	87	82			72	87	120	79	84	65	50	64	52		70	64	66	75	55	65	62		71		6
5	74	52	65	79	75	120	97	67	79	112	72	76	59	48	59	48	90	64	59	62	69	52	60	57	86	66	75	5
4	68	47	60	72	68	109	86	61	71	99	66	69	54	45	54	45	81	58	53	57	63	49	55	52	77	61	68	4
3	61	43	55	64	61	93	75	56	64	85	60	61	49	42	49	42	71	52	47	53	57	46	50	47	68	56	60	3
2	55	38	50	56	54	77	64	50	56	71	54	54	44	39	45	39	61	46	41	48	51	43	45	42	59	51	53	2
1	48	34	45	49	47	61	54	45	48	57	47	47	39	36	40	36	51	40	36	43	45	40	40	38	50	46	46	1
0	42	30	40	41	40	45	43	39	40	44	41	39	33	34	35	33	42	34	30	39	39	37	35	33	41	41	38	0

Raw Score	FRS1	FRS2	DEP1	DEP2	DEP3	DEP4	HEA1	HEA2	HEA3	BIZ1	BIZ2	ANG1	ANG2	CYN1	CYN2	ASP1	ASP2	TPA1	TPA2	LSE1	LSE2	SOD1	SOD2	FAM1	FAM2	TRT1	TRT2	Raw Score

TABLE A.9 Linear T Score Conversions for Additional Validity Scales

Raw Score	F(p)	S	So	Ds	Men Ds-r	FBS	ODec	IR	Sd	F(p)	S	So	Ds	Women Ds-r	FBS	ODec	IR	Sd	Raw Score
55																			55
54																			54
53																			53
52																			52
51																			51
50		79									80		120						50
49		78									78		118						49
48		76		120							77		116						48
47		75		119							76		115						47
46		74		118							75		113						46
45		73		116							74		111						45
44		72		114							72		109						44
43		71		112							71		108		120				43
42		70		110							70		106		118				42
41		68		108							69		104		116				41
40		67		106							68		102		113				40
39		66		104	120						66		100		111				39
38		65		102	119						65		99		109				38
37		64	65	101	116						64	66	97		106				37
36		63	63	99	114						63	64	95		104				36
35		61	61	97	111						61	62	93		101				35
34		60	58	95	109						60	60	92		99				34
33		59	56	93		106	96		105		59	58	90	118	96	106		114	33
32		58	54	91		103	94		102		58	56	88	116	94	103		111	32
31		57	52	89	120	101	91		100		57	54	86	113	92	101		108	31
30		56	50	87	119	98	89		97		55	53	84	111	89	98		105	30
29		55	47	86	116	95	87		94		54	51	83	108	87	95		102	29
28		53	45	84	113	93	85		92		53	49	81	105	84	93		99	28
27		52	43	82	110	90	82		89		52	47	79	103	82	90		95	27
26		51	41	80	107	88	80		86		51	45	77	100	80	88		92	26
25		50	39	78	105	85	78		83		49	43	76	98	77	85		89	25
24		49	36	76	102	82	75		81		48	41	74	95	75	83		86	24
23		48	34	74	99	80	73		78		47	39	72	92	72	80		83	23
22		47	32	72	96	77	71		75		46	37	70	90	70	78		80	22
21		45	30	71	93	74	68		73		45	35	68	87	67	75		77	21
20		44		69	90	72	66		70		43	33	67	85	65	73		74	20
19		43		67	87	69	64		67		42	31	65	82	63	70		71	19
18		42		65	85	67	62		64		41	30	63	79	60	67		68	18
17		41		63	82	64	59		62		40		61	77	58	65		65	17
16		40		61	79	61	57		59		39		60	74	55	62		62	16
15		38		59	76	59	55		56		37		58	72	53	60		59	15
14		37		57	73	56	52		53		36		56	69	51	57		56	14
13		36		55	70	53	50		51		35		54	67	48	55		53	13
12		35		54	67	51	48		48		34		53	64	46	52		50	12
11	120	34		52	65	48	45		45		33		51	61	43	50		47	11
10	113	33		50	62	46	43		43	120	31		49	59	41	47		43	10
9	106	32		48	59	43	41	120	40	113	30		47	56	39	45		40	9
8	99	30		46	56	40	39	114	37	105			45	54	36	42	120	37	8
7	94			44	53	38	36	105	34	97			44	51	34	39	118	34	7
6	84			42	50	35	34	96	32	89			42	48	31	37	108	31	6
5	77			40	47	32	32	87	30	81			40	46	30	34	97	30	5
4	70			39	45	30	30	78		73			38	43		32	86		4
3	63			37	42			69		65			37	41		30	75		3
2	56			35	39			60		57			35	38			65		2
1	48			33	36			50		49			33	35			54		1
0	41			31	33			41		41			31	33			43		0
Raw Score	F(p)	S	So	Ds	Ds-r Men	FBS	ODec	IR	Sd	F(p)	S	So	Ds	Ds-r Women	FBS	ODec	IR	Sd	Raw Score

TABLE A.10   Linear T Score Conversions for Personality Psychopathology Five (*PSY-5*) Scales

Raw Score	AGG	PSY	Men CON	NEN	PEE	AGG	PSY	Women CON	NEN	PEE	Raw Score
40											40
39											39
38											38
37											37
36											36
35											35
34					75					76	34
33				93	73				88	73	33
32				91	70				86	71	32
31				90	68				85	68	31
30				88	66				83	66	30
29			86	86	64			78	81	64	29
28			83	84	61			75	79	61	28
27			81	82	59			73	78	59	27
26			78	80	57			70	76	57	26
25			76	79	55			67	74	54	25
24			73	77	52			64	72	52	24
23		120	70	75	50		120	62	71	49	23
22		117	68	73	48		117	59	69	47	22
21		114	65	71	46		114	56	67	45	21
20		110	63	69	43		110	54	65	42	20
19		106	60	68	41		106	51	64	40	19
18	83	103	58	66	39	90	103	48	62	38	18
17	80	99	55	64	37	86	99	45	60	35	17
16	76	95	53	62	34	83	96	43	58	33	16
15	73	92	50	60	32	79	92	40	57	30	15
14	70	88	47	58	30	76	88	37	55		14
13	66	84	45	57		72	85	35	53		13
12	63	81	42	55		69	81	32	51		12
11	59	77	40	53		65	77	30	50		11
10	56	73	37	51		61	74		48		10
9	53	70	35	49		58	70		46		9
8	49	66	32	47		54	67		44		8
7	46	62	30	46		51	63		43		7
6	43	59		44		47	59		41		6
5	39	55		42		44	56		39		5
4	36	52		40		40	52		37		4
3	32	48		38		36	48		36		3
2	30	44		36		33	45		34		2
1		41		35		30	41		32		1
0		37		33			38		30		0
Raw Score	AGG	PSY	CON Men	NEN	PEE	AGG	PSY	CON Women	NEN	PEE	Raw Score

TABLE A.11 Linear T Score Conversions for Personality Disorder Scales

Nonoverlapping Scales

Men

Raw Score	HST	NAR	BDL	ANT	DEP	CPS	AVD	PAG	PAR	STY	SZD	Raw Score
20												20
19												19
18				87								18
17			92	84								17
16			89	80	96							16
15			85	77	92				110	108		15
14		81	82	74	88		84	83	105	103		14
13	73	77	78	71	84		80	79	100	98		13
12	68	72	74	68	81		77	75	95	93		12
11	64	68	71	65	77	76	73	72	90	89	88	11
10	59	63	67	62	73	71	69	68	85	84	84	10
9	55	59	63	59	69	66	66	64	80	79	79	9
8	50	54	60	56	65	62	62	61	75	74	74	8
7	46	50	56	53	61	57	58	57	70	69	69	7
6	41	45	52	49	57	53	55	53	65	65	64	6
5	37	41	49	46	54	48	51	50	61	60	59	5
4	32	37	45	43	50	43	47	46	56	55	55	4
3	30	32	42	40	46	39	44	42	51	50	50	3
2		30	38	37	42	34	40	38	46	45	45	2
1			34	34	38	30	36	35	41	41	40	1
0			31	31	34		33	31	36	36	35	0
Raw Score	HST	NAR	BDL	ANT	DEP	CPS	AVD	PAG	PAR	STY	SZD	Raw Score

Women

Raw Score	HST	NAR	BDL	ANT	DEP	CPS	AVD	PAG	PAR	STY	SZD	Raw Score
20												20
19												19
18				96								18
17			85	93								17
16			82	89	87							16
15			78	86	83				110	111		15
14		83	75	82	80		78	85	105	106		14
13	73	79	72	78	77		75	81	100	101		13
12	68	74	68	75	73		71	77	96	96		12
11	64	70	65	71	70	75	68	73	91	91	92	11
10	60	66	62	68	67	71	65	70	86	86	87	10
9	55	61	58	64	63	66	61	66	81	81	82	9
8	51	57	55	61	60	61	58	62	76	76	77	8
7	46	53	52	57	57	56	55	58	71	71	72	7
6	42	48	48	54	53	51	51	55	66	66	67	6
5	37	44	45	50	50	47	48	51	62	61	62	5
4	33	40	41	47	47	42	45	47	57	56	57	4
3	30	36	38	43	43	37	41	43	52	51	52	3
2		31	35	40	40	32	38	40	47	46	46	2
1		30	31	36	36	30	34	36	42	41	41	1
0			30	33	33		31	32	37	36	36	0
Raw Score	HST	NAR	BDL	ANT	DEP	CPS	AVD	PAG	PAR	STY	SZD	Raw Score

(continued)

TABLE A.11   Linear T Score Conversions for Personality Disorder Scales (continued)

Overlapping Scales

Raw Score	HST	NAR	BDL	ANT	DEP	Men CPS	AVD	PAR	STY	SZD	Raw Score
40											40
39											39
38							88				38
37							87				37
36							85				36
35							84		105		35
34							82		103		34
33							81		101		33
32							79		99		32
31		84					78		96		31
30		81					76		94		30
29		79					75		92		29
28		76					73		90		28
27		74					72		88		27
26		71					70		86		26
25		68					69		84		25
24		66					67		82		24
23		63		88			66		80		23
22		61	92	86			64	105	78		22
21		58	89	83			63	101	76		21
20	72	56	86	80	99		61	98	73	92	20
19	69	53	83	78	95		60	95	71	89	19
18	66	51	80	75	92		58	92	69	86	18
17	63	48	77	73	89		57	88	67	83	17
16	60	46	74	70	86		55	85	65	79	16
15	57	43	71	67	82		54	82	63	76	15
14	54	41	69	65	79		52	79	61	73	14
13	51	38	66	62	76	77	51	75	59	70	13
12	49	36	63	60	72	73	49	72	57	67	12
11	46	33	60	57	69	69	48	69	55	64	11
10	43	31	57	54	66	65	46	66	52	61	10
9	40		54	52	63	61	45	62	50	58	9
8	37		51	49	59	57	43	59	48	55	8
7	34		48	47	56	53	42	56	46	52	7
6	31		45	44	53	49	40	53	44	49	6
5			42	42	50	45	39	49	42	46	5
4			39	39	46	41	37	46	40	43	4
3			36	36	43	37	36	43	38	40	3
2			33	34	40	34	34	40	36	37	2
1			30	31	37	30	33	36	34	34	1
0					33		31	33	31	31	0
Raw Score	HST	NAR	BDL	ANT	DEP	CPS	AVD	PAR	STY	SZD	Raw Score

Overlapping Scales

Raw Score	HST	NAR	BDL	ANT	DEP	Women CPS	AVD	PAR	STY	SZD	Raw Score
40											40
39											39
38							84				38
37							82				37
36							81				36
35							79		105		35
34							78		103		34
33							77		101		33
32							75		99		32
31		85					74		97		31
30		83					72		95		30
29		80					71		93		29
28		78					70		90		28
27		76					68		88		27
26		73					67		86		26
25		71					66		84		25
24		68					64		82		24
23		66		98			63		80		23
22		63	88	95			61	106	78		22
21		61	85	92			60	102	76		21
20	72	58	82	90	89		59	99	74	98	20
19	69	56	79	87	86		57	96	72	94	19
18	66	54	76	84	83		56	92	69	91	18
17	63	51	73	81	80		54	89	67	88	17
16	60	49	71	78	77		53	86	65	84	16
15	57	46	68	75	75		52	83	63	81	15
14	54	44	65	72	72		50	79	61	78	14
13	51	41	62	69	69	77	49	76	59	75	13
12	48	39	59	66	66	73	47	73	57	71	12
11	46	36	56	63	63	69	46	69	55	68	11
10	43	34	53	60	61	65	45	66	53	65	10
9	40	32	50	57	58	61	43	63	51	61	9
8	37		47	54	55	57	42	59	48	58	8
7	34		45	51	52	53	40	56	46	55	7
6	31		42	48	49	49	39	53	44	52	6
5			39	46	46	44	38	50	42	48	5
4			36	43	44	40	36	46	40	45	4
3			33	40	41	36	35	43	38	42	3
2			30	37	38	32	33	40	36	39	2
1				34	35		32	36	34	35	1
0				31	32		31	33	32	32	0
Raw Score	HST	NAR	BDL	ANT	DEP	CPS	AVD	PAR	STY	SZD	Raw Score

TABLE A.12   Linear T Score Conversions for Wiggins Content Scales

Raw Score	HEA	DEP	ORG	FAM	AUT	Men FEM	HOS	MOR	PHO	PSY	HYP	SOC	Raw Score
40													40
39													39
38										120			38
37										119			37
36										117			36
35										115			35
34										112			34
33		111								110			33
32		109								108			32
31		107								105			31
30		105								103			30
29		102	120							101			29
28		100	117							98			28
27		98	114							96			27
26		95	111						108	94		81	26
25		93	108				89		105	91		79	25
24		91	106				87		103	89		77	24
23		89	103			100	84		100	87	84	75	23
22		86	100			96	82	88	97	84	81	74	22
21		84	97			93	80	86	94	82	78	72	21
20		82	94		77	89	77	83	91	80	75	70	20
19	111	80	91		75	86	75	81	88	77	73	68	19
18	107	77	88		72	83	73	79	85	75	70	66	18
17	103	75	86		70	79	71	76	82	73	67	64	17
16	99	73	83	97	67	76	68	74	80	70	64	62	16
15	95	71	80	93	65	73	66	72	77	68	61	60	15
14	92	68	77	89	62	69	64	69	74	66	59	58	14
13	88	66	74	85	60	66	61	67	71	63	56	57	13
12	84	64	71	82	58	62	59	64	68	61	53	55	12
11	80	62	68	78	55	59	57	62	65	59	50	53	11
10	76	59	66	74	53	56	54	60	62	56	48	51	10
9	72	57	63	70	50	52	52	57	59	54	45	49	9
8	68	55	60	66	48	49	50	55	56	52	42	47	8
7	64	52	57	62	45	45	47	53	54	49	39	45	7
6	60	50	54	58	43	42	45	50	51	47	37	43	6
5	56	48	51	54	40	39	43	48	48	45	34	41	5
4	53	46	48	50	38	35	40	46	45	42	31	39	4
3	49	43	46	46	36	32	38	43	42	40	30	38	3
2	45	41	43	42	33	30	36	41	39	38		36	2
1	41	39	40	38	31		33	39	36	35		34	1
0	37	37	37	34	30		31	36	33	33		32	0
Raw Score	HEA	DEP	ORG	FAM	AUT	FEM	HOS	MOR	PHO	PSY	HYP	SOC	Raw Score

Raw Score	HEA	DEP	ORG	FAM	AUT	FEM	HOS	MOR	PHO	PSY	HYP	SOC	Raw Score
						Women							
55													55
54													54
53													53
52													52
51													51
50													50
49													49
48													48
40													40
39													39
38													38
37										120			37
36										118			36
35										115			35
34										113			34
33		103								111			33
32		101	120							108			32
31		99	118							106			31
30		97	115							104			30
29		95	113							101			29
28		93	110							99			28
27		91	108							96			27
26		89	105						94	94		80	26
25		87	102				93		91	92		78	25
24		85	100				91		89	89		76	24
23		83	97			78	88		86	87	86	75	23
22		81	95			74	86	80	84	85	83	73	22
21		79	92			70	83	78	81	82	80	71	21
20		76	89		83	67	81	76	78	80	77	69	20
19	104	74	87		80	63	78	74	76	78	74	67	19
18	100	72	84		78	59	76	72	73	75	71	65	18
17	97	70	81		75	55	73	70	71	73	68	63	17
16	93	68	79	91	72	51	71	68	68	70	65	62	16
15	90	66	76	88	70	48	68	66	66	68	62	60	15
14	86	64	74	84	67	44	66	64	63	66	59	58	14
13	82	62	71	80	65	40	63	62	61	63	56	56	13
12	79	60	68	77	62	36	61	59	58	61	53	54	12
11	75	58	66	73	59	32	58	57	56	59	51	52	11
10	72	56	63	69	57	30	56	55	53	56	48	51	10
9	68	54	61	65	54		53	53	51	54	45	49	9
8	65	52	58	62	51		51	51	48	52	42	47	8
7	61	50	55	58	49		48	49	46	49	39	45	7
6	57	47	53	54	46		46	47	43	47	36	43	6
5	54	45	50	51	44		43	45	41	44	33	41	5
4	50	43	48	47	41		41	43	38	42	30	39	4
3	47	41	45	43	38		38	41	36	40		38	3
2	43	39	42	40	36		36	38	33	37		36	2
1	39	37	40	36	33		33	36	31	35		34	1
0	36	35	37	32	30		31	34	28	33		32	0
Raw Score	HEA	DEP	ORG	FAM	AUT	FEM	HOS	MOR	PHO	PSY	HYP	SOC	Raw Score

TABLE A.13   Linear T Score Conversions for Martin and Finn Masculinity-Femininity Subscales

Raw Score	Mf$_1$	Mf$_2$	Mf$_3$	Mf$_4$	Men Mf$_5$	Mf$_6$	Mf$_7$	F-M	Raw Score
22								104	22
21								101	21
20								97	20
19								94	19
18								90	18
17								87	17
16								83	16
15								80	15
14								76	14
13		80						73	13
12		76						69	12
11	76	72						66	11
10	72	69						63	10
9	67	65						59	9
8	63	61						56	8
7	59	57						52	7
6	54	54	87	63			66	49	6
5	50	50	79	56	69	83	59	45	5
4	46	46	71	49	63	74	52	42	4
3	41	42	63	42	56	65	45	38	3
2	37	39	55	35	49	56	39	35	2
1	33	35	47	28	42	47	32	31	1
0	28	31	39	21	36	38	25	28	0
Raw Score	Mf$_1$	Mf$_2$	Mf$_3$	Mf$_4$	Mf$_5$	Mf$_6$	Mf$_7$	F-M	Raw Score

Women

Raw Score	Mf₁	Mf₂	Mf₃	Mf₄	Mf₅	Mf₆	Mf₇	F-M	Raw Score
22								73	22
21								70	21
20								66	20
19								63	19
18								60	18
17								56	17
16								53	16
15								50	15
14								46	14
13		76						43	13
12		72						40	12
11	64	68						37	11
10	59	65						33	10
9	54	61						30	9
8	49	57						27	8
7	44	53						23	7
6	39	50	70	61			63	20	6
5	33	46	63	54	67	57	55	17	5
4	28	42	56	47	60	46	48	13	4
3	23	38	49	39	52	35	40	10	3
2	18	34	42	32	45	24	33	7	2
1	13	31	35	24	38	13	26	3	1
0	8	27	28	17	31	2	18	0	0
Raw Score	Mf₁	Mf₂	Mf₃	Mf₄	Mf₅	Mf₆	Mf₇	F-M	Raw Score

Item Composition of the Scales

Note. Means and standard deviations provided for each scale are based on the contemporary normative sample of 1,138 males and 1,462 females.

TABLE B.1 Basic Scales

L — Lie (15 items)

True

False

| 16 | 29 | 41 | 51 | 77 | 93 | 102 | 107 | 123 | 139 | 153 | 183 | 203 | 232 | 260 |

Males: Mean 3.53; S.D. 2.28.   Females: Mean 3.57; S.D. 2.08.

F – Infrequency (60 items)

True

18	24	30	36	42	48	54	60	66	72	84	96	114	138
144	150	156	162	168	180	198	216	228	234	240	246	252	258
264	270	282	288	294	300	306	312	324	336	349	355	361	

False

| 6 | 12 | 78 | 90 | 102 | 108 | 120 | 126 | 132 | 174 | 186 | 192 | 204 | 210 |
| 222 | 276 | 318 | 330 | 343 | | | | | | | | | |

Males: Mean 4.53; S.D. 3.24.   Females: Mean 3.66; S.D. 2.91.

K – Correction (30 items)

True

83

False

29	37	58	76	110	116	122	127	130	136	148	157	158	167
171	196	213	243	267	284	290	330	338	339	341	346	348	356
365													

Males: Mean 15.30; S.D. 4.76.   Females: Mean 15.03; S.D. 4.58.

---

1 Hs – Hypochondriasis (32 items)

True

| 18 | 28 | 39 | 53 | 59 | 97 | 101 | 111 | 149 | 175 | 247 |

False

| 2 | 3 | 8 | 10 | 20 | 45 | 47 | 57 | 91 | 117 | 141 | 143 | 152 | 164 |
| 173 | 176 | 179 | 208 | 224 | 249 | 255 | | | | | | | |

Raw scores without K:
Males: Mean 4.92; S.D. 3.87.   Females: Mean 5.93; S.D. 4.51.
Raw scores with K:
Males: Mean 12.84; S.D. 3.82.   Females: Mean 13.70; S.D. 4.05.

(continued)

TABLE B.1   Basic Scales (continued)

---

2 D – Depression (57 items)

True

5	15	18	31	38	39	46	56	73	92	117	127	130	146
147	170	175	181	215	233							

False

2	9	10	20	29	33	37	43	45	49	55	68	75	76
95	109	118	134	140	141	142	143	148	165	178	188	189	212
221	223	226	238	245	248	260	267	330				

Males: Mean 18.32; S.D. 4.59.   Females: Mean 20.14; S.D. 4.97.

---

3 Hy – Conversion Hysteria (60 items)

True

11	18	31	39	40	44	65	101	166	172	175	218	230

False

2	3	7	8	9	10	14	26	29	45	47	58	76	81
91	95	98	110	115	116	124	125	129	135	141	148	151	152
157	159	161	164	167	173	176	179	185	193	208	213	224	241
243	249	253	263	265								

Males: Mean 20.87; S.D. 4.73.   Females: Mean 22.08; S.D. 4.73.

---

4 Pd – Psychopathic Deviate (50 items)

True

17	21	22	31	32	35	42	52	54	56	71	82	89	94
99	105	113	195	202	219	225	259	264	288			

False

9	12	34	70	79	83	95	122	125	129	143	157	158
160	167	171	185	209	214	217	226	243	261	263	266	267

Raw scores without K:
Males: Mean 16.57; S.D. 4.60.   Females: Mean 16.21; S.D. 4.65.
Raw scores with K:
Males: Mean 22.69; S.D. 4.63.   Females: Mean 22.22; S.D. 4.52.

---

5 Mf-m – Masculinity-Femininity (Masculine) (56 items)

True

4	25	62	64	67	74	80	112	119	122	128	137	166	177
187	191	196	205	209	219	236	251	256	268	271		

False

1	19	26	27	63	68	69	76	86	103	104	107	120	121
132	133	163	184	193	194	197	199	201	207	231	235	237	239
254	257	272										

Males: Mean 26.01; S.D. 5.08.

5 Mf-f – Masculinity-Femininity (Feminine) (56 items)

True

4	25	62	64	67	74	80	112	119	121	122	128	137	177
187	191	196	205	219	236	251	256	271					

False

1	19	26	27	63	68	69	76	86	103	104	107	120	132
133	163	166	184	193	194	197	199	201	207	209	231	235	237
239	254	257	268	272									

Females: Mean 35.94; S.D. 4.08.

6 Pa – Paranoia (40 items)

True

16	17	22	23	24	42	99	113	138	144	145	146	162	234
259	271	277	285	305	307	333	334	336	355	361			

False

81	95	98	100	104	110	244	255	266	283	284	286	297	314
315													

Males: Mean 10.10; S.D. 2.87.   Females: Mean 10.23; S.D. 2.97.

7 Pt – Psychasthenia (48 items)

True

11	16	23	31	38	56	65	73	82	89	94	130	147	170
175	196	218	242	273	275	277	285	289	301	302	304	308	309
310	313	316	317	320	325	326	327	328	329	331			

False

3	9	33	109	140	165	174	293	321

Raw scores without K:
Males: Mean 11.24; S.D. 6.61.   Females: Mean 12.69; S.D. 7.19.
Raw scores with K:
Males: Mean 26.54; S.D. 4.82.   Females: Mean 27.72; S.D. 5.07.

8 Sc – Schizophrenia (78 items)

True

16	17	21	22	23	31	32	35	38	42	44	46	48	65
85	92	138	145	147	166	168	170	180	182	190	218	221	229
233	234	242	247	252	256	268	273	274	277	279	281	287	291
292	296	298	299	303	307	311	316	319	320	322	323	325	329
332	333	355											

False

6	9	12	34	90	91	106	165	177	179	192	210	255	276
278	280	290	295	343									

Raw scores without K:
Males: Mean 11.20; S.D. 7.12.   Females: Mean 11.24; S.D. 7.57.
Raw scores with K:
Males: Mean 26.50; S.D. 5.73.   Females: Mean 26.27; S.D. 5.93.

(continued)

TABLE B.1 Basic Scales (continued)

---

9 Ma – Hypomania (46 items)

True

13	15	21	23	50	55	61	85	87	98	113	122	131	145
155	168	169	182	190	200	205	206	211	212	218	220	227	229
238	242	244	248	250	253	269							

False

88	93	100	106	107	136	154	158	167	243	263

Raw scores without K:
Males: Mean 16.88; S.D. 4.51.   Females: Mean 16.07; S.D. 4.49.
Raw scores with K:
Males: Mean 19.95; S.D. 4.28.   Females: Mean 19.09; S.D. 4.26.

---

0 Si – Social Introversion (69 items)

True

31	56	70	100	104	110	127	135	158	161	167	185	215	243
251	265	275	284	289	296	302	308	326	328	337	338	347	348
351	352	357	358	364	367	368	369						

False

25	32	49	79	86	106	112	131	181	189	207	209	231	237
255	262	267	280	321	335	340	342	344	345	350	353	354	359
360	362	363	366	370									

Males: Mean 24.74; S.D. 8.84.   Females: Mean 26.90; S.D. 9.46.

TABLE B.2 Harris-Lingoes Subscales

D_1 – Subjective Depression (32 items)

True

31	38	39	46	56	73	92	127	130	146	147	170	175	215
233													

False

2	9	43	49	75	95	109	118	140	148	178	188	189	223
260	267	330											

Males: Mean 6.86; S.D. 3.79.   Females: Mean 7.65; S.D. 4.21.

D_2 – Psychomotor Retardation (14 items)

True

38	46	170	233

False

9	29	37	49	55	76	134	188	189	212

Males: Mean 5.34; S.D. 1.82.   Females: Mean 5.74; S.D. 1.83.

D_3 – Physical Malfunctioning (11 items)

True
18   117   175   181

False
2   20   45   141   142   143   148
Males: Mean 2.89; S.D. 1.23.   Females: Mean 3.22; S.D. 1.36.

D_4 – Mental Dullness (15 items)

True
15   31   38   73   92   147   170   233

False
9   10   43   75   109   165   188
Males: Mean 2.42; S.D. 2.09.   Females: Mean 2.55; S.D. 2.21.

D_5 – Brooding (10 items)

True
38   56   92   127   130   146   170   215

False
75   95
Males: Mean 1.83; S.D. 1.77.   Females: Mean 2.50; S.D. 1.95.

Hy_1 – Denial of Social Anxiety (6 items)

True
none

False
129   161   167   185   243   265
Males: Mean 3.89; S.D. 1.86.   Females: Mean 3.85; S.D. 1.87.

Hy_2 – Need for Affection (12 items)

True
230

False
26   58   76   81   98   110   124   151   213   241   263
Males: Mean 6.69; S.D. 2.58.   Females: Mean 6.88; S.D. 2.44.

(continued)

TABLE B.2 Harris-Lingoes Subscales (continued)

Hy₃ – Lassitude-Malaise (15 items)

True

31	39	65	175	218

False

2	3	9	10	45	95	125	141	148	152

Males: Mean 2.55; S.D. 2.20.   Females: Mean 2.73; S.D. 2.48.

Hy₄ – Somatic Symptoms (Somatic Complaints) (17 items)

True

11	18	40	44	101	172

False

8	47	91	159	164	173	176	179	208	224	249

Males: Mean 2.50; S.D. 2.06.   Females: Mean 3.22; S.D. 2.53.

Hy₅ – Inhibition of Aggression (7 items)

True

False

7	14	29	115	116	135	157

Males: Mean 3.29; S.D. 1.32.   Females: Mean 3.46; S.D. 1.29.

Pd₁ – Familial Discord (9 items)

True

21	54	195	202	288

False

83	125	214	217

Males: Mean 1.79; S.D. 1.52.   Females: Mean 2.05; S.D. 1.65.

Pd₂ – Authority Problems (8 items)

True

35	105

False

34	70	129	160	263	266

Males: Mean 3.48; S.D. 1.50.   Females: Mean 2.55; S.D. 1.29.

Pd_3 – Social Imperturbability (6 items)

True
none

False
| 70 | 129 | 158 | 167 | 185 | 243 | , |

Males: Mean 3.83; S.D. 1.69.　　Females: Mean 3.58; S.D. 1.71.

Pd_4 – Social Alienation (13 items)

True
| 17 | 22 | 42 | 56 | 82 | 99 | 113 | 219 | 225 | 259 |

False
| 12 | 129 | 157 |

Males: Mean 3.93; S.D. 1.90.　　Females: Mean 4.18; S.D. 1.89.

Pd_5 – Self-Alienation (12 items)

True
| 31 | 32 | 52 | 56 | 71 | 82 | 89 | 94 | 113 | 264 |

False
| 9 | 95 |

Males: Mean 3.39; S.D. 2.08.　　Females: Mean 3.35; S.D. 2.07.

Pa_1 – Ideas of External Influence (Persecutory Ideas) (17 items)

True
| 17 | 22 | 42 | 99 | 113 | 138 | 144 | 145 | 162 | 234 | 259 | 305 | 333 | 336 |
| 355 | 361 |

False
314

Males: Mean 1.74; S.D. 1.66.　　Females: Mean 1.79; S.D. 1.67.

Pa_2 – Poignancy (9 items)

True
| 22 | 146 | 271 | 277 | 285 | 307 | 334 |

False
| 100 | 244 |

Males: Mean 2.36; S.D. 1.43.　　Females: Mean 2.57; S.D. 1.58.

(continued)

TABLE B.2   Harris-Lingoes Subscales (continued)

Pa₃ – Naïveté (9 items)

True
16

False
| 81 | 98 | 104 | 110 | 283 | 284 | 286 | 315 |

Males: Mean 4.84; S.D. 2.09.   Females: Mean 4.95; S.D. 2.09.

Sc₁ – Social Alienation (21 items)

True
| 17 | 21 | 22 | 42 | 46 | 138 | 145 | 190 | 221 | 256 | 277 | 281 | 291 | 292 |
| 320 | 333 |

False
| 90 | 276 | 278 | 280 | 343 |

Males: Mean 2.72; S.D. 2.42.   Females: Mean 3.11; S.D. 2.59.

Sc₂ – Emotional Alienation (11 items)

True
| 65 | 92 | 234 | 273 | 303 | 323 | 329 | 332 |

False
| 9 | 210 | 290 |

Males: Mean 1.05; S.D. 1.04.   Females: Mean 1.12; S.D. 1.09.

Sc₃ – Lack of Ego Mastery, Cognitive (10 items)

True
| 31 | 32 | 147 | 170 | 180 | 299 | 311 | 316 | 325 |

False
165

Males: Mean 1.31; S.D. 1.66.   Females: Mean 1.18; S.D. 1.62.

Sc₄ – Lack of Ego Mastery, Conative (14 items)

True
| 31 | 38 | 48 | 65 | 92 | 233 | 234 | 273 | 299 | 303 | 325 |

False
| 9 | 210 | 290 |

Males: Mean 2.13; S.D. 1.85.   Females: Mean 2.17; S.D. 1.95.

Sc$_5$ – Lack of Ego Mastery, Defective Inhibition (11 items)

True

23   85   168   182   218   242   274   320   322   329   355

False

Males: Mean 1.42; S.D. 1.43.   Females: Mean 1.57; S.D. 1.57.

Sc$_6$ – Sensorimotor Dissociation (Bizarre Sensory Experiences) (20 items)

True

23   32   44   168   182   229   247   252   296   298   307   311   319   355

False

91   106   177   179   255   295

Males: Mean 1.90; S.D. 2.04.   Females: Mean 2.07; S.D. 2.20.

Ma$_1$ – Amorality (6 items)

True

131   227   248   250   269

False

263

Males: Mean 1.97; S.D. 1.29.   Females: Mean 1.56; S.D. 1.20.

Ma$_2$ – Psychomotor Acceleration (11 items)

True

15   85   87   122   169   206   218   242   244

False

100   106

Males: Mean 5.29; S.D. 2.07.   Females: Mean 5.07; S.D. 1.99.

Ma$_3$ – Imperturbability (8 items)

True

155   200   220

False

93   136   158   167   243

Males: Mean 3.51; S.D. 1.66.   Females: Mean 3.06; S.D. 1.56.

(continued)

TABLE B.2 Harris-Lingoes Subscales (continued)

Ma_4 – Ego Inflation (9 items)

True

| 13 | 50 | 55 | 61 | 98 | 145 | 190 | 211 | 212 |

False

Males: Mean 3.04; S.D. 1.53.   Females: Mean 3.09; S.D. 1.64.

TABLE B.3 Wiener-Harmon Subtle-Obvious Subscales

D-O – Depression, Obvious (39 items)

True

| 15 | 18 | 31 | 38 | 39 | 46 | 56 | 73 | 92 | 127 | 130 | 146 | 147 | 170 |
| 175 | 215 | 233 |

False

| 2 | 9 | 10 | 20 | 33 | 43 | 45 | 49 | 75 | 95 | 109 | 118 | 140 | 141 |
| 142 | 165 | 188 | 223 | 245 | 248 | 260 | 330 |

Males: Mean 7.72; S.D. 4.29.   Females: Mean 8.75; S.D. 4.88.

D-S – Depression, Subtle (18 items)

True

| 5 | 117 | 181 |

False

| 29 | 37 | 55 | 68 | 76 | 134 | 143 | 148 | 178 | 189 | 212 | 221 | 226 | 238 |
| 267 |

Males: Mean 10.60; S.D. 2.61.   Females: Mean 11.39; S.D. 2.44.

Hy-O – Hysteria, Obvious (32 items)

True

| 11 | 18 | 31 | 39 | 40 | 44 | 65 | 101 | 166 | 172 | 175 | 218 |

False

| 2 | 3 | 8 | 9 | 10 | 45 | 47 | 91 | 95 | 115 | 125 | 141 | 152 | 159 |
| 164 | 173 | 179 | 208 | 224 | 249 |

Males: Mean 4.78; S.D. 3.61.   Females: Mean 5.67; S.D. 4.21.

Hy-S – Hysteria, Subtle (28 items)

True

230

False

| 7 | 14 | 26 | 29 | 58 | 76 | 81 | 98 | 110 | 116 | 124 | 129 | 135 | 148 |
| 151 | 157 | 161 | 167 | 176 | 185 | 193 | 213 | 241 | 243 | 253 | 263 | 265 |

Males: Mean 16.09; S.D. 4.31.   Females: Mean 16.41; S.D. 4.09.

Pd-O – Psychopathic Deviate, Obvious (28 items)

True

17	22	31	32	35	42	52	54	56	71	82	94	99	105
195	202	225	259	264	288								

False

9	12	34	79	95	125	261	266

Males: Mean 6.16; S.D. 3.74.   Females: Mean 5.40; S.D. 3.72.

Pd-S – Psychopathic Deviate, Subtle (22 items)

True

21	89	113	219

False

70	83	122	129	143	157	158	160	167	171	185	209	214	217
226	243	263	267										

Males: Mean 10.41; S.D. 2.58.   Females: Mean 10.80; S.D. 2.48.

Pa-O – Paranoia, Obvious (23 items)

True

17	22	23	24	42	99	138	144	146	162	234	259	277	285
305	307	333	336	355	361								

False

255	266	314

Males: Mean 2.55; S.D. 2.19.   Females: Mean 2.76; S.D. 2.33.

Pa-S – Paranoia, Subtle (17 items)

True

16	113	145	271	334

False

81	95	98	100	104	110	244	283	284	286	297	315

Males: Mean 7.55; S.D. 2.36.   Females: Mean 7.47; S.D. 2.34.

Ma-O – Hypomania, Obvious (23 items)

True

15	23	50	61	85	87	145	155	168	182	190	205	218	227
229	238	242	250	253	269								

False

100	106	107

Males: Mean 6.84; S.D. 2.95.   Females: Mean 6.38; S.D. 2.97.

(continued)

TABLE B.3 Wiener-Harmon Subtle-Obvious Subscales (continued)

Ma-S – Hypomania, Subtle (23 items)

True

13	21	55	98	113	122	131	169	200	206	211	212	220	244
248													

False

88	93	136	154	158	167	243	263

Males: Mean 10.04; S.D. 2.68.   Females: Mean 9.69; S.D. 2.60.

TABLE B.4 Si Subscales

Si_1 – Shyness/Self-Consciousness (14 items)

True

158	161	167	185	243	265	275	289

False

49	262	280	321	342	360

Males: Mean 4.80; S.D. 3.44.   Females: Mean 5.31; S.D. 3.69.

Si_2 – Social Avoidance (8 items)

True

337	367

False

86	340	353	359	363	370

Males: Mean 3.12; S.D. 2.33.   Females: Mean 2.75; S.D. 2.19.

Si_3 – Alienation—Self and Others (17 items)

True

31	56	104	110	135	284	302	308	326	328	338	347	348	358
364	368	369											

False

Males: Mean 4.99; S.D. 3.35.   Females: Mean 5.23; S.D. 3.59.

TABLE B.5 Supplementary Scales

A – Anxiety (39 items)

True

31	38	56	65	82	127	135	215	233	243	251	273	277	289
301	309	310	311	325	328	338	339	341	347	390	391	394	400
408	411	415	421	428	442	448	451	464	469				

False

388

Males: Mean 10.02; S.D. 7.10.   Females: Mean 11.64; S.D. 7.90.

R – Repression (37 items)

True

False

1	7	10	14	37	45	69	112	118	120	128	134	142	168
178	189	197	199	248	255	256	297	330	346	350	353	354	359
363	365	422	423	430	432	449	456	465

Males: Mean 15.18; S.D. 4.53.   Females: Mean 16.34; S.D. 3.81.

Es – Ego Strength (52 items)

True

| 2 | 33 | 45 | 98 | 141 | 159 | 169 | 177 | 179 | 189 | 199 | 209 | 213 | 230 |
| 245 | 323 | 385 | 406 | 413 | 425 |

False

23	31	32	36	39	53	60	70	82	87	119	128	175	196
215	221	225	229	236	246	307	310	316	328	391	394	441	447
458	464	469	471

Males: Mean 37.34; S.D. 4.46.   Females: Mean 34.37; S.D. 4.90.

MAC-R – MacAndrew Alcoholism-Revised (49 items)

True

7	24	36	49	52	69	72	82	84	103	105	113	115	128
168	172	202	214	224	229	238	257	280	342	344	387	407	412
414	422	434	439	445	456	473	502	506	549

False

| 73 | 107 | 117 | 137 | 160 | 166 | 251 | 266 | 287 | 299 | 325 |

Males: Mean 20.81; S.D. 4.37.   Females: Mean 18.85; S.D. 3.69.

F_B – Back F (40 items)

True

281	291	303	311	317	319	322	323	329	332	333	334	387	395
407	431	450	454	463	468	476	478	484	489	506	516	517	520
524	525	526	528	530	539	540	544	555

False

| 383 | 404 | 501 |

Males: Mean 1.86; S.D. 2.44.   Females: Mean 1.94; S.D. 2.58.

(continued)

TABLE B.5 Supplementary Scales (continued)

VRIN – Variable Response Inconsistency (67 item-response pairs)
   For each of the following response pairs add one point.

3 T – 39 T	125 T – 195 T	349 T – 515 F
6 T – 90 F	125 F – 195 F	349 F – 515 T
6 F – 90 T	135 F – 482 T	350 F – 521 T
9 F – 56 F	136 T – 507 F	353 T – 370 F
28 T – 59 F	136 F – 507 T	353 F – 370 T
31 T – 299 F	152 F – 464 F	364 F – 554 T
32 F – 316 T	161 T – 185 F	369 F – 421 T
40 T – 176 T	161 F – 185 T	372 T – 405 F
46 T – 265 F	165 F – 565 F	372 F – 405 T
48 T – 184 T	166 T – 268 F	380 T – 562 F
49 T – 280 F	166 F – 268 T	395 T – 435 F
73 T – 377 F	167 T – 243 F	395 F – 435 T
81 T – 284 F	167 F – 243 T	396 T – 403 F
81 F – 284 T	196 F – 415 T	396 F – 403 T
83 T – 288 T	199 T – 467 F	411 T – 485 F
84 T – 105 F	199 F – 467 T	411 F – 485 T
86 T – 359 F	226 T – 267 F	472 T – 533 F
95 F – 388 T	259 F – 333 T	472 F – 533 T
99 F – 138 T	262 F – 275 F	491 T – 509 F
103 T – 344 F	290 T – 556 F	506 T – 520 F
110 T – 374 F	290 F – 556 T	506 F – 520 T
110 F – 374 T	339 F – 394 T	513 T – 542 F
116 T – 430 F		

Males: Mean 5.07; S.D. 2.62.   Females: Mean 5.04; S.D. 2.51.

TRIN – True Response Inconsistency (23 item-response pairs)

1) For each of the following response pairs *add* one point:

3 T – 39 T	65 T – 95 T	209 T – 351 T
12 T – 166 T	73 T – 239 T	359 T – 367 T
40 T – 176 T	83 T – 288 T	377 T – 534 T
48 T – 184 T	99 T – 314 T	556 T – 560 T
63 T – 127 T	125 T – 195 T	

2) For each of the following response pairs *subtract* one point:

9 F – 56 F	140 F – 196 F	262 F – 275 F
65 F – 95 F	152 F – 464 F	265 F – 360 F
125 F – 195 F	165 F – 565 F	359 F – 367 F

3) Then add 9 points to the total raw score.

Males: Mean 8.95; S.D. 1.41.   Females: Mean 9.00; S.D. 1.32.

O-H – Overcontrolled Hostility (28 items)

True

67	79	207	286	305	398	471

False

1	15	29	69	77	89	98	116	117	129	153	169	171	293	344
390	400	420	433	440	460									

Males: Mean 12.51; S.D. 2.94.   Females: Mean 13.53; S.D. 2.74.

Do – Dominance (25 items)

True

| 55 | 207 | 232 | 245 | 386 | 416 |

False

| 31 | 52 | 70 | 73 | 82 | 172 | 201 | 202 | 220 | 227 | 243 | 244 | 275 | 309 | 325 |
| 399 | 412 | 470 | 473 |

Males: Mean 16.62; S.D. 2.95.   Females: Mean 16.27; S.D. 2.89.

Re – Social Responsibility (30 items)

True

| 100 | 160 | 199 | 266 | 440 | 467 |

False

| 7 | 27 | 29 | 32 | 84 | 103 | 105 | 145 | 164 | 169 | 201 | 202 | 235 | 275 | 358 |
| 412 | 417 | 418 | 430 | 431 | 432 | 456 | 468 | 470 |

Males: Mean 20.09; S.D. 3.89.   Females: Mean 21.02; S.D. 3.36.

Mt – College Maladjustment (41 items)

True

| 15 | 16 | 28 | 31 | 38 | 71 | 73 | 81 | 82 | 110 | 130 | 215 | 218 | 233 | 269 |
| 273 | 299 | 302 | 325 | 331 | 339 | 357 | 408 | 411 | 449 | 464 | 469 | 472 |

False

| 2 | 3 | 9 | 10 | 20 | 43 | 95 | 131 | 140 | 148 | 152 | 223 | 405 |

Males: Mean 11.30; S.D. 6.44.   Females: Mean 12.31; S.D. 6.99.

GM – Gender Role-Masculine (47 items)

True

| 8 | 20 | 143 | 152 | 159 | 163 | 176 | 199 | 214 | 237 | 321 | 350 | 385 | 388 | 401 |
| 440 | 462 | 467 | 474 |

False

| 4 | 23 | 44 | 64 | 70 | 73 | 74 | 80 | 100 | 137 | 146 | 187 | 289 | 331 | 351 |
| 364 | 392 | 395 | 435 | 438 | 441 | 469 | 471 | 498 | 509 | 519 | 532 | 536 |

Males: Mean 37.87; S.D. 4.87.   Females: Mean 28.83; S.D. 6.51.

GF – Gender Role-Feminine (46 items)

True

| 62 | 67 | 119 | 121 | 128 | 203 | 263 | 266 | 353 | 384 | 426 | 449 | 456 | 473 | 552 |

False

| 1 | 27 | 63 | 68 | 79 | 84 | 105 | 123 | 133 | 155 | 197 | 201 | 220 | 231 | 238 |
| 239 | 250 | 257 | 264 | 272 | 287 | 406 | 417 | 465 | 477 | 487 | 510 | 511 | 537 | 548 |
| 550 |

Males: Mean 27.93; S.D. 4.72.   Females: Mean 37.68; S.D. 3.88.

(continued)

TABLE B.5 Supplementary Scales (continued)

PK – Post Traumatic Stress Disorder-Keane (46 items)

True

16	17	22	23	30	31	32	37	39	48	52	56	59	65	82
85	92	94	101	135	150	168	170	196	221	274	277	302	303	305
316	319	327	328	339	347	349	367							

False

2	3	9	49	75	95	125	140

Males: Mean 8.01; S.D. 5.99.   Females: Mean 8.52; S.D. 6.57.

PS – Post Traumatic Stress Disorder-Schlenger (60 items)

True

17	21	22	31	32	37	38	44	48	56	59	65	85	94	116
135	145	150	168	170	180	218	221	273	274	277	299	301	304	305
311	316	319	325	328	377	386	400	463	464	469	471	475	479	515
516	565													

False

3	9	45	75	95	141	165	208	223	280	372	405	564

Males: Mean 10.49; S.D. 7.98.   Females: Mean 11.82; S.D. 8.96.

MDS – Marital Distress Scale (14 items)

True

21	22	135	195	219	382	484	563

False

12	83	95	125	493	494

Males: Mean 2.79; S.D. 2.17.   Females: Mean 2.90; S.D. 2.33.

APS — Addiction Potential Scale (39 items)

True

7	29	41	89	103	113	120	168	183	189	196	217	242	260	267
341	342	344	377	422	502	523	540							

False

4	43	76	104	137	157	220	239	306	312	349	440	495	496	500
504														

Males: Mean 23.37; S.D. 3.69.   Females: Mean 23.13; S.D. 3.71.

AAS – Addiction Admission Scale (13 items)

True

172	264	288	362	387	487	489	511	527	544

False

266	429	501

Males: Mean 2.86; S.D. 2.05.   Females: Mean 1.98; S.D. 1.76.

TABLE B.6   Content Scales

ANX – Anxiety (23 items)

True

| 15 | 30 | 31 | 39 | 170 | 196 | 273 | 290 | 299 | 301 | 305 | 339 | 408 | 415 | 463 |
| 469 | 509 | 556 |

False

140   208   223   405   496

Males: Mean 5.53; S.D. 4.17.   Females: Mean 6.53; S.D. 4.51.

FRS – Fears (23 items)

True

| 154 | 317 | 322 | 329 | 334 | 392 | 395 | 397 | 435 | 438 | 441 | 447 | 458 | 468 | 471 |
| 555 |

False

115   163   186   385   401   453   462

Males: Mean 3.80; S.D. 2.96.   Females: Mean 6.59; S.D. 3.60.

OBS – Obsessiveness (16 items)

True

| 55 | 87 | 135 | 196 | 309 | 313 | 327 | 328 | 394 | 442 | 482 | 491 | 497 | 509 | 547 |
| 553 |

False

Males: Mean 4.93; S.D. 3.06.   Females: Mean 5.50; S.D. 3.32.

DEP – Depression (33 items)

True

| 38 | 52 | 56 | 65 | 71 | 82 | 92 | 130 | 146 | 215 | 234 | 246 | 277 | 303 | 306 |
| 331 | 377 | 399 | 400 | 411 | 454 | 506 | 512 | 516 | 520 | 539 | 546 | 554 |

False

3   9   75   95   388

Males: Mean 4.79; S.D. 4.62.   Females: Mean 5.86; S.D. 5.02.

HEA – Health Concerns (36 items)

True

| 11 | 18 | 28 | 36 | 40 | 44 | 53 | 59 | 97 | 101 | 111 | 149 | 175 | 247 |

False

| 20 | 33 | 45 | 47 | 57 | 91 | 117 | 118 | 141 | 142 | 159 | 164 | 176 | 179 | 181 |
| 194 | 204 | 224 | 249 | 255 | 295 | 404 |

Males: Mean 5.29; S.D. 3.91.   Females: Mean 6.16; S.D. 4.47.

(continued)

TABLE B.6 Content Scales (continued)

BIZ – Bizarre Mentation (23 items)

True

24	32	60	96	138	162	198	228	259	298	311	316	319	333	336
355	361	466	490	508	543	551								

False

427

Males: Mean 2.30; S.D. 2.50.   Females: Mean 2.21; S.D. 2.49.

ANG – Anger (16 items)

True

29	37	116	134	302	389	410	414	430	461	486	513	540	542	548

False

564

Males: Mean 5.63; S.D. 3.31.   Females: Mean 5.68; S.D. 3.08.

CYN – Cynicism (23 items)

True

50	58	76	81	104	110	124	225	241	254	283	284	286	315	346
352	358	374	399	403	445	470	538							

False

Males: Mean 9.50; S.D. 5.35.   Females: Mean 8.73; S.D. 5.16.

ASP – Antisocial Practices (22 items)

True

26	35	66	81	84	104	105	110	123	227	240	248	250	254	269
283	284	374	412	418	419									

False

266

Males: Mean 7.91; S.D. 4.19.   Females: Mean 6.17; S.D. 3.70.

TPA – Type A (19 items)

True

27	136	151	212	302	358	414	419	420	423	430	437	507	510	523
531	535	541	545											

False

Males: Mean 8.08; S.D. 3.68.   Females: Mean 7.41; S.D. 3.34.

LSE – Low Self-Esteem (24 items)

True

70	73	130	235	326	369	376	380	411	421	450	457	475	476	483
485	503	504	519	526	562									

False

61   78   109

Males: Mean 4.25; S.D. 3.69.   Females: Mean 5.16; S.D. 4.24.

SOD – Social Discomfort (24 items)

True

46   158   167   185   265   275   281   337   349   367   479   480   515

False

49   86   262   280   321   340   353   359   360   363   370

Males: Mean 7.65; S.D. 4.77.   Females: Mean 7.53; S.D. 4.80.

FAM – Family Problems (25 items)

True

21	54	145	190	195	205	256	292	300	323	378	379	382	413	449
478	543	550	563	567										

False

83   125   217   383   455

Males: Mean 5.32; S.D. 3.52.   Females: Mean 6.14; S.D. 3.77.

WRK – Work Interference (33 items)

True

15	17	31	54	73	98	135	233	243	299	302	339	364	368	394
409	428	445	464	491	505	509	517	525	545	554	559	566		

False

10   108   318   521   561

Males: Mean 7.30; S.D. 4.98.   Females: Mean 8.51; S.D. 5.45.

TRT – Negative Treatment Indicators (26 items)

True

22	92	274	306	364	368	373	375	376	377	391	399	482	488	491
495	497	499	500	504	528	539	554							

False

493   494   501

Males: Mean 4.70; S.D. 3.71.   Females: Mean 5.02; S.D. 3.98.

TABLE B.7   Content Component Scales

FRS1 - Generalized Fearfulness (12 items)										

True

| 317 | 322 | 329 | 334 | 395 | 435 | 441 | 447 | 468 | 471 | 555 |

False

186

Men: Mean .65; SD 1.11 Women: Mean 1.21; SD 1.52

FRS2 - Multiple Fears (10 items)						

True

| 154 | 392 | 438 | 458 |

False

| 115 | 163 | 385 | 401 | 453 | 462 |

Men: Mean 3.59; SD 2.04 Women: Mean 5.54; SD 2.27

DEP1 - Lack of Drive (12 items)								

True

| 38 | 71 | 92 | 399 | 400 | 512 | 516 | 539 | 554 |

False

| 3 | 9 | 75 |

Men: Mean 1.72; SD 1.82 Women: Mean 1.98; SD 1.99

DEP2 - Dysphoria (6 items)			

True

| 56 | 65 | 146 | 215 |

False

| 95 | 388 |

Men: Mean .87; SD 1.17 Women: Mean 1.07; SD 1.33

DEP3- Self-Depreciation (7 items)

True

52   82   130   234   246   377   411

False

Men: Mean 1.21; SD 1.41 Women: Mean 1.30; SD 1.43

DEP4 - Suicidal Ideation (5 items)

True

303   454   506   520   546

False

Men: Mean .25; SD .60 Women: Mean .27; SD .63

HEA1 - Gastrointestinal Symptoms (5 items)

True

18   59   111

False

20   47

Men: Mean .45; SD .77 Women: Mean .62; SD .93

HEA2 - Neurological Symptoms (12 items)

True

44   53   101   149   247

False

91   142   159   164   179   255   295

Men: Mean 1.40; SD 1.50 Women: Mean 1.86; SD 1.83

HEA3 - General Health Concerns (6 items)

True

175

False

33   45   118   141   224

Men: Mean 1.15; SD 1.24 Women: Mean 1.18; SD 1.29

(continued)

TABLE B.7   Content Component Scales (continued)

BIZ1 - Psychotic Symptomatology (11 items)

True

24	60	96	138	162	228	336	355	361	508	551

False

Men: Mean .50; SD .85 Women: Mean .42; SD .73

BIZ2 - Schizotypal Characteristics (9 items)

True

32	259	298	311	316	319	333	466	543

False

Men: Mean 1.36; SD 1.54 Women: Mean 1.33; SD 1.60

ANG1 - Explosive Behavior (7 items)

True

37	134	389	414	540	548

False

564

Men: Mean 1.68; SD 1.57 Women: Mean 1.40; SD 1.34

ANG2 - Irritability (7 items)

True

116	302	430	461	486	513	542

False

Men: Mean 2.71; SD 1.91 Women: Mean 3.09; SD 1.92

CYN1 - Misanthropic Beliefs (15 items)

True

58	76	81	104	110	241	254	283	284	286	352	374
470	538										

False

Men: Mean 6.16; SD 3.68 Women: Mean 5.71; SD 3.57

CYN2 - Interpersonal Suspiciousness (8 items)

True

| 50 | 124 | 225 | 315 | 346 | 358 | 403 | 445 |

False

Men: Mean 3.34; SD 2.17 Women: Mean 3.02; SD 2.10

ASP1 - Antisocial Attitudes (16 items)

True

| 26 | 66 | 81 | 104 | 110 | 123 | 227 | 248 | 250 | 254 | 269 | 283 |
| 284 | 374 | 418 | 419 |

False

Men: Mean 6.22; SD 3.49 Women: Mean 5.33; SD 3.27

ASP2 - Antisocial Behavior (5 items)

True

| 35 | 84 | 105 | 412 |

False

266

Men: Mean 1.63; SD 1.39 Women: Mean .80; SD 1.03

TPA1 - Impatience (6 items)

True

| 302 | 420 | 430 | 507 | 523 | 535 |

False

Men: Mean 2.74; SD 1.73 Women: Mean 2.62; SD 1.64

TPA2 - Competitive Drive (9 items)

True

| 27 | 151 | 212 | 358 | 419 | 423 | 510 | 531 | 545 |

False

Men: Mean 3.81; SD 1.95 Women: Mean 3.41; SD 1.74

(continued)

TABLE B.7   Content Component Scales (continued)

LSE1 - Self-Doubt (11 items)

True

73	130	326	411	450	483	485	504

False

61	78	109

Men: Mean 2.06; SD 1.97 Women: Mean 2.33; SD 2.19

LSE2 - Submissiveness (6 items)

True

70	369	421	457	503	519

False

Men: Mean 1.25; SD 1.41 Women: Mean 1.78; SD 1.68

SOD1 - Introversion (16 items)

True

46	265	281	337	349	367	480	515

False

49	86	280	340	353	359	363	370

Men: Mean 4.7; SD 3.46 Women: Mean 4.23; SD 3.27

SOD2 - Shyness (7 items)

True

158	167	185	275

False

262	321	360

Men: Mean 2.51; SD 1.84 Women: Mean 2.93; SD 2.04

FAM1 - Family Discord (12 items)

True

21	54	190	205	256	323	378	382	449	478	563

False

83

Men: Mean 2.86; SD 2.01 Women: Mean 3.47; SD 2.07

FAM2 - Familial Alienation (5 items)

True

195 550

False

217 383 455

Men: Mean 1.06; SD 1.13 Women: Mean .97; SD 1.10

TRT1 - Low Motivation (11 items)

True

92 364 368 376 491 497 500 528 539 554

False

494

Men: Mean 1.26; SD 1.70 Women: Mean 1.72; SD 1.98

TRT2 - Inability to Disclose (5 items)

True

274 373 375 391 495

False

Men: Mean 1.62; SD 1.31 Women Mean 1.52; SD 1.35

TABLE B.8 Additional Validity Scales

DS – Dissimulation (58 items)

True

11	17	18	19	22	28	30	31	40	42	44
54	61	72	81	85	92	111	166	190	195	205
221	252	258	268	274	287	292	294	300	307	310
320	329	362	395	412	419	421	425	431	433	435
436	451	458	463							

False

57	75	83	108	125	188	278	318	404	429

Males: Mean 10.08; S.D. 5.32. Females: Mean 10.57; S.D. 5.64.

DS-r – Dissimulation—Revised (32 items)

True

11	18	22	28	30	31	40	44	81	85	92
111	205	221	274	292	300	320	329	362	395	419
433	451	458	463							

False

57	75	83	108	278	318

Men: Mean 5.89; S.D. 3.50. Women: Mean 6.63; S.D. 3.86.

FBS – Fake Bad (43 items)

True

11	18	28	30	31	39	40	44	59	111	252
274	325	339	464	469	505	506				

False

12	41	57	58	81	110	117	152	164	176	224
227	248	249	250	255	264	284	362	373	374	419
433	496	561								

Men: Mean 11.67; S.D. 3.81. Women: Mean 13.76; S.D. 4.14.

F(p) – Infrequency Psychopathology (27 items)

True

66	114	162	193	216	228	252	270	282	291	294
322	323	336	371	387	478	555				

False

51	77	90	93	102	126	192	276	501

Men: Mean 1.16; S.D. 1.38. Women: Mean 1.03; S.D. 1.26.

IR – Inconsistent Response (16 items)

True

114	182	228	234	322	332	336	355	407	478	511
527	530									

False

51	77	93

Men: Mean 0.95; S.D. 1.10. Women: Mean 0.63; S.D. 0.93.

ODecp – Other Deception (33 items)

True

49	100	133	184	194	201	206	207	211	220	239
257	261	345	350	356	416	439				

False

21	29	41	77	89	93	183	196	203	232	290
326	341	428	442							

Men: Mean 12.99; S.D. 4.34.   Women: Mean 11.15; S.D. 3.93.

S – Superlative (50 items)

True

121	148	184	194	534	560

False

15	50	58	76	81	87	89	104	110	120	123
154	196	205	213	225	264	279	284	290	302	337
341	346	352	373	374	403	420	423	428	430	433
442	445	449	461	486	487	523	538	542	545	547

Men: Mean 25.02; S.D. 8.69.   Women: Mean 25.48; S.D. 8.29.

Sd – Wiggins Social Desirability (33 items)

True

25	49	80	100	131	133	184	194	201	206	207
211	220	249	257	263	345	351	354	356	366	402
416	439									

False

29	41	77	93	183	203	232	326	341

Men: Mean 12.72; S.D. 3.68.   Women: Mean 12.14; S.D. 3.27.

So – Edwards Social Desirability (37 items)

True

8	20	78	95	152	186	318	335

False

31	39	48	54	127	136	146	158	168	172	221
238	243	270	273	288	289	299	300	301	306	320
324	338	349	368	415	420	469				

Men: Mean 30.16; S.D. 4.56.   Women: Mean 28.70; S.D. 5.16.

Note. Means and standard deviations are based on the MMPI-2 normative group (Butcher et al., 1989).

TABLE B.9 Personality Psychopathology Five (PSY-5) Scales (continued)

AGG – Aggressiveness (18 items)

True

27	50	85	134	239	323	324	346	350	358	414
423	452	521	548							

False

70	446	503

Men: Mean 8.20; S.D. 2.97.   Women: Mean 6.80; S.D. 2.81.

PSY – Psychoticism (25 items)

True

24	42	48	72	96	99	138	144	198	241	259
315	319	336	355	361	374	448	466	490	508	549
551										

False

184	247

Men: Mean 3.58; S.D. 2.74.   Women: Mean 3.42; S.D. 2.76.

CON – Constraint (29 items)

True

34	100	121	126	154	263	266	309	351	402	497

False

35	84	88	103	105	123	209	222	250	284	344
362	385	412	417	418	431	477				

Men: Mean 15.01; S.D. 3.90.   Women: Mean 18.68; S.D. 3.67.

NEN – Neuroticism/Negative Emotional Experience (33 items)

True

37	52	82	93	116	166	196	213	290	301	305
329	375	389	390	395	397	407	409	415	435	442
444	451	513	542	556						

False

63	223	372	405	496	564

Men: Mean 9.44; S.D. 5.45.   Women: Mean 11.26; S.D. 5.72.

PEE – Positive Emotional Experience (34 items)

True

9	49	61	75	78	86	95	109	131	174	188
189	207	226	231	244	267	318	330	340	342	343
353	356	359	370	460	531	534				

False

38	56	233	515	517

Men: Mean 22.98; S.D. 4.44.   Women: Mean 23.26; S.D. 4.21.

Note. Means and standard deviations are based on the MMPI-2 normative group (Butcher et al., 1989).

TABLE B.10 Morey, Waugh, and Blashfield Personality Disorder Scales

---

Nonoverlapping

HST – Histronic (13 items)

True

86	112	169	262	342	363	389	422

False

100	167	220	275	281

Men: Mean 7.97; S.D. 2.21.   Women: Mean 7.84; S.D. 2.26.

NAR – Narcissistic (14 items)

True

61	153	227	248	254	286	321	345	350	358	452

False

130	158	243

Men: Mean 7.02; S.D. 2.24.   Women: Mean 6.36; S.D. 2.32.

BDL – Borderline (17 items)

True

37	62	102	116	134	146	150	189	213	215	264
271	430	469								

False

34	372	388

Men: Mean 5.32; S.D. 2.75.   Women: Mean 6.55; S.D. 2.97.

ANT – Antisocial (18 items)

True

21	35	41	66	81	84	105	123	156	240	284
412	418	428	431	433						

False

266	429

Men: Mean 6.17; S.D. 3.23.   Women: Mean 4.88; S.D. 2.85.

DEP – Dependent (16 items)

True

70	129	326	347	368	369	398	411	421	450	457

False

109	157	239	318	440

Men: Mean 4.09; S.D. 2.59.   Women: Mean 5.04; S.D. 2.98.

(continued)

TABLE B.10 Morey, Waugh, and Blashfield Personality Disorder Scales (continued)

CPS – Obsessive-Compulsive (11 items)

True

| 77 | 87 | 120 | 136 | 196 | 290 | 309 | 313 | 356 | 402 | 442 |

False
none

Men: Mean 5.42; S.D. 2.17. Women: Mean 5.69; S.D. 2.10.

PAG – Passive-Aggressive (14 items)

True

| 31 | 38 | 55 | 98 | 135 | 212 | 214 | 233 | 308 | 325 | 419 |
| 423 | 461 | 472 | | | | | | | | |

False
none

Men: Mean 5.13; S.D. 2.72. Women: Mean 4.74; S.D. 2.67.

PAR – Paranoid (15 items)

True

| 19 | 99 | 110 | 124 | 144 | 145 | 151 | 216 | 225 | 228 | 251 |
| 270 | 300 | 424 | | | | | | | | |

False
314

Men: Mean 2.85; S.D. 2.04. Women: Mean 2.62; S.D. 2.06.

STY – Schizotypal (15 items)

True

| 24 | 32 | 42 | 72 | 138 | 162 | 241 | 259 | 265 | 285 | 311 |
| 315 | 316 | 337 | 466 | | | | | | | |

False
none

Men: Mean 2.97; S.D. 2.08. Women: Mean 2.81; S.D. 2.00.

AVD – Avoidant (14 items)

True

| 73 | 127 | 185 | 277 | 289 | 310 | 386 | 446 |

False

| 63 | 79 | 335 | 340 | 359 | 360 |

Men: Mean 4.74; S.D. 2.73. Women: Mean 5.62; S.D. 2.97.

SZD – Schizoid (11 items)

True

| 46 | 291 | 337 | 349 | 367 | 405 |

False

| 49 | 78 | 280 | 353 | 370 |

Men: Mean 3.04; S.D. 2.07. Women: Mean 2.69; S.D. 1.97.

Overlapping

HST – Histrionic (20 items)

True

86	112	169	262	321	340	342	353	359	363	370
389	422									

False

100	158	167	220	275	281	349

Men: Mean 12.51; S.D. 3.48.　　Women: Mean 12.52; S.D. 3.46.

NAR – Narcissistic (31 items)

True

19	61	109	110	112	153	227	239	248	254	262
270	286	318	321	345	350	358	359	370	398	452

False

73	79	130	158	167	243	275	289	450

Men: Mean 17.68; S.D. 3.96.　　Women: Mean 16.54; S.D. 4.09.

BDL – Borderline (22 items)

True

37	62	86	102	116	134	146	150	169	189	213
215	264	271	359	363	389	430	469			

False

34	372	388

Men: Mean 7.69; S.D. 3.41.　　Women: Mean 8.88; S.D. 3.47.

ANT – Antisocial (23 items)

True

21	35	41	66	81	84	105	110	123	134	156
214	240	264	284	412	418	428	431	433		

False

34	266	429

Men: Mean 8.27; S.D. 3.86.　　Women: Mean 6.52; S.D. 3.41.

DEP – Dependent (20 items)

True

70	73	129	326	347	368	369	398	411	421	450
457										

False

109	120	157	214	239	318	335	440

Men: Mean 5.10; S.D. 3.07.　　Women: Mean 6.27; S.D. 3.55.

(continued)

TABLE B.10   Morey, Waugh, and Blashfield Personality Disorder Scales (continued)

CPS – Obsessive-Compulsive (13 items)

True

55	77	87	120	135	136	196	290	309	313	356
402	442									

False
none

Men: Mean 6.17; S.D. 2.53.   Women: Mean 6.37; S.D. 2.48.

PAR – Paranoid (22 items)

True

19	42	99	110	120	124	127	144	145	151	216
228	225	241	251	259	270	285	300	423	424	

False
314

Men: Mean 5.21; S.D. 3.07.   Women: Mean 5.13; S.D. 3.03.

STY – Schizotypal (35 items)

True

24	32	42	72	99	124	127	138	144	145	162
167	216	241	243	251	259	265	285	311	315	316
337	367	466								

False

49	63	79	280	340	342	353	359	360	370

Men: Mean 8.83; S.D. 4.77.   Women: Mean 8.74; S.D. 4.76.

AVD – Avoidant (38 items)

True

46	73	127	130	157	167	185	243	251	265	275
277	285	289	310	326	337	367	386	411	446	

False

49	63	78	79	86	109	157	262	280	321	335
340	342	353	359	360	370					

Men: Mean 12.51; S.D. 6.68.   Women: Mean 13.85; S.D. 7.18.

SZD – Schizoid (20 items)

True

46	79	157	265	270	281	291	337	349	367	405

False

49	78	86	280	340	342	353	359	370

Men: Mean 6.36; S.D. 3.27.   Women: Mean 5.50; S.D. 3.05.

Note. Means and standard deviations are based on the MMPI-2 normative group (Butcher et al., 1989).

TABLE B.11 Wiggins Content Scales

HEA – Poor Health (19 items)

True

11	28	36	59	111	253	464				

False

2	20	33	45	47	117	141	143	152	181	194
208										

Men: Mean 3.36; S.D. 2.56.   Women: Mean 3.94; S.D. 2.79.

DEP – Depression (33 items)

True

38	52	56	65	82	92	94	146	196	233	234
246	252	277	301	303	305	341	364	396	400	407
408	450	451	454	463						

False

9	63	75	188	388	405

Men: Mean 5.90; S.D. 4.42.   Women: Mean 7.23; S.D. 4.82.

ORG – Organic Symptoms (32 items)

True

18	40	97	101	147	149	168	172	175	229	247
296	299	472								

False

43	57	91	106	142	159	164	165	173	176	177
179	204	224	249	255	295	404				

Men: Mean 4.57; S.D. 3.50.   Women: Mean 4.95; S.D. 3.83.

FAM – Family Problems (16 items)

True

21	190	195	202	205	219	288	292	297	413	449

False

83	90	125	276	455

Men: Mean 4.09; S.D. 2.51.   Women: Mean 4.83; S.D. 2.70.

AUT – Authority Conflict (20 items)

True

50	58	81	103	104	105	110	227	241	250	254
269	283	284	286	344	346	352	418			

False

266

Men: Mean 8.91; S.D. 4.08.   Women: Mean 7.45; S.D. 3.81.

(continued)

TABLE B.11 Wiggins Content Scales (continued)

FEM – Feminine Interests (23 items)

True

62	64	67	74	80	112	119	128	137	187	236
426	473									

False

1	69	197	199	201	257	272	417	467	474

Men: Mean 8.36; S.D. 2.95.   Women: Mean 15.65; S.D. 2.62.

HOS – Manifest Hostility (25 items)

True

27	37	68	76	98	116	134	150	151	256	270
302	323	324	332	358	386	406	410	414	419	423
430	437	461								

False
none

Men: Mean 8.16; S.D. 4.31.   Women: Mean 7.62; S.D. 4.00.

MOR – Poor Morale (22 items)

True

71	73	127	130	225	289	326	331	339	347	348
368	390	394	399	409	411	415	457	469		

False

109	239

Men: Mean 5.83; S.D. 4.26.   Women: Mean 7.51; S.D. 4.77.

PHO – Phobias (26 items)

True

154	170	317	320	329	334	367	392	395	397	435
438	441	442	458	468						

False

115	118	163	186	261	321	385	401	453	462

Men: Mean 5.75; S.D. 3.47.   Women: Mean 8.63; S.D. 3.99.

PSY – Psychoticism (45 items)

True

17	22	23	24	32	42	48	60	61	72	96
99	113	124	138	144	162	180	182	198	211	216
228	251	259	271	281	285	298	307	311	315	316
319	333	336	345	355	361	424	448	466		

False

184	314	427

Men: Mean 7.30; S.D. 4.29.   Women: Mean 7.35; S.D. 4.23.

HYP – Hypomania (23 items)

True

15	122	156	169	206	210	213	218	226	242	244
267	304	308	330	366	389	393	420	422	428	439
444										

False
none

Men: Mean 10.84; S.D. 3.62.   Women: Mean 10.82; S.D. 3.41.

SOC – Social Maladjustment (26 items)

True

46	158	161	167	185	243	265	275	337	357	391
446										

False

49	79	86	262	280	335	340	342	353	359	360
365	370	452								

Men: Mean 9.57; S.D. 5.27.   Women: Mean 9.71; S.D. 5.41.

Note. Means and standard deviations are based on the MMPI-2 normative group (Butcher et al., 1989).

TABLE B.12   Cripe's Neurological Symptom Scales

AM – Attention/Mental Control (6 items)

True

31	122	299	325	341	475	525

False
none

Men: Mean 2.14; S.D. 1.43.   Women: Mean 2.26; S.D. 1.49.

BB – Biobehavioral (6 items)

True

166	253

False

12	20	143	208

Men: Mean 1.23; S.D. 1.17.   Women: Mean 1.45; S.D. 1.25.

EB – Emotional/Behavioral Control (22 items)

True

23	37	38	93	102	116	146	213	226	233	271
301	302	389	400	430	469	513				

False

223	372	405	564

Men: Mean 6.84; S.D. 3.80.   Women: Mean 8.13; S.D. 4.23.

(continued)

TABLE B.12   Cripe's Neurological Symptom Scales (continued)

FE – Fatigue/Lack of Energy (6 items)

True
175   366   464

False
152   330   561

Men: Mean 0.90; S.D. 1.07.   Women: Mean 1.11; S.D. 1.21.

GC – General Cognitive (10 items)

True
32   135   170   180   309   482   491

False
43   109   206

Men: Mean 1.70; S.D. 1.55.   Women: Mean 1.88; S.D. 1.77.

HD – Headaches (6 items)

True
40   97   101   149

False
57   176

Men: Mean 0.67; S.D. 0.98.   Women: Mean 0.94; S.D. 1.22.

HE – Health (4 items)

True
none

False
33   45   141   148

Men: Mean 1.11; S.D. 0.99.   Women: Mean 1.10; S.D. 1.03.

ME – Memory (5 items)

True
308   472   533   565

False
165

Men: Mean 1.07; S.D. 1.29.   Women: Mean 1.07; S.D. 1.29.

MT – Motor (6 items)

True
172   476

False
91   177   295   404

Men: Mean 0.52; S.D. 0.84.   Women: Mean 0.58; S.D. 0.92.

PN – Pain (2 items)

True
 none

False
 47   224

Men: Mean 0.37; S.D. 0.61.   Women: Mean 0.34; S.D. 0.59.

SB – Seizures/Blank Episodes (5 items)

True
 168   182   229

False
 142   159

Men: Mean 0.54; S.D. 0.81.   Women: Mean 0.68; S.D. 0.79.

SD – Sleep Disturbance (6 items)

True
 5   39   258   293

False
 3   140

Men: Mean 1.36; S.D. 1.11.   Women: Mean 1.57; S.D. 1.17.

SE – Sensory (13 items)

True
 44   53   198   247   252   298   307

False
 8   173   194   204   249   255

Men: Mean 2.37; S.D. 1.63.   Women: Mean 2.66; S.D. 1.76.

SL – Speech/Language (3 items)

True
 147   296

False
 106

Men: Mean 0.45; S.D. 0.67.   Women: Mean 0.43; S.D. 0.69.

SO – Social (5 items)

True
 367   480   507

False
 83   86

Men: Mean 1.64; S.D. 1.18.   Women: Mean 1.67; S.D. 1.17.

(continued)

TABLE B.12   Cripe's Neurological Symptom Scales (continued)

VN – Vertigo/Nausea (3 items)

True
  18

False
  164   179

Men: Mean 0.17; S.D. 0.44.   Women: Mean 0.28; S.D. 0.57.

VO – Vocational (2 items)

True
  517

False
  10

Men: Mean 0.19; S.D. 0.41.   Women: Mean 0.16; S.D. 0.38.

Note. Means and standard deviations are based on the MMPI-2 normative group (Butcher et al., 1989).

TABLE B.13   Martin and Finn Subscales for Scale 5 (Masculinity-Femininity)

Mf$_1$ – Denial of Stereotypical Masculine Interests (11 items)

True
  none

False
  1   69   133   197   199   201   417   465   467   474   477

Men: Mean 4.98; S.D. 2.29.   Women: Mean 8.20; S.D. 1.96.

Mf$_2$ – Hypersensitivity/Anxiety (13 items)

True
  166   196   205   219   251   256   268   271

False
  63   184   194   237   239

Men: Mean 5.04; S.D. 2.66.   Women: Mean 6.12; S.D. 2.65.

Mf$_3$ – Stereotypical Feminine Interests (6 items)

True
  4   64   74   80   119   236

False
  none

Men: Mean 1.35; S.D. 1.25.   Women: Mean 3.15; S.D. 1.40.

Mf$_4$ – Low Cynicism (6 items)

True
none

False

26	27	76	104	193	254

Men: Mean 4.13; S.D. 1.44.   Women: Mean 4.44; S.D. 1.35.

Mf$_5$ – Aesthetic Interests (5 items)

True

25	67	112	187	191

False
none

Men: Mean 2.12; S.D. 1.48.   Women: Mean 2.67; S.D. 1.37.

Mf$_6$ – Feminine Gender Identity (5 items)

True

62	371	384	426

False
272

Men: Mean 1.32; S.D. 1.10.   Women: Mean 3.55; S.D. 0.75.

Mf$_7$ – Restraint (6 items)

True
none

False

19	68	86	207	209	231

Men: Mean 3.68; S.D. 1.48.   Women: Mean 4.26; S.D. 1.35.

Mf$_{10}$ – Composite Femininity-Masculinity (22 items)

True

4	62	64	74	80	119	236	371	384	426		

False

1	69	133	197	199	201	272	417	465	467	474	477

Men: Mean 8.93; S.D. 2.98.   Women: Mean 8.69; S.D. 2.59.

Note. Means and standard deviations are based on the MMPI-2 normative group (Butcher et al.,1989).

Appendix C

Critical Item Sets

TABLE C.1 Koss-Butcher Critical Items Sets, Revised

Acute Anxiety State

2F	28T	208F	463T
3F	39T	218T	469T
5T	59T	223F	
10F	140F	301T	
15T	172T	444T	

Depressed Suicidal Ideation

9F	92T	233T	411T	520T
38T	95F	273T	454T	524T
65T	130T	303T	485T	
71T	146T	306T	506T	
75F	215T	388F	518T	

Threatened Assault

37T
85T
134T
213T
389T

Situational Stress Due to Alcoholism

125F	511T
264T	518T
487T	
489T	
502T	

Mental Confusion

24T	180T	325T
31T	198T	
32T	299T	
72T	311T	
96T	316T	

Persecutory Ideas

17T	144T	241T	361T
42T	145T	251T	
99T	162T	259T	
124T	216T	314F	
138T	228T	333T	

TABLE C.2 Lachar-Wrobel Critical Item Sets

Anxiety and Tension

15T	261F	463T
17T	299T	
172T	301T	
218T	320T	
223F	405F	

Depression and Worry

2F	75F	273T	454T
3F	130T	303T	
10F	150T	339T	
65T	165F	411T	
73T	180T	415T	

Sleep Disturbance

5T	471T
30T	
39T	
140F	
328T	

Deviant Beliefs

42T	162T	333T
99T	216T	336T
106F	228T	355T
138T	259T	361T
144T	314F	466T

Deviant Thinking and Experience

32T	298T
60T	307T
96T	316T
122T	319T
198T	427F

Substance Abuse

168T
264T
429F

Antisocial Attitude

27T	240T
35T	254T
84T	266F
105T	324T
227T	

Family Conflict

21T
83F
125F
288T

Problematic Anger

85T
134T
213T
389T

Sexual Concern and Deviation

12F	268T
34F	
62T/F	
121F	
166T	

Somatic Symptoms

18T	47F	111T	176F	255F
28T	53T	142F	182T	295F
33F	57F	159F	224F	464T
40T	59T	164F	229T	
44T	101T	175T	247T	

Appendix D

Prototypic Scores for Specific Codetypes in Clinical Settings

Appendix D-1

Prototypic Scores for Spike 1 Codetypes (N = 483)

Demographics

Demographics		M	SD	Marital Status		%
	Age	41.4	14.6		Never Married	29.3
	Education	11.6	5.6		Married	50.0
	Gender	%			Separated	2.1
	Men	54.5			Divorced	16.4
	Women	44.5			Widowed	2.1

Test-Taking Scales

Omissions		M	SD	Consistency	M	SD
	?	1.2	3.3	VRIN	50.1	9.9
				|F - FB|	2.7	1.9
				TRIN	49.7	9.7

Accuracy of Item Endorsement

Underreporting		M	SD	Overreporting		M	SD
	False %	63.5	6.0		True %	35.3	6.0
Impression	L	58.5	12.0	Infrequency	F	49.8	7.8
Management	ODecp	57.5	10.2		FB	49.1	8.4
	Sd	57.2	10.3		F[p]	51.8	11.1
Superlative	S	53.7	8.8	Critical Items	K & B	12.2	6.4
Adjustment					L & W	21.3	8.0
Self-Deception	K	54.5	9.0	Dissimulation	F - K	-13.2	5.5
	So	51.5	7.8		Ds	49.5	8.3
					O - S	5.5	47.2

Scales

Validity and Clinical / Supplementary / Morey et al. Overlapping Personality Disorder

Scale	M	SD	Scale	M	SD	Scale	M	SD
?	1.2	3.3	A	45.6	7.0	PAR	48.8	9.1
L	58.5	12.0	R	55.1	9.3	SZD	48.9	9.4
F	49.8	7.8	Es	46.5	8.8	STY	47.0	8.7
K	54.5	9.0	TRIN	49.7	9.7	ANT	46.7	8.8
1(Hs)	68.3	3.5	VRIN	50.1	9.9	BDL	46.1	8.5
2(D)	55.6	6.1	O-H	56.6	10.9	HST	48.7	9.3
3(Hy)	58.6	4.6	Do	48.1	9.3	NAR	51.9	8.5
4(Pd)	50.9	7.0	Re	50.8	9.4	AVD	46.1	7.7
5(Mf)	47.9	8.8	GM	47.8	9.1	DEP	46.6	7.9
6(Pa)	49.6	8.3	GF	49.7	8.5	CPS	46.0	9.1
7(Pt)	51.0	6.9	Mt	50.1	7.3	Personality		
8(Sc)	51.8	6.4	PK	48.2	7.2	Psychopathology Five		
9(Ma)	49.4	7.1	PS	49.2	7.1	Scale	M	SD
0(Si)	48.3	7.7	MAC-R	50.6	8.9	AGG	50.0	8.3
			APS	45.6	11.3	PSY	48.5	9.0
			AAS	46.3	8.6	CON	52.2	9.2
			MDS	46.9	7.5	NEN	47.6	8.2
			Ho	48.3	8.4	PEE	50.1	7.9
			CAL-R	45.4	10.3			

Content / Content Component

Scale	M	SD	Scale	M	SD	Scale	M	SD
ANX	51.8	8.0	FRS1	50.7	12.3	ASP1	49.1	9.2
FRS	50.6	10.9	FRS2	49.8	10.4	ASP2	49.5	10.4
OBS	45.7	8.1	DEP1	49.5	7.4	TPA1	45.8	9.5
DEP	48.7	7.2	DEP2	48.1	8.5	TPA2	47.1	9.9
HEA	63.3	6.6	DEP3	46.4	7.4	LSE1	45.0	6.6
BIZ	48.8	8.1	DEP4	47.6	8.2	LSE2	46.7	7.9
ANG	46.8	8.3	HEA1	60.6	13.2	SOD1	48.1	8.3
CYN	50.7	9.4	HEA2	60.2	11.4	SOD2	47.7	9.1
ASP	49.5	8.8	HEA3	61.1	10.4	FAM1	44.7	8.3
TPA	46.4	9.3	BIZ1	47.7	7.6	FAM2	48.6	9.1
LSE	46.2	7.4	BIZ2	47.0	7.3	TRT1	47.5	7.5
SOD	48.0	8.2	ANG1	47.2	8.0	TRT2	46.3	8.5
FAM	46.2	7.9	ANG2	46.9	8.9			
WRK	48.1	7.5	CYN1	50.7	9.8			
TRT	47.5	7.8	CYN2	49.4	9.9			

Note. All scores are T scores except: Cannot Say, K & B and L & W critical items which are raw scores; True % and False % which are the percentage of items endorsed "true" or "false;" and \|F - FB\|, F - K, and O - S which are difference scores.

Appendix D-2

Prototypic Scores for 1-2/2-1 Codetypes (N = 1,676)

Demographics

Demographics		M	SD	Marital Status	%
Age		42.5	13.6	Never Married	22.5
Education		11.4	5.1	Married	53.0
Gender		%		Separated	3.8
	Men	40.0		Divorced	17.7
	Women	60.0		Widowed	3.0

Test-Taking Scales

Omissions		M	SD	Consistency		M	SD
	?	1.6	3.8		VRIN	54.7	10.7
					|F - FB|	3.7	2.8
					TRIN	50.9	11.8

Accuracy of Item Endorsement

Underreporting		M	SD	Overreporting		M	SD
	False %	57.7	7.0		True %	41.0	7.0
Impression	L	56.5	11.2	Infrequency	F	65.0	13.9
Management	ODecp	48.2	10.5		FB	64.8	17.7
	Sd	49.6	11.0		F[p]	55.6	12.2
Superlative	S	45.4	8.9	Critical Items	K & B	29.4	11.0
Adjustment					L & W	40.7	12.7
Self-Deception	K	45.7	8.8	Dissimulation	F - K	-4.5	6.8
	So	34.3	10.9		Ds	62.5	11.8
					O - S	101.7	62.1

Scales

Validity and Clinical			Supplementary			Morey et al. Overlapping Personality Disorder		
Scale	M	SD	Scale	M	SD	Scale	M	SD
?	1.6	3.8	A	61.0	10.1	PAR	57.1	10.9
L	56.5	11.2	R	60.5	10.3	SZD	58.7	11.4
F	65.0	13.9	Es	28.2	11.5	STY	61.1	11.1
K	45.7	8.8	TRIN	50.9	11.8	ANT	49.0	9.0
1(Hs)	81.5	9.2	VRIN	54.7	10.7	BDL	52.6	9.1
2(D)	83.7	10.9	O-H	51.3	10.3	HST	39.8	10.2
3(Hy)	73.8	10.8	Do	36.9	10.3	NAR	42.2	10.7
4(Pd)	58.5	10.8	Re	48.2	9.2	AVD	59.5	10.0
5(Mf)	50.4	9.4	GM	37.8	9.7	DEP	56.6	11.1
6(Pa)	61.5	12.8	GF	49.2	8.9	CPS	54.4	9.6
7(Pt)	69.0	11.3	Mt	69.8	10.0	Personality Psychopathology Five		
8(Sc)	67.6	12.1	PK	67.3	12.2	Scale	M	SD
9(Ma)	49.3	8.4	PS	69.3	12.2	AGG	47.9	9.7
0(Si)	62.3	9.6	MAC-R	47.5	10.0	PSY	56.6	11.7
			APS	48.5	9.9	CON	55.9	9.4
			AAS	48.4	9.6	NEN	59.1	9.6
			MDS	59.3	12.0	PEE	33.4	12.0
			Ho	55.0	9.2			
			CAL-R	45.0	10.8			

Content			Content Component					
Scale	M	SD	Scale	M	SD	Scale	M	SD
ANX	68.9	11.3	FRS1	58.9	15.4	ASP1	52.0	9.0
FRS	56.8	12.1	FRS2	53.5	10.1	ASP2	49.1	10.1
OBS	56.6	10.8	DEP1	68.4	14.1	TPA1	54.1	10.6
DEP	66.2	10.8	DEP2	66.2	12.0	TPA2	50.6	9.9
HEA	77.4	10.5	DEP3	58.4	10.3	LSE1	58.6	11.9
BIZ	54.6	9.8	DEP4	61.3	22.9	LSE2	53.6	10.8
ANG	54.6	10.8	HEA1	74.9	16.4	SOD1	60.1	11.6
CYN	56.1	10.3	HEA2	74.6	15.5	SOD2	55.5	9.2
ASP	51.6	8.5	HEA3	75.6	10.0	FAM1	50.1	10.7
TPA	52.4	10.7	BIZ1	52.4	11.7	FAM2	52.1	12.3
LSE	59.5	11.3	BIZ2	52.9	10.6	TRT1	63.8	15.0
SOD	60.0	11.3	ANG1	52.0	10.6	TRT2	53.3	10.1
FAM	52.5	11.1	ANG2	55.5	10.3			
WRK	64.6	11.2	CYN1	55.8	9.9			
TRT	62.7	12.5	CYN2	54.3	9.8			

Note. All scores are T scores except: Cannot Say, K & B and L & W critical items which are raw scores; True % and False % which are the percentage of items endorsed "true" or "false;" and |F - FB|, F - K, and O - S which are difference scores.

Appendix D-3

Prototypic Scores for 1-3/3-1 Codetypes (N = 5,223)

Demographics

		M	SD	Marital Status		%
Age		41.6	12.8	Never Married		24.2
Education		12.0	5.3	Married		51.5
Gender		%		Separated		4.1
	Men	39.0		Divorced		17.9
	Women	61.0		Widowed		2.3

Test-Taking Scales

Omissions

		M	SD	Consistency	M	SD
	?	1.5	3.4	VRIN	51.3	10.4
				|F - FB|	3.3	2.4
				TRIN	47.6	11.4

Accuracy of Item Endorsement

Underreporting

		M	SD	Overreporting		M	SD
	False %	63.3	6.9		True %	35.4	6.9
Impression	L	58.8	11.5	Infrequency	F	57.2	12.4
Management	ODecp	53.2	10.2		FB	55.4	13.8
	Sd	52.8	10.3		F[p]	52.5	11.4
Superior	S	53.5	9.6	Critical Items	K & B	21.2	10.9
Adjustment					L & W	33.3	13.4
Self-Deception	K	54.5	9.6	Dissimulation	F - K	-11.0	7.0
	So	44.3	10.9		Ds	54.9	11.6
					O - S	37.3	64.9

Scales

Validity and Clinical			Supplementary			Morey et al. Overlapping Personality Disorder		
Scale	M	SD	Scale	M	SD	Scale	M	SD
?	1.5	3.4	A	51.7	9.7	PAR	48.0	10.2
L	58.8	11.5	R	59.2	10.3	SZD	49.5	9.8
F	57.2	12.4	Es	35.6	12.0	STY	48.5	9.9
K	54.5	9.6	TRIN	47.6	11.4	ANT	44.9	9.4
1(Hs)	82.6	10.3	VRIN	51.3	10.4	BDL	48.7	9.7
2(D)	70.0	12.2	O-H	57.4	10.1	HST	47.6	9.6
3(Hy)	85.3	12.2	Do	45.7	10.0	NAR	48.7	9.1
4(Pd)	58.6	10.0	Re	52.5	9.6	AVD	47.7	8.9
5(Mf)	50.7	9.3	GM	44.0	10.2	DEP	48.8	9.2
6(Pa)	60.0	12.2	GF	49.6	9.0	CPS	48.0	9.9
7(Pt)	64.0	11.7	Mt	60.4	11.0	Personality Psychopathology Five		
8(Sc)	64.4	12.0	PK	57.4	12.2	Scale	M	SD
9(Ma)	52.3	9.4	PS	59.7	12.3	AGG	49.5	8.7
0(Si)	49.9	9.1	MAC-R	48.3	9.7	PSY	50.2	11.0
			APS	48.4	10.8	CON	54.0	9.6
			AAS	47.2	9.0	NEN	51.5	10.0
			MDS	52.3	10.7	PEE	43.3	10.8
			Ho	46.3	8.8			
			CAL-R	43.8	10.6			

Content			Content Component					
Scale	M	SD	Scale	M	SD	Scale	M	SD
ANX	61.0	12.1	FRS1	53.6	13.3	ASP1	44.8	8.8
FRS	52.3	10.9	FRS2	50.7	10.2	ASP2	48.8	10.2
OBS	48.5	9.6	DEP1	58.3	11.9	TPA1	47.4	10.3
DEP	56.8	10.6	DEP2	57.4	13.3	TPA2	46.1	9.6
HEA	75.2	11.6	DEP3	51.3	9.5	LSE1	49.1	9.5
BIZ	51.4	10.0	DEP4	53.7	17.0	LSE2	46.3	8.1
ANG	49.1	10.5	HEA1	69.5	17.8	SOD1	50.4	9.6
CYN	47.5	9.1	HEA2	74.1	16.6	SOD2	45.9	8.7
ASP	45.8	8.3	HEA3	72.2	11.2	FAM1	45.6	9.8
TPA	46.5	9.4	BIZ1	50.2	10.6	FAM2	49.9	10.8
LSE	49.6	9.1	BIZ2	49.5	9.8	TRT1	52.3	11.7
SOD	48.9	9.0	ANG1	49.4	9.8	TRT2	46.3	9.0
FAM	47.7	10.3	ANG2	49.0	10.4			
WRK	54.0	9.6	CYN1	46.7	9.7			
TRT	51.2	10.4	CYN2	47.9	9.5			

Note. All scores are T scores except: Cannot Say, K & B and L & W critical items which are raw scores; True % and False % which are the percentage of items endorsed "true" or "false;" and \|F - FB\|, F - K, and O - S which are difference scores.

Appendix D-4					

Prototypic Scores for 1-4/4-1 Codetypes (N = 224)

Demographics		M	SD	Marital Status	%
Age		36.6	12.3	Never Married	32.1
Education		11.2	5.3	Married	40.4
Gender		%		Separated	6.2
	Men	43.3		Divorced	19.2
	Women	56.7		Widowed	2.1

Test-Taking Scales

Omissions		M	SD	Consistency		M	SD
	?	1.1	2.9	VRIN		53.2	10.7
				|F - FB|		3.8	2.8
				TRIN		46.7	11.2

Accuracy of Item Endorsement

Underreporting		M	SD	Overreporting		M	SD
	False %	60.8	7.3	True %		38.0	7.3
Impression	L	55.0	12.1	Infrequency	F	61.2	13.5
Management	ODecp	49.8	9.5		FB	57.9	14.9
	Sd	51.0	9.1		F[p]	54.5	13.4
Superior	S	48.1	10.2	Critical Items	K & B	22.1	11.9
Adjustment					L & W	32.1	13.2
Self-Deception	K	53.5	10.4	Dissimulation	F - K	-9.4	7.8
	So	45.3	11.4		Ds	59.2	11.9
					O - S	36.2	68.8

Scales

Validity and Clinical			Supplementary			Morey et al. Overlapping Personality Disorder		
Scale	M	SD	Scale	M	SD	Scale	M	SD
?	1.1	2.9	A	52.0	10.5	PAR	54.1	11.4
L	55.0	12.1	R	54.1	9.7	SZD	48.1	10.5
F	61.2	13.5	Es	41.3	11.0	STY	51.5	10.6
K	53.5	10.4	TRIN	46.7	11.2	ANT	55.4	10.0
1(Hs)	73.4	6.9	VRIN	53.2	10.7	BDL	52.1	11.0
2(D)	62.6	9.3	O-H	54.4	10.8	HST	50.3	9.1
3(Hy)	65.8	8.2	Do	44.9	10.3	NAR	50.8	9.1
4(Pd)	75.5	7.6	Re	43.8	10.1	AVD	48.9	8.8
5(Mf)	51.3	10.0	GM	44.6	10.0	DEP	52.1	9.2
6(Pa)	58.8	10.8	GF	44.8	9.7	CPS	48.3	10.3
7(Pt)	60.4	9.0	Mt	58.4	11.1	Personality Psychopathology Five		
8(Sc)	63.1	8.9	PK	58.2	12.8			
9(Ma)	54.1	8.8	PS	58.6	12.5	Scale	M	SD
0(Si)	50.6	9.4	MAC-R	56.0	10.9	AGG	50.2	9.8
			APS	50.6	11.6	PSY	54.6	11.6
			AAS	55.4	11.5	CON	45.7	10.2
			MDS	60.3	12.2	NEN	53.8	10.7
			Ho	52.2	9.5	PEE	45.4	10.8
			CAL-R	53.1	11.0			

Content			Content Component					
Scale	M	SD	Scale	M	SD	Scale	M	SD
ANX	58.1	11.6	FRS1	52.2	12.6	ASP1	50.5	8.9
FRS	50.8	10.5	FRS2	49.5	10.2	ASP2	59.6	12.5
OBS	49.7	10.7	DEP1	58.1	12.9	TPA1	48.3	11.0
DEP	58.4	11.3	DEP2	56.8	12.1	TPA2	48.7	9.7
HEA	68.3	9.4	DEP3	56.1	11.9	LSE1	51.0	10.4
BIZ	53.9	9.8	DEP4	54.5	18.4	LSE2	48.4	8.8
ANG	52.2	11.1	HEA1	66.5	15.1	SOD1	50.4	9.5
CYN	53.5	10.6	HEA2	63.5	13.6	SOD2	45.8	7.9
ASP	53.6	9.0	HEA3	65.6	11.1	FAM1	54.3	10.5
TPA	48.5	10.2	BIZ1	51.0	10.9	FAM2	60.3	14.0
LSE	51.7	9.6	BIZ2	52.1	10.3	TRT1	53.6	12.7
SOD	49.1	8.6	ANG1	52.8	11.0	TRT2	49.2	10.1
FAM	58.6	11.8	ANG2	50.9	10.5			
WRK	54.4	11.1	CYN1	53.0	10.1			
TRT	53.6	11.4	CYN2	52.3	10.8			

Note. All scores are T scores except: Cannot Say, K & B and L & W critical items which are raw scores; True % and False % which are the percentage of items endorsed "true" or "false;" and |F - FB|, F - K, and O - S which are difference scores.

Appendix D-5

Prototypic Scores for 1-5/5-1 Codetypes (N = 145)

Demographics

Demographics		M	SD	Marital Status	%
Age		39.6	13.7	Never Married	35.5
Education		10.7	5.7	Married	43.8
Gender		%		Separated	0.8
	Men	13.1		Divorced	15.7
	Women	86.9		Widowed	4.1

Test-Taking Scales

Omissions		M	SD	Consistency		M	SD
	?	2.6	5.5	VRIN		53.6	10.8
				|F - FB|		3.1	2.5
				TRIN		51.1	13.9

Accuracy of Item Endorsement

Underreporting		M	SD	Overreporting		M	SD
	False %	62.0	7.3		True %	36.5	7.3
Impression	L	60.9	12.1	Infrequency	F	56.5	13.6
Management	ODecp	59.9	11.6		FB	52.8	12.1
	Sd	57.2	11.3		F[p]	58.3	16.1
Superior	S	52.0	9.1	Critical Items	K & B	16.3	8.8
Adjustment					L & W	26.7	10.9
Self-Deception	K	52.9	10.2	Dissimulation	F - K	-10.7	7.4
	So	48.7	8.8		Ds	53.1	10.4
					O - S	30.1	58.2

Scales

Validity and Clinical			Supplementary			Morey et al. Overlapping Personality Disorder		
Scale	M	SD	Scale	M	SD	Scale	M	SD
?	2.6	5.5	A	48.0	8.3	PAR	51.0	9.7
L	60.9	12.1	R	56.2	9.4	SZD	51.8	9.9
F	56.5	13.6	Es	43.7	10.1	STY	49.0	9.3
K	52.9	10.2	TRIN	51.1	13.9	ANT	49.6	9.5
1(Hs)	71.0	5.6	VRIN	53.6	10.8	BDL	48.2	9.4
2(D)	58.1	7.7	O-H	55.4*	10.2	HST	47.5	9.8
3(Hy)	61.4	6.9	Do	44.5	10.1	NAR	52.5	9.3
4(Pd)	53.0	8.3	Re	49.5	10.2	AVD	46.8	8.5
5(Mf)	72.0	5.7	GM	49.3	9.1	DEP	45.7	8.2
6(Pa)	50.1	9.3	GF	41.7	12.4	CPS	46.0	9.2
7(Pt)	52.4	8.1	Mt	52.8	8.2	Personality Psychopathology Five		
8(Sc)	56.4	8.4	PK	52.3	9.8	Scale	M	SD
9(Ma)	52.0	8.4	PS	53.0	9.5	AGG	51.5	9.9
0(Si)	50.1	8.6	MAC-R	52.6	9.7	PSY	52.4	11.4
			APS	42.3	10.5	CON	50.3	9.8
			AAS	49.1	8.9	NEN	49.3	9.7
			MDS	49.2	9.1	PEE	47.4	9.3
			Ho	50.9	9.3			
			CAL-R	45.1	11.6			

Content			Content Component					
Scale	M	SD	Scale	M	SD	Scale	M	SD
ANX	53.0	9.3	FRS1	52.5	12.9	ASP1	52.3	10.1
FRS	50.6	10.6	FRS2	48.7	9.8	ASP2	51.6	11.7
OBS	46.0	8.2	DEP1	54.0	9.9	TPA1	47.0	10.8
DEP	52.2	8.7	DEP2	50.5	9.4	TPA2	48.3	9.2
HEA	66.2	8.8	DEP3	48.2	9.9	LSE1	46.4	8.3
BIZ	51.2	9.8	DEP4	49.3	12.4	LSE2	48.0	8.1
ANG	49.0	10.2	HEA1	63.1	14.2	SOD1	50.1	9.9
CYN	53.3	10.2	HEA2	64.2	12.9	SOD2	48.0	9.3
ASP	52.9	9.5	HEA3	62.5	11.3	FAM1	46.0	9.4
TPA	48.0	9.8	BIZ1	49.8	10.6	FAM2	51.5	10.2
LSE	48.4	8.3	BIZ2	48.6	8.7	TRT1	48.5	9.0
SOD	49.4	9.1	ANG1	50.7	10.5	TRT2	48.7	9.4
FAM	48.1	9.1	ANG2	48.0	10.2			
WRK	49.8	8.2	CYN1	54.3	11.1			
TRT	50.0	9.2	CYN2	49.9	9.7			

Note. All scores are T scores except: Cannot Say, K & B and L & W critical items which are raw scores; True % and False % which are the percentage of items endorsed "true" or "false;" and \|F - FB\|, F - K, and O - S which are difference scores.

Appendix D-6
Prototypic Scores for 1-6/6-1 Codetypes (N = 383)

Demographics

Demographics		M	SD	Marital Status		%
Age		40.1	12.2		Never Married	26.0
Education		11.7	5.1		Married	48.0
Gender		%			Separated	3.9
	Men	49.1			Divorced	19.8
	Women	50.9			Widowed	2.2

Test-Taking Scales

Omissions		M	SD	Consistency	M	SD
	?	1.6	3.2	VRIN	55.9	10.4
				|F - FB|	4.5	3.2
				TRIN	51.9	12.8

Accuracy of Item Endorsement

Underreporting		M	SD	Overreporting		M	SD
	False %	55.8	7.5		True %	43.0	7.5
Impression	L	56.7	10.3	Infrequency	F	68.8	16.7
Management	ODecp	52.6	9.4		FB	65.9	18.2
	Sd	54.8	9.8		F[p]	59.7	15.2
Superior	S	46.8	8.8	Critical Items	K & B	30.4	12.2
Adjustment					L & W	42.6	14.8
Self-Deception	K	46.1	8.8	Dissimulation	F - K	-3.4	8.1
	So	36.7	11.6		Ds	64.2	13.1
					O - S	97.0	72.4

Scales

Validity and Clinical			Supplementary			Morey et al. Overlapping Personality Disorder		
Scale	M	SD	Scale	M	SD	Scale	M	SD
?	1.6	3.2	A	58.7	10.4	PAR	65.3	11.9
L	56.7	10.3	R	54.3	9.7	SZD	53.0	10.9
F	68.8	16.7	Es	30.7	14.1	STY	61.9	11.4
K	46.1	8.8	TRIN	51.9	12.8	ANT	48.7	10.0
1(Hs)	79.5	9.8	VRIN	55.9	10.4	BDL	54.2	10.1
2(D)	68.0	11.5	O-H	54.6	10.3	HST	45.7	10.3
3(Hy)	71.5	11.2	Do	41.6	10.8	NAR	48.8	9.9
4(Pd)	60.4	10.2	Re	45.5	10.2	AVD	54.5	9.8
5(Mf)	51.2	8.7	GM	38.7	11.5	DEP	52.8	10.5
6(Pa)	82.2	11.4	GF	47.2	9.8	CPS	53.2	9.7
7(Pt)	64.5	12.2	Mt	64.4	11.0	Personality Psychopathology Five		
8(Sc)	67.9	12.8	PK	66.5	13.3			
9(Ma)	55.8	10.1	PS	66.9	13.4	Scale	M	SD
0(Si)	55.0	9.5	MAC-R	54.1	10.0	AGG	52.7	9.8
			APS	50.0	10.4	PSY	67.2	16.0
			AAS	49.6	9.7	CON	53.1	10.6
			MDS	58.7	11.3	NEN	58.6	10.0
			Ho	56.5	9.6	PEE	43.8	10.7
			CAL-R	47.1	10.8			

Content			Content Component					
Scale	M	SD	Scale	M	SD	Scale	M	SD
ANX	66.9	11.5	FRS1	62.3	17.8	ASP1	49.4	9.2
FRS	57.7	13.4	FRS2	52.7	10.6	ASP2	51.3	11.5
OBS	55.1	11.4	DEP1	62.1	12.9	TPA1	50.6	10.9
DEP	62.9	10.3	DEP2	63.1	13.1	TPA2	53.9	10.5
HEA	76.8	11.8	DEP3	56.8	11.3	LSE1	53.0	10.6
BIZ	64.5	13.7	DEP4	58.5	19.3	LSE2	51.9	10.6
ANG	54.7	11.9	HEA1	76.4	17.3	SOD1	53.9	10.6
CYN	55.6	10.7	HEA2	76.2	16.7	SOD2	51.3	9.6
ASP	50.4	8.9	HEA3	68.4	12.3	FAM1	51.3	10.8
TPA	52.7	11.2	BIZ1	66.5	20.0	FAM2	51.7	12.2
LSE	54.9	10.4	BIZ2	60.8	13.4	TRT1	58.1	13.3
SOD	53.9	10.1	ANG1	53.8	11.0	TRT2	51.8	10.5
FAM	54.3	11.0	ANG2	54.0	10.7			
WRK	59.3	11.0	CYN1	53.6	10.0			
TRT	58.7	11.5	CYN2	56.4	10.1			

Note. All scores are T scores except: Cannot Say, K & B and L & W critical items which are raw scores; True % and False % which are the percentage of items endorsed "true" or "false;" and |F - FB|, F - K, and O - S which are difference scores.

Appendix D-7

Prototypic Scores for 1-7/7-1 Codetypes (N = 202)

Demographics

Demographics		M	SD	Marital Status		%
Age		39.3	13.1		Never Married	33.0
Education		11.9	4.6		Married	44.9
Gender		%			Separated	3.2
	Men	55.9			Divorced	15.7
	Women	44.1			Widowed	3.2

Test-Taking Scales

Omissions		M	SD	Consistency	M	SD
	?	1.6	3.4	VRIN	55.6	10.1
				|F - FB|	3.4	2.8
				TRIN	53.2	11.7

Accuracy of Item Endorsement

Underreporting		M	SD	Overreporting		M	SD
	False %	53.7	6.9		True %	45.0	6.8
Impression	L	51.5	10.2	Infrequency	F	64.4	13.1
Management	ODecp	45.1	8.9		FB	67.5	17.2
	Sd	48.0	8.7		F[p]	55.5	13.5
Superior	S	42.9	8.3	Critical Items	K & B	30.2	9.6
Adjustment					L & W	42.6	11.9
Self-Deception	K	46.0	9.0	Dissimulation	F - K	-4.7	6.9
	So	31.7	10.4		Ds	66.4	11.3
					O - S	103.0	59.5

Scales

Validity and Clinical			Supplementary			Morey et al. Overlapping Personality Disorder		
Scale	M	SD	Scale	M	SD	Scale	M	SD
?	1.6	3.4	A	65.8	9.3	PAR	58.2	10.0
L	51.5	10.2	R	52.8	9.8	SZD	52.8	10.7
F	64.4	13.1	Es	27.8	12.6	STY	59.2	8.9
K	46.0	9.0	TRIN	53.2	11.7	ANT	52.0	9.7
1(Hs)	79.6	8.9	VRIN	55.6	10.1	BDL	57.2	9.8
2(D)	71.5	8.9	O-H	50.3	9.8	HST	44.0	10.3
3(Hy)	70.6	10.7	Do	35.0	11.2	NAR	42.8	10.4
4(Pd)	59.3	10.0	Re	43.3	10.5	AVD	60.1	8.6
5(Mf)	50.3	9.7	GM	33.2	10.7	DEP	63.2	10.4
6(Pa)	61.9	11.5	GF	48.1	9.1	CPS	57.7	9.0
7(Pt)	80.1	9.3	Mt	71.2	9.2	Personality Psychopathology Five		
8(Sc)	70.9	10.4	PK	69.8	11.1	Scale	M	SD
9(Ma)	54.7	9.3	PS	72.0	11.0	AGG	47.8	10.7
0(Si)	60.5	8.3	MAC-R	51.8	10.9	PSY	59.4	11.7
			APS	54.7	10.7	CON	52.3	9.7
			AAS	52.2	10.5	NEN	63.7	9.6
			MDS	58.7	10.1	PEE	41.5	9.6
			Ho	55.7	8.9			
			CAL-R	47.0	12.1			

Content			Content Component					
Scale	M	SD	Scale	M	SD	Scale	M	SD
ANX	71.3	10.0	FRS1	65.7	17.9	ASP1	52.2	8.9
FRS	59.5	12.6	FRS2	53.8	9.9	ASP2	51.4	11.2
OBS	63.4	10.6	DEP1	66.2	12.9	TPA1	54.8	9.9
DEP	66.0	9.5	DEP2	65.1	11.2	TPA2	53.7	10.1
HEA	77.6	10.3	DEP3	61.6	10.6	LSE1	60.9	10.5
BIZ	59.1	10.8	DEP4	59.7	20.1	LSE2	59.1	10.1
ANG	57.9	11.6	HEA1	74.9	15.8	SOD1	54.6	10.3
CYN	55.8	10.3	HEA2	75.6	16.1	SOD2	57.0	9.2
ASP	52.7	9.4	HEA3	71.1	11.1	FAM1	53.4	10.3
TPA	54.0	10.8	BIZ1	54.0	12.6	FAM2	52.4	11.6
LSE	63.3	10.0	BIZ2	59.0	12.0	TRT1	64.6	13.4
SOD	56.5	10.2	ANG1	55.0	11.6	TRT2	55.9	9.9
FAM	55.3	10.2	ANG2	57.7	10.3			
WRK	65.5	9.5	CYN1	55.0	9.9			
TRT	63.6	10.6	CYN2	54.8	9.5			

Note. All scores are T scores except: Cannot Say, K & B and L & W critical items which are raw scores; True % and False % which are the percentage of items endorsed "true" or "false;" and |F - FB|, F - K, and O - S which are difference scores.

Appendix D-8

Prototypic Scores for 1-8/8-1 Codetypes (N = 508)

Demographics

Demographics		M	SD	Marital Status		%
Age		39.6	14.2		Never Married	36.5
Education		10.1	5.6		Married	44.5
Gender		%			Separated	4.3
	Men	53.5			Divorced	11.6
	Women	46.5			Widowed	3.0

Test-Taking Scales

Omissions		M	SD	Consistency	M	SD
	?	1.8	3.9	VRIN	57.4	11.0
				|F - FB|	4.9	3.7
				TRIN	54.7	13.0

Accuracy of Item Endorsement

Underreporting		M	SD	Overreporting		M	SD
	False %	50.0	9.0		True %	48.7	9.0
Impression	L	53.1	11.3	Infrequency	F	84.2	19.3
Management	ODecp	47.9	10.7		FB	85.3	25.2
	Sd	50.4	11.1		F[p]	68.9	17.7
Superior	S	40.5	9.8	Critical Items	K & B	38.3	14.1
Adjustment					L & W	54.4	17.0
Self-Deception	K	43.0	10.0	Dissimulation	F - K	3.0	9.5
	So	26.8	13.0		Ds	76.7	14.8
					O - S	154.4	79.3

Scales

Validity and Clinical			Supplementary			Morey et al. Overlapping Personality Disorder		
Scale	M	SD	Scale	M	SD	Scale	M	SD
?	1.8	3.9	A	67.0	11.2	PAR	66.3	12.9
L	53.1	11.3	R	53.4	11.2	SZD	57.3	12.5
F	84.2	19.3	Es	20.4	13.6	STY	66.9	13.0
K	43.0	10.0	TRIN	54.7	13.0	ANT	57.2	10.9
1(Hs)	85.6	10.2	VRIN	57.4	11.0	BDL	59.1	10.2
2(D)	75.2	12.6	O-H	49.8*	10.4	HST	42.9	11.1
3(Hy)	75.9	12.2	Do	33.3	11.1	NAR	46.2	10.4
4(Pd)	66.2	12.1	Re	40.3	11.2	AVD	60.0	10.4
5(Mf)	52.5	9.8	GM	32.7	11.5	DEP	59.5	11.1
6(Pa)	71.0	14.7	GF	42.8	10.8	CPS	58.3	10.1
7(Pt)	75.4	12.2	Mt	72.5	11.9	Personality Psychopathology Five		
8(Sc)	88.1	13.1	PK	77.2	15.6			
9(Ma)	62.5	11.2	PS	79.8	14.6	Scale	M	SD
0(Si)	61.6	10.3	MAC-R	56.7	11.2	AGG	53.2	11.4
			APS	50.4	11.9	PSY	71.8	17.1
			AAS	55.5	12.0	CON	49.6	11.6
			MDS	66.7	12.8	NEN	64.6	10.7
			Ho	61.5	9.9	PEE	38.1	13.2
			CAL-R	51.0	10.9			

Content			Content Component					
Scale	M	SD	Scale	M	SD	Scale	M	SD
ANX	72.3	12.6	FRS1	70.4	20.3	ASP1	57.1	9.3
FRS	62.4	14.3	FRS2	54.5	10.8	ASP2	55.7	12.5
OBS	63.4	12.2	DEP1	73.3	15.6	TPA1	55.5	10.8
DEP	70.9	12.6	DEP2	66.3	12.4	TPA2	56.6	11.5
HEA	85.4	12.5	DEP3	64.1	12.3	LSE1	61.4	12.8
BIZ	70.2	14.5	DEP4	73.0	29.2	LSE2	56.2	10.7
ANG	61.1	12.1	HEA1	80.9	16.5	SOD1	59.1	12.5
CYN	62.4	10.8	HEA2	89.4	16.1	SOD2	54.7	9.5
ASP	58.6	10.8	HEA3	73.8	12.2	FAM1	58.9	12.0
TPA	57.4	12.8	BIZ1	67.6	20.9	FAM2	57.9	13.5
LSE	63.8	12.1	BIZ2	69.1	14.6	TRT1	68.9	16.0
SOD	59.4	12.2	ANG1	59.3	12.1	TRT2	58.3	11.0
FAM	62.7	12.8	ANG2	59.5	10.0			
WRK	69.3	12.4	CYN1	60.0	9.1			
TRT	68.8	13.5	CYN2	60.1	9.5			

Note. All scores are T scores except: Cannot Say, K & B and L & W critical items which are raw scores; True % and False % which are the percentage of items endorsed "true" or "false;" and \|F - FB\|, F - K, and O - S which are difference scores.

Appendix D-9

Prototypic Scores for 1-9/9-1 Codetypes (N = 158)

Demographics

		M	SD	Marital Status		%
	Age	35.7	13.5		Never Married	46.3
	Education	11.3	5.5		Married	35.3
	Gender	%			Separated	3.7
	Men	48.7			Divorced	14.0
	Women	51.3			Widowed	0.7

Test-Taking Scales

Omissions		M	SD	Consistency		M	SD
	?	1.4	3.4		VRIN	51.3	9.9
					|F - FB|	3.6	2.5
					TRIN	53.8	12.3

Accuracy of Item Endorsement

Underreporting		M	SD	Overreporting		M	SD
	False %	54.5	6.3		True %	44.2	6.3
Impression	L	53.8	10.7	Infrequency	F	59.7	12.9
Management	ODecp	54.7	9.7		FB	57.0	13.0
	Sd	56.7	9.4		F[p]	54.4	11.8
Superior	S	42.9	8.1	Critical Items	K & B	23.3	10.1
Adjustment					L & W	36.3	12.1
Self-Deception	K	46.4	9.0	Dissimulation	F - K	-6.4	7.2
	So	43.5	10.1		Ds	60.8	11.1
					O - S	66.2	60.1

Scales

Validity and Clinical			Supplementary			Morey et al. Overlapping Personality Disorder		
Scale	M	SD	Scale	M	SD	Scale	M	SD
?	1.4	3.4	A	54.2	9.1	PAR	58.7	10.0
L	53.8	10.7	R	45.4	7.9	SZD	46.5	8.9
F	59.7	12.9	Es	37.8	10.5	STY	50.3	8.6
K	46.4	9.0	TRIN	53.8	12.3	ANT	55.9	9.3
1(Hs)	73.3	6.5	VRIN	51.3	9.9	BDL	57.3	10.2
2(D)	57.0	9.0	O-H	52.4	9.6	HST	55.4	8.6
3(Hy)	63.4	8.1	Do	44.4	11.2	NAR	60.1	7.7
4(Pd)	56.8	9.8	Re	41.1	11.1	AVD	45.1	7.3
5(Mf)	49.9	9.2	GM	45.3	8.3	DEP	48.4	8.7
6(Pa)	54.9	10.3	GF	42.2	10.3	CPS	55.5	9.0
7(Pt)	57.8	8.6	Mt	60.5	9.6	Personality Psychopathology Five		
8(Sc)	61.8	9.1	PK	60.3	11.6			
9(Ma)	74.4	7.1	PS	62.3	11.1	Scale	M	SD
0(Si)	46.2	7.2	MAC-R	60.1	9.2	AGG	59.9	9.5
			APS	53.4	11.9	PSY	59.9	11.7
			AAS	52.2	10.8	CON	43.8	10.9
			MDS	54.9	10.2	NEN	56.1	9.8
			Ho	59.0	8.1	PEE	53.7	8.1
			CAL-R	47.9	11.8			

Content			Content Component					
Scale	M	SD	Scale	M	SD	Scale	M	SD
ANX	61.7	10.7	FRS1	55.2	12.9	ASP1	58.5	8.6
FRS	52.3	10.6	FRS2	49.7	10.1	ASP2	54.8	11.7
OBS	54.9	9.5	DEP1	57.6	10.8	TPA1	51.6	10.7
DEP	56.4	8.7	DEP2	54.6	11.5	TPA2	56.6	9.8
HEA	71.9	8.7	DEP3	52.4	10.3	LSE1	48.9	8.6
BIZ	59.0	9.7	DEP4	51.7	13.9	LSE2	49.7	8.8
ANG	57.8	11.9	HEA1	67.9	16.1	SOD1	46.3	8.5
CYN	61.3	10.7	HEA2	71.2	14.1	SOD2	44.3	7.8
ASP	59.4	9.9	HEA3	67.5	10.3	FAM1	55.0	10.8
TPA	55.8	11.6	BIZ1	55.3	12.0	FAM2	50.6	10.7
LSE	50.9	7.9	BIZ2	56.8	11.4	TRT1	52.2	11.3
SOD	45.7	8.2	ANG1	57.4	12.5	TRT2	50.0	9.4
FAM	55.8	10.1	ANG2	55.3	9.9			
WRK	56.3	9.5	CYN1	59.3	8.8			
TRT	54.1	9.3	CYN2	59.4	9.3			

Note. All scores are T scores except: Cannot Say, K & B and L & W critical items which are raw scores; True % and False % which are the percentage of items endorsed "true" or "false;" and \|F - FB\|, F - K, and O - S which are difference scores.

583

Appendix D-10

Prototypic Scores for 1-0/0-1 Codetypes (N = 65)

Demographics

Demographics			M	SD	Marital Status		%
	Age		40.0	12.9		Never Married	20.7
	Education		11.1	4.7		Married	53.4
	Gender		%			Separated	3.4
		Men	50.8			Divorced	17.2
		Women	49.2			Widowed	5.2

Test-Taking Scales

Omissions		M	SD	Consistency	M	SD
	?	0.9	2.3	VRIN	52.1	9.9
				|F - FB|	2.7	2.2
				TRIN	53.3	9.9

Accuracy of Item Endorsement

Underreporting		M	SD	Overreporting		M	SD
	False %	56.4	7.0		True %	42.4	7.1
Impression	L	54.8	9.4	Infrequency	F	59.7	11.7
Management	ODecp	46.5	7.7		FB	62.2	14.8
	Sd	47.9	9.1		F[p]	53.8	10.6
Superior	S	43.6	9.2	Critical Items	K & B	23.4	9.0
Adjustment					L & W	34.0	11.0
Self-Deception	K	41.0	8.9	Dissimulation	F - K	-3.7	7.0
	So	35.2	10.5		Ds	60.7	11.5
					O - S	94.2	56.0

Scales

Validity and Clinical			Supplementary			Morey et al. Overlapping Personality Disorder		
Scale	M	SD	Scale	M	SD	Scale	M	SD
?	0.9	2.3	A	61.1	9.8	PAR	58.7	10.0
L	54.8	9.4	R	59.4	9.8	SZD	46.5	8.9
F	59.7	11.7	Es	33.4	9.9	STY	50.3	8.6
K	41.0	8.9	TRIN	53.3	9.9	ANT	55.9	9.3
1(Hs)	72.1	5.5	VRIN	52.1	9.9	BDL	57.3	10.2
2(D)	63.9	6.6	O-H	48.7	10.0	HST	55.4	8.6
3(Hy)	60.1	6.5	Do	36.4	10.2	NAR	60.1	7.7
4(Pd)	49.9	7.5	Re	46.2	9.5	AVD	45.1	7.3
5(Mf)	49.4	9.8	GM	35.7	10.1	DEP	48.4	8.7
6(Pa)	53.6	10.9	GF	49.8	8.5	CPS	55.5	9.0
7(Pt)	59.1	8.2	Mt	64.2	8.9	Personality Psychopathology Five		
8(Sc)	56.9	10.3	PK	62.8	10.6	Scale	M	SD
9(Ma)	45.6	7.8	PS	64.6	10.8	AGG	47.1	12.1
0(Si)	71.4	5.1	MAC-R	46.8	10.6	PSY	56.2	10.5
			APS	46.9	9.0	CON	55.7	9.2
			AAS	48.5	9.3	NEN	59.5	10.9
			MDS	57.0	10.4	PEE	35.7	8.6
			Ho	59.0	8.1			
			CAL-R	47.9	11.8			

Content			Content Component					
Scale	M	SD	Scale	M	SD	Scale	M	SD
ANX	62.2	10.3	FRS1	59.3	14.5	ASP1	53.9	9.2
FRS	58.5	11.7	FRS2	55.9	10.6	ASP2	50.6	9.9
OBS	57.8	11.0	DEP1	59.5	11.9	TPA1	55.3	10.3
DEP	60.9	9.8	DEP2	60.7	12.8	TPA2	53.8	10.6
HEA	72.7	8.8	DEP3	56.3	10.2	LSE1	59.2	12.2
BIZ	54.0	8.7	DEP4	58.7	22.7	LSE2	58.6	10.1
ANG	57.8	11.9	HEA1	67.5	16.1	SOD1	68.1	7.8
CYN	59.2	11.4	HEA2	71.3	14.2	SOD2	64.6	5.6
ASP	54.0	10.3	HEA3	66.3	10.2	FAM1	54.2	11.5
TPA	55.8	12.9	BIZ1	51.2	9.4	FAM2	52.5	13.1
LSE	62.2	11.8	BIZ2	52.0	10.4	TRT1	62.0	15.1
SOD	70.7	8.0	ANG1	55.2	12.3	TRT2	58.1	10.5
FAM	55.4	11.3	ANG2	58.0	10.2			
WRK	63.0	9.5	CYN1	58.6	10.0			
TRT	63.0	11.9	CYN2	55.7	10.1			

Note. All scores are T scores except: Cannot Say, K & B and L & W critical items which are raw scores; True % and False % which are the percentage of items endorsed "true" or "false;" and \|F - FB\|, F - K, and O - S which are difference scores.

Appendix D-11

Prototypic Scores for Spike 2 Codetypes (N = 402)

Demographics

Demographics		M	SD	Marital Status	%
Age		40.9	14.3	Never Married	26.5
Education		12.5	5.4	Married	57.7
Gender		%		Separated	3.9
	Men	52.7		Divorced	9.7
	Women	47.3		Widowed	2.2

Test-Taking Scales

Omissions

Omissions		M	SD	Consistency	M	SD
	?	1.2	3.3	VRIN	54.3	9.7
				|F - FB|	3.1	2.1
				TRIN	49.8	11.7

Accuracy of Item Endorsement

Underreporting		M	SD	Overreporting		M	SD
	False %	61.1	6.0	True %		37.7	6.0
Impression	L	54.5	11.6	Infrequency	F	53.1	8.6
Management	ODecp	49.4	9.7		FB	51.4	8.7
	Sd	51.5	10.3		F[p]	51.2	10.0
Superior	S	49.3	8.4	Critical Items	K & B	17.6	6.6
Adjustment					L & W	22.5	7.4
Self-Deception	K	47.3	9.1	Dissimulation	F - K	-8.8	5.7
	So	44.6	7.8		Ds	51.1	8.1
					O - S	29.6	44.8

Scales

Validity and Clinical			Supplementary			Morey et al. Overlapping Personality Disorder		
Scale	M	SD	Scale	M	SD	Scale	M	SD
?	1.2	3.3	A	54.0	8.0	PAR	51.4	8.9
L	54.5	11.6	R	56.6	9.6	SZD	53.3	9.5
F	53.1	8.6	Es	44.1	7.9	STY	53.5	7.8
K	47.3	9.1	TRIN	49.8	11.7	ANT	48.2	8.7
1(Hs)	55.0	7.0	VRIN	54.3	9.7	BDL	50.3	9.5
2(D)	69.6	4.1	O-H	50.6	10.9	HST	44.5	8.1
3(Hy)	54.2	6.7	Do	43.9	9.4	NAR	44.9	8.7
4(Pd)	52.0	7.2	Re	50.2	8.8	AVD	54.9	7.7
5(Mf)	49.2	8.4	GM	45.0	8.7	DEP	54.3	10.0
6(Pa)	52.1	7.7	GF	51.8	8.5	CPS	51.7	9.4
7(Pt)	55.9	6.0	Mt	58.6	7.9	Personality Psychopathology Five		
8(Sc)	51.2	6.8	PK	55.1	8.1	Scale	M	SD
9(Ma)	44.9	6.8	PS	55.9	7.8	AGG	46.3	8.7
0(Si)	55.7	6.2	MAC-R	46.0	8.7	PSY	49.1	8.5
			APS	49.8	11.1	CON	53.5	8.9
			AAS	47.3	9.1	NEN	54.2	8.9
			MDS	53.2	9.9	PEE	41.5	8.5
			Ho	50.3	8.4			
			CAL-R	49.8	10.0			

Content			Content Component					
Scale	M	SD	Scale	M	SD	Scale	M	SD
ANX	59.0	8.4	FRS1	50.8	10.9	ASP1	49.5	8.6
FRS	51.4	10.1	FRS2	51.0	10.1	ASP2	48.0	8.4
OBS	51.3	8.5	DEP1	57.2	10.9	TPA1	49.3	9.8
DEP	58.0	7.9	DEP2	59.4	10.7	TPA2	49.0	10.0
HEA	54.7	7.2	DEP3	53.6	9.3	LSE1	53.1	9.6
BIZ	48.3	7.5	DEP4	50.5	11.9	LSE2	50.8	9.8
ANG	50.3	9.4	HEA1	53.0	10.5	SOD1	53.6	9.2
CYN	50.5	9.0	HEA2	49.8	8.9	SOD2	53.6	9.0
ASP	49.2	7.9	HEA3	58.8	10.9	FAM1	48.1	9.5
TPA	49.2	9.3	BIZ1	47.6	7.9	FAM2	51.3	11.2
LSE	53.6	8.3	BIZ2	47.1	7.1	TRT1	54.7	10.9
SOD	54.2	8.3	ANG1	48.1	8.6	TRT2	48.6	9.7
FAM	50.1	9.4	ANG2	51.7	10.2			
WRK	55.8	8.0	CYN1	51.1	9.6			
TRT	54.0	9.3	CYN2	48.8	9.1			

Note. All scores are T scores except: Cannot Say, K & B and L & W critical items which are raw scores; True % and False % which are the percentage of items endorsed "true" or "false;" and |F - FB|, F - K, and O - S which are difference scores.

585

Appendix D-12

Prototypic Scores for 2-3/3-2 Codetypes (N = 2,841)

Demographics

Demographics		M	SD	Marital Status		%
Age		41.5	12.3		Never Married	24.1
Education		12.6	4.9		Married	50.4
Gender		%			Separated	4.3
	Men	32.0			Divorced	18.7
	Women	68.0			Widowed	2.6

Test-Taking Scales

Omissions		M	SD	Consistency	M	SD
	?	1.6	3.9	VRIN	54.1	9.8
				|F - FB|	3.4	2.5
				TRIN	47.4	11.2

Accuracy of Item Endorsement

Underreporting		M	SD	Overreporting		M	SD
	False %	61.4	6.4		True %	37.3	6.4
Impression	L	57.5	10.8	Infrequency	F	62.5	13.2
Management	ODecp	47.0	9.3		FB	63.9	17.3
	Sd	48.1	10.3		F[p]	52.1	10.5
Superior	S	50.5	8.8	Critical Items	K & B	29.6	9.8
Adjustment					L & W	38.7	12.3
Self-Deception	K	49.6	8.8	Dissimulation	F - K	-7.3	6.6
	So	36.0	10.2		Ds	58.9	11.5
					O - S	70.9	59.6

Scales

Validity and Clinical | Supplementary | Morey et al. Overlapping Personality Disorder

Scale	M	SD	Scale	M	SD	Scale	M	SD
?	1.6	3.9	A	60.4	8.7	PAR	50.6	10.4
L	57.5	10.8	R	63.4	10.6	SZD	56.1	11.6
F	62.5	13.2	Es	30.2	11.5	STY	56.1	11.1
K	49.6	8.8	TRIN	47.4	11.2	ANT	45.4	9.0
1(Hs)	76.8	10.5	VRIN	54.1	9.8	BDL	51.3	8.7
2(D)	87.0	10.8	O-H	54.5	10.2	HST	40.8	10.5
3(Hy)	87.1	11.3	Do	39.5	10.0	NAR	40.9	10.2
4(Pd)	63.7	10.2	Re	51.9	9.2	AVD	56.6	10.1
5(Mf)	50.4	9.0	GM	40.4	9.7	DEP	56.4	10.6
6(Pa)	65.6	12.1	GF	50.7	8.3	CPS	52.0	8.8
7(Pt)	73.1	10.9	Mt	70.5	8.7	Personality Psychopathology Five		
8(Sc)	69.0	11.9	PK	67.1	11.3	Scale	M	SD
9(Ma)	48.2	8.5	PS	69.2	11.2	AGG	45.7	9.3
0(Si)	58.5	9.9	MAC-R	43.2	9.9	PSY	51.5	11.2
			APS	49.9	9.6	CON	56.4	9.5
			AAS	47.6	8.9	NEN	57.3	9.3
			MDS	59.7	11.2	PEE	30.6	11.7
			Ho	48.1	8.8			
			CAL-R	46.6	10.5			

Content | Content Component

Scale	M	SD	Scale	M	SD	Scale	M	SD
ANX	70.7	10.1	FRS1	56.2	14.9	ASP1	45.3	8.9
FRS	54.1	11.7	FRS2	51.6	10.3	ASP2	48.1	9.3
OBS	54.1	9.6	DEP1	70.1	13.6	TPA1	51.3	10.7
DEP	68.0	9.9	DEP2	70.2	10.2	TPA2	45.9	9.4
HEA	70.9	11.3	DEP3	58.7	9.2	LSE1	58.6	11.4
BIZ	51.5	9.8	DEP4	65.1	24.5	LSE2	50.0	10.0
ANG	51.8	10.4	HEA1	65.1	16.5	SOD1	58.6	11.6
CYN	48.4	8.9	HEA2	66.8	15.9	SOD2	50.6	9.8
ASP	45.9	8.3	HEA3	73.5	11.6	FAM1	48.0	10.7
TPA	48.1	9.5	BIZ1	50.0	10.7	FAM2	51.6	12.2
LSE	57.5	10.4	BIZ2	50.1	9.8	TRT1	63.4	14.6
SOD	56.6	11.2	ANG1	50.3	9.7	TRT2	49.3	10.0
FAM	50.5	11.0	ANG2	52.9	10.6			
WRK	62.9	10.2	CYN1	48.0	9.7			
TRT	60.3	11.8	CYN2	48.2	9.5			

Note. All scores are T scores except: Cannot Say, K & B and L & W critical items which are raw scores; True % and False % which are the percentage of items endorsed "true" or "false;" and |F - FB|, F - K, and O - S which are difference scores.

Appendix D-13

Prototypic Scores for 2-4/4-2 Codetypes (N = 855)

Demographics

Demographics		M	SD	Marital Status	%
Age		36.0	11.4	Never Married	41.1
Education		12.5	4.8	Married	35.0
Gender		%		Separated	6.4
	Men	36.6		Divorced	16.5
	Women	63.4		Widowed	1.0

Test-Taking Scales

Omissions		M	SD	Consistency	M	SD
	?	0.9	2.5	VRIN	54.4	9.8
				|F - FB|	4.1	2.8
				TRIN	47.3	10.6

Accuracy of Item Endorsement

Underreporting		M	SD	Overreporting		M	SD
	False %	57.3	6.5		True %	41.6	6.5
Impression	L	50.4	9.4	Infrequency	F	69.3	15.0
Management	ODecp	41.5	8.4		FB	67.7	18.1
	Sd	44.4	9.7		F[p]	55.7	12.6
Superior	S	43.6	8.5	Critical Items	K & B	31.8	10.5
Adjustment					L & W	37.2	12.2
Self-Deception	K	31.1	6.4	Dissimulation	F - K	-3.4	7.2
	So	34.3	10.7		Ds	65.0	12.3
					O - S	79.4	59.9

Scales

Validity and Clinical			Supplementary			Morey et al. Overlapping Personality Disorder		
Scale	M	SD	Scale	M	SD	Scale	M	SD
?	0.9	2.5	A	63.6	8.9	PAR	59.2	10.8
L	50.4	9.4	R	57.1	10.5	SZD	56.4	12.1
F	69.3	15.0	Es	36.3	10.8	STY	61.1	10.8
K	45.8	8.8	TRIN	47.3	10.6	ANT	57.4	10.5
1(Hs)	61.9	10.5	VRIN	54.4	9.8	BDL	56.9	10.0
2(D)	80.4	9.7	O-H	48.5	10.4	HST	43.6	10.8
3(Hy)	64.5	10.3	Do	37.4	10.6	NAR	41.5	10.2
4(Pd)	80.5	8.9	Re	41.2	10.9	AVD	60.8	9.8
5(Mf)	50.2	9.7	GM	41.3	8.6	DEP	63.1	10.9
6(Pa)	64.9	10.6	GF	46.2	10.4	CPS	54.0	8.6
7(Pt)	69.2	9.5	Mt	70.4	9.0	Personality Psychopathology Five		
8(Sc)	67.2	10.5	PK	69.8	11.0			
9(Ma)	49.9	8.6	PS	69.3	11.1	Scale	M	SD
0(Si)	61.0	9.4	MAC-R	50.4	11.3	AGG	47.0	10.2
			APS	53.2	10.1	PSY	55.5	10.8
			AAS	57.7	12.1	CON	46.8	10.1
			MDS	71.7	11.0	NEN	61.8	9.4
			Ho	55.5	9.3	PEE	30.9	11.7
			CAL-R	57.0	10.7			

Content			Content Component					
Scale	M	SD	Scale	M	SD	Scale	M	SD
ANX	68.4	10.2	FRS1	53.1	12.4	ASP1	51.8	9.4
FRS	50.6	10.3	FRS2	48.6	9.8	ASP2	58.6	13.2
OBS	57.0	10.3	DEP1	72.2	14.4	TPA1	53.0	10.7
DEP	72.1	10.3	DEP2	71.6	9.6	TPA2	51.2	10.1
HEA	60.5	10.0	DEP3	67.9	10.6	LSE1	64.6	12.2
BIZ	53.5	9.2	DEP4	66.9	26.3	LSE2	54.1	11.0
ANG	56.4	11.7	HEA1	57.8	13.4	SOD1	59.0	12.0
CYN	54.0	9.4	HEA2	53.5	11.5	SOD2	53.0	9.9
ASP	54.6	10.3	HEA3	65.1	12.6	FAM1	60.1	11.4
TPA	52.1	10.8	BIZ1	49.1	10.0	FAM2	64.0	14.5
LSE	62.8	11.3	BIZ2	53.6	10.5	TRT1	65.8	13.9
SOD	58.4	11.7	ANG1	54.3	11.4	TRT2	53.7	11.2
FAM	64.3	11.7	ANG2	56.2	10.6			
WRK	66.0	11.5	CYN1	53.8	9.5			
TRT	64.4	12.0	CYN2	53.0	9.8			

Note. All scores are T scores except: Cannot Say, K & B and L & W critical items which are raw scores; True % and False % which are the percentage of items endorsed "true" or "false;" and \|F - FB\|, F - K, and O - S which are difference scores.

Appendix D-14

Prototypic Scores for 2-5/5-2 Codetypes (N = 113)

Demographics

Demographics		M	SD	Marital Status		%
Age		38.9	11.6		Never Married	42.7
Education		12.3	6.0		Married	33.3
Gender		%			Separated	7.3
	Men	43.4			Divorced	15.6
	Women	56.6			Widowed	1.0

Test-Taking Scales

Omissions		M	SD	Consistency		M	SD
	?	2.5	5.3		VRIN	56.4	9.7
					|F - FB|	3.6	2.3
					TRIN	51.1	11.8

Accuracy of Item Endorsement

Underreporting		M	SD	Overreporting		M	SD
	False %	58.1	6.6		True %	40.4	6.8
Impression	L	53.6	11.8	Infrequency	F	58.9	10.4
Management	ODecp	48.5	13.1		FB	57.4	13.2
	Sd	49.8	12.5		F[p]	54.5	13.0
Superior	S	45.8	8.5	Critical Items	K & B	23.5	8.3
Adjustment					L & W	30.1	10.0
Self-Deception	K	31.1	6.4	Dissimulation	F - K	-6.2	5.7
	So	39.7	9.1		Ds	57.7	9.8
					O - S	59.6	52.8

Scales

Validity and Clinical | Supplementary | Morey et al. Overlapping Personality Disorder

Scale	M	SD	Scale	M	SD	Scale	M	SD
?	2.5	5.3	A	58.2	8.6	PAR	54.8	9.3
L	53.6	11.8	R	57.1	9.5	SZD	56.3	9.8
F	58.9	10.4	Es	39.9	9.6	STY	57.8	8.6
K	45.2	8.0	TRIN	51.1	11.8	ANT	51.4	9.3
1(Hs)	57.8	9.6	VRIN	56.4	9.7	BDL	53.6	10.1
2(D)	73.5	6.4	O-H	50.6	12.1	HST	43.4	9.2
3(Hy)	57.9	9.8	Do	39.8	11.1	NAR	45.4	10.5
4(Pd)	56.2	8.5	Re	46.6	10.5	AVD	58.0	9.8
5(Mf)	73.3	5.5	GM	41.4	12.6	DEP	57.6	12.4
6(Pa)	56.4	10.5	GF	48.6	15.8	CPS	53.6	9.5
7(Pt)	61.3	8.3	Mt	63.7	9.0	Personality		
8(Sc)	59.5	10.0	PK	61.5	9.0	Psychopathology Five		
9(Ma)	48.2	8.2	PS	61.7	9.5	Scale	M	SD
0(Si)	58.0	9.2	MAC-R	46.4	9.1	AGG	47.7	10.1
			APS	49.0	11.0	PSY	52.9	9.5
			AAS	50.1	8.5	CON	50.6	10.8
			MDS	58.6	10.3	NEN	57.3	9.1
			Ho	54.4	9.6	PEE	38.0	9.4
			CAL-R	50.5	10.1			

Content | Content Component

Scale	M	SD	Scale	M	SD	Scale	M	SD
ANX	62.8	9.3	FRS1	54.4	11.6	ASP1	52.8	10.4
FRS	53.0	10.9	FRS2	50.9	10.7	ASP2	51.0	9.8
OBS	53.9	9.8	DEP1	62.8	12.5	TPA1	53.0	10.0
DEP	63.0	10.2	DEP2	65.0	12.9	TPA2	50.5	9.6
HEA	58.6	9.2	DEP3	58.0	10.5	LSE1	58.4	10.7
BIZ	52.4	8.7	DEP4	54.4	19.4	LSE2	53.2	11.2
ANG	52.9	11.0	HEA1	56.4	12.9	SOD1	57.1	10.2
CYN	54.6	11.0	HEA2	54.9	12.6	SOD2	53.5	10.3
ASP	53.3	10.5	HEA3	61.5	11.5	FAM1	51.8	10.5
TPA	52.0	9.6	BIZ1	49.9	8.9	FAM2	53.8	12.1
LSE	57.9	9.6	BIZ2	51.6	9.3	TRT1	59.4	13.9
SOD	57.1	10.2	ANG1	50.4	10.5	TRT2	52.5	10.2
FAM	54.2	10.2	ANG2	54.5	10.3			
WRK	59.6	9.9	CYN1	54.6	11.1			
TRT	59.2	11.5	CYN2	52.6	10.2			

Note. All scores are T scores except: Cannot Say, K & B and L & W critical items which are raw scores; True % and False % which are the percentage of items endorsed "true" or "false;" and |F - FB|, F - K, and O - S which are difference scores.

Appendix D-15

Prototypic Scores for 2-6/6-2 Codetypes (N = 1,104)

Demographics

Demographics		M	SD	Marital Status	%
Age		38.2	11.8	Never Married	32.3
Education		12.2	5.4	Married	40.8
Gender		%		Separated	5.9
	Men	36.1		Divorced	19.4
	Women	63.9		Widowed	1.6

Test-Taking Scales

Omissions		M	SD	Consistency		M	SD
	?	1.7	4.3		VRIN	55.2	10.6
					|F - FB|	3.9	2.9
					TRIN	50.7	11.6

Accuracy of Item Endorsement

Underreporting		M	SD	Overreporting		M	SD
	False %	54.8	7.1		True %	43.9	7.1
Impression	L	54.0	10.4	Infrequency	F	73.3	18.2
Management	ODecp	44.6	9.3		FB	75.3	22.0
	Sd	47.5	10.4		F[p]	57.7	14.3
Superior	S	44.1	8.7	Critical Items	K & B	37.2	11.8
Adjustment					L & W	44.5	14.6
Self-Deception	K	31.1	6.4	Dissimulation	F - K	-0.6	7.8
	So	30.0	10.7		Ds	66.5	13.2
					O - S	118.4	68.5

Scales

Validity and Clinical

Scale	M	SD
?	1.7	4.3
L	54.0	10.4
F	73.3	18.2
K	42.5	8.1
1(Hs)	68.0	13.1
2(D)	84.6	11.3
3(Hy)	68.8	12.6
4(Pd)	66.0	10.5
5(Mf)	51.0	9.3
6(Pa)	85.2	12.0
7(Pt)	72.5	11.0
8(Sc)	71.8	13.7
9(Ma)	49.6	8.4
0(Si)	64.9	10.0

Supplementary

Scale	M	SD
A	66.5	9.1
R	59.3	10.6
Es	28.1	13.1
TRIN	50.7	11.6
VRIN	55.2	10.6
O-H	50.3*	10.1
Do	36.4	11.0
Re	45.3	9.8
GM	37.5	10.0
GF	47.8	9.1
Mt	72.7	9.2
PK	74.6	12.2
PS	74.7	12.3
MAC-R	47.2	10.2
APS	51.2	9.6
AAS	51.5	11.3
MDS	66.3	12.0
Ho	57.4	9.8
CAL-R	51.2	10.9

Morey et al. Overlapping Personality Disorder

Scale	M	SD
PAR	66.2	12.6
SZD	61.6	12.0
STY	69.8	12.5
ANT	49.9	10.0
BDL	56.4	9.0
HST	38.1	10.9
NAR	38.7	10.1
AVD	64.9	9.7
DEP	62.2	11.5
CPS	56.9	8.7

Personality Psychopathology Five

Scale	M	SD
AGG	47.5	10.3
PSY	65.7	15.7
CON	54.7	10.0
NEN	63.6	9.1
PEE	29.3	12.4

Content

Scale	M	SD
ANX	73.8	9.8
FRS	56.2	13.3
OBS	60.4	10.6
DEP	73.7	10.6
HEA	67.4	12.7
BIZ	61.5	12.6
ANG	57.5	11.3
CYN	55.1	10.6
ASP	50.1	9.2
TPA	53.9	10.8
LSE	64.2	11.7
SOD	63.9	12.1
FAM	56.5	12.1
WRK	68.9	11.8
TRT	67.9	13.0

Content Component

Scale	M	SD	Scale	M	SD
FRS1	60.7	18.3	ASP1	49.5	9.4
FRS2	51.7	10.4	ASP2	50.4	10.8
DEP1	74.5	15.1	TPA1	54.8	10.3
DEP2	73.5	9.4	TPA2	52.7	10.1
DEP3	65.5	10.9	LSE1	65.0	11.8
DEP4	72.5	26.7	LSE2	55.8	11.5
HEA1	64.7	16.9	SOD1	63.8	12.0
HEA2	62.4	15.7	SOD2	57.4	9.6
HEA3	68.3	13.0	FAM1	53.0	11.8
BIZ1	61.6	18.6	FAM2	55.1	13.2
BIZ2	59.9	12.9	TRT1	69.5	15.7
ANG1	54.8	11.4	TRT2	54.8	10.7
ANG2	57.8	10.1			
CYN1	53.4	10.3			
CYN2	55.7	10.2			

Note. All scores are T scores except: Cannot Say, K & B and L & W critical items which are raw scores; True % and False % which are the percentage of items endorsed "true" or "false;" and \|F - FB\|, F - K, and O - S which are difference scores.

589

Appendix D-16

Prototypic Scores for 2-7/7-2 Codetypes (N = 1,934)

Demographics

Demographics		M	SD	Marital Status		%
Age		38.6	13.0		Never Married	32.6
Education		12.5	5.1		Married	48.0
Gender		%			Separated	3.6
	Men	45.9			Divorced	14.2
	Women	54.1			Widowed	1.5

Test-Taking Scales

Omissions		M	SD	Consistency		M	SD
	?	1.3	3.5		VRIN	53.9	9.7
					|F - FB|	3.4	2.6
					TRIN	51.0	10.7

Accuracy of Item Endorsement

Underreporting		M	SD	Overreporting		M	SD
	False %	55.7	6.5		True %	43.1	6.5
Impression	L	51.6	10.1	Infrequency	F	67.1	14.1
Management	ODecp	40.5	8.3		FB	72.1	19.6
	Sd	43.5	9.7		F[p]	54.4	11.6
Superior	S	44.6	8.4	Critical Items	K & B	33.7	9.7
Adjustment					L & W	40.0	12.0
Self-Deception	K	31.1	6.4	Dissimulation	F - K	-3.8	6.7
	So	28.6	10.0		Ds	64.6	12.1
					O - S	103.5	58.7

Scales

Validity and Clinical			Supplementary			Morey et al. Overlapping Personality Disorder		
Scale	M	SD	Scale	M	SD	Scale	M	SD
?	1.3	3.5	A	69.4	8.4	PAR	57.5	10.9
L	51.6	10.1	R	60.9	10.7	SZD	60.9	11.5
F	67.1	14.1	Es	28.3	12.1	STY	65.3	10.7
K	45.6	8.3	TRIN	51.0	10.7	ANT	50.6	10.2
1(Hs)	67.3	11.1	VRIN	53.9	9.7	BDL	55.3	9.1
2(D)	85.7	10.5	O-H	48.1	10.3	HST	36.8	10.3
3(Hy)	68.4	11.3	Do	33.0	9.9	NAR	34.5	10.3
4(Pd)	64.0	10.4	Re	45.9	10.0	AVD	67.6	9.3
5(Mf)	51.0	9.5	GM	35.3	9.7	DEP	68.7	11.1
6(Pa)	66.0	11.0	GF	50.0	9.0	CPS	57.1	8.5
7(Pt)	82.8	9.4	Mt	74.9	8.1	Personality Psychopathology Five		
8(Sc)	72.0	11.0	PK	73.5	11.6	Scale	M	SD
9(Ma)	47.4	8.5	PS	75.3	11.2	AGG	41.3	10.2
0(Si)	67.5	9.3	MAC-R	44.6	10.2	PSY	56.8	11.6
			APS	52.4	9.4	CON	55.0	10.1
			AAS	51.3	11.1	NEN	63.9	9.1
			MDS	63.8	11.6	PEE	27.5	12.3
			Ho	54.0	9.4			
			CAL-R	50.3	11.3			

Content			Content Component					
Scale	M	SD	Scale	M	SD	Scale	M	SD
ANX	74.5	9.5	FRS1	61.3	17.3	ASP1	50.2	9.6
FRS	56.8	12.4	FRS2	52.5	10.4	ASP2	50.2	11.1
OBS	63.5	10.1	DEP1	75.0	14.3	TPA1	55.2	10.2
DEP	73.7	9.9	DEP2	73.8	9.6	TPA2	50.0	9.7
HEA	64.8	11.0	DEP3	66.4	9.8	LSE1	68.6	11.3
BIZ	54.7	10.2	DEP4	69.8	26.0	LSE2	60.1	11.8
ANG	55.5	11.1	HEA1	60.8	15.1	SOD1	63.7	11.7
CYN	52.6	9.9	HEA2	59.2	14.1	SOD2	60.3	9.2
ASP	50.7	9.6	HEA3	67.5	13.0	FAM1	52.4	11.1
TPA	51.9	10.2	BIZ1	50.9	11.4	FAM2	53.9	12.7
LSE	68.7	11.6	BIZ2	54.9	11.3	TRT1	71.8	15.0
SOD	65.1	11.9	ANG1	52.1	10.9	TRT2	55.7	10.7
FAM	55.1	11.2	ANG2	57.3	10.4			
WRK	70.9	10.3	CYN1	52.4	10.2			
TRT	68.8	12.4	CYN2	51.4	9.6			

Note. All scores are T scores except: Cannot Say, K & B and L & W critical items which are raw scores; True % and False % which are the percentage of items endorsed "true" or "false;" and |F - FB|, F - K, and O - S which are difference scores.

Appendix D-17
Prototypic Scores for 2-8/8-2 Codetypes (N = 1,075)

Demographics

Demographics		M	SD	Marital Status	%
Age		38.9	13.2	Never Married	34.4
Education		11.4	5.1	Married	40.9
Gender		%		Separated	3.1
	Men	33.3		Divorced	18.8
	Women	66.7		Widowed	2.8

Test-Taking Scales

Omissions		M	SD	Consistency		M	SD
	?	1.4	3.6	VRIN		55.0	10.8
				|F - FB|		4.2	3.1
				TRIN		52.4	11.7

Accuracy of Item Endorsement

Underreporting		M	SD	Overreporting		M	SD
	False %	49.8	6.9	True %		49.0	7.0
Impression	L	51.5	10.6	Infrequency	F	87.9	18.0
Management	ODecp	41.3	9.1		FB	94.1	23.9
	Sd	44.0	10.2		F[p]	68.1	16.9
Superior	S	38.9	8.0	Critical Items	K & B	43.8	11.1
Adjustment					L & W	54.9	14.5
Self-Deception	K	31.1	6.4	Dissimulation	F - K	5.2	8.0
	So	21.7	10.6		Ds	79.2	13.7
					O - S	165.6	64.0

Scales

Validity and Clinical

Scale	M	SD
?	1.4	3.6
L	51.5	10.6
F	87.9	18.0
K	40.0	7.6
1(Hs)	75.4	12.4
2(D)	89.7	10.5
3(Hy)	73.4	12.7
4(Pd)	71.0	11.2
5(Mf)	53.0	9.6
6(Pa)	74.3	12.9
7(Pt)	80.4	10.5
8(Sc)	90.1	11.6
9(Ma)	55.4	9.6
0(Si)	70.4	9.3

Supplementary

Scale	M	SD
A	72.6	8.3
R	59.6	10.5
Es	19.8	12.7
TRIN	52.4	11.7
VRIN	55.0	10.8
O-H	46.0	9.9
Do	29.9	10.5
Re	41.0	10.4
GM	33.4	10.3
GF	43.6	10.3
Mt	78.3	8.0
PK	84.3	12.3
PS	85.1	11.1
MAC-R	49.5	11.1
APS	49.8	9.7
AAS	55.7	12.5
MDS	74.3	11.8
Ho	62.9	9.4
CAL-R	53.6	11.0

Morey et al. Overlapping Personality Disorder

Scale	M	SD
PAR	67.4	12.0
SZD	67.2	11.0
STY	74.4	11.7
ANT	56.9	10.5
BDL	58.5	8.8
HST	34.7	10.3
NAR	36.9	10.0
AVD	69.3	9.2
DEP	67.4	11.9
CPS	59.2	8.5

Personality Psychopathology Five

Scale	M	SD
AGG	48.8	10.7
PSY	70.4	15.7
CON	52.0	11.0
NEN	67.6	9.4
PEE	23.6	12.3

Content

Scale	M	SD
ANX	77.1	10.0
FRS	61.6	14.6
OBS	66.4	10.8
DEP	80.2	10.2
HEA	75.5	13.0
BIZ	67.1	12.7
ANG	61.8	10.8
CYN	61.8	10.5
ASP	57.4	10.2
TPA	58.4	11.4
LSE	72.5	12.5
SOD	69.7	11.4
FAM	66.7	12.8
WRK	76.6	10.7
TRT	77.4	12.3

Content Component

Scale	M	SD	Scale	M	SD
FRS1	70.0	20.6	ASP1	56.6	9.2
FRS2	53.3	10.2	ASP2	54.0	12.2
DEP1	84.2	13.3	TPA1	59.2	9.5
DEP2	73.9	9.2	TPA2	55.8	10.6
DEP3	71.0	10.7	LSE1	71.6	12.0
DEP4	87.4	29.0	LSE2	60.3	11.5
HEA1	69.1	17.2	SOD1	69.7	11.2
HEA2	75.4	17.3	SOD2	59.7	8.7
HEA3	72.9	12.4	FAM1	62.0	11.7
BIZ1	62.7	18.9	FAM2	62.5	15.0
BIZ2	68.4	13.4	TRT1	78.8	14.6
ANG1	58.8	11.5	TRT2	61.2	10.2
ANG2	61.3	8.8			
CYN1	60.4	9.2			
CYN2	59.0	9.4			

Note. All scores are T scores except: Cannot Say, K & B and L & W critical items which are raw scores; True % and False % which are the percentage of items endorsed "true" or "false;" and |F - FB|, F - K, and O - S which are difference scores.

Appendix D-18

Prototypic Scores for 2-9/9-2 Codetypes (N = 36)

Demographics

Demographics		M	SD	Marital Status	%
Age		35.0	10.8	Never Married	32.4
Education		10.3	6.0	Married	52.9
Gender		%		Separated	5.9
	Men	33.3		Divorced	8.8
	Women	66.7		Widowed	0.0

Test-Taking Scales

Omissions		M	SD	Consistency	M	SD
	?	1.8	4.1	VRIN	54.4	7.3
				|F - FB|	3.6	2.9
				TRIN	56.3	13.3

Accuracy of Item Endorsement

Underreporting		M	SD	Overreporting		M	SD
	False %	53.1	6.4	True %		45.6	6.2
Impression	L	55.4	11.3	Infrequency	F	61.0	10.7
Management	ODecp	51.9	9.8		FB	59.0	10.7
	Sd	55.2	9.4		F[p]	55.2	12.2
Superior	S	41.9	6.7	Critical Items	K & B	26.5	8.2
Adjustment					L & W	36.1	10.6
Self-Deception	K	31.1	6.4	Dissimulation	F - K	-3.6	6.3
	So	37.4	10.1		Ds	61.3	10.9
					O - S	85.0	48.6

Scales

Validity and Clinical			Supplementary			Morey et al. Overlapping Personality Disorder		
Scale	M	SD	Scale	M	SD	Scale	M	SD
?	1.8	4.1	A	60.7	9.5	PAR	58.9	9.7
L	55.4	11.3	R	49.2	8.8	SZD	50.7	10.2
F	61.0	10.7	Es	34.2	10.8	STY	55.2	9.0
K	41.1	7.6	TRIN	56.3	13.3	ANT	55.1	8.3
1(Hs)	61.2	8.0	VRIN	54.4	7.3	BDL	59.2	9.4
2(D)	72.5	4.5	O-H	46.2	11.1	HST	51.8	8.4
3(Hy)	59.2	10.0	Do	35.2	10.9	NAR	52.8	6.9
4(Pd)	57.1	9.6	Re	42.9	11.5	AVD	51.3	7.8
5(Mf)	51.0	10.7	GM	43.2	9.5	DEP	52.3	11.5
6(Pa)	54.6	10.0	GF	43.1	9.0	CPS	55.7	9.1
7(Pt)	59.9	8.4	Mt	66.4	8.0	Personality Psychopathology Five		
8(Sc)	61.9	6.8	PK	65.2	10.4	Scale	M	SD
9(Ma)	72.9	6.3	PS	67.1	11.0	AGG	54.8	8.3
0(Si)	53.0	7.0	MAC-R	55.1	9.2	PSY	60.5	10.2
			APS	52.1	13.1	CON	46.0	10.0
			AAS	49.3	9.0	NEN	59.2	9.6
			MDS	61.1	11.7	PEE	46.3	8.6
			Ho	58.9	9.0			
			CAL-R	53.8	11.4			

Content			Content Component					
Scale	M	SD	Scale	M	SD	Scale	M	SD
ANX	64.3	9.8	FRS1	54.9	11.2	ASP1	59.4	7.5
FRS	51.8	11.0	FRS2	49.3	11.5	ASP2	52.1	10.7
OBS	55.9	10.5	DEP1	65.8	11.4	TPA1	54.7	6.7
DEP	63.9	7.6	DEP2	66.1	11.9	TPA2	57.4	11.6
HEA	63.1	9.8	DEP3	58.6	11.2	LSE1	55.4	8.6
BIZ	56.3	9.0	DEP4	52.6	12.4	LSE2	52.9	11.0
ANG	58.5	10.7	HEA1	58.0	15.4	SOD1	50.8	9.0
CYN	61.0	9.9	HEA2	61.3	11.4	SOD2	48.7	9.1
ASP	59.1	8.0	HEA3	67.1	12.8	FAM1	55.8	12.5
TPA	57.7	11.0	BIZ1	53.9	10.4	FAM2	52.6	12.6
LSE	56.4	8.4	BIZ2	54.5	10.5	TRT1	58.2	12.4
SOD	50.8	8.1	ANG1	56.1	9.7	TRT2	52.8	10.0
FAM	55.2	11.4	ANG2	57.9	10.0			
WRK	63.1	9.2	CYN1	60.8	8.2			
TRT	59.6	9.6	CYN2	57.1	8.7			

Note. All scores are T scores except: Cannot Say, K & B and L & W critical items which are raw scores; True % and False % which are the percentage of items endorsed "true" or "false;" and \|F - FB\|, F - K, and O - S which are difference scores.

Appendix D-19

Prototypic Scores for 2-0/0-2 Codetypes (N = 665)

Demographics

Demographics		M	SD	Marital Status		%
Age		39.7	12.7		Never Married	30.1
Education		12.5	5.2		Married	49.7
Gender		%			Separated	3.5
	Men	51.0			Divorced	15.1
	Women	49.0			Widowed	1.7

Test-Taking Scales

Omissions / Consistency

Omissions		M	SD	Consistency	M	SD
	?	1.0	2.7	VRIN	53.1	9.8
				|F - FB|	3.6	2.6
				TRIN	50.3	11.0

Accuracy of Item Endorsement

Underreporting		M	SD	Overreporting		M	SD
	False %	57.2	5.8		True %	41.7	5.9
Impression	L	51.6	9.9	Infrequency	F	62.5	11.8
Management	ODecp	40.7	8.3		FB	63.0	15.6
	Sd	43.1	9.0		F[p]	52.6	10.6
Superior	S	43.0	7.5	Critical Items	K & B	27.4	9.3
Adjustment					L & W	32.1	10.2
Self-Deception	K	31.1	6.4	Dissimulation	F - K	-2.9	6.0
	So	31.5	9.4		Ds	60.7	10.2
					O - S	94.2	51.5

Scales

Validity and Clinical / Supplementary / Morey et al. Overlapping Personality Disorder

Scale	M	SD	Scale	M	SD	Scale	M	SD
?	1.0	2.7	A	66.0	8.5	PAR	58.3	10.0
L	51.6	9.9	R	62.1	8.9	SZD	68.4	7.5
F	62.5	11.8	Es	35.4	10.3	STY	70.0	7.4
K	40.8	7.4	TRIN	50.3	11.0	ANT	51.7	8.6
1(Hs)	58.3	10.6	VRIN	53.1	9.8	BDL	51.9	8.4
2(D)	77.6	8.5	O-H	46.0*	10.2	HST	30.4	6.7
3(Hy)	55.7	10.1	Do	35.6	9.4	NAR	31.9	7.6
4(Pd)	56.8	9.1	Re	47.6	8.9	AVD	72.0	6.0
5(Mf)	50.7	8.7	GM	36.8	9.2	DEP	66.6	10.8
6(Pa)	57.0	9.7	GF	49.8	8.6	CPS	57.0	8.6
7(Pt)	65.1	8.4	Mt	69.8	8.9	Personality Psychopathology Five		
8(Sc)	60.2	9.4	PK	67.5	10.4	Scale	M	SD
9(Ma)	42.5	7.0	PS	68.0	10.4	AGG	40.7	9.3
0(Si)	74.7	5.7	MAC-R	41.5	9.8	PSY	54.8	9.5
			APS	49.0	8.7	CON	55.6	9.0
			AAS	49.6	9.8	NEN	61.6	8.8
			MDS	64.2	11.5	PEE	26.5	9.5
			Ho	57.0	8.5			
			CAL-R	49.1	11.0			

Content / Content Component

Scale	M	SD	Scale	M	SD	Scale	M	SD
ANX	68.0	9.9	FRS1	54.4	12.4	ASP1	53.1	8.4
FRS	53.7	10.3	FRS2	52.2	9.8	ASP2	49.6	9.9
OBS	59.7	9.5	DEP1	68.5	14.8	TPA1	55.9	10.2
DEP	68.8	9.9	DEP2	70.3	11.3	TPA2	50.5	9.1
HEA	59.8	10.5	DEP3	63.3	9.8	LSE1	66.7	11.5
BIZ	50.9	8.5	DEP4	61.1	21.7	LSE2	61.0	11.5
ANG	55.2	10.7	HEA1	55.8	13.1	SOD1	70.4	7.5
CYN	56.3	9.5	HEA2	54.9	13.1	SOD2	65.4	6.0
ASP	52.7	8.5	HEA3	61.8	13.0	FAM1	54.0	10.7
TPA	52.8	9.8	BIZ1	48.4	8.8	FAM2	56.1	12.9
LSE	67.1	10.9	BIZ2	50.5	9.4	TRT1	68.6	14.5
SOD	72.9	7.7	ANG1	51.4	10.5	TRT2	56.7	10.6
FAM	56.4	10.5	ANG2	57.4	10.0			
WRK	67.9	9.9	CYN1	56.6	9.1			
TRT	67.1	11.8	CYN2	53.6	9.1			

Note. All scores are T scores except: Cannot Say, K & B and L & W critical items which are raw scores; True % and False % which are the percentage of items endorsed "true" or "false;" and |F - FB|, F - K, and O - S which are difference scores.

Appendix D-20

Prototypic Scores for Spike 3 Codetypes (N = 784)

Demographics

Demographics		M	SD	Marital Status	%
	Age	40.9	12.3	Never Married	21.9
	Education	13.6	5.7	Married	47.1
	Gender	%		Separated	11.3
	Men	47.4		Divorced	17.5
	Women	52.6		Widowed	2.2

Test-Taking Scales

Omissions		M	SD	Consistency		M	SD
	?	1.2	3.1		VRIN	45.1	9.5
					|F - FB|	2.4	1.7
					TRIN	46.5	9.3

Accuracy of Item Endorsement

Underreporting		M	SD	Overreporting		M	SD
	False %	67.4	4.6		True %	31.4	4.6
Impression	L	57.1	10.5	Infrequency	F	46.8	6.4
Management	ODecp	53.9	9.4		FB	45.6	4.9
	Sd	52.3	9.8		F[p]	47.4	7.6
Superior	S	59.5	8.3	Critical Items	K & B	8.7	5.5
Adjustment					L & W	15.2	6.8
Self-Deception	K	31.1	6.4	Dissimulation	F - K	-16.3	4.9
	So	55.5	6.6		Ds	44.2	6.8
					O - S	-43.8	39.4

Scales

Validity and Clinical			Supplementary			Morey et al. Overlapping Personality Disorder		
Scale	M	SD	Scale	M	SD	Scale	M	SD
?	1.2	3.1	A	43.0	5.9	PAR	41.4	6.3
L	57.1	10.5	R	57.3	8.5	SZD	45.8	7.6
F	46.8	6.4	Es	51.4	7.0	STY	42.4	6.4
K	59.0	8.5	TRIN	46.5	9.3	ANT	42.2	7.5
1(Hs)	58.3	4.7	VRIN	45.1	9.5	BDL	43.4	7.9
2(D)	53.2	6.5	O-H	58.6	9.3	HST	50.2	8.2
3(Hy)	68.3	3.3	Do	53.1	7.6	NAR	50.4	7.4
4(Pd)	54.3	6.1	Re	55.7	8.1	AVD	43.0	6.0
5(Mf)	49.7	7.4	GM	52.3	7.3	DEP	47.1	6.9
6(Pa)	52.4	6.7	GF	52.9	7.9	CPS	43.8	8.5
7(Pt)	51.7	6.3	Mt	46.1	7.1	Personality Psychopathology Five		
8(Sc)	50.5	6.2	PK	45.1	6.2	Scale	M	SD
9(Ma)	47.6	6.3	PS	45.4	6.2	AGG	46.7	7.2
0(Si)	43.9	6.5	MAC-R	45.4	7.7	PSY	43.6	6.3
			APS	47.0	9.9	CON	53.0	8.6
			AAS	45.6	7.8	NEN	44.9	7.7
			MDS	47.2	8.0	PEE	49.8	7.6
			Ho	40.6	6.3			
			CAL-R	49.6	9.0			

Content			Content Component					
Scale	M	SD	Scale	M	SD	Scale	M	SD
ANX	49.8	7.8	FRS1	46.7	6.5	ASP1	40.5	6.8
FRS	47.9	7.9	FRS2	48.6	9.5	ASP2	47.5	8.6
OBS	42.9	6.6	DEP1	47.0	6.4	TPA1	43.0	8.7
DEP	46.2	7.2	DEP2	47.4	8.8	TPA2	42.1	8.0
HEA	52.3	7.1	DEP3	45.1	6.6	LSE1	43.6	5.9
BIZ	45.7	6.9	DEP4	46.3	5.1	LSE2	44.5	6.8
ANG	43.6	8.1	HEA1	49.3	8.4	SOD1	46.0	7.0
CYN	41.8	6.4	HEA2	48.6	8.1	SOD2	43.0	6.6
ASP	42.0	6.6	HEA3	54.2	10.8	FAM1	43.2	8.2
TPA	42.4	7.1	BIZ1	45.8	6.0	FAM2	49.4	9.9
LSE	43.5	6.8	BIZ2	44.6	5.6	TRT1	45.2	5.9
SOD	44.7	6.4	ANG1	44.7	7.2	TRT2	42.4	6.6
FAM	45.5	8.6	ANG2	43.5	8.6			
WRK	44.4	6.9	CYN1	41.0	7.0			
TRT	43.0	6.4	CYN2	42.6	7.3			

Note. All scores are T scores except: Cannot Say, K & B and L & W critical items which are raw scores; True % and False % which are the percentage of items endorsed "true" or "false;" and |F - FB|, F - K, and O - S which are difference scores.

Appendix D-21

Prototypic Scores for 3-4/4-3 Codetypes (N = 752)

Demographics

Demographics		M	SD	Marital Status		%
Age		37.6	11.1		Never Married	31.2
Education		13.2	5.1		Married	38.5
Gender		%			Separated	11.2
	Men	39.6			Divorced	17.3
	Women	60.4			Widowed	1.9

Test-Taking Scales

Omissions		M	SD	Consistency		M	SD
	?	1.1	3.1		VRIN	51.3	9.7
					|F - FB|	3.6	2.6
					TRIN	43.9	10.7

Accuracy of Item Endorsement

Underreporting		M	SD	Overreporting		M	SD
	False %	63.8	6.6		True %	35.0	6.7
Impression	L	52.6	10.3	Infrequency	F	58.0	12.8
Management	ODecp	46.7	8.5		FB	54.8	13.5
	Sd	47.8	9.2		F[p]	51.1	10.8
Superior	S	52.5	10.1	Critical Items	K & B	20.7	11.5
Adjustment					L & W	28.6	13.3
Self-Deception	K	31.1	6.4	Dissimulation	F - K	-11.4	7.4
	So	46.5	10.8		Ds	55.1	12.3
					O - S	6.2	64.4

Scales

Validity and Clinical			Supplementary			Morey et al. Overlapping Personality Disorder		
Scale	M	SD	Scale	M	SD	Scale	M	SD
?	1.1	3.1	A	51.8	9.8	PAR	48.0	10.3
L	52.6	10.3	R	55.7	9.7	SZD	46.2	9.4
F	58.0	12.8	Es	44.2	10.5	STY	47.5	8.4
K	55.8	9.9	TRIN	43.9	10.7	ANT	51.7	10.9
1(Hs)	65.2	8.9	VRIN	51.3	9.7	BDL	51.6	10.6
2(D)	63.9	10.6	O-H	55.4	10.0	HST	51.1	8.7
3(Hy)	76.5	9.0	Do	47.6	10.0	NAR	49.0	8.5
4(Pd)	77.5	9.1	Re	47.7	10.5	AVD	47.3	7.4
5(Mf)	50.6	9.2	GM	47.6	8.6	DEP	53.1	9.0
6(Pa)	61.6	9.6	GF	47.9	10.4	CPS	47.1	9.3
7(Pt)	62.7	9.6	Mt	58.2	11.9	Personality Psychopathology Five		
8(Sc)	62.4	9.9	PK	57.7	12.2			
9(Ma)	52.7	9.5	PS	57.7	12.2	Scale	M	SD
0(Si)	47.7	7.6	MAC-R	49.5	10.2	AGG	48.0	9.0
			APS	52.2	9.8	PSY	48.6	9.8
			AAS	54.2	11.5	CON	47.0	10.0
			MDS	62.1	11.6	NEN	53.0	10.2
			Ho	45.6	8.9	PEE	43.0	10.0
			CAL-R	54.9	10.9			

Content			Content Component					
Scale	M	SD	Scale	M	SD	Scale	M	SD
ANX	59.1	11.4	FRS1	49.2	8.7	ASP1	44.0	8.9
FRS	48.8	8.3	FRS2	48.6	9.5	ASP2	56.4	12.6
OBS	48.0	9.3	DEP1	58.4	13.3	TPA1	46.5	10.2
DEP	59.3	11.4	DEP2	60.9	12.6	TPA2	45.3	9.5
HEA	59.3	10.9	DEP3	55.9	11.8	LSE1	51.5	10.7
BIZ	50.4	9.1	DEP4	54.4	18.4	LSE2	46.5	8.1
ANG	51.0	11.7	HEA1	54.9	12.8	SOD1	48.5	8.9
CYN	45.4	8.2	HEA2	55.0	12.6	SOD2	43.1	6.9
ASP	47.5	9.1	HEA3	60.5	12.8	FAM1	53.6	11.2
TPA	45.8	9.3	BIZ1	47.7	8.8	FAM2	59.4	13.8
LSE	50.5	9.5	BIZ2	49.8	9.4	TRT1	52.1	11.4
SOD	46.6	7.9	ANG1	51.4	11.6	TRT2	46.4	9.2
FAM	57.7	11.5	ANG2	49.8	10.8			
WRK	52.7	10.8	CYN1	44.6	9.0			
TRT	51.2	10.8	CYN2	45.8	8.9			

Note. All scores are T scores except: Cannot Say, K & B and L & W critical items which are raw scores; True % and False % which are the percentage of items endorsed "true" or "false;" and |F - FB|, F - K, and O - S which are difference scores.

Appendix D-22

Prototypic Scores for 3-5/5-3 Codetypes (N = 114)

Demographics

Demographics		M	SD	Marital Status	%
Age		39.1	12.4	Never Married	40.4
Education		12.8	6.2	Married	45.5
Gender		%		Separated	6.1
	Men	36.8		Divorced	8.1
	Women	63.2		Widowed	0.0

Test-Taking Scales

Omissions		M	SD	Consistency		M	SD
	?	1.9	4.7	VRIN		48.1	10.9
				|F - FB|		2.7	2.0
				TRIN		47.9	11.1

Accuracy of Item Endorsement

Underreporting		M	SD	Overreporting		M	SD
	False %	66.0	5.5	True %		32.7	5.5
Impression	L	58.8	11.1	Infrequency	F	49.7	7.8
Management	ODecp	56.2	11.5		FB	47.3	5.9
	Sd	54.5	9.9		F[p]	50.7	10.6
Superior	S	57.6	10.1	Critical Items	K & B	11.9	7.6
Adjustment					L & W	19.3	9.5
Self-Deception	K	31.1	6.4	Dissimulation	F - K	-15.2	6.1
	So	52.9	8.2		Ds	47.1	9.1
					O - S	-27.5	49.6

Scales

Validity and Clinical			Supplementary			Morey et al. Overlapping Personality Disorder		
Scale	M	SD	Scale	M	SD	Scale	M	SD
?	1.9	4.7	A	45.2	7.9	PAR	43.9	7.5
L	58.8	11.1	R	57.3	8.6	SZD	45.9	8.2
F	49.7	7.8	Es	50.0	8.9	STY	43.3	6.6
K	58.5	9.4	TRIN	47.9	11.1	ANT	44.3	9.5
1(Hs)	62.0	6.0	VRIN	48.1	10.9	BDL	45.1	8.4
2(D)	55.5	7.8	O-H	58.9*	10.2	HST	51.3	8.1
3(Hy)	70.4	5.6	Do	50.5	8.9	NAR	51.3	8.3
4(Pd)	56.1	7.5	Re	53.9	9.1	AVD	43.2	6.9
5(Mf)	70.4	4.6	GM	51.6	10.5	DEP	46.9	9.9
6(Pa)	52.6	9.1	GF	48.6	13.1	CPS	43.8	9.0
7(Pt)	54.2	8.0	Mt	49.8	9.6	Personality Psychopathology Five		
8(Sc)	54.4	7.5	PK	47.3	8.0	Scale	M	SD
9(Ma)	49.9	7.3	PS	48.1	8.2	AGG	48.4	9.2
0(Si)	43.9	6.3	MAC-R	49.1	10.1	PSY	46.6	7.6
			APS	47.9	10.6	CON	50.1	8.0
			AAS	47.1	8.8	NEN	46.2	8.7
			MDS	47.7	8.9	PEE	50.1	8.2
			Ho	42.7	8.0			
			CAL-R	49.6	9.6			

Content			Content Component					
Scale	M	SD	Scale	M	SD	Scale	M	SD
ANX	52.1	9.4	FRS1	46.9	6.8	ASP1	43.2	8.7
FRS	47.3	9.1	FRS2	47.7	10.5	ASP2	48.6	9.7
OBS	43.6	8.1	DEP1	49.0	7.7	TPA1	43.6	8.9
DEP	48.4	8.6	DEP2	49.3	10.8	TPA2	44.7	9.6
HEA	55.8	7.8	DEP3	47.3	8.5	LSE1	44.4	7.1
BIZ	48.1	7.7	DEP4	47.6	7.2	LSE2	43.9	6.5
ANG	45.4	8.6	HEA1	51.9	9.0	SOD1	46.6	8.4
CYN	43.7	8.1	HEA2	52.3	9.9	SOD2	42.3	6.7
ASP	44.4	8.4	HEA3	56.6	10.6	FAM1	43.7	10.0
TPA	44.1	9.0	BIZ1	47.0	7.7	FAM2	51.0	11.6
LSE	44.6	7.3	BIZ2	46.2	6.5	TRT1	46.4	7.2
SOD	44.7	7.2	ANG1	47.2	7.6	TRT2	43.1	7.7
FAM	46.2	10.8	ANG2	45.2	9.2			
WRK	46.6	7.7	CYN1	43.3	9.1			
TRT	44.5	7.7	CYN2	44.3	8.4			

Note. All scores are T scores except: Cannot Say, K & B and L & W critical items which are
raw scores; True % and False % which are the percentage of items endorsed "true" or
"false;" and |F - FB|, F - K, and O - S which are difference scores.

596

Appendix D-23

Prototypic Scores for 3-6/6-3 Codetypes (N = 734)

Demographics

		M	SD	Marital Status		%
Age		38.7	11.1	Never Married		23.3
Education		12.7	5.3	Married		45.7
Gender		%		Separated		10.2
	Men	42.4		Divorced		19.8
	Women	57.6		Widowed		1.1

Test-Taking Scales

Omissions		M	SD	Consistency	M	SD
	?	1.7	4.4	VRIN	52.7	10.5
				|F - FB|	3.7	2.8
				TRIN	48.2	11.3

Accuracy of Item Endorsement

Underreporting		M	SD	Overreporting		M	SD
	False %	59.5	7.0		True %	39.2	7.0
Impression	L	54.6	10.1	Infrequency	F	63.9	17.1
Management	ODecp	49.2	9.0		FB	63.6	20.1
	Sd	50.8	9.7		F[p]	54.1	12.6
Superior	S	50.7	9.0	Critical Items	K & B	29.2	13.7
Adjustment					L & W	39.1	16.8
Self-Deception	K	31.1	6.4	Dissimulation	F - K	-6.9	8.2
	So	39.5	12.1		Ds	59.8	13.8
					O - S	59.1	77.3

Scales

Validity and Clinical

Scale	M	SD
?	1.7	4.4
L	54.6	10.1
F	63.9	17.1
K	50.1	8.9
1(Hs)	72.2	12.8
2(D)	69.9	13.6
3(Hy)	83.0	12.5
4(Pd)	65.9	11.2
5(Mf)	51.1	9.5
6(Pa)	84.1	12.9
7(Pt)	67.7	12.3
8(Sc)	68.6	14.8
9(Ma)	55.6	10.1
0(Si)	50.7	10.0

Supplementary

Scale	M	SD
A	57.3	10.4
R	56.4	9.8
Es	33.8	14.4
TRIN	48.2	11.3
VRIN	52.7	10.5
O-H	56.0	10.3
Do	45.3	11.3
Re	48.5	9.5
GM	41.9	10.9
GF	48.8	9.5
Mt	63.9	12.2
PK	65.3	14.1
PS	65.8	14.8
MAC-R	49.8	10.3
APS	53.0	9.5
AAS	50.7	10.6
MDS	58.7	12.1
Ho	49.3	9.1
CAL-R	50.3	10.4

Morey et al. Overlapping Personality Disorder

Scale	M	SD
PAR	57.0	12.1
SZD	49.1	10.6
STY	55.8	11.8
ANT	46.5	9.7
BDL	54.1	10.0
HST	48.0	10.0
NAR	47.5	9.1
AVD	51.0	9.1
DEP	53.4	10.3
CPS	51.7	9.0

Personality Psychopathology Five

Scale	M	SD
AGG	50.5	9.6
PSY	59.7	15.5
CON	52.5	9.7
NEN	57.4	10.2
PEE	42.3	11.4

Content

Scale	M	SD
ANX	67.8	12.1
FRS	53.7	11.6
OBS	52.7	10.0
DEP	63.9	12.2
HEA	68.5	14.2
BIZ	59.8	12.9
ANG	53.1	10.9
CYN	47.4	8.7
ASP	45.2	8.0
TPA	49.2	9.9
LSE	52.9	10.8
SOD	49.9	9.6
FAM	53.0	11.7
WRK	57.7	11.5
TRT	55.7	12.8

Content Component

Scale	M	SD
FRS1	56.4	15.6
FRS2	51.0	10.1
DEP1	63.2	15.1
DEP2	66.2	12.9
DEP3	56.9	12.0
DEP4	62.8	24.4
HEA1	64.1	18.1
HEA2	66.2	17.9
HEA3	65.8	14.0
BIZ1	59.8	18.0
BIZ2	57.3	12.8
ANG1	52.5	10.8
ANG2	52.5	10.5
CYN1	45.3	9.2
CYN2	50.0	9.7

Scale	M	SD
ASP1	43.2	8.1
ASP2	51.3	11.2
TPA1	49.4	10.7
TPA2	49.1	9.6
LSE1	52.9	11.2
LSE2	48.6	9.5
SOD1	51.6	10.5
SOD2	46.0	8.5
FAM1	49.6	11.0
FAM2	51.6	12.4
TRT1	57.2	14.4
TRT2	48.9	10.2

Note. All scores are T scores except: Cannot Say, K & B and L & W critical items which are raw scores; True % and False % which are the percentage of items endorsed "true" or "false;" and \|F - FB\|, F - K, and O - S which are difference scores.

Appendix D-24

Prototypic Scores for 3-7/7-3 Codetypes (N = 442)

Demographics

		M	SD	Marital Status	%
Age		38.7	12.1	Never Married	33.4
Education		12.6	5.3	Married	46.7
Gender		%		Separated	2.9
	Men	54.1		Divorced	16.0
	Women	45.9		Widowed	1.0

Test-Taking Scales

Omissions

		M	SD	Consistency	M	SD
	?	1.1	2.8	VRIN	54.1	9.6
				|F - FB|	3.0	2.3
				TRIN	49.1	10.8

Accuracy of Item Endorsement

Underreporting		M	SD	Overreporting		M	SD
	False %	59.2	6.8	True %		39.6	6.8
Impression	L	52.4	10.0	Infrequency	F	59.8	12.4
Management	ODecp	44.1	8.8		FB	62.9	18.0
	Sd	46.7	9.5		F[p]	50.8	9.7
Superior	S	49.3	9.2	Critical Items	K & B	28.1	10.8
Adjustment					L & W	36.9	13.5
Self-Deception	K	31.1	6.4	Dissimulation	F - K	-9.0	6.9
	So	35.4	12.0		Ds	59.9	12.5
					O - S	58.7	66.2

Scales

Validity and Clinical / Supplementary / Morey et al. Overlapping Personality Disorder

Scale	M	SD	Scale	M	SD	Scale	M	SD
?	1.1	2.8	A	62.5	10.2	PAR	50.4	9.6
L	52.4	10.0	R	57.4	10.5	SZD	50.0	10.8
F	59.8	12.4	Es	32.2	13.7	STY	52.8	10.2
K	52.1	9.3	TRIN	49.1	10.8	ANT	47.8	9.5
1(Hs)	72.4	10.7	VRIN	54.1	9.6	BDL	54.8	10.0
2(D)	73.7	11.2	O-H	53.1	10.1	HST	46.5	10.3
3(Hy)	83.7	11.2	Do	39.9	10.5	NAR	42.9	9.9
4(Pd)	65.2	10.2	Re	47.7	10.0	AVD	55.2	10.1
5(Mf)	51.5	10.0	GM	38.1	11.5	DEP	60.9	11.2
6(Pa)	66.1	10.9	GF	50.6	8.9	CPS	54.0	8.9
7(Pt)	82.0	10.7	Mt	69.0	10.7	Personality Psychopathology Five		
8(Sc)	71.1	11.6	PK	66.7	12.9	Scale	M	SD
9(Ma)	52.9	9.3	PS	69.4	12.8	AGG	45.3	9.4
0(Si)	54.7	9.8	MAC-R	46.3	10.0	PSY	52.1	11.0
			APS	56.3	9.6	CON	53.2	9.4
			AAS	50.5	10.7	NEN	60.1	10.7
			MDS	57.6	11.1	PEE	39.1	11.4
			Ho	47.1	8.8			
			CAL-R	49.4	10.9			

Content / Content Component

Scale	M	SD	Scale	M	SD	Scale	M	SD
ANX	70.9	11.4	FRS1	59.5	16.3	ASP1	44.2	8.5
FRS	55.7	11.9	FRS2	52.3	10.1	ASP2	50.6	10.8
OBS	58.3	10.5	DEP1	65.7	13.8	TPA1	52.2	10.6
DEP	66.1	10.7	DEP2	68.3	13.1	TPA2	47.7	9.3
HEA	67.6	12.3	DEP3	59.6	10.4	LSE1	59.0	11.9
BIZ	53.5	10.3	DEP4	61.4	23.4	LSE2	52.7	10.8
ANG	53.8	11.4	HEA1	61.5	16.4	SOD1	52.6	10.8
CYN	46.4	8.1	HEA2	63.2	16.8	SOD2	49.7	9.4
ASP	45.8	8.0	HEA3	67.8	12.4	FAM1	49.7	10.4
TPA	49.3	9.3	BIZ1	50.1	10.4	FAM2	51.5	11.5
LSE	59.0	11.0	BIZ2	53.4	11.0	TRT1	61.8	15.1
SOD	52.1	10.5	ANG1	51.7	10.6	TRT2	49.5	9.9
FAM	52.4	10.6	ANG2	54.4	11.4			
WRK	62.6	10.8	CYN1	45.3	8.8			
TRT	58.8	12.0	CYN2	47.2	9.4			

Note. All scores are T scores except: Cannot Say, K & B and L & W critical items which are
raw scores; True % and False % which are the percentage of items endorsed "true" or
"false;" and |F - FB|, F - K, and O - S which are difference scores.

Appendix D-25

Prototypic Scores for 3-8/8-3 Codetypes (N = 439)

Demographics

Demographics		M	SD	Marital Status	%
Age		38.2	12.7	Never Married	34.9
Education		12.0	5.0	Married	44.1
Gender		%		Separated	4.2
	Men	50.6		Divorced	14.5
	Women	49.4		Widowed	2.2

Test-Taking Scales

Omissions		M	SD	Consistency		M	SD
	?	1.9	4.3		VRIN	57.0	10.2
					|F - FB|	4.7	3.4
					TRIN	49.4	12.2

Accuracy of Item Endorsement

Underreporting		M	SD	Overreporting		M	SD
	False %	54.0	7.6		True %	44.7	7.5
Impression	L	54.0	10.5	Infrequency	F	80.4	19.2
Management	ODecp	45.6	9.4		FB	83.3	24.6
	Sd	47.6	9.9		F[p]	65.4	16.8
Superior	S	44.0	9.2	Critical Items	K & B	38.2	13.2
Adjustment					L & W	52.6	16.3
Self-Deception	K	31.1	6.4	Dissimulation	F - K	0.5	8.7
	So	28.9	12.3		Ds	73.3	14.5
					O - S	123.5	73.3

Scales

Validity and Clinical / Supplementary / Morey et al. Overlapping Personality Disorder

Scale	M	SD	Scale	M	SD	Scale	M	SD
?	1.9	4.3	A	65.5	10.1	PAR	59.4	12.2
L	54.0	10.5	R	55.9	11.4	SZD	56.0	12.1
F	80.4	19.2	Es	22.7	14.9	STY	62.4	12.8
K	45.7	9.2	TRIN	49.4	12.2	ANT	54.6	10.3
1(Hs)	80.7	12.7	VRIN	57.0	10.2	BDL	58.2	10.4
2(D)	78.0	13.1	O-H	51.8	9.9	HST	43.8	11.3
3(Hy)	90.0	12.5	Do	36.5	10.7	NAR	44.8	10.6
4(Pd)	70.9	11.6	Re	43.9	10.7	AVD	57.2	10.6
5(Mf)	53.4	9.5	GM	35.7	12.4	DEP	58.5	11.5
6(Pa)	74.0	15.2	GF	44.3	10.5	CPS	56.2	9.4
7(Pt)	78.2	12.6	Mt	72.8	10.6			
8(Sc)	89.3	13.1	PK	77.5	15.0			
9(Ma)	61.6	11.2	PS	79.6	14.2	Scale	M	SD
0(Si)	58.2	10.4	MAC-R	51.9	10.6	AGG	52.8	10.8
			APS	52.4	10.6	PSY	67.0	15.9
			AAS	55.7	12.4	CON	50.1	11.8
			MDS	68.3	12.5	NEN	63.3	11.1
			Ho	55.3	9.7	PEE	35.4	13.1
			CAL-R	52.6	11.2			

(Personality Psychopathology Five for AGG, PSY, CON, NEN, PEE)

Content / Content Component

Scale	M	SD	Scale	M	SD	Scale	M	SD
ANX	72.9	12.4	FRS1	67.6	21.5	ASP1	50.8	9.8
FRS	60.2	14.4	FRS2	53.4	10.5	ASP2	54.9	12.4
OBS	60.1	11.2	DEP1	75.4	15.8	TPA1	54.7	10.2
DEP	72.5	12.7	DEP2	69.5	12.6	TPA2	51.8	11.0
HEA	79.6	13.9	DEP3	63.5	11.7	LSE1	61.4	12.9
BIZ	67.3	13.4	DEP4	77.2	29.6	LSE2	52.3	10.4
ANG	60.2	11.9	HEA1	69.3	18.4	SOD1	59.0	12.3
CYN	54.7	10.8	HEA2	83.7	18.3	SOD2	49.7	9.3
ASP	52.8	10.0	HEA3	72.7	12.3	FAM1	58.6	12.3
TPA	53.8	11.1	BIZ1	63.7	18.7	FAM2	58.6	14.8
LSE	61.5	11.6	BIZ2	66.4	13.7	TRT1	67.6	16.0
SOD	57.0	11.5	ANG1	59.5	11.8	TRT2	54.5	10.8
FAM	62.4	13.6	ANG2	58.2	10.4			
WRK	66.9	11.6	CYN1	53.3	10.3			
TRT	66.2	13.4	CYN2	54.6	10.3			

Note. All scores are T scores except: Cannot Say, K & B and L & W critical items which are raw scores; True % and False % which are the percentage of items endorsed "true" or "false;" and |F - FB|, F - K, and O - S which are difference scores.

Appendix D-26
Prototypic Scores for 3-9/9-3 Codetypes (N = 116)

Demographics

Demographics		M	SD	Marital Status	%
	Age	37.9	10.5	Never Married	26.4
	Education	12.7	5.2	Married	52.8
	Gender	%		Separated	6.6
	Men	32.8		Divorced	11.3
	Women	67.2		Widowed	2.8

Test-Taking Scales

Omissions		M	SD	Consistency		M	SD
	?	1.4	3.6		VRIN	53.3	11.7
					|F - FB|	3.8	2.5
					TRIN	49.2	10.8

Accuracy of Item Endorsement

Underreporting		M	SD	Overreporting		M	SD
	False %	58.4	5.7		True %	40.4	5.6
Impression	L	52.4	9.9	Infrequency	F	58.0	12.8
Management	ODecp	51.4	7.6		FB	52.2	10.6
	Sd	53.7	8.5		F[p]	51.0	11.2
Superior	S	48.1	8.7	Critical Items	K & B	20.5	9.8
Adjustment					L & W	31.3	12.4
Self-Deception	K	31.1	6.4	Dissimulation	F - K	-8.5	6.1
	So	46.1	9.5		Ds	57.5	10.1
					O - S	25.7	52.7

Scales

Validity and Clinical			Supplementary			Morey et al. Overlapping Personality Disorder		
Scale	M	SD	Scale	M	SD	Scale	M	SD
?	1.4	3.6	A	52.3	8.6	PAR	51.4	9.4
L	52.4	9.9	R	47.6	7.9	SZD	44.4	7.3
F	58.0	12.8	Es	42.5	10.9	STY	46.6	7.6
K	49.4	7.5	TRIN	49.2	10.8	ANT	52.8	9.8
1(Hs)	64.6	9.5	VRIN	53.3	11.7	BDL	54.2	10.1
2(D)	56.9	9.1	O-H	51.1	9.4	HST	55.9	6.9
3(Hy)	74.8	8.2	Do	47.6	8.9	NAR	56.1	7.0
4(Pd)	59.5	9.5	Re	47.5	9.0	AVD	44.5	5.9
5(Mf)	50.1	8.7	GM	47.7	7.6	DEP	49.8	8.4
6(Pa)	57.4	9.8	GF	44.5	9.6	CPS	53.0	8.9
7(Pt)	58.7	8.9	Mt	57.4	9.6	Personality Psychopathology Five		
8(Sc)	62.2	10.0	PK	57.0	9.9	Scale	M	SD
9(Ma)	75.0	7.8	PS	58.4	10.0	AGG	55.2	8.4
0(Si)	43.7	6.0	MAC-R	54.7	10.9	PSY	55.1	11.9
			APS	56.2	9.8	CON	44.8	10.6
			AAS	53.0	11.8	NEN	53.7	8.8
			MDS	55.7	11.4	PEE	53.5	7.3
			Ho	50.8	8.1			
			CAL-R	54.1	11.9			

Content			Content Component					
Scale	M	SD	Scale	M	SD	Scale	M	SD
ANX	59.9	10.1	FRS1	48.5	7.6	ASP1	50.1	9.5
FRS	48.3	8.2	FRS2	48.3	9.5	ASP2	52.9	11.4
OBS	52.5	9.1	DEP1	55.8	11.3	TPA1	48.2	9.9
DEP	54.9	9.0	DEP2	54.0	11.7	TPA2	49.8	9.5
HEA	63.1	10.0	DEP3	52.4	9.2	LSE1	48.6	8.7
BIZ	56.2	10.0	DEP4	49.6	10.5	LSE2	47.7	8.4
ANG	53.4	10.8	HEA1	56.6	13.1	SOD1	45.8	7.6
CYN	50.1	8.4	HEA2	61.1	13.2	SOD2	42.4	7.5
ASP	51.5	9.1	HEA3	61.3	12.2	FAM1	53.7	10.6
TPA	49.3	8.8	BIZ1	54.1	12.2	FAM2	53.2	13.1
LSE	49.7	7.9	BIZ2	52.9	10.6	TRT1	50.6	9.1
SOD	44.2	6.8	ANG1	53.0	11.7	TRT2	46.8	9.0
FAM	55.7	11.8	ANG2	52.6	9.6			
WRK	53.6	8.6	CYN1	48.8	9.0			
TRT	50.5	9.0	CYN2	51.6	9.3			

Note. All scores are T scores except: Cannot Say, K & B and L & W critical items which are raw scores; True % and False % which are the percentage of items endorsed "true" or "false;" and \|F - FB\|, F - K, and O - S which are difference scores.

Appendix D-27
Prototypic Scores for 3-0/0-3 Codetypes (N = 14)

Demographics

Demographics		M	SD	Marital Status		%
Age		39.1	12.7	Never Married		8.3
Education		12.3	5.7	Married		83.3
Gender		%		Separated		0.0
	Men	50.0		Divorced		8.3
	Women	50.0		Widowed		0.0

Test-Taking Scales

Omissions		M	SD	Consistency	M	SD
	?	0.2	0.4	VRIN	51.1	6.8
				|F - FB|	3.0	3.1
				TRIN	48.7	9.8

Accuracy of Item Endorsement

Underreporting		M	SD	Overreporting		M	SD
	False %	59.6	5.3		True %	39.4	5.3
Impression	L	56.6	10.2	Infrequency	F	59.6	8.3
Management	ODecp	40.2	6.7		FB	61.1	12.3
	Sd	41.7	7.7		F[p]	48.7	7.3
Superior	S	47.4	8.5	Critical Items	K & B	23.7	7.2
Adjustment					L & W	32.5	9.9
Self-Deception	K	31.1	6.4	Dissimulation	F - K	-5.7	5.5
	So	34.5	8.4		Ds	59.6	6.9
					O - S	66.1	61.9

Scales

Validity and Clinical

Scale	M	SD
?	0.2	0.4
L	56.6	10.2
F	59.6	8.3
K	45.0	8.5
1(Hs)	63.9	8.8
2(D)	67.4	7.8
3(Hy)	74.5	8.1
4(Pd)	59.1	5.7
5(Mf)	45.4	7.4
6(Pa)	58.5	8.0
7(Pt)	66.4	8.8
8(Sc)	61.3	9.7
9(Ma)	44.7	5.4
0(Si)	74.0	7.3

Supplementary

Scale	M	SD
A	64.0	9.6
R	63.0	8.2
Es	37.3	10.2
TRIN	48.7	9.8
VRIN	51.1	6.8
O-H	52.7	9.8
Do	34.5	10.9
Re	49.0	8.9
GM	36.2	9.1
GF	48.9	9.4
Mt	64.7	8.2
PK	65.1	8.8
PS	65.5	9.8
MAC-R	43.0	8.7
APS	45.9	10.0
AAS	48.6	6.0
MDS	63.8	14.9
Ho	50.9	9.7
CAL-R	45.0	8.5

Morey et al. Overlapping Personality Disorder

Scale	M	SD
PAR	51.6	9.1
SZD	67.6	6.1
STY	66.3	6.4
ANT	49.5	8.6
BDL	49.1	8.8
HST	28.6	5.7
NAR	29.5	10.7
AVD	69.4	7.1
DEP	65.3	12.0
CPS	54.5	9.8

Personality Psychopathology Five

Scale	M	SD
AGG	41.1	13.6
PSY	50.5	8.2
CON	54.5	8.9
NEN	60.4	8.1
PEE	28.3	7.0

Content

Scale	M	SD
ANX	68.2	7.8
FRS	51.1	9.3
OBS	60.6	8.9
DEP	65.9	8.3
HEA	63.1	12.5
BIZ	50.5	8.0
ANG	53.5	13.0
CYN	51.1	11.7
ASP	50.3	10.4
TPA	48.9	10.6
LSE	67.4	11.2
SOD	70.6	9.4
FAM	58.1	11.2
WRK	65.1	8.8
TRT	67.0	11.5

Content Component

Scale	M	SD	Scale	M	SD
FRS1	51.7	7.2	ASP1	47.5	10.0
FRS2	49.8	10.3	ASP2	54.6	11.8
DEP1	63.8	12.6	TPA1	51.4	12.2
DEP2	65.8	10.7	TPA2	50.2	9.9
DEP3	61.5	10.4	LSE1	63.6	12.4
DEP4	59.1	20.3	LSE2	60.3	11.8
HEA1	54.2	11.5	SOD1	69.4	7.1
HEA2	63.4	18.7	SOD2	63.0	8.6
HEA3	58.4	11.2	FAM1	54.6	10.3
BIZ1	47.4	6.6	FAM2	57.9	13.0
BIZ2	49.6	8.3	TRT1	69.6	13.2
ANG1	52.4	13.2	TRT2	56.9	10.8
ANG2	54.1	12.2			
CYN1	49.4	10.9			
CYN2	50.9	11.3			

Note. All scores are T scores except: Cannot Say, K & B and L & W critical items which are raw scores; True % and False % which are the percentage of items endorsed "true" or "false;" and \|F - FB\|, F - K, and O - S which are difference scores.

Appendix D-28
Prototypic Scores for Spike 4 Codetypes (N = 1,268)

Demographics

Demographics		M	SD	Marital Status	%
Age		34.5	10.9	Never Married	36.2
Education		12.7	5.2	Married	33.9
Gender		%		Separated	12.1
	Men	54.0		Divorced	17.3
	Women	46.0		Widowed	0.5

Test-Taking Scales

Omissions		M	SD	Consistency	M	SD
	?	0.7	2.3	VRIN	47.4	10.5
				|F - FB|	3.0	2.0
				TRIN	47.2	9.3

Accuracy of Item Endorsement

Underreporting		M	SD	Overreporting		M	SD
	False %	64.6	5.9		True %	34.3	5.9
Impression	L	53.7	10.9	Infrequency	F	51.1	8.0
Management	ODecp	51.2	9.4		FB	48.7	7.7
	Sd	52.0	9.9		F[p]	49.0	8.4
Superior	S	55.8	10.1	Critical Items	K & B	11.0	7.1
Adjustment					L & W	16.7	7.7
Self-Deception	K	31.1	6.4	Dissimulation	F - K	-14.5	6.4
	So	54.8	8.2		Ds	48.1	8.5
					O - S	-33.3	51.7

Scales

Validity and Clinical			Supplementary			Morey et al. Overlapping Personality Disorder		
Scale	M	SD	Scale	M	SD	Scale	M	SD
?	0.7	2.3	A	44.8	7.6	PAR	46.5	9.3
L	53.7	10.9	R	52.1	9.1	SZD	45.7	8.4
F	51.1	8.0	Es	53.6	7.6	STY	45.3	8.1
K	58.1	10.3	TRIN	47.2	9.3	ANT	51.6	9.9
1(Hs)	51.0	6.8	VRIN	47.4	10.5	BDL	47.4	9.6
2(D)	51.3	6.8	O-H	56.1*	9.6	HST	52.4	8.4
3(Hy)	54.0	6.7	Do	49.6	10.2	NAR	52.1	7.7
4(Pd)	70.3	4.4	Re	47.4	10.1	AVD	44.7	7.5
5(Mf)	48.5	7.9	GM	53.0	7.4	DEP	49.2	7.9
6(Pa)	53.8	7.1	GF	48.0	9.3	CPS	44.1	9.3
7(Pt)	52.4	6.2	Mt	46.8	8.5	Personality Psychopathology Five		
8(Sc)	53.4	5.7	PK	47.7	8.1	Scale	M	SD
9(Ma)	50.1	6.5	PS	46.9	7.7	AGG	48.1	7.9
0(Si)	45.2	7.5	MAC-R	52.7	9.7	PSY	46.3	8.2
			APS	48.8	10.2	CON	45.9	9.3
			AAS	53.2	10.1	NEN	47.1	9.2
			MDS	54.0	10.0	PEE	48.9	8.0
			Ho	45.1	8.9			
			CAL-R	56.8	9.1			

Content			Content Component					
Scale	M	SD	Scale	M	SD	Scale	M	SD
ANX	49.1	8.3	FRS1	47.0	7.5	ASP1	45.1	9.4
FRS	46.5	8.6	FRS2	46.7	9.5	ASP2	58.0	11.4
OBS	44.1	8.0	DEP1	48.6	8.7	TPA1	43.7	9.2
DEP	49.2	8.9	DEP2	49.7	9.5	TPA2	44.5	9.4
HEA	46.9	7.4	DEP3	49.6	9.6	LSE1	45.6	8.0
BIZ	47.6	7.8	DEP4	47.2	7.1	LSE2	45.3	7.4
ANG	47.0	9.9	HEA1	47.6	7.2	SOD1	46.6	7.9
CYN	45.7	9.0	HEA2	45.4	6.7	SOD2	43.5	7.6
ASP	48.8	9.2	HEA3	49.4	8.5	FAM1	49.7	10.6
TPA	44.2	8.9	BIZ1	46.2	6.4	FAM2	55.8	12.6
LSE	45.3	8.2	BIZ2	47.0	7.5	TRT1	46.9	8.0
SOD	45.3	7.6	ANG1	48.3	9.7	TRT2	45.3	9.1
FAM	52.4	10.6	ANG2	45.8	9.6			
WRK	45.6	8.3	CYN1	45.7	9.7			
TRT	46.0	9.0	CYN2	45.2	9.1			

Note. All scores are T scores except: Cannot Say, K & B and L & W critical items which are raw scores; True % and False % which are the percentage of items endorsed "true" or "false;" and |F - FB|, F - K, and O - S which are difference scores.

Appendix D-29
Prototypic Scores for 4-5/5-4 Codetypes (N = 204)

Demographics

Demographics		M	SD	Marital Status		%
Age		33.3	11.6	Never Married		50.3
Education		11.5	6.3	Married		26.6
Gender		%		Separated		6.9
	Men	38.7		Divorced		16.2
	Women	61.3		Widowed		0.0

Test-Taking Scales

Omissions		M	SD	Consistency	M	SD
	?	1.0	3.0	VRIN	51.3	11.3
				|F - FB|	3.4	2.4
				TRIN	48.1	10.2

Accuracy of Item Endorsement

Underreporting		M	SD	Overreporting		M	SD
	False %	61.7	6.8		True %	37.2	6.8
Impression	L	53.5	11.5	Infrequency	F	56.2	11.9
Management	ODecp	51.2	12.4		FB	53.7	12.7
	Sd	51.9	11.4		F[p]	54.2	12.2
Superior	S	51.6	11.1	Critical Items	K & B	16.0	9.4
Adjustment					L & W	22.0	10.7
Self-Deception	K	31.1	6.4	Dissimulation	F - K	-11.3	7.5
	So	50.8	10.1		Ds	53.3	11.1
					O - S	-3.6	59.9

Scales

Validity and Clinical			Supplementary			Morey et al. Overlapping Personality Disorder		
Scale	M	SD	Scale	M	SD	Scale	M	SD
?	1.0	3.0	A	48.6	9.4	PAR	50.6	10.7
L	53.5	11.5	R	50.5	9.1	SZD	47.9	9.2
F	56.2	11.9	Es	51.7	9.5	STY	48.8	9.4
K	54.4	10.6	TRIN	48.1	10.2	ANT	55.8	12.1
1(Hs)	51.5	7.7	VRIN	51.3	11.3	BDL	50.5	10.5
2(D)	53.3	8.5	O-H	54.4	11.1	HST	51.8	8.0
3(Hy)	54.0	8.7	Do	47.0	10.9	NAR	52.4	8.7
4(Pd)	72.3	6.7	Re	43.6	12.5	AVD	47.2	9.2
5(Mf)	71.4	6.0	GM	52.0	10.8	DEP	50.2	10.3
6(Pa)	55.6	8.5	GF	42.9	17.2	CPS	46.9	10.1
7(Pt)	54.4	7.9	Mt	51.1	10.4	Personality Psychopathology Five		
8(Sc)	58.1	7.6	PK	52.5	10.2			
9(Ma)	54.0	8.4	PS	51.9	9.8	Scale	M	SD
0(Si)	47.1	8.4	MAC-R	54.9	11.5	AGG	49.8	9.6
			APS	49.5	11.4	PSY	49.9	9.4
			AAS	56.0	11.2	CON	42.0	10.6
			MDS	58.1	12.0	NEN	49.8	10.4
			Ho	49.2	10.5	PEE	48.2	9.2
			CAL-R	58.1	10.3			

Content			Content Component					
Scale	M	SD	Scale	M	SD	Scale	M	SD
ANX	52.1	9.9	FRS1	48.5	8.5	ASP1	49.2	11.0
FRS	46.2	8.8	FRS2	45.3	9.7	ASP2	60.8	14.9
OBS	47.5	10.1	DEP1	53.5	11.1	TPA1	46.0	10.4
DEP	54.3	10.2	DEP2	53.8	11.6	TPA2	46.5	10.2
HEA	49.0	8.7	DEP3	53.9	11.5	LSE1	50.0	10.9
BIZ	50.7	8.4	DEP4	50.9	13.1	LSE2	46.6	9.4
ANG	49.9	11.0	HEA1	49.3	9.4	SOD1	48.6	9.1
CYN	49.1	10.8	HEA2	47.9	8.8	SOD2	44.1	7.6
ASP	53.1	11.7	HEA3	50.4	9.5	FAM1	54.1	11.8
TPA	46.5	10.7	BIZ1	47.2	7.6	FAM2	59.4	14.4
LSE	49.1	10.1	BIZ2	50.4	9.1	TRT1	51.0	11.9
SOD	47.3	8.4	ANG1	50.5	11.1	TRT2	48.0	9.7
FAM	57.0	12.3	ANG2	48.7	10.7			
WRK	49.5	11.1	CYN1	49.2	11.3			
TRT	50.6	11.0	CYN2	48.4	10.2			

Note. All scores are T scores except: Cannot Say, K & B and L & W critical items which are raw scores; True % and False % which are the percentage of items endorsed "true" or "false;" and \|F - FB\|, F - K, and O - S which are difference scores.

603

Appendix D-30

Prototypic Scores for 4-6/6-4 Codetypes (N = 1,104)

Demographics

Demographics		M	SD	Marital Status	%
Age		33.6	11.0	Never Married	40.5
Education		12.0	5.0	Married	31.1
Gender		%		Separated	9.0
	Men	51.2		Divorced	18.4
	Women	48.8		Widowed	0.9

Test-Taking Scales

Omissions		M	SD	Consistency		M	SD
	?	1.1	3.2		VRIN	53.4	10.4
					|F - FB|	4.1	2.9
					TRIN	48.7	11.1

Accuracy of Item Endorsement

Underreporting		M	SD	Overreporting		M	SD
	False %	56.1	8.1		True %	42.7	8.0
Impression	L	51.2	10.0	Infrequency	F	68.1	17.2
Management	ODecp	47.1	9.2		FB	66.3	19.5
	Sd	50.2	9.8		F[p]	57.2	14.2
Superior	S	45.3	9.8	Critical Items	K & B	29.1	13.1
Adjustment					L & W	36.2	14.5
Self-Deception	K	31.1	6.4	Dissimulation	F - K	-4.0	8.9
	So	39.2	12.5		Ds	63.1	13.6
					O - S	63.5	73.0

Scales

Validity and Clinical			Supplementary			Morey et al. Overlapping Personality Disorder		
Scale	M	SD	Scale	M	SD	Scale	M	SD
?	1.1	3.2	A	58.8	11.2	PAR	63.8	13.2
L	51.2	10.0	R	50.2	9.8	SZD	49.3	11.0
F	68.1	17.2	Es	39.9	11.9	STY	59.3	11.9
K	46.8	10.1	TRIN	48.7	11.1	ANT	57.5	11.2
1(Hs)	56.3	11.1	VRIN	53.4	10.4	BDL	58.2	11.1
2(D)	62.6	11.1	O-H	51.9	10.5	HST	50.1	10.2
3(Hy)	59.8	10.9	Do	41.5	12.3	NAR	49.3	9.9
4(Pd)	79.3	10.0	Re	39.0	11.7	AVD	54.0	10.3
5(Mf)	51.7	9.5	GM	43.7	10.0	DEP	57.0	11.0
6(Pa)	80.7	10.6	GF	44.6	10.5	CPS	53.4	9.2
7(Pt)	62.8	10.8	Mt	62.0	11.9	Personality Psychopathology Five		
8(Sc)	65.8	11.6	PK	65.9	14.0	Scale	M	SD
9(Ma)	56.8	10.7	PS	64.4	13.7	AGG	52.2	10.4
0(Si)	52.8	10.2	MAC-R	56.9	10.5	PSY	62.4	14.8
			APS	54.7	10.0	CON	44.1	10.7
			AAS	58.9	12.4	NEN	60.0	10.5
			MDS	67.5	13.0	PEE	43.6	10.9
			Ho	55.8	10.8			
			CAL-R	58.7	10.4			

Content			Content Component					
Scale	M	SD	Scale	M	SD	Scale	M	SD
ANX	64.1	11.3	FRS1	53.4	12.7	ASP1	50.2	10.7
FRS	51.0	9.8	FRS2	49.1	9.6	ASP2	61.5	12.9
OBS	54.6	11.0	DEP1	62.6	15.3	TPA1	50.5	10.9
DEP	65.3	12.6	DEP2	65.2	12.9	TPA2	52.7	11.2
HEA	57.4	11.0	DEP3	63.3	13.7	LSE1	56.7	12.6
BIZ	61.3	12.2	DEP4	61.1	23.0	LSE2	51.7	10.4
ANG	56.7	12.5	HEA1	55.1	13.2	SOD1	51.7	10.8
CYN	53.8	11.3	HEA2	54.2	12.6	SOD2	48.0	9.7
ASP	54.5	11.6	HEA3	57.0	11.9	FAM1	58.8	12.5
TPA	52.2	11.5	BIZ1	59.3	17.2	FAM2	61.4	15.0
LSE	56.6	12.0	BIZ2	60.5	12.8	TRT1	58.5	14.6
SOD	51.1	10.6	ANG1	56.4	12.9	TRT2	52.4	11.4
FAM	63.4	13.4	ANG2	54.8	10.9			
WRK	58.6	12.3	CYN1	52.0	10.8			
TRT	58.8	13.7	CYN2	54.2	10.6			

Note. All scores are T scores except: Cannot Say, K & B and L & W critical items which are raw scores; True % and False % which are the percentage of items endorsed "true" or "false;" and |F - FB|, F - K, and O - S which are difference scores.

Appendix D-31
Prototypic Scores for 4-7/7-4 Codetypes (N = 446)

Demographics

Demographics		M	SD	Marital Status	%
Age		32.1	10.8	Never Married	50.0
Education		12.5	4.8	Married	30.3
Gender		%		Separated	5.9
	Men	52.9		Divorced	13.1
	Women	47.1		Widowed	0.7

Test-Taking Scales

Omissions		M	SD	Consistency	M	SD
	?	0.8	2.2	VRIN	54.5	9.6
				|F - FB|	3.6	2.4
				TRIN	49.1	10.9

Accuracy of Item Endorsement

Underreporting		M	SD	Overreporting		M	SD
	False %	54.8	7.6		True %	44.0	7.6
Impression	L	47.3	8.6	Infrequency	F	65.7	13.2
Management	ODecp	41.6	8.0		FB	67.1	19.3
	Sd	46.1	9.1		F[p]	54.0	11.3
Superior	S	43.6	9.5	Critical Items	K & B	30.7	11.2
Adjustment					L & W	36.2	13.2
Self-Deception	K	31.1	6.4	Dissimulation	F - K	-5.4	7.4
	So	34.5	11.8		Ds	65.3	13.1
					O - S	67.5	65.9

Scales

Validity and Clinical			Supplementary			Morey et al. Overlapping Personality Disorder		
Scale	M	SD	Scale	M	SD	Scale	M	SD
?	0.8	2.2	A	65.6	10.5	PAR	58.4	11.6
L	47.3	8.6	R	50.4	10.1	SZD	49.5	11.3
F	65.7	13.2	Es	38.3	11.7	STY	57.9	11.0
K	48.2	9.6	TRIN	49.1	10.9	ANT	58.8	10.8
1(Hs)	58.0	10.3	VRIN	54.5	9.6	BDL	60.0	11.0
2(D)	67.7	9.1	O-H	47.7	10.2	HST	48.7	10.7
3(Hy)	61.0	10.2	Do	36.1	11.0	NAR	44.7	10.0
4(Pd)	80.2	8.7	Re	38.6	10.9	AVD	58.4	9.8
5(Mf)	51.3	9.9	GM	40.9	9.4	DEP	65.2	11.0
6(Pa)	65.1	9.7	GF	45.2	10.9	CPS	55.1	9.5
7(Pt)	78.0	8.4	Mt	69.1	10.4	Personality Psychopathology Five		
8(Sc)	69.6	9.4	PK	70.2	12.3	Scale	M	SD
9(Ma)	55.7	10.0	PS	69.9	12.5	AGG	48.2	10.9
0(Si)	57.0	9.5	MAC-R	54.0	11.0	PSY	56.5	11.7
			APS	57.9	9.7	CON	44.4	10.3
			AAS	59.1	12.4	NEN	63.4	10.1
			MDS	67.9	11.6	PEE	39.3	10.4
			Ho	54.3	10.0			
			CAL-R	57.9	10.7			

Content			Content Component					
Scale	M	SD	Scale	M	SD	Scale	M	SD
ANX	68.9	10.9	FRS1	55.1	13.1	ASP1	52.2	9.9
FRS	51.5	9.8	FRS2	48.8	9.4	ASP2	59.4	13.0
OBS	60.4	11.6	DEP1	68.5	14.0	TPA1	53.5	10.8
DEP	69.9	10.3	DEP2	69.5	11.7	TPA2	52.3	10.6
HEA	56.8	11.0	DEP3	67.9	10.4	LSE1	62.8	11.6
BIZ	56.5	9.8	DEP4	63.2	23.7	LSE2	56.3	11.9
ANG	58.7	12.4	HEA1	54.7	13.4	SOD1	52.5	11.1
CYN	52.6	10.2	HEA2	51.8	11.6	SOD2	51.4	10.2
ASP	55.6	11.2	HEA3	57.7	11.8	FAM1	59.9	11.8
TPA	53.0	11.0	BIZ1	50.8	10.2	FAM2	60.6	13.6
LSE	62.8	11.6	BIZ2	57.7	12.0	TRT1	64.8	14.8
SOD	53.1	11.0	ANG1	57.0	12.9	TRT2	53.5	10.7
FAM	62.9	12.0	ANG2	57.8	10.6			
WRK	65.3	11.9	CYN1	52.3	10.1			
TRT	63.0	12.3	CYN2	51.4	10.3			

Note. All scores are T scores except: Cannot Say, K & B and L & W critical items which are raw scores; True % and False % which are the percentage of items endorsed "true" or "false;" and |F - FB|, F - K, and O - S which are difference scores.

Appendix D-32

Prototypic Scores for 4-8/8-4 Codetypes (N = 692)

Demographics

Demographics		M	SD	Marital Status	%
Age		31.7	12.1	Never Married	52.5
Education		11.7	5.1	Married	29.5
Gender		%		Separated	6.0
	Men	49.0		Divorced	11.1
	Women	51.0		Widowed	1.0

Test-Taking Scales

Omissions

Omissions		M	SD	Consistency	M	SD
	?	1.0	2.7	VRIN	55.9	10.5
				|F - FB|	4.9	3.3
				TRIN	51.5	11.4

Accuracy of Item Endorsement

Underreporting		M	SD	Overreporting		M	SD
	False %	51.5	8.8		True %	47.3	8.8
Impression	L	47.6	9.4	Infrequency	F	82.0	19.6
Management	ODecp	43.4	9.1		FB	82.8	26.5
	Sd	46.3	9.9		F[p]	67.1	17.3
Superior	S	40.3	10.5	Critical Items	K & B	36.2	14.9
Adjustment					L & W	45.6	18.0
Self-Deception	K	31.1	6.4	Dissimulation	F - K	1.3	9.9
	So	31.8	14.4		Ds	74.9	15.4
					O - S	107.9	80.8

Scales

Validity and Clinical			Supplementary			Morey et al. Overlapping Personality Disorder		
Scale	M	SD	Scale	M	SD	Scale	M	SD
?	1.0	2.7	A	65.2	12.2	PAR	65.4	13.6
L	47.6	9.4	R	50.3	10.7	SZD	55.0	12.0
F	82.0	19.6	Es	33.8	13.8	STY	64.0	12.8
K	44.9	10.6	TRIN	51.5	11.4	ANT	65.5	11.2
1(Hs)	62.7	13.1	VRIN	55.9	10.5	BDL	60.5	11.9
2(D)	67.9	12.5	O-H	48.0	10.8	HST	47.3	11.1
3(Hy)	62.8	13.2	Do	35.7	11.7	NAR	47.7	10.4
4(Pd)	83.8	10.4	Re	34.6	12.0	AVD	58.0	11.0
5(Mf)	54.7	9.9	GM	40.4	11.0	DEP	62.0	12.1
6(Pa)	70.0	12.7	GF	39.1	11.7	CPS	55.1	10.5
7(Pt)	71.4	11.6	Mt	69.0	12.5	Personality Psychopathology Five		
8(Sc)	82.8	12.6	PK	75.7	15.8	Scale	M	SD
9(Ma)	61.7	11.5	PS	74.9	15.6	AGG	54.2	11.7
0(Si)	58.2	10.7	MAC-R	57.0	11.4	PSY	66.8	15.7
			APS	53.8	11.0	CON	39.7	10.7
			AAS	64.3	14.0	NEN	62.9	12.1
			MDS	73.9	12.8	PEE	36.7	12.3
			Ho	61.1	11.2			
			CAL-R	58.7	10.9			

Content			Content Component					
Scale	M	SD	Scale	M	SD	Scale	M	SD
ANX	67.6	13.5	FRS1	58.6	15.1	ASP1	58.1	10.8
FRS	53.8	11.3	FRS2	49.8	10.2	ASP2	64.4	12.5
OBS	60.7	13.2	DEP1	73.8	16.9	TPA1	54.3	10.8
DEP	72.2	13.8	DEP2	66.9	12.9	TPA2	56.5	11.8
HEA	63.7	13.8	DEP3	68.3	13.2	LSE1	63.4	13.5
BIZ	65.6	13.0	DEP4	74.3	28.7	LSE2	55.2	11.4
ANG	61.1	13.9	HEA1	58.9	15.7	SOD1	57.1	12.3
CYN	60.1	11.9	HEA2	63.3	16.4	SOD2	50.1	9.8
ASP	63.1	12.9	HEA3	60.5	13.8	FAM1	66.5	12.2
TPA	56.8	13.0	BIZ1	59.1	17.2	FAM2	67.4	14.0
LSE	63.8	13.2	BIZ2	67.3	14.2	TRT1	68.2	17.0
SOD	56.0	11.7	ANG1	61.0	14.2	TRT2	57.7	11.1
FAM	71.3	13.0	ANG2	57.7	11.1			
WRK	67.1	13.7	CYN1	58.9	10.7			
TRT	68.5	14.8	CYN2	56.9	10.3			

Note. All scores are T scores except: Cannot Say, K & B and L & W critical items which are
raw scores; True % and False % which are the percentage of items endorsed "true" or
"false;" and |F - FB|, F - K, and O - S which are difference scores.

Appendix D-33

Prototypic Scores for 4-9/9-4 Codetypes (N = 440)

Demographics

		M	SD	Marital Status		%
Age		28.3	10.5		Never Married	58.4
Education		11.2	5.0		Married	20.2
Gender		%			Separated	7.9
	Men	53.9			Divorced	12.3
	Women	46.1			Widowed	1.3

Test-Taking Scales

Omissions

		M	SD	Consistency	M	SD
	?	0.9	2.5	VRIN	52.7	10.4
				|F - FB|	4.2	3.1
				TRIN	50.5	10.3

Accuracy of Item Endorsement

Underreporting / Overreporting

Underreporting		M	SD	Overreporting		M	SD
	False %	54.4	7.2		True %	44.4	7.2
Impression	L	49.0	9.9	Infrequency	F	63.8	14.8
Management	ODecp	50.4	8.6		FB	60.3	14.8
	Sd	53.6	9.0		F[p]	57.5	14.7
Superior	S	43.2	9.0	Critical Items	K & B	23.6	10.3
Adjustment					L & W	31.4	11.6
Self-Deception	K	47.0	9.2	Dissimulation	F - K	-5.4	7.8
	So	45.0	10.7		Ds	61.9	11.5
					O - S	39.7	61.7

Scales

Validity and Clinical / Supplementary / Morey et al. Overlapping Personality Disorder

Scale	M	SD	Scale	M	SD	Scale	M	SD
?	0.9	2.5	A	54.6	9.9	PAR	60.0	12.0
L	49.0	9.9	R	42.6	8.7	SZD	43.3	8.0
F	63.8	14.8	Es	46.2	10.1	STY	50.5	8.9
K	47.0	9.2	TRIN	50.5	10.3	ANT	64.1	10.8
1(Hs)	51.6	9.0	VRIN	52.7	10.4	BDL	59.8	10.4
2(D)	52.4	9.1	O-H	48.1*	10.1	HST	58.4	7.2
3(Hy)	52.6	9.0	Do	41.2	11.5	NAR	59.2	7.7
4(Pd)	75.4	8.1	Re	34.6	11.4	AVD	45.6	6.9
5(Mf)	50.4	10.3	GM	48.6	8.7	DEP	52.1	9.6
6(Pa)	59.2	9.8	GF	37.6	11.0	CPS	53.5	9.4
7(Pt)	56.7	9.1	Mt	57.9	10.3			

Personality Psychopathology Five

Scale	M	SD	Scale	M	SD	Scale	M	SD
8(Sc)	61.9	9.1	PK	60.8	11.7	AGG	59.5	10.1
9(Ma)	75.2	7.9	PS	60.1	11.2	PSY	58.9	12.5
0(Si)	45.1	7.6	MAC-R	63.0	10.3	CON	36.0	10.2
			APS	56.2	10.5	NEN	56.6	10.2
			AAS	61.1	11.9	PEE	52.9	7.9
			MDS	63.4	10.9			
			Ho	58.1	9.9			
			CAL-R	59.9	10.2			

Content / Content Component

Scale	M	SD	Scale	M	SD	Scale	M	SD
ANX	57.9	10.1	FRS1	51.0	10.2	ASP1	58.7	10.8
FRS	47.3	9.5	FRS2	45.5	9.9	ASP2	64.4	12.7
OBS	54.3	10.3	DEP1	58.9	12.4	TPA1	50.7	10.4
DEP	59.2	9.8	DEP2	56.5	11.2	TPA2	55.9	11.2
HEA	53.7	9.0	DEP3	59.1	11.6	LSE1	51.4	9.6
BIZ	58.8	10.3	DEP4	52.8	15.9	LSE2	49.9	9.5
ANG	58.9	12.2	HEA1	52.4	11.6	SOD1	44.5	7.3
CYN	58.0	10.9	HEA2	51.6	10.1	SOD2	42.3	7.0
ASP	63.6	12.8	HEA3	53.3	9.9	FAM1	62.5	11.0
TPA	54.8	11.7	BIZ1	54.2	13.0	FAM2	60.5	14.0
LSE	52.0	9.0	BIZ2	58.0	12.0	TRT1	54.5	12.1
SOD	43.6	7.1	ANG1	59.6	12.9	TRT2	50.6	10.3
FAM	64.4	11.6	ANG2	55.3	10.2			
WRK	56.1	10.2	CYN1	56.9	10.1			
TRT	55.4	11.7	CYN2	56.3	9.8			

Note. All scores are T scores except: Cannot Say, K & B and L & W critical items which are raw scores; True % and False % which are the percentage of items endorsed "true" or "false;" and \|F - FB\|, F - K, and O - S which are difference scores.

Appendix D-34

Prototypic Scores for 4-0/0-4 Codetypes (N = 70)

Demographics

Demographics		M	SD	Marital Status		%
Age		35.6	12.0	Never Married		40.7
Education		11.3	5.8	Married		35.6
Gender		%		Separated		8.5
	Men	58.6		Divorced		15.3
	Women	41.4		Widowed		0.0

Test-Taking Scales

Omissions		M	SD	Consistency		M	SD
	?	1.3	2.9		VRIN	53.3	10.8
					|F - FB|	3.0	2.4
					TRIN	49.6	12.2

Accuracy of Item Endorsement

Underreporting			M	SD	Overreporting		M	SD
		False %	54.8	6.6		True %	43.9	6.5
Impression		L	48.7	8.2	Infrequency	F	64.0	11.4
Management		ODecp	40.5	8.2		FB	68.0	18.2
		Sd	43.2	9.6		F[p]	54.4	11.3
Superior		S	40.1	8.0	Critical Items	K & B	27.3	9.3
Adjustment						L & W	32.1	9.2
Self-Deception		K	31.1	6.4	Dissimulation	F - K	-2.3	6.2
		So	32.5	9.7		Ds	65.0	10.9
						O - S	87.9	51.5

Scales

Validity and Clinical			Supplementary			Morey et al. Overlapping Personality Disorder		
Scale	M	SD	Scale	M	SD	Scale	M	SD
?	1.3	2.9	A	64.6	8.5	PAR	62.8	10.8
L	48.7	8.2	R	54.6	10.2	SZD	66.7	9.1
F	64.0	11.4	Es	38.8	9.9	STY	70.9	7.2
K	40.9	8.2	TRIN	49.6	12.2	ANT	61.6	9.5
1(Hs)	50.5	9.9	VRIN	53.3	10.8	BDL	55.1	9.3
2(D)	63.3	8.3	O-H	46.1	9.3	HST	33.0	7.6
3(Hy)	47.8	9.9	Do	35.4	10.7	NAR	36.4	8.9
4(Pd)	74.0	6.8	Re	38.7	10.8	AVD	70.8	6.4
5(Mf)	50.8	10.0	GM	38.8	10.0	DEP	64.6	10.6
6(Pa)	60.6	8.4	GF	44.7	10.7	CPS	54.9	8.2
7(Pt)	61.3	8.4	Mt	66.0	8.6	Personality		
8(Sc)	60.1	8.4	PK	69.1	10.8	Psychopathology Five		
9(Ma)	47.7	8.8	PS	65.9	9.3	Scale	M	SD
0(Si)	72.7	5.6	MAC-R	51.3	10.9	AGG	47.1	10.6
			APS	49.9	9.1	PSY	57.1	10.3
			AAS	59.2	12.7	CON	45.5	9.4
			MDS	71.1	11.4	NEN	64.2	9.2
			Ho	60.7	9.2	PEE	30.9	9.7
			CAL-R	57.7	8.7			

Content			Content Component					
Scale	M	SD	Scale	M	SD	Scale	M	SD
ANX	64.0	10.2	FRS1	53.7	11.7	ASP1	57.9	8.8
FRS	52.9	10.4	FRS2	51.5	10.6	ASP2	61.1	12.6
OBS	59.3	10.7	DEP1	66.3	14.5	TPA1	56.0	9.5
DEP	68.6	9.8	DEP2	68.1	10.3	TPA2	53.3	10.3
HEA	54.8	8.3	DEP3	67.2	10.2	LSE1	65.8	11.0
BIZ	52.4	9.9	DEP4	60.6	21.5	LSE2	59.0	10.9
ANG	61.1	11.5	HEA1	51.4	10.5	SOD1	69.1	8.6
CYN	60.6	10.5	HEA2	52.1	10.0	SOD2	64.3	6.7
ASP	61.0	9.9	HEA3	54.2	10.2	FAM1	63.6	12.1
TPA	54.5	10.7	BIZ1	47.3	6.9	FAM2	66.1	13.6
LSE	65.5	10.8	BIZ2	54.1	12.0	TRT1	66.5	15.4
SOD	71.5	8.7	ANG1	59.4	12.9	TRT2	59.5	10.2
FAM	66.9	12.4	ANG2	59.5	9.5			
WRK	65.5	10.7	CYN1	60.0	9.3			
TRT	68.0	11.3	CYN2	57.0	9.8			

Note. All scores are T scores except: Cannot Say, K & B and L & W critical items which are raw scores; True % and False % which are the percentage of items endorsed "true" or "false;" and |F - FB|, F - K, and O - S which are difference scores.

Appendix D-35

Prototypic Scores for Spike 5 Codetypes (N = 1,365)

Demographics

Demographics		M	SD	Marital Status	%
Age		34.4	11.3	Never Married	40.4
Education		12.6	5.7	Married	34.7
Gender	%			Separated	7.1
	Men	21.5		Divorced	16.7
	Women	78.5		Widowed	1.1

Test-Taking Scales

Omissions		M	SD	Consistency		M	SD
	?	1.2	3.2	VRIN		45.4	10.6
				|F - FB|		2.2	1.7
				TRIN		49.9	8.7

Accuracy of Item Endorsement

Underreporting		M	SD	Overreporting		M	SD
	False %	64.5	6.1	True %		34.3	6.0
Impression	L	57.9	12.7	Infrequency	F	47.0	7.6
Management	ODecp	60.4	12.7		FB	46.1	6.6
	Sd	58.2	12.0		F[p]	50.7	10.2
Superior	S	58.3	10.5	Critical Items	K & B	7.4	6.0
Adjustment					L & W	12.2	7.7
Self-Deception	K	31.1	6.4	Dissimulation	F - K	-15.1	6.0
	So	56.7	7.6		Ds	44.8	8.5
					O - S	-29.2	50.3

Scales

Validity and Clinical			Supplementary			Morey et al. Overlapping Personality Disorder		
Scale	M	SD	Scale	M	SD	Scale	M	SD
?	1.2	3.2	A	42.4	7.1	PAR	45.6	9.3
L	57.9	12.7	R	52.7	9.2	SZD	47.8	8.8
F	47.0	7.6	Es	56.1	8.1	STY	44.0	8.7
K	56.5	10.2	TRIN	49.9	8.7	ANT	45.9	9.5
1(Hs)	48.3	6.9	VRIN	45.4	10.6	BDL	44.1	8.9
2(D)	46.5	6.8	O-H	57.5	9.9	HST	50.9	8.7
3(Hy)	48.8	7.5	Do	50.6	9.0	NAR	54.0	7.9
4(Pd)	50.0	6.9	Re	52.6	9.7	AVD	43.2	8.3
5(Mf)	69.0	4.6	GM	56.1	10.3	DEP	44.3	8.6
6(Pa)	47.8	7.8	GF	46.3	12.1	CPS	42.9	10.0
7(Pt)	46.3	6.9	Mt	43.1	7.5	Personality Psychopathology Five		
8(Sc)	48.0	6.6	PK	44.0	6.8	Scale	M	SD
9(Ma)	48.8	6.7	PS	43.7	6.6	AGG	50.3	8.2
0(Si)	44.4	7.9	MAC-R	50.3	9.0	PSY	46.0	8.3
			APS	42.9	10.9	CON	49.5	9.1
			AAS	46.1	8.3	NEN	43.3	9.2
			MDS	45.6	7.9	PEE	52.4	8.2
			Ho	45.9	9.4			
			CAL-R	51.9	8.2			

Content			Content Component					
Scale	M	SD	Scale	M	SD	Scale	M	SD
ANX	45.5	8.2	FRS1	46.6	8.3	ASP1	47.5	10.4
FRS	45.6	9.5	FRS2	45.4	10.6	ASP2	49.5	10.4
OBS	42.6	8.5	DEP1	45.5	6.5	TPA1	42.9	8.8
DEP	44.0	7.9	DEP2	45.1	7.7	TPA2	45.0	9.3
HEA	45.7	8.1	DEP3	44.9	7.6	LSE1	43.6	6.6
BIZ	46.7	7.9	DEP4	46.4	5.8	LSE2	44.6	7.6
ANG	44.1	8.5	HEA1	47.2	7.0	SOD1	46.2	8.4
CYN	47.6	10.3	HEA2	45.3	7.1	SOD2	45.0	8.5
ASP	48.2	10.0	HEA3	49.0	8.3	FAM1	43.2	9.3
TPA	44.2	8.9	BIZ1	46.6	7.3	FAM2	49.4	9.3
LSE	43.5	7.6	BIZ2	45.6	6.9	TRT1	45.0	6.7
SOD	45.4	8.4	ANG1	45.7	8.0	TRT2	44.2	8.1
FAM	44.6	8.9	ANG2	43.6	8.8			
WRK	42.9	8.3	CYN1	48.0	11.0			
TRT	44.0	8.3	CYN2	46.1	9.5			

Note. All scores are T scores except: Cannot Say, K & B and L & W critical items which are raw scores; True % and False % which are the percentage of items endorsed "true" or "false;" and |F - FB|, F - K, and O - S which are difference scores.

Appendix D-36

Prototypic Scores for 5-6/6-5 Codetypes (N = 154)

Demographics

		M	SD	Marital Status		%
	Age	36.2	12.7		Never Married	38.7
	Education	12.7	5.9		Married	28.5
	Gender	%			Separated	10.2
	Men	54.5			Divorced	21.2
	Women	45.5			Widowed	1.5

Test-Taking Scales

Omissions		M	SD	Consistency		M	SD
	?	1.0	3.0		VRIN	53.6	10.9
					|F - FB|	3.1	2.3
					TRIN	50.5	11.5

Accuracy of Item Endorsement

Underreporting		M	SD	Overreporting		M	SD
	False %	58.8	6.8		True %	40.0	6.8
Impression	L	53.0	11.4	Infrequency	F	55.8	12.0
Management	ODecp	49.6	11.0		FB	55.7	13.7
	Sd	51.6	10.8		F[p]	55.2	13.3
Superior	S	48.5	8.6	Critical Items	K & B	19.4	8.9
Adjustment					L & W	26.4	10.0
Self-Deception	K	31.1	6.4	Dissimulation	F - K	-8.1	6.9
	So	46.3	10.0		Ds	55.3	10.6
					O - S	33.4	62.0

Scales

Validity and Clinical			Supplementary			Morey et al. Overlapping Personality Disorder		
Scale	M	SD	Scale	M	SD	Scale	M	SD
?	1.0	3.0	A	52.6	9.4	PAR	58.6	11.9
L	53.0	11.4	R	50.8	9.2	SZD	49.8	10.3
F	55.8	12.0	Es	45.7	9.7	STY	55.4	10.2
K	47.4	9.0	TRIN	50.5	11.5	ANT	51.5	8.9
1(Hs)	50.2	8.9	VRIN	53.6	10.9	BDL	54.5	10.1
2(D)	53.9	9.2	O-H	54.7	9.6	HST	49.9	9.7
3(Hy)	53.0	9.1	Do	48.0	12.1	NAR	50.5	8.8
4(Pd)	57.9	8.1	Re	45.5	10.7	AVD	52.2	9.4
5(Mf)	70.9	5.1	GM	45.0	11.4	DEP	51.9	9.6
6(Pa)	73.1	6.4	GF	48.8	13.9	CPS	51.4	9.1
7(Pt)	54.7	8.9	Mt	54.0	9.8	Personality Psychopathology Five		
8(Sc)	57.1	8.7	PK	55.5	9.7	Scale	M	SD
9(Ma)	52.8	8.7	PS	54.8	9.7	AGG	50.0	8.4
0(Si)	50.3	9.9	MAC-R	50.9	10.0	PSY	56.9	12.1
			APS	51.3	11.1	CON	48.1	8.9
			AAS	50.8	9.5	NEN	54.6	9.7
			MDS	56.5	11.3	PEE	49.0	9.2
			Ho	52.7	10.3			
			CAL-R	53.6	9.3			

Content			Content Component					
Scale	M	SD	Scale	M	SD	Scale	M	SD
ANX	57.4	9.2	FRS1	51.9	12.2	ASP1	48.8	9.9
FRS	51.4	10.2	FRS2	50.0	10.3	ASP2	54.7	10.6
OBS	50.6	9.2	DEP1	52.7	10.3	TPA1	48.5	9.7
DEP	55.9	9.1	DEP2	58.2	12.9	TPA2	51.5	10.3
HEA	53.6	8.6	DEP3	53.6	10.7	LSE1	50.3	10.4
BIZ	57.8	10.0	DEP4	50.3	10.9	LSE2	49.2	9.8
ANG	51.5	10.0	HEA1	49.8	9.3	SOD1	50.6	10.2
CYN	51.4	10.7	HEA2	51.1	9.5	SOD2	49.5	9.6
ASP	51.0	9.3	HEA3	52.7	9.6	FAM1	53.0	11.1
TPA	50.3	9.8	BIZ1	55.0	12.8	FAM2	53.4	14.0
LSE	51.0	10.4	BIZ2	57.1	11.7	TRT1	51.5	11.0
SOD	50.9	9.9	ANG1	51.0	10.1	TRT2	49.3	10.4
FAM	55.3	11.2	ANG2	51.4	9.7			
WRK	51.5	9.8	CYN1	50.3	11.2			
TRT	51.4	11.2	CYN2	51.2	10.4			

Note. All scores are T scores except: Cannot Say, K & B and L & W critical items which are raw scores; True % and False % which are the percentage of items endorsed "true" or "false;" and |F - FB|, F - K, and O - S which are difference scores.

610

Appendix D-37

Prototypic Scores for 5-7/7-5 Codetypes (N = 68)

Demographics

		M	SD	Marital Status		%
	Age	35.1	11.9		Never Married	62.9
	Education	13.1	5.8		Married	24.2
	Gender	%			Separated	0.0
	Men	75.0			Divorced	11.3
	Women	25.0			Widowed	1.6

Test-Taking Scales

Omissions / Consistency

Omissions		M	SD	Consistency	M	SD
	?	1.0	3.3	VRIN	56.8	10.5
				|F - FB|	3.1	2.1
				TRIN	52.0	11.8

Accuracy of Item Endorsement

Underreporting		M	SD	Overreporting		M	SD
	False %	57.0	6.3		True %	41.8	6.3
Impression	L	48.1	10.0	Infrequency	F	56.5	9.4
Management	ODecp	40.8	10.4		FB	57.6	12.0
	Sd	45.1	9.9		F[p]	51.2	10.2
Superior	S	45.9	9.4	Critical Items	K & B	23.7	8.7
Adjustment					L & W	29.6	8.9
Self-Deception	K	31.1	6.4	Dissimulation	F - K	-7.7	6.2
	So	38.6	10.3		Ds	59.5	11.3
					O - S	46.8	61.4

Scales

Validity and Clinical			Supplementary			Morey et al. Overlapping Personality Disorder		
Scale	M	SD	Scale	M	SD	Scale	M	SD
?	1.0	3.3	A	62.5	11.5	PAR	53.9	9.6
L	48.1	10.0	R	52.2	12.3	SZD	50.2	10.0
F	56.5	9.4	Es	41.9	9.4	STY	55.9	9.0
K	47.5	9.2	TRIN	52.0	11.8	ANT	52.6	9.3
1(Hs)	52.2	9.3	VRIN	56.8	10.5	BDL	57.5	10.9
2(D)	62.7	8.1	O-H	50.5	9.9	HST	46.1	10.2
3(Hy)	55.0	7.7	Do	43.2	8.9	NAR	42.8	10.5
4(Pd)	59.2	8.1	Re	47.9	9.2	AVD	59.5	9.7
5(Mf)	72.3	5.3	GM	38.6	12.0	DEP	65.0	14.0
6(Pa)	57.7	8.3	GF	54.5	12.9	CPS	55.4	9.5
7(Pt)	73.3	6.5	Mt	64.2	9.6	Personality Psychopathology Five		
8(Sc)	63.0	6.9	PK	62.6	10.7	Scale	M	SD
9(Ma)	53.6	9.9	PS	64.7	11.5	AGG	44.6	11.6
0(Si)	57.3	9.6	MAC-R	45.9	10.1	PSY	52.9	10.6
			APS	55.3	9.9	CON	49.9	10.4
			AAS	55.1	12.3	NEN	60.8	9.9
			MDS	57.3	10.3	PEE	42.9	10.5
			Ho	50.6	9.6			
			CAL-R	53.4	9.2			

Content			Content Component					
Scale	M	SD	Scale	M	SD	Scale	M	SD
ANX	64.8	10.5	FRS1	53.9	11.3	ASP1	48.9	9.6
FRS	52.8	9.0	FRS2	51.0	9.5	ASP2	49.7	10.3
OBS	60.4	12.6	DEP1	63.4	12.4	TPA1	51.2	11.0
DEP	64.6	9.2	DEP2	65.0	13.2	TPA2	49.8	10.4
HEA	53.8	9.6	DEP3	60.6	11.1	LSE1	59.0	11.5
BIZ	52.7	8.6	DEP4	56.3	16.4	LSE2	55.6	13.6
ANG	54.3	10.2	HEA1	51.8	10.2	SOD1	52.9	9.6
CYN	49.4	9.3	HEA2	49.9	9.2	SOD2	56.0	10.5
ASP	49.4	8.8	HEA3	53.8	10.0	FAM1	54.6	11.5
TPA	50.9	11.6	BIZ1	48.5	8.3	FAM2	54.1	12.2
LSE	60.0	11.9	BIZ2	52.0	8.8	TRT1	61.0	12.2
SOD	55.0	10.5	ANG1	51.7	10.0	TRT2	52.9	9.6
FAM	56.9	10.7	ANG2	55.5	10.7			
WRK	61.6	12.0	CYN1	49.2	9.9			
TRT	58.8	9.8	CYN2	48.9	10.5			

Note. All scores are T scores except: Cannot Say, K & B and L & W critical items which are raw scores; True % and False % which are the percentage of items endorsed "true" or "false;" and |F - FB|, F - K, and O - S which are difference scores.

Appendix D-38

Prototypic Scores for 5-8/8-5 Codetypes (N = 76)

Demographics

Demographics		M	SD	Marital Status		%
Age		34.5	14.9	Never Married		50.0
Education		9.7	6.4	Married		33.3
Gender		%		Separated		3.3
	Men	30.3		Divorced		13.3
	Women	69.7		Widowed		0.0

Test-Taking Scales

Omissions		M	SD	Consistency		M	SD
	?	2.6	5.1		VRIN	61.3	11.6
					|F - FB|	4.0	3.1
					TRIN	56.5	17.1

Accuracy of Item Endorsement

Underreporting		M	SD	Overreporting		M	SD
	False %	52.7	9.9		True %	45.9	9.8
Impression	L	52.1	12.4	Infrequency	F	68.6	18.3
Management	ODecp	52.2	11.7		FB	70.8	25.2
	Sd	54.4	12.8		F[p]	67.1	20.2
Superior	S	45.4	10.8	Critical Items	K & B	24.9	10.4
Adjustment					L & W	34.3	13.1
Self-Deception	K	31.1	6.4	Dissimulation	F - K	-3.2	9.0
	So	39.0	11.2		Ds	64.7	14.0
					O - S	77.7	74.2

Scales

Validity and Clinical			Supplementary			Morey et al. Overlapping Personality Disorder		
Scale	M	SD	Scale	M	SD	Scale	M	SD
?	2.6	5.1	A	58.8	10.1	PAR	59.5	13.2
L	52.1	12.4	R	49.3	9.3	SZD	55.3	9.5
F	68.6	18.3	Es	38.4	11.3	STY	59.4	10.7
K	44.9	10.4	TRIN	56.5	17.1	ANT	56.4	10.5
1(Hs)	55.1	9.3	VRIN	61.3	11.6	BDL	54.5	10.5
2(D)	55.8	8.8	O-H	50.1	11.9	HST	46.4	9.3
3(Hy)	52.1	9.9	Do	37.6	12.5	NAR	50.5	8.8
4(Pd)	58.0	8.7	Re	40.4	12.3	AVD	54.4	9.3
5(Mf)	73.2	6.9	GM	44.9	9.8	DEP	54.4	11.1
6(Pa)	59.5	10.1	GF	39.0	16.7	CPS	53.4	9.5
7(Pt)	60.4	8.9	Mt	59.8	9.2	Personality Psychopathology Five		
8(Sc)	72.2	7.9	PK	63.5	12.0			
9(Ma)	57.3	9.2	PS	63.9	11.0	Scale	M	SD
0(Si)	54.6	7.9	MAC-R	54.0	12.7	AGG	52.6	10.3
			APS	48.3	10.0	PSY	62.8	13.8
			AAS	54.2	12.6	CON	45.7	10.1
			MDS	59.7	9.6	NEN	56.9	10.3
			Ho	57.5	12.3	PEE	45.3	9.5
			CAL-R	53.6	11.5			

Content			Content Component					
Scale	M	SD	Scale	M	SD	Scale	M	SD
ANX	58.8	10.1	FRS1	60.2	17.4	ASP1	56.3	12.6
FRS	54.8	13.1	FRS2	49.4	9.3	ASP2	55.6	12.2
OBS	58.6	12.1	DEP1	62.0	12.2	TPA1	50.8	11.4
DEP	61.4	10.2	DEP2	55.9	10.5	TPA2	54.4	12.5
HEA	58.0	9.7	DEP3	59.6	14.2	LSE1	56.0	12.3
BIZ	63.3	11.0	DEP4	59.9	19.8	LSE2	53.0	10.3
ANG	54.2	11.8	HEA1	53.5	10.7	SOD1	54.6	9.3
CYN	58.5	13.3	HEA2	60.4	12.7	SOD2	51.7	9.0
ASP	58.0	12.8	HEA3	52.9	9.8	FAM1	57.4	12.5
TPA	53.5	13.5	BIZ1	59.1	16.0	FAM2	56.9	13.9
LSE	57.7	12.4	BIZ2	62.4	13.4	TRT1	60.1	13.8
SOD	54.4	8.8	ANG1	56.2	12.8	TRT2	56.2	11.5
FAM	59.4	12.4	ANG2	52.3	10.2			
WRK	60.3	11.5	CYN1	57.9	12.6			
TRT	61.5	13.0	CYN2	54.8	11.1			

Note. All scores are T scores except: Cannot Say, K & B and L & W critical items which are raw scores; True % and False % which are the percentage of items endorsed "true" or "false;" and |F - FB|, F - K, and O - S which are difference scores.

612

Appendix D-39

Prototypic Scores for 5-9/9-5 Codetypes (N = 187)

Demographics

Demographics		M	SD	Marital Status	%
Age		32.3	12.6	Never Married	47.7
Education		11.0	6.2	Married	30.1
Gender	%			Separated	5.2
	Men	23.5		Divorced	15.0
	Women	76.5		Widowed	2.0

Test-Taking Scales

Omissions		M	SD	Consistency	M	SD
	?	1.1	3.2	VRIN	51.6	11.1
				|F - FB|	3.2	2.4
				TRIN	54.8	11.5

Accuracy of Item Endorsement

Underreporting		M	SD	Overreporting		M	SD
	False %	55.7	7.1		True %	43.1	7.0
Impression	L	53.8	11.9	Infrequency	F	55.1	12.1
Management	ODecp	58.7	12.4		FB	53.1	12.6
	Sd	59.4	12.5		F[p]	55.9	13.4
Superior	S	46.9	9.0	Critical Items	K & B	15.5	8.2
Adjustment					L & W	23.4	9.9
Self-Deception	K	31.1	6.4	Dissimulation	F - K	-8.8	7.0
	So	50.0	9.3		Ds	55.0	9.7
					O - S	22.8	58.8

Scales

Validity and Clinical			Supplementary			Morey et al. Overlapping Personality Disorder		
Scale	M	SD	Scale	M	SD	Scale	M	SD
?	1.1	3.2	A	49.1	8.7	PAR	55.8	11.5
L	53.8	11.9	R	44.3	8.7	SZD	46.4	8.3
F	55.1	12.1	Es	50.4	10.3	STY	48.5	9.7
K	48.0	9.6	TRIN	54.8	11.5	ANT	57.0	10.9
1(Hs)	48.9	8.5	VRIN	51.6	11.1	BDL	53.9	9.3
2(D)	45.8	8.7	O-H	51.5	9.5	HST	55.9	7.6
3(Hy)	46.4	8.6	Do	45.7	11.5	NAR	60.2	7.6
4(Pd)	53.9	8.5	Re	41.5	11.0	AVD	44.4	7.9
5(Mf)	71.1	5.8	GM	51.5	11.4	DEP	47.1	7.9
6(Pa)	51.2	9.2	GF	38.8	16.0	CPS	51.9	9.9
7(Pt)	49.6	8.1	Mt	50.0	8.3	Personality Psychopathology Five		
8(Sc)	54.2	7.7	PK	51.5	8.9			
9(Ma)	70.5	5.6	PS	52.4	9.0	Scale	M	SD
0(Si)	44.3	8.4	MAC-R	59.8	11.1	AGG	58.7	9.2
			APS	49.3	10.6	PSY	56.0	11.6
			AAS	52.5	10.5	CON	41.7	10.3
			MDS	52.1	9.3	NEN	51.1	9.8
			Ho	57.3	10.5	PEE	56.9	7.5
			CAL-R	53.5	10.0			

Content			Content Component					
Scale	M	SD	Scale	M	SD	Scale	M	SD
ANX	52.0	9.5	FRS1	50.9	11.3	ASP1	58.6	11.5
FRS	48.4	11.1	FRS2	46.6	11.3	ASP2	57.5	14.0
OBS	51.5	9.8	DEP1	51.2	9.7	TPA1	48.4	9.8
DEP	50.2	9.3	DEP2	48.7	9.1	TPA2	55.0	11.9
HEA	52.1	8.8	DEP3	49.7	10.1	LSE1	46.4	7.1
BIZ	56.1	10.2	DEP4	48.0	8.9	LSE2	48.8	9.0
ANG	53.0	10.8	HEA1	51.9	10.6	SOD1	45.0	8.2
CYN	58.1	11.7	HEA2	50.9	9.2	SOD2	44.8	7.7
ASP	60.7	12.8	HEA3	51.8	9.4	FAM1	53.4	10.7
TPA	53.1	11.9	BIZ1	54.1	13.2	FAM2	52.2	10.5
LSE	48.3	8.2	BIZ2	53.8	10.7	TRT1	48.8	9.8
SOD	44.9	7.8	ANG1	54.1	11.0	TRT2	49.0	9.8
FAM	54.2	10.3	ANG2	51.0	10.2			
WRK	49.7	9.0	CYN1	57.4	11.7			
TRT	50.3	10.3	CYN2	55.7	10.2			

Note. All scores are T scores except: Cannot Say, K & B and L & W critical items which are raw scores; True % and False % which are the percentage of items endorsed "true" or "false;" and \|F - FB\|, F - K, and O - S which are difference scores.

Appendix D-40
Prototypic Scores for 5-0/0-5 Codetypes (N = 42)

Demographics

Demographics		M	SD	Marital Status	%
	Age	35.4	10.5	Never Married	42.5
	Education	13.9	5.3	Married	42.5
	Gender	%		Separated	7.5
	Men	64.3		Divorced	5.0
	Women	35.7		Widowed	2.5

Test-Taking Scales

Omissions		M	SD	Consistency	M	SD
	?	0.7	2.0	VRIN	56.2	9.2
				|F - FB|	3.5	2.6
				TRIN	51.2	13.8

Accuracy of Item Endorsement

Underreporting		M	SD	Overreporting		M	SD
	False %	57.6	6.4		True %	41.2	6.4
Impression	L	49.3	9.0	Infrequency	F	57.7	10.0
Management	ODecp	41.0	8.7		FB	58.0	13.6
	Sd	42.9	9.2		F[p]	55.8	10.0
Superior	S	43.6	7.7	Critical Items	K & B	18.4	7.2
Adjustment					L & W	24.4	7.4
Self-Deception	K	31.1	6.4	Dissimulation	F - K	-4.3	4.4
	So	37.6	7.6		Ds	60.4	9.7
					O - S	58.8	37.5

Scales

Validity and Clinical			Supplementary			Morey et al. Overlapping Personality Disorder		
Scale	M	SD	Scale	M	SD	Scale	M	SD
?	0.7	2.0	A	60.4	8.6	PAR	57.6	10.1
L	49.3	9.0	R	57.4	8.9	SZD	64.6	9.7
F	57.7	10.0	Es	42.5	8.5	STY	67.2	7.2
K	41.0	5.4	TRIN	51.2	13.8	ANT	51.5	10.0
1(Hs)	45.1	9.0	VRIN	56.2	9.2	BDL	51.9	10.5
2(D)	58.5	6.1	O-H	49.9	11.2	HST	35.5	7.1
3(Hy)	44.9	9.3	Do	39.5	11.0	NAR	37.2	9.1
4(Pd)	51.5	7.3	Re	47.1	9.6	AVD	69.8	6.3
5(Mf)	70.8	5.2	GM	37.5	12.6	DEP	65.0	12.2
6(Pa)	52.3	8.8	GF	53.5	12.3	CPS	54.1	8.2
7(Pt)	55.1	9.2	Mt	58.9	6.8	Personality Psychopathology Five		
8(Sc)	52.8	9.9	PK	59.6	6.9			
9(Ma)	44.4	6.8	PS	58.3	7.5	Scale	M	SD
0(Si)	69.7	4.0	MAC-R	41.2	11.6	AGG	43.7	10.4
			APS	50.3	7.3	PSY	54.5	9.4
			AAS	49.6	12.0	CON	53.3	9.4
			MDS	59.0	10.1	NEN	59.8	7.1
			Ho	57.3	8.2	PEE	37.2	7.1
			CAL-R	52.0	9.3			

Content			Content Component					
Scale	M	SD	Scale	M	SD	Scale	M	SD
ANX	59.7	7.1	FRS1	57.5	15.1	ASP1	54.2	9.8
FRS	57.0	13.5	FRS2	54.3	12.2	ASP2	47.0	7.9
OBS	55.3	10.1	DEP1	54.5	8.1	TPA1	53.3	11.1
DEP	60.1	7.1	DEP2	61.3	11.0	TPA2	52.9	10.0
HEA	52.4	7.9	DEP3	60.1	9.4	LSE1	58.6	10.3
BIZ	51.4	9.0	DEP4	50.9	11.4	LSE2	58.1	12.6
ANG	54.0	10.8	HEA1	50.7	8.3	SOD1	66.1	8.8
CYN	54.8	10.0	HEA2	48.4	8.9	SOD2	65.0	6.5
ASP	52.9	9.7	HEA3	52.4	9.0	FAM1	56.6	10.5
TPA	53.3	11.2	BIZ1	49.2	9.1	FAM2	56.4	13.7
LSE	60.2	8.6	BIZ2	50.2	10.2	TRT1	58.0	11.5
SOD	69.3	8.7	ANG1	50.9	11.6	TRT2	58.8	10.6
FAM	57.5	9.9	ANG2	55.1	10.2			
WRK	59.7	6.8	CYN1	55.4	10.6			
TRT	60.1	9.5	CYN2	52.6	10.0			

Note. All scores are T scores except: Cannot Say, K & B and L & W critical items which are raw scores; True % and False % which are the percentage of items endorsed "true" or "false;" and |F - FB|, F - K, and O - S which are difference scores.

Appendix D-43

Prototypic Scores for 6-8/8-6 Codetypes (N = 1,929)

Demographics

Demographics		M	SD	Marital Status		%
Age		34.0	12.4		Never Married	47.5
Education		11.0	4.9		Married	33.2
Gender		%			Separated	5.2
	Men	56.4			Divorced	13.1
	Women	43.6			Widowed	1.0

Test-Taking Scales

Omissions		M	SD	Consistency	M	SD
	?	1.6	3.7	VRIN	55.8	11.5
				|F - FB|	5.6	4.2
				TRIN	56.2	13.0

Accuracy of Item Endorsement

Underreporting		M	SD	Overreporting		M	SD
	False %	44.1	8.0		True %	54.6	8.0
Impression	L	50.5	10.0	Infrequency	F	99.0	19.3
Management	ODecp	44.6	9.7		FB	105.4	27.5
	Sd	48.5	10.7		F[p]	78.4	20.0
Superior	S	37.1	8.3	Critical Items	K & B	49.4	12.6
Adjustment					L & W	63.6	16.5
Self-Deception	K	31.1	6.4	Dissimulation	F - K	11.4	9.7
	So	19.5	12.5		Ds	85.5	14.8
					O - S	195.9	71.5

Scales

Validity and Clinical / Supplementary / Morey et al. Overlapping Personality Disorder

Scale	M	SD	Scale	M	SD	Scale	M	SD
?	1.6	3.7	A	74.0	9.4	PAR	78.2	11.6
L	50.5	10.0	R	51.5	11.4	SZD	61.8	12.5
F	99.0	19.3	Es	17.2	13.9	STY	78.7	12.6
K	37.7	7.5	TRIN	56.2	13.0	ANT	61.5	11.8
1(Hs)	73.6	15.2	VRIN	55.8	11.5	BDL	63.8	9.7
2(D)	77.3	14.0	O-H	47.2	10.3	HST	40.5	11.6
3(Hy)	70.8	15.8	Do	29.2	11.0	NAR	42.7	11.5
4(Pd)	73.9	12.1	Re	34.0	11.6	AVD	66.7	10.6
5(Mf)	54.1	9.4	GM	29.9	12.3	DEP	66.7	12.5
6(Pa)	96.5	13.4	GF	40.0	11.6	CPS	62.1	8.6
7(Pt)	80.9	12.9	Mt	76.7	9.7	Personality Psychopathology Five		
8(Sc)	95.0	13.9	PK	88.0	13.6	Scale	M	SD
9(Ma)	64.4	11.4	PS	87.9	12.9	AGG	55.8	11.3
0(Si)	66.1	10.7	MAC-R	59.0	11.7	PSY	89.3	18.2
			APS	53.1	10.5	CON	47.4	12.1
			AAS	60.8	14.4	NEN	70.7	9.6
			MDS	76.3	12.3	PEE	33.0	14.3
			Ho	67.1	9.0			
			CAL-R	56.7	11.1			

Content / Content Component

Scale	M	SD	Scale	M	SD	Scale	M	SD
ANX	77.5	10.3	FRS1	78.1	23.1	ASP1	58.5	9.9
FRS	65.2	15.4	FRS2	54.3	10.8	ASP2	59.2	13.4
OBS	69.9	11.2	DEP1	81.7	15.0	TPA1	59.0	9.3
DEP	80.4	11.6	DEP2	74.1	10.8	TPA2	60.9	11.3
HEA	77.9	14.6	DEP3	73.6	12.2	LSE1	70.4	13.4
BIZ	84.4	15.7	DEP4	90.0	30.2	LSE2	61.8	11.8
ANG	66.7	11.8	HEA1	71.6	18.6	SOD1	64.3	12.5
CYN	64.9	10.8	HEA2	81.3	18.6	SOD2	57.8	9.8
ASP	61.6	12.3	HEA3	69.1	13.4	FAM1	65.8	12.2
TPA	62.6	12.7	BIZ1	91.3	27.3	FAM2	62.3	14.6
LSE	72.3	13.1	BIZ2	80.4	12.8	TRT1	78.4	16.3
SOD	65.0	12.9	ANG1	65.3	12.5	TRT2	62.5	10.2
FAM	70.8	13.3	ANG2	62.7	8.7			
WRK	76.0	11.6	CYN1	61.6	9.0			
TRT	77.9	13.3	CYN2	62.4	8.5			

Note. All scores are T scores except: Cannot Say, K & B and L & W critical items which are raw scores; True % and False % which are the percentage of items endorsed "true" or "false;" and |F - FB|, F - K, and O - S which are difference scores.

Appendix D-44

Prototypic Scores for 6-9/9-6 Codetypes (N = 356)

Demographics

Demographics		M	SD	Marital Status	%
Age		32.1	11.9	Never Married	52.7
Education		11.6	5.3	Married	28.1
Gender		%		Separated	7.6
	Men	58.1		Divorced	11.7
	Women	41.9		Widowed	0.0

Test-Taking Scales

Omissions		M	SD	Consistency		M	SD
	?	0.9	2.6		VRIN	52.8	11.8
					|F - FB|	4.2	3.3
					TRIN	55.6	12.2

Accuracy of Item Endorsement

Underreporting		M	SD	Overreporting		M	SD
	False %	52.0	8.0		True %	46.8	8.0
Impression	L	50.5	10.4	Infrequency	F	64.3	16.6
Management	ODecp	53.9	9.2		FB	62.3	17.9
	Sd	57.5	9.3		F[p]	60.0	15.6
Superior	S	43.7	9.2	Critical Items	K & B	25.3	10.7
Adjustment					L & W	34.3	13.0
Self-Deception	K	31.1	6.4	Dissimulation	F - K	-3.8	8.6
	So	42.6	11.1		Ds	61.4	12.0
					O - S	60.3	66.9

Scales

Validity and Clinical			Supplementary			Morey et al. Overlapping Personality Disorder		
Scale	M	SD	Scale	M	SD	Scale	M	SD
?	0.9	2.6	A	56.5	10.4	PAR	65.7	12.6
L	50.5	10.4	R	43.0	8.6	SZD	45.3	8.6
F	64.3	16.6	Es	42.3	11.0	STY	56.0	10.1
K	44.3	9.3	TRIN	55.6	12.2	ANT	57.7	11.3
1(Hs)	52.5	10.6	VRIN	52.8	11.8	BDL	60.5	10.4
2(D)	50.7	9.4	O-H	49.4	10.4	HST	56.7	7.8
3(Hy)	51.6	10.3	Do	43.5	12.2	NAR	58.6	7.3
4(Pd)	59.7	9.0	Re	37.8	10.7	AVD	47.8	8.0
5(Mf)	50.7	9.1	GM	46.0	9.4	DEP	52.1	10.1
6(Pa)	75.3	8.0	GF	41.3	11.0	CPS	55.6	9.4
7(Pt)	57.0	9.2	Mt	57.2	10.4	Personality Psychopathology Five		
8(Sc)	62.3	9.7	PK	60.9	11.4			
9(Ma)	75.4	8.0	PS	60.9	11.6	Scale	M	SD
0(Si)	45.8	8.5	MAC-R	60.8	10.1	AGG	59.0	9.7
			APS	55.1	10.2	PSY	67.5	15.6
			AAS	55.6	11.3	CON	41.7	10.1
			MDS	57.2	10.7	NEN	58.1	10.2
			Ho	59.4	10.2	PEE	56.3	7.1
			CAL-R	55.5	10.2			

Content			Content Component					
Scale	M	SD	Scale	M	SD	Scale	M	SD
ANX	60.7	10.2	FRS1	54.8	14.1	ASP1	56.2	11.0
FRS	50.4	10.5	FRS2	47.3	9.6	ASP2	57.7	12.0
OBS	56.2	11.0	DEP1	56.9	12.4	TPA1	51.3	10.3
DEP	58.4	10.4	DEP2	57.0	11.5	TPA2	57.8	11.4
HEA	56.9	10.3	DEP3	56.4	12.0	LSE1	50.7	9.4
BIZ	66.6	12.6	DEP4	53.6	15.8	LSE2	52.0	10.9
ANG	58.4	12.2	HEA1	53.9	12.3	SOD1	45.8	8.1
CYN	58.1	11.8	HEA2	56.9	13.3	SOD2	45.2	8.4
ASP	59.0	12.5	HEA3	54.3	10.8	FAM1	57.1	11.4
TPA	56.3	12.0	BIZ1	66.0	19.0	FAM2	52.8	12.7
LSE	52.9	10.1	BIZ2	64.2	12.8	TRT1	54.5	12.9
SOD	45.5	8.1	ANG1	57.9	12.5	TRT2	51.4	10.3
FAM	59.0	11.5	ANG2	55.9	10.4			
WRK	55.9	10.6	CYN1	55.6	10.9			
TRT	55.3	11.6	CYN2	57.9	9.5			

Note. All scores are T scores except: Cannot Say, K & B and L & W critical items which are raw scores; True % and False % which are the percentage of items endorsed "true" or "false;" and \|F - FB\|, F - K, and O - S which are difference scores.

Appendix D-45

Prototypic Scores for 6-0/0-6 Codetypes (N = 139)

Demographics

Demographics		M	SD	Marital Status	%
Age		37.6	10.9	Never Married	28.0
Education		12.8	4.4	Married	49.6
Gender		%		Separated	8.0
	Men	64.0		Divorced	13.6
	Women	36.0		Widowed	0.8

Test-Taking Scales

Omissions		M	SD	Consistency	M	SD
	?	1.0	2.8	VRIN	52.3	9.2
				|F - FB|	3.5	2.8
				TRIN	53.7	11.1

Accuracy of Item Endorsement

Underreporting		M	SD	Overreporting		M	SD
	False %	54.0	6.7		True %	44.8	6.8
Impression	L	52.1	9.0	Infrequency	F	64.9	15.1
Management	ODecp	44.7	8.4		FB	67.1	17.7
	Sd	47.8	9.0		F[p]	55.9	12.3
Superior	S	42.3	7.9	Critical Items	K & B	28.3	9.6
Adjustment					L & W	33.7	10.5
Self-Deception	K	31.1	6.4	Dissimulation	F - K	-0.9	7.3
	So	31.6	9.7		Ds	62.2	10.8
					O - S	97.5	54.6

Scales

Validity and Clinical			Supplementary			Morey et al. Overlapping Personality Disorder		
Scale	M	SD	Scale	M	SD	Scale	M	SD
?	1.0	2.8	A	65.0	8.1	PAR	67.5	11.3
L	52.1	9.0	R	54.8	8.4	SZD	66.4	7.6
F	64.9	15.1	Es	37.2	9.9	STY	74.3	7.3
K	38.8	7.3	TRIN	53.7	11.1	ANT	52.4	9.2
1(Hs)	50.7	9.6	VRIN	52.3	9.2	BDL	54.9	9.0
2(D)	64.2	6.6	O-H	46.4	10.5	HST	32.9	6.5
3(Hy)	48.5	8.6	Do	36.7	10.1	NAR	36.3	8.8
4(Pd)	57.8	8.6	Re	43.7	10.0	AVD	72.3	5.3
5(Mf)	49.9	8.6	GM	37.3	9.1	DEP	64.2	10.0
6(Pa)	75.1	7.6	GF	47.8	9.1	CPS	57.6	7.5
7(Pt)	59.7	8.5	Mt	64.9	8.9	Personality Psychopathology Five		
8(Sc)	59.1	9.3	PK	67.3	10.2	Scale	M	SD
9(Ma)	46.7	7.6	PS	66.9	10.7	AGG	46.4	10.3
0(Si)	72.2	5.0	MAC-R	47.8	10.5	PSY	63.5	13.0
			APS	48.8	9.8	CON	54.8	9.2
			AAS	51.3	10.7	NEN	63.9	8.4
			MDS	66.0	12.0	PEE	34.9	8.8
			Ho	60.9	9.5			
			CAL-R	52.2	8.9			

Content			Content Component					
Scale	M	SD	Scale	M	SD	Scale	M	SD
ANX	66.0	9.2	FRS1	56.7	13.5	ASP1	52.8	10.1
FRS	54.3	10.7	FRS2	51.5	10.8	ASP2	52.5	10.8
OBS	59.7	9.0	DEP1	63.7	14.5	TPA1	56.0	9.7
DEP	66.8	10.2	DEP2	66.5	12.4	TPA2	55.8	10.1
HEA	57.1	9.4	DEP3	64.3	12.2	LSE1	62.8	11.9
BIZ	59.4	9.8	DEP4	58.6	19.4	LSE2	61.3	10.9
ANG	59.6	11.3	HEA1	54.5	12.2	SOD1	68.5	7.5
CYN	58.3	11.3	HEA2	55.0	11.1	SOD2	65.5	6.6
ASP	53.6	10.4	HEA3	54.8	9.2	FAM1	57.1	10.6
TPA	56.4	11.9	BIZ1	58.1	14.7	FAM2	58.3	14.2
LSE	65.1	10.9	BIZ2	57.4	10.6	TRT1	66.0	14.2
SOD	71.6	7.4	ANG1	55.9	11.7	TRT2	57.1	11.0
FAM	60.7	11.7	ANG2	60.0	9.8			
WRK	64.4	9.5	CYN1	56.1	10.6			
TRT	65.9	12.2	CYN2	57.9	9.5			

Note. All scores are T scores except: Cannot Say, K & B and L & W critical items which are raw scores; True % and False % which are the percentage of items endorsed "true" or "false;" and |F - FB|, F - K, and O - S which are difference scores.

Appendix D-46

Prototypic Scores for Spike 7 Codetypes (N = 185)

Demographics

Demographics		M	SD	Marital Status		%
	Age	34.3	12.3		Never Married	43.0
	Education	12.7	6.0		Married	40.1
	Gender	%			Separated	2.9
	Men	64.3			Divorced	13.4
	Women	35.7			Widowed	0.6

Test-Taking Scales

Omissions		M	SD	Consistency		M	SD
	?	1.1	2.9		VRIN	52.9	9.8
					|F - FB|	2.9	2.0
					TRIN	50.4	9.7

Accuracy of Item Endorsement

Underreporting		M	SD	Overreporting		M	SD
	False %	58.7	6.6		True %	40.2	6.6
Impression	L	50.3	10.0	Infrequency	F	51.2	6.9
Management	ODecp	46.6	9.0		FB	52.4	10.4
	Sd	49.3	9.4		F[p]	49.2	8.1
Superior	S	48.7	9.5	Critical Items	K & B	17.9	8.0
Adjustment					L & W	23.1	9.0
Self-Deception	K	31.1	6.4	Dissimulation	F - K	-11.1	5.9
	So	44.5	8.1		Ds	52.9	9.3
					O - S	21.5	52.4

Scales

Validity and Clinical			Supplementary			Morey et al. Overlapping Personality Disorder		
Scale	M	SD	Scale	M	SD	Scale	M	SD
?	1.1	2.9	A	57.1	8.7	PAR	51.3	9.3
L	50.3	10.0	R	51.2	9.7	SZD	48.6	9.1
F	51.2	6.9	Es	45.9	8.5	STY	51.6	8.3
K	51.0	10.3	TRIN	50.4	9.7	ANT	49.8	9.8
1(Hs)	52.2	7.3	VRIN	52.9	9.8	BDL	52.2	10.0
2(D)	57.5	5.3	O-H	49.3	10.3	HST	48.2	7.6
3(Hy)	52.3	7.0	Do	41.6	9.7	NAR	44.2	8.4
4(Pd)	54.3	6.8	Re	46.6	9.4	AVD	55.5	7.6
5(Mf)	50.0	8.3	GM	44.5	7.7	DEP	60.5	9.0
6(Pa)	54.1	7.1	GF	50.2	8.6	CPS	54.1	9.9
7(Pt)	68.6	3.3	Mt	58.5	8.6	Personality Psychopathology Five		
8(Sc)	55.9	5.6	PK	56.4	9.4	Scale	M	SD
9(Ma)	49.7	6.9	PS	56.8	9.2	AGG	45.6	9.3
0(Si)	53.5	6.5	MAC-R	48.1	9.5	PSY	49.9	8.3
			APS	55.7	9.5	CON	51.0	9.3
			AAS	50.2	9.7	NEN	55.4	9.6
			MDS	52.0	9.7	PEE	47.4	8.1
			Ho	49.3	9.2			
			CAL-R	50.9	10.9			

Content			Content Component					
Scale	M	SD	Scale	M	SD	Scale	M	SD
ANX	59.2	9.2	FRS1	51.4	10.2	ASP1	48.2	9.8
FRS	50.3	9.7	FRS2	49.1	10.2	ASP2	50.0	9.4
OBS	57.6	10.8	DEP1	55.2	11.0	TPA1	50.6	10.5
DEP	57.7	8.0	DEP2	56.6	10.6	TPA2	50.2	9.9
HEA	51.2	8.9	DEP3	57.2	9.8	LSE1	57.2	9.7
BIZ	50.8	8.0	DEP4	49.6	11.3	LSE2	54.2	10.2
ANG	51.6	11.2	HEA1	51.5	10.4	SOD1	49.8	8.6
CYN	48.6	9.5	HEA2	47.8	8.7	SOD2	53.6	8.4
ASP	49.0	9.5	HEA3	51.8	9.4	FAM1	48.6	9.6
TPA	50.0	9.9	BIZ1	47.7	7.9	FAM2	50.1	10.9
LSE	57.6	8.9	BIZ2	50.0	9.4	TRT1	55.1	11.3
SOD	51.4	7.2	ANG1	50.0	10.6	TRT2	48.9	9.9
FAM	49.8	9.0	ANG2	52.5	10.8			
WRK	56.6	9.2	CYN1	48.3	10.0			
TRT	53.8	9.1	CYN2	48.2	9.6			

Note. All scores are T scores except: Cannot Say, K & B and L & W critical items which are raw scores; True % and False % which are the percentage of items endorsed "true" or "false;" and \|F - FB\|, F - K, and O - S which are difference scores.

Appendix D-47

Prototypic Scores for 7-8/8-7 Codetypes (N = 1,263)

Demographics

Demographics		M	SD	Marital Status		%
Age		34.9	12.6		Never Married	45.5
Education		11.3	5.2		Married	36.1
Gender		%			Separated	5.0
	Men	67.9			Divorced	12.0
	Women	32.1			Widowed	1.4

Test-Taking Scales

Omissions		M	SD	Consistency	M	SD
	?	1.2	3.2	VRIN	56.0	11.1
				|F - FB|	4.2	3.2
				TRIN	55.0	12.6

Accuracy of Item Endorsement

Underreporting		M	SD	Overreporting		M	SD
	False %	46.9	7.5		True %	51.9	7.5
Impression	L	47.8	9.4	Infrequency	F	84.6	18.3
Management	ODecp	40.9	8.8		FB	93.5	26.1
	Sd	45.2	10.0		F[p]	67.6	17.3
Superior	S	38.1	8.1	Critical Items	K & B	42.3	11.6
Adjustment					L & W	54.0	14.8
Self-Deception	K	31.1	6.4	Dissimulation	F - K	4.5	8.5
	So	20.7	12.1		Ds	80.5	13.9
					O - S	162.8	71.0

Scales

Validity and Clinical			Supplementary			Morey et al. Overlapping Personality Disorder		
Scale	M	SD	Scale	M	SD	Scale	M	SD
?	1.2	3.2	A	75.3	9.1	PAR	67.8	11.7
L	47.8	9.4	R	52.4	11.0	SZD	59.7	12.4
F	84.6	18.3	Es	20.6	13.8	STY	71.2	12.2
K	40.8	8.2	TRIN	55.0	12.6	ANT	59.9	10.8
1(Hs)	71.1	14.3	VRIN	56.0	11.1	BDL	62.7	9.8
2(D)	76.9	12.3	O-H	46.1	9.6	HST	40.8	11.4
3(Hy)	68.4	14.7	Do	29.1	10.4	NAR	39.5	10.9
4(Pd)	70.1	11.2	Re	37.2	11.0	AVD	68.1	10.4
5(Mf)	54.7	9.9	GM	29.4	11.9	DEP	71.7	11.6
6(Pa)	73.7	13.2	GF	44.6	11.0	CPS	61.5	8.4
7(Pt)	88.3	10.8	Mt	77.5	9.3	Personality Psychopathology Five		
8(Sc)	90.7	13.1	PK	84.8	13.3			
9(Ma)	60.5	11.0	PS	85.9	12.8	Scale	M	SD
0(Si)	67.2	10.6	MAC-R	53.6	11.7	AGG	49.5	11.6
			APS	55.6	10.1	PSY	72.2	15.4
			AAS	59.2	12.9	CON	48.6	11.5
			MDS	72.2	12.8	NEN	70.1	9.7
			Ho	62.5	9.5	PEE	33.0	13.6
			CAL-R	55.0	11.2			

Content			Content Component					
Scale	M	SD	Scale	M	SD	Scale	M	SD
ANX	77.3	10.3	FRS1	73.7	23.0	ASP1	57.2	9.8
FRS	63.2	15.0	FRS2	54.5	10.7	ASP2	56.3	12.6
OBS	71.3	10.4	DEP1	80.0	15.1	TPA1	58.9	9.3
DEP	78.2	11.1	DEP2	74.0	11.2	TPA2	57.2	11.0
HEA	73.5	14.0	DEP3	71.9	10.9	LSE1	71.4	12.3
BIZ	70.9	13.3	DEP4	80.7	29.7	LSE2	64.7	11.6
ANG	63.7	11.7	HEA1	67.5	17.4	SOD1	62.5	12.4
CYN	61.0	11.1	HEA2	74.6	18.9	SOD2	59.9	9.8
ASP	59.1	11.5	HEA3	67.9	13.4	FAM1	63.7	11.7
TPA	59.1	12.0	BIZ1	65.3	19.2	FAM2	60.0	13.7
LSE	73.9	12.3	BIZ2	72.8	13.4	TRT1	78.0	16.1
SOD	64.6	12.9	ANG1	61.0	12.3	TRT2	61.3	10.4
FAM	67.3	12.4	ANG2	62.1	9.2			
WRK	75.7	10.6	CYN1	59.2	9.8			
TRT	75.6	13.1	CYN2	58.6	9.2			

Note. All scores are T scores except: Cannot Say, K & B and L & W critical items which are raw scores; True % and False % which are the percentage of items endorsed "true" or "false;" and \|F - FB\|, F - K, and O - S which are difference scores.

Appendix D-48

Prototypic Scores for 7-9/9-7 Codetypes (N = 98)

Demographics

Demographics		M	SD	Marital Status		%
Age		31.0	12.0	Never Married		56.7
Education		11.8	5.7	Married		20.0
Gender		%		Separated		3.3
	Men	59.2		Divorced		16.7
	Women	40.8		Widowed		3.3

Test-Taking Scales

Omissions		M	SD	Consistency	M	SD
	?	0.6	1.4	VRIN	54.9	10.7
				|F - FB|	4.2	2.8
				TRIN	53.1	11.6

Accuracy of Item Endorsement

Underreporting		M	SD	Overreporting		M	SD
	False %	49.4	6.9		True %	49.5	6.9
Impression	L	45.3	7.8	Infrequency	F	63.5	14.1
Management	ODecp	47.5	7.7		FB	62.0	14.9
	Sd	52.8	9.0		F[p]	55.1	13.9
Superior	S	39.6	8.0	Critical Items	K & B	29.3	9.3
Adjustment					L & W	38.2	11.5
Self-Deception	K	31.1	6.4	Dissimulation	F - K	-3.5	7.2
	So	36.3	10.3		Ds	66.4	11.1
					O - S	80.9	57.5

Scales

Validity and Clinical			Supplementary			Morey et al. Overlapping Personality Disorder		
Scale	M	SD	Scale	M	SD	Scale	M	SD
?	0.6	1.4	A	64.8	8.2	PAR	62.4	11.4
L	45.3	7.8	R	41.9	7.9	SZD	46.2	8.2
F	63.5	14.1	Es	35.8	11.4	STY	55.7	8.7
K	43.2	7.7	TRIN	53.1	11.6	ANT	59.6	11.1
1(Hs)	57.6	10.2	VRIN	54.9	10.7	BDL	63.3	9.8
2(D)	59.2	8.9	O-H	45.5	8.8	HST	56.2	7.7
3(Hy)	56.5	11.2	Do	37.3	10.8	NAR	54.6	7.6
4(Pd)	61.2	8.1	Re	36.4	11.0	AVD	52.9	7.7
5(Mf)	53.7	9.3	GM	40.7	9.4	DEP	60.7	9.5
6(Pa)	60.4	9.7	GF	44.2	11.0	CPS	60.4	8.0
7(Pt)	74.1	6.6	Mt	67.4	8.0	Personality Psychopathology Five		
8(Sc)	67.4	7.8	PK	68.7	10.3	Scale	M	SD
9(Ma)	77.0	6.9	PS	69.7	9.3	AGG	56.9	9.7
0(Si)	49.9	8.3	MAC-R	58.4	11.0	PSY	62.4	11.7
			APS	60.8	10.2	CON	42.4	10.1
			AAS	54.8	11.6	NEN	63.3	8.7
			MDS	60.5	9.3	PEE	52.5	7.8
			Ho	60.4	9.3			
			CAL-R	52.6	10.8			

Content			Content Component					
Scale	M	SD	Scale	M	SD	Scale	M	SD
ANX	68.2	9.6	FRS1	57.9	15.2	ASP1	57.9	9.3
FRS	53.7	11.8	FRS2	50.2	9.8	ASP2	55.4	11.8
OBS	63.4	9.8	DEP1	62.7	10.7	TPA1	56.3	9.4
DEP	63.7	7.9	DEP2	62.5	12.0	TPA2	58.7	10.5
HEA	61.2	9.9	DEP3	61.3	9.9	LSE1	57.9	9.1
BIZ	63.1	10.6	DEP4	53.1	15.5	LSE2	56.6	9.9
ANG	62.2	10.6	HEA1	55.0	11.4	SOD1	47.3	7.8
CYN	59.5	11.1	HEA2	57.9	13.9	SOD2	46.6	7.8
ASP	59.3	11.2	HEA3	60.8	10.6	FAM1	60.0	9.6
TPA	59.2	11.6	BIZ1	60.1	14.4	FAM2	52.7	11.2
LSE	59.5	8.5	BIZ2	62.5	12.1	TRT1	58.4	12.4
SOD	47.2	7.6	ANG1	60.0	10.9	TRT2	54.0	10.2
FAM	60.3	9.3	ANG2	59.7	8.6			
WRK	63.0	9.4	CYN1	56.6	9.9			
TRT	59.1	10.4	CYN2	59.9	8.2			

Note. All scores are T scores except: Cannot Say, K & B and L & W critical items which are raw scores; True % and False % which are the percentage of items endorsed "true" or "false;" and |F - FB|, F - K, and O - S which are difference scores.

Appendix D-49

Prototypic Scores for 7-0/0-7 Codetypes (N = 147)

Demographics

Demographics		M	SD	Marital Status	%
Age		35.5	11.4	Never Married	37.3
Education		13.4	4.7	Married	51.4
Gender	%			Separated	2.8
	Men	73.5		Divorced	7.7
	Women	26.5		Widowed	0.7

Test-Taking Scales

Omissions		M	SD	Consistency	M	SD
	?	0.7	2.0	VRIN	53.0	10.2
				|F - FB|	3.3	2.5
				TRIN	51.6	9.6

Accuracy of Item Endorsement

Underreporting		M	SD	Overreporting		M	SD
	False %	55.0	5.9		True %	43.9	5.9
Impression	L	48.7	9.6	Infrequency	F	60.7	11.4
Management	ODecp	39.0	7.6		FB	62.0	14.5
	Sd	42.0	8.7		F[p]	51.7	9.0
Superior	S	43.2	8.4	Critical Items	K & B	27.2	9.1
Adjustment					L & W	32.3	9.7
Self-Deception	K	31.1	6.4	Dissimulation	F - K	-3.7	6.5
	So	30.0	10.4		Ds	62.7	10.6
					O - S	92.3	53.1

Scales

Validity and Clinical			Supplementary			Morey et al. Overlapping Personality Disorder		
Scale	M	SD	Scale	M	SD	Scale	M	SD
?	0.7	2.0	A	69.6	9.0	PAR	58.6	9.4
L	48.7	9.6	R	57.1	9.3	SZD	65.5	7.7
F	60.7	11.4	Es	34.6	10.1	STY	70.1	7.0
K	42.0	8.4	TRIN	51.6	9.6	ANT	52.3	9.6
1(Hs)	54.3	9.9	VRIN	53.0	10.2	BDL	54.7	9.6
2(D)	66.9	7.4	O-H	44.4	10.1	HST	31.6	7.5
3(Hy)	52.3	8.9	Do	33.8	9.1	NAR	32.2	7.5
4(Pd)	57.9	9.3	Re	46.3	9.4	AVD	73.9	5.8
5(Mf)	52.0	8.6	GM	35.8	9.8	DEP	72.2	11.4
6(Pa)	57.7	8.9	GF	50.0	9.2	CPS	57.9	8.7
7(Pt)	75.4	7.4	Mt	69.7	9.8	Personality Psychopathology Five		
8(Sc)	63.1	8.8	PK	69.1	10.7			
9(Ma)	45.4	6.7	PS	69.8	11.1	Scale	M	SD
0(Si)	74.9	5.8	MAC-R	43.3	10.2	AGG	38.8	9.4
			APS	52.3	9.3	PSY	56.2	10.7
			AAS	51.9	9.9	CON	54.4	9.5
			MDS	62.7	12.6	NEN	63.5	9.3
			Ho	56.3	8.5	PEE	31.9	8.8
			CAL-R	51.2	10.2			

Content			Content Component					
Scale	M	SD	Scale	M	SD	Scale	M	SD
ANX	68.6	9.9	FRS1	56.2	13.7	ASP1	52.1	8.6
FRS	53.6	10.6	FRS2	51.3	9.9	ASP2	51.0	10.3
OBS	64.4	10.0	DEP1	65.1	13.6	TPA1	56.0	9.8
DEP	67.7	9.2	DEP2	70.4	12.2	TPA2	52.4	9.1
HEA	57.3	9.8	DEP3	64.8	10.6	LSE1	66.7	11.2
BIZ	53.9	9.3	DEP4	56.2	16.4	LSE2	66.2	11.5
ANG	56.2	10.7	HEA1	53.3	12.6	SOD1	68.3	7.8
CYN	54.0	9.4	HEA2	53.6	11.0	SOD2	67.4	6.0
ASP	52.2	9.0	HEA3	56.0	11.5	FAM1	55.3	11.4
TPA	53.7	10.0	BIZ1	50.3	9.9	FAM2	56.2	12.6
LSE	69.7	11.2	BIZ2	54.6	10.1	TRT1	68.8	15.0
SOD	72.6	8.2	ANG1	52.2	10.6	TRT2	58.7	10.5
FAM	57.0	10.8	ANG2	58.3	10.0			
WRK	67.8	9.7	CYN1	54.1	9.1			
TRT	67.3	11.8	CYN2	52.5	9.9			

Note. All scores are T scores except: Cannot Say, K & B and L & W critical items which are raw scores; True % and False % which are the percentage of items endorsed "true" or "false;" and \|F - FB\|, F - K, and O - S which are difference scores.

623

Appendix D-50

Prototypic Scores for Spike 8 Codetypes (N = 145)

Demographics

Demographics		M	SD	Marital Status	%
Age		32.8	14.1	Never Married	65.6
Education		10.9	6.3	Married	23.8
Gender		%		Separated	1.6
	Men	60.0		Divorced	6.6
	Women	40.0		Widowed	2.5

Test-Taking Scales

Omissions		M	SD	Consistency		M	SD
	?	1.6	4.0	VRIN		54.9	11.1
				|F - FB|		4.0	2.9
				TRIN		52.2	12.6

Accuracy of Item Endorsement

Underreporting		M	SD	Overreporting		M	SD
	False %	57.5	8.4		True %	41.3	8.3
Impression	L	52.5	11.3	Infrequency	F	61.3	11.8
Management	ODecp	51.3	9.7		FB	58.3	13.4
	Sd	51.8	9.9		F[p]	59.7	14.0
Superior	S	49.0	9.7	Critical Items	K & B	18.1	8.9
Adjustment					L & W	25.5	9.6
Self-Deception	K	31.1	6.4	Dissimulation	F - K	-7.2	8.3
	So	45.0	9.9		Ds	58.0	9.7
					O - S	37.2	59.0

Scales

Validity and Clinical			Supplementary			Morey et al. Overlapping Personality Disorder		
Scale	M	SD	Scale	M	SD	Scale	M	SD
?	1.6	4.0	A	53.6	9.7	PAR	53.1	11.1
L	52.5	11.3	R	50.0	9.7	SZD	52.6	10.1
F	61.3	11.8	Es	44.9	9.7	STY	53.4	9.9
K	49.3	11.9	TRIN	52.2	12.6	ANT	54.2	9.8
1(Hs)	53.4	7.4	VRIN	54.9	11.1	BDL	51.5	9.7
2(D)	52.9	7.0	O-H	53.1	10.6	HST	48.1	9.0
3(Hy)	50.5	8.1	Do	43.1	10.8	NAR	50.1	8.5
4(Pd)	55.5	7.2	Re	45.8	9.4	AVD	51.7	8.9
5(Mf)	50.7	8.5	GM	45.4	9.8	DEP	52.6	9.0
6(Pa)	53.5	6.7	GF	46.9	9.6	CPS	48.9	10.6
7(Pt)	56.0	5.5	Mt	54.4	9.3	Personality Psychopathology Five		
8(Sc)	67.4	2.8	PK	57.1	10.8	Scale	M	SD
9(Ma)	53.2	6.3	PS	58.0	10.4	AGG	49.6	10.1
0(Si)	52.1	7.7	MAC-R	50.5	10.3	PSY	56.2	12.0
			APS	47.4	10.4	CON	48.3	9.0
			AAS	51.3	10.4	NEN	52.0	10.0
			MDS	56.8	10.6	PEE	47.5	8.7
			Ho	53.3	10.1			
			CAL-R	53.2	9.9			

Content			Content Component					
Scale	M	SD	Scale	M	SD	Scale	M	SD
ANX	53.1	9.3	FRS1	54.3	13.6	ASP1	52.8	10.8
FRS	52.0	11.7	FRS2	49.7	10.2	ASP2	54.3	11.1
OBS	51.6	9.6	DEP1	56.2	11.8	TPA1	47.7	9.8
DEP	55.6	10.3	DEP2	52.2	10.3	TPA2	49.7	10.6
HEA	54.6	7.7	DEP3	54.6	11.4	LSE1	51.4	10.3
BIZ	57.0	11.0	DEP4	52.0	14.3	LSE2	52.1	9.9
ANG	51.9	10.6	HEA1	51.5	9.8	SOD1	52.3	9.8
CYN	53.3	11.0	HEA2	55.9	11.1	SOD2	50.5	9.0
ASP	54.3	11.1	HEA3	50.2	8.8	FAM1	55.2	11.0
TPA	49.0	10.5	BIZ1	52.7	11.4	FAM2	55.0	12.9
LSE	54.0	9.6	BIZ2	57.2	11.8	TRT1	53.3	10.8
SOD	52.2	9.2	ANG1	52.2	10.4	TRT2	53.8	10.7
FAM	56.5	10.5	ANG2	51.6	10.1			
WRK	53.4	9.8	CYN1	53.7	10.7			
TRT	55.3	10.3	CYN2	50.8	10.8			

Note. All scores are T scores except: Cannot Say, K & B and L & W critical items which are raw scores; True % and False % which are the percentage of items endorsed "true" or "false;" and |F - FB|, F - K, and O - S which are difference scores.

624

Appendix D-51

Prototypic Scores for 8-9/9-8 Codetypes (N = 424)

Demographics

Demographics		M	SD	Marital Status		%
Age		27.4	13.1	Never Married		68.5
Education		9.8	5.4	Married		18.0
Gender		%		Separated		3.9
	Men	60.4		Divorced		7.9
	Women	39.6		Widowed		1.7

Test-Taking Scales

Omissions		M	SD	Consistency	M	SD
	?	1.5	3.7	VRIN	59.1	10.9
				|F - FB|	5.2	3.6
				TRIN	57.3	13.6

Accuracy of Item Endorsement

Underreporting		M	SD	Overreporting		M	SD
	False %	47.1	7.9		True %	51.6	7.8
Impression	L	49.3	10.4	Infrequency	F	77.9	18.0
Management	ODecp	51.6	9.8		FB	76.8	21.5
	Sd	55.1	10.3		F[p]	68.9	17.9
Superior	S	39.5	8.1	Critical Items	K & B	31.7	10.7
Adjustment					L & W	43.4	13.1
Self-Deception	K	31.1	6.4	Dissimulation	F - K	1.8	8.4
	So	34.3	11.4		Ds	72.6	12.0
					O - S	108.0	61.7

Scales

Validity and Clinical			Supplementary			Morey et al. Overlapping Personality Disorder		
Scale	M	SD	Scale	M	SD	Scale	M	SD
?	1.5	3.7	A	63.0	10.0	PAR	66.6	11.0
L	49.3	10.4	R	42.9	9.4	SZD	50.7	10.4
F	77.9	18.0	Es	34.1	11.6	STY	59.3	9.7
K	41.5	8.1	TRIN	57.3	13.6	ANT	64.6	10.7
1(Hs)	59.2	11.3	VRIN	59.1	10.9	BDL	62.0	10.2
2(D)	56.1	10.8	O-H	46.6	10.2	HST	53.7	8.7
3(Hy)	54.3	11.9	Do	35.4	11.2	NAR	56.8	8.8
4(Pd)	62.5	10.5	Re	33.3	10.6	AVD	52.2	9.0
5(Mf)	51.4	10.6	GM	41.1	10.0	DEP	56.2	10.9
6(Pa)	63.2	11.5	GF	37.1	11.7	CPS	58.4	9.4
7(Pt)	65.0	9.8	Mt	64.6	9.6	Personality Psychopathology Five		
8(Sc)	78.1	10.2	PK	70.7	12.6			
9(Ma)	80.1	9.0	PS	71.4	11.7	Scale	M	SD
0(Si)	52.1	8.9	MAC-R	61.8	11.0	AGG	60.5	9.8
			APS	54.0	11.0	PSY	70.9	13.7
			AAS	59.7	13.4	CON	39.5	10.7
			MDS	64.2	11.4	NEN	61.3	9.9
			Ho	64.1	8.5	PEE	50.6	9.2
			CAL-R	56.6	10.6			

Content			Content Component					
Scale	M	SD	Scale	M	SD	Scale	M	SD
ANX	63.8	10.8	FRS1	62.9	16.3	ASP1	63.2	8.7
FRS	54.8	12.0	FRS2	48.8	10.4	ASP2	59.9	13.0
OBS	62.1	11.5	DEP1	66.5	13.3	TPA1	55.1	9.8
DEP	64.7	10.6	DEP2	59.2	11.6	TPA2	61.4	10.8
HEA	64.1	10.8	DEP3	61.7	12.9	LSE1	57.1	11.0
BIZ	70.1	11.5	DEP4	62.7	22.0	LSE2	56.9	11.3
ANG	61.9	11.7	HEA1	58.9	13.9	SOD1	51.0	9.8
CYN	64.6	10.4	HEA2	67.1	15.3	SOD2	48.5	9.2
ASP	66.6	11.8	HEA3	58.0	11.2	FAM1	64.2	11.0
TPA	60.6	11.9	BIZ1	66.6	18.9	FAM2	57.2	13.8
LSE	60.3	10.7	BIZ2	69.8	12.4	TRT1	62.5	14.7
SOD	50.9	9.0	ANG1	61.6	12.0	TRT2	57.7	10.9
FAM	66.0	11.3	ANG2	58.4	9.8			
WRK	63.6	11.0	CYN1	62.2	8.1			
TRT	63.9	12.6	CYN2	60.8	8.6			

Note. All scores are T scores except: Cannot Say, K & B and L & W critical items which are raw scores; True % and False % which are the percentage of items endorsed "true" or "false;" and |F - FB|, F - K, and O - S which are difference scores.

Appendix D-52
Prototypic Scores for 8-0/0-8 Codetypes (N = 96)

Demographics

Demographics		M	SD	Marital Status		%
Age		34.1	10.8	Never Married		52.3
Education		12.1	4.8	Married		33.0
Gender		%		Separated		3.4
	Men	67.7		Divorced		10.2
	Women	32.3		Widowed		1.1

Test-Taking Scales

Omissions		M	SD	Consistency	M	SD
	?	1.1	2.6	VRIN	55.6	10.4
				|F - FB|	3.9	2.6
				TRIN	57.8	13.2

Accuracy of Item Endorsement

Underreporting		M	SD	Overreporting		M	SD
	False %	49.6	6.5	True %		49.1	6.3
Impression	L	47.8	8.4	Infrequency	F	76.0	13.1
Management	ODecp	40.3	9.1		FB	80.8	17.9
	Sd	42.7	9.8		F[p]	64.5	12.4
Superior	S	37.3	7.0	Critical Items	K & B	32.9	9.9
Adjustment					L & W	40.8	10.8
Self-Deception	K	31.1	6.4	Dissimulation	F - K	3.4	6.3
	So	24.9	9.4		Ds	73.7	9.4
					O - S	133.1	47.9

Scales

Validity and Clinical			Supplementary			Morey et al. Overlapping Personality Disorder		
Scale	M	SD	Scale	M	SD	Scale	M	SD
?	1.1	2.6	A	71.4	9.2	PAR	65.9	9.3
L	47.8	8.4	R	53.9	9.5	SZD	70.2	7.1
F	76.0	13.1	Es	31.0	11.4	STY	74.0	7.3
K	37.3	7.4	TRIN	57.8	13.2	ANT	61.0	10.3
1(Hs)	55.9	10.1	VRIN	55.6	10.4	BDL	58.5	9.9
2(D)	66.2	7.7	O-H	42.5	10.3	HST	31.7	8.6
3(Hy)	50.3	8.6	Do	32.5	9.7	NAR	35.6	10.4
4(Pd)	60.9	9.3	Re	39.7	10.6	AVD	73.0	6.9
5(Mf)	54.4	8.5	GM	35.1	10.2	DEP	68.5	12.1
6(Pa)	61.0	9.9	GF	43.4	10.7	CPS	59.3	9.2
7(Pt)	67.0	8.8	Mt	71.2	8.5	Personality Psychopathology Five		
8(Sc)	76.8	8.1	PK	75.2	9.9			
9(Ma)	52.0	9.0	PS	75.6	10.0	Scale	M	SD
0(Si)	75.2	6.6	MAC-R	47.3	11.9	AGG	47.5	9.7
			APS	48.9	11.5	PSY	64.7	11.2
			AAS	58.3	12.5	CON	49.1	11.2
			MDS	69.2	12.0	NEN	65.8	9.1
			Ho	63.9	8.1	PEE	31.8	10.2
			CAL-R	53.5	11.7			

Content			Content Component					
Scale	M	SD	Scale	M	SD	Scale	M	SD
ANX	68.6	10.2	FRS1	62.1	17.4	ASP1	59.4	8.1
FRS	56.6	13.7	FRS2	51.5	10.6	ASP2	57.7	13.3
OBS	63.6	10.8	DEP1	71.6	15.0	TPA1	57.4	9.1
DEP	72.2	10.6	DEP2	69.2	11.7	TPA2	57.7	8.5
HEA	61.9	9.4	DEP3	68.7	10.8	LSE1	68.5	13.2
BIZ	62.2	10.9	DEP4	68.1	24.8	LSE2	63.7	12.0
ANG	61.4	10.8	HEA1	57.4	12.2	SOD1	71.3	8.0
CYN	63.1	10.3	HEA2	62.7	13.4	SOD2	65.3	7.4
ASP	61.2	11.0	HEA3	56.0	10.7	FAM1	63.8	10.7
TPA	58.1	10.9	BIZ1	54.6	12.2	FAM2	64.9	13.6
LSE	71.4	12.0	BIZ2	64.9	14.3	TRT1	73.9	16.3
SOD	74.0	8.5	ANG1	57.6	11.9	TRT2	62.9	9.5
FAM	68.3	11.2	ANG2	61.8	8.9			
WRK	71.4	10.0	CYN1	61.9	8.4			
TRT	73.6	13.1	CYN2	58.4	9.7			

Note. All scores are T scores except: Cannot Say, K & B and L & W critical items which are raw scores; True % and False % which are the percentage of items endorsed "true" or "false;" and \|F - FB\|, F - K, and O - S which are difference scores.

Appendix D-53

Prototypic Scores for Spike 9 Codetypes (N = 1,025)

Demographics

Demographics		M	SD	Marital Status	%
Age		33.1	12.5	Never Married	45.5
Education		12.0	5.6	Married	30.4
Gender		%		Separated	7.1
	Men	57.6		Divorced	15.7
	Women	42.4		Widowed	1.3

Test-Taking Scales

Omissions		M	SD	Consistency	M	SD
	?	0.8	2.4	VRIN	48.3	9.9
				|F - FB|	2.6	2.0
				TRIN	52.3	9.4

Accuracy of Item Endorsement

Underreporting		M	SD	Overreporting		M	SD
	False %	58.2	6.1		True %	40.7	6.1
Impression	L	53.0	10.7	Infrequency	F	50.0	8.9
Management	ODecp	56.9	10.0		FB	49.4	8.9
	Sd	58.5	10.4		F[p]	50.9	9.7
Superior	S	49.9	9.4	Critical Items	K & B	12.5	7.2
Adjustment					L & W	19.4	8.5
Self-Deception	K	31.1	6.4	Dissimulation	F - K	-11.2	6.1
	So	52.9	8.6		Ds	51.0	8.5
					O - S	-3.4	51.5

Scales

Validity and Clinical

Scale	M	SD
?	0.8	2.4
L	53.0	10.7
F	50.0	8.9
K	50.3	9.1
1(Hs)	48.0	7.6
2(D)	45.2	7.8
3(Hy)	48.0	7.7
4(Pd)	52.4	6.6
5(Mf)	47.5	8.8
6(Pa)	50.1	8.0
7(Pt)	48.6	7.1
8(Sc)	50.8	6.7
9(Ma)	69.3	5.3
0(Si)	41.8	7.3

Supplementary

Scale	M	SD
A	47.1	7.9
R	44.3	7.8
Es	52.4	9.2
TRIN	52.3	9.4
VRIN	48.3	9.9
O-H	52.0	10.0
Do	48.5	10.0
Re	44.5	9.9
GM	51.8	8.0
GF	44.4	9.6
Mt	48.2	8.2
PK	49.1	8.1
PS	49.3	7.8
MAC-R	56.7	8.8
APS	50.5	9.9
AAS	49.9	10.0
MDS	49.9	8.3
Ho	53.0	9.1
CAL-R	53.4	9.1

Morey et al. Overlapping Personality Disorder

Scale	M	SD
PAR	52.1	9.8
SZD	44.0	7.2
STY	44.9	7.9
ANT	52.5	10.4
BDL	51.9	8.6
HST	57.7	6.9
NAR	59.6	7.4
AVD	42.3	6.8
DEP	46.5	8.2
CPS	50.1	9.4

Personality Psychopathology Five

Scale	M	SD
AGG	56.2	8.3
PSY	52.7	10.1
CON	44.0	9.7
NEN	49.4	9.1
PEE	58.2	6.6

Content

Scale	M	SD
ANX	51.2	8.6
FRS	47.1	8.8
OBS	48.9	8.8
DEP	48.7	7.9
HEA	49.5	8.3
BIZ	53.7	9.2
ANG	50.8	10.0
CYN	53.7	10.4
ASP	55.0	10.6
TPA	50.0	9.9
LSE	46.4	8.0
SOD	42.5	6.8
FAM	51.4	9.6
WRK	48.0	8.2
TRT	47.2	8.8

Content Component

Scale	M	SD	Scale	M	SD
FRS1	48.8	8.7	ASP1	54.0	10.2
FRS2	46.4	9.4	ASP2	53.3	11.4
DEP1	49.4	8.5	TPA1	46.2	9.6
DEP2	47.7	8.1	TPA2	52.3	10.2
DEP3	47.8	8.5	LSE1	45.3	7.2
DEP4	47.0	6.9	LSE2	47.6	8.6
HEA1	49.2	9.0	SOD1	43.2	6.4
HEA2	48.5	8.9	SOD2	42.6	7.1
HEA3	50.3	8.1	FAM1	51.1	10.2
BIZ1	51.2	10.1	FAM2	49.9	10.4
BIZ2	51.7	9.8	TRT1	47.1	8.0
ANG1	51.0	10.0	TRT2	46.6	9.2
ANG2	49.6	9.6			
CYN1	52.9	10.3			
CYN2	52.9	9.7			

Note. All scores are T scores except: Cannot Say, K & B and L & W critical items which are raw scores; True % and False % which are the percentage of items endorsed "true" or "false;" and |F - FB|, F - K, and O - S which are difference scores.

Prototypic Scores for 9-0/0-9 Codetypes (N = 8)

Demographics

Demographics		M	SD	Marital Status	%
Age		29.9	9.0	Never Married	71.4
Education		11.8	5.7	Married	28.6
Gender		%		Separated	0.0
	Men	75.0		Divorced	0.0
	Women	25.0		Widowed	0.0

Test-Taking Scales

Omissions		M	SD	Consistency	M	SD
	?	0.6	1.1	VRIN	54.5	9.1
				|F - FB|	3.0	1.7
				TRIN	56.5	18.6

Accuracy of Item Endorsement

Underreporting		M	SD	Overreporting		M	SD
	False %	49.6	9.1		True %	49.1	8.9
Impression	L	49.9	10.3	Infrequency	F	59.3	12.5
Management	ODecp	46.7	8.5		FB	62.1	21.3
	Sd	48.4	8.3		F[p]	52.8	10.3
Superior	S	39.1	6.1	Critical Items	K & B	26.9	7.7
Adjustment					L & W	35.3	5.9
Self-Deception	K	31.1	6.4	Dissimulation	F - K	-1.5	7.3
	So	34.1	9.1		Ds	67.7	8.4
					O - S	102.8	57.0

Scales

Validity and Clinical			Supplementary			Morey et al. Overlapping Personality Disorder		
Scale	M	SD	Scale	M	SD	Scale	M	SD
?	0.6	1.1	A	67.6	6.3	PAR	65.3	9.1
L	49.9	10.3	R	47.0	12.6	SZD	62.6	8.2
F	59.3	12.5	Es	39.4	6.2	STY	68.1	9.0
K	37.0	8.0	TRIN	56.5	18.6	ANT	59.3	9.9
1(Hs)	46.8	10.8	VRIN	54.5	9.1	BDL	58.6	10.4
2(D)	58.9	6.3	O-H	43.1	10.9	HST	37.8	9.5
3(Hy)	45.8	9.9	Do	28.1	12.6	NAR	46.6	6.9
4(Pd)	55.6	6.6	Re	35.1	11.4	AVD	68.4	7.6
5(Mf)	48.8	5.7	GM	39.5	6.2	DEP	63.1	8.8
6(Pa)	58.1	10.6	GF	41.9	8.9	CPS	59.3	11.6
7(Pt)	61.3	4.9	Mt	68.6	7.1	Personality Psychopathology Five		
8(Sc)	62.3	4.2	PK	69.1	8.4	Scale	M	SD
9(Ma)	70.6	3.5	PS	70.0	8.6	AGG	57.5	4.7
0(Si)	71.9	4.5	MAC-R	54.4	13.4	PSY	60.3	6.4
			APS	52.3	12.8	CON	43.5	6.2
			AAS	55.4	18.7	NEN	65.5	9.8
			MDS	59.4	11.9	PEE	39.5	7.4
			Ho	64.0	9.2			
			CAL-R	53.0	11.5			

Content			Content Component					
Scale	M	SD	Scale	M	SD	Scale	M	SD
ANX	66.8	8.8	FRS1	52.0	7.4	ASP1	58.1	8.7
FRS	48.4	6.4	FRS2	46.9	5.5	ASP2	62.8	10.7
OBS	63.1	14.1	DEP1	58.8	8.8	TPA1	57.9	8.7
DEP	65.0	7.3	DEP2	67.4	11.3	TPA2	63.0	9.9
HEA	56.6	7.4	DEP3	65.3	11.1	LSE1	59.8	11.2
BIZ	58.9	8.9	DEP4	53.4	17.8	LSE2	59.0	9.7
ANG	64.6	13.7	HEA1	54.0	10.5	SOD1	64.4	10.6
CYN	61.3	11.5	HEA2	56.8	10.3	SOD2	62.8	6.9
ASP	62.1	12.0	HEA3	53.0	9.5	FAM1	62.4	8.2
TPA	62.3	12.3	BIZ1	53.3	7.6	FAM2	45.9	10.9
LSE	62.0	8.2	BIZ2	59.9	15.5	TRT1	63.5	16.1
SOD	67.0	9.7	ANG1	63.1	12.3	TRT2	59.1	10.5
FAM	58.4	8.4	ANG2	60.9	9.9			
WRK	67.8	10.4	CYN1	58.9	9.2			
TRT	65.0	14.3	CYN2	61.1	7.2			

Note. All scores are T scores except: Cannot Say, K & B and L & W critical items which are raw scores; True % and False % which are the percentage of items endorsed "true" or "false;" and \|F - FB\|, F - K, and O - S which are difference scores.

Appendix D-55

Prototypic Scores for Spike 0 Codetypes (N = 388)

Demographics

Demographics		M	SD	Marital Status	%
Age		39.5	13.0	Never Married	23.4
Education		12.5	5.3	Married	54.9
Gender	%			Separated	7.4
	Men	61.9		Divorced	13.7
	Women	38.1		Widowed	0.6

Test-Taking Scales

Omissions		M	SD	Consistency		M	SD
	?	0.9	2.5		VRIN	53.3	9.7
					|F - FB|	3.1	2.3
					TRIN	50.1	10.9

Accuracy of Item Endorsement

Underreporting		M	SD	Overreporting		M	SD
	False %	59.3	6.7		True %	39.5	6.7
Impression	L	53.8	10.5	Infrequency	F	53.7	9.4
Management	ODecp	47.0	9.2		FB	52.7	10.8
	Sd	48.2	9.6		F[p]	50.1	9.6
Superior	S	47.2	8.6	Critical Items	K & B	14.9	7.8
Adjustment					L & W	19.9	8.6
Self-Deception	K	31.1	6.4	Dissimulation	F - K	-6.9	6.1
	So	42.5	8.2		Ds	53.2	9.3
					O - S	43.3	46.7

Scales

Validity and Clinical			Supplementary			Morey et al. Overlapping Personality Disorder		
Scale	M	SD	Scale	M	SD	Scale	M	SD
?	0.9	2.5	A	55.2	8.5	PAR	54.5	10.0
L	53.8	10.5	R	57.8	10.0	SZD	64.6	8.0
F	53.7	9.4	Es	45.3	8.5	STY	64.4	6.1
K	43.9	9.0	TRIN	50.1	10.9	ANT	49.8	9.5
1(Hs)	47.9	8.3	VRiN	53.3	9.7	BDL	47.2	10.0
2(D)	56.3	6.4	O-H	50.2	10.4	HST	33.2	7.2
3(Hy)	44.1	7.4	Do	39.5	10.2	NAR	37.7	8.2
4(Pd)	48.5	7.4	Re	47.9	9.6	AVD	66.0	5.2
5(Mf)	48.0	8.3	GM	41.7	8.6	DEP	59.1	10.1
6(Pa)	49.6	8.4	GF	49.5	8.6	CPS	53.4	9.4
7(Pt)	51.8	7.3	Mt	55.0	8.2	Personality Psychopathology Five		
8(Sc)	49.2	8.0	PK	54.7	8.2			
9(Ma)	43.2	6.8	PS	54.1	8.3	Scale	M	SD
0(Si)	68.4	3.3	MAC-R	44.4	10.4	AGG	42.8	10.0
			APS	46.0	10.8	PSY	51.6	9.1
			AAS	47.5	8.7	CON	54.7	9.3
			MDS	54.5	10.1	NEN	54.8	9.2
			Ho	54.8	9.0	PEE	38.7	7.5
			CAL-R	49.8	9.7			

Content			Content Component					
Scale	M	SD	Scale	M	SD	Scale	M	SD
ANX	55.4	8.5	FRS1	52.5	11.3	ASP1	51.8	9.3
FRS	52.3	10.3	FRS2	51.3	10.3	ASP2	50.0	10.7
OBS	53.6	9.5	DEP1	52.4	9.8	TPA1	51.7	10.2
DEP	55.5	8.1	DEP2	54.7	10.4	TPA2	50.6	10.3
HEA	51.6	8.6	DEP3	54.1	10.6	LSE1	55.3	10.4
BIZ	49.5	8.7	DEP4	49.4	11.9	LSE2	57.7	10.8
ANG	51.2	10.3	HEA1	50.4	9.2	SOD1	65.1	8.0
CYN	54.9	10.2	HEA2	50.0	9.8	SOD2	63.6	6.3
ASP	51.8	9.4	HEA3	50.2	8.8	FAM1	51.1	10.5
TPA	51.0	10.6	BIZ1	48.0	8.0	FAM2	53.7	12.3
LSE	58.1	9.1	BIZ2	48.9	8.8	TRT1	55.7	11.1
SOD	67.5	7.6	ANG1	48.8	9.5	TRT2	53.8	10.4
FAM	53.1	10.2	ANG2	52.9	10.3			
WRK	56.3	7.9	CYN1	55.3	9.9			
TRT	56.7	9.6	CYN2	52.0	9.6			

Note. All scores are T scores except: Cannot Say, K & B and L & W critical items which are raw scores; True % and False % which are the percentage of items endorsed "true" or "false;" and |F - FB|, F - K, and O - S which are difference scores.

APPENDIX E

Item Overlap among MMPI-2 Scales

TABLE E.1   Item Overlap among MMPI-2 Scales

ITEM	TRUE	FALSE
1		Mfm Mff R OH GF
2	Es	Hs D Hy Mt PK
3	VRIN TRIN	Hs Hy Pt Mt PK PS DEP DEP1
4	Mfm Mff	GM APS
5	D	
6	VRIN	F Sc VRIN
7	MAC-R APS	Hy R Re
8	GM	Hs Hy VRIN
9		D Hy Pd Pt Sc Mt PK PS DEP DEP1 VRIN TRIN
10		Hs D Hy R Mt WRK
11	Hy Pt HEA	
12	TRIN	F Pd Sc MDS
13	Ma	
14		Hy R
15	D Ma Mt ANX WRK	OH
16	Pa Pt Sc Mt PK	L
17	Pd Pa Sc PK PS WRK	
18	F Hs D Hy HEA HEA1	
19	Ho	Mfm Mff
20	GM	Hs D Mt HEA HEA1
21	Pd Sc Ma PS FAM FAM1 MDS	
22	Pd Pa Sc PK PS TRT MDS	
23	Pa Pt Sc Ma PK	Es GM
24	F Pa MAC-R BIZ BIZ1	
25	Mfm Mff	Si
26	ASP ASP1	Hy Mfm Mff
27	TPA TPA2	Mfm Mff Re GF
28	Hs Mt HEA VRIN	CAL-R
29	ANG APS	L K D Hy OH Re
30	F PK ANX	
31	D Hy Pd Pt Sc Si A Mt PK PS ANX WRK VRIN	Es Do
32	Pd Sc PK PS BIZ BIZ2 VRIN	Si Es Re
33	Es	D Pt HEA HEA3
34		Pd Sc
35	Pd Sc ASP ASP2	
36	F MAC-R HEA	Es
37	PK PS ANG ANG1	K D R

ITEM	TRUE	FALSE
38	D Pt Sc A Mt PS DEP DEP1	
39	Hs D Hy PK ANX VRIN TRIN	Es
40	Hy HEA VRIN TRIN	
41	APS	L
42	F Pd Pa Sc	
43		D Mt APS CAL-R
44	Hy Sc PS HEA HEA2	GM
45	Es	Hs D Hy R PS HEA HEA3
46	D Sc Ho SOD SOD1 VRIN	
47		Hs Hy HEA HEA1
48	F Sc PK PS VRIN TRIN	
49	MAC-R VRIN	D Si PK SOD SOD1
50	Ma Ho CYN CYN2	
51		L F(p)
52	Pd MAC-R PK DEP DEP3 CAL-R	Do
53	Hs HEA HEA2	Es CAL-R
54	F Pd FAM FAM1 WRK	
55	Ma Do OBS	D CAL-R
56	D Pd Pt Si A PK PS DEP DEP2	VRIN TRIN
57		Hs HEA
58	Ho CYN CYN1	K Hy
59	Hs PK PS HEA HEA1	VRIN
60	F BIZ BIZ1	Es
61	Ma	LSE LSE1
62	Mfm Mff GF	
63	TRIN	Mfm Mff GF
64	Mfm Mff	GM
65	Hy Pt Sc A PK PS DEP DEP2 TRIN	TRIN
66	F ASP ASP1 F(p)	
67	Mfm Mff OH GF	
68		D Mfm Mff GF
69	MAC-R	Mfm Mff R OH
70	Si LSE LSE2	Pd Do Es GM
71	Pd Mt DEP DEP1	
72	F MAC-R	
73	D Pt Mt LSE LSE1 WRK VRIN TRIN	MAC-R Do GM
74	Mfm Mff	GM
75		D PK PS DEP DEP1
76	Ho CYN CYN1	K D Hy Mfm Mff APS
77		L OH F(p)
78		F LSE LSE1
79	OH	Pd Si GF
80	Mfm Mff	GM
81	Mt Ho CYN CYN1 ASP ASP1	Hy Pa VRIN
82	Pd Pt A MAC-R Mt PK DEP DEP3	Es Do
83	K VRIN TRIN	Pd FAM FAM1 MDS

(continued)

TABLE E.1 Item Overlap among MMPI-2 Scales (continued)

ITEM	TRUE	FALSE
84	*F MAC-R ASP ASP2 VRIN*	*Re GF*
85	*Sc Ma PK PS*	
86	*VRIN*	*Mfm Mff Si SOD SOD1*
87	*Ma OBS*	*Es*
88		*Ma*
89	*Pd Pt APS*	*OH*
90	*VRIN*	*F Sc VRIN F(p)*
91		*Hs Hy Sc HEA HEA2*
92	*D Sc PK DEP DEP1 TRT TRT1*	
93		*L Ma F(p) CAL-R*
94	*Pd Pt PK PS*	
95	*TRIN*	*D Hy Pd Pa Mt PK PS DEP DEP2 VRIN TRIN MDS*
96	*F BIZ BIZ1*	
97	*Hs HEA*	
98	*Ma Es WRK*	*Hy Pa OH*
99	*Pd Pa Ho TRIN*	*VRIN*
100	*Si Re*	*Pa Ma GM*
101	*Hs Hy PK HEA HEA2*	
102		*L F F(p)*
103	*MAC-R VRIN APS*	*Mfm Mff Re*
104	*Si Ho CYN CYN1 ASP ASP1*	*Mfm Mff Pa APS*
105	*Pd MAC-R ASP ASP2*	*Re GF VRIN*
106		*Sc Ma Si*
107		*L Mfm Mff Ma MAC-R*
108		*F WRK*
109		*D Pt LSE LSE1*
110	*Si Mt Ho CYN CYN1 ASP ASP1 VRIN*	*K Hy Pa VRIN*
111	*Hs HEA HEA1*	
112	*Mfm Mff*	*Si R*
113	*Pd Pa Ma MAC-R APS CAL-R*	
114	*F F(p)*	
115	*MAC-R*	*Hy FRS FRS2*
116	*PS ANG ANG2 VRIN*	*K Hy OH*
117	*D*	*Hs MAC-R OH HEA*
118		*D R HEA HEA3*
119	*Mfm Mff GF*	*Es*
120	*APS*	*F Mfm Mff R*
121	*Mff GF CAL-R*	*Mfm*
122	*Mfm Mff Ma*	*K Pd*
123	*ASP ASP1*	*L GF*
124	*Ho CYN CYN2*	*Hy*
125	*VRIN TRIN*	*Hy Pd PK FAM VRIN TRIN MDS CAL-R*
126		*F F(p)*
127	*D Si A TRIN*	*K*
128	*Mfm Mff MAC-R GF*	*R Es*
129		*Hy Pd OH*

ITEM	TRUE	FALSE
130	D Pt Mt DEP DEP3 LSE LSE1	K
131	Ma	Si Mt
132		F Mfm Mff
133		Mfm Mff GF
134	ANG ANG1	D R
135	Si A PK PS OBS WRK MDS	Hy VRIN
136	Ho TPA VRIN	K Ma VRIN
137	Mfm Mff	MAC-R GM APS
138	F Pa Sc BIZ BIZ1 VRIN	
139		L
140		D Pt Mt PK ANX TRIN
141	Es	Hs D Hy PS HEA HEA3
142		D R HEA HEA2
143	GM	Hs D Pd
144	F Pa	
145	Pa Sc Ma PS Ho FAM	Re
146	D Pa DEP DEP2 CAL-R	GM
147	D Pt Sc	
148	CAL-R	K D Hy Mt
149	Hs HEA HEA2	
150	F PK PS	
151	TPA TPA2	Hy
152	GM	Hs Hy Mt VRIN TRIN
153		L OH
154	FRS FRS2	Ma
155	Ma	GF
156	F	
157		K Hy Pd APS
158	Si SOD SOD2	K Pd Ma
159	Es GM	Hy HEA HEA2
160	Re	Pd MAC-R
161	Si VRIN	Hy VRIN
162	F Pa BIZ BIZ1 F(p)	
163	GM	Mfm Mff FRS FRS2
164	CAL-R	Hs Hy Re HEA HEA2
165		D Pt Sc PS VRIN TRIN
166	Hy Mfm Sc VRIN TRIN	Mff MAC-R VRIN
167	Si SOD SOD2 VRIN	K Hy Pd Ma VRIN
168	F Sc Ma MAC-R PK PS APS CAL-R	R
169	Ma Es	OH Re
170	D Pt Sc PK PS ANX	
171	Ho CAL-R	K Pd OH
172	Hy MAC-R AAS	Do
173		Hs Hy
174		F Pt
175	Hs D Hy Pt HEA HEA3	Es CAL-R

(continued)

TABLE E.1   Item Overlap among MMPI-2 Scales (continued)

ITEM	TRUE	FALSE
176	GM VRIN TRIN CAL-R	Hs Hy HEA
177	Mfm Mff Es	Sc
178		D R
179	Es	Hs Hy Sc HEA HEA2 CAL-R
180	F Sc PS	
181	D	Si HEA
182	Sc Ma	
183	APS	L
184	VRIN TRIN	Mfm Mff
185	Si SOD SOD2 VRIN	Hy Pd VRIN
186		F FRS FRS1
187	Mfm Mff	GM
188		D
189	Es APS	D Si R
190	Sc Ma FAM FAM1	
191	Mfm Mff	
192		F Sc F(p)
193	F(p)	Hy Mfm Mff
194		Mfm Mff HEA
195	Pd FAM FAM2 VRIN TRIN MDS	VRIN TRIN
196	Mfm Mff Pt PK ANX OBS APS	K Es VRIN TRIN
197		Mfm Mff R GF
198	F BIZ	
199	Es Re GM VRIN	Mfm Mff R VRIN
200	Ma	
201		Mfm Mff Do Re GF
202	Pd MAC-R	Do Re
203	GF	L
204		F HEA
205	Mfm Mff Ma Ho FAM FAM1	
206	Ma	
207	OH Do	Mfm Mff Si
208		Hs Hy PS ANX
209	Mfm Es TRIN	Pd Mff Si
210		F Sc
211	Ma	
212	Ma TPA TPA2	D
213	Es	K Hy
214	MAC-R GM	Pd
215	D Si A Mt DEP DEP2	Es
216	F F(p)	
217	APS	Pd Ho FAM FAM2
218	Hy Pt Sc Ma Mt PS	
219	Pd Mfm Mff MDS	
220	Ma	Do GF APS

ITEM	TRUE	FALSE
221	Sc PK PS	D Es
222		F
223		D Mt PS ANX
224	MAC-R	Hs Hy HEA HEA3
225	Pd Ho CYN CYN2	Es
226	VRIN	D Pd
227	Ma Ho ASP ASP1	Do
228	F BIZ BIZ1 F(p)	
229	Sc Ma MAC-R	Es
230	Hy Es	Ho
231		Mfm Mff Si GF
232	Do	L
233	D Sc A Mt WRK	
234	F Pa Sc DEP DEP3	
235	LSE	Mfm Mff Re
236	Mfm Mff	Es
237	GM	Mfm Mff Si
238	Ma MAC-R	D GF
239	TRIN	Mfm Mff GF APS
240	F ASP	
241	Ho CYN CYN1	Hy
242	Pt Sc Ma APS	
243	Si A WRK VRIN	K Hy Pd Ma Do VRIN
244	Ma	Pa Do
245	Do Es	D
246	F DEP DEP3	Es
247	Hs Sc HEA HEA2	
248	Ma Ho ASP ASP1	D R
249		Hs Hy HEA
250	Ma ASP ASP1	GF
251	Mfm Mff Si A Ho	MAC-R
252	F Sc F(p)	
253	Ma CAL-R	Hy
254	Ho CYN CYN1 ASP ASP1	Mfm Mff
255		Hs Pa Sc Si R HEA HEA2
256	Mfm Mff Sc FAM FAM1	R
257	MAC-R	Mfm Mff GF
258	F CAL-R	
259	Pd Pa Ho BIZ BIZ2	VRIN
260	APS	L D
261		Pd
262		Si SOD SOD2 VRIN TRIN
263	GF	Hy Pd Ma
264	F Pd AAS CAL-R	GF
265	Si Ho SOD SOD1	Hy VRIN TRIN
266	Re GF	Pd Pa MAC-R ASP ASP2 AAS

(continued)

TABLE E.1 Item Overlap among MMPI-2 Scales (continued)

ITEM	TRUE	FALSE
267	APS	K D Pd Si VRIN
268	Mfm Sc VRIN	Mff VRIN
269	Ma Mt ASP ASP1	
270	F F(p)	CAL-R
271	Mfm Mff Pa	
272		Mfm Mff GF
273	Pt Sc A Mt PS ANX	
274	Sc PK PS TRT TRT2	
275	Pt Si SOD SOD2	Do Re VRIN TRIN
276		F Sc F(p)
277	Pa Pt Sc A PK PS DEP	
278		Sc
279	Sc	
280	MAC-R	Sc Si PS SOD SOD1 VRIN
281	Sc FB SOD SOD1	
282	F F(p)	
283	CYN CYN1 ASP ASP1	Pa
284	Si CYN CYN1 ASP ASP1 VRIN	K Pa VRIN
285	Pa Pt	
286	OH Ho CYN CYN1	Pa CAL-R
287	Sc	MAC-R GF
288	F Pd VRIN TRIN AAS	
289	Pt Si A	GM
290	ANX VRIN	K Sc VRIN
291	Sc FB F(p)	
292	Sc FAM	
293		Pt OH
294	F F(p)	
295		Sc HEA HEA2
296	Sc Si	
297		Pa R
298	Sc BIZ BIZ2	
299	Sc Mt PS ANX WRK	MAC-R VRIN
300	F FAM	
301	Pt A PS ANX	
302	Pt Si Mt PK ANG ANG2 TPA TPA1 WRK	
303	Sc FB PK DEP DEP4	
304	Pt PS	
305	Pa OH PK PS ANX	
306	F Ho DEP TRT	APS
307	Pa Sc	Es
308	Pt Si	
309	Pt A OBS	Do
310	Pt A	Es
311	Sc A FB PS BIZ BIZ2	
312	F	APS

ITEM	TRUE	FALSE
313	Pt OBS	
314	TRIN	Pa
315	Ho CYN CYN2	Pa
316	Pt Sc PK PS BIZ BIZ2 VRIN	Es
317	Pt FB FRS FRS1	
318		F WRK
319	Sc FB PK PS BIZ BIZ2	
320	Pt Sc	
321	GM	Pt Si SOD SOD2
322	Sc FB FRS FRS1 F(p)	
323	Sc Es FB FAM FAM1 F(p)	
324	F	
325	Pt Sc A Mt PS	MAC-R Do
326	Pt Si LSE LSE1	
327	Pt PK OBS	
328	Pt A PK PS OBS	Si Es
329	Pt Sc FB FRS FRS1	
330		F K D R
331	Pt Mt DEP	GM
332	Sc FB	
333	Pa Sc FB BIZ BIZ2 VRIN	
334	Pa FB FRS FRS1 CAL-R	
335		Si
336	F Pa BIZ BIZ1 F(p)	
337	Si SOD SOD1	
338	Si A Ho	K
339	A Mt PK ANX WRK	K VRIN
340		Si SOD SOD1
341	A APS	K
342	MAC-R APS	Si
343		F Sc
344	MAC-R APS	Si OH VRIN
345		Si
346	Ho CYN CYN2	K R
347	Si A PK Ho	
348	Si	K
349	F PK SOD SOD1 VRIN	VRIN APS
350	GM	Si R VRIN
351	Si TRIN	GM
352	Si Ho CYN CYN1	
353	GF VRIN	Si R SOD SOD1 VRIN
354		Si R
355	F Pa Sc BIZ BIZ1	
356		K
357	Si Mt Ho	
358	Ho CYN CYN2 TPA TPA2	Si Re
359	TRIN CAL-R	Si R SOD SOD1 VRIN TRIN

(continued)

TABLE E.1 Item Overlap among MMPI-2 Scales (continued)

ITEM	TRUE	FALSE
360		Si SOD SOD2 TRIN
361	F Pa BIZ BIZ1	
362	AAS	Si
363		Si R SOD SOD1
364	Si WRK TRT TRT1	GM VRIN
365		K R
366		Si
367	Si PK SOD SOD1 TRIN	TRIN
368	Si WRK TRT TRT1	
369	Si LSE LSE2	VRIN
370	VRIN	Si SOD SOD1 VRIN
371	F(p)	
372	VRIN	PS VRIN
373	TRT TRT2	
374	CYN CYN1 ASP ASP1 VRIN	VRIN
375	TRT TRT2	
376	LSE TRT TRT1	
377	PS DEP DEP3 TRT TRIN APS	VRIN
378	FAM FAM1	
379	FAM	
380	LSE VRIN	
381		
382	FAM FAM1 MDS	
383		FB FAM FAM2
384	GF	
385	Es GM	FRS FRS2
386	Do PS Ho	
387	FB MAC-R AAS F(p)	
388	GM VRIN	A DEP DEP2
389	ANG ANG1	
390	A	OH
391	A TRT TRT2	Es
392	FRS FRS2	GM
393	Ho	
394	A OBS WRK VRIN	Es
395	FB FRS FRS1 VRIN	GM VRIN
396	VRIN	VRIN
397	FRS	
398	OH Ho	
399	DEP DEP1 CYN TRT	Do
400	A PS DEP DEP1	OH
401	GM	FRS FRS2
402		
403	CYN CYN2 VRIN	VRIN
404		FB HEA
405	VRIN	Mt PS ANX VRIN

ITEM	TRUE	FALSE
406	Es Ho	GF
407	MAC-R FB	
408	A Mt ANX	
409	WRK	
410	ANG	
411	A Mt DEP DEP3 LSE LSE1 VRIN	VRIN
412	MAC-R ASP ASP2	Do Re
413	Es FAM	
414	MAC-R Ho ANG ANG1 TPA	
415	A ANX VRIN	
416	Do	
417		Re GF
418	ASP ASP1	Re
419	Ho ASP ASP1 TPA TPA2	
420	TPA TPA1	OH
421	A LSE LSE2 VRIN	
422	MAC-R APS	R
423	Ho TPA TPA2	R
424		
425	Es Ho	
426	GF	
427		BIZ
428	A WRK	
429		AAS
430	ANG ANG2 TPA TPA1	R Re VRIN CAL-R
431	FB	Re
432		R Re
433		OH
434	MAC-R	
435	FRS FRS1 VRIN	GM VRIN
436	Ho	
437	TPA	
438	FRS FRS2	GM
439	MAC-R	
440	Re GM	OH APS
441	FRS FRS1	Es GM
442	A OBS	
443	Ho	
444		
445	MAC-R Ho CYN CYN2 WRK	
446		
447	FRS FRS1	Es
448	A	
449	Mt GF FAM FAM1	R
450	FB LSE LSE1	
451	A	
452	Ho	

(continued)

TABLE E.1 Item Overlap among MMPI-2 Scales (continued)

ITEM	TRUE	FALSE
453		FRS FRS2
454	FB DEP DEP4	
455		FAM FAM2
456	MAC-R GF	R Re
457	Ho LSE LSE2	
458	FRS FRS2	Es
459		
460		OH
461	ANG ANG2	
462	GM	FRS FRS2
463	FB PS ANX	
464	A Mt PS WRK	Es VRIN TRIN CAL-R
465		R GF
466	Ho BIZ BIZ2 CAL-R	
467	Re GM VRIN	VRIN
468	FB FRS FRS1	Re
469	A Mt PS ANX	Es GM
470	Ho CYN CYN1	Do Re
471	OH PS FRS FRS1	Es GM
472	Mt VRIN	VRIN
473	MAC-R GF	Do
474	GM	
475	PS LSE	
476	FB LSE	
477		GF
478	FB FAM FAM1 F(p)	
479	PS SOD	
480	SOD SOD1	
481		
482	OBS TRT VRIN	
483	LSE LSE1	
484	FB MDS	
485	LSE LSE1 VRIN	VRIN
486	ANG ANG2	
487	AAS	GF
488	TRT	
489	FB AAS	
490	BIZ	
491	OBS WRK TRT TRT1 VRIN	
492		
493		TRT MDS
494		TRT TRT1 MDS
495	TRT TRT2	APS
496		ANX APS
497	OBS TRT TRT1	
498		GM

ITEM	TRUE	FALSE
499	*TRT*	
500	*TRT TRT1*	*APS*
501		*FB TRT AAS F(p)*
502	*MAC-R APS*	
503	*LSE LSE2*	
504	*LSE LSE1 TRT*	*APS*
505	*WRK*	
506	*MAC-R FB DEP DEP4 VRIN*	*VRIN*
507	*TPA TPA1 VRIN*	*VRIN*
508	*BIZ BIZ1*	
509	*ANX OBS WRK*	*GM VRIN*
510	*TPA TPA2*	*GF*
511	*AAS*	*GF*
512	*DEP DEP1*	
513	*ANG ANG2 VRIN*	
514		
515	*PS SOD SOD1 VRIN*	*VRIN*
516	*FB PS DEP DEP1*	
517	*FB WRK*	
518		
519	*LSE LSE2*	*GM*
520	*FB DEP DEP4 VRIN*	*VRIN*
521	*VRIN*	*WRK*
522		
523	*TPA TPA1 APS*	
524	*FB*	
525	*FB WRK*	
526	*FB LSE*	
527	*AAS*	
528	*FB TRT TRT1*	
529		
530	*FB*	
531	*TPA TPA2*	
532		*GM*
533	*VRIN*	*VRIN*
534	*TRIN*	
535	*TPA TPA1*	
536		*GM*
537		*GF*
538	*CYN CYN1*	
539	*FB DEP DEP1 TRT TRT1*	
540	*FB ANG ANG1 APS*	
541	*TPA*	
542	*ANG ANG2*	*VRIN*
543	*BIZ BIZ2 FAM*	
544	*FB AAS*	
545	*TPA TPA2 WRK*	

(continued)

TABLE E.1 Item Overlap among MMPI-2 Scales (continued)

ITEM	TRUE	FALSE
546	DEP DEP4	
547	OBS	
548	ANG ANG1	GF
549	MAC-R	
550	FAM FAM2	GF
551	BIZ BIZ1	
552	GF	
553	OBS	
554	DEP DEP1 WRK TRT TRT1 VRIN	
555	FB FRS FRS1 F(p)	
556	ANX VRIN TRIN	VRIN
557		
558		
559	WRK	
560	TRIN	
561		WRK
562	LSE	VRIN
563	FAM FAM1 MDS	
564		PS ANG ANG1
565	PS	VRIN TRIN
566	WRK	
567	FAM	

K- and Non-K-Corrected T Score Values for the MMPI-2 Basic Scales Based on the Original Minnesota Normative Group (N = 225 Males, 315 Females)

The following tables make it possible to score an MMPI-2 protocol using the original Hathaway/McKinley norms. This may be useful, for example, if one wants to compare an individual's MMPI-2 profile with that same individual's profile obtained earlier with the original MMPI. The T score values are identical to the values originally published, except for those MMPI-2 basic scales (*F, 1, 2, 0*) that are slightly shorter than the original scales; values for these scales were recomputed on the original normative samples. Scale *5* was also shortened, but since the original normative data are not available for this scale, the original values have been adjusted by a type of prorating.

TABLE F.1 K-Corrected T Score Values for the MMPI-2 Basic Scales Based on the Original Minnesota Normative Group (N = 225 Males, 315 Females)

Males

RAW SCORE	L	F	K	Hs +.5K	D	Hy	Pd +.4K	Mf	Pa	Pt +1K	Sc +1K	Ma +.2K	Si	RAW SCORE
72														72
71														71
70														70
69													96	69
68													95	68
67													94	67
66													93	66
65													92	65
64													91	64
63													90	63
62													89	62
61													88	61
60													87	60
59											120		86	59
58											119		85	58
57										120	117		84	57
56										118	115		83	56
55						120				116	113		82	55
54						118		120		114	111		81	54
53						116		118		112	109		80	53
52						115		116		110	107		79	52
51						113		114		107	105		78	51
50						111		112		105	103		77	50
49						109	120	110		103	101		76	49
48						107	119	108		101	99		75	48
47						106	116	106		99	97		74	47
46						104	114	104		97	96		73	46
45						102	111	102		95	94	120	72	45
44					120	100	109	100		93	92	118	71	44
43					118	98	107	98		91	90	116	70	43
42					116	96	104	96		89	88	113	69	42
41					113	95	102	94		87	86	111	68	41
40					111	93	100	92		85	84	108	67	40
39				120	108	91	97	90		83	82	106	66	39
38				118	106	89	95	88		81	80	103	65	38
37				116	104	87	93	86		79	78	101	64	37
36				113	101	86	90	84		77	76	98	63	36

Females

RAW SCORE	L	F	K	Hs +.5K	D	Hy	Pd +.4K	Mf	Pa	Pt +1K	Sc +1K	Ma +.2K	Si	RAW SCORE
72														72
71														71
70														70
69											120		96	69
68										120	119		95	68
67										118	118		94	67
66										117	116		93	66
65										115	115		92	65
64										114	113		91	64
63										112	112		90	63
62										110	110		89	62
61										109	109		88	61
60										107	107		87	60
59										106	106		86	59
58						120				104	104		85	58
57						118				102	103		84	57
56						116				101	101		83	56
55					120	114				99	100		82	55
54					119	112				98	98		81	54
53					117	110				96	97		80	53
52					115	109				94	95		79	52
51					113	107				93	94		78	51
50					111	105				91	92		77	50
49					109	103	120			89	91		76	49
48					107	101	119			88	89		75	48
47				119	105	100	116			86	87		74	47
46				117	103	98	114			84	86		73	46
45				115	102	96	111			83	84	120	72	45
44				113	100	94	109			81	83	118	71	44
43				111	98	93	107	30		79	81	116	70	43
42				109	96	91	104	32		78	80	113	69	42
41				107	94	89	102	34		76	78	111	68	41
40				105	92	87	100	37		74	77	108	67	40
39				103	90	86	97	39		73	75	106	66	39
38				101	88	84	95	41		71	74	103	65	38
37				99	86	82	93	43		69	72	101	64	37
36				97	84	80	90	45		68	71	98	63	36

Males

RAW SCORE	L	F	K	Hs +.5K	D	Hy	Pd +.4K	Mf	Pa	Pt +1K	Sc +1K	Ma +.2K	Si
35		120		111	99	84	88	82		75	74	96	62
34		118		108	96	82	86	80		73	73	93	61
33		116	83	106	94	80	83	78	120	71	71	91	60
32		114	81	103	92	78	81	76	117	69	69	88	58
31		112	79	100	89	76	79	74	114	66	67	86	56
30		110	77	98	87	75	76	73	111	64	65	83	55
29		108	75	95	84	73	74	71	108	62	63	81	54
28		106	74	93	82	71	71	69	105	60	61	78	53
27		104	72	90	80	69	69	67	102	58	59	75	52
26		102	70	88	77	67	67	64	100	56	57	73	51
25		100	68	85	75	65	64	61	97	54	55	70	50
24		98	66	82	72	64	62	59	94	52	53	68	49
23		96	64	80	70	62	60	57	91	50	51	65	48
22		94	62	77	68	60	57	55	88	48	50	63	47
21		92	61	75	65	58	55	53	85	46	48	60	46
20		90	59	72	63	56	53	51	82	44	46	58	45
19		88	57	70	60	55	50	49	79	42	44	55	44
18		86	55	67	58	53	48	47	76	40	42	53	43
17		84	53	65	56	51	46	45	73	38	40	50	42
16		82	51	62	53	49	43	43	70	36	38	48	41
15	86	80	49	59	51	47	41	41	67	34	36	45	40
14	83	78	48	57	48	45	39	39	65	32	34	43	39
13	80	76	46	54	46	44	36	37	62	30	32	40	38
12	76	73	44	52	44	42	34	35	59		30	38	37
11	73	70	42	49	41	40	32	32	56			35	36
10	70	68	40	47	39	38	30	30	53			33	35
9	66	66	38	44	36	36			50			30	34
8	63	64	36	41	34	35			47				33
7	60	62	35	39	32	33			44				32
6	56	60	33	36	30	31			41				30
5	53	58	31	34		30			38				
4	50	55	30	31					35				
3	46	53		30					33				
2	44	50							30				
1	40	48											
0	36	46											

Females

RAW SCORE	L	F	K	Hs +.5K	D	Hy	Pd +.4K	Mf	Pa	Pt +1K	Sc +1K	Ma +.2K	Si
35		120		95	82	79	88	48		66	69	96	62
34		118		93	80	77	86	51		65	67	93	61
33		116	83	91	78	75	83	53	120	63	66	91	60
32		114	81	89	76	73	81	55	117	61	64	88	58
31		112	79	87	75	72	79	57	114	60	63	86	56
30		110	77	85	73	70	76	59	111	58	61	83	55
29		108	75	82	71	68	74	61	108	56	60	81	54
28		106	74	80	69	66	71	63	105	55	58	78	53
27		104	72	78	67	64	69	66	102	53	57	75	52
26		102	70	76	65	63	67	68	100	51	55	73	51
25		100	68	74	63	61	64	70	97	50	54	70	50
24		98	66	72	61	59	62	72	94	48	52	68	49
23		96	64	70	59	57	60	74	91	46	51	65	48
22		94	62	68	57	56	57	76	88	45	49	63	47
21		92	61	66	55	54	55	78	85	43	47	60	46
20		90	59	64	53	52	53	80	82	41	46	58	45
19		88	57	62	51	50	50	82	79	40	44	55	44
18		86	55	60	49	49	48	84	76	38	43	53	43
17		84	53	58	47	47	46	86	73	36	41	50	42
16		82	51	56	45	45	43	88	70	35	40	48	41
15	86	80	49	54	44	43	41	90	67	33	38	45	40
14	83	78	48	52	42	42	39	92	65	32	37	43	39
13	80	76	46	50	40	40	36	94	62	30	35	40	38
12	76	73	44	48	38	38	34	96	59		34	38	37
11	73	70	42	46	36	36	32	98	56		32	35	36
10	70	68	40	44	34	34	30	100	53		31	33	35
9	66	66	38	42	32	33		103	50		30	30	34
8	63	64	36	39	30	31		105	47				33
7	60	62	35	37		30		107	44				32
6	56	60	33	35				109	41				30
5	53	58	31	33				111	38				
4	50	55	30	31				113	35				
3	46	53		30				115	33				
2	44	50						117	30				
1	40	48						119					
0	36	46						120					

Males

RAW SCORE	L	F	K	Hs +.5K	D	Hy	Pd +.4K	Mf	Pa	Pt +1K	Sc +1K	Ma +.2K	Si

Females

RAW SCORE	L	F	K	Hs +.5K	D	Hy	Pd +.4K	Mf	Pa	Pt +1K	Sc +1K	Ma +.2K	Si

TABLE F.2 Non-*K*-Corrected T Score Values for the MMPI-2 Basic Scales Based on the Original
Minnesota Normative Group
(*N* = 225 Males, 315 Females)ψ

Females

RAW SCORE	L	F	K	Hs	D	Hy	Pd	Mf	Pa	Pt	Sc	Ma	Si	RAW SCORE
72														72
71														71
70														70
69													96	69
68													95	68
67											120		94	67
66											119		93	66
65											118		92	65
64											117		91	64
63											116		90	63
62											114		89	62
61											113		88	61
60											112		87	60
59											111		86	59
58						120					109		85	58
57						118					108		84	57
56						116					107		83	56
55					120	114					106		82	55
54					119	112					104		81	54
53					117	110					103		80	53
52					115	109					102		79	52
51					113	107					101		78	51
50					111	105					99		77	50
49					109	103					98		76	49
48					107	101					97		75	48
47					105	100				95	96		74	47
46					103	98				94	94	120	73	46
45					102	96				93	93	119	72	45
44					100	94				91	92	117	71	44
43					98	93	120	30		90	91	115	70	43
42					96	91	117	32		88	89	112	69	42
41					94	89	115	34		86	88	110	68	41
40					92	87	113	37		85	87	108	67	40
39					90	86	110	39		84	86	106	66	39
38					88	84	108	41		82	84	104	65	38
37					86	82	106	43		81	83	101	64	37
36					84	80	103	45		80	82	99	63	36

Males

RAW SCORE	L	F	K	Hs	D	Hy	Pd	Mf	Pa	Pt	Sc	Ma	Si	RAW SCORE
72														72
71														71
70														70
69													96	69
68													95	68
67													94	67
66													93	66
65													92	65
64											120		91	64
63											118		90	63
62											117		89	62
61											115		88	61
60											114		87	60
59											113		86	59
58											111		85	58
57											110		84	57
56											109		83	56
55						120					107		82	55
54						118		120			106		81	54
53						116		118			105		80	53
52						115		116			103		79	52
51						113		114			102		78	51
50						111		112			101		77	50
49						109		110		103	99		76	49
48						107		108		102	98		75	48
47						106		106		100	97		74	47
46						104		104		99	96	120	73	46
45						102		102		98	95	119	72	45
44					120	100		100		96	94	117	71	44
43					118	98		98		95	93	115	70	43
42					116	96	120	96		93	92	112	69	42
41					113	95	119	94		92	91	110	68	41
40					111	93	116	92		91	90	108	67	40
39					108	91	114	90		90	89	106	66	39
38					106	89	111	88		89	88	104	65	38
37					104	87	108	86		88	87	101	64	37
36					101	86	106	84		86	86	99	63	36

646

Males

RAW SCORE	L	F	K	Hs	D	Hy	Pd	Mf	Pa	Pt	Sc	Ma	Si
35		120			99	84	103	82	120	85	84	97	62
34		118			96	82	101	80	117	84	83	95	61
33		116			94	80	98	78	114	82	82	93	60
32		114		113	92	78	96	76	111	81	80	90	58
31		112		110	89	76	93	74	108	79	79	88	56
30		110	83	108	87	75	91	73	105	78	78	86	55
29		108	81	106	84	73	88	71	102	77	76	84	54
28		106	79	104	82	71	86	69	100	75	75	81	53
27		104	77	101	80	69	83	67	97	74	74	79	52
26		102	75	99	77	67	81	64	94	73	72	77	51
25		100	74	97	75	65	78	61	91	71	71	75	50
24		98	72	94	72	64	75	59	88	70	70	72	49
23		96	70	92	70	62	73	57	85	68	68	70	48
22		94	68	90	68	60	70	55	82	67	67	68	47
21		92	66	88	65	58	68	53	79	66	65	66	46
20		90	64	85	63	56	65	51	76	64	64	63	45
19		88	62	83	60	53	63	49	73	63	63	61	44
18		86	61	81	58	51	60	47	70	61	61	59	43
17		84	59	78	56	49	58	45	67	60	60	57	42
16		82	57	76	53	47	55	43	65	57	59	54	41
15	86	80	55	74	51	45	53	41	62	56	57	52	40
14	83	78	53	72	49	44	50	39	59	54	56	50	39
13	80	76	51	69	46	42	47	37	56	53	55	48	38
12	76	73	49	67	44	40	45	35	53	52	53	45	37
11	73	70	48	65	41	38	42	34	50	50	51	43	36
10	70	68	46	62	39	36	40	32	47	48	49	41	35
9	66	66	44	60	36	35	37	30	44	46	48	39	34
8	63	64	42	58	34	33	35		41	45	47	37	33
7	60	62	40	56	32	31	32		38	43	44	34	32
6	56	60	38	53	30	30	30		35	42	43	32	30
5	53	58	36	51					33	41	41	30	
4	50	55	35	49					30	39	40		
3	46	53	33	47						38	38		
2	44	50	31	44						36	37		
1	40	48	30	42									
0	36	46		40									

Females

RAW SCORE	L	F	K	Hs	D	Hy	Pd	Mf	Pa	Pt	Sc	Ma	Si
35		120			82	79	101	48		78	80	97	62
34		118			80	77	99	51		77	79	95	61
33		116			78	75	96	53		76	78	93	60
32		114		97	76	73	94	55		75	77	90	58
31		112		96	75	72	91	57	120	73	75	88	56
30		110	83	94	73	70	89	59	117	72	74	86	55
29		108	81	92	71	68	87	61	114	71	73	84	54
28		106	79	90	69	66	84	63	111	69	72	81	53
27		104	77	88	67	64	82	66	108	68	70	79	52
26		102	75	86	65	63	80	68	105	67	69	77	51
25		100	74	84	63	61	77	70	102	65	68	75	50
24		98	72	82	61	59	75	72	100	64	67	72	49
23		96	70	80	59	57	73	74	97	63	65	70	48
22		94	68	79	57	56	70	76	94	62	64	68	47
21		92	66	77	55	54	68	78	91	60	63	66	46
20		90	64	75	53	52	65	80	88	59	62	63	45
19		88	62	73	51	50	63	82	85	58	60	61	44
18		86	61	71	49	49	61	84	82	56	59	59	43
17		84	59	69	47	47	58	86	79	55	58	57	42
16		82	57	67	46	45	56	88	76	54	57	54	41
15	86	80	55	65	45	43	53	90	73	52	55	52	40
14	83	78	53	63	44	42	51	92	70	51	54	50	39
13	80	76	51	62	42	40	49	94	67	50	53	48	38
12	76	73	49	60	40	38	47	96	65	49	52	45	37
11	73	70	46	58	38	36	44	98	62	47	50	43	36
10	70	68	44	56	36	34	42	100	59	46	49	41	35
9	66	66	42	54	34	33	40	103	56	45	48	39	34
8	63	64	40	52	32	31	37	105	53	43	47	37	33
7	60	62	38	50	30	30	35	107	50	42	45	34	32
6	56	60	36	48			32	109	47	41	44	32	30
5	53	58	35	46			30	111	44	39	43	30	
4	50	55	33	45				113	41	38	42		
3	46	53	31	43				115	38	37	40		
2	44	50	30	41				117	35	36	39		
1	40	48		39				119	33	34	38		
0	36	46		37				120	30	33	37		

APPENDIX G

MMPI-2 to MMPI Conversion Tables

TABLE G.1 Conversion from MMPI Group Form to MMPI-2*

1-1	51-45	101-88	151-162	201-185	251-229	301-273
2-2	52-46	102-89	152-140	202-234	252-306	302-34
3-3	53-	103-91	153-141	203-187	253-230	303-274
4-4	54-78	104-92	154-142	204-191	254-231	304-275
5-5	55-47	105-93	155-143	205-240	255-232	305-277
6-7	56-84	106-94	156-168	206-	256-312	306-278
7-8	57-49	107-95	157-145	207-188	257-318	307-279
8-9	58-	108-97	158-146	208-189	258-	308-21
9-10	59-50	109-98	159-147	209-246	259-233	309-280
10-11	60-51	110-99	160-148	210-252	260-235	310-12
11-13	61-52	111-100	161-149	211-258	261-236	311-35
12-14	62-53	112-120	162-151	212-190	262-237	312-281
13-15	63-	113-126	163-152	213-193	263-238	313-283
14-	64-55	114-101	164-174	214-194	264-239	314-16
15-16	65-90	115-132	165-153	215-264	265-241	315-17
16-17	66-96	116-103	166-154	216-195	266-242	316-284
17-6	67-56	117-104	167-155	217-196	267-243	317-285
18-20	68-57	118-105	168-180	218-270	268-244	318-9
19-19	69-	119-106	169-186	219-197	269-324	319-286
20-12	70-	120-107	170-157	220-276	270-245	320-287
21-21	71-58	121-138	171-158	221-199	271-248	321-289
22-23	72-59	122-109	172-161	222-200	272-330	322-290
23-18	73-61	123-144	173-160	223-201	273-247	323-32
24-22	74-62	124-110	174-159	224-202	274-249	324-291
25-25	75-102	125-111	175-164	225-203	275-336	325-292
26-26	76-65	126-112	176-163	226-205	276-343	326-23
27-24	77-64	127-113	177-192	227-282	277-250	327-297
28-27	78-67	128-115	178-165	228-206	278-251	328-31
29-28	79-63	129-116	179-166	229-207	279-253	329-293
30-29	80-68	130-117	180-167	230-208	280-254	330-295
31-30	81-69	131-118	181-169	231-209	281-255	331-42
32-31	82-70	132-119	182-170	232-211	282-256	332-296
33-32	83-108	133-121	183-171	233-212	283-257	333-22
34-36	84-71	134-122	184-198	234-213	284-259	334-298
35-42	85-114	135-123	185-204	235-214	285-260	335-299
36-33	86-73	136-124	186-172	236-215	286-349	336-302
37-34	87-74	137-125	187-177	237-217	287-261	337-301
38-35	88-75	138-127	188-173	238-218	288-18	338-305
39-37	89-76	139-150	189-175	239-219	289-263	339-303
40-48	90-77	140-128	190-176	240-220	290-15	340-304
41-38	91-79	141-129	191-178	241-221	291-355	341-307
42-54	92-80	142-130	192-179	242-223	292-265	342-308
43-39	93-81	143-131	193-181	243-224	293-361	343-309
44-40	94-82	144-133	194-182	244-225	294-266	344-310
45-41	95-	145-134	195-183	245-288	295-	345-311
46-43	96-83	146-156	196-210	246-294	296-267	346-313
47-44	97-85	147-135	197-216	247-300	297-268	347-314
48-60	98-	148-136	198-184	248-226	298-269	348-315
49-66	99-86	149-137	199-222	249-	299-271	349-316
50-72	100-87	150-139	200-228	250-227	300-272	350-319

(continued)

TABLE G.1 Conversion from MMPI Group Form to MMPI-2* (continued)

351-317	382-390	413-407	444-	475-433	506-444	537-
352-320	383-338	414-408	445-422	476-	507-445	538-
353-321	384-391	415-350	446-344	477-434	508-	539-462
354-322	385-392	416-409	447-423	478-	509-446	540-
355-323	386-393	417-410	448-424	479-360	510-447	541-
356-325	387-	418-411	449-353	480-435	511-448	542-
357-326	388-395	419-412	450-359	481-362	512-	543-463
358-327	389-394	420-	451-363	482-342	513-	544-464
359-328	390-396	421-413	452-	483-	514-	545-
360-329	391-340	422-	453-	484-	515-	546-
361-331	392-397	423-	454-	485-436	516-449	547-370
362-285	393-	424-	455-357	486-	517-450	548-
363-332	394-398	425-	456-	487-364	518-451	549-368
364-333	395-399	426-414	457-	488-	519-	550-465
365-334	396-400	427-351	458-425	489-	520-452	551-466
366-277	397-339	428-	459-	490-	521-262	552-467
367-385	398-348	429-	460-	491-	522-453	553-468
368-386	399-372	430-	461-356	492-438	523-	554-
369-	400-345	431-415	462-	493-	524-	555-469
370-	401-401	432-416	463-426	494-441	525-458	556-
371-335	402-402	433-	464-427	495-437	526-454	557-
372-	403-	434-417	465-428	496-	527-455	558-470
373-	404-403	435-	466-429	497-	528-	559-471
374-341	405-404	436-352	467-	498-	529-456	560-472
375-	406-346	437-418	468-430	499-442	530-	561-
376-	407-405	438-419	469-358	500-439	531-457	562-473
377-337	408-	439-420	470-	501-440	532-459	563-474
378-	409-	440-354	471-431	502-365	533-	564-369
379-388	410-406	441-	472-432	503-	534-460	565-
380-	411-347	442-	473-367	504-443	535-	566-
381-389	412-	443-421	474-	505-366	536-461	

*Missing numbers represent items from the original MMPI not included in the MMPI-2 booklet. The 16 items duplicated in the original MMPI are not duplicated in MMPI-2; hence, they occur in only one location in MMPI-2 (e.g., items 8 and 318 are not equivalent to item 9).

TABLE G.2 Conversion from MMPI-2 to MMPI Group Form*

1-1	65-76	129-141	193-213	257-283	321-353	385-367
2-2	66-49	130-142	194-214	258-211	322-354	386-368
3-3	67-78	131-143	195-216	259-284	323-355	387-
4-4	68-80	132-115	196-217	260-285	324-269	388-379
5-5	69-81	133-144	197-219	261-287	325-356	389-381
6-17	70-82	134-145	198-184	262-521	326-357	390-382
7-6	71-84	135-147	199-221	263-289	327-358	391-384
8-7	72-50	136-148	200-222	264-215	328-359	392-385
9-8,318	73-86	137-149	201-223	265-292	329-360	393-386
10-9	74-87	138-121	202-224	266-294	330-272	394-389
11-10	75-88	139-150	203-225	267-296	331-361	395-388
12-20,310	76-89	140-152	204-185	268-297	332-363	396-390
13-11	77-90	141-153	205-226	269-298	333-364	397-392
14-12	78-54	142-154	206-228	270-218	334-365	398-394
15-13,290	79-91	143-155	207-229	271-299	335-371	399-395
16-15,314	80-92	144-123	208-230	272-300	336-275	400-396
17-16,315	81-93	145-157	209-231	273-301	337-377	401-401
18-23,288	82-94	146-158	210-196	274-303	338-383	402-402
19-19	83-96	147-159	211-232	275-304	339-397	403-404
20-18	84-56	148-160	212-233	276-220	340-391	404-405
21-21,308	85-97	149-161	213-234	277-305,366	341-374	405-407
22-24,333	86-99	150-139	214-235	278-306	342-482	406-410
23-22,326	87-100	151-162	215-236	279-307	343-276	407-413
24-27	88-101	152-163	216-197	280-309	344-446	408-414
25-25	89-102	153-165	217-237	281-312	345-400	409-416
26-26	90-65	154-166	218-238	282-227	346-406	410-417
27-28	91-103	155-167	219-239	283-313	347-411	411-418
28-29	92-104	156-146	220-240	284-316	348-398	412-419
29-30	93-105	157-170	221-241	285-317,362	349-286	413-421
30-31	94-106	158-171	222-199	286-319	350-415	414-426
31-32,328	95-107	159-174	223-242	287-320	351-427	415-431
32-33,323	96-66	160-173	224-243	288-245	352-436	416-432
33-36	97-108	161-172	225-244	289-321	353-449	417-434
34-37,302	98-109	162-151	226-248	290-322	354-440	418-437
35-38,311	99-110	163-176	227-250	291-324	355-291	419-438
36-34	100-111	164-175	228-200	292-325	356-461	420-439
37-39	101-114	165-178	229-251	293-329	357-455	421-443
38-41	102-75	166-179	230-253	294-246	358-469	422-445
39-43	103-116	167-180	231-254	295-330	359-450	423-447
40-44	104-117	168-156	232-255	296-332	360-479	424-448
41-45	105-118	169-181	233-259	297-327	361-293	425-458
42-35,331	106-119	170-182	234-202	298-334	362-481	426-463
43-46	107-120	171-183	235-260	299-335	363-451	427-464
44-47	108-83	172-186	236-261	300-247	364-487	428-465
45-51	109-122	173-188	237-262	301-337	365-502	429-466
46-52	110-124	174-164	238-263	302-336	366-505	430-468
47-55	111-125	175-189	239-264	303-339	367-473	431-471
48-40	112-126	176-190	240-205	304-340	368-549	432-472
49-57	113-127	177-187	241-265	305-338	369-564	433-475
50-59	114-85	178-191	242-266	306-252	370-547	434-477
51-60	115-128	179-192	243-267	307-341	371-	435-480
52-61	116-129	180-168	244-268	308-342	372-399	436-485
53-62	117-130	181-193	245-270	309-343	373-	437-495
54-42	118-131	182-194	246-209	310-344	374-	438-492
55-64	119-132	183-195	247-273	311-345	375-	439-500
56-67	120-112	184-198	248-271	312-256	376-	440-501
57-68	121-133	185-201	249-274	313-346	377-	441-494
58-71	122-134	186-169	250-247	314-347	378-	442-499
59-72	123-135	187-203	251-278	315-348	379-	443-504
60-48	124-136	188-207	252-210	316-349	380-	444-506
61-73	125-137	189-208	253-279	317-351	381-	445-507
62-74	126-113	190-212	254-280	318-257	382-	446-509
63-79	127-138	191-204	255-281	319-350	383-	447-510
64-77	128-140	192-177	256-282	320-352	384-	448-511

(continued)

651

TABLE G.2   Conversion from MMPI-2 to MMPI Group Form* (continued)

449-516	466-551	483-	500-	517-	534-	551-
450-517	467-552	484-	501-	518-	535-	552-
451-518	468-553	485-	502-	519-	536-	553-
452-520	469-555	486-	503-	520-	537-	554-
453-522	470-558	487-	504-	521-	538-	555-
454-526	471-559	488-	505-	522-	539-	556-
455-527	472-560	489-	506-	523-	540-	557-
456-529	473-562	490-	507-	524-	541-	558-
457-531	474-563	491-	508-	525-	542-	559-
458-525	475-	492-	509-	526-	543-	560-
459-532	476-	493-	510-	527-	544-	561-
460-534	477-	494-	511-	528-	545-	562-
461-536	478-	495-	512-	529-	546-	563-
462-539	479-	496-	513-	530-	547-	564-
463-543	480-	497-	514-	531-	548-	565-
464-544	481-	498-	515-	532-	549-	566-
465-550	482-	499-	516-	533-	550-	567-

*Missing numbers represent items that did not appear in the original MMPI. Pairs of numbers refer to the two locations in which duplicate items appeared in the original MMPI.

TABLE G.3   Conversion from MMPI Form R to MMPI-2*

367-335	396-262	425-	454-	483-	512-	541-
368-341	397-370	426-414	455-389	484-	513-	542-
369-337	398-368	427-	456-	485-436	514-	543-463
370-338	399-369	428-	457-	486-	515-	544-464
371-340	400-385	429-	458-425	487-396	516-449	545-
372-339	401-401	430-	459-	488-	517-450	546-
373-348	402-402	431-415	460-	489-	518-451	547-399
374-345	403-	432-416	461-390	490-	519-	548-
375-346	404-403	433-	462-391	491-	520-452	549-400
376-347	405-404	434-417	463-426	492-438	521-398	550-465
377-350	406-386	435-	464-427	493-	522-453	551-466
378-351	407-405	436-	465-428	494-441	523-	552-467
379-352	408-	437-418	466-429	495-437	524-	553-468
380-354	409-	438-419	467-	496-	525-458	554-
381-344	410-406	439-420	468-430	497-	526-454	555-469
382-353	411-	440-	469-392	498-	527-455	556-
383-359	412-	441-	470-	499-442	528-	557-
384-363	413-407	442-	471-431	500-439	529-456	558-470
385-357	414-408	443-421	472-432	501-440	530-	559-471
386-356	415-	444-	473-393	502-397	531-457	560-472
387-	416-409	445-422	474-	503-	532-459	561-
388-358	417-410	446-	475-433	504-443	533-	562-473
389-367	418-411	447-423	476-	505-	534-460	563-474
390-360	419-412	448-424	477-434	506-444	535-	564-372
391-362	420-	449-	478-	507-445	536-461	565-
392-342	421-413	450-388	479-	508-	537-	566-
393-364	422-	451-	480-435	509-446	538-	
394-365	423-	452-	481-395	510-447	539-462	
395-366	424-	453-	482-394	511-448	540-	

*Conversion of items 1-366 is identical to Table G.1. Missing numbers represent items from MMPI Form R not included in the MMPI-2 booklet.

TABLE G.4   Conversion of MMPI-2 to MMPI Form R*

262-396	344-381	354-380	364-393	374-	384-	394-482
335-367	345-374	355-291	365-394	375-	385-400	395-481
336-275	346-375	356-386	366-395	376-	386-406	396-487
337-369	347-376	357-385	367-389	377-	387-	397-502
338-370	348-373	358-388	368-398	378-	388-450	398-521
339-372	349-286	359-383	369-399	379-	389-455	399-547
340-371	350-377	360-390	370-397	380-	390-461	400-549
341-368	351-378	361-293	371-	381-	391-462	
342-392	352-379	362-391	372-564	382-	392-469	
343-276	353-382	363-384	373-	383-	393-473	

*Conversion of items 1-334, with the exception of item 262 and items 401-567, is identical to Table G.2. Missing numbers represent items from MMPI Form R not included in the MMPI-2 booklet.

Aaronson, A. L., Dent, O. B., & Kline, C. D. (1996). Cross-validation of MMPI and MMPI-2 predictor scales. *Journal of Clinical Psychology, 52,* 311–315.

Aaronson, A. L., Dent, O. B., Webb, J. T., & Kline, C. D. (1996). Graying of the critical items: Effects of aging on responding to MMPI-2 critical items. *Journal of Personality Assessment, 66,* 169–176.

Aaronson, B. S. (1959). A comparison of two MMPI measures of masculinity-femininity. *Journal of Clinical Psychology, 15,* 48–50.

Aaronson, B. S., & Grumpelt, H. R. (1961). Homosexuality and some MMPI measures of masculinity-femininity. *Journal of Clinical Psychology, 17,* 245–247.

Alfano, D. P., Finlayson, M. A. J., Stearns, G. M., & Neilson, P. M. (1990). The MMPI and neurologic dysfunction: Profile configuration and analysis. *The Clinical Neurologist, 4,* 69–79.

Alfano, D. P., Neilson, P. M., Paniak, C. E., & Finlayson, M. A. J. (1992). The MMPI and closed head injury. *The Clinical Neuropsychologist, 6,* 134–142.

Allen, J. (1998). Personality assessment with American Indians and Alaska Natives: Instrument considerations and service delivery style. *Journal of Personality Assessment, 70,* 17–42.

Allen, J. P. (1991). Personality correlates of the Mac-Andrew alcoholism scale: A review of the literature. *Psychology of Addictive Behavior, 5,* 59–65.

Almada, S. J., Zonderman, A. B., Shekelle, R. B., Dyer, A. R., Daviglus, M. L., Costa, P. T., Jr., & Stamler, J. (1991). Neuroticism and cynicism and risk of death in middle-aged men: The Western Electric study. *Psychosomatic Medicine, 53,* 165–175.

Alperin, J. J., Archer, R. P., & Coates, G. D. (1996). Development and effects of a *K*-correction procedure for the MMPI-A. *Journal of Personality Assessment, 67,* 155–168.

American Psychiatric Association (1980). *Diagnostic and statistical manual of mental disorders* (3rd ed.). Washington: Author.

American Psychiatric Association (1987). *Diagnostic and statistical manual of mental disorders* (3rd ed. Revised). Washington: Author.

American Psychiatric Association (1994). *Diagnostic and statistical manual of mental disorders* (4th ed.). Washington: Author.

Anastasi, A. (1968). *Psychological testing* (3rd ed.). New York: Macmillan.

Anderson, W. (1956). The MMPI: Low *Pa* scores. *Journal of Counseling Psychology, 3,* 226–228.

Anderson, W. P., & Kunce, J. T. (1984). Diagnostic implications of markedly elevated MMPI *Sc* scores for non-hospitalized clients. *Journal of Clinical Psychology, 40,* 925–930.

Anthony, N. (1976). Malingering as role taking. *Journal of Clinical Psychology, 32,* 32–41.

Apfeldorf, M. (1978). Alcoholism scales and the MMPI: Contributions and future directions. *International Journal of the Addictions, 13,* 17–55.

Arbisi, P., & Ben-Porath, Y. S. (1993, March). *Interpreting the F scales of inpatients: Moving from art to science.* Paper presented at the 28th Annual Symposium on Recent Developments in the Use of the MMPI/MMPI-2/MMPI-A, St. Petersburg, FL.

Arbisi, P. A., & Ben-Porath, Y. S. (1995). An MMPI-2 infrequent response scale for use with psychopathological populations: The Infrequency Psychopathology scale, *F(p)*. *Psychological Assessment, 7,* 424–431.

Arbisi, P. A., & Ben-Porath, Y. S. (1997). Characteristics of the MMPI-2 *F(p)* scale as a function of diagnosis in an inpatient sample of veterans. *Psychological Assessment, 9,* 102–105.

Arbisi, P. A., & Ben-Porath, Y. S. (1998). The ability of MMPI-2 validity scales to detect fake-bad responses in psychiatric patients. *Psychological Assessment, 10,* 221–228.

Arbisi, P. A., Ben-Porath, Y. S., & McNulty, J. (1998, August). *The impact of ethnicity on the MMPI-2 in inpatient psychiatric settings.* Paper presented at the annual meeting of the American Psychological Association, San Francisco.

Archer, R. P. (1984). Use of the MMPI with adolescents: A review of salient issues. *Clinical Psychology Review, 4,* 241–251.

Archer, R. P. (1987). *Using the MMPI with adolescents.* Hillsdale, NJ: Erlbaum.

Archer, R. P. (1988). Using the MMPI with adolescents. In C. D. Spielberger & J. N. Butcher (Eds.), *Advances in personality assessment* (Vol. 7, pp. 103–126). Hillsdale, NJ: Erlbaum.

Archer, R. P. (1992). *The MMPI-A: Assessing adolescent psychopathology.* Hillsdale, NJ: Erlbaum.

Archer, R. P. (1997a). Future directions for the MMPI-A: Research and clinical issues. *Journal of Personality Assessment, 68,* 95–109.

Archer, R. P. (1997b). *The MMPI-A: Assessing adolescent psychopathology* (2nd ed.). Mahwah, NJ: Erlbaum.

Archer, R. P., Aiduk, R., Griffin, R., & Elkins, D. E. (1996). Incremental validity of the MMPI-2 Content scales in a psychiatric sample. *Assessment, 3,* 79–90.

Archer, R. P., Belevich, J. K., & Elkins, D. E. (1994). Item-level and scale-level factor structures of the MMPI-A. *Journal of Personality Assessment, 62,* 332–345.

Archer, R. P., Elkins, D. E., Aiduk, R., & Griffin, R. (1997). Incremental validity of MMPI-2 Supplementary scales. *Assessment, 4,* 193–205.

Archer, R. P., Fontaine, J., & McCrae, R. R. (1998). Effects of two MMPI-2 validity scales on basic scale relations to external criteria. *Journal of Personality Assessment, 70,* 87–102.

Archer, R. P., & Gordon, R. A. (1994). Psychometric stability of MMPI-A item modifications. *Journal of Personality Assessment, 62,* 416–426.

Archer, R. P., Gordon, R. A., Anderson, G. L., & Giannetti, R. A. (1989). MMPI special scale correlates for adolescent inpatients. *Journal of Personality Assessment, 53,* 654–664.

Archer, R. P., Gordon, R. A., Giannetti, R. A., & Singles, J. M. (1988). MMPI scale clinical correlates for adolescent inpatients. *Journal of Personality Assessment, 52,* 707–721.

Archer, R. P., Griffin, R., & Aiduk, R. (1995). MMPI-2 clinical correlates for ten common codes. *Journal of Personality Assessment, 65,* 391–407.

Archer, R. P., & Jacobson, J. M. (1993). Are critical items "critical" for the MMPI-A? *Journal of Personality Assessment, 61,* 547–556.

Archer, R. P., & Krishnamurthy, R. (1994). A structural summary approach for the MMPI-A: Development of empirical correlates. *Journal of Personality Assessment, 63,* 554–573.

Archer, R. P., & Krishnamurthy, R. (1997). MMPI-A scale-level factor structure: Replication in a clinical sample. *Assessment, 4,* 337–349.

Archer, R. P., Krishnamurthy, R., & Jacobson, J. M. (1994). *MMPI-A casebook.* Odessa, FL: Psychological Assessment Resources.

Archer, R. P., Pancoast, D. L., & Gordon, R. A. (1994). The development of the MMPI-A Immaturity scale: Findings for normal and clinical samples. *Journal of Personality Assessment, 62,* 145–156.

Archer, R. P., Pancoast, D. L., & Klinefelter, D. (1989). A comparison of MMPI code types produced by traditional and recent adolescent norms. *Psychological Assessment, 1,* 23–29.

Arita, A. A., & Baer, R. A. (1998). Validity of selected MMPI-A Content scales. *Psychological Assessment, 10,* 59–63.

Armentrout, J. A., & Hauer, A. L. (1978). MMPIs of rapists of adults, rapists of children, and non-rapist sex offenders. *Journal of Clinical Psychology, 34,* 330–332.

Arthur, G. (1944). An experience in examining an Indian twelfth-grade group with the MMPI. *Mental Hygiene, 28,* 243–250.

Artzy, G. (1994). *Correction factors for the MMPI-2 in head injured men and women.* Unpublished doctoral dissertation, University of Victoria, British Columbia, Canada.

Ashby, H. U., Jr., Lee, R. R., & Duke, E. H. (1979, September). *A Narcissistic Personality Disorder MMPI scale.* Paper presented at the annual meeting of the American Psychological Association, New York.

Astin, A. W. (1959). A factor study of the MMPI Psychopathic Deviate scale. *Journal of Consulting Psychology, 23,* 550–554.

Astin, A. W. (1961). A note on the MMPI Psychopathic Deviate scale. *Educational and Psychological Measurement, 21,* 895–897.

Austin, J. S. (1992). The detection of fake good and fake bad on the MMPI-2. *Educational and Psychological Measurement, 52,* 669–674.

Baer, R. A., Ballenger, J., Berry, D. T. R., & Wetter, M. W. (1997). Detection of random responding on the MMPI-A. *Journal of Personality Assessment, 68,* 139–151.

Baer, R. A., Wetter, M. W., & Berry, D. T. R. (1992). Detection of underreporting of psychopathology on the MMPI: A meta-analysis. *Clinical Psychology Review, 12,* 509–525.

Baer, R. A., Wetter, M. W., & Berry, D. T. R. (1995). Effects of information about validity scales on underreporting of symptoms on the MMPI-2: An analogue investigation. *Assessment, 2,* 189–200.

Baer, R. A., Wetter, M. W., Nichols, D. S., Greene, R. L., & Berry, D. T. R. (1995). Sensitivity of MMPI-2 validity scales to underreporting of symptoms. *Psychological Assessment, 4,* 419–423.

Bagby, R. M., Rogers, R., & Buis, T. (1994). Detecting malingered and defensive responding on the MMPI-2 in a forensic inpatient sample. *Journal of Personality Assessment, 62,* 191–203.

Bagby, R. M., Rogers, R., Buis, T., & Kalemba, V. (1994). Malingered and defensive response styles on the MMPI-2: An examination of validity scales. *Assessment, 1,* 31–38.

Bagby, R. M., Rogers, R., Buis, T., Nicholson, R. A., Cameron, S. L., Rector, N. A., Schuller, D. R., & Seeman, M. V. (1997). Detecting feigned depression and schizophrenia on the MMPI-2. *Journal of Personality Assessment, 68,* 650–664.

Bagby, R. M., Rogers, R., Nicholson, R., Buis, T., Seeman, M. V., & Rector, N. (1997a). Does clinical training facilitate feigning schizophrenia on the MMPI-2? *Psychological Assessment, 9,* 106–112.

Bagby, R. M., Rogers, R. A., Nicholson, R., Buis, T., Seeman, M. V., & Rector, N. (1997b). Effectiveness of the MMPI-2 validity indicators in the detection of defensive responding in clinical and nonclinical samples. *Psychological Assessment, 9,* 406–413.

Baldesserini, R. J., Finkelstein, S., & Arana, G. W. (1983). The predictive power of diagnostic tests and the effects of prevalence of illness. *Archives of General Psychiatry, 40,* 569–573.

Baldwin, M. J. V. (1952). A clinico-experimental investigation into the psychologic aspects of multiple sclerosis. *Journal of Nervous and Mental Disease, 115,* 299–342.

Ball, J. C. (1960). Comparison of MMPI profile differences among Negro-white adolescents. *Journal of Clinical Psychology, 16,* 304–307.

Ball, J. C. (1962). *Social deviancy and adolescent personality.* Lexington: University of Kentucky Press.

Barefoot, J. C., Dahlstrom, W. G., & Williams, R. B., Jr. (1983). Hostility, CHD incidence, and total mortality: A 25-year follow-up study of 255 physicians. *Psychosomatic Medicine, 45,* 59–63.

Barefoot, J. C., Dodge, K. A., Peterson, B. L., Dahlstrom, W. G., & Williams, R. B., Jr. (1989). The Cook-Medley Hostility scale: Item content and ability to predict survival. *Psychosomatic Medicine, 51,* 46–57.

Barefoot, J. C., Peterson, B. L., Dahlstrom, W. G., Siegler, I. C., Anderson, N. B., & Williams, R. B., Jr. (1991). Hostility patterns and health implications: Correlates of Cook-Medley Hostility scale scores in a national survey. *Health Psychology, 10,* 18–24.

Barley, W. D., Sabo, T. W., & Greene, R. L. (1986). MMPI normal K^+ and other unelevated profiles. *Journal of Consulting and Clinical Psychology, 54,* 502–506.

Barron, F. (1953). An ego-strength scale which predicts response to psychotherapy. *Journal of Consulting Psychology, 17,* 327–333.

Bathurst, K., Gottfried, A. W., & Gottfried, A. E. (1997). Normative data for the MMPI-2 in child custody litigation. *Psychological Assessment, 9,* 205–211.

Baucom, D. H. (1976). Independent masculinity and femininity scales on the California Psychological Inventory. *Journal of Consulting and Clinical Psychology, 44,* 876.

Baughman, E. E., & Dahlstrom, W. G. (1968). *Negro and white children: A psychological study in the rural South.* New York: Academic Press.

Beck, A. T. (1987). *Beck Depression Inventory.* San Antonio, TX: The Psychological Corporation.

Beck, A. T. (1988). *Beck Hopelessness Scale.* San Antonio, TX: The Psychological Corporation.

Ben-Porath, Y. S. (1994). The ethical dilemma of coached malingering research. *Psychological Assessment, 6,* 14–15.

Ben-Porath, Y. S., & Butcher, J. N. (1989). Psychometric stability of rewritten MMPI items. *Journal of Personality Assessment, 53,* 645–653.

Ben-Porath, Y. S., Butcher, J. N., & Graham, J. R. (1991). Contribution of the MMPI-2 Content scales to the differential diagnosis of schizophrenia and major depression. *Psychological Assessment, 3,* 634–640.

Ben-Porath, Y. S., Hostetler, K., Butcher, J. N., & Graham, J. R. (1989). New subscales for the MMPI-2 Social Introversion (*Si*) scale. *Psychological Assessment, 1,* 169–174.

Ben-Porath, Y. S., McCully, E., & Almagor, M. (1993). Incremental validity of the MMPI-2 Content scales in the assessment of personality and psychopathology by self-report. *Journal of Personality Assessment, 61,* 557–575.

Ben-Porath, Y. S., & Sherwood, N. E. (1993). *The MMPI-2 content component scales: Development, psychometric characteristics, and clinical application.* Minneapolis: University of Minnesota Press.

Ben-Porath, Y. S., Shondrick, D. D., & Stafford, K. P. (1995). MMPI-2 and race in a forensic diagnostic sample. *Criminal Justice and Behavior, 22,* 19–32.

Ben-Porath, Y. S., Slutske, W. S., & Butcher, J. N. (1989). A real-data simulation of computerized adaptive administration of the MMPI. *Psychological Assessment, 1,* 18–22.

Benarick, S. J., Guthrie, G. M., & Snyder, W. U. (1951). An interpretive aid for the *Sc* scale of the MMPI. *Journal of Consulting Psychology, 15,* 142–144.

Bence, V. M., Sabourin, C., Luty, D. T., & Thackrey, M. (1995). Differential sensitivity of the MMPI-2 depression scales and subscales. *Journal of Clinical Psychology, 51,* 375–377.

Berg, I. A. (1955). Response bias and personality: The deviation hypothesis. *Journal of Psychology, 40,* 61–72.

Berg, I. A. (1957). Deviant responses and deviant people: The formulation of the deviation hypothesis. *Journal of Counseling Psychology, 4,* 154–161.

Bernreuter, R. G. (1933). The theory and construction of the personality inventory. *Journal of Social Psychology, 4,* 387–405.

Bernstein, I. H., & Garbin, C. P. (1985). A comparison of alternative proposed subscale structures for MMPI Scale 2. *Multivariate Behavioral Research, 20,* 223–235.

Berry, D. T. R. (1995). Detecting distortion in forensic evaluations with the MMPI-2. In Y. S. Ben-Porath, J. R. Graham, G. C. N. Hall, R. D. Hirschman, & M. S. Zaragoza (Eds.), *Forensic applications of the MMPI-2* (pp. 82–102). Thousand Oaks, CA: Sage.

Berry, D. T. R., Adams, J. J., Clark, C. D., Thacker, S. R., Burger, T. L., Wetter, M. W., Baer, R. A., & Borden, J. W. (1996). Detection of a cry for help on the MMPI-2: An analog investigation. *Journal of Personality Assessment, 67,* 26–36.

Berry, D. T. R., Adams, J. J., Smith, G. T., Greene, R. L., Sekirnjak, G. C., Wieland, G., & Tharpe, B. (1997). MMPI-2 clinical scales and 2-point code types: Impact of varying levels of omitted items. *Psychological Assessment, 9,* 158–160.

Berry, D. T. R., Baer, R. A., & Harris, M. J. (1991). Detection of malingering on the MMPI: A meta-analysis. *Clinical Psychology Review, 11,* 585–598.

Berry, D. T. R., & Butcher, J. N. (1998). Detection of feigning of head injury symptoms on the MMPI-2. In C. R. Reynolds (Ed.), *Detection of malingering during head injury litigation* (pp. 209–238). New York: Plenum.

Berry, D. T. R., Lamb, D. G., Wetter, M. W., Baer, R. A., & Widiger, T. A. (1994). Ethical considerations in research on coached malingering. *Psychological Assessment, 6,* 16–17.

Berry, D. T. R., Wetter, M. W., Baer, R. A., Larsen, L., Clark, C., & Monroe, K. (1992). MMPI-2 random responding indices: Validation using a self-report methodology. *Psychological Assessment, 4,* 340–345.

Berry, D. T. R., Wetter, M. W., Baer, R. A., Widiger, T. A., Sumpter, J. C., Reynolds, S. K., & Hallam, R. A. (1991). Detection of random responding on the MMPI-2: Utility of *F,* Back *F,* and *VRIN* scales. *Psychological Assessment, 3,* 418–423.

Berry, D. T. R., Wetter, M. W., Baer, R. A., Youngjohn, J. R., Gass, C. S., Lamb, D. G., Franzen, M. D., MacInnes, W. D., & Buchholz, D. (1995). Overreporting of closed-head injury symptoms on the MMPI-2. *Psychological Assessment, 7,* 517–523.

Bertelson, A. D., Marks, P. A., & May, G. D. (1982). MMPI and race: A controlled study. *Journal of Consulting and Clinical Psychology, 50,* 316–318.

Bieliauskas, L. A., & Shekelle, R. B. (1983). Stable behaviors associated with high-point D MMPI profiles in a nonpsychiatric population. *Journal of Clinical Psychology, 39,* 422–426.

Bieliauskas, V. J. (1965). Recent advances in psychology of masculinity and femininity. *Journal of Psychology, 60,* 255–263.

Blais, M. A. (1995). MCMI-II personality traits associated with the MMPI-2 Masculinity-Femininity scale. *Assessment, 2,* 131–136.

Block, J. (1965). *The challenge of response sets: Unconfounding meaning, acquiescence, and social desirability in the MMPI.* New York: Appleton-Century-Crofts.

Block, J. (1977). An illusory interpretation of the first factor of the MMPI: A reply to Shweder. *Journal of Consulting and Clinical Psychology, 45,* 930–935.

Bloomquist, M. I., & Dossa, D. E. (1988). Assessing family functioning with the MMPI family scales. *International Journal of Family Psychiatry, 9,* 19–27.

Blumberg, S. (1967). MMPI *F* scale as an indicator of severity of psychopathology. *Journal of Clinical Psychology, 23,* 96–99.

Boerger, A. R., Graham, J. R., & Lilly, R. S. (1974). Behavioral correlates of single-scale MMPI code types. *Journal of Consulting and Clinical Psychology, 42,* 398–402.

Bolla-Wilson, K., & Bleecker, M. L. (1989). Absence of depression in elderly adults. *Journal of Gerontology, 44,* p53–p55.

Bollinger, A. R. (1997). *Validity of the MMPI-2 and MCMI-II Personality Disorder scales among combat veterans with Posttraumatic Stress Disorder.* Unpublished doctoral dissertation, Pacific Graduate School of Psychology, Palo Alto, CA.

Boone, D. E. (1994). Validity of the MMPI-2 Depression Content scale with psychiatric patients. *Psychological Reports, 74,* 159–162.

Boone, D. E. (1995). Differential validity of the MMPI-2 subtle and obvious scales with psychiatric inpatients: Scale 2. *Journal of Clinical Psychology, 51,* 526–531.

Bornstein, R. A., & Kozora, E. (1990). Content bias of the MMPI *Sc* scale in neurological patients. *Neuropsychiatry, Neuropsychology, and Behavioral Neurology, 3,* 200–205.

Brauer, B. A. (1992). The signer effect on MMPI performance of deaf respondents. *Journal of Personality Assessment, 58,* 380–388.

Brauer, B. A. (1993). Adequacy of a translation of the MMPI into American Sign Language for use with deaf individuals: Linguistic equivalency issues. *Rehabilitation Psychology, 38,* 247–260.

Brems, C., & Johnson, M. E. (1991). Subtle-obvious scales of the MMPI: Indicators of profile validity in a psychiatric population. *Journal of Personality Assessment, 56,* 536–544.

Brems, C., & Lloyd, P. (1995). Validation of the MMPI-2 Low Self-Esteem Content scale. *Journal of Personality Assessment, 65,* 550–556.

Broughton, R. (1984). A prototype strategy for construction of personality scales. *Journal of Personality and Social Psychology, 47,* 1334–1346.

Brower, D. (1947). The relation between intelligence and MMPI scores. *Journal of Social Psychology, 25,* 243–245.

Brown, J. B., & Dunbar, P. W. (1978). MMPI differences between fee-paying and non-fee-paying psychotherapy clients. *Journal of Clinical Psychology, 34,* 953–954.

Brown, M. N. (1950). Evaluating and scoring the MMPI "Cannot Say" items. *Journal of Clinical Psychology, 6,* 180–184.

Brozek, J. (1955). Personality changes with age: An item analysis of the MMPI. *Journal of Gerontology, 10,* 194–206.

Brulot, M. M., Strauss, E., & Spellacy, F. (1997). Validity of the MMPI-2 correction factors for use with patients with suspected head injury. *The Clinical Neuropsychologist, 11,* 391–401.

Brunetti, D. G., Schlottmann, R. S., Scott, A. B., & Hollrah, J. L. (1998). Instructed faking and MMPI-2 response latencies: The potential for assessing response validity. *Journal of Clinical Psychology, 54,* 143–153.

Buck, J. A., & Graham, J. R. (1978). The *4-3* MMPI profile type: A failure to replicate. *Journal of Consulting and Clinical Psychology, 46,* 344.

Burish, T. G., & Houston, B. K. (1976). Construct validity of the Lie scale as a measure of defensiveness. *Journal of Clinical Psychology, 32,* 310–314.

Burkhart, B. R., Christian, W. L., & Gynther, M. D. (1978). Item subtlety and faking on the MMPI: A paradoxical relationship. *Journal of Personality Assessment, 42,* 76–80.

Burkhart, B. R., Gynther, M. D., & Fromuth, M. E. (1980). The relative predictive validity of subtle versus obvious items on the MMPI depression scale. *Journal of Clinical Psychology, 36,* 748–751.

Buros, O. K. (Ed.). (1978). *The eighth mental measurements yearbook.* Highland Park, NJ: Gryphon Press.

Burton, A. (1947). The use of the Masculinity-Femininity scale of the MMPI as an aid in the diagnosis of sexual inversion. *Journal of Psychology, 24,* 161–164.

Butcher, J. N. (1985). Current developments in MMPI use: An international perspective. In C. D. Spielberger & J. N. Butcher (Eds.), *Advances in personality assessment* (Vol. 4, pp. 83–94). Hillsdale, NJ: Erlbaum.

Butcher, J. N. (1990). Education level and MMPI-2 measured psychopathology: A case of negligible influence. *MMPI-2 News and Profiles, 1,* 3.

Butcher, J. N. (1994). Psychological assessment of airline pilot applicants with the MMPI-2. *Journal of Personality Assessment, 62,* 31–44.

Butcher, J. N. (Ed.) (1972). *Objective personality assessment: Changing perspectives.* New York: Academic Press.

Butcher, J. N. (Ed.) (1987). *Computerized psychological assessment: A practitioner's guide.* New York: Basic.

Butcher, J. N. (Ed.) (1996). *International adaptations of the MMPI-2: Research and clinical applications.* Minneapolis: University of Minnesota Press.

Butcher, J. N., Aldwin, C. M., Levenson, M. R., Ben-Porath, Y. S., Spiro, A., & Bosse, R. (1991). Personality and aging: A study of the MMPI-2 among older men. *Psychology and Aging, 6,* 361–370.

Butcher, J. N., Ball, B., & Ray, E. (1964). Effects of socioeconomic level on MMPI differences in Negro-white college students. *Journal of Counseling Psychology, 11,* 83–87.

Butcher, J. N., Braswell, L., & Raney, D. (1983). A cross-cultural comparison of American Indian, black, and white inpatients on the MMPI and presenting symptoms. *Journal of Consulting and Clinical Psychology, 51,* 587–594.

Butcher, J. N., & Clark, L. A. (1979). Recent trends in cross-cultural MMPI research and application. In J. N. Butcher (Ed.), *New developments in the use of the MMPI* (pp. 69–111). Minneapolis: University of Minnesota Press.

Butcher, J. N., Dahlstrom, W. G., Graham, J. R., Tellegen, A., & Kaemmer, B. (1989). *MMPI-2: Manual for administration and scoring.* Minneapolis: University of Minnesota Press.

Butcher, J. N., Graham, J. R., & Ben-Porath, Y. S. (1995). Methodological problems and issues in MMPI,

MMPI-2, and MMPI-A research. *Psychological Assessment, 7,* 320–329.

Butcher, J. N., Graham, J. R., Dahlstrom, W. G., & Bowman, E. (1990). The MMPI-2 with college students. *Journal of Personality Assessment, 54,* 1–15.

Butcher, J. N., Graham, J. R., Williams, C. L., & Ben-Porath, Y. S. (1990). *Development and use of the MMPI-2 Content scales.* Minneapolis: University of Minnesota Press.

Butcher, J. N., & Han, K. (1995). Development of an MMPI-2 scale to assess the presentation of self in a superlative manner: The *S* scale. In J. N. Butcher & C. D. Spielberger (Eds.), *Advances in personality assessment* (Vol. 10, pp. 25–50). Hillsdale, NJ: Erlbaum.

Butcher, J. N., & Hostetler, K. (1990). Abbreviating MMPI item administration: What can be learned from the MMPI for the MMPI-2? *Psychological Assessment, 2,* 12–21.

Butcher, J. N., Jeffrey, T., Cayton, T. G., Colligan, S., DeVore, J. R., & Minegawa, R. (1990). A study of active duty military personnel with the MMPI-2. *Military Psychology, 2,* 47–61.

Butcher, J. N., Kendall, P. C., & Hoffman, N. (1980). MMPI short forms: Caution. *Journal of Consulting and Clinical Psychology, 48,* 275–278.

Butcher, J. N., Morfitt, R. C., Rouse, S. V., & Holden, R. R. (1997). Reducing MMPI-2 defensiveness: The effect of specialized instructions on the retest validity in a job applicant sample. *Journal of Personality Assessment, 68,* 385–401.

Butcher, J. N., & Pancheri, P. (1976). *A handbook of cross-cultural MMPI research.* Minneapolis: University of Minnesota Press.

Butcher, J. N., & Rouse, S. V. (1996). Personality: Individual differences and clinical assessment. *Annual Review of Psychology, 47,* 87–111.

Butcher, J. N., & Tellegen, A. (1966). Objections to MMPI items. *Journal of Consulting Psychology, 30,* 527–534.

Butcher, J. N., & Tellegen, A. (1978). Common methodological problems in MMPI research. *Journal of Consulting and Clinical Psychology, 46,* 620–628.

Butcher, J. N., & Williams, C. L. (1992). *Essentials of MMPI-2 and MMPI-A interpretation.* Minneapolis: University of Minnesota Press.

Butcher, J. N., Williams, C. L., Graham, J. R., Archer, R. P., Tellegen, A., Ben-Porath, Y. S., & Kaemmer, B. (1992). *MMPI-A (Minnesota Multiphasic Personality Inventory—Adolescent): Manual for administration, scoring, and interpretation.* Minneapolis: University of Minnesota Press.

Byrne, D., Barry, J., & Nelson, D. (1963). Relation of the revised Repression-Sensitization scale to measures of self-description. *Psychological Reports, 13,* 323–334.

Caldwell, A. B. (1969). *MMPI critical items.* Unpublished mimeograph. (Available from Caldwell Report, 1545 Sawtelle Boulevard, Los Angeles, CA 90025.)

Caldwell, A. B. (1985). *MMPI clinical interpretation.* Paper presented at the Advanced Psychological Studies Institute, Los Angeles.

Caldwell, A. B. (1988). *MMPI supplemental scale manual.* Los Angeles: Caldwell Report.

Caldwell, A. B. (1990, August). *MMPI, MMPI-2, and the measurement of the human condition.* Paper presented at the annual meeting of the American Psychological Association, Boston.

Caldwell, A. B. (1991). [Review of the book *Development and use of the MMPI-2 content scales*]. *Contemporary Psychology, 36,* 560–561.

Caldwell, A. B. (1997a). [MMPI-2 data research file for clinical patients.] Unpublished raw data.

Caldwell, A. B. (1997b). [MMPI-2 data research file for personnel applicants.] Unpublished raw data.

Caldwell, A. B. (1997c). Whither goest our redoubtable mentor, the MMPI/MMPI-2? *Journal of Personality Assessment, 68,* 47–68.

Caldwell, A. B. (1998a). *MMPI-2 critical items.* Unpublished mimeograph. (Available from Caldwell Report, 1545 Sawtelle Boulevard, Los Angeles, CA 90025.)

Caldwell, A. B. (1998b). [MMPI-2 data research file for pain patients.] Unpublished raw data.

Caldwell, M. G. (1953). The youthful male offender in Alabama: A study in delinquency causation. *Sociology and Social Research, 37,* 236–243.

Canul, G. D., & Cross, H. J. (1994). The influence of acculturation and racial identity attitudes on Mexican-Americans' MMPI-2 performance. *Journal of Clinical Psychology, 50,* 736–745.

Carlin, A. S., & Hewitt, P. L. (1990). The discrimination of patient-generated and randomly generated MMPIs. *Journal of Personality Assessment, 54,* 24–29.

Carson, R. C. (1969). Interpretative manual to the MMPI. In J. N. Butcher (Ed.), *MMPI: Research development and clinical applications* (pp. 279–296). New York: McGraw.

Castlebury, F. D., & Durham, T. W. (1997). The MMPI-2 *GM* and *GF* scales as measures of psychological well-being. *Journal of Clinical Psychology, 53,* 879–893.

Castlebury, F. D., Hilsenroth, M. J., Handler, L., & Durham, T. W. (1997). Use of the MMPI-2 Personality Disorder scales in the assessment of DSM-IV Antisocial,

Borderline, and Narcissistic Personality Disorders. *Assessment, 4,* 155–168.

Chatham, P. M., Tibbals, C. J., & Harrington, M. E. (1993). The MMPI and MCMI in the evaluation of narcissism in a clinical sample. *Journal of Personality Assessment, 60,* 239–251.

Chisholm, S. M., Crowther, J. H., & Ben-Porath, Y. S. (1997). Selected MMPI-2 scales' ability to predict premature termination and outcome from psychotherapy. *Journal of Personality Assessment, 69,* 127–144.

Christian, W. L., Burkhart, B. R., & Gynther, M. D. (1978). Subtle-obvious ratings of MMPI items: New interest in an old concept. *Journal of Consulting and Clinical Psychology, 46,* 1178–1186.

Clark, C. G., & Miller, H. L. (1971). Validation of Gilberstadt and Duker's 8-6 profile type on a black sample. *Psychological Reports, 29,* 259–264.

Clark, M. E. (1994). Interpretive limitations of the MMPI-2 Anger and Cynicism Content scales. *Journal of Personality Assessment, 63,* 89–96.

Clark, M. E. (1996). MMPI-2 Negative Treatment Indicators Content and Content component scales: Clinical correlates and outcome prediction for men with chronic pain. *Psychological Assessment, 8,* 32–38.

Clopton, J. R. (1974). A computer program for MMPI scale development with contrasted groups. *Educational and Psychological Measurement, 34,* 161–163.

Clopton, J. R. (1975). Automated MMPI interpretation based on a modification of Gilberstadt's codebook. *Journal of Clinical Psychology, 31,* 648–651.

Clopton, J. R. (1978a). Alcoholism and the MMPI: A review. *Journal of Studies on Alcohol, 39,* 1540–1558.

Clopton, J. R. (1978b). MMPI scale development methodology. *Journal of Personality Assessment, 42,* 148–151.

Clopton, J. R. (1979a). Development of special MMPI scales. In C. S. Newmark (Ed.), *MMPI: Clinical and research trends* (pp. 354–372). New York: Praeger.

Clopton, J. R. (1979b). The MMPI and suicide. In C. S. Newmark (Ed.), *MMPI: Clinical and research trends* (pp. 149–166). New York: Praeger.

Clopton, J. R. (1982). MMPI scale development methodology reconsidered. *Journal of Personality Assessment, 46,* 143–146.

Clopton, J. R., & Baucom, D. H. (1979). MMPI ratings of suicide risk. *Journal of Personality Assessment, 43,* 293–296.

Clopton, J. R., & Jones, W. C. (1975). Use of the MMPI in the prediction of suicide. *Journal of Clinical Psychology, 31,* 52–54.

Clopton, J. R., & Klein, G. L. (1978). An initial look at the redundancy of specialized MMPI scales. *Journal of Consulting and Clinical Psychology, 46,* 1436–1438.

Clopton, J. R., & Neuringer, C. (1977a). FORTRAN computer programs for the development of new MMPI scales. *Educational and Psychological Measurement, 37,* 783–786.

Clopton, J. R., & Neuringer, C. (1977b). MMPI Cannot Say scores: Normative data and degree of profile distortion. *Journal of Personality Assessment, 41,* 511–513.

Clopton, J. R., Pallis, D. J., & Birtchnell, J. (1979). MMPI profile patterns of suicide attempters. *Journal of Consulting and Clinical Psychology, 47,* 135–139.

Clopton, J. R., Post, R. D., & Larde, J. (1983). Identification of suicide attempters by means of MMPI profiles. *Journal of Clinical Psychology, 39,* 868–871.

Cofer, C. N., Chance, J., & Judson, A. J. (1949). A study of malingering on the MMPI. *Journal of Psychology, 27,* 491–499.

Cohen, J. (1988). *Statistical power analyses for the behavioral sciences* (2nd ed.). Hillsdale, NJ: Erlbaum.

Colby, F. (1989). Usefulness of the *K* correction in the MMPI profiles of patients and nonpatients. *Psychological Assessment, 1,* 142–145.

Colligan, R. C., Davis, L. J., Jr., Morse, R. M., & Offord, K. P. (1988). Screening medical patients for alcoholism with the MMPI: A comparison of seven scales. *Journal of Clinical Psychology, 44,* 582–592.

Colligan, R. C., Morey, L. C., & Offord, K. P. (1994). The MMPI/MMPI-2 Personality Disorder scales: Contemporary norms for adults and adolescents. *Journal of Clinical Psychology, 50,* 168–200.

Colligan, R. C., & Offord, K. P. (1986). [MMPI data research tape for Mayo Clinic patients referred for psychiatric evaluations.] Unpublished raw data.

Colligan, R. C., & Offord, K. P. (1987a). Resiliency reconsidered: Contemporary MMPI normative data for Barron's Ego Strength Scale. *Journal of Clinical Psychology, 43,* 467–471.

Colligan, R. C., & Offord, K. P. (1987b). The MacAndrew alcoholism scale applied to a contemporary normative sample. *Journal of Clinical Psychology, 43,* 291–293.

Colligan, R. C., & Offord, K. P. (1988a). Changes in MMPI factor scores: Norms for the Welsh A and R dimensions from a contemporary normal sample. *Journal of Clinical Psychology, 44,* 142–148.

Colligan, R. C., & Offord, K. P. (1988b). The risky use of the MMPI Hostility scale in assessing risk for coronary heart disease. *Psychosomatics, 29,* 188–196.

Colligan, R. C., & Offord, K. P. (1989). The aging MMPI: Contemporary norms for contemporary teenagers. *Mayo Clinic Proceedings, 64,* 3–27.

Colligan, R. C., & Offord, K. P. (1992). Age, stage, and the MMPI: Changes in response patterns over an 85-year age span. *Journal of Clinical Psychology, 48,* 476–493.

Colligan, R. C., Osborne, D., & Offord, K. P. (1980). Linear transformation and the interpretation of MMPI *T* scores. *Journal of Clinical Psychology, 36,* 162–165.

Colligan, R. C., Osborne, D., Swenson, W. M., & Offord, K. P. (1983). *The MMPI: A contemporary normative study.* New York: Praeger.

Colligan, R. C., Osborne, D., Swenson, W. M., & Offord, K. P. (1985). Using the 1983 norms for the MMPI: Code type frequencies in four clinical samples. *Journal of Clinical Psychology, 41,* 629–633.

Colligan, R. C., Osborne, D., Swenson, W. M., & Offord, K. P. (1989). *The MMPI: A contemporary normative study of adults* (2nd ed.). Odessa, FL: Psychological Assessment Resources.

Comrey, A. L. (1957a). A factor analysis of items on the MMPI Hypochondriasis scale. *Educational and Psychological Measurement, 17,* 568–577.

Comrey, A. L. (1957b). A factor analysis of items on the MMPI Depression scale. *Educational and Psychological Measurement, 17,* 578–585.

Comrey, A. L. (1957c). A factor analysis of items on the MMPI Hysteria scale. *Educational and Psychological Measurement, 17,* 586–592.

Comrey, A. L. (1958a). A factor analysis of items on the MMPI Psychopathic Deviate scale. *Educational and Psychological Measurement, 18,* 91–98.

Comrey, A. L. (1958b). A factor analysis of items on the MMPI Paranoia scale. *Educational and Psychological Measurement, 18,* 99–107.

Comrey, A. L. (1958c). A factor analysis of items on the MMPI Psychasthenia scale. *Educational and Psychological Measurement, 18,* 293–300.

Comrey, A. L. (1958d). A factor analysis of items on the MMPI Hypomania scale. *Educational and Psychological Measurement, 18,* 312–323.

Comrey, A. L., & Marggraff, W. M. (1958). A factor analysis of items on the MMPI Schizophrenia scale. *Educational and Psychological Measurement, 18,* 301–311.

Constantinople, A. (1973). Masculinity-femininity: An exception to a famous dictum? *Psychological Bulletin, 80,* 389–407.

Cooke, G., Pogany, E., & Johnston, N. G. (1974). A comparison of blacks and whites committed for evaluation of competency to stand trial on criminal charges. *Journal of Psychiatry and Law, 2,* 319–337.

Cook, W. W., & Medley, D. M. (1954). Proposed hostility and Pharisiac-virtue scales for the MMPI. *Journal of Applied Psychology, 39,* 123–129.

Cord, E. L. J., Sajwaj, T. E., Tolliver, D. K., & Ford, T. W. (1997, June). *Normative update on MMPI-2 data for a large federal power utility.* Paper presented at the 32nd annual symposium on Recent Developments in the Use of the MMPI-2 and MMPI-A, Minneapolis.

Costa, P. T., Jr., & McCrae, R. R. (1985). *The NEO Personality Inventory manual.* Odessa, FL: Psychological Assessment Resources.

Costello, R. M. (1973). Item level racial differences on the MMPI. *Journal of Social Psychology, 91,* 161–162.

Costello, R. M. (1977). Construction and cross-validation of an MMPI black-white scale. *Journal of Personality Assessment, 41,* 514–519.

Costello, R. M., Fine, H. J., & Blau, B. I. (1973). Racial comparisons on the MMPI. *Journal of Clinical Psychology, 29,* 63–65.

Costello, R. M., Tiffany, D. W., & Gier, R. H. (1972). Methodological issues and racial (black-white) comparisons on the MMPI. *Journal of Consulting and Clinical Psychology, 38,* 161–168.

Cowan, M. A., Watkins, B. A., & Davis, W. E. (1975). Level of education, diagnosis and race-related differences in MMPI performance. *Journal of Clinical Psychology, 31,* 442–444.

Coyle, F. A., Jr., & Heap, R. F. (1965). Interpreting the MMPI *L* scale. *Psychological Reports, 17,* 722.

Craig, R. J. (1984). A comparison of MMPI profiles of heroin addicts based on multiple methods of classification. *Journal of Personality Assessment, 48,* 115–120.

Cramer, K. M. (1995). Comparing three new MMPI-2 randomness indices in a novel procedure for random profile derivation. *Journal of Personality Assessment, 65,* 514–520.

Cripe, L. I. (1996). The MMPI in neuropsychological assessment. *Applied Neuropsychology, 3/4,* 97–103.

Cripe, L. I. (1997). Personality assessment of brain-impaired patients. In M. E. Maruish & J. A. Moses, Jr. (Eds.), *Clinical neuropsychology: Theoretical foundations for practitioners* (pp. 119–142). Mahwah, NJ: Erlbaum.

Cripe, L. I. (1999). Using the MMPI with mild traumatic brain injured patients. In N. R. Varney & R. J. Roberts (Eds.), *Evaluation and treatment of mild traumatic brain injury.* Mahwah, NJ: Erlbaum.

Cripe, L. I., Maxwell, J. K., & Hill, E. (1995). Multivariate discriminant function analysis of neurologic, pain, and psychiatric patients with the MMPI. *Journal of Clinical Psychology, 51,* 258–268.

Cuellar, I. (1998). Cross-cultural clinical psychological assessment of Hispanic Americans. *Journal of Personality Assessment, 70,* 71–86.

Cuellar, I., Arnold, B., & Maldonado, R. (1995). Acculturation rating scale for Mexican Americans—II: A revision of the original ARSMA scale. *Hispanic Journal of Behavioral Sciences, 17,* 275–304.

Cuellar, I., Harris, L. C., & Jasso, R. (1980). An acculturation scale for Mexican-American normal and clinical populations. *Hispanic Journal of Behavioral Science, 2,* 199–217.

Dahlstrom, W. G. (1991, July). *Correlates of each of the subtle and obvious subscales of D, Hy, Pd, Pa, and Ma (Wiener & Harmon).* Paper presented at the MMPI-2 Summer Institute, Colorado Springs, CO.

Dahlstrom, W. G. (1992). Comparability of two-point high-point code patterns from original MMPI norms to MMPI-2 norms for the restandardizations sample. *Journal of Personality Assessment, 59,* 153–164.

Dahlstrom, W. G. (1993). *The items in the MMPI-2: Alterations in wording, patterns of interrelationship, and changes in endorsement.* Minneapolis: University of Minnesota Press.

Dahlstrom, W. G., Archer, R. P., Hopkins, D. G., Jackson, E., & Dahlstrom, L. E. (1994). *Assessing the readability of the Minnesota Multiphasic Inventory Instruments—the MMPI, MMPI-2, MMPI-A.* Minneapolis: University of Minnesota Press.

Dahlstrom, W. G., Lachar, D., & Dahlstrom, L. E. (1986). *MMPI patterns of American minorities.* Minneapolis: University of Minnesota Press.

Dahlstrom, W. G., & Tellegen, A. (1993). *Socioeconomic status and the MMPI-2: The relation of MMPI-2 patterns to levels of education and occupation.* Minneapolis: University of Minnesota Press.

Dahlstrom, W. G., Welsh, G. S., & Dahlstrom, L. E. (1972). *An MMPI handbook: Vol. I. Clinical interpretation* (rev. ed.). Minneapolis: University of Minnesota Press.

Dahlstrom, W. G., Welsh, G. S., & Dahlstrom, L. E. (1975). *An MMPI handbook: Vol. II. Research applications* (rev. ed.). Minneapolis: University of Minnesota Press.

Dana, R. H. (1990). Cross-cultural and multi-ethnic assessment. In J. N. Butcher & C. D. Spielberger (Eds.), *Advances in personality assessment* (Vol. 8, pp. 1–26). Hillsdale, NJ: Erlbaum.

Dana, R. H. (1993). *Multicultural assessment perspectives for professional psychology.* Boston: Allyn & Bacon.

Dana, R. H. (1995). Culturally competent MMPI assessment of Hispanic populations. *Hispanic Journal of Behavioral Sciences, 17,* 305–319.

Dana, R. H. (1998). Cultural identity assessment of culturally diverse groups: 1997. *Journal of Personality Assessment, 70,* 1–16.

Dannenbaum, S. E., & Lanyon, R. I. (1993). The use of subtle items in detecting deception. *Journal of Personality Assessment, 61,* 501–510.

Davis, K. R., & Sines, J. O. (1971). An antisocial behavior pattern associated with a specific MMPI profile. *Journal of Consulting and Clinical Psychology, 36,* 229–234.

Davis, L. J., Jr., Colligan, R. C., Morse, R. M., & Offord, K. P. (1987). Validity of the MacAndrew scale in a general medical population. *Journal of Studies on Alcohol, 48,* 202–206.

Davis, L. J., Jr., & Offord, K. P. (1997). Logistic regression. *Journal of Personality Assessment, 68,* 497–507.

Davis, L. J., Jr., Offord, K. P., Colligan, R. C., & Morse, R. M. (1991). The CAL: An MMPI alcoholism scale for general medical patients. *Journal of Clinical Psychology, 47,* 632–646.

Davis, R. D., Wagner, E. E., & Patty, C. C. (1994). Maximized split-half reliabilities for Harris-Lingoes subscales: A followup with larger Ns. *Perceptual and Motor Skills, 78,* 881–882.

Davis, W. E. (1972). Age and the discriminative "power" of the MMPI with schizophrenic and nonschizophrenic patients. *Journal of Consulting and Clinical Psychology, 38,* 151.

Davis, W. E. (1975). Race and the differential "power" of the MMPI. *Journal of Personality Assessment, 39,* 138–140.

Davis, W. E., Beck, S. J., & Ryan, T. A. (1973). Race-related and educationally related MMPI profile differences among hospitalized schizophrenics. *Journal of Clinical Psychology, 29,* 478–479.

Davis, W. E., & Jones, M. H. (1974). Negro versus Caucasian psychological test performance revisited. *Journal of Consulting and Clinical Psychology, 42,* 675–679.

Dawes, R. M. (1994). *House of cards: Psychology and psychotherapy built on myth.* New York: Free Press.

Dean, R. B., & Richardson, H. (1964). Analysis of MMPI profiles of forty college-educated overt male homosexuals. *Journal of Consulting Psychology, 28,* 483–486.

Deiker, T. E. (1974). A cross-validation of MMPI scales of aggression on male criminal criterion groups. *Journal of Consulting and Clinical Psychology, 42,* 196–202.

Denny, N., Robinowitz, R., & Penk, W. E. (1987). Conducting applied research on Vietnam combat-related Post-traumatic Stress Disorder. *Journal of Clinical Psychology, 43,* 56–66.

Derogatis, L. R. (1983). SCL-90-R. *Administration, scoring, and procedures manual.* Towson, MD: Clinical Psychometric Research.

Dolan, M. P., Roberts, W. R., Penk, W. E., Robinowitz, R., & Atkins, H. G. (1983). Personality differences among black, white, and Hispanic-American male heroin addicts on MMPI content scales. *Journal of Clinical Psychology, 39,* 807–813.

Drake, L. E. (1946). A social I-E scale for the MMPI. *Journal of Applied Psychology, 30,* 51–54.

Drake, L. E., & Oetting, E. R. (1959). *An MMPI codebook for counselors.* Minneapolis: University of Minnesota Press.

Dubinsky, S., Gamble, D. J., & Rogers, M. L. (1985). A literature review of subtle-obvious items on the MMPI. *Journal of Personality Assessment, 49,* 62–68.

Dubro, A. F., & Wetzler, S. (1989). An external validity study of the MMPI Personality Disorder scales. *Journal of Clinical Psychology, 45,* 570–575.

Dubro, A. F., Wetzler, S., & Kahn, M. W. (1988). A comparison of three self-report questionnaires for the diagnosis of DSM-III personality disorders. *Journal of Personality Disorders, 2,* 256–266.

Duckworth, J. C., & Anderson, W. (1986). *MMPI interpretation manual for counselors and clinicians* (3rd ed.). Muncie, IN: Accelerated Development.

Duckworth, J. C., & Barley, W. D. (1988). Within-Normal-Limit profiles. In R. L. Greene (Ed.), *The MMPI: Use in specific populations* (pp. 278–315). San Antonio: Grune & Stratton.

Dunn, J. T., & Lees-Haley, P. R. (1995). The MMPI-2 correction factor for closed-head injury: A caveat for forensic cases. *Assessment, 2,* 47–51.

Durham, T. W. (1994, April). *The CAL-R and MMPI-2 relationships with inpatient substance abusers.* Paper presented at the annual meeting of the Southeastern Psychological Association, New Orleans.

Dush, D. M., Simons, L. E., Platt, M., Nation, P. C., & Ayres, S. Y. (1994). Psychological profiles distinguishing litigating and nonlitigating pain patients: Subtle, and not so subtle. *Journal of Personality Assessment, 62,* 299–313.

Dye, C. J., Bohm, K., Anderten, P., & Won Cho, D. (1983). Age group differences in depression on MMPI *D* Scale. *Journal of Clinical Psychology, 39,* 227–234.

Eaddy, M. L. (1962). An investigation of the Cannot Say scale of the group MMPI. *Dissertation Abstracts, 23,* 1070.

Edinger, J. D. (1981). MMPI short forms: A clinical perspective. *Psychological Reports, 48,* 627–631.

Edwards, A. L. (1957). *The social desirability variable in personality assessment and research.* New York: Dryden.

Edwards, A. L. (1959). *Edwards Personal Preference Schedule manual.* New York: Psychological Corporation.

Edwards, A. L. (1977). Comments on Shweder's "Illusory correlation and the MMPI controversy." *Journal of Consulting and Clinical Psychology, 45,* 925–929.

Edwards, A. L., & Diers, C. J. (1962). Social desirability and the factorial interpretation of the MMPI. *Educational and Psychological Measurement, 22,* 501–509.

Edwards, D. W., Morrison, T. L., & Weissman, H. N. (1993a). The MMPI and MMPI-2 in an outpatient sample: Comparisons of code types, validity scales and clinical scales. *Journal of Personality Assessment, 61,* 1–18.

Edwards, D. W., Morrison, T. L., & Weissman, H. N. (1993b). Uniform versus linear T scores on the MMPI-2/MMPI in an outpatient psychiatric sample: Differential contributions. *Psychological Assessment, 5,* 499–500.

Edwards, E. L., Holmes, C. B., & Carvajal, H. H. (1998). Oral and booklet presentation of MMPI-2. *Journal of Clinical Psychology, 54,* 593–596.

Ehrenworth, N. V., & Archer, R. P. (1985). A comparison of clinical accuracy ratings of interpretive approaches for adolescent MMPI responses. *Journal of Personality Assessment, 49,* 413–421.

Eichman, W. J. (1962). Factored scales for the MMPI: A clinical and statistical manual. *Journal of Clinical Psychology, 18,* 363–395.

Elion, V. H., & Megargee, E. I. (1975). Validity of the MMPI *Pd* scale among black males. *Journal of Consulting and Clinical Psychology, 43,* 166–172.

Endicott, N. A., Jortner, S., & Abramoff, E. (1969). Objective measures of suspiciousness. *Journal of Abnormal Psychology, 74,* 26–32.

Endler, N. S., Parker, J. D. A., & Butcher, J. N. (1993). A factor analytic study of coping styles and the MMPI-2 content scales. *Journal of Clinical Psychology, 49,* 523–527.

Erdberg, S. P. (1975). MMPI differences associated with sex, race, and residence in a southern sample. In W. G. Dahlstrom, G. S. Welsh, & L. E. Dahlstrom, *An MMPI handbook: Vol. II. Research applications* (pp. 155–157). Minneapolis: University of Minnesota Press.

Erickson, W. D., Luxenberg, M. G., Walbek, N. H., & Seely, R. K. (1987). Frequency of MMPI two-point code types among sex offenders. *Journal of Consulting and Clinical Psychology, 55,* 566–570.

Evans, C., & McConnell, T. R. (1941). A new measure of introversion-extroversion. *Journal of Psychology, 12,* 111–124.

Evans, R. G. (1984a). Normative data for two MMPI critical item sets. *Journal of Clinical Psychology, 40,* 512–515.

Evans, R. G. (1984b). Utility of the MMPI-168 with men inpatient alcoholics. *Journal of Studies on Alcohol, 45,* 371–373.

Evans, R. G., & Dinning, W. D. (1983). Response consistency among high F scale scorers on the MMPI. *Journal of Clinical Psychology, 39,* 246–248.

Exner, J. E., Jr. (1993). *The Rorschach: A comprehensive system.* Vol. 1: *Basic foundations* (3rd ed.). New York: Wiley.

Exner, J. E., Jr., McDowell, E., Pabst, J., Stackman, W. & Kirk, L. (1963). On the detection of willful falsifications in the MMPI. *Journal of Consulting Psychology, 27,* 91–94.

Eyman, J. R., & Eyman, S. K. (1991). Personality assessment in suicide prediction. *Suicide and Life Threatening Behaviors, 21,* 37–55.

Eyman, J. R., & Eyman, S. K. (1992). Psychological testing for potentially suicidal individuals. In B. Bongar (Ed.), *Suicide: Guidelines for assessment, management, and treatment* (pp. 127–143). New York: Oxford.

Fairbank, J. A., McCaffrey, R. J., & Keane, T. M. (1985). Psychometric detection of fabricated symptoms of posttraumatic stress disorder. *American Journal of Psychiatry, 142,* 501–503.

Farberow, N. L. (1956). Personality patterns of suicidal mental hospital patients. In G. S. Welsh and W. G. Dahlstrom (Eds.), *Basic readings on the MMPI in psychology and medicine* (pp. 427–432). Minneapolis: University of Minnesota Press.

Farberow, N. L., & Devries, A. G. (1967). An item differentiation analysis of MMPIs of suicidal neuropsychiatric hospital patients. *Psychological Reports, 20,* 607–617.

Farr, S. P., & Martin, P. W. (1988). Neuropsychological dysfunction. In R. L. Greene (Ed.), *The MMPI: Use with specific populations* (pp. 214–245). San Antonio: Grune & Stratton.

Faschingbauer, T. R. (1974). A 166-item written short form of the group MMPI: The FAM. *Journal of Consulting and Clinical Psychology, 42,* 645–655.

Faschingbauer, T. R. (1979). The future of the MMPI. In C. S. Newmark (Ed.), *MMPI: Clinical and research trends* (pp. 373–398). New York: Praeger.

Faschingbauer, T. R., & Newmark, C. S. (1978). *Short forms of the MMPI.* Lexington, MA: Heath.

Faust, D. (1984). *The limits of scientific reasoning.* Minneapolis: University of Minnesota Press.

Faust, D. (1995). The detection of deception. Special issue: Malingering and conversion reactions. *Neurology Clinics, 13,* 255–265.

Fekken, G. C., & Holden, R. R. (1987). Assessing the person reliability of an individual MMPI protocol. *Journal of Personality Assessment, 51,* 123–132.

Ferguson, G. A. (1971). *Statistical analysis in psychology and education* (3rd ed.). New York: McGraw-Hill.

Fillenbaum, G. G., & Pfeiffer, E. (1976). The Mini-Mult: A cautionary note. *Journal of Consulting and Clinical Psychology, 44,* 698–703.

Finger, M. S., & Ones, D. S. (1998, August). *Equivalence of the computer and booklet MMPI forms: A meta-analytic investigation.* Paper presented at the annual meeting of the American Psychological Association, San Francisco.

Finn, S. E. (1996). *Using the MMPI-2 as a therapeutic intervention.* Minneapolis: University of Minnesota Press.

Finn, S. E., & Kamphuis, J. H. (1995). What a clinician needs to know about base rates. In J. N. Butcher (Ed.), *Clinical personality assessment: Practical approaches* (pp. 224–235). New York: Oxford.

Fischer, C. T. (1994). *Individualizing psychological assessment.* Hillsdale, NJ: Erlbaum.

Fjordbak, T. (1985). Clinical correlates of high *Lie* scale elevations among forensic patients. *Journal of Personality Assessment, 49,* 252–255.

Flanagan, J., & Lewis, G. (1969). Comparison of Negro and white lower class men on the general aptitude test battery and the MMPI. *Journal of Social Psychology, 78,* 289–291.

Forgac, G. E., Cassel, C. A., & Michaels, E. J. (1984). Chronicity of criminal behavior and psychopathology in male exhibitionists. *Journal of Clinical Psychology, 40,* 827–832.

Forsyth, D. R. (1967). MMPI and college populations. *Journal of College Student Personnel, 8,* 90–96.

Fow, N., Sittig, M., Dorris, G., Breisinger, G., & Anthony, K. (1994). An analysis of the relationship of gender and age to MMPI scores of patients with chronic pain. *Journal of Clinical Psychology, 50,* 537–554.

Fowler, R. D., & Coyle, F. A. (1968). A comparison of two MMPI actuarial systems used in classifying an alcoholic out-patient population. *Journal of Clinical Psychology, 24,* 434–435.

Fox, D. D., Gerson, A., & Lees-Haley, P. R. (1995). Interrelationships of MMPI-2 validity scales in personal injury claims. *Journal of Clinical Psychology, 51,* 42–47.

Fraboni, M., Jackson, D. N., & Helmes, E. (1993, August). *Discriminant properties of the MMPI-2 Content scales.* Paper presented at the annual meeting of the American Psychological Association, Toronto.

Frank, J. G., Velasquez, R. J., Reimann, J. O., & Salazar, J. (1997, June). *MMPI-2 profiles of Latino, black, and white rapists and child molesters on parole.* Paper presented at the 32nd annual symposium on Recent Developments in the Use of the MMPI (MMPI-2 and MMPI-A), Minneapolis.

Franzen, M. D., Iverson, G. L., & McCracken, L. M. (1990). The detection of malingering in neuropsychological assessment. *Neuropsychology Review, 1,* 247–279.

Frederick, R. I. (1998, August). *Characteristics of the Infrequency-Psychopathology scale, F(p), among a sample of criminal forensic examinees.* Paper presented at the annual meeting of the American Psychological Association, San Francisco.

Friberg, R. R. (1967). Measures of homosexuality: Cross-validation of two MMPI scales and implications for usage. *Journal of Consulting Psychology, 31,* 88–91.

Friedman, A. F., Webb, J. T., & Lewak, R. (1989). *Psychological assessment with the MMPI.* Hillsdale, NJ: Erlbaum.

Friedman, H. S., & Booth-Kewley, S. (1988). Personality, Type A behavior, and coronary heart disease: The role of emotional expression. *Journal of Personality and Social Psychology, 53,* 783–792.

Friedrich, W. N. (1988). Child abuse and sexual abuse. In R. L. Greene (Ed.), *The MMPI: Use in specific populations* (pp. 246–258). San Antonio: Grune & Stratton.

Frueh, B. C., Gold, P. B., de Arellano, M. A., & Brady, K. L. (1997). A racial comparison of combat veterans evaluated for PTSD. *Journal of Personality Assessment, 68,* 692–702.

Frueh, B. C., Smith, D. W., & Libet, J. M. (1996). Racial differences on psychological measures in combat veterans seeking treatment for PTSD. *Journal of Personality Assessment, 66,* 41–53.

Fry, F. D. (1949). A study of the personality traits of college students and of state prison inmates as measured by the MMPI. *Journal of Psychology, 28,* 439–449.

Gallen, R. T., & Berry, D. T. R. (1996). Detection of random responding in MMPI-2 protocols. *Assessment, 3,* 171–178.

Gallen, R. T., & Berry, D. T. R. (1997). Partially random MMPI-2 protocols: When are they interpretable? *Assessment, 4,* 61–68.

Gallucci, N. T. (1984). Prediction of dissimulation on the MMPI in a clinical field setting. *Journal of Consulting and Clinical Psychology, 52,* 917–918.

Gallucci, N. T. (1985). Influence of dissimulation on indexes of response consistency for the MMPI. *Psychological Reports, 57,* 1013–1014.

Gallucci, N. T. (1997). On the identification of patterns of substance abuse with the MMPI-A. *Psychological Assessment, 9,* 224–232.

Gallucci, N. T., Kay, D. C., & Thornby, J. I. (1989). The sensitivity of 11 substance abuse scales from the MMPI to change in clinical status. *Psychology of Addictive Behaviors, 3,* 29–33.

Ganellen, R. J., & Harlem, A. (1997, August). *Race and MMPI-2 performance.* Paper presented at the annual

meeting of the American Psychological Association, Chicago.

Gass, C. S. (1991). MMPI-2 interpretation and closed head injury: A correction factor. *Psychological Assessment, 3,* 27–31.

Gass, C. S. (1996). MMPI-2 interpretation and stroke: Cross-validation of a correction factor. *Journal of Clinical Psychology, 52,* 569–572.

Gass, C. S., & Lawhorn, L. (1991). Psychological adjustment following stroke: An MMPI study. *Psychological Assessment, 3,* 628–633.

Gass, C. S., & Russell, E. W. (1991). MMPI profiles of closed head trauma patients: Impact of neurologic complaints. *Journal of Clinical Psychology, 47,* 253–260.

Gaston, L., Brunet, A., Koszycki, D., & Bradwejn, J. (1996). MMPI profiles of acute and chronic PTSD in a civilian sample. *Journal of Traumatic Stress, 9,* 817–832.

Gaston, L., Brunet, A., Koszycki, D., & Bradwejn, J. (1998). MMPI scales for diagnosing acute and chronic PTSD in a civilian sample. *Journal of Traumatic Stress, 11,* 355–365.

Gauron, E., Severson, R., & Englehart, R. (1962). MMPI *F* scores and psychiatric diagnosis. *Journal of Consulting Psychology, 26,* 488.

Gayton, W. F., Burchstead, G. N., & Matthews, G. R. (1986). An investigation of the utility of an MMPI Posttraumatic Stress Disorder subscale. *Journal of Clinical Psychology, 42,* 916–917.

Gearing, M. L. (1979). The MMPI as a primary differentiator and predictor of behavior in prison: A methodological critique and review of the recent literature. *Psychological Bulletin, 86,* 929–963.

Geisinger, K. F. (Ed.) (1992). *Psychological testing of Hispanics.* Washington, D.C.: American Psychological Association.

Genthner, R. W., & Graham, J. R. (1976). Effects of short-term public psychiatric hospitalization for both black and white patients. *Journal of Consulting and Clinical Psychology, 44,* 118–124.

Giannetti, R. A., Johnson, J. H., Klingler, D. E., & Williams, T. A. (1978). Comparison of linear and configural MMPI diagnostic methods with an uncontaminated criterion. *Journal of Consulting and Clinical Psychology, 46,* 1046–1052.

Gilberstadt, H. (1970). *Comprehensive MMPI code book for males.* Minneapolis: MMPI Research Laboratory, Veterans Administration Hospital.

Gilberstadt, H., & Duker, J. (1965). *A handbook for clinical and actuarial MMPI interpretation.* Philadelphia: Saunders.

Goldberg, L. R. (1965). Diagnosticians vs. diagnostic signs: The diagnosis of psychosis vs. neurosis from the MMPI. *Psychological Monographs, 79* (Whole No. 602).

Goldberg, L. R. (1969). The search for configural relationships in personality assessment: The diagnosis of psychosis vs. neurosis from the MMPI. *Multivariate Behavioral Research, 4,* 523–536.

Golden, C. J., Sweet, J. J., & Osmon, D. C. (1979). The diagnosis of brain-damage by the MMPI: A comprehensive evaluation. *Journal of Personality Assessment, 43,* 138–142.

Goldman, V. J., Cooke, A., & Dahlstrom, W. G. (1995). Black-white differences among college students: A comparison of MMPI and MMPI-2 norms. *Assessment, 2,* 293–299.

Gonen, J. Y., & Lansky, L. M. (1968). Masculinity, femininity, and masculinity-femininity: A phenomenological study of the *Mf* scale of the MMPI. *Psychological Reports, 23,* 183–194.

Good, P. K., & Brantner, J. P. (1961). *The physician's guide to the MMPI.* Minneapolis: University of Minnesota Press.

Good, P. K., & Brantner, J. P. (1974). *A practical guide to the MMPI.* Minneapolis: University of Minnesota Press.

Goodstein, L. D. (1954). Regional differences in MMPI responses among male college students. *Journal of Consulting Psychology, 18,* 437–441.

Gordon, N. G., & Swart, E. C. (1973). A comparison of the Harris-Lingoes subscales between the original standardization population and an inpatient Veterans Administration hospital population. *VA Newsletter for Research in Mental Health and Behavioral Sciences, 15,* 28–31.

Gottesman, I. I., Hanson, D. R., Kroeker, T. A., & Briggs, P. F. (1987). New MMPI normative data and power-transformed *T*-score tables for the Hathaway-Monachesi Minnesota cohort of 14,019 15-year-olds and 3,674 18-year-olds. In R. P. Archer, *Using the MMPI with adolescents* (pp. 241–297). Hillsdale, NJ: Erlbaum.

Gottesman, I. I., & Prescott, C. A. (1989). Abuses of the MacAndrew MMPI alcoholism scale: A critical review. *Clinical Psychology Review, 9,* 223–242.

Gough, H. G. (1947). Simulated patterns on the MMPI. *Journal of Abnormal and Social Psychology, 42,* 215–225.

Gough, H. G. (1950). The *F* minus *K* dissimulation index for the MMPI. *Journal of Consulting Psychology, 14,* 408–413.

Gough, H. G. (1954). Some common misconceptions about neuroticism. *Journal of Consulting Psychology, 18,* 287–292.

Gough, H. G. (1957). *California Psychological Inventory manual.* Palo Alto, CA: Consulting Psychologists Press.

Gough, H. G., McClosky, H., & Meehl, P. E. (1951). A personality scale for dominance. *Journal of Abnormal and Social Psychology, 46,* 360–366.

Gough, H. G., McClosky, H., & Meehl, P. E. (1952). A personality scale for social responsibility. *Journal of Abnormal and Social Psychology, 47,* 73–80.

Graham, J. R. (1987). *The MMPI: A practical guide* (2nd ed.). New York: Oxford.

Graham, J. R. (1990a). Congruence between MMPI and MMPI-2 codetypes. *MMPI-2 News and Profiles, 1,* 1–2, 12.

Graham, J. R. (1990b). *MMPI-2: Assessing personality and psychopathology.* New York: Oxford.

Graham, J. R. (1993). *MMPI-2: Assessing personality and psychopathology* (2nd ed.). New York: Oxford.

Graham, J. R., Ben-Porath, Y. S., & McNulty, J. L. (1997). Empirical correlates of low scores on the MMPI-2 scales in an outpatient mental health setting. *Psychological Assessment, 9,* 386–391.

Graham, J. R., & Butcher, J. N. (1988, March). *Differentiating schizophrenic and major affective disorders with the revised form of the MMPI.* Paper presented at the 23rd Annual Symposium on Recent Developments in the Use of the MMPI, St. Petersburg, FL.

Graham, J. R., & Mayo, M. A. (1985, March). *A comparison of MMPI strategies for identifying black and white male alcoholics.* Paper presented at the 20th Annual Symposium on Recent Developments in the Use of the MMPI, Honolulu.

Graham, J. R., & Schroeder, H. E. (1972). Abbreviated *Mf* and *Si* scales for the MMPI. *Journal of Personality Assessment, 36,* 436–439.

Graham, J. R., Schroeder, H. E., & Lilly, R. S. (1971). Factor analysis of items on the Social Introversion and Masculinity-Femininity scales of the MMPI. *Journal of Clinical Psychology, 27,* 367–370.

Graham, J. R., Smith, R. L., & Schwartz, G. F. (1986). Stability of MMPI configurations for psychiatric inpatients. *Journal of Consulting and Clinical Psychology, 54,* 375–380.

Graham, J. R., & Strenger, V. E. (1988). MMPI characteristics of alcoholics: A review. *Journal of Consulting and Clinical Psychology, 56,* 197–205.

Graham, J. R., Timbrook, R. E., Ben-Porath, Y. S., & Butcher, J. N. (1991). Code-type congruence between MMPI and MMPI-2: Separating fact from artifact. *Journal of Personality Assessment, 57,* 205–215.

Graham, J. R., & Tisdale, M. J. (1983, April). *Interpretation of low Scale 5 scores for women of high educational levels.* Paper presented at the 18th Annual

Symposium on Recent Developments in the Use of the MMPI, Minneapolis.

Graham, J. R., Watts, D., & Timbrook, R. E. (1991). Detecting fake-good and fake-bad MMPI-2 profiles. *Journal of Personality Assessment, 57,* 264–277.

Gravitz, M. A. (1967). Frequency and content of test items normally omitted from MMPI scales. *Journal of Consulting Psychology, 31,* 642.

Gravitz, M. A. (1968). Normative findings for the frequency of MMPI critical items. *Journal of Clinical Psychology, 24,* 220.

Gravitz, M. A. (1970). Validity implications of normal adult MMPI "*L*" scale endorsement. *Journal of Clinical Psychology, 26,* 497–499.

Gravitz, M. A. (1971). Declination rates on the MMPI validity and clinical scales. *Journal of Clinical Psychology, 27,* 103.

Gravitz, M. A. (1987). An empirical study of MMPI *F* scale validity. *Psychological Reports, 60,* 389–390.

Grayson, H. M. (1951). *A psychological admissions testing program and manual.* Los Angeles: Veterans Administration Center, Neuropsychiatric Hospital.

Greene, R. L. (1977). Student acceptance of generalized personality interpretations: A reexamination. *Journal of Consulting and Clinical Psychology, 45,* 965–966.

Greene, R. L. (1978a). An empirically derived MMPI carelessness scale. *Journal of Clinical Psychology, 34,* 407–410.

Greene, R. L. (1978b). Can clients provide valuable feedback to clinicians about their personality interpretations? Greene replies. *Journal of Consulting and Clinical Psychology, 46,* 1496–1497.

Greene, R. L. (1980). *The MMPI: An interpretive manual.* New York: Grune & Stratton.

Greene, R. L. (1982). Some reflections on "MMPI short forms: A literature review." *Journal of Personality Assessment, 46,* 486–487.

Greene, R. L. (1987). Ethnicity and MMPI performance: A review. *Journal of Consulting and Clinical Psychology, 55,* 497–512.

Greene, R. L. (1988a). Assessment of malingering and defensiveness by objective personality measures. In R. Rogers (Ed.), *Clinical assessment of malingering and deception* (pp. 123–158). New York: Guilford.

Greene, R. L. (1988b). Summary. In R. L. Greene (Ed.), *The MMPI: Use with specific populations* (pp. 316–321). Boston: Allyn & Bacon.

Greene, R. L. (Ed.). (1988c). *The MMPI: Use in specific populations.* San Antonio: Grune & Stratton.

Greene, R. L. (1989). *Assessing the validity of MMPI profiles in clinical settings. Clinical Notes on the MMPI,* No. 11. Minneapolis: National Computer Systems.

Greene, R. L. (1990). Stability of MMPI scale scores within four codetypes over four decades. *Journal of Personality Assessment, 55,* 1–6.

Greene, R. L. (1991). *The MMPI-2/MMPI: An interpretive manual.* Boston: Allyn & Bacon.

Greene, R. L. (1994). Relationships among MMPI codetype, gender, and setting and the MacAndrew Alcoholism scale. *Assessment, 1,* 39–46.

Greene, R. L. (1997). Assessment of malingering and defensiveness by multiscale inventories. In R. Rogers (Ed.), *Clinical assessment of malingering and defensiveness* (2nd ed.) (pp. 169–207). New York: Guilford.

Greene, R. L., Arredondo, R., & Davis, H. G. (1990, August). *The comparability between the MacAndrew Alcoholism Scale—Revised (MMPI-2) and the MacAndrew Alcoholism scale (MMPI).* Paper presented at the annual meeting of the American Psychological Association, Boston.

Greene, R. L., & Brown, R. C. (1998). *MMPI-2 adult interpretive system* [Computer software] (2nd ed.). Lutz, FL: Psychological Assessment Resources.

Greene, R. L., Brown, R. C., & Kovan, R. E. (1998). *MMPI-2 Adult Interpretive System professional manual.* Lutz, FL: Psychological Assessment Resources.

Greene, R. L., & Clopton, J. R. (1999). MMPI-2. In M. Maruish (Ed.), *Use of psychological testing for treatment planning and outcome* (2nd ed.) (pp. 1023–1049). Hillsdale, NJ: Erlbaum.

Greene, R. L., Davis, L. J., Jr., & Morse, R. P. (1993, March). *Stability of MMPI codetypes in alcoholic inpatients.* Paper presented at the midwinter meeting of the Society for Personality Assessment, San Francisco.

Greene, R. L., & Garvin, R. D. (1988). Substance abuse/dependence. In R. L. Greene (Ed.), *The MMPI: Use in specific populations* (pp. 159–197). San Antonio: Grune & Stratton.

Greene, R. L., Gwin, R., & Staal, M. (1997) Current status of MMPI-2 research: A methodologic overview. *Journal of Personality Assessment, 68,* 20–36.

Greene, R. L., & Nichols, D. S. (1995). *MMPI-2 Structural Summary* [Computer software]. Lutz, FL: Psychological Assessment Resources.

Greene, R. L., & Schinka, J. A. (1995). [MMPI-2 data research file for psychiatric inpatients and outpatients.] Unpublished raw data.

Greene, R. L., Weed, N. C., Butcher, J. N., Arredondo, R., & Davis, H. G. (1992). A cross-validation of MMPI-2 substance abuse scales. *Journal of Personality Assessment, 58,* 405–410.

Greiffenstein, M. F., Gola, T., & Baker, W. J. (1995). MMPI-2 validity scales versus domain specific measures in detection of factitious traumatic brain injury. *The Clinical Neuropsychologist, 9,* 230–240.

Griffith, A. V., & Fowler, R. D. (1960). Psychasthenic and Hypomanic scales of the MMPI and reaction to authority. *Journal of Counseling Psychology, 7,* 146–147.

Griffith, A. V., Upshaw, H. S., & Fowler, R. D. (1958). The Psychasthenic and Hypomanic scales of the MMPI and uncertainty in judgments. *Journal of Clinical Psychology, 14,* 385–386.

Gripshover, D. L., & Dacey, C. M. (1994). Discriminative validity of the MacAndrew scale in settings with a high base rate of substance abuse. *Journal of Studies on Alcohol, 55,* 303–308.

Gross, L. R. (1959). MMPI *L-F-K* relationships with criteria of behavioral disturbance and social adjustment in a schizophrenic population. *Journal of Consulting Psychology, 23,* 319–323.

Grossman, L. S., Haywood, T. W., Ostrov, E., Wasyliw, O., & Cavanaugh, J. L., Jr. (1990). Sensitivity of MMPI validity scales to motivational factors in psychological evaluations of police officers. *Journal of Personality Assessment, 55,* 551–561.

Grossman, L. S., & Wasyliw, O. E. (1988). A psychometric study of stereotypes: Assessment of malingering in a criminal forensic group. *Journal of Personality Assessment, 52,* 549–563.

Gudjonsson, G. H., Petursson, H., Sigurdardottir, H., & Skulason, S. (1991). Overcontrolled hostility among prisoners and its relationship with denial and personality scores. *Personality and Individual Differences, 12,* 17–20.

Gumbiner, J. (1997). Comparison of scores on the MMPI-A and MMPI-2 for young adults. *Psychological Reports, 81,* 787–794.

Gumbiner, J. (1998). MMPI-A profiles of Hispanic adolescents. *Psychological Reports, 82,* 659–672.

Guthrie, P. C., & Mobley, B. D. (1994). A comparison of the differential diagnostic efficiency of three personality disorder inventories. *Journal of Clinical Psychology, 50,* 656–665.

Gynther, M. D. (1961). The clinical utility of "invalid" MMPI *F* scores. *Journal of Consulting Psychology, 25,* 540–542.

Gynther, M. D. (1972). White norms and black MMPIs: A prescription for discrimination? *Psychological Bulletin, 78,* 386–402.

Gynther, M. D. (1979). Ethnicity and personality: An update. In J. N. Butcher (Ed.), *New developments in the use of the MMPI* (pp. 113–140). Minneapolis: University of Minnesota Press.

Gynther, M. D. (1983). MMPI interpretation: The effects of demographic variables. In C. D. Spielberger & J. N. Butcher (Eds.), *Advances in personality assessment* (Vol. 3, pp. 175–193). New York: Erlbaum.

Gynther, M. D. (1989). MMPI comparisons of blacks and whites: A review and commentary. *Journal of Clinical Psychology, 45,* 878–883.

Gynther, M. D., Altman, H., & Sletten, I. W. (1973). Replicated correlates of MMPI two-point code types: The Missouri actuarial system. *Journal of Clinical Psychology, 29,* 263–289.

Gynther, M. D., Altman, H., & Warbin, R. (1973a). Behavioral correlates for the MMPI 4-9, 9-4 codetypes: A case of the emperor's new clothes? *Journal of Consulting and Clinical Psychology, 40,* 259–263.

Gynther, M. D., Altman, H., & Warbin, R. (1973b). Interpretation of uninterpretable MMPI profiles. *Journal of Consulting and Clinical Psychology, 40,* 78–83.

Gynther, M. D., & Brilliant, P. J. (1968). The MMPI *K*+ profile: A reexamination. *Journal of Consulting and Clinical Psychology, 32,* 616–617.

Gynther, M. D., & Burkhart, B. R. (1983). Are subtle MMPI items expendable? In J. N. Butcher & C. D. Spielberger (Eds.), *Advances in personality assessment* (Vol. 2, pp. 115–132). Hillsdale NJ: Erlbaum.

Gynther, M. D., Burkhart, B. R., & Hovanitz, C. (1979). Do face-valid items have more predictive validity than subtle items? The case of the MMPI *Pd* scale. *Journal of Consulting and Clinical Psychology, 47,* 295–300.

Gynther, M. D., Fowler, R. D., & Erdberg, P. (1971). False positives galore: The application of standard MMPI criteria to a rural, isolated, Negro sample. *Journal of Clinical Psychology, 27,* 234–237.

Gynther, M. D., & Green, S. B. (1980). Accuracy may make a difference, but does a difference make for accuracy? A response to Pritchard and Rosenblatt. *Journal of Consulting and Clinical Psychology, 48,* 268–272.

Gynther, M. D., Lachar, D., & Dahlstrom, W. G. (1978). Are special norms for minorities needed? Development of an MMPI *F* scale for blacks. *Journal of Consulting and Clinical Psychology, 46,* 1403–1408.

Gynther, M. D., & Petzel, T. P. (1967). Differential endorsement of MMPI *F* scale items by psychotics and behavior disorders. *Journal of Clinical Psychology, 23,* 185–188.

Gynther, M. D., & Shimkunas, A. M. (1965a). Age, intelligence, and MMPI *F* scores. *Journal of Consulting Psychology, 29,* 383–388.

Gynther, M. D., & Shimkunas, A. M. (1965b). More data on MMPI *F* > 16 scores. *Journal of Clinical Psychology, 21,* 275–277.

Gynther, M. D., & Witt, P. H. (1976). Windstorms and important persons: Personality characteristics of black educators. *Journal of Clinical Psychology, 32,* 613–616.

Hale, G., Zimostrad, S., Duckworth, J., & Nicholas, D. (1986, March). *The abusive personality: MMPI profiles of male batterers.* Paper presented at the 21st Annual Symposium on Recent Developments in the Use of the MMPI, Clearwater, FL.

Hall, G. C. N., Mauiro, R. D., Vitaliano, P. P., & Proctor, W. C. (1986). The utility of the MMPI with men who have sexually assaulted children. *Journal of Consulting and Clinical Psychology, 54,* 493–496.

Haller, D. L., Knisely, J. S., Elswick, R. K., Jr., Dawson, K. S., & Schnoll, S. H. (1997). Perinatal substance abusers: Factors influencing treatment retention. *Journal of Substance Abuse Treatment, 14,* 513–519.

Hamilton, J. M., Finlayson, M. A. J., & Alfano, D. P. (1995). Dimensions of neurobehavioral dysfunction: Cross-validation using a head-injured sample. *Brain Injury, 9,* 479–485.

Hampton, P. J. (1953). The development of a personality questionnaire for drinkers. *Genetic Psychological Monographs, 48,* 55–115.

Han, K., Weed, N. C., Calhoun, R. F., & Butcher, J. N. (1995). Psychometric characteristics of the MMPI-2 Cook-Medley Hostility scale. *Journal of Personality Assessment, 65,* 567–585.

Harding, C. F., Holz, W. C., & Kawakami, D. (1958). The differentiation of schizophrenic and superficially similar reactions. *Journal of Clinical Psychology, 14,* 147–149.

Hare, R. D. (1985). Comparison of procedures for the assessment of psychopathy. *Journal of Consulting and Clinical Psychology, 53,* 7–16.

Harkness, A. R., & McNulty, J. L. (1994). The Personality Psychopathology Five (PSY-5): Issue from the pages of a diagnostic manual instead of a dictionary. In S. Strack & M. Lorr (Eds.), *Differentiating normal and abnormal personality* (pp. 291–315). New York: Springer.

Harkness, A. R., McNulty, J. L., & Ben-Porath, Y. S. (1995). The Personality Psychopathology Five (PSY-5): Constructs and MMPI-2 scales. *Psychological Assessment, 7,* 104–114.

Harrell, T. H., Honaker, L. M., & Parnell, T. (1992). Equivalence of the MMPI-2 with the MMPI in psychiatric patients. *Psychological Assessment, 4,* 460–465.

Harris, R. E., & Lingoes, J. C. (1955). *Subscales for the MMPI: An aid to profile interpretation.* Unpublished manuscript, University of California.

Harris, R. J., Wittner, W., Koppell, B., & Hilf, F. D. (1970). MMPI scales vs. interviewer ratings of paranoia. *Psychological Reports, 27,* 447–450.

Harrison, R. H., & Kass, E. H. (1967). Differences between Negro and white pregnant women on the MMPI. *Journal of Consulting Psychology, 31,* 454–463.

Harrison, R. H., & Kass, E. H. (1968). MMPI correlates of Negro acculturation in a northern city. *Journal of Personality and Social Psychology, 10,* 262–270.

Hartshorne, H., & May, M. A. (1928). *Studies in deceit.* New York: Macmillan.

Haskell, A. (1996). *Mexican-American and Anglo-American endorsement of items on the MMPI-2 Scale 2, the Center for Epidemiological Studies Depression scale, and the Cohen-Hoberman Inventory of Physical Symptoms.* Unpublished doctoral dissertation, Texas Tech University, Lubbock.

Hathaway, S. R. (1956). Scales 5 (Masculinity-Femininity), 6 (Paranoia), and 8 (Schizophrenia). In G. S. Welsh & W. G. Dahlstrom (Eds.), *Basic readings on the MMPI in psychiatry and medicine* (pp. 104–111). Minneapolis: University of Minnesota Press.

Hathaway, S. R., & Briggs, P. F. (1957). Some normative data on new MMPI scales. *Journal of Clinical Psychology, 13,* 364–368.

Hathaway, S. R., & McKinley, J. C. (1940). A multiphasic personality schedule (Minnesota): I. Construction of the schedule. *Journal of Psychology, 10,* 249–254.

Hathaway, S. R., & McKinley, J. C. (1942). A multiphasic personality schedule (Minnesota): III. The measurement of symptomatic depression. *Journal of Psychology, 14,* 73–84.

Hathaway, S. R., & McKinley, J. C. (1951). *MMPI manual.* New York: Psychological Corporation.

Hathaway, S. R., & McKinley, J. C. (1967). *MMPI manual* (rev. ed.). New York: Psychological Corporation.

Hathaway, S. R., & McKinley, J. C. (1983). *Manual for administration and scoring of the MMPI.* Minneapolis: National Computer Systems.

Hathaway, S. R., & Meehl, P. E. (1951). *An atlas for the clinical use of the MMPI.* Minneapolis: University of Minnesota Press.

Hathaway, S. R., & Monachesi, E. D. (1963). *Adolescent personality and behavior: MMPI patterns of normal, delinquent, dropout, and other outcomes.* Minneapolis: University of Minnesota Press.

Hays, R. D., & Revetto, J. P. (1992). Old and new MMPI-derived scales and the short-MAST as screening tools for alcohol disorder. *Alcohol & Alcoholism, 27,* 685–695.

Hearn, M. D., Murray, D. M., & Luepker, R. V. (1989). Hostility, coronary heart disease, and total mortality: A 33-year follow-up study of university students. *Journal of Behavioral Medicine, 12,* 105–121.

Hedayat, M. M., & Kelly, D. B. (1994). Relationship of MMPI Dependency and Dominance scale scores to staff's ratings, diagnoses, and demographic data for day-treatment clients. *Psychological Reports, 68,* 259–266.

Hedlund, J. L. (1977). MMPI clinical scale correlates. *Journal of Consulting and Clinical Psychology, 45,* 739–750.

Hedlund, J. L., & Won Cho, D. (1979). [MMPI data research tape for Missouri Department of Mental Health patients.] Unpublished raw data.

Hedlund, J. L., Won Cho, D., & Powell, B. J. (1975). Use of MMPI short forms with psychiatric patients. *Journal of Consulting and Clinical Psychology, 43,* 924.

Heilbrun, A. B. (1961). The psychological significance of the MMPI *K* scale in a normal population. *Journal of Consulting Psychology, 25,* 486–491.

Heilbrun, A. B. (1963). Revision of the MMPI *K* correction procedure for improved detection of maladjustment in a normal college population. *Journal of Consulting Psychology, 27,* 161–165.

Heilbrun, A. B. (1979). Psychopathy and violent crime. *Journal of Consulting and Clinical Psychology, 47,* 509–516.

Helmes, E., & McLaughlin, J. D. (1983). A comparison of three MMPI short forms: Limited clinical utility in classification. *Journal of Consulting and Clinical Psychology, 51,* 786–787.

Helmes, E., & Reddon, J. R. (1993). A perspective on developments in assessing psychopathology: A critical review of the MMPI and MMPI-2. *Psychological Bulletin, 113,* 453–471.

Henderson, M. (1983). Self-reported assertion and aggression among violent offenders with high or low levels of overcontrolled hostility. *Personality and Individual Differences, 4,* 113–115.

Henrichs, T. F. (1964). Objective configural rules for discriminating MMPI profiles in a psychiatric population. *Journal of Clinical Psychology, 20,* 157–159.

Henrichs, T. F. (1966). A note on the extension of MMPI configural rules. *Journal of Clinical Psychology, 22,* 51–52.

Herreid, C. F., & Herreid, J. R. (1966). Differences in MMPI scores in native and nonnative Alaskans. *Journal of Social Psychology, 70,* 191–198.

Hibbs, B. J., Kobos, J. C., & Gonzalez, J. (1979). Effects of ethnicity, sex, and age on MMPI profiles. *Psychological Reports, 45,* 591–597.

Hill, H. E., Haertzen, C. A., & Glaser, R. (1960). Personality characteristics of narcotic addicts as indicated by the MMPI. *Journal of General Psychology, 62,* 127–139.

Hills, H. A. (1995). Diagnosing personality disorders: An examination of the MMPI-2 and MCMI-II. *Journal of Personality Assessment, 65,* 21–34.

Hilsenroth, M. J., Handler, L., & Blais, M. A. (1996). Assessment of Narcissistic Personality Disorder: A multi-method review. *Clinical Psychology Review, 16,* 655–683.

Hiner, D. L., Ogren, D. J., & Baxter, J. C. (1969). Ideal-self responding on the MMPI. *Journal of Projective Techniques and Personality Assessment, 33,* 389–396.

Hjemboe, S., Butcher, J. N., & Almagor, M. (1992). Empirical assessment of marital distress: The Marital Distress scale for the MMPI-2. In C. D. Spielberger & J. N. Butcher (Eds.), *Advances in Personality Assessment* (Vol. 9, p. 141–152). Hillsdale, NJ: Erlbaum.

Hodo, G. L., & Fowler, R. D. (1976). Frequency of MMPI two-point codes in a large alcoholic sample. *Journal of Clinical Psychology, 32,* 487–489.

Hoffmann, H., Loper, R. G., & Kammeier, M. L. (1974). Identifying future alcoholics with MMPI alcoholism scales. *Quarterly Journal of Studies on Alcohol, 35,* 490–498.

Hoffmann, N. G., & Butcher, J. N. (1975). Clinical limitations of three MMPI short forms. *Journal of Consulting and Clinical Psychology, 43,* 32–39.

Hokanson, J. E., & Calden, G. (1960). Negro-white differences on the MMPI. *Journal of Clinical Psychology, 16,* 32–33.

Holcomb, W. R., & Adams, N. (1982). Racial influences on intelligence and personality measures of people who commit murder. *Journal of Clinical Psychology, 38,* 793–796.

Holcomb, W. R., Adams, N. A., & Ponder, H. M. (1984). Are separate black and white MMPI norms needed? An IQ-controlled comparison of accused murderers. *Journal of Clinical Psychology, 40,* 189–193.

Holden, R. R., & Kroner, D. G. (1992). Relative efficacy of differential response latencies for detecting faking on a self-report measure of psychopathology. *Psychological Assessment, 4,* 170–173.

Holland, T. R. (1979). Ethnic group differences in MMPI profile pattern and factorial structure among adult offenders. *Journal of Personality Assessment, 43,* 72–77.

Holland, T. R., & Levi, M. (1983). Personality correlates of extent versus type of antisocial behavior among adult offenders: A multivariate analysis. *Multivariate Behavioral Research, 18,* 391–400.

Hollrah, J. L., Schlottmann, R. S., Scott, A. B., & Brunetti, D. G. (1995). Validity of the MMPI subtle items. *Journal of Personality Assessment, 65,* 278–299.

Holmes, G. R., Sabalis, R. F., Chestnut, E., & Khoury, L. (1984). Parent MMPI critical item and clinical scale changes in the 1970s. *Journal of Clinical Psychology, 40,* 1194–1198.

Holmes, W. O. (1953). *The development of an empirical MMPI scale for alcoholism.* Unpublished Master's thesis, San Jose State College.

Honaker, L. M. (1988). The equivalency of computerized and conventional MMPI administration: A critical review. *Clinical Psychology Review, 8,* 561–577.

Honaker, L. M., Harrell, T. H., & Buffaloe, J. D. (1988). Equivalency of microtest computer MMPI administration for standard and special scales. *Computers in Human Behavior, 4,* 323–337.

Hoppe, C. M., & Singer, R. D. (1976). Overcontrolled hostility, empathy, and egocentric balance in violent and nonviolent psychiatric offenders. *Psychological Reports, 39,* 1303–1308.

Horn, J. M., & Turner, R. G. (1976). MMPI profiles among subgroups of unwed mothers. *Journal of Consulting and Clinical Psychology, 44,* 25–33.

Horowitz, L. M., Wright, J. C., Lowenstein, E., & Parad, H. W. (1981). The prototype as a construct in abnormal psychology: 1. A method for deriving prototypes. *Journal of Abnormal Psychology, 90,* 568–574.

Hovanitz, C. A., & Gynther, M. D. (1980). The prediction of impulsive behavior: Comparative validities of obvious versus subtle MMPI hypomania (*Ma*) items. *Journal of Clinical Psychology, 36,* 422–427.

Hovey, H. B., & Lewis, E. G. (1967). Semi-automatic interpretation of the MMPI. *Journal of Clinical Psychology, 23,* 123–134.

Hoyt, D. P., & Sedlacek, G. M. (1958). Differentiating alcoholics from normals and abnormals with the MMPI. *Journal of Clinical Psychology, 14,* 69–74.

Hryckowian, M. J., & Gynther, M. D. (1988). MMPI item subtlety: Another look. *Journal of Clinical Psychology, 44,* 148–152.

Hsu, L. M., & Betman, J. A. (1986). MMPI *T*-score conversion tables, 1957–1983. *Journal of Consulting and Clinical Psychology, 54,* 497–501.

Huba, G. J. (1986). The use of the runs test for assessing response validity in computer scored inventories. *Educational and Psychological Measurement, 46,* 929–932.

Huber, N. A., & Danahy, S. (1975). Use of the MMPI in predicting completion and evaluating changes in a long-term alcoholism treatment program. *Journal of Studies on Alcohol, 36,* 1230–1237.

Huesmann, L. R., Lefkowitz, M. M., & Eron, L. D. (1978). Sum of MMPI Scales *F, 4,* and *9* as a measure of aggression. *Journal of Consulting and Clinical Psychology, 46,* 1071–1078.

Hunt, H. F. (1948). The effect of deliberate deception on MMPI performance. *Journal of Consulting Psychology, 12,* 396–402.

Hunt, H. F., Carp, A., Cass, W. A., Jr., Winder, C. L., & Kantor, R. E. (1948). A study of the differential diagnostic efficiency of the MMPI. *Journal of Consulting Psychology, 12,* 331–336.

Hutton, H. E., Miner, M. H., Blades, J. R., & Langfeldt, V. C. (1992). Ethnic differences on the MMPI Overcontrolled-Hostility scale. *Journal of Personality Assessment, 58,* 260–268.

Hyer, L., Boudewyns, P., Harrison, W. R., O'Leary, W. C., Bruno, R. D., Saucer, R. T., & Blount, J. B. (1988). Vietnam veterans: Overreporting versus acceptable reporting of symptoms. *Journal of Personality Assessment, 52,* 475–486.

Ingram, J. C., Marchioni, P., Hill, G., Caraveo-Ramos, E., & McNeil, B. (1985). Recidivism, perceived problem-solving abilities, MMPI characteristics, and violence: A study of black and white incarcerated male adult offenders. *Journal of Clinical Psychology, 41,* 425–432.

Iverson, G. L., Franzen, M. D., & Hammond, J. A. (1995). Examination of inmates' ability to malinger on the MMPI-2. *Psychological Assessment, 7,* 118–121.

Jackson, D. N. (1968). *Personality Research Form manual.* Goshen, NY: Research Psychologists Press.

Jackson, D. N. (1971). The dynamics of structured personality tests: 1971. *Psychological Review, 78,* 229–248.

Jackson, D. N. (1967). [Review of J. Block: *The challenge of response sets.*] *Educational and Psychological Measurement, 27,* 207–219.

Jackson, D. N., Fraboni, M., & Helmes, E. (1997). MMPI-2 Content scales: How much content do they measure? *Assessment, 4,* 111–117.

Janus, M. D., Tolbert, H., Calestro, K., & Toepfer, S. (1996). Clinical accuracy ratings of MMPI approaches for adolescents: Adding ten years and the MMPI-A. *Journal of Personality Assessment, 67,* 364–383.

Jarnecke, R. W., & Chambers, E. D. (1977). MMPI content scales: Dimensional structure, construct validity, and interpretive norms in a psychiatric population. *Journal of Consulting and Clinical Psychology, 45,* 1126–1131.

Jenkins, C. D., Rosenman, R. H., & Friedman, M. (1967). Development of an objective psychological test for the determination of the coronary-prone behavior pattern in employed men. *Journal of Chronic Diseases, 20,* 371–379.

Jenkins, G. (1985). *Response sets and personality measures: The K scale of the MMPI.* Unpublished doctoral dissertation, Texas Tech University, Lubbock.

Johnson, J. H., Null, C., Butcher, J. N., & Johnson, K. N. (1984). Replicated item level factor analysis of the full MMPI. *Journal of Personality and Social Psychology, 47,* 105–114.

Johnson, M. E., Jones, G., & Brems, C. (1996). Concurrent validity of the MMPI-2 Feminine Gender role (*GF*) and Masculine Gender role (*GM*) scales. *Journal of Personality Assessment, 66,* 153–168.

Jones, E. E. (1978). Black-white personality differences: Another look. *Journal of Personality Assessment, 42,* 244–252.

Kamerow, D. B., Pincus, H. A., & Macdonald, D. I. (1986). Alcohol abuse, other drug abuse, and mental disorders in medical practice. *Journal of the American Medical Association, 255,* 2054–2057.

Kammeier, M. L., Hoffmann, H., & Loper, R. G. (1973). Personality characteristics of alcoholics as college freshmen and at time of treatment. *Quarterly Journal of Studies on Alcohol, 34,* 390–399.

Karol, R. L. (1985). MMPI omitted items: A method for quickly determining individual scale impact. *Journal of Consulting and Clinical Psychology, 53,* 134–135.

Kawachi, I., Sparrow, D., Kubzansky, L. D., Spiro, A., Vokonas, P. S., & Weiss, S. T. (1998). Prospective study of a self-report Type A scale risk of coronary heart disease: Test of the MMPI-2 Type A scale. *Circulation, 98,* 405–412.

Kawachi, I., Sparrow, D., Spiro, A., Vokonas, P., & Weiss, S. T. (1996). A prospective study of anger and coronary heart disease: The normative aging study. *Circulation, 94,* 2090–2095.

Kazan, A. T., & Sheinberg, I. M. (1945). Clinical note on the significance of the validity score (*F*) in the MMPI. *American Journal of Psychiatry, 102,* 181–183.

Keane, T. M., Malloy, P. F., & Fairbank, J. A. (1984). Empirical development of an MMPI subscale for the assessment of combat-related posttraumatic stress disorder. *Journal of Consulting and Clinical Psychology, 52,* 888–891.

Keiller, S. W., & Graham, J. R. (1993). The meaning of low scores on MMPI-2 clinical scales of normal subjects. *Journal of Personality Assessment, 61,* 211–223.

Kelch, L. W., & Wagner, E. E. (1992). Maximized split-half reliabilities and distributional characteristics for Harris-Lingoes subscales with few items: A reevaluation for the MMPI-2. *Perceptual and Motor Skills, 75,* 847–850.

Kelley, C. K., & King, G. D. (1978). Behavioral correlates for within-normal-limit MMPI profiles with and without elevated *K* in students at a university mental health center. *Journal of Clinical Psychology, 34,* 695–699.

Kelley, C. K., & King, G. D. (1979a). Behavioral correlates of infrequent two-point MMPI code types at a university mental health center. *Journal of Clinical Psychology, 35,* 576–585.

Kelley, C. K., & King, G. D. (1979b). Behavioral correlates of the *2-7-8* MMPI profile type in students at a university mental health center. *Journal of Consulting and Clinical Psychology, 47,* 679–685.

Kelley, C. K., & King, G. D. (1979c). Cross-validation of the *2-8/8-2* MMPI code type for young adult psychiatric outpatients. *Journal of Personality Assessment, 43,* 143–149.

Kelley, C. K., & King, G. D. (1980). Two- and three-point classification of MMPI profiles in which Scales *2, 7,* and *8* are the highest elevations. *Journal of Personality Assessment, 44,* 25–33.

Kessler, R. C., McGonagle, K. A., Zhao, S., Nelson, C. B., Hughes, M., Eshleman, S., Wittchen, H., & Kendler, K. S. (1994). Lifetime and 12-month prevalence of DSM-II-R psychiatric disorders in the United States. *Archives of General Psychiatry, 51,* 8–19.

Kincannon, J. C. (1968). Prediction of the standard MMPI scale scores from 71 items: The Mini-Mult. *Journal of Consulting and Clinical Psychology, 32,* 319–325.

King, G. D., & Kelley, C. K. (1977a). Behavioral correlates for Spike-*4,* Spike-*9,* and *4-9/9-4* MMPI profiles in students at a university mental health center. *Journal of Clinical Psychology, 33,* 718–724.

King, G. D., & Kelley, C. K. (1977b). MMPI behavioral correlates of Spike-*5* and two-point code types with Scale *5* as one elevation. *Journal of Clinical Psychology, 33,* 180–185.

King, H. F., Carroll, J. L., & Fuller, G. B. (1977). Comparison of nonpsychiatric blacks and whites on the MMPI. *Journal of Clinical Psychology, 33,* 725–728.

Kirk, A. R., & Zucker, R. A. (1979). Some sociopsychological factors in attempted suicide among urban black males. *Suicide and Life Threatening Behavior, 9,* 76–86.

Kleinmuntz, B. (1960). Identification of maladjusted college students. *Journal of Counseling Psychology, 7,* 209–211.

Kleinmuntz, B. (1961a). The college maladjustment scale (Mt): Norms and predictive validity. *Educational and Psychological Measurement, 21,* 1029–1033.

Kleinmuntz, B. (1961b). Screening: Identification or prediction? *Journal of Counseling Psychology, 8,* 279–280.

Kleinmuntz, B. (1963). MMPI decision rules for the identification of college maladjustment: A digital computer approach. *Psychological Monographs, 77,* 14 (Whole No. 577).

Kline, J. A., Rozynko, V. V., Flint, G., & Roberts, A. C. (1973). Personality characteristics of male Native American alcoholic patients. *International Journal of the Addictions, 8,* 729–732.

Klinge, V., & Strauss, M. E. (1976). Effects of scoring norms on adolescent psychiatric patients' MMPI profiles. *Journal of Personality Assessment, 40,* 13–17.

Knapp, R. R. (1960). A reevaluation of the validity of MMPI scales of dominance and social responsibility. *Educational and Psychological Measurement, 20,* 381–386.

Knowles, E. E., & Schroeder, D. A. (1990). Concurrent validation of the MacAndrew Alcoholism scale: Mixed-group validation. *Journal of Studies on Alcohol, 51,* 257–262.

Kohutek, K. J. (1992a). The location of items of the Wiggins content scales on the MMPI-2. *Journal of Clinical Psychology, 48,* 617–620.

Kohutek, K. J. (1992b). Wiggins Content scales and the MMPI-2. *Journal of Clinical Psychology, 48,* 215–218.

Kornfield, A. D. (1995). Police officer candidate MMPI-2 performance: Gender, ethnic, and normative factors. *Journal of Clinical Psychology, 51,* 536–540.

Koss, M. P., & Butcher, J. N. (1973). A comparison of psychiatric patients' self-report with other sources of clinical information. *Journal of Research in Personality, 7,* 225–236.

Koss, M. P., Butcher, J. N., & Hoffmann, N. G. (1976). The MMPI critical items: How well do they work? *Journal of Consulting and Clinical Psychology, 44,* 921–928.

Krakauer, S. Y., Archer, R. P., & Gordon, R. A. (1993). The development of Items-easy (*Ie*) and Items-Difficult (*Id*) scales for the MMPI-A. *Journal of Personality Assessment, 60,* 561–571.

Kroger, R. O., & Turnbull, W. (1975). Invalidity of validity scales: The case of the MMPI. *Journal of Consulting and Clinical Psychology, 43,* 48–55.

Kwan, K. K. (1994, August). *MMPI/MMPI-2 performance of the Chinese: Cross-cultural applicability.* Paper presented at the annual meeting of the American Psychological Association, Los Angeles.

Lachar, D. (1974). *The MMPI: Clinical assessment and automated interpretation.* Los Angeles: Western Psychological Services.

Lachar, D., & Alexander, R. S. (1978). Veridicality of self-report: Replicated correlates of the Wiggins MMPI content scales. *Journal of Consulting and Clinical Psychology, 46,* 1349–1356.

Lachar, D., Klinge, V., & Grisell, J. L. (1976). Relative accuracy of automated MMPI narratives generated from adult norm and adolescent norm profiles. *Journal of Consulting and Clinical Psychology, 44,* 20–24.

Lachar, D., & Wrobel, T. A. (1979). Validating clinicians' hunches: Construction of a new MMPI critical item set. *Journal of Consulting and Clinical Psychology, 47,* 277–284.

Lacks, P. B., Rothenberg, P. J., & Unger, B. L. (1970). MMPI scores and marital status in male schizophrenics. *Journal of Clinical Psychology, 26,* 221–222.

Ladd, J. S. (1996). MMPI-2 critical item norms in chemically dependent inpatients. *Journal of Clinical Psychology, 52,* 367–372.

Ladd, J. S. (1997). The *F*(*p*) Infrequency-Psychopathology scale with chemically dependent inpatients. *Journal of Clinical Psychology, 54,* 655–671.

Lamb, D. G., Berry, D. T. R., Wetter, M. W., & Baer, R. A. (1994). Effects of two types of information on malingering of closed head injury on the MMPI-2: An analog investigation. *Psychological Assessment, 6,* 8–13.

Landis, C., & Katz, S. E. (1934). The validity of certain questions which purport to measure neurotic tendencies. *Journal of Applied Psychology, 18,* 343–356.

Lane, P. J., & Kling, J. S. (1979). Construct validation of the Overcontrolled Hostility scale of the MMPI. *Journal of Consulting and Clinical Psychology, 47,* 781–782.

Lanyon, R. I. (1967). Simulation of normal and psychopathic MMPI personality patterns. *Journal of Consulting Psychology, 31,* 94–97.

Lanyon, R. I. (1968). *A handbook of MMPI group profiles.* Minneapolis: University of Minnesota Press.

Lanyon, R. I., & Lutz, R. W. (1984). MMPI discrimination of defensive and nondefensive felony sex offenders. *Journal of Consulting and Clinical Psychology, 52,* 841–843.

Lapham, S. C., Skipper, B. J., Owen, J. P., Kleyboecker, K., Teaf, D., Thompson, B., & Simpson, G. (1995). Alcohol abuse screening instruments: Normative test data collected from a first DWI offender screening program. *Journal of Studies on Alcohol, 56,* 51–59.

Lawson, H. H., Kahn, M. W., & Heiman, E. M. (1982). Psychopathology, treatment outcome and attitude toward mental illness in Mexican American and European patients. *International Journal of Social Psychology, 28,* 20–26.

Leary, T. (1956). *Multilevel measurement of interpersonal behavior.* Berkeley, CA: Psychological Consultation Service.

Leary, T. (1957). *The interpersonal diagnosis of personality.* New York: Ronald Press.

Lees-Haley, P. R. (1992). Efficacy of MMPI-2 validity scales and MCMI-II modifier scales for detecting spurious PTSD claims: F, F - K, Fake Bad scale, Ego Strength, subtle-obvious subscales, DIS, and DEB. *Journal of Clinical Psychology, 48,* 681–688.

Lees-Haley, P. R. (1997). MMPI-2 base rates for 492 personal injury plaintiffs: Implications and challenges for forensic assessment. *Journal of Clinical Psychology, 53,* 745–755.

Lees-Haley, P. R., English, L. T., & Glenn, W. J. (1991). A fake bad scale on the MMPI-2 for personal-injury claimants. *Psychological Reports, 68,* 203–210.

Lees-Haley, P. R., & Fox, D. D. (1990). MMPI subtle-obvious scales and malingering: Clinical versus simulated scores. *Psychological Reports, 66,* 907–911.

Leiker, M. A., & Hailey, B. J. (1988). A link between hostility and disease: Poor health habits? *Behavioral Medicine, 14,* 129–133.

Leon, G. R., Finn, S. E., Murray, D., & Bailey, J. M. (1988). Inability to predict cardiovascular disease from Hostility scores or MMPI items related to Type A behavior. *Journal of Consulting and Clinical Psychology, 56,* 597–600.

Leon, G. R., Gillum, B., Gillum, R., & Gouze, M. (1979). Personality stability and change over a 30-year period—middle age to old age. *Journal of Consulting and Clinical Psychology, 47,* 517–524.

Leonard, C. V. (1977). The MMPI as a suicide predictor. *Journal of Consulting and Clinical Psychology, 45,* 367–377.

Lester, D., & Clopton, J. R. (1979). Suicide and overcontrol. *Psychological Reports, 44,* 758.

Levenson, M. R., Aldwin, C. M., Butcher, J. N., De Labry, L., Workman-Daniels, K., & Bosse, R. (1990). The *MAC* scale in a normal population: The meaning of "false positives." *Journal of Studies on Alcohol, 51,* 457–462.

Levitt, E. E. (1978). A note on "MMPI scale development methodology." *Journal of Personality Assessment, 42,* 503–504.

Levitt, E. E. (1989). *The clinical application of MMPI special scales.* Hillsdale, NJ: Erlbaum.

Levitt, E. E. (1990). A structural analysis of the impact of MMPI-2 on the MMPI-1. *Journal of Personality Assessment, 55,* 562–577.

Levitt, E. E., & Gotts, E. E. (1995). *The clinical application of MMPI special scales* (2nd ed.). Hillsdale, NJ: Erlbaum.

Levy, L. H. (1963). *Psychological interpretation.* New York: Holt, Rinehart, & Winston.

Lichenstein, E. & Bryan, J. H. (1966). Short-term stability of MMPI profiles. *Journal of Consulting Psychology, 30,* 172–174.

Lilienfeld, S. O. (1996). The MMPI-2 Antisocial Practices Content scale: Construct validity and comparison with the Psychopathic Deviate scale. *Psychological Assessment, 8,* 281–293.

Lim, J., & Butcher, J. N. (1996). Detection of faking on the MMPI-2: Differentiation among faking-bad, denial, and claiming extreme virtue. *Journal of Personality Assessment, 67,* 1–25.

Lindsey, M. L. (1998). Culturally competent assessment of African American clients. *Journal of Personality Assessment, 70,* 43–53.

Lingoes, J. C. (1960). MMPI factors of the Harris and the Wiener subscales. *Journal of Consulting Psychology, 24,* 74–83.

Liske, R., & McCormick, R. (1976). MMPI profiles compared for black and white hospitalized veterans. *Newsletter for Research in Mental Health and Behavioral Sciences, 18,* 30–32.

Little, K. B., & Fisher, J. (1958). Two new experimental scales of the MMPI. *Journal of Consulting Psychology, 22,* 305–306.

Livesley, W. J. (1986). Trait and behavioral prototypes of personality disorders. *American Journal of Psychiatry, 143,* 728–732.

Long, K. A., & Graham, J. R. (1991). The Masculinity-Femininity scale of the MMPI-2: Is it useful with normal men? *Journal of Personality Assessment, 57,* 46–51.

Long, K. A., Graham, J. R., & Timbrook, R. E. (1994). Socioeconomic status and MMPI-2 interpretation. *Measurement and Evaluation in Counseling and Development, 27,* 158–177.

Loper, R. G., Kammeier, M. L., & Hoffmann, H. (1973). MMPI characteristics of college freshman males who later became alcoholics. *Journal of Abnormal Psychology, 82,* 159–162.

Lubin, B., Larsen, R. M., Matarazzo, J. D., & Seever, M. (1985). Psychological test usage patterns in five professional settings. *American Psychologist, 40,* 857–861.

Lucio, E., Reyes-Lagunes, I., & Scott, R. L. (1994). MMPI-2 for Mexico: Translation and adaptation. *Journal of Personality Assessment, 63,* 105–116.

MacAndrew, C. (1965). The differentiation of male alcoholic outpatients from nonalcoholic psychiatric outpatients by means of the MMPI. *Quarterly Journal of Studies on Alcohol, 26,* 238–246.

MacAndrew, C. (1981). What the *MAC* scale tells us about men alcoholics: An interpretive review. *Journal of Studies on Alcohol, 42,* 604–625.

MacAndrew, C. (1986). Toward the psychometric detection of substance misuse in young men: The *SAP* scale. *Journal of Studies on Alcohol, 47,* 161–166.

MacAndrew, C. (1987). An examination of the applicability of the Substance Abuse Proclivity scale to young adult males. *Psychology of Addictive Behaviors, 1,* 140–145.

MacAndrew, C. (1988). Differences in the self-depictions of female alcoholics and psychiatric outpatients: Towards a depiction of the modal female alcoholic. *Journal of Studies on Alcohol, 49,* 71–77.

MacAndrew, C., & Geertsma, R. H. (1964). A critique of alcoholism scales derived from the MMPI. *Quarterly Journal of Studies on Alcohol, 25,* 68–76.

Malinchoc, M., Offord, K. P., Colligan, R. C., & Morse, R. M. (1994). The Common Alcohol Logistic—Revised scale (*CAL-R*): A revised alcoholism scale for the MMPI and MMPI-2. *Journal of Clinical Psychology, 50,* 436–445.

Mallory, C. H., & Walker, C. E. (1972). MMPI *O-H* scale responses of assaultive and nonassaultive prisoners and associated life history variables. *Educational and Psychological Measurement, 32,* 1125–1128.

Maloney, M. P., Duvall, S. W., & Friesen, J. (1980). Evaluation of response consistency on the MMPI. *Psychological Reports, 46,* 295–298.

Manosevitz, M. (1971). Education and MMPI *Mf* scores in homosexual and heterosexual males. *Journal of Consulting and Clinical Psychology, 36,* 395–399.

Marks, P. A., & Briggs, P. F. (1972). Adolescent norm tables for the MMPI. In W. G. Dahlstrom, G. S. Welsh, & L. E. Dahlstrom, *An MMPI Handbook: Vol. I. Clinical interpretation* (rev. ed., pp. 388–399). Minneapolis: University of Minnesota Press.

Marks, P. A., & Seeman, W. (1963). *The actuarial description of abnormal personality.* Baltimore: Williams & Wilkins.

Marks, P. A., Seeman, W., & Haller, D. L. (1974). *The actuarial use of the MMPI with adolescents and adults.* Baltimore: Williams & Wilkins.

Marsella, A. J., Sanborn, K. O., Kameoka, V., Shizuru, L., & Brennan, J. (1975). Cross-validation of self-report measures of depression among normal populations of Japanese, Chinese, and Caucasian ancestry. *Journal of Clinical Psychology, 31,* 281–287.

Marsh, G. G., Hirsch, S. H., & Leung, G. (1982). Use and misuse of the MMPI in multiple sclerosis. *Psychological Reports, 51,* 1127–1134.

Martin, E. H. (1993). *Masculinity-femininity and the MMPI-2.* Unpublished doctoral dissertation: University of Texas, Austin.

Matarazzo, J. D. (1955). MMPI validity scores as a function of increasing levels of anxiety. *Journal of Consulting Psychology, 19,* 213–217.

McCaffrey, R. J., Hickling, E. J., & Marrazo, M. J. (1989). Civilian-related post-traumatic stress disorder: assessment-related issues. *Journal of Clinical Psychology, 45,* 72–76.

McCann, J. T. (1989). MMPI Personality Disorder scales and the MCMI: Concurrent validity. *Journal of Clinical Psychology, 45,* 365–369.

McCann, J. T. (1991). Convergent and discriminant validity of the MCMI-II and MMPI Personality Disorder scales. *Psychological Assessment, 3,* 9–18.

McCranie, E. W., Watkins, L. O., Brandsma, J. M., & Sisson, B. D. (1986). Hostility, coronary heart disease (CHD) incidence, and total mortality: Lack of association in a 25-year follow-up of 478 physicians. *Journal of Behavioral Medicine, 9,* 119–125.

McCreary, C. (1975). Personality profiles of persons convicted of indecent exposure. *Journal of Clinical Psychology, 31,* 260–262.

McCreary, C., & Padilla, E. (1977). MMPI differences among Black, Mexican-American, and White male offenders. *Journal of Clinical Psychology, 33,* 171–177.

McDonald, R. L., & Gynther, M. D. (1962). MMPI norms for southern adolescent Negroes. *Journal of Social Psychology, 58,* 277–282.

McDonald, R. L., & Gynther, M. D. (1963). MMPI differences associated with sex, race, and class in two adolescent samples. *Journal of Consulting Psychology, 27,* 112–116.

McFall, M. E., Moore, J. E., Kivlahan, D. R., & Capestany, F. (1988). Differences between psychotic and nonpsychotic patients on content dimensions of the MMPI *Sc* scale. *The Journal of Nervous and Mental Diseases, 176,* 732–736.

McGill, J. C. (1980). MMPI score differences among Anglo, Black, and Mexican-American welfare recipients. *Journal of Clinical Psychology, 36,* 147–151.

McGrath, R. E., & O'Malley, W. B. (1986). The assessment of denial and physical complaints: The validity of the *Hy* scale and associated MMPI signs. *Journal of Clinical Psychology, 42,* 754–760.

McGrath, R. E., Powis, D., & Pogge, D. L. (1998). Code type-specific tables for interpretation of MMPI-2 Harris and Lingoes subscales: Consideration of gender and code type definition. *Journal of Clinical Psychology, 54,* 655–664.

McGrath, R. E., Sapareto, E., & Pogge, D. L. (1998). A new perspective on gender orientation measurement with the MMPI-2: Development of the Masculine-

Feminine Pathology scale. *Journal of Personality Assessment, 70,* 551–563.

McGrath, R. E., Sweeney, M., O'Malley, W. B., & Carlton, T. K. (1998). Identifying psychological contributions to chronic pain complaints with the MMPI-2: The role of the *K* scale. *Journal of Personality Assessment, 70,* 448–459.

McKegney, F. P. (1965). An item analysis of the MMPI *F* scale in juvenile delinquents. *Journal of Clinical Psychology, 21,* 201–205.

McKenna, T., & Butcher, J. N. (1987, March). *Continuity of the MMPI with alcoholics.* Paper presented at the 22nd Annual Symposium on Recent Developments in the Use of the MMPI, Seattle.

McKinley, J. C., & Hathaway, S. R. (1940). A multiphasic personality schedule (Minnesota): II. A differential study of hypochondriasis. *Journal of Psychology, 10,* 255–268.

McKinley, J. C., & Hathaway, S. R. (1942). A multiphasic personality schedule (Minnesota): IV. Psychasthenia. *Journal of Applied Psychology, 26,* 614–624.

McKinley, J. C., & Hathaway, S. R. (1944). The MMPI: V. Hysteria, hypomania, and psychopathic deviate. *Journal of Applied Psychology, 28,* 153–174.

McKinley, J. C., Hathaway, S. R., & Meehl, P. E. (1948). The MMPI: VI. The *K* scale. *Journal of Consulting Psychology, 12,* 20–31.

McLaughlin, J. D., Helmes, E., & Howe, M. G. (1983). Note on the reliability of three MMPI short forms. *Journal of Personality Assessment, 47,* 357–358.

McNulty, J. L., Graham, J. R., Ben-Porath, Y. S., & Stein, L. A. R. (1997). Comparative validity of MMPI-2 scores of African American and Caucasian mental health center clients. *Psychological Assessment, 9,* 464–470.

McNulty, J. L., Harkness, A. R., Ben-Porath, Y. S., & Williams, C. L. (1997). Assessing the Personality Psychopathology Five (PSY-5) in adolescents: New MMPI-A scales. *Psychological Assessment, 9,* 250–259.

Meehl, P. E. (1945). An investigation of a general normality or control factor in personality testing. *Psychological Monographs, 59* (Whole No. 274).

Meehl, P. E. (1956). Wanted—A good cookbook. *American Psychologist, 11,* 263–272.

Meehl, P. E. (1959). A comparison of clinicians with five statistical methods of identifying psychotic MMPI profiles. *Journal of Counseling Psychology, 6,* 102–109.

Meehl, P. E., & Dahlstrom, W. G. (1960). Objective configural rules for discriminating psychotic from neurotic MMPI profiles. *Journal of Consulting Psychology, 24,* 375–387.

Meehl, P. E., & Hathaway, S. R. (1946). The *K* factor as a suppressor variable in the MMPI. *Journal of Applied Psychology, 30,* 525–564.

Megargee, E. I. (1972). *The California Psychological Inventory handbook.* San Francisco: Jossey-Bass.

Megargee, E. I. (1985). Assessing alcoholism and drug abuse with the MMPI: Implication for employment screening. In C. D. Spielberger & J. N. Butcher (Eds.), *Advances in personality assessment* (Vol. 5, pp. 1–39). Hillsdale, NJ: Erlbaum.

Megargee, E. I., & Cook, P. E. (1975). Negative response bias and the MMPI overcontrolled-hostility scale: A response to Deiker. *Journal of Consulting and Clinical Psychology, 43,* 725–729.

Megargee, E. I., Cook, P. E., & Mendelsohn, G. A. (1967). Development and validation of an MMPI scale of assaultiveness in overcontrolled individuals. *Journal of Abnormal Psychology, 72,* 519–528.

Megargee, E. I., & Mendelsohn, G. A. (1962). A cross-validation of twelve MMPI indices of hostility and control. *Journal of Abnormal and Social Psychology, 65,* 431–438.

Megargee, E. I., Mercer, S. J., & Carbonell, J. L. (1999). MMPI-2 with male and female state and federal prison inmates. *Psychological Assessment,* in press.

Mehlman, B., & Rand, M. E. (1960). Face validity of the MMPI. *Journal of General Psychology, 63,* 171–178.

Meikle, S., & Gerritse, R. (1970). MMPI "cookbook" pattern frequencies in a psychiatric unit. *Journal of Clinical Psychology, 26,* 82–84.

Meyerink, L. H., Reitan, R. M., & Selz, M. (1988). The validity of the MMPI with multiple sclerosis patients. *Journal of Clinical Psychology, 44,* 764–769.

Mezzich, J. E., Damarin, F. L., & Erickson, J. R. (1974). Comparative validity of strategies and indices for differential diagnosis of depressive states from other psychiatric conditions using the MMPI. *Journal of Consulting and Clinical Psychology, 42,* 691–698.

Miller, C., Knapp, S. C., & Daniels, C. W. (1968). MMPI study of Negro mental hygiene clinic patients. *Journal of Abnormal Psychology, 73,* 168–173.

Miller, C., Wertz, C., & Counts, S. (1961). Racial differences on the MMPI. *Journal of Clinical Psychology, 17,* 159–161.

Miller, H. R., Goldberg, J. O. & Streiner, D. L. (1995). What's in a name? The MMPI-2 PTSD scales. *Journal of Clinical Psychology, 51,* 626–631.

Miller, H. R., & Streiner, D. L. (1985). The Harris-Lingoes subscales: Fact or fiction? *Journal of Clinical Psychology, 41,* 45–51.

Miller, H. R., & Streiner, D. L. (1986). Differences in MMPI profiles with the norms of Colligan et al. *Journal of Consulting and Clinical Psychology, 54,* 843–845.

Miller, H. R., Streiner, D. L., & Parkinson, A. (1992). Maximum likelihood estimates of the ability of the

MMPI and MCMI Personality Disorder scales and the SIDP to identify personality disorders. *Journal of Personality Assessment, 59,* 1–13.

Millon, T. (1983). *Millon Clinical Multiaxial Inventory manual* (3rd ed.). Minneapolis: National Computer Systems.

Millon, T. (1987). *Manual for the Millon Clinical Multiaxial Inventory-II (MCMI-II)* (2nd ed.). Minneapolis: National Computer Systems.

Monroe, J. J., Miller, J. S., & Lyle, W. H., Jr., (1964). The extension of psychopathic deviancy scales for the screening of addict patients. *Educational and Psychological Measurement, 24,* 47–56.

Montgomery, G. T., & Orozco, S. (1985). Mexican Americans' performance on the MMPI as a function of level of acculturation. *Journal of Clinical Psychology, 41,* 203–212.

Moore, C. D., & Handal, P. J. (1980). Adolescents' MMPI performance, cynicism, estrangement, and personal adjustment as a function of race and sex. *Journal of Clinical Psychology, 36,* 932–936.

Moreland, K. L. (1984). Comparative validity of the MMPI and two short forms: Psychiatric ratings. *Journal of Personality Assessment, 48,* 265–270.

Moreland, K. L. (1996). Persistent issues in multicultural assessment of social and emotional functioning. In L. A. Suzuki, P. J. Meller, & J. G. Ponterotto (Eds.), *Handbook of multicultural assessment: Clinical, psychological, and educational applications* (pp. 51–76). San Francisco: Jossey-Bass.

Morey, L. C., & Le Vine, D. J. (1988). A multitrait-multimethod examination of MMPI and MCMI. *Journal of Psychopathology and Behavioral Assessment, 10,* 333–344.

Morey, L. C., & Smith, M. R. (1988). Personality disorders. In R. L. Greene (Ed.), *The MMPI: Use with specific populations* (pp. 110–158). Philadelphia: Grune & Stratton.

Morey, L. C., Waugh, M. H., & Blashfield, R. K. (1985). MMPI scales for DSM-III personality disorders: Their derivation and correlates. *Journal of Personality Assessment, 49,* 245–251.

Morrison, T. L., Edwards, D. W., Weissman, H. N., Allen, R., & DeLaCruz, A. (1995). Comparing MMPI and MMPI-2 profiles: Replication and integration. *Assessment, 2,* 39–46.

Mueller, S. R., & Grace, M. (1988). Use and misuse of the MMPI: A reconsideration. *Psychological Reports, 63,* 483–491.

Muller, B. P., & Bruno, L. N. (1988, March). *The effects of ethnicity on personality assessment in police candidates.* Paper presented at the 23rd Annual Symposium on Recent Developments in the Use of the MMPI, St. Petersburg, FL.

Muller, B. P., & Bruno, L. N. (1990, August). *The myth of ethnic effects on the MMPI/MMPI-2.* Paper presented at the annual meeting of the American Psychological Association, Boston.

Mundt, J. E. (1992). Construct analysis and relative efficacy of two versions of the MacAndrew Alcoholism scale in a correctional population. (Unpublished doctoral dissertation, 1992). *Dissertation Abstracts International, 53,* 5989.

Munley, P. H., & Busby, R. M. (1994). MMPI-2 Negative Treatment Indicators scale and irregular discharge. *Psychological Reports, 74,* 903–906.

Munley, P. H., Busby, R. M., & Jaynes, G. (1997). MMPI-2 findings in schizophrenia and depression. *Psychological Assessment, 9,* 508–511.

Murphree, H. B., Karabelas, M. J., & Bryan, L. L. (1962). Scores of inmates of a federal penitentiary on two scales of the MMPI. *Journal of Clinical Psychology, 18,* 137–139.

Murray, J. B., Munley, M. J., & Gilbart, T. E. (1965). The *Pd* scale of the MMPI for college students. *Journal of Clinical Psychology, 21,* 48–51.

Murray, R. P., Barnes, G. E., & Patton, D. (1994). The relative performance of diverse measures of alcohol abuse and dependence in a community sample. *Journal of Studies on Alcohol, 55,* 72–80.

Nakamura, C. Y. (1960). Validity of *K* scale (MMPI) in college counseling. *Journal of Counseling Psychology, 7,* 108–115.

Negy, C., Leal-Puente, L., Trainor, D. J., & Carlson, R. (1997). Mexican American adolescents' performance on the MMPI-A. *Journal of Personality Assessment, 69,* 205–214.

Nelson, D. V., Novy, D. M., Averill, P. M., & Berry, L. A. (1996). Ethnic comparability of the MMPI in pain patients. *Journal of Clinical Psychology, 52,* 485–497.

Nelson, L. D. (1987). Measuring depression in a clinical population using the MMPI. *Journal of Consulting and Clinical Psychology, 55,* 788–790.

Nelson, L. D., & Cicchetti, D. (1991). Validity of the MMPI Depression scale for outpatients. *Psychological Assessment, 3,* 55–59.

Nelson, L. D., Pham, D., & Uchiyama, C. (1996). Subtlety of the MMPI-2 Depression scale: A subject laid to rest? *Psychological Assessment, 8,* 331–333.

Newmark, C. S., Gentry, L., Simpson, M., & Jones, T. (1978). MMPI criteria for diagnosing schizophrenia. *Journal of Personality Assessment, 42,* 366–373.

Newmark, C. S., Ziff, D. R., Finch, A. J., Jr., & Kendall, P. C. (1978). Comparing the empirical validity of the standard form with two abbreviated MMPIs. *Journal of Consulting and Clinical Psychology, 46,* 53–61.

Newton, J. R. (1968). Clinical normative data for MMPI special scales: Critical items, manifest anxiety, and repression-sensitization. *Journal of Clinical Psychology, 24,* 427–430.

Nichols, D. S. (1987). *Interpreting the Wiggins MMPI Content scales. Clinical notes on the MMPI,* No. 10. Minneapolis: National Computer Systems.

Nichols, D. S. (1988). Mood disorders. In R. L. Greene (Ed.), *The MMPI: Use in specific populations* (pp. 74–109). San Antonio: Grune & Stratton.

Nichols, D. S. (1992). [Review of the book *Development and use of the MMPI-2 content scales*]. *Journal of Personality Assessment, 58,* 434–437.

Nichols, D. S., & Greene, R. L. (1991, March). *New measures for dissimulation on the MMPI/MMPI-2.* Paper presented at the 26th Annual Symposium on Recent Developments in the Use of the MMPI (MMPI-2/MMPI-A), St. Petersburg Beach, FL.

Nichols, D. S., & Greene, R. L. (1995). *MMPI-2 Structural Summary interpretive manual.* Lutz, FL: Psychological Assessment Resources.

Nichols, D. S., & Greene, R. L. (1997). Dimensions of deception in personality assessment: The example of the MMPI-2. *Journal of Personality Assessment, 68,* 251–266.

Nichols, D. S., Greene, R. L., & Schmolck, P. (1989). Criteria for assessing inconsistent patterns of endorsement on the MMPI: Rationale, development, and empirical trials. *Journal of Clinical Psychology, 45,* 239–250.

Nicholson, R. A., Mouton, G. J., Bagby, R. M., Buis, T., Peterson, S. A., & Buigas, R. A. (1997). Utility of MMPI-2 indicators of response distortion: Receiver operating characteristic analysis. *Psychological Assessment, 9,* 471–479.

O'Connor, J. P., & Stefic, E. C. (1959). Some patterns of hypochondriasis. *Educational and Psychological Measurement, 19,* 363–371.

Okazaki, S. (1998). Psychological assessment of Asian Americans: Research agenda for cultural competency. *Journal of Personality Assessment, 70,* 54–70.

Okazaki, S., & Sue, S. (1995a). Cultural considerations in psychological assessment of Asian-Americans. In J. N. Butcher (Ed.), *Clinical personality assessment: Practical approaches* (pp. 107–119). New York: Oxford.

Okazaki, S., & Sue, S. (1995b). Methodological issues in assessment research with ethnic minorities. *Psychological Assessment, 7,* 367–375.

O'Laughlin, S., & Schill, T. (1994). The relationship between self-monitored aggression and the MMPI-2 *F, 4, 9* composite and Anger Content scale scores. *Psychological Reports, 74,* 733–734.

Olmsted, D. W., & Monachesi, E. D. (1956). A validity check on MMPI scales of responsibility and dominance. *Journal of Abnormal and Social Psychology, 53,* 140–141.

Osborne, D., Colligan, R. C., & Offord, K. P. (1986). Normative tables for the *F-K* index of the MMPI based on a contemporary normal sample. *Journal of Clinical Psychology, 42,* 593–595.

O'Sullivan, M. J., & Jemelka, R. P. (1993). The *3-4/4-3* MMPI codetype in an offender population: An update on levels of hostility and violence. *Psychological Assessment, 5,* 493–498.

Otto, R. K., Lang, A. R., Megargee, E. I., & Rosenblatt, A. I. (1988). Ability of alcoholics to escape detection by the MMPI. *Journal of Consulting and Clinical Psychology, 56,* 452–457.

Overall, J. E., & Gomez-Mont, F. (1974). The MMPI-168 for psychiatric screening. *Educational and Psychological Measurement, 34,* 315–319.

Overall, J. E., & Gorham, D. R. (1962). The Brief Psychiatric Rating Scale. *Psychological Reports, 10,* 799–812.

Pace, T. M., Choney, S. K., Blair, G. M., Hill, J. S. H., & Lacey, K. (1997, August). *Evaluating the MMPI-2 American Indian norms.* Paper presented at the annual meeting of the American Psychological Association, Chicago.

Padilla, E. R., Olmedo, E. L., & Loya, F. (1982). Acculturation and the MMPI performance of Chicano and Anglo college students. *Journal of Behavioral Sciences, 4,* 451–466.

Page, J., Landis, C., & Katz, S. E. (1934). Schizophrenic traits in the functional psychoses and in normal individuals. *American Journal of Psychiatry, 90,* 1213–1225.

Page, R. D., & Bozlee, S. (1982). A cross-cultural MMPI comparison of alcoholics. *Psychological Reports, 50,* 639–646.

Pancoast, D. L., & Archer, R. P. (1989). Original adult MMPI norms in normal samples: A review with implications for future developments. *Journal of Personality Assessment, 53,* 376–395.

Pancoast, D. L., & Archer, R. P. (1992). MMPI response patterns of college students: Comparisons to adolescents and adults. *Journal of Clinical Psychology, 48,* 47–53.

Panton, J. H. (1959a). Inmate personality differences related to recidivism, age, and race as measured by the MMPI. *Journal of Correctional Psychology, 4,* 28–35.

Panton, J. H. (1959b). The response of prison inmates to MMPI subscales. *Journal of Social Therapy, 5,* 233–237.

Paolo, A. M., & Ryan, J. J. (1992). Detection of random response sets on the MMPI-2. *Psychotherapy in Private Practice, 11,* 1–8.

Paolo, A. M., Ryan, J. J., & Smith, A. J. (1991). Reading difficulty of MMPI-2 subscales. *Journal of Clinical Psychology, 47,* 529–532.

Patalano, F. (1978). Personality dimensions of drug abusers who enter a drug-free therapeutic community. *Psychological Reports, 42,* 1063–1069.

Patterson, E. T., Charles, H. L., Woodward, W. A., Roberts, W. R., & Penk, W. E. (1981). Differences in measures of personality and family environment among black and white alcoholics. *Journal of Consulting and Clinical Psychology, 49,* 1–9.

Pauker, J. D. (1966). Identification of MMPI profile types in a female, inpatient, psychiatric setting using the Marks and Seeman rules. *Journal of Consulting Psychology, 30,* 90.

Paulhus, D. L. (1984). Two-component models of socially desirable responding. *Journal of Personality and Social Psychology, 46,* 598–609.

Paulhus, D. L. (1986). Self-deception and impression management in test responses. In A. Angleitner & J. S. Wiggins (Eds.), *Personality assessment via questionnaires: Current issues in theory and measurement* (pp. 143–165). Berlin: Springer-Verlag.

Paulson, M. J., Afifi, A. A., Thomason, M. L., & Chaleff, A. (1974). The MMPI: A descriptive measure of psychopathology in abusive parents. *Journal of Clinical Psychology, 30,* 387–390.

Payne, F. D., & Wiggins, J. S. (1972). MMPI profile types and the self-report of psychiatric patients. *Journal of Abnormal Psychology, 79,* 1–8.

Pendleton, L., Tisdale, M. J., Moll, S. H., & Marler, M. R. (1990). The *4-5-6* configuration on the MMPI in bulimics vs. controls. *Journal of Clinical Psychology, 46,* 811–816.

Penk, W. E., Keane, T., Robinowitz, R., Fowler, D. R., Bell, W. E., & Finkelstein, A. (1988). Post-traumatic stress disorder. In R. L. Greene (Ed.), *The MMPI: Use in specific populations* (pp. 198–213). San Antonio: Grune & Stratton.

Penk, W. E., Roberts, W. R., Robinowitz, R., Dolan, M. P., Atkins, H. G., & Woodward, W. A. (1982). MMPI differences of black and white polydrug abusers seeking treatment. *Journal of Consulting and Clinical Psychology, 50,* 463–465.

Penk, W. E., Robinowitz, R., Roberts, W. R., Dolan, M. P., & Atkins, H. G. (1981). MMPI differences of male Hispanic-American, black, and white heroin addicts. *Journal of Consulting and Clinical Psychology, 49,* 488–490.

Penk, W. E., Woodward, W. A., Robinowitz, R., & Hess, J. L. (1978). Differences in MMPI scores of black and white compulsive heroin users. *Journal of Abnormal Psychology, 87,* 505–513.

Pepper, L. J., & Strong, P. N. (1958). *Judgmental subscales for the Mf scale of the MMPI.* Unpublished manuscript.

Persons, R. W., & Marks, P. A. (1971). The violent *4-3* MMPI personality type. *Journal of Consulting and Clinical Psychology, 36,* 189–196.

Peteroy, E. T., & Pirrello, P. E. (1982). Comparison of MMPI scales for black and white hospitalized samples. *Psychological Reports, 50,* 662.

Peterson, C. D., & Dahlstrom, W. G. (1992). The derivation of gender-role scales *GM* and *GF* for the MMPI-2 and their relationship to Scale 5 (*Mf*). *Journal of Personality Assessment, 59,* 486–499.

Peterson, D. R. (1954). The diagnosis of subclinical schizophrenia. *Journal of Consulting Psychology, 18,* 198–200.

Phillips, G. A., & McCord, D. M. (1998, August). *The continuing usefulness of the MMPI-2 College Maladjustment scale.* Poster presented at the annual meeting of the American Psychological Association, San Francisco.

Pincus, T., Callahan, L. F., Bradley, L. A., Vaughn, W. K., & Wolfe, F. (1986). Elevated MMPI scores for Hypochondriasis, Depression, and Hysteria in patients with rheumatoid arthritis reflect disease rather than psychological status. *Arthritis and Rheumatism, 29,* 1456–1466.

Plemons, G. (1977). A comparison of MMPI scores of Anglo- and Mexican-American psychiatric patients. *Journal of Consulting and Clinical Psychology, 45,* 149–150.

Pollack, D., & Shore, J. H. (1980). Validity of the MMPI with Native Americans. *American Journal of Psychiatry, 137,* 946–950.

Popham, S. M., & Holden, R. R. (1990). Assessing MMPI constructs through the measurement of response latencies. *Journal of Personality Assessment, 54,* 469–478.

Posey, C. D., & Hess, A. K. (1984). The fakability of subtle and obvious measures of aggression by male prisoners. *Journal of Personality Assessment, 48,* 137–144.

Posey, C. D., & Hess, A. K. (1985). Aggressive response sets and subtle-obvious MMPI scale distinctions in male offenders. *Journal of Personality Assessment, 49,* 235–239.

Post, R. D., Clopton, J. R., Keefer, G., Rosenberg, D., Blyth, L. S., & Stein, M. (1986). MMPI predictors of mania among psychiatric patients. *Journal of Personality Assessment, 50,* 248–256.

Post, R. D., & Gasparikova-Krasnec, M. (1979). MMPI validity scales and behavioral disturbance in psychiatric inpatients. *Journal of Personality Assessment, 43,* 155–159.

Poythress, N. G., & Blaney, P. H. (1978). The validity of MMPI interpretations based on the Mini-Mult and the FAM. *Journal of Personality Assessment, 42,* 143–147.

Priest, W., & Meunier, G. F. (1993). MMPI-2 performance of elderly women. *Clinical Gerontologist, 14,* 3–11.

Pritchard, D. A., & Rosenblatt, A. (1980a). Racial bias in the MMPI: A methodological review. *Journal of Consulting and Clinical Psychology, 48,* 263–267.

Pritchard, D. A., & Rosenblatt, A. (1980b). Reply to Gynther and Green. *Journal of Consulting and Clinical Psychology, 48,* 273–274.

Project MATCH Research Group (1993). Project MATCH: Rationale and methods for multisite clinical trial matching alcoholism patients to treatment. *Alcoholism: Clinical and Experimental Research, 17,* 1130–1145.

Prokop, C. K. (1986). Hysteria scale elevations in low back pain patients: A risk factor for misdiagnosis? *Journal of Consulting and Clinical Psychology, 54,* 558–562.

Prokop, C. K. (1988). Chronic pain. In R. L. Greene (Ed.), *The MMPI: Use with specific populations* (pp. 22–49). San Antonio: Grune & Stratton.

Putnam, S. H., Kurtz, J. E., & Houts, D. C. (1996). Four-month test-retest reliability of the MMPI-2 with normal male clergy. *Journal of Personality Assessment, 67,* 341–353.

Quay, H., & Rowell, J. T. (1955). The validity of a schizophrenic screening scale of the MMPI. *Journal of Clinical Psychology, 11,* 92–93.

Quereshi, M. Y., & Kleman, R. (1996). Validation of selected MMPI-2 basic and content scales. *Current Psychology, 15,* 249–253.

Quinsey, V. L., Maguire, A., & Varney, G. W. (1983). Assertion and overcontrolled hostility among mentally disordered murderers. *Journal of Consulting and Clinical Psychology, 51,* 550–556.

Rader, C. M. (1977). MMPI profile types of exposers, rapists, and assaulters in a court services population. *Journal of Consulting and Clinical Psychology, 45,* 61–69.

Rand, S. W. (1979). Correspondence between psychological reports based on the Mini-Mult and the MMPI. *Journal of Personality Assessment, 43,* 160–163.

Raskin, R., & Novacek, J. (1989). An MMPI description of the narcissistic personality. *Journal of Personality Assessment, 53,* 66–80.

Reilley, R. R., & Knight, G. E. (1970). MMPI scores of Mexican-American college students. *Journal of College Student Personnel, 11,* 419–422.

Reitan, R. M., & Wolfson, D. (1997). Emotional disturbance and their interaction with neuropsychological deficits. *Neuropsychology Review, 7,* 3–19.

Rich, C. C., & Davis, H. G. (1969). Concurrent validity of MMPI alcoholism scales. *Journal of Clinical Psychology, 25,* 425–426.

Ries, H. A. (1966). The MMPI *K* scale as a predictor of prognosis. *Journal of Clinical Psychology, 22,* 212–213.

Robin, R. W., Greene, R. L., Albaugh, B., & Caldwell, A. B. (1999). Application and validity of the MMPI-2 to American Indian populations. Unpublished manuscript.

Robins, L. N., Helzer, J. E., Weisman, M. M., Orvaschel, H., Gruenberg, E., Burke, J. D., Jr., & Regier, D. A. (1984). Lifetime prevalence rates of specific psychiatric disorders in three sites. *Archives of General Psychiatry, 41,* 949–958.

Rodevich, M. A., & Wanlass, R. L. (1995). The moderating effect of spinal cord injury on MMPI-2 profiles: A clinically derived T score correction procedure. *Rehabilitation Psychology, 40,* 181–190.

Rogers, R. (1983). Malingering or random? A research note on obvious vs. subtle subscales of the MMPI. *Journal of Clinical Psychology, 39,* 257–258.

Rogers, R. (1988). Researching dissimulation. In R. Rogers (Ed.), *Clinical assessment of malingering and deception* (pp. 309–327). New York: Guilford.

Rogers, R., Bagby, R. M., & Chakraborty, D. (1993). Feigning schizophrenic disorders on the MMPI-2: Detection of coached simulators. *Journal of Personality Assessment, 60,* 215–226.

Rogers, R., Dolmetsch, R., & Cavanaugh, J. L., Jr., (1983). Identification of random responders on MMPI protocols. *Journal of Personality Assessment, 47,* 364–368.

Rogers, R., Gillis, J. R., & Dickens, S. E. (1989). A research note on the MMPI *Pd* scale and sociopathy. *International Journal of Offender Therapy and Comparative Criminology, 33,* 21–25.

Rogers, R., Sewell, K. W., & Salekin, R. T. (1994). A meta-analysis of malingering on the MMPI-2. *Assessment, 1,* 227–237.

Rogers, R., Sewell, K. W., & Ustad, K. L. (1995). Feigning among chronic outpatients on the MMPI-2: A systematic examination of fake-bad indicators. *Assessment, 2,* 81–89.

Rohan, W. P., Tatro, R. L., & Rotman, S. R. (1969). MMPI changes in alcoholics during hospitalization. *Quarterly Journal of Studies on Alcohol, 30,* 389–400.

Roper, B. L., Ben-Porath, Y. S., & Butcher, J. N. (1991). Comparability of computerized and conventional testing with the MMPI-2. *Journal of Personality Assessment, 57,* 278–290.

Roper, B. L., Ben-Porath, Y. S., & Butcher, J. N. (1995). Comparability and validity of computerized adaptive testing with the MMPI-2. *Journal of Personality Assessment, 65,* 358–371.

Rosen, A. (1954). Detection of suicidal patients: An example of some limitations in the prediction of infrequent events. *Journal of Consulting Psychology, 18,* 397–403.

Rosen, A. C. (1974). Brief report of MMPI characteristics of sexual deviation. *Psychological Reports, 35,* 73–74.

Rosenberg, M. (1965). *Society and the adolescent self-image.* Princeton, NJ: Princeton University Press.

Rosenblatt, A. I., & Pritchard, D. A. (1978). Moderators of racial differences on the MMPI. *Journal of Consulting and Clinical Psychology, 46,* 1572–1573.

Rothke, S. E., Friedman, A. F., Dahlstrom, W. G., Greene, R. L., Arredondo, R., & Mann, A. W. (1994). MMPI-2 normative data for the *F-K* index: Implications for clinical, neuropsychological, and forensic practice. *Assessment, 1,* 1–15.

Rowell, R. K. (1992). *Differences between black, Mexican-American, and white probationers on the revised MacAndrew Alcoholism scale of the MMPI-2.* Unpublished doctoral dissertation, Texas A & M University, College Station.

Rubin, H. (1954). Validity of a critical-item scale for schizophrenia on the MMPI. *Journal of Consulting Psychology, 18,* 219–220.

Ruch, F. L., & Ruch, W. W. (1967). The *K* factor as a (validity) suppressor variable in predicting success in selling. *Journal of Applied Psychology, 51,* 201–204.

Saunders, T. R., Jr., & Gravitz, M. A. (1974). Sex differences in the endorsement of MMPI critical items. *Journal of Clinical Psychology, 30,* 557–558.

Sawrie, S. M., Kabat, M. H., Dietz, C. B., Greene, R. L., Arredondo, R., & Mann, A. W. (1996). Internal structure of the MMPI-2 Addiction Potential scale in alcoholic and psychiatric inpatients. *Journal of Personality Assessment, 66,* 177–193.

Scagnelli, J. (1975). The significance of dependency in the paranoid syndrome. *Journal of Clinical Psychology, 31,* 29–34.

Schenkenberg, T., Gottfredson, D. K., & Christensen, P. (1984). Age differences in MMPI scale scores from 1,189 psychiatric patients. *Journal of Clinical Psychology, 40,* 1420–1426.

Schill, T., & Wang, S. (1990). Correlates of the MMPI-2 Anger Content scale. *Psychological Reports, 67,* 800–802.

Schinka, J. A., & Borum, R. (1993). Readability of adult psychopathology inventories. *Psychological Assessment, 5,* 384–386.

Schinka, J. A., & LaLone, L. (1997). MMPI-2 norms: Comparisons with a census-matched subsample. *Psychological Assessment, 9,* 307–311.

Schinka, J. A., LaLone, L., & Greene, R. L. (1998). Effects of psychopathology and demographic characteristics on MMPI-2 scale scores. *Journal of Personality Assessment, 70,* 197–211.

Schlenger, W. E., & Kulka, R. A. (1987, August). *Performance of the Keane-Fairbank MMPI scale and other self-report measures in identifying post-traumatic stress disorder.* Paper presented at the annual meeting of the American Psychological Association, New York.

Schmidt, H. O. (1948). Notes on the MMPI: The *K* factor. *Journal of Consulting Psychology, 12,* 337–342.

Schneck, J. M. (1948). Clinical evaluation of the *F* scale on the MMPI. *American Journal of Psychiatry, 104,* 440–442.

Schotte, C., De Doncker, D., Maes, M., Cluydts, R., & Cosyns, P. (1993). MMPI assessment of the DSM-III-R Histrionic Personality Disorder. *Journal of Personality Assessment, 60,* 500–510.

Schretlen, D. J. (1988). The use of psychological tests to identify malingered symptoms of mental disorder. *Clinical Psychology Review, 8,* 451–476.

Schretlen, D. J. (1990). A limitation of using the Wiener and Harmon obvious and subtle scales to detect faking on the MMPI. *Journal of Clinical Psychology, 46,* 782–786.

Schuldberg, D. (1992). Ego-Strength revised: A comparison of the MMPI-2 and MMPI-1 versions of the Baron Ego-Strength scale. *Journal of Clinical Psychology, 48,* 500–505.

Schuler, C. E., Snibbe, J. R., & Buckwalter, J. G. (1994). Validity of the MMPI Personality Disorder scales (MMPI-PD). *Journal of Clinical Psychology, 50,* 220–227.

Schwartz, M. F., & Graham, J. R. (1979). Construct validity of the MacAndrew alcoholism scale. *Journal of Consulting and Clinical Psychology, 47,* 1090–1095.

Schwartz, M. S. (1969). "Organicity" and the MMPI *1-3-9* and *2-9* codes. *Proceedings of the 77th Annual Convention of the APA, 4,* 519–520.

Schwartz, M. S., & Krupp, N. E. (1971). The MMPI "conversion V" among 50,000 medical patients: A study of incidence, criteria, and profile elevation. *Journal of Clinical Psychology, 27,* 89–95.

Schwartz, M. S., Osborne, D., & Krupp, N. E. (1972). Moderating effects of age and sex on the association of medical diagnoses and *1-3/3-1* MMPI profiles. *Journal of Clinical Psychology, 28,* 502–505.

Sepaher, I., Bongar, B., & Greene, R. L. (1999). Codetype base rates for the "I mean business" suicide items on the MMPI-2. *Journal of Clinical Psychology,* in press.

Serkownek, K. (1975). *Subscales for Scales 5 and 0 of the MMPI.* Unpublished manuscript.

Sewell, K. W., & Rogers, R. (1994). Response consistency and the MMPI-2: Development of a simplified screening scale. *Assessment, 1,* 293–299.

Shaevel, B., & Archer, R. P. (1996). Effects of MMPI-2 and MMPI-A norms on T-score elevations for 18-year-olds. *Journal of Personality Assessment, 67,* 72–78.

Shekelle, R. B., Gale, M., Ostfeld, A. M., & Paul, O. (1983). Hostility, risk of coronary heart disease, and mortality. *Psychosomatic Medicine, 45,* 109–114.

Sheppard, D., Smith, G. T., & Rosenbaum, G. (1988). Use of MMPI subtypes in predicting completion of a residential alcoholism treatment program. *Journal of Consulting and Clinical Psychology, 56,* 590–596.

Shore, R. E. (1976). A statistical note on "Differential misdiagnosis of blacks and whites by the MMPI." *Journal of Personality Assessment, 40,* 21–23.

Shultz, T. D., Gibeau, P. J., & Barry, S. M. (1968). Utility of MMPl "cookbooks." *Journal of Clinical Psychology, 24,* 430–433.

Shweder, R. A. (1977a). Illusory correlation and the MMPI controversy. *Journal of Consulting and Clinical Psychology, 45,* 917–924.

Shweder, R. A. (1977b). Illusory correlation and the MMPI controversy: Reply to some of the allusions and elusions in Block's and Edwards' commentaries. *Journal of Consulting and Clinical Psychology, 45,* 936–940.

Sieber, K. O., & Meyers, L. S. (1992). Validation of the MMPI-2 Social Introversion subscales. *Psychological Assessment, 4,* 185–189.

Silver, R. J., & Sines, L. K. (1962). Diagnostic efficiency of the MMPI with and without the *K* correction. *Journal of Clinical Psychology, 18,* 312–314.

Simon, W., & Gilberstadt, H. (1958). Analysis of the personality structure of 26 actual suicides. *Journal of Nervous and Mental Disease, 127,* 555–557.

Sines, J. O. (1966). Actuarial methods in personality assessment. In B. A. Maher (Ed.), *Progress in experimental personality research* (pp. 133–193). New York: Academic Press.

Sines, J. O. (1977). M-F: Bipolar and probably multidimensional. *Journal of Clinical Psychology, 33,* 1038-1041.

Sines, L. K., Baucom, D. H., & Gruba, G. H. (1979). A validity scale sign calling for caution in the interpretation of MMPIs among psychiatric inpatients. *Journal of Personality Assessment, 43,* 604–607.

Singer, M. I. (1970). Comparison of indicators of homosexuality on the MMPI. *Journal of Consulting and Clinical Psychology, 34,* 15–18.

Sivec, H. J., Hilsenroth, M. J., & Lynn, S. J. (1995). Impact of simulating borderline personality disorder on the MMPI-2: A cost-benefits model employing base rates. *Journal of Personality Assessment, 64,* 295–311.

Sivec, H. J., Lynn, S. J., & Garske, J. P. (1994). The effect of somatoform disorder and paranoid psychotic role-related dissimulations as a response set on the MMPI-2. *Assessment, 1,* 69–81.

Smith, C. P., & Graham, J. R. (1981). Behavioral correlates for the MMPI standard *F* scale and for a modified *F* scale for black and white psychiatric patients. *Journal of Consulting and Clinical Psychology, 49,* 455–459.

Smith, E. E. (1959). Defensiveness, insight, and the *K* scale. *Journal of Consulting Psychology, 23,* 275–277.

Snyter, C. M., & Graham, J. R. (1984). The utility of subtle and obvious MMPI subscales based on scale-specific ratings. *Journal of Clinical Psychology, 40,* 981–985.

Spielburger, C. D. (1987). *State-Trait Anger Inventory manual.* Palo Alto, CA: Consulting Psychologists Press.

Spielburger, C. D., Gorsuch, R. L., Lushene, R., Vagg, P. R., & Jacobs, G. A. (1984). *Manual for the State-Trait Anxiety Inventory.* Palo Alto, CA: Consulting Psychologists Press.

Spirito, A., Faust, D., Myers, B., & Bechtel, D. (1988). Clinical utility of the MMPI in the evaluation of adolescent suicide attempters. *Journal of Personality Assessment, 52,* 204–211.

Spiro, R., Butcher, J. N., Levenson, M., Aldwin, C., & Bosse, R. (1993, August). *Personality change over five years: The MMPI-2 in older men.* Paper presented at the annual meeting of the American Psychological Association, Toronto.

Sprock, J., & Bienek, J. (1998). Barron's Ego Strength and Welsh's Anxiety and Repression scales: A comparison of the MMPI and MMPI-2. *Journal of Personality Assessment, 70,* 506–513.

Stanton, J. M. (1956). Group personality profile related to aspects of antisocial behavior. *Journal of Criminal Law, Criminology, and Police Science, 47,* 340–349.

Stein, K. B. (1968). The TSC scales: The outcome of a cluster analysis of the 550 MMPI items. In P. McReynolds (Ed.), *Advances in psychological assessment* (Vol. I, pp. 80–104). Palo Alto CA: Science & Behavior Books.

Stevens, M. J., Kwan, K., & Graybill, D. (1993). Comparison of MMPI-2 scores of foreign Chinese and Caucasian-American students. *Journal of Clinical Psychology, 49,* 23–27.

Stevens, M. R., & Reilley, R. R. (1980). MMPI short forms: A literature review. *Journal of Personality Assessment, 44,* 368–376.

Strassberg, D. S., Clutton, S., & Korboot, P. (1991). A descriptive and validity study of the MMPI-2 in an elderly Australian sample. *Journal of Psychopathology and Behavioral Assessment, 13,* 301–311.

Strauss, M. E., Gynther, M. D., & Wallhermfechtel, J. (1974). Differential misdiagnosis of blacks and whites by the MMPI. *Journal of Personality Assessment, 38,* 55–60.

Streiner, D. L., & Miller, H. R. (1986). Can a good short form of the MMPI ever be developed? *Journal of Clinical Psychology, 42,* 109–113.

Streiner, D. L., & Miller, H. R. (1988). Validity of the MMPI scales for DSM-III Personality Disorders: What are they measuring? *Journal of Personality Disorders, 2,* 238–242.

Streit, K., Greene, R. L., Cogan, R., & Davis, H. G. (1993). Clinical correlates of MMPI Depression scales. *Journal of Personality Assessment, 60,* 390–396.

Sue, S., Keefe, K., Enomoto, K., Durvasula, R. S., & Chao, R. (1996). Asian American and white college students' performance on the MMPI-2. In J. N. Butcher (Ed.), *International adaptations of the MMPI-2: Research and clinical applications* (pp. 206–218). Minneapolis: University of Minnesota Press.

Sue, S., & Sue, D. W. (1974). MMPI comparisons between Asian-American and non-Asian students utilizing a student health psychiatric clinic. *Journal of Counseling Psychology, 21,* 423–427.

Suinn, R. M., Ahuna, C., & Khoo, G. (1992). The Suinn-Lew Asian Self-Identity Acculturation Scale: Concurrent and factorial validation. *Educational and Psychological Measurements, 52,* 1041–1046.

Suinn, R. M., Khoo, G., & Ahuna, C. (1995). The Suinn-Lew Asian Self-Identity Acculturation Scale: Cross-cultural information. *Journal of Multicultural Counseling and Development, 23,* 139–148.

Suinn, R. M., Rikard-Figueroa, K., Lew, S., & Virgil, P. (1987). The Suinn-Lew Asian Self-Identity Acculturation scale: An initial report. *Educational and Psychological Measurement, 47,* 401–407.

Super, D. E. (1942). The Bernreuter Personality Inventory: A review of research. *Psychological Bulletin, 39,* 94–125.

Sutker, P. B., Archer, R. P., & Allain, A. N. (1978). Drug abuse patterns, personality characteristics, and relationships with sex, race, and sensation seeking. *Journal of Consulting and Clinical Psychology, 46,* 1374–1378.

Sutker, P. B., Archer, R. P., & Allain, A. N. (1980). Psychopathology of drug abusers: Sex and ethnic considerations. *The International Journal of the Addictions, 15,* 605–613.

Sutker, P. B., & Kilpatrick, D. G. (1973). Personality, biographical, and racial correlates of sexual attitudes and behavior. *Proceedings of the American Psychological Association, 8,* 261–262.

Svanum, S., & Ehrmann, L. C. (1992). Alcoholic subtypes and the MacAndrew Alcoholism scale. *Journal of Personality Assessment, 58,* 411–422.

Svanum, S., & Ehrmann, L. C. (1993). The validity of the MMPI in identifying alcoholics in a university setting. *Journal of Studies on Alcohol, 54,* 722–729.

Svanum, S., McGrew, J., & Ehrmann, L. C. (1994). Validity of the substance abuse scales of the MMPI-2 in a college student sample. *Journal of Personality Assessment, 62,* 427–439.

Swain-Holcomb, B., & Thorne, B. M. (1984). A comparison of male and female alcoholics with an MMPI classification system. *Journal of Personality Assessment, 48,* 392–397.

Sweetland, A., & Quay, H. (1953). A note on the *K* scale of the MMPI. *Journal of Consulting Psychology, 17,* 314–316.

Swenson, W. M. (1961). Structured personality testing in the aged: An MMPI study of the gerontic population. *Journal of Clinical Psychology, 17,* 302–304.

Swenson, W. M., Pearson, J. S., & Osborne, D. (1973). *An MMPI source book: Basic item, scale, and pattern data on 50,000 medical patients.* Minneapolis: University of Minnesota Press.

Tamkin, A. S., & Scherer, I. W. (1957). What is measured by the "Cannot Say" scale of the group MMPI? *Journal of Consulting Psychology, 21,* 370.

Tanner, B. A. (1990a). Composite descriptions associated with rare MMPI two-point code types: Codes that involve Scale *5. Journal of Clinical Psychology, 46,* 425–431.

Tanner, B. A. (1990b). Composite descriptions associated with rare MMPI two-point code types in an urban psychiatric setting: Codes that involve Scale *0. Journal of Clinical Psychology, 46,* 791–795.

Tarter, R. E., & Perley, R. N. (1975). Clinical and perceptual characteristics of paranoids and paranoid schizophrenics. *Journal of Clinical Psychology, 31,* 42–44.

Taulbee, E. S., & Sisson, B. D. (1957). Configurational analysis of MMPI profiles of psychiatric groups. *Journal of Consulting Psychology, 21,* 413–417.

Taylor, G. P., Jr. (1970). Moderator-variable effect on personality-test item endorsements of physically disabled patients. *Journal of Consulting and Clinical Psychology, 35,* 183–188.

Taylor, J. R., Strassberg, D. S., & Turner, C. W. (1989). Utility of the MMPI in a geriatric population. *Journal of Personality Assessment, 53,* 665–676.

Tellegen, A. (1992, July). *Unigender norms for the MMPI-2.* Paper presented at the MMPI-2 Summer Institute, Colorado Springs, CO.

Tellegen, A., & Ben-Porath, Y. S. (1992). The new uniform T scores for the MMPI-2: Rationale, derivation, and appraisal. *Psychological Assessment, 4,* 145–155.

Terman, L. M., & Miles, C. C. (1938). *Manual of information and directions for use of Attitude-Interest Analysis Test.* New York: McGraw-Hill.

Thackston-Hawkins, L., Compton, W. C., & Kelly, D. B. (1994). Correlates of hopelessness on the MMPI-2. *Psychological Reports, 75,* 1071–1074.

Timbrook, R. E., & Graham, J. R. (1994). Ethnic differences on the MMPI-2? *Psychological Assessment, 6,* 212–217.

Timbrook, R. E., Graham, J. R., Keiller, S. W., & Watts, D. (1993). Comparison of the Wiener-Harmon subtle-obvious scales and the standard validity scales in detecting valid and invalid MMPI-2 profiles. *Psychological Assessment, 5,* 53–61.

Todd, A. L., & Gynther, M. D. (1988). Have MMPI *Mf* scale correlates changed in the past 30 years? *Journal of Clinical Psychology, 44,* 505–510.

Trull, T. J. (1991). Discriminant validity of the MMPI Borderline Personality Disorder scale. *Psychological Assessment, 3,* 232–238.

Trull, T. J., Useda, J. D., Costa, P. T., Jr., & McCrae, R. R. (1995). Comparison of the MMPI-2 Personality Psychopathology Five (PSY-5), the NEO-PI, and the NEO-PI-R. *Psychological Assessment, 7,* 508–516.

Truscott, D. (1990). Assessment of Overcontrolled Hostility in adolescence. *Psychological Assessment, 2,* 145–148.

Tsushima, W. T., & Onorato, V. A. (1982). Comparison of MMPI scores of white and Japanese-American medical patients. *Journal of Consulting and Clinical Psychology, 50,* 150–151.

Tyler, F. T. (1951). A factorial analysis of fifteen MMPI scales. *Journal of Consulting Psychology, 15,* 451–456.

Tyler, F. T., & Michaelis, J. U. (1953). K-scores applied to MMPI scales for college women. *Educational and Psychological Measurement, 13,* 459–466.

Uecker, A. E., Boutilier, L. R., & Richardson, E. H. (1980). "Indianism" and MMPI scores of men alcoholics. *Journal of Studies on Alcohol, 41,* 357–362.

Van Balen, H. G. G., Van Limbeek, J., & De Mey, H. R. A. (1997). The identification of neurologically relevant items in the MMPI-2. *International Journal of Rehabilitation Research, 20,* 355–370.

Velasquez, R. J. (1984). *An atlas of MMPI group profiles on Mexican Americans.* Los Angeles: Spanish Speaking Mental Health Research Center.

Velasquez, R. J. (1992). Hispanic-American MMPI research (1949–1992): A comprehensive bibliography. *Psychological Reports, 70,* 743–754.

Velasquez, R. J. (1995). Personality assessment of Hispanic clients. In J. N. Butcher (Ed.), *Clinical personality assessment: Practical approaches* (pp. 120–139). New York: Oxford.

Velasquez, R. J., & Callahan, W. J. (1990a). MMPI comparisons of Hispanic- and White-American veterans seeking treatment for alcoholism. *Psychological Reports, 67,* 95–98.

Velasquez, R. J., & Callahan, W. J. (1990b). MMPIs of Hispanic, black, and white DSM-III schizophrenics. *Psychological Reports, 66,* 819–822.

Velasquez, R. J., Callahan, W. J., & Carrillo, R. (1989). MMPI profiles of Hispanic-American inpatient and outpatient sex offenders. *Psychological Reports, 65,* 1055–1058.

Velasquez, R. J., Callahan, W. J., & Young, R. (1993). Hispanic-white MMPI comparisons: Does psychiatric diagnosis make a difference? *Journal of Clinical Psychology, 49,* 528–534.

Velasquez, R. J., & Gimenez, L. (1987). MMPI differences among three diagnostic groups of Mexican-American state hospital patients. *Psychological Reports, 60,* 1071–1074.

Venn, J. (1988). Low scores on MMPI Scales *2* and *0* as indicators of character pathology in men. *Psychological Reports, 62,* 651–657.

Vesprani, G. J., & Seeman, W. (1974). MMPI *X* and zero items in a psychiatric outpatient group. *Journal of Personality Assessment, 38,* 61–64.

Vestre, N. D., & Watson, C. G. (1972). Behavioral correlates of the MMPI Paranoia scale. *Psychological Reports, 31,* 851–854.

Vincent, K. R., Castillo, I. M., Houser, R. I., Zapata, J. A., Stuart, H. J., Cohn, C. K., & O'Shanick, G. J. (1984). *MMPI-168 codebook.* Norwood, NJ: Ablex.

Vincent, N. M. P., Linsz, N. L., & Greene, M. I. (1966). The *L* scale of the MMPI as an index of falsification. *Journal of Clinical Psychology, 22,* 214–215.

Wales, B., & Seeman, W. (1968). A new method for detecting the fake good response set on the MMPI. *Journal of Clinical Psychology, 24,* 211–216.

Wales, B., & Seeman, W. (1972). Instructional sets and MMPI items. *Journal of Personality Assessment, 36,* 282–286.

Walker, C. E., & Ward, J. (1969). Identification and elimination of offensive items from the MMPI. *Journal of Projective Techniques and Personality Assessment, 33,* 385–388.

Walters, G. D. (1984). Identifying schizophrenia by means of Scale *8* (*Sc*) of the MMPI. *Journal of Personality Assessment, 48,* 390–391.

Walters, G. D. (1985). Scale *4* (*Pd*) of the MMPI and the diagnosis Antisocial Personality. *Journal of Personality Assessment, 49,* 474–476.

Walters, G. D. (1986). Screening for psychopathology in groups of black and white prison inmates by means of the MMPI. *Journal of Personality Assessment, 50,* 257–264.

Walters, G. D. (1988a). Assessing dissimulation and denial on the MMPI in a sample of maximum security, male inmates. *Journal of Personality Assessment, 52,* 465–474.

Walters, G. D. (1988b). Schizophrenia. In R. L. Greene (Ed.), *The MMPI: Use in specific populations* (pp. 50–73). San Antonio: Grune & Stratton.

Walters, G. D., & Greene, R. L. (1988). Differentiating between schizophrenic and manic inpatients by means of the MMPI. *Journal of Personality Assessment, 52,* 91–95.

Walters, G. D., Greene, R. L., & Jeffrey, T. B. (1984). Discriminating between alcoholic and nonalcoholic blacks and whites on the MMPI. *Journal of Personality Assessment, 48,* 486–488.

Walters, G. D., Greene, R. L., Jeffrey, T. B., Kruzich, D. J., & Haskin, J. J. (1983). Racial variations on the MacAndrew Alcoholism scale of the MMPI. *Journal of Consulting and Clinical Psychology, 51,* 947–948.

Walters, G. D., & Solomon, G. S. (1982). Methodological note on deriving behavioral correlates for MMPI profile patterns: Case of the female *4-5-6* configuration. *Psychological Reports, 50,* 1071–1076.

Walters, G. D., White, T. W., & Greene, R. L. (1988). Use of the MMPI to identify malingering and exaggeration of psychiatric symptomatology in male prison inmates. *Journal of Consulting and Clinical Psychology, 56,* 111–117.

Ward, L. C. (1986). MMPI item subtlety research: Current issues and directions. *Journal of Personality Assessment, 50,* 73–79.

Ward, L. C. (1997). Confirmatory factor analyses of the Anxiety and Depression content scales of the MMPI-2. *Journal of Personality Assessment, 68,* 678–691.

Ward, L. C., & Dillon, E. A. (1990). Psychiatric symptoms of MMPI Masculinity-Femininity scale. *Psychological Assessment, 2,* 286–288.

Ward, L. C., & Jackson, D. B. (1990). A comparison of primary alcoholics, secondary alcoholics, and nonalcoholic psychiatric patients on the MacAndrew Alcoholism scale. *Journal of Personality Assessment, 54,* 729–735.

Ward, L. C., Kersh, B. C., & Waxmonsky, J. A. (1998). Factor structure of the Paranoia scale of the MMPI-2 in relation to the Harris-Lingoes subscales and Comrey factor analysis. *Psychological Assessment, 10,* 292–296.

Ward, L. C., & Perry, M. S. (1998). Measurement of Social Introversion by the MMPI-2. *Journal of Personality Assessment, 70,* 171–182.

Warman, R. E., & Hannum, T. E. (1965). MMPI pattern changes in female prisoners. *Journal of Research in Crime and Delinquency, 2,* 72–76.

Wasyliw, O. E., Grossman, L. S., Haywood, T. W., & Cavanaugh, J. L., Jr. (1988). The detection of malingering in criminal forensic groups: MMPI validity scales. *Journal of Personality Assessment, 52,* 321–333.

Watkins, C. E., Jr., Campbell, V. L., Nieberding, R., Hallmark, R. (1995). Contemporary practice of psychological assessment by clinical psychologists. *Professional Psychology: Research and Practice, 26,* 54–60.

Watson, C. G., Klett, W. G., Walters, C., & Vassar, P. (1984). Suicide and the MMPI: A cross-validation of predictors. *Journal of Clinical Psychology, 40,* 115–119.

Watson, C. G., Manifold, V., Klett, W. G., Brown, J., Thomas, D., & Anderson, D. Comparability of computer- and booklet-administered Minnesota Multiphasic Personality Inventories among primarily chemically dependent patients. *Psychological Assessment, 2,* 276–280.

Watson, C. G., Thomas, D., & Anderson, P. E. D. (1992). Do computer-administered Minnesota Multiphasic Personality Inventories underestimate booklet-based scores? *Journal of Clinical Psychology, 48,* 744–748.

Wechsler, D. (1980). *Wechsler Adult Intelligence Scale—Revised manual.* New York: Psychological Corporation.

Weed, N. C., Ben-Porath, Y. S., & Butcher, J. N. (1990). Failure of Wiener and Harmon MMPI subtle scales as personality descriptors and as validity indicators. *Psychological Assessment, 2,* 281–285.

Weed, N. C., & Butcher, J. N. (1992). The MMPI-2: Development and research issues. In J. C. Rosen & P. McReynolds (Eds.), *Advances in psychological assessment* (Vol. 8, pp. 131–163). San Francisco: Jossey-Bass.

Weed, N. C., Butcher, J. N., & Ben-Porath, Y. S. (1995). MMPI-2 measures of substance abuse. In J. N. Butcher & C. D. Spielberger (Eds.), *Advances in personality assessment.* (Vol. 10, pp. 121–145). Hillsdale, NJ: Erlbaum.

Weed, N. C., Butcher, J. N., McKenna, T., & Ben-Porath, Y. S. (1992). New measures for assessing alcohol and drug abuse with the MMPI-2: The APS and AAS. *Journal of Personality Assessment, 58,* 389–404.

Weed, N. C., Butcher, J. N., & Williams, C. L. (1994). Development of MMPI-A Alcohol/Drug Problem scales. *Journal of Studies on Alcohol, 55,* 296–302.

Weinstein, J., Averill, J. R., Opton, E. M., Jr., & Lazarus, R. S. (1968). Defensive style and discrepancy between self-report and physiological indexes of stress. *Journal of Personality and Social Psychology, 10,* 406–413.

Weiss, R. W., & Russakoff, S. (1977). Relationship of MMPI scores of drug-abusers to personal variables and type of treatment program. *Journal of Psychology, 96,* 25–29.

Welsh, G. S. (1956). Factor dimensions *A* and *R.* In G. S. Welsh & W. G. Dahlstrom (Eds.), *Basic readings on the MMPI in psychology and medicine* (pp. 264–281). Minneapolis: University of Minnesota Press.

Welsh, G. S. (1965). MMPI profiles and factor scales *A* and *R. Journal of Clinical Psychology, 21,* 43–47.

Werner, P. D., Becker, J. M. T., & Yesavage, J. A. (1983). Concurrent validity of the Overcontrolled Hostility scale for psychotics. *Psychological Reports, 52,* 93–94.

Wetter, M. W., Baer, R. A., Berry, D. T. R., & Reynolds, S. K. (1994). The effect of symptom information on faking on the MMPI-2. *Assessment, 1,* 199–207.

Wetter, M. W., Baer, R. A., Berry, D. T. R., Robison, L. H., & Sumpter, J. (1993). MMPI-2 profiles of motivated fakers given specific symptom information: A comparison to matched patients. *Psychological Assessment, 5,* 317–323.

Wetter, M. W., Baer, R. A., Berry, D. T. R., Smith, G. T., & Larsen, L. H. (1992). Sensitivity of MMPI-2 validity scales to random responding and malingering. *Psychological Assessment, 4,* 369–374.

Wetzler, S., Khadivi, A., & Moser, R. K. (1998). The use of the MMPI-2 for the assessment of depressive and psychotic disorders. *Assessment, 5,* 249–261.

White, A. J., & Heilbrun, K. (1995). The classification of overcontrolled-hostility: Comparison of two diagnostic methods. *Criminal Behaviour and Mental Health, 5,* 106–123.

Whitworth, R. H. (1988). Anglo- and Mexican-American performance on the MMPI administered in Spanish or English. *Journal of Clinical Psychology, 44,* 891–897.

Whitworth, R. H., & McBlaine, D. D. (1993). Comparison of the MMPI and MMPI-2 administered to Anglo- and Hispanic-American university students. *Journal of Personality Assessment, 61,* 19–27.

Whitworth, R. H., & Unterbrink, C. (1994). Comparison of MMPI-2 clinical and content scales administered to Hispanic and Anglo-Americans. *Hispanic Journal of Behavioral Sciences, 16,* 255–263.

Widiger, T. A., & Corbitt, E. M. (1993). The MCMI-II Personality Disorder scales and their relationship to DSM-III-R diagnosis. In R. J. Craig (Ed.), *The Millon Clinical Multiaxial Inventory* (pp. 181–201). Hillsdale, NJ: Erlbaum.

Wiederholt, J. L., & Bryant, B. R. (1992). *Gray Oral Reading Test (GORT-3)* (3rd ed.). Austin, TX: Pro-Ed, Inc.

Wiener, D. N. (1948). Subtle and obvious keys for the MMPI. *Journal of Consulting Psychology, 12,* 164–170.

Wiggins, J. S. (1959). Interrelationships among MMPI measures of dissimulation under standard and social desirability instructions. *Journal of Consulting Psychology, 23,* 419–427.

Wiggins, J. S. (1964). Convergences among stylistic response measures from objective personality tests. *Educational and Psychological Measurement, 24,* 551–562.

Wiggins, J. S. (1966). Substantive dimensions of self-report in the MMPI item pool. *Psychological Monographs, 80* (Whole No. 630).

Wiggins, J. S. (1973). *Personality and prediction: Principles of personality assessment.* Reading, MA: Addison-Wesley.

Wiggins, J. S., Goldberg, L. R., & Appelbaum, M. (1971). MMPI content scales: Interpretive norms and correlations with other scales. *Journal of Consulting and Clinical Psychology, 37,* 403–410.

Wiggins, N., & Hoffman, P. J. (1968). Three models of clinical judgment. *Journal of Abnormal Psychology, 73,* 70–77.

Wilcox, P., & Dawson, J. G. (1977). Role-played and hypnotically induced simulation of psychopathology on the MMPI. *Journal of Clinical Psychology, 33,* 743–745.

Williams, C. L. (1983). Further investigation of the *Si* scale of the MMPI: Reliabilities, correlates, and subscale utility. *Journal of Clinical Psychology, 39,* 951–957.

Williams, C. L. (1986). MMPI profiles from adolescents: Interpretive strategies and treatment considerations. *Journal of Child and Adolescent Psychotherapy, 3,* 179–193.

Williams, C. L., Ben-Porath, Y. S., & Hevern, V. W. (1994). Item level improvements for use of the MMPI with adolescents. *Journal of Personality Assessment, 63,* 284–293.

Williams, C. L., & Butcher, J. N. (1989a). An MMPI study of adolescents: I. Empirical validity of the standard scales. *Psychological Assessment, 1,* 251–259.

Williams, C. L., & Butcher, J. N. (1989b). An MMPI study of adolescents: II. Verification and limitations of code type classifications. *Psychological Assessment, 1,* 260–265.

Williams, C. L., Butcher, J. N., Ben-Porath, Y. S., & Graham, J. R. (1992). *MMPI-A content scales: Assessing psychopathology in adolescents.* Minneapolis: University of Minnesota Press.

Williams, R. B., Jr., Haney, T. L., Lee, K. L., Kong, Y. H., Blumenthal, J. A., & Whalen, R. E. (1980). Type A behavior, hostility, and coronary atherosclerosis. *Psychosomatic Medicine, 42,* 539–549.

Wilson, R. L. (1980). *A comparison of the predictive validities of subtle versus obvious MMPI items: Predicting the elusive neurosis.* Unpublished Master's thesis, Auburn University.

Wimbish, L. G. (1984). *The importance of appropriate norms for the computerized interpretations of adolescent MMPI profiles.* Unpublished doctoral dissertation, Ohio State University, Columbus.

Wink, P., & Gough, H. G. (1990). New narcissism scales for the California Psychological Inventory and the MMPI. *Journal of Personality Assessment, 54,* 446–462.

Winter, W. D., & Stortroen, M. (1963). A comparison of several MMPI indices to differentiate psychotics from normals. *Journal of Clinical Psychology, 19,* 220–223.

Winters, K. D., Newmark, C. S., Lumry, A. E., Leach, K., & Weintraub, S. (1985). MMPI codetypes characteristic of DSM-III schizophrenics, depressives, and bipolars. *Journal of Clinical Psychology, 41,* 382–386.

Wise, E. A. (1996). Comparative validity of the MMPI-2 and MCMI-II Personality Disorder classifications. *Journal of Personality Assessment, 66,* 569–582.

Witt, P. H., & Gynther, M. D. (1975). Another explanation for black-white MMPI differences. *Journal of Clinical Psychology, 31,* 69–70.

Wolf, A. W., Schubert, D. S. P., Patterson, M., Grande, T., & Pendleton, L. (1990). The use of the MacAndrew Alcoholism scale in detecting substance abuse and antisocial personality. *Journal of Personality Assessment, 54,* 747–755.

Wong, M. R. (1984). MMPI Scale Five: Its meaning, or lack thereof. *Journal of Personality Assessment, 48,* 279–284.

Woodworth, R. S. (1920). *Personal data sheet.* Chicago: Stoelting.

Wooten, A. J. (1984). Effectiveness of the *K* correction in the detection of psychopathology and its impact on profile height and configuration among young adult men. *Journal of Consulting and Clinical Psychology, 52,* 468–473.

Worthington, D. L., & Schlottmann, R. S. (1986). The predictive validity of subtle and obvious empirically derived psychological test items under faking conditions. *Journal of Personality Assessment, 50,* 171–181.

Woychyshyn, C. A., McElheran, W. G., & Romney, D. M. (1992). MMPI validity measures: A comparative study of original with alternative indices. *Journal of Personality Assessment, 58,* 138–148.

Wrobel, T. A. (1992). Validity of Harris and Lingoes MMPI subscale descriptors in an outpatient sample. *Journal of Personality Assessment, 59,* 14–21.

Wrobel, T. A., & Lachar, D. (1982). Validity of the Wiener subtle and obvious scales for the MMPI: Another example of the importance of inventory-item content. *Journal of Consulting and Clinical Psychology, 50,* 469–470.

Yonge, G. D. (1966). Certain consequences of applying the *K* factor to MMPI scores. *Educational and Psychological Measurement, 26,* 887–893.

Youngjohn, J. R., Burrows, L., & Erdal, K. (1995). Brain damage or compensation neurosis? The controversial post-concussion syndrome. *The Clinical Neuropsychologist, 9,* 112–123.

Youngjohn, J. R., Davis, D., & Wolf, I. (1997). Head injury and the MMPI-2: Paradoxical severity effects and the influence of litigation. *Psychological Assessment, 9,* 177–184.

Zalewski, C., & Greene, R. L. (1996). Multicultural usage of the MMPI-2. In L. A. Suzuki, P. J. Meller, & J. G. Ponterotto (Eds.), *Handbook of multicultural assessment: Clinical, psychological, and educational applications* (pp. 77–114). San Francisco: Jossey-Bass.

Zalewski, C., Schatz, C. T., Gottesman, I. I., & Nichols, D. S. (1997). Discriminant validity of the MMPI Depression Subtle (D-S) and Depression Obvious (D-O) scales. *Assessment, 4,* 311–319.

Zelin, M. L. (1971). Validity of the MMPI scales for measuring twenty psychiatric dimensions. *Journal of Consulting and Clinical Psychology, 37,* 286–290.

CREDITS